BURMA

Louis Allen served as a Japanese speaking intelligence officer in South East Asia during and after the Second World War, and has a thorough understanding of Japanese language and culture. He writes from his own experiences and draws upon exhaustive research from Japanese, British and US official histories, apologias, reminiscences, generals' biographies, diaries and newspaper reports. He taught French literature at the University of Durham, was a theatre and literary critic, and a frequent broadcaster on both radio and television.

Also by Louis Allen

Prisoner of the British: A Japanese Soldier's Experiences in Burma, by Yuji Aida (trans. Louis Allen and Hidé Ishiguro)

Japan: The Years of Triumph. From Feudal Isolation to Pacific Empire

Sittang: The Last Battle. The End of the Japanese in Burma, July–August 1945

Singapore, 1941–1942

The End of the War in Asia

BURMA
The Longest War
1941–1945

Louis Allen

PHOENIX
PRESS

PHOENIX PRESS
5 UPPER SAINT MARTIN'S LANE
LONDON WC2H 9EA

A PHOENIX PRESS PAPERBACK

First published in Great Britain
by J.M. Dent in 1984
This paperback edition published in 2000
by Phoenix Press,
a division of The Orion Publishing Group Ltd,
Orion House, 5 Upper St Martin's Lane,
London WC2H 9EA

Third impression 2001

Copyright © Louis Allen, 1984
Maps © J.M. Dent & Sons Ltd, 1984

A CIP catalogue record for this book is available
from the British Library.

Printed in Great Britain by
Butler & Tanner Ltd, Frome and London

ISBN 1 84212 260 6

Contents

List of Illustrations

List of Maps

For Brigid, Mark and Toby

Acknowledgments

I have many acknowledgments to make. First, for permission to refer to their books and quote from them, I would like to thank General Sir Geoffrey Evans for *The Desert and the Jungle* and *Imphal*, the latter written in collaboration with Antony Brett-James, on whose *Ball of Fire*, the history of 5 Indian Division, I have also drawn, as well as his autobiographical account, *Report My Signals*; Bryan Perrett for *Tanks to Rangoon* and Miles Smeeton for *A Change of Jungles*, both of which gave me a clear notion of the use of armour in Burma; Michael Calvert for *Prisoners of Hope*, *The Chindits*, and *Fighting Mad*; Shelford Bidwell for *The Chindit Campaign* and also authorization to make use of manuscript material collected by him for that book and now stored in the Imperial War Museum; Lord Ballantrae for his father's *Beyond the Chindwin*, *The Wild Green Earth* and *Trumpet in the Hall*; Charles Romanus and Riley Sunderland for their three volumes on Stilwell (a magnificent personal gift to me from Riley Sunderland himself); Barbara Tuchman for *Sand Against the Wind*; Viscount Slim for his father's *Defeat into Victory* and Mrs Ronald Lewin for her late husband's brilliant biography *Slim*; the estates of John Connell for *Auchinleck* and *Wavell, Supreme Commander*, of John Masters for *Road Past Mandalay* and of Compton Mackenzie for *Eastern Epic*; Richard Rhodes James for *Chindit*; James Baggaley for *A Chindit Story* and David Halley for *With Wingate in Burma*; David Rissik for *The DLI At War* and Lieutenant-Colonel O. G. White for *Straight on for Tokyo*; Brian Bond for *Chief of Staff* (Lieutenant-General Sir Henry Pownall's diaries); the estate of the late Arthur Swinson for *Kohima* and *Four Samurai*; Arthur Campbell for *The Siege*; Lieutenant-Colonel Tony Mains for *The Retreat from Burma* and the estate of Sir John Smyth for *Before the Dawn*; HMSO for Vols II – V of *The War Against Japan* by Major-General W. Kirby and the first volume of *Burma, The Struggle for Independence*; Theda Maw Sturtevant and William C. Sturtevant for Ba Maw's *Breakthrough in Burma*; Cedric Dover for *Hell in the Sunshine*. Of the Japanese authors whose work I have found most useful I would like to mention Lieutenant-General Fujiwara Iwaichi, whose *F Kikan* is now available in an English version by Professor Yoji Akashi, whom I would also like to thank for discussions and papers on the Japanese occupation of Burma; Takagi Toshirō for his book on Arakan, *Senshi*, and his series on the Imphal and Kohima battles, *Inpāru*, *Kōmei*, *Funshi* and *Zenmetsu*; Kojima Noboru for *Taiheiyō Sensōshi* and *Eirei no tani*; Hamachi Toshio for *Biruma Saizensen*; Sagara Shunsuke for *Kiku to Tatsu*; Itō Keiichi for *Heitaitachi no rikugunshi*; Kikuchi Hitoshi for *Kyōfū Inpāru Saizensen*; Kuzuma Yasuji for *Sakimori no shi*; Professor Asai Tokuichi for *Biruma Sensen Fūdoki*; Hatakeyama Seigyō for *Hiroku Rikugun Nakano Gakkō*: Ushiro Masaru for *Biruma senki*; Katakura Tadashi for *Inpāru Sakusen Hishi*; Senda Natsumitsu for *Jūgun Ianfu*; Tsutsumi Shinzō for *Tenshin* and *Kikoku Shūshū*.

Others have been generous with documents and personal accounts. Jack Scollen and Colonel Alastair Tuck gave me their narratives of the battle of Meiktila, and Mr Cecil Goodman let me use his account of the retreat from Burma in 1942; I owe my knowledge of the existence of that document to George ('Sam') Shepperson, Professor of History in the University of Edinburgh, who also gave me some notion of the role of the East Africans in Burma. To Roy Hudson, of Chiangmai, in Thailand, I owe generous hospitality and a Kiplingesque evening at the old British consulate as the Union Jack was flown there for the last time; and I thank him, too, for a gift of the Malerkotla Sappers and Miners' War Diary, which enabled me to fix the details of the blowing of the Sittang Bridge. His colleague Major Bashir Ahmed Khan (BAK) sent me from Lahore many precious documents and his narrative of the actual blowing, which fixed the timing. Tsutsumi Shinzō, at the time Vice-President of Mitsui and Co., was my host at a memorable *tempura* dinner in Tokyo where he entertained Majors Hachisuka Mitsuo and Wakō Hisanori, who told me about the Sittang breakout and the intelligence organizations of 28 Army, subjects discussed often with the late Lieutenant-Colonel Tsuchiya Eiichi, who also kept me supplied with copies of his 28 Army bulletin, *Nanso*, and all the latest publications on Burma in Japanese, whether available in the bookshops or privately printed. One of the most skilful of Japanese agents in Burma, Kayabuki Nobumasa, told me, during a visit to Durham in 1979, about his work in Arakan. Pat Woodward talked about the Battle of the Sittang Bend from the RAF viewpoint, and Arthur Adamson from the artillery angle, as well as annotating and correcting my account of that episode.

For criticisms of my chapter on Meiktila I am indebted to Stanley Charles, of Balliol, Meiktila, and the Welsh Office, with whom, in Payagyi Camp, I had endless profitable discussions on the whole Burma campaign as we interrogated and translated and produced the first accounts of the war from the Japanese side. I owe him thanks for warm encouragement in my writing ever since, as I do also to my late friend, Dick Storry, Professor of Japanese in the University of Oxford. In terms of information and stimulus, my debt to him is simply unrepayable; but the number of those who can say that is legion. Through his invitations to give seminars at Oxford's Far East Centre, I owe the privilege of having a paper on the war in the Far East criticized by Michael Howard, Regius Professor of History at Oxford, from whose detailed understanding of the role of China in the strategy of the Far East I have profited. I have also quite unashamedly taken advantage of Mr C. R. Escritt's expert knowledge of the Burma-Siam Railway, which he acquired the hard way; and of Bill Edge's experiences as an officer in the King's Liverpool Regiment during the first Wingate expedition. He has read my chapter on that episode and corrected errors both of fact and judgment. On both Wingate expeditions, I have been lucky enough to have corresponded with Brigadier Peter Mead, and to use the memorandum on the lacunae of the Official History in relation to Wingate prepared by himself and Sir Robert Thompson. Mr F. H. Thomas gave me precious information on Wingate's last flight and Mr D. C. Wilson on photo reconnaissance over Burma. On clandestine warfare, I have also been lucky enough to have corresponded with Lieutenant-Colonel Ritchie Gardiner, former head of Burma Section, Force 136; and Sir Leslie Glass and Mr F. S. V. Donnison commented on a paper on Burma I presented to the Far East Centre in Oxford. But what I know of Burmese politics and clandestine warfare has its roots much earlier, and I should now thank Lieutenant-Colonel Bill Tibbetts of V Force, for notions of that unit's activities derived from shared curried chicken legs and chapattis in Penwegon. My friend Hugh Toye is an inexhaustible mine of information on the Indian National Army and Subhas Chandra Bose, and he has treated my enquiries with great patience; while Bose's nephew, Dr Sisir K. Bose, of the Netaji Bhawan in Calcutta, has sent me copies of the *Oracle* and kept me in touch with research on the INA. Hugh Tinker has let me use his paper on the exodus of civilian refugees in 1942 – and all writers on Burma are in his debt for the splendid edition of the political papers relating to the campaign and the transfer of power. My former colleague, Lieutenant-Colonel L. Slater, once Master of University College, Durham, has answered queries on Burmese topography from his unrivalled experience on the ground in the 1930s and in the mapping rooms of the Inter-Services Topographical Department in Delhi. Major Pat Rome allowed me to use his account of the DLI at Kohima.

On the Japanese side, I have received from Mr Hirakubo Masao precious details about the siege of Kohima, and the loan of his manuscript account of his adventures as a supply captain under Miyazaki during the battle. I have talked to Professor Aida Yūji on a number of occasions on his experiences as a prisoner in British hands, after I co-authored the translation of his book *Āron shūyōjo*. I have been his guest at one of Kyoto's most famous traditional Japanese restaurants; and I have enjoyed similar hospitality at the Defence Agency club at Ichigaya, when ex-officers of the Japanese 28 Army gave a dinner to celebrate the Japanese translation of my book *Sittang*, which gave me a chance to talk about Arakan and the breakout, and life in the Pegu Yomas, with Major (later

Lieutenant-General) Yamaguchi Tatsuru and Major (later Lieutenant-General) Fukutomi Shigeru, and a former staff captain (now an Anglican minister in Tokyo), the Reverend Isaiah Taka Sakurai. At lunch in the Imperial Hotel in Tokyo, Lieutenant-General Sugita Ichiji talked to me both about his moment of triumph at Singapore in February 1942 and about his verdict on the Imphal battle two years later. Professor Eto Jun of the Tokyo University of Technology discussed the literature of war with me, and debated the subject with me in the columns of the *Mainichi Shimbun*. Lieutenant-General Fujiwara, my friend now for close on forty years, and my host on a number of occasions in Tokyo and Kyoto, not only answered endless questions about F Kikan and the Imphal battles, but guided me personally through the Defence Agency archives and read through the Mutaguchi and Kawabe diaries with me. I also owe a debt to his learned and co-operative nephew, Professor Yokoyama Toshio of St Antony's, Oxford, and the University of Kyoto, for keeping me up-to-date with recent publications and periodicals, and for introducing me to Mr Kuzuma Yasuji, of the *Kyoto Shimbun*, from whom I first heard of the Japanese use of poison gas in at least one incident in the campaign.

It is a pleasure to thank General Toga Hiroshi, head of the War History Room at Ichigaya, for putting documents at my disposal; and the staff at the Public Record Office at Kew for their generously given expertise and helpfulness. I warmly acknowledge the debt I owe to Dr Roderic Suddaby and Mr Philip Reed, of the Imperial War Museum, who unearthed countless documents, Japanese and British, printed and manuscript, to help this work forward; to Miss Jenny Wood who showed me the vast range of paintings and drawings the Museum holds from wartime commissions to artists; and to Miss Julia Sheppard, and Dr Angus, the Librarian of the Liddell Hart Centre for Military Archives at King's College, London, who helped me with the papers of Sir Robert Brooke-Popham and Generals Gracey and Hutton. For financial assistance in visiting various archives I am indebted to the Durham University Research Fund and the Japan Foundation.

Mrs Lilian McDonough has kept me domestically afloat, and made writing possible. My indefatigable typist, Mrs Krys Stenhouse, made a smooth typescript from the morass of my illegible scrawls, even when she was on the very verge of parturition. My old friend P. J. M. Fry ('Roger'), who began the study of Japanese with me on the same day at the School of Oriental Studies, and whose close friendship I have valued ever since, has done more than friendship bargained for in correcting the proofs of this book; just as Peter Shellard, my publisher, must be thanked for showing tolerance and forbearance well beyond the call of duty and the threat of deadlines. My sons Felix and Toby helped me, with statistics and charts, to make some sense of the often discrepant evidence about casualties. Last but far from least, I thank Jean Davies, who taught me, forty years after I first put the SEAC insignia on my shoulders, the true significance of the Phoenix.

Preface

I think I should say why I wanted to write this book and how my idea of it
has changed as I have written it. First, the war in Burma is not just a
magnificent story, it is a whole host of magnificent stories. Fantastic
individuals are their heroes and, at times, their narrators. Some of the
stories have been told by soldiers who were writers, including XIV Army
commander himself, Field-Marshal Viscount Slim. Indeed, few campaigns
have been so meticulously recorded by the general who won them, with
such an eye for the salient details of a battle, the qualities of soldiers, and
the turn of a phrase. But Slim is in distinguished company: the Wingate
expeditions have been brilliantly narrated by column commanders like
Fergusson, Calvert and Masters; the 'Admin Box' and the Irrawaddy
crossings have been unforgettably described by General Evans, who has
also, with Antony Brett-James, written of the invasion of India; in the
intervals of sailing round the Horn, Miles Smeeton has written a crisp and
fascinating account of what it was like to lead tanks into battle at Meiktila;
novelists like H. E. Bates and Walter Baxter have turned the horrors of the
first retreat into memorable fiction, just as Richard Mason has depicted the
throat-catching excitement of the first encounters at Imphal. And there are
countless others, Japanese as well as British, who, in the narrating of a
personal adventure or disaster, have made stories out of the story.

A great variety of races and motivations was involved: British, Japanese,
Chinese, American, Indian, Gurkha, East and West African, Burmese,
Karen, Kachin. So, too, was a great variety of military operations, as the
Japanese Colonel Fuwa has noted: the war in Burma was a combination of
jungle war, mountain war, desert war, and naval war; hand-to-hand combat appropriate to the Stone Age; and air transportation of whole divisions
with their artillery and vehicles with a speed and efficiency that seemed
improbable even in the twentieth century. Landings by glider took place in
remote jungle-strips, naval craft probed through mangrove swamps to land
commandos along the coast of Arakan; soldiers marched under a curtain of
snow flakes through hills as remote from Japan as they were from Britain
or through acres of muddy paddy-fields under solid sheets of monsoon rain
that rotted their boots as they moved. The place and its climate were as

much an enemy as the man you were sent to kill. Burma is one of the most beautiful countries in the world, its green depths as you fly over them are a benison to the eye after the parched tracts of India; but they harbour diseases that can decimate a division and wreck a campaign, a mite that carries lethal scrub typhus, a mosquito that fells thousands of the unwary with malaria, leeches that penetrate the tightest boot and trousers and live on blood until smoked off with a lighted cigarette. So the war was a medical war as well as a war of bayonets, guns and aircraft, a war of transportation, too, in which decisions were often reached because of the supply – or more often the lack – of aircraft and landing craft. It was a very cruel war. It was often better to be killed outright than to be taken prisoner. Commanders' despair drove men to suicide tactics, punishment for breaches of military discipline sometimes reverted to the savagery of the nineteenth century.

It saw the farthest westward advance of the militarized Japan of the 1930s and 1940s and the greatest defeat on land her army has ever known. That defeat was the work, too, of a unique military symbiosis, now gone for ever: largely officered by Britons but manned by every race from the sub-continent, not just those selected by a post-Mutiny panic as 'the martial races of India', the Indian Army was the instrument of victory in Burma, fed by all kinds of diet and speaking a bewildering variety of tongues, often reduced to the universal British other ranks' Urdu which became the pidgin of the battlefield.

It is difficult not to see a tragic twist in the upshot of what turned out to be the longest campaign fought by the British in the Second World War, from the dark December days of 1941 when nothing seemed to go right, to the weary but apocalyptic triumph of 1945. Ostensibly, it was fought for two things: to keep open the road to China and ensure she stayed in the war against Japan and held down a mass of Japanese divisions that might otherwise have been used against the Allies; and to reconquer a province of the British Empire. Yet by the time the road was safely pushed through to Kunming, it was too late: the war was nearly over, and aircraft could carry more supplies than the road did anyway. And the country which was so bitterly fought for was the first, after the grant of independence, to leave the British Commonwealth, three short years after XIV Army had driven the Japanese from it.

The stone raised in memory of the dead at Kohima says, with brief poignancy,

> When you go home
> Tell them of us, and say,
> For your tomorrow
> We gave our today.

But for whose tomorrow were those lives given? For an Empire on the verge of voluntary dissolution, knowing it could not hold on much longer to its rich dominions by a military force which it was both too poor and too self-doubting to exercise. Yet it is too facile to suggest they died for nothing. What if the dreams of Lieutenant-General Mutaguchi, one of Japan's most ambitious generals, had been realized, if there had been no barrier to his invasion of India? He saw the possibility of wresting India from the British, thereby completing the collapse of British power in the East, entailing perhaps withdrawal from the war. Combined with a link-up with triumphant German forces through the Caucasus and Persia, the Japanese might have achieved, not a defeat of the United States, but an isolation from her Allies that might in the end have compelled a separate peace, a compromise with the worst elements in recent German and Japanese history that might have resulted in a world of authoritarian, militarised darkness. No doubt all this seems fanciful when we look at our present reality; but that is precisely because the battle was won in the way it was.

So the story covers a great deal more than the military narration of the bravery and cowardice of individuals or units, the stupidity, ambition, or genius of generals. Politics is essential to it, not only in the decisions which sent the armies this way and that, but in the final efforts of the Burmese people to be masters in their own house. British and Japanese armies fought twice across the whole length and breadth of their country, for purposes little identifiable with those of the Burmese people, each promising liberation, each on their own terms. Problems of race are part of the fabric, implicit in the composition of the opposing armies and in the motivations to which they appealed. Sex matters, too, either as nostalgia and deprivation or as the conscription of women's bodies for *le repos du guerrier*.

I have tried to set these things down as I learned them then, and later, as I felt the nature of the mutual antagonisms and gulfs of language and bitter prejudice dividing peoples who had once been close allies. I have no difficulty, though much shame, in recalling my naivety and ignorance as a young soldier of twenty-two; but I have tried to revise my unconscious assumptions by devouring everything that has been written about Burma, in Japanese and English – official histories, generals' apologias, journalists' accounts, private soldiers' reminiscences, diaries and narratives buried in archives – as well as engaging in endless conversation with those on both sides who either shared or disputed my memories of what happened. The eerie progress of modern electronics has even made it possible for me to hear again the sounds of battle in Burma: at the pressure of a switch, I can listen in the comfort of my study, under the shadow of Durham Cathedral, to the sounds of machine-guns hammering at Church Knoll at Kohima, the voice of General Rees directing the assault on Fort Dufferin in Mandalay, or an awe-struck BBC war correspondent watching a Japanese soldier burst out from a roadside cliff near Imphal and blow himself up with a grenade in the stomach.

The Japanese say Java was their happiest station in Asia, Burma their worst; and the latter verdict might well be shared by the British soldiers who fought there. Farthest away from home, often for years at a stretch, at the end of a long and often rickety supply-line, they remained largely unnoticed by a public in the United Kingdom for whom the war was, by its very nature, remote from everyday experience. They were fighting a people more difficult to understand than the Germans, seemingly much more cruel, though the Japanese were never guilty of the pitiless genocide planned by the Germans in Europe. Unfamiliarity and linguistic distance were formidable barriers to comprehension; and the mutual views of British and Japanese have been one of my constant intellectual preoccupations ever since.

Of the people who remember any or all of this, only the very youngest will be under sixty. But I don't think old men forget. Many of them will admit that their time in Burma, however faded and indistinct the intervening decades may have rendered it, was a form of extreme experience they might otherwise never have known. If they are honest with themselves they will confess that they shared in a great, if puzzling and tragic enterprise, the dimensions of which they probably never realized at the time and may not have descried since. I don't think it matters whether they recall the bitterness of cruelty, deprivation, sickness and bloodshed; the discomfort, misery or boredom; or the zest of adventure. They will be marked by it, one way or another, and this is as true of Japanese as of British: the books about Burma which come without a break from the presses of one of the world's biggest publishing industries are ample proof of this.

I have written this book with the desire to tell what the war was like, and what I thought it meant, to discern the underlying political structure and also to narrate the variety of direct personal experience of a strange and complex battlefield. I have also wanted to tell it from both sides. It is forty years since the battles of Imphal and Kohima were fought and it is long overdue that both sides should see their wartime enemies not as stereotypes from a cartoon but as fellow human beings, as diverse as they are themselves, plain and simple, subtle and sophisticated, capable of the grossest cruelty, as human beings are, but also of invincible courage. As they also are.

Louis Allen
Durham, February 1984

MAPS ACKNOWLEDGMENTS

We acknowledge, with thanks, Orient Longman Ltd for the use of certain maps from Khera and Prasad, *Indian Armed Forces in World War Two: Reconquest of Burma*; Macmillan Ltd for a map from *Imphal*, by Geoffrey Evans and Antony Brett-James; the Controller of Her Majesty's Stationery Office for maps from S.W. Kirby, *The War Against Japan*, vols 2–5; and the Kirkham Studios for maps specially made for this book.

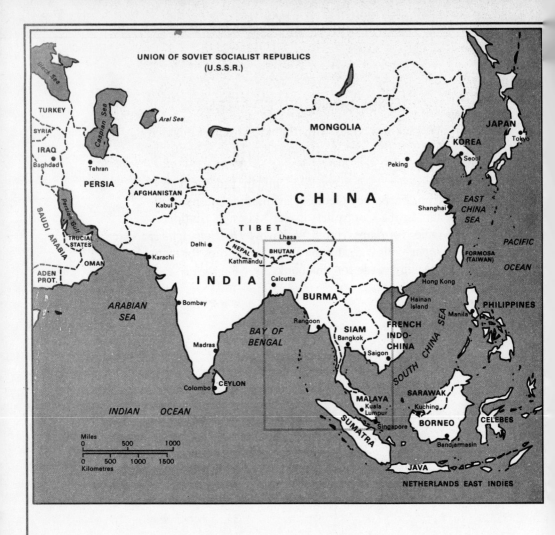

BURMA AND SURROUNDING COUNTRIES
(1940 - 1945)

Key

------- International bounderies

——— Roads

----------- Tracks

□ Allied airfields, December 1941

⊠ Japanese airfields, December 1941

+++++++ Railways

Land over 500 metres
(1640 feet)

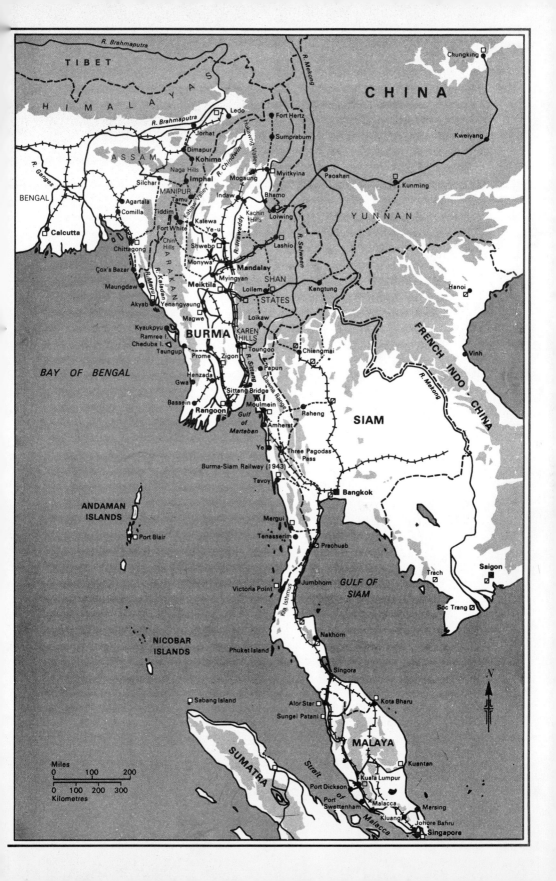

1. THE BRIDGE

The Japanese take Burma

A bridge too few — Japan's farthest reach —
'Ourselves alone', Burmese version — White man's
burden — Gaoling the PM — Colonel Suzuki and the
Thirty Comrades — Colonel Suzuki as Miss
Lonelyhearts — General Smyth looks westward to the
sea — By the old Moulmein pagoda — War comes to
Mi Mi Khaing and Daw Sein — Bashir blows the bridge
— The forsaken city — The skin of General
Alexander's teeth — The longest retreat: Slim
improves on Sir John Moore — Exodus

A bridge too few

The time: before dawn, on the morning of 23 February 1942. The place: the bridge spanning the Sittang River in Lower Burma. The area is controlled by 17 Indian Division, which has two brigades on the east bank and one on the west; but the Japanese invaders, after three weeks in Burma, have broken through on the east bank, and are in the jungle beyond the village of Mokpalin. The bridge is wired to go up to prevent the Japanese seizing it. They have not tried to bomb it yet, because it is the easiest way for them to reach Rangoon, the capital city of Burma, the immediate objective of what has been so far a lightning and highly successful invasion.

The bridgehead on the east bank is formed by the 3rd Burma Rifles, a battalion already sapped by desertions, and about to disintegrate. The Japanese are so close that a light machine gunner is spraying the whole length of the bridge with bullets. The British sapper whose job it is to blow the bridge has told his brigadier that if the Japanese machine gunner keeps up his fire, he cannot guarantee the setting-off of the fuses. They will have to be fired at two or three points along the bridge to ensure its collapse. Even silencing the machine gun will offer only temporary respite, because the bridge is in easy range of Japanese mortar fire.

1

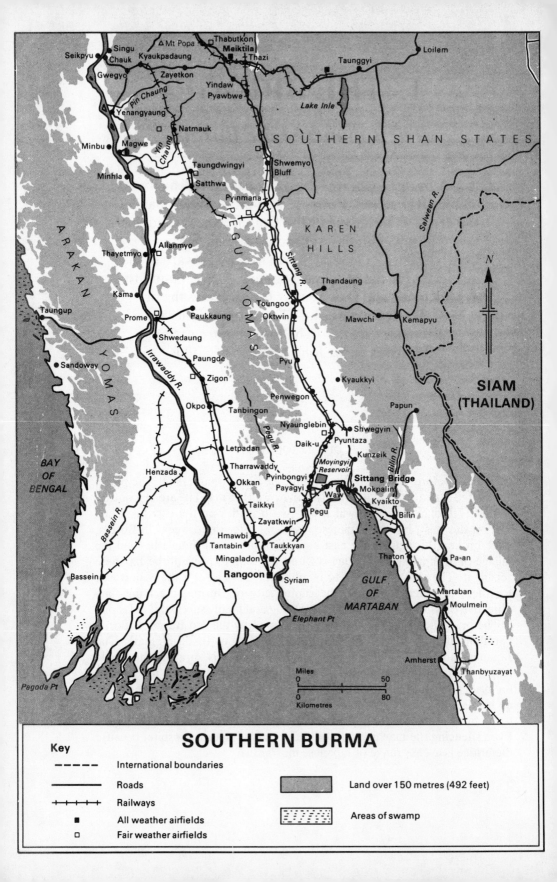

SOUTHERN BURMA

Key

- – – – International boundaries
- ——— Roads
- +++++ Railways
- ■ All weather airfields
- □ Fair weather airfields
- ▨ Land over 150 metres (492 feet)
- ▨ Areas of swamp

The Bridge

At 4.30 am – as Major-General Smyth remembers it – the Brigadier of 48 Brigade, Noel Hugh-Jones, calls a conference at the bridgehead. The Army commander, Lieutenant-General Tom Hutton, has already given orders that the Japanese are to be kept on the east bank of the Sittang for as long as possible. If they manage to seize the bridge after dawn, the way to Rangoon is open to them. It is clear, Hugh-Jones tells the assembled unit commanders and staff officers, that if the bridge is to be blown at all, it must be before daylight, otherwise no sapper will survive the Japanese automatic weapons. There are not enough troops on the other side to stop them.

Hugh-Jones tells his divisional commander, Major-General J. G. Smyth, VC, that he cannot guarantee to hold the bridge any longer against the likelihood of a Japanese onslaught. He wants a definite order from Smyth as to whether he should blow the bridge or not . . . 'If we blow', Smyth thinks, 'it is in the knowledge that two-thirds of the division is left on the far bank. If we do not blow, a complete Japanese division can march straight on to Rangoon.' Smyth knows that the decision is his alone. He makes it, and the responsibility for doing so remains with him for the rest of his life. It takes him less than five minutes to make up his mind: 'Hard though it is, there is very little doubt as to what is the correct course: I give the order that the bridge shall be blown immediately.'[1]

At the western end of the bridge, a group of staff officers armed with tommy-guns acts as rearguard as the covering troops, 1/4 Gurkha Rifles,[2] withdraw across the 1650-foot steel span. By the time everything seems ready, there are only two sections of riflemen in the sand-bagged emplacements on the bridge. Fortunately the Japanese do not probe through the night to see how strongly the bridgehead is being held. Then word comes from the sapper officer: he is not yet ready, the two sections must hang on. Finally the commanding officer of the Gurkhas and one rifleman with an LMG cover the demolition party.

Dawn is fingering the sky as a series of awesome explosions tears the air apart; a blinding flash, a rush of hot air through the darkness, and a shower of steel fragments. Then follows an equally awesome silence. The Japanese have ceased firing. Some of the staff officers on the west bank decide to check the result. As they move forward over what is left of the bridge, their heavy nailed boots clang against the girders, the first sounds to break the silence. Two spans are down, but as they look into the swirling waters, they can see the tops of the girders of the fallen spans. The Malerkotla Field Company have broken the bridge, but not completely, and not irrevocably.

---

[1] J. G. Smyth, *Before the Dawn*, p. 189

[2] C. Mackenzie, *Eastern Epic*, p. 446; 3 Queen Alexandra's Own Gurkha Rifles, in B. Prasad, ed., Official History of the Indian Armed Forces. *Retreat of Burma*, I, 1958, p. 177

Then the sound of Japanese voices is borne along the wind to the officers on the bridge, voices chattering in excitement.

Among the British, Indian and Gurkha troops still on the east bank of the Sittang, there is no excitement. Rage, despair, bitterness at being – as they see it – abandoned to the enemy; these are their first emotions when the meaning of that explosion percolates through. Without their leaders, tired and defeated, some Indian troops surrender tamely to the Japanese. Others reconcile themselves to the only recourse available: if they are to survive, they will have to swim the Sittang. Fearfully, they begin to wade out into the swirling waters . . .

Japan's farthest reach

What did the Japanese want in Burma in the first place? For most of their history, they had been a martial race, administered by a warrior caste with a fierce and unrelenting code of chivalry – the Way of the Samurai – which demanded absolute loyalty and exacted the penalty of painful suicide for failure. But the warriors of that caste fought each other: before the late nineteenth century, only once in Japan's violent history had that violence been directed to the outside world. In 1592, the shogun Hideyoshi had attempted to set himself on the throne of the Chinese Empire, by an invasion of Korea. The invasion had been thwarted, and Japan had re-turned to its accustomed role of seclusion and isolation. Christian mis-sionaries were expelled, and Christian converts massacred, in the sixteenth century, because they were thought to be the spearheads of aggressive Spanish and Portuguese designs on Japan. From 1636, Japan became *sakoku* – 'the closed country' – and, with the exception of a foothold for Dutch merchants on the island of Deshima in Nagasaki harbour, remained so until the mid-nineteenth century.

In 1853, the American admiral Perry compelled the Japanese to accept the overtures of the outside world for trade and diplomacy, an invasion of privacy which ultimately led to the overthrow of the Tokugawa shoguns as incapable of preserving the country against the foreign barbarian; an overthrow followed by the restoration of the Imperial power, and the shift of the capital from Kyoto to Edo (Tokyo). The feudal clans who had operated this overthrow were not partisans of foreign trade. Quite the contrary. But, even in its seclusion, news had penetrated into Japan of the European seizure of most of the countries of East Asia, either by direct annexation – India, Lower Burma, Java, Indo-China, the Philippines – or by commercial pressure. The vast Empire of China had been humiliated by defeat at the hands of the British in the Opium War and compelled to allow trade and the foreigners' presence on their own terms: every nation in Europe seemed to have a foothold on the Chinese coast and in her vast river-basins. The Japanese saw they would go the same way, unless they defended themselves. So western teachers and technicians were employed to teach the Japanese the use and manufacture of the most sophisticated European weapons. French and German instructors helped create a modern army out of conscripts who showed their mettle by defeating the last samurai uprising in 1878, in Kyushu. The British built ships and trained Japanese sailors. Then Japan began to look overseas. Those countries like China and Korea who shared her mode of civilization – in many ways, China was the origin of it – must be made to realize what awaited them if they continued to allow the Europeans to do whatever they wanted. If they would not listen, they must be compelled, even if this meant Japan using force against them. Hence the Sino-Japanese war of 1895, and the annexation of Formosa (Taiwan); and that of Korea in 1910. Japan began to see herself as the only country in Asia with both wit and muscle enough to resist European and American incursions. Was she not intended, at some future date, wrote Field-Marshal Yamagata in 1914, to take over the leadership of the coloured peoples of the world against the aggression of the white races?

Japan's liberal and democratic governments of the 1920s slowed down this process, for a time. Then the economic upheavals of the 1930s revived the belief in military short-cuts to Japanese aims, and soon Japanese officers were pressing the government towards more drastic action in China and, ultimately, to guarantee the possibility of Japanese settlement overseas by occupying Manchuria, invading North China and establishing a puppet government there, and planning the security of Japan's raw materials by conquering those parts of East Asia which were already used for the same purpose by the western colonial powers.

At first, British business interests – the most extensive and powerful in China – had not been uniformly hostile towards Japanese intentions. After all, the presence of the Japanese Army in Manchuria and North China acted as a *cordon sanitaire* against Soviet Russian ambitions in the Far East; and Japanese troops might succeed in imposing a semblance of orderly government on the anarchical chaos which had developed in the Chinese Republic, once the Empire was overthrown in 1911. But this mood did not last, particularly when the Japanese made it clear that their new economic order in East Asia would make it impossible for western companies to trade. And Japan's barbaric methods of imposing her will in China aligned her naturally enough, in western minds, with the fascist and nazi aggressions of Italy and Germany.

The defeat of the colonial powers – France, Belgium, Holland – in 1940, and the comparative helplessness of Great Britain, reduced for a moment to the status of beleaguered island, offered Japan a heaven-sent chance to apply pressure on French Indo-China, where she managed to have the installation of her troops accepted, however unwillingly, by the French authorities (in the North in 1940, in the South in 1941). She applied similar pressure on the Dutch to increase oil exports to Japan from the Dutch East Indies. The Dutch held out, and refused concessions; and America had begun to stir. Throughout the 1930s, American opinion, which had long had a sentimental attachment to China, viewed Japan's behaviour on the international scene with horror; and began to put that horror into a practical form by applying an economic embargo on Japan and finally, in the summer of 1941, by freezing Japanese assets in the US.

As the Japanese saw it, their legitimate ambitions in East Asia were being strangled by those already in economic possession of its wealth, and if necessary they would use force to break out of that stranglehold. As the Americans, British and Dutch saw it, *their* legitimate economic interests were being threatened by a group of military fanatics similar to those who had already, in Germany, begun to take over the continent of Europe. They had seen what had happened when you failed to unite effectively to stop Hitler. So something had to be done to stop the Japanese. Garrisons began to be reinforced, extra troops were raised, ships were sent to naval bases. But never enough. There was no question, for instance, of Britain being able to defend herself against the Germans in Europe and the Middle East, and at the same time to fight a full-scale war against the Japanese in Asia. So an immense bluff was undertaken called 'Fortress Singapore', the myth of whose invincibility was, as the C-in-C Far East told an American correspondent in Malaya, intended to deter the Japanese from even starting hostilities.

The Japanese were not fooled. They knew exactly what strength would be deployed against them, and they were confident they could cope with it. If the Americans refused to relax their stranglehold, then Japan must go out and seize those raw materials denied her. In essence, she must seize the Dutch East Indies, and ensure that she had, as a result, enough oil to keep her industries and navy going. But if she were to ship that oil back to Japan, her ships would be vulnerable to the two powers whose presence dominated the sea lanes: Great Britain, from Malaya and Borneo, and the US, from the Philippines. In other words, Japan would need not merely to annex the Dutch East Indies, but conquer Malaya and the Philippines as well. Basically, that was the Japanese plan for South-East Asia.

It did not include Burma. And indeed, early Japanese planning never envisaged the conquest of Burma. It *did* anticipate that Great Britain, once Japanese armies were deployed down the Malay Peninsula on the way to assault Singapore, would try to counter-attack from South-West Burma, from which it would be quite possibie to cut the Kra Isthmus and the railway from Bangkok to Singapore; and also to send reinforcements by air from India, for which purpose Burma held vital staging-points at Akyab and Victoria Point. Japanese Imperial General Headquarters had therefore planned a limited campaign to secure her Malayan flank against British reprisals from Burma. It would be enough, for this purpose, to seize Tenasserim and its airfields, and the port of Rangoon.

But there was another factor in the Burma situation. From Rangoon to the Chinese border at Wanting ran the Burma Road, one of the two surviving lifelines of supply to Nationalist China. Japan had managed to block China's coastline and occupy her major cities, which should have been enough to bring the Chinese to their knees. Unaccountably, the Chinese fought on, and drew their capital and headquarters back, far into the interior, to Chungking. They could still receive supplies from the Russians, across the vastnesses of Central Asia, through Urumchi; and from the West, which could feed them through French Indo-China – along the railway which led from the port of Haiphong to Yunnan Province – and through Burma. Diplomatic pressure was exerted on Britain to close the Burma Road, and indeed for a few months in 1940, when Britain was in no state to answer back, this pressure succeeded briefly in its aim. But not for long, and while the road remained, it was a continual source of irritation. Was it not possible to close the road, if not by diplomatic means, then by making things difficult for the British among the Burmese population? Japanese agents began to explore the sentiments of dissident Burmese party leaders and those young Burmese, ex-students for the most part, whose party of Thakins ('Masters') had as its avowed purpose to drive the British out of Burma. So, long before there was any precise thought of a military campaign, Japanese agents were active in Rangoon and elsewhere, stirring up what mischief they could.

'Ourselves alone', Burmese version

In 1941, Burma was – as it still is – largely an agricultural country, its economy based on rice and timber, though it was also rich in minerals, with oil wells at Yenangyaung on the banks of the Irrawaddy and the wolfram mines at Mawchi in the Karen Hills, which produced a third of the world's wolfram. Its population had reached 17,000,000: 10,000,000 Burmans, 4,000,000 Karens, 2,000,000 Shans, and 1,000,000 hill tribesmen – Nagas, Chins and Kachins. There were also sizeable minorities of Indians and Chinese.

The country is bigger than France but elongated in shape, and from Fort Hertz in the north to Rangoon extends about as far as the distance from Biarritz to Newcastle-on-Tyne. Then there is a long finger of territory of the same length stretching down into the Malay Peninsula. The country is watered by four main rivers. The Irrawaddy is 1300 miles long, up to three miles wide in parts and navigable from the sea to Bhamo, a distance of 800 miles, which was regularly served by the Irrawaddy Flotilla Company steamers twice a week. You then went on as far as Myitkyina by country boat. Its tributary, the Chindwin, roughly marked the border with India, and was navigable by shallow draught steamers. The much shorter Sittang ran east of the Pegu Yomas, and was crossed at Sittang/Mokpalin by a railway bridge on the line going from Rangoon into Tenasserim (there was a railway line, but no road, for much of this distance between Waw and Kyaikto). The Sittang was also characterized by a tidal bore, which made crossing it difficult. The mighty Salween for some of its length – it actually rose in China – marked the frontier with Siam (Thailand). It is longer than the Irrawaddy, not navigable, and no bridges crossed it, so you had to use ferries.

All these rivers ran roughly north and south, and that is how communications ran in Burma, since most Burmese had always travelled and traded by water. Some parts of Burma were really only reachable by water anyway. The Arakan coastal strip on the Bay of Bengal was more easily reachable by boat from Calcutta or Chittagong than from the interior of Burma itself: only one track ran into the central plain from Arakan, via Taungup and Prome, but this was not suitable for cars. The situation in the Tenasserim finger was a little better, but not much. There was no complete road from Rangoon to Moulmein – the gap between Waw and Kyaikto interrupted it; but the railway went down as far as Ye, provided you were prepared to cross the mouth of the Salween by ferry between Martaban and Moulmein. Cart-tracks, not roads, connected Thailand with Burma across Tenasserim.

With India, across the Chindwin and Chin Hills, there were also tracks, nothing more. With China, the case was different. Japan had seized most of China's coastline by 1938, and cut the Hankow-Canton railway. This left two possible entries for goods and munitions into China, one via French Indo-China (Haiphong to Yunnan), the other via the so-called Burma Road, which the Chinese had built with handtools from Kunming to the border with Burma at Wanting, where it met the road which led from Lashio to Mandalay and Rangoon. The Burma Road was 750 miles long, and the journey took five days; it did not carry much, in comparison with the lifeline from Haiphong, but it was better than nothing. This was Burma's main road; many of the other roads were roads only in name, and in the rainy season could be impassable because of flooded *chaungs* (streams and rivers) or because the heavy rains had washed away a hillside and the road with it. The hills rose to 3000 feet in some areas, but to 8000 in the Chin Hills and to 12000 in the Naga Hills on the Indian border. So Burma was a country of immense topographical contrasts: high jungles, swampy coastal plains, alluvial deltas, a central plain with a dry triangle (Mandalay-Magwe-Toungoo) in the middle, the whole walled in by high mountains which separated it from India in the west, China in the north, and Siam in the east.

The southwest monsoon blows for five months from mid-May to mid-October, and turns vast areas of the country into swamp and quagmire – parts of Arakan have an annual rainfall of 200 inches. From October to March, however, the climate is delightful, even in the crowded town streets.

8

Not that large towns were a feature of Burmese landscape – only Rangoon and Mandalay really qualified for the term 'large' – otherwise Burma was made up of small towns and villages. Many of the names made famous by the battles of 1942–5 were nothing but a few streets of wooden houses and shops, with a pagoda. The jungles were, of course, teeming with wildlife. You could hunt tiger in Arakan, and have timber dragged to the river by herds of elephants.

How had the British come into this beautiful country in the first place? In 1824, the Burmese had begun to disturb the peace of the East India Company by forays on the Indian frontier. When the fighting was over, Britain annexed the parts of Burma more obviously controllable from the sea: the two coastal strips, Arakan and Tenasserim. In a second war in 1852, the Burmese were again defeated and Britain annexed Pegu the following year. King Thibaw made war against Britain in 1885, and this was followed by the capture of Mandalay and the annexation of Upper Burma in 1886. There was no sudden peace. Thibaw's army dispersed and took to brigandage (dacoity) and it took 30,000 troops five years to suppress it. A beginning of self-government (excluding law and order, finance, defence) was given to Burma in 1923, as it had been to other Indian provinces after the Government of India Act of 1919. It was little enough, and the Burmese people, particularly the students of Rangoon University, grew increasingly restive after the First World War; there were riots in 1930 and 1938, partly anti-British, partly anti-Indian. Indian chettyars (money-lenders) had begun to acquire vast amounts of Burmese land. The Government of Burma Act (1935) separated Burma from India, effectively from April 1937, though many spheres were still reserved to the Governor and his advisers and were not the province of elected representatives: the scheduled areas, the hill tracts to west, north and east, did not come under their jurisdiction. For minds longing for complete independence, and impressed by the achievements of the Indian Congress Party and the romantic rebelliousness of Sinn Fein, there was still a long way to go. Perhaps the Japanese would help?

*   *   *

That question was in the minds of many among the more politically articulate sections of the Burmese people. Students of Rangoon University staged a strike in 1936, just before their final examinations. Six hundred students camped on the slopes of Shwe Dagon Pagoda Hill to win public support, then returned to the University every morning to picket candidates who turned up for the examinations and were thus considered as blacklegs. The technique was devastingly simple: the strikers lay across the entrances to the building, and since it was an unpardonable insult to a male Buddhist to have his body trodden on, and no Burmese dare inflict such an insult, the blockade was effective.[1] The attractive moment for staging the strike was no doubt a factor in its popularity, even though there were students who could not afford to spend another year waiting to graduate; but in theory the strike was against the autocratic nature of the Principal's administration of the college, as it was held desirable that he should be 'more accountable to Burmese political leaders'.[2] The strike was therefore, ultimately, based on nationalism.

Two and a half years later, the novelist H. G. Wells, on a world lecture tour to convince audiences of the desirability of a confederation of free people sustaining a world law, found to his distress that Burmese ears were ill-attuned to his idealistic message. He breakfasted with U Ba Llang (Wells's spelling), recently released from gaol for sedition, who listened to him impatiently and burst out, 'Tell that to your English friends.' U Ba Llang's ideas, Wells noted, seemed to be 'a mix-up of resentful nationalism, a sort of crude communism – communism of sentiment rather than organization – and what I might call insurrectionism at large. All the negative stuff in the world.' He was distressed that U Ba Llang did not wish to listen to Wells pleading for help to a Free China: 'He cared no more for the freedom of the Chinese than he cared for the future of an ant-hill in Patagonia.'

Wells was sure that the existing Imperial system in the East was paralysed, and he listened with attention when the PEN Club of Burma gave him tea in a boat club by the river, where the young men and women were deliberately wearing Burmese dress: 'Many of the men had those round pink silk caps with a coquettish pink ribbon bow at the side, a little yellow jacket and a gay undivided trouser, so to speak, which is the normal costume of a sober and serious man in Rangoon.' He spoke to them of his conception of a broad-based English-linked world community, which would transcend the squabbles of their petty militant nationalisms. They countered by showing him snapshots of a police *lathi* charge on students a few months before, and by telling him of press censorship, of an education system meant to train them to become nothing better than clerks or salesmen. He proclaimed a future in which the two sides of the question, imperialism and nationalism, would be transcended. 'There is another world,' he told them, 'the free-thinking, free-speaking, liberal world. Belong to that.'

He got the answer he should have expected: 'But our government won't let us. Our censorship won't let us. Our schools prevent us. The past stands in our way. Our boys are learning more by striking, argument and reading forbidden literature, than by sitting in class-rooms. They are learning to feel responsible for Burma.'[3]

---

[1] Mi Mi Khaing, *Burmese Family*, 1946, p. 97

[2] ibid.

[3] H. G. Wells, *Travels of a Republican Radical In Search of Hot Water*, 1939, pp. 84–8

Paradoxically, the very man who, as Burma's first Premier after separation from India, had to refuse the Rangoon students' demands, Dr Ba Maw, felt uncomfortable as he did so, and in the same month – January 1939 – as he finally rejected them (a few weeks before Wells's visit) he had welcomed an approach by the Japanese who saw the possibility of using the resentments of frustrated Burmese nationalism as a weapon against the British. The Japanese consulate in Rangoon was, of course, *au fait* with Dr Ba Maw's anti-British sentiments, and approaches were made to him after he became Prime Minister – in 1938 and again in 1939 – to do something to stop the traffic of munitions into China along the Burma Road from the port of Rangoon. He was offered a substantial sum of money, but told his Japanese visitors that decisions on the Road were out of Burmese hands. There was no question, either, of Ba Maw himself engineering an armed revolt against the British, which would immobilize traffic on the Road: the Burmese were not ready for insurrection.

It was easy enough for the Japanese to make the initial contact with Ba Maw. His family doctor for many years was a Japanese, Dr Suzuki, who had close relations with the Japanese consulate in Rangoon and also with Japanese agents then active in Burma. It seems clear that Ba Maw approached *him* rather than the other way round: convenient monsoon-induced lumbago caused Ba Maw to call upon Dr Suzuki's ministrations fairly frequently, and during the regular treatment visits Ba Maw sounded him out on what Japan could do for the Burmese independence movement. Nothing loath, Suzuki contacted his consul. This set wheels in motion. In the company of Thein Maung, Ba Maw had a few meetings with the consul, and Japanese naval officers also called on him. Ba Maw gathered that they had already been in touch with some of the young Thakins. Thein Maung, with Japanese assistance, went to Tokyo in November 1939, and returned with a guarantee that financial aid would be forthcoming when Ba Maw started his proposed agitation for independence. The idea was political, though, not military: no armed insurrection was hinted at at this stage.

That it should be naval officers who met Ba Maw is not surprising. South-East Asia, with its British naval bases, was first and foremost a naval problem for the Japanese; only later, when a campaign of conquest was positively envisaged, did the Army begin to carry out preparatory tasks such as espionage and subversion. One reserve naval officer, whose wife practised dentistry in Rangoon, had come to know the Burmese very well and moved about Burma with a self-assurance born of a conviction that the British would not harm him, since they were obviously eager not to cross swords with Japan while fully occupied in Europe. Kokubu Shōzō had published books and articles about Burma, and his knowledge was not the superficial pragmatic knowledge of the secret agent. It was real. But Kokubu's confidence led him astray. By and large the Japanese consulate was wary of him, since they felt he would put his foot in it some time. He did.

In the company of a highly-placed Japanese diplomat,Ohashi Chūichi, Kokubu went up to Upper Burma to 'visit' the famous Gokteik Viaduct, a railway bridge on the Road leading from Burma to Yunnan. The British had been told that a Japanese general called Tsuchihashi was going to blow up this vital bridge. There *was* such a general, in command of the Japanese forces in neighbouring French Indo-China, but either because the British confused him with Ohashi, or because they did not like the idea of Japanese snooping round a sensitive viaduct, they arrested Kokubu and his companion. The outwardly mild-mannered Kokubu suggested to Ohashi that they should seize the rifle of the sentry guarding them, shoot him, and escape, but Ohashi calmed him down and pointed out that an incident of that kind would put a damper on any Japanese activities in Burma from that time on. The Japanese consulate was contacted, the consul apologized for the misdemeanour, and the two were freed. The episode had consequences for the future of Burma. The Japanese consulate warned Ba Maw off Kokubu, as a dangerous contact, and although Kokubu visited Ba Maw in gaol several times after the British arrested him for sedition in August 1940, there was no question of entrusting Kokubu with further contacts. On the other hand, his friendships in Thakin Ba Sein's party began to bear unexpected fruit, also through failure. Ba Sein's group was a splinter party, which had not joined the coalition between Ba Maw and the Thakins, called the Freedom Bloc. Kokubu recommended Ba Sein to his headquarters in Tokyo, and was told to smuggle him out of Burma to make contact with the man at the centre of all Japanese espionage in South-East Asia, Colonel Tamura, military attaché at the Bangkok Embassy. Ba Sein made for the Thai border, but was arrested just before entering Thailand, while having what he thought would be his last sleep on Burmese soil. The resonance of Ba Sein's escape attempt was what counted: the young Thakin leader Aung San heard of it, and it turned his mind towards help from the Japanese.

White man's burden

The fact that many young Burmese, idealists or narrow nationalists (however one chooses to regard them), could so easily be recruited against British rule, is perhaps hardly surprising. Many British in Burma were devoted both to the country and its people, and had made great strides in providing educational opportunities and establishing a system of law and order. But Britain's main motive for her presence in Burma, as seen by Maurice Collis, for example, was mercantile. Of his merchant companions on the way to Rangoon by ship in 1912, 'Their aim', he wrote, ' . . .was to buy cheap in Asia and sell dear in Europe. As it was rarely necessary for these people to know the Burmese language, they were ignorant of it and so had never spoken to a Burman except in English or Hindustani . . . Their prejudices were very marked, their opinions jejune, but they felt themselves to be the most patriotic of men, for their lives were devoted, not like the Indian civilians, to giving the Burmese a sound administration . . . but to conducting to London the stream of profits, on which the very existence of England depended.'[1] 'You will get your independence,' an American oil driller at Yenangyaung once said to U Pu, a member of Ba Maw's Freedom Bloc, 'when your country ceases to produce a single drop of earth-oil and when there is not a single teak in your forests and when your paddy fields have become barren. These British have come out to Burma just to make money.'[2]

The effect of British rule had been to bring considerable material improvements to Burmese life, of that there can be no question: modern education, good roads, hospitals, irrigation. But the development of Burma's resources in oil, timber and minerals was the work of British, Chinese or Indian capital. The Burmese, whatever their role in the legislature since separation from India in 1937, had no control over the economy of their country. Their capital city, Rangoon, was more than half Indian in population. The Indians, through their grip on land, had become a hated minority, and, as the Burmese saw it, only existed under the umbrella of British rule. Saya San's rebellion of 1936 had been in part directed against the Indian minority as much as against the British (it was at his trial that Ba Maw first achieved eminence, as defence counsel, and earned the dislike of many British residents, who saw him as a man misusing a European legal education, a person of 'immense vanity, who looked and behaved like a film star').[3]

Even the armed forces of Burma were hardly Burmese at all. In 1939 the Burma Defence Force contained only 472 Burmans as against 3,197 Karens, Chins and Kachins – hill tribes with a lower stage of political development, and therefore safer from the British point of view. It was imprudent to enlist Burmans 'in a force which might have to be used against their fellow countrymen'.[4]

Shortly after the outbreak of war with Japan, the C-in-C, Far East, Air Chief Marshal Sir Robert Brooke-Popham, who had his hands full with the invasion of Malaya, but who was still responsible for Burma, set down his thoughts on the problem in a few 'Notes on Burma'. 'Most of the hill country in the East', he observed, 'consists of the Shan States; the

[1] M. Collis, *The Journey Outward*, 1952, pp. 121–2

[2] Ba Maw, *Breakthrough in Burma*, 1968, p. 78

[3] F. Tennyson Jesse, *The Story of Burma*, p. 169

[4] D. G. Hall, *Burma*, 1950, p. 167

population is loyal to the British Empire, several battalions and other units were raised, and in some cases the local rulers were paying for them.' A satisfactory state of affairs, due largely, he thought, to the credit of the Commissioner, Mr Fogarty. The population of central Burma was another kettle of fish, and caused anxiety:

> First, there was a frequent cry for independence, starting perhaps with Dominion status. Secondly, there was hostility against In-dians in Burma. This was mainly due to the question of land; the Indians had advanced money on mortgage and were gradually acquiring ownership of a large proportion of the fertile lands in the river valleys; the possibility of a general attack on the Indian population had always to be kept in mind.

But there was something deeper than this. Religion was a factor, too. Like the Japanese, the Burmese were Buddhists, though from a different branch; and religion and politics were mingled: 'Some of the leading priests were loyal to Great Britain, but a great many were not, and inculcated the idea of independence.'

These were all, in one way or another, security issues. But Brooke-Popham went on, in a mood of wondering disbelief:

> Apart from this, it is rather disheartening, after all the years we have been in Burma and the apparent progress that has taken place under our rule, to find that the majority of the population want to be rid of us and that some of the leaders, for instance the late [sic] Prime Minister, U Saw, were actually in communication with the Japanese at a time when they were our potential, if not our actual, enemies. We pride ourselves on being worthy to be trusted with mandates and talk of regarding ourselves as trustees for the advancement of backward peoples. If we are to prove ourselves worthy of this it is up to everyone, especially to those on whom the burden of Empire will fall after the war, to consider what was wrong in Burma.

Brooke-Popham had considered this already, and as the Japanese armies were drilling their way into Burma, aided and abetted by the youth of the Burma Independence Army, he drew his conclusions:

> I can only suggest three things that are, at any rate, worthy of investigation. First, a tendancy [sic] among Englishmen to regard themselves as naturally superior in every way to any coloured race, without taking steps to ensure that this is always a fact. Secondly, a failure to develop a sympathetic understanding with

14

the Burmese, to know what they were really thinking all the time, what were their particular difficulties and aspirations. Thirdly, the fact that the majority of non-official Englishmen in Burma were more concerned with making money and getting high dividends from their investments than of benefiting the native population.[1]

Racialism, arrogance, aloofness, greed. There was more in the picture of the British presence in Burma than this; but enough of the accusation was true (and the source is no prejudiced witness) to allow it to be understood why the Japanese impact on Burma was what it was.

Gaoling the PM

Japanese infiltration into Burma's ruling classes had gone even further than the flirtation with Ba Maw suggests. His premiership came to an end in March 1939. His successor, U Pu, expressed open support for Britain in her war against Germany, since she was, he said, fighting a just war against tyranny. It was a decent gesture, and hard enough to make politically, since Burma had been dragged willy-nilly into the war, her legislature not having been consulted: to be at war or peace was the Governor's decision alone under the terms of the 1936 Act. Burmese opinion was far from solidly behind this affirmation, and one of his ministers, U Ba Thi, passed through the legislature, in March 1940, a motion that support for Britain should be conditional on the promise of early Dominion status for Burma. U Pu's government fell in September 1940.

The third Premier since separation from India, U Saw, has been described by a civil servant with long experience of Burma as a 'demagogue of mediocre education, ambitious for himself and without scruples'.[2] But the Governor, Dorman-Smith, who had more and more the feeling that Burma had been run in a stuffy and rigid way, rather took to U Saw's openly disreputable style. U Saw was crafty, he could see that, but he was also warm, human and amusing: at a party in Government House, the Governor taxed him openly with charging 10,000 rupees for an appointment in Mandalay. U Saw indignantly denied selling government patronage, then added disarmingly that the figure was, in fact, 15,000 and he would stop it.[3]

Like Ba Maw, U Saw was passionately dedicated to Burmese independence. He had raised a private army of youths, the Galon Army, to back this demand, and also controlled a leading newspaper. But that was on the surface. Five years before the premiership he had visited Japan, and rumour

---

[1] Brooke-Popham Papers, Liddell-Hart Archive, File V, No. 7/18/2

[2] M. Collis, *Last and First in Burma*, 1956, p. 22

[3] ibid. p. 25

had it that on his return he was in Japanese pay. When it became obvious that, in spite of Dorman-Smith's urgings, the British Cabinet would not give a definite promise of Dominion status in exchange for popular co-operation in the war effort which U Saw had provided, Dorman-Smith suggested that he should go to London to present his case in person. U Saw agreed to go, provided the reason for his visit was described as being 'with a view to declaring full self-government for Burma after victory'.[1] Churchill refused to use this phrase, but U Saw nonetheless set off for London in October 1941 with the Secretary of the Defence Council, U Tin Tut. As a parting gesture, the Premier flew his private plane round and round the spire of the Shwe Dagon Pagoda – a gesture of prayer which the more pious Buddhists of Rangoon found offensive, disrespectful, and completely in character.

After conversations with Churchill and Leopold Amery, the Colonial Secretary, who would promise nothing but a vaguely liberal treatment for Burma after the war, and refused to discuss constitutional issues while locked in battle with Germany, U Saw began his journey home in November, angry and disillusioned. The original route was to be across America and the Philippines, but the attack on Pearl Harbour interrupted westward passenger traffic across the Pacific. U Saw had got as far as Hawaii on 8 December, and saw the shattered US Pacific Fleet still burning after the Japanese raid.

He and U Tin Tut were then re-routed via Portugal, and on his way through Lisbon he called on the Japanese Consul-General. The next day the Japanese Ambassador in Lisbon cabled to Tokyo an account of the interview in which he said the Burmese Premier had promised that if Japan invaded Burma, the Burmese would rebel against the British and help the Japanese to drive them out.

The British had, as it happens, broken the Japanese diplomatic code, and messages from the Lisbon embassy were regularly intercepted and decoded. The information was soon on Amery's desk in Whitehall. Even if the Ambassador had been exaggerating, it was going to be an unacceptable risk to let U Saw go back to Burma. He and U Tin Tut were therefore arrested in Haifa, as they touched down on the next leg eastward. U Tin Tut had not been involved, and was later released. U Saw was interned for the duration.

So two of Burma's three Premiers since the separation with India had made subversive overtures to the Japanese; and an entire party of student extremists was being actively trained by the Japanese for political and military collaboration.

[1] ibid. p. 32

Colonel Suzuki and the Thirty Comrades

In May 1940, a representative of the Japanese newspaper *Yomiuri Shimbun*, calling himself Minami Masuyo, arrived in Rangoon. His quiet, smiling, inconspicuous demeanour was a great contrast to Kokubu's self-assurance, and he spent his time, as a good journalist should, listening carefully and watching the course of events. He was accompanied by Sugii Mitsuru, a member of the Economic Bureau of a Japanese corporation acting from Shanghai, the East Asia Development Organization (Kōa-in), and Sugii's colleague, Mizutani. Minami's quiet manner was as much of a disguise as his name and function. He was, in fact, Colonel Suzuki Keiji, of Imperial General Headquarters, and his real role was to sound out Burmese political opinion and assess how it could be used to carry out his assignment: cutting the Burma Road and its arms supplies to China. Sugii and Mizutani were his assistants in this project.[1]

Colonel Suzuki was to play a considerable role in the future of Burma. A swashbuckler, he had already been returned to Tokyo from Shanghai where he had embroiled himself in a local dispute between the Japanese army and navy. When Imperial General Headquarters decided to make some army contacts in Burma, as a balance to Kokubu's naval sources, the job was given to Suzuki and he threw himself into it with characteristic zeal and vigour. He became secretary of the Japan-Burma Association in Tokyo, one of many groups which Japan had instituted in order to link herself to various Asian countries with a cultural bond that might later have a political pay-off. Late in 1939, Ba Maw's friend, the politician Thein Maung, visited Tokyo and made contacts with the Japan-Burma Association. Thein Maung ran a newspaper, *New Burma*, which for some time had been preaching the ideal of looking to the East for political inspiration. He was the vital contact through whom Suzuki could forge a link with political parties in Burma.

A more colourful figure acted as a go-between once Suzuki reached Rangoon. This was the Japanese Buddhist monk, Nagai, who had lived in Burma for many years, and was a familiar sight in the pagodas, chanting sutras and ringing bells (he was a member of the Nichiren sect which specializes in bell-ringing). Like the Burmese *pongyis* (monks) Nagai lived by begging food from door to door, and so could call freely anywhere in Rangoon without arousing suspicion, a useful accomplishment for

---

[1] On Suzuki, see *Biruma Kōryaku Sakusen* (The taking of Burma), pp. 8–12, pp. 117–34; Hatakeyama Seikō, *Hiroku Rikugun Nakano Gakkō* (The Army's secret school at Nakano), continuation, 1971, pp. 154–64; another 'continuation' of the same title, pp. 26–49; Yamamoto Masayoshi, *Biruma kōsaku to bōryaku shōkō* (An intelligence officer in the Burma operation), 1978; Kawashima Takenobu, 'Biruma dokuritsu giyūgun to Minami Kikan' (The BIA and the Minami Organization), in *Rekishi to Jinbutsu* (Man and History), special issue on the Nakano School, October, 1980, pp. 134–43; Joyce Lebra, *Japanese-trained armies in Southeast Asia*, 1977; Louis Allen, *End of the War in Asia*, 1976.

someone who was in the service of Japanese Intelligence. Nagai acted as go-between for Thein Maung and Suzuki, who made some useful contacts among the young Thakins. His aim, at the time, was quite simple: an armed insurrection would be one way of closing the Burma Road, and help to the Thakins was one way of achieving this. So whereas the diplomats in the Japanese consulate were wary of upsetting British political sensibilities by overtures to dissidents, Suzuki had no such inhibitions. More than this, he came to believe in the inevitability of Burmese independence from Britain, not just as an element in Japan's political campaigns in East Asia, but as a thing in itself. This belief, which he held with genuine passion, was later to be the cause of fierce disputes with Japanese Army commanders.

Like many Eastern politicians who were eagerly awaiting the moment to emancipate themselves from the European colonial powers, Dr Ba Maw watched events in Europe in the summer of 1940 with electrified anticipation. Surely this was Burma's chance? He had several meetings with his Japanese doctor, Suzuki (not to be confused with the colonel – the name is as common as Smith) and the Japanese consul, Kuga. Kuga told him that the Japanese knew India was in pretty much the same condition, and that Subhas Chandra Bose, the militant Congress leader, who had been Mayor of Calcutta, and was an admirer of Mussolini, had already contacted the Japanese for help. Bose had demanded financial aid – 10,000,000 rupees – and 10,000 rifles. 'We want half that amount in Burma to begin with,' Ba 'Maw told him, 'and we shall also want Japanese instructors.'[1]

The British were not unaware of these pro-Japanese conspiracies going on under their noses. They arrested Ba Maw on 6 August 1940, and sentenced him to a year's imprisonment for infringing the Defence of Burma Act. A recent declaration by the Governor had affirmed that Britain intended to grant Dominion status to Burma after the war, but in his new capacity as leader of the Freedom Bloc, a union between his own party, the Sinyetha (Proletariat) Party, and the rebellious young Thakins of Rangoon University, Ba Maw had no intention of settling for that. One of the young Thakins, Aung San, had already been to Chungking, and had received encouragement from the Nationalist Chinese. In May 1940, he had gone to Ramgarh, in India, to attend the Indian National Congress, as one of a Thakin delegation. It seemed unlikely that the Thakins, with this kind of encouragement, would ever turn to Japan, which was, after all, the fascist aggressor against Nationalist China and the very opposite of Gandhi's pacifist ideals. On the other hand, Japan and her Axis partners were the most likely sources of help against Britain, and other Burmese had already made contacts with the Japanese. At any rate, the British were cracking down on the Thakins, and as they had not hesitated to arrest an ex-Premier, Aung San knew that if he did not get out of Burma his days as

[1] Ba Maw, *Breakthrough in Burma*, 1968, pp. 114–15

18

a free man were numbered. Eight days after Ba Maw had been gaoled, Aung San with another Thakin, Bo Yan Aung, stowed away in a Norwegian freighter, the *Hai Lee*, carrying rice to Amoy on the southern coast of China, then under Japanese military occupation.

It was not a Japanese ship. The Japanese vice-consul in Rangoon, Fuki, had already conveyed to Ba Maw, who had told the Japanese of Aung San's intended escape, that no Japanese ship would dare to carry him out of Rangoon harbour: the British surveillance was too strict. He should go to China on a boat belonging to a country that was friendly to the British, Fuki told Ba Maw. 'To Amoy. From there we will take him to Japan.'[1] There was no question, then, of directly associating the Japanese with the first part of the escape, but Ba Maw's Sinyetha Party had the answer to that. Tun Shwe, one of its members, was a labour contractor to the ships of the British India Steam Navigation Company. Aung San and Yan Aung could be smuggled into the docks as dock labourers.

Once they reached Amoy the two Thakins found themselves stranded and alone, with their money running out, and no sign of help forthcoming. They had assumed that their contacts with the Rangoon consulate would have guaranteed an immediate and favourable reception by the Japanese authorities on the China coast, but Aung San had not told the consulate exactly when he was going. It is likely, too, that the Japanese army in China had little connection with diplomats in Burma, and Fuki's messages would have gone through the usual, slow, channels. Aung San fell ill and, almost destitute, went to live in a sleazy lodging house in a village called Kun Long Su outside Amoy. Suzuki heard about Aung San's predicament, and acted at once.

With Sugii, he flew to Bangkok and went to the Japanese Embassy. From there, he sent off photographs of the two Thakins to Kempei GHQ on Formosa, with the full story and a request for the Kempei (Military Police) to scour the China coast and pick up the boys. Major Kanda, of the Amoy Kempei, finally traced them to the lodging house in Kun Long Su, where he found Aung San very weak, suffering from dysentery, and very downhearted. The encounter decided Aung San's destination for him. In November 1940, he and Yan Aung were flown to Tokyo, and met at the airport by Suzuki.

It was at last the opportunity Suzuki had been waiting for. Here was direct evidence of the possibility of active intervention in Burma which he could show to Imperial General Headquarters. He put forward a plan for an organization which would take young Thakins out of Burma, give them military training, and infiltrate them back into Burma through Thailand. So the Minami Kikan (Minami Organization), with Suzuki at its head, was officially set up in February 1941, with its headquarters in Tokyo and

[1] ibid. p. 120

operational centre in Bangkok. In four towns along the Thai border with Burma – Chiengmai, Rahaeng, Kanburi, and Ranaung – branches were established under the guise of commercial undertakings. The towns were selected as possible jumping-off points for a Japanese invasion of Burma, and the heads of the branches undertook work in the area which enabled them to survey territory. In Rahaeng, for instance, the officer in charge was Lt Takahashi Hachirō who explored the roads and tracks leading to the border, in the guise of a forestry expert; Lt Noda Takeshi at the branch at Kanchanaburi operated a grocer's shop and used river transport up the River Khwae Noi (of later, and more sinister, fame). This offered the shortest route to Tavoy. The head of the Ranaung branch, feigning forestry and fishing interests, surveyed the area leading to Victoria Point, the southernmost village in Burma, and the site of a crucial airfield on the reinforcement route from India to Singapore.

From these various points on the border, young Burmans were infiltrated back into their home country, after training by the Japanese. The Japanese officers themselves had already received a thorough training in espionage techniques in Japan, since over half of them were graduates of the army espionage school, the Nakano School in Tokyo. Even so, Suzuki put an unfamiliar edge on their training. He despised old-fashioned warnings to steer clear of drink and women. Drink as much as you like, he told the Minami Kikan neophytes, and have women; but don't get uncontrollably drunk and don't lose your head when you're with a woman. 'Don't wage war as if what matters is promotion and medals. That's what soldiers tend to do, they wage war looking backwards, as if the General Staff and War Ministry were breathing down their necks. Well, as far as I'm concerned, the enemy's in front. *Teki wa tsune ni mae ni iru.*'[1]

In point of fact, the enemy *was* behind, in his own Army headquarters, as he and the Thakins of the Burma Independence Army in the end discovered. But in the meanwhile, his enthusiasm carried everything before it. The Japanese would bring thirty members of his party out of Burma, he told Aung San, give them training, supply them with arms, and infiltrate them back. Then they could begin guerrilla action against the British. This would free southern Burma and an independent government could be set up by the Burmese themselves. It was not long before Suzuki managed to assemble his thirty candidates in Tokyo, and from there they were sent to Hainan Island for rigorous military training under Capt Kawashima Takenobu, a Military Academy graduate and product of the Nakano School. The young Thakins were soon exhausted by the stiff military discipline and drills of their jungle training camp – 'We ended each day limp and dazed with fatigue', said Tun Oke[2] – but their intense

[1] Hatakeyama, op.cit., p. 32
[2] Ba Maw, op.cit., p. 133

patriotism and the feeling they would soon be going into battle for their country made them endure. Imperial General Headquarters was not as quick to use them as Suzuki had hoped, and, in contravention of distinct orders *not* to send them to Burma yet, Suzuki despatched four Thakins via Bangkok and across the border. At the same time, he purged his Kikan of Japanese navy influences, partly because he and Kokubu did not get on, partly from traditional Army-Navy rivalry. In August 1941 the Japanese Navy formally withdrew from the Kikan and the Army was on its own. This had repercussions many years later in Burmese politics: just as the entire Japanese aid was channelled through Suzuki and his organization, so the fact that it was Aung San and his friends among the Thakins who were the first recipients of aid and training gave them a foothold in the future of Burma which members of the other parties failed to achieve.

The emotional bond between Suzuki and the Thakins was confirmed by dramatic oath-taking. Suzuki himself adopted the Burmese name Bo Mogyo ('Thunderbolt') and a story was spread about him that he was the descendant of a Burmese prince, the fulfilment in person of a prophecy to drive the British out of Burma. The other members of the Kikan took Burmese names as well, and the Thakins gave themselves fresh titles with the prefix 'Bo' ('officer'). Then followed the ceremony known as 'thwe thauk' ('blood drinking'). The Thirty Comrades gathered round a silver bowl, each slit a finger till blood dripped into the bowl, mixed it with strong liquor, and drank. All then swore, in unison, an oath 'to be indissolubly bound together by this bond of blood when fighting the British enemy'. It left the young men, as Ba Maw claims, 'taut and inflamed'.[1]

On 31 December 1941, three weeks after Japan declared war on Great Britain and the US, the *Shutsu-jin-shiki* (ceremony on leaving for the front) was performed in Bangkok. The Thirty Comrades had recruited other young Burmese from the Burmese settlements round Bangkok and areas near the Burmese border. About 300 lined up in front of Colonel Suzuki. He read out the order dissolving his own organization, the Minami Kikan, and inaugurating the Burma Independence Army. He named himself as its first commander, with Captain Kawashima – under his Burmese name of Bo Aye – as second in command. Aung San, calling himself Bo Te Za, was given the rank of major-general, and all the other comrades and the Japanese instructors were similarly exalted. The army was to split into six columns. Suzuki, with Aung San, would lead the first two through the Thai towns of Rahaeng and Mae Sot with the main Japanese invasion force. Bo Ne Win (the present head of state in Burma) with a Japanese lieutenant, would act as a sabotage unit once the border was crossed. The fourth column would act as a liaison unit for the Japanese 55th Division in Tenasserim, and columns five and six would be combat formations, one to

[1] Ba Maw, op. cit., p. 139

invade Burma from Kanchanaburi, through Tavoy, the other to reach
Victoria Point from Ranaung and then move north through Tenasserim.
The first unit left that night, and by mid-January 1942 the rest were either
over the border or poised ready to strike. In their eyes, it was the beginning
of the war of Burmese independence or, for the historically minded among
them, 'the fourth and final Anglo-Burmese War'.[1]

Colonel Suzuki as Miss Lonelyhearts

At the Rahaeng branch of the Minami Kikan, Lt Takahashi Hachirō was in
command, as a forestry technician, buying teak and pine resin and reconnoitring the Menado track to the frontier. British spies and Thai government officials made precautions necessary. The majority of the inhabitants were of Burmese descent (in fact only four of them were Thais),
but Takahashi was solidly built and easily spotted as a Japanese. He tried
to make friends among the locals, but they were leery of him and never
came to his house. Takahashi felt he needed to install himself without
question in the community, since he had to check roads, rivers and
topography – the Rahaeng-Menado road would be a principal invasion
route for the Japanese Army. It was the road to Moulmein.

Suzuki came to see him, and gave him a characteristic piece of advice.
'In a dangerous spot, the best thing to do is to get married. If the worst
comes to the worst, your wife's family will be on your side, and her
relatives will look after you. If you want to look as if you're settling down,
pick yourself a bride. *Onna wo mote. Kekkon shiro . . .* Get hold of a
woman. Get married.'[2]

Takahashi started to look over possible candidates among the women of
Rahaeng. He came across one with a passable face and figure, a teacher at
the local school who spoke English. She was a little past what was locally
regarded as marriageable age but when he proposed, her answer was
immediate and unhesitating: 'OK'. Takahashi used the wedding ceremony
to issue invitations to the important people among the locals, the headman,
the police chief, etc. Whereas they had ignored him before, now they all
turned up, bearing presents for his wife. He was offered a house just
opposite the police station and moved in his kit and furniture.

As they were carrying in the chairs and tables, a young man walked past.
He wore a dirt-stained *longyi*, and dragged his feet with exhaustion, as if
he had been walking along endless roads. Takahashi met his gaze, waited
for him to go past, and followed behind. The youth stopped when
Takahashi spoke to him, and muttered, 'I am Thakin member'.

[1] ibid. p. 141

[2] Hatakeyama, op.cit., p. 32

There was no question of taking him into the house since it was right in front of the police station. 'Wait for me at the temple,' Takahashi said. He went back to finish the removal of his furniture and when he got to the temple at the edge of the village found the youth squatting on the pavement waiting for him. He went up to him, and said 'S'. The youth made no reply. 'S' repeated Takahashi, but the youth merely stared at him. 'S' was a password for Thakin escapees, and the youth should have answered 'K'.

'If he doesn't know the password,' thought Takahashi, 'then he's a British spy. He must have a shrewd idea who I am, though, and there's only one way of shutting his mouth.' Takahashi had no great taste for murder, and the possibility of an enquiry revealing who and what he was did not appeal. He decided after a sleepless night to kill him. At breakfast, Takahashi took up a piece of paper that was lying to hand, and scribbled 'S' on it in pencil. The youth looked at the paper, took the pencil, and wrote 'K'. Takahashi's tension snapped, and he gave a great sigh of relief. This was the first of the Thakin escapees, Than Zu In.[1]

Very soon Rahaeng had to get used to the idea of Japanese in even greater numbers. Under its commander Lieutenant-General Takeuchi, 55 Division moved up from Pitsanuloke and established its headquarters at Rahaeng, which was to be the springboard for the invasion of Burma.

One thing 55 Division was short of was accurate maps. The Division concentrated in Bangkok on 22 December 1941, and there Takeuchi issued operation orders for the crossing of the Burma frontier and the capture of Moulmein. When he asked 15 Army for maps, he was told that none were to be had, and he had better simply 'go and see'. Army GHQ finally came up with some very inadequate maps of Thailand and some operational maps of Tenasserim. The Thailand maps proved to be quite inaccurate and difficult to compare with the reality of the terrain, despite assistance in interpreting them from members of the Minami Kikan in Mae Sot. The Burma maps were comparatively accurate.

The difficulties of the frontier area demanded a change in methods of transport. Motorized units switched to mules and oxen, and mountain guns were reallocated, one to a company. Heavy artillery simply had to be left behind in Bangkok, to be forwarded later by road and sea after Moulmein had been taken. On 1 January 1942, the divisional commander left Bangkok for Pitsanuloke, set up a divisional liaison office there, and moved on to Rahaeng. The Thais were very helpful, and the Prefectural Governor of Pitsanuloke and the headman at Sukhotai received certificates of appreciation from Takeuchi. The Thai Army sent a staff officer to help the Japanese in their contacts with the locals. There were large supplies of horses and cattle to be procured, for one thing. The Japanese began

[1] ibid. pp. 26–9

23

breaking them in, but the animals fled when they started to harness them to sledges. By the time 55 Division reached the Burmese frontier, almost no cattle were left. Once west of Sukhotai, the jungle began to close in. The Japanese moved for the first time through virgin forests and climbed what seemed to be endless mountains. The columns began to thin out. The men were afraid of tigers which, they had been told, roamed in the forests; but the main hazards were the precipices. The pack horses slipped and fell to the valley floor and many horses died. By the time they reached Mae Sot, only a third of the horses survived. 'Two or three days after we left Pitsanuloke on 11 January', wrote Captain Honjō Seikei (143 Infantry Regiment) in his diary,

the ground was hilly but the slope comparatively gentle, and covered with thickets of bamboo. From 4 January, the going became much steeper and we were soon swallowed up in a deep jungle sea.

We moved ahead in single file, watching for rocks and tree roots: if you missed your footing, you'd be engulfed in the bottomless jungle floor. We climbed up painfully, step by step, hauling ourselves up by holding on to creepers. By day, the temperature was over 100°, and by night the cold pierced your skin. Gradually our unit began to spin out, until it stretched like an endless belt from one peak to the next. We only made about ten miles a day, and finally reached Rahaeng on 17 January.

The steep peaks went on and on – they were up to about four and a half thousand feet – like a succession of walls between Rahaeng and Mae Sot. We had three very rough days after leaving Rahaeng and then, on 22 January, in the afternoon of the fourth day, the column was swallowed up in the darkness of teak forest. Finally we came to Mae Sot, and the frontier.[1]

General Takeuchi reached Mae Sot on 17 January, and on the following day issued orders for the division to move on Kawkareik and attack Moulmein.

General Smyth looks westward to the sea

Takeuchi had already marched his men to the Burmese frontier when the new commander of 17 Indian Division surveyed his responsibilities about 100 miles to the west. Major-General Smyth was inwardly appalled at what he saw, but he put a brave face on it. He had already met a number of old

[1] *Biruma Kōryaku Sakusen*, pp. 85–6

friends, some of whom cheered him up. Others had the opposite effect. Smyth left Calcutta by flying-boat on 9 January 1942, and after arrival in Rangoon had talks with the Army Commander, General Tom Hutton, and the Governor of Burma, Sir Reginald Dorman-Smith, who had once been a subaltern in Smyth's battalion (15th Sikhs), and who radiated a quite misplaced confidence in the probability of the Burmese population rising up in anger against the Japanese invader (the Japanese 143 Infantry Regiment had already taken Victoria Point, the southernmost tip of Burma). After taking leave of the Governor, Smyth and Hutton flew to Mergui and Tavoy. The commander of 2 Burma Rifles at Mergui was another old friend, who had the impossible job of protecting the airfield, the town and its people, and at the same time watching for possible Japanese forces from the south, the north, and the mass of tiny islands of the Mergui archipelago. The next battalion at Tavoy was an hour's flying time away: 6th Burma Rifles, a police battalion only recently converted into a regular force and quite untrained. On 10 January, Hutton flew back to Rangoon, and Smyth stayed in Moulmein to organize his divisional headquarters.

He had not liked the Army Commander's insistence on placing isolated pockets of troops as far forward as possible, and on guarding the Tenasserim airfields. Smyth attributed it to the fact that Hutton had been Wavell's Chief of Staff at India Command, and did whatever Wavell wanted; and what Wavell wanted was not to cede an inch of ground unnecessarily to the Japanese, whom he considered to be inferior troops (the same mistake he made in Malaya and Singapore). Smyth saw the issue as a contest between a political decision – holding on to Burmese territory whatever its strategic value – and a military decision – retreating to a spot selected by him as a suitable battleground on which to concentrate his forces, and fight the Japanese on his terms and not theirs. Hutton never saw it in that light. His reasons for wanting to fight the Japanese as far forward as possible were military not political: if one reason for defending Burma were to keep the Burma Road going, then the Japanese had to be kept at a distance from it, and that road for many miles ran close to the River Sittang, hence its vulnerability. If the Japanese seized the Tenasserim airstrips, that made the bombing of Rangoon and convoys approaching it so much easier for the Japanese. If it became necessary to evacuate from Lower Burma, then Rangoon was the port of evacuation, and the same reasoning applied. Lastly, the effect of withdrawal on the Chinese would be considerable. Smyth was therefore told to fight the Japanese as far forward as possible, and not to withdraw unless given specific permission to do so.

Hutton needed time. Given enough time, he could move 46 Brigade into Tenasserim from Rangoon, ensure that 48 Brigade landed without hazard, and enable 1st Burma Division to come down from the Shan States to the Toungoo area; that is, provided the offer of help from Chiang Kai Shek's

Chinese Nationalist army to take over the defence of the Shan States materialized (even then, the offer itself contained innumerable snags, logistic and political). To gain time, Hutton insisted that Smyth fight his battle as far forward into Tenasserim as possible. On the very tip of that finger pointing down into Malaya, Mergui (2 Burma Rifles), Tavoy (6 Burma Rifles) and Victoria Point could obviously not be held, and their garrisons must be withdrawn, even if that meant (and it did) leaving the civilian population and police to the tender mercies of the invader. But surely the Japanese could be stopped where the River Salween met the sea at Moulmein, where it was a mile-and-a-half wide?

Smyth did not think so. In fact he found the proposition, militarily speaking, absurd. He was being asked to fight a superior force, with his back to a wide river estuary, at the end of an impossible line of communications, a mixture of river steamer, rail and road, the road itself far from complete. 'The long line of communications,' he later wrote, 'from Moulmein northwards towards Bilin and Sittang . . . was an absolute nightmare . . . From Moulmein northwards there was a somewhat anti-quated steamer ferry service over the 7000 yards of open water which lay between Moulmein and Martaban. From the railhead at Martaban a good metal road and single track railway ran back through Thaton over the Bilin River to Kyaikto. Thence a dusty unmade track led to the broad Sittang river railway bridge, where his responsibility ended.'[1]

When Smyth looked round the defences of Moulmein, he felt like withdrawing at once. It was his first visit to Burma, though his parents had spent many years there. His father had been in the Indian Civil Service. Smyth went up to the pagoda-studded ridge above the town. The river was partly hidden by the morning mist, as his eyes turned north and then west, towards the sea: the Gulf of Martaban, across which lay Rangoon. The coastal plain, shaded by water palms along the shore, was criss-crossed by a myriad little creeks, and oxen champed slowly in the brilliant green grass. Huge, magnificent butterflies flitted across the water to the sampans off-shore, egrets swarmed on the warm sand, and here and there a vulture spread its wings over the water's edge. The pagodas on the ridge gleamed white in the sun.

Moulmein itself, a prosperous teak- and rice-exporting town of well over 50,000 inhabitants, retained a flavour of an earlier colonial period, with its three parallel main streets. Long before the British arrived in Lower Burma in 1821 the Portuguese had been here, and in spite of the ubiquitous corrugated iron roofs, some of the old stone houses with the mango trees in their gardens, their spacious proportions, their double columns flanking doors and windows, and wrought-iron balconies, where crows perched and picked at the potted flowers, were reminiscent of that mingling of

[1] Smyth, op.cit., p. 140

Portuguese Renaissance style with native Indian architecture that recalls the baroque settlements of Goa and Malacca.

Below him, Smyth watched the roofs of the houses, glittering in the early sunlight, then gazed southward, and east. There lay the jungle, thick, dense jungle, as far as he could see. In the town, its inhabitants were already about their daily concerns, unaware of what lay in store for them as they passed through the streets in their gaily coloured *longyis*, puffing away – men and women alike – at enormous cheroots. Just behind him on the ridge squatted the great golden Buddha of the main pagoda.

'Sitting up on my hillside,' he later wrote, 'I gazed down on Moulmein. What an impossible place to defend with a small force! And what an even more impossible place from which to withdraw, as the only line of withdrawal was by river steamer across a broad expanse of water.'[1] The solitary 8th Burma Rifles battalion which was all there was of British military power in the town at that moment was without barbed wire, sandbags, or the usual equipment for defence, and no attempt had been made to dig positions. A perimeter to cover *all* the positions he needed to cover – riverside quays, supply and ammunition depots, aerodrome – would, as he found out when he drove round them later that evening, measure at least twenty-five miles. Three days later he drove to the forward positions of 16 Indian Infantry Brigade (Brigadier J. K. Jones) in the Dawna Hills. The road to Kawkareik was good, but entailed ferry crossings of two wide rivers. It took an hour to get one car across, and there was (of course) no bridging equipment in Burma. As Smyth impatiently waited for his car to reach the far side, he wondered what on earth would happen if the crossing had to be made under attack by enemy aircraft.

16 Brigade was only two battalions strong (1/7 Gurkhas and 4 Burma Rifles) and 400 of the Burma Rifles were already malaria casualties. The troops were tied to the road, with inadequate lorry transport, and the Brigade had only one wireless set, which had to be carried in a lorry, and was in use most of the time for communication with division. Jones himself was a tall, handsome Indian Army officer whose experience had been on the North-West Frontier. He was over fifty but, Smyth judged, he was fitter than most of his officers. Smyth messed with the brigade that night and, as they dined, a tiger roared endlessly in the nearby jungle: as accurate an omen as any for the days that were to come. The Brigade intelligence officer, who was better informed than the staff at Army HQ in Rangoon, told Smyth that a Japanese division, with ancillary Thai troops, would invade Burma within a week, through Kawkareik. Reconnaissance aircraft did not provide much advance news. This did not surprise Smyth, who had gazed across the endless sea of treetops and realized that an army could hide there easily, safe from prying aircraft overhead. The Brigade

---

[1] ibid. p. 136

27

intelligence officer was a man who had been in business in the area for years, hence his fuller information. Smyth took a leaf out of 16 Brigade's book, and took on to his staff a Moulmein businessman who began to provide the information he needed.

In contrast, as Smyth ruefully remarks in *Before the Dawn*, the Japanese were fully informed of everything beforehand. 'They not only got information of our every movement, but they got guides, rafts, ponies, elephants, and all the things which we could not get for love, and only with great difficulty, for money.'[1] The reasons for the contrast were political. Lt Takahashi and his organization were using, against Smyth, the results of years of resentment by young Burmese against British rule.

Back in Moulmein, Smyth surveyed his lines of communication and wrote out an appreciation for Hutton. The area required at least two divisions to defend it. Hutton was not likely to disagree. He simply did not have two divisions for the defence of Tenasserim alone. Later, he often thought Burma might have been saved if the Chinese had moved quickly into action to hold the area north of 17 Division, and if the War Office had sent 18 Division to Rangoon instead of diverting it to Singapore (where it was put into the bag by the Japanese a few days after it landed). Be that as it may, Smyth had to make do with what he had.

Hutton put under Smyth's command 46 Indian Infantry Brigade – still only partially trained – which was sent to the Bilin area, Burma Brigade – the Burma Rifles battalions garrisoning Tenasserim – and 16 Brigade which had been moved from Mandalay to Moulmein. Nobody really believed the isolated Tenasserim garrisons could hold on for long, however desirable it might be to keep the Japanese air force at a distance from Rangoon; so when the Tavoy garrison was extruded by III Battalion, 112 Infantry Regiment of the Japanese 55 Division, on 19 January, and Mergui to the south of it was therefore cut off, Hutton ordered the Mergui garrison to withdraw. By 23 January 1942, the three important airstrips in southern Tenasserim – Tavoy, Mergui, Victoria Point – were all in Japanese hands, and fighter cover could now be provided for every bombing raid on Rangoon.

On 22 January Hutton had warned the Governor that the fate of Rangoon might be decided in ten days if reinforcements failed to reach Burma immediately. That same day Mergui was evacuated, and Smyth sent Hutton a message to say that the Japanese had appeared in force on the frontier – perhaps a division in strength, 10,000 men, with artillery and air support. Smyth's 16 Brigade had only recently been transferred to Moulmein from the Mandalay area, under command of 1st Burma Division, which was supposed to protect Burma from an attack through the Shan States. Hutton believed this would not be the attack route. He was right: it

---

[1] ibid. pp. 139–40

would come through Tenasserim. Four days before, 46 Indian Brigade had landed in Rangoon to join Smyth's division, but it was weak, only half-trained and without its transport. A Brigade of Gurkhas, 48 Brigade, was on its way, but was not expected to arrive until the end of January.

From his distant GHQ in Java, preoccupied as he was by the Japanese triumphs in Malaya, Wavell answered Hutton's request for more infantry battalions to stem the Japanese invasion: 'I have no resources with which I can assist you . . . Cannot understand why with troops at your disposal you should be unable to hold Moulmein and trust you will do so. Nature of country and resources must limit Japanese effort.'[1] That signal was sent on 22 January. The following day, Wavell decided to go and have a look himself, and flew to Rangoon where Hutton was not awaiting him. He was forward, with Smyth, the news that Wavell was coming never having reached him. He had authorized Smyth to bring his HQ fifty miles further north, to Kyaikto, but Moulmein was to be held with one brigade and denied to the Japanese as long as possible. Hutton then returned to Rangoon to see Wavell. After a discussion with Hutton and Dorman-Smith, Wavell returned by flying-boat to Sumatra the following day.

He sent the Chief of the Imperial General Staff, by signal, his views on the situation in Burma:

> Japanese advance in Tenasserim should not have results it did. Trouble started at Tavoy where indifferent battalion Burmese Rifles . . . apparently allowed itself to be surprised and then gave in without putting up fight. Troops at Mergui were never attacked but were withdrawn rather hastily for fear they might be cut off.[2]

Wavell added that he thought that the Japanese were attacking in small parties and should have been held easily, but troops were being de-moralised by infiltration tactics. He had a word of praise for Smyth as a 'good fighting divisional commander' – a verdict he was to revise in weeks to come. The Burma Rifles were unreliable, he thought, and even good Indian troops seemed bewildered once they were away from roads.

In fact, the Japanese 55 Division, two (instead of three) regiments strong, was making for Moulmein from the south, from the south-east through the Three Pagodas Pass, and straight across the Dawna Hills through Kawkareik. Smyth's presentiment about the ferry on the Kawkareik road was realized. By what the Official History chooses to call an 'unfortunate accident', an overloaded ammunition truck sank the ferry over the Kyaing River in midstream as 16 Brigade retreated towards Moulmein, forcing the Brigadier to abandon all his transport on the wrong

---

[1] J. Connell, *Wavell, Supreme Commander*, p. 117

[2] ibid. p. 122

side of the river and send his men on foot. Two days later they were harbouring in Martaban. Their losses had not been great, but most of their supporting weapons – and nearly all of their morale – had disappeared. Jones had, as Smyth was later to comment, 'retired too soon'.[1]

Fourteen Japanese bombers had raided Moulmein on 17 January catching the divisional commander in his pyjamas, raging with impotence at the inability of the four ancient ack-ack guns to answer back, and at the total lack of British aircraft at Moulmein itself. Not much damage was done, but the shops closed and the civil labour force melted away, as it did in Rangoon. The Army had to take over banks, post and telegraph office, and the railway and ferry service. The Japanese bombed Moulmein twice the day after Tavoy fell and set the bazaar ablaze. Smyth had already put it to Hutton that all his forces should leave Moulmein and concentrate in the Bilin-Kyaikto-Sittang area. Hutton knew that Smyth meant to retire across the Sittang, in fact, which he considered to be a major obstacle, and also because once on the other side he was relatively free of jungle and could fight in open country which would suit his troops better.

Hutton was having none of this. A forward defence policy was still to be maintained, and, in particular, Moulmein was to be held. Smyth was furious, not merely at the refusal itself, but at the fact that he was not empowered to make *any* withdrawals on his own initiative. Everything had to be countenanced by the Army Commander back in Rangoon, and Smyth felt he should have been given more latitude, since he was the commander who had to fight the battle.

Both in relation to Moulmein, and to the order to fight on the Bilin River line, from which he also wished to withdraw, Smyth's case seems to have been upheld by the Official Historian, who writes, 'Hutton might have been wiser, once action had been joined on the Bilin, to leave Smyth a free hand.'[2] Hutton rejected this completely, and pointed out that if Smyth had been left a free hand he would have scuttled back across the River Sittang as quickly as possible, after putting up a mere token resistance on the Bilin River.[3] Hutton had been given definite orders by Wavell that there were to be no further withdrawals, and he felt that if there were going to be withdrawals in spite of this, then he as Army Commander should accept the responsibility for them directly. It was a well-known principle, he pointed out to the Official Historian, that an order should be disobeyed only if the Supreme Commander is not available for reference and one is satisfied that, if present, he would have agreed; the Official Historian accepted this and offered to publish an amendment

[1] Smyth, op.cit., p. 151

[2] S. W. Kirby, *War Against Japan*, I, p. 76

[3] Lieutenant-General Sir Thomas Hutton, *Rangoon 1941–2. A Personal Record*, Postscript, p. 4. TS in Liddell-Hart Archive.

deleting the reference to giving Smyth a free hand (though this was never done).

By the old Moulmein pagoda

From his Supreme ABDA (American-British-Dutch-Australian) Command headquarters in Java, General Wavell flew to Rangoon to visit the Burma front. He spent 25 January in Burma and flew back to Java during the night. Already oppressed by the impending loss of Malaya and the threat to Singapore, he did not believe that the situation in Burma warranted too pessimistic a view. 'I found the situation better than I expected,' he later wrote, 'and did not consider it immediately serious provided the reinforcement of Burma with land and air forces proceeded without delay.'[1] Whether the soldiers believed him or not is one thing; at any rate the Governor was very bucked by his optimistic visitor and wired that same night to Leopold Amery in London that, after seeing Wavell, he could not believe the worst could happen.

That same day, after being routed by the Japanese at Kawkareik, the battered 16 Indian Brigade came into Moulmein. What was left of the Brigade – *sans* animal transport, signal equipment, and all its vehicles – was ferried across the river Salween and posted along the line of the river between Martaban and Pa-an, with orders to hold it. Meanwhile, 2 Burma Brigade awaited the advance of the Japanese 55 Division. Moulmein had proved itself too exposed a spot for a divisional headquarters, so Smyth moved back fifty miles up the coast to Kyaikto, leaving Brigadier Bourke to defend Moulmein with three battalions of Burma Rifles, 3rd and 7th having come to reinforce the 8th. There was also now a battalion of the Frontier Force Regiment, 12 Mountain Battery's four howitzers and four Bofors guns, the sole A/A defence – around 3000 men in all. Moulmein also held 2000 men of the division's administrative tail, clerks, supply staff, hospital orderlies and so on. Few of the men in the Burma Rifles battalions had more than two years service; many of them had been soldiers only for a matter of months – in some cases weeks.

The Japanese came at Moulmein in small parties, not *en masse*. For four days, 26–29 January, they infiltrated the area methodically. Patrols went out to find them, and villagers' reports made it obvious that they were coming closer. But no contacts were made, no prisoners taken, so Brigadier Bourke was in the dark about how they proposed to attack.

Then, on 30 January, they put in a very heavy attack on the perimeter, from the south and south-east. Bourke moved his HQ to the ridge overlooking the town at 8 am. At 9.30 am the Japanese shelled the ridge and

[1] Collis, op.cit., p. 72

launched an attack from the east. Bourke's men held these attacks and by noon the fighting seemed to have died down, apart from desultory sniping.

During the lull in the fighting, Brigadier Roger Ekin, the commander of 16 Brigade, which was assembling in Kyaikto, arrived in Moulmein. Smyth had received orders from Hutton to put Ekin in charge of the town's defences and so, although Bourke had the situation in hand, there was a change of command halfway through the battle. Ekin was, writes Maurice Collis, 'a man of charming character and his intervention at so inopportune a moment did no harm'.[1] As Ekin had had no previous knowledge of the troops or the terrain, it did not do much good, either.[2]

The Japanese attacked again at 4 pm and the Burma Rifles battalions east of the town withdrew and shortened their perimeter so that Ekin could form a box, leaving a detachment to hold the airfield. This guard was composed of Sikhs recruited in Burma, and was commanded by an Indian officer from the 15th Sikhs who had seen service with Smyth in the First World War. The Sikhs did magnificently, and held the airfield for twenty-four hours when completely cut off. They then broke through the Japanese encirclement to make their way back to Martaban. The defection of a Burma Rifles battalion left a gap in the box, and by evening a withdrawal seemed necessary; but Ekin, who thought only 1000 Japanese were involved, told Smyth over the telephone (one of the communication links in Burma which *did* work) that it was still possible to hold the town, and he would delay his decision to quit. Ekin held out during the night. From 7 pm the pressure increased but in the morning his own HQ was directly under attack. It had been sited on the Ridge where the Moulmein Pagoda stands looking *west*ward to the sea, and was later shifted to the Public Works bungalow in Salween Park. A party of Japanese infiltrated the defences and stormed the bungalow. Brigade HQ then moved to the Telephone Exchange near the Mission Street jetty. The Japanese had, in fact, pressed the defenders back and back until there was almost no perimeter left, and the buildings on the river front were all ablaze.

Parties of Japanese disguised as Burmans had landed near the Timber Yard and mingled with the Burma Rifles as they withdrew. This party surprised the Bofors gunners in the northern part of the town and bayoneted them; the guns were abandoned. Ekin phoned Smyth, and said he must now withdraw. Smyth was not only prepared for this request, but welcomed it. He knew that, sentimentally and from the point of view of civilian morale, it was an extremely important Burmese town[3] and he must

---

[1] ibid. p. 78

[2] Nor could it, given the superiority of the forces attacking Moulmein. The Japanese 55 Division had five infantry battalions, five field artillery batteries (with twenty 75 mm guns), two troops of cavalry, and two companies of engineers, a total of 7–8000 men.

[3] Smyth, op.cit., p. 156

have known that Wavell had telegraphed Hutton only a week before, with some asperity, 'Cannot understand why with troops at your disposal you should be unable to hold Moulmein and trust you will do so.'[1] Hutton had visited Moulmein on 28 January, convinced himself the situation was quiet, that the attack on Kawkareik had not been in great force, and that casualties were few – the rapid withdrawal and loss of transport by 16 Indian Brigade had not, therefore, been justified, and he reported in that sense to Wavell, adding that there was no question of evacuating Moulmein.

Smyth thought differently. Jones's hasty retreat from Kawkareik, and the loss of the Brigade's transport and weapons, had reinforced him in his view that he should be allowed, as the local forward commander, to order his own withdrawals as and when he thought fit. There was no corps commander interposed between him and Hutton, the army commander in Rangoon, who insisted on controlling the withdrawals himself – an insistence which, in Smyth's view, disregarded the vital factor of timing in a fast rearguard action such as the campaign had become. Smyth made no secret of his differences of opinion with Hutton. His senior commanders knew of them, and so did the Brigadier General Staff ('Taffy' Davies) at Army HQ, who supported Smyth against his own Commander-in-Chief.

An American woman journalist, Eve Curie, passed through the front at this time, and later rhetorically compared Moulmein to Stalingrad. It was picturesque, and ludicrous. Hutton had finally agreed with Smyth that a rearguard action should be fought there, with one brigade, to deny it to the Japanese as long as possible. There was no question of a last-ditch stand.

It was just as well. The morale of the troops was poor, Smyth observed, Indian and Burmese defenders mutually distrusted each other, and were keenly aware of the artillery and air support they did not have. So when Ekin phoned to ask permission to withdraw, Smyth gave it.

The Japanese were closing in on the river frontage, where the boats were lined up to take the survivors across to Martaban. The commander of 12 Mountain Battery found one of his sections missing, took a party of gunners and Frontier Force Regiment back through the Japanese lines and brought out the missing guns. Although the few Bofors were captured, an Indian officer, noticing that the Japanese had left them unguarded, swam ashore, from the ferry which was taking him to safety, in order to spike the guns. He was taken prisoner as a result. As the Japanese closed in on the quayside, the defenders began to cross the Salween under a hail of shelling and machine-gun fire.

None too soon. By 10 am, the Post Office and Telephone Exchange had been destroyed, and Brigade HQ and the rearguard just got away in the ferry steamer as the Japanese reached the jetty. Not all the steamers managed to cross without incident – one was sunk by Japanese shellfire; and

---

[1] Connell, op.cit., p. 117

some men escaped by raft, or swam across. Many of the civilian operators of the ferry steamers, understandably, had fled. Their place was taken by Indian sappers and miners who moved the retreating garrison across the wide stream at 9 am on the 31st, under intense fire, without panic or confusion. It took Ekin forty minutes to get across in a launch. Brigadier Bourke and 12 Mountain Battery crossed on the last ferry. At Martaban, Ekin went off to rejoin his own Brigade at Kyaikto. The brief battle for Moulmein was over.

Smyth always viewed the defence of Moulmein as a grave tactical error. Hutton himself put the question whether it was necessary to evacuate it, but finally came to the conclusion that with the Japanese established both to north and south of the town, it would have been impossible to relieve it, even had any troops been available for the purpose. He admitted that at least two infantry brigades were needed to hold the perimeter, and there was a snag about water: the only supply lay outside the perimeter. Besides, even though only one Japanese regiment had been involved in the fighting, both Hutton and Smyth were sure that another one was available to be called in. Hutton was forced to send Wavell a telegram announcing the fall of Moulmein. It must have been very hard to write, three days after his initial show of confidence, because he was a shrewd and cautious man, accustomed to a correct analysis:

> In spite of effort to gain contact and delay enemy he attacked Moulmein yesterday from all directions. Situation in hand till afternoon when counter-attack necessary. Commander consolidated small bridgehead during night and Divisional Commander has decided on evacuation while still possible. With one exception troops seem to have fought well.[1]

The one exception was the behaviour of the 3rd and 7th Burma Rifles. 'I fear these battalions of Burma Rifles are unreliable', Wavell had signalled to the Chief of the Imperial General Staff on 26 January.[2] As a general judgment, this was far too sweeping. Some of the Burma Rifles fought hard and well, and later on, as Hutton points out,[3] some of them did very well in both Chindit campaigns. But men of the 3rd and 7th Battalions began to desert during the battle and in its last phase rushed the jetties at Moulmein to get on the ferries first. They had to be held back by officers at gun point.

So Moulmein was lost to the enemy. The Japanese had achieved their first major objective, and the district of Burma which had been longest in British hands (since 1826) passed out of them. It was the only part of Burma,

[1] ibid. p. 133

[2] ibid. p. 122

[3] Hutton, op.cit.

Compton Mackenzie later thought when visiting Moulmein to prepare his war history, *Eastern Epic*, where the welfare of the people had not been sacrificed to commercial interests, and where prosperity under British rule could be contrasted with a previous period of continuous warfare. In the rest of Burma (he was writing in 1947) there was a strong and unanimous desire to see the last of the British rulers, but in Tenasserim he felt many would regret their departure. It is perhaps ironical that the Burmese of Tenasserim were the first to come under Japanese rule.

War comes to Mi Mi Khaing and Daw Sein

Even those Burmese who were not politically anti-British felt that the war had descended on them at someone else's bidding. Mi Mi Khaing had been a student at Rangoon University, and was twenty-five when war came. Most nations which declare war, or have war declared on them, she later wrote, can feel a call to sacrifice for their nation or for an ideal. 'But how could this apply in the case of Burma,' she asked, 'a country which had lost proud sovereignty fifty-five years before, which had not yet gained a modern replacement for it, and which felt itself to be only incidentally in the path of the war monster's appetite?'[1]

The idea was mooted of her whole family returning to Thaton, their ancestral home, to shelter from the bombing in Rangoon. A young cousin objected, pointing out that Thaton was in the direct path of the Japanese invasion. 'Well, what if it is?' answered Mi Mi Khaing's mother. 'Do we go to the middle of the roadway, and stand, looking up with our mouth open to receive the cannon balls? We are human beings, eating rice . . . We can reason like human beings and move aside, avoid a little, and the menace will go straight down the road, and after a time leave us behind.'[2]

It did not work that way in practice, of course. The panic which hit the Rangoon population when the Japanese air-raids began almost emptied the city. A Burmese midwife, Daw Sein, recalls that she had heard vaguely about a war, but wasn't sure who was fighting whom. So the day the bombs began to fall, she thought the booming sounds were the onset of a storm, until her husband Maung Ba Swe burst in and yelled 'Out! Quick! We must get away!'

Daw Sein fled the house and was halfway to the station before she realized she had no *longyi* on, and was half-naked. Her husband stopped, tore his own *longyi* in half and gave her the torn piece of cloth. Clutching it to herself, she sprinted to the station, and they tumbled into a train which was just leaving for Moulmein. Packed to the doors, the train left, then

[1] Mi Mi Khaing, *A Burmese Family*, p. 130

[2] ibid.

after an hour stopped to let people get off. An old man began to vomit over her, children sobbed, women shouted. She got down from the train and found her husband picking wild bananas – there was nothing to eat or drink on the train itself. They waited for hours. Then a man walked along beside the stationary coaches calling out 'Moulmein has been destroyed! Moulmein has been destroyed! Bombs are falling everywhere! The train isn't going any further!'

The rumour went round that Rangoon had been destroyed, too. So there was no going forward, and no going back. 'Why not try and make for India?' her husband suggested. 'The Japanese will take everything here.' Daw Sein did not want to go, she thought she would never see her children again (they were with relatives at Tandwai, near Sandoway in Arakan). So they reached a compromise: they would make for Mandalay. Her husband would try to reach India from there, and she would go on to Tandwai.

They set off northwards, along the line of the railway, on foot. Finally they reached a spot where another train was waiting. It took that train three days to reach Mandalay, stopping everywhere. It was even more crowded than the first train, even the lavatories were full, so that passengers had to clamber out and use the trackside to relieve themselves whenever the train stopped. Inevitably, some got left behind, and in spite of the tragedy of the occasion, Daw Sein laughed when they tried to sprint after the train, their toilet half-completed, with their *longyis* hitched up to their hips. One woman lost her husband like that. Daw Sein heard her weeping in the carriage. He had caught diarrhoea from contaminated food he must have eaten *en route*. 'You don't lose a man so easily!' Daw Sein chaffed at her – she was quite hard-bitten by this time – 'If he's not killed, you'll meet him again sooner or later.'[1]

When Mandalay in turn was bombed, recalls U Hla Pe, one woman was so terrified and hysterical with fear that she left for Shwebo with all her worldly goods and only realized, half-an-hour after she had arrived, that she had left her two-year-old child behind her on the platform in Mandalay. He doesn't know whether she ever saw the child again.[2]

Bashir blows the bridge

The blowing of the Sittang Bridge with two brigades still on the wrong side of the river was the turning-point in the first Burma campaign.[3]

---

[1] Claude Delachet Guillon, *Daw Sein. Les dix mille vies d'une femme birmane*, 1978, pp. 152–55

[2] U Hla Pe, *Narrative of the Japanese Occupation of Burma*, p. 3

[3] The rights and wrongs of the decision have been endlessly debated. 'I'd like to meet the man who blew the bridge,' an officer of the 8th Burma Rifles told Compton Mackenzie after the war. 'He had a ghastly decision to make, and I'd like to tell him that I think he was right, and

The sapper officer who set the charges to blow the Sittang bridge and the sapper officer who pressed the exploder and blew it are still alive.[1] Roy Hudson, now managing director of Hudson Enterprises at Chiangmai in Thailand, was a lieutenant in the Royal Engineers attached to a Field Company of the Malerkotla Sappers and Miners, under the command of Major Richard Orgill. The Malerkotlas were sent to Burma in November 1941 and joined 1st Burma Brigade at Taunggyi in the Shan States. When the Japanese invaded Tenasserim, they formed part of the reinforcements sent from 1st Burma Division to 17 Indian Division at Kyaikto.

Roy Hudson spent a good deal of time in demolitions behind the Bilin River line and in Kyaikto, and then moved on to Mokpalin, his men being attacked for three hours by the RAF – and suffering two casualties – as they withdrew to the line of the Sittang.

At dawn on 22 February, Roy Hudson went to the main road in a 15 cwt. truck to obtain firing orders. There was a long queue of trucks, so he got out of the truck and went towards the Sittang Bridge on foot. Hudson learned that a 3-tonner Officers' Mess truck belonging to the CRE of 17 Indian Division had stuck on the bridge with one wheel over the decking which had been put down to make the railway bridge temporarily usable for road traffic. It had taken over two hours to shift it.

He went back to his own truck and when they were within 200 yards of the bridge he heard small arms fire (this was the start of the Japanese 33 Division's attempt on the bridgehead). Hudson was determined to get his truck on to the west bank of the Sittang, and once it was over the bridge he handed over to the driver, and walked back over the immense structure on foot, clutching a tommy gun. An officer he didn't know was already at the far end armed with a bren gun. They took up a defensive point north of the Bridge, anticipating that the Japanese would soon attack. They were quite close by this time. Hudson saw some Burmese villagers trying to escape to the west bank by swimming

---

that by his courage he probably saved us from being in far worse plight... I was almost the last man across, and so can't be accused of being an armchair critic, but I salute the man who made that courageous and ghastly decision.' The issue has been hotly debated ever since, see Appendix 2.

[1] This section is based on conversations with Roy Hudson (Chiangmai, 1980), correspondence with him and Major Bashir Ahmed Khan (Retd) of the Malerkotla Sappers and Miners, and the following documents: 'Notes by Roy Hudson on the Battle of Sittang River' 22 February 1942 (TS); 'War Diary of Malerkotla Field Company Sappers and Miners, Indian State Forces' (32 pp); 'Nambu Biruma sakusen sentō yōhō' (Record of operations in South Burma), the War Diary of 215 Infantry Regiment, 33 Division, by Colonel Harada Munaji, (56 pp) in Imperial War Museum; B. A. Khan, *History of the Malerkotla Sappers and Miners* (draft sections communicated privately); Colonel E. W. Sandes, *The History of Indian Engineers 1939–1947*, Institute of Royal Engineers; *Hohei Dai-215 Rentai Dai-3 Chūtai Senki* (War History of 3 Coy., 215 Infantry Regiment) pub. by Dai-3 chūtai hensan iinkai (Pubn. Cttee of No 3 Coy), Tokyo, 1979.

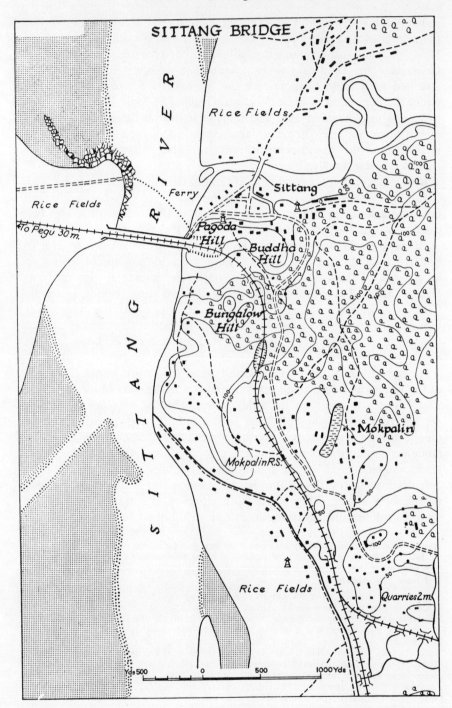

across. There was a sudden burst of small arms fire, and the Burmese were hit, and sank into the waters.

Hudson looked back at the bridge and saw Richard Orgill, his CO. An officer patrol was covering the eastern end, all of them with drawn revolvers to prevent any disorderly rushing of the bridge by stragglers. He had to convince them of who he was before he could join Orgill, then they set about organizing parties to prepare the bridge for demolition.

To this day, Hudson cannot understand why *they* had to do it. The CRE of 17 Indian Division, Tuffett Armitage, had three field companies of engineers of his own who should already have undertaken this task. It was hardly suitable for a last-minute improvisation. All three companies had passed back over the Sittang through the Malerkotlas, who had been demolishing the Kyaikto bridges.

The organization of the ferry service to evacuate the Moulmein garrison had taken its toll of Armitage. Smyth had noticed that 'he was worked off his feet and eventually had to be carried off to hospital'.[1] The strain had already begun to show. Not only had he omitted to order the engineer field companies under his command to ready the Sittang Bridge for demolition, he ordered Hudson to take a small detachment of Malerkotlas to blow up a small bridge which was said to be between the Sittang River and Mokpalin Station. Hudson dutifully went along the line to Mokpalin, found there was no such bridge, and prepared a length of track for demolition instead. That done, he took his 15 cwt. truck back to the bridge. He was one of the last to cross.

Orgill told him to get the preparations moving. It was quite a formidable job. The work of modifying the bridge for road traffic had only just been completed, and the planking was dangerously narrow. Two junior sapper subalterns, Macklin and Mills, spent the night loading charges into wooden boxes which had previously been fixed to the girders. The Japanese put in an attack on the bridgehead while this was going on, but failed to break through.

All the Malerkotlas' stores had been used up in the Kyaikto demolitions, so they had to make do with what they could find: a store of explosives and fuses which lay a hundred yards from the west end of the bridge. The spans to be demolished were the fourth, fifth and sixth, counting from the east bank. There was no explosive equipment for more, and even these three spans would have to be dealt with separately. Only the fifth span was prepared with electric detonators and instantaneous fuse, the others were set with long lengths of safety fuse to individual girders, with sympathetic detonation.

Japanese sniped at the sappers as they worked, and bullets kept pinging off the girders, but no one was hit – in fact more nerve was needed to

[1] Smyth, *Before the Dawn*, p. 151

clamber on top of the bridge to set the charges than to face the Japanese fire. Not all the men had a head for heights. Preparations were completed by 3 pm.

Hudson then ran into another problem. He ran out the wire from Number 5 span and found there wasn't enough to reach the safe bank. The exploder box had therefore to be sited on a flange of the crossbeam transom under the bridge, about three spans from the brink. He tested the circuit, found that it worked, and reported Number 5 span as ready for firing.

The Japanese began to shell and mortar the bridgehead on the east bank with increasing accuracy, so orders were given to withdraw across the bridge. About 500 troops came over, leaving the Malerkotla firing parties and a Vickers gun, crewed by three officers crouched behind a sandbag emplacement on the railway track of the bridge, next to Hudson who was squatting on the track with his hand on the plunger of the exploder box, ready to blow when the Japanese rushed the bridge. Nothing happened. In ones and twos, stragglers, including some men from the Duke of Wellington's Regiment, reached the bridge and crossed over.

The decision was then taken to form the bridgehead again. The commander of 48 Brigade, Brigadier Hugh-Jones, obviously thought there was still a chance that 16 Brigade, which was moving to the Sittang with 46 Brigade in its wake, might reach the bridge before dark.

In the early hours of 23 February, Hugh-Jones asked Major Orgill if he could guarantee the blowing of the bridge during daylight the following day, assuming the Japanese held the east bank and had the bridge under fire. 'Orgill could give no such guarantee,' the Official History says, the possible implication being that the casualties to the sappers would prevent this, an impression confirmed by a statement in Tim Carew's *The Longest Retreat*: 'his answer was guided more by humanitarian than tactical motives: he had lost a dozen sappers killed and wounded during the hazardous operation of placing the explosive charges on the bridge. If the bridge were blown in daylight, the men whose duty it was to touch off the instantaneous fuses would be clearly visible to the enemy machine-gunners who had the entire length of the bridge squarely in their sights and would undoubtedly exploit this advantage to the full.'[1]

This does make it sound as if Orgill were weighing up his men's lives against the possibility of keeping the bridge open for the two stranded brigades. In fact, says Hudson, Orgill's motives were purely technical. His sappers had, to start with, sustained no casualties at all as they were placing the charges. He knew that two brigades were still on the wrong side of the Sittang – so too was one of his own detachments,[2] so he was well aware of

[1] Carew, *The Longest Retreat*, p. 123

[2] Under a Jemadar. They were caught on the wrong side, and swam to safety.

the need to keep the bridge open and intact as long as possible. But the shortage of explosives, wire and fuses meant that the charges to Spans Numbers 4 and 6 would have to be fired by long lengths of safety fuse, which would have to be lighted by several sappers using fuzee matches. These sappers would then have to dash smartly off the bridge before Span Number 5 was demolished by the simpler procedure of pushing down the plunger on the exploder-box. Any casualties to these sappers would mean, quite simply, that the fuses to 4 and 6 might not be lit. Hence Orgill could not guarantee an *effective* daylight demolition for any more than one span. He could be sure of blowing Number 5, but not more. Hudson, sitting behind the sandbags in the afternoon of the 22nd, was prepared to do just that if the Japanese rushed the Bridge. In fact, in Hudson's view – and as one of the engineers on the spot his view commands respect – Hugh-Jones should not have asked Orgill for that guarantee. He should have accepted the risk of a partial demolition in daylight, for the sake of the rest of the Division, and he should have given that advice to Smyth, by this time at a new HQ some eight miles west of the bridge.

By the time the bridgehead had been re-established, Hudson was beginning to show signs of extreme fatigue, as he crouched behind the exploder-box. Orgill came up and told him to hand over to Lt Mills, R.E., of 17 Division Field Company. 'I made my way back,' he recalls, 'found our HQ, had a wash, ate some chicken, and returned to the bridge at about 10 pm. Everything was quiet, and in pitch darkness I walked up and down the length of the bridge, looking for Richard Orgill. I eventually found him, with a group of a dozen sleeping sappers. He was his usual calm self, and told me to get back to have some sleep at HQ, as everything at the bridge was under control. This I did. I was awakened by the sound of the demolition in the early hours.'

In the event, the professional engineer in Hudson still winces at the improvised demolition of the Sittang Bridge. Only Number 5 Span – the one of which the charge was electrically detonated – fell out, and dropped into the river. The girders of Spans 4 and 6 were blown in parts, but neither span collapsed.[1]

A bizarre coincidence brought about a later encounter between Hudson, then a Major commanding 77 Indian Field Company, and the first Japanese to inspect the damaged bridge. Hudson was in Thailand in 1945, after the Japanese surrender, and had working under him a party of Japanese from the 33rd Engineer Battalion of 33 Division. The Japanese

[1] So his notes to Carew (letter dated 9 July 1970). **But the Malerkotla War Diary** p. 9 says 5 and 6 were 'demolished successfully'. 'Only one air photo is available at the Imperial War Museum, used by Smyth and Carew,' writes Roy Hudson. 'From it one can see that only Span No. 5 was completely demolished. No. 6 has a shadow indicating part of the span is up in the air... Stragglers *were* able to cross the bridge by clambering over the broken steelwork, and I heard that a rope was strung across to assist, as they had to wade through water in the centre of Span No. 5.' (Letter to the author, 2 xi '78)

captain in command of the Bridge Building Company had been a subaltern in the same battle in 1942, and, he told Hudson, 'it was possible for me to clamber over the tangled mass of steel girders at low tide'. So, like the demolition of the Johore Causeway leading into Singapore, that of the Sittang Bridge was only partially successful. Hudson and the Malerkotlas accompanied the retreating Army, cheerfully blowing bridges and oil installations until they came out of Burma at the end of May 1942.

Inevitably, in the case of such a traumatic event, there are discrepancies in the accounts of the last hours of the Sittang Bridge.

The man who actually blew the bridge has his own version of events. Lieutenant (later Major) Bashir Ahmed Khan, like Roy Hudson an officer in the Malerkotla Sappers and Miners, says that Smyth's assumption about the previous preparation of the charges was wrong, that the exploder was not in the end sited on the bridge itself, that Orgill was not there when the order was given, and that the bridge was blown an hour-and-a-half before the time given in the official history. In a letter to Roy Hudson (10 March 1981) and in a letter to the *Times* (31 January 1981) Smyth said that the bridge was prepared for demolition by Hutton's Burma Sappers, weeks before the battle, three times over. This may well be true, says Bashir Khan, but these charges were later removed and stacked in a spot where the Malerkotlas found them on 21/22 February in the custody of the Artisan Works Company. The final preparation for the demolition, he adds, was carried out by the Malerkotlas on 22 February, after the conversion of the railway bridge into a rail-cum-road bridge by the same Artisan Works Company.

Bashir Khan was put in charge of the firing point, and he readjusted the circuit in such a way that the exploder could be placed inside a foxhole by the side of the abutment wall, instead of over the bridge itself. This was a very sensible precaution, because the previous plan, with the exploder held on the bridge roadway side, carried a great risk for the firing officer. If he became a casualty, Khan points out, confusion might arise among the sapper other ranks of the firing party which could ruin a second attempt if the first failed. The circuits of the three spans to be blown, 4, 5 and 6, were linked together to make a stronger detonation and eliminate possibilities of a misfire. Orgill impressed on Bashir Khan the need to be strictly punctual and to avoid risk of failure at all costs, and then left for Abya with a detachment of No 2 Platoon Sappers some time before the demolition.

I lighted the small length of safety-fuze before exploding electrically (according to CO's instructions) [says Khan]. The FID-cum-electric circuit worked successfully, as could be seen from the results, in spite of the fact that span 6 had a far lesser quantity of explosives. The blowing-up was carried out as soon as I received a pre-arranged signal from the Gurkha officer with the

Vickers gun on the bridge. The gun was emplaced and mounted on the bridge, ahead of span 6, with a strong sand-bags parapet and parados. The explosion took place immediately after a quick pullout by the last Gurkha bridgehead detachment, clear of the bridge, just after 0400 am – in the early hours of 23 February 1942, while it was still dark.'[1]

The Malerkotlas were given the responsibility for the demolition of the Sittang Bridge at 7.30 pm on 21 February 1942, Khan emphasizes, while they were still engaged in denial action in the Mokpalin area. No one except the Malerkotlas was present at the time and site of the demolition, he adds, not even the Gurkhas, who had so tenaciously held the bridge for 21 hours and 30 minutes (6.30 am 22 February to 4.00 am 23 February).

Lieutenant Khan reported the demolition to Orgill at Abya later in the morning of the 23rd.

The moment of unbearable decision and tragic loss has inevitably become the enduring myth of the campaign, from the British point of view. Once the Sittang Bridge had gone and 17 Division rendered powerless, the road to Rangoon was open, and the fate of Burma sealed. Yet the episode does not figure in the same way in Japanese accounts. Colonel Hattori, in his general account of the Pacific War, does not even mention it. The official Japanese war history, *Biruma Kōryaku Sakusen* (p. 146), prints a photograph of Japanese troops with a machine gun covering the approaches to the bridge, of which one span is seen to be blown, while officers stand nearby looking through binoculars at the far bank.[2] A short account of the Japanese units reaching the bridgehead is given, and then the bald statement that the British continued fiercely resisting but blew the bridge at 6.00 am on 23 February; that some men were taken prisoners, and others plunged into the river, of whom many were drowned, while yet others took boats from a point south of Mokpalin: 'in this way the battle on the banks of the Sittang ended in a great victory'. A section of the contemporary war record of Harada's 215 Regiment of 33 Division devotes ten pages to it, much of which is concerned with the march to the Sittang rather than the action at the bridge, which was blown, this account says, at 6.30 am on 23 February.

The Japanese historian is interested by something else. Great victory though it undoubtedly was, he indicates that it was also a moment of great anxiety for General Iida. In the general's words,

It will naturally be thought that the command of 15 Army functioned very well because a great deal of booty was captured

---

[1] Letter to the author, and draft preface to 2nd edition, Part I, of Major B. A. Khan's *History of the Malerkotla Sappers and Miners*, 26 May 1982.

[2] *Biruma Kōryaku Sakusen*, pp. 147–8.

43

and we inflicted heavy casualties on the enemy, particularly in the battle on the banks of the Sittang, where they were destroyed wherever they came into contact with the two Japanese divisions. But it was not really like this at all. 15 Army tried to maintain control of the advance of its two front-line formations as best it could, but we were unable to do it properly, right up to the Sittang.

I was very worried at the time about the battle efficiency of the two divisions. They had to cross the mountains of the Thai-Burma frontier, where the going was difficult even with pack-horses, and as a result they were both deficient in equipment. They were divisions in name only, since from the point of view of the normal divisional organization they were weak. Both of them had two infantry regiments (*i.e. instead of three*) and only two battalions of mountain artillery; and their supply and transport set-up was pathetic.

There was some doubt about how fast they could operate, and we naturally feared the enemy might slip away from under our noses, just as we caught him in the trap.

The forsaken city

By 4 March, Rangoon was a city of the dead. The streets and bazaars were still and empty, the silence shattered periodically by the howling of pi-dogs, with nothing left to scavenge. Along the length of the main business centre, Phayre Street, doors were barred, nothing moved. The silk market of the Indian Moslems in Dalhousie Street was in ruins, smoke rising idly from the remnants. Fires began to fill the night sky in the residential areas, where bands of hooligans looted the houses of the wealthy and set them ablaze when they had taken what they wanted. To the confusion and vandalism was added the sheer terror of roaming bands of convicts and lunatics: the prisoners had been set free on the first night of the evacuation from the city, and the lunatics from the asylum were loose. The press photographer George Rodger was warned not to go out into the streets at night for fear of snipers, but he had to see the city's death throes, and wandered through the blazing suburbs, revolver in hand, to see whole streets alight. In one place a temple wall had collapsed, and a row of twenty Buddhas, twelve feet high, glowed red-hot against the darkness.

Incredibly, there remained pockets of order imposed by a small group of British Field Security men. The police, who were not Burmese but largely Indian – Sikhs and Punjabi Mussulmans – were disliked by the townspeople, and panicked on the approach of the Japanese. They had heard that in Tenasserim the Japanese had turned the police over to the mob. Tony Mains, a Field Security officer, had to threaten to shoot a crowd of over 100 uniformed policemen who were trying to storm the railway barrier in the station in order to catch the last train out of the city. They were finally calmed down and put on the train for Prome. Each one had arrived equipped with his own private store of loot from the shops and bazaars: new bolts of cloth, sheets, towels, whatever they could lay their hands on, and Mains promptly told his Field Security men to set about them with *lathis* until they relinquished their hoards. While this was going on, the Police Commissioner, Prescott, arrived, and angrily demanded to know why the Field Security men were beating the police.

At this, Mains lost his temper completely. Why, he wanted to know, had Prescott sent this disorderly mob up to the station without warning anyone beforehand? Why had his men looted the cloth market? What was the difference between them and any other mob of disorderly thieves and hooligans? He should be glad Mains had not ordered his men to open fire. Mains was all the more irate because the conduct of the police contrasted strongly with the cool courage of the Anglo-Burmese train drivers and firemen, who took their trains north without escort – and this meant in many cases driving across territory through which Japanese troops were passing – and then returned to rescue more people from the abandoned city.

The GSO I at Army Headquarters summoned Mains to his office. As he was going up the stairs, he heard the Police Commissioner's voice raised in fury: 'You have sold me out to the Army!' What was meant by this Mains learnt when he went in. 'You are to go back into the city, and take charge of law and order. Churchill has ordered Rangoon to be held, and we have to bring an Australian Division in through the docks.'[1] Mains learnt that Hutton had been superseded by General Alexander, and that the city was to be fought for, like Tobruk. The commanding officer of the garrison troops – the Gloucesters – was made Military Governor,[2] and Mains was termed his Assistant, to put Rangoon under 'military control'. This did not involve martial law, but looters were to be shot at sight. The Official History speaks of the imposition of a curfew, but Mains affirms there was none: there was no point, since nearly all the inhabitants had left, and those remaining were either servicemen, civilians on essential maintenance, or undesirables.

With these, Mains was ruthless. He fired on a mob of looters in the main market, and cleared it; and the rumour of what had happened scared off looters elsewhere (Mains's men had killed about half-a-dozen of them). He

[1] Lt-Colonel Tony Mains, *The Retreat from Burma: an Intelligence Officer's Personal Story*, 1973, p.49

[2] Sir Reginald Dorman-Smith, the Governor, objected to the title as derogatory to his authority, and it was changed to 'Military Commandant'. (Mains, op.cit., p. 51)

also had to rid the docks of corpses, the result not of air-raids but of warfare between rival gangs of looters.[1] Normally corpses would be disposed of by Indian sweepers, but these had fled. He could not order Indian troops to do the work, for reasons of caste, so his own British Field Security men had to set about it. Later, with some ingenuity, he organized a small van, covered with disinfectant, to act as a hearse, with two British NCOs in charge, the undertaker labour being provided by captured looters who were given this nauseating chore as an alternative to being shot.

Surprisingly, many of the essential services were still running: the power station functioned, there was light and power until the very last afternoon; the sewage works kept going, and drinking water still came through the taps. The Government Telephone Exchange and two private exchanges were still getting numbers.[2] And one team of Auxiliary Fire Servicemen did its best with the impossible problem of city-wide arson. Men of the Indian Pioneer Corps were working down at the docks to assemble trucks on the quayside, load them and get them away before the Japanese arrived. Sadly, the American Technical Group and their Chinese technicians, organizing supplies to Chungking, had anticipated that the city would be taken earlier than it was, and, conscientiously following a 'scorched earth' policy, had destroyed their entire stocks of military supplies, including 1000 trucks, the charred skeletons of which still smouldered on the wharves.

Mains and his Field Security men were to be ferried from the wharves early in the afternoon of 7 March to ships which would take them to India. At 2 pm the Military Commandant arrived and told him the ships were full and they would have to go north by road. They would wait for a company of Gloucesters which had been garrisoning the oil refinery across the river at Syriam, and move north with them and the rest of the 'last ditchers' of the Rangoon garrison. Mains was furious at this change of plan, since his men had been promised evacuation by sea, but there was no help for it. He sat and waited with the fuming Prescott, the Police Commissioner with whom he had crossed swords earlier. At 3 pm the fan which had been cutting cool swathes through the rising heat suddenly stopped. Then there was the sound of an explosion. The power station had been blown.

George Rodger of *Life* Magazine and a colleague from Movietone News decided they should leave Rangoon before the Japanese reached the junction of the roads to Pegu and Prome, twenty-one miles north of the city, so they drove out in a convoy of vehicles heading for Prome. Rodger turned round in the vehicle for one last look at the burning city, and saw

---

[1] Not all Burmese by any means. 'On the water front, warehouses were being rifled by soldiers, sailors and coolies.' *The Retreat from Burma*, Prasad, ed., p. 208

[2] So Mains affirms. The Official Indian History says that the telephone system had ceased to function on 21 February.

the gleaming gold of the Shwe Dagon Pagoda pointing skywards, like a lone and forlorn sentry, against the swirling black smoke clouds.

As they drove on, they realized they had left one kind of chaos for another. Seventy miles north of Rangoon, passing through the village of Okkan, rifle shots spat at them from the jungle running along the roadside. In Tharawaddy, riots had broken out between Burmans and Indians, and mobs armed with clubs and *dahs* (machetes) filled the streets, shouting and throwing stones as Rodger and Tozer drove through. Further still, where they crawled past columns of weary refugees on foot, corpses littered the edge of the road. Cholera and typhoid had already broken out, and no one stayed to tend the dying.[1]

Mains took his small party down to the riverside area. To his amazement, he was greeted by a British lieutenant seconded to the Royal Indian Navy. The peak of his cap had been blown off – he had been carrying out demolitions – and the last launch had left without him. Mains invited him to join his party, and the invitation was accepted unhesitatingly. 'HMS Hindustan' was the lieutenant's contribution to the transport available: a jeep painted battleship grey. He told Mains that there was no point in leaving to the Japanese the store of refrigerated beer in the fridge of the Port Trust Club. Nothing loath, Mains – who had spent many hours staving in casks of Chinese spirit and loading whisky into the vaults of the Reserve Bank of India to prevent the victorious Japanese becoming inflamed with drink – collected chairs from the fire station and sat with his men on the dockside, quaffing cold beer and waiting for the Gloucesters' launch to appear from Syriam.

There was no longer any question of holding Rangoon to await the arrival of the promised Australian Division from the Middle East, which everyone, from Wavell downwards, had hoped would reverse the defeats of the past month and drive the Japanese back. The Australian Prime Minister, Curtin, needed every Australian who could be spared to defend Australia against the Japanese, who were driving south towards it from several quarters at once. And little he had read of the defence of Burma so far gave him confidence that his highly trained troops would be anything other than chaff thrown into the flames at the last minute. 'It is of infinite importance to us to know whether Australian Division will arrive,' the Governor of Burma telegraphed to Winston Churchill. 'Please say yes or no.' 'We have made every appeal,' came back the dusty answer, ' . . . but Australian Government absolutely refuses. Fight on.'[2]

Fighting on had its limits, as Dorman-Smith signalled to the Viceroy of India on 27 February:

[1] G. Rodger, *Red Moon Rising*, 1943, pp. 66–7

[2] Carew, op.cit., p. 149

This is the last message I will send from Rangoon until we have recaptured it . . . Our troops have fought very well but they are worn out . . . Unless some miracle happens I propose to start demolition at or about 7 hours on 1st March . . . I bitterly regret that we must go from here . . . I can see nothing in sight which can save Rangoon but by going now we may be able to retain a whole lot which may help you in your effort on some other Far Eastern Front . . . I think we will be very fortunate if we live to fight in Upper Burma . . . Still no telegram from you which makes it imperative for me as man on the spot to make decision. I intend to leave 08 hours March 1st after demolition order has been given.[1]

Even at this juncture Wavell still thought reinforcements might save Rangoon. 63 Indian Infantry Brigade was turned away from Rangoon on the same day that Dorman-Smith sent his telegram to Delhi. It was the Army Commander, Hutton, who did this, knowing the brigade was not fit to fight. He urged that it should be sent back to Calcutta or landed at Akyab. Wavell countermanded his decision, and the brigade was ordered to disembark at Rangoon. Sensing that Hutton was prepared already to evacuate the city and move north, Wavell flew to Magwe, on the Irrawaddy, from Calcutta on 28 February. Dorman-Smith, Hutton, and the AOC Air Vice-Marshal Stevenson were there to meet him.

It was a fraught meeting. Wavell lost control of himself completely. He stormed at Hutton in front of the Governor and the AOC, and a number of officers and civilian officials. Hutton was, needless to say, mortified and humiliated at this public assault from one whose Chief of Staff he had been until a matter of a few months ago, not on his conduct of the campaign but on what Wavell thought was his defeatist attitude; but he said nothing, feeling that the most dignified rejoinder was silence.[2]

Wavell ordered Rangoon to be held as long as possible, to pass the maximum number of troops in through the port while there was still time. He flew on to Rangoon, taking Hutton with him. When they reached Army Headquarters, there was a signal awaiting Hutton from Smyth, whose 17 Divisional HQ was then at the village of Hlegu, about halfway between Rangoon and Pegu. Smyth wanted to withdraw his forces from Pegu at once. Exasperated by yet another demand from Smyth to with-

---

[1] Connell, *Wavell, Supreme Commander*, pp. 201–2

[2] 'It was the only time I have seen him completely lose control of himself. He stormed at me in front of the Governor, the AOC and a number of Officers and Civilians in a most excited way and I felt the only dignified thing to do was to make no reply. I certainly felt then, and still feel, that if he had had his way the whole army and a large number of Civilians would have been captured in Rangoon by the Japanese. In fact by holding up the evacuation and ordering Alexander to counter-attack at Pegu he very nearly achieved that result.' (Lt .-General Sir Thomas Hutton, op.cit., p. 56)

draw, Wavell decided to drive up the hot dusty road the same evening, to see Smyth at his HQ. 'I little knew,' Smyth wrote later, 'that Sunday, 1st March, would be my last day's soldiering. But it was so.'[1] Wavell saw that Smyth was a sick man. The injections of strychnine and arsenic seemed no longer able to dampen the pain from his agonizing anal fissure. He was fighting the Japanese and dire sickness at one and the same time, and it was proving too much. Wavell told Cowan, Smyth's Chief of Staff, to take over the division. Smyth was packed off back to India.

Many personal tragedies were involved in the fall of Lower Burma, but none worse than Smyth's. Through a cloud of pain, he had been fighting in pursuance of a strategy he totally disbelieved in, with quite inadequate resources. His humiliation at being relieved of his command was reinforced when he reached Delhi. An official letter awaited him from the Military Secretary: by General Wavell's command he was to be deprived of his rank of Major-General forthwith, and immediately retired from the service. Not only did he, at one fell swoop, lose rank and pension, he was charged with two offences, of not having a medical inspection when ordered to Burma – thus disregarding Medical Regulations (India) paragraph 86 – and of applying for leave after having been passed fit by a medical board.

Here the Sittang River battle pursued Smyth to the bitter end. His ADMS, Lieutenant-Colonel Mackenzie, who had examined him in Burma just before the bridge was blown, and had told him to go on leave as soon as possible,[2] had been taken prisoner by the Japanese (he spent the rest of the war in Rangoon Jail). The recommendation of Mackenzie's medical board on Smyth had obviously not been seen by Wavell. Utterly drained and exhausted, Smyth asked to see Wavell and was refused an interview. Hutton, he was sure, had put all the blame for the loss of Rangoon and Burma upon him.[3]

Whether Wavell ever saw Smyth's medical board report and its recommendations for leave or not will never be known; Hutton knew of it on 25 February, but there was no need for him to say anything further about it to Wavell when they saw Smyth a week later at his HQ. As Wavell signalled to the Chiefs of Staff, Smyth was 'definitely a sick man' – no report was needed to prove that; and Hutton had no control over what happened to Smyth when he was back in India. He had, in any case, no part in Smyth's removal from the command of 17 Indian Division. The decision was

[1] Smyth, *Before the Dawn*, p. 195

[2] To recommend a commander to take leave in the midst of an arduous operation may seem curious anyway but, Smyth later wrote, 'I may have looked a bit strained, the operations had been a great strain, particularly as I was constantly ordered to do things which I knew were militarily very wrong. But I was perfectly capable of continuing.' Archive Material, Imperial War Museum.

[3] In the usual way, Wavell thanks a number of subordinate commanders in his despatch on the sorry defeat in Burma. Smyth's name is not in the list.

justifiable on medical grounds, but it was Wavell's decision. He did not consult Hutton at all.

The irony was, of course, that Hutton himself had already been superseded as Army Commander. His successor, Lieutenant-General Sir Harold (later Field-Marshal Lord) Alexander had not yet arrived, but Hutton knew that he had lost his command and was to remain on the spot to act as Alexander's Chief of Staff. He and Alexander had a friendly personal relationship but it was a humiliating position all the same, particularly since he disagreed with Alexander's view of how to fight what little of the campaign was left.

The editor of Lord Alanbrooke's diaries, Sir Arthur Bryant, describes Alexander as 'the finest general the CIGS could recommend'.[1] The view was not universally held, at any rate among Indian Army generals who later fought under Alexander in North Africa. In this connection, Lieutenant-General Sir Francis Tuker's caustic note puts weight in another pan of the balance. 'I think he is quite the least intelligent commander I have ever met in a high position,' Tuker wrote, 'I cannot imagine his ever producing a plan, let alone a good plan. I don't think he ever did. Certainly in Italy I am sure he never really took charge of operations. He had no tactical policy of his own. Everything just drifted.'[2]

That verdict was passed years after Alexander's performance in Burma. But even then, the plans he put forward were Wavell's, not his own, and the view he took of the situation could have lost not merely the capital city but the entire Burma Army.

In his favour, it must be said he was faced with a situation which had begun to deteriorate ungovernably long before he arrived. Hutton's supersession, for one thing, does not seem to have been caused by a failure in conducting operations; it was more the result of a cold-eyed pessimism, which saw things blackly, as they were, and put forward no view to relieve the inspissated gloom. Had he confined these views to Wavell, whom he knew well enough to feel that his confidence was respected, it would have been risky enough at a time when Wavell was looking in every direction for crumbs of comfort about British morale in the Far East. But Hutton's signals to Wavell were read by other eyes. They were shown to the Viceroy. Prompted (so Hutton believed) by General Sir Alan Hartley, acting C-in-C India, the Viceroy feared for the security of India, and cabled to London, 'Our troops in Burma are not fighting with proper spirit. I have not the least doubt that this is in great part due to lack of drive and inspiration from the top.' Hutton was a good Chief of Staff, he went on,

---

[1] Sir Arthur Bryant, *The Turn of the Tide*, p. 256

[2] MS notes, Tuker Papers, Imperial War Museum.

but not fitted to be a commander in the field. The text of Linlithgow's telegram was sent by Churchill to Wavell, with a request that he should tell Lieutenant-General Sir Alan Brooke, Chief of the Imperial General Staff, what he thought. If Wavell agreed with the Viceroy, Churchill added, he was prepared to send Alexander out to Burma at once. A signal from Wavell to both Churchill and Alan Brooke left the same day, and supported Linlithgow's melancholy suspicions:

> I am very disturbed altogether at lack of real fighting spirit in our troops shown in Malaya and so far in Burma. Neither British, Australians or Indians have shown real toughness of mind or body . . . Causes go deep, softness of last twenty years, lack of vigour in peace training, effects of climate and atmosphere of East. Leaders of real drive and inspiration are few. I looked for one in Malaya and Singapore and could not find him. Hutton has plenty of determination behind quiet manner and will never get rattled but lacks power of personal inspiration. At time I selected him reorganization of whole military machine in Burma was imperative, I knew he would do this excellently and considered also he would be resolute and skilful commander. I have no reason to think otherwise but agree that Alexander's forceful personality might act as stimulus to troops.[1]

Wavell was reluctant to change commanders, but agreed that Hutton should stay as CGS (or return to India as CGS), and added that if Alexander were to be sent, then he should be in Burma within a week. Early in the afternoon of 22 February, while the Sittang Bridge was still being fought for, Hutton received a signal from Wavell which he was instructed to decipher personally:

> War Cabinet has decided in view large proposed increase army in Burma that General Alexander should be appointed C-in-C Burma. You will remain CGS in Burma after his arrival. You should inform Governor. Otherwise keep appointment secret till arrival Alexander.[2]

It proved an awkward time for Hutton, even after Alexander arrived. Except at Army HQ, everyone thought Hutton was still in command. He was the same rank as Alexander (who was promoted acting General in April 1942), so he naturally got very tired of explaining that he no longer was in command; and he recalled with some bitterness a phrase he had

[1] Connell, *Wavell, Supreme Commander*, p. 181–2

[2] ibid. p. 191

read in a life of Wellington: 'Of all the awkward situations in the world that which is most so is to serve in a subordinate capacity in an Army which one has commanded.'[1]

Alexander's arrival on 5 March did nothing to save Rangoon. Even the landing of a new division might not have achieved that. The last train puffed northwards from the abandoned, burning city on 7 March, at 7.30 pm. A few minutes later, the column of Gloucesters, with Mains's Field Security jeeps and trucks, left by the Prome Road. The following morning around noon[2] the Japanese marched in.

As it happened, the end of a period of imperial history had already been italicized by the Governor of Burma's ADC. Before the Governor left, on 1 March, a final dinner was held in Government House. When the few diners rose from the table, and moved to the billiard room, an unaccountable mood of high spirits seized the ADC, Eric Battersby. Taking hold of a billiard ball, he hurled it at one of the portraits of past imperial glory staring down, in mute criticism, from their gilded frames. 'Don't you think, H.E., that we ought to deny them also to the Japs?' he shouted, as the ball went through the canvas. The mood was catching. In a few seconds, the others grabbed billiard balls and threw them at the pictures all over the room. The following morning, 1 March 1942, Sir Reginald Dorman-Smith left his capital city behind and drove north to Maymyo.

When Lieutenant-General Sir Harold Alexander arrived in Burma to take over command, he naturally determined to hold on to the capital at all costs. It was certainly with that in mind that the Chief of the Imperial General Staff, Lieutenant-General Sir Alan Brooke, sent Alexander out in the first place: 'If we had concentrated on reinforcing Rangoon,' he wrote later, ' . . .Burma might have been held.'[3] But in his diary, at the time, the CIGS noted on 18 February 1942, 'Burma news bad. If the Army cannot fight better than it is doing at present we shall deserve to lose our Empire.' He gloomily noted on 27 February, 'I cannot see how we are going to go on holding Rangoon much longer.'[4]

Wavell was back in India on 3 March and saw Alexander in Calcutta, and gave him verbal instructions how to conduct his campaign:

> The retention of Rangoon is a matter of vital importance to our position in the Far East and every effort must be made to hold it. If however that is not possible, the British force must not be allowed to be cut off and destroyed, but must be withdrawn from

[1] Hutton, *Rangoon 1941–2*, p. 56

[2] 'Before dawn' in Prasad, op.cit., p. 213

[3] Bryant, op.cit., p. 255

[4] ibid. p. 256

the Rangoon area for the defence of upper Burma. This must be held as long as possible in order to safeguard the oil-fields at Yenangyaung, keep contact with the Chinese and protect the construction of the road from Assam to Burma.[1]

Alexander arrived in Rangoon at noon on 5 March, went up to Hlegu, and cancelled Hutton's orders for 48 Brigade to withdraw from Pegu to Hlegu and 16 Brigade to withdraw from Hlegu to Taukkyan. Instead, 1st Burma Division was to attack south from Nyaunglebin towards Pegu, and 17 Division, backed by the newly arrived 63 Brigade and 7th Armoured Brigade, was to mount an offensive against the Japanese east of Pegu at Waw. In this way Alexander hoped to restore the situation and stem the advance of General Iida's two divisions, 33 and 55, on the capital. The attempt failed, the Japanese put a ring round Pegu and infiltrated commando parties by sea to take the oil refineries at Syriam, across the river from Rangoon. It was not going to be possible to hold Rangoon after all, Alexander realized after exactly one day in Burma, and he ordered demolitions to go ahead and the city to be abandoned, with the intention of regrouping his forces in the Irrawaddy Valley to the north.[2]

Cranes on the dockside were thrown into the river or blown up, warehouses were blasted, supplies left in Rangoon station were set on fire, Field Security fired the telegraph office using Chinese explosives, the power station was blown up, police headquarters set ablaze and, most vivid of all, the oil refineries at Syriam were dynamited and clouds of black smoke, thousands of feet high, poured over the stricken city. The so-called 'last-ditchers' who volunteered to do the demolitions were taken off by launch down the Rangoon River to three ships which were waiting to take them to Calcutta.[3]

The garrison marched north. 17 Division was holding Hlegu until the garrison had cleared the road junction at Taukkyan, where the road from Pegu and Mandalay met the road leading to Rangoon from the Irrawaddy. An advance guard of the garrison passed through Taukkyan at dawn on 7 March and made for Tharawaddy, which had been fixed as the line on which any Japanese moving north from Rangoon were to be held. Once the garrison passed through Taukkyan, 17 Division was to come up behind them and act as rearguard as they moved up the Irrawaddy Valley to protect the oil-fields.

[1] Kirby, *War Against Japan*, II, p. 86

[2] Kirby, *War Against Japan*, II, p. 94

[3] Alfred Wagg, *A Million Died*, 1943, p. 53

The skin of General Alexander's teeth

That was the theory. But the Japanese established a road block five miles north of Taukkyan, and despite repeated attacks by the Rangoon garrison, the block held. Alexander and his forces were trapped. 7th Armoured Brigade was sent against the block, but by 4 pm on 7 March they had made no impression. 2 Frontier Force Rifles of 63 Brigade were brought in from Hlegu to Taukkyan, but the Japanese threw them back and inflicted heavy casualties. Alexander and his headquarters staff spent the night in a rubber plantation near Taukkyan. The perimeter was ringed by tanks and infantry, but it was as well the Japanese never attacked it: the core of the position consisted of administrative and office staffs from Rangoon, including some women who had disobeyed the earlier orders to leave the city.[1]

Alexander ordered the block to be attacked at dawn, with 63 Brigade's 1/10 Gurkhas on the west, 1st Sikh Regiment on the east, and the tanks of the 7th Hussars charging straight up the road after an artillery barrage. The attack was doomed almost before it began. The Gurkhas got lost in the jungle and split up, the Sikhs were bombed by Japanese planes as they concentrated in open country.

Nothing seemed able to shift the Japanese and their stranglehold on Alexander. Then suddenly they weren't there any more. The block was lifted, Alexander and his garrison passed through. Writing as historian of the Indian Army, Compton Mackenzie speaks of 'the enemy's whimsical abandonment of the block' and adds that 'no explanation put forward for his astonishing mistake is satisfactory'.[2] The British official historians were perplexed by the episode and one of them, Colonel G. T. Wards, himself an expert on the Japanese Army and a former military attaché in Japan, sent a post-war enquiry to Tokyo to find out what the Japanese motivation had been. After all, they were within an ace of putting in the bag not only the Rangoon garrison but 17 Division, too, as it withdrew from Pegu through Hlegu, Taukkyan and up the Prome road; and, of course, the Commander-in-Chief himself.

> Two questions at once present themselves [wrote Colonel Wards]. It may be that HQ 33 Division did not know or realize that they had such a large and important body of enemy in the bag if they wished to hold the net closed, and again it may be that this division had been given the primary role of capturing Rangoon and putting the capture of enemy troops secondly. It is on this latter assumption that, as it stands at present, criticism is

[1] Mackenzie, *Eastern Epic*, p. 455

[2] ibid., pp. 455–6

being made of Japanese leadership at this time, pointing out that to go for a geographical object rather than your enemy's army is bad strategy. It also occurs to me that perhaps such a mistake on the part of the Japanese might be due to the rigidity of their military methods and actions. Orders were very often detailed and binding, encouraging a tendency to stick to them too closely and thus at times (as in the present instance) miss opportunities which if taken by the man on the spot would lead to success and victory.[1]

The man on the spot was Colonel Sakuma Takanobu, commanding 214 Infantry Regiment of 33 Division. 33 Division had been given the task of crossing the Sittang north of the shattered bridge, at Kunzeik, on 3 March, and then making for a line connecting Hlegu and Hmawbi. From that line it was to descend on Rangoon. The divisional commander, Lieutenant-General Sakurai Shōzō, took it that this order, issued on 27 February, meant he was to conserve his forces for the capture of Rangoon and not be deflected in any way by minor skirmishes, because he anticipated a battle in the northern outskirts of the city and then in the city streets. He wanted above all to avoid a long fight for Rangoon which might hold up the Japanese use of the port, and possibly allow the British to mount an attack on him from the direction of Prome. He knew elements of the garrison were withdrawing from the city, but did not understand that this was a complete evacuation.

The order he received from 15 Army on 6 March seemed to be telling him to do something very different from the earlier one. He was at Wapange, a village just east of the road leading from Hlegu into the Pegu Yomas, when he was told, 'You will advance on Rangoon, seek out the enemy and destroy him.'[2] When the order came in, Sakurai had very uncertain notions not only of enemy strength but also of what was happening on the front of his neighbouring division, 55, then engaged with 17 Division in the battle for Pegu. He decided the best thing to do was to aim at the city at all costs and absolutely avoid contact with the British. He summoned regimental and battalion commanders at noon on the 7th and told them that the advance on Rangoon would begin at nightfall that day. The advance would go ahead in two columns, 214 Infantry Regiment on the left and 215 Regiment on the right. When they began to move, they did everything possible to keep out of the way of British observers, bypassing the larger villages, crossing dried paddy and moving along jungle tracks. In this way, after crossing the Prome road between Taukkyan and Hmawbi, the division would come out north-west of Rangoon.

[1] Letter to British Embassy, Tokyo, dated 26 Feb. 1953, Imperial war Museum.
[2] OCH *Biruma shinkō sakusen* p. 90

Then the battalion in the van was bumped by what the Japanese took to be an armoured unit retreating from Pegu. The battalion commander, Major Takanobu, was badly wounded almost at once, and the casualties began to mount. The regimental commander, Colonel Sakuma, realized that this encounter went clean against the principles on which the division was moving, but he gathered the rest of his regiment south of the main road and decided for the time being to watch how the battle developed.

Meanwhile, as the British were involved in this engagement, 215 Regiment (Colonel Harada Munaji) crossed the Prome road without incident. General Sakurai, informed of the encounter, told Sakuma that his prime duty was to conform to previously issued orders and make for Rangoon at all costs. Sakuma acted on this, and at 10 am on 7 March told Takanobu not to develop the battle further. In fact, the encounter was undoubtedly Takanobu's fault. A patrol of platoon strength had observed the British retreating along the main road while the rest of the battalion was halted a mile east of it. The patrol reported to Takanobu who decided to attack the retreating British without more ado. He then reported to Sakuma what he had done.[1]

It was, of course, quite feasible for Sakurai to grasp the opportunity of destroying whatever force this happened to be, but Sakuma came to divisional HQ at 10.20 am, told the Chief of Staff what had happened, and recommended that his regiment should not pursue the action which had been begun by Takanobu's rashness, but should push on to Rangoon. When consulted, Harada concurred.

Sakurai thought that the British, alerted to the presence of Japanese on the Prome road by Takanobu's attack, might take the hint and strengthen Rangoon's north and north-west defences. He agreed with his two regimental commanders that the dash into Rangoon was the foremost priority, and told Sakuma to make Takanobu disengage and move on.

Sakuma was back at his regimental HQ at 3 pm and issued orders to move on at 5 pm. When the main body of the regiment reached the Prome road, they found Takanobu wounded and his men not yet able to break contact. Sakuma decided to continue his advance without his 3rd Battalion, and told Takanobu to break contact as soon as he could and follow on. At dawn on 8 March Sakuma was on Mingaladon airfield.[2]

His fellow regimental commander, Harada, was by this time already in the northern suburbs. Harada had anticipated a great battle for Rangoon, and the comparative quiet in the villages as his men moved through the Pegu Yomas, across the Prome road, and then turned south, he took to be the calm before the storm. His men were buoyed up by the thought that

[1] ibid., p. 92

[2] ibid. pp. 90–4; US Historical Section, Tokyo, reply to Colonel Wards, 30 April 1953, Imperial War Museum Archives.

they had already cut the supply route to Chiang Kai-shek, and so helped their comrades in the 'Holy War' on the battlefields of China. By 10 am on 8 March his advance guard was in the deserted streets. Two hours later Sakurai set up his divisional tactical headquarters on the edge of Victoria Lake.

Wards's criticism was not entirely otiose, nevertheless. His view echoes that of Terauchi and Southern Army at the time. Five days before 15 Army's two divisions crossed the Sittang, Southern Army told Iida that his main effort should be to win a decisive engagement against the Chinese forces coming down from North Burma, rather than the early capture of Rangoon, which could be taken by part of his force. Iida, sensibly enough, thought otherwise. Neither 33 nor 55 Division had received supplies since they crossed the border with Thailand, and their ammunition stocks were perilously low. If Iida took Rangoon, he could at once be supplied by sea from Singapore, which had been in Japanese hands since 15 February. And if his campaign were to expand into Central and Upper Burma, he would need the port to land extra divisions. So while Iida was sorry Sakurai had allowed 17 Indian Division to escape the net, he was satisfied that Rangoon was in his hands.

Neither the regimental commander at Taukkyan, nor the divisional commander, nor the Army commander, nor the Japanese historians who have since written about it, seem to have been aware they almost had General Alexander in the bag. The Japanese Official History and the version produced for officer training in the Self-Defence Force still speak of the body attacking the Taukkyan roadblock as if it were part of 17 Indian Division retreating from Pegu via Hlegu. It is true that 63 Brigade units were involved. But the initial clash of Takanobu's battalion of 214 Infantry Regiment was with the withdrawing Rangoon garrison, as the British Official History makes clear. That history was in print in 1958, and the Japanese historians made use of it when they wrote their own which was printed nine years later. But this particular revelation seems to have escaped their notice. As Hutton later commented, 'Alex never had a greater stroke of luck in his life.'[1] Owing to Sakurai's unwavering eye on the target, a city rather than a man, Alexander was spared the next three years in a Japanese prison camp.

The longest retreat: Slim improves on Sir John Moore

The Chinese intervention in the first Burma campaign is a complex and controversial episode. It was in Chiang Kai-shek's interest to keep open his supply route from the Western powers and vital to ensure the safety of the

---

[1] See Hutton obituary, *The Times*, 20 Jan. 1981

port of Rangoon on which that depended. Its air defence was in large part
the work of the American pilots of the American Volunteer Group ('Flying
Tigers') of Major-General Claire Chennault. Wavell accepted the offer of
two Chinese divisions, 49 and 93 (two-thirds of Chinese VI Army) and
asked that V Army, which had also been offered, should be kept in reserve
at Kunming. The fact that he did not welcome both V and VI Armies with
open arms is understandable.[1] The Chinese had no supply system and lived
off the land like locusts. There was profound mistrust between them and
the Burmese, and their command arrangements were chaotic. As a sop to
Roosevelt, on the recommendation of Marshall, the Chief of Staff, Chiang
accepted the US general Stilwell in 'command' of Chinese forces in
Burma. Stilwell was to act as Chiang's Chief of Staff, but when he visited
Alexander and told him he was in command of the Chinese in Burma, he
found that General Tu Lü Ming, GOC V Army, had already introduced
himself in that capacity.[2] The Governor of Burma, Dorman-Smith, was
puzzled by this dual phenomenon but, Tu told him, 'the American general
only thinks he is commanding. In fact he is doing no such thing. You see,
we Chinese think that the only way to keep the Americans in the war is to
give them a few commands on paper. They will not do much harm as long
as we do the work!'[3]

Stilwell thought he had mastered the situation when Chiang visited
Alexander at Maymyo on April 5th, assembled the Chinese commanders
and told them Stilwell had full powers over them and promised Stilwell the
official seal or *kuan fang* to show this. Without its red stamp no order
would be valid. But when the *kuan fang* arrived its device was not 'Commander-in-Chief, Burma Expeditionary Force' but 'Chief of Staff, Allied
Armies' and no letter of authority came with it. To the Chinese generals
this clearly indicated that, whatever Chiang said in Maymyo, Stilwell was
an advisor, not a commander.[4]

On 13 March 1942 (noted as an unlucky Friday 13th in his diary) Stilwell
met Alexander for the first time. Predictably, impressions were not favourable: 'Very cautious. Long sharp nose. Rather brusque and *yang ch'i*
(stand-offish). Let me stand around waiting for Shang Chen (Director of

---

[1] 'As regards the Chinese, Wavell made it quite clear to me when I met him in Rangoon after
his return from Chungking that he did not want the Chinese in Burma which in his opinion
was not immediately threatened and for which he supposed he would have ample British
Indian and African troops available. These views may well have tended to slow up the
advance of the Chinese when this help was called for.' (Hutton, op. cit., p. 4)

[2] Variously misspelt in books about the period: Tu Yu Ming in *The Stilwell Papers*; Tu Li
Ming in Barbara Tuchman, *Sand Against the Wind,* Tu Li-min in *US Foreign Relations, 1945,*
VII

[3] Romanus & Sunderland, *Stilwell's Mission to China,* 1953, p. 120. Tu emphasized that
General Lo Ying-ching was in command. Lo had been given to Stilwell by Chiang as his
'executive'.

[4] ibid., p. 280

Foreign Affairs Bureau of Chinese general staff) to come. Uninterested when Shang did come. Astonished to find *me* – mere me, a goddam American – in command of Chinese troops. "Extrawdinery!" Looked me over as if I had just crawled out from under a rock.'[1]

The situation was further complicated by Chiang's belief that Stilwell should command both British and Chinese troops in Burma, since after the loss of Singapore and Rangoon he had no faith in British strategy or morale.[2] A compromise was achieved by Wavell's agreement with the Chiefs of Staff that Alexander should 'co-ordinate British and Chinese forces in Burma on Wavell's behalf'.[3] Meanwhile 200 Division (Chinese V Army) was to garrison the Toungoo area. V Army's other two divisions (22, 96) would not advance further south than Mandalay. Stilwell pushed these two divisions into Burma as soon as he took over, and obtained Chiang's consent to 22 Division reinforcing 200 Division at Toungoo.

200 Division was to relieve 1st Burma Division (Major-General Bruce Scott) of the defence of Toungoo. 1st Burma Division was then to move back through the Chinese to Yedashe and on to Taungdwingyi, a nodal point for rail and road traffic north of the Pegu Yomas. It was to come under the newly constituted Burcorps, consisting of 1st Burma Division, 17 Indian Division and 7 Armoured Brigade, and a newly appointed Corps Commander, who, more than any other soldier in the theatre, was to imprint his will on the course of the war: Lieutenant-General William Slim.

Burcorps would fight for the oil-fields area round Yenangyaung. The Chinese would be responsible for the road and railway to Mandalay up the Sittang Valley.

They were dealing with vastly increased Japanese forces. The threat of the Chinese coming down from Yunnan compelled the Japanese to double their bid for Burma. In March and April an extra regiment arrived for 33 Division (213 Infantry Regiment), and 18 and 56 Divisions came into Rangoon by sea. The strengthened 33 Division was to drive north up the Irrawaddy Valley through Prome and take Yenangyaung. 55 Division would continue to advance north from the Pegu-Nyaunglebin area by taking Toungoo and move on to Pyinmana and Mandalay. 56 Division would make a wide hook east through Taunggyi and advance north through the Shan States to cut the roads to China. 18 Division would be the reserve in the Sittang Valley and follow 55 Division.

200 Chinese Division (Tai An-lan) was about 8500 men strong, much bigger than the other two divisions of V Army which had about 6000 men each or than those of VI Army which only had around 5700. But the figures are deceptive. They include coolies for labour and transportation. The

---

[1] *Stilwell Papers*, p. 78

[2] Kirby, *War Against Japan*, II, p. 154

[3] ibid., p. 155

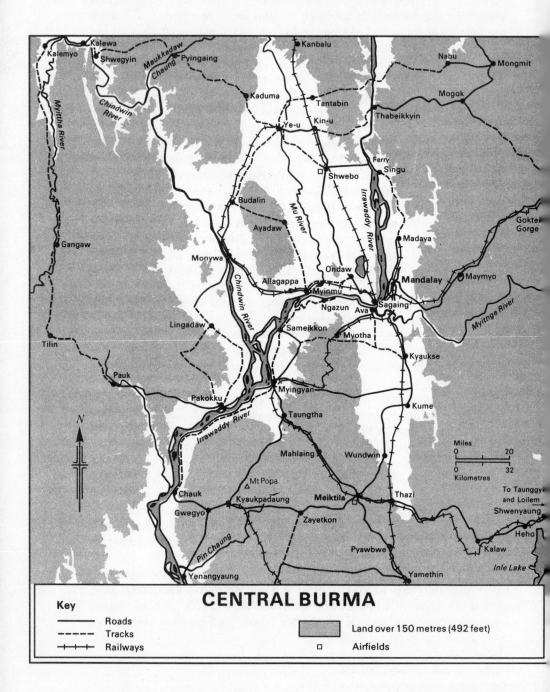

Kalemyo
Kalewa
Shwegyin
Maukkadaw Chaung
Pyingaing
Kanbalu
Nabu
Mongmit
Chindwin River
Myittha River
Kaduma
Tantabin
Mogok
Ye-u
Kin-u
Thabeikkyin
Shwebo
Ferry
Singu
Budalin
Mu River
Irrawaddy River
Ayadaw
Madaya
Gangaw
Monywa
Ondaw
Mandalay
Maymyo
Allagappa
Myinmu
Sagaing
Chindwin River
Ngazun
Ava
Myitnge River
Lingadaw
Sameikkon
Myotha
Tilin
Kyaukse
Pauk
Myingyan
Kume
Pakokku
Taungtha
Irrawaddy River
N
Mahlaing
Wundwin
Miles
0   20
0   32
Kilometres
Mt Popa
Chauk
Kyaukpadaung
Meiktila
Thazi
To Taunggyi
and Loilem
Gwegyo
Zayetkon
Shwenyaung
Pin Chaung
Pyawbwe
Heho
Yenangyaung
Yamethin
Kalaw
Inle Lake
Gokte Gorge

Key

——	Roads
- - -	Tracks
+++	Railways

CENTRAL BURMA

Land over 150 metres (492 feet)

□ Airfields

division was motorized, had some armour, and with recent lend-lease equipment its artillery possessed 36 75mm howitzers and a motorized battalion of 105mm. But its medical services were non-existent, and it had no interpreters to make contact with the British – a handicap on both sides throughout the campaign.

By a happy coincidence, Slim knew both his divisional commanders very well. All three had been officers together in the same battalion, 1/6 Gurkhas, and were old friends of more than twenty years' standing. Slim needed all the moral support he could get. Wavell had not minced matters when he told him why Singapore had fallen and Burma looked as if it would go the same way. He had not been told what the campaign was *for*, whether to retain part of Burma or get the Army back intact to India. His Corps HQ was short of transport and wireless and soon after he reached HQ at Prome he lost all his air support: the Japanese raided the airfield at Magwe on 21 March and destroyed RAF and AVG planes on the ground, in reprisal for a bombing raid on Rangoon.[1] By the end of the afternoon of 22 March, six Blenheims, three Tomahawks and eleven Hurricanes were all that were left, and these were promptly withdrawn, the RAF to Akyab – still in British hands – and the AVG to Loiwing and Lashio near the Chinese border. Slim could not have been very much surprised by the RAF at Magwe being caught on the hop. When he arrived there en route to Prome, he found the aircraft completely unguarded and the RAF blithely convinced it was the Army's job to look after their planes. From then on, as Slim pointed out, his Corps had no air reconnaissance, defence or support. Anything in the sky was Japanese.[2]

When Bruce Scott handed over to General Tai An-lan at Toungoo, it was almost impossible to explain the situation for lack of interpreters and the Chinese lack of maps. In the end Scott gave up and extricated his Divisional HQ just in time. The Chinese had set it ablaze, along with many other buildings in Toungoo, on the theory that that was the best way to defend the town. Tu wanted 1st Burma Division out of the way, whereas Stilwell desperately wanted it to stay put until 22 Chinese Division came south.[3]

Toungoo came under attack by Takeuchi's 55 Division on 24 March. Tai An-lan's men resisted fiercely but the airfield was taken and the town surrounded by the 27th. The nearest help was 22 Division (Liao Yao-shang) which was sixty miles north at Pyinmana, but Chiang Kai-shek asked Alexander to attack the Japanese in the Irrawaddy Valley and relieve the pressure at Toungoo that way. (Stilwell believed, wrongly, that the Japanese facing 200 Division were being reinforced from the Irrawaddy Valley.) Slim did not want to attack while his forces were still concentrat-

---

[1] Slim, *Defeat into Victory*, p. 19

[2] ibid., pp. 21–2, 42

[3] Romanus & Sunderland, op. cit., p. 106

ing and was not convinced, anyway, that anything he did would divert the Japanese from Toungoo. He told Cowan to make a sortie towards Okpo, sixty miles south-east of Prome, and a scratch force was sent under Brigadier Anstice (7 Armoured Brigade) to take Paungde as a preliminary measure. Anstice had a tank regiment, an artillery battery and three infantry battalions, but after entering Paungde and inflicting heavy casualties on the Japanese he was forced out again. One of his liaison officers returning to Cowan's HQ found that the town of Shwedaung, ten miles south of Prome, was already in Japanese hands. Major Sato Misao's II/215 Regiment (33 Division) had occupied it at 9.00 am on 29 March.

Anstice looked like being cut off, and Cowan sent two battalions (4 Frontier Force Regt., 2 Frontier Force Rifles) to clear Shwedaung and let him through. With Anstice's force – thirty tanks, twenty guns, 200 vehicles – attacking from the southern entrance to the town and two infantry battalions from the north, successive road blocks on the main artery were hammered through by two companies of 1 Gloucester and a troop of 7 Hussars, while Japanese aircraft machine-gunned the attackers. What was significant about this battle was the comparatively large numbers of Burma National Army engaged on the side of the Japanese, under Bo Yan Naing and two Japanese officers, Hirayama and Ikeda. The Japanese took up positions on the right side of the Prome road, the Burmese on the left. The BNA vanguard battalion (Bo Tun Shein) was surrounded and practically wiped out, in part due to their sheer ignorance of modern war. Ba Maw describes them scornfully as 'raw young peasants with plenty of guts but little else'; they had never seen a tank before, came too close to one, and were promptly blown to pieces.[1]

Yan Naing and 400 BNA blocked the retreat of Anstice's force in the fields outside the town, where the battle spread after a lucky shot from the only anti-tank gun in Japanese hands knocked out a British tank on a vital bridge and stopped all movement across it. Yan Naing saw a group of seventy Indian troops under their British officers come forward to surrender, with raised hands. He and Hirayama ordered the Burmese to stop firing, and he shouted to the Indians to lay down their arms. While the surrender was being negotiated, firing came from the British side and cut down the Japanese officers, leaving Yan Naing unharmed. He at once ordered his men to open fire on the Indians until the last man was killed, a barbarous ending to a hard day's fighting as Ba Maw observes. 'I had to act at once,' Yan Naing told him later, 'It was no time to weigh things too long or nicely. And the sight of my two closest comrades lying crumpled and dead maddened me.'[2]

By the time Yan Naing withdrew from Shwedaung, his men had lost

---

[1] Ba Maw, *Breakthrough in Burma* p. 167

[2] ibid., p. 168

more than half their numbers. Of 1300, sixty were killed, around sixty made prisoner, 300 were wounded and 350 had deserted in panic. Even when some of these shamefacedly returned at nightfall, the BNA at Shwedaung only mustered around 600 men. They collected the bodies of Hirayama and Ikeda and gave them a ceremonial funeral: petrol was poured over the Japanese corpses and set alight, while the Burmese wept and prayed for their reincarnation in a higher life. The battle of Shwedaung gave the BNA a sense of discipline and fulfilment, Ba Maw implies; but the Japanese Official History never even mentions them.[1]

Cowan's losses were heavy, too. The battle at Shwedaung cost him ten tanks, two guns and over 350 killed and wounded.[2] In the upshot, it had no impact on the Toungoo battle. Stilwell urged 22 Division to leave Pyinmana and the commander promised an attack for 28 March, but nothing happened. After ten days of bitter fighting, 200 Chinese Division fought its way out of encirclement and reached Yedashe, but in the retreat it forgot to blow the bridge over the upper reaches of the Sittang and so left intact for the Japanese the road to Mawchi and the Southern Shan States. The Japanese 56 Division had sent its vanguard to join 55 Division in the battle and it seized the opportunity offered by the intact bridge and began to move up towards Taunggyi and Lashio. The way was open for a loop through the Shan States right to the Chinese frontier. The Japanese of 148 Regiment, 56 Division, after a five-hour battle, occupied Lashio on 29 April and found themselves the owners of over 40,000 tons of stores.

The loss of Toungoo left Slim's Burcorps much too far forward down the Irrawaddy Valley. The decision was taken to withdraw fifty miles north and cover the Yenangyaung oil-fields directly. 17 Division was sent to control the area of Taungdwingyi and keep contact with the Chinese on the east side of the Yomas. Yenangyaung itself was at the time fairly lightly held by the tired remnants of 1st Gloucesters, now numbering no more than seven officers and 170 men, and lacking their CO, Col Bagot, who had been evacuated to hospital.

Japanese infiltration forced 1st Burma Division back until it stood on the line of the Yin Chaung, an almost dry watercourse running into the Irrawaddy from north of Taungdwingyi. The next watercourse was forty miles further north, the Pin Chaung just north of Yenangyaung. Delaying actions were fought on this line at great risk. 2 KOYLI were surrounded at Myingun on 14 April and only just managed to break the Japanese ring round them and reach Magwe, a few miles further north. But the risk had a point. It was vital to keep the oil-fields producing fuel for the Allied forces as long as possible. There was now, simply, no other source.[3]

---

[1] *Biruma Kōryaku Sakusen*, pp. 300–6

[2] *Eight* tanks according to Mackenzie, *Eastern Epic*, p. 464; *twenty-two* says *Biruma Kōryaku Sakusen*, p. 304. These casualty discrepancies are commonplace.

[3] Kirby, *War Against Japan*, II, p. 167

Slim himself gave the signal for demolitions to start at 1 pm on 15 April.[1] W. L. Forester, a civil engineer who had already demolished installations in Rangoon, and a 23-year-old RE Captain, Walter Scott, who had blown up Syriam, turned the parched landscape of oil derricks into a sheet of fire, fed by millions of gallons of oil, and the sky into a thunderstorm of explosions.

When the oil wells went up, 1st Burma Division was still south of Yenangyaung, making for the crossing at the Pin Chaung which would allow them to retreat further north, and expecting some relief from the Chinese coming across the hills north of Taungdwingyi. 1 Burma Brigade was on the banks of the Yin Chaung on 16/17 April and after some resistance was forced to retreat to the Magwe-Yenangyaung road. The Japanese of 33 Division were infiltrating between 17 Division at Taungdwingyi and 1st Burma Division, in spite of 48 Brigade's desperate attempt to fling them back at Kokkogwa, described by Slim as 'one of the bitterest fought actions of the whole campaign'.[2] In fact, since the Chinese were far to the north-east of Taungdwingyi, and 1st Burma Division was being forced further up the Irrawaddy, there was no point in keeping 17 Division there in a forward position which was being constantly eroded. Slim was eager to pull 17 Division out, but Alexander insisted on retaining it where it was since its withdrawal, he feared, might adversely affect the Chinese in the Sittang Valley. Even supply of the division would have been a problem if the sappers, with amazing industry and ingenuity, had not turned the railway between Taungdwingyi and the Irrawaddy into a motor road leading north to Natmauk.

Slim's fears for 17 Division might well have been realized had it not been for the Chinese. In fact his entire Burcorps might have been trapped. Sakurai's 214 Regiment (Sakuma), with a mountain artillery battalion, found what he took to be the only motorable exit north of Yenangyaung, the ford across the Pin Chaung, and set themselves up there to block further northward moves by Burcorps. At midnight on 16 April, advanced elements of 1st Burma Division bumped this block, while the main body of the division was still twelve miles south. Burcorps was immediately warned, and Slim, knowing how shattered his forces were, decided to call on the Chinese. 66 Army's 38 Division (Sun Li-jen), originally intended for the defence of Mandalay, was already on its way to the Irrawaddy as a result of a change of mind and a direct order by Chiang Kai-shek.[3]

Contemptuous of the British withdrawal from Allanmyo, north of Prome, to the line Minhla-Taungdwingyi, and of the pessimistic picture

---

[1] '1 am' in Mackenzie, op.cit., p. 470; '0100 on 15 April', Romanus & Sunderland op.cit., p. 125; '1 pm', Tim Carew, op.cit., p. 229

[2] Slim, *Defeat into Victory*, p. 55

[3] Romanus & Sunderland, op.cit., p. 125

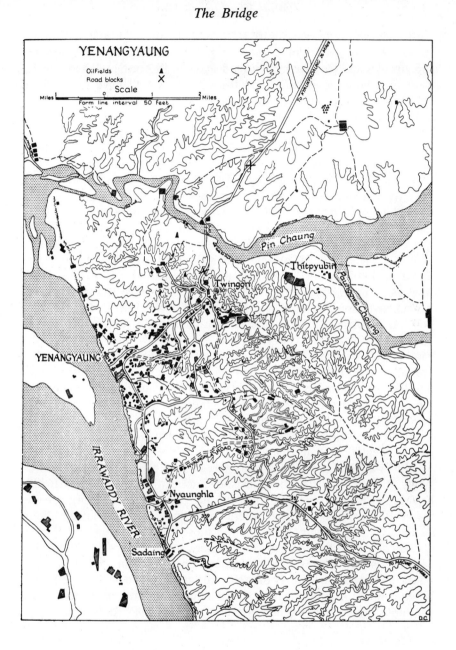

painted by a British liaison officer at Stilwell's HQ of the strength of the
British battalions – down to 3–400 men each – and the inability of tanks to
operate off the roads without previous reconnaissance, Chiang decided on
9 April to send no more than a single battalion to help the British. The next

day, obviously made more aware of the real situation – his information was always several days behind events – he agreed to send 'a strong division' in support of Slim.[1] He changed his mind again on 15 April, saying the British were in a hopeless position and the Chinese would have to act independently; and again five days later he switched once more and told Stilwell to rescue the British. Whether the 10,000 men and thirty-six guns now at Slim's disposal could have held any line between the Irrawaddy and the Sittang Valley is dubious. Sakurai had 15,000 men of three regiments against him, and was aggressively infiltrating through any gaps he could find. A static line was no defence at all. The Japanese were constantly on the move even though, like the British, they were short of water and fazed by the intense heat of Central Burma's desert zone, where even at night the temperature rarely went below 90°.

Such conditions did not move Stilwell at all. All he saw was the debacle of the British Army: 'Riot among British soldiers at Yenangyaung', he noted in his diary for 28 March and, quite inaccurately on that date, '*British destroying the oil fields*. GOOD GOD. What are we fighting for?'[2] 'Complete demoralization' was how General Tu described the British position at Magwe after a brief visit, and a flight to Maymyo to see Alexander at Army HQ confirmed Stilwell in his view: 'Did Aleck have the wind up! Disaster and gloom. No fight left in the British.'[3] These verdicts are all of a piece with his opinion of his own Chinese troops as 'pusillanimous bastards',[4] part of his generalized contempt for all allies. In the event, both British and Chinese together put up a display of courage in adversity which would have surprised him had he deemed it worth more than a dismissive line: '38th retook Yenangyaung. Got 400 Japs. Burmese out to Gwegyo. So that's cleared up.'[5]

'38th' was Sun Li-jen's division, part of Lt-General Chang Chen's 66 Army and, like most Chinese divisions, about the strength of a British brigade (a Chinese 'Army' was the equivalent of a British division). Sun was the very best type of Chinese general, a graduate of the Virginia Military Academy and – an incredible boon in those days – an excellent English speaker. Later in the campaign, the American missionary doctor Gordon Seagrave, attached to Stilwell for the duration, noted Sun's 'tall, handsome figure, looking much younger than his years, going round his wounded in the hospital wards, listening patiently, treating the enlisted men much more courteously than their sergeants or lieutenants would have done.'[6]

[1] ibid., p. 124

[2] *Stilwell Papers*, p. 88. Emphasis Stilwell's.

[3] ibid., p. 99

[4] Tuchman, *Sand Against the Wind*, p. 277

[5] 20 April, 1942, *Stilwell Papers*, p. 103

[6] G. Seagrave, *Burma Surgeon Returns*, 1946, p. 30

Sun made an immediate impression on Slim. Though by this time very much in need of solace from any quarter, Slim knew perfectly well that the Chinese bore Greek gifts. Time meant nothing to them, and they were inveterate thieves and pillagers; but he grimly realized they had good reason to be:

> After all, if I had belonged to an army that had been campaigning for four or five years without any supply, transport or medical organization worth the name and had only kept myself alive by collecting things from other people, I should either have had much the same ideas on property or have been dead.[1]

Slim put his plan for an attack by the Chinese on the Pin Chaung, while 1st Burma Division broke out of Yenangyaung, to Sun's 113 regimental commander at Kyaukpadaung. The tough and intelligent colonel accepted it, then refused to bring his men in the lorries Slim offered, until Sun himself gave the order. After an hour-and-a-half's exasperated discussion, the colonel finally agreed to move his men. Sun himself turned up later in the day. Slim found him alert and energetic, cool and aggressively minded and 'completely straightforward' in his dealings.[2]

Sun was at first on his guard, suspecting that the British were going to manipulate him, but Slim melted his mistrust by putting under his command all the Burcorps guns north of the Pin Chaung and that most precious of assets, Brigadier Anstice's 7 Armoured Brigade. A glance at Anstice's pained countenance made Slim realize how far he had gone in Allied collaboration, but he made amends by telling Sun to consult Anstice before employing the armour. In the event, Sun's intervention saved Burcorps.

1st Burma Division to the south of Yenangyaung had to fight its way through the town and break through the road block at Twingon, a village almost on the edge of the Pin Chaung. North of the *chaung*, the Japanese had put another road block, so the approach was doubly barred. The Inniskillings attacked Twingon, to find it a hive of machine-gun nests. 'Our men were worn out', said an Inniskilling major to an American reporter, 'but they had guts. They crouched low with bayonets fixed and charged forward like the Guards on a parade ground – or, at least, they thought they did. The plain fact is they were so worn out that they stumbled forward like drunken men hardly able to hold their rifles. But they gave them hell. . . and drove the bastards out of Twingon.'[3]

---

[1] Slim, op.cit., p. 64

[2] ibid., p. 65

[3] Darrell Berrigan in A. Wagg, *A Million Died*, p. 90

The reporter, Darrell Berrigan, was standing by the radio truck and heard Bruce Scott say, 'We are surrounded. My troops are tired and without water. Water is our chief problem. We will not advance beyond Twingon. I am warning all troops not to shoot at the Chinese.' It was a sensible warning. The British, Indians and Gurkhas might easily mistake Sun's Chinese for the enemy, and even though he and the British agreed on a signal to show troops were Chinese and not Japanese – sticking a Chinese cap on the end of a rifle and raising it in the air – it did not take the Japanese long to discover what this meant and to mimic it for their own purposes. Two companies of Inniskillings which moved round Twingon and reached the Pin Chaung mistook the Japanese for Chinese and were taken prisoner after what they had assumed to be fraternizing.[1]

Sitting under a locust tree on the edge of a stud farm in the blistering heat, Bruce Scott directed his attack on 18 April to take the little suburb north and east of Yenangyaung where the roads converged at Twingon to lead to the ford. But the attack got no further. Sun's 38 Division left Kyaukpadaung on the 17th and by 10 am on the 18th had cleared a section of the Pin Chaung and then halted.

Slim pressed Sun to attack again, but Sun refused to do so before he had made adequate reconnaissance. Every Allied engagement in Burma so far, he confided to Frank Merrill, Stilwell's aide, had failed because the reconnaissance was inadequate. Nonetheless Slim told Bruce Scott to hold on. Scott had proposed abandoning his transport and fighting his way across country. The Chinese would attack the following day, Slim told him, and Bruce Scott harboured in a defensive perimeter for the night of 18/19 April, without water (the demolition parties destroyed Yenangyaung's water tanks as well as the oil wells), his men exhausted by the furnace-like heat. 'We'll hang on,' he told Slim, 'but for God's sake, Bill, make those Chinese attack.'[2]

Scott was now under pressure from the south, too, where Harada's 215 Regiment – the same troops that had taken Rangoon – was moving up as one claw of a pincer. They came up the Irrawaddy in landing craft and cut into Yenangyaung from the west. The other was provided by Sakuma's men of 214 Regiment, who moved in from the east on the night of 16 March (it was one of Sakuma's battalions which set up the road block north of the Pin Chaung on the morning of the 17th). A false report that the Japanese were in Kyaukpadaung sent Slim's forces – a squadron of tanks and West Yorks infantry which had crossed the Pin Chaung to help Scott in default of the Chinese – back north to Gwegyo to deal with a problem that did not exist (it was the Chinese who were in Kyaukpadaung).

[1] Kirby, *War Against Japan*, II, p. 171.

[2] Slim, op.cit., p. 68

At 2 pm on the 19th, Bruce Scott decided not to wait any longer and took his transport east along a track to the Pin Chaung, guns in front, wounded in lorries to the rear. The Japanese guns found him and pounded his column, knocking out a tank and some trucks. The rest then got bogged down in the sand. Scott's men had already begun to die of heat exhaustion, and he decided to abandon his vehicles and put his guns out of action.[1] The tanks were sent across the *chaung*, with the wounded lying on top of them, and the others following on foot. The mules moved fastest. Maddened by the approach to water, they dashed into the *chaung* and the thirsty men flung themselves in after them.[2] By dusk they were five miles north-east of the ford on the way to Yenangyaung. Scott's two brigades were already at half-strength when he reached Kyaukpadaung. When he left it, he had lost a fifth of his men and most of his equipment.[3] 1st Burma Division had practically ceased to exist as a fighting force. 'The enemy's fighting spirit suddenly collapsed,' says the Japanese Official History. 'He abandoned his vehicles and retreated northwards. Soon he went to pieces. It was a rout.'[4] A very early history of 33 Division says that the British destruction of the oil-fields prevented it achieving its main objective, but the damage it inflicted on the British and Indian forces was the decisive factor in the fighting in Central Burma.[5]

The Chinese attack, promised for dawn on the 19th, then for 12.30 pm, then postponed to 2.00 pm, then again to 4.00 pm, was – at Slim's insistence – finally begun at 3.00 pm.[6]

Supported by Burcorps artillery and Anstice's tanks, Sun fought his way into Twingon, and rescued the captured Inniskillings. He attacked again on the 20th, right into Yenangyaung, inflicting heavy casualties on the Japanese. A counter-attack was expected the next day, and Slim, not wanting to fritter away a division of what had turned out to be courageous Chinese soldiers – there being no point in defending Yenangyaung once the oil was blown – told Sun to retire to the Pin Chaung and later make for Gwegyo. He had impressed Slim enormously: when the time came for the Allied armies to retreat finally from Burma, Slim asked that Burcorps be allowed to take Sun's 38 Division back into India.

[1] Mackenzie, op.cit., p. 475

[2] Slim, op.cit., p.71

[3] Kirby, *War Against Japan*, II, p. 172

[4] *Biruma Kōryaku Sakusen*, p. 354

[5] Major Misawa, *History of Japanese 33 Division*, English version by Interpreter Section, HQ Burma Area Army, SEATIC Detachment, HQ Burma Command, Aug. 1946

[6] There are discrepancies between the British accounts of this timetable and the US histories. Romanus and Sunderland speak of a Chinese attack at 0800 hrs on the 19th, continuing to 1130. But there is a lack of logic in their assertion that one of the results of the 1500 hrs attack was to make the Japanese shift their men to fill a gap, which was then exploited for its escape by lst Burma Division, at *1300* hrs. (ibid. p. 126)

Two things were now crystal clear. Alexander's Burma Army could not hold a line across North Burma indefinitely. The road from Assam could bring in no more than thirty tons a day, and there were only two months' reserves in North Burma. Deprived of a supply port at Rangoon, then of its source of fuel at Yenangyaung, the question was no longer whether to retreat, but where to? It is a sign of the resilience of the higher command that, four days before the shambles at Yenangyaung, Wavell gave instructions to Lieutenant-General Sir Edwin Morris, his Chief of Staff, to begin planning at once for an offensive to reoccupy Burma.[1]

Alexander later declared that he received no directive from above after the initial one to save Rangoon. This is patently untrue – in fact two days before Slim withdrew Burcorps from the oil-fields, Wavell wrote to Alexander to maintain contact with the Chinese, to cover the Kalewa-Tamu route back to India, and keep a force in being. Alexander issued an operation instruction on 23 April to ensure that all Chinese forces east of the railway Pyawbwe – Mandalay withdrew north-east to defend the road through Lashio, and that British forces, plus Sun's 38 Division, should not be involved in the defence of Mandalay but would protect routes to India via Shwebo and the Chindwin. He ordered his Army to move across the Irrawaddy on the night of 25 April, the Japanese of 18 Division being held off by 48 Brigade's artillery at Kyaukse. A conference on 29 April decided that a line Kalewa – Katha – Bhamo – Hsenwi should be held. If it broke, then the bulk of Burma Army would make for India. He was not going to let his troops be trapped by a long drawn-out defence of Mandalay.[2]

On 30 April, the massive Ava Bridge across the Irrawaddy below Mandalay was demolished. Wavell seized the opportunity to send Peter Fleming, the author, by this time a lieutenant-colonel in the Grenadier Guards, to carry out a deception tactic like that worked by Major (later Colonel) Richard Meinertzhagen at the battle of Gaza in 1917. Meinertzhagen rode in full view of the Turks, carrying a despatch case, then ostentatiously withdrew, pretended to be wounded when fired on, and made a show of dropping the despatch case. It was full of forged documents purporting to be Allenby's plan of attack, which the Turks took at face value. Wavell – later Allenby's biographer – always felt that the ruse played a great part in the victory at Gaza, and Fleming arranged a similar stratagem. A car was crashed over a thirty-foot drop beyond the Ava Bridge just after it was blown. In the car was left a letter case, apparently Wavell's own, in which some scribbled 'Notes for Alexander' gave vastly inflated figures of British reinforcements on their way to Burma. It was never possible to verify, says Wavell's biographer, whether the ruse had any effect on Japanese plans or

---

[1] Major-General Sir John Kennedy, *The Business of War*, p. 209

[2] Connell, *Wavell, Supreme Commander*, p. 211; Romanus & Sunderland, *Stilwell's Mission to China*, pp. 136–7

not, but it is possible, he thinks, that their decision not to extend their advance into India in 1942 was not unaffected by the Meinertzhagen re-enactment.[1]

Slim was far more worried by the possibility that, in obedience to Wavell's directive, Alexander might take maintaining contact with the Chinese so seriously that he would want some of Burma Army to withdraw into China. His fears were far from groundless. A plan drawn up as early as the end of March envisaged a brigade group of 17 Division and – unthinkable! – 7 Armoured Brigade to make for Lashio and go out to China with the Chinese V Army. The rest of 17 Division and 1st Burma Division would withdraw into India. Not only would administration be impossible, in what Slim took to be a famine-stricken area, but the state in which the troops arrived in China would hardly be the best advertisement for maintaining an alliance with Great Britain. He asked that Burcorps should come out through Kalewa into India, and take Sun's 38 Division with it.[2]

Even at the end of April, Slim was still full of offensive plans. He envisaged pulling 1st Burma Division together, and then using his Burcorps with 200 Chinese Division to defeat Sakurai's 33 Division, then cross to the Sittang Valley and take 55 Division in the flank while the Chinese hit it frontally. It was not without merit, but it bore no relation to current reality. Within days, the Japanese reinforcements brought about the disintegration of Chinese VI Army (Stilwell asked for a reprimand for its commander, General Kan, and for one of his generals to be sacked), and hooked through the Northern Shan States to Loilem. General Kan picked up the broken pieces of his command and led them into Kengtung, then into China. Kengtung was promptly occupied by units of the Thai Army in collaboration with the Japanese.[3]

Stilwell's agreement to let Slim have 200 Division evaporated with the news from VI Army. No sooner had the Chinese arrived at Kyaukpadaung, HQ Burcorps, than an order came from Stilwell to get back in their trucks and make for North-East Burma at once. Stilwell used the 200th to good effect, retaking Taunggyi from the Japanese on 24 April and then going on to retake Loilem. It was, as Slim generously admits, 'a magnificent achievement', but in the end it petered out and the Chinese moved on into Yunnan along the Loilem-Lashio road.[4]

Stilwell himself meant to move out to China, and on 5 May was still planning to go to Myitkyina when the news came in that the railway north and south of Indaw was blocked and that the Japanese were already in

[1] I think not, myself. I asked every Japanese general left in Burma and Thailand in 1945 about this, and none of them had even heard of it, let alone used it.

[2] Slim, op.cit., p. 75

[3] Romanus & Sunderland, op.cit., p. 130

[4] Slim, op.cit., p. 77–9

Bhamo. That was too near Myitkyina for comfort so Stilwell left his vehicles on 6 May and marched west. It was sensible enough: the Japanese occupied Myitkyina on the 8th. Stilwell's party was a motley group of Chinese, British officers, newspapermen, his own staff, and Seagrave's ambulance unit with its Kachin nurses. Several of his party fell out with heat exhaustion, but they were revived and marched on, along jungle trails, splashing through streams where the tracks came to an end, building rafts where the streams broadened into rivers. The party crossed the Chindwin on 13 May, the Indian frontier at Saiyapaw on the 15th, and on the 20th was in safety at Imphal, where Stilwell delivered himself of his oft-quoted laconic summary of the campaign: 'We got a hell of a beating. It was as humiliating as hell. We ought to find out why it happened and go back!'[1]

Sun's 38 Division reached India in the next ten days and was on the verge of being disarmed and confined by the Governor of Assam as a 'mere rabble', had Brigadier-General Gruber, Stilwell's representative in India, not intervened with Wavell.[2] 22 Division also came out into India, with remnants of 28, 96 and 200. Stilwell's deputy, Brigadier-General Boatner, reported that soldiers of 96 Division looted and murdered among the civilian refugees and Kachin tribesmen but their odyssey was a long and adventurous one. Instead of turning west to India at Taro, they went north to Shingbwiyang, on to Fort Hertz and through the largely unexplored mountain masses of North Burma into China.

Six Chinese divisions, with the Japanese 18 and 56 divisions snapping at their heels, escaped into Yunnan. Had they wished to push on into Yunnan there is no doubt nothing could have stopped the Japanese, but Iida ordered them on 26 April to halt on the line of the Salween, a resolution simplified by Chennault's AVG pilots who bombed 56 Division's supply convoys.[3]

Alexander's Burma Army retreated towards the Chindwin, but not without incident and further loss. His notion that 7 Armoured Brigade and one of Cowan's brigades should accompany the Chinese was viewed with horror both by Slim and the War Office in London. 'Wavell telegraphed his advice that Alexander should be directed to fall back into China', wrote (somewhat inaccurately) the Director of Military Operations, Major-General Sir John Kennedy. 'If this had been accepted, our troops would have been almost entirely cut off from supplies, and could have had nothing more than a guerilla value. We felt that Alexander should make for Assam, and that, if we were given a few months' respite, roads could be put through from there to Northern Burma.'[4]

[1] Romanus & Sunderland, op.cit., p. 143

[2] ibid., p. 140

[3] ibid., p. 143

[4] Kennedy, *The Business of War*, p. 210

Slim's Chief Staff Officer, Brigadier Davies, was also appalled by the idea, and was sure Slim never intended letting any of his troops go to China, though it was not clear how he could avoid this if he received a direct order.[1]

In the upshot, Alexander agreed with General Lin Wei, chief liaison officer for Chiang Kai-shek, that no British troops would be evacuated through China, and Burcorps would cover the withdrawal routes through Kalewa to India, while 7 Armoured Brigade would cover the retreat of those Chinese forces moving up west of Mandalay through Shwebo. Troops south of the Irrawaddy would withdraw across the Ava Bridge before it was blown. In the case of 1st Burma Division, it was the vehicles which used the bridge: the men were ferried across further downstream at Sameikkon.[2] They were across by 30 April and moved west across Central Burma to Monywa on the Chindwin, preceded by demoralised deserters from some units, metamorphosed by defeat into robbers and looters who were to create an appalling – and false – impression of the state of Burcorps when they came (first) over the frontier of India in May.

A rumour that the Japanese had moved up the west bank of the Irrawaddy, with the intention of sending a force up the Myittha Valley (Pauk-Gangaw-Kalemyo) to cut off the British retreat even when they were west of the Chindwin, caused Alexander to send the whole of 2 Burma Brigade, not merely a detachment, up the valley, 1 Burma Brigade being ordered to go by boat up the Chindwin to Kalewa and on to Kalemyo by road. This would leave 1st Burma Division's remaining 13 Brigade at Monywa, reinforced by 63 Brigade from 17 Division. Monywa was an important river port, and the last place on the Chindwin from which a large body of troops could go by water up to Shwegyin, only six miles from Kalewa, on the east bank.

17 Division and 7 Armoured Brigade were to use another route, one followed later by the XIV Army coming back into Burma in 1944. From Shwebo and Kinu, reachable by road and rail from Mandalay – now a burned-out ruin – tracks led to Yeu and beyond it, west, to Pyingaing. Yeu to the Chindwin, as the crow flies, is about eighty miles; between Yeu and the Mu River and Monywa on the Chindwin is about fifty, with Budalin just over halfway between Yeu and Monywa. Slim decided to set up his Corps HQ, for the withdrawal, near Budalin. As the Army walked, however, it was nearer 140 miles, most of it, after Kaduma, through jungle, a steep, narrow, waterless track.

There was now more to worry about than the Japanese advance. The monsoon would probably break around 20 May. It would solve the problem of thirst, but create another: rivers would become unfordable, tracks would slip and slither away into nothingness.

[1] Ronald Lewin, *Slim*, p. 97

[2] ibid., p. 98

At the end of April, 17 Division was strung out along the banks of the Irrawaddy from Sagaing to Allagappa, while 1st Burma Division was at Ma-u four miles south of Monywa with a tiny force (a few Gloucesters and Royal Marines) in Monywa itself. It was at this moment that Slim made a crucial error of judgment.[1] 1 Brigade and 13 Brigade of 1st Burma Division were not yet in Monywa but coming up towards it slowly, twenty miles to the south. 2 Burma Brigade was to start for the Myittha Valley on the night of 28/29 April and Slim wanted it to move fast because there were rumours of Japanese and hostile Burmese in the valley. So he let the brigade go even though he knew it meant leaving Monywa uncovered for at least a day.

Slim's Burcorps HQ was in a grove of trees attached to a Buddhist monastery a few miles north of Monywa. He was upbraiding a hapless staff officer from Alexander's HQ after dinner on the evening of 30 April when news was brought in that the Japanese had taken Monywa. As they sat, they could hear the distant sounds of mortar fire.

The Japanese had not yet, in fact, occupied Monywa. 33 Division's advance guard, Harada's 215 Regiment, came up the Chindwin in boats, landed at Ywashe opposite Monywa, and began to shell and mortar 1st Burma Division's tiny garrison. In the early hours of 1 May, Japanese and some Burmese rebels attacked 1st Burma Division HQ at Ma-u and over-ran it, after setting up a roadblock between HQ and Monywa itself. The HQ defence platoon of Burma Rifles evaporated, and Scott and his HQ staff had to fight their way out, losing several officers and men killed and wounded in the process, as well as much of the divisional equipment although, as Slim recalls, they rescued their ciphers and secret documents.[2] After Japanese air reconnaissance, the landing stage area at Monywa was heavily shelled and the Gloucesters and Marines were too few to prevent the landing of three launch-loads of Japanese troops, each launch holding around 200 men, at 8 am on 1 May. The town was in their hands within an hour and the British withdrew to Budalin. The rest of 1st Burma Division and 17 Division would be forced to bypass the town to reach Yeu.[3]

Slim rapidly whistled up 1 and 13 Brigades of 1st Burma Division to Chaung-u, fifteen miles south of Monywa, and sent back most of his own Corps HQ to Yeu. He told Cowan to detach 63 Brigade and send it to Chaung-u. Alexander was asked to remove 7 Armoured Brigade from its

---

[1] Slim, op.cit., pp 91–2

[2] Not according to the US historians. 'The 215th Regiment, 33rd Division, occupied Monywa... overrunning the Burma Division headquarters and taking all its codebooks' (*Stilwell's Mission to China*, p. 139.) Kirby says Scott's HQ took all its documents with it (*War Against Japan*, II, p. 201), and the Japanese official cadet history echoes this. The larger official Japanese history, *Biruma Kōryaku Sakusen*, does not refer to an attack on a headquarters at all.

[3] *Dai-San Chūtai Senki* (History of 3 Coy, 215 Regiment), p. 240

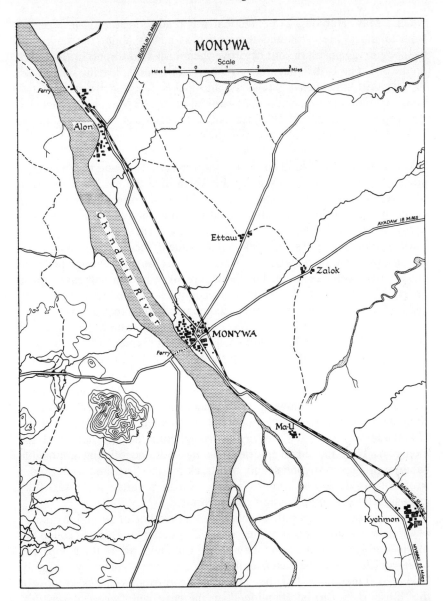

job of escorting 38 Chinese Division east of the Mu River. Yeu was now positively seething with HQs: Alexander's Burma Army, Slim's Burcorps, Cowan's 17 Division were all there. All were obsessed by the problem of Monywa. In Japanese hands, it threatened the river routes to the Shwegyin-Kalewa crossing, and so put in jeopardy the whole withdrawal plan.

On 2 May, Harada's 215 Regiment was ready for attacks on Monywa from all sides. He estimated the British as having about ten tanks and twenty guns against him, but he drove them back and turned to the attack on the 3rd. The British began to withdraw northwards, leaving behind 403 POWs, thirty-one heavy MGs, six anti-tank guns, 158 trucks and two tanks. Harada followed them north on the night of 3 May, and attacked a Burcorps force of about 700 men and a dozen tanks near Budalin. He entered Budalin just before noon on the 4th.

Sakurai sent forward 214 Regiment (Sakuma) as reinforcements. Sakuma crossed the Chindwin on the morning of 2 May and had reached a point south of Monywa on the 3rd, by which time the battle for the town was over. II/213 Regiment (Isagoda) was also sent from Meiktila to share in the pursuit of Burcorps and joined the main body of the division at Monywa without coming into contact with the British at all.

Meanwhile Slim had sent forward 16 Brigade to secure his crossing-point on the Chindwin, the village of Shwegyin. There was still enough petrol to move all the vehicles there, but the troops were put on half-rations as a precaution, to save stocks. There were about 2300 casualties to transport, and refugees by the hundred accompanied the retreating troops.[1] Alexander asked for air strikes on vessels moving up from Monywa on 3, 4 and 5 May. He was also told by Wavell not to halt his men at Kalewa but to take them right through to Tamu in the Kabaw Valley, to ease the supply problem.[2]

So the Burma Army retreated, its rearguard of 48 Brigade and 7 Armoured Brigade following up through forest tracks, from Yeu to Kaduma and on to Pyingaing (inevitably christened 'Pink Gin'), over the Maukkadaw Chaung, to Shwegyin, racing both the Japanese and the monsoon. They moved over dried *chaung* beds, negotiating impossible bamboo bridges. 'Anyone seeing this track for the first time,' Alexander wrote in his despatch, 'would find it difficult to imagine how a fully mechanized force could possibly move over it.'[3]

They entered Shwegyin through a hollow horseshoe of ground, a quarter of a mile wide, surrounded by steep cliffs 200 feet high. This was called the 'Basin' and gave on to a sandy bay on the Chindwin where the troops and what vehicles could be taken embarked. Six river steamers were used, holding 600 men each; but they could only carry four vehicles so most of the transport had to be abandoned on the east bank, where it was destroyed.[4]

---

[1] Kirby, *War Against Japan*, II, 205

[2] ibid., p. 206

[3] Mackenzie, op.cit., p. 494

[4] ibid., p. 495

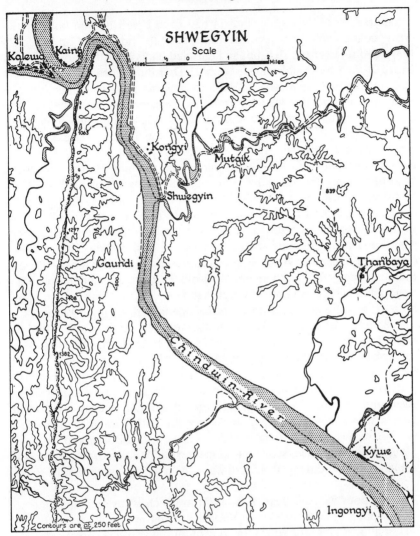

The boom placed across the Chindwin below Shwegyin to stop Japanese boats moving up was bombed and broken on 7 May. Two days later, Japanese aircraft bombed Shwegyin itself. The same day, Sakurai's divisional vanguard came up the river in landing craft. Jitter parties had already attacked Cowan's and Slim's HQs at Yeu on the night 3/4 May, on which occasion Slim's Burma Rifles defence platoon, like Scott's at Monywa, melted away, and the HQ staff stood to all night. As Slim himself later wrote, 'If somebody brings me a bit of good news, I shall burst into tears', adding drily, 'I was never put to the test.'[1]

[1] Slim, op.cit., p. 97

Sakurai's speed up the Chindwin had been urged on him both by the Army commander, Iida, and the Chief of Staff. Iida called on him on 9 May at Kinu, north of Shwebo, and outlined plans of further advances into North Burma he would require from 33 Division, which Sakurai greeted with less than enthusiastic silence, feeling his men had already done enough and wondering why the fresher 56 Division should not be asked to do the sweeping-up of North Burma which Iida wanted. He thought 33 Division should confine itself to cutting Alexander's retreat on the Irrawaddy and Chindwin fronts.[1] His rapid advance up-river had, in fact, caught Alexander and Slim – personally – on the hop. In the early hours of 10 May, Slim landed at Shwegyin jetty, having come down from Kalewa to put some hustle into the turn-round of the river steamers and speed the evacuation. As he stepped from the deck to the jetty, tracer bullets spat overhead and to his right, on the south rim of the Basin – supposedly guarded – machine guns searched him out, and mortars and artillery opened up. This was Araki Force, composed of 33 Divisional HQ, 213 Infantry Regiment and a mountain artillery battalion under the direct command of Sakurai himself, which had come up the Chindwin in about forty vessels and landed south of Shwegyin during the night of 9 May.

The basin was crowded with men and vehicles. Sakurai saw within his grasp the possibility of fulfilling what his diary noted he had been asked by the Army Chief of Staff on 5 May: 'Not one Allied soldier is to get back to India.'[2] He had an ideal target for a massacre, once the groups of sentries posted round the ridge were overcome. The Japanese began to mortar the Basin and to infiltrate through its forward defence screen, bringing up snipers when they were temporarily repulsed, then a small field-piece which became engaged – to its own detriment – with a Bofors gun.

The loading of the steamers went steadily on amid the firing and fusillades. So too did the agonies of war, which did not escape Slim's eye:

> One poor woman, near the tank from which I was speaking, lay propped against the side of the track dying in the last stages of smallpox. Her little son, a tiny boy of four, was trying pathetically to feed her with milk from a tin a British soldier had given him. One of our doctors, attending wounded at the jetty, found time to vaccinate the little chap,, but nothing could be done for his mother. She died, and we bribed an Indian family with a blanket and a passage on the steamer to take the boy with them.[3]

Smith Dun, a Karen officer attached to 17 Division (who was later to

---

[1] *Biruma Kōryaku Sakusen* p. 426

[2] ibid., p. 426

[3] Slim, op.cit., p. 105

become post-war Commander-in-Chief of the Burmese Army) heard moans from a stranded lorry, and found a young woman in labour pains, giving birth to a baby, the emergence of life in the midst of death.[1]

Cowan had held 17 Division two miles short of the Basin to avoid congestion, but hastened his men towards it when he heard firing. They fought their way in, but by that time the native crews of the steamers had had enough, and nothing would induce them to risk the Shwegyin trip again. So the weary men of Burcorps, having shot off the guns to the last round, footslogged another six miles to Kaing, directly opposite Kalewa.

The Japanese did not pursue them. There was far too much booty to be got in the Basin, hundreds of vehicles, guns, and even tanks, the loss of which grieved Slim sorely, but there was no way of getting them over the Chindwin. Only one, a Stuart tank named 'The Curse of Scotland', came across in the steamer in place of a lorry. It led the armour back into Burma two years later. This does not seem consistent with Sakurai's instruction not to let a single soldier return to India; but he received orders to go further north up the Chindwin and block every possible route across it, so Araki Force moved on up-river, reaching Tamanthi, 250 miles north, at the end of May. General Iida noted with satisfaction in his diary the booty gained at Burma Army's crossing of the Chindwin, once the Japanese occupied Kalewa on 12 May. They counted 1200 bodies, 2000 vehicles, 110 tanks, and forty guns. To achieve this reward, Sakurai's division had marched for 127 days, taken part in thirty-four battles, and covered over 1500 miles, some of it – on foot – at the rate of thirty miles a day. They had roundly defeated the British, and taken from their Empire a rich and prosperous country and its capital city.[2]

Slim took his men on through Kalemyo and up to Tamu. He even let his own beard grow for a time, as so many of the men did – but hastily reverted to shaving when he noticed the hairs were coming out white.[3] He was joined in Imphal on 24 May by Sun Li-jen, who had taken his 38 Division north until the Japanese occupation of Myitkyina cut him off from China. He turned west, and reached Assam. On one occasion the Japanese surrounded and destroyed his 138 Regiment, but Slim points out that he brought his men into Imphal as a fighting formation. The other Chinese looted and plundered their way north and east until they found themselves back in Yunnan.

Burma Army was given a very sorry welcome in Imphal. Slim saw his men trudge into bivouac areas made into swamps by the monsoon, now fully upon them, with no tents or blankets awaiting them, no water supply, no medical arrangements. So, after their escape from the Japanese they were still harried, even in the safety of Manipur State, by the malaria and

---

[1] General Smith Dun, *Memoirs of the Four-Foot Colonel*, 1980, p. 33

[2] *Biruma Kōryaku Sakusen*, pp. 440–42

[3] Slim, op.cit., p. 108

dysentery which battened on their sodden and exhausted bodies. Nearly one in ten fell sick, and many of them died.

Slim noted the balance sheet. Alexander's Army had lost 13,000 men, killed, wounded and missing, against a Japanese total of 4000 killed and wounded. He handed over what was left of his command to IV Corps (Irwin) on 20 May, and Burcorps ceased to exist. He had watched them come out of Burma, and was proud to see that even in their utmost extremity, they were more than just survivors:

> On the last day of that nine-hundred mile retreat I stood on a bank beside the road and watched the rearguard march into India. All of them, British, Indian and Gurkha, were gaunt and ragged as scarecrows. Yet, as they trudged behind their surviving officers in groups pitifully small, they still carried their arms and kept their ranks, they were still recognisable as fighting units. They might look like scarecrows, but they looked like soldiers too.[1]

Exodus

As the Burma Army fought its way north, the exodus of the civilian refugees began. There were British – occasional businessmen or officials unlucky to have stayed too long – and some Burmese who followed in their wake; but the exodus was really Indian. The last pre-war census (1931) showed Burma had an Indian population of over 1,000,000, three-fifths of whom were Indian-born. In the days when Burma was a province of British India, this was of little consequence. But with the separation of Burma and India in 1937, and the Japanese sponsorship of extreme forms of Burmese nationalism, the Indians, who were concentrated in the larger towns and cities of the south and the Delta – Rangoon, Pegu, Syriam, Moulmein, Pyapon, Bassein, Prome, Taungup, Akyab – naturally feared for their status, their property and their lives and began to go back to India once the air-raids on Rangoon began on 23 December 1941. As long as Rangoon remained in British hands, a not too intolerable week-long sea-journey of

---

[1] Slim, op.cit., pp 109–10. The Japanese figures are somewhat different. From the beginning of the campaign to 10 June 1942, they claim 27,454 dead and 4918 prisoners. This figure must include the Chinese, whose numbers they vastly over-estimate, on the assumption a Chinese division numbered 11,000 men, whereas some of the Chinese divisions in Burma had a strength only half that. They captured 270 tanks, they say, though an earlier typescript of 33 Division history in my possession puts the figure at 126. They took over 100 guns, 6000 lorries and over 7000 cars. Their own killed in battle numbered 1896, died of wounds 108, and other casualties 438, a total of 2431. Not a heavy price to pay for such a victory, against a British force they judged to be 28,000 to start with and increased with reinforcements to 45,000; apart from the Chinese, whom they over-estimate as 100,000 odd – *Biruma Kōryaku Sakusen*, pp. 439–41. (There are mistakes in the additions at this point even on the printed page, but they do not make a radical difference to the overall picture)

750 miles to Calcutta was involved – or 1000 miles to Madras. Seventy thousand left by this route before the Japanese occupied Rangoon. It was then the problems began.

Using very often the roads, tracks and rivers traversed by the retreating armies, the Indians moved overland at first by car, or bullock-cart, then on foot, seeking the gateways into India. The most obvious route, in the early days, was up to Prome, then across the Irrawaddy and the track over the pass in the Arakan hills to Taungup on the Bay of Bengal, whence a motor-boat could reach Akyab. From Akyab, coastal vessels plied to Chittagong, on the other side of the border. Not everyone could afford a passage by motor-boat, but a country boat could make the journey in a week, and G. S. Bozman of the Indian Overseas Department traced a track through the hills which took three weeks on foot.

But there were snags before the journey began. Original instructions to the Indian community in Rangoon had been to stand fast, because the docks and the municipal services of Rangoon would come to a halt without them. Officials went up and down the Rangoon-Prome road persuading the Indians to return and promising them billeting in government camps outside the city. In addition, Burmese police were ordered to stop Irrawaddy crossings at Prome and to tell intending refugees that the pass to Taungup was dangerous. Orders were also issued forbidding adult Indians to travel as deck passengers from Rangoon, which effectively allowed wealthy merchants who could pay for cabins to use the ships, but not those who could only afford to sleep on deck. It was a segregation that some Indian politicians and officials found perfectly natural. Indeed, one of the complaints echoed by Rajagopalachari was that persons of the middle-class, like clerks and teachers, should not be herded with labourers, even in this extremity.[1]

When the evacuation began in real earnest, orders to the Burmese police at Prome remained uncancelled, and they added a few embellishments of their own. You could only cross the Irrawaddy if you paid two rupees. You had to show an inoculation certificate. It cost you up to six rupees if you did not have one. When you got to Taungup, it cost you three rupees to clamber on board a boat. At Akyab, the shipping firm Mackinnon Mackenzie ran five extra ships to Chittagong, and some hundreds of refugees were flown out by the US pilots of China National Airways. But these were a drop in the ocean. There is a 100% discrepancy in the figures of those who succeeded in reaching India by this route, many of whom died on the way. Some sources give 100,000, some 200,000, by mid-May 1942, and in the nature of things, accuracy can hardly be expected.[2]

[1] Hugh Tinker,'The Indian Exodus from Burma 1942', *Journal of South-East Asian Studies*, Vol. VI, No. 1, March 1975, p. 5, n. 7

[2] Tinker, op.cit., p. 6

The Government of India's representative in Rangoon, known as the Agent, was Robert Hutchings, and he urged the Government to speed up the process on the Indian side, setting up a headquarters at Sagaing, west of Mandalay, from where he intended to direct the stream of refugees from Lower and Central Burma on to Monywa, Kalewa, Tamu and Imphal. From Kalewa to Tamu there was a motorable road, but after Tamu only an old mule track to Palel. From Palel there was a dry-season road to Imphal and an all-weather road from there to Dimapur, the Assam railhead, an overall distance of 200 miles. The Government of India, unable to cope with the new influx into Manipur State, told Hutchings to limit the number of Indians moving through Tamu to 500 a day, not realizing that the Government of Burma, in its hill-station at Maymyo, had long ceased to control the means of enforcing orders, and could hardly help Hutchings in any way.

Hutchings did as he was told, and herded up to 100,000 refugees in camps in the Mandalay area under the control of J. S. Varley, who had organized the Rangoon camps. Many of these were killed in a Japanese air-raid on Mandalay on Good Friday, 1942, and the rest fled. Varley himself compiled a highly critical report of the way in which government seemed to have washed its hands of the problem, no copies of which, significantly, have survived in the archives either of London or Delhi.

In March, motor convoys began to shorten the two or three week trip to Tamu from the Mandalay area, mainly for Europeans, Anglo-Burmans or Anglo-Indians employed by the Burmah Oil Company, but when protests of racial discrimination were voiced, some of the convoys took on Indians. The route ceased to be numerically controlled during March, and up to 30,000 refugees reached Imphal in that month.[1]

Six weeks remained before the Japanese entered Kalewa, and in that period the Indians and Alexander's retreating forces trod the same purgatorial 132 miles to Palel. 'Months later', writes Roy McKelvie,

> when the first British returned to Tamu, they found skeletons sitting, lying or propped up, just as they had been before dying. In the Post Office, twenty skeletons were around the counter and one hung round the broken telephone. It is not difficult to imagine the agony and desolation of the exodus from Burma. Disease, under-nourishment and weariness had broken down the will to live. The prospect of one last drag over the cold, rain-soaked mountains was more than they could stand. Only the strong survived. Yet nearly 200,000 refugees crossed from Tamu to Imphal, some to die of strain, others to die in hospitals so crowded that the staffs were incapable of handling the patients.

[1] Tinker, op.cit., p. 8

Over ninety per cent of the army and civilians who tried to cope with their mass trek suffered from malaria.[1]

Even when some of the army were transported by lorry to Kanglatongbi, north of Imphal, their reception was not of the best. 24 Field Company, Indian Engineers, found itself allocated a camp site, in torrential rain, with no tents, and few ground sheets. Already racked with malaria and dysentery, the men bivouacked in the mud. 70 Field Company was little better off when it reached Kanglatongbi on 18 May 1942. It was given a strip of scrub jungle as a camp site, again without tents. The men had mosquito nets, but no ground sheets and no blankets. 'It was indeed', wrote Major (later Major-General) Lyall-Grant, 'a cold and miserable reception to India.' The engineers built themselves shelters with brushwood and tarpaulins over the next three days, but they could not get their clothes dry and there was no comfort for them until they moved into Imphal on 22 May, by which time one man in five was in hospital.[2]

They were the lucky ones. Palel and the road to Imphal were strewn with decomposing bodies which the survivors had no time or energy to bury. The natural scavenger of the dead was no help, either: there were no vultures in the area.

According to Major-General Wood, a sapper officer who was named Administrator-General of Eastern Frontier Communications and who reached Tamu on 10 March, the Burma Government had abdicated its responsibilities to the refugees. With little earth-moving equipment and a few engineers, Wood built fifty-four miles of dry-weather road between Tamu and Palel as his first priority, as the most practical thing he could do. But it took eight weeks, and in those weeks the stricken Indian civilians kept moving and dying in the mountains. Hutchings met Wood on 22 April at Tamu, and asked that all transport for a fortnight should be devoted to getting the refugees out of Kalewa. Wood referred the request to the Government of India, which rejected it.[3]

Not without reason, heartless as it may seem. Alexander took the decision to move the Burma Army back into India on 26 April. They were to evacuate through Kalewa and military priorities along the road became paramount. Added to the natural hazards of the route was the ill-treatment of the refugees. They were looted and robbed, and Indians stranded in North Burma had to pay an air fare of 280 rupees to be airlifted from Magwe and Shwebo – in other words, only the professional

[1] Roy McKelvie, *The War in Burma*, pp. 44–5

[2] Colonel E. W. C. Sandes, *The Indian Sappers and Miners*, Institution of Royal Engineers, Chatham, p. 237

[3] Tinker, op.cit., p. 8

and business families got out. Even this route was closed on 9 May, by which time over 14,000 people had been flown out, of whom not quite 5000 were Indians.[1]

Wood was ready to lift the civilians by lorry along his new road when a signal arrived from Alexander's Headquarters on 28 April telling him not to expect refugees but to concentrate on gathering in the troops of the Burma Army. Wood sent supplies along to Kalewa to feed the soldiers, leaving the refugees in their improvised camps at Tamu. Then he was relieved of the problem on 4 May when IV Corps took over responsibility for all military transport. Wood's duties still included moving the refugees, but he was not to use the road, and he no longer had any trucks anyway.

Then the Army began to arrive. As Hugh Tinker remembers it, there was a vast difference in morale from one unit to the next. Some were still in good order and discipline was kept: the 7 Armoured Brigade, which had formed the rearguard, was still combative, though they had managed to land only one Stuart tank at Kalewa. Other units 'were demoralised and had almost disintegrated. Senior officers seemed to be leading in the manner of the Duke of Plaza Toro: at the head of the retreat. At Tamu, a cynical British NCO set up a betting shop on 'the Tamu Stakes': giving odds on the numbers of Brigadiers who would go through in a day.'[2] The Army took three weeks to pass through, and after it had gone, an Indian civil servant, T. S. Atkinson, stayed in Kalewa until 10 May to continue the civilian evacuation.

As a young officer, Hugh Tinker worked the road from Palel to Tamu, picking up refugees, a driving hazard in itself along the dusty dirt road, and heartbreaking at the end of the journey:

> The young drivers had to push back the shouting men who rushed their lorries and try to find room for the women, the children and the sick. It was all hopelessly chaotic, and all too often families were separated, people lost their belongings, those most in need were left behind. The convoys shuttled back and forward again. The Indian drivers were at the wheel for eighteen hours every day. But at least they could look forward to a meal when they reached their destination at ten or eleven at night. The refugees could expect nothing.[3]

Even in this desperate situation, there were moments of tragic humour. As the rains settled in, at first clearing the dust-dry atmosphere, then cascading down until the roads became quagmires and the Seaforth Highlanders

[1] Tinker, op.cit., p. 9

[2] ibid., p. 10

[3] ibid., p. 10

stood to in waterlogged trenches on the Shenam Saddle, awaiting the first Japanese probes into India, a group of Tamils presented themselves, all wearing pith helmets and retaining a semblance of forlorn smartness. They were the Rangoon Fire Brigade and when Government left, they left. Here, on the edge of India, in the first monsoon, they looked round in bewilderment for orders.

Mostly, discipline had been an early casualty, and as the rains increased, epidemic diseases began to spread, dysentery, smallpox, malaria and – by mid-June – the dreaded cholera. Even the organization in Imphal was badly hit by Japanese air-raids on 10 and 16 May, when Wood's civilian employees scarpered, much as they had done in Rangoon and Mandalay.

Up as far as Imphal, the planters of the Indian Tea Association ran trucks to bring up supplies, but did not operate beyond it. And in resentment at complaints from Government of India envoys, official and otherwise, that the rescue of the refugees was exclusively controlled by Europeans and that there was preferential treatment for Europeans and Anglo-Indians, they withdrew their rescue workers.

Further north than Imphal, where even Chinese soldiers who had escaped into Manipur refused to enter the camps because they were so filthy, were the high passes out of the Hukawng Valley, the Pangsau Pass to Ledo, the Chaukan Pass, and the Diphu Pass. Those who were caught in Northern Burma by the swiftness of the Japanese advance, and could not be flown from Myitkyina, made for these passes. The Government of Burma signalled to India on 1 May 1942 that 500 Europeans and 10,000 Indians were making for Ledo. Wood got together 6500 porters, with elephants, mules and ponies to bring them in, but the rains stopped them going down into the Hukawng Valley, and the swollen rivers began to block the refugees' progress.

Perhaps one European's account will serve as illustration for all.[1] Lieutenant C. J. Goodman was a sapper officer who had been building an airfield at Heho when they were told the Japanese had broken through the road to Loikaw. The unit packed up quickly and moved off in two large trucks and two cars: four officers, two sergeants and twenty Indian orderlies and cooks. They took along with them two English women stranded at the nearby hill-station of Kalaw, the widow of a colonel, and her niece, married to an officer fighting elsewhere in the campaign. Goodman's Austin 20 went like a bird, and they passed through Hsipaw – teeming with Chinese soldiers – Lashio and Kutkai. At one point, the Chinese driver of a six-wheeler kept trying to overtake him and finally edged him over. Goodman got out and swung at him with his fist. The

---

[1] 'Personal experiences of the retreat to India in 1942, by motor transport from Heho to Myitkyina (April 20 to May 6) and then on foot via the Hukawng Valley and Pangsau Pass to Ledo in Assam (May 7 to June 16) of C. J. Goodman, Capt., R. E.', 12pp. TS, written in Ceylon, July 1943.

Chinese ducked, and came back at him with a foot-long spanner. He missed, Goodman seized the loaded rifle in the car and threatened to fire at the six-wheeler's tyres before the Chinese driver reluctantly allowed them to go ahead.

After two days at Bhamo, they left the trucks behind at the Kazu ferry. They burnt the trucks, and their kit with them, though absurdly they were given a case of Gordon's Gin, six bottles of which were consumed in the next twenty-four hours. Then they were in Myitkyina, and arranged for the two women and Goodman's major to fly out on the first plane the next day.

At 6.30 am they were on the airfield, and waited hour after hour in the increasingly unbearable heat until two Dakotas landed, loaded up with Indian casualties and a few civilians, including Goodman's party. As the engines revved, and Goodman stood waving goodbye, two Japanese fighters buzzed the airfield and began dropping bombs and machine-gunning the runway. Goodman went flat, but felt painfully vulnerable on the undefended strip, and got up to find the place a shambles.

The transports were scenes of carnage. The younger of the two women was already dead, and her aunt and the sapper major were badly wounded. The major died the next day. What had been an eventful but not unenjoyable adventure had turned into tragedy.

Goodman picked up the remnants of his unit, burned his car when the road petered out, and started to walk. He packed food, a half blanket, a spare shirt, shorts and socks, and set out for the Mogaung-Mainkwang road, which he reckoned to be thirty or forty miles away, hoping to get a lift to Mainkwang. That would save about ninety miles of walking. But it turned out to be a vain hope.

They hit the road eventually, having loaded their packs on bullock carts their Brigadier bought in a Burmese village. (Their mules broke loose at night and bolted.) At Mainkwang the road ended and turned into a jungle track, just wide enough for the bullock carts: 'there was a long stream of people for miles – British officers and Indian and Burmese troops, and all sorts of civilians, from British civil servants to Indian coolies. One very nice Anglo-Burmese couple were a pathetic sight; the wife was seven months gone with a baby.'

They reached the Chindwin in a few days, the only means of crossing being a bamboo raft, pulled from bank to bank by a bamboo rope. Hundreds of people gathered on the beach, and with every crossing the raft became more and more overloaded so that finally the rope snapped under the strain. Goodman realized the raft wouldn't take the bullock-carts anyway, so these went the same way as the trucks and cars. They made a vast bonfire, a blaze eight feet high round which everyone sat throughout the night. It rained the entire time.

Two young Anglo-Burmese officers swam the river and tried to repair the rope, and when that proved fruitless induced the village headman to bring out his dug-out canoes. He refused at first, since some troops had let their rifles off in his village and scared the wits out of his people. Finally, a ferry service started, the bullocks swam across, and after a day's rest in the village, Goodman and what was left of his unit pushed on.

> One evening we saw the welcome sight of a large village, and looked forward to shelter and sleep. When we reached it, however, it seemed curious that nobody else had decided to camp there... the smell, however, soon told us the reason – dead bodies were all over the place, so we just had to go on further and sleep in the open – and did we swear when it started raining! We soon got used to the sight of dead, and many of them were a far from pleasant sight. The civilian evacuation had started some weeks before us, and many of the deceased had been dead for a considerable time – I never realized before the full meaning of the word 'decomposition'! Some, I suppose, had died from starvation, and others from disease – practically all were Indians of the lower class type. Without any exaggeration, I saw hundreds of those corpses, and it was surprising how one became hardened to it. I also actually saw several lying or sitting by the wayside on the point of death, but there was nothing we could do about it, and we just said 'Poor –', and hoped we wouldn't come to it. Of course, any Britisher who died was buried by his pals to the best of their ability, but luckily they were not very numerous – I only knew of two.
>
> We jogged along, the weather getting worse, and the track becoming a quagmire seldom less than ankle deep, frequently knee-deep, and it was weary work doing a sort of goose-step in the mud. We rested from time to time, but it took a hell of an effort to get started again.

Their humour and dreams of beer and civilization had not left them yet, and their Indian cooks managed to keep some sort of diet going, tea and a small portion of porridge being the morning staple, with a biscuit at midday and 'almost a blow-out' of rice and bully beef at night until the latter ran out. Then it was just rice. 'Luckily, we weren't short of water, in fact, at times we had too much of it, frequently having to wade across rivers, and walk for hours feeling as though you had "wet" yourself.'

Then the tiredness began to tell, the food to grow short, until they began to disbelieve in the rumours of the RAF dropping rations. But they found new energy from the sound of large aircraft flying low over a village with a large open clearing. Here a British party was issuing the rations the planes had dropped, and Goodman's party agreed to let them move on and take over the distribution. For three days they fed a pitiful breadline of hundreds of Indians, including mothers with babies and young children: rice, condensed milk, tinned fruit, and corned beef for themselves, packets of figs and dried apricots.

Goodman had by this time done half his journey, but the hills were still in front, and they set off again, their spirits raised by the food and damped by the monsoon:

> Oh, those—hills. Up and up you went, till you had no breath to curse with, and when you reached the top (the highest was reputed to be about 6000 feet) there was nothing but more hills as far as the eye could reach, so down you went again into the next valley, and up the next ascent. The track was seldom more than three or four feet wide, with churned up mud, so that you slipped and slid all over the place, and if you weren't careful you'd fall the wrong way and go rolling over the edge. One fell down in the mud several times a day, and it required a great effort to try and wash the muck off when we camped at night.

The party split into smaller groups, which usually assembled again at the night stop. Goodman went down with fever, and was nursed through it by his Indian orderly, who fed him spoonfuls of rice between his spasms of temperature and shivering:

> The days dragged on, everybody on the trail was looking haggard and weary. I had a lovely beard, and must have looked a beautiful sight with a sodden topee resembling a badly mauled haggis. Of my party, a Major Cooke of the Burma ASC and I had dropped behind – he had a cocker spaniel, and we couldn't help laughing at the grand little dog, all caked with mud! But it was game, and trotted ahead and came back to look for us as if it was a Sunday afternoon walk.

By the time they had been on the move for five weeks, Goodman developed sores on his feet, with the mud rubbing down from the top of his boots. He urged Cooke to go on without him, but Cooke refused, and always waited a little ahead on the track until one day Goodman had no energy to get up after a rest, and they separated. He had heard the Assam tea-planters had set up camps at intervals to meet them, and that one was not far off, so he started off on the road hoping to find one:

> By now my leg was swollen almost to my knee, and slipping and sliding up and down the track was very painful work. I probably

fell over a dozen times that day, and as the hours went by and no camp or village appeared, things did not look too good, and for the first time I began to have serious doubts of my 'making the grade'. The only food I had left was a tin of cheese which I had kept intact, and a little bit of tea. Late in the afternoon a little native hut built upon posts came in sight, and under it were three Indian soldiers. They had a little fire, and I just couldn't resist the thought of human companionship and the chance of making a cup of tea, so I crawled in with them – they had two pals in the room overhead, one of whom was ill. They had a few biscuits, so we ate them with my cheese, and pooled the little water in our bottles and had a drop of 'char'... they pointed out a dead body to me, lying about 15 feet away, but I was too browned off to worry about a detail like that!

But his insouciance did not last the night. The next morning he was filled with panic at the thought of becoming like that corpse, and tried to induce the Indians to come with him. They wanted to stay put, so he made a colossal effort and set out again by himself, dragging himself along:

My leg was giving me hell, my right hand was getting paralysed through gripping a stick so much, and it was no use deluding myself any longer that if I didn't get some help soon there was little likelihood of me ever seeing Blighty again. I just do not know how I kept going that day, but for once rumour was not a lying jade, and some time in the afternoon, a good-sized camp of bamboo huts came into view. I felt like blubbing like a kid, and can't describe how I felt when, as I reached the first hut, a cheery Englishman welcomed me and gave me a cup of tea. The place was a sea of mud, and it was pouring with rain, but it looked like heaven.

His leg was twice its normal size and he was sent onwards on a bamboo stretcher, suspended by ropes from a pole carried on the shoulders of two coolies. They stumbled and dropped him once or twice, but he was past caring, knowing the worst was over. His youth and resilience – and the occasional friendliness shown him – had brought him through.

The general picture of those who arrived at Ledo was grimmer: 'Complete exhaustion, physical and mental, with disease superimposed, is the usual picture', one Brigadier reported. 'All social sense is lost... they suffer from bad nightmares and their delirium is a babble of rivers and crossings, of mud and corpses... Emaciation and loss of weight is universal.'[1]

[1] Tinker, op.cit., p.14

The exodus of the Indian refugees reflected little credit on the foresight or compassion of the governments of India or Burma. Had it not been for the gallant and selfless work of volunteers like the Assam tea planters, many thousands more refugees would have died. Over 500,000 reached India safely, according to the Indians Overseas Department of the Government of India. Estimates of the dead are as high as 100,000, but Tinker regards such a figure as grossly exaggerated: 10–50,000 may have died. About half of those who reached India went back to Burma to resume their former lives, with varying success. Tinker claims that the exodus of 1942 brought Burma's Indian community to an end. In a sense this is true, but not all Indians left Rangoon, and an observer there in 1944, under the Japanese occupation, said that Indian traders were working as Japanese contractors, collecting produce for sale to Japanese firms who then re-sold it to the Japanese Army. Bose was a factor here. Although the Japanese had to ensure that Ba Maw thought he was getting a good deal out of independence they also had to sweeten Bose, and his Indian Independence League looked after the interests of Indian property-owners in Rangoon. The Japanese considered abandoned Indian land as 'enemy property' and refused to hand it over to the Burmese, saying it had to be conveyed to the Provisional Government of Free India. So a community *did* remain, but obviously in very straitened circumstances.

Perhaps, though, they had chosen the better part? An officer making one of the last searches for Indian stragglers on the road out of Burma describes one of their resting-places, the Tagun Hill on the way to Ledo:

> The clearing was littered with tumble-down huts, where often whole families stayed and died together. I found the bodies of a mother and child locked in each other's arms. In another hut were the remains of another mother who had died in childbirth, with the child only half-born. In this one *jhum* (clearing) more than fifty people had died. Sometimes pious Christians placed little wooden crucifixes in the ground before they died. Others had figures of the Virgin Mary still clutched in their skeleton hands. A soldier had expired wearing his side cap, all his cotton clothing had rotted away, but the woollen cap sat smartly on his grinning skull. Already the ever-destroying jungle had overgrown some of the older huts, covering up the skeletons and reducing them to dust and mould.[1]

[1] Geoffrey Tyson, *Forgotten Frontier*, p. 79

2. THE BALANCE

The first Arakan battles;
the first Wingate expedition

The first Arakan battles

'There were few less desirable places in which to fight a campaign', writes General Evans of Arakan.[1] It is the conditions, not the distances, which make it so. The term 'Arakan' covers a great distance from the Chin Hills on the edge of Manipur right down to the south-western corner of Burma at Cape Negrais, but from the campaigning point of view in 1942–5 the area concerned ran from the Indian frontier to the island and town of Akyab. Cox's Bazar, just over the frontier, was 120 miles north of Akyab, and Chittagong, the supply port on the Bay of Bengal for the British forces, was another forty-five miles further north. To Kaladan on the Kaladan River, which flows down west of the Arakan Yomas, across to the Bay of Bengal is around sixty-five miles. The Mayu Range of hills, rising to 2000 feet, which runs from near the frontier along the peninsula ending at Foul Point, just opposite Akyab Island, is about eighty miles in length. Foul Point to Akyab Town is fifteen miles.

So the distances were not great. The operational conditions, on the other hand, were appalling. Arakan is a land of creeks and *chaungs*[2], where transport is largely by water. There are tracks, but only one real road in the accepted sense of the term, which runs across the Mayu range from the little port of Maungdaw on the Naf River to the town of Buthidaung on the Kalapanzin; and it runs through two tunnels en route. The Mayu hills are covered with dense jungle, but to their west runs a coastal strip two miles wide at Maungdaw and a few hundred yards wide at Foul Point. The coast is part sandy beach, part mangrove swamp, and some of the *chaungs* are tidal. In the flat valleys are hillocks covered with peepul trees and bamboo. Grisly though much of the combat had been, the Arakan scenery turned Cecil Beaton lyrical when he saw it in 1944:

[1] Evans, *Slim as Military Commander*, p. 86

[2] small rivers

The landscape is pastoral; so lush, sylvan and peaceful is the general aspect in the brilliant sun or moonlight that, in spite of the intermittent thuds of gunfire, one cannot quite believe that deadly warfare is being carried on nearby.[1]

Lt-Commander Tsutsumi Shinzō, of the Imperial Japanese Navy, agreed. He was paymaster to a unit responsible for coastal defence from Akyab round to the Irrawaddy Delta, and he loved Arakan, the screaming monkeys flying from branch to branch, the resplendent plumage of the birds, the sound of his shots (there was big game, even tiger, in the hills) reverberating and echoing until they were swallowed up by the thickly cushioned forest slopes. If he looked inland, at nightfall, he could contemplate endlessly receding waves of mountains stretching across Burma to India or China, disappearing into the purple velvet of the tropical night. If he turned west, he could watch the darkening sea, the last light of day over the Bay of Bengal.[2]

The climate presents great contrasts. In the dry, or campaigning season – October to May – the heat is not oppressive, the nights can be chill, and the mornings covered in thick mist. The monsoon changes all this. The Arakan coastal strip, from just north of Akyab, shows deep purple on the rainfall maps: it receives up to 200 inches of rain a year, and that brings everything except boats on the *chaungs* to a standstill. It is highly malarial, and a paradise for leeches. It made sense therefore to operate only in the dry season. The question is, naturally enough, why campaign here at all?

The answer lies in Akyab. If the capital of Burma, Rangoon, were one day to be re-taken, the best way to it was across the Bay of Bengal and round the Delta with a seaborne operation. Failing this, the appalling prospect of an overland re-conquest opened up; and was not taken very seriously until it was on the verge of happening. But either way, air cover to Rangoon would be needed, and only the airfields at Akyab provided it. Aircraft flying from it were just over 330 miles from Rangoon, and a radius of 250 miles swept Central Burma from Mandalay through Toungoo to Henzada in the Delta.

The Japanese were well aware of this, and pushed on as far as Akyab on 4 May 1942. It was not out of the question that they might even go on into India, and British forces in Chittagong had withdrawn a hundred miles north to Feni, leaving behind a small garrison, which would be withdrawn if the Japanese came up that far. As a result of the withdrawal, the dock installations at Chittagong were destroyed, and many of the inhabitants sought a safer spot. It was not, therefore, in the dry season of 1942–3, the most cheerful of places. But it was from here that a counter-offensive had to be launched.

[1] Cecil Beaton, *Far East*, p. 29
[2] Louis Allen, *Sittang: the last battle*, p. 196

The Commander-in-Chief, India, General Sir Archibald (later Lord) Wavell, had abolished the peacetime India commands – Northern, Eastern and Southern – and turned them into Armies with headquarters supposed to be operational rather than administrative. Eastern Army had its headquarters at Ranchi, and was responsible for Assam, Bengal, Orissa and Bihar, as well as for repelling any Japanese invasion up the coast of Arakan; or, for that matter, across the Bay of Bengal into the mouths of the Hoogly. It had two Corps, IV (70 British Division, 23 Indian Division) and XV (14 and 26 Indian Divisions) and a brigade in Assam. Throughout much of the latter half of 1942, the threat to internal security from the Congress Party's 'Quit India' campaign was stronger than that from the Japanese. And 70 Division spent a good deal of its time split up into penny packets patrolling disaffected areas on behalf of the civil power.

But Wavell, who always underestimated the Japanese, had already begun planning to re-take Burma as early as April 1942, before the long retreat was over. And a thrust down to Akyab seemed the obvious choice. IV Corps' front was to receive the battered remnants of the Burma Army in the summer and would be confining its activities to patrolling and sheltering refugees, or at any rate passing them on. The Corps Commander was Lieutenant-General N. M. S. Irwin, who had commanded the British forces at the abortive expedition against Dakar, and who greeted the returning soldiers from Burma with less than cordiality. That the men had come through a nightmare was beside the point. He was convinced they should have come out in better order, and told their commanders so. One of these was Lieutenant-General William Slim, who had taken over command of Burcorps on 19 March 1942 in the middle of the fighting retreat. Slim knew that the men preceding the fighting units into India were a mob, and a disreputable mob at that:

> No longer organized units, without any supply arrangements, having deserted their officers, they banded together in gangs, looting, robbing, and not infrequently murdering the unfortunate villagers on their route. They were almost entirely Indians and very few belonged to combatant units of the Army.[1]

It is perhaps understandable that Irwin should greet the appearance of this mob with some asperity. But Slim obviously felt he should have differentiated between them and the soldiers who came back in some order. Instead, Irwin was rude to him personally. 'I never thought an officer whose command I was about to join could be so rude to me,' Slim said. 'I can't be rude,' was Irwin's retort. 'I'm senior.'[2]

[1] Slim, op.cit., p. 86
[2] Lewin, *Slim*, p. 105

Slim's biographer, Ronald Lewin, while prepared to concede considerable intellectual gifts to Irwin, nonetheless says they were marred 'by a dictatorial and egocentric temperament'. Irwin treated subordinates 'like indentured coolies deserving neither trust nor consideration'.[1] Because he could trust no one but himself, he was unable to decentralize. He was always on his commanders' backs, looking into the small details of operations, interfering instead of leaving them to carry out a plan. On the other hand, it is fair to say that his major concern was in no sense different from Wavell's or Slim's. They were all obsessed with what they saw as the crumbling morale of their troops in the face of the Japanese.

There were basically three attempts to dent the Japanese hold on Burma in the year and a half between their completion of their conquest and the authorization of the plan to invade Manipur State. One was in Arakan, a constantly renewed attempt to take Akyab. Another was Stilwell's road from Ledo, originally a British idea to push a way across the Pangsau Pass and enlarge it to use the Chinese forces evacuated from Burma and re-trained in India. They were to fight a way through North Burma to Myitkyina, 275 miles away, and have US Army Engineers build a road and a pipeline behind them. The third was Operation LONGCLOTH, in February 1943, the first Wingate Expedition behind Japanese lines.

Akyab was the real focus of British efforts for many months. It became Irwin's target when he was promoted from IV Corps to the command of Eastern Army. Slim, the man he had insulted at Imphal, he found in command of XV Corps (Slim had handed over his Burcorps command on 20 May), and saw that he was faced with another job of improvisation. To protect the mouths of the Hoogly, that vast pattern of inland waterways called the Sunderbans, Slim devised a fleet of old paddle-steamers armed with Maxim guns and screw guns from the Bengal Artillery and some two-pounder anti-tank guns. Some of the weaponry had been in the Calcutta Arsenal since the days of Lord Roberts, and it is perhaps as well that the Sunderbans Flotilla was never put to the test of staving off a Japanese battle fleet. But it was characteristic of Slim not to moan about what he did not have and to get on with what was on the spot.

Of his divisions, 26 was immobile through lack of transport, and only 14 Division was operational on the frontier. This was the force which would carry out Wavell's plan to seize Akyab, Operation CANNIBAL, or at least what was left of it by the time a seaborne component had been cancelled (27 February 1943).

Wavell had issued a directive in September 1942 to capture Akyab and the northern sector of Arakan. 29 Brigade, with assault craft, fresh from the Madagascar landings, would be the chief force, and 14 Division would provide what was essentially a landward diversion. In the end, 29 Brigade

[1] ibid., p. 105

could not be available in time, air support would be less than expected, and orders were changed. Irwin was to take the whole of the Mayu Peninsula with 14 Division only, advancing over land. When they reached Foul Point they would make the assault across the channel dividing it from Akyab Island. The operation would begin on 21 December 1942.

Slim's XV Corps headquarters was almost entirely involved with static duties in support of the sorely tried civil power. Irwin did not bring him into play to control 14 Division's movements. It was a grave mistake, because Major-General Lloyd soon had under his command nine brigades, a force three times the size of the normal division, enough to justify a Corps control; and Irwin's responsibilities, from Calcutta to Fort Hertz in North Burma, were too far-flung for him to exercise operational control. Yet this is just what he tried to do. Slim's headquarters were moved from Barrackpore near Calcutta to Ranchi in Bihar, and Irwin set up his Eastern Army headquarters in Barrackpore in August 1942. From here he not only had to supervise operations in Arakan and the Manipur-Chindwin front, and the engineering plans at Ledo, but also to see to the refugee problem in Imphal and – vital in a tropical zone – to bring up to date a sleepy and inadequate military hospital system. All this, against a background of civil strife, during which the RAF and close on sixty battalions of infantry were deployed to repress rebellion.

Yet roads as much as anything else were what Irwin deemed essential. XV Corps had to build one south from Chittagong. IV Corps was making a two-way road from Dimapur to Imphal and a fairweather road on as far as Tiddim, as well as another road to Tamu and the Kabaw Valley. An ambitious plan was drafted to turn the Silchar-Bishenpur track into a modern road, but Irwin dismissed this as not feasible for at least a year, because it would need a new alignment. So the track, 'jeepable with difficulty', had to stay.[1]

By the end of the cold weather, early in 1943, Irwin planned to have a motor road as far as the Pangsau Pass, and to extend it as far south as Shingbwiyang. It was accepted that road construction took priority over everything, even over a battle.

But he was not content with motor roads. Irwin was forward-looking enough to see that the future of the war in Burma lay with transport planes. He wrote to Wavell asking that the whole resources of the UK and the US be called upon to produce transport planes, and he saw clearly the sensible way back to Mandalay:

> If I can jump the gap between the Chindwin and, say, Shwebo in
> one hop, if I can get troops into an area of relatively good

---

[1] Irwin to Wavell, *Notes for the C-in-C*, appended to letter dated 14 November 1942, Irwin Papers.

communications and there we could fight on, monsoon or no monsoon, until we've driven an M.T. road through. I realize this means a force of probably 150 aircraft. But April is a long way away yet and I live in hopes that by then perhaps an Armada of transport planes might come to our help.[1]

'I only wish I could get you more transport planes,' Wavell replied:

They do not appear to be making any at all at home and we are entirely dependent on the Americans, who also appear to be in short supply, at any rate they are not producing many for us, and the prospect is not encouraging.[2]

With this diversity of anxieties on his mind, Irwin should never have become bogged down in the tactical details of Lloyd's battalions. Yet this is precisely what occurred.

Until the first week in January, Lloyd's 14 Division was opposed by two battalions of 33 Division, then responsible for garrisoning Arakan. The two battalions were under the command of Colonel Miyawaki Kōsuke, regimental commander of 213 Regiment, who also had a battalion of mountain artillery, a company of engineers, field, A/A and anti-tank guns, an airfield battalion, a signals section, an L of C hospital, Kempei, and an intelligence detachment from the Hikari Kikan to liaise with Indian agents. This composite group was known as Miyawaki Force, with an approximate strength of 3600. Miyawaki was anxious about Lloyd's direction and strengths, but since he was commanding seasoned troops from Sendai in northern Japan, who had fought in China and conquered Burma, he was not unduly worried about the quality of the force facing him. He knew, as his men did, that the British were weaker than the Chinese.[3]

His Isagoda Battalion (II/213) was fifty-five miles north of the main body, and occupied Buthidaung and Maungdaw on 24 October 1942. These two towns were around ten miles apart, on either side of the Mayu Range, joined by a road driven across the range, which went through two tunnels, East and West, to carry the rice from Arakan's rich alluvial plains. It was a good road, a strategic prize, therefore, and Isagoda spent fifty days to 16 December 1942 building defensive positions around it and reconnoitring the Indian frontier. He was lucky enough to capture British maps of the area, and had them flown at once to Japan, where they were copied and the copies flown back to Arakan. Japanese operations for the next two years in Arakan relied on these maps.

[1] ibid.
[2] Wavell to Irwin, 16 November 1942, Irwin Papers.
[3] OCH *Arakan Sakusen*, p. 25

Lloyd decided to attack the Buthidaung-Maungdaw line on 2 December 1942, but Irwin told him to delay until his lines of communication had improved. They were quite appallingly difficult. Supplies came by rail as far as Dohazari, twenty miles south of Chittagong. South of Dohazari a metalled road ran for ten miles then became a four-foot wide earth track (unusable in the wet weather). Motor transport ran from Cox's Bazar to Tumbru at the head of the Naf River, whence supplies could be ferried down to Teknaf near the river mouth. Sampans were used for this and brought loads to Bawli Bazar and Teknaf, whence they were carried further on by packs and porters. Lloyd improved on this rickety structure part of the way by having supplies sent by sea to Cox's Bazar. Engineers were told to build a road to Ramu and Cox's Bazar and in spite of the lack of local stone this was done by mid-October 1942, good enough for animal transport and light vehicles. But it was like fighting a modern war along stone-age tracks.

Heavy rain on 7 December closed all the tracks and stopped road-work, so Lloyd further postponed his offensive until mid-December. On the 17th, he began to move. 123 Brigade (Hammond) was to approach Rathedaung along the east bank of the Mayu River, while 47 Brigade (Blaker) moved south down the peninsula on Foul Point, two battalions west of the Mayu Range, one battalion east. In reserve at Chittagong, Lloyd kept 55 Brigade, and he knew that to complete the operation he could call on 6 Brigade with five motor launches, seventy-two landing craft and three paddle steamers to negotiate the crossing to Akyab Island. He also had more or less complete air supremacy, and considerable numerical superiority.

The Japanese knew this, and to avoid wasteful casualties, Miyawaki withdrew Isagoda's battalion from the Buthidaung-Maungdaw line on 22 December. When Lloyd's men arrived there the next day, they found the line empty. Isagoda had withdrawn down the east side of the Mayu Range, to a line Kondan-Gwedauk, on the opposite side of the river from Rathedaung. V Force (agents behind the Japanese lines) sent Lloyd an absurdly inflated figure of the Japanese presence here. About 800 Japanese, they reported, were in Kondan, building defensive positions. Air reconnaissance tried hard to find these positions, but the Kondan area is covered with thick jungle and they saw nothing. In fact, there was not very much to see. A single platoon of Isagoda Battalion was in occupation of Kondan, between fifty and sixty men. When 1/7 Rajput reported they were held up by Japanese at Kondan, this, in Lloyd's view, confirmed V Force's estimate. On the other hand, without meeting any Japanese, a carrier patrol from 47 Brigade went as far as Foul Point.

Miyawaki was operating under direct command of 15 Army, whose headquarters were in Rangoon. He was told on 3 January to take Donbaik and Rathedaung, in anticipation of the arrival that week of 55 Division in

Arakan to take over the defence of south-west Burma. Miyawaki told Isagoda to take Rathedaung and send a small force to occupy Laung-chaung, a village near the end of the Mayu River on the west bank. Itō's III Battalion was to send one company to forward positions at Donbaik, the rest of the battalion to garrison Akyab. By sunset on 4 January 1943, a mixed company under Lt Watanabe Sadao was in place. On the 5th, he tangled with 5/8 Punjab and though the Punjabis were repulsed, Watanabe was killed in the fight and his place taken by 2/Lt Asano Genjirō.[1]

The Japanese moved forward to positions over a mile north of Donbaik, along what is called the 'F.D.L. Chaung', which is a natural anti-tank defensive position, with steep sides up to nine feet high. The company had the Bay of Bengal on its left, and the foothills of the Mayu Range on its right. The only snag in the position was the difference of tides on the coastal strip. At low tide, vehicles and men can use the hard sand of the beach and the position might be outflanked. In this spot, for fifty days, the Japanese stood off attack after attack by massed battalions of 14th Indian Division. This was, in part, due to the careful reconnaissance Miyawaki had insisted on, along the Mayu ridge and the coastal plain. He had an excellent eye for terrain, and the position was perfectly chosen. And the Japanese had a defensive system that the British had not come upon before, largely because it was they who had been on the defensive. This was the bunker.

The bunker is basically a pill-box using natural materials. It can hold up to twenty men and is dug into the ground or, if the water-table is too high to allow this, it can be built up to six feet above ground. The revetment is built of logs and earth up to five feet thick, and the roof is secure from bombing and shelling. Many bunkers survived even direct hits from bombs and shells, and were so sited as to give crossfire from one bunker to another. Infantry attacking them would find that they came under fire from two or more other bunkers as they sought to attack one. In the early stages of the fighting in Arakan, British artillerymen assumed that concrete had been used in bunker construction, so effective were the log walls and roofs. It was defences of this kind which brought Lloyd's offensive to a halt, not once but time after time.

The Inniskillings of 47 Brigade tried to take Donbaik on 7 January. The attack was in company strength. It failed. The next day, an attack was put in, in battalion strength. That failed too. The next two days, 8 and 9 January, the Inniskillings threw themselves at the defenders of Donbaik and were repulsed each time, with a total of 100 casualties.

123 Brigade was making as little progress on the east bank of the Mayu River. Hammond had sent out a patrol of the 10th Lancashire Fusiliers, who went into Rathedaung on Christmas Day and found it empty. They repor-

[1] OCH *Arakan Sakusen*, pp. 53–4

ted back at once, and Hammond decided to send more of the Fusiliers down by river craft to Htizwe, seven miles north of Rathedaung; they could make the rest of the journey easily along the track. They did, and arrived in Rathedaung on 28 December to be greeted by machine-gun and mortar fire. The next day, the rest of the battalion arrived, attacked again, and were repulsed with heavy losses. The RAF bombed and machine-gunned the Japanese positions on 9 January, and two mountain batteries joined in, to soften the Japanese up for another assault by the Lancashire Fusiliers. They made some headway, but by nightfall they had been driven back to where they started. Blaker's reserve battalion, 1/15 Punjab, was then sent in and took Temple Hill some hundreds of yards to the north of Rathedaung, but got no further. On both sides of the Mayu, by 10 January, the British offensive was at a standstill.

Wavell and Irwin came down to visit Lloyd on 10 January. It was vital, he was told, to take the Donbaik position. 'Can I have tanks for the bunkers?' he asked, and was assured they would be forthcoming. Here Slim objected, when he was told how they would be used. The tanks were Valentines, from 50 Tank Brigade, under Slim's XV Corps, and the brigadier protested when only one troop was asked for. He knew the risks to tanks of being used in penny packets, and Slim supported him, on the principle 'the more you use, the fewer you lose'.[1] When it was pointed out to Slim that the front on the Mayu Peninsula was extremely narrow, he answered that even on that front you could deploy a regiment of tanks. He was overruled, .and the tanks were sent, half a squadron of them in the event, from C Squadron 146 Regiment RAC. Captain da Costa and his two troop leaders, Lt Carey and Lt Thornton, recce-ed the position as soon as they arrived, and their conclusions were predictable: they had eight tanks and – Slim was right – the job called for a regiment.[2]

Lloyd ordered an attack for 1 February, with 55 Brigade (Hunt), now brought forward and supported by the eight tanks and most of the divisional artillery, to attack Donbaik, while 123 Brigade would go for Rathedaung two days later. The tanks were to sortie twice, once from the foothills along F.D.L.Chaung to a spot called 'Wooded Village', and back again, and next in support of 1/7 Dogra also along the *chaung* but moving further south to 'Wadi Junction' and then again towards the foothills, to the height called South Knob.

Thornton took his troop as far as the *chaung*, swung right and continued along westward, firing at the Japanese as they went. Then the leading tank hit a ditch, as did the two following. Smoke was put down to hide the tanks. Carey's tank fell into a ditch, and while his driver was reversing out of it a shell killed the gunner and wounded Carey. But they got back to the

---

[1] Slim, op.cit., p. 152

[2] B. Perrett, *Tank Tracks to Rangoon*, p. 80

beach. Da Costa took three tanks along the beach to rescue Thornton's troop, but had no luck; the Japanese gunners opened up on them and brought them to a halt. The remains of five bodies were found near the tanks when they were examined in 1945, by which time the Mayu Peninsula was clear of Japanese.[1]

At Rathedaung, Hammond's battalions made a slight impression during 3 February, but by the end of the day he was forced to withdraw to a position on two small hills, West Hill and Temple Hill, north of the town. The Japanese still held it.

They were by no means complacent about their success. Miyawaki had been told to hold on to Donbaik and Rathedaung until Koga's 55 Division could take over, and he meant to do that. But Koga, who flew up to Akyab with his staff on 24 January, knew that his division would not be fully concentrated until the end of February, and even when it was, it would only be two-thirds of its strength: its 144 Infantry Regiment, 4300 strong, had been sent to Eastern New Guinea as the Nankai ('South Seas') Force, under direct command of Imperial Headquarters. When Koga took over from Takeuchi at the end of 1942, the division did not have quite such a high reputation in the eyes of higher command – 15 Army in Rangoon – as its sister divisions, 18 and 33, which had shared the first Burma campaign. The Chief of Staff had been dismissed, and the regimental commander of 112 Regiment had had a nervous breakdown in March 1942 because of the high casualties sustained against the British. Nonetheless, its record was quite impressive. It had done nearly 1600 operational miles, during nearly 160 operational days, and been in combat above battalion strength fifty times. So it had quite a confidence in its own ability.

To reach Arakan, its forces would have to move over 600 miles, cross the Arakan Yomas – which went up to 8000 feet – and avoid Allied air attacks as they did so. Iida realized how desperate the situation might become, and told Koga he would put another battalion from 213 Regiment into Arakan to link up with Miyawaki Force. I/213 was then at Pakokku, and it was ordered to take a mountain battery and make for Paletwa in the Kaladan Valley, the area V Force was operating in. If Miyawaki could hold off Lloyd, then Koga's division could take over by the end of the month.[2]

Irrepressible as ever, and still certain the Japanese were being over-estimated, Wavell wrote to Irwin on 7 March 1943 to say he was sure Irwin would be able to deal with the threat that now seemed to be posed by a long-range penetration against the lines of communication from the direction of the Kaladan: 'a strong blow on the Mayu Peninsula and a real

---

[1] Kirby, *War Against Japan*, II, p. 267, says the tank men did not carry out a reconnaissance and so mistook the side of the *chaung* they were to traverse. But Perrett speaks of three tank officers recce-ing the ground.

[2] ibid., II, p. 266

success here will do more than anything to help the situation. I should like to finish up this campaigning season with a real success which will show both our own troops and the Jap that we can and mean to be top dog.'[1]

The day that wish was expressed, the Japanese struck in the Kaladan Valley and at 123 Brigade north of Rathedaung.Within a week the situation was critical enough for Lloyd to move 71 Brigade from the coastal plain to the Mayu River valley to help withdraw the two battalions at Rathedaung. The 1st Lincolns of 71 Brigade were left with 6 Brigade, which also took under its wing 5/8 Punjab from 47 Brigade. 6 Brigade (Cavendish) was therefore six battalions strong, a very powerful infantry force indeed, and Irwin ordered Lloyd to have it attack Donbaik on 18 March.

He had already brusquely overruled Lloyd's plan of attack, using 6 Brigade on the coastal plain and 71 Brigade clearing the high ground to the top of the Mayu Ridge, on the grounds that 6 Brigade's attack would be exactly like all the others which had failed before. He preferred a highly concentrated attack on a limited objective, he told Wavell, and he had made the plan after sitting on top of a hill for an hour overlooking enemy territory and walking through one battalion area. He resented having to do it:

> It is a monstrous thought that it should be necessary to undertake in this way the duties which should be properly carried out by the Divisional, Bde and Bn Commanders, but not only in this instance but also as a result of the day I spent on the Rathedaung Front, I am left in no doubt that we are most weakly served by our relatively senior commanders and by the lack of training and, unpleasant as it is to have to say so, the lack of determination of many of our troops... and I must take the responsibility personally for our results.[2]

The threat from the Kaladan materialized. A Japanese battalion marched over the Kansauk Pass and struck at the rear of 55 Brigade at Htizwe, north of Rathedaung, forcing it to withdraw across the Mayu River. By the time the attack of 18 March on Donbaik went in, the Japanese were in control of much of the eastern side of the Mayu River valley. They crossed the Mayu itself on the 24th, and then the ridge, threatening the lines of communication to all Lloyd's forces on the Mayu Peninsula. The Durham Light Infantry and the Royal Welch Fusiliers opened up the new attack on Donbaik, preceded by a curtain of shellfire

[1] Wavell to Irwin, 7 March 1943, Irwin Papers.

[2] Irwin to Wavell., 9 March 1943, Irwin Papers.

in the early hours of the morning, during which 140 tons of shells were fired into the F.D.L. Chaung area.

6 Brigade was not facing Miyawaki. Koga's 55 Division had arrived and settled in, and the defence of Donbaik was now the responsibility of Colonel Uno, of 143 Infantry Regiment. Donbaik was now a strong fortress, and 6 Brigade spent itself against it in vain, losing 300 men before being brought to a standstill, after Cavendish had put in a night attack the following day.

The next day, 20 March, Wavell, Irwin and Lloyd conferred at 14 Divisional Headquarters. Each man was nagged at by private griefs. Wavell was being harried by the Metropolitan of Calcutta in the Diocesan Record about brothels, and disturbed by reports that patrols on IV Corps' front had begun executing village headmen and burning villages in the Chindwin Valley presumably on suspicion of collaboration with the Japanese;[1] Irwin was sure the morale of his commanders and their men was crumbling; and Lloyd had lost his daughter in February – she had died at home in England – and he was still suffering great distress. It was an unhappy meeting, and its upshot was an admission of defeat. No ground was to be given up until the onset of the monsoon, it was decided, but 'positions in depth' should be taken up in preparation for a withdrawal to the Maungdaw-Buthidaung line.[2]

Irwin was still convinced his method of overwhelming infantry power on narrow fronts was correct:

> the 6 Brigade attack... failed obviously because – although the local commanders think otherwise – there were not enough troops following each other up. It was not, in my mind, the frontages that were wrong, but the depths.[3]

Wavell replied that he thought the only way to upset the Japanese was to take the whole of the Mayu Peninsula, controlling the river mouth and threatening Akyab. On the other hand, Lloyd seemed to be bogged down at Donbaik, and strength concentrated there might mean being outflanked further east. He could not see what role the force east of the Mayu was playing, and although he saw no good alternative to Irwin's proposals, he did not like them. They had let the Japanese get the initiative and he did not see how they could regain it. His exasperation with the stalemate erupted in the final paragraph, bristling with suggestions:

---

[1] As he heard it, it was a rumour, but he said if true it must be stopped at once and disciplinary action taken. There was nothing more damaging to future operations than troops getting a reputation for reprisals against inhabitants. (Wavell to Irwin, 15 January 1943)

[2] Connell, *Wavell, Supreme Commander*, p. 252

[3] Irwin to Wavell, 20 March 1943, Irwin Papers.

I was, as you probably realize, most disappointed at the Donbaik attack. It seemed to me to show a complete lack of imagination, and was neither one thing nor the other. An attack in real depth with determined soldiers like the 6th Brigade would, I am sure, have accomplished something, though it might have cost us casualties. But to use one battalion at a time, and that usually only deploying one company, seems to me to be poor tactics. With the Japanese in a pocket like that, I cannot believe that a plan could not have been made to eat them up; it looked to me practically ideal for covering machine-gun and mortar fire from a flank. I should now like to see what can be done by way of a very gradual point by point advance, using a little imagination and originality. For instance, is it not possible to bring up a 25 pr gun to point-blank range to the nearest of those strong points? Would it not be possible to put one or two low-flying fighter aircraft over the Japanese forward positions and under cover of the noise and distraction make a night advance? Is there any possibility of damming up the *chaung* and then flooding the Japanese positions? Can we concentrate the fire of, say, 20 mortars and some artillery on one of their strong points and pound it to pieces, and then quickly move the mortars to escape retaliation? I am told that there is a kind of fougasse, made of tar and petrol, I think, which was devised for use against tanks and is guaranteed to set practically anything alight; do you, or your Engineer-in-Chief, know anything about this? I am told there are some in the Calcutta area. I cannot think the Japanese should be allowed to exist in a pocket like they are on that front without very heavy losses indeed.[1]

Three days later, while approving harassing action at Donbaik, and hoping to 'clean it up' if possible before the monsoon, he expressed lack of confidence in Lloyd: 'I feel it is no use ordering it while Lloyd is in command, since he obviously does not believe in it. But if Lomax takes over and after examination thinks it can be done, I am quite prepared to support another attempt.'[2] The invitation to get rid of Lloyd could hardly have been put more clearly.

Wavell wrote this only a fortnight after Irwin had commented both favourably and unfavourably on Lloyd:

In some ways I have been disappointed because Lloyd has not shown that determination of command which I had expected and

---

[1] Wavell to Irwin 22 March 1943, Irwin Papers.

[2] Wavell to Irwin, 25 March 1943, Irwin Papers; Kirby, *War Against Japan*, II, p. 339

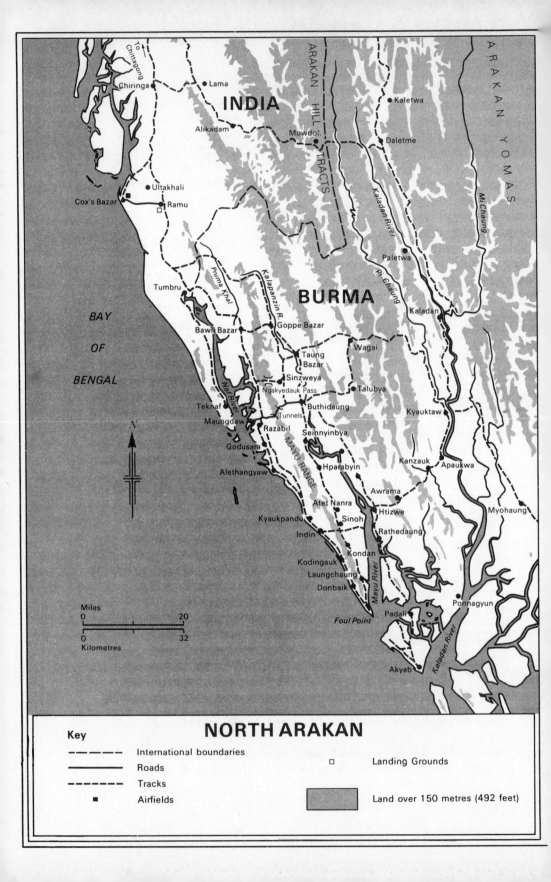

NORTH ARAKAN

Key

- – – – – International boundaries
- ——— Roads
- – – – – Tracks
- ■ Airfields

□ Landing Grounds

▨ Land over 150 metres (492 feet)

Miles
0   20

Kilometres
0   32

BAY OF BENGAL

INDIA

BURMA

ARAKAN HILL TRACTS

ARAKAN YOMAS

To Chittagong
Chiringa
Lama
Alikadam
Mowdok
Kaletwa
Daletme
Kaladan River
Mi Chaung
Ultakhali
Cox's Bazar
Ramu
Paletwa
Pi Chaung
Tumbru
Pruma Khal
Kalapanzin R.
Kaladan
Bawli Bazar
Goppe Bazar
Wagai
Taung Bazar
Sinzweya
Talubya
Ngakyedauk Pass
Kyauktaw
Teknaf
Naf River
Buthidaung
Maungdaw
Tunnels
Razabil
Seinnyinbya
Godusara
Kanzauk
Apaukwa
Hparabyin
Alethangyaw
MAYU RANGE
Awrama
Myohaung
Atet Nanra
Htizwe
Kyaukpandu
Sinoh
Rathedaung
Indin
Kodingauk
Kondan
Laungchaung
Mayu River
Donbaik
Foul Point
Padali
Ponnagyun
Akyab
Kaladan River

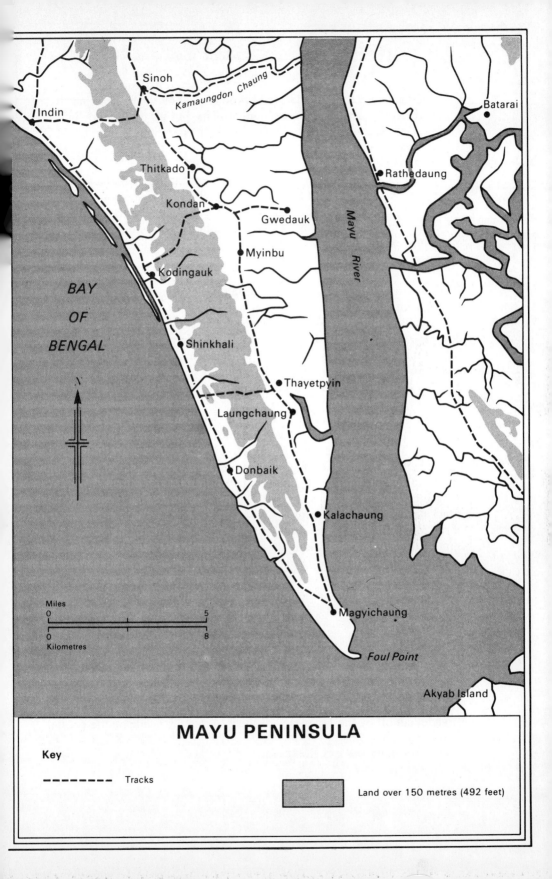

BAY

OF

BENGAL

Sinoh

Indin

Kamaungdon Chaung

Batarai

Rathedaung

Thitkado

Kondan

Gwedauk

Myinbu

Mayu River

Kodingauk

Shinkhali

Thayetpyin

Laungchaung

Donbaik

Kalachaung

Magyichaung

Foul Point

Akyab Island

Miles
0   5

0   8
Kilometres

MAYU PENINSULA

Key

– – – – – – –   Tracks

⬛   Land over 150 metres (492 feet)

is more prone to wait for suggestions or requests from his subordinate commanders than to impose his will on them. He is not
sufficiently meticulous in examining plans put up by them or in
supervising the detailed conduct of their operations – long distances account for this to a considerable extent. I have warned
him to this effect.

On the other hand he has undertaken a great task with the very
limited resources that I have been able to place at his disposal and
possibly because we were too successful or too impetuous initially
he is finding himself in awkward situations with tired, and, to
some extent, demoralised troops. I believe it would be a mistake
even to suggest a change at this moment.[1]

It is true that Irwin was convinced the Japanese could be overwhelmed by
numbers on a narrow front, an idea rich in casualties, as we have seen. But
Lloyd believed this too, as Slim found out when Irwin requested him to go
down to Arakan and visit Lloyd. As XV Corps commander, Slim found the
request ambiguous. Was he to take his headquarters staff with him, i.e.
was he to assume control? No, Irwin replied, a corps headquarters was not
necessary, he was not being asked to take operational control, just to see
and report.

Slim was in Maungdaw on 10 March and visited the forward brigades.
The divisional headquarters was unable to cope with running nine
brigades, he saw at once; and, in any case, he was committed to that view
before he left. He also saw that unit morale was very low, there was a great
deal of futile ammunition expenditure by panicky troops, and Lloyd's plan
for using 6 Brigade seemed wrong. Lloyd said he *had* to make a frontal
attack because he had no ships to hook down the coast and the jungle ridge
of the Mayu Range was impassable to a flanking force. 'I told him,' writes
Slim, 'I thought he was making the error that most of us had made in 1942
in considering any jungle impenetrable and that it was worth making a
great effort to get a brigade, or at least part of one, along the spine of the
ridge.'[2] Lloyd told him he had given this much thought, had concluded it
was not feasible, and his brigadiers agreed. Slim had no operational authority to alter Lloyd's verdict, and he simply went back and reported to
Irwin. Under pressure from Wavell to put in another attack, and convinced
by the men on the spot that to use the Mayu Ridge was impossible, Irwin
accepted Lloyd's verdict, with the result we have seen.

The last straw came when Lloyd, under pressure from a new Japanese
attack developing from the east against the Mayu Valley, directed 47
Brigade, cut off by the Japanese advance, to join 6 Brigade on the coastal

---

[1] Irwin to Wavell, 9 March 1943, Irwin Papers.

[2] Slim, op.cit., pp. 153–4

plain and retreat northwards. This was on 25 March, less than a week after
Irwin had made it clear that no ground was to be given up before the
monsoon made movement impossible for British and Japanese alike. Irwin
countermanded Lloyd's order, and took command of 14 Division in person
on 29 March, sending Lloyd back to India on leave. 'Stand fast' he told 47
Brigade, and ordered 4 Brigade (26 Division) to establish contact with it.[1]

Lomax was ordered forward, and arrived in Maungdaw to take command, ahead of his staff. Slim's XV Corps was told to be ready to take
higher command of the battle. Irwin told him to set up his Corps
Headquarters in Chittagong, though he was not to take operational control
until Irwin said so; and even then would not have administrative control, a
decision Slim clearly thought foolish, since a Corps Headquarters could
relieve the forward division of a large administrative burden and allow it to
get on with the battle. Slim briefed himself from both sides: he saw Irwin in
Calcutta on the morning of 5 April, having been recalled from leave in the
small hours; and he dined with the dismissed Lloyd that night in the Bengal
Club, found him 'quite without bitterness' and heard his side of the story.
He flew to Chittagong the following day, met Lomax later at forward
divisional headquarters, and was much impressed by his calm
level-headedness.[2]

He was going to need every ounce of it. The same day Irwin handed over
to Lomax, 3 April, General Koga's forces completed their trek across
Arakan from the east, crossing the ridge of the Mayu Range and coming
out on the coastal strip. They emerged at Indin, through which 6 Brigade
was withdrawing after its failure to take Donbaik. The attackers were 112
Infantry Regiment, under Colonel Tanahashi. This is how Tanahashi reported what followed, when he returned to 55 Division headquarters:

> On 3rd April, my column had successfully cut the road on the
> coastal strip NW of Indin, and was gradually tightening its
> stranglehold from the coast road with the main body, and from
> the foothills of the Mayu Range with the rest. At dawn on the
> 6th, we burst into the village of Indin. A lightning attack was put
> in on 6 Brigade headquarters, and the 6 Brigade commander, his
> adjutant and staff, five or six men in all, surrendered. I was
> interrogating them through an interpreter when, immediately
> afterwards, the British began to pour a fierce concentration of
> artillery fire into Indin, from both north and south. Our mountain
> artillery in the Mayu Range and Uno Column's artillery began
> firing at the British guns, and the Indin area was turned into a
> crucible of gun smoke and shells.

[1] Connell, op.cit., p. 252

[2] Slim, op.cit., p. 156

My column's wireless was smashed, I was wounded, and five of my regimental headquarters staff were wounded too. Brigadier Cavendish and five or six of his men were all killed at this time. As the shelling was so fierce, the main body of the column was pinned down in Indin and unable to attack the British and Indian troops escaping north along the coast road.[1]

The news of what happened reached the Durham Light Infantry at seven that morning – the Japanese had attacked the Royal Scots and Cavendish's headquarters during the night – and command of the brigade was taken over by the DLI's colonel, Theobalds, who was senior commanding officer in 6 Brigade. The Durham battalion moved into Indin to find that the Royal Scots had suffered heavily, and that the Japanese were in position among clumps of bamboo round the huts which formed the village of Indin itself – it was all the cover there was. The acting CO ordered the battalion to make for Kyaukpandu, three miles along the coast road to the north, where they were to concentrate by five in the evening. Before they went, they brought down artillery and mortar fire to bear on the Japanese round Indin who had not had time to dig in properly. They had the choice of being killed by shells or shot down as they ran for it. The DLI took a heavy toll of Tanahashi's column and Uno column, and repeated the shelling when they passed Japanese gun positions on the Mayu Range, as they withdrew to Kyaukpandu. The guns unhooked from their limbers and fired smoke and high explosive to protect the retreating infantry. The Japanese guns on the hills seemed to be firing at extreme range, 'so that the shells fell wearily on the wet sand and bounced slowly across the path of the marching columns'.[2]

But 6 Brigade was not the only brigade to be trapped by Koga's offensive. The route leading from 47 Brigade's area east of the Mayu Range ran through a village called Sinoh across to Indin. When 6 Brigade withdrew, the Japanese controlled this track and cut off 47 Brigade. Wimberley ordered his brigade to move across to Indin at dawn on the 6th, found it impossible to get through and decided to leave the area of the track and go across country to the village of Kwason, south of Indin, assuming 6 Brigade to be there. He soon found he was in country where his brigade could no longer move as a single force, so he abandoned his heavy equipment, including his 3" mortars, and went back up to the summit to find another escape route. The Japanese were already in Kwason, a patrol informed him, so he split his brigade up into small groups and told them to find their way back as best they could. Most succeeded in doing so, and joined up with 6 Brigade by 14 April. But they were little use to Lomax by

[1] OCH *Arakan Sakusen*, p. 110; *Inpāru Sakusen*, p. 42
[2] D. Rissik, *The D.L.I. at War*, p. 180

this time, disorganized and without their equipment. As the Official History puts it, 'As a fighting formation, 47th Brigade had temporarily ceased to exist.'[1] The survivors were sent back to India.

'I have rarely been so unhappy on a battlefield', is how Slim remembers the events of that week. 'Things had gone wrong, terribly wrong, and we should be hard put to it to avoid worse.'[2] He was sorely tempted to take over tactical command from Lomax and would have done so had he not been impressed by the way the 26th Divisional commander handled the situation, steady, confident, competent, regrouping his rear brigades to cover the Maungdaw-Buthidaung road and reorganizing his shattered forward brigades. Slim and he saw how the disaster had weakened a morale that was already low. They excepted 6 Brigade, who had had a hammering, but were still staunch. Some other units had behaved far from well. Irwin, always ready to criticize, was far more specific. He had already told Wavell how dissatisfied he was with some British units on the IV Corps front. Writing to Wavell about 17 Division, whose spirit he described as 'excellent', he nevertheless indicated that certain units were having 'domestic difficulties':

...for example, the Gloucesters appear to me to be generally good but they, like the K.O.Y.L.I. have some men which we have asked to be removed to some other theatre of war – they are the worst type of rascal. The Gloucesters too have a few senior officers who have reached their 6 years service abroad who are applying for re-patriation. This seems to me to show not a very good spirit at this moment, but the matter is being gone into on the spot.[3]

After the most recent debacle, his wrath fell on 47 Brigade, and he excoriated

the evident failure of the Inniskillings to fight. I believe a great many of them who have come out, have done so without their weapons, and a captured Jap document indicates that the British troops on the writer's front – and this could only be on the Inniskilling front – were surrendering readily. I'll have courts of enquiry all ready for such cases, including the loss of equipment when I get the 14 Div. troops out.

He was writing to a man who shared his grave doubts about the condition of the troops. 'I am more worried about the morale aspect both of the troops and to (sic) India as a whole, than anything else,' Wavell wrote, in a letter

[1] Kirby, *War Against Japan*, II, p. 345
[2] Slim, op.cit., p. 157
[3] Irwin to Wavell, 9 April 1943, Irwin Papers.

that crossed Irwin's.[1] Yet neither man seems as concerned about the fate of Cavendish as about the documents his headquarters was carrying. The loss of Cavendish 'and evidently the files of secret papers and codes of 6 Bde' were among the more disturbing features of the operation, Irwin commented, and Wavell saw it no differently. 'The Japanese capture of 6 Brigade HQ is unfortunate as I suppose it will probably have given him a very good idea of our dispositions and strength.'[2]

The Japanese regarded Cavendish's capture as a notable event. It was flashed to divisional HQ, thence to Rangoon, thence to Southern Army, and on to Imperial General Headquarters in Tokyo. The 'destruction of six enemy brigades' was featured in the Japanese press, with the fanciful figure of '20,000 enemy casualties'.[3] Koga was disappointed, then, when Tanahashi had to report Cavendish's death during the British shelling. And ugly rumours began to circulate. The British Official History merely mentions in a footnote that, 'According to Japanese reports he was killed shortly afterwards by British artillery fire.'[4] Slim is a little more specific: 'Brigadier Cavendish was captured,' he writes, 'only to be killed a little later by his guards or by our own artillery fire.[5]

Slim's doubts about how Cavendish met his death were shared by the Japanese military historian Takagi Toshirō, whose attention was drawn to the episode by the announcement of Tanahashi's suicide in 1946 after he had been summoned to GHQ SCAP in Tokyo. Takagi at first assumed Tanahashi was wanted for enquiries by MacArthur's headquarters into Cavendish's death, and indeed Tanahashi himself may have believed this. In fact, he was merely going to be asked to contribute his knowledge of the campaigns in Burma to a history of the war. His motives for suicide may be complex, involving a feeling of remorse at having failed in the Arakan battles of 1944. Takagi's book *Senshi* (*Death in Battle*) (Asahi Shimbunsha, Tokyo, 1967) leaves the reader with the impression of a non-proven verdict, but other accounts of Cavendish's death have appeared since, including one by the Japanese medical officer who saw the corpse and signed the death certificate, Ogawa Tadahiro ('*Inden senki*' – The battle at Indin – , *Nanso*, No. 39, privately printed, Tokyo, July 1972). Ogawa points out that no eye-witnesses of the death survive, but from the position and posture of the body and that of Japanese bodies near it, he is convinced Cavendish was killed by shell fragments from British artillery fire.

This was certainly the story given to me by survivors of 112 Regiment in Payagyi Camp in 1945, when I interrogated them about Cavendish's death at the request of the then C-in-C ALFSEA, Lieutenant-General Sir Miles

---

[1] Wavell to Irwin, 9 April 1943, Irwin Papers.

[2] ibid.

[3] OCH *Arakan Sakusen*, p. 117

[4] Kirby, *War Against Japan*, II, p. 344, n. 1.

[5] Slim, op. cit., p.156

Dempsey, a friend of the Cavendish family. One of the men I – and later Takagi – questioned was the interpreter Matsumura, also responsible for beating Major Turrall during the surrender period (see p.542). He was an unsavoury looking piece of work, but – in the nature of things – his account was no different from anyone else's.

Koga gave orders for the capture of Buthidaung and Maungdaw on 20 April. The attack was to start on 24 April and he would use Uno Force (143 Infantry Regiment and II/214 Regiment), Matsukihira Battalion (I/112 Regiment), Miyawaki Force (213 Infantry Regiment), Tanahashi Force (112 Regiment) and divisional artillery. Uno Force had the hard task of advancing north along the Mayu Range and was harassed throughout by difficulties of supply. Without trucks, or horses, food had to be man-handled by a detachment from Tanahashi. Colonel Uno was moved to verse by his predicament:

Kate tsukite	Our food is exhausted;
sude ni nanuka wo	already for seven days
banana ki no	we have been gnawing at
shin wo kajirite	the banana tree's core:
hita ni tatakau	into battle.

Back in the gloomy desolation of Chittagong, Slim deduced that Koga's next move must be on Buthidaung-Maungdaw and the Tunnels, and Lomax agreed. 6 Brigade, after its recent battering at the hands of Uno and Tanahashi, was dug in in the Mayu foothills and coastal strip further north, and Lomax had a second brigade in reserve behind it. He was sure that Koga would make a move east of the ridge. Lomax devised a fly-trap for them, a box into which the attacking forces would move, and which would have a lid to close on them. The box involved six battalions. Two would be massed on the ridges of the Mayu Range, two along the Mayu River, two on the hills just south of the Maungdaw-Buthidaung road, which would be the bottom of the box. The lid was a force of nearly a brigade, which would close in on the Japanese as they penetrated into the box, making for the Tunnels. As Slim said later, it sounds very simple and geometrical. But he and Lomax were using tired men who had already taken a beating.

Uno made for Buthidaung and bumped 55 Brigade near two hills, 297 and 275, where a fierce mountain battle ensued. Allied aircraft joined in on the 28th, bombing and strafing Uno Force, permitting 55 Brigade to counter-attack. Tanahashi rescued Uno, and the hills were re-taken. Uno forged on, and on 4 May cut the Buthidaung-Maungdaw road at MS 27 and MS 55. The Japanese thrust north had happened just as Slim and Lomax planned it would. The plan failed because the bottom dropped out of the box. The two battalions in the 'bottom' position failed to hold. 71 Brigade had sent forward a detachment of 10th Lancashire Fusiliers to hold Point 551, a hill overlooking the East Tunnel. The Japanese moved forward on 2 May, and on the afternoon of the 3rd drove the Lancashire Fusiliers off the hill. Slim saw Lomax on the 5th and permitted him to sacrifice Buthidaung if he thought it necessary, to allow 55 Brigade and the troops east of the tunnels to be extricated; but Maungdaw must be held. The Japanese had destroyed the bridge across the Letwedet Chaung at MS 4 from Buthidaung, which compelled 55 Brigade and 1st Lincolnshire to wreck their vehicles and march across country on the night of the 6th. Two days later, Lomax disposed his forces round Maungdaw, to obey Slim's orders – and those of Irwin, who reiterated that Maungdaw must be held. The Japanese air force put in appearance on the 8th, bombing Maungdaw and Bawli Bazar, and putting civilian labour to flight. Miyawaki Force came round the Mowdok Hills and was east of Buthidaung by 9 April. The box had simply fallen apart. At 7pm on 8 May, Uno Force moved east and occupied Buthidaung, a more than military triumph because it was the headquarters of military government for Arakan. Matsukihira Battalion marched north from Godusara and took Maungdaw on the 14th. 'It was too much like 1942 over again,' says Slim, 'with the added bitterness that this time we had been defeated by forces smaller than our own.'[1]

It was Slim's pressure, much against Irwin's reluctant judgment, that allowed Lomax to abandon Maungdaw. A siege of it, still unstocked, and held by troops who, he was now sure, 'could not be relied on to hold anything', would invite disaster. It did not matter that V Force reports led to Maungdaw being abandoned rather hastily, on the assumption that a Japanese force was looping round to come in from the east and prevent any sort of ordered withdrawal. It would probably not have been possible to hold it anyway. So, after months of heavy and dispiriting fighting, the British forces were back where they started in October 1942.

In an irritable postscript to Slim, Irwin totted up the casualty list for the week ending 8 May. 'For ARAKAN they totalled Br. and Ind. all ranks: 10 killed, 40 wounded, 3 missing and for that loss, 17 Bns. have been chased about by possibly 6, a sad but realistic commentary on the present fighting.'[2]

Looking over the campaign as a whole, Slim did not think the cost in men had been high. 'Our actual losses in killed, wounded and missing were not high, about 2500, and, while we had not inflicted as many on the enemy, he had suffered too.'[3] Slim's reckoning tallies well enough with the official British figures:

[1] Slim, op.cit., p. 160
[2] OCH Irwin to Slim, 10 May 1943, Irwin Papers.
[3] Slim, op.cit., p. 161

Killed: 916
Wounded: 2889
Missing: 1252
Total: 5057.[1]

But they are very much at variance with the Japanese statistics:

British losses:
Killed: approx. 4789 (this figure is qualified by the phrase
iki shitai, 'abandoned corpses')
POW: 483 (including 3 officers).
(No figures are given for wounded)
Japanese losses:
Killed: 611
Wounded: 1165
Total: 1775 (30% of the forces taking part).[2]

'The greatest gain from the campaign,' Wavell proclaimed in his despatch, 'was experience of the enemy's methods and of our own defects in training and organization. The serious loss was in prestige and morale. On balance I shall certainly never regret that I ordered the campaign to take place in spite of lack of resources.'[3]

Slim was more specific. In a letter to Irwin (18 April 1943) he commented on morale:

All Brigadiers, Hopkins, Lowther and Curtis are worried about the state of their troops. This is the most serious aspect of the whole show. If our troops were in first-class fighting form and health we should have little to worry about. The British troops are tired and they are 'browned off' with the operations in Arakan as a whole. Their health is deteriorating. The recent rain has added to the malaria and the three Bns and att troops in 6 Bde are now evacuating 50 men a day. None of the Bns is much over 500 and several lower.

The Indian troops, except 4 Bde, are tired too, but with them the fault is the inferior quality in physique, training and spirit of the men, especially of the drafts that have joined in Arakan...

I think the troops, both British and Indian, will fight on the whole well, for one more time, but won't go on much after that. Whatever happens in Arakan it is imperative that the highest authorities get down to improving the quality of men in our

[1] Kirby, *War Against Japan*, V, p. 543
[2] *OCH Inpāru Sakusen*, pp. 45–6
[3] Connell, op.cit., p. 255

infantry, and raising their powers of endurance. We are fighting
an army in which the best men go into the Infantry, and we shan't
make much progress until we follow suit.

Perhaps naturally, Irwin was perturbed lest the blame be firmly fixed on
the higher command. He admitted its faults, but felt the blame lay
elsewhere, as he confided to Wavell on 8 May in a MOST SECRET AND
PERSONAL letter:

> We are about to be faced with the difficult problem of how to
> explain away the loss of Buthidaung and Maungdaw. From the
> public's point of view, undoubtedly it will be the Commanders
> who will go through it and will be held responsible for the defeat.
> In fact, although the Commanders are far from being much good,
> the cause unquestionably lies in the inability of troops to fight.

He followed this up with a MOST SECRET set of 'Notes on the Army in India
and Army problems relevant to operations on the India/Burma Border'. 'I
can say,' he averred, 'that troops practically without exception are not
worth 50% of Jap infantryman in jungle country. . . It is for this reason that
I emphasize the absolute necessity of "letting" troops "in" lightly and
slowly. I have available reports on the poor quality of troops and I am
personally able to quote instances of behaviour which ordinarily would be
regarded as "scandalous conduct and cowardice in the face of the enemy"
which in the operations in Arakan reached such proportions that there was
no alternative but to accept the fact that the standard of troops was not up
to the task.'

A liaison officer was sent from Slim's headquarters during the first half
of May, when the fighting for the Buthidaung-Maungdaw road was reaching a climax. He visited 4, 6 and 71 Brigades, and came away with the
impression 'gained from personal observation and conversations with
senior and junior officers, NCOs., men and escaped POW that on this
front the Japanese soldier, with the notable exception of the gunners, was
definitely superior to the troops forming the bulk of our forces in this area.'

> Outstanding was the fact [he continued] that our troops were
> either exhausted, browned off or both, and that both Indian and
> British troops did not have their hearts in the campaign. The
> former were obviously scared of the Jap and generally de-
> moralised by the nature of the campaign, i.e. the thick jungle and
> the subsequent blindness of movement, the multiple noises of the
> jungle at night, the terror stories of Jap brutality, the undermin-
> ing influence of fever, and the mounting list of failures; the latter
> also fear the jungle, hate the country and see no object in fighting

for it, and also have the strong feeling that they are taking part in a forgotten campaign in which no one in authority is taking any real interest...

Some units, especially the Lancashire Fusiliers, have been in the battle since the beginning of operations in Oct 42, they feel that they have a grouse in that most units have been changed over and that they have been ordered to stay...

Reinforcements that have arrived have consisted mostly of untrained men, many of whom according to the CO of the L.F. had never even seen a Bren Gun...

To sum up the man-to-man situation – the seasoned and highly trained Jap troops are confronted by a force which, though impressive on paper, is little better, in a large number of cases, than a rather unwilling band of levies. This cardinal factor, especially in jungle warfare, completely nullifies our estimated 5–3 superiority.

Specific examples were then adduced: the 8/13 Frontier Force Regiment failing to hold Hill 551 because they blazed away all their ammunition at noises during the night and by morning had none left and were compelled to retire; the Sikh company of the same battalion refusing to obey orders – 'during the course of the attack itself the O.C.Coy and the 2nd-in-Comd found themselves on the 551 feature while their coy was fast moving in the opposite direction.' The Brigade Major of 71 Brigade told him that it was no uncommon thing for the British officer in charge of a patrol, at the threat of contact with the enemy, to find himself suddenly alone without his patrol.

Morale was linked with training:

It was most noticeable that the majority of C.Os. and the staff of 26 Div had little or no confidence in the men under their command and that one and all considered the fault lay in training and lack of training, i.e. troops being sent to a theatre of war for which they had no practical preparation whatever, together with a large percentage of almost raw recruits.[1]

Irwin's papers contain reports dated 22 May, 1943, described as being from 'a young Liaison Officer on Arakan front', which tell the same story in even franker fashion; the directness, and the fact that they are contained in a letter, suggest they may have been written by Irwin's son, Anthony, who acted for a while as liaison officer in Arakan before joining V Force:

The troops that I came in contact with, and they were the most forward units and their Commanders, were gutless. That is the

---

[1] 'Report on Visit to Maungdaw Front from 4/5/43–9/5/43', Irwin Papers.

only word I can find for them. They were disinterested (sic), indisciplined, untrained in many cases. In all they were gutless. For example I cannot do better than tell you again of the fellow, the British Corporal, who said 'Don't shoot, sir, they'll only shoot back.'

...I saw the impossibility of any form of success with the present force, and those that sit at home in comfort only have the knowledge to read the black and white of the Sitreps [Situation Reports]. What do they know of the Jungle, and what would be their answer if you were to tell them that the British soldier is a rotten and gutless fighter after he has spent a little while against the Jap. What would they say if you told them of the spirit of the men who come here to fight. They come, hating the powers that sent them, they come only hoping to return on the morrow, and they come praying that they may not have to fight. Those were the men of your Army.'[1]

From whatever source, the melancholy tale of defeat and its cause, shattered morale, could be repeated. The Army in Burma undoubtedly needed roads, weapons, comforts, air support and so on. But most of all it needed an immense uplifting of the spirit. It needed Orde Wingate.

The first Wingate expedition

A vast literature has grown up about the personality and strategic ideas of Orde Wingate and his two long-range penetrations into Burma behind the Japanese lines. They have attracted more attention than the rest of the campaigns put together and this has led to an unjust under-estimation of the strategic value and achievements of other formations. On the other hand, the animus Wingate aroused in fellow commanders and distant staffs has also led to determined efforts to denigrate him and to reduce the impact of what he did. Even now, to do him – and his enemies – justice, requires a fair amount of dexterous tight-rope walking.

'Impact' is what matters, at least as far as the first Wingate expedition is concerned. When it started out, the original plan on which it had been based was already scrapped. It could not therefore, by definition, achieve the original purpose for which it was formed. The idea was to send Wingate's 3000 men, supplied by air, into Burma as a kind of extended cavalry raid, an accompaniment to an invasion by a much larger force. The larger force was not forthcoming. Should the raid be cancelled, or should it go ahead? Largely with Wavell's support, it went ahead, and the skilful publicity with which Wingate's return to life was stage-managed was of

[1] Irwin papers, Imperial War Museum

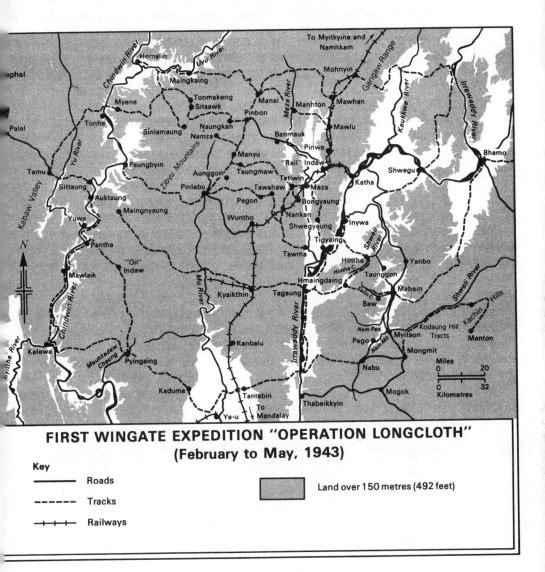

FIRST WINGATE EXPEDITION "OPERATION LONGCLOTH"
(February to May, 1943)

Key

———— Roads

------ Tracks

+-+-+-+ Railways

Land over 150 metres (492 feet)

incalculable profit to future operations in Burma, often for those who disliked most his military notions and aggressive personality. The expedition gave British morale a boost. That the boost was needed, the account of the first Arakan campaign will already have indicated. When the soldiers' morale was at its lowest, when the notion – against which all commanders struggled – that the Japanese infantryman was a kind of jungle superman, who could not be defeated save by overwhelming superiority in numbers and massive fire-power, was almost universally prevalent, here was someone who demonstrated that the Japanese could be beaten at those things they were thought to be best at: physical endurance, secret and swift movement, and inventive use of jungle tactics.

Military historians will no doubt continue to deride some of Wingate's pretensions and prove, quite correctly, that what in the end won the Burma campaign were the Indian divisions who broke the Japanese at Imphal and Meiktila. Devotees of the dull and staid will decry his flamboyance, histrionic procedures and the publicity which attended them. They miss the point. What the press and world opinion made of Wingate's initial exploits infused a new spirit into the affairs of Burma. Whatever the strategic upshot, whatever Wingate's psychological faults – *on a les défauts de ses qualités* – that renewal of the spirit cannot be gainsaid.

The codename for the first Expedition was Operation LONGCLOTH. It went into Burma on 13 February 1943, a day on which Lloyd's unhappy forays into Arakan were futilely battering away at Donbaik and Rathedaung. It returned in May, when Eastern Army and XV Corps had accepted defeat at the hands of numerically inferior Japanese forces and glumly gone back to Square One. The two operations were simultaneous. But the spirit and energy behind them were totally different, and although First Wingate also ended in defeat, it was a defeat full of promise for the future. LONGCLOTH had panache, it had glamour, it had cheek, it had everything the successive Arakan failures lacked. It was the perfect psychological medicine for an Army sadly devoid of confidence in its methods, its purposes and its ability to fulfil them.

Orde Charles Wingate was a gunner officer – Charterhouse and Woolwich – who served in pre-war Palestine where he achieved notable success against the Arab rebellion of 1936 by organizing 'night squads' of Jewish settlers to defend their *kibbutzim*. It earned him a DSO and also a transfer from an area where his pronounced pro-Zionist views were felt to be a political embarrassment, as well as somewhat peculiar in an Army officer. In these operations lie the roots of Haganah, the Israeli force which later fought the British and the Arabs to establish the State of Israel in 1948, by which time Wingate had been dead four years. At a time when anti-semitism was fashionable in the upper echelons of the British Army, and the schoolboy Arabophilia engendered by hasty misreadings of Lawrence's *Seven Pillars of Wisdom* seemed much more acceptable, Wingate's dedication to the people of the Old Testament – his parents were strict Plymouth Brethren – made the return of the Jews to Israel a passionate cause.

He kicked his heels at home for the first few months of the Second World War, but with the entry of Italy into the war in June 1940 his expertise in guerrilla warfare and service with the Sudan Defence Force made him a natural choice for the elimination of the Italians from their conquests in Abyssinia. The British had around 40,000 men in North Africa, the Italians 400,000, a discrepancy which rather ruled out the virtues of head-on frontal attack and put a premium on guile and ruses. At the suggestion of an Englishman, A. D. Sandford, with long experience of Abyssinia, the exiled Emperor Haile Selassie was introduced into his former domain and a rebellion fomented. With the support of regular forces operating from the Sudan, the rebellion triumphed, and Wingate's 'Gideon Force' – about 2000 Sudanese and Abyssinian regulars, 1000 Abyssinia guerrillas, a sprinkling of British officers and NCOs – defeated 36,000 Italians complete with armoured cars, field guns, bombers and fighter-planes. Wingate entered the capital, Addis Ababa, with the restored Haile Selassie, and flew back to Khartoum and on to Cairo.[1]

It had not been roses all the way. He had quarrelled with Sandford, he had got across the British Commander-in-Chief, Sir William Platt, partly because Wingate believed the British government were lukewarm about the guerrilla achievements, wanting British regular forces to enter the capital first and so diminish the Emperor's prestige, making him amenable to British plans for East Africa. There was some foundation for this, but it became an obsession with Wingate, his resentment made him enemies, and on his return to Cairo a fit of depression made him attempt to cut his throat in an hotel bedroom. That was in July 1941. He was saved from his own foolishness by an officer in the next room who heard him fall to the floor, and from his career coming to an abrupt end by Wavell's sympathetic treatment. Wavell had been impressed by the performance of Gideon Force, and when he became Commander-in-Chief, India, he remembered Wingate. Deeply perturbed by the declining morale of the British Army in the Far East, Wavell summoned Wingate to see what chestnuts unorthodox warfare could save from the fire that was consuming Burma.

He flew to Delhi, and then on to Maymyo, where General Hutton told this somewhat morose young Colonel that shortages of men and aircraft and the swift Japanese advance offered little hope for the expansion of guerrilla activities. He recommended him to see Michael Calvert, a bellicose sapper officer, who was running the Bush Warfare School to train British officers to run bands of Chinese guerrillas in China against the Japanese. Calvert knew China, had seen the Japanese operating in Shanghai, and in between bouts of boxing for the Army had fought the Germans in Norway and helped run the commando training centre at Lochailort. Calvert's 'School' was not merely instructional. He mounted raids from it, and Wingate discussed these with him, and was introduced by Calvert to Slim, by then commander of Burcorps at Prome, and to Chiang Kai-shek, with whom he flew to Chungking to discuss the possibilities of

---

[1] Abyssinia and Eritrea were a proving ground for many of the generals who later commanded in Burma: Slim, Messervy, Briggs, Lloyd, Rees.

long-range penetration from China. The situation deteriorated too rapidly for Wingate to be able to assert his authority over the various guerrilla units that had sprung up in Burma, and he returned to Delhi at the end of April 1942.

Bernard Fergusson, on the Joint Planning Staff at GHQ, remembers any number of people offering suggestions for the re-taking of Burma, but only one that made a real impression, 'a broad-shouldered, uncouth, almost simian officer who used to drift gloomily into the office for two or three days at a time, audibly dream dreams, and drift out again . . . as we became aware that he took no notice of us . . . but that without our patronage he had the ear of the highest, we paid more attention to his schemes. Soon we had fallen under the spell of his almost hypnotic talk; and by and by we – some of us – had lost the power of distinguishing between the feasible and the fantastic.'[1]

There was nothing particularly fantastic about the real basis of Wingate's notions. It was air power. British defeat in Malaya and Burma had been at the hands of numerically inferior forces because the British were road-bound. If their L of C was cut – a standard, reiterated Japanese ploy – then they seemed incapable of fighting back. So they always fought with one eye over their shoulder, fearful of enemy road blocks, of being cut off from hospitals and supplies. In an age of air transport, Wingate saw that this could change radically. Most of what lorries could bring up, aircraft could carry in or, if they could not land, could drop in by parachute. At one stroke this destroyed the soldier's dependence on a land L of C. He could have everything, food, water, post, mules, jeeps, guns, ferried through the skies to wherever he happened to be. The only requisite was an efficient wireless system to signal dropping-points with accuracy. When surrounded, instead of being compelled to fight his way back to base through a Japanese road-block, or jettison his equipment and flee through the jungle, he could stay and fight it out on the spot. And the air could also provide the long-range heavy artillery he could not carry with him. Air-strikes from fighter bombers would become the cannon of the modern age. It sounds so terribly trite now. It is only so because men like Wingate made it a practical reality.[2]

But Wingate did not want simply a strategy that rescued beleaguered units and turned them into successful garrisons. He wanted movement. In a country like Burma – bigger than France – in which the Japanese at the time had only four divisions with some garrison brigades, most of them occupying frontier defences against a possible invasion, there were vast areas of L of C relatively unprotected and sparsely defended. A force

[1] Fergusson, *Beyond the Chindwin*, p. 20

[2] For a criticism of Wingate's ideas on aircraft in an artillery role, see Terence O'Brien, 'Wingate – a flawed hero', *Sunday Telegraph*, March 11, 1984, p. 9

which could act on this L of C would achieve results out of all proportion to its size. It would not be quite the same as Abyssinia. There, he could rely on the local inhabitants' hostility to the Italian occupation and their friendliness to anyone promising to overthrow it. The case of Burma was different. In 1943, the Japanese were still the liberators, and the gesture of political independence was only just round the corner. It would not do to assume the Burmese wanted the British back. On the other hand, the Burma Rifles men who had come out in 1942 still existed as a military unit. They were hill tribesmen, Karens, Chins, Kachins, and they would act as guides, interpreters, and reconnaissance platoons. 'They were our eyes and ears', Fergusson said, 'and our foragers, too.'[1]

It was enough that Wavell believed in him for Wingate to be given the brigade he would need for his first attempt. But he was faced with problems. So were the officers he commanded. Wingate was forty when his first expedition went into Burma. Careless of his appearance, yet attentive to the impact he created, he grew a beard in Abyssinia and on the march in Burma (though not in the training stages in India) and sported a sola topee of the kind which used to be Army tropical issue but went out of use with the advent of the more serviceable and infinitely more picturesque Australian bush hat. An Ancient Mariner in speech, holding his hapless interlocutor with piercing blue eyes and a numbing fund of recondite information, given to harangues, quarrelsome of personality and yet strangely persuasive, he was the perfect image of the unconventional and unorthodox soldier beloved of Wavell and also, as Shelford Bidwell calls him, 'a romantic and patriot'.[2] He also refers to him, quite correctly I think, as a 'cyclothyme', a manic-depressive passing from moods of profound despair in which he believed that God (who had chosen him for some great work) had abandoned him, to a zestful euphoria in which everything pointed to fulfilment.

He was given a British battalion which, on the surface, could hardly have been worse suited to the task he had in mind. This was the 13th King's Liverpool. They had been on coastal defence duties in England before being drafted out to serve as garrisons in India. They were city-bred men, not only from Liverpool but from Glasgow and Manchester; most of them were married, and many were over thirty. The average age was over thirty until some younger recruits were drafted in. 'Ordinary, and in some cases third-rate... nondescript' is how Bidwell sums up Wingate's British troops.[3] Through no fault of their own, says one of Calvert's officers, Jeffrey Lockett, many were physically incompetent for the task or 'had no liking for what lay ahead.' Wingate himself noted their 'marked lack of enthusiasm'.[4]

[1] Fergusson, *Trumpet in the Hall*, p. 143

[2] Bidwell, *The Chindit War*, p. 39

[3] ibid., p. 25

[4] Major-General Derek Tulloch, *Wingate in Peace and War*, p. 71. C. Sykes, *Orde Wingate*, p. 372

There was inevitably a good deal of shedding. The Force was meant to be eight columns strong, each column being based on an infantry company. In the event, there were four Gurkha columns, and three British columns, so ruthless had been the weeding-out process during the training in the Central Provinces: it included the King's battalion commander as well as 250 of his men. The rest found their pale flesh turning tanned and hardening, and their chests filling out. They also found that any tendency to hypochondria had to be firmly controlled. With the co-operation of his medical officers, Wingate decided to cut the percentage of men going sick, which had reached 70%. Attending sick parade without cause became a punishable offence. All slight ailments were to be treated by platoon commanders (as would often happen on the march anyway). The officers had to inspect the men's stools in the latrines to see if complaints of dysentery were justified.[1] By the time the training was over, only 3% of men were reporting sick.

The 3/2 Gurkha Rifles were Wingate's other infantry component. They were raised in wartime and were short of specialized officers. Only one officer had been on active service and only two had a thorough knowledge of Gurkhali.[2] In fact the Gurkha officers thought they already knew a fair amount about the type of warfare for which Wingate was training them, and never really – in Calvert's view – accepted Wingate's ideas.[3] He and Calvert believed that senior officers at their depots and in Delhi encouraged in them a tendency to insubordination. That senior Gurkha officers disliked Wingate is certainly true. W. D. Lentaigne, who was then raising 111 Brigade as a long-range penetration force, and who was later even to succeed Wingate in command of the Chindits, is said to have loathed him and despised his ideas. And a nameless Indian Army general, a former Gurkha officer, is quoted as saying, 'He brought off what must be an all-time record in rotting out a Gurkha battalion, a young one withal.'[4] It should be noted that Wingate continued to ask for Gurkhas when he raised his second expedition, in spite of his known contempt for the Indian Army as a whole.

The survivors of Calvert's Bush Warfare School were incorporated as the 142 Commando Company. They would carry out the sabotage and demolitions which were one of the purposes of the expedition. Calvert had had some hardened roughnecks under his command in the last days of the 1942 retreat, including even some deserters who had been serving time in a detention camp. On one occasion he had found their sentries asleep, and a gang of them absconding in a truck. He hunted for the men and never

[1] Information from Lt. W. Edge.
[2] Sykes, op.cit., p. 371
[3] Calvert, *Fighting Mad*, p. 123
[4] Connell, *Auchinleck*, p. 743, n. 1

found them, so chaotic were conditions at the time; but he later acquired the reputation of having gone after them and killed them in person, which did him no harm at all with the wild ones left behind. He hadn't put a high price on their loyalty anyway.[1]

Each column, commanded by a major, would have fifteen horses and a hundred mules, and was armed with Vickers medium MGs as well as the usual infantry weapons and Thompson sub-machine guns. Heavy transport was by mule, and supply by airdrop, so an RAF section was attached to each column to signal suitable dropping zones. Rations were rarely adequate, even so. The rigours of jungle training prepared the men for hardship. They were often on short commons, often appallingly thirsty, gnawed by insects, battened on by leeches, and exhaustion became a customary condition. This made sense of the medical discipline imposed at Saugor: a sick man isolated in the Burmese jungle, like the wounded, would have to be abandoned, and that meant being taken prisoner or dying. Both officers and men cursed Wingate as he drove them through the relentless weeks of exercise, but they admired him, too, and his very eccentricities made him more acceptable: he might be found stark-naked scrubbing himself down with a stiff hairbrush, consuming buffalo milk, or devouring raw onions, the virtues of which he was prepared to preach to all and sundry.

The day began at six, with half-an-hour's bayonet drill, and unarmed combat. Breakfast was followed by jungle craft lectures, use of the compass, and map-reading. They rested during the period of most intense heat, did fatigues between 3 pm and 5 pm. There were no buildings to sweep out, so these consisted mainly of digging latrines and clearing jungle for mule lines. They finished at 5 pm, at least during the normal working day. Most often they would be out on exercises, blowing bridges, attacking airfields, or laying ambushes.[2] Calvert easily justified the excessive stresses of the training programme:

> Most Europeans do not know what their bodies can stand; it is the mind and willpower which so often give way first. Most soldiers never realized that they could do the things they did, and hardly believe it now. One advantage of exceptionally hard training is that it proves to a man what he can do and suffer. If you have marched thirty miles in a day, you can take twenty-five miles in your stride.[3]

Ever sensitive to propaganda values, Wingate improved on the numerical title of his force. In conversation with one of his Burmese officers, he misheard the Burmese word for 'lion', 'chinthe', as 'chindit'. The word

[1] Calvert, op.cit., p. 116

[2] David Halley, *With Wingate in Burma*, pp. 30–2

[3] Calvert, *Prisoners of Hope*, 1971, p. 12

stuck, and it has since entered military history. This is in large part due to the impact of books written by two of his column commanders, Michael Calvert and Bernard Fergusson (later Lord Ballantrae). Calvert had finally escaped from Burma after strangling a Japanese officer during a naked man-to-man truggle while swimming in the Chindwin, and later disguised as an Indian woman with a party of Indian refugees. He was irrepressible, and as soon as Wingate heard he was alive, he recruited him.

Fergusson was impressed by Wingate's ideas even in the hothouse atmosphere of GHQ (India) but he had in fact met Wingate before. A monocled Old Etonian from the Black Watch with a patrician drawl which later had the expected, if perhaps not intended, effect on General Stilwell, Fergusson had led on the whole a privileged Army life, having been ADC to Wavell and instructor of cadets at Sandhurst. Fergusson had also, like Wingate, developed an *engouement* for the Near East, and like him, too, had been engaged in intelligence work in Palastine in 1936. He was not put off a passionate desire to escape the cloistered atmosphere of Lutyens's Secretariat and join Wingate, either by his fellow staff officers who told him not to touch it with a bargepole or by the indignant major he met changing trains at the junction before Saugor, who was leaving the Force and told him, 'My advice to you is to turn round and go straight back to Delhi. Wingate's crackers, and I'm off.'[1]

Fergusson had not been happy in Delhi, where he had had the only job in which he found himself 'continuously and thoroughly miserable'. He was vexed by GHQ, not only for himself, but also for his former Chief, Wavell, now C-in-C India. Fergusson recalled the brilliant staffs who had served Wavell in Aldershot and Cairo, and compared them with the Second XI by whom he was served in Delhi. He was glad to get away.[2]

Unlike Lawrence, who wrote his own *apologia*, Wingate's ideas survive only as letters and official memoranda. His reputation has therefore come down in books written by those who served under him or, in one case, commanded him. And in the case of Fergusson it has known some ups and downs. *Beyond the Chindwin* is the panegyric of a convert. *Trumpet in the Hall*, his last book, though it repeats the praise of the former, adds qualifications that the younger Fergusson would have hesitated to make, that the national press 'inflated him to a ridiculous degree'[3] and that 'at times the truth was simply not in him'.[4]

It will not do to treat the first Wingate expedition simply as collaboration between Wavell and Wingate. As GOC Eastern Army, Irwin also had a say in it, his only proviso being that the idea would only work if a larger

[1] Fergusson, *Beyond the Chindwin*, p. 24

[2] Fergusson, *Wavell: Portrait of a Soldier*, p. 72

[3] Fergusson, *Trumpet in the Hall*, p. 179

[4] ibid p. 177. Later still (*Radio Times; 16. vii. 76*) he regretted, to some extent, the verdict in this book.

force invaded Burma at the same time, which was the initial premise anyway:

> I may say... [he wrote to the Official Historian, Major-General Kirby, in January 1956] that Wavell sent Wingate down to me in 1942 to discuss his organizations and possible role. As a result of his visit I supported the whole idea and actually wrote out the C-in-C's Operation Instruction which GHQ accepted and subsequently issued in their name. The time was to come, however, for a decision whether or not to send the Chindits into Burma in default of any major operation developing alongside them. In short my advice to the C-in-C was that from the operational value and the inevitable disclosure of the whole idea Wingate should *not* be used yet. From the training point of view and the experience to be gained from ground/air cooperation, however, the enterprise might be well worth while. I did not feel competent to weigh these alternatives against the bigger issues involved and so asked Wavell to go up to Assam, see Wingate and Scoones and decide on the spot. This he did, in the manner known.[1]

As we have seen, the idea had been fleetingly raised of using Wingate's men in Arakan, as a long-range hook against the Japanese L of C, to match a proposed seaborne landing. When the landing was not forthcoming, for lack of landing craft, the operation was reduced to Lloyd's overland advance. Perhaps, for the future of Wingate's columns, it was just as well that he did not become involved in the morass of Arakan, though the end-product in casualties might have been no worse.

Wavell opted for the operation to go ahead, after Wingate had been told on 3 February 1943 that it was to be postponed. Wavell went up to Imphal to talk it over with Wingate. For the Force could now not achieve a strategic aim, since it was going in alone. Lives would be lost for nothing, and – Irwin's point – the Japanese would be made aware of what was brewing for North Burma (a real fear, as Mutaguchi's reactions were to prove). Wingate argued that long-range penetration would continue to be merely theory, and dismissable as such, if he could not try it out. There was also, he had been told, a Japanese threat to the tiny British force holding the last foothold in the far north of Burma at Fort Hertz. His men would divert Japanese attention from Fort Hertz.

But these were not the real reasons. 'The Brigade had been raised and trained for operations in the winter of 42/43,' wrote Wingate in his *Report*, 'and the whole tempo, physical and psychological, set to that tune. Not to use it was to lose it.'[2]

---

[1] Irwin to Kirby, 4 January 1956, p. 4, Irwin Papers.

[2] Prasad, ed., *Reconquest of Burma*, I, p. 99

'I had to balance the inevitable losses – the larger since there would be no other operation to divide the enemy's forces – to be sustained without strategical profit, against the experience to be gained of Wingate's new method and organization. I had little doubt in my own mind of the proper course, but I had to satisfy myself also that Wingate had no doubts and that the enterprise had a good chance of success and would not be a senseless sacrifice: and I went into Wingate's proposals in some detail before giving the sanction to proceed for which he and his brigade were so anxious.' That was how Wavell saw it himself. Irwin is convinced that Wavell's decision to go ahead was based on the incurable optimism he always had about the nature of the Japanese as enemy, an optimism which consorted ill with his pessimism about the morale of his own soldiers. When Irwin asked him what opposition he expected from the Japanese, Wavell replied, 'I have a hunch that the Jap is pulling out and that the appearance of Wingate may just turn the doubt into a reality.'[1]

There was also the point that some people in Manipur feared the Japanese would try the same trick as Wingate. Brigadier Teague, CO of the L of C area behind Imphal, with his headquarters at Kohima, believed in the possibility of a Japanese advance across the Naga Hills to cut the British L of C between Kohima and Imphal. Irwin accepted this but GHQ India and Scoones rejected it. It is, of course, precisely what happened twelve months from Wingate's First Expedition.

So Wavell weighed his motives and Wingate's, and turned to Lieutenant-General Somervell, USAAF, who had accompanied him to Imphal, to ask his views. 'Well, I guess I'd let them roll' was the only possible answer, and Somervell gave it.

Wavell uttered a few embarrassed phrases of farewell to the assembled columns outside Imphal, beside a stream between two hills. He saluted them as they made off westward. Wingate wrote an Order of the Day, in his style which echoes scriptural language and the half-forgotten rhetoric of an earlier age. Some of the officers affected to scorn this high-flown view of the war, but even on the toughest of the men it sometimes had astonishing results:

Today we are on the threshold of battle [he told them]. The time of preparation is over and we are moving on the enemy to prove ourselves and our methods... Our motives may be taken to be the desire to serve our day and generation in the way that seems nearest to our hand. The battle is not always to the strong, nor the race to the swift. Victory in war cannot be counted on, but what can be counted on is that we shall go forward determined to do what we can to bring this war to an end which we believe best

[1] Irwin, loc. cit.

for our friends and comrades-in-arms; without boastfulness or forgetting our duty, resolved to do the right so far as we can see the right.

...knowing the vanity of man's effort and the confusion of his purpose, let us pray God may accept our services and direct our endeavours so that when we shall have done all, we shall see the fruit of our labours and be satisfied.

O. C. WINGATE, *Commander*.

Jeffrey Lockett led the Commando Group in No 3 Column (Calvert), and passed it round to each of them in turn. Finally he handed it to the Sergeant-Major, Blain, a tough regular soldier, aged thirty-seven, who had served in the Argylls and been court-martialled five times. Blain burst into tears. 'It did gather up the sentiments of most of us', Fergusson remembered, 'and I can imagine no more fitting committal to a great enterprise...'[1]

On the night of 13 February 1943, Wingate's First Expedition began to cross the Chindwin. The strategic aim had been removed, but they had been allotted a number of specific tasks. They were to demolish the railway line between Mandalay and Myitkyina at several points, to cut supplies to the two divisions in North Burma. They were to harass the Japanese in the Shwebo area, north-west of Mandalay. If circumstances allowed, they were to cut the railway between Mandalay and Lashio.

The brigade was split into two groups. The first group, or Southern Group, Columns 1 and 2, was to carry out deception measures to mislead the Japanese about Wingate's real intentions. The Northern Group, Brigade HQ and Columns 3, 4, 5, 7 and 8 were to carry out the demolitions. This group crossed at or around Tonhe, while the feint south to Auktaung drew the patrolling Japanese parties on the Chindwin east bank further south. The Commando CO, Major Jeffries, made sure he was very visible near Auktaung, wearing the rank badges of a Brigadier, to ensure reports went back to the Japanese that Wingate had crossed there. After pulling the wool over the eyes of the Japanese patrols, the group was then to make for the Irrawaddy at Tagaung, cross it, reach the hills in the area of Mongmit and await the arrival of the main body of the Force. That meant marching around 250 miles across enemy-occupied territory, and the group did precisely that.

Once over the Chindwin, the columns had to cross the Zibyu Range, down into a wide valley and up again, across the Mangin Range, rising to nearly 4000 feet, then dip down again into the valley of the Meza River. The

---

[1] Fergusson, *Beyond the Chindwin*, p. 59. Cf. Lt. Edge on the impression made during training: 'I remember once when he assembled the whole unit after a demoralising period of training in the jungles near Saugor, when a very large proportion of the men were down with jungle sores, malaria, dysentery etc – and made the kind of Victorian rallying speech, playing on their patriotism, sense of duty, honour, etc – after a sticky start, he carried the day, and had everybody with him.' Letter to the author.

Meza flowed into the Irrawaddy, and the north-south railway crossed it at Meza. Above Meza lay the important town of Indaw, sometimes known as Rail Indaw to differentiate it from Oil Indaw further east. A few miles further on was Katha on the Irrawaddy itself. A crow flying across the map would make it around 100 miles or more. A man on foot, laden with more than sixty pounds of equipment in single file – 'Column Snake' as it was called – up and down the slopes, would probably settle for double that mileage. The highest points of the Zibyu Taungdan could be avoided by making straight from Tonhe through Myene and Tonmakeng and across to Pinbon, after which there was a slight break in the Mangin Range. Moving south-east from Pinbon, the Northern Group would then fall upon the stretch of line between Bongyaung and Nankan which it was to blow.

The main body crossed unopposed at Tonhe, and took four days to get to Myene, not quite ten miles away. It found its supplies there: HQ 2 Burma Rifles had gone on ahead and taken the supply drop of 70,000 lbs in the course of three nights dropping by the RAF. It took sixteen sorties to finish the drop, after which the Northern Group kept on going to Tonmakeng, around thirty miles further east, reaching it on 22 February.

Fifteen miles south of Tonmakeng lay the village of Sinlamaung, where the Japanese were reported to be. Three columns, 3 (Calvert), 7 (Gilkes) and 8 (Scott) were sent south, since Wingate wanted to start on the offensive once the supply drops were distributed. They arrived to find the locals had been conscripted into preparing a meal for the Japanese, who had just gone out on patrol, presumably looking for the Chindits. Calvert was not unaware of the piquancy of the situation, his men devoured the food, and the column set off back to Tonmakeng plus one horse and one elephant complete with oozie (or mahout).

It was known there was a garrison at Pinlebu also, about thirty miles south down the Mu Valley. To draw the attention of the Japanese away from the railway, Wingate ordered 7 and 8 columns to mount an attack on Pinlebu and Pinbon, at the northern head of the Mu Valley. At the same time 4 Column (Bromhead) was to appear to be making for Indaw. If IV Corps were to make an advance from the Chindwin at Sittaung, Pinlebu is exactly where they were likely to head for (it was the way 19 Indian Division came through in 1944) and Wingate hoped the Japanese would assume his Force intended to lay siege to Pinlebu, as the advance party of a larger body. Then Wingate heard that the track leading from the Mu Valley just north of Pinlebu, via Aunggon and Pegon, right to the railway at Nankan, was not guarded by the Japanese. He therefore changed his plan for Bromhead, and told him to go south towards Pinlebu to link up with Gilkes and Scott.

Bromhead did this, and found his way blocked by a superior Japanese force. He gave battle, but found his column being overwhelmed. He promptly ordered them to disperse. There was a previously fixed operational rendezvous, but Bromhead's cipher and wireless were lost in the fighting, and he found himself isolated from the main body of the Force, with no means of getting in touch. He did the only sensible thing, and told the men to make their way back to the Chindwin, which most of them did.

Disaster also befell 2 Column of the Southern Group. No 1 Column was almost into Kyaikthin, on the railway south of Wuntho, and forty miles south of where the main body of the Brigade was operating, on 3 March. 2 Column arrived in the Kyaikthin area on the night of 2 March, and concentrated three miles outside it, at the foot of a hill. But Burnett had marched his men in broad daylight from about six miles out of Kyaikthin and they had been spotted. A Japanese infantry company was rushed up from Wuntho, twenty-five miles away to the north. This company was already in position as 2 Column moved out at 9.30 pm to attack the railway. They plastered Burnett's column with mortar fire, and Burnett gave the order to disperse and reorganize to the rear of the position, but his order was not transmitted to all his units, some of whom simply pushed on to the Irrawaddy, on the assumption that the rest of the Brigade would be there sooner or later, the others making for the Chindwin under Major Emmett. Emmett was in the same situation as Bromhead. Most of his animals were dead, his wireless set was lost, and his ciphers had fallen into enemy hands. 'The disaster to No 2 Column,' wrote Wingate later (*Report*, p. 20) 'was easily avoidable and would never have taken place had the commander concerned [Burnett] understood the doctrines of penetration.'[1]

Of the seven columns that had set out, two were now written off. But 3 (Calvert) and 5 (Fergusson) had profited from the diversion round Pinlebu and made for the railway, where they were to carry out demolitions. Calvert was west of Nankan on 5 March, and sent out a patrol to reconnoitre. There were no Japanese there, he was told, but about sixty were at Wuntho. This was the cue for RAF co-operation. A signal from Calvert's RAF Section brought bombers on the scene. That gave Calvert an idea. If the same bombers could be induced to plaster Wuntho, and Katha the next day, he could put in his attack on Nankan with the minimum interference. So he settled down for the night two miles out of Nankan Station.

Further north, about ten miles away, Fergusson reached Bongyaung. Near here the railway line ran through a gorge, and his job was to blow the gorge and block the line with the debris. Either side of Bongyaung, he was told by the locals, there were small garrison units in the stations – at Meza to the north and Nankan to the south. There was nothing in Bongyaung itself. In his bivouac, three miles from Bongyaung Station, Fergusson contacted Wingate by wireless. The news was not good. He was told of the

---

[1] Prasad, op.cit., I, p. 107

loss of Bromhead's ciphers, but although he realized that meant 4 Column had walked into disaster, he was filled with pleasurable anticipation himself. He had been on the move for eighteen days since he crossed the Chindwin and had not seen a single Japanese the entire time. Yet here they were, right by a vital railway, ready to blow it the next day. Day, not night. Fergusson had begun to find the constant movement by night an irritation. There were no Japanese to watch them, so why not use the daylight for the demolitions? His Engineer officer, Lt Whitehead, told him that debris could be cleared from the gorge pretty easily, and that the sensible thing was to blow the bridge at the railway station. Why not do both, was Fergusson's reaction. Strong patrols up and down the road were meant to allow the demolition to go on without interference, and one of them found a lorry-load of Japanese and fired on it. The Japanese fired back as the lorry sped off, carrying away its own dead. Fergusson's party had two dead and – the thing Fergusson feared most – six wounded including Lt John Kerr. Wingate had made it clear to everyone before the march started that wounded had to be left. No one would slow down the march for walking wounded. If they could not keep up, they too had to be left. Only one of this group survived, some being killed by the locals, the rest in Japanese hands.[1]

Charges were laid along 140 feet of the bridge and in the cliff side overlooking the track. At nine o'clock the bridge was blown. 'The mules plunged and kicked,' wrote Fergusson, 'the hills for miles around rolled the noise of it about their hollows and flung it to their neighbours. Mike Calvert and John Fraser heard it away in their distant bivouacs; and all of us hoped that John Kerr and his little group of abandoned men whose sacrifice had helped to make it possible, heard it also, and knew that we had accomplished that which we had come so far to do.'[2] Heavy-hearted at the loss of Kerr and the other wounded, Fergusson nonetheless inwardly exulted at the explosion. 'All my life I've wanted to blow up bridges!' And there was more to come. Half his Commando platoon, under Lt Harman, had made for the gorge. As the rest of the column were about to bivouac that night, they heard another enormous explosion, and knew the gorge had gone, too.

There were three spans on the bridge, one of which was blown off its piers, another, 100 feet long, was resting with one end in the bottom of the gorge and twisted like a corkscrew. And some of the piers had blown away. Fergusson signalled this to Wingate at a noon halt the next day.

Calvert's column was similarly successful at Nankan. They moved on the railway on 6 March (it was Calvert's thirtieth birthday) and blew up two railway bridges, one of which was 300 feet long, and destroyed the line in

---

[1] Fergusson, *Beyond the Chindwin*, p. 96–7; *Trumpet in the Hall*, p. 148

[2] Fergusson, *Beyond the Chindwin*, p. 99

no fewer than seventy places. To ensure the Commando party had an uninterrupted session, Calvert had placed ambush parties on the road north and south. Two lorry-loads of Japanese were ambushed coming up from Wuntho, but they put up a stiff fight against Calvert's small party which was armed with an anti-tank rifle, a bren gun, and mines. They heard the explosions on the railway around 3.30 pm. The Japanese were reinforced, but in the end they broke off and fled into the jungle north of Nankan. To Calvert's great joy, he had not lost a single man. He moved off promptly to the Irrawaddy.

Fergusson had taken the precaution of sending a party down towards the river, since he had heard there was a river steamer station at Tigyaing. It should be possible to cross there. As it happened, Wingate was by no means sure that they should. While the demolitions had been going on he had been on a hillside overlooking the railway just north of Nankan. He was still unsure of the fate of his Southern Group and 4 Column was on its way back to the Chindwin. He signalled Fergusson:

> Owing no news received from No 1 Group for ten days crossing of Irrawaddy possibly hazardous stop no news Four Column stop leave it your own discretion whether you continue movement or make safe bivouac in Gangaw Hills to harass reconstruction railway.[1]

Fergusson learned that the Tigyaing crossing was feasible, and he calculated that the Japanese would expect him, now his mission was accomplished, to turn back and make for the Chindwin again. He asked Wingate for a few hours to think it over, and when one of his patrols that he had assumed was lost turned up he decided to chance it. He signalled Wingate he would cross the Irrawaddy and attempt to blow the Shweli bridge on the road leading up to Bhamo. Tigyaing was full of boats, and the chief of police there was a Karen of friendly disposition (he asked to be locked in his office, to prove to the returning Japanese he had not connived with Fergusson), so Fergusson decided to march his column through in style. They marched in threes, rifles at the slope, very parade-ground in manner, to such effect that an old man watching them from his balcony called out repeatedly 'God Save the King! God Save the King!' Fergusson had scruples enough to warn him that they were only raiders, not a returning force, and that he ought to be prudent in case someone informed on him. (He did, in fact, survive, as Fergusson found out when he met him nearly twenty years later in Mandalay.)[2]

[1] ibid. p. 101

[2] Fergusson, *Trumpet in the Hall*, p. 350

They paddled across, mortars, machine guns, wireless sets, and re-calcitrant mules, the latter taking more time than anything else. It took till dusk, and they had two boatloads to go when they realized the boatmen had vanished. This was a sure sign the Japanese had arrived in the neighbourhood, and the flashes of their rifles soon began to light up the darkness. The fall of mortar bombs in the sand added a certain haste to the proceedings, and the last thirty men crossed in boats weighed down to the gunwales, with Fergusson himself literally bringing up the rear: he had waded waist-deep to push the boat off and had to be heaved on board by his pack and the seat of his trousers:

> Every time I tried to shift so that I could sit the boat rolled frighteningly and everybody hissed at me to keep still, so I remained on my hands and knees with my stern sticking out towards the enemy. Hence my favourite boast, of being the only British officer ever to have crossed the Irrawaddy on all fours.[1]

Calvert's move to the Irrawaddy was soon through twelve-foot-high elephant grass and painfully slow. It occurred to Calvert that he had the remedy and should have thought of it earlier: the column's elephant. He brought it forward, and put one of his corporals on top with the oozie. Calvert called out the directions, the corporal tapped the oozie on the relevant shoulder, and the party moved forward. Calvert walked behind, reading his compass as he went, and when the elephant came to a sudden stop he blundered into its hind-quarters. The elephant had stopped for its own personal reasons, and Calvert found himself thoroughly soaked. His men found the sight, inevitably, hilarious, since it is not, as he was aware, every soldier who has the joy of seeing such a thing happen to his commanding officer. But the stench remained with him even after he washed his clothes in the Meza River after more hours of uncomfortable and malodorous marching.[2]

Calvert was going to make for Tigyaing, too, but one of his patrols learned that the Japanese, alerted by his demolitions, were now in occupation there and at the village of Tawma, some eight miles west. He decided to slip between Tawma and Tigyaing and sneak across the river, a procedure he found galling. The Japanese caught them as they crossed, but the rearguard held them off. Leaving ammunition and medical supplies behind – they could be replenished by supply drop – Calvert got across with his weapons and wireless, at the cost of seven men killed and six wounded. He was luckier with them than Fergusson with his. He left them with Burmese villagers, to whom he gave a note for the Japanese, reminding

---

[1] ibid., p. 151

[2] Calvert, *Fighting Mad*, p. 134–5

them that their tradition of Bushido should cause them to treat the wounded as well as they would treat their own. And in fact that is what occurred.[1]

The Japanese were, naturally, not passive spectators of these events. One of the best divisions in the Japanese Army garrisoned the area through which Wingate's columns moved. This was 18 Division, under the command of Lt-General Mutaguchi Renya, which had taken Singapore. The men were from the Nagasaki and Fukuoka areas of Kyushu, an island which has a reputation for producing hardy and bellicose fighters. The division's codename was Kiku – 'Chrysanthemum' – which was the Imperial flower, and it had a fine conceit of itself.

Its 55 Infantry Regiment under Colonel Koba was responsible for the area west of the Zibyu Range, roughly Homalin to Mawlaik, the northern part of which was I Battalion's responsibility, the southern half that of III Battalion, down to the 33 Divisional zone which started just north of Kanbalu. Regimental HQ and half of I Battalion was at Katha on the Irrawaddy, and II Battalion at Bhamo. From Katha to the Chindwin was the 'Katha Area' and, until they crossed the Irrawaddy, this was where the Chindits operated.

The first news of the Chindits came from Major Nagano Shigemi. He was the CO of I/55 Regiment, and signalled his regimental commander at noon on 17 February (three days after the Tonhe crossings): 'According to local reports, enemy about three to four thousand strong on march eastward from area Paungbyin.'[2] It was a totally unexpected piece of intelligence and Koba was sceptical. Then further reports came in, both from Nagano again and from local sources, so Koba ordered his I and III Battalions to find the force and destroy it, reporting to the divisional commander what he had done.

The next report spoke of the force as being split in three as it approached the Zibyu Range. Then five columns were reported. When the various sightings were put together, the impression given was of a force that was avoiding contact with the Japanese, slipping through gaps in its defences, and moving by night. The fact that the nature of this large force, as it penetrated deeper into their area, was not known to Koba's men, had a deeply disturbing effect. On indications that the force was making for Pinlebu, Koba moved his own HQ there from Katha and concentrated III Battalion with him, around 25 February.

In divisional HQ at Maymyo, Mutaguchi received Koba's early reports on the evening of 17 February, and was unable to make sense of the conflicting information. To see for himself, he went to Katha at the

[1] ibid., p. 137

[2] *Inpāru Sakusen* p. 57

end of February and visited Pinlebu with his Chief of Staff, Yokoyama Akira.

Meanwhile the situation was becoming clearer. Prisoners captured by III Battalion north-west of Pinlebu said that the force was advancing on Pinbon from the area of I Battalion. As it happened, wireless contact with I Battalion failed at this time, and Koba decided to switch III Battalion to Indaw on the railway line, about six miles west of Katha. They were unlucky. There were no trucks available so, like the men they were hunting, they had to go on foot. Koba decided to move to Indaw himself with half of I Battalion under his command. Mutaguchi, who by this time clearly did not think the force much of a threat, returned to Maymyo and told Koba he left the situation in his hands.

Reports then came in from south of 18 Division's area, from 33 Division. II Battalion of 215 Regiment had bumped an enemy force, strength unknown, as it was moving through its district on policing and propaganda. This was Wingate's Southern Group. They were moving east at the end of February, west of Kanbalu, about sixty-five miles south-east of Pinlebu. In this engagement the battalion commander, Major Nasu Ichirō, was killed. 33 Division described the enemy as 'a Gurkha unit', which afterwards made off in the direction of the Irrawaddy.

Putting this report together with the rest, 15 Army in Rangoon began to puzzle out what kind of a force was moving across north Burma. It was split into two groups, apparently, the main body to the north coming through I/55 Regiment's area to Pinbon, and the smaller southern group moving east along the boundary between 18 and 33 Divisions. But 15 Army was still vague about its strength, movements and intentions.

On the night 5/6 May south-west of Indaw, III/55 clashed with British troops after moving to Indaw from Pinlebu. They took prisoner around 100 men. The enemy there split into further columns and crossed the railway between Nankan and Bongyaung in the direction of the Irrawaddy. When Koba learned this, he took two companies of I/55 under command and hurried from Indaw to the Irrawaddy and inflicted great damage, he believed, on the rearguard of a unit crossing the river near Tigyaing. But the enemy's main body crossed the river and vanished on the opposite bank.

Information from prisoners now led Koba to believe that the whole force was 77 Brigade, led by Brigadier Wingate who was himself in command of the northern group. It was clear he had crossed the Irrawaddy at Inywa. But Koba could not guess where he was making for, or what his purpose was, on the other bank.

15 Army assumed the force was supplied overland, but no traces of this could be found. It seemed that the force filtered through Japanese positions at night and received air-dropped supplies by day. The whole thing suddenly started to look like a more ambitious venture than had at first

seemed to be the case, and Lieutenant-General Iida Shōjirō, at 15 Army headquarters in Rangoon, decided that 18 Division and 33 Division should cooperate to crush the force. When reports indicated that after crossing the Irrawaddy it was moving further east, Iida brought another of his divisions into play. This was 56 Division (Lieutenant-General Matsuyama Yūzō), which could trap 77 Brigade from the east while 18 and 33 Divisions moved in on it from the west and south. The three divisions would act as a *tōbatsu* ('punitive expedition').[1]

So the area south-west of Bhamo was to be swept by II/55 stationed there, while two battalions of 56 Regiment (II Battalion at Kyaukme, III Battalion at Maymyo) sought Wingate's men on both banks of the Shweli. At the same time Matsuyama directed III/146 Regiment in Namkham to move south down the course of the Shweli to trap them there.

These efforts began to bear fruit. Wingate's columns were compelled to split up into smaller parcels, and systematic movement became impossible. By the end of March, all it could do was send these parcels westward to escape. Its condition of extreme fatigue was, in the event, completely matched by that of the Japanese units pursuing it. On the other hand, Wingate's forces' dependence on the air began to tell against them, because air drops could only be made to large groups, the Japanese believed, and as they scattered the less likely was it that their air supplies could reach them. They would become more and more distressed through having to leave behind more and more wounded, and would grow weaker as their food grew less.

That is the Japanese picture, as their Official History sees it. What the Japanese could not know at the time was that Wingate was basically improvising the return journey, and changing plans as he thought fit. He had crossed the Irrawaddy with two columns a week after Fergusson brought 5 Column over. Wingate crossed at Inywa, and, as Fergusson puts it, when they met again after a month, and the columns were brought together, they realized they were caught in a bag. The rivers were on three sides of them, the Shweli and the Irrawaddy. At the base of this quasi-triangle, a motor-road ran which, if the Japanese used enough troops along it, would seal the bag. They had already begun to confiscate boats on the side of the rivers where 77 Brigade was. Fergusson wondered why Wingate had waited so long – a week – before crossing the Irrawaddy eastwards after 5 Column, when the maps showed it could become a trap. One reason was that Wingate was buoyed up by the news that 1 Column had not met the fate of its sister column in the Southern Group, but had demolished the railway line at Kyaikthin and gone straight east to the Irrawaddy at Tagaung in conformity with the original plan.

Wingate instructed Calvert and Fergusson to combine their efforts and

[1] *Inpāru Sakusen,* p.60

destroy the famous Gokteik Viaduct. This huge structure, crossing the Nam Tu at the Gokteik Gorge, and bearing the road north-east from Mandalay to Lashio, was a sore point with Calvert. He had had the opportunity to demolish it several times with his scallywags of the Bush Warfare School in 1942, and each time his request was turned down. He had in fact been a week in Gokteik hoping to be given the go-ahead, until he was forced to withdraw his men. When he met General Alexander, then in command of the forces retreating through Burma, Alexander asked, 'Did you blow up the viaduct?' No, replied Calvert, completely baffled. Alexander explained that 'political' reasons, the nature of which he did not clarify for Calvert, prevented him giving an order for the viaduct to be blown, but he had wanted it blown just the same and had sent Calvert to the spot because he had heard Calvert was the sort of man who would disobey orders if a good demolition could be had. Alexander seemed very disappointed that this time Calvert decided to behave himself.[1]

Now, in 1943, here was the chance again. Gokteik was the final objective Wavell had given Wingate.[2] The latter still had 2200 men under command, and 1000 pack-animals. The supply drop system was working, and so was the signals system. The railway he had been sent to demolish had been demolished. Thus far, LONGCLOTH was a success. Now was to begin what Wingate's *Report* called 'the second and more fruitful phase' of the campaign. In fact, it was the start of the disasters which split his force up. He was entering a zone far less suitable to Chindit operations, intersected by motor roads along which Japanese reinforcements could easily travel, dry, hot, almost waterless forest. Calvert turned south towards Myitson, and Fergusson followed. 5 Column intelligence then informed Fergusson that there were several hundred Japanese in Myitson and he passed this on to the Brigade Air Base. RAF bombers promptly put in a raid on it. At the same time Wingate cancelled the order to Fergusson to act with Calvert and help destroy the Gokteik Viaduct. He was to turn back and act as advance group for the movement of the main body instead. On 25 March Fergusson rejoined the rest of the Brigade on the Hehtin Chaung, to be told that Wingate had taken the decision to return to India.

Calvert did not yet know this. He moved close to Myitson, but knew his force was nowhere near strong enough to take a town of that size. The Nam Mit flowed into the Shweli there, and to cross this tributary he had to move his column further south and west. As he did so, he was told the Japanese regularly patrolled the Nam Mit between Myitson and Nabu, and at once he saw the opportunity for an ambush. Perhaps he should have

[1] Calvert, *Fighting Mad*, p. 85

[2] So Tulloch, op.cit. p. 66, but Irwin spoke of it as being 'an enterprising effort but rather against orders... I have told Scoones to be sure that Wingate complies generally with the Directive given to him which is to feint southwards and withdraw northward and westward back into 4 Corps.' Irwin to Wavell, 26 March 1943, Irwin Papers.

ignored the chance, but he convinced himself that, since he had to cross the Nam Mit anyway, he might as well have a go at this patrol as he did so. Three ambushes were set in line, one leading to the other, and a few hours later a company of Japanese walked into them. It was, says Calvert, one of the most one-sided actions he ever fought in. About 100 Japanese were killed for the loss of a Gurkha NCO.[1] He then went up into the hills to rest his tired men before pushing on to Gokteik. He was well supplied, after taking a ten-ton supply drop on 19 March, the biggest drop of the whole expedition, about 100 miles north of the Burma Road. Blowing the Gokteik would sever that celebrated artery for a considerable time, but Calvert was to be thwarted of it yet again. IV Corps had been in touch with Wingate, who had proposed moving east into the Kachin Hills towards Lashio. It made very good sense in terms of moving through a friendly population, making a wide sweep to the north via Bhamo and Indawgyi. But not in terms of air drops. He would be moving beyond effective supply range, he was told; so would Calvert, at Gokteik.

Wingate thought it over, decided he could not risk out-marching his air drops, and the order to return to India was given. Calvert, by then far south of the main body, was told to come out by himself. Wingate was at this time about twenty miles north of Calvert, near the village of Baw, a few miles west of the Shweli and directly east of the Irrawaddy crossing-point at Tagaung. He had two columns with him, the men were desperately short of food, and Wingate decided he needed a supply drop. It was unwise, because there were Japanese in Baw, but the situation overruled prudence. The Japanese in Baw would have to be held in by men from the columns blocking all exits from the village. At which point an understandable human failing let him down. One officer was told to take his men to the far side of Baw to block a main track. He was not under any circumstances to cross any part of the village but to keep to the jungle. Secrecy was of the essence. The going turned out to be very tough for tired and hungry men, the officer decided to take a risk, and cut through the outskirts of the village. He ran into a Japanese sentry. He reacted fast, and killed him, but the other Japanese in the village heard the shot and manned their defensive posts. Another party failed to block the road leading into Baw from Mabein on the Shweli to the east.[2] As the battle began, Wingate reached the scene and realized that the supply drop could not take place on the open paddy, as planned, and fires would have to be lit in the jungle to guide the planes in. Lieutenant-Colonel 'Sam' Cooke, the commander of the Northern Group, tried to clear the village, but it was far from easy and the fighting went on for several hours, with heavy casualties on both sides.

[1] So Calvert, *Fighting Mad*, p. 139; but *Reconquest of Burma*, I, p. 122, says 'three dead and two missing'.

[2] 'Jeffery Lockett's Account' in Tulloch, op.cit., p. 85

8 Column (Scott) succeeded in getting into Baw and drove out the Japanese from a group of houses. They promptly took up positions in foxholes astride the track to Mabein and the fight might have taken a worse turn if a message had not come through from HQ to say the drop had taken place and Scott's Column should withdraw.

It is a sign of how hungry the men had become that their normal wariness about booby traps had eased. The village, about fifteen houses, seemed to be deserted as 8 Column moved in, and one of the men spotted a large ham hanging from the doorpost of a hut. An NCO told him not to go near it, it was probably booby-trapped, but the sight of the ham was too much for him. He broke ranks and ran to the *basha*. The corporal ran after him to stop him, and as he reached the ham a fusillade of machine-gun bullets killed them both. The machine gun was sited in a house larger than the rest, the headman's house, and 8 Column pasted it with mortar and machine-gun fire until the remnants of the garrison who had holed up there were dead.[1]

Jeffrey Lockett says that the supply drop was interfered with and some of it had to be abandoned, and 1000 men went hungry as a result. Whether or not this is an exaggeration, Wingate punished the culprit. The officer who had gone into Baw and shot the Japanese sentry was reduced to the ranks at once and sent to Fergusson's column as a private.[2] There *were* draconian punishments on the march. Little justification as there may be for assuming, as the men did, that Wingate had been given special powers of punishment by C-in-C, India, some column commanders certainly used them. One found a sentry asleep, which of course endangered the security of the entire column. Lockett records that he gave the culprit three choices, to be shot, to be flogged, to be banished from the column and set off alone back to the Chindwin, eighty miles away. Lockett saw nothing unusual about this, and had men flogged himself during the 1944 expedition.[3]

Wingate decided to re-cross the Irrawaddy at Inywa, on the assumption that the Japanese would not believe he would use the same crossing-point twice. It was decided, against Fergusson's protests, to leave most of the pack-animals on the east bank of the Irrawaddy, and abandon six tons of

---

[1] Halley, op.cit., p. 96

[2] Lockett reports he was later re-instated, and Fergusson says the punishment was for not reaching his position in time. (*Beyond the Chindwin*, p. 142). In fact each of them seems to have referred to half the story. The platoon (17 of 8 Column) was halted by the Platoon Commander and lay up till first light. One of its attached Burma Riflemen shot a Japanese sentry as they moved towards the village, after which the Japanese opened up with mortars. (Cf. Sergeant Tony Aubrey's account in Halley, *With Wingate in Burma*, pp. 89–91.)

[3] Tulloch, op.cit., p. 85. '"Flogging" wasn't always very severe. More like a caning.' (Edge). Cf. 5 Column War Diary (Fergusson) for 30 March 1943: 'Party now consisted of 9 Officers, 109 ORs, of which 3 Officers 2 ORs wounded. All weak and hungry in varying degrees. Addressed all ranks and told them: – (a) Only absolute discipline would get us out. I would shoot anybody who pilfered comrades or villages, or who grumbled. (b) Anybody who lost his rifle or equipment I would expel from the party, unless I was satisfied with excuse. (c) Only chance was absolute trust and implicit obedience. (d) No stragglers.'

equipment. Fergusson moved on ahead and advanced on the village of Hintha on 28 March, his function being to delay any Japanese follow-up and set ambushes. Then came one of those perfect moments of crystallized action which Fergusson describes so well. They saw the reflection of a fire and made for it:

> Round it, symmetrically, one on each side, sat four men. They looked so peaceful and innocent that I immediately concluded that they were Burmese; and in that tongue (of which my knowledge was limited to a few sentences) I asked, 'What is the name of this village?'
>
> The men on the far side looked up, and those on this side looked round: I was only three yards from them. They were Japs. Resisting a curious instinct which was prompting me to apologize for interrupting them, I pulled the pin out of my grenade, which had suddenly become sticky with sweat, and lobbed it – oh so neatly – into the fire. I just caught the expression of absolute terror on their faces; they were making no attempt to move; and ran. It was a four-second grenade, and went off almost at once.[1]

The Japanese whom Fergusson so neatly killed were part of Koba's three-line plan to catch the Chindits as they made their way back to India. He proposed three lines running north-south along which his forces would patrol: the line of the Irrawaddy; the line Mansi-Pinbon-Manyu-Taungmaw-Pinlebu (i.e. the valley of the Mu River); and the line of the Chindwin. South of Inywa, about forty to fifty miles, and in the Shwegu area, as his patrols closed in, they destroyed around a hundred of Wingate's Brigade. His three lines, he believes, compelled Wingate to disperse his men in small groups to infiltrate through the gaps in the Japanese defence positions. Fergusson queried this policy. Since they had concentrated the columns once again, he argued, would they not have a greater chance of success in breaking through as a united force? The Japanese they encountered would not be likely to accumulate a much greater force than their own.

Wingate's decision to disperse the Brigade was reinforced by what happened to 7 Column (Gilkes) as it began to cross the Irrawaddy at Inywa. About twenty boats were collected, the troops went across, and as they landed on the other side firing broke out. The Japanese opened up on the landing position with mortar fire of great accuracy, as was their wont, and sank one of the boats. Their snipers joined in. The column adjutant, David Hastings (son of the well-known lawyer Sir Patrick Hastings) was walking up the bank making for the jungle, when the first shots rang out,

[1] Fergusson, *Beyond the Chindwin*, p. 151

and was seen to fall. The Japanese were obviously in full control of the landing site on the opposite bank – Wingate's assumptions had played him false – and there was no question of the Brigade as a whole getting over.

The column commanders conferred, 'a short and sad meeting', as Wingate's *Report* called it.[1] Those who had succeeded in getting across would have to make it back to India on their own. The other columns would turn east and make for a safe rendezvous. Ten miles east-south-east from Pyinlebin Wingate arranged for a massive air drop to equip the columns before they broke out on their own. Extra maps, compasses, rations and boots were dropped. Wingate did not contact Fergusson as he moved back, but John Fraser, Fergusson's second-in-command, arrived at Wingate's HQ on 29 March and described the encounter at Hintha. Wingate told him to get to the supply drop. It took Fergusson more time than he had bargained for to find the Brigade, and when he reached the spot the birds had flown. All that was left were the depressions in the grass where they had been sleeping. Wingate's own skill defeated Fergusson here. The woodcraft learned in the long training had perfected the art of covering up exits from bivouacs, and Fergusson could not make out where they had gone. So Fergusson did not get his share of the supply drop and decided to make for India at once. During the battle at Hintha his wireless mule had been shot and fallen into a gully. Neither the mule nor the set was recuperable, so Fergusson was unable to summon supply drops, and Koba's policy of ensuring the villages had bodies of Japanese infantry on the look-out meant that foraging was almost out of the question. He determined to turn north and east away from the Inywa crossing-point, to cross the Shweli and move into the Kachin Hills where he expected his men would find sanctuary.

The Shweli proved a hard nut. He could find no boats, and he found Japanese in a village opposite staring at him through binoculars as he stared at them. But it was the Shweli itself which proved his undoing:

> There is no word for it but 'nightmare'. The roaring of the waters, the blackness of the night, the occasional sucking of a quicksand were bad enough, but the current was devilish. At its deepest, I suppose it was about four feet six or a little more: I am over six feet one, and it was more than breast high on me. The current must have been four to five knots. It sought to scoop the feet from under you and at the same time thrust powerfully against your chest. . . If once you lost your vertical position, you knew as a black certainty that you would disappear down the stream for ever.[2]

[1] p. 34; in Prasad, op.cit., I, p. 127

[2] Fergusson, *Trumpet in the Hall*, p. 158

It was seventy to eighty yards across, and the smaller men were going to find it hard going. They were distributed in platoons, ready to wade across; the few boats that had been scrounged would not be adequate for the whole column. Four or five of the men lost their footing and were swept downstream at once. They were never seen again. Even linking hands didn't help: you couldn't retain the grip of the next man. A horse tried to cross with them, they tried to get it up the bank, and failed. It, too, gave up the struggle and the waters took it.

When the men reached a bank, it was not the further side. A sandbank lay in midstream, and the rest of the crossing lay ahead, with the water scooping steep cliffs out of the side. Then, at 4 am, when the second stage was due to start, Fergusson was told that a boat had capsized and two boatmen had gone off with their craft. There were now no boats for the trip from the sandbank. The men had been waiting on it for hours, cold and hungry, and unnerved by the swirling waters, the screams, the cries for help. Fergusson, quite practically, knew their main weakness was lack of food: 'morale depends more on food than anything else'.[1] His second-in-command, Fraser, lost his footing in the water and disappeared. He was sighted, and rescued, but the incident had an effect on those who remained.

Fergusson now had to make a decision which weighed on him for the rest of his life. Little over an hour remained to dawn, when the Japanese might easily hit upon the crossing-point. Lights of Japanese lorries could be seen in the distance on a motorable road on the east bank.[2] If he stayed, he risked the lives of those who had got across. At any rate, the wounded were over, and so were some Gurkhas, who had managed the crossing in spite of their diminutive proportions. There were nine officers and sixty-five men on the right side of the Shweli. That left forty-six who had either been drowned or were still on the sandbank – mostly the latter.

> I made the decision to come away. I have it on my conscience for
> as long as I live; but I stand by that decision and believe it to have
> been the correct one. Those who think otherwise may well be
> right. Some of my officers volunteered to stay, but I refused them
> permission to do so...
> ...to my mind the decision which fell on me there was as cruel
> as any which could fall on the shoulders of a junior commander.[3]

It was not the end of Fergusson's anguish. Two days later, when they were stocking up with food in a Kachin village, the Japanese arrived, and as his

[1] Fergusson, *Beyond the Chindwin*, p. 173
[2] Information from Lt. W. Edge.
[3] Fergusson, *Beyond the Chindwin*, p. 174

seventy-odd men were in no condition for a pitched battle, they left. His great friend, the Australian Duncan Menzies, entered the village on patrol the next day, was captured, tied to a tree, and bayonetted. He was found by the Burma Rifles HQ under Lieutenant-Colonel Wheeler the following day. He gave Wheeler his watch for his parents, and asked for a lethal dose of morphia. Wheeler gave it to him, and was himself killed the next instant by a Japanese sniper.

The remnant of 5 Column forged on, obsessed by food, Fergusson himself by the torment of remembered coffee-cream pâtisserie in Tours as a schoolboy (they were particularly short of sugar). Fifteen days after crossing the Irrawaddy, they reached the Chindwin on 24 April, and were in Imphal two days later. Fergusson's Burma Rifles had long since gone home to their villages, and one of his men died of cerebral malaria in Imphal. Others of his column got out through China, others again through Fort Hertz, but he had lost two-thirds of the men he commanded: of the 318 with whom he had gone into Burma, ninety-five survived. There were moments of both eerie strangeness and cruel testing on the way back, when the Force suffered far more casualties than when it was making its way through Koba's scattered pair of battalions. An example of the first is Jeffrey Lockett's account of the only casualty of his Commando section:

> We had halted for about ten minutes for our hourly halt, and I sent Private Brown about 100 yards forward of the main body on the other side of a small hillock to act as sentry. It was after we had started again and marched no more than a couple of minutes that we found he was missing. First I sent back Sergeant-Major Blain to find him and then went myself, while the rest of the party waited. We searched for over an hour and shouted ourselves hoarse, but never found him. There were no Japs in the area, and to this day I do not know what became of him. He just disappeared into thin air.[1]

Sergeant Tony Aubrey of 8 Column recalls the tragedy of the wounded and those who simply could march no more:

> That night one man, whose feet were in a very bad state, made up his mind he could go no further. He lay down. His mates, worn out as they were, tried to carry him. But he wouldn't allow them to. All he wanted was to be left alone with as many hand grenades as we could spare. So we gave him the grenades and left him. There wasn't anything else to do.

[1] Tulloch, op.cit., p. 88

Another man, the same night, took a false step, and fell over the khud (Urdu, 'edge'). He didn't fall far, but he landed awkwardly, and ruptured himself. We had no M.O. with us now, he having gone on with Captain Whitehead, but we bandaged his hernia up as well as we could with a shell dressing, and he marched on. He was soon at the rear of the column. Sometimes he was ten yards behind us, sometimes a hundred, sometimes he was lost to view altogether. At first we worried about him, 'How's so-and-so making out?' we asked each other. But after a time we forgot him. He was just another bit of the landscape.

This must sound like a case of man's inhumanity to man, but it wasn't, you know. We were just too tired to care.[1]

Calvert's men returned in dribs and drabs, the main body crossing the Chindwin between Tonhe and Auktaung, familiar ground. En route, Calvert had cheekily done a little more demolition on the railway and would no doubt have created further mayhem had Wingate not signalled him that it was now important to bring out as many survivors as possible: 'We can get new equipment and wireless sets. But it will take twenty-five years to get another man. These men have done their job, their experience is at a premium.'[2] Calvert's party were at the Chindwin on 14 April, the first out of Burma, a success mainly due, the Indian Army Official History says, 'to Calvert's acumen and training'.[3]

Koba was sure he had trapped Wingate himself. He had a patrol north of Paungbyin on the banks of the Chindwin, one night towards the end of April. About ten men began to swim across. The Japanese patrol spotted them, and started to fire. The night was too dark, and they missed.[4] There is no doubt that Japanese patrols in the area were expecting the arrival of 'the Commander of the British Forces in Burma'. The story is that an old monk guided them across the Mu Valley and through the elephant tracks and mountain streams beyond. They lived on rice and buffalo – which Wingate is reputed to have killed with a slash from a scalpel he carried in his surgical kit. It did his signals officer, Lt Spurlock, no good. Spurlock had had severe diarrhoea ever since, during the halt in the Shweli 'bag', the HQ group had spent a week resting and stuffing itself on horse flesh and mule meat to gather strength for the march ahead. Wingate, against all the rules, waited forty-eight hours to see if Spurlock would be fit enough to go on, but in the end they had to leave him behind in a village, with some food, a map, and a compass.[5]

[1] D. Halley, op.cit., pp. 136–7

[2] Rolo, *Wingate's Raiders*, p. 113

[3] Prasad, *Reconquest of Burma*, I, p. 130

[4] *Inpāru Sakusen*, p. 62

[5] W. G. Burchett, *Wingate's Phantom Raiders*, p. 154–6

At any rate, when they were close to the Chindwin, the old monk scouted around and found a villager who told them there were Japanese in his village nearby who had been searching for them. Wingate decided to cross without more ado. Wingate had caught a small live turtle, and the old man asked for it. 'The Burmese word for turtle is *leik*,' his interpreter told him, 'and for English it is *Inglei*. The old man wants you to release the turtle to bring you luck.' The turtle was put into the water and swam off, but the omen didn't seem to come right at first. They had hoped for guides, but no one came, and by 3.30 am Wingate decided to go back into the shelter of the forest. He split his party into swimmers and non-swimmers. HQ Group consisted of 220 officers and men when they set out. The final dispersal group which came to the Chindwin with Wingate numbered forty-three. The swimmers were his Burmese interpreter, Aung Thin, Major John Jeffries of the Commando Section, and three other ranks. The rest were told to wait with Major Anderson until the swimmers crossed and sent boats for them.

The trek back to the river bank began. The exhausted men hacked their way through elephant grass, making 300 yards in three hours, walking by compass, and bleeding from the knife-edges of the reeds. Wingate had worn corduroy trousers throughout the expedition and they had been torn to shreds. His legs were streaming with blood when he finally pushed his head and shoulders through the last screen of the terrible reeds and looked out across the Chindwin.[1]

It was midday. Normally they would not have dreamed of venturing out on to a river bank in the open sunlight, particularly with the sure knowledge of Japanese patrols in the vicinity. But Anderson's party would be expecting boats that night, and Wingate and Jeffries opted for swimming at once. With bamboo in his pack to make it float, Wingate fastened boots and revolver to a webbing belt and dashed with the rest across the beach, after making sure the Japanese patrol was not hiding in the reeds (they were reputed to be half-a-mile downstream).

Wingate, the great apostle of swimming, found his strength ebbing after only a hundred yards. Jeffries was soon floundering. Willshaw, one of the NCOs, was only saved by a Mae West which he had been lucky enough to have brought along, an incredible piece of foresight in the circumstances. Wingate turned on his back to float, and heard Jeffries cry out, 'How much farther is it? I'm finished!' 'Keep going, you're nearly there', Wingate shouted, and soon their feet touched bottom. Jeffries collapsed on the hot sand, groaning to himself, 'My God! I was sure I'd never make it.' But they were in luck. A Burmese fisherman on the other side said there was a British outpost four miles upstream, and took them to a village where they were given a meal. A guide led them to a Gurkha post, and the CO and Wingate went back for Anderson.

[1] ibid. p. 157

When it was dark, Anderson had gone to the river bank and cautiously signalled, a lighted match cupped in his hand. No response. He tried at fixed intervals until after midnight. Still nothing. He began to think Wingate and his party must have drowned or been shot. Four men, none of them good swimmers, volunteered to have a go and cross in the dark. Half-an-hour later, one of them came back. The man next to him had been grabbed by the current and drowned. He didn't know what had become of the other two. Anderson began signalling again, every hour, then, with gloom settling on all and sundry, went back through the reeds.[1]

It looked as if the only chance was to get boats from some village. With the HQ party was an Indian official observer, a man of some experience who had already been decorated for gallantry in Libya. He was Captain Motilal Katju, a nephew of Pandit Jawaharlal Nehru, who had come to the column straight from the Middle East, had not had the training the rest had, and had kept up with the best marchers without complaining. Katju volunteered to take a Burmese *havildar* (Sergeant) with him and explore the nearest village. Given the reports they had had, it was a great risk. Anderson warned him there were most likely Japanese in the village, but Katju's mind was made up. He had a premonition he was going to die. He ordered the *havildar* to stay on the edge of the village while he went in. A few minutes later the *havildar* heard a volley of shots. He waited ten minutes, but Katju did not emerge, and he rushed back to tell Anderson.[2]

Anderson decided to try signalling again, after dusk. This time he was sure he saw a flicker on the opposite bank, and boats began to move across the Chindwin. The men, tired as they were, clambered in at once, and pushed off from the hostile shore. The Japanese had been waiting for them to leave. Mortar fire was aimed at the boats and the previous night's bivouac, and automatic fire ripped across the sand and round the boats. The Japanese were about half-a-mile away and closing in, when Gurkhas on the other side fired back and halted them. The men were extraordinarily lucky. By the time the boat grounded on the other bank, not a man had been hit. 'Many happy returns' said Wingate, as Anderson stepped ashore. It was his birthday, 29 April.

Throughout the campaign, the Japanese were unsure, not of the strength of Wingate's forces – they deduced this soon enough – but of what exactly he was after. Their first instinct was to think the Chindits were merely trouble-makers, out to raid and disturb Japanese-occupied areas. Then it was thought that perhaps something had been planned in collaboration with Chiang Kai-shek, once Wingate decided to cross the Irrawaddy. Then

---

[1] Wingate had gone back to wait for Anderson's signal, but the presence of the Japanese forced Anderson a mile off the rendezvous, and the signal light was too dim for Wingate to make it out at that distance. Rolo, *Wingate's Raiders*, p. 144

[2] Prasad, *Reconquest of Burma*, I, p. 133

when he switched west and made for India again, they drew the conclusion that he was preparing for a new offensive in North and Central Burma, carrying out topographical reconnaissance and sounding out the positions of the Japanese Army. It was taken for granted that the Burma Rifles men were part of a vast spy network the British intended to leave behind in the villages. An early Japanese account speaks of more than half the Force being taken prisoner, which is of course quite untrue. They were, though, struck by the age of some of the prisoners, over thirty in many cases; there were even some over forty. 'Wingate's mad', the prisoners said. 'We've had enough of jungle marches. We're browned off with the war (*mō senso wa iya da*).' Others, 'our officers were rotten (*shōkō wa keshikaran*) – they had folding camp-beds taken on horse-back on the march.' The Japanese thought the men poor-spirited (*seni ni toboshii*) and the intelligence officer who talked to them felt the strange contrast between what they were saying and the evident fighting spirit of the officers.[1]

Even before Wingate returned, GHQ (India) realized that from the publicity point of view he was going to be a hot potato. On 3 April the Director of Public Relations sent a MOST SECRET note, forwarded to Irwin by Wavell, about how it was to be handled:

> Reference publicity about LONGCLOTH. When the moment for release arrives it is very desirable, in order to control that publicity carefully and to ease censorship problems, to have the material issuing from G.H.Q. It would, therefore, be extremely helpful if H.E. the C-in-C would ask the GOC-in-C Eastern Army to arrange that the Commander of LONGCLOTH when, as we hope, he re-emerges from Burma, should be warned not to talk to the Press and should be brought without delay, by air, straight to Delhi. Here he could most valuably give a suitably controlled Press Conference.

But the war correspondents assembled in Delhi were not dealing with a novice in the world of propaganda. The news was released to the outside world on 21 May. Had the campaign gone according to plan, Wingate was asked? 'In war, nothing ever goes according to plan', was the natural answer, 'not in this kind of war. A campaign may be planned meticulously, yet there will be changes as fighting progresses. All you can do is allow for the changes when you make your plans.' All that was trite enough. Then he added, 'I am quite satisfied with the results. The expedition was a complete success.'[2]

---

[1] Fujio Masayuki, 'Biruma no ryūko' ('Rivals in Burma'), *Hiroku Dai Tōa Senshi*, Biruma-hen, p. 141

[2] Rolo, op.cit., p. 148

That was indeed putting a brave face on it. The cost had been high. Of the 3000 officers and men who had crossed the Chindwin on 14 February, 2182 were back in India by the first week in June. Nearly all the mules had been lost, and most of the equipment, except personal arms, had been lost or destroyed. Of the nearly 1000 men missing, around 450 had been killed in battle with the Japanese. A hundred and twenty men of 2 Burma Rifles had been permitted to shed their uniforms and remain in Burma in their home areas. Most of the remaining 430 were prisoners in Japanese hands.[1]

The men who came back had marched at least 750 miles; most of them had done 1000 miles. Many of them were by this time mere skin and bone, with inward-caving stomachs and visible rib-cages, suffering from beri-beri and malaria. Some of them were unfit for rigorous military duty for a long time to come, others knew they had experience which, once their physical condition improved, they could use again.

'The strategic value of the campaign was nil,' writes the Indian Official Historian.[2] In sum, what their arduous efforts achieved was to put the Mandalay-Myitkyina railway out of action for four weeks, and make the Japanese use a longer L of C, via Bhamo. They acquired much valuable topographical information. They killed quite a number of Japanese troops, and directed RAF bombers onto large concentrations of them. They loosened the Japanese grip on the Kachin Levies north of Myitkyina, and gave the Japanese something to think about other than infiltrating patrols across the Chindwin. But, of course, since there was no follow-up by main forces, the expedition was 'an engine without a train'.[3]

But this is battle accountancy of the wrong kind. At a moment when a glance at the British performance in Burma could only have induced the utmost gloom in the observer, the Press, sensing there was something vastly different here, of a different moral dimension from what had been happening in Arakan, amplified. Even Fergusson's self-dismissive summing-up does not detract from the impact that was made:

> What did we accomplish? Not much that was tangible. What there was became distorted in the glare of publicity soon after our return. We blew up bits of railway, which did not take long to repair; we gathered some useful intelligence; we distracted the Japanese from some minor operations, and possibly from some bigger ones; we killed a few hundreds of an enemy which numbers eighty millions; we proved that it was feasible to maintain a force by supply dropping alone.[4]

---

[1] Connell, *Wavell, Supreme Commander*, p. 262; and Prasad, *Reconquest of Burma*, I, p. 135

[2] Prasad, op.cit., p. 136

[3] Burchett, op. cit., p.180

[4] Fergusson, *Beyond the Chindwin*, p. 240

That last sentence is the most important. The RAF officers, under Squadron-Leader (later Sir) Robert Thompson, who marched with the columns and shared all their hardships, put into practice with the signals teams an effective way of taking the British Army off the roads and into the air. The appalling hardships were striking when the newspapers introduced Wingate to world opinion, and the impact was reinforced by the press photographs of gaunt, bearded men who had, in Wingate's own words, 'endured severities to which there are few parallels in our compaigns'.[1] But that was strictly *décor*. The hard fact was that Wingate had changed the nature of jungle campaigning for good.

In his *Report* he points out that the troops were not picked men, but the only men available. The Gurkhas suffered from a shortage of Gurkhali-speaking officers and from the Gurkha's slowness in learning. The 2 Burma Rifles were first-rate and maintained excellent health by living on local produce, such as snakes and frogs. The King's Liverpool were on the whole too old and not sufficiently tough, intelligent, educated or adaptable; this applied particularly to the officers, during training. The average Englishman, Wingate wrote, 'is in general far too apt to take minor ailments too seriously'. Generally speaking, 'the quality of existing infantry is bad'. That was the reason why he wanted to take men from other arms, such as the artillery and the RAC where, in his view, they would not be wanted for the war against Japan. He was nonetheless, in spite of these sweeping views, later to describe the British infantryman as best suited to the Chindit type of warfare.[2]

He was sensible enough to spread the achievement to the ordinary soldier. The unit which suffered most was the 13th King's Liverpool, which lost over a third of its men. Of the 721 who went in, 384 came back to India. Seventy-one survived imprisonment (including Lt Spurlock). Wingate emphasized the *ordinariness* of these men. Oddly enough, the statement which stressed this was made in February, before the Brigade went into Burma, to the *Daily Express* correspondent, Alaric Jacob, and kept for use later:

> If this operation succeeds, it will save thousands of lives. Should we fail, most of us will never be heard of again.
>
> If we succeed, we shall have demonstrated a new style of warfare to the world, bested the Jap at his own game, and brought nearer the day when the Japanese will be thrown bag and baggage out of

---

[1] *Report*, p. 37, in *Reconquest of Burma*, I, p. 135

[2] Wingate's Report on Long Range Penetration Groups, 3 August 1943, PRO, WO 231/13. The comment on armour and artillery is an illustration of how Wingate was limited by the *part* of the theatre he operated in. His view that as long as Burma was 'forest, hill, and marsh', the war would be exclusively an 'infantry-cum-air' war was undoubtedly true of North Burma but absolutely untrue of the way the campaign later developed in the Central Burma plain, where the tank was master.

Burma. Most of my Chindits are not in their first youth, but married men between twenty-eight and thirty-five, who have previously done coastal defence and internal security work and never dreamt they would serve as shock troops, doing one of the toughest jobs any soldiers have undertaken in this war.

If ordinary family men from Liverpool and Manchester can be trained for this specialized jungle war behind the enemy's lines, then any fit man in the British Army can be trained to do the same, and we show ourselves to the world as fighting men second to none, which I believe we are.[1]

It was the kind of language the British public longed to hear from a theatre where the news had been almost uniformly depressing for too long. The man who had wondered if a court-martial were awaiting him on his return, for the loss of a third of his brigade, was suddenly a national hero. The Prime Minister, acutely aware of the value of propaganda, and appalled by the endless delays in the offensives in Arakan, was overjoyed. He also overshot the mark. Some young, imaginative commander was needed to lift British fortunes out of the rut in the Far East. Now here he was, to hand. On 24 July 1943, Churchill issued a directive:

> There is no doubt that in the welter of inefficiency and lassitude which has characterized our own operations on the Indian front, this man, his force and his achievements stand out; and no question of seniority must obstruct the advance of real personalities in their proper station in war.[2]

To those for whom Slim alone is the *chevalier sans peur et sans reproche* of the Burma campaign, Churchill's verdict must seem – did seem – almost sacrilegious. But that is to forget the context of the times. When Churchill wrote those words, Slim was still largely unknown, certainly in the top echelons of British politics; he had commanded a brigade in East Africa, had led, with great courage, a Corps in retreat, and later commanded another Corps which had also – quite recently – been forced to retreat. Those who knew the man might well realize there was an enormous unfulfilled potential in Slim. But on paper, at an impersonal distance, the record was by no means brilliant. Wingate, abrasive oddity though he might be, had succeeded in everything he had put his hand to. Churchill, who was about to elevate a young naval officer, admittedly well-connected, to high command in the Far East, saw in Wingate a man of similar calibre and, even more effective, of similar good fortune.

[1] Burchett, op. cit., p. 179

[2] M. Howard, *Grand Strategy*, IV, p. 548

3. THE BOX

The Japanese plan to invade India; the battle of the Admin Box

The invasion of India — War games: Mutaguchi tries it on — Subhas Chandra Bose — The Box — British plans

The invasion of India

There was one person on whom the first Wingate expedition made an even greater impression than on Churchill. That was Lt-General Mutaguchi Renya, GOC 18 Division in Northern Burma. Mutaguchi despised the British Army. His division had fought and defeated them in Singapore. Now here they were, breaking into his back yard, making their way in along routes he had already decided were impossible. When the Japanese completed their occupation of Burma in the summer of 1942, a colonel on General Terauchi's Southern Army staff, Colonel Hayashi Akira, thought the Japanese should not halt, but follow through into Assam and take Dimapur and Tinsukia.[1] Imperial GHQ in Tokyo was consulted, and 'Operation 21' was devised, in which a force of two divisions would approach India through the Hukawng Valley in northernmost Burma, another two divisions would take Imphal, the capital of Manipur State, and a third force, one division only, would move along the shores of the Bay of Bengal to take Chittagong.

There would have been little to stop them if they had carried out Operation 21. But it was regarded as positively dangerous, or at any rate inopportune, by a vigorous and influential figure, Major Fujiwara Iwaichi, an officer on Terauchi's staff. Fujiwara had personally raised an anti-British force – the Azad Hind Fauj or Indian National Army – from among the thousands of prisoners captured in Malaya and Singapore, and from his contacts with Indians in South-East Asia he judged that Gandhi and Nehru would oppose an invasion by the Japanese. In his view, the training and

---

[1] Cf. *The Japanese Account of their operations in Burma*, ed. HQ XII Army, 1945, p. 3

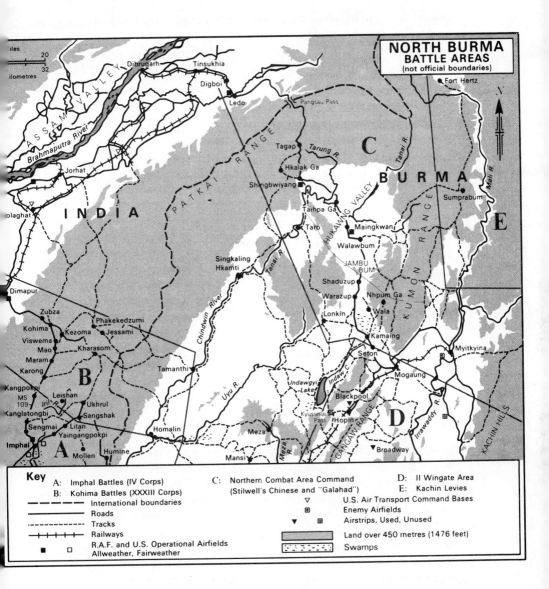

Key

A:	Imphal Battles (IV Corps)	**C:**	Northern Combat Area Command
B:	Kohima Battles (XXXIII Corps)		(Stilwell's Chinese and "Galahad")

D: II Wingate Area

E: Kachin Levies

- – – – – – International boundaries
- ———— Roads
- - - - - - - - Tracks
- +++++ Railways
- ■ □ R.A.F. and U.S. Operational Airfields
  Allweather, Fairweather

- ▽ U.S. Air Transport Command Bases
- ▣ Enemy Airfields
- ▼ ▣ Airstrips, Used, Unused
- Land over 450 metres (1476 feet)
- Swamps

equipping of the Indian National Army was the first step to a successful entry into India. Imperial GHQ brushed these objections aside, and the order to study Operation 21 was given on 22 July 1942.[1] If successful, it would cut the air route which supplied Chiang Kai-shek from Calcutta via Ledo in Northern Assam and Kunming in South-West China, but if it was

---

[1] Author's conversations with Lt-General Fujiwara, Singapore 1946, and Tokyo 1978, 1980

151

to work it had to have the backing of the Japanese divisions then occupying Burma.

These were sounded out by the victorious commander of 15 Army, Lt-General Iida Shōjirō. He travelled up to Taunggyi in the Shan States in September 1942 to talk to his subordinate divisional commanders about the feasibility of the undertaking. Opposition came immediately from Mutaguchi, whose 18 Division was garrisoning the Shan States. He told Iida that the terrain in North Burma was so forbidding – endless jungles and mountains – that no large-scale force could cross the mountains into Assam or be supported there. The idea that 18 Division should advance on Tinsukia through the Hukawng Valley (to cut Chiang Kai-shek's air supply route) was just not on.

Iida went on to Kalaw to call on Lieutenant-General Sakurai Shōzō, GOC 33 Division, who had captured Rangoon. 33 Division's role, in conjunction with 18 Division, was to move into Imphal and on to Dimapur, cutting the line of retreat of the British and Indian troops who would be moving back after 18 Division had taken Tinsukia. In this way, the two divisions would secure northern Assam. Sakurai also opposed the plan, and Iida, endorsing his divisional commanders' views, urged Southern Army to think again. Iida was listened to. On 25 October 1942 he was told to stop preparations for Operation 21.[1]

Caution seemed indicated for later developments by the British advance on Akyab at the end of 1942. It was a failure but it showed that the British were capable of mounting an offensive. The impression was confirmed when a battalion of 33 Division was bumped while on the march on the evening of 19 February 1943. A battle developed with a strong British unit during which the Japanese sustained many casualties including the death in action of the battalion commander. This was the first contact with Wingate's Operation LONGCLOTH – intelligence reports on which had started to come in from Burmese sources on 16 February.

At first Mutaguchi could not understand Wingate's intentions. Was the incursion connected with Chungking? Was he setting up an espionage network? Was it a 'survey campaign', checking Japanese tactics and pre-parations for an offensive? One thing he did not consider: was it a prepara-tion for a much larger campaign later? And he disregarded Fujiwara's interpretation, namely that Wingate's adventure indicated a new strength in the British Army. Fujiwara had, on elephant-back, gone round the expedition's tracks and picked up prisoners. They did not know much, but the name Wingate cropped up again and again.

Fujiwara was forty days on Wingate's tracks, from April to the beginning of May 1943, between Homalin and Kalewa, up and down the Chindwin,

---

[1] Fujiwara to author, conversation of September 1978. But Kojima Noboru gives this date as 23 November 1942

gathering a total of 360 prisoners.

But Mutaguchi's puzzlement did not disguise the major impact upon him of this intelligence. Contrary to what he had supposed, a large force could cross the hills separating India and Burma. If the British could do it, then he, Mutaguchi, who had thrashed the British in Singapore and Burma, could certainly do it. His passion to invade India dates from the time of Wingate's first expedition. There was something else. When he first rejected the notion, he thought it was simply his Army commander's, or at most that of the GOC Southern Army, Terauchi, then in Singapore. When he learned the idea had been mooted much higher up, at Imperial General Headquarters, he began to feel he had not only sown in the minds of Imperial GHQ and Southern Army the seeds of doubt about 15 Army's willingness to fight, but possibly even spurned a suggestion emanating ultimately from the Emperor himself. So his mind began to work along Imperial as well as strategic patterns. He attempted to enlist the Emperor's brother, Prince Takeda, in support of his plan, and thought in terms of bringing off the taking of Imphal by 29 April 1944, the Emperor's birthday (*Tenchōsetsu*).

His ambitions were wider even than this. As regimental commander in China at the time of the Marco Polo Bridge Incident near Peking in 1937, he believed he had sparked off the war in China which led ultimately to Pearl Harbour and the Pacific War. As divisional commander of 18 Division he had taken part in the conquest of Malaya from the British and been a major element in the surrender of Singapore. That was his second triumph. The third, crowning them all, would be the wresting of India from the British Empire. And, with that, the inevitable consequences to Great Britain, and her ability to prosecute the war, which must follow. A weakened Britain would either withdraw from the conflict, or acquiesce in a stalemate. America would be forced into isolation, and compelled to make terms. He, Mutaguchi, had it in his power to achieve all this.

Mutaguchi was promoted to GOC 15 Army on 18 March 1943, and on 15 April set up his headquarters in Maymyo, the delightful hill station in the Shan States, with its red-brick villas and luxuriant gardens, a place of outstanding natural beauty away from the heat and dust of the plains. The Japanese were then closing in on the retreating columns of Wingate's first expedition as they made speed to the Chindwin. But 15 Army's duties were far more extensive than this. They had to cover the Salween front, facing the Chinese in Yunnan who were supplied by the US, and then to put a ring round Burma through Myitkyina, Kamaing and the Zibyu Mountains, passing through Kalewa and Gangaw in central Burma: more than a thousand kilometres of front 'line'. Three divisions held that ring, 18, 56, and 33, though 31 and 15 were soon to reinforce them (15 Division was ordered to join the order of battle of 15 Army on 17 June

1943 but was held up on road-building chores in Thailand for months on end, by order of Southern Army).

Mutaguchi was aware that he was facing three possible Allied offensives: from Yunnan, from the Hukawng Valley, from Arakan, i.e. from the north-east, the north-west and the west. Reports had reached the Japanese of massive Allied preparations for a counter-offensive, and one or two airborne divisions were said to be training inside India. That meant another anxiety. The air balance which until then had been in Mutaguchi's favour whenever he had been at war, had now swung against him. Air supremacy was back in Allied hands.

So a new defence line had to be established to pre-empt an Allied invasion of Burma. The line the Japanese held, along the Zibyu Mountains, should be pushed westwards to the line of the Chindwin. On the other hand, in the dry season, the Chindwin was no great obstacle to a determined army, so moving the defence line that far would not be a basic stroke against an Allied offensive, merely a stoppage. The best plan was to move into the Imphal Plain, there destroy the Allied base and seize the supply dumps which would be the springboard for an offensive.

The plan grew in his mind. It would no longer simply be substituting a positive approach for the negative approach he had shown before as a divisional commander. It would be more grandiose, transcending the mere establishment of a defence line. He would thrust right into Assam. His diary reveals this quite clearly:

> I started off the Marco Polo Incident, which broadened out into the China Incident, and then expanded until it turned into the Great East Asia War. If I push into India now, by my own efforts, and can exercise a decisive influence on the Great East Asia War, I, who was the remote cause of the outbreak of this great war, will have justified myself in the eyes of our nation.[1]

What would a successful invasion of India do? If Mutaguchi moved far enough into Assam, destroying the British base at Imphal as he did so, he could provide a launching-pad for the Bengali leader, Subhas Chandra Bose, then collaborating with the Japanese, to raise Bengal against the British. From Bengal the flames of rebellion would spread – it was only a year since Gandhi's 'Quit India' campaign had shaken the unquiet *raj* – India would become unstable as a base for any offensive against the Japanese in East Asia and might even win her independence. Such a blow would take Great Britain out of the war, and if this happened the isolation of America would force them to make peace. Germany and Japan might even join hands in Persia...

[1] *Inpāru Sakusen*, pp. 90–1

That Japanese minds were moving in this direction was known to Wavell, Commander-in-Chief, India, and later Viceroy, in 1943, but he discounted the possibility of them arousing India to rebellion. When Slim looked back on that time, much later, he was not so sure: 'They were right in thinking that victory in Assam would resound far beyond the remote jungle land; it might, indeed, as they proclaimed in exhortations to their troops, change the whole course of the world war.'[1]

Convinced of this, the converted Mutaguchi began to preach the invasion of India to all and sundry. He started with the newly appointed Commander-in-Chief of Burma Area Army, Lieutenant-General Kawabe Masakazu, who interviewed him on 1 April 1943. After leaving his post as Chief of Staff to the China Expeditionary Force in Nanking, Kawabe passed through Tokyo where on 22 March he saw Tojo, then both Prime Minister and War Minister. He also spoke to the head of the Burmese Provisional Government, Dr Ba Maw. 'The measures we take in relation to Burma', Tojo had told him, 'are really the first steps in our policy towards India. I'd like to stress that our main objective lies there, in India.'[2]

Primed in this way, he found Mutaguchi's views fitted perfectly with his own. And he knew Mutaguchi well. He had been his brigade commander in Peking in 1937, that fateful moment when everything began. It was essential, though, to focus the striking force, and he decided to concentrate on Imphal. Arakan was a sideshow. A battle there would serve to draw in British reserves, but it had little other purpose. And he thought he could contain the US-commanded Chinese forces on the northern front, whether they came along Stilwell's new road from Ledo or across the Chinese frontier from Yunnan. The crucial battle would be fought on the central front.

Slim thought so too. He also knew that there was no point in trying to break up a Japanese offensive during its preparation, as he would be extending his communications for over a hundred miles across impossible country. His best plan was to draw in his horns. He would pull in his outlying divisions, then in contact with the Japanese at various points along the Burmese perimeter, and concentrate them in the Imphal Plain. If the Japanese pursued him there, as he was sure they must, *he* would be drawing *them* into a situation where *their* lines of communication were intolerably extended. Admittedly, it meant sacrificing country and none of his divisional commanders would accept that without an argument. But it was *reculer pour mieux sauter*. 'I wanted a battle *before* we went into Burma,' he later wrote, 'and I was as eager as Kawabe to make it decisive'.[3] For both British and Japanese, Imphal was to be the killing-ground.

[1] Slim, *Defeat into Victory*, p. 285

[2] *Inpāru Sakusen*, pp. 91–2

[3] Slim, *Defeat into Victory*, p. 286

Half a year after the Japanese, the British began to re-organize themselves for their war in Asia. The Japanese were quite right to believe the Allies intended to take the offensive in Burma, but their puzzlement as to the direction this offensive was to take, and its extent, was shared by the Allies themselves. Stilwell wanted to take enough of North Burma to enable him to push through his road from Assam into China. He was little concerned with the British need to recapture their lost territory, and the British high command, both in India and in London, was convinced that little useful could be done by advancing across Central Burma to Rangoon. It seemed much more sensible to take Akyab and Rangoon from the sea. Churchill's eyes were set on Singapore and Hong Kong and he was much more inclined to put a force into the northern tip of Sumatra and by-pass Burma completely.

South-East Asia Command was created in September 1943 to carry out a seaborne invasion. That explains why Lord Louis Mountbatten was considered by Churchill to be the appropriate Supreme Commander in the theatre. His reputation as chief of Combined Operations indicated the kind of offensive that would be expected from him, and the Japanese concluded that the appointment meant they would have to watch the sea-coasts of their conquests.

Mountbatten also had the authority derived from his royal connections, and considerable personal panache, although, as the Chief of the Imperial General Staff noted caustically in his diary, he had never commanded anything more than destroyers.[1] Brooke admitted, though, that he had boundless energy and drive and added that this would require the steadying influence of a carefully selected Chief of Staff. Lieutenant-General Sir Henry Pownall was this Chief of Staff, and that is exactly how he saw his brief. After serving in that very same capacity under Wavell during the short-lived ABDA Command in 1942, Pownall had been put in command of the Army in Ceylon. He did not particularly want to end his career in Asia, nor to take over staff duties instead of an operational command, but he knew India Command well and felt he would be useful in balancing an effervescent and dynamic Supremo with Auchinleck, who could be mulish at times and on whom Mountbatten's forces would have to rely for training and supplies. Pownall appreciated Mountbatten's gifts. He was less generous about Wingate:

> He has extraordinarily narrow views, runs in blinkers and can see no good except in his own chosen path... he is distinctly *unst-able*... Until he can be taken in hand and Mountbatten educated to see him in the right light we shall have trouble. G.H.Q. here loathe the sight of him...[2]

[1] Bryant, *The Turn of the Tide*, 1958, p. 568

[2] *Chief of Staff: The Diaries of Lieutenant-General Pownall*, ed. Brian Bond, 1974, II, pp. 111-12

So the image of Wingate continued to haunt both friend and foe, incubus to his own commanders and colleagues, irritation and inspiration to his Japanese enemies. The way the war in Burma was won would, in the end, be quite different from the way he had planned it. But that result itself was, paradoxically, derived from the possibility of invading India that he had, *malgré lui*, introduced into the mind of a Japanese general.

War Games : Mutaguchi tries it on

A number of studies were made on the Japanese side of the aims and methods of the operation against Imphal or, as it became known, Operation U-GO.[1] Of all of these, the most important was the one held in Rangoon at headquarters Burma Area Army between 24 and 27 June 1943.

Mutaguchi had some reconnaissance made before the conference began. One of his staff majors, Fujiwara Iwaichi, took fourteen graduates of the Nakano School, the Tokyo institution which trained apt pupils for espionage and political subversion in Asia, with a younger colleague, Lieutenant Izumiya, to explore the territory between the Irrawaddy and the Chindwin, particularly the Zibyu Mountains, a range stretching a hundred miles north to south and about thirty miles across. Fujiwara used trucks, elephants and horses (he had been Mutaguchi's riding companion in Maymyo) and while Izumiya stayed in a village near Homalin carrying out propaganda, Fujiwara moved on to the Chindwin to check crossing-points. He saw it was feasible to cross by making rafts, swam in the river to check its depth, calculated from the fields in the area that there was enough food available for a battalion, and gazed in wonder at the groups of monkeys chattering and climbing their way through the thick forest. The people of this part were not Nagas but Shans, who seemed friendly towards the Japanese and brought them food when they stopped overnight in a temple. Some of Wingate's men were still wandering about in the area, and Fujiwara rounded them up and handed them over to a Japanese Army unit. They were mostly Gurkhas, as he remembers it. He returned to Maymyo in mid-May and reported. It was possible to cross the Chindwin in the dry season, it was possible to get to the Chindwin if the roads were repaired, the Shans were co-operative, and five or six battalions could be self-sufficient in supplies in the area of Homalin. On the other hand, he could not give any information about what it was like in the rainy season, or what circumstances were like west of the Chindwin.[2]

---

[1] It may seem quaint, but it is not. U is the Japanese equivalent of C in one reading of the Japanese syllabary, so we could call it OPERATION C

[2] Conversations with Lieutenant-General Fujiwara

Enthusiastic over this report, Mutaguchi gave the details to Major-General Inada, the Vice-Chief of General Staff of the Southern Army, who visited Maymyo on 17 May 1943. He spoke to Inada of storming into India. 'You remember when you were on a tour of inspection in Manchuria in 1939?' he asked Inada. 'I was Chief of Staff of 4 Army then, and I told you I felt deeply the responsibility of having, as regimental commander, fired the first shot at the Marco Polo Bridge two years before. I begged you to use me somewhere where I could die for my country. I feel now exactly as I did then. Let me go into Bengal! Let me die there!'

'It would no doubt satisfy you,' Inada drily replied, 'to go to Imphal and die there. But Japan might be overthrown in the process.'[1]

The idea of going into Assam was absurd, Inada obviously thought. In any case, the whole thing needed investigation by Burma Area Army as well as by Mutaguchi's own staff. So both staffs came to Rangoon, with staff officers from 15 Army divisions, 55 and 56 Divisions, 5 Air Division and 3 Air Army. Southern Army headquarters in Singapore was represented by Inada, and Imperial General Headquarters in Tokyo by two lieutenant-colonels, Kondō Gonpachi and the Emperor's brother, Prince Takeda (Takeda no Miya Tsunenori). It was an impressive turnout.

The war game ran into difficulties from the start. When everyone was seated, Mutaguchi's Chief of Staff, Major-General Kunomura, handed over a pile of documents to the presiding officer, Lieutenant-General Naka, Chief of Staff of Burma Area Army. Fujiwara, who was present, glanced at their general title and was surprised: '15 Army Appreciation of the Situation', it read. This had been prepared at Mutaguchi's instigation at an overnight stop in Pyinmana, on the journey from Maymyo to Rangoon. It strongly advocated Mutaguchi's own cherished views, with the conclusion: '15 Army wishes to attack and destroy the enemy in the Arakan Mountains and advance at once into Assam'.[2] Fujiwara gave a sideways look at Naka. How would he take this forestalling of the entire purpose of the war game? 'Not a good idea,' thought Fujiwara, 'the documents should have been handed in afterwards', because the avowed purpose of the meeting was to sound out the concept put forward by Burma Area Army: to drive forward the defence line for Burma inside the mountains west of the Chindwin. If Kunomura, at Mutaguchi's behest, was urging the crossing of those hills in order to invade Assam, instead of just establishing a new defence line, he risked being counterproductive. But of course he was Mutaguchi's pliant instrument, that was

---

[1] Takagi Toshirō, *Kōmei*, p. 71

[2] This does not mean what it seems to mean to British readers, for whom 'Arakan Mountains' are the Arakan Yomas, in Arakan itself. The Japanese always referred incorrectly to the mountains separating India and Burma on the central front as 'the Arakan Mountains'.

why he had been appointed. His predecessor, Major-General Obata, had opposed Mutaguchi's notions and been sacked for his pains.

In the event, Kunomura met his match in Rangoon. Naka's senior staff officer, Colonel Katakura Tadashi, who had come to Rangoon from China with a great reputation for efficiency, stretched out a hand, took one look at the documents, struck the table with them, and bawled out at the top of his voice, 'What's all this? We don't have to take nonsense like this!' The loud voice was Katakura's trademark and everybody in the room froze. It was not an unrehearsed reaction. Katakura had a suspicion that something of the kind was going to be tried. 'I heard, the day before the war game began,' he later recalled, 'that Mutaguchi had worked out a plan for an offensive into north-east India and had pressed this on to Prince Takeda, and tried to present it to the GOC Burma Area Army.[1] I both saw to it that Kawabe did not accept it, and went to Kondō's place and asked him to ensure that Prince Takeda didn't accept it either. At the very start of the war game, I bawled Kunomura out, and said, "Just as we are about to investigate the question of a western defence line, in the presence of officers from Imperial GHQ and Southern Army, your 15 Army, without the prior knowledge or consent of Burma Area Army (its immediate superior) has attempted to propose its own plan to these officers, which goes completely against the chain of command. Please withdraw it at once." A chill of embarrassment ran through the whole assembly, but Naka smoothed things over.'[2]

Katakura's outburst had not been purely splenetic. Kunomura *had* offended against the principle of chain of command by trying to pre-empt the conference decision. And Katakura found Kawabe's sympathy with Mutaguchi hard to follow. But Kawabe had already told Naka not to be harsh with Mutaguchi for pushing his own views with such fervent conviction. 'I know Mutaguchi', he told him. 'So long as the supreme command is not upset, in other words so long as the final decision is mine, have some regard for his positive way of looking at things.'

The war game, in the event, went forward under Naka's supervision, on the basis of Mutaguchi's plan. Colonel Kinoshita Hideaki, his senior staff officer, who was no friend of Kunomura, was nonetheless loyal to 15 Army and stated bluntly that the objective of the operation was Imphal. 33 Division was to attack from the south, 15 Division from the east, and the whole of 31 Division was to take Kohima in the north to cut the enemy's retreat and reinforcements. Hard fighting was anticipated, but the decision

[1] Kawabe knew the Prince had been approached, but did not disapprove. 'I hear Mutaguchi asked for an audience with H.I.H. because he wanted to clarify to him personally how he saw the operation' he wrote in his diary (29 June 1943). 'I love that man's enthusiasm. You can't help admiring his almost religious fervour.' (OCH, *Inpāru sakusen*, I, 61.)

[2] Katakura Tadashi, *Inpāru Sakusen hishi* (Secret history of the Imphal operation) p. 67; and Kojima Noboru, *Eirei no tani* (Valley of heroes) pp. 29–30

was taken to go ahead. The reason was plain enough. Given the preparations the British were making for a return to Burma, even if the Japanese
intended no more than to advance their defence line to the west bank of
the Chindwin, the result would be a decisive battle between the two
armies. In that case, the Japanese might as well aim at the enemy base of
Imphal from the start. Neither Inada, from Southern Army, nor Kondō,
from Imperial GHQ, dissented from the rationale of the campaign. But
doubts were expressed about 15 Army's methods.

Naka said that Burma Area Army's view was that to use three divisions
from three different directions and, in addition, to divide them into two,
was to disperse too much. There was a further risk in sending 15 and 31
Divisions through the mountains to begin their assault. Burma Area
Army recommended that both 33 and 15 Divisions should approach
Imphal from the south and that only four battalions of 31 Division should
make for Kohima, the main body being held in reserve.

Inada said more thought would have to be given to supply. To attack
with men carrying their food and ammunition and afterwards rely on
stores taken from the enemy was 'to skin the raccoon before you caught
him'. He absolutely rejected the notion of 'dashing into Assam' from
Imphal. Prince Takeda had deeper reservations and made no secret of
them when he returned to Tokyo. He was obviously furious that
Mutaguchi had tried to nobble him during the conference. Mutaguchi had
called on him privately, as Katakura realized, and asked his support in
obtaining Tokyo's authorization. Prince Takeda replied that he saw no
hope of setting up a large-scale operation, from the point of view of
supply alone. He reported to Colonel Masada, the chief of No. 1 Bureau
of 2 Section (Operations) at Army GHQ when he went back to Tokyo.
'The army which is to occupy the front line', he told him, 'has no control
of the situation in its rear. As things look from the state of preparations, I
think the Imphal operation is definitely not on.' Masada listened, but
drew a different conclusion, because there were political pressures to find
a victory in the west after Japan's setbacks in the Pacific. Tojo was still
smarting from defeats at Guadalcanal and Midway. 'If we investigate the
rear set-up thoroughly' he concluded, 'we can certainly get as far as
Imphal.'[1]

At Southern Army in Singapore, Inada accepted the political implications, even though he had doubts about the strategy. He supported
Kawabe's interpretation of what should happen, and 'even if we do not
carry out the Imphal operation to its fullest extent, we could establish
Subhas Chandra Bose in a corner of India and raise the flag of free India.
That alone would be an adequate political result. It will be an
embellishment for Tojo's war leadership.'

[1] Kojima, *Eirei no tani*, p. 31

All these various levels of command had their own understanding of what the Imphal operation was about, what it would achieve, how it would be done. But none of them squared exactly with Mutaguchi's conception. As he was the commander of the Army which was to carry out the operation, in the end he got his own way, partly because of the vacuum of ideas above him. When Naka expressed his disquiet, 'Burma Area Army's job', Kawabe told him, 'is to indicate to its subordinate commanders the objective they are to attain. How to achieve it is left to them. And Mutaguchi is a commander in whom I have the greatest confidence. We will make it clear that the object of the operation is to take the Imphal area. What happens after that remains in my hands. But there will be no mad rush into Assam.'[1]

That may have been clear enough in Kawabe's mind. But he was a taciturn man, and he never made it clear enough to Mutaguchi. Neither Naka nor any other member of his staff really knew what was in Kawabe's mind. And, as we shall see, at a crucial moment in the battle, neither he nor Mutaguchi could communicate to each other what was uppermost in their minds. Their soldiers continued to die because of their silence.

Similarly, Inada saw his own reservations as curbs upon Mutaguchi. But there was little in the way of sanctions for them. Tokyo and Singapore were far away, and preoccupied with other less promising fields of battle. Mutaguchi never wavered. He was going into Assam.

On 12 August 1943, Mutaguchi held his own 'tactical exercise without troops' at his GHQ in Maymyo, under the chairmanship of his Chief of Staff, Major-General Kunomura. From Burma Area Army came Lieutenant-General Naka who had presided over the table manoeuvres in Rangoon. The odd thing is, he does not seem to have had the force of character to intervene when Kunomura, obviously at Mutaguchi's bidding, went against a clear Rangoon decision *not* to invade Assam but to consider the operation as a defensive one to destroy the British base and then hold a line Kohima-Imphal-Chin Hills. Instead, the Maymyo war game made the decision to use not just one regiment of 31 Division to take Kohima, but the whole division, and it was evident that Mutaguchi's reason for this was to have enough strength in the Kohima area, once the town had been taken, to move fast on Dimapur and break into Assam from there. Naka had been the main mover in the decision to forbid an invasion of India as the objective of the Imphal operation. Now Naka was a pleasant, affable but indecisive character and not particularly gifted as a Chief of Staff. In the event his failure to insist that Mutaguchi's plan was

[1] ibid., pp. 61–2

ultra vires was to have fatal consequences for thousands of Japanese soldiers.

A further conference – this time of the Chiefs of Staff of Southern Army's higher formations – was held at General Count Terauchi's residence in Singapore on 12 September 1943 (it was the former British governor-general's house). Naka brought with him Kunomura and Fujiwara, neither of whom were entitled to be present. But Naka ensured that a special order was made out granting his request that their presence be permitted. In the intervals of the discussion, Naka talked with the Chief of Staff of Southern Army, Inada, and pressed upon him the case for a speedy follow-through for the Imphal operations. 'I've brought Kunomura and Fujiwara with me,' he told Inada. 'Won't you see them? Fujiwara knows the Imphal terrain better than anyone.' Inada was both puzzled and furious. He was puzzled that Naka should be so evidently swapping horses, since three months earlier he had been the lynch-pin of the stop-Mutaguchi campaign at the Rangoon conference. Inada was furious because his suspicions were gradually being confirmed that Kawabe and Naka were now doing their best to get rid of Katakura who, at Rangoon, had openly rebuked 15 Army's efforts to get a favourable hearing even before the conference began and was known not to favour Imphal, at least as Mutaguchi intended to use it.

Kunomura and Inada were old school friends and Inada was two years senior to Kunomura in the Military Academy. Kunomura knew he could speak uninhibitedly, but he was taken aback by Inada's hostility. There was something else, too, which had clinched Inada's suspicions that Burma Area Army, which should have acted as a brake on Mutaguchi on behalf of Southern Army, had gone over to Mutaguchi's views. He had had a note from Kawabe about Katakura: 'he is extremely abusive with anyone who does not agree with his notions', Kawabe had written, 'and as a result there is an unpleasantly oppressive atmosphere inside Burma Area Army HQ, not conducive to fully utilizing the resources of that HQ and planning operations.'[1] Kawabe wanted Katakura transferred.

At first, Inada saw nothing unusual about the request. After all, the smooth running of personal relationships was the basis of running an army. Mutual antagonisms were often at work, and to solve them was one of Inada's concerns. Katakura was simply one example of this. But then Naka and Kunomura came to see him, together, and it soon became obvious that for both of them Katakura was an obstacle to the Imphal operation. Inada began to be aware that a conspiracy was afoot to get rid of Katakura not because of any discord inside Burma Area Army HQ, but because he was a stumbling block to Mutaguchi. Kunomura was Mutaguchi's creature, and Kawabe and Naka were pliant instruments of his ambition, though in

[1] Takagi, *Kōmei*, p. 60

theory one was the Commander-in-Chief and the other Chief of Staff of the higher command which was supposed to give Mutaguchi his orders.

Kunomura presumed on old acquaintance to press Mutaguchi's plan. 'Do me a favour, Inada, authorize it!' But it was the same plan which the Rangoon war game had accepted only on condition it was revised and adjusted, and none of the revisions and adjustments had been made. 'I can't authorize it unless you revise it,' Inada replied. 'Does Naka approve it?'

'If he didn't, he wouldn't be here with me now,' Kunomura said. Inada couldn't fathom this. Either Kawabe and Naka had been won over by Mutaguchi's persistent and eloquent pleading, which argued a certain lack of consistency and fibre in the higher command in Burma; or some hint had been passed down from much higher up – from Tojo himself? – and the time-servers in Rangoon were intent on ingratiating themselves with him. The trend to sycophancy was certainly there. Whatever the reason, Inada would not go along with the plan. 'If you don't revise it, I can't authorize it, and that's flat. Katakura will be furious if he hears about this. Let's take it I've heard nothing.' 'Don't be obdurate, Inada', pleaded Kunomura. 'I must be', was Inada's answer. 'If you go into India and it misfires, it could be an irretrievable mistake for Japan as a whole, not just for Burma Area Army and Mutaguchi. We are not in the ascendant anywhere now, apart from Burma. Think what that means.' It was in this impasse that Kunomura decided to play the Fujiwara card.

'If you don't let Operation C go forward', Fujiwara insisted when he was brought in, 'the whole of 15 Army will go stale.'[1]

'There must be a better reason for the operation than helping out 15 Army. And if you don't want to go stale, then why Imphal particularly? Why not south-west China? Why not Yunnan?'

'Yunnan?' Fujiwara was nonplussed.

'Sure. Why not go into China and pick up a few girls?' Inada was known to be flippant and Fujiwara was not sure how to take this. 'Sounds fine,' he countered, 'but isn't Imphal a better bet than Yunnan?'

It was the opportunity Inada had been looking for. He knew Fujiwara was given to grandiose and ambitious planning, and began to discourse on the possibility of the Japanese armies in Burma withdrawing into Yunnan and linking up in China with Japan's Expeditionary Force, to prevent the US and the British keeping China in the war. It wouldn't matter then if the British *did* re-take Burma, they would still find strong Japanese armies between them and Chiang Kai-shek. He offered Fujiwara a view of how the war might develop half-a-decade ahead. 'We have to think in terms of a *jikyū-sen*, a war of attrition. We may have to withdraw into China from South-East Asia. The first step might well be Yunnan. In the long run, a much better bet than Imphal.'

---

[1] He used the word *kusaru*, 'to rot', 'to decay'.

Fujiwara had not anticipated that the interview would take this course, and was reduced to repeating his advocacy of Mutaguchi's plans for India. Inada tried another tack. 'Mutaguchi wants to go ahead,' he told Fujiwara, 'but I've spoken to his divisional commanders and not a single one of them wants to. What kind of a campaign will you have when the three divisional commanders fundamentally disagree with what the army commander's after?'

This was true. Yanagida, the 33 Division commander, a cultivated and well-informed general, was scathing about Mutaguchi and was convinced the operation against Imphal was impossible. He had gone further. 'What's going to happen to us, with a moron like Mutaguchi as our Commander-in-Chief?'[1]

Yamauchi, of 15 Division, was very much the intellectual, a man of fine distinctions, not really fit for the hurly-burly of battle command. Only Satō, of 31 Division, who had fought the Russians at Changkufeng, was as tough as Mutaguchi. But, for reasons buried deep in the past of the army factionalism of the 1930s, the two loathed each other. That these three men should have become Mutaguchi's subordinate commanders in the first place was an illustration of the ineptitude of the Personnel Bureau of Imperial General Headquarters and of its chief, the Vice War-Minister, Lieutenant-General Tominaga. Mutaguchi and his generals were, to say the least of it, ill-suited. Inada summed it up for Kunomura: 'Whichever way you look at it, there are disadvantages. But if you want to go into India, you've got to alter that plan!'[2]

It was clear that not only Katakura but Inada would continue to oppose the Imphal operation, and it seemed as if Mutaguchi would have to withdraw, or await a fresh opportunity in the future. Then fate took a hand.

In 1943, the Japanese Government and Imperial General Headquarters decided on an Outline Plan for Policy Guidance in Greater East Asia (*Dai Tōa Seiryaku Shidō Taikō*), the purpose of which was to bind the countries of Asia closer to Japan so that together they would form a defensive ring against the return of the Allied armies. A link in this ring was a Greater Thailand. On 4 July 1943, Tojo visited Field Marshal Pibun Songkram, Prime Minister and Regent of Thailand, and promised that Thailand's 'lost' provinces would be restored. Japan had already intervened in the Franco-Thai dispute of 1940 as a result of which a large part of Cambodia had been handed over to the Thais. Now he was offering the Malay provinces of Perlis, Kedah, Kelantan, and Trengganu as well as a consider-

---

[1] '*Anna wake no wakaran gun-shireikan wa dōmo naran ne?*' (Takagi, *Kōmei*, p. 65). In private and not-so-private conversations, Mutaguchi was known to return the compliment: 'What can you do with a gutless bastard (*yowamushi*) like that?'

[2] Takagi, *Kōmei*, p. 66

able slice of Burma. At first sight, it is far from clear why Japan should alienate possible goodwill from three countries, Burma, Malaya and French Indo-China, in order to ensure the goodwill of a fourth. But Burma was a battlefield, and had not yet obtained her independence, Malaya was under Japanese military occupation and likely to remain so, and French Indo-China, though nominally administered still by the Vichy Government, was in the firm grasp of the Japanese Army. In a real sense, Thailand was the 'core' country of the South-East Asian peninsula, and central to any plan for creating a redoubt against an Allied counter-offensive. So Tojo wooed Pibun with these proposals and instructed Southern Army to go ahead with a new frontier demarcation. As it happened, the lines drawn did not conform to the promises made to Pibun by Tojo, who was furious, and demanded a scapegoat. Inada was not responsible, but as Deputy Chief of Staff he had signed and sealed the diplomatic documents and Tojo asked for his head on a charger.

At least, that was how things appeared at the time. Later, it became clear that Inada had been set up. Tominaga, as head of Personnel in Tokyo, had found Inada awkward and refractory at Southern Army, and induced Tojo to have him removed. The Thai imbroglio was no more than a means to this end. On 11 October 1943, Inada was transferred to HQ 19 Army. His successor was Lieutenant-General Ayabe, chief of No. 1 Bureau (Operations) at Army Staff GHQ (Sanbō Honbu).

When Inada handed over to Ayabe, he warned him, among other things, to sit firmly on Mutaguchi whenever he put forward his wild schemes for an invasion of India through Imphal. During drinks after the official handing over, Ayabe told Inada that he had received his orders at a most awkward time, halfway through a tour of inspection of Rabaul in the South Pacific. There had been no hint of a move before he set off, and he was indignant at the cavalier treatment he had received. It was the height of arbitrariness, Inada agreed, and he saw in it the hand of both Tojo and Tominaga, removing officers they couldn't get on with. It indicated a deep *malaise* at the very summit of Japan's command structure.

We can leave Inada and Ayabe to their drunken denunciation of Tojo. They were, in fact, right. But the end product, in the local sense, was that, with Inada out of the way, there was no one at Southern Army HQ to put a bridle on Mutaguchi. And whatever he may have said to Inada in his cups, once Ayabe was drawn into the atmosphere of Singapore, and discovered that his staff were not really opposed to going ahead with *some* plan for Imphal, and that General Terauchi himself simply said, 'Yes, get on with it, but be quick about it,' he found himself unable to stem the tide. In Rangoon, even Katakura ceased to oppose the operation, though no one understood why.

So, when the final war game was held in Rangoon on 23 December 1943, in the presence of Ayabe and Naka, neither of them uttered a word of protest. Yesterday's antagonists had become the protagonists of today. Terauchi approved, and dispatched Ayabe to Tokyo to urge Imperial General Headquarters to give its authorization. Six months before, Ayabe had been Tokyo's envoy, transmitting the decision to halt the planning. Now he was an emissary to Tokyo, urging its approval.

For three days and nights Ayabe was grilled at Army Staff HQ. He gave an account of 15 Army's preparations and morale and expressed Southern Army's confidence that the operation would be completed – i.e. that a new and better defence line would be established – before the monsoon. On 31 December 1943, Imperial General Headquarters gave its approval, but the final word rested with Tojo himself.

The head of the Military Affairs Bureau, Colonel Nishiura Susumu, hurried to the Prime Minister's official residence.[1] Tojo had just got into the bath, but when it was represented to him that the matter was urgent, he summoned Nishiura to the dressing-room and spoke to him through the glass partition. When Nishiura said he'd come for the authorization of the Imphal operation, Tojo called, 'Wait a minute!' and began to fire questions at him from the steaming tub. Was the supply set-up all right? Were there any flaws in Mutaguchi's operational thinking? Since only inferior air-power was available, were any measures planned against the enemy's ground-air co-operation? Was there any likelihood that reinforcements would be needed after breaking into the Imphal Plain? Would any snags occur later in the overall defence of Burma as a result of pushing the defence line forward into Indian territory? Were any counter-measures planned in the event of an Allied attack from the sea against Southern Burma?

Without a note, squatting stark naked in his bath, Tojo put these queries to Nishiura, who was amazed at how Tojo immediately recalled all the major problems that had been raised in the past six months. 'Confirm all these points with the Operations Bureau,' Tojo shouted through the noise of the water gurgling away, 'then come back and report.' Nishiura went to a telephone, got through to Army General Headquarters and relayed Tojo's questionnaire to his staff officers. He came back to the bathroom and called out, 'No need to worry. All points dealt with.' Tojo came out, affixed his seal to the document, and with a final admonition to Nishiura – 'impress on Ayabe he's not to attempt the impossible!' – brought the interview to a close.[2]

So, in the end, everyone had come round to Mutaguchi's way of thinking; or at least had decided that silence was the better part. Only Mutaguchi's steadfast confidence in his own plan, since Wingate had converted him to the

---

[1] Itō Masanori, *Teikoku rikugun no saigo*, III, p. 113

[2] ibid., p. 113

possibility of crossing the Chindwin and the Naga Hills, had remained unchanged. Authorization came from Tokyo on 7 January 1944, in the form of Imperial General Headquarters Army Order No. 1776: 'For the defence of Burma, the Commander-in-Chief Southern Army shall destroy the enemy on that front at the appropriate juncture and occupy and secure a strategic zone in North-East India in the area of Imphal.' Whatever limits were implied in the wording ('for the defence of Burma', 'in the area of Imphal'), Mutaguchi took it as his green light. He could now get on with the invasion of India.

Subhas Chandra Bose

India was on his side, he thought. So was Genghis Khan. Every staff officer at the conference had made a fuss about the supply problems. But Mutaguchi remembered that when Genghis Khan conquered Asia and much of Europe, he had solved these problems by taking along with him meat on the hoof. Mutaguchi would do the same, and the order went out to assemble cattle, buffalo and goats ready to be taken through the hills and collected at the crossing points on the Chindwin: Tonhe for 15 Division, Homalin for 31 Division.

India was on his side because India, for him, meant Subhas Chandra Bose. On the last day of the Rangoon war game, 27 June 1943, Bose arrived in Singapore from Tokyo, to open a congress of the Indian Independence League. The conference opened in the Dai Tōa Theatre on 4 July, and the League's president, Rash Behari Bose (no relation), who had taken refuge in Japan after an attempt to assassinate the Viceroy of India, Lord Hardinge, over forty years before, proposed Subhas Chandra Bose as his successor.

A Cambridge graduate, Subhas Chandra Bose spurned the chance of becoming one of the 'heaven-born' of the Indian Civil Service for a career in politics, and gradually moved away from the Congress Party and Gandhi's *ahimsa* (non-violence) to a firm conviction that India would only be freed from the British by the use of military force. In the 1930s, Bose visited Europe and was received by Hitler and Mussolini. He even married an Austrian girl – secretly, though, because he had sworn to his followers that he would never marry until India was free. A Bengali, he had been Lord Mayor of Calcutta and President of Congress and his new breakaway party, Forward Bloc, had a strong power base in Bengal. The British arrested him on a charge of sedition on 2 July 1940, but he escaped and walked out of India.

His escape is pure John Buchan. His trial was fixed for 26 January 1941 but a week earlier he left Calcutta disguised as a Muslim. Two hundred miles west of Calcutta, he caught a train to Peshawar, where he turned into a Pathan, with the added precaution of pretending to be a deaf-mute since he knew no Pushtu. He left by car for Kabul, in Afghanistan, then when the car broke down completed the journey on foot, accompanied by two Pathan guides. Kabul had the perfectly deserved reputation of being a nest of British spies and after unsuccessful attempts to get help from the Japanese and Soviet embassies, Bose prevailed on the Italian ambassador, Luigi Quarini, to give him an Italian passport. As 'Signore Mazzotta' he crossed into Soviet territory, passed through Bokhara and Samarkand, and took the train to Moscow. The Nazi-Soviet Pact still had a few months to run before Hitler's invasion of Russia in June 1941, so on 28 March Bose was able to travel from Moscow to Berlin. It was a natural terminus. Bose was no democrat and proclaimed unashamedly his extreme authoritarian characteristics. 'You cannot have a democratic system', he declared in 1939, 'if that system has to put through economic reforms on a socialistic basis. Therefore, we must have a political system – a State – of an authoritarian character... with a democratic system we cannot solve the problem of Free India.'[1]

Given his sneaking admiration for the British Empire, Hitler was lukewarm about proclaiming unconditional support for Bose, and Ciano, Mussolini's foreign minister, was no more forthcoming. Bose had to content himself with broadcasting anti-British propaganda from Berlin and with building the 3000-strong 'Indian Legion' from POWs captured in North Africa. After a German victory at Stalingrad, the Legion was to accompany the German armies through Central Asia and sweep into India from the north-west. Unfortunately for Bose, Stalingrad did not fall, the victory failed to materialize, and he turned to the Japanese.

The Japanese ambassador in Berlin was General Oshima Hiroshi, a fervent pro-Nazi, and his military attaché, Colonel Yamamoto Bin, was instructed by Tokyo to contact Bose, but to offer no firm commitment. After endless discussion between one foreign ministry and another, permission was granted early in 1943 for Bose to leave Germany. The second part of his odyssey began, no less adventurous than the first.

With his Indian secretary, Hassan, he left by submarine in February. On 26 April, a Japanese submarine from Penang rendezvoused with the German submarine in the Indian Ocean south-east of Madagascar. Bose transferred to it, and landed on Sabang Island, off the coast of Sumatra, some days later. By 16 May he was in Tokyo and on 10 June was received by Tojo.

Tojo's first experience with the anti-British movement among the Indians of South-East Asia had not been a happy one. The first 'Indian National Army' (Azad Hind Fauj) was founded in Singapore from Indian POWs taken in Malaya and at the British surrender of the city on 15

---

[1] Joyce Lebra, *Jungle Alliance*, p. 106

February 1942. Its leader, Captain Mohan Singh, co-operated with the Indian Independence League, civilians under Rash Behari Bose, but wrangles and disputes were sparked off between the civil and military sides of the movement and the Japanese, who supported Rash Behari Bose, finally put Mohan Singh under arrest. He promptly retorted by dissolving the INA.

In Subhas Chandra Bose's view, it was vital to have an Indian National Army as well as a civilian organization and he intended to use it, in a military alliance with Japan, to take power in India. His oratory took on a somewhat Nazi style and he raised the crowds at the Dai Tōa theatre to fever pitch. The hall shook with applause as he outlined his plans to put an end to the British Raj. He proclaimed the Free India Provisional Government and made a declaration of war against Great Britain. In tearful raptures, the audience promised contributions and undying allegiance to the cause. The next day, on a dais in front of the Singapore Municipal Buildings, Bose took the salute at an INA march-past. By a happy chance, Tojo was in Singapore on that day and attended the parade. To pay him honour, Bose stood one step behind him at the saluting base. 'Your Excellency,' murmured Bose, seeing the satisfaction with which Tojo gazed at the force of 10,000 Indian troops, 'I'd like to increase my army three-fold, five-fold!' Regrettably, Tojo's English was not up to much, and he did not understand what Bose had said. So he kept silent and returned the troops' salute. It was only later, when what Bose had said was reported to him, that he opened his eyes wide in astonishment.

Yet it echoed an idea in his mind. Just before leaving Tokyo for Singapore, he had received a private signal from Mutaguchi, strongly advocating the need for an operation to invade Assam and for an increase in the number of Japanese divisions in Burma. Perhaps, thought Tojo, Bose should be told of the plans for an operation against Imphal?

When he learned what was afoot, Bose went wild with enthusiasm. He had met Kawabe, en route to his new appointment as Commander-in-Chief in Burma, in Tokyo three months before, and Kawabe had already taken Tojo's hint that India was the logical extension of Japan's campaigns in South-East Asia. Bose paid a call on the imprisoned Mohan Singh, who asked him how he could be convinced of a Japanese victory in Assam. 'My name carries enough weight,' replied Bose. 'When I appear in Bengal everyone will revolt. Wavell's whole army will join me.'[1]

At the Greater East Asia Conference, held in Tokyo in November 1943, Bose was the outstanding politician among those in Asia who collaborated with the Japanese, though he was the only one who ruled over no territory. (Tojo conceded the Andaman and the Nicobar Islands to him but it was a

[1] Lebra, op. cit., p. 124. Mohan Singh avers he listened to this with some scepticism (Singh, *Soldier's Contribution to Indian Independence*, 1974, p. 266)

fairly empty gesture. The islands were penal colonies in the Bay of Bengal, and the Japanese Navy intended to keep on using them.) It was his prestige, rather than his administration of territory, which gave him the confidence to resist General Terauchi's views on the use of the INA. Terauchi saw the Indians merely as guerrilla, sabotage and intelligence units scattered piecemeal in attachment to the Japanese divisions in Burma. Bose demanded that the INA be considered as an autonomous army acting in alliance with the Japanese and under overall Japanese command. Lieutenant-General Sugiyama, chief of the Japanese Imperial General Staff, agreed with Bose. 'If the Japanese Army once sets foot in India,' he thought, 'the whole of India will submit.'[1] The assurances that a large portion of the INA – the Subhas Brigade – would be employed in the Imphal campaign, that it would not be split into forces smaller than a battalion, that it would be treated as the army of an ally, that it would not be subject to Japanese military law, and that it would spearhead the advance into India, were concessions wrung from Kawabe, much against his will, when Bose arrived in Rangoon on 4 January 1944.

The Box

Arakan was a sideshow for Kawabe. But a sudden threat against British positions there would distract attention from the Imphal front and, with luck, keep British divisions now in the Maungdaw-Buthidaung area away from the central area of operations at Imphal. The British had been soundly beaten in Arakan by the Japanese in early 1943, but by the end of the year were beginning to creep southward again, with the ultimate – and usual – objective of taking Akyab and its airfields.

The Japanese 28 Army was intended to protect Arakan from a seaborne British invasion, but it had no intention of sitting tight and waiting for the British to hit it. The British southward thrust could be stopped; and, on this front too, there was at least one Japanese general who would not be satisfied with that, but intended to thrust into Bengal from Chittagong. The Imphal operation was christened in the usual Japanese syllabary code U-GO, or 'Operation C'. The Arakan operation was termed HA-GO, 'Operation Z'. Its function was not only to destroy XV Corps, it was to draw off reserves into the Arakan so that the Imphal front would be naked to Mutaguchi's offensive. It was timed to begin on 4 February, 1944. U-GO was at first planned to start at the beginning of March 1944, about three weeks after HA-GO had begun, bringing an even closer relation between the two operations than actually occurred; but it was delayed because of

[1] Nukada Hiroshi, *Jinji kyokuchō no kaisō* (Recollections of the Chief of the Personnel Bureau), Fuyō Shōbō, p. 139

the slow arrival of one of its three component divisions, 15 Division, and did not begin, as a result, until 9 March.

The limits of the penetration in Arakan authorized by the 28 Army GOC-in-C, Lieutenant-General Sakurai Shōzō, were fixed with a mind to the power of its main force, 55 Division, and the British strength. 55 Infantry Group, under the command of Sakurai's namesake, Major-General Sakurai Tokutarō, was to lead 55 Division's main force on 3 February through the British lines north-east of the village of Buthidaung, make for Taung Bazar and occupy it by dawn on the 4th. It was then to attack 7 Indian Division from the rear, surround and destroy it. After that, Sakurai was to cross the Mayu Range and destroy 5 Indian Division in the area of Maungdaw. Sakurai also intended, for his part, to make for the actual divisional headquarters of 7 Division and capture its commander.

The additional aim was very much in character. 'Tokuta', as Sakurai was affectionately nicknamed, was a boisterous personality who had come to 55 Division with a considerable reputation. Like the new commander, Hanaya, he was an old China hand and stories of his bravery and dash were common currency in the division. When he was an intelligence major on the staff of the China Expeditionary Force he negotiated a ceasefire with Sung Che-yuan's army in Peking. The negotiations took place on the wall of a fortification, by the Kuang An Gate, and 'Tokuta' spotted the Chinese closing the gate and getting ready to fire on the Japanese party. To stop them, he leaped straight down from the high wall.

He had the reputation of always being in front of his men and in particular was a specialist in night combat. He was also something of an eccentric, of the kind the Japanese army seemed to foster. He had got into hot water in China for using unscrupulous Japanese roughnecks, *Shinagoro* as they were called, who were little better than gangsters, on intelligence missions. Their violence did a great deal of harm to the Japanese army's public relations and 'Tokuta' was hauled over the coals.

By August 1943 he was a major-general and given the command of 55 Division Infantry Group. When he arrived in Akyab to take over, Colonel Tanahashi sent a young officer to welcome him. Lt Uehara was astonished to see the general wearing a long pearl necklace. 'Don't look so surprised,' 'Tokuta' rebuked him, 'they're my Buddhas.' Uehara's astonishment was not diminished by the Chinese folk dance that 'Tokuta' insisted on performing for the regimental officers at the mess dinner they gave him that night. 'Tokuta' stripped naked and puffed away, during his gyrations, at lighted cigarettes protruding from his nostrils and the corners of his mouth – cigarettes which were promptly handed to the nearest officer to smoke when the dance was at an end. 'Tokuta's' striptease act soon became legendary throughout the entire Burma army.

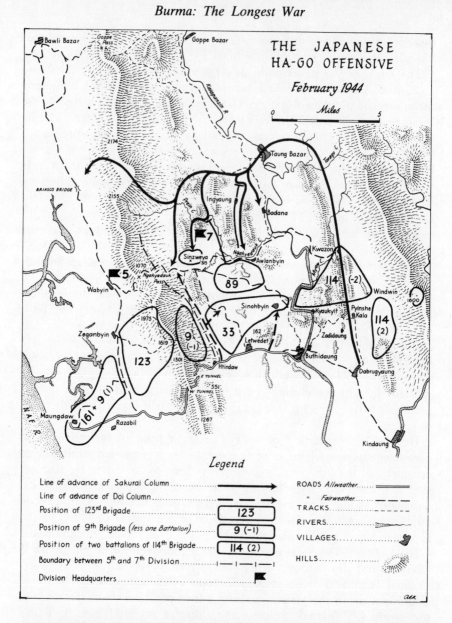

THE JAPANESE HA-GO OFFENSIVE

February 1944

Legend

Line of advance of Sakurai Column .... ➡
Line of advance of Doi Column .... ⇢
Position of 123rd Brigade .... [123]
Position of 9th Brigade *(less one Battalion)* ...... [9 (-1)]
Position of two battalions of 114th Brigade .... [114 (2)]
Boundary between 5th and 7th Division ..... ┆—┆—┆—┆
Division Headquarters .... 🚩

ROADS *Allweather* ....
"   *Fairweather* ....
TRACKS ....
RIVERS ....
VILLAGES ....
HILLS ....

He didn't think much of Lieutenant-General Christison's attempt to move south in Arakan once the rains were over. 'It's child's play,' remarked 'Tokuta', 'to smash the enemy in the Mayu Peninsula. Give me one battalion, I'll show you, I'd be in Chittagong by now.'

The divisional commander, Lieutenant-General Koga Takeshi, had led the division triumphantly through the early stages of the Burma campaign, from the Thai border to the Indian frontier. Now, in November 1943, he was to be replaced by a notorious bully and brute, Lieutenant-General Hanaya, an old China hand who was convinced that he had created Japan's puppet state of Manchukuo single-handed during his days as a major in a special intelligence section in Manchuria. On the least provocation Hanaya had been known to slap the faces of quite senior officers in front of their men, and would frequently tell subalterns to commit suicide, offering them the use of his own sword if they hesitated.

The conjunction of Hanaya and 'Tokuta' had been the design of Burma Area Army's Chief Staff Officer, Katakura Tadashi. Like them, a soldier with experience in China, he felt that if he had a team made up of these two tough generals in 55 Division he could rest secure about Burma Area Army's seaward defences against attack from the Bay of Bengal, which seemed the most likely form of incursion by the allied armies, particularly since the new Supreme Commander, Lord Louis Mountbatten, was not only an admiral but, as former Chief of Combined Operations in Europe, an expert in commando and landing operations.

But the first British moves were not seaward at all. Christison planned, ultimately, to take Akyab. It was the natural ambition of every general in Arakan, because the Akyab airfields would at once provide a vastly increased radius for Allied aircraft to cover parts of Burma out of reach of the airfields in Bengal. It was an essential stage in the recapture of Rangoon, itself only a staging point in the ultimate desirability, the retaking of Singapore from the Japanese. So Christison pulled back 26 Division to rest and sent forward two divisions, 5 and 7 Indian Divisions, with orders to capture the road running between Buthidaung and Maungdaw and so obtain easy communications from the sea inland across Arakan. On 9 January 1944, the British were in Maungdaw. Two days later, Hanaya gave instructions for Operation HA-GO to begin.

His division was to destroy the British-Indian forces on the right bank of the Kalapanzin (i.e. the upper reaches of the Mayu River) north of Buthidaung. Hanaya did not simply wish to clear the British out of Arakan. He had another objective. He was to support the forthcoming invasion of India. On 7 January 1944 Imperial General Headquarters in Tokyo finally gave its approval to Operation U-GO which authorized the 15 Army commander, Mutaguchi, to cross the Burma border into the state of Manipur, and take its capital Imphal, centre of the Allied build-up for a counter-offensive to retake Burma. Hanaya was to draw into Arakan British reserves and hold them there, either destroying them in battle or at any rate preventing them from reinforcing the British IV Corps on the Imphal Plain. 'Tokuta' was given the task of applying the old Japanese formula of attack to the British and Indian troops in Arakan; encirclement, cutting of communications, withering the enemy on the branch, terrifying him by sudden attacks at night. He was told to take his force as far as Bawli Bazar, which was inside Burma, but he and his men had no intention of stopping there. The Allied base was over the border in Chittagong and he intended to take it, whether it was named in his orders or not.

Whatever campaigns were planned to retake Rangoon, a forward air base was essential, since transport aircraft had an average flying radius of 250 miles, which only brought within reach parts of Central Burma. Down the Arakan coast, Akyab's airfield offered a better springboard than anything on IV Corps' front at Manipur. There had been an amphibious operation ('Bullfrog') planned for the capture of Akyab, but 'Bullfrog' perished for lack of landing craft. The less ambitious 'Pigstick', a seaborne operation against the Mayu Peninsula, with Akyab as a later objective, was called off in January 1944. It was still possible, of course, to take Akyab by sheer slog: in other words, an overland advance by XV Corps, with no seaborne operation to back it, provided, as Mountbatten's Chief of Staff noted in his diary for 6 January 1944, that the Chiefs of Staff were not told of this, 'for it seems we have only to tell them of an operation for them promptly to remove the resources we need for it!'[1]

Christison had in fact begun to move his XV Corps forward from 1 November 1943, with the objective of easing communications across the northern part of Arakan. A sixteen-mile long metalled road ran between Maungdaw and Buthidaung. The Japanese had taken this road and the British were compelled to use a jeep track between the Naf River and the village of Ngakyedauk. 7 Indian Division moved over this track on 29 November, to occupy positions east of the Mayu Range from which, with 5 Indian Division, they would mount an assault on the Japanese 'front' of the Maungdaw-Buthidaung road. This road passed under the Mayu Range in a series of tunnels which the Japanese had converted into a kind of fortress, with other strong positions close by, including Razabil, three miles east of Maungdaw.

In the 'Pigstick' plan, 2 British Division was to land on the Mayu Peninsula in February 1944 to trap the Japanese 55 Division between themselves and XV Corps. When 'Pigstick' was cancelled, Christison went ahead on his own and by 9 January 1944, 5 Division had taken Maungdaw. Razabil still held out but Christison decided to move south down the spine of the Mayu Range and by the end of January 1944 had taken most of the area, apart from Razabil itself. Christison set up a supply zone and administrative area for his corps near the village of Sinzweya, in a clearing on the Ngakyedauk Pass road, where vast stocks were accumulated in support of the next stage of the offensive. Once he could use the cross-Arakan route of the metalled road between Maungdaw and Buthidaung, he intended to move on to Akyab and take its airfields.

[1] Bond, ed., op.cit., p. 130

Then the Japanese struck. Colonel Tanahashi, the man whose troops had defeated the British attempt to take Donbaik earlier in 1943, and who had captured the Brigadier of 6 Brigade, Cavendish, was in the van. It was close to dawn on 6 February but the mist had thickened as his Force moved through the darkness. Major Matsukihira's II Battalion was in front, followed by Regimental Headquarters, the Mountain Gun Company, and a Transport Unit. They debouched into a flat clearing cut by low hills. Calculating the distance they had marched, Tanahashi judged they must be close to the main British position.

A report came back that Matsukihira Battalion had bumped the British forces, and Tanahashi called up 2/Lieutenant Murase, the wireless section commander of the signals company. 'The vanguard of II Battalion has got hold of a British W/T set. Go and bring it in.' Murase went forward a hundred yards to the foot of a hill. Four or five British soldiers lay there, all dead. Murase found the W/T set in the shelter of a rock. It was massive, not a portable set. He couldn't budge it, so he took its clock out and told his men to destroy the set. As he started on his way back to regimental headquarters, he glanced down into the valley. The mist briefly lifted and a shock ran through him: he saw line upon line of tents. It was a huge encampment; with more than tents. There were tanks. Then the white mist came down again and covered everything.

When Tanahashi heard this, he sent a runner off at once to bring in Matsukihira and his II Battalion. There was no sign of them anywhere. II Battalion was the only combat unit available to Tanahashi at that crucial moment. I Battalion had moved west of Sinzweya to cut the British retreat. III Battalion (Sugiyama) was still some way behind. Tanahashi was concerned for his regimental flag which would be endangered if his headquarters was attacked, and it now seemed to lie naked to the British. He had just over 200 men: 60 in the flag escort company, 80 in the signals telephone section and fifty in the W/T section, with another score as headquarters defence. The signallers were commanded by a captain, Midorigawa, who had been with 55 Division since the invasion of Burma two years before, was known for his bravery and had a fund of battle experience. His first thought was for the safety of his set, which he buried in earth near the river bank.

The flag escort company moved uphill, through jungle, then halted. They did not know it, but they were on the very verge of 7 Indian Division's headquarters. Major-General Frank Messervy had sited his headquarters at Launggyaung, two miles north of the XV Corps administrative area known for convenience – and later to history – as the 'Admin Box'. When it became obvious that the Japanese were on the move, had slipped through one of his brigades and were turning south to come at them in an enveloping movement of the old familiar kind, Messervy began to wonder how exposed he was. On the other hand, he himself had been insisting that when the Japanese carried out their well-worn tactic of coming round the flank, the thing to do was to stay put and fight. His headquarters was not composed of infantrymen but if his clerks and signallers could stick it out it would show he meant what he said. He had at his disposal part of an engineer battalion and the divisional signals, together with the usual HQ assortment of orderlies and clerks.

It was upon this motley crew that Tanahashi's regimental headquarters fell, itself quite unprotected by combat troops. Light automatic fire poured on them from the hilltop and soon two tanks came into view. The flag escort company was only armed with small arms and had no means of standing up to tanks. Lt Uehara sped back to Tanahashi. He was concealed in the jungle close to the river bank, protecting the regimental flag with NCOs and men attached to HQ. 'What are the signals doing?' he asked angrily. 'Get them up on this hill fast!'

Uehara sprinted to the signals company. They turned him down flat. 'We're not coming out!' 'You have to, it's critical!' Uehara burst out, with the fierce firing on the hillside in his ears. 'Not on your life,' came the reply. 'If *our* signals sets get bust, *you* can't fight. Doesn't Tanahashi know anything about the importance of signals?' 'All right,' said Uehara. 'Do you want to see the flag escort company massacred?' 'Tell that to Tanahashi!' was the blunt retort.

Then a staff captain, Arata, came up. 'Midorigawa, what the hell do you think you're playing at? This is an order from the regimental commander. You will attack *now*!' Grumbling but obedient, Midorigawa came out and split his men into two groups. They charged the hilltop. 2/Lieutenant Murase, who had spotted the British position earlier in the mist, sprinted up the slope and fell. His orderly picked him up, but his right big toe felt as if it were broken. He blenched as the orderly carried out first-aid. He raised his head and saw a British tank come to a halt twenty yards in front of him. Troops clambered down from it. 'Shall I fire?' whispered his orderly. 'Don't be a fool, get the hell out of it!' Murase then crawled out of sight. He could hear Midorigawa shouting and yelling on the hilltop. The signallers had taken it. 'That saves *me*,' thought Murase.

He was not the only one who was relieved. When Tanahashi heard that Uehara had taken the hill, he went up it with the flag. He could see half his flag escort company lying dead on the slope as he reached the summit. His men fired into a group of tents and rushed in. They discovered later that it was Messervy's headquarters. So this battle produced the quaint situation of the regimental HQ signallers of one side – 200 men in all, armed with small arms only – acting as infantrymen against the divisional HQ of the other. One of Tanahashi's men picked up a general's hat – which had fallen off as Messervy escaped – tried it on, felt pleased with the effect and continued to wear it.

This was the result that the infantry group commander, 'Tokuta', had longed for. As the battle was being planned, every time he visited Burma Area Army GHQ in Rangoon he kept asking Lieutenant-Colonel Fuwa, on the staff, what the latest news was about the position of 7 Indian Division HQ. He was intent on capturing the divisional commander, and almost succeeded. He did at any rate capture some of the division's liquor, and as he saw Tanahashi's flag go up on what the Japanese later christened 'Flag Hill', he raised his glass aloft. It was perhaps, as a Japanese historian has pointed out, the zenith of his triumph.

Its edge, however, was soon to be blunted. The British histories say that all code books and important documents were burned before 7 Division HQ retreated from Launggyaung. In fact, the Japanese came across a number of vital documents, including some in Japanese. These proved to be a copy of Sakurai's own operation instructions, the operation order for HA-GO itself, no doubt removed from a Japanese officer's body. So the entire plan of operations – all the unit formations, the names of commanding officers, the notion of breaking through to Taung Bazar and then reversing south on to 7 Division – was known to the British already; as was Sakurai's desire to go further than the operational limits (a line east-west of Taung Bazar) cautiously assigned by 28 Army, and capture Chittagong. This British knowledge of their dispositions and plans was undoubtedly one of the causes of the Japanese defeat at Sinzweya.

Further down the hill, the Japanese heard a whistle being blown and took it to be the signal for a British counter-attack. It was not. The British were withdrawing, partly because heavy rain made it impossible for the tanks of 25 Dragoons to manoeuvre on the hill slopes. But the real battle, for the Sinzweya Basin itself, on which the Japanese could now gaze down unhindered, was just about to begin. And although the tiny area involved led to fierce hand-to-hand fighting, this was not the decisive factor. The battle of the Admin Box was won by tanks and aircraft, and by enormous British material superiority in both.

But it would be unfair to attribute the British victory later in the battle merely to material advantage. The British *used* their material superiority with intelligence and skill, and their victory was also – at last – one of morale and ideas. It was a real pointer away from the past eighteen months of frustration and defeat in Arakan.

The Japanese realized that they had to achieve their objectives quickly because they were so lightly armed. Apart from a few mountain guns they had nothing with which to compete with the British artillery. They had no tanks of their own and little with which to counter the British tanks, though the 55 Divisional commander, Hanaya, had been told the British had tanks on the divisional front. And although they put up a surprising number of fighter aircraft as a protective screen in the first few days of the battle, the British knocked those aircraft out of the skies when it became necessary to do so.

Indeed, it became necessary by 8 February. Slim had already ensured that enough parachutes would be ready for the supply drop, by using jute – nearly all of which is produced in Bengal – to make them with, as there were not enough silk parachutes to go round. The wind passed through tiny vents in them instead of through one large vent at the top and although they would not have done for dropping paratroops or fragile equipment they were adequate for the task in hand and, as Slim proudly pointed out in his memoirs, they cost the British taxpayer one-twentieth of the cost of a silk parachute.[1]

There was another problem. The Japanese air force had been active over Arakan. The front was swept by 100 aircraft on the first day of the offensive and on later days as many as 60 planes were in the air, not only Zeros but the newer and more manoeuvrable Tojos, but they did not match the three forward squadrons of Spitfires which took a toll of Japanese fighters at a disproportionate rate. The Japanese were pushed out of the skies, 65 fighters being lost in the first thirteen days of the battle for the loss of three Spitfires. This did not mean air supply was without danger. Light anti-aircraft fire and small arms fire from the ground could be effective against aircraft compelled to fly low to make an accurate drop. Eventually the drops had to be made at night to reduce even that risk. Everything came through the air: rations, ammunition, petrol, medical supplies, Frank Owen's newspaper *SEAC*, socks, spectacles, toothbrushes, razors, the lot. Only one item of replacement could not be obtained: Messervy's hat (Messervy's head was unusually large). But then, by an incredible coincidence, among a group of Japanese who attacked the Admin Box in captured British uniforms was the very soldier who had appropriated Messervy's hat and had been nicknamed 'Shōgun' ('The General') by his comrades as a result. The hat was removed from 'Shōgun's' body and returned to its rightful owner.

When the air supply tactics began to switch the hard battle in the Box in favour of the British, the Japanese 28 Army Chief of Staff, who had a gift for coining phrases, termed what was happening the '*entō jinchi sakusen*', or 'the cylinder position operation'. Down into Sinzweya, like liquid through a cylinder or funnel, poured the munitions of war.

The site itself was like a big flat piece of common, about 1200 yards square, consisting of dried-up paddy fields surrounded by low wooded hills. A smaller hillock about 150 feet high stood in its centre, with a growth of scrub covering it, round which were stacked ammunition boxes, enough for an entire corps. This was known – it was hardly the

---

[1] Slim, op.cit., p. 220

moment for originality – as Ammunition Hill. To the east lay another conspicuous hill, Artillery Hill.

Along the southern edge of the clearing ran the road from the Ngakyedauk Pass to Ngakyedauk village. At the western entrance, the road to the Pass began. It was still dangerous going and the road was screened – to stop men falling over the precipice – with strips of sacking tied here and there to dead trees. The road saw a constant traffic of barefoot coolies carrying tree trunks to make bridges or yoke poles with baskets suspended from them. Beyond the road stretched a beautiful landscape of low hills into the distance. To the photographer Cecil Beaton, moving along the Pass a few weeks before the Japanese burst through, the screened trees gave a curious unreal effect against the elaborate panorama of more distant hills, as if he were looking at a background for a Leonardo. The impact of battle did not, though, change Sinzweya permanently. 'Nothing now remains,' wrote Compton Mackenzie when he visited it only three years later (1947), 'to recall that desperate struggle in the Admin Box except a few tanks and the slit trenches gradually filling up. Cattle are grazing tranquilly. We sat beneath a tree and surveyed a scene of Arcadian peace... one could see the road our Sappers had cut through the Ngakyedauk Pass, but it is rapidly falling to pieces so that even its trace will hardly be discernible after another couple of monsoons.'[1]

When Geoffrey Evans came over the Pass on 6 February 1944 he found it tough to negotiate. In the warm dry weather of the previous few days it would have been all right, but rain had been falling for two or three hours and his tracked carrier slipped and slithered along the narrow path. Finally, half a mile from Sinzweya, the carrier jibbed at an uphill slope. Evans decided to finish the journey on foot through the dripping jungle, locking himself onto the track with his steel-tipped mountain stick. By 11.30 am on 6 February, he reached XV Corps Administrative Area, the 'Admin Box'.

The Box contained more than ammunition. There was a hospital, an officers' shop, a dressing station, a mule company, and petrol and supply dumps of all kinds. This was the supply core for the offensive by 5 and 7 Divisions. Evans had arrived in Arakan only two days before from his job as Brigadier General Staff, IV Corps, in the Imphal Plain, to take command of 9 Infantry Brigade of 5 Indian Division, west of the Mayu Range. 7 Division lay east of the Range, and the Ngakyedauk Pass linked them. Lieutenant-General Briggs, whom Evans had last seen in the Western Desert in North Africa in 1942, was both pleased and surprised to see him. Evans set off to join his new command. 9 Brigade HQ was positioned behind its two battalions, 3/14 Punjab and 2 West Yorks, and at 11 pm that night shells and mortar bombs began to fall around Brigade HQ. The

[1] Compton Mackenzie, *All Over The Place*, p. 143

179

commander of the Mountain Artillery Regiment, Humphry Hill, told Evans he thought it was harassing fire but information came through the following morning that the Japanese had been sighted at Taung Bazar, twelve miles north of Buthidaung, well behind 7 Division's front, and Evans noted that Japanese aircraft were more active than usual. He was ordered to send a company of West Yorks to the Admin Box and at 9.30 am on 6 February he was called to the phone. It was Briggs: 'Early this morning the Japs overran Frank Messervy's HQ at Launggyaung. Nobody knows whether he or anybody else got away. The situation is obscure, to say the least of it, but obviously a large enemy force has got round behind 7 Division.' It turned out that the Corps Commander, Christison, wanted Evans to leave his Brigade, go to the Admin Box with his West Yorks (less one company) and take command of the area. 'Put it into a state of defence,' he was told, 'and hold it at all costs.'

The bemused Evans handed his Brigade over to Brigadier Salomons and pushed on to Sinzweya. He did not know where the Corps Administrative Area was, nor what were the detailed dispositions of 7 Indian Division, though he knew Crowther's 89 Brigade was on his left flank. He told Salomons to join him in the Box as soon as he could, with Brigade HQ, and ordered Major Hugh Ley, second in command of 25 Dragoons who had come across Ngakyedauk Pass two days before, to do likewise. 'And bring a troop of tanks with you,' he added. He never gave a more vital order in his life.

On the very day that Tanahashi Force slipped through 7 Indian Division and on to Taung Bazar, Mountbatten's Chief of Staff in SEAC headquarters in Kandy, Ceylon, was gloomily summing up the prospects for Burma. A deputation headed by the US Major-General Albert Wedemeyer had that day left for London and Washington to put Mountbatten's views on the future of operations in the Far East. The ideas reached at QUADRANT (the Quebec Conference) in 1943 about recapturing Burma and opening the Ledo Road to China were to be squashed: 'We cannot recapture Burma by advances only from the north and west', wrote Pownall in his diary, thus defining as impossible exactly what the XIV Army was to carry out in the next eighteen months. Instead, SEAC's appreciation was that Burma should be bypassed in favour of Sumatra, bursting through to Malaya or the Sunda Straits afterwards and opening a port in South China long before the Ledo Road could be finished. Not that Pownall thought much of the need to keep up China's fighting capacity, but a southward thrust would support MacArthur in the South-West Pacific and Nimitz in the Central Pacific. And Churchill was a strong supporter of the notion of bypassing Burma in favour of Sumatra. On the other hand, Pownall realized, such a *coup* depended on landing craft, of which there was a shortage, and even when the war in Europe was over he was sure they would all go to the Pacific and not to South-East Asia. So, he lugubriously concluded, 'If. . . we are relegated to mucking about in Burma they may as well wind up this unlucky S.E. Asia command, leave here, if you like, a few figureheads, a good deception staff and plenty of press men to write it up. Our practical value will disappear and the Burma operations turned back to India to run indifferently well.'[1]

Even when, nearly a week later, he was able to observe that the Japanese offensive in Arakan had not gone as the Japanese had confidently anticipated – 'We've learned now to fight where we stand and not to be frightened of the bogey of infiltration' – he was still convinced the end product would not help much: 'But all this is putting our timings back and our chances of getting to Akyab before the monsoon swell begins are down to next to nothing. It's just as well we have never proclaimed Akyab as our next objective – if we had done so we should have been hauled over the coals for failure to get there!'[2] It was just as well, too, that the men who were doing the fighting did not know the vacillations of their high command. In effect, they were creating a new situation which that command and its planners would have to take into account, in spite of themselves; and so the soldiers would have Burma in the end, whether Churchill and Mountbatten wanted it or not.

[1] Bond, ed., op.cit., p. 139

[2] ibid., p. 140

While Pownall was wondering what, if anything, the British were going to do in Burma, Messervy was more perturbed about his position on a Burmese hill. When Tanahashi's HQ Force burst in on 7 Division headquarters, tearing the sky asunder with their yells and screams, the Signals office came under attack and Messervy's own quarters were threatened. He recognized the situation at once. He had been here before: years previously, in the North African desert, he had been taken prisoner when his headquarters had been overrun by the Afrika Corps, and had escaped. History seemed to be about to repeat itself. The Japanese cut his telephone wires, and various parts of the HQ position ceased to communicate with each other. Messervy and his staff were pinned down on a steep hillock by light machine-gun fire and he finally decided to abandon the position without being able to convey his decision to those of his staff who were not on the spot, or to the divisional HQ signallers. He broke through the Japanese lines, losing his hat in the process, as we have seen, waded down a *chaung* and through jungle and at 12.45 pm he reached the Regimental HQ of 25 Dragoons at Sinzweya, a general without a division.

Colonel Pat Hobson, commanding 7 Division Signals, decided to fight on, though his sets were being destroyed and the Japanese had set up machine guns on a ridge which dominated the British strong points. At 10.30 am operators on the divisional wireless net heard someone say, 'put a pick through that set'. Then silence. The division's Commander Royal Artillery, Brigadier Hely, gave the order to evacuate the position, and the signallers, HQ clerks and orderlies were told to rendezvous at the eastern end of Ngakyedauk Pass. But the signallers did not reach the Admin Box unscathed: they lost seven officers, with eight British other ranks and ninety Indian other ranks killed or missing.

Under Evans's supervision, the Box rapidly became a nest of HQs. After contacting his scattered divisional units with the wireless sets of 25 Dragoons, Messervy established a new Divisional HQ south of Ammunition Hill, Salomons brought 5 Division's 9 Brigade HQ to the same spot, and to the west of it the Admin Box itself was situated. HQ 89 Brigade lay just south of the Ngakyedauk Road, near the eastern exit from the Box.

So the defence of the Box began. Half an hour after Messervy had supped tea with whisky to revive him after his ordeal, Japanese Zeros strafed the Box, killing a number of troops and two mules close to Evans's HQ. The stench from these corpses gradually made life in the Box GHQ intolerable. 'Your job is to stay put and keep the Japanese out', Evans told his unit commanders. Evans was not the easiest of men to get on with and he grated on one or two of his subordinates, but he had little choice other than to impose his personality quickly and ruthlessly because morale in the Box, at the start, was poor. The troops had had a rough time in the rain making their way there, slipping up and down muddy slopes and heaving transport mules along, and as lorries became bogged down in their tracks and bren carriers flailed through the mud and played havoc with the paths, men held on to the dripping branches of trees to heave themselves forward and finally collect in bewildered, dispirited groups.

On the night of 7 February, the Japanese were beaten off at the eastern entrance to the Box by the shelling of the tanks' 75 mm guns and a counter-attack by the West Yorks. They then began to move in again in the darkness from the south-west. The direction indicates that they belonged to a battalion of 112 Infantry Regiment. Rifle and automatic fire came in bursts, 300 yards from Box HQ. Then came screams and cries for help. 'Good God!' Evans heard someone say, 'They've got into the hospital!'

The hospital was defended by a section of West Yorks and a score of walking wounded. Evans realized there was little he could do to help, because artillery and mortar shelling would be indiscriminate, and the West Yorks he had in reserve did not know the hospital lay-out. A carrier was sent in, but the Japanese used grenades to drive it back.

In the hospital itself, the orderly medical officer, Lieutenant Basu of the Indian Medical Service, was interrogated by the Japanese commander. They had taken many of the patients prisoner and had bound them, hands tied tightly behind their backs. They also compelled the Indian medical officers to hand over the drugs, quinine, morphine, anti-tetanus, throwing away the rest. The following morning, the prisoners were dragged out of the medical inspection room and mown down by automatic weapons fired from a carrier. Others were bayoneted in their beds. A party of twenty who were told, 'come and get treatment', were taken to a dried-up watercourse by a Japanese officer and then shot. Three survived. Lieutenant Basu was shot at twice and had the incredible luck merely to be stunned by the experience. He put out his hand where he lay and touched the body of a friend, whose blood he then smeared over his face and head and down his shirt so that the Japanese would think he was already finished. He slid into a trench and survived, unnoticed. When the West Yorks finally cleared the hospital area on 9 February they found the bodies of thirty-one patients and four doctors.

Awful as it was, then and in retrospect, the ferocity of Matsukihira's men is explainable: they were in a hurry. Their overall timetable was very short. After 'Tokuta' and Tanahashi annihilated 7 Division, they were to cross the Mayu Range and do the same with 5 Division which by then would be cut off from XV Corps Headquarters at Bawli Bazar by Kubo Force, a battalion from the Japanese 33 Division which had swept across from the east and gripped the north-south road back to India with a stranglehold on 8 February. Two days later Tanahashi Force was in touch with elements of Doi Force from the main body of 55 Division, thus effectively encircling 7 Indian Division. Messervy brought into the Admin Box area two of his outlying battalions and the men in the Box dug in, prepared to resist to the last. The Box perimeter was not continuously held but defended by a mixture of odds and sods and a few infantry companies: the 2 West Yorks and a battalion of 4/8 Gurkhas from 89 Brigade of 7 Division (less two companies). These infantry companies were given the most vital spots to cover: the western entrance and eastern exit to the Box of the Ngakyedauk Pass Road. The odds and sods – officers' shop troops, clerks, transport troops – were formed in small boxes at fixed intervals round the perimeter.

Sometimes the Japanese inability to change a plan once they decided on it brought them needless casualties in their attempt to gain and keep an entrance into the Box. Evans describes how RSM Maloney of the West Yorks was in command of a defence post covering a bend in a *chaung* which came down from the hills south of the Box. After the siege had been under way for four nights, Maloney and his party heard footsteps coming along the *chaung* bed, which was overhung by high banks. Two Japanese were moving towards the Box and were promptly despatched. The following night a larger group of Japanese took exactly the same direction. Maloney was on the alert and told his men to do nothing until he gave the command. They had four grenades each and their rifles. Slowly the Japanese came into view. The West Yorks began to count. 'Christ!' thought one of them, 'there must be more than forty of the buggers!'[1] Maloney waited until they reached the bend in the *chaung*. His men then hurled their grenades from the high bank. Rifle fire finished off most of the few survivors who scrambled up the bank, apart from a Japanese officer who brought up the rear. He leaped into a trench, to find himself confronted by a West Yorks sergeant. The officer tried to slice him in two with his sword, which the sergeant parried with his rifle butt. A West Yorks corporal then jumped into the trench and the two of them bayoneted the officer to death. The body was searched for documents which were sent off to 7 Division HQ. One of these was a map showing rendezvous points where parties were to concentrate before attacking the Box. The bend in the *chaung* was one of these points and in spite of the disaster which had wiped out several score of them already, the Japanese kept coming on. In the end, 110 bodies were counted at the spot.

In contrast to that relatively inexpensive encounter, other infantry combat was fierce, hard-fought and ruthless. A Japanese medical officer looking over the types of wound suffered by men of 112 Infantry Regiment noticed that they were chiefly bullet wounds and stab wounds from bayonets, indicating the ferocity of close-quarter fighting. The Japanese were stoical about the results of this, as about much else. A tough and robust sergeant was taken prisoner during the siege with a

[1] Geoffrey Evans, *The Desert and the Jungle*, p. 109

bullet wound in his left shoulder. When the British medical officer came to examine it, he saw the wound was crawling with maggots. The Japanese sergeant was totally unconcerned.

But what swayed the battle was not infantry engagements. The massed artillery and tanks in the Box did that. The tanks were scattered during the day and hidden among the hills at night, acting as mobile bunkers against Japanese infiltrators. When the Sugiyama Battalion put in a night attack against the southern end of the Box from Hill 315 it was the tanks which finally repulsed them. The only solution, as far as Sugiyama could see, was to send in suicide squads, which he did. Three NCOs with three or four men each hurled themselves against the Lees of 25 Dragoons, but to no purpose. They were all wiped out before they reached their objective.

This was the pattern of many attacks. On both 14 and 16 February, Tanahashi carried out a night-raid – 'Tokuta's' favourite tactic – with three battalions, Matsukihira, Matsuo, Sugiyama. They burst into the Box at 10.20 pm, yelling and shouting. The night throbbed with screams, rifle fire and shell fire, but Tanahashi could wrest no decisive victory in the face of determined British resistance. His men were held up on the barbed wire, the night was brilliant with star shells and the tanks poured machine-gun fire into the Japanese until their casualties forced them back. The British knew the attack was coming, as Sakurai's wireless order for a general all-out attack at 1400 hours on the 14th had been intercepted.

The Japanese did succeed in capturing a height known as C Company Hill which guarded the western gate to the Box. They swept a company of West Yorks off the hill, and found they could overlook the new position of the hospital; a thought which, when he was told what had happened, gave Evans the horrors – he had not forgotten the events of 7 February. In addition, the Japanese on C Company Hill were only 300 yards from Box HQ.

The Box was so crammed with men, vehicles and stores that it was difficult for the Japanese fire *not* to find a target. So the hospital filled up with casualties. Two grimy unshaven surgeons, their rubber aprons dripping blood, worked away, as one infantry officer described it, 'like a pair of knackers'.[1] Stores had been hit, too. Seventy-five Zero fighters of 5 Air Division had twice set ablaze dumps on Ammunition Hill, and sent heavy shells bursting through the flaming night.

Evans knew he had to get back C Company Hill. Ten tanks of 25 Dragoons directed the fire of their 75s against it and continued to blaze away while Major O'Hara of A Company of the West Yorks took his men up the slope. The tanks' high explosive tore the jungle to shreds until a Very light from O'Hara went up into the sky a short distance from the hilltop. The tank gunners instantly changed from high explosive to solid shot,

[1] ibid., p. 113

which enabled the infantry to advance close behind the curtain of fire without fear of shell bursts wounding them instead of the Japanese. Fifteen yards behind the shells, O'Hara sent up another Very light to tell the tanks to stop. Then the West Yorks went in with the bayonet. The hill was back in British hands.

Not with impunity, however. The two companies, A and B, of the West Yorks, which had acted as Evans's mobile reserve, were down to half their strength and could only boast around 100 men each. But Tanahashi's units had suffered too. In his diary 'Tokuta' noted that the strength of Tanahashi Force on 11 February was 2190 men. On the 21st, it was down to 400, and most of those casualties were the result of that night attack.

No wonder Tanahashi cut wireless communication with his force commander on 22 February. 'The British are cutting through the jungle,' wrote 'Tokuta' that day, 'they seem to be no more than fifty yards away. I hope and pray Tanahashi's attack tonight succeeds.' But Tanahashi did not attack. It was no use Sakurai insisting that if men did not resolve to die, they would not defeat the enemy. Tanahashi had pushed his men as far as they would go, and was on edge himself. He ordered an attack on 19 February, and gave a fire plan to Ohara, the commander of his mountain artillery. 'We can't mount an attack of that kind,' Ohara told him. Before Ohara knew what was happening Tanahashi was roaring at him, 'Are you saying I don't know what artillery can do and what it cannot do?' and he struck the gunner commander on the head with his clenched fist until the blood came.

The postponement by two days of the attack timed for 22 February was not Tanahashi's first or last despairing gesture. He had already put off an attack due on the 19th to the 20th. When the 20th came, he proposed the 22nd. He was down to 400 men and each of his companies could muster no more than forty or fifty men apiece. The mountain guns had no ammunition left, and his men had nothing to eat except unhulled rice collected locally in their steel helmets. In the end, he cut wireless contact with 'Tokuta' from 2 pm on the 22nd and, ignoring Hanaya's furious order to put in an attack, made no move that night. Two days later, without waiting for 'Tokuta's' authorization, he began to shift his men south, back to their starting line, dissolving the encirclement of Sinzweya. He broke wireless silence to tell 'Tokuta' what he was going to do: 'I regret this, but am determined to do it; there is no alternative. Have decided to retreat tonight.' 'Tokuta' could not stop him. Two days later, after consulting with Sakurai, Hanaya permitted Phase One of the Sinzweya operation to come to an end.

Worst off, when the order to withdraw finally came through, was Kubo Force which had been operating between 5 Division and XV Corps at Bawli Bazar, raiding outposts, cutting the road down which British reinforcements passed. Kubo had forty miles to make through the British positions and he recalls passing through a British encampment where the troops, in astonished silence, watched the exhausted lines of Japanese infantry march south, bathed in moonlight, through gaps in the jungle. Kubo himself was wounded and his men carried him back the whole way on a stretcher.

In his diary for 26 February, 'Tokuta' jotted down the reasons for his failure. The operation had begun well, his men had moved fast, they had caught the British on the hop, they had surrounded 7 Division. But they had failed to destroy it. Inadequate communications and intelligence had not helped, nor had the impossibility of keeping open the supply roads. Even though he was an apostle of the night attack, he had to admit that darkness had been such that movement by night was at times almost impossible. His men needed more training in close combat with grenades and a more effective treatment of casualties.

But, as a later Japanese historian has seen, the most important factor was the altered geometry of the battlefield. The *flat* encirclement by the Japanese at Sinzweya, unaccompanied by adequate fire-power, was countered by the *cubic* tactics (*rittai senpō*) adopted by the British. The multi-directional defence made possible by air supply congealed the initial fluidity into a hardness which could only have been countered by stronger fire-power, which the Japanese simply did not have.[1] 'Tokuta' had four mountain guns and four medium howitzers, no more. The British cubic tactic could also have been countered by a strong fighter screen and harassing anti-aircraft fire. In fact the first supply planes were so heavily engaged on 8 February that they turned back, and it was not until the flight was taken charge of personally, by their commander, the US Brigadier General Old, who flew a plane himself, that they came through; an indication that if the Japanese had been able to put up a constant stream of fighter aircraft the British cubic tactics might not have worked.

Again, with strong firepower directed on the fuel and ammunition dumps in the crowded box, the Japanese could have caused chaos and destruction. If they had had anti-tank weapons, they could have countered the 25 Dragoons' Lees. As it was, they had bargained on the success of their traditional lightning attack and encirclement, which had never so far failed them, and always demoralised an enemy like the British who clung to their supply roads.

This is perhaps where the greatest change of all lay, and why Evans, Slim and Mountbatten regard the Battle of the Admin Box as the turning-point of *their* war against Japan. In his *March on Delhi* Colonel A. J. Barker says rather disparagingly, 'In Delhi... there was much congratulation... but the battle was not of the magnitude which the fuss at Delhi suggested it was. A total of five divisions and an enormous air effort

---

[1] OCH *Arakan Sakusen*, pp. 245–6

had held off an invasion of one third their strength.'[1] This is perfectly true, and as Mountbatten indicates in his *Report* (p. 44) the scope of the Arakan battlefield was limited, though the enemy left 5000 dead on the field. Nonetheless, he goes on to say, its significance must be judged by its effect on morale. It *was* a turning-point in the campaign for Burma because, in Slim's words,

> For the first time a British force had met, held and decisively defeated a major Japanese attack, and followed this up by driving the enemy out of the strongest possible natural positions that they had been preparing for months and were determined to hold at all costs. British and Indian soldiers had proved themselves, man for man, the masters of the best the Japanese could bring against them... It was a victory, a victory about which there could be no argument and its effect, not only on the troops engaged, but on the whole XIV Army, was immense.[2]

British plans

The Japanese plan for Imphal was not difficult to forecast, in outline, and Lieutenant-General Geoffrey Scoones, GOC IV Corps, knew fairly precisely what they would attempt: an approach through Tiddim, breaking into the Imphal Plain at Torbung, in the south-west corner; an attack through Tamu and Palel, in the south-east corner; and attempts to cut the British supply road from Dimapur into Imphal, most probably at Kohima.

The British had their own plans, and it suited Slim and Scoones that the Japanese should put Imphal under siege. The British would then withdraw their outlying troops, close in on themselves like a box, and allow the Japanese to advance at the end of difficult lines of communication, with their supply problems getting worse day by day. If cut off, IV Corps would be supplied by air from bases further back in Assam. The Japanese did not have mastery of the air, and air supply was therefore out of the question for them. And although the Chindwin was navigable as far north as Tamanthi, and supplies could be brought by water as well as by rail from Rangoon, once the Japanese had entered the mountains between the Chindwin and Imphal they were going to find supply the most acute problem of all. Some at any rate of their forces – in the upshot, 15 and 31 Divisions – would have to cross the grain of the country, up and down murderously steep jungle-clad slopes for 150 miles or more. The rest – in the upshot, 33 Division –

---

[1] Barker, *March on Delhi*, p. 92

[2] Slim, op.cit., pp. 246–7

would approach from the south along the grain of the hills and would therefore be able to bring up heavy guns and tanks. Tanks would be used, too, in the Kabaw Valley, treacherous though the terrain was.

The British got their facts about forces and directions nearly right. They got the timing wrong, a mistake which nearly proved fatal to 17 Division, whose HQ was at Milestone 102 on the Imphal-Tiddim Road, well across the frontier into Burma. The date on which the British expected the Japanese to move was 15 March 1944, and that was indeed the date on which 15 and 31 Divisions crossed the Chindwin at a number of points north of Tamu. But the Japanese 33 Division, south of Kalemyo, began to move on 8 March from the Fort White area which it had seized from 17 Indian Division in November 1943.

IV Corps was scattered. 23 Division, which had been involved in operations continuously since June 1942 without a break – and for much of the time had been ravaged by malaria – had been withdrawn from Tamu to rest in the Imphal Plain, and 20 Division had taken over the Tamu area.[1] 50 Indian Parachute Brigade was posted north-east of Imphal, covering the approaches to the plain from the Chindwin via Sangshak and Ukhrul. As Slim had only anticipated that a single Japanese regiment was likely to attack Kohima, it was 'defended' by units from 202 L of C area.

It was not easy to pass from one IV Corps division to another. There were no lateral communications between 17 and 20 Division, for instance, so to travel from one to the other meant going into the Plain and out again, a possible journey of 250 miles. Scoones knew his forces were too dispersed to fight a major battle and ran the risk of being eaten up piecemeal by a Japanese offensive. When the time came, then, they would have to concentrate. That time would be when more than one battalion of Japanese were observed crossing the Chindwin, and when that happened, 20 Division was instructed to move up the Palel Road from Tamu, fighting delaying actions, and then stop definitively at Shenam.[2]

Now 20 Division, after much effort and intensive patrolling, had established domination of the Tamu and Kabaw Valley area during the winter months. Its commanding general, Douglas Gracey, was confident of being able to handle any Japanese assault, and intensely grieved when Scoones indicated to him that he might have to relinquish positions which his men had fought hard months to win, simply in order to concentrate on the Imphal Plain. Scoones had been persuading Gracey of the need to build roads in his divisional area, but wrote in a different tune on 7 February 1944, telling him of the Arakan battle, hinting that Japanese infiltration round Gracey's 20 Division positions was also a possibility, hoping that his

---

[1] In November 1942, Lieutenaut-General Reginald Savory's 23 Division was 5000 men short of a strength of 17,000 (cf Evans and Brett-James, *Imphal*, p. 33).

[2] Lewin, *Slim*, p. 169

defences were sound and finally – a sinister addendum – that he had made 'all arrangements for destroying documents in an emergency'.[1]

A MOST SECRET letter was despatched a week later telling Gracey that the Japanese had outflanked 17 Division. It repeated the order to 17 Division to withdraw to the Imphal Plain. Later still, when Gracey himself received orders to withdraw into Imphal from his long-prepared positions, he naturally jibbed, and wondered whether Scoones was giving him all the information about the coming battle he should have.

[1] Gracey Papers, 40, 150, Liddell Hart Archive.

4. THE BASE

Imphal and Kohima: March – July 1944

Imphal — Black Cats vs. White Tigers (Round One):
Tiddim, Tongzang, Torbung — Shenam-Palel (i) —
The taking of Sangshak — Shenam-Palel (ii) —
Kohima Phase One: the assault and the siege —
Black Cats vs. White Tigers (Round Two): on to
Bishenpur — The Battle for Nungshigum — The
Inspector from Tokyo — General Kawabe goes to
see for himself — Kohima Phase Two: Durhams
and Dorsets on Garrison Hill; cavalry to the rescue
— Black Cats vs. White Tigers (Round Three): the
Silchar track, Potsangbam and Ninthoukhong —
Kohima Phase Three: Sato vs. Mutaguchi — 'The
Road is Open' — Yamauchi's swansong — Uehara's
poison gas — the adventures of Lt Shima —
Shenam-Palel (iii) — Kohima Phase Four: Sato
dismissed — U-GO comes to an end

Imphal was not a single engagement but a complex series of battles lasting five months, ranging from the banks of the Chindwin to the road beyond Kohima, well inside Assam. The operation was, after much discussion, authorized by Imperial General Headquarters in Tokyo on 7 January 1944. As we have seen, the Japanese attacked first in Arakan, where Sakurai's 28 Army tried to prevent reserves from XV Corps reinforcing the central front at Imphal, an attempt which failed.

Mutaguchi's 15 Army began its offensive in the first week in March. 33 Division (Yanagida) struck at 17 Indian Division (Cowan) from the south, aiming at Imphal along the road from Tiddim to Bishenpur. A week later, 33 Division's Infantry Group, Yamamoto Force, came up

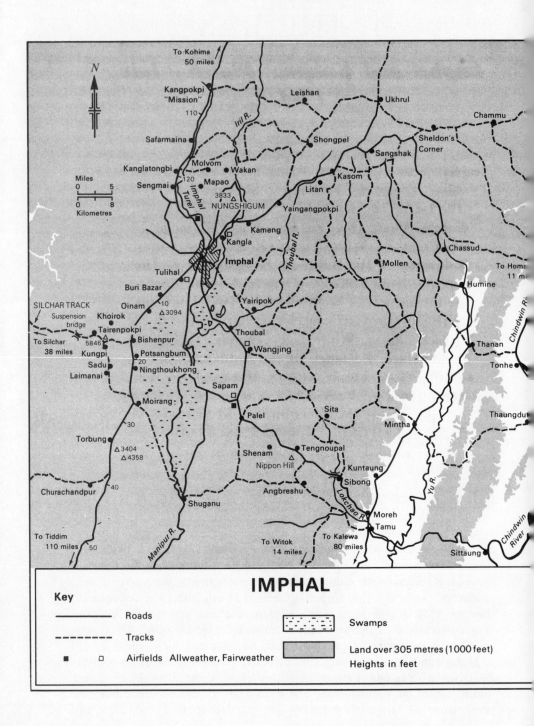

IMPHAL

Key

————————	Roads
- - - - - - - - -	Tracks
■ □	Airfields Allweather, Fairweather

Swamps

Land over 305 metres (1000 feet)

Heights in feet

the Kabaw Valley against 20 Indian Division (Gracey) and tried to force a way into the Imphal Plain across the hills to Palel. They were stopped at the group of hills called the Shenam Saddle. A very much depleted 15 Division (Yamauchi) marched across the mountains north-east of Imphal and cut the main road to Kohima north of Kanglatongbi. They remained astride the road until they were forced off it in early June. Further north still, 31 Division (Sato) marched from the Chindwin to Kohima, took all but a few hill patches of the little town, and blocked IV Corps' reinforcements from the railhead at Dimapur, completing the isolation of Imphal. In some of the bitterest fighting of the war, Sato was finally prised out of Kohima in June. Lt-General Kawabe, the Commander-in-Chief of Burma Area Army in Rangoon, conceded defeat in July, bringing the operation officially to a close.

Mutaguchi had planned a brief three weeks' campaign. His men were to be supplied first with meat on the hoof, then with rations and arms captured from the British. But the cattle died, and the dumps at Imphal remained in British hands. Lacking air cover and outgunned on the ground, the battered, starving and diseased remnants of Mutagachi's three divisions crawled back into Burma, bringing with them the Indians of Bose's Indian National Army. Slim's defeat of 15 Army meant that Central Burma was open to him, and a campaign to retake Burma overland, which the British high command had flinched from for two years, became a real possibility. It was the biggest defeat the Japanese Army had sustained in its whole history.

Imphal

Imphal is the capital of Manipur State, India's easternmost province, the boundary state between India and Burma. Four hundred miles from Calcutta and seventy miles from the Burmese border, it is really a group of villages surrounded by groves of plantain and bamboo. The Manipuris are Hindus, ruled in 1944 by a Maharajah. One-tenth of the population is Muslim. The hill peoples of the state are the nomadic Kukis, and the Nagas who live in semi-fortified villages on the hilltops. Some of them are Christians, converted by the efforts of an American Baptist mission in the nineteenth century. The Manipuris rebelled against British rule in 1891 but since the quelling of that rebellion the state had been at peace – partly, no doubt, because of its isolation. Imphal is cut off from the outside world in a basin – the Imphal Plain – thirty miles long and twenty miles across, lying 2600 feet above sea-level, on all sides of which lie jungle-covered mountains. To the north and east the Naga Hills rise to 5000 feet in height. To the south, the Chin Hills can rise to 6000 feet, with some peaks reaching 9000 feet.

Between hills and town lies the Logtak Lake, a low-lying swamp ablaze with flowers, as are the hedges and riverbanks. Embedded in bougainvillea, snapdragon and lupin, the neat bungalows of the cantonment contained, in pre-war days, around a dozen members of the European community, in whose lives golf, tennis and duck-shooting loomed large. The brickwalled old citadel and the ruined Palace stood along the shallow brown Manipur River, in contrast with the bright white of the new Palace built outside the town, and the gold-leaf of temple domes.

Administratively, Manipur was a Native State, and the nearest outpost of British India lay to the west at Cachar, in Assam. Silchar, the headquarters station of Assam, could be reached by a track from Imphal which wandered across rivers and through mountain passes for 130 miles. It is monsoon country. In May, rivers, swampland and the parched stubble of the rice-paddies change their nature. The torrential rains turn paths to mud, streams to maelstroms and ricefields into little lakes. When the sun strikes through the grey or purple storm clouds, the landscape gleams with reflections from surface water or temple roof, and from the rich green of the forests on the steep mountain slopes.

Imphal's remoteness conceals both beauty and terror.[1] Apart from the western foothills, which are treeless, around the Plain there are green wooded ridges and deep ravines, made magnificent by trees of all shapes and sizes, like the huge peepul tree outside the town, which separates the traffic on either side, peach trees rising to a height of twenty feet, oak scrub, teak, wild banana trees, and feathery bamboos. And there are flowers: purple iris, white jasmine, the maroon and gold of African marigolds, festoons of lilac creepers, primulas and asters clinging to brown grass on the slopes, and row upon row of terraced rice paddy spread out like fans on the hillsides. These hills, and the Plain itself, shelter a great variety of bird life, from the commonplace wagtail and pigeon to the glamour of the golden oriole. Game birds – snipe, duck, geese – are plentiful on Logtak Lake and its islets. Animals too: deer, flying foxes, elephants, and now and then an occasional marauding tiger or leopard. There are snakes of all kinds, cobras, kraits, hamadryads; and insect life in abundance – tiger mosquitoes, leeches, and, lower down in the scale but more important for man, the amoebas which bring dysentery. East of the Plain, where the road to Tamu runs across the Shenam Saddle through magnificent countryside, a hill named Typhus Hill testifies to the deceptive beauty of the landscape. A hundred men of the Devon Regiment found this an attractive camp site where green bamboo was growing afresh after being cut. But the hill was infested with the mite that carries scrub typhus. Seventy of the hundred were infected, and fifteen died.

---

[1] Not everyone saw it so: to the historian of the Dorset Regiment, it was a 'collection of bashas in a hot, malarial plain', (Lieutenant-Colonel O. G. White, *Straight on for Tokyo*, p. 155.)

Imphal was a hunter's paradise, the last place on earth one would choose as the venue of a vast military campaign. Yet it was here that Japanese, British, Indians, Gurkhas, arrived in 1944 to kill each other in their thousands. The Japanese were driven by the dream of invading India: the others by the need to stop them.

Black Cats vs. White Tigers (Round One):
Tiddim, Tongzang, Torbung[1]

33 Division's plan to destroy 17 Indian Division made good sense and came within an ace of success. It followed the classic Japanese pattern of encirclement which had worked against British forces so often before. But in Arakan, in February 1944, the British stopped behaving according to the Malaya and early Burma pattern: retreating when surrounded, and being forced to fight through road blocks set up behind them. Instead, they stood and fought where they were, since they no longer needed to rely on a road. Food and ammunition were dropped from the skies. Mutaguchi's plan was drawn up in 1943, before the Japanese could learn this lesson.

17 Indian Division was distributed between Tongzang, just over 110 miles south of Imphal, and Tiddim, about forty miles further south. Just north of Tongzang, at MS 109, lay a huge dump where stocks had been built up in preparation for the proposed British invasion of Burma.

The division was not supposed to stay and fight at Tiddim. It was no part of Lieutenant-General Scoones's strategy to fight with his units parcelled out along the roads leading from Imphal into Burma. When the expected Japanese onslaught came, the divisions were to withdraw into the Imphal Plain, shortening communications and forming a hard core of tanks and guns round 'the Citadel' – the town of Imphal itself – against which the Japanese, their lines of communication stretched to the utmost, would batter in vain. But this plan depended on good intelligence, swift reaction to it, and swifter action to follow. None of these were forthcoming in the first weeks of March 1944. In the event, the detailed intelligence was patchy, the reaction to it slow, and the action delayed just long enough to put the whole of 17 Division at risk.

Against 17 Division, Yanagida and his 33 Division sent three prongs: a

---

[1] The 'Black Cat' was 17 Division's divisional emblem, and the Japanese recognized it, and sometimes referred to the division as *Kuroneko Shidan*, 'The Black Cat Division'. The term 'White Tigers' is how 33 Division referred to itself, and a white tiger figures on some of its flags. The reference is to one of the groups of warriors of the Aizu clan during the disturbances of 1868, the tiger being one of four animals placed by Chinese astrology at the four points of the compass: red sparrow, green dragon, black tortoise and white tiger. The White Tigers were seventeen-year-old sons of samurai, forced to retreat into the castle of Wakamatsu by the imperial forces. Twenty of them committed suicide when they believed the castle had fallen. Wakamatsu is part of 33 Divisional district.

central column straight up the main road to Tiddim from Fort White, which the Japanese had occupied in November 1943; a left column hooking up through the hills west of the road and coming in on the road around MS 100; and a right column starting from Yazagyo along tracks through Phaitu, ending up just east of Tongzang and then hooking north to take the dump at MS 109. 33 Division was timed to move on 'Y-Day' (7/8 March 1944), a week before 'X-Day', the date of departure for the main body of 15 Army. The discrepancy misled Slim and Scoones, who had calculated that the Japanese forces would be on the move around 15 March. Nonetheless, Scoones had taken what he thought was a reasonable precaution. Slim had left him to decide exactly when he should withdraw his divisions back into Imphal and he determined to give the signal only when he was convinced a major offensive had begun; when, say, a force a battalion strong had crossed the Chindwin and moved west.

The commander of 17 Division, Major-General 'Punch' Cowan, was still under orders to march on Kalemyo as a preliminary to re-entering Central Burma, but he was aware that if the Japanese pre-empted his advance he was to move back, so he regrouped his two brigades.[1]

63 Brigade (Burton) acted as mobile reserve between Kennedy Peak and Tiddim and 48 Brigade (Cameron) was between Kennedy Peak and Vangte. A force of two battalions, with artillery, covered Tongzang and the bridge at MS 126 over the Manipur River, a vital link on Cowan's retreat road from Tiddim to Imphal. Division HQ was at Tiddim.

The warning was in fact given soon enough. A patrol from 1/10 Gurkhas (63 Brigade) spotted movement across the Manipur River near Mualbem, about twelve miles south of Tiddim, on 8 March. They counted 2000 men[2] with guns and pack animals, in effect the main body of Colonel Sasahara's 215 Infantry Regiment. The Japanese moved north from Mualbem through Kaptel (where locals reported their movement to the British) from which they were bound for the village of Singgel at MS 100, where they intended to cut 17 Division's passage north.

Now the eyes of IV Corps, a body of British officers and local agents called V Force, and other forces operating behind the Japanese lines or in the areas between the armies, patrolled the area west of the Manipur River. If a large body of Japanese was on the move in the hills west of the road, they should have been spotted, but no confirmation of the Gurkhas' report was forthcoming from this source. And as only two Gurkha sepoys had seen the Japanese crossing, the report was not acted upon.

Then, three days after the Gurkhas, V Force sent a message. Two columns of Japanese, about 1500 strong, had been sighted near Mualnuam,

---

[1] Kirby, *War Against Japan*, III, p. 193

[2] Kirby, op.cit., III, p. 193; but '50' according to the official Indian Army History, *Reconquest of Burma*, I, p. 187

moving north. Mualnuam was about twenty miles north of the crossing point where the Gurkhas had their sighting. V Force's report was sent on 11 March. Scoones received it the next day, and almost at once came the news that a strong force of Japanese had reached the hills west of the Tiddim Road, near MS 108. These reports were surely indicative of the movement of the same Japanese unit, which was obviously bound for the dump at MS 109 and the bridge across the Manipur River.

Alarmed by the information, Scoones ordered his corps machine gun company, 9 Jats, down to guard the bridge, but as Tonforce (two battalions detached by Cowan to defend Tongzang) was already on the spot, the Jats were set to guard the dump, then defended only by administrative troops. This was on 13 March. With Sasahara's appearance on the heights west of 17 Division's lifeline, Scoones realized how critical the situation had suddenly become, and he resolved to send 37 Brigade from 23 Division down the Tiddim Road to help Cowan's men back. This was stripping 'the Citadel' with a vengeance. It left a single brigade inside Imphal.

On 13 March, Scoones finally gave Cowan the order to move back.[1] The Japanese were already across the road in several places so it was late enough. But, inexplicably, Cowan took his time. He only issued orders to move at 1 pm the following day, and told the division to start out at 5 pm. It was a massive operation. From a twenty-mile area, Cowan pulled in 16,000 troops, 2500 vehicles, and 3500 mules and set them off northwards. Tiddim was booby-trapped. Unhindered, the Division reached Tongzang, where a very different picture was revealed.

On 13 March Cowan told 63 Brigade to cover Tongzang which was then under attack by Colonel Sakuma's 214 Infantry Regiment. But Tonforce had not been able to stop the Japanese bypassing the village – they slipped round through the jungle to the north – and blocking the road at Tuitum Saddle, at MS 132, which put them between Cowan and the Manipur River bridge.

The column of 33 Division which was to capture the positions of 17 Division was 214 Infantry Regiment commanded by Colonel Sakuma Takanobu. He sent one force straight up the main road to Imphal under the command of the Division's Engineer Colonel, Hagi. His second battalion (Major Ogawa Sadao) attacked south of Tongzang, and his first battalion (Captain Saito) put in an attack on Tuitum, north of Tongzang. Colonel Sasahara (215 Infantry Regiment), commanding Yanagida's left column, slipped into the hills on the right bank of the Manipur River and made for Singgel, north of Tongzang, at MS 100 from Imphal. In this way Yanagida expected to cut the path of 17 Division in several places, as it made for the plain.

---

[1] 'during the morning of the 13th', Kirby, *The War Against Japan*, III, p. 194 (1961); 'soon after half past eight on the evening of March 13th', Evans and Brett-James, *Imphal*, p. 114 (1962); 'At 2040 hours on 13 March', *Reconquest of Burma*, I, p. 190 (1958).

On 14 March, Yanagida received a report that 17 Division had been surrounded. Overjoyed, his fears about the offensive momentarily stilled, he decided to move his headquarters forward to the village of Khamzang on the following day. The staff officer who had been attached to him from Mutaguchi's headquarters, Major Fujiwara, was sure things were going well, and returned to report the great initial success to Army headquarters in Maymyo. Then things began to go very wrong.

Saito Battalion (1/214) was responsible for cutting the road by occupying the Tuitum Saddle and reached it at dawn on 14 March, having lost their battalion gun down a precipice en route. Saito's men found they couldn't dig in very effectively, as the rockbed was close to the soil surface, and in the daylight, when they were fired on by artillery and mortars from the north bank of the Manipur River and Tongzang, they sustained heavy casualties. They repulsed an attack at noon on 15 March by about 300 British and Indian troops and managed to secure their position by sunset but only just. Saito knew he would not be able to hold after the next day, and he decided to put in a night attack.

Advancing along a ridge to the hill-top, his men were met by heavy machine-gun fire from the flank. Bodies tumbled into the valley, the battalion broke up in disorder and Saito and his orderly were cut off. They made their way south to regimental HQ, and the other survivors reached Luntak on 18/19 March, although Saito was unable to bring them all under command before the 26th. 17 Indian Division was enabled to withdraw through Tuitum as a result.

Cowan's orders to 63 Brigade (Burton) on the night of 16 March were crisp and clear: 'Forget those bloody Japs and keep your eye on the ball.' In other words, clear the division's road north back to Imphal. Burton called down an air-strike and most of the divisional artillery upon the Japanese. The artillery fired over open sights and the 1/3 Gurkhas then charged their hill-top position to find that half the Japanese battalion had been destroyed. Sasahara's third battalion, under Major Sueki, was attacked by 48 Brigade of 17 Division, under a Brigadier who had scores to settle. Cameron was a Gurkha battalion commander at the battle for the Sittang bridge two years before, and when the bridge was blown, had had to make the decision to leave behind Gurkhas he had known from the day of their recruitment twenty years before. His hair went white in a single night. He had no intention of being trounced a second time by 33 Division, and put in a fierce attack on Sueki. In the fight, Sueki lost three company commanders, and half his battalion were either killed or wounded.

The Japanese tried to rectify the situation by sending in tanks. Six light tanks of 14 Tank Regiment led an advance through the thick darkness of the night of 22 March. Suddenly the Japanese infantry heard the sound of explosions. The six tanks had been destroyed by land mines. The attack came to a halt. The next day, north of Singgel, Lt-Col. Irie fell to cannon shell fired from a British fighter plane.[1] His death hit the battalion hard. What little fighting spirit they had left after their pounding vanished, and both officers and men made for the shelter of the wooded hills. Sasahara relied on Irie. Of all his battalion commanders Irie was the one he trusted most. Two days after Irie's death, on 25 March, Sasahara received a signal from Sueki on Hill 3299. 'The battalion is burning its code books and destroying its W/T sets, resolved to fight to the last man.' Sasahara saw his whole regiment facing annihilation, and sent his Operations Staff Officer, Lt Katayama Tōru, to both first and third battalions. They were to relax their grip on the road. There was no point in attempting to hold 17 Division in the face of such losses. Sasahara should not have given that order without reference to the divisional commander. Instead, he sent him a signal saying what was happening, and asserting, as Sueki had done, his resolve to fight to the last.

That signal was incorrectly received, and the mistake had a crucial effect on the battle. When he had sent it, Sasahara gathered the officers and men of his regimental headquarters and told them what he had done. 'The last hour has come. When the enemy puts in his attack, we will fight, and I will be in front. I know you will fight bravely to the end.' He poured some *sake* in a mess-tin lid, took a sip, and handed round the cup of farewell to his men. Where they drank it, on the mountain slope, a pink flower like a rhododendron grew here and there. Lt Ueda, one of his young officers, thought briefly and without regret what it would be like to die among the flowers on the mountain.

The signal, as Yanagida received it, said nothing about resolving to fight to the end. It simply said Sasahara was destroying his code books and burning the flag. Clearly, Yanagida thought, his force was being destroyed. He summoned his signals officer and told him to address a MOST SECRET telegram to XV Army. There is no question of taking Imphal in three weeks, he wired to Mutaguchi. With the onset of the monsoon, and supply problems, we are inviting a tragedy; and the British airborne forces dropped in central Burma have rendered the defence of Burma critical. Mutaguchi was furious. He summoned every angry reprimand in his vocabulary and signalled back to Yanagida to get on with his advance. Fujiwara was told to get back to 33 Division and see Yanagida complied with the order.

Yanagida may seem volatile. Lt Sugimoto, his adjutant, had already had his suspicions about the general's firmness of purpose. On the way to Khamzang, the headquarters had passed through Fort Peacock, which the division had taken a few days before. Traces of the battle were still visible, and the bodies of the defenders still lay in the heat, swollen corpses rotting fast, with maggots crawling in and out of eyeballs. 'Look, maggots, Your

---

[1] OCH, *Inpāru Sakusen*, I, p. 184, says it was from heavy artillery gunfire.

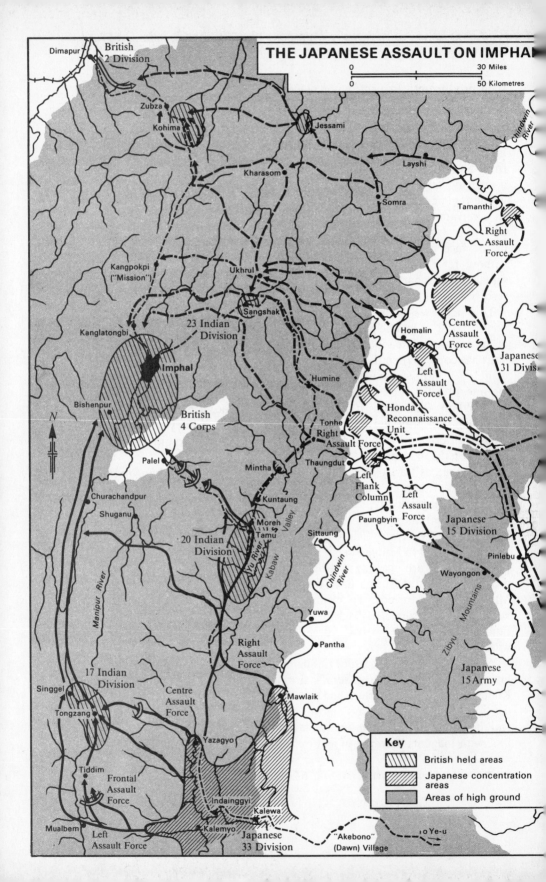

Excellency!' Sugimoto called out. He had been a platoon commander in China and was no stranger to corpses. However, it was the first time Yanagida had been on a battlefield. He glanced, turned away, and passed by. Later on, when the division's casualties were passing through the headquarters area, pitiful blood-soaked figures, covered in mud, Yanagida shut himself up in his tent. He was, Sugimoto thought, unable to endure the tragic condition of his men. He had already crossed swords with Colonel Tanaka, his Chief of Staff, and Sugimoto had heard Yanagida, in his tent with voice raised, proclaiming 'I am the divisional commander. The command of the division is my job.' And Tanaka replying: 'I am Chief of Staff. The divisional staff is *my* responsibility and *I* carry out the operations.' Tanaka was a tough character, very much in sympathy with Mutaguchi. He was wild with rage when Yanagida reacted as he did to Sasahara's signal.

The reaction was, in fact, precipitate. Things were bad. But Sueki's battalion had *not* been annihilated. Miura, a divisional staff officer who had been in the Tongzang area, had a W/T set in his truck and heard Sasahara's signal coming in, and the impression *he* got from it was that Sueki and Sasahara were simply intimating their resolve to fight on. But the situation was disturbing enough for Miura to go into Tongzang and climb a tower, about fifty feet high, in the middle of the village. He took his binoculars and scanned the countryside. Tongzang itself was on a height, so he had a good view. He could not see Singgel, to the north-west, because of the hills, but looking east he could make out Hill 3299, or at any rate its western slope. White smoke was rising from it, and the flash of mountain guns. Sueki was still holding out.

The details of the complicated and bloody fighting on the Tiddim road can best be summed up in Slim's own image: 'a Neapolitan ice of layers of our own troops alternating with Japanese.' Reading from north to south, 23 Division's two brigades, 37 (transferred from the Kohima-Dimapur road area), and 49 (transferred from the Ukhrul area), were pressing down the road to the relief of 17 Indian Division, the leading brigade of which, on 15 March, was at MS 82 south of Imphal. Next there was an area from MS 100 to MS 109 (17 Division's supply depot) blocked by Japanese infiltrators. Then a small British force was at the depot. Japanese were again in Tongzang once 17 Division had passed through that village. Then again came 17 Division moving north, and lastly the Japanese in hot pursuit coming up from Tiddim.

The depot at MS 109 was a problem. Thousands of non-combatant troops left it during 18 March, but the force left behind could not hold it against Sasahara's battalions and the Japanese took it and gleefully re-ported their seizure of enough food, ammunition and vehicles to run a division for two months. Watchers from the hill-tops saw them careering round the dump in captured jeeps. But the Manipur River bridge had been held and 17 Division crossed it safely on 17 March. 48 Brigade was then put in to clear the road block intercepting the division's route back to the plain. Marching along the ridges from the village of Sakawng (north of Tongzang) to a position above MS 109, Cameron's men attacked the Japanese on 21 and 22 March, helped by a strike of RAF fighter bombers. These were unopposed by Japanese aircraft, who later put in one brief appearance over the battlefield ('five minutes' reported one disgusted Japanese observer) but did not intervene again. The depot was recaptured from the Japanese on the 25th and much of the equipment recovered.

Among the signs of a rapid Japanese departure were unmade beds and scattered bottles of gin. And more grisly indications: the bodies of two Indian POWs were discovered, hanging naked. They had been used for bayonet practice, and although 17 Division was not unused to Japanese atrocities by this time, 'It was', remarked one staff officer, 'quite the most horrifying sight I saw during the entire war.'

During the battle, Allied air superiority was clearly demonstrated. Cowan's men were supplied by air when the road from Imphal was blocked, and the Japanese planes only flew over once. This was on 25 March when 5 Air Division was asked to co-operate in the battle near Tongzang. The request was made at noon, and in the afternoon ten Japanese fighters and three light bombers appeared overhead and bombed the Manipur River crossing-point. The Japanese were overjoyed to see the red-spot markings they had missed for so long, and jumped up and down in glee as the planes came in. Seizing the opportunity, the Japanese mountain and heavy artillery began to fire simultaneously, the mountain artillery on British positions north of Tongzang and the heavy guns at a motorized unit hidden near the road and gun positions on the other bank of the Manipur River. But the heavy artillery had only twenty rounds per gun, and when the planes flew off, the British artillery began to shoot once more.[1]

On 26 March, 63 Brigade followed the division across the Manipur River bridge. The Japanese heard the sound of a huge explosion, and saw black smoke rising into the sky. 17 Division were over the river, and had blown up the bridge behind them.

When Miura returned to the division to report, he found Tanaka sunk in gloom because of Yanagida's signal to Army. 'The divisional commander has signalled a recommendation to stop the operation. Bloody fool! How can you start an operation like this and then tell everybody, About turn? Mutaguchi's sent back a real rocket. And of course he'll blame me.' 'I'd better report,' ventured Miura. 'Don't listen to his whining,' was Tanaka's parting shot.[2] Puzzled, Miura went to the divisional signals office and

---

[1] No. 1 Mountain Artillery Bn (Mizawa) had received a supply of 300 rounds on the night of 24 March.

[2] Takagi, *Inpāru*, p. 70

checked the telegram. It was as he suspected. Only half the text he had heard got through, possibly because the set didn't work well back to division across the steep hills. At any rate, when he saw Yanagida's face, grim and pale, he tried to clear up the business of the signal, but it was too late. Yanagida was convinced that 'fight to the last man' was a fact not a resolve.[1] The confident mood of a few days before had gone. In its place was doubt and the fear of losing his men. Perhaps he had seized upon the occasion to pour forth to Mutaguchi his true opinion of the likely failure of the operation.

After the battle for Tongzang, Yanagida talked to his staff officer (Intelligence) Major Okamoto Iwao, and told him he expected the battle to be tough from then on, but wondered what Okamoto thought. Okamoto knew that Yanagida was keen on slowing down the advance, and felt distressed by this. Leaving the divisional commander's tent, he was called over by Colonel Tanaka, the Chief of Staff. 'What have you been talking to the divisional commander about? Don't listen to his complaints,' he said, in a loud voice that was intended to carry to Yanagida's tent. Okamoto felt keenly the unhappy mood in HQ, and asked to be transferred to a front line unit.

The following evening, at Burma Area Army headquarters in Rangoon, Lieutenant-General Kawabe looked gloomily through his window at the night sky. The meteorology section had reported that the monsoon was likely to break earlier that year. Three days before, Rangoon had been visited by a heavy thunderstorm. He turned to Naka, his Chief of Staff. 'Tell Mutaguchi not to let his front line divisions idle!' Mutaguchi needed no urging. He impressed on Fujiwara the need to get Yanagida moving, and fast. 'No question of marching on Imphal at one fell swoop,' was Yanagida's retort. 'Clearly, the enemy is ready for us. It's madness to advance without enough ammunition, food supplies, and adequate reconnaissance.' 'Your Excellency,' replied Fujiwara, 'the Army commander thinks differently. 15 Division is already pressing on Imphal from the north, 31 Division is approaching Kohima. You are the main assault division. If you don't push ahead, you're putting 15 and 31 Divisions at risk.'

In fact, Yanagida's caution was by this time quite justifiable. Sasahara's third battalion (Sueki) was down to a third of its strength after its rough handling by Cameron's 48 Brigade, and that picture was characteristic of

---

[1] No copy survives of the signal. Miura recalls it as '*Rentai wa gunki wo hōshō shi, angōsho wo yaku yōi wo shi, zen-in gyokusai wo kakugo de nimmu ni maishin su.*' 'The regiment is pushing on to fulfil its duty, resolved to die to the last man, burning code books and the regimental flag.' The order of words is almost the opposite in Japanese, and the signal ended at *zenin gyokusai*, 'die to the last man', omitting the last seven words which proclaimed Sasahara's will to fight on. Other versions of the signal story speak of it being delivered in two parts, with the latter part arriving too late. This is equally possible, given Japanese army signal practice of not sending a signal entire in one transmission.

the whole of 215 Regiment. When Fujiwara moved up to Mualkai to Sasahara's HQ, he found that the losses around Singgel were twenty officers and over 250 men. The wounded were three times that number. Fujiwara estimated Sasahara's battle strength to be a half of what it had been two weeks before. But it was his job to convince Yanagida that he must press on.

Fujiwara went to see Tanaka. 'I must apologize to Army for what's happened, but there was nothing I could do.' Tanaka told him what the division now planned: a double-pronged assault up the road, Sasahara on the left, Sakuma on the right, until they reached Torbung, where the road breaks out of the mountains into the plain. At that point they expected a counter-attack and intended to move at the speed of what was called 'controlled advance' (*tōsei zenshin*). When he heard the phrase, Fujiwara groaned. The Army plan demanded a 'swift onslaught' (*totsushin*) not movement in which you checked and secured each point of your advance. Fujiwara knew that Yanagida's decision corresponded to the fears of other staff officers, whatever Tanaka thought. Officers and men were exhausted by the struggle with 17 Division. Sakuma proved stubborn about rations. He wanted rice for his men and insisted on going right back to Falam to get it. Wheat flour had been captured at Tiddim and Sakuma was told to make do with that and the tins of food. He tasted it, said 'It's noodle flour, isn't it?' and rejected it, insisting his men should have rice or he would not budge.[1] Okamoto (Intelligence) had talked to Horiba (Operations) who told him that the British at Tongzang had not been broken in any way by the Japanese onslaught. They had left supplies behind, but no bodies, and no ammunition. They might turn and stand at any point. And the Japanese themselves were exhausted. The living flopped down beside corpses in the rain, and some were on the edge of suicide. Captain Katayama Tōru, on a visit to Sasahara Regiment, heard a soldier shoot himself by setting a rifle against his chest and pulling the trigger with his toe. The man failed in his attempt and said to Katayama, as he was carried off on a blood-soaked stretcher, 'I'm very sorry, sir!' Furious, Katayama bellowed 'What do you mean, sorry?' but his eyes filled with tears. He could see from the expressions of the other men round him that the unlucky stretcher case was not the only one who had thought of opting out.

Some Japanese historians have seen Yanagida as greatly at fault at this juncture. Whatever his view about the feasibility of the operation, once it had begun he should have done his best to make it succeed. He seems to have watched the battle develop rather than impose a leadership from above. The captured depot should have been better utilized, too, and that was too big a responsibility for a battalion commander to handle. And even when a battalion was in such straits as Sueki's, the target for four battalions

[1] Kojima Noboru, *Eirei no tani* (Valley of heroes), 1970, pp. 156–7

of Allied troops, it must be remembered that the topography rendered the deployment of 17 Division artillery against Sueki difficult, and no tanks were used against him. Was it impossible for him to maintain his position for a week against the British? Kojima Noboru, one of the historians of the Imphal battle, says briskly, 'The duty allotted to the regiment was to cut the enemy's retreat. Should they not have striven to do just that, even if it meant being annihilated?'[1]

These historians' voices are echoing Mutaguchi's post-war justifications of himself, of course. He recalled that he had termed Yanagida a 'defeatist' (*senkyō hikansha*): 'The divisional commander finally began to move north, but was afraid of enemy counter-attacks and so advanced with caution (*tōsei zenshin*). The result was that the Army's initial plan to storm into Imphal collapsed like a bubble. Had I been the 33 Divisional commander, even after the mistake of opening the road of retreat to 17 Indian Division, I would have got in among the enemy, and reached Bishenpur in one fell swoop. If the division had shown spirit and guts at that moment, I believe he could have followed them up, and taken the initiative on the battlefield.'[2]

It is easy to understand Mutaguchi's exasperation. But he was not at 33 Divisional headquarters. As Miura recalls, 'Div HQ was sited in a valley, next to the road. The wounded kept passing endlessly to the rear along the road, in front of HQ. A stream came out near HQ, and the wounded stopped to drink there, and the sight of these men and their blood-soaked bandages filled the HQ with gloom. Yanagida was particularly susceptible to the sight of wounded men. And there was something else: because they were in a valley, W/T contact with the forward columns was liable to be interrupted. And Irie's death depressed him, as it saddened Sasahara.'[3]

Finally, the exhausted columns began to move, Sasahara on 29 March and Sakuma the next day. He was still waiting for his rice. Isagoda Battalion (II/213 Regiment) was given the task of blocking the road at MS 72 from 24 March, but was attacked by 48 Brigade as it moved up from Singgel and was finally forced to open the road on 2 April. Isagoda Battalion came under the command of Sasahara's column, and between 6 and 8 April, the two columns reached MS 38, just south of Torbung. They were at the gates of the Imphal Plain, and had paid a high price to get there. Sakuma had already lost half his men. 17 Indian Division, too, despite its massive firepower, had sustained heavy losses. But by 4 April, it was finally in harbour, its supplies dropped in by aircraft, its wounded evacuated, its morale high. The Black Cats were licking their wounds and getting ready for the next round.

---

[1] Kojima Noboru, *Eirei no tani*, p. 159

[2] OCH, *Inpāru Sakusen*, I, p. 187

[3] ibid., p. 188

It's easy to say this with hindsight, but it is true: reactions were slow all along the line. The C-in-C 11 Army Group (Lieutenant-General Giffard) seems to have felt no urgency to ensure the build-up of reserves to feed into the battle. Slim was too slow in shifting his strength from Arakan, perhaps because he wanted to guarantee a complete success in the area of his old Corps (XV Corps) where he had in the past planned to overcome the Japanese by the use of overwhelming numerical superiority. In command of IV Corps, Scoones was slow in ordering 17 Division to move out of Tiddim into the Imphal Plain. And Cowan, in command of that division, was slow in getting his men on the move after receiving the order.

On the Japanese side, the faults shown in the initial assault from the south in Imphal were to bedevil the whole campaign: deep-seated quarrels between various levels of command, disorganization and an inadequate supply system, overweening contempt for their opponents, inability to compete with Allied air strength, frequent cruelty to prisoners (which in the end rebounded on the Japanese themselves) and a belief that *Yamato-damashii* (Japanese spirit) would overcome material deficiencies. It is all there in these preliminary engagements.

Shenam — Palel (i)

The Japanese division had a rank control system different from its British counterpart. Under the commander, a lieutenant-general, there was an infantry group commanded by a major-general. It was usually he who commanded any large force or column split off from the main body of the division, and in the case of 33 Division this infantry group was commanded by Major-General Yamamoto Tsunoru. In accordance with Japanese custom, when code words were not used for a formation, it was known by the commander's name. Indeed, it might be known both by his name and a code name. So the extreme right column of 33 Division was known as Yamamoto Force. It was this force which faced Major-General Douglas Gracey's 20 Indian Division, and from the point of view of firepower it was the best equipped in the whole of 15 Army. Based on III Battalion, 213 Infantry Regiment, it had 5 and 7 companies from 215 Regiment, heavy and medium artillery, 33 Engineer Regiment and thirty light tanks, with eighty-four 7 mm machine-guns and eight 10 cm cannon. Two battalions from 15 Division (II/51 and III/60) were also attached to Yamamoto from the start of the battle. There was a good reason for this concentration of firepower. The road Yamamoto was to take, through Tamu and Palel, was the shortest motorable route from the Chindwin into Imphal, and the airfield at Palel was a vital component of Imphal's defence system.

On the map, it looks as if Yamauchi's 15 Division aimed most directly for the plain: it is sixty miles as the crow flies from the crossing-point on the Chindwin, near Tonhe, to Kangpokpi ('Mission' to the Japanese) and Kanglatongbi on the Imphal-Kohima road. But 15 Division's route was across the grain of the country and the tracks it followed were far less easily negotiable than the road from Tamu to Palel which had been widened by Gracey's division in preparation for its entry into Burma. Segment by segment, Yamamoto's distances were quite short: from the Chindwin to Tamu is 20 miles; from Tamu to Tengnoupal is 14 miles; from Tengnoupal to Shenam is 4 miles; a further 5 miles and you are in Palel, on the edge of the Imphal Plain, with Imphal itself only 25 miles away. Another track from Palel runs south along the hillside at Shuganu, down through Mombi, to join the north-south track from Humine to Kalewa near Htinzin.

At the close of 1943, Scoones's policy had been to push 20 Division on towards the villages on the banks of the Chindwin and prepare for a thrust into Central Burma by making roads and piling up stores. A large dump was set up at Moreh where the road from Palel debouched from the hills into the Kabaw Valley, and from the end of the 1943 monsoon Gracey's brigades (32, 80, 100) began intense patrol activity up and down the Kabaw Valley and on to the Chindwin.

The patrols did well and Gracey felt they gave a good account of themselves whenever they encountered the probings of Yanagida's 33 Division moving north towards the Kabaw Valley from Yazagyo, where the Japanese started to accumulate stocks for *their* offensive. He was therefore not much taken with the strategy of turning tail and withdrawing on Imphal in anticipation of a Japanese assault and told Scoones so in no measured terms. Why build roads and stockpile supplies only to leave them for the enemy to use?

In the end, of course, Gracey had to conform to Scoones's plan but he left behind a screen of patrols of 9/12 Frontier Force Regiment between Tamu and the Chindwin. It was an officer of this regiment, Lt Walton, who warned Gracey that the Japanese were crossing the Chindwin in force on 15 March. Walton was at a spot called Myaingtha on the east bank of the Chindwin south of Tonhe, around 6.30 pm. It was getting dark, and he heard shouting below him and the noise of hammering, and boats being pushed together, and saw lighted torches going to and fro. He lay up during the 16th to avoid Japanese patrols and then found himself a point of vantage where a large red stone twenty yards square and twenty feet high offered him a perch.

At about 1830 hours (he reported on his return) men were seen going north up the bank to collect boats, which were spaced at approximately twenty yard intervals along the bank, and brought down. These boats were approximately eight feet long and four

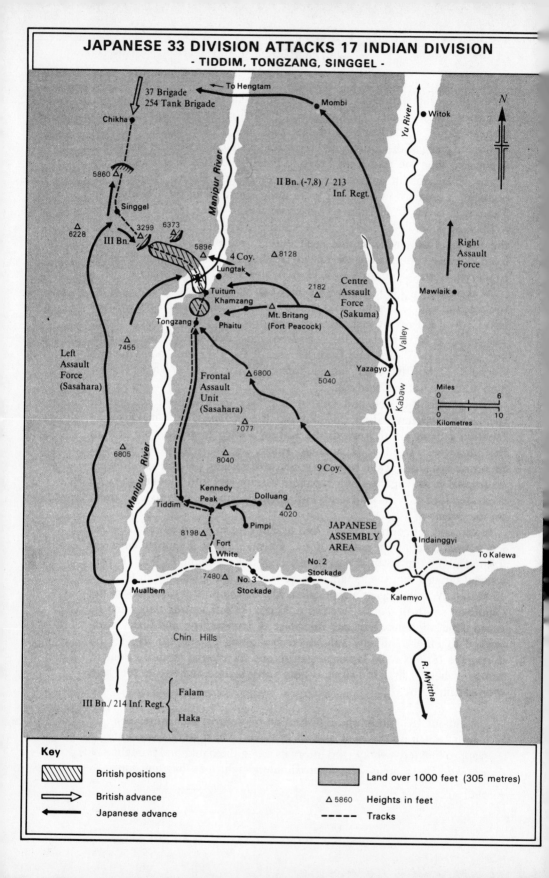

JAPANESE 33 DIVISION ATTACKS 17 INDIAN DIVISION
- TIDDIM, TONGZANG, SINGGEL -

N

To Hengtam

37 Brigade
254 Tank Brigade

Mombi

Witok

Yu River

Chikha

△ 5860

Singgel

II Bn. (-7,8) / 213
Inf. Regt.

△ 6228

△ 3299   △ 6373

III Bn.

△ 5896

4 Coy.

Lungtak

△ 8128

Right
Assault
Force

Tuitum

Khamzang

2182 △

Centre
Assault
Force
(Sakuma)

Mawlaik ●

Tongzang

Phaitu

Mt. Britang
(Fort Peacock)

△ Khamzang

Left
Assault
Force
(Sasahara)

△ 7455

Yazagyo

Manipur River

Frontal
Assault
Unit
(Sasahara)

△ 6800

△ 5040

Miles
0   6

0   10
Kilometres

Kabaw

Valley

△ 7077

△ 6805

△ 8040

9 Coy.

Manipur River

Kennedy
Peak

Dolluang

Tiddim

△ 4020

Pimpi

JAPANESE
ASSEMBLY
AREA

Indainggyi

To Kalewa

8198 △

Fort
White

7480 △   No. 3
Stockade

No. 2
Stockade

Kalemyo

Mualbem

Chin   Hills

R. Myittha

III Bn./ 214 Inf. Regt.   { Falam

Haka

Key

▨ British positions	▨ Land over 1000 feet (305 metres)
⇨ British advance	△ 5860 Heights in feet
⬅ Japanese advance	- - - - Tracks

feet wide with sharp prows and appeared to have a mounting for an outboard motor. After darkness fell six of these boats were collated together, lashed with bamboos and then lengths of decking placed on top. Various lengths were then put together and one end fixed to the bank. The other end was allowed to swing with the current across the river until it hit the bank on the opposite side – a distance of approximately 300 yards. Almost immediately a number of men crossed the bridge with ammunition boxes and these were followed by bullocks, horses, ponies and more bullocks. The ponies were seen to be carrying what looked like dismantled mountain guns. These were followed by approximately 100 men carrying white and green boxes, and each man made at least two journeys... This traffic continued, to my knowledge, until approximately 0200 hours, and almost certainly until daylight. As daylight broke, a motor boat dragged the far end of the bridge up stream back to the East bank, where it was dismantled and the decking removed and about half the boats taken upstream to the end of the sandbank north of Myaingtha and dispersed on the river bank. As soon as daylight came all noise and most movement ceased.[1]

So the Japanese were using portable pontoon bridges, carefully concealed during the hours of daylight from marauding RAF fighters. What Walton saw were elements of 15 Division crossing to reinforce Yamamoto further south. At the same time Yamamoto's main force was coming up the Kabaw Valley from Yazagyo. In the early hours of 14 March, Japanese medium artillery began to shell 9 Field Regiment's guns, and Yamamoto's tanks and infantry moved up to assault Witok, defended by Gurkhas and the Border Regiment. The defenders heard the Japanese tanks withdraw briefly, then, early on 15 March, they came north again and bivouacked seventy yards from the Gurkhas' perimeter. That day, six Lee tanks from the Carabiniers (Pettit) reinforced the infantry, and five days later rescued some ambushed Indian troops whose wounded could not move. Pettit's force was ambushed in turn by Japanese 95-type tanks, and one of the Lees was set ablaze. Pettit burst through the ambush into a clearing, turned about, and brought his guns to bear on the Japanese ambush position. The Japanese infantry sprinted into the jungle, where their tanks could not go. In this situation they should have reversed into cover, but the drivers evidently panicked and tried to break away through the Carabiniers' Lees. Five tanks were hit and a sixth captured. This was the only occasion in the entire campaign in which roughly equal numbers of tanks on either side produced a tank battle as such.

[1] Gracey Papers, Liddell-Hart Archives.

But the Japanese were not to be held back. They were in Witok on 19 March and made for Gracey's base at Moreh. 20 Division's plan was not to go right back into the Imphal Plain. Instead, it was to move along the Tamu-Palel road through Tengnoupal and hold the Japanese at the 5000-feet-high Shenam Saddle. From it you can overlook Palel. As the road leads up from Shenam, the eye traverses a magic vision of gorges and ravines and mountain ridges, with the green Imphal Plain spread out below, bounded by a horizon of distant grey-blue mountains. The Saddle is really a complex of hills strung out between Shenam and Tengnoupal and these have survived in Army histories – British, Indian and Japanese – as nicknames, the British derived largely from the Mediterranean, the Japanese often from the names of officers who captured them. From west to east they are: Gibraltar (not unlike its namesake in configuration), Malta, Scraggy, Crete West, Crete East, and Cyprus; the Japanese equivalents being Laimatol Hill – a local name – sometimes referred to by its height as 5185, then Yajima or Futago Hill, Itō Hill, Kawashima Hill, Ikkenya Hill. On the other side of the road lies what the British called Nippon Hill, a tribute to the ferocity with which the Japanese fought for it. They themselves called it Maejima after the company commander who first took it.

On 25 March 1944 Gracey scanned a note from the Brigadier General Staff at IV Corps, sent from Imphal. Bayley told Gracey that the main Japanese thrust, then ten days old, was coming along the Litan road through Sangshak, as Corps HQ saw it. Whether this decreased the threat against Imphal which was being launched through Gracey's area, he wasn't sure, but at any rate it meant Corps would want help from 20 Division, and quickly.

Gracey signalled back that if any troops were to be taken from his division it would mean withdrawing to the position Tengnoupal-Shenam at once and destroying the supplies built up at Moreh. He followed this with a MOST SECRET AND PERSONAL letter to Scoones the next day in which he let his chagrin flow:

> My orders have been to defend the Shenam-Moreh road with their boxes, and though I have been, and am being, helped by various units – a squadron of tanks and some Engineer units – it must be remembered that I am missing one Battalion 14 FF Rifles in the hills and am carrying one dud battalion – 4 Madras – which fills spaces but has no offensive value at all, and that I am now expected to keep the road open as well. If I am to keep the road open in addition to defending the three boxes in it, I cannot spare one single soldier more back...
>
> This Division has fought magnificently so far and all the troops have been fully aware of the necessity of withdrawing to their present position, with the Army Commander's assurance that behind them is a pile-up of reserves rapidly being reinforced to

deal with the situation behind them. Our morale is sky high, as we have beaten the enemy and given him a real bloody nose everywhere. Everyone is prepared to hang on where they are now like grim death. It is their Verdun.

It will be most shattering to morale if they are now asked to assist in the Imphal Plain and they will feel that someone has let them down.[1]

Gracey knew he would have to obey, though, and offered some alternatives: stop keeping the road open and just defend boxes, abandon Moreh ('a dreadful admission of defeat to my mind') or make further withdrawals to hold Tengnoupal and Shenam with five battalions.

The base at Moreh had been built up to supply two divisions for an invasion of Burma. Hidden in the jungle to the left of the Shenam-Moreh road, it was two and a half miles long by a mile and a half wide, harboured 200 head of cattle and vast quantities of oil, petrol and ammunition. As Yamamoto Force moved up the Kabaw Valley and 15 Division's Yoshioka Battalion approached from the north, some stores had been shifted back, from 17 March onwards. On 31 March 32 Brigade (Mackenzie) received orders to withdraw from Moreh the following day. Like Gracey, he preferred to stay and fight, but the answer was 'No'. Mackenzie boobytrapped everything he could think of, then realized he still had 200 head of cattle on his hands. He could not leave them to the Japanese, and if he released them from their pens they might move east and alert the Japanese to the fact that Moreh was being evacuated. So he asked the Northamptons to provide an army butcher, who slaughtered the cattle with knives (shooting them would have alerted the Japanese, too). 'With the blood all over the place, and the flies,' thought Mackenzie, 'it'll help to make Moreh very unpleasant for the Japanese.'[2]

Finally he gave the order, 'Fire the oil!' and within five minutes a thick pall of smoke began to rise from the jungle. The Japanese started to shell, but 32 Brigade lost no men in the withdrawal, as they moved silently out of their positions and up the road to Shenam. They had destroyed close on a million pounds' worth of supplies.

By the end of April, 32 Brigade was back in reserve at Palel, and 80 and 100 Brigades were on the Shenam Saddle, holding a series of fortified positions overlooking the stretch of road between Tengnoupal and Palel, a distance of roughly five miles. The course of the battle for the next two months was briefly this: the Japanese tried to force their way through the network of hills, took some of them and failed to take others. The British and Indian troops recaptured some of the hills and failed to recapture

---

[1] Gracey Papers, Liddell Hart Archive.

[2] Evans and Brett-James, op.cit., p. 178

others. The Japanese then tried to break the deadlock by moving round the hill network along the track into the hills to the north, through which they tried to reach out at Palel through jungle paths. At the end of April, with a unit of the Indian National Army, they put in a commando-type raid on Palel airfield, which failed. In June they repeated the attempt, and succeeded in destroying a number of aircraft on the ground and put paid to some supply depots. But they could not take and hold the airfield, and finally withdrew.

The Taking of Sangshak

On the northern front of the Imphal battle, the crucial struggle took place at the little town of Kohima. But there was a fierce and bloody curtain-raiser to Kohima, the battle for the village of Sangshak. Neither of the units, British or Japanese, which fought that battle, was initially supposed to be there at all. Although IV Corps had estimated that the Japanese would send only one regiment against Kohima, a screen of defensive positions had been flung out west of it, and 49 Brigade of 23 Division was at Sangshak to watch movement from the Chindwin towards Ukhrul, which the Japanese would need to take as it lay astride their path. Ukhrul was eight miles north of Sangshak, which itself lay on the road leading through Litan from the Imphal Plain to Humine and the Chindwin River.

But the predicament of 17 Division compelled Scoones to remove 49 Brigade and send it south to the Tiddim Road as part of the plan to rescue Cowan and his men as they extricated themselves from the Japanese pincers at Tongzang. To replace it, Scoones put in the 3000-strong 50 Indian Parachute Brigade, which had arrived in the Kohima area a few weeks before from north-west India. There was no question of an airborne role. They would simply have to stand and fight as they were.

The brigade commander was Brigadier M. Hope-Thomson, thirty-two years old at the time, ten years younger than Wingate, but lacking Wingate's varied combat experience. He had 152 (Gurkha) and 153 (Indian) Parachute Battalions under command, a medium machine-gun company, artillery, engineers and a field ambulance. Hope-Thomson's orders to move came five days before the Japanese crossed the Chindwin on 15 March, but he was short of vehicles and his men were barely in position before news came of the Japanese presence in the hills to the east.

152 Battalion (Lieutenant-Colonel P. Hopkinson) reached Sangshak on 14 March, ahead of the main body. 49 Brigade then moved out, leaving behind the 4/5 Mahratta Light Infantry (Lieutenant-Colonel J. H. Trim) and two companies from the Nepalese Army. Hope-Thomson put the Mahrattas in reserve at Kidney Camp, just north of Sangshak, and 152 Battalion took over their positions. Two companies were sent forward, one

to a hill covering the approaches to Ukhrul – Point 7378 – another to Sheldon's Corner, a fork in the road about six miles east of Sangshak. The machine-gun company was in Ukhrul.

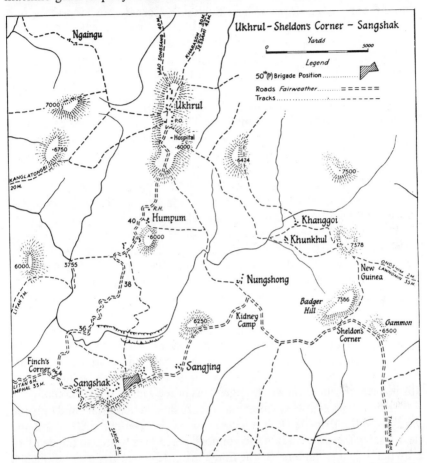

On the afternoon of 18 March, Naga tribesmen came into Sangshak from the village of Pushing, about a dozen or more miles east. The Japanese had occupied their village and were moving west. Early next morning, an officer's patrol counted around 200 Japanese moving towards Sangshak, but Trim and Hopkinson at Sheldon's Corner judged the Japanese force to be in battalion strength, up to 900 men.

The Japanese attacked C Company at Point 7378 and by the morning of 20 March, the only surviving British officer of that company decided to withdraw his men – only twenty were left – to Sheldon's Corner.

Colonel Abbott, the brigade second-in-command, walked from Sangshak to Sheldon's Corner to confer with Hopkinson. It was a distance of nine miles and he did it back again, in the sweltering heat, convinced that to distribute the Brigade's forces in penny-packets as a defensive fringe across the hills was asking for trouble. Hope-Thomson took his advice and began to pull in his companies and concentrate them.[1] On 21 March the greater part of his force was at Sheldon's Corner, but Hope-Thomson signalled, around noon, that he wanted them to withdraw on Kidney Camp. As it happened, Hopkinson had asked for an air-drop of food, water and ammunition and this order had not been cancelled. So the supplies began to drop in from the skies just as it was getting dark, by which time the troops were ready to move. But they could hardly leave the drop to be picked up by the Japanese, and had to blow all the new ammunition.

They arrived in Sangshak, exhausted by the hot march and the carrying of heavy equipment, at 4.30 pm, to learn that the Japanese were advancing south on them from Ukhrul and had cut the road leading back to Imphal through Litan. Hope-Thomson decided to stand at Sangshak, where he could deal with the Japanese approaching from the east. It seemed a good position, an empty village at the end of a grassy, flower-covered hill overlooked by an American missionary church at its northern end.

Hope-Thomson then went into reverse. He had had his forces scattered all over the countryside. Now he concentrated them, with a vengeance. Into an area 400 by 800 yards, he assembled three battalions of infantry, his two Nepalese companies, a mortar battery, a mountain battery and his field ambulance, about 1,850 men all told. Not only men, but mules also, which had carried the mountain guns. It was, certainly, a concentration of strength, but also of vulnerability, made worse by the fact that bedrock was only three feet down, as the men discovered when they began to dig trenches. Once the Japanese began to use guns and mortars, they could hardly miss. And Hope-Thomson had chosen his perimeter without regard for its lack of water. He was to regret this bitterly in the days to come.

The fighting was at very close quarters. A shell hit a mortar sited only ten yards from the Brigade HQ trenches, which were spattered with blood and flesh. A Japanese attack into the gunners' positions resulted in the death of both battery commanders. By the time the battle was nearly over, about 300 wounded lay in shallow trenches near Brigade HQ, the worst cases drugged by morphia, since the position was too open to carry out operations. As the water ran short, and the parachute drops landed among the enemy, the defenders drank from puddles left by the heavy rain, their thirst more powerful than any distaste they might feel for the blood- and mud-stained liquid. It was impossible to sleep and men fell exhausted even in the midst of shelling.

When Hope-Thomson saw a column moving his way from Ukhrul on 22 March, he naturally supposed it was his own 153 Battalion withdrawing on Sangshak. It was in fact 11 Battalion, 58 Infantry Regiment of 31 Division,

---

[1] Evans and Brett-James, op.cit., p. 163

under the command of Captain Nagaya. At least Nagaya was nominally in command, but the force commander, Major-General Miyazaki, the commander of 31 Division Infantry Group based on 58 Regiment, was with him, and Miyazaki was the reason why Nagaya suddenly cut down the track from Ukhrul instead of pushing straight ahead for Kohima.

Sangshak was not in Miyazaki's operational zone at all. It was in the area assigned to 15 Division, and the left column of that division, 60 Infantry Regiment (Matsumura), was to take it on its way to cut the Imphal-Kohima road at Kangpokpi[1] and Kanglatongbi. Miyazaki was uneasy about this presence of a sizeable British force just ten miles south of his line of march, and although he knew 15 Division was supposed to deal with it, they seemed to be moving slowly. On 22 March, he intercepted a signal from Mutaguchi to the GOC 15 Division: 'Regret delay in your advance. Your division must move bravely and fiercely, without hesitation.' So it sounded as if they needed to be urged on.

In contrast, the morale of Miyazaki's own group was high, and II Battalion had routed the British at Ukhrul in one fell swoop. He learned from his intelligence officer, Lt Hama Tetsurō, that the British were in Sangshak in brigade strength, and he thought he could tackle them. He sent a company round behind Sangshak to block the Imphal road to reinforcements, and decided to attack when his regimental and mountain guns caught up with him.

Nagaya begged him not to wait for the guns. 'Put in a night attack!' he implored the general, and Miyazaki consented. He was both brave and energetic and felt that, tactically, the sooner he took Sangshak the better.

At 1.30 am on 23 March, Nagaya's 8 Company (Lieutenant Naka) followed by 5 and 6 Companies, raced for the positions of 50 Parachute Brigade. But speed was no substitute for artillery support, and it was a dreadful miscalculation. Hope-Thomson had mountain guns and 3-in mortars, a total of 46 pieces. The Japanese were attacking on the simple basis of the belief 'strength lies in the soldier'. Lt Naka was taken aback by the concentration of British artillery fire, but hurled himself forward, brandishing his sword as he screamed '*Tsukkome!*' (Charge!). With the sword in one hand, he hacked down four Indian soldiers, and as he was about to slay a fifth his body was torn to pieces by machine-gun bullets and shell fragments. 'Don't let the company commander down!' yelled the platoon commanders as 8 Company hurled its grenades into the British positions and fired their LMGs from the hip. Trim remembered being filled with fear as he heard the Japanese yelling encouragement to one another, with shrieks that sounded barely human. But fear didn't stop the men of 50 Parachute Brigade returning the Japanese fire, and in the gun smoke and scream of shells the officers and men of Nagaya's 8 Company fell, one after

---

[1] Always referred to in Japanese texts as 'Mission', because of the church there.

the other. Nagaya ordered 5 and 6 Companies to press the attack, but the British fire turned them back. Distraught at the loss of Naka, Nagaya himself told the adjutant, Lieutenant Kameyama, to take over, saying, 'I must go and find Naka's bones, I must find his bones!' as the blood streamed from a bullet wound in his jaw. But the dawn brought British aircraft into the skies over Sangshak, and Kameyama knew there was no question of renewing the attack.

The day brought something else. Coloured parachutes floated down from the sky as transport aircraft droned over, hundreds of them dancing in the heavens and then landing like outspread flowers blossoming on the hillsides. Many fell into Japanese hands, and they realized what the colour code meant: blue for rations, white for water, red for ammunition. Gleefully, the Japanese soldiers took charge of these 'Churchill rations' as they called them. Then the Gurkhas put in an attack, supported not only by Hope-Thomson's artillery but also by the fighter planes which had escorted the transport aircraft. The Japanese repulsed the attack, but at a price. 5 Company commander, Lieutenant Saitō, was badly wounded, and Lieutenant Watanabe, 6 Company commander, was decapitated by a mortar bomb fragment as he was reconnoitring the British positions.

An attack on 24 March by 6 Company succeeded in breaking into the south-west corner of the hill area and Nagaya, the II Battalion commander, came through the perimeter with them. As they burst into the enemy lines, two grenades landed near him and the adjutant. Kameyama kicked one hard and sent it flying, hurling himself to the ground. Nagaya picked up the other and threw it ahead, yelling 'Charge! Charge!' They held their gains, but got no further, as a curtain of shellfire came down.

Then Miyazaki's III Battalion arrived on the field of battle, commanded by Major Shimanoe. Colonel Fukunaga, 58 Regiment commander, was with him. Miyazaki was watching the battle from a height north of Sangshak, and ordered Shimanoe to attack at once, but his men were brought to a halt in front of the British positions.

So the battle wore on. Hardest hit was Nagaya's II Battalion. In attack after counter-attack, he lost more than 400 killed and wounded. As Nagaya numbered his depleted companies, with bloodshot eyes, heavy with bitter self-reproach and crushed by fatigue, he knew his battalion had almost ceased to exist as a fighting force. There were moments when he was on the edge of madness.

The exhausted defenders were also oppressed by the smell of decomposing mules and men. The hillside was littered with rotting corpses, friend and foe decomposing indiscriminately under the same hot sun. And the air supply on 24 March dropped rations and ammunition, but not water, which was what he needed most. On 23 March he had rationed his men to a bottle a day, and on the 24th, it became necessary to make this a bottle every other day. Scuffles arose between Indian troops and Gurkhas

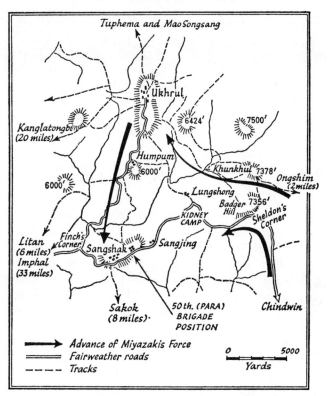

Tuphema and Mao Songsang

Ukhrul

6424'

7500'

Kanglatongbi
(20 miles)

Humpum
6000'

6000'

Khunkhul 7378'

Ongshim
(2 miles)

Lungshong

Badger 7356'
Hill

KIDNEY
CAMP

Sheldon's
Corner

Litan
(6 miles)
Imphal
(33 miles)

Finch's
Corner

Sangshak

Sangjing

Sakok
(8 miles)·

50th. (PARA)
BRIGADE
POSITION

Chindwin

➤ Advance of Miyazakis Force
═══ Fairweather roads
▬ ▬ ▬ Tracks

0   5000

Yards

The battle of Sangshak, March 1944

looking for water. The defenders' nerves were on edge from lack of sleep, but there was to be no respite. Japanese shelling from a new direction began to range in on them on the evening of 25 March.

The shelling came from east of Sangshak. It was not Miyazaki's guns, but two old mountain guns belonging to Lieutenant Tōjō's battery of 21 Field Artillery Regiment, attached to 60 Regiment of 15 Division. In other words, the Japanese who should have taken Sangshak in the first place had reached the field of battle.

In fact, III Battalion, 60 Regiment arrived at a point east of Sangshak on the morning of 23 March, heard the sounds of rifle and gun-fire, and deduced that 31 Division must be attacking. The regimental commander, Colonel Matsumura, told the CO III Battalion, Major Fukushima, to support the attack.

But Fukushima was a perfectionist. Instead of acting like Nagaya, like a bull at a gate, he told his company commanders to study their method of attack, 'Reconnoitre until you're sure of your ground. You're the ones who'll be doing the fighting, so make sure.' They were further slowed down by the dense jungle east of Sangshak, and night marching by compass merely meant they lost their way. On the morning of 25 March, they came to a spot from which they could see Sangshak on its hill and watch the fall of shot of Tōjō's mountain guns as he skilfully blew up, one after another, Hope-Thomson's entrenchments. Fukushima ordered his attack for just before dawn on 26 March. He reckoned he was one valley distant from Sangshak, and the battalion cheerfully made its way into the jungle, only to find the valley unexpectedly deep and, under the trees, dark. They could not even make out the lettering on the compasses. They threshed their way through the jungle night, and when they came out, as dawn broke, they were only 200 yards in front of 50 Parachute Brigade's position.

They were pinned down at once by fierce fire from the weary but vigilant defenders of Sangshak, and the regimental commander ordered Fukushima to postpone his attack for twenty-four hours. In the meanwhile, Fukushima decided he should co-ordinate his attack with whatever Fukunaga, CO 58 Regiment, had planned. If he was to attack by dawn on the 27th, he did not want his men fired on by Fukunaga from the other side of Sangshak hill. He told Lieutenant Asai to contact 31 Division. 'You're to speak to Fukunaga himself, understand? No subordinates. Without fail.' Lieutenant Asai took five men and made for the heights north of Sangshak.

There was no sign of Fukunaga, so Asai decided to go to the top and contact Miyazaki. He stammered out Fukushima's plan of attack, and was appalled when Miyazaki bellowed at him down the field telephone, 'What's the matter with you? Don't you know the meaning of "the soldier's compassion"?'

Miyazaki was grieving over the loss of young officers. Every platoon commander in 11 Company had been killed in a fierce engagement at dawn on 26 March, at the same time as the men of 15 Division had prudently decided to postpone their attack. The commander, Lieutenant Nishida Susumu[1], had been wounded, and the assault force of 150 men reduced to twenty.

Miyazaki was not angry with Asai for being absent from the battle. It was a little more complicated than that. The CO 58 Regiment, Colonel Fukunaga, was at that very moment planning one final all-out attack to take Sangshak, with himself carrying the regimental flag at the head of II Battalion and III Battalion, now reduced to half their strength. Miyazaki intended them to have the full glory of the assault, since in his view they had borne the brunt of the battle. He had no time for late-comers in the field. 'Colonel Fukunaga is taking the battle flag into Sangshak! Don't you know what "the soldier's compassion" is?' He repeated the phrase he'd used before, a well-known samurai expression: *bushi no nasake. Nasake*

---

[1] The former Lieutenant Nishida is now president of the 58 Regiment Veterans' Association, *Go-Hachi Kai*.

means sympathy, compassion, fellow-feeling and is the instinctive, intuitive feeling one samurai or *bushi* should have for the predicament of another. Miyazaki was telling Asai that he did not want 58 Regiment's last glorious fight for its honour interfered with by any other unit. 'Go back and tell Colonel Matsumura this! If we take Sangshak tonight, I'll let him have as much booty as he wants, ammunition, rations, the lot. But if we've not captured it by 6 am, he can assume 58 Regiment has been annihilated, and he can do whatever he likes. "*Bushi no nasake*"' Miyazaki said "'*Bushi no nasake*".' And rang off.

That night, snow fell on the battlefield. 58 Infantry Regiment was a Niigata unit, from northern Japan, used to snow, and amazed to find it in India. As the men felt the snow trickle down from their helmets, they looked up at the night sky, and felt unbearably homesick: 'The snow has come from Echigo to meet us', said one of them. They opened their mouths wide, and, waiting for the order to attack, drank the snow flakes as they fell.

Quailing under Miyazaki's onslaught, Asai nevertheless had enough presence of mind to confirm the attack details with the officers of 58 Regiment HQ, and returned to his own HQ at four in the morning.

Both Matsumura and Fukushima thought the general's attitude odd, but they decided to carry on as planned with the battalion attack, and moved out at 4.30 am. But they found Sangshak empty. Apart, that is, from the dead and dying. Hope-Thomson had received 23 Division's order to move out at 6 pm the previous day. It was decided to move out at 10.30 pm, through a rearguard provided by Trim's 4/5 Mahrattas. In a state of collapse from battle exhaustion, Hope-Thomson left with a small detachment from Brigade HQ, and on arrival in Imphal was admitted at once to hospital with a nervous breakdown. (Cf. Appendix 2b, p. 653).

The firing stopped, and silence settled over Sangshak. The Japanese sent an officer patrol to find out why everything was suddenly so quiet. They came back and reported there was no sign of the enemy.

Nagaya stormed onto the hill, his frantic eyes looking everywhere for the bones of 8 Company, for Lieutenants Naka and Baba. The hill was an appalling sight. The charred ruins of the missionary church looked down on the burned grass and few trees. Discarded weapons lay everywhere, and scattered shell fragments. The white bodies of British troops lay with the brown and black bodies of the dead Indians, exposed to the sun or lying in heaps in foxholes; corpses with bellies scooped out, or headless, among the mules swelling and heaving with putrefaction.

Nagaya and his men walked through it all, turning over the corpses, looking for comrades they could recognize. He could see no sign of Naka anywhere, and questioned the Indian prisoners. A Japanese officer, they told him, had been buried by the order of a British battalion commander, for his bravery. They showed Nagaya where, and he told his men to start digging. It was true. Naka lay there. His sword had not been looted, but had been buried with him.

Lieutenant-General Miyazaki came up, bowed his head over the Japanese corpses, and joined his hands together. 'Thank you,' he murmured, 'You did well'. He saluted Naka's body, then turned briskly to the survivors. The tinned food, cigarettes and whisky left behind by 50 Parachute Brigade were to be distributed, and the battlefield cleared. There was other booty, too, from Sangshak and the dumps leading to the Chindwin; trucks, wireless sets, mortars.

At least that was how it seemed to Miyazaki and his men at the time, as he ordered the advance on Kohima to begin again, on 28 March. But the balance is not so simple. Among those casualties were more than half the company and platoon commanders of 58 Regiment's II and III Battalions, a loss which had its effect on the fight for Kohima. So, more important, did the delay in getting there. 50 Parachute Brigade had been shattered in the battle for Sangshak, but it had put Miyazaki's timetable out by a week, and his timetable was very tight indeed. That week was invaluable for the British. It enabled a scratch garrison to move into Kohima. It gave Scoones time to fly in 5 Indian Division from Arakan into the Imphal Plain and, although Miyazaki did not know this, it gave Scoones the Japanese plans for Kohima and the road south from it to Imphal.

Among the young infantry officers who hurled themselves through 50 Parachute Brigade's perimeter in the first flush of the assault, was one whose dispatch case contained marked maps and plans. Hope-Thomson's HQ had with it a Burmese who understood some Japanese, enough to make him aware of the vital importance of these papers. The brigadier decided it was worth risking one of his officers to get them back to Scoones. The maps were copied, one set given to a member of the Intelligence section, another to the Brigade Intelligence Officer. Risking capture throughout almost the length of their journey, these two made their way from Sangshak after nightfall and took the documents to Corps HQ. They showed quite clearly that Slim and Scoones had guessed wrongly about Mutaguchi's plans for Kohima. The Japanese were sending 15 Division across the hills to cut the Imphal road at Mission and Kanglatongbi. That had been predicted. But it was not a regiment, as had been supposed, but the whole of 31 Division, that was making for Kohima. In the preliminary stages of the battle, it was a priceless piece of information.[1]

---

[1] There is still disagreement among the Japanese as to the correctness of Miyazaki's decision to attack Sangshak in the first place, and also of his imperious rejection of help from 60 Regiment of 15 Division. There is no doubt that that regiment's approach was leisurely, and 58 Regiment bore the major weight of the battle. But Lieutenant Tōjō's artillery helped, and 15 Division Infantry completed the encirclement of the British positions. The official Japanese history finds it necessary to append an author's note to its account of Sangshak, to exonerate Miyazaki from the charge of arrogant poaching on 15 Division's preserves. His

Shenam — Palel (ii)
(see map facing p. 314)

15 Division's reinforcements for Yamamoto were drawn from the battle against the Chindits. Major Takemura's battalion broke off contact with Calvert at Mawlu, came down the Irrawaddy as far as Yeu and then crossed to Kalewa. He had 400 men with him. Pack transport and some of his heavy weapons were still on the way. He was met at Sibong by the Force adjutant and taken by car to Force HQ at Chamol. He could see firing on a number of hilltops, from the car window, and at the same time sounds from the countryside that were not at all war-like: the eerie chatter of monkeys and the occasional roar of a tiger deep in the hills. In his mind, too, lingered the image of the Indian National Army troops he had passed on his way to Sibong, wild with enthusiasm as they walked on Indian soil, holding their rifles aloft and yelling *'Jai Hind! Chalo Delhi!'* (India for ever! On to Delhi!). These were men of Kiani's No. 2 Guerrilla Regiment of the 1st INA Division, also attached to Yamamoto Force, and soon to be involved in Takemura's own battle.

'Our vital strength in the front line has reached rock bottom,' was the welcome he received from Yamamoto when he reported. 'Itō of 213 Regiment pays no attention to what I say. I simply tell him to take enemy

record at Kohima, and later as GOC 54 Division in Arakan and on the Irrawaddy, shows that he was not only a brave but unselfish leader and acted sensibly on the interception of Mutaguchi's signal to the GOC 15 Division, Yamauchi, accusing him of delay in advancing on the Kohima-Imphal road. With a British force ten miles to the south of him, Miyazaki naturally wanted to eliminate the threat it presented. He was successful, but took the risk of being delayed in his march on Kohima, and paid for that risk.

On the other hand, it has also been pointed out that most accounts of Sangshak are based on 58 Infantry Regiment records and reminiscences, those of a unit with a proper pride in its achievements, and this has prevented any other version gaining currency. Itō Keiichi, the military historian, in his book *Heitaitachi no rikugunshi (Army history from the soldier's point of view)* (Tokyo, 1969) has a section entitled 'The Mystery of Sangshak' (pp. 303–06) in which he makes a case for 60 Regiment of 15 Division. Miyazaki's men reached Sangshak on the evening of 22 March, 1944, and Matsumura's men were there a day later, on the morning of the 23rd. Matsumura was astonished that Miyazaki, on a wrong course, was attacking Sangshak from the north, but at once deployed his regimental guns and field guns in support. At the same time, he had the Uchibori Battalion attack from the south. As a result, 50 Indian Parachute Brigade was under attack from the north (Miyazaki), the east (Matsumura) and the south (Uchibori) and was therefore more or less surrounded by Japanese forces, being compelled to retreat on 26 March. Uchibori Battalion took prisoner around a hundred of the retreating enemy.

15 Division therefore claims it *did* play a part in the British defeat at Sangshak, while freely admitting the preponderant role of 58 Infantry Regiment. On the other hand, it puts forward the following queries:

1. Why did Miyazaki move south from Ukhrul and bring about, by the five-day battle at Sangshak, a crucial delay in the march on Kohima?
2. Why, after the war, did Miyazaki accuse Matsumura of misjudgment?
3. Why is 15 Division's contribution passed over in silence?

15 Division veterans acknowledge that if 15 Division had attacked Sangshak by itself, as it was intended to do, at least five days would have been required to take it, and many men would have been lost. It was for them a stroke of luck that Miyazaki should have attacked first, but they would have taken Sangshak in the end, as they were supposed to do.

positions, he goes and raises the flag and has everyone slaughtered.'
Yamamoto was overjoyed to have Takemura's battalion, and intended to
use him at once. 'You are to take part in an attack at dawn tomorrow,' he
told him. 'You will be under the command of Lieutenant-Colonel Mitsui,
of No. 3 Heavy Field Artillery Regiment.' Takemura next went to Mitsui's
HQ, where he was shown the fireplan, what was known about British
positions, and given an objective. Takemura could see that Mitsui, however expert a gunner he might be, had no conception of what was involved
in commanding an infantry unit in the field, and was blithely giving orders
when he himself would be two or three miles away in a safe zone, beyond
the reach of enemy artillery. 'Your battalion will take part in the attack on
Point 4562, Itō Hill (Scraggy) tomorrow morning' was the order. 'My men
are still on the march from Sibong to Tengnoupal', Takemura protested.
'They are not yet under command, and I would like to recce the area after
daybreak and have time to prepare the attack.' 'Out of the question!'
Mitsui rapped back. 'Attack at once!' Takemura left the HQ with murder
in his heart and waited in the jungle for his men to arrive. It turned cold,
and the mist seemed to penetrate his skin. Then the sky grew pale, the mist
cleared, and the advanced positions at Palel looked almost within a hand's
reach.

There could be no immediate attack unless he knew what the British
positions were, and he intended, in spite of Mitsui, to find out for himself.
Takemura took a patrol out and moved along just below the road. Later in
the day he heard the sound of engines and caterpillar tracks, a rhythmic
roar which seemed to crawl and climb up the Tengnoupal road. It was the
tanks of 14 Tank Regiment, under Colonel Ueda Nobuo. Takemura and
his men counted twelve of them, spaced out along the road. Then something seemed to go wrong. The leading tank swung left, and in the dusk a
streak of light moved towards it. At that instant came the sound of anti-
tank guns firing from the British positions, and the noise of splintering
metal echoed among the hills. Shrapnel came whizzing over the heads of
the patrol. The tank advance came to a halt.

This was obviously part of the attack Takemura was to participate in.
What had happened was simple and tragic. Given the precipitous terrain,
the twelve Japanese tanks could not move off the road. When they moved
up towards the British positions, artillery and anti-tank guns opened up on
the column. The leading 97 medium tank was destroyed in an instant. The
tank company commander was badly wounded, and the tanks behind him
came to a standstill. The second tank had no time to engage the enemy fire
point and itself became a target for concentrated British gun fire which
played up and down the column for twenty minutes as the regimental
commander attempted to extricate his tanks. The attack was then
abandoned and the tanks withdrew. Ueda did not want his tanks to be
caught stationary on the road by enemy aircraft.

Next morning, Ueda was summoned to the Force Commander's HQ. Yamamoto was furious. 'You are a coward!' he bellowed at Ueda. 'Why did you retreat?' It was an unheard-of accusation for Ueda. He went livid, but kept his temper. 'The method of employing tanks in combat is to return to your starting point when the combat is over. That is the principle.' Yamamoto was not interested: 'If you were afraid of enemy aircraft, what have you got tank guns for? Use your guns and shoot them down!' 'They'd be on to us while we swivelled the turrets,' retorted Ueda, 'and smash us into smithereens (*koppa mijin*).' His three captains were listening and knew he was right. They were in the hands of an idiot who knew nothing about tank deployment, that was clear. Tanks were useless in narrow defiles. But Yamamoto was unimpressed and continued to mock Ueda in front of the assembled officers. Perhaps, Ueda suggested, the Force commander should go up to the front line and see for himself? He had overstepped the mark. His dismissal was certain from that point on, but he had been pushed too far to care. 'If this happens again, I'll cut my belly open in front of Yamamoto!' he told his officers.

Yamamoto was no less brusque with his infantry commanders, as the fight for Maejima Hill and Itō Hill showed. The battles for the hills resulted from Gracey's decision after he had withdrawn from Moreh. He still had too much territory to cover, about 25 miles of front, and his policy was to defend a number of fortified boxes and keep the road open, rather than hold the area in its entirety. This meant intensive patrolling and a determined effort to secure the chain of hills leading to Shenam. The struggle for Maejima Hill (Nippon Hill) is characteristic of the fierce fighting between Tengnoupal and Shenam which derived from Gracey's plan. The hill lies slightly south of the road and was one of Yamamoto's first objectives. At his HQ in Khonkhang he put together the intelligence available on Gracey's front, and on 8 April ordered an attack on the Tengnoupal position, using III Battalion 213 Regiment, with regimental and mountain guns, and Mitsui's heavy field artillery in support.

These heavy guns caused the greatest problems in deployment. To keep them from being spotted, Mitsui used the workmen's huts left behind by Gracey's road-building parties and brought his heavy artillery up at night, piece by piece, and hid them in the huts. His positions were not discovered until the end of the battle, and he did not lose a single gun.

Major Itō commanded the assault force and covered his battalion's left flank by sending 11 Company under Lt Maejima Yōichi to take the hill south-west of Tengnoupal. Maejima took it and was subjected to fierce counter-attacks in battalion strength, with artillery shelling and bombing from the air. 4/10 Gurkha rifles were ordered to retake the hill on 2 April, with help from guns and mortars but no aircraft. The Japanese held the crest, a crater thirty yards across. On the first part of the climb, the Gurkhas could shelter in trees and scrub, but as they approached the crater the steep slope offered no cover. A bayonet charge was countered by a shower of grenades by Maejima's men, and the Gurkhas were thrown back. When night fell they attacked again, but failed to take the crest.[1]

On 11 April, the Brigade commander (Brigadier 'Sam' Greeves) put in the 1st Devonshire Regiment (Lieutenant-Colonel G. A. Harvest) and this time assured there was not simply a concentrated artillery barrage but a Hurribomber strike by the RAF. The whole hill-top was turned into a ploughed field and Major Itō, from a nearby summit, watched the annihilation of Maejima's men, in a helpless rage, powerless to support him. C and D Companies of the Devons watched as the aircraft zoomed in and bombed the labyrinth of bunkers which Maejima's men had spent the past nine days tunnelling into the hill. At half-past ten they moved up and – even after that bombardment – were met by a tornado of machine-gun fire and grenades. Artillery was again called up to shell the machine-gun positions, and D Company finally took the crest.

Maejima's entire company had been wiped out. But the Devons had paid a price, too. They had 87 casualties, all three company commanders were wounded and two officers killed. Leaving A Company in possession, the rest of the Devons went back to their original positions on Patiala Ridge, to the north-west. They were a little previous. The Japanese badly wanted that hill. Yamamoto ordered another attempt to take it, preceded by artillery bombardment and a hail of machine-gun fire. Two attacks were driven back, but the third broke through A Company's perimeter. Only the gunners saved them, firing on the perimeter where over three score Japanese dead were counted the following morning.

The conditions in which the infantry fought were as appalling as anything at Kohima or on the Somme in the First World War. The distance between friend and foe was often as little as six yards. Under close observation it was impossible to wire the positions, or to dig. The dead lay in the sun and putrefied until the stench of rotting flesh became unbearable.[2] In some places the tension was such that men had to be relieved every twenty minutes. The trees that had covered the hillsides were now shattered stumps, shell-bursts had turned the slopes into a desert where nothing grew. And, as in the case of Sangshak, there were no water-points and water had to be dragged up in canvas *chagals* by the men themselves. Until the monsoon broke, that is. But when that happened, conditions changed to provide further horrors. The troops were almost submerged in rain and, at 4000 feet, in cloud for weeks on end, so that visibility was reduced to 100 yards, and the sun itself became invisible. Trenches collapsed in the incessant downpour, dugouts were ankle-deep in mud.

[1] Evans and Brett-James, op.cit., p. 233
[2] Major T. G. Picard, 3/3 Gurkhas, in Evans and Brett-James, op.cit., p. 291

9/12 Frontier Force Regiment took over from the Devons' A Company. This was the same battalion that had provided the screen of patrols when the Japanese first crossed the Chindwin, but Nippon Hill was a tougher proposition. Ueda brought up his tanks and shelled the hill-top again and again. Within a few days the Punjabis of 9/12 FFR were pushed off the slopes. Major Itō took the hill by storm on 16 April, avenging the loss of Lieutenant Maejima and his company. So the Japanese ruled the crest once more, and had a magnificent platform from which they overlooked the entire stretch of road from Tengnoupal to Shenam. Gracey decided to let things stand. He could afford to lose no more men over a single hill-top – the Japanese had already started on the other hills – and he let Yamamoto's men control Nippon Hill until the end of July.

Five nights after he took Nippon Hill, Itō's men captured Ikkenya Hill (Crete East), set up an HQ there and pressed on the attack to Kawamichi Hill (Crete West) but failed to take it. In the attack, Itō sustained heavy losses, but Yamamoto insisted he try again. 'Give 1 Company to your adjutant, Captain Yazu, to take Kawamichi', he told Itō, 'then take your whole unit on to Itō Hill (Scraggy)'. 'I've been ordered to put in two attacks,' Itō protested, 'but last night's was a failure and we are still collecting the dead and wounded. I'd like to wait until we can prepare an attack properly and recce the enemy positions.' 'What's that?' Yamamoto stormed at him. 'You coward! Didn't you hear my orders? They are the Emperor's orders!'[1]

But Itō had had enough, and was past caring. 'The Emperor couldn't possibly give orders as stupid as these!' Relations between Yamamoto and Itō, as Japanese accounts politely put it, were strained. But, like Ueda, Itō went too far, and military law was harsh on him. The Force Commander removed him from his command at once.[2]

Itō's attacks had made an impact on the British. Early in the morning of 22 April, the Devons' commander, Colonel Harvest, telephoned his Brigade HQ to report the attack on Crete. Unless a counter-attack were mounted at once he thought the hill would be overrun. Sam Greeves heard the report with some scepticism because, although he had always considered Harvest to be a good CO, he thought him inclined to be unduly elated by success and unduly depressed by failure.[3] Greeves then went across to HQ 3/1 Gurkha Rifles to see if a counter-attack was feasible, discussed matters with the CO, Colonel Wingfield, and went off to HQ 1 Devon. A battle was raging as he arrived, with heavy shelling and mortar fire. Harvest seemed depressed, and said the Japanese were coming at Crete from all sides, his forward posts on Crete East had been driven in,

---

[1] Military command was assumed to derive its ultimate authority from the Emperor.

[2] Hamachi Toshio, *Inpāru saizensen* (*Imphal front-line*), Tokyo, 1980, p. 120

[3] Gracey Papers, 182, Greeves to Gracey, 23 April 1944

and the position was becoming untenable from enemy shell fire and tank guns. He had already had heavy casualties. Only a counter-attack on a large scale, perhaps at brigade strength, would save the situation.

Greeves disagreed, and told Harvest that even if he could not hold the forward edge of Crete East, he must on no account abandon the summit. C Company, which had been Harvest's deep concern – he thought it completely cut off and without water – could find water from the stream in front of its position by using fighting patrols at night; and, far from being cut off, Greeves did not think it had even been attacked. If Crete were taken by the Japanese then C Company would withdraw under cover of darkness. Wingfield then arrived and they discussed again the idea of a counter-attack, which Greeves finally vetoed. 'I told Colonel Harvest,' he later noted, 'that as far as I knew, his casualties had not been unduly heavy and that this was now a matter of guts and his fellows must hold on.'[1]

This was rough medicine, particularly since Greeves had used the Devons to pick his chestnuts out of the fire on Nippon Hill a few days before, and they had paid a heavy price for it. But Harvest later agreed that he had misappreciated the situation and blamed this on incorrect information from his company commanders. He placed the company commander who had withdrawn from Crete East in direct contradiction to his orders under arrest, as Greeves advised. Another was deprived of command of his company. Harvest told Greeves that he missed his more experienced officers – casualties in the recent battles – as so much in this type of fighting depended on company and platoon commanders. Greeves agreed: it was 50% of the battle, jungle training and defences being 'only the other half.' Greeves reported all this to Gracey and added that the Japanese themselves must be very tired and suffering heavy casualties. Greeves's guess was right. The Devons had paid a high price. But so had Itō's battalion. By the time the fight was over it was down to eighty men.

While the dingdong exchange of hills was going on along the main road to Palel, Yoshioka and Takemura were leading their battalions through the hills to the north against the airfield. This first attempt to put Palel airfield out of action, at the end of April, was a failure, and it involved Kiani's Indians, too.

Under pressure from Fujiwara, then visiting Yamamoto Force, Kiani was taken in by Japanese optimism about the imminent fall of Imphal. Speed was of the essence, he was told, if his men were to share in the triumph of taking this capital of an Indian province, so his men left behind their heavy baggage at Kalewa, including their grenades and machine-guns. They set off for battle with blankets, rifles and fifty rounds apiece.

---

[1] ibid.

The raid on the airfield was assigned to a striking force of 300 men under Major Pritam Singh. Carrying only one day's rations, they covered forty miles until they reached the outskirts of Palel on 28 April. The attack was timed for midnight, so they hid in thick shrubs until nightfall.

Moving up to the airfield perimeter, Pritam Singh found it heavily defended, with strong picquets posted on the surrounding heights. Captain Sadhu Singh was told to take one of the picquets and his men fixed bayonets, moved up to it under cover of darkness and charged. The defenders – Indians themselves – were taken by surprise and put up their hands. '*Sathi ham ko mat maro*! (Comrade, don't kill us!)' they called out to the INA men, and the picquet commander asked one of the INA officers, Lt Lal Singh, what he wanted. Lal Singh was carrying a Naga spear and shouted, 'I want the blood of those two English officers who are hiding in that corner!' He charged at them with his spear, but the Indian troops in the picquet reacted against this attack on their British officers, opened fire on him and riddled him with bullets. Major Pritam Singh, who had be- lieved the Indians in the picquet were about to surrender, retreated with his men in disorder.

Another INA party had better luck and infiltrated the picquet line on the airfield but found no Japanese at the rendezvous to hold it. They withdrew after carrying out demolitions.[1] The British exacted retribution. When dawn came, artillery opened up on the Gandhi Brigade positions. The one day's rations proved foolhardy, and the guns were punishing. In one day, Gandhi Brigade lost 250 men.

Kohima Phase One: assault and siege

On 5 April, the day after Scoones regrouped his forces in the Imphal Plain, the Japanese closed in on Kohima, eighty miles further north. At 5 pm that day, Hugh Richards, a former Chindit colonel, the commander of the small Kohima garrison, listened to a report from a Naga tribesman. The Japanese had appeared, in battalion strength, near Mao Songsang to the south of Kohima and were marching towards Kohima along the main road from Imphal. This was Major-General Miyazaki's 58 Infantry Regiment, fresh from the victory at Sangshak. Miyazaki was on horseback – the horse had been taken at Sangshak – and carried his little pet monkey Chibi ('Tich') on his shoulder. He had been given it as a present by the village

---

[1] According to Shah Nawaz Khan, whose account this is (*INA and its Netaji*, pp. 114–15) they destroyed RAF aircraft on the ground, but Slim records no damage was done (*Defeat into Victory*, p. 327) and it is possible there is a confusion with the later and more successful raid in June 1944. Hugh Toye says the raid was on 2 May, not on the airfield perimeter but on a Gurkha platoon position five miles away (*Springing Tiger*, pp. 226–7).

headman at Mao Songsang, where the notables had welcomed Miyazaki, giving him five pigs, ten chickens and a hundred eggs for his men.[1]

Richards did not know what unit was moving against him, but it had been taken for granted in the planning of the Imphal battle that the Japanese would attempt to sever communications with the rest of India at the village of Kohima. The neat bungalows and tidy red-roofed lines of Kohima stand 5000 feet above sea-level where the road from Imphal makes a sudden turn westward towards Dimapur forty-six miles away. At Dimapur the road ends and joins the railway running between Ledo and Calcutta. The village is set in an ocean of peaks and ridges crossed by bridle-paths. Its importance lay in the fact that it was at the summit of a pass; to its west rose a steep massif reaching to 10,000 feet, to its north and east ranges reaching to nearly 8000 feet. This pass was, in effect, the best route between Assam, Manipur, and ultimately Burma. The ridge slopes at Kohima were steep and thickly wooded, and although the terraces of the town itself were cleared for cultivation, the trees on the ridges were tall and (until artillery fire destroyed them) dense enough to create pitch darkness underneath during the cold nights, and a hot and sweaty place during the day.[2]

Kohima was the peacetime headquarters of the Deputy Commissioner, who at the time was Charles Pawsey, much beloved by the Naga tribesmen and devoted to their welfare. His bungalow, with its tennis court, was situated in the right angle bend of the main road. To the north-east stood the Naga village proper, just beyond the hill called Treasury Hill. South of the bungalow stretched a series of small hills, on which stood warehouses and shacks housing supplies. These hills saw what Compton Mackenzie later described as 'fighting as desperate as any recorded in history'.[3]

Slim and Scoones miscalculated about Kohima. Naturally enough. Given the impossible nature of the terrain between it and the Chindwin, miles to the east, a landscape endlessly filled with high jungle ridges, they judged that the Japanese would certainly try to take Kohima, but that they would send a regiment against it, no more. The Japanese sent a division.

Richards arrived in Kohima on 22 March 1944 to find the place in chaos. He was supposed to have 1st Assam Regiment as garrison troops, but only some rear details were there, with a few Assam Rifles platoons (3 Naga Hills Bn.) and the Shere Regiment, raw troops from the Royal Nepalese Army. Richards was delighted when the West Yorks were sent in, as part of 5 Division's reinforcement of the Dimapur-Kohima area. But they were despatched elsewhere almost at once. The 4 Battalion Royal West Kents arrived and were then in turn ordered back to Dimapur. Fortunately for the

---

[1] Kojima, *Eirei no tani*, p. 173

[2] Kirby, *War Against Japan*, III, p. 300; A. Campbell, *The Siege*, p. 57

[3] Mackenzie, *All Over The Place*, p. 77

Kohima garrison they were ordered back again from the relative comforts of Dimapur to Kohima. They were the last British troops to get into the town before the Japanese surrounded it. Richards knew he ought to build fortifications, but he could not get barbed wire from Dimapur. There was an administrative regulation forbidding the use of barbed wire in the Naga Hills and the Dimapur quartermaster observed it to the letter.[1] Ahead of Kohima, in the hills leading to the Chindwin, troops of the Assam Regiment held the outposts of Jessami and Kharasom, with orders to hold to the last man.

The 4 Royal West Kents had been flown in from Arakan, under their commander Lt-Colonel John ('Danny') Laverty, and they were in Dimapur when the fighting began. In overall command of both Dimapur and Kohima was Major-General Ranking, commander of 202 Area, in other words the head of an administrative division, not the chief of a fighting force, and with no staff to handle a battle. In 1943, Dimapur and Kohima were both rear echelon locations. It was an odd appointment, made for an emergency. Scoones at IV Corps in Imphal could not control affairs so far back, and Slim had arranged for a fresh Corps and its commander to run the battle, i.e. XXXIII Corps under Lieutenant-General (later Sir) Montagu Stopford, who would also have under his command 7 Indian Division (Messervy) which was following 5 Division out of Arakan and 2 Division (Major-General John Grover), a regular British division then scattered in jungle camps throughout India. 2 Division consisted of some of the best infantry regiments in the British Army: Camerons, Royal Scots, Royal Welch Fusiliers, Norfolks, Dorsets, Berkshires, Durham Light Infantry, with the 2nd Manchester Machine Gun Battalion, three regiments of field artillery and an anti-tank regiment. It was a formidable force, furnished to European standards with motor transport, highly trained and well-equipped, but originally destined for combined operations rather than jungle warfare. Four of its battalions had already been engaged in Arakan during the 1943 campaign but the division as a whole had not been in action since Dunkirk.

Ranking had ordered 161 Brigade (Warren) to Kohima, but when Stopford took over he told Ranking that the defence of Dimapur was first priority.[2] Odd as this may seem in retrospect, it was not so at the time: Kohima was, in essence, a roadblock. Dimapur, the railhead, was a vast storehouse of supplies and ammunition. The dump there was eleven miles long and at least a mile wide, and its loss would have put paid to any Allied offensive into Burma.[3] But Warren saw the risk involved in letting the

[1] Swinson, 'Kohima', *Purnell's History of the Second World War*, p. 1693

[2] Swinson, op.cit., but Slim, *Defeat into Victory*, pp. 309–10, implies he himself gave the order.

[3] Compton Mackenzie visited Dimapur in 1947, and was amused to notice the old ruined fort nearby with its score of huge stones, shaped like enormous button mushrooms and called by British troops, inevitably, 'Prick Park'. (*All Over the Place* p. 69)

Japanese into Kohima by default, and he was furious when he was told to leave it; as were Pawsey and Richards. Pawsey naturally thought the Army was leaving his Nagas to the tender mercies of the advancing Japanese, and Richards that his garrison was being given up for lost long before the battle had even begun. Ranking explained to them that an RAF report showed the Japanese to be outflanking Kohima and making for Dimapur. Pawsey poured scorn on this: 'If the Japanese were there, then my Nagas would have told me so!'[1] But given Slim's emphasis on holding Dimapur, Ranking insisted. Warren had no option but to withdraw his men, even though he knew that once the Kohima ridge was occupied by the Japanese a major battle would be needed to retake it. The two forward positions at Jessami and Kharasom were soon overrun. Richards had managed to have the 'last man last round' order rescinded, since it seemed a pointless waste of lives, and the cancellation got through to 1st Bn. Assam Regiment at Jessami, from where the surviving defenders withdrew on the night of 31 March/1 April. The news never reached Kharasom. Captain Young, the commander, realizing how hopeless the situation was, sent all his men back to Kohima and fought on alone until he was killed.

During the night of 3 April, the advance guard (11 Coy, III Bn, 58 Inf. Regt.) of 31 Division reached the outskirts of the Naga village. 11 Company's leading platoon was commanded by Kobayashi Naoji, who was the first Japanese into Kohima. They had covered about 160 miles, across the grain of the country, over endless ridges reaching to 8000 feet or more above sea-level, in twenty days, bringing with them animals (for food) and guns, broken up and manhandled over the mountains. It was an epic march by any standards. 'When my platoon reached the fork in the road close to where you go into Kohima village', remembers Kobayashi,

> the dawn was about to break and the order to rest came from Company HQ. The men were dead beat after marching night and day and flopped down to sleep. I couldn't sleep, not being sure of the lay-out of Kohima and feeling responsible as platoon commander. I prospected ahead, wondering whether to take the right fork or the left. The sky lightened, and I could see a number of figures moving up the slope on the hill opposite. And what looked like soldiers... I looked harder. It was the enemy all right. But they seemed to be completely unaware that the Japanese were coming. I roused the platoon, told them to keep absolutely quiet, and reported to the company commander, who soon had every platoon commander converging on my position. The company commander distributed the men, who moved smartly... So we were the first into Kohima, we fired the first

---

[1] Swinson, op.cit., p. 1964

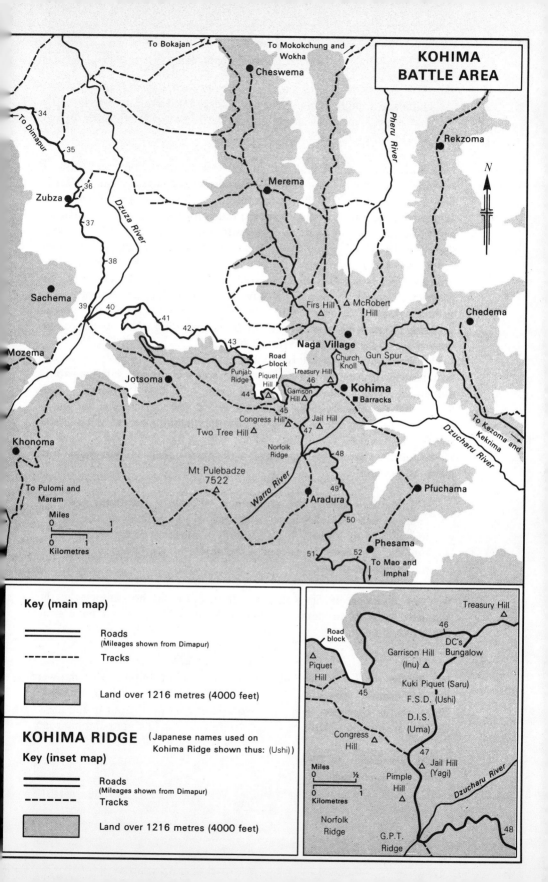

KOHIMA BATTLE AREA

To Bokajan

To Mokokchung and Wokha

Cheswema

To Mokokchung and Wokha

Pheru River

34

To Dimapur

35

Rekzoma

36

Zubza

N

37

Dzuza River

Merema

38

Sachema

39 40

41

42

Chedema

43

Mozema

Firs Hill

McRobert Hill

Naga Village

Church Knoll

Gun Spur

Jotsoma

Road block

Punjab Ridge

Piquet Hill

Treasury Hill

46

Kohima

Barracks

44

45

Garrison Hill

To Kezoma and Kekrima

Dzucharu River

Congress Hill

Jail Hill

Two Tree Hill

47

Norfolk Ridge

48

Khonoma

Mt Pulebadze 7522

Warro River

Aradura

49

Pfuchama

To Pulomi and Maram

50

Phesama

Miles
0   1

51   52

To Mao and Imphal

Kilometres
0   1

Key (main map)

Roads
(Mileages shown from Dimapur)

- - - - - Tracks

Land over 1216 metres (4000 feet)

KOHIMA RIDGE

(Japanese names used on Kohima Ridge shown thus: (Ushi))

Key (inset map)

Roads
(Mileages shown from Dimapur)

- - - - - Tracks

Land over 1216 metres (4000 feet)

Treasury Hill

Road block

46

DC's Bungalow

Garrison Hill (Inu)

Piquet Hill

Kuki Piquet (Saru)

45

F.S.D. (Ushi)

D.I.S. (Uma)

Congress Hill

47

Jail Hill (Yagi)

Miles
0   ½

Pimple Hill

Kilometres
0   1

Dzucharu River

Norfolk Ridge

G.P.T. Ridge

48

shot. Even though the battle ultimately ended in defeat, I still claim the honour of being the first man of III Battalion to go into that place, where the most fearful battles were fought, and of being the first to catch sight of the enemy.

Like Kobayashi, the rest of the Japanese were tense, but confident. Lt Nishida, also of 11 Company, III Battalion, had already carried out a secret reconnaissance of the terrain leading to Kohima and as he drew up his men on the banks of the Chindwin ready for the midnight crossing, he had something to say to them. They were 110 strong, and after checking their equipment, he paced slowly between the ranks and stopped, his voice low but powerful as it broke the silence: 'Let us now take farewell of our country.' His sword flew from its scabbard, flashed in the moonlight: 'Fix bayonets! Present... arms!' The bayonets looked like the crest of a wave as hands slapped the rifles. No one moved. Nishida was aware of the blood coursing through his veins and of the tears trembling in his eyelids, as his men swore to die for their distant motherland.[1]

The divisional commander, Lieutenant-General Satō Kōtoku, also said his farewells. But he did it without heroics and was not very sanguine about the future. When the order to move came – 'X-Day 15 March' – Satō assembled the officers of his divisional HQ at the spot deep in the jungle west of Maungaing where he lived during the planning period. It was about eight miles from HQ, and Satō did the trip on foot every day to keep fit. He hoped they would be successful, and drank a glass of champagne with them, but added:

> I'll take the opportunity, gentlemen, of making something quite clear to you. Miracles apart, everyone of you is likely to lose his life in this operation. It isn't simply a question of the enemy's bullets. You must be prepared for death by starvation in these mountain fastnesses.

Not the cheeriest of farewells, but then Satō did not indulge in the Japanese habit of euphemism. The battle for Kohima might have gone differently if he had.

The British official historian points out that, unlike Imphal, Kohima was not deliberately chosen by the British commanders as a battleground.[2] There was no question of any garrison defending every spot in the area. The key position was Kohima Ridge itself, since the Dimapur-Imphal road

---

[1] OCH, *Biruma sensen*, pp. 209–11

[2] Kirby, *War Against Japan*, III, p. 299

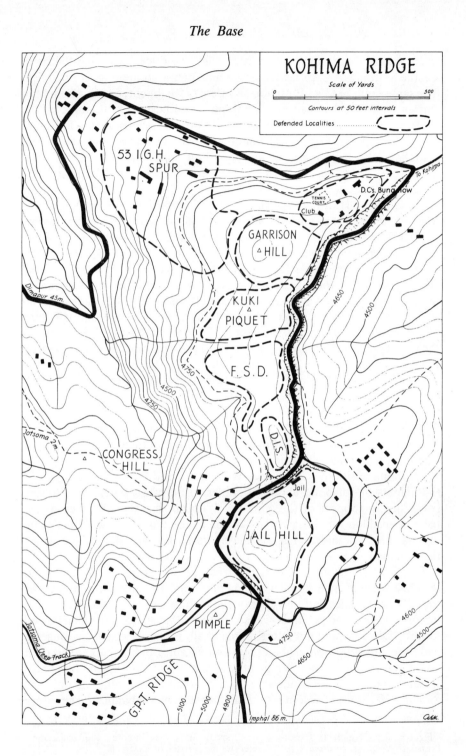

KOHIMA RIDGE

Scale of Yards

0 ———————————— 500

Contours at 50 feet intervals

Defended Localities .... ⌒⌒⌒

53 I.G.H. SPUR

D.C's. Bungalow

To Kohima

TENNIS COURTS

Club

GARRISON HILL

Dimapur 45 m.

KUKI PIQUET

4650

4500

F.S.D.

4750

4500

4250

D.I.S.

Jotsoma 2 m.

CONGRESS HILL

Jail

JAIL HILL

4600

PIMPLE

Jotsoma (Jeep Track)

4750

4650

G.P.T. RIDGE

5100

5000

4900

4500

Imphal 86 m.

made a loop round it. Whoever controlled the ridge controlled the road. On the morning of 4 April, Richards's men prepared the ridge for defence. The same night Satō's I Battalion 58 Infantry Regiment, coming from Mao further south on the road to Imphal, put in an unsuccessful attack on the southern end of the defences at General Purpose Transport (GPT) Ridge. The following morning they had another go and gained a foothold. The III Battalion, also from Mao, worked round into the Naga village north-east of Kohima ridge on 4 April. They were then ordered to march on Cheswema, a report having been received that other Japanese units had taken Garrison Hill, the implication being the Kohima was taken and that it might be possible to push the advance further. The report was erroneous, and III/58 was ordered to return to Naga village on 6 April, at the same time as I/138 came into it.

The Royal West Kents (Laverty) moved on Kohima on 5 April as the advance guard of 161 Brigade of 5 Division. With some engineers and a mountain battery they were in place that afternoon as the Japanese began their assault from the south on the positions along the ridge: Jail Hill, east of the road, DIS (Detail Issue Store), FSD (Field Supply Depot), Kuki Picquet, Garrison Hill, DC's Bungalow, to the west of it. It was just as well Laverty's men had the mountain battery with them. The first scratch garrison had only a 25-pounder which was knocked out a few minutes after battle started on the morning of the 5th.

Then the siege began. It lasted for a fortnight, during which the Japanese inched up the ridge, from one fiercely contested position to the next, sometimes driven off, but always returning to the attack. They had put a ring round Kohima which prevented the rest of 161 Brigade coming into the Kohima position, so Brigadier Warren decided to establish himself on the heights of Jotsoma, about two miles to the west, where his artillery could fire in support of the garrison. Without that support, they would have been done for, because two of their mountain guns went the same way as the 25-pounder. The Japanese overlooked any place from which they could fire.

The West Kents were under 500 strong as they went into Kohima and they lost some of their numbers trying to occupy Treasury Hill (on the way to the Naga village) and to withdraw the men isolated on GPT Ridge. The fighting at these two positions was so confused that some of the men retired towards Dimapur and not into Kohima at all. Richards's garrison, once he had evacuated 200 wounded and non-combatants, and taking into account the men from the Assam Regiment who had been withdrawn in time from Jessami, and the 5/7 Rajputs sent from Jotsoma by Warren, amounted to around 2500 men, of whom a thousand were non-combatants.[1] They were

---

[1] Figures vary. Campbell, *The Siege*, p. 53, speaks of 'fifteen hundred non-combatants.' Prasad, *Reconquest of Burma*, I, p. 276, refers to 'the garrison of 3500 men.'

facing, not, as Slim and Scoones had planned, a Japanese regiment (say 3000 men), but almost the whole weight of two regiments of 31 Division, well over 6000 men. And the garrison, like the men at Sangshak, corralled into a triangular area 700 yards by 900 by 1100, found that although there was plenty of food and ammunition, they were short of water.

An officer from the West Kents, after noting with disgust that the position held only one gun, described the medical arrangements as 'utterly inefficient' and the water supply as dire.[1] A pipeline led in from the hills but, apart from the west side, the Japanese were all around on the hills and ridges, and that pipe would be cut. Both the Indian General Hospital and the Field Supply Depot had canvas tanks, which should have been sunk into the ground to preserve them under gunfire; and they should have been filled. But they weren't.

From 6 April onwards, the Japanese mortared and shelled the garrison every evening at dusk. When it grew dark, they sent in wave after wave of infantry. Inevitably, the defenders gave ground, and the Japanese re- morselessly began to crawl and bomb and bayonet their way along Kohima Ridge. First GPT Ridge fell, and its defenders withdrew, demoralised, along the road to Dimapur, instead of moving into Kohima to strengthen the box. It was the loss of this ridge which gave the Japanese control of Kohima's water supply. They then attacked Jail Hill and were repulsed. Frontal attacks were tried, and also the classic tactic of infiltration: on the night 6/7 April a Japanese party infiltrated into *bashas* (huts) between the FSD and DIS. When they got through and the *bashas* were fired on by the West Kents, the Japanese hid in brick ovens in the FSD, and it was on this occasion that one of the West Kents, L/Cpl Harman, carried out one of the actions that later led to his (posthumous) VC.

To get into the FSD shacks, the platoon commander of the Indian Sappers and Miners, Lt Wright, offered the use of pole charges to blow down the walls of the windowless FSD bakery where the Japanese were hiding in the brick ovens, sheltered by the heavy iron lids. Wright used slabs of guncotton tied to the tops of ammunition boxes, the lot being fixed to the end of a bamboo pole. Under covering fire from the infantry, his men would dash to the bakery walls and detonate the charges. As the walls blew down, the infantry would charge in.

That was the theory. In fact the West Kents D Company were cut down by automatic fire and grenades hurled from.the bakery buildings. And on their flank two machine guns raked the area and kept the attackers pinned down. Harman decided to have a go himself. A big burly lad of 19, recently promoted to lance-corporal, Harman was the son of the owner of Lundy Island. He was a natural fighter and had already proved his courage under fire. This time he walked out of his slit trench under the covering fire of

---

[1] Campbell, op.cit., p. 55

Bren guns, lobbed two grenades into the bakery, sprinted to the shelter of the wall, shot one machine-gun crew and came back with the machine gun across his shoulders. His bravery inspired his own section to get up off the ground, the sappers dashed to the walls and exploded their charges, and the infantry rushed the ruined buildings.[1]

One building did not fall to the main assault. Harman went in, counted ten ovens and narrowly missed being shot at from them. He returned, dragging a case of hand grenades, and went round all the ovens, one by one, counting three before lifting the lid and popping in the 4-second grenade. He brought two wounded Japanese, one under each arm, back to his section. The whole bakery position was by this time an inferno and Indians who had been taken prisoner by the Japanese ran for their lives from the flaming *bashas*, followed by the Japanese themselves, who were picked off by D Company's reserve platoon. The West Kents counted forty-four Japanese dead when the attack was over. That action was characteristic of much of the fighting on Kohima Ridge itself. The actions were hand-to-hand combat, fierce and ruthless, by filthy, bedraggled, worn-out men, whose lungs were rarely free of the noxious smell of decaying corpses inside and outside the perimeter, who were dependent on air-drop supplies even for water, and desperate on seeing the long-desired parachutes often fall into the Japanese positions; unable to use the little artillery left to them because no positions could be found from which the Japanese could not spot them. Once the circle had closed, the wounded could not be evacuated, and were often wounded again as they lay, helpless, in the restricted space available to the frantically over-worked medical officers, one of whom, Lieutenant-Colonel John Young (75 Indian Field Ambulance) had marched in from Dimapur, on foot and alone, to be with the garrison. Fortunately for the wounded – and for the garrison as a whole – the water position was slightly relieved when a pipe fed by a spring[2] was found on the road north-west of the box. But it was exposed to Japanese fire, and water could only be drawn in the hours of darkness.

'Many of the wounded, I feel sure,' said Major Donald Easten, commander of D Company, 'died in the last few days because they had given up hope.'[3] One historian of the battle hints that wounded officers contemplated suicide:

> The officers from whom pistols had been removed when they were first carried in on stretchers, insisted on having their weapons back; some, at least, had decided in the long hours and

---

[1] Campbell, op.cit., p. 81

[2] So Prasad, p. 279. Kirby describes it as 'a seepage on the north face of Garrison Hill' (*War Against Japan*, III, p. 303).

[3] Brett-James, *Ball of Fire*, p. 314.

days of anxiety and fear that, if badly wounded again, they would shoot and be finished with it all.[1]

By 15 April, the garrison had been shepherded into an even more confined area by Japanese encroachments and by the shelling from Japanese gun positions on the slopes above Kohima, using in some cases ammunition parachuted to them in error. On 16 April two medical officers were killed and a third wounded when Japanese artillery hit the Medical Inspection Room. The following day pressure built up in the FSD area and the DC's bungalow, a pleasant spot reduced to a smoking ruin by the battle. Between it and the Kohima Club – now a pile of rubble – lay a tennis court. In no time, it became the front line between attacker and defender, and where tennis balls had been idly lobbed by the few Europeans in more placid times, grenades whizzed back and forth across the width of the court.

Outside Kohima, the 161 Brigade box at Jotsoma, on which the garrison relied for its artillery cover and for counter-battery fire against the Japanese guns in the heights above the Naga village, was itself cut off from Dimapur. The arrival of 2 British Division in Dimapur had allowed Stopford to send 161 Brigade (which belonged to 5 Indian Division) to Jotsoma in the first place. The Brigade stayed in communication with 2 Division by telephone, but patrols checking broken lines on 8 April found that the Japanese had cut the road to Dimapur near Zubza, only thirty-six miles from the railhead. These were elements of 138 Infantry Regiment which had been ordered to stop reinforcements reaching the Kohima garrison. A detachment of Punjabis tried to clear the block on the 9th but failed, and the road remained closed until 14 April.

On 17 April, the exhausted West Kents in the FSD area needed to be relieved, and two platoons of Assam Rifles and one of the Assam Regiment took over.[2] Indian troops repelled several attacks on the bungalow area but were finally forced to give way when darkness came. Then Richards realized that Kuki Picquet, the position lying between Garrison Hill and FSD, was at risk. In the early hours of 18 April the Japanese swarmed on it and by 3 am it was in their hands. They had cut the garrison in two. They then opened heavy fire on Garrison Hill, a few yards to the north, and Richards had no reserves to stop them.

'The whole defence of Kohima was about to crumble,' records the Indian Official History. 'It all seemed over, and the brave garrison waited with their hearts in their mouths. But the Japanese knew not how near they came to success. The minutes lengthened into hours and the night wore off (*sic*), but the final vicious assault did not come. With the first faint glimmer

---

[1] ibid., p. 316

[2] Prasad, *Reconquest of Burma*, p. 279

of dawn, a ray of hope was born in the battle-weary garrison again. A new day, Thursday, 18 April, was coming, and with it came help at last.'[1]

The garrison had expected help on a number of occasions, and each time had felt the bitterness of hope deferred. Now the help was real. 161 Brigade, finally enabled to move out of its Jotsoma box by the advance of 2 Division from Dimapur, sent in a battalion of Punjabis (1/1 Punjab) and a tank detachment. First they relieved Hospital Ridge, where 300 wounded were waiting to be evacuated with the disconsolate and harried non-combatants who had been forced to remain during the siege. A company of Punjabis took over the West Kents' positions facing Kuki Picquet, another the defence positions at the DC's bungalow, and another, with the battalion's HQ, set itself up on Summerhouse Hill. By the time 161 Brigade took over, Kohima had been changed beyond recognition. Most of its buildings were in ruins, walls still standing were pockmarked with shell bursts or bullet holes, the trees were stripped of leaves and parachutes hung limply from the few branches that remained. It was the nearest thing to a battlefield of the First World War in the whole Burma campaign. 'The liberators saw little groups of grimy and bearded riflemen standing at the mouths of their bunkers and staring with blood-shot sleep-starved eyes as the relieving troops came in. They had not had a wash for a week. With the boom of the guns and the screech of shells always in their ears, they had fought and lived in their trenches for almost a fortnight. For rest they had thrown themselves on the ground with their boots on, ready to fight at a moment's notice.'[2]

That was 20 April. The garrison had been relieved. The siege of Kohima was over. But the battle for Kohima was about to begin. The tough little Miyazaki and his 58 Infantry Regiment were still in possession of most of it, and of the surrounding ridges, and would have to be prised out, bunker by bunker, ridge by ridge, before the road to Imphal could be re-opened. Stopford was receiving further reinforcements. 7 Indian Division had followed 5 Division from Arakan, and one of its brigades was now deploying to the north of Kohima, to strike down and cut at Satō's tracks from the Chindwin. 2 Division was moving up the road from Dimapur to the help of 161 Brigade. The most gruesome fortnight of the war had come to an end. But fighting was to continue in and around Kohima for two more months before the Japanese were winkled out; and it was internal dissension among their commanders, every bit as much as the powerful British onslaught, which in the end freed the road.

---

[1] ibid., p. 280

[2] Prasad, op.cit., p. 281; and Major Donald Easten, in Brett-James, *Ball of Fire*, p. 320

Black Cats vs. White Tigers (Round Two): on to Bishenpur

After destroying the British at Torbung, Yanagida planned to advance along the road through Bishenpur into Imphal and also to strike the road above Bishenpur by passing Sakuma's regiment through the hills west of the road and moving down from Ngaranjial. At the same time he needed to be sure that the British could not attack him along the track from Silchar. A commando raid was planned to ensure this: 2/Lt Abe Toshio, a platoon commander from II Company in Sasahara's regiment (215), was given command of a volunteer unit (*teishintai*) to sever the track. Twenty men, including engineers, left Singgel on 29 March and, without any preliminary reconnaissance, penetrated deep into the Indian hills for about 120 miles to fall upon the bridge over the Ilang River on 14 April. The bridge spanned a gorge seventy-five feet deep and was ninety yards long;[1] after a brisk exchange with troops guarding the bridge Abe's men blew it and were back with their regiment on the 26th. 'One Japanese jumped to his death in the gorge,' wrote Slim later, 'the other two went up with the bridge.'[2] But the others got away, and Abe returned to a triumphal welcome. Sasahara gave him and his men five days' leave.

Then began a struggle for the heights to the west of Bishenpur. Yanagida's men began their assault on Bishenpur by attacking the HQ of 49 Brigade at MS 27, and failed. But Yanagida was not relying on a frontal assault. His men were already in the hills west of the road, cutting the Silchar track. The British then began to change their dispositions. After the fighting of the past few weeks, 49 Brigade had earned a rest and was withdrawn through Bishenpur and Imphal. Its place was taken by 32 Brigade of 20 Division, which concentrated at Bishenpur. The brigade faced elements – now much depleted – of all of Yanagida's three regiments, 213, 214 and 215 with medium and field artillery in support. Between 15 April and the end of the first week in May, the brigade tried to prevent the Japanese bypassing its strongpoints in the hills, but here and there parties broke through and Indian patrols discovered them at the villages of Khoirok and Nunggang north-west of Bishenpur. At the same time, just west of MS 22, the village of Ninthoukhong was entered by Japanese on 20 April and in spite of a fierce attack by two Gurkha companies, two troops of 3 Dragoon Guards and an air-strike, they could not be budged. The British force was met by machine gun fire and sustained seventy casualties. One Lee tank was hit and burnt out. The

---

[1] So the Japanese figures. 'This was a three-hundred-foot suspension bridge over an eighty-foot deep gorge and its destruction made a complete break in the track.' Slim, *Defeat into Victory*, p. 329

[2] Slim, op.cit., p. 239

attack went in again on 25 April but failed again, this time with the loss of four tanks. The Japanese were left in occupation of the village.

Sakuma's 214 Regiment moved into the hills from Churachandpur and a company of his I Battalion took a hill position (Mori Hill, or 'Forest Hill') about a mile south-west of Hill 5846 which was occupied by Gurkhas and the Northamptons (Taunton). About a hundred yards east was another hill where two old wireless aerials stood – Wireless Hill. The Japanese took this, too, but concentrated artillery shelling from Bishenpur cut them off from their regimental HQ. The brigadier commanding 32 Brigade (Mackenzie) concentrated all his artillery in the village, eight 25-pounders, four 3.7 howitzers, six 6-pounders, and three A/A guns, twenty-one pieces in all, and poured fire into the Japanese positions in the hills.[1]

32 Brigade only beat the Japanese to its own defence line in the hills by a matter of hours. They were just in position by 16 April, but rapidly built and strengthened a line of positions Bishenpur-Ngaranjial-Forest Hill, behind which ran another line, the Outer Bishenpur Line. The Japanese made desperate attempts to break through these lines and rush Imphal. Even Japanese fighter aircraft joined in on the night of 24 April, striking British positions on Forest Hill. But some Japanese units had already lost appetite for the battle. Four days before, when Sueki Battalion of Sasahara Regiment (III/215) moved into positions in front of Wireless Hill in readiness for a dawn attack on the 21st, as the arrowhead of a regimental thrust, it was shelled in error by its own mountain guns and many men were killed. The battalion withdrew to the valley in its rear.

The Northamptons had suffered, too. Having taken over a hundred casualties defending Hill 5846, they found themselves cut off by intense machine gun and artillery fire from Bishenpur. Supply convoys from Bishenpur only got through by picqueting the track into the hills. By 27 April the Japanese were so firmly lodged on the Silchar track that the convoys could not get through at all. An attempt to clear a way through to the Northamptons' water point – visible to Japanese artillery on a height near the village of Kokadan – was repulsed, even though it was supported by a troop of tanks from 3 Carabiniers, one of which got stuck, and a second fell into a nullah.

---

[1] The British official war history sees the artillery balance in a different light. 'The artillery supporting 32nd Brigade (twelve field and four mountain guns)' writes Kirby (*War Against Japan*, III, p. 311) 'was quite inadequate to deal with the Japanese artillery, which included a heavy field artillery regiment. In consequence the British medium tanks, boldly handled in support of the brigade's attempt to clear the area, although superior to the Japanese tanks, began to incur such heavy losses as to cause some anxiety.' As long as the road to the railhead at Dimapur was cut at Kohima, these losses could not be made good and the tank crews of 150 Squadron RAC were evacuated to India, handing over what was left of their tanks to the Carabiniers to make up their losses. (ibid., p. 311, n. 1)

This close, fierce fighting hardly seems the kind of warfare in which propaganda might be of use. But the war of attrition which was gradually whittling down the strength and vitality of Sakuma and Sasahara Regiments decided the British to put in wireless broadcasts. The newspaper *Gunjin Shimbun* ('The Soldiers' Daily News'), edited in Calcutta by an American of Japanese descent called Oka Shigeki, was showered on the Japanese positions, while loudspeakers called on 'the brave warriors of 33 Division' to listen while the shelling stopped. Japanese popular songs then came over the air, and, at the end, an announcement came: 'We are going to start shelling again. Soldiers, go back into your foxholes. Leave your officers outside.'

The Japanese sniped the track along which the Northamptons sent their mule-drivers for water, and the Northamptons sniped back. One of them, Sergeant Kelly of Peterborough, later Regimental Sergeant-Major, would watch for hours until a target offered itself and then notch his rifle butt. Ultimately, it held 23 such notches. One of his rifles was blown to pieces by a grenade, but Kelly went on sniping with another. The water fatigue used him as its shield until a wound put him out of action. A Japanese historian wonders whether the official regimental account of the Northamptons was 'making heroes' when it described Kelly's performance, and says it is hard to accept blindly the *ude* or skill of what he calls '*Koroshiya Kerii*' – 'Killer Kelly'.[1] If it is true, he adds, then one-fifth of the casualties sustained by 215 Regiment at Ngaranjial were the result of Kelly's markmanship. On 1 May, the regiment had under 500 men, and of these, only two-thirds were fit to fight. It had lost half its fighting strength in the battle for Tongzang, and then at Ngaranjial it lost close on another 500 in killed and wounded.

Sakuma was in little better state. In attacks on Forest Hill he had 289 casualties. His freshest troops, 9 Company, put in a night attack on Forest Hill on 24 April under an umbrella of fire from one 150 mm howitzer and five mountain guns. They attacked the British positions from the west but were greeted with such concentrated mortar fire under the artificial daylight of bursting star shells, and from tanks, that they took very heavy casualties, the attack failed, and by the end of it they were down to less than forty men.

British losses were heavy, too. At one stage, when 17 Indian Division in this sector had just one brigade under command (32 Brigade), one of its battalions lost three-quarters of its officers and men. At great cost, they had brought 33 Division's thrust on Imphal finally to a standstill: the Japanese in the hills were ten miles away, but they got no further.

A mood of crisis enveloped both higher commands for most of March and April. 17 Division's beleaguered retreat from Tiddim had deprived Scoones of his Corps reserve when he was compelled to send 23 Division to

[1] Kojima op.cit., p. 217

the rescue. And the threat in the centre from 15 Division and to Kohima in the north from 31 Division emphasized how vulnerable IV Corps had suddenly become. It had originally been mooted to bring in 5 Division from Arakan to reinforce Imphal, and move up 26 and 36 Divisions into Arakan. The move had been planned by road and rail but such leisurely means of transport might have lost the battle. The decision was taken to fly them in. War-experienced as 5 Division was, it had never been flown out *en masse* before, but the operation went without a serious hitch – involving a 100-mile journey to the airfield at Dohazari and a flight of over 250 miles over territory some of which was already in the hands of the Japanese. General Evans quotes an instance of an artillery regiment moved out of action on a Monday at 2.00 pm, guns dismantled for flight at Dohazari on the Tuesday, guns reassembled at the airfield on the Wednesday, and in action on the Thursday.[1] It was a fast and brilliant piece of management.

But it had only been possible as a result of drive from the top. Lieutenant-General Sir George Giffard, Commander-in-Chief 11 Army Group, under whose orders Slim's XIV Army operated, thought Slim could run the battle without too much interference from him, and had enough force at his disposal to do so. Giffard, to put it mildly, did not get on with Mountbatten, and when he was upbraided for his slowness in moving the reserves, he sulked. According to Mountbatten's Chief of Staff, Lieutenant- General Sir Henry Pownall, Slim did not show much sense of urgency, either, and Mountbatten acted at once off his own bat to get the aircraft needed for the fly-in. This entailed borrowing transport aircraft from the flight over the Hump to China. And as they had been borrowed already for the fly-in of supplies to XV Corps in Arakan and of men, mules and guns to Wingate's landing grounds after 5 March, Mountbatten was in a quandary. It had taken seventeen days[2] to get the aircraft before, 'through channels' (i.e. via Stilwell, who controlled the China operation, to the Combined Chiefs of Staff in Washington) and Mountbatten had been told by Roosevelt himself that it was not to happen again. The Americans were committed to building up air bases in China for heavy bombers to support an air offensive from carrier-based aircraft in the Pacific against the Philippines and Formosa. As they saw it, those bases were the sole *raison d'être* of the entire Burma campaign and *nothing* was to interfere with them. Nevertheless, Mountbatten went ahead, and commandeered the aircraft.

As it happened, he was in a parlous state himself. On a visit to Ledo to confer with Stilwell, a sharp bamboo entered his eye during a jeep drive.[3] There was a possibility he might lose his sight and the doctors

---

[1] Purnell's *History of the Second World War*, p. 1688

[2] Ten days, according to Ronald Lewin, *Slim*, p. 174

[3] In his role of tough no-nonsense Yankee paying host to an effete aristocratic Limey dude, Stilwell showed Mountbatten Japanese corpses on his front: 'Louis has been up but didn't like the smell of corpses.' He added, though, 'Louis and I get on famously even if he does have curly eyelashes.' (*The Stilwell Papers*, p. 263)

forbade him to read for two days. These were the early days of the battle, when the Japanese were pouring over the Chindwin on all fronts, so Mountbatten was forced to be more, not less, active. He was back at his GHQ on 18 March, having called to see Slim at XIV Army on the way. Slim realized in the course of conversation how slowly his back-up would come, as Pownall had found out from Giffard when Mountbatten was still in Ledo:

I had sounded a warning here to Giffard (*Pownall noted in his diary for 18 March*)[1] who was extremely cagey on the subject and disturbingly complacent about the whole situation. He said that Slim had plenty of troops and could move them as he wanted. It was clear that he didn't propose to intervene himself or give the spur to Slim and he made it plain that he would regard intervention by Mountbatten as being unwelcome.

When Mountbatten came back Giffard was still unduly complacent, for it was quite clear to everyone else that the situation was just on the point of boiling up (it did so within 28 hours) and the IV Corps would then find themselves in a jam for lack of reserves. And that is precisely what has happened. Despite Giffard, however, Mountbatten insisted on an acceleration of the movement of 5 Division from Arakan to Imphal. The only way that could be done was by flying the personnel of 5 Division, with the light equipment, from Arakan. So he took the bull by the horns and, with fine support from Sultan and Stratemeyer[2] of CBI [*China-Burma-India Theater*, as designated by the US], ordered thirty aircraft off the Hump and reported to Washington what he had done to meet the emergency. Luckily we were immediately backed up for Washington agreed within 36 hours – admirable. All this initiative came from Mountbatten – neither Slim nor Giffard had shown any at all.[3]

So the 76 US and British aircraft at the disposal of SEAC for North Burma were reinforced by 20 from the Hump. The discrepancy with Pownall's figures is that the 20 were 'Commandos' (C 46), bigger than the

[1] *Chief of Staff: The Diaries of Lieutenant-General Sir Henry Pownall*, ed. Brian Bond, II, p. 151

[2] Lt-General Daniel Sultan was Stilwell's deputy, and Lt-General G. E. Stratemeyer C-in-C Eastern Air Command. Both were Americans.

[3] This comment squares ill with the timetable of the request as given in Lewin's *Slim*, p. 174, according to which Slim asked Mountbatten at Comilla on 14 March for extra aircraft from the Hump route. On 15 March Slim learned from Scoones at Imphal that all IV Corps reserves had been committed, and signalled to Mountbatten that he needed 25 to 30 Dakotas between 18 March and 20 April. The same evening Mountbatten said he could have the aircraft at once. Authorization was confirmed by Washington on 17 April.

Dakota (C 47) and capable of carrying a load equivalent to that of thirty Dakotas.[1]

But Mountbatten had the sense not to be satisfied with this, impertinent and peremptory though it must have seemed in Washington. He asked for a further seventy Dakotas as well, because the fly-in of 5 Division, though spectacular, was not enough. Once the Japanese had closed the ring round Imphal – on 29 March – IV Corps would have to be supplied exclusively by air. That meant Scoones reducing his Corps rations by one-third, for 150,000 men, which he did. And he evacuated 43,000 non-combatants from the battle zone. These were taken out by aircraft, as were 13,000 casualties during the battle. At the same time, aircraft flew in 14,000,000 lbs of rations, nearly 1,000,000 gallons of petrol, over a thousand bags of mail and more than 40,000,000 cigarettes.[2] IV Corps required 540 tons of supplies per *day*, and until Air Marshal Baldwin's reorganization of his transport command was fully effective there was always a shortfall. Baldwin needed to bring out six of the seven RAF squadrons for safety into airfields in Assam and Eastern Bengal.[3] There were only two airfields in the Plain, one at Palel and the other on the outskirts of the town of Imphal itself. Occasional Japanese commando parties infiltrated Palel airfield and destroyed aircraft on the ground, and the runway surface later began to break up under the weight of the C 46s, so that in the end Scoones was forced to rely on the strip at Imphal.[4]

In his North Burma fastness, Stilwell's reactions to the initial setbacks on XIV Army's front were predictably splenetic. 'After lunch *bad news from Imphal*', his diary notes on 16 March 1944. 'Limeys have wind up.' 'Imphal threatened,' he wrote two days later. 'This ties a can to us and finishes up the glorious 1944 spring campaign.' On 3 April, 'Jap astride Imphal road in two places. Very serious now. Slim wants help.'

Slim wanted nothing of the kind, at any rate from Stilwell. Indeed, had the well-trained twenty battalions of Wingate's Special Force been diverted to come west and south and catch Mutaguchi's XV Army from the rear, Slim might well have been able to finish the Imphal battle a great deal sooner. But Wingate's force was committed to helping Stilwell by harassing the lines of communication leading to north Burma, and its impact on the Imphal front – still, forty years later, a matter of controversy – was coincidental. Pownall noted in his diary rather wistfully, 'If Wingate can be induced (ordered is hardly the word with him!) to come westwards towards the Chindwin and if we also hold the Jap in front, we should be in a very good way to eat up at least two Jap divisions.'[5] Slim told Brigadier M. R.

---

[1] Mountbatten, *Report*, p. 55, n. 2

[2] Evans, in *Purnell*, op.cit., p. 1773

[3] Evans, *Slim*, p. 162

[4] Mountbatten, op.cit., p. 59

[5] *Chief of Staff*, ed. B. Bond, pp. 152–3

Roberts (commanding 114 Brigade, 7 Division) who saw him at XIV Army HQ in March that he was under pressure to turn Wingate south to disrupt Mutaguchi's communications and indicated that he would not do so.[1] It was the wrong decision, as he was later to acknowledge; but he kept his word to Stilwell in the end. I say 'in the end' because at an afternoon conference with Mountbatten on 3 April at Jorhat, it was decided that two of Special Force's brigades (14 and 111) should operate in XIV Army rear, a decision which was reversed six days later at a meeting between Mountbatten, Slim and Lentaigne, Wingate's successor.[2] At Jorhat, on the morning of 3 April, Slim had talked with Stilwell, and to the latter's amazement refused his offer of 38 Chinese Division to protect the Dimapur-Ledo supply line. Stilwell's advance on Myitkyina would be brought to a halt by Japanese seizure of Dimapur, so it was not an entirely disinterested offer. 'Much to my surprise,' Stilwell confided to his diary, 'no question of help from us. On contrary, Slim and Supreme Commander said to go ahead.'[3]

That conference at Jorhat took place the day before the date which Sir Geoffrey Evans, himself a notable historian of the Burma campaign and one of Slim's generals, considers to be the turning point of the Imphal battle: 4 April. By that date 17 Division had completed its withdrawal and Scoones could revert to his original plan. 5 Division had been flown in and covered the approaches from Ukhrul while one of its brigades had gone to Dimapur. 20 Division had withdrawn to Shenam as planned. 23 Division was in Corps reserve, with one of its brigades blocking the Japanese advance from the south.

For the Japanese the crucial date was 19 April, according to General Kirby, at least as far as the front north of Imphal was concerned. The Japanese of 15 Division failed to break through at Sengmai and were ordered on the defensive.[4] And although Mutaguchi kept urging on his divisional commanders, imploring them to take Imphal for the date of

---

[1] Lewin, *Slim*, p. 181; Slim, *Defeat into Victory*, p. 268

[2] Lewin, *Slim*, p. 184

[3] *Stilwell Papers*, p. 267. Mountbatten's use of aircraft had made this possible, and fortunately he had Churchill's support: 'Let nothing go from the battle that you need for victory,' came a signal from London that evening. 'I will not accept denial of this from any quarter, and will back you to the full.' (Kirby, *War Against Japan*, III, p. 324) In the exchange between Slim and Stilwell, the latter's biographer, Barbara Tuchman, sees calculation on both sides. Stilwell's offer of 38 Chinese Division she terms 'a manoeuvre of some risk to test the situation' and adds '. . . to give up the hardened 38th might have slowed if not halted his entire campaign and cost the hope of taking Myitkyina, but it is doubtful if he expected the British to accept Chinese assistance. He was frequently caustic on the subject of the Indian Army divisions kept to guard India's North-West Frontier and his offer may have been conceived as a form of smoking them out. If Slim had accepted the offer, the necessity would have allowed Stilwell no choice, for a Japanese breakthrough behind him would have ended his campaign in any event.' (Tuchman, *Sand Against the Wind*, p. 441)

[4] *War Against Japan*, III, p. 310

Tenchōsetsu, the Emperor's birthday (29 April), the butter of the British army, which he thought he would slice through, had turned to hard stone.

His commanders were a cross for him, too. Yamauchi of 15 Division was a sick man and half his force was late on to the battlefield. Satō of 31 Division was an old political enemy from the days of army factional wrangling in the 1930s and had already made it clear that he would do his prescribed duty and no more. Yanagida, quite simply, was a coward. When he received Yanagida's signal on 25 March, Mutaguchi swore to have him court-martialled for lack of guts. He decided to bypass him and operate the division through Colonel Tanaka Tetsujirō, the Chief of Staff.

On the other fronts, things went well at first, then came to a standstill. 15 Division cut the Imphal-Kohima road just north of Imphal at Kanglatongbi on 7/8 April, but its battle strength was much reduced by the fighting at Nungshigum and night attacks in the hills east of Sengmai on 12 and 16 April. Yamamoto Force's drive on Palel through the Shenam Pass had been blocked by 20 Division. By mid-April, Mutaguchi's offensive had ceased to expand.

He himself was still remote from the battle. Whereas his opposite number, Scoones, was in the heart of the offensive at Imphal, Mutaguchi's HQ was still in Maymyo, and the interposition of Wingate's forces made overland communication with his front line hazardous and also distracted him – to some extent – as a commander. It was no good directing the battle by signal and staff officer from a hill station hundreds of miles away in the Shan States, and he finally moved his tactical HQ to Indainggyi (five miles north-east of Kalemyo) on 29 April – thirty-six days after the start of his offensive.

The day before Mutaguchi left, General Kawabe in Rangoon noted in his diary, 'XV Army moves west tomorrow. I can understand their feelings, not wanting to stay [in Maymyo]. I've sent a signal to Mutaguchi and pray for a continual series of successes as he marches off. And I said he should give his undivided attention to Imphal.' In fact, Mutaguchi did not move all that fast and his attention was by no means given undivided to Imphal. He made a halt *en route* at Shwebo, where he set up his geisha house. He was not all that keen on leaving the cool air of Maymyo for a bamboo shack in the jungle of Manipur, and his fondness for geishas was shared by his staff, each of whom had his preferred geisha in the *Seimeisō* at Maymyo. Life was not at all bad in HQ. They left work at around five in the evening, and the nights offered agreeable diversions. Indainggyi was a great deal more spartan...

The battle for Nungshigum

So the Japanese of 31 Division had cut off Imphal from India at Kohima, though their grip on the little town was not secure since British 2 Division was on its way to retake it. And to the south, the Japanese of 33 Division had approached to within ten miles of Imphal and were probing north-west of Bishenpur to find a way through IV Corps defences. We must now look at what was happening in the centre. Here, Imphal was under assault from two directions. From the south-east, the very strong force called Yamamoto Force, better equipped with artillery than any other element in Mutaguchi's army, and with a regiment of tanks, was attempting the short-cut from the Kabaw Valley through Witok and Tamu, to force its way along the road between Shenam and Palel. The distance between Tamu and Palel was only twenty-five miles; Palel overlooked the Imphal Plain and was only twenty-five miles from Imphal itself. A battalion (II/60 Regiment) from 15 Division crossed at another point on the Chindwin and made for the Tamu-Palel road in support of Yamamoto. The main body of 15 Division crossed the grain of the country to the south of Satō's 31 Division and made for the road between Kohima and Imphal, which it cut at Kangpokpi, the place the Japanese called 'Mission', from a mission station twenty-three miles north of Imphal, on 3 April, just over two weeks after crossing the Chindwin at Thaungdut.

But 15 Division was already in hot water with the army commander and was seriously under strength. The divisional commander, Major-General Yamauchi, a sensitive and gentle-spirited Japanese, had lived abroad a good deal as military attaché and had served in Washington. His personality contrasted sharply with the rough-and-ready flamboyance of the coarse and burly Mutaguchi, and the two failed to hit it off from the start. Yamauchi was mortally ill from tuberculosis. He had a special western-style latrine made for him, and one of his orderly's jobs was to see that this accompanied the general in the most out-of-the-way spots. The division had previously been in central China, where it was equipped with motor transport, and on the way to the Burma front it was compelled to change to pack transport – no lorries could negotiate the routes planned for it. And it was both under-gunned and under-manned. On the way through Thailand, Southern Army had detailed it for pioneer labour and it had spent months building a road between Chiengmai in northern Thailand and Toungoo in Burma. A useful road no doubt, but the troops would have been more profitably employed in getting to the Chindwin on time.

The guns they used in China were changed for mountain guns which could be dismantled and manhandled across the hills west of the Chindwin. But most of the anti-tank component was missing. They would not encounter tanks, they were comfortingly told by Lieutenant-General Naka, the Chief of Staff of Burma Area Army, who had come up from Rangoon to discuss the operation. And at the last table manoeuvres before it began, the operation was treated as if British tanks would simply not put in an appearance (this was a conference at Maymyo from 22 to 26 December 1943, at which neither Satō nor Yanagida were present).

Just as 15 Division was about to begin its move across the Chindwin, a crestfallen Naka came up to the front again and admitted he was wrong. The British *would* be employing tanks after all. By then it was too late to modify the division's equipment, and the offensive began with six under-strength battalions instead of the usual nine, and inadequate artillery support.[1] The Infantry Gun Company of 60 Regiment (Matsumura) had two 41-type mountain guns[2] with 200 rounds each and two anti-tank guns with 700 rounds each. Even so, the Gun Company commander, Captain Yamanaka, feared that his men would not have the strength to manhandle all this equipment across the Mintami Mountains and then across the next range, so he left behind, hidden in the village of Tonhe on the banks of the Chindwin, one mountain gun with 100 rounds. One battalion of the di-vision (II/51) had been sent to join the composite force at Indaw to deal with the Second Wingate Expedition. 67 Infantry Regiment (less III/67), 21 Field Artillery Regiment, and most of the divisional transport, were still in Thailand. So 15 Division started off the campaign with a strength of six battalions and 18 guns. In spite of these drawbacks, Yamauchi's men soon began to pose a serious threat to IV Corps.[3]

His right reconnaissance force, or *teishintai* (two companies of III/67 Regiment under Captain Honda), passed through Ukhrul on 24 March and four days later cut the Imphal-Kohima road at 'Mission'. The right assault column, or *totsushintai* (II/60 and III/60), also looped north from the Chindwin, split into two in the hills, crossed the Iril River and reached the road near Safarmanai, then crossed it and moved down on Imphal in the hills west of the road towards Karakul and Kulaopokpi. The left assault column (51 Infantry Regiment) attacked British positions at Hill 3524 north-west of Imphal on 27 March and in a few more days was at Mapao (Hill 4950). By the end of March, Yamauchi's men had cut the main road and were astride the hills looking down on IV Corps Headquarters, the 'Keep'.

Honda was to blow up the two iron bridges near 'Mission' and cut the road, along which he observed 120–130 trucks and jeeps an hour passing to Imphal, when he reached it at 10 pm on 28 March. He was fearfully impressed by what the traffic implied of material supply and mechanical force available to the British. He had never seen anything like it in Japan, he noted in his diary. He blew the bridges, cut the telephone wires and broke communication between Kohima and Imphal.

After 51 Regiment (Omoto) and 60 Regiment (Matsumura) had reached the road and cut it, a dispute arose between Yamauchi and his Chief of Staff, Lieutenant-General Okada. 51 and 60 Regiments were to switch

[1] Takagi Toshirō, *Funshi* (Death in Anger), Bungei Shunjū, Tokyo, 1969, pp. 126–31
[2] The type refers to the date, the 41st year of Meiji, i.e. 1908!
[3] Kirby, *War Against Japan*, III, p. 190

roles. Hitherto, 51's role had been to reach an east-west line running through the village of Sengmai, about twelve miles north of Imphal. The divisional commander now wanted it shifted to an objective further east, Hill 3833 (this is how the Japanese histories refer to the hill known in British and Indian accounts as Nungshigum). Matsumura (60 Regiment) would take over the Sengmai line.

The transfer seemed pointless, but Yamauchi had been impressed by a report from Captain Honda to the effect that the Kohima-Imphal road was now cut. Yamauchi noted this in his diary, but added that British-Indian forces might well still escape along the Silchar track (this was in any case in 33 Division's zone, not his). An all-out attack by small units, now, might achieve an encirclement of the enemy which would be impossible if he waited to assemble his forces into larger formations. Okada disagreed. All that had happened was that the Japanese had succeeded in cutting the *main* road. But on the Sangshak-Imphal road 51 Regiment had been under attack. The British were *not* on the run. Of course they were, countered Yamauchi. They had been surrounded, they were trying to get away. It was standard form for them. Okada could not believe his ears. This was exactly the kind of language used by Mutaguchi at his Maymyo conference: 'The British Army is weaker than the Chinese. If you surround them, they run away!' How could Yamauchi share this view, when he had suffered from Mutaguchi's contempt of his own division, and had dismissed Mutaguchi as a *wakarazuya*, a blockhead, unfit to be in command of an army? But Yamauchi persisted. Couldn't Okada see this was a *senki*, an opportunity of war? Okada could not see how switching Omoto to Hill 3833 helped matters anyway. He thought Yamauchi wanted to bring Omoto closer to divisional HQ, now 25 miles from Imphal, and add strength to the push along the road from Ukhrul.[1]

On 1 April, there occurred an episode which Yamauchi took as confirmation of his views. Six tanks with infantry came up to Japanese positions at Hill 3524 north-east of Yaingangpokpi and the CO of 10 Company, Captain Nakanishi, ordered his grenade section to attack them. One of the grenades struck a tank amidships and the six tanks changed course and made off towards Yaingangpokpi. Nakanishi was jubilant. It *was* possible to use grenade launchers to repel tanks! When a staff officer from divisional HQ called on his company, Nakanishi described what had happened. 'Perhaps they just came to recce?' the staff officer, Imaoka, wondered, but he passed the news on to the general. Yamauchi was impressed. Clearly the British *were* weak. 'Order Nakanishi to move on Kameng', he told Imaoka.

Nakanishi was less than overjoyed with the new order which his own optimism had engendered. 'Wait until we've completed a reconnaissance of the enemy', he asked, 'otherwise we're asking for heavy casualties.' Imaoka

[1] Takagi, *Funshi*, pp. 190–1

urged him on, and with the knowledge that this was the divisional commander's intention, Nakanishi reluctantly set out against Kameng. 'This
daft order from a staff officer,' recalls Second Lieutenant Nakamura
Shūichirō, 'was the direct cause of 10 Company being wiped out.' At 8 pm
on 3 April, the company set off towards a hill south of Kameng. The moon
was cloudy, there was nothing like a road, and it was 4 am on 4 April
before they slithered down a hillside on to the plain. They had covered
about nine miles, and were deep into enemy territory. Second-Lieutenant
Maeda, at point, using compass and map, hurried on ahead. As the sky
lightened in the east, Nakanishi sent runners to each platoon, telling them
to hug the foothills. He was afraid they would be caught in the open once
dawn came.

The sound of rifle fire was heard halfway up the hillside as Satouchi
Platoon of 11 Company reached the skirt of a hill. 'Next, firing came from
in front. Then the shelling started. The shelling and firing grew more
intense as the sky lightened, and when I ran up to the company commander, the men in the vanguard seemed to be trapped at the enemy lines. We
were very close by now. The company commander ordered us to attack at
once, but our men began to fall, the vanguard commander was severely
wounded, and we could make no headway against the enemy positions.
The attack failed, and we lost half our strength. I myself was wounded by
two grenade fragments in front of the enemy positions at exactly 5.10 am.'

The company commander tried to whip up enthusiasm among the
twenty-odd men who were still on their feet, but his face was a tragic mask
as he saw, in the now clear light of day, the bodies of his men heaped up as
they had fallen. He glared, speechless, at the enemy positions. The crackle
of rifle fire and the scream of shells continued to break the silence of the
hillsides. Then the British came out, counter-attacked, and drove the
company back.

Around 10 am, when the British could no longer be seen round the skirts
of the hill, tanks came into view, opening up with their guns and MGs.
Nakanishi was killed. Lieutenant Kuwayama, commander of 1 Platoon,
took over command of the company:

> There were no trees on the slopes where we could take cover, and
> the tank guns went on shelling us for an hour.
>
> Evening came, and the shelling stopped. But whenever one of
> us survivors budged, rifles cracked. Of a company which had
> eighty men to start with, we were now no more than ten, and
> everyone of us had been wounded. As the night drew on, we
> escaped. We hadn't even the strength to bury the dead. The
> lightly wounded helped the rest, but two of the more severe
> casualties died on the way across the plain. It took the remaining
> eight of us three days and nights to get back to our starting point

by the same track we'd travelled in a single night. So we retreated, on the edge of death.[1]

In the same retreat, Sergeant Ueda adds a touch of horror when he remembers that after four of the British tanks had shelled them, flamethrowers were directed on to one of the Japanese and burned him alive.[2]

Kameng was 15 Division's first encounter with British tanks, and from then on the tanks would make all the difference. On this front, covering the road which led from Imphal to Litan in the north-east, Scoones realized that the Japanese route was the shortest, and that he might be in danger very rapidly. So, as soon as 5 Indian Division began arriving from Arakan (less 161 Brigade which was near Kohima), he ordered its commander, Lieutenant-General Briggs, to halt the Japanese advance. At the same time, 23 Division was to move up the road to Kasom, where the Japanese 15 Division HQ was thought to be located. 9 Brigade of 5 Division was to advance on Mapao, the strongly-held flank position covering Yamauchi's forces attacking Sengmai. Briggs sent 123 Brigade (Evans) to a position at the village of Yaingangpokpi, twenty-three miles north of Imphal, the point at which the road debouches from the hills and slopes down a saddle to the Plain. Evans's brigade consisted of 1/17 Dogra Regiment, 2/1 Punjab, and 2 Suffolk, who had been sent up to Kohima as soon as they landed at Imphal from Arakan on 18 March. A week later, they were sent back to rejoin their brigade. 9 Brigade (Salomons) was to move up the Iril Valley, which lies roughly at right angles to the road Imphal-Kameng-Sangshak- Ukhrul.

A hill dominated the northern end of the Imphal Plain, and offered an ideal observation platform for all these movements: the height called Nungshigum. It was this hill that Yamauchi wanted his 51 Regiment to secure, bringing them uncomfortably close to the very heart of the British defences of Imphal. IV Corps HQ, in its 'Keep', was only six miles away, and the petrol and ammunition dumps, and the airfield at Kangla, were even nearer.

They had come close along the main road, too. A raiding party had already forced the evacuation of the stores depot at the village of Kangla-tongbi before 9 Brigade came to the rescue. Another blew up the controls of the filtration plant of the water supply in the hills north-west of Imphal. (Fortunately for the defenders, there was a reserve plant which could be switched on, so the water supply was not affected.) Scoones was under no illusion. His 'Keep' was under a direct threat from forces closer to Imphal than the Japanese had ever been, and it was imperative to clear the area.

---

[1] From *Hohei 67 Rentai Bunshū,* (Records of 67 Regiment), in Takagi, *Funshi*, p. 199
[2] ibid., p. 200

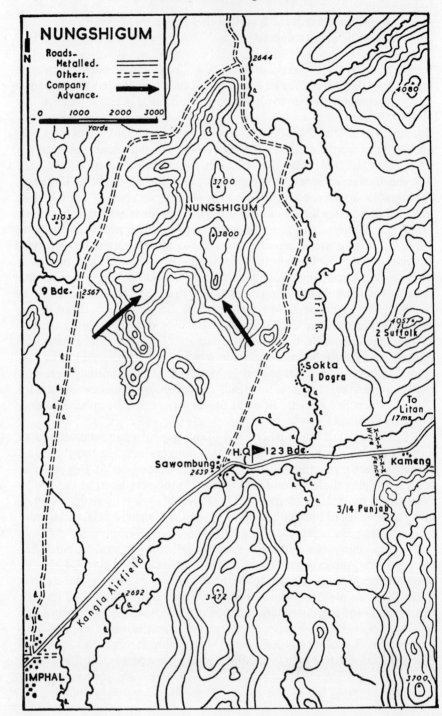

NUNGSHIGUM

Roads—
Metalled.
Others.
Company
Advance.

0   1000   2000   3000
yards

2644

4080

3700

NUNGSHIGUM

3103

3800

9 Bde. *2567*

Iril R.

4057
2 Suffolk

Sokta
1 Dogra

To
Litan
17 ms.

H.Q. 123 Bde.

Sawombung
2639

Kameng

Wire
Fence

3/14 Punjab

Kangla Airfield

2692

3172

3700

IMPHAL

In command of 9 Brigade, Salomons was heavily involved in backloading the stores from Kanglatongbi and could only allot two platoons – about sixty men – of the 3/9 Jat for Nungshigum. The hill was not thickly wooded, but covered with tall grass and scrub. At the top, the trees thinned out, and red earth and bare rock showed through. The summit was not a single peak but a ridge about four miles long, a number of hills linked by cols, and about a third of a mile across at its widest point. It was an hour's stiff climb, and on 6 April the 3/9 Jats sweated up the slopes in intense heat, but evening was upon them before they could dig in at the Imphal side of the hill. In the small hours of the next day, III Battalion, 51 Regiment (Major Morikawa) attacked the hill during a rain storm and in three hours the Jats lost nearly half their men and were told to withdraw. One of their *havildars* was left for dead, and his body was thrown down the hillside by the Japanese. In fact, though wounded in both hand and foot, he was still alive, and managed to reach his battalion HQ, only to die later of his wounds.

The Jat commander, Lieutenant-Colonel Gerty, sent up another of his companies to retake the hill. The Japanese position had been softened up by a Hurribomber air-strike, and this time the Jats took the hill with ease, only to find themselves attacked again on 8 and 9 April, and on the 10th, on the last occasion by 75 mm guns. On the morning of the 11th, the Jats were compelled to retreat again, and lost a company commander and many men in an unsuccessful counter-attack. It looked as if the Japanese were on Nungshigum to stay, and only an assault in very great strength would shift them.

Such an assault was planned at a conference summoned by Briggs on 12 April. Wing-Commander Archer of 221 Group HQ RAF, which provided air support for XIV Army, was in attendance, with Brigadier Geoffrey Evans, the advance of whose 123 Brigade was threatened by Omoto's men on Nungshigum, and the Corps Commander's brother, Brigadier Reginald ('Cully') Scoones, in command of 254 Tank Brigade. The Jats were clearly played out, and the infantry role devolved on one of Evans's battalions, 1st Dogra, commanded by Lieutenant-Colonel E. J. (Lakri) Woods.[1] The Dogras are Rajputs, heirs of a proud warrior tradition, and small in stature, so the Japanese historians (even now) confuse them with Gurkhas. Woods's men were then south of the road, and would have to be relieved by 3/14 Punjab of 9 Brigade before they could move, so the attack could not be timed before the morning of 13 April. Archer promised three RAF squadrons in support, two of Vengeance dive-bombers and one of Hurribombers, twenty-four aircraft in all. The hill would also be shelled by the massed artillery of 5 Division, with an additional medium artillery

---

[1] *Lakri*, Urdu for 'Wood' is the inevitable nickname for any Indian Army officer called Wood or Woods.

regiment to back it up. Scoones offered B Squadron of 3 Carabiniers. Against one Japanese battalion, with little artillery and no air strength, this was an unambiguous example of Slim's doctrine of the use of overwhelming power.

The tanks faced an almost impossible task, and doubt was cast on their ability to reach the summit up the steep slope at the top. Scoones was convinced they could do it. So was Ralph Younger, commander of the Carabiniers. In the event, the machines and men proved more than equal to the demands made on them, but the angle of climb near the summit had unfortunate consequences for the tank commanders. Woods planned that his Dogra companies should move out at 10.30 am with a tank escort, A Company (Major L. A. Jones) to take the west side of the hill and B Company (Captain H. Alden) the east side. With A Company went No. 5 Troop Carabiniers (Lieutenant H. N. Neale), HQ tanks (Major Sanford), and with B Company the Forward Observation Officer and No. 4 Troop (Lieutenant C. T. V. Fitzherbert). The other two troops, No. 6 (Lieutenant A. Weir) and No. 7 (Lieutenant L. A. Stewart), were to stay down in the Plain to provide overhead support from their guns during the ascent.

The Dogras moved to their starting point in the darkness, across the hard surface of the dried-up paddy fields. They kept wireless contact with Woods in the village of Sokta on the banks of the Iril which flowed along past the east flank of Nungshigum. He in turn was in touch with Evans at 123 Brigade HQ, set up in the village of Sawombung on the Imphal-Litan Road. Like the stage in a theatre, the entire southern flank of the hill was in full view of all the British commanders.

The Japanese saw all this activity beneath their eyes, as they looked down on the Plain on the morning of 13 April. They could also see the streets and houses of Imphal. They noticed the tanks as they arrived in the Iril Valley, and saw them stop at the foot of the hill. They were not at the time particularly perturbed by their presence. None of them believed for an instant that the tanks could actually come at them up the hill. The general wisdom of the Japanese army was that tanks could not climb hills. At Nungshigum – as later at Kohima – it was to prove a costly wisdom.

Morikawa's III Battalion was dug in at the lowest col and his Machine Gun Company was sited near the summit. The digging was hard, and it took HQ troops a couple of hours to dig the command trench three feet deep. One of the diggers, Superior Private Yamamoto Yutaka, recalled later that they also had to dig trenches for the adjutant and the sergeant-major, so that by the time it came to dig their own, they were exhausted and merely piled up earth between tree trunks instead. Later, when there was time to dig, after they had repulsed the first attack, some one said, 'We're probably digging our own graves, so make a decent job of it.' Yamamoto dug deep enough to be able to squat. They could tell from the busy battalion telephone that an attack was brewing, but no one answered the tracer bullets which flew over their heads.

Yamamoto's thoughts were elsewhere: perhaps he was not the kind of soldier the Japanese Army required? He remembered looking through the carriage window of a train on his way to China, passing through Osaka and Kobe, when he was first conscripted: he thought of people who had helped him, girls, the joys of a green spring. He had felt the very opposite of brave himself, and had been opposed to the war in his innermost heart. But that was buried deep, it was not something, as a Japanese, he could permit to be seen. 'I didn't fear death', he wrote later. 'Death was only the destruction of the flesh. Man has an immortal soul and in that soul there was always peace.' Towards dawn, Yamamoto dozed off.[1]

When he awoke, the morning sun was blazing down on the hillside. It was such a splendid day, he could hardly believe he was on a field of battle. But he could see the groups of lorries in the valley below, something was afoot. Then suddenly he heard the sound of aircraft, bombs exploded below him, and he pressed himself to the floor of his foxhole, 'stuck like a trapped octopus' (the Japanese called their foxholes 'octopus pots', *takotsubo*).

It was the RAF. Dive-bombers came in first, then peeled off back to Imphal. The Hurribombers followed, pouring machine gun fire into the Japanese on the hill crest, their bombs blowing trees and bodies into the air. The time was 10.30 am. Twenty minutes later the artillery of 5 Division opened up, eighty-eight guns blazing away on to a single hill. To Yamamoto's ears it sounded like a hundred thunder claps echoing round his own trench. He quivered further into the ground, covered with earth, sand and fragments of rock.

Down in the valley floor, the Dogras began to move. 'When I first saw the hill that morning', Hugh Alden, B Company commander remembers,

> my impression was that it was very high. It was really quite open, covered with sparse bushes about two or three feet high, and a few scraggy trees. You could see the men moving about quite easily. It wasn't steep to begin with, but became so as we climbed higher. We advanced with one platoon leading accompanied by one tank, the infantry moving well to the flanks to avoid any fire that was aimed at the tank and any ricochets that might bounce off it. The troop commander's tank moved with my company headquarters, but as we were not tied up with their wireless, if we wanted to talk to them inside the tank we had either to shout or use the tank telephone attached to the

[1] Takagi, *Funshi*, p. 219

back. It was awfully hot, and we sweated pints. Until more water
was sent up after the battle, we would have to rely on our water
bottles only.[1]

It was hotter still inside the tanks, which moved up the slopes in low gear,
making about one mile an hour. They reached the feature known as The
Pyramid, on the western side of the summit, at 11.15 am. Fitzherbert came
to the Twin Bumps and followed Neale and Sanford along the razorbacked
col linking them with the Northern Bump. The ridge was so narrow at this
point that the tanks had to move, agonizingly slowly, in single file. The gun
fire from 5 Divisional artillery had ceased and the air strike was over.

'Tanks! Tanks!' Japanese voices cried out on the hilltop. Yamamoto
peeped out briefly from his foxhole, saw nothing, then risked emerging a
little further. He saw two tanks climbing up towards him from the slope
below. 'Bring up the LMGs! Prepare to fire! Bring the guns forward!'
yelled the battalion commander, Major Morikawa. The tanks pushed the
trees aside, and came to within a hundred yards below Yamamoto. He
could see the Indian troops moving after each tank. The Japanese could
not bring their battalion gun to bear on them, it was sited too low on the
southern slope. 'Let me have that gun!' the company commander shouted
to Yamamoto. 'Put in armour piercing shot!' 'None here,' Yamamoto
answered, 'must have been left behind.' 'Use whatever's there!' The company commander started firing, and Yamamoto began to use his rifle,
aiming at the Dogras. The tank guns opened up on his position, earth shot
up in showers around him, the air was full of smoke, the sound of groans
enveloped him. Nearer and nearer the tanks came, fifty yards, thirty yards.
One tank climbed to the hill-top. Yamamoto rammed his head into the
earth, clutching his rifle. He felt the tank stop, about a foot to his right.
'I'm going to die,' he thought, 'there's nothing I can do about it.' Then he
began to slide down the slope, still pressed firmly into the ground. A
second tank climbed up. Japanese engineers ran towards it with 'tortoise'
mines, fragmentation mines with magnets fixed at four corners, giving the
outward appearance of an ungainly tortoise. Two of them ran up to the
tank and pushed the mine on, below the track. Nothing happened. The
tank turret opened like a lid, and the tank commander thrust his head out,
fired his pistol at them, then threw grenades. Two or three Japanese took
aim at him, and uncannily the tank gun began to swivel towards them.

Yamamoto looked round, saw other Japanese lying some distance away
with shattered intestines, others with their heads blown off. The corpses
reminded him, oddly, of potato peelings thrown away. When he stopped
screaming, he noticed another Superior Private, unwounded as he was,
and with him began to collect water bottles from their dead comrades.

[1] Evans and Brett-James, *Imphal*, p. 220

They made a stretcher and took one of the wounded down the hillside. He met a dozen others, by the stream in the valley, and they decided to wait there, by the water, until sundown.

The British tank commanders pushed on, but they had to observe from their turrets and this made them very vulnerable. On the west slope, Sanford was hit (he died later) and Younger from his command post down on the Imphal road told Fitzherbert to assume command. One of the reserve troops was despatched to the Pyramid. Fitzherbert told Neale's and Sanford's tanks to clear the way ahead, then Sergeant Doe, in command of the leading tank of Neale's troop, was shot dead. Corporal Hubbard took his place and was himself shot through the head. Fitzherbert slowed down, but eventually brought his three tanks in front of the Northern Bump, where the Japanese had built themselves bunkers. Squadron Quarter-Master Sergeant Branston, in the tank just ahead of Fitzherbert, was shot, his body falling down into the turret. His gunner, Trooper Hopkins, took over the tank and was killed instantly. The Japanese began to swarm round the tanks and Fitzherbert himself was killed.

Because of the vulnerability of their commanders, the tanks had been brought to a standstill. Younger told Squadron Sergeant-Major Craddock to take over command of the troops, but insisted the attack go on. At this point the battle might well have gone against the British. The Dogras had lost their two company commanders, and casualties had been heavy. The senior VCO, Subadar Ranbir Singh, agreed to go on with the attack, after consulting with Craddock. Craddock was to close in on the bunkers while two platoons of Dogras went in with the bayonet.

When the Japanese regimental commander, Colonel Omoto, heard that tanks were moving up Nungshigum, he refused to believe it. His veterinary officer, Lieutenant Tabe, had been watching the battle through binoculars, and saw the tanks bury the Japanese alive as they crunched over bodies. He told Omoto what he had seen. 'Don't be a fool! How could they? Give me those glasses!' Omoto firmly believed tanks could only operate on the flat. Then he saw for himself. He yelled with grief and rage, 'We're done for! That's it!' He put down the binoculars, tears streaming from his eyes.

The British brigadiers and colonels were watching the battle, too, as if they were sitting in the stalls. From Brigade HQ at Sawombung, Evans and Scoones watched the infantry disappear in the long grass, saw the tanks move towards the hill and slowly negotiate the slopes. Enemy troops moved along the ridge. The divisional general, Briggs, came along to join the audience, and all three, Briggs, Evans and Cully Scoones, sat alongside 'Lakri' Woods by the edge of a dried-up paddy field as the attack progressed.

Some of the most crucial episodes were out of their sight. When Hugh Alden went to look for the company commander of B Company, 'Jonah' Jones, he was nowhere to be seen. Alden made his way up forward through the leading Dogras and found Jones, grey-faced and bleeding, in a ditch. He sent him back, took command of the attacking infantry, and moved off to arrange covering fire from the tanks. He could make no sense through the tank telephone and clambered on to it to speak directly to the commander. One by one, he showed him the positions of the Japanese bunkers, and the tank began to range on them. Alden was asking for trouble, but there seemed to be no alternative. He stayed perched on top of the tank to direct its fire, and as the tank gun spat out its second round, a Japanese bullet hit him in the chest and knocked him off the tank. In this way, in the course of the battle for Nungshigum, every single tank and infantry officer was either killed or wounded.[1]

This in no way dimmed the courage of the attackers. When Squadron Sergeant-Major Craddock decided to move closer to the bunkers, he ordered Fitzherbert's tank to get out of his path. Fitzherbert's dead body was still slumped in the turret, but the tank gun was firing at the bunkers. The driver, Trooper Smith, found he could not obey Craddock's order because his starting button had jammed, and though the Japanese were throwing everything they had at the tanks, he clambered down with a tow rope, fixed it to the tank and had it towed away.

The first of Craddock's charges failed. The Dogras got to within five yards of the bunker defences and were driven back. Craddock then determined on an almost preposterous manoeuvre: while he worked his way round the flank, he ordered another tank (Sergeant Hannan) to climb right on top of the Northern Bump in which the bunkers had been dug. This time it worked, the two tanks pulverized the bunkers, the Dogras moved in with grenades and bayonets, killed the Japanese inside, and were home.[2]

A few miles to the east, in his divisional HQ at Kasom, General Yamauchi had heard the bombardment of Nungshigum, but the result of the battle came first to Omoto's Regimental HQ. About 3 pm, a tottering figure, his tattered uniform black with smoke, appeared. He was on the verge of collapse, and Lieutenant Tabe recognized him as one of the regimental medical officers, Second Lieutenant Kihira Masao, attached to the III Battalion. He had been sent to make contact with the regimental commander. Kihira stood before Omoto, hollow-eyed, breathing in gasps. 'Kihira! Control yourself!' bellowed Omoto. Kihira straightened up. But for a long time he could not speak. He just stood there with tears streaming down his cheeks. 'The Battalion has been overrun[3] by enemy tanks, and

---

[1] Evans and Brett-James, op.cit., p. 223

[2] A commemoration of this feat occurs annually on the anniversary of Nungshigum; B Squadron of the Royal Scots Dragoon Guards (the unit made up from the amalgamation of the 3 Carabiniers and the Royal Scots Greys) parades on that day without officers, under the command of the Squadron Sergeant-Major and NCOs. Cf. Bryan Perrett, *Tank Tracks to Rangoon*, p. 117, and Evans and Brett-James, op.cit., p. 225

[3] He actually used the word *jūrin* which means 'trampled on'.

annihilated.' The words began to jumble in his mouth and he collapsed in front of Omoto. Omoto's face was furious. He had suffered defeat after defeat – by this time his regimental fighting strength, shorn, from the start, of his second battalion away in North Burma, had been whittled down to almost nothing. All that he had left was to protect the honour of his regiment. 'Tabe!' he called, 'we will make straight for Hill 3833! We will defend that hill until everyone of us is dead!' Tabe was cooler. He realized Omoto had been knocked off balance by the tanks' destruction of his men, and said quietly that no purpose would be served by throwing themselves into the same cauldron. Practically, they could effect nothing; much better to withdraw and try to think out how to rectify the situation. As if all the strength had left his body, Omoto sank down. He stayed like this for a long time without moving, then whispered in a low voice to Tabe, 'It was inevitable, wasn't it? Let's go down.'

Like the British, the Japanese losses in officers had been severe: Major Morikawa, the III battalion commander, was killed, so was the adjutant, the battery commander of the field artillery battery, the gun section commander, 12 Company commander, and other officers of III battalion. Not a single surviving officer was unwounded. Inevitably, then, when what remained of Omoto's force tried to counter-attack at 7 pm, by which time the whole of the Dogra battalion was on the hill, they were easily shelled off. The following morning, the Dogras counted 100 Japanese dead, making a total of 250 dead since the fight for Nungshigum had started on 6 April. Five machine guns and two 75s were taken.[1]

Large, organized Japanese forces never got nearer to Imphal than this. Not only did the loss of Nungshigum blunt one of Yamauchi's prongs thrust at Imphal, it threatened communications with 60 Regiment (Matsumura) astride the main Imphal-Kohima road, which was trying to force its way through 63 Brigade's defences at Sengmai. It was this factor which made 15 Division's Chief of Staff, Major-General Okada, reluctant to accede to Omoto's request to withdraw from the Nungshigum position completely. Of course, the request was not framed as such. After his defeat, Omoto signalled to Divisional HQ: 'Enemy retaken front line south of Hill 3833. Difficult to hold in face of tanks. Decided attack all strength Hill 4057.' Hill 4057 was a little distance to the east across the Iril Valley and in the hands of 2 Suffolk, one of Evans's battalions. And although the signal was phrased in terms of an attack on this position, Okada knew that Omoto was saying he wanted permission to withdraw from the impossible situation at Nungshigum. With 31-type mountain guns, he could not fight tanks. The survivors would be totally destroyed, unless they made for a spot where tanks could not reach them. But would Okada authorize the opening of such a gap? It would mean Matsumura Regiment being cut off at Sengmai.

---

[1] Evans and Brett-James, op.cit., p. 224

He felt he could not decide this alone, and made for Yamauchi's tent, and showed him the signal. 'I feel I cannot reply to this. It's too important. Please take the decision personally.' Worn out as much by the disease that was slowly killing him as by the stress of battle, Yamauchi pondered for a long time. Of all three of his regimental commanders, he trusted Omoto most. The request would not have been made if the situation was not irretrievable.

'According to a report from Staff Officer Naruse,' Yamauchi wrote in his diary that day, 'Matsumura is being excessively cautious and his advance has slowed down. He is a first-class regimental commander, but lacks experience, so there's nothing to be done. On the other hand, Omoto is an old and seasoned commander, and although at first I did wonder if he was not being overcautious, he later pushed on with great courage, and always seemed to move faster than the right column.'[1] In the end, Yamauchi authorized Omoto to withdraw from Hill 3833.

With his few survivors, Omoto left the area of Nungshigum, and sent his I Battalion against the Suffolks on Hill 4057. They fared no better than III Battalion had done. Not only did they lose around 100 men, food and ammunition ran short, and amoebic dysentery began to spread. Soon only about fifty men could stand on their feet. Yamauchi's men had weeks ahead of bitter fighting against 5 Division, 20 and 23 Divisions, in the hills north-east of Imphal, but it was with diminished strength and resilience. His three regiments had set off under-strength in the first place, IV Corps' resolute counter-attacks had cut them down pitilessly (at great cost to themselves) and Mutaguchi's Genghis Khan rations had failed to material- ize, since most of the cattle that set off with the division never reached the front line. But the main cause of the near-destruction of 15 Division was its inability to cope with the British tanks. It was this despair in the face of the overwhelming onslaught of the tanks that led, a few weeks later, to the use by the Japanese of poison gas. As Takagi Toshirō points out, Naka's mistake was the direct cause of the deaths of the thousands of Japanese soldiers whose rotting corpses littered the hillsides and jungle west of the Chindwin in the summer of 1944.[2]

The Inspector from Tokyo

The date considered by the British Official History as the turning-point in the Battle for Imphal is 19 April 1944. By then, the Japanese offensives had come to a halt, the Kohima garrison had been relieved, 17 Division had been withdrawn safely into the Plain, and the Japanese from the east and south-east had been blocked. It was precisely on that day, too, that

---

[1] Takagi, *Funshi*, pp. 229–30   [2] ibid p. 230

Major Ushiro Masaru, a staff officer at the headquarters of Burma Area Army in Rangoon, decided that he ought to see what was happening at the front. He went as far as Kinu with his colleague, Kitagawa, who had been sent up to Mawlu to help 24 Independent Mixed Brigade in its battle against Wingate's airborne forces. When they separated, Kitagawa turned and said to him, 'I wonder which of us will survive this? At any rate, let's do our best. No regrets.' Ushiro never saw him again.[1]

He took the road west. The bridge at Yeu had been destroyed by RAF bombing, but a boat had been told to wait for him, and dawn was breaking as he neared the Jupi Mountains. He had been this way with Lieutenant-General Naka, the Chief of Staff, two months before, on a pre-battle inspection of Mutaguchi's three divisions. He noticed one difference: enemy aircraft were now more active. They swooped down on the road like eagles on their prey, sweeping it with machine-gun fire. Ushiro shot from his car seat and took refuge in the jungle. 'This is really Yasukuni Avenue,[2] sir,' said the soldier sheltering with him, 'You'd better watch yourself.'

It was soon blisteringly hot, and Ushiro couldn't see water anywhere. He tried nibbling a biscuit, but his throat was so dry, he couldn't swallow. He got back into the car and drove on, seeing soldiers huddled by the roadside all the way. Halfway through the night, he reached the crossing-point on the Chindwin, east of Kalewa. The river was 600 yards across, and boats were ferrying munitions under the flickering light of torches. The road soon deteriorated, and along it came apparently endless files of casualties from the front line. At dawn the next day, Ushiro was at 15 Army Tactical Headquarters at Indainggyi. Some of the staff were away with the divisions, others were still at Maymyo, but he obtained a clear picture from Kunomura and the others. The British were reinforcing their strength by flying in troops from Arakan, and they were thought to have the equivalent of three divisions and a great number of tanks. Using 80 to 100 aircraft, they must be getting at least 100 tons of supplies daily, and there was still aircraft enough to drop and sustain the airborne forces lying across the rear lines of communication of 31 Division; all this, in contrast with the pitiable 10–15 tons a day supplied to 15 Army. It looked as if there were only one division – 33 – which had any chance of breaking through to Imphal, and Ushiro decided to visit it. Ushiro went through the files and read every signal that had passed between 15 Army and its three divisions. The plight of these divisions, unknown to Burma Area Army, was revealed to him in full as he read on.

Then, on 28 April, a signal came from Rangoon. 'Vice COS expected arrive Rangoon 30 April to observe situation Burma Area Army. Bring details of 15 Army plans for Imphal return Rangoon 30 April.' It would

[1] Ushiro Masaru, *Biruma senki* (The War in Burma), 1953, p.26.
[2] The long road in Tokyo by the Yasukuni Shrine, where the ashes of dead soldiers are revered.

take him four days there and back to see 33 Division, so he reluctantly gave up the idea. The Vice Chief of Staff from Imperial GHQ Tokyo obviously had precedence. Lieutenant-General Hata Hikosaburō was on a visit to the Southern Regions, which took in the campaigns against the Americans in the South-West Pacific, and he was to report to the Prime Minister, Tojo, on his return. Viewed against the losses in the Pacific, with the threat they implied to the Philippines and then to the islands of Japan itself, Burma was not a major issue. But it was important because it seemed to offer a chance of success, and Tojo badly needed *some* good news from the battlefronts. Field-Marshal Terauchi had moved his GHQ Southern Army to Manila to be closer to the fighting in the Pacific, and Hata had conferred with him there. He obviously could not stay in Burma long, and it was unlikely he would have travelled to the battlefield himself, so he would rely on reports from staff officers. Ushiro went round 15 Army Tactical Headquarters to say goodbye. 'Victory seems only a hair's breadth away,' Mutaguchi told him. 'But we simply have not got the strength. I regret to say it, but it's true. At any rate, look after yourself.' He scribbled on a couple of visiting cards, one for Kawabe, the Commander in Chief Burma Area Army, and another for Naka, the Chief of Staff. Ushiro's eyes caught the phrase on the card destined for Naka: 'Thinking of distant Tokyo, I am overwhelmed with shame.'

So that was what the man responsible for the whole of the Imphal operation really thought of the possibility of success. Ushiro drove his jeep towards the Kalemyo airfield, the rain lashing at the sides and canvas roof. As he drove, the road turned into a river, the jeep began to slip, and he lost control for a while. It was halfway through the night before he reached the airfield, and as he came down at Rangoon on 2 May, he saw a big plane just taking off. He had a sudden hunch it must be the Vice Chief of Staff on his way back to Tokyo.

He was right. When he returned to GHQ Burma Area Army, Hata had gone, leaving behind some of his staff, including a high-ranking staff officer from the Operations Section of Imperial GHQ, Matsuda. Ushiro was asked to give an account of his trip. Not suspecting that his opinion might decide the fate of 15 Army – even Burma Area Army itself – he described Mutaguchi's battle strength, the efficiency (or otherwise) of the supply system, the effect the monsoon was having, and the fact that the operation, successful or not, needed to be concluded by May at the latest. The staff of Burma Area Army GHQ, who listened to all this, grew more and more restive as time passed. All their optimism seemed to dissolve. Matsuda took the measure of the atmosphere, and sent a signal to Imperial GHQ in Tokyo.

But Ushiro's reports had another effect. Staff officers flew to Burma from Southern Army, and reported – they were meant to – that the Imphal operation could still succeed. This news was transmitted to Tokyo, where

Hata was interviewed by Tojo on his return. Hata had been subjected to a good deal of propaganda during his tour of inspection. On arrival at Southern Army GHQ, he had been told that they believed the Imphal operation had a 90% hope of success, but he noted wryly that they had not so far sent a single staff officer to Burma to see how things were going. Two were despatched on 1 May.[1]

Hata flew to Rangoon on 1 May and called on Kawabe the following day. For Kawabe and his Chief of Staff and Senior Staff Officer (Naka and Aoki) the expectation of success was 80–85%. Hata nonetheless broached the cancellation of the operation. 'There is only one way, and that is to stick it out,' Kawabe answered. 'Give me a little more time.'[2]

Hata was puzzled. The GHQ nearer the battle seemed slightly less optimistic over the outcome (although the Southern Army Chief of Staff, Major-General Iimura, agreed with his views about cancellation). Logically, he should have visited 15 Army, but he made no attempt to do so, as he was expected back at Southern Army on 5 May for a conference of army group commanders. He left for Singapore, but arranged for Colonel Sugita, a member of his staff, to stay behind and listen to Ushiro's report. After hearing what Ushiro had to say about 15 Army, Sugita flew up to Maymyo where the newly created 33 Army had put its HQ from which to conduct the battle in North Burma against Wingate and the US-trained Chinese (thus leaving Mutaguchi free to concentrate on Imphal). The Chief of Staff of the new Army was Major-General Katakura (kicked upstairs from Burma Area Army) who knew all about the conflicts between Mutaguchi and his three divisional commanders and did not hesitate to enlighten Sugita on that score; adding that he felt the success of the Imphal operation was pretty doubtful. Sugita thought it an odd attitude to take, because he knew that Katakura, as a colonel on Burma Area Army's staff, had been one of those responsible for planning the operation. Sugita returned to Singapore with the conviction that success at Imphal was doubtful. He returned to Tokyo with Hata on 11 May. The Chief of the Operation Section at Imperial GHQ, Colonel Hattori, asked him to call the following day. 'Reports from the front line situation have come in from two staff officers of Burma Area Army, the contents of which indicate that there have been people on tours of inspection who are pessimistic about the outcome of the operation, and that this is most improper. Does that not mean there might be something to consider, from this angle, in Hata's report to the Chief of the General Staff (Tojo)?' 'There's no particular need,' replied Sugita, 'to alter the contents of his report.' And, he added, 'There's no doubt he judges Imphal will fail.'

---

[1] Recollections of Colonel Sugita, OCH, *Inpāru Sakusen*, II, p. 68
[2] Kawabe's diary, ibid., p. 69

Hata's report was given to Tojo in the presence of a great number of staff officers of all kinds from Bureau Chiefs to representatives from Air Force Headquarters. 'I do not positively assert,' he concluded, 'that the Imphal operation will end in failure, but it is proving to be extremely difficult.' He softened the impact of his verdict by circumlocution. Tojo could not forget his audience. 'The battle must be fought to the end. What do you mean with all this feeble talk?' Hata said nothing. There was silence and an air of tension in the room. 'You have reached your conclusion on the basis of a report by a callow and inexperienced staff officer!' (Tojo obviously had learned that Hata's source was Ushiro, via Sugita.) Tojo promised action. Thirty-eight aircraft would be earmarked to fly supplies to Burma, but only twenty-four tons of material were made available, the opportunity to bring the operation to a stop was lost, and the decision taken to encourage 15 Army to go on. An envoy from Imperial GHQ (Major-General Itō) later relayed the message in a visit to Burma: 'The Imphal operation is now a problem not just for Burma but on the world stage. Whatever sacrifice is required, Burma Area Army must make it to take Imphal.'

Ushiro frequently advocated the cessation of the operation, even after that, but no one listened. Another staff officer who accompanied Kawabe on his tour of inspection at the beginning of June told Ushiro, with some sarcasm, that 15 Army 'wished to ensure that no staff officers were sent to the front if they were likely to report that the Imphal operation was going to fail.'

General Kawabe goes to see for himself

At the very time Satō's 31 Division was bitterly resisting XXXIII Corps' attempts to retake Kohima, the Commander-in-Chief in Rangoon was already becoming reconciled to losing it. He had anxieties elsewhere, too. The Chinese had begun a counter-offensive on the Salween front on 11 May, and pressure was increasing on the Hukawng front where 18 Division faced Stilwell's forces. A week later Myitkyina airfield was taken. It looked as if the whole North Burma situation might collapse, and Kawabe could not rush forces to hold the gap unless Mutaguchi took Imphal quickly. And he still feared the British Navy might attempt a landing south of Akyab across the Bay of Bengal. On 21 May, he issued an order declaring that the moment of decision in the Imphal battle had arrived. Imphal *must* be taken, even if that meant removing units from the battle at Kohima. He decided to see Mutaguchi himself and set off for Indainggyi with two staff officers on 25 May through Mandalay, Shwebo and Kalewa.

It was not an auspicious journey. After leaving Kalewa on 31 May, he met Lieutenant-General Yanagida, whom Mutaguchi had relieved of his command of 33 Division. The two men exchanged pained greetings, and Kawabe

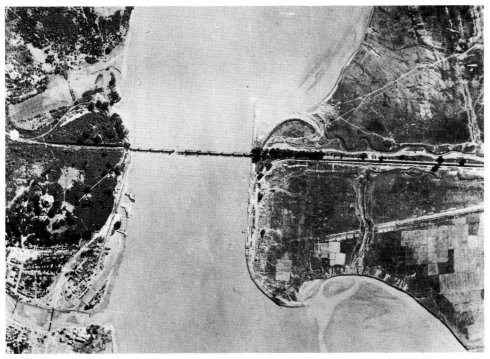

The Sittang Bridge from the air. *(Imperial War Museum)*

The man who blew the bridge – Lieutenant (later Major) Bashir Ahmed Khan, 369 (Malerkotla) Field Company of Engineers of Corps of Bengal Sappers and Miners. *(Major B. A. Khan)*

Snapshots from an Occupation: a. Japanese supervisor and Indian servants;
b. Japanese soldier photographed against a Burmese pagoda. *(Author)*

Major (later Lieutenant-General) Fujiwara Iwaichi. Founder, with Mohan Singh, of the pro-Japanese Indian National Army, and later on Mutaguchi's staff at Imphal. *(Lieutenant-General Fujiwara)*

Subhas Chandra Bose in his uniform as Commander-in-Chief, Indian National Army.

The Burmese Adipadi (Leader), Ba Maw, in conversation with Subhas Chandra Bose, Tokyo 1943. (in Ba Maw, *Breakthrough in Burma*)

Colonel Suzuki Keiji (Minami Masuyo; in Burmese, Bo Mo Gyo). Head of the Minami Kikan and founder of the pro-Japanese Burma National Army. (in Ba Maw, *Breakthrough in Burma*)

Aung San, leader of the 'Thirty Comrades', later Commander-in-Chief of the Burma National Army. *(Imperial War Museum)*

British soldier and Japanese prisoner on Arakan front. Drawing by Feliks Topolski. *(Imperial War Museum)*

Inniskilling Fusiliers on the beach at Donbaik, Arakan, 18 February 1943. Painting by Anthony Gross. *(Imperial War Museum)*

Medical Dressing Station at Indin, Arakan, 1943. British troops and a Japanese prisoner on a stretcher. Painting by Anthony Gross. *(Imperial War Museum)*

Inside the Admin Box. *(Imperial War Museum)*

Kohima. District Commissioner's Bungalow in centre foreground. Garrison Hill right foreground, with white flecks showing parachutes. FSD Hill, DIS Ridge, and Jail Hill alongside road leading south. Aradura Spur in background. *(Imperial War Museum)*

The Kohima tennis court, scene of the solo efforts of Sergeant Waterhouse of B Squadron, 149 Tank Regiment. *(Imperial War Museum)*

Part of the short Palel-Tamu road, crucial in the battles for Imphal during 1944.
(Imperial War Museum)

Lieutenant-General Sir George Giffard (left), Commander-in-Chief 11 Army
Group, with warrant officer (centre) and Lieutenant-Colonel John Laverty
(right) commanding the Royal West Kents at the siege of Kohima.
(Imperial War Museum)

pressed on. When he arrived at 15 Army Headquarters, Mutaguchi was away. He had not returned from inspecting 33 Division, so Kawabe took the opportunity to see what was happening on the Palel front. Fujiwara acted as his guide, and he saw Yamamoto on 2 June. There was no diminishing of Yamamoto's own spirit of attack, he could see that, but there was an admission that the morale of officers and men had taken a beating and the inevitable promise that the stalemate could be broken if only he had reinforcements. On the way back to Indainggyi his party met Major Usui, on his way to Ukhrul to advise on 15 Army's new plan: 31 Division was to deploy on the left flank of 15 Division, and attack Imphal. This was in line with Kawabe's thinking, but it had no basis in fact, as we shall see.

He met Mutaguchi on 5 June. 'Mutaguchi was in good health', he noted in his diary, 'but his eyes were filled with tears. "We are at the crossroads (*kangami*), but have no fears", he greeted me. I did not touch on the situation then, but postponed it until the afternoon. I rested in the morning, and Colonel Kinoshita gave me a report on the situation at 4 pm.'[1] (This was not idleness on Kawabe's part. He was suffering from amoebic dysentery, was very weak, and lacked the strength to argue.)[2] After the report, the policy.

There was no way of taking Imphal now other than by transferring 31 Division from the Kohima front; but Imphal would be taken, Kinoshita was convinced. Kinoshita knew at that time, of course, that Satō had already begun to retreat, and 15 Army's plan was to stop him at Ukhrul and turn him onto Imphal from there. In this way, Mutaguchi intended to conceal the facts of Satō's withdrawal.

On 6 June, the two generals had a formal meeting. Mutaguchi reported that he had removed Yamauchi from command of 15 Division, on the grounds that the burden of command was too much for him, and that his sickness had got worse. Kawabe accepted the decision as unavoidable, but mentally registered that Mutaguchi was showing poor man-management (*mazui jinji*).

Mutaguchi then pleaded for reinforcements, Kawabe promised to do his best, and the conversation came to an end. But Kawabe sensed Mutaguchi had something else to say, and could not find the words to say it. He knew what Mutaguchi had in his mind, but made no attempt to confirm this. There is an interesting phenomenon in Japanese life called *hara-gei* –'belly-art' – which is a way of describing the Japanese capacity for non-verbal communication. By a glance, a stiffening of the facial muscles, a twitch, you can convey to your equally well-trained protagonist the burden of your ideas without actual words intervening in the process.

---

[1] *Kawabe Nikki*, Defence Agency Archives, Tokyo.

[2] Conversation with Fujiwara, OCH, *Inpāru Sakusen*, II, p. 111

It was *hara-gei* that Mutaguchi was trying on with Kawabe, as he recalled in post-war days:

> I guessed Kawabe's real purpose (*ma no hara*) in coming was to sound out my views on the possibility – or otherwise – of continuing the Imphal operation. The sentence, 'The time has come to give up the operation as soon as possible' got as far as my throat; but I could not force it out in words. But I wanted him to get it from my expression.

Kawabe called Mutaguchi and his staff officers together on the evening of 6 June and said, 'I'm going back to Rangoon with confidence in you, and with peace of mind.' He reached Maymyo on 9 June and sent a report on his tour of the front to Southern Army and Imperial GHQ in which he gave a factual appraisal of what was happening at Imphal and made it clear that difficulties ahead would increase with the onset of the monsoon. But he made no request for authority to cancel the operation.

When he returned to Rangoon, he found piles of signals from higher HQs hoping for the success of the operation and encouraging him to be patient.They were the last thing he needed. He was already convinced there was no hope of success and that the time to cancel the operation had already come. But the signals gave him no choice. He had to order his armies to fight to the end.

Kohima Phase Two:
Durhams and Dorsets on Garrison Hill;
cavalry to the rescue

After the first siege had been lifted, Miyazaki's further attempts to take Garrison Hill fell on the second battalion of the Durham Light Infantry. As part of 6 Brigade of 2 Division, they had already had to fight their way into Kohima. They were two miles away on 17 April 1944, the day before 161 Brigade made contact with the besieged Royal West Kents, and B Company of the battalion was ordered to make the road safe for 2 Division transport threatened by the Japanese on Terrace Hill, just below Two Tree Hill which had been turned into a strong point by II/124 Infantry Regiment. The Durham Light Infantry inflicted fifty casualties on the Japanese, for the loss of their own company commander. They then rejoined A and C companies who had gone into the village itself, to occupy the south and west portions of Garrison Hill. The garrison had – most of it – been withdrawn by this time, but the relics of the first siege were everywhere, broken ammunition and water containers, splintered tree stumps festooned with parachutes from the supply drops, and the unburied dead. The Japanese were still holding the hillock – Kuki Picquet – to the south of Garrison Hill, which they called 'Saru' (Monkey); Garrison Hill was 'Inu' (Dog). In full view of the Japanese, who were only fifty yards away, the Durham Light Infantry began to scavenge round for spare food left behind by the Royal West Kents, and accumulated a dump load of tins of milk, bacon, corned beef and fruit. It looked for a moment as if life on Garrison Hill was going to be festive.

With the pious hope of getting a night's sleep, D Company found holes in their hillside and settled in. At 1.30 am on the 18th the Japanese showered C Company with mortars and grenades. D Company commander, Major 'Tank' Waterhouse, turned over in his foxhole, told himself it had nothing to do with him, and tried to get to sleep again. The noise increased, and the shells and bombs woke one of his platoon commanders, Lieutenant Pat Rome, who stuck his head out of his hole and found the whole area covered in smoke and flame, and the smell of cordite everywhere. An ammunition dump on the hill above him was ablaze, and a ration dump was burning. The dull thud of bursting tins of bully beef mingled with the crack of blazing pines and exploding ammunition.

Rome suddenly heard yelling and a high-pitched scream, then Bren guns opened on his perimeter. Everything seemed to be sounding off at once, Japanese screaming '*Banzai!*', LMGs crackling, grenades exploding, with figures dashing madly through the firelit smoke. Rome and the sergeant he shared the hole with clambered out, got the platoon together and made for Company HQ. They had gone twenty yards when Rome heard the sergeant groan and then crumple. He was dead, so Rome pushed on. It was clear that some Japanese had broken into the Durham Light Infantry position and more were massing for an attack. Waterhouse realized it was not possible to bring up artillery support. Nearly all the W/T sets had gone, the telephone lines had been severed by the shelling and the gunner officer attached to them was dead. It was two hours before any defensive fire came down, but around 4 am a counter-attack was mounted. Waterhouse's second-in-command, Lockhart, was killed by a burst from an automatic as he lay beside Rome. But that was quick. Rome remembers others not so quick, an infantryman hit in the stomach cursing and screaming with pain, one of the officers' batmen crying out that both his legs were broken, Corporal Worthy calling out to his platoon commander 'Mr Rome! Come and fetch me, I'm blind!' Rome went out and dragged him back. Then Rome was hit himself. He stood up for a brief moment and was knocked round. His arm hung limply beside him, useless and numb. He picked up a rifle sling, wrapped it round his neck and hung the broken arm in it.

In a lull in the fighting, Waterhouse chatted to C Company commander, Roger Stock. They smoked a cigarette and talked about leave. Rome talked to him too. Five minutes later Stock was dead. The battalion commander decided to send in a platoon of A Company under Captain

Sean Kelly, the company commander, to retake the lost ground. Kelly and his men fixed bayonets and crawled over the heaped bodies of British and Japanese dead. One of Kelly's sergeants was wounded in the legs, but went on firing his sten gun from a sitting position and giving orders to his section until a bursting mortar shell killed him. A second platoon was brought up, but the platoon commander was killed and a whole section wiped out by Japanese fire from Kuki Picquet. As day dawned, the Durham Light Infantry in the open on a forward slope were in full view of the Japanese who opened up on them with machine guns. Rome took a bren gunner and tried to spot the Japanese positions, but failed, and decided it was time to take cover when his bren gunner's hair was parted by a burst of fire. Rome ducked down behind a Japanese corpse. The eyes were open and kept staring at him. One of A Company's officers, Peter Stockton, came up to Rome and asked what the situation was. He was about to lead a counter-attack which went right into the Japanese trenches, Stockton leading with a *kukri*. He was killed almost at once, the Japanese proved too strong, and the wounded began to straggle back to the British lines, the Japanese peppering them with LMG fire on the way. The stretcher-bearers knelt in the open and patched up the wounded, carried them back, then went out again – two were recommended for a Victoria Cross during this single night. Around 8 am, things died down, Rome reported to Waterhouse and was told to take a rest. He sat in a foxhole and dozed off until it was time to sprint down to the ambulances.

It had been a costly night. Only four officers of the three forward companies remained, out of fifteen. In one night, A Company had shrunk from 136 men to 60. The Durham Light Infantry had been blooded in another way, too. They found one of their officers after the battle. He had been wounded and taken prisoner. The Japanese had tied him to a tree and bayoneted him. The quality of mercy ran very short in Kohima.

At the same time that Pat Rome was chatting about Teesdale with his friend Roger Stock – so soon to die – similar nostalgia was being felt on the other side of the hill. The men of 10 Company, 124 Regiment were cutting their hair and nails to make memorial packages of them in case they were killed, and they composed memorial notes, taking farewell of their families, by the light of a candle in a foxhole. The letters used simple, often rehearsed phrases: 'Dear father and mother, what is life like in Japan now? Soon I shall be going to a faraway place. For some time, I'll not be able to send you any news, but don't worry, there's no need!' To a beloved wife, or a beloved child, there was no way of saying: 'I'm going to die now.'

'All memorials and letters are to be handed in to Battalion HQ,' came the order. 'When they're finished, collect them. Then, so the enemy can't say, after you're dead, that you're unmanly and sentimental, burn all your photographs and family letters.'

Captain Yoshifuku, who had given the order, looked at the photo of his eldest son. 'Daddy, I'm top of the class now' – he saw his son's writing, and on the snapshot the smiling face in first year at school, proudly thrusting forward the arm with the 'top of the class' badge on it. 'So you're top of the class,' he wrote back. 'You've done well. Even when daddy's not there, keep it up!' He started to talk to the photograph, realized what he was doing, and set fire to it. His eye caught that of Corporal Kamikado Isamu, who was doing the same thing. They exchanged smiles. Yoshifuku's company was to lead the attack. They took off badges of rank, and the men threw away their bayonet scabbards. They would not need them again. If Garrison Hill did not fall, they would not be coming back.

Zero hour was 5 am for this assault. The second platoon commander, 2nd Lieutenant Umeda, was first up the ladder, hurled himself into the dead ground in front of him, and drove in the pin of his grenade. At once he felt a burning sensation in his chest. He tumbled down the slope onto the Imphal road, wounded in the throat.

Captain Yoshifuku was wounded in eleven places and collapsed, his whole body soaked in blood. 'Don't mind about me, get on to those buildings!' he ordered his men. One of the British soldiers prepared to throw a grenade in his direction, and Private Ochiai smashed at him from the side with the hilt of his bayonet. The soldier threw back his head and screamed, dropping the grenade. 'Look out!' – a grenade fragment scooped a hole in Ochiai's back as he dived to the ground. His men half-dragged, half-lifted Captain Yoshifuku to the edge of the slope, and rolled him from there into safety. Gouts of blood came from his wounds as he fell twenty feet to the road.[1]

The severance from the past was not the only way the Japanese at Kohima kept their courage up. Superstition helped, in some cases – the angels of Mons will never die. After the Japanese withdrew from Kohima Ridge, a Gurkha prisoner captured in the fighting at Hill 5120 in the Naga village told them how the ghost of a Japanese soldier appeared every night after the Japanese retreated. When it grew dark, a battle-cry sounded, and the soldier, steel helmet tied firmly on his head, would come charging through them like a demon. 'When we fired, it vanished in front of our position, like a ghost!' The Japanese of III/58 Regiment heard the story repeated after the surrender when they were acting as a labour unit near Prome. The British unit there had fought against them at Kohima. 'We do not think it odd,' writes one of the compilers of 58 Regiment's History, 'when we think of the tenacity of the many hundreds and thousands of our comrades who went to their deaths on those hills. We can think that their spirits might become a phantom assault unit.'[2]

[1] *Kyōdo butai senki* (War reports of our regiments) in *Biruma Sensen*, pp. 158–9
[2] *Biruma Sensen* (Recollections of 58 Infantry Regiment), 1964, p. 405

Lieutenant Kameyama Seisaku, HQ, II Battalion, 58 Infantry Regiment, found an even odder, but perhaps more traditional way, of appealing to the courage of his men. He remembered a novel by Satō Kōroku in which older members of a baseball team got the players who were without a box to grasp their testicles. (The story is also told of Admiral Togo at the battle of Tsushima.)

'Don't flap!' he called out to his men who were finding it hard to dig in on the slopes where the ground was hard, and were sniped at whenever they showed themselves. 'No point in panicking. Calm down. Everyone, grab your balls! Right? If they're hanging loose, you're OK!'

He tried to suit his own actions to his words and found to his dismay that, far from hanging loose, his scrotum was contracted hard. Thirty or so of his men were gazing at him demonstrating, all of them with their hands between their crotch. He brazened it out. 'Well, what are they like? *Mine* are dangling!'

Not even the imminent terrors of the battle prevented the whole group bursting out laughing when a young private in front of him, face red with the effort of search, said 'Sir, I can't find my balls. . .'[1]

Stopford's forces for the retaking of Kohima easily outnumbered the Japanese. He retained 161 Brigade from 5 Division, which was sent forward of MS 32. Coming down on the old Naga village from the hills to the north was 7 Division, recently air-freighted from Arakan. Further east in the hills beyond the village, one of Wingate's long-range penetration units, 23 LRP Brigade (Perowne), was cutting supplies and communications on the tracks leading to the Chindwin. And 2 Division (Grover) was to assault Kohima Ridge and open the road to Imphal.

On 22 April, after nightfall, Grover sent his 5 Brigade (Hawkins) against Merema Ridge, occupied by Satō's 6 Company, 138 Infantry Regiment. It was a wide left hook three miles north of Kohima Ridge, carried out in pouring rain, first in single file along the Dzuza valley and then up again on to the Ridge itself. The Ridge was the strong point of Sato's Right Area. He had split his command into three zones, Right Area stretching from Merema to the fringe of Naga village, Centre Area being Naga village itself, in and around which he had four battalions (2/138, 3/138, 3/124 and 3/58) and the Left Area consisting of Kohima Ridge and the surrounding heights, the most heavily defended of all, where he concentrated four battalions and where the HQs of 58 and 124 Regiments, and of 31 Division Infantry Group, were situated.

Hawkins's Brigade, with 1st Cameron Highlanders leading the way and Naga porters carrying supplies, went up a steep spur 2000 feet. This put

---

[1] ibid., p. 308

them in a position from which they could come up behind the Japanese in the Naga village, which they attacked on 4 May. The Japanese counter-attacked during the night and retook some ground from the Camerons, but on 5 May 5 Brigade was still holding the west side of the village, and began to send out fighting patrols towards Treasury Hill.

From Garrison Hill the land fell a hundred feet in four terraces, the drop from one to the next varying from ten to forty feet. The topmost terrace was a club badminton court, below that the tennis court, then the DC's bungalow – a drop of over thirty feet – then a garden twenty feet above the road junction. It was impossible to see what was happening in any one terrace from the one above.

In spite of the fact that all this area was part of the DC's bungalow, the British troops attacking it were not all sure of its detailed topography. It took an attack by the 2nd Battalion Dorsetshire Regiment to establish the site of the tennis court, which had previously been assumed to be on the club square.[1] The Dorsets and the Royal Berkshires were the next to bear the brunt of Miyazaki's attacks. The Dorsets' Commanding Officer recognized from the start that he would need the help of tanks to blast the Japanese out of their bunkers in the DC's bungalow area, and several attempts were made to manoeuvre a tank on to the club square from where the tennis court could be dominated. On 28 April, a bulldozer driver from the Royal Engineers drove his vehicle along the main road, right round the Japanese positions, and tried to haul a Lee tank behind him up the steep slope towards the bungalow compound. With incredible coolness, he first made a track up the slope and then went to hitch on the tank. As he dismounted to make an adjustment, the tank he was towing went into reverse by mistake, pulled the bulldozer back down on itself and crashed down the slope. Two days later, an attempt was made with a Honey tank. First its internal communication system went haywire, then it ran out of petrol. The driver had another go the following day, though he had a profound mistrust of the drop from the club square to the tennis court. An officer of the Dorsets went with him and agreed it was impossible to drop the tank down onto the court. As they were manoeuvring in the very limited space, the Honey had a near miss from a Japanese 75 mm gun only 600 yards away – they were devastating at close range – and as it pulled back into cover, it was squarely hit by a 3.7" anti-tank gun and put out of action – without casualties.[2]

The Dorsets' inability to descry what was happening in the bungalow area was partly their own fault: a thick screen of trees hid Japanese movement and the outline of the buildings from them. Then the Rajputs

---

[1] White, *Straight on for Tokyo, the War History of the 2nd Battalion, the Dorsetshire Regiment (54th Foot)*, 1948, p. 193

[2] ibid, p. 101

moved into the Garrison Hill perimeter and, with the laudable intention of giving themselves as much cover as possible, started to chop down the trees for dug-outs. The reaction of the Dorsets' Commanding Officer was immediate: 'A day or two later, on my way to visit B Company, I noticed that something seemed to be different. The forest was much thinner and sure enough, on glancing down the hill towards the club square, I saw a sight which stirred me as much as Cortes must have been excited at his first view of the Pacific – I could see the District [sic] Commissioner's bungalow! I could not only see the bungalow but also expanses of the compound! The few square yards thus made visible by the Rajputs' jungle-clearing activities seemed vast to us who had tried every possible way to get just a little peek into this hitherto closed territory.'[1]

It was time to think of using tanks again. The Japanese had managed to construct a honeycomb of positions in the area of GPT Ridge and Jail Hill, with underground tunnels and strong revetments which were almost impervious to British shelling. By mid-May, the Japanese had been at the rough end of the British guns to the extent of 3000 rounds from thirty-eight 3.7″ howitzers, 7000 rounds from forty-eight 25 pounders, 1500 rounds medium (from two 5.5s – the only two available in the whole of XXXIII Corps), quite apart from mortar concentrations and daily bombing and machine-gunning by the RAF. Yet nothing seemed to shift them. When the tornado was over, the Japanese infantry were ready to fight back, with nothing in the air to help them, and little from their own guns, short of ammunition.

It was vital to eliminate their last hold on Kohima Ridge before the battle could be taken further into the Naga village and down towards Aradura, and the sappers were called in again to bulldoze a track for a tank up Hospital Hill Spur to break into the perimeter from behind. By evening on 12 May, the sappers had done the impossible in spite of the gradient and wet ground. The Dorsets gleefully got ready to go in with the tank and asked the Mountain Artillery to heave a 3.7″ gun into a position from which it could fire at the tin hut alongside the tennis court and the water tank next to it, both of which were strongly held by the Japanese.

At 10 am on 13 May, Sergeant Waterhouse, of B Squadron 149 Tank Regiment, edged his Lee tank slowly towards the steep slope from the club bank. The forward infantry platoon commander had been unable to give Waterhouse any ideas of the ground ahead and he and Waterhouse had recce-ed the position the previous evening just before dusk. Waterhouse took one of the Dorset's officers inside the tank, and moved over the edge. "Old on!' his driver called out, but it was too late. The tank was on the tennis court crashing right on top of a Japanese position and burying the defenders alive. With what seemed like agonizing slowness to the watching

[1] ibid, pp. 110–11

Dorsets it steadied itself on the court and swung its gun round. Waterhouse found himself in front of the steel water tower which was sheltered by sandbags. The Japanese began to pour rifle and LMG fire, hopelessly, at the Lee. Then Waterhouse's 75 began to pump shells into them. They dropped their weapons and fled, only to be met by fire from the Dorsets, whose signal to attack was the first round from Waterhouse. At the same time, the Mountain Artillery 3.7″ howitzer shot fifty rounds into the rear of the Japanese position. Sergeant Given of the Dorsets moved round the tennis court and reported what was happening on the tank telephone to the Dorset officer inside. For twenty minutes, Waterhouse raked the Japanese machine-gun positions and trenches round the tennis court, and then took his tank to the edge of the drop overlooking the Deputy Commissioner's bungalow and fired his 75 into it. The Dorsets went in when the shelling stopped and took the bungalow with only one casualty. Waterhouse reported, 'The infantry again went in and took over without a casualty.'[1] In fact, the Dorsets' only death on 13 May was at this time, when Corporal Signett, of the Battalion Police, was killed leading his section into the bungalow.[2]

The whole action had lasted forty minutes. The Dorsets had been on Garrison Hill eighteen days, at a cost of seventy-five men killed. It was a good day for 2 Division elsewhere, too. 6 Brigade linked up with 33 Brigade (7 Division) and 4 Brigade and drove the Japanese back on to Aradura Spur. Between 4 and 7 May, Miyazaki had successfully repulsed attacks on Kuki Picquet, FSD Hill and DIS Hill by 6 Brigade and 33 Brigade, but five days later, 33 Brigade tried again and compelled the Japanese to withdraw. With the Dorsets' capture of the Deputy Commissioner's bungalow on 13 May, Kohima Ridge was clear.

The remaining Japanese were in two strong positions: in Naga village north of the Ridge and Aradura Spur to the south of it. To cut off Miyazaki's men in Aradura, Grover had ordered his 4 Brigade (Goschen) to carry out the same pincer movement on the right as 5 Brigade had achieved on the left. But 4 Brigade had to tackle harder terrain. The huge peak of Mount Pulebadze, nearly 8000 feet high, lay two miles south-west of Kohima and 4 Brigade would have to go round it and come upon Miyazaki from the south-west. The Brigade set off with the 1st Royal Norfolks (Scott) in front, led by Naga guides, in heavy rain, along muddy tracks, through deep valleys peopled with giant trees and a vegetation that sunlight barely penetrated. Rations were short and, in order to achieve surprise, cooking fires were forbidden and no supply air drops were made. 4 Brigade slithered and hacked their way through and on 4 May came out near GPT (General Purposes Transport) Ridge. The Japanese called this

---

[1] Perrett, *Tank Tracks to Rangoon*, p. 143

[2] White, op.cit., p. 114

Heisha Kōchi (Barrack Hill) and it was here that Miyazaki had set up his Headquarters and was directing the battle for Kohima Ridge. The original plan had been to make directly for Aradura Spur by 28 April but the hard going made this impossible, and the turning movement was shortened.

The Norfolks were supposed to halt at the edge of the jungle and wait for an artillery barrage to saturate GPT Ridge before they went in, but Scott wanted to use the surprise he had achieved and took his battalion straight in with fixed bayonets. They took the Ridge and Scott got on the phone to his Headquarters.

'I am on GPT and am consolidating.'

'But you can't be on GPT,' came the astonished reply. 'You haven't had the fire plan yet.'

'I am, I tell you. Send someone up to see.'

In fact, the Norfolks had not taken the whole position. The Japanese held a group of bunkers north of the Ridge, and their snipers were still lethally installed in the jungle overlooking it.

The bunkers were a menace. 33 Brigade (Loftus-Tottenham, 7 Division) had been loaned to Grover for the assault on the central Kohima position starting on 4 May, during which 4 Brigade on the right was to co-operate with 6 Brigade in taking Jail Hill by 7 May, while 3 Brigade moved down into Naga village. But Loftus-Tottenham, who arrived on 5 May, had a look at the route his men were to take and saw at once that fire from the Japanese bunkers left on GPT Ridge would catch him on the right flank. 4 Brigade were asked to clear the ridge, and 2 Norfolk captured the north-east spur after the bunkers had been subjected to a fierce artillery barrage. In an act of almost unbelievable gallantry, one of the Norfolks' officers, Captain Randle, blocked a bunker aperture with his own body to allow his men to take it, but the Japanese held out, and machine-gun fire sprayed the attackers from Aradura Spur. Two 6-pounder guns brought up on 9 May to shell the bunker at point-blank range failed to make an impression either (the bunkers were proof against anything except 5.5″ medium guns and 75 mm guns at close range).

On the morning of 7 May, Gurkhas attacked the bunkers on GPT Ridge, but had no better luck than the Norfolks. Their commanding officer was killed, and in an attempt to bring him in, Brigadier Goschen's batman was killed, then Goschen himself was killed while on reconnaissance. It is an indication of the nature of the close combat for Kohima that British casualties included two Brigadiers killed. And at the other end of the scale of ranks, by 7 May, II Battalion Durham Light Infantry was reduced to a strength of six platoons. Fire from GPT Ridge, just as Loftus-Tottenham had feared, caught the 1st Queen's (West Surreys) in the flank as they moved towards Jail Hill after half-an-hour's bombardment from the division's guns. The Japanese then ranged on them with a 75 mm gun and drove them back. It was, as Arthur Swinson, the historian of Kohima, says, 'a bitter defeat'.[1] Four days later, at 4.30 am on 11 May, the Queens, with the 4/15 Punjab, attacked Jail Hill again, and the Japanese on GPT Ridge hit them again in exactly the same way. But this time the Queens pressed on and took the summit.

Between 8–10 May, 2 Division licked its wounds and prepared to attack again. By 12 May, the Gurkhas had cleared Jail Hill, the 4/15 Punjab took DIS Hill and 1st Royal Berkshires captured FSD Ridge. The Japanese evacuated the few remaining positions on DIS Hill during the night of 12 May. The following day, 4/1 Gurkha Rifles infiltrated on to Treasury Hill and found it almost empty. 5 Brigade, with tanks which had reached them along the road from Kohima Ridge, pushed south and joined up with the Gurkhas on 15 May. This left the high ground east of Naga village still to be taken – Church Knoll, Hill 5120, Gun Spur – and Aradura to the south.

By this time, Stopford was receiving fresh reinforcements. 7 Division (Messervy) with its 114 Brigade, followed 33 Brigade into the Kohima area in early May, and 161 Brigade was placed under its command in lieu of 89 Brigade which had been flown to Imphal. 268 Brigade was used to provide reliefs for units of 2 Division, which allowed brigades to be in action for three or four days only and then brought back to Dimapur for a rest period.[2]

The contrast with the Japanese could hardly have been more striking. Their casualties had been colossal, they received no reinforcements, they had no air support, no tanks, and even for their inadequate artillery, ammunition was running low. No rations were coming through from the depots on the Chindwin, and the only relief they could expect was death. Nonetheless, when Stopford ordered the second phase of the retaking of Kohima to start on 16 May 1944, they rose to meet him.

Black Cats vs. White Tigers (Round Three): the Silchar track, Potsangbam and Ninthoukhong

Major-General Tanaka Nobuo became acting commander of 33 Division in May 1944,[3] and was promoted to full command in the rank of Lieutenant-General in June when, to all intents and purposes, the battle had already been lost. But Tanaka never behaved as if it had. A burly, impressive figure, six-foot tall, with a striking luxuriant moustache, the tips

---

[1] Swinson, op.cit., p. 1702

[2] *Reconquest of Burma*, I, p. 296

[3] Mutaguchi signalled for authority to replace Yanagida on 9 May, and on the next day Tanaka was ordered to leave 29 IMB in Thailand and was in Rangoon en route to the front on 13 May. Colonel Tanaka Tetsujirō, Chief of Staff, ran the division until Tanaka took over. (OCH, *Inpāru Sakusen*, II, p. 56)

of which reached his ears, he issued a rousing summons to his men on 2 June:

> Now is the time to capture Imphal. Our death-defying infantry group expects certain victory when it penetrates the main force of the enemy. The coming battle is a turning point. It will decide the success or failure of the Greater East Asia War... It must be expected that the Division will be almost annihilated. I have confidence in your courage and devotion, and believe that you will do your duty... On this one battle rests the fate of the Empire. All officers and men, fight courageously![1]

Stirring stuff. But the same day, he confided thoughts to his diary in a much lower key:

> The officers and men look dreadful. They've let their hair and beards grow, and look just like wild men of the mountains. More than a hundred days have passed since the operation began and in all that time there's been almost nothing to eat and there's not an ounce of fat left on any of them. They all look pale and skinny from undernourishment. People at home would not even be able to imagine what they've gone through.
>
> We've had two or three days of clear skies, but last night it sheeted down. A few comforts and some rations have come through. Up to now, we've been short of candles and so have had no light except when it was absolutely vital. Afterwards we've been in total darkness – time for meditation! Now we'll be able to read our maps even at night.
>
> I was particularly pleased to get the pickled plums. Jungle greens taste bitter and have a grassy smell – we eat them because we must. But even with one plum each, the taste of food's taken a turn for the better.
>
> I've not used a watch since the 15th of June. Watches are useless on the battlefield. Although the rain pours down endlessly, enemy planes are active. There's no let-up for twenty-four hours when the skies are clear...[2]

Tanaka, on that day, was planning an attack to break the stalemate on the Bishenpur front between himself and 17 Indian Division. Cowan had 32 Brigade (Mackenzie) of 20 Division under command, and gave it the task of resisting Tanaka's encroachments in the area of the Silchar track. 63

---

[1] Evans and Brett-James, op.cit., pp. 105–6
[2] OCH, *Inpāru Sakusen*, II, p. 134

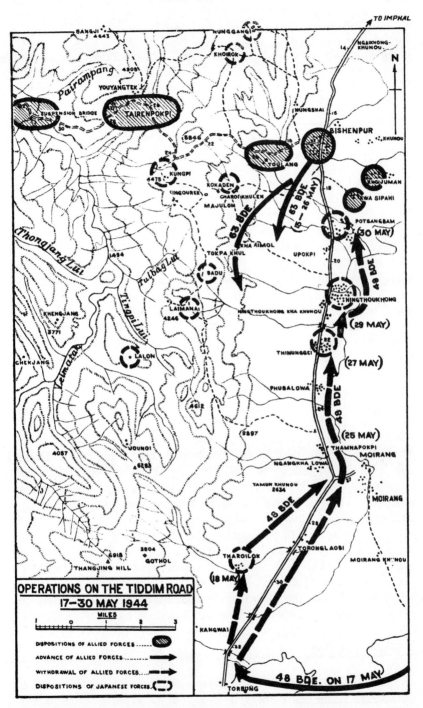

OPERATIONS ON THE TIDDIM ROAD
17–30 MAY 1944

MILES

DISPOSITIONS OF ALLIED FORCES......
ADVANCE OF ALLIED FORCES.........
WITHDRAWAL OF ALLIED FORCES.....
DISPOSITIONS OF JAPANESE FORCES..

Brigade would take over 32 Brigade's positions on the main road south to Tiddim and seize the village of Ninthoukhong which straddled the road and had been occupied by the Japanese in April. They had even pressed further north into the next village, Potsangbam, in the first week in May. Mackenzie had already tried to winkle the Japanese out of Ninthoukhong at the end of April, and had failed, with the loss of three tanks and 130 casualties.

63 Brigade (Burton) was to have another go, while 48 Brigade (Cameron) took a circuitous route east of Logtak Lake down a track leading to Shuganu – it brought him almost to the edge of the fighting at Palel – and swung west across country (and the Manipur River) towards MS 33 and Torbung. He was to establish road-blocks there and strangle Tanaka's supply route from the south. Cameron set out on 13 May,[1] marching by night, and reached Hill 3404 from which he could look down at the Japanese positions at the Torbung defile, at 6 am on 16 May. He took an air drop at Hill 3404, then sent his Gurkhas to cut the road, where they destroyed three Japanese tanks. Early on the morning of 18 May, two Japanese convoys approached the block, three lorries from the north and eight from the south. Eight of the eleven were destroyed. Further road-blocks were set up, at MS 28 and MS 36. Tanaka's men hurled themselves in vain at the blocks and at Cameron's brigade headquarters, losing over 200 men.[2] But it was essential to Cowan's plan that 63 Brigade should push through the Japanese positions, mopping up the infantry battalion and engineer regiment thought to be positioned between Potsangbam and Torbung, and meet 48 Brigade as it came up the road. Instead of which, 63 Brigade was held up by Japanese resistance in the Kha Aimol area west of Potsangbam, though it took the saddle west of Tokpa Khul which the Japanese called *Mitsukobu Kōchi* (Three Pimple Height), only a couple of miles north of Tanaka's 33 Division Headquarters at Laimanai, thus cutting communications between Tanaka and his forward regiments. The upshot was that 48 Brigade became increasingly isolated, and, in a kind of replay of 17 Division's retreat from Tiddim in March, moved up the road in box-formation, Gurkhas to the front and Gurkhas to the rear, fighting off Tanaka's attempts to encircle. Cameron's advance guard – 1/7 Gurkha Rifles – was at Ninthoukhong on the morning of 29 May, and fought all day to pierce a way through. But the Japanese held firm, and in the end the village was bypassed. The next day, Cameron was in contact with elements of 63 Brigade. The hook hadn't worked, and 48 Brigade had lost heavily; but they forced a heavy price out of Tanaka – a thousand casualties.

---

[1] A. J. Barker, *March on Delhi*, p. 139; 14 May according to *Reconquest of Burma*, I, p. 227

[2] The Gurkhas lost five men. But nearly three times that number and thirty-seven mules were lost when the RAF shot up the roadblock by mistake. Kirby, *War against Japan*, III, p. 347

While Cowan was using 48 Brigade to look for Tanaka's jugular, Tanaka was doing the same to him. He sent Sakuma's 214 Regiment north to Nunggang, where Sakuma was to split his force, sending II Battalion (Sueda) against 17 Division's position at Hill 2926 north of MS 12 from Imphal, and I Battalion (Moritani) to cross the road below MS 14 and come down on Bishenpur from the north.

This attack was carried out on 20 May in conjunction with an assault on Bishenpur by Sasahara's 215 Infantry Regiment from the hills to the west, and a probe by II Battalion/213 Regiment (Isagoda), which was to come up from Ninthoukhong, bypass Potsangbam, and hit Bishenpur from the south-east across the plain.

The impetus of Sakuma's attack brought his men almost on top of Cowan's headquarters at the village of Chingphu. On 20 May they came out of the hills west of Buri Bazar at MS 10 from Imphal, and took a hill which dominated the road (Point 2926, or 'Red Hill'). Or, at least, they took most of it. A pimple defended by twenty sepoys from 7/10 Baluch resisted the onslaught; and the Japanese did not occupy the part of the hill which overlooked HQ 17 Indian Division. They were simply cutting the road from Imphal and did not know Cowan was there. Cowan, rather naturally, objected to conducting his battle in the very shadow of the Japanese offensive, and after a scratch force from Divisional HQ and a number of infantry companies had failed to dislodge the Japanese, 50 Parachute Brigade (Woods)[1] was brought in. With the assistance of 3/1 Gurkha Rifles (Wingfield) from 20 Division and two troops of tanks (3 Carabiniers), the Japanese were forced off Red Hill by the end of May. Sakuma watched the battle from Regimental HQ at Nunggang. When it was over, Sueda's II Battalion, 500 strong when he set out, was down to forty men.

At 2 am on 20 May Moritani brought his 380 men to the road fork just north of Bishenpur and dug in with his machine guns. The British reacted swiftly and tanks, brought up the next day, overran Captain Matsumura's positions and he and his entire company were killed. Sakuma then sent in seventy men of 7 Company under Captain Yamori to have another crack at Bishenpur. They stormed in on the 26th, and not a single one returned.

For Sakuma's two battalions the net result of the fight was that I Battalion lost 360 out of its strength of 380, and II Battalion 460 out of its 500. Isagoda's II/213 Battalion lost the chance of breaking into Bishenpur from the south-east, and Sasahara's main attack with his 215 Regiment was completely thwarted by 63 Indian Brigade's incursion into the rear of his positions and the establishment of a strongpoint at Three Pimple Hill in the very heart of 33 Division.

---

[1] Battalion commander of I Dogras at the battle for Nungshigum described earlier.

That was the situation when Tanaka took over his new responsibilities. He made his impact at once: 'I believe', he announced, 'that the only way to serve our country is to carry out duties positively, with an iron will. War is a contest of wills. Whining complaints about orders, and expressions of opinions which show softness are strictly forbidden.'[1] He reached 15 Army's new tactical headquarters at Molloh on 22 May, reported to Mutaguchi, and arrived at his own headquarters at Laimanai the same night. As Yanagida handed over to him, he gave vent to his anger: 'The situation is completely in the enemy's favour. Annihilation is only a matter of time!' Tanaka had known Yanagida as head of the Officers' School and a member of the Military Academy's sword team; also that he was perhaps over-sensitive. At any rate, he had no sympathy for such pessimism, and turned to the task in hand. He had to take back Three Pimple Hill and Kha Aimol from 63 Brigade and restore communications with his front line regiments.

A composite force from 215 Regiment under Captain Shinohara was ordered to attack Observatory Hill from the north on the night of 24 May, but the headquarters party stumbled on a mine which exploded and killed them all, and this attack came to nothing. Isagoda was ordered to lead his battalion against Kha Aimol, which he did on the night of 25 May. His men occupied the British positions, but at a cost of thirty-eight casualties, including two company commanders, so they withdrew.

Sasahara Regiment's assault on Three Pimple Hill (using II and III Battalions) lasted from 22 to 28 May, but this too was a disaster. The two battalion commanders were among the many casualties. The regimental figures now made nonsense. Its main force, I Battalion, was 100 men strong. Other battalions had around forty men apiece. Companies were down to seven or eight men. The same was true of 214 Regiment under Sakuma. II Battalion (Sueda) was made up of companies numbering three to eight men each, with not a single officer in command of any of them. From the start of the campaign to 23 May, the division as a whole had suffered 3500 casualties (including 1200 killed). And only two battalion commanders in the entire division were unwounded.

In the main road area, 4 Independent Engineer Regiment (Taguchi) took over the position left by Isagoda Battalion in Ninthoukhong. The regiment had sixty survivors from the recent fighting, but 14 Tank Regiment (now Colonel Ise), having broken through 48 Brigade's encirclement, brought its two battalions (Seko, Iwasaki) into Ninthoukhong to strengthen it, on the night of 31 May. Ise had no intention of sitting in the village, though. Taking Taguchi's Engineers under command, he started to prepare yet another attack on Bishenpur. There should have been reinforcements for 214 Regiment also, but the commander of III

[1] OCH, *Inpāru Sakusen*, II, p. 72

battalion took his time moving up from the Haka-Falam area, reached the Torbung defile only on 25 May and reported at 33 Division headquarters at Sado (Tanaka had moved his tactical headquarters nearer to Bishenpur) after taking four days when he should only have needed one.

Tanaka's first instinct was to court-martial him but he decided there might be more point in using him and ordered him to skirt round Three Pimple Hill and report to Sakuma. But Tanaka began to reflect on Yanagida's views, which at first he scorned. What had he been told when he was going to take over? Yanagida was a 'talented grouser'. But Yanagida had told him how he had been continually urged to take Bishenpur at all costs, regardless of casualties. 15 Army would be responsible. Now Tanaka looked at the results: two battalions of 214 Regiment annihilated in the fight for Bishenpur and Red Hill. 215 Regiment's I Battalion down to 100 men, and getting ready to burn the regimental flag. Had Yanagida been right? He himself was out of touch with his regimental commanders, because of the British occupation of Three Pimple Hill, a mere 600 yards away. Mutaguchi had misjudged the strength of XIV Army, and it was wrong to put the blame exclusively on Yanagida's negative command. Slowly, his sympathy for Yanagida increased.

But there was no disguising the fact that he was still under Mutaguchi's command, and Mutaguchi planned a new offensive. Annihilation or not, Tanaka would obey.

Between 5 and 7 June Tanaka cleared the British positions in his vitals – Kha Aimol, Tokpa Khul, Observatory Hill – and was able to put supplies through to what remained of 214 and 215 Regiments. At the same time, he used recently arrived reinforcements from Arakan, II/154 Regiment (Iwasaki) of 54 Division, to advance north from Ninthoukhong in a wide westward arc to bring it into Potsangbam on 7 June at 6 am, where Iwasaki managed to get a foothold on the edge of the village, the price being a hundred men.

But Ninthoukhong was no sure base from which to mount an attack. The village was divided in two. A muddy stream ran through it, with steep-sided banks. The Japanese held the southern end of the village, which had plenty of trees and hedges for cover. The north side was held by 17 Division's Support Battalion, I West Yorkshires (Cooper) who were comparatively uncovered and vulnerable to sniping. The ground was flat and boggy behind them, and it was useless digging foxholes since they filled with water both from the incessant heavy rain and seepage from Logtak Lake. This meant more than discomfort: footrot set in.

The Japanese attacked a West Yorkshire platoon, twenty men strong, on the morning of 7 June, and drove them back from their perimeter with a shower of grenades and machine-gun fire. That they could not advance further was due to the single-handed courage of the West Yorkshire platoon sergeant, Victor Turner, who was awarded a posthumous VC for charging the Japanese six times, loaded with grenades, and hurling them into the Japanese machine guns. Under attack from tank guns and artillery, the Japanese paused and before dawn the next day Seko withdrew the men of his battalion (I/67 on loan from 15 Division) with a loss of sixty men out of eighty, including the acting battalion commander, Lieutenant Kaneko. But the West Yorkshires had been plastered too, and had taken fifty casualties including two officers. So 2/5 Gurkha Rifles (Townsend, then Eustace) were brought in to replace them.

Throughout June, while 15 and 31 Divisions were relaxing their grip on IV Corps, General Tanaka was still intent on cutting the Silchar track (a useless aim once XXXIII Corps linked up with IV Corps on 22nd June) and taking Bishenpur, from which Imphal was only a stone's throw away.

He decided to use recent reinforcements from North Burma, Colonel Hashimoto's 151 Infantry Regiment of 53 Division, against Forest Hill, approaching it from the west. It would then move east against 'Plum Hill' (a height north of Ngaranjial) and attack towards Bishenpur. From the south, Sasahara (215 Regiment) would attack British positions east of Ngaranjial to take pressure off Hashimoto. Sakuma (214 Regiment) would send a commando party to raid the British A/A gun positions at Nunggang the day before the division's general assault. British counter-attacks against Hashimoto would be halted by Japanese artillery (Hashimoto in fact had one regimental gun, which had had to be broken up and man-handled to the front line).

Admittedly, Hashimoto's troops were fresher than those Tanaka had been using. But they had not had an easy time at Mawlu against Calvert, and had marched through heavy rain to reach positions where the monsoon was at its height. Men lived in soaking wet conditions without relief, sickness was on the increase, and they took ten hours to march what healthy men in dry conditions would cover in two. The attack was postponed from 20 June by one day.

Both commando raids were a success, and British artillery was silent. The raiders had also laid mines which wrecked four light tanks. Hashimoto's 300 men took the defenders of Forest Hill by surprise while they were breakfasting, and occupied the position. It took them an hour, at the cost of six casualties, to achieve what Sasahara's repeated assaults – and fearful casualties – had failed to do. All the more humiliating for the White Tigers was the fact that the 33 Division thought themselves – and were thought by many others – to be among the best in the Japanese Army, whereas 53 Division, to which Hashimoto belonged, was largely a conscript formation of town dwellers from Kyoto.

But Hashimoto's ammunition was low, and he could not capture his next objective, 'Plum Hill'. And the British artillery at Bishenpur, untouched by any raids, poured shells into his force on the hillside as they came up for the attack, and in a matter of minutes he lost a battalion commander and

205 men, and had half his guns destroyed. Nor could Hashimoto consolidate.

15 Army instructed him not to bring engineering equipment, and 151 Regiment was sadly lacking in tools when they were most required. Okamoto (I/215) took Triangle Hill from the south, but Isagoda (II/213) failed to take Bare Hill east of Ngaranjial on the 22nd, hardly surprising since the 'battalion' consisted of Isagoda and eighteen men. But they took it the following day, Isagoda himself being wounded in the attempt.

On 4 June, the British appeared to the north of Nunggang and infiltrated into Khoirok, and Sakuma shifted his headquarters to Laimaton, a little way into the hills to the north-west. The front then quietened down, to allow Sakuma's men to contemplate their malaria, dysentery and skin diseases, which were multiplying by leaps and bounds in their sodden foxholes, or 'octopus pots' (*tako tsubo*). But Sakuma did not let the monsoon make him idle. He put together two or three commando teams for advance patrolling and sabotage. One such team, with six engineers, set off east across the hills to Bunte and blew up an A/A gun (used by the British for horizontal firing) and a tented camp. Another, consisting of 47 men from No. 9 Company penetrated deep behind the British lines for over a week and put in a blitz attack on a British artillery position at Buli Bazar (seven miles north-east of Bishenpur), and destroyed four tanks and six trucks into the bargain. They approached to within four miles of Imphal – the closest any Japanese ever came to the town (and spotted a signpost to prove it).

Sakuma was also lucky enough to capture some British plans. On 23 June, Pfc. Watanabe Yasuhira, a sentry at the mountain gun position near Khoirok, saw a figure appear unexpectedly out of the thick morning mist. He recovered enough to use his bayonet; the corpse proved to be that of a British major carrying a brigade order: 'You will attack Tairenpokpi on 24 June and cut the road to the Japanese forces.' Sakuma shifted his II Battalion to Tairenpokpi at once, but there was no attack that day. The next day, 25 June, the British sent 200 men against Laimaton and 400 against Khoirok.

Tanaka pressed his weary regimental commanders into fresh efforts. When Sasahara's 215 Regiment was clearly exhausted, he ordered it to attack British gun positions, which he knew were the core of Cowan's ability to hit him in the hills west of Bishenpur. At a pinch, Sasahara was to split his men up, make two commando formations and send them out *daily* against the British guns.

Cowan's 17 Division had suffered heavily in these latest battles with 33 Division, and 32 Brigade detached from 20 Division was still locked in battle with two battalions of Japanese infantry and tanks at Ninthoukhong on the main road – the scene of battles in which two VCs were awarded in these monsoon months, both to Gurkhas.

The Japanese tanks were the forlorn remnants of the famous 14 Tank Regiment which had ridden so proudly down the Malayan Peninsula to Singapore. Now all that was past, and they found their 47 mm guns no match for the 75s of the British medium tanks which dominated the road south of Bishenpur. The British divisional commander was so confident of success that while Tanaka was planning to storm Bishenpur from all sides, Noel Coward was in the village entertaining the troops.

Cowan's confidence, of course, was justified. His artillery, tanks and air support were overwhelming. Sakuma, in contrast, worked out that his regiment had lost, in the fighting around Bishenpur, 791 men killed, 241 wounded, and 22 missing, a total of 1054 casualties. Tanaka did the same sums for his division on 30 June. In killed and wounded, they had lost 7000 men, and 5000 more from sickness, a total of 12,000 – in other words, 70% of the divisional strength.

With staggering losses like this, and with the monsoon at its height, Tanaka nevertheless intended to stop IV Corps pushing him out of the way. When 5 Division took over from 17 Division, sent back to India to refit, Tanaka put up the best show he could. The other divisional commanders walked back to the Chindwin. He fought his way there. It may have been a hopeless struggle, as Slim was later to point out, and as no doubt Tanaka knew at the time, but we can agree with Slim's verdict on Sakuma's commando raids: 'There can have been few examples of a force as reduced, battered and exhausted as 33 Japanese Division delivering such furious assaults. . . . Whatever one may think of the military wisdom of thus pursuing a hopeless object, there can be no question of the supreme courage and hardihood of the Japanese soldiers who made the attempts. I know of no army that could have equalled them.'[1]

Kohima Phase Three: Satō vs. Mutaguchi

Satō and Mutaguchi had met long before. In the 1930s the Japanese Army was split by a number of warring factions, most of which aimed at overthrowing parliamentary government and differed chiefly about methods. The 'Control Faction' (Tōsei-ha) were officers who were prepared to work with politicians and capitalism, provided the politicians would do as they asked. The 'Imperial Way Faction' (Kōdō-ha) was more radical, saw Soviet Russia as the prime enemy, and was prepared to assassinate politicians and businessmen to achieve its aims. Fanatical young officers sympathetic to the aims of the Kōdō-ha mutinied on 26 February 1936 and assassinated a number of senior officers. The mutiny was only quelled by direct intervention of the Emperor.

[1] Slim, *Defeat into Victory*, pp. 336–7

Two years before the mutiny, while the Kōdō-ha was still in the ascendant, Satō, whose allegiance was to Tojo and the officers of the Tōsei-ha (though his diary shows he thought the dichotomy Kōdō-ha/Tōsei-ha an oversimplification), found that he was being spied on and that his movements were being reported to the Kōdō-ha and to a certain bureau chief of the General Affairs Bureau at Army GHQ – a colonel, named Mutaguchi Renya.

So, when Satō was appointed to command 31 Division in 1943, he and Mutaguchi were not exactly strangers. The mutual feeling of intense mistrust was to survive in both of them. Satō was always convinced that Mutaguchi was using the Imphal campaign to further his own megalomaniac dreams and he did not want to see his men die on the altar of Mutaguchi's ambitions. On the other hand, he loyally carried out the purposes of the campaign because it was his duty to do so, and he made a public show of sharing the desire for success, declaring to his men in an order of the day that millions of people in India were awaiting the Japanese invasion to throw off the hated British rule. He was governed by *shōshō hikkin* ('implicit obedience to an imperial order'), but if the operation were to fail, he saw no disgrace in withdrawing, and thought voluntary acceptance of annihilation was stupid. He also tried to ensure that his men would stand a fair chance in the battle. The key to this was supply.

Lieutenant-General Naka, Chief of Staff of Burma Area Army, visited 31 Division on 12 February 1944. He had been a year senior to Satō at the Sendai Military Academy, and Satō felt he could speak freely. Giving him a parting gift of two peacocks and an elephant's tooth, he urged on him a re-examination of the entire business of supply. When he said goodbye, Satō decided in his own mind that if his demands were not met, and Burma Area Army and 15 Army failed to provision his men, he would withdraw them from the battle.[1]

Two weeks before his division was due to set off, Satō received confirmation of his suspicions that Mutaguchi was, in his usual grandiose way, aiming beyond the strategic limits of the operation. Lieutenant-General Kunomura, Mutaguchi's Chief of Staff – and malleable puppet – came to see him. 'I have a special request to pass on from the Army commander,' he said. 'If 31 Division sees the opportunity, he wants you to advance to Dimapur. It is his most earnest wish.'

Southern Army and Burma Area Army had countenanced the Imphal operation as a defensive operation, as we have seen. An advance to Dimapur would turn it into an offensive one, into an invasion of India, in fact. 'I cannot accept that,' Satō replied. 'My orders from 15 Army itself are to occupy Kohima. I will do my utmost to achieve that. But how can I move on to Dimapur at a moment's notice? What is the enemy strength

[1] Takagi, *Kōmei*, p. 97

there? What supplies will I have? Just saying "Go to Dimapur" without examining any of these factors is foolish.' Satō was furious with Kunomura for having transmitted the order and acting as Mutaguchi's messenger-boy. It was the job of a good Chief of Staff to see his Commander-in-Chief didn't make a fool of himself.

To mollify Satō, Kunomura and his Rear Staff Officer, Major Usui, guaranteed that 31 Division would get ten tons a day after the operation began, and 250 tons up to 25 March. But nothing came. By 5 April, the three weeks' rations the men had carried with them were nearly exhausted and only local foraging spun them out. But the men could not do this at random. Miyazaki's Left Assault Column had strict rules. Propaganda squads were sent on ahead into the Naga villages along the Ukhrul-Kharasom track to win over the locals and it was strictly forbidden to rough up the villages. Planned foraging was carried out under the supervision of intendance officers. As a result, Miyazaki's units – 58 Regiment, chiefly – were not in such a precarious situation. Nor, for that matter, were the men of 138 Regiment, the Central Column. It was 124 Regiment, the main body of the divisional advance, including HQ itself, which was worst off.

As far as ammunition went, the battle at Sangshak had proved generous to Miyazaki. But it was then used up in the fighting at Kohima Ridge, and although Miyazaki's men captured depots on the ridge, most of the ammunition was lost in fires and bombing during British counter-attacks. There was *some* attempt to bring up supplies. At the end of April, Lieutenant-Colonel Hattori, of 5 Field Transport GHQ, took a convoy of seventeen jeeps with 500 rounds of mountain gun ammunition, *sake* and cigarettes. Five jeeps went to Chakhabama (Divisional Tactical HQ) with 160 rounds of special armour-piercing shells (*tadan*). They were greeted frostily with 'Why didn't you bring rice and salt?' The second load, two tons of mountain-gun shells on twelve jeeps, went to Tohema. Major-General Takeda, using three jeeps, reached Chakhabama on 24 May, but his load was mainly 'camp comforts' (*jinchū mimai-hin*). So supplies came through twice, and the amount was insignificant.[1] At the start, the mountain artillery allocation was 150 rounds per gun. There were seventeen guns in all, and Hattori's contribution meant an extra thirty rounds per gun, so each gun could fire 180 rounds apiece. No proper artillery battle was possible at that rate, and most of the ammunition was exhausted by the end of May. (In contrast, during one engagement, the Japanese reckoned the British artillery hit them with 11,500 rounds in the space of two days.) Miyazaki later pointed out that Perowne's Long Range Penetration Brigade which cut the division's rear lines of communication east of Kohima restricted the fighting area. So did British propaganda which succeeded in encouraging ill-will towards the Japanese among the

[1] OCH, *Inpāru Sakusen*, II, p. 95

Nagas. Again, it was Satō and divisional HQ which most directly felt the impact of this.

On 17 April, Satō received an order from Mutaguchi to take Kohima by 29 April. He was then to transfer three infantry battalions and one mountain artillery battalion, in lorries captured from the British, to the Imphal front under Miyazaki's command. Satō was astonished, because he could see no way of carrying out this order when his forces were fully committed and Miyazaki himself was in tactical command of the battle in his HQ on GPT Ridge. But he realized he would have to do what he could. For one thing, the order made sense, in terms of an earlier concept of the battle. If only one regiment had been told to cut off the road at Kohima, and the rest of 31 Division sent against Imphal from the north, as originally planned in 1943, it is quite possible that Imphal would have fallen. But now was not the time to strip 31 Division of men when it was locked in battle for Kohima Ridge.

Slim is very disparaging about Satō: 'Without exception the most unenterprising of all the Japanese generals I encountered.'[1] And he relates how he dissuaded the RAF from bombing Satō's HQ because he wanted him kept alive, wasting away his division on the impossible heights of Kohima when he might so easily have brought disruption to XIV Army by moving on to Dimapur. But Satō was neither stupid nor unenterprising. He had come nearer to doing what he set out to do than any other of Mutaguchi's divisional commanders, and he was concerned that his men should neither starve to death nor be wasted in Mutaguchi's capricious adventures, which he judged Dimapur to be. So although he made preliminary moves towards instructing a force to be ready to move from Kohima to Imphal, it is highly unlikely he would ever have let the transfer become reality.[2] The strength required by Mutaguchi amounted to the whole of Satō's Left Area unit, and they were anyway down to almost half their number. And if he moved them, how would they be supplied? If they spent their time looking for food, how could they fight? Where was the ammunition coming from? And why was Mutaguchi insisting on 29 April – the Emperor's birthday – as the terminal date for the capture of Imphal? Another example of his insatiable craving for publicity, for which he was prepared to sacrifice his troops. Satō was not. So Satō first of all employed the technique of *mokusatsu*, treating the order with disdainful silence. Then, when the demand was repeated, he said the move was impossible. The order was finally cancelled by 15 Army on 29 April, to the dissatisfaction of Mutaguchi's staff, who felt he had let himself be pushed around by a divisional commander.

From the middle of May, Satō was more and more concerned with preserving the fighting strength of his division. Hence, after 12/13 May, 2 Division found it possible to take the hills of Kohima Ridge when previously

[1] Slim, *Defeat into Victory*, p. 311
[2] Takagi, *Kōmei*, p. 153

its attacks had come to naught against raging fire from well-sited bunkers. As still no supplies were forthcoming, Satō's resolve to withdraw his men from the battle hardened, by the end of May, into a desperate decision. If he notified the Army beforehand, he would be stopped, he knew that. And if he conferred with the other divisional commanders, he would inevitably draw them in, willy-nilly. So he decided to act alone, and by 24/25 May, his decision was taken.[1]

Some indication of what might happen was given by a signal Satō sent to Burma Area Army on 16 May, describing the appalling supply situation, then acidly criticizing 15 Army's conduct of the battle. Kawabe was, to put it mildly, displeased by Satō's going over the Army commander's head, and brought the signal to Mutaguchi's attention.[2]

On 24/25 May, during Major-General Takeda's visit, Satō learnt from him that the transport of reinforcements to 33 Division was using up trucks, and that there could be no question of supplying 31 Division. Hearing this, Satō spoke to Colonel Hashimoto, a staff officer who accompanied Takeda, of his anger at the lack of supplies, and insinuated that he was thinking of taking his men out of the battle on his own initiative. On 25 May, he sent the following signal to 15 Army:

> My Division's rations are now exhausted. We have completely used up ammunition for mountain artillery and heavy infantry weapons. The Division will therefore withdraw from Kohima by 1st June at the latest and move to a point where it can receive supplies.[3]

Hashimoto left Satō after spending the night at Chakhabama, and arrived at 15 Division HQ on 27 May. He confided to 15 Division Chief of Staff, Major-General Okada, his fears that Satō would take his men out of the line and abandon Kohima. He also signalled to Burma Area Army in Rangoon that the best way to extract 31 Division from its present crisis was to pull it back to Ukhrul and thereby shorten its supply routes.[4]

The reception of Satō's signal, and Hashimoto's on 28 May, alerted Mutaguchi to the closeness of the crisis. Characteristically, instead of blaming the problem of supply, he had Kunomura send a signal urging Satō to reconsider:

> I am deeply pained that, forgetful of the brave deeds of your division, and adducing difficulties of supply, you have decided on

---

[1] Satō's recollections in OCH, *Inpāru Sakusen*, II, p. 96

[2] Fuwa's recollections, OCH, *Inpāru Sakusen*, II, p. 96

[3] Hashimoto's recollections, OCH, *Inpāru Sakusen*, II, p. 97

[4] Yamauchi's diary; Hashimoto's recollections, OCH, *Inpāru Sakusen*, II, p. 97

a withdrawal from Kohima. I want you to maintain your present position for ten more days.

The Army will take Imphal and reward the distinguished service of your division.

The signal ended with a well-known proverb: '*Danjite okonoeba kishin mo saku*' – 'before a resolute will even the gods give way'.[1]

Satō was angry when he received this. 'It was completely impossible to carry out this order, and it was urging me to reconsider by a mixture of discourtesy and threats', he remembered. 'It seems Army cannot grasp the real situation: no supplies and men wounded and sick', he signalled. 'I wish to inform you that, according to the situation, the divisional commander will act on his own initiative.'[2]

On the night of the day he sent that signal (31 May) Satō received a farewell telephone message from Colonel Shiraishi, his contemporary at the Military Academy, commander of the Central Area (Naga village). It seemed to be the signal he was waiting for. He at once ordered Left and Right Area units to leave Kohima for Chedema (2 miles east of Kohima) at midnight on 31 May. It was the first step in the retreat. To 15 Army he sent a further signal: We have fought for two months with the utmost courage, and have reached the limits of human fortitude. Our strength is exhausted (literally: 'our swords are broken and our arrows gone'). Shedding bitter tears, I now leave Kohima. The very thought is enough to break a general's heart.' Satō sealed the signal with his own chop, to make it clear that the responsibility was his.

15 Army sent an answer: '31 Division will withdraw to line 0000[3] if the situation is unavoidable. Time of withdrawal notified separately.'[4] Satō did not answer it. In order to protect the Division's right flank, he withdrew I/138 Regiment from Miyazaki and sent it to Kharasom (twenty-seven miles ESE of Kohima) and ordered it to secure the vital points on the withdrawal.

However, on 9 June, he received a change-of-direction[5] order from Army:

31 Division main force will move with all speed to Ukhrul area and after receiving supplies will link up with left flank of 15 Division and prepare to attack towards Imphal. At the same time

---

[1] OCH, *Inpāru Sakusen*, II, p. 97

[2] Satō's notes. OCH, *Inpāru Sakusen*, II, p. 98

[3] Satō is not clear what the line was, but believes it was a line east/west through Kekrema, not an adequate withdrawal at all.

[4] OCH, *Inpāru Sakusen*, II, p. 99

[5] '*Tenshin*'. It was the standard Japanese military euphemism for 'retreat'.

4 Infantry Battalions and 1 Mountain Artillery Battalion under command Major-General Miyazaki (to come under direct command of Army) will secure Aradura Height and Sojiema (ESE Kohima, 25 kilometres) and halt the advance to Imphal of the enemy in that area. Preparation for attack to be completed by 10th June.

To complete such dispositions by 10 June was an impossibility and the order merely confirmed Satō's mistrust of Army's ability to command.[1]

Besides signalling Satō, Mutaguchi sent his Chief of Staff, Major-General Kunomura, and Usui, the staff officer responsible for Rear L of C, to call on Satō. Usui was told to see that supplies were moved up from Humine to Ukhrul. He left Indainggyi on 4 June, went north up the Kabaw Valley, and crossed the GOC, Burma Area Army, on the way. He took the opportunity to explain Mutaguchi's new plan for a threat by 15 and 31 Divisions on Imphal along the Ukhrul – Sangshak axis, and hurried on to Humine. When he got there, he found the monsoon rains had made the road to Ukhrul impassable for lorries, and he set about loading rations on to pack-frames for porterage. The amount he managed to get to Ukhrul was therefore small and, as men of 15 Division removed it, it was impossible to keep the stocks for 31 Division. Kunomura had come up from Humine with him, and they managed to get a jeep along the appalling tracks in the midst of the monsoon rains, and at a place called Nunshong, at dawn on 21 June, six miles south-east of Ukhrul, they came across 31 Division HQ by the roadside. Kunomura asked to see Satō, who was in his tent. Satō refused: 'I see no need to meet the Army Chief of Staff.' Kunomura swallowed his pride, and handed over the Army order to Katō, 31 Division Chief of Staff.

As Katō recalls the order, it had three items:

1. 1 Infantry Battalion and 1 Artillery Battalion under a regimental commander to reinforce Miyazaki along the road Ukhrul-'Mission' (on the main Imphal-Kohima road).
2. 900 men to be sent to Humine to transport food and ammunition for the Division's offensive.
3. The Divisional Commander to deploy the remaining strength on the left flank of 15 Division and take the offensive against Imphal from south-west of Sangshak.[2]

To send two battalions to Miyazaki and 900 men to Humine meant – it was obvious – leaving next to no men under Satō's direct command. Katō

---

[1] Satō's recollections, OCH, *Inpāru Sakusen*, II, p. 100

[2] OCH, *Inpāru Sakusen*, II, p. 577

patiently explained to Kunomura that there was no way of reinforcing Miyazaki since the British had already cut the Ukhrul-'Mission' road (forty-seven miles south of Kohima) on 19 June, and there had been no news since. The Army order ignored the real state of the divisional strength. The first job was to get rations to the men.

Kunomura then insisted strongly on seeing Satō himself, and finally, and reluctantly, Satō agreed. As Kunomura and Usui entered his tent, Satō abruptly began to shout at Usui. 'No preparations for supply at Kharasom! None at Ukhrul! Why not? What became of your promises to the Division? Well, Usui, what have you to say?'

Usui said nothing. Kunomura intervened. If there were any complaints to be made, Satō should address them directly to him, and not to one of his staff. Usui and Katō then left the tent. Kunomura recalls the dialogue between himself and Satō, and his account is followed in the official Japanese history. But Takagi Toshirō's version, derived from Satō's notebooks (*Kōmei*, p. 209 et seq.) is a fuller one and what follows combines the two.

Satō	In this operation, the major factor is supply. 15 Army's attitude towards it so far has been completely irresponsible. It is impossible for this division to take part in any further operations until it receives supplies.
Kunomura	You cannot say 'impossible' in that sweeping fashion. As Army has signalled you, it is determined to switch 31 Division against Imphal. That has not changed. Burma Area Army has requested this.
Satō	You mean to say that when you get a requirement from Burma Area Army, you push your subordinate commands around without making a plan?
Kunomura	No, we'll make a proper study.
Satō	You must stock rations at Ukhrul, to go onto Imphal from there. But there's absolutely nothing there; nor to the north of it. How can you talk of a proper study when you don't know *that*? Has any 15 Army staff ever been sent here? [Usui had been told to see supplies reached Sangshak but he had never been there once. And this was Kunomura's first visit to that part of the front.] We are in an appalling situation through lack of supplies. To attack Imphal as we are is the height of absurdity (*muri da*). Please acquaint the Army command with this fact.

Kunomura	You say there were no supplies at Ukhrul. I think 15 Division took them. As Usui said, your division can restore its fighting strength by getting supplies at Humine, where there are stocks. Then I'd like you to rectify your situation and move north. 15 Division's rear is open, and we will be in a mess if 31 Division does not hold firm.
Satō	I have no objection to rectifying the situation in the north, but first we have to eat (*sore yori mazu kuu koto da*). I am still determined to move somewhere we can be sure to eat.
Kunomura	Where do you intend to retreat to?
Satō	It's not a question of 'where to?' We will simply go where there's something to eat. We can probably get rations at Humine.
Kunomura	At all events, if you have no intention of moving on Imphal there's no more to be said. Do you intend to carry out Army orders, or to disobey?[1]
Satō	I have not said I will not carry out Army orders. But *first* we must eat. Carrying out Army orders comes after that.

At 11 pm, the conversation came to an end. Kunomura indicated he would like to stay the night before returning to 15 Army HQ at Kuntaung (it had moved there on 7 June), but Satō said he had no intention of stopping there, and meant to press on through the darkness.

Satō took his leave and 31 Division pushed on through the night, but only made about three miles along the narrow track in the pouring rain. An order then came from 15 Army on 23 June. '31 Division will leave its casualties at Humine L of C Hospital and assemble its main force at Mintha.' Harried by hunger, fever and diarrhoea, Satō's men moved on, urged along only by the thought that, at last, at Humine there would be rice.

There was indeed rice at Humine, as Kunomura had said. But only enough for two days – sixteen tons. Satō at once sent men out to see what lay to the south. They came back with the news that between Humine and Tamu there were absolutely no stocks of rations at all. How could Kunomura have got him to assemble his men at such a spot, knowing the

---

[1] 'During this conversation, I said absolutely nothing about a retreat', Satō later revealed. 'I was afraid they would accuse me of "lack of fighting spirit", so I spoke with circumspection.' Article 42 of Japanese Military Law states that a commander who flees in the face of the enemy while in command of troops and who does not exhaust every possible means of continuing the fight shall be put to death. (OCH, *Inpāru Sakusen*, p. 167.)

inadequacy of the stocks? It was that fearful lack of responsibility, that awesome stupidity of 15 Army again.[1]

So Satō split his men into packs to forage in the mountain villages west of Humine. At least there would be unhulled rice there. There was a little, and endless corpses on the sides of the track to guide them to it . . .

'The Road is Open'

Captain Nishida Susumu of 58 Infantry Regiment, Miyazaki Force, reached the hill north-east of Safarmaina on the evening of 18 June. He reported to Colonel Matsumura, commanding 60 Infantry Regiment. The

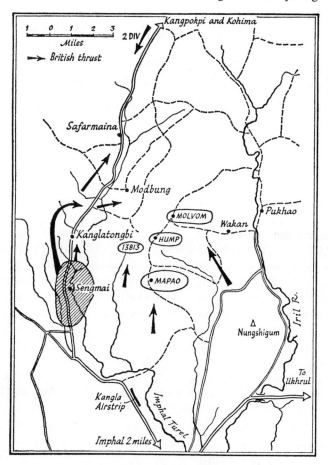

'Breaking the ring' to reopen the Kohima road

[1] Takagi, *Kōmei*, p. 217

main body of 31 Division was in retreat of its own volition, and abandoning the Kohima front. A force consisting of one battalion under Miyazaki's command was moving south along the Kohima-Imphal road, occupying successive strong points to hold up the British advance. Matsumura heard him out, then said, 'That's the oddest report I've ever received. How can a formation commander, off his own bat, do anything so stupid as to stop his operation and retreat, without an Army order – however difficult the situation?'

The retreat, of course, directly affected Matsumura. He was wedged in between enemy attacks from north and south. He was about six miles south of 'Mission' (Kangpokpi) which the British would reach in a few days. Miyazaki's planned withdrawal was to be as follows:

Viswema	— 4–13 June
Mao Songsang	— 13–17 June (the India/Burma frontier)
Maram	— 17–20 June[1]
Karong	— as long as possible after 20 June.

But he had already been pushed back on Karong – about 38 miles away – so Matsumura sent his intelligence officer, Lieutenant Takenoya, with Sergeant-Major Yamada, to go back to Karong with Nishida and find out what the score was. Takenoya came through the hills at night and was back on the 19th. Miyazaki didn't think he could hold at Karong beyond 22 June; then he'd come down to 'Mission'. Given the pressure of 2 Division, he would be lucky to hold 'Mission' for more than three days. 'Ask Matsumura from me to put up a good fight', the indomitable Miyazaki had asked.

Matsumura did not wait. He told his units to withdraw up the road towards 'Mission'. The casualties who were in No. 1 Field Hospital, which had been set up on an eminence west of the road at 'Mission', were to be moved to Hill 5797. Honda Battalion – which had been the advance guard of the entire division in March – was soon the target of concentrated mortar fire. Then tanks broke through Matsumura's positions at Safarmaina. Uchibori's men were shelled from the north on 21 June. 2 Division's tanks moved south after breaking through Miyazaki's blocks at Karong (MS 95) on 20 June and started pumping shells into Hill 5797 south-east of 'Mission' where it was known that Matsumura's 60 Regiment was concentrated. A few miles west of MS 112, 123 Brigade Headquarters was perched on a hill from which the Intelligence Section kept an eye open for movement on the road.

Lance-Corporal Canning used a tree as his observation post, and reported back to Brigade Headquarters by telephone. He knew the leading elements of 2 Division would have been at MS 103 – eight miles distant from IV Corps'

---

[1] i.e. three days, not ten, as stated in the Indian Army Official History, *Reconquest of Burma*, I, p. 308

perimeter – on the evening of 21 June. At 10.30 am on the 22nd, Canning scanned the road with his binoculars. He could see a troop of Lee tanks with infantry riding on them. It was 149 Regiment, Royal Armoured Corps, with II Battalion Durham Light Infantry in the van of 2 Division's final breakthrough. There had been a mild brush with some of Matsumura's men before they retreated into the hills, but now the road was clear.

Not to be outdone, IV Corps' tanks had been told to push up the road that morning. C Squadron, 3 Carabiniers (Major Dimsdale) led the column, with C Squadron 7 Light Cavalry behind. They had met two road-blocks, the first simply a large tree which they towed out of the way, the second a barricade of loose stones, which the leading troop was about to demolish by knocking a way through it, when the leading tank commander, Sergeant Reed, brought his tank to a halt. He was fifteen feet from the wall, and was about to drive through when he noticed a glint of metal between the stones. The wall had been stuffed with about forty 37 mm shells pointing towards the tanks. The Carabiniers stopped while sappers dealt with the wall, only to find, to their chagrin, that just as they were ready to start up again, 7 Cavalry swept past them northwards, making for the double bridge at MS 169. 1/17 Dogras were there before them. They had moved through the hills west of the road, coming back on to it at MS 109, where at 10.30 am they shook hands with 2 Division's leading tanks.[1]

It was a meeting of generals, too. Salomons, commanding 9 Brigade, drove his jeep through the marching columns until he saw Brigadier Smith of 6 Brigade walking along with General Grover. 'Good to see you, Smithy.' 'Glad we made it.' Stopford and Briggs arrived later to arrange divisional boundaries.[2]

The Japanese who had been told to help the No. 1 Field Hospital casualties across the road and into the hills in many cases abandoned them on the hillside when they heard tanks approaching along the road from both north and south. 'Take us with you!' the wounded implored the departing stretcher-bearers. Others took it as their cue to make an end of themselves with a hand-grenade. Watching from up on the hillside, Sergeant-Major Inoue Takeo of 60 Regimental Headquarters saw a motor cycle and side-car combination drive up from the south and stop in front of the tanks. Officers climbed down from the tanks and shook hands with the side-car's rider and passenger. 'We've been beaten!' Inoue thought. The idea had never entered his head before, but there was the evidence on the road in front of him.

Sergeant-Major Tochihira, on the hillside, watched the road where the hospital casualties had been lined up and abandoned. He counted about 120 men in all, including some who had fallen as they tried to make their way to the road bridge. As he stared, an Indian sepoy[3] came up to the casualties

---

[1] Perrett, *Tank Tracks to Rangoon*, p. 144

[2] Evans and Brett-James, *Imphal*, p. 327

[3] 'A British soldier' (Ei-hei) according to Kojima Noboru, *Eirei no tani*, p. 266

with a container and began to pour water over them. 'He's brought them water from the river,' Tochihira thought. It looked like water. At that moment, the Indian took the cigarette from his mouth, bent forward and applied the tip to the liquid. A tongue of flame licked across the wounded and sick Japanese. Shouts of wild anger rolled up the hillside, frightened moans, shrieking, yelling voices. The scene reminded Tochihira of paintings he had often seen in Japan of Buddhist hells, huge flames licking round distorted bodies and grimacing faces. He was seeing that hell now, as the flames licked higher, and a strange black smoke began to rise from the burning bodies.[1]

Sean Kelly, A Company commander of the Durham Light Infantry simply knew that Imphal had been relieved. 'We sat alone in the sunshine and smoked and ate,' he remembers. 'Soon the staff cars came purring both ways. The road was open again. It was a lovely day.'[2]

Yamauchi's swansong

The general commanding 15 Division fared little better than his men, though he had been fairly coddled to start with. Yamauchi was already a sick man when U-GO began and insisted on a special diet. His service abroad had accustomed him to western styles of eating, and he preferred bread to rice. Not just any bread, and certainly not in the form of *kanpan* or hard biscuit that was part of the Japanese ration. When he commanded the Division in China, bread was brought specially to his headquarters in Nanking from Shanghai. So even in the Imphal campaign, his headquarters staff baked his bread. Not without difficulty, of course, and when the intendance department reported that they were being asked to do the impossible, one of his staff officers, Imaoka, suggested that they should, in the absence of wheat flour, use a powder made from ground barley. Oatmeal, too, was scoured from stocks looted from British depots, and milk was obtained from the few cattle which had survived the crossing of the Chindwin and the journey into the hills.[3]

Yamauchi's western tastes extended not merely to the ingestion of food. He preferred the western style lavatory-seat to crouching over the traditional Japanese *benjo*. Even when his headquarters was escaping the clutches of Scoones's divisions, the adjutant ordered Yamauchi's orderly, Corporal Sakahara, to carry Yamauchi's specially constructed portable latrine – not something to encourage admiration and devotion among the men...

[1] Hamachi Toshio, *Inpāru sai-zensen*, pp. 243–4
[2] David Rissik, *The D.L.I. at War*, p. 197
[3] Takagi, *Funshi*, p. 236

But Yamauchi was already living in a world of his own. One day he sent his orderly to call on one of the war correspondents attached to his division, Iizuka Masaji, deputy head of Yomiuri Shimbun's East Asian bureau. 'The divisional commander has asked me to give you this,' said the orderly. Iizuka took the proferred lump of meat, already covered with a black lustre, and asked why it was sent. When a cow was killed, the orderly told him, the heart and tongue were always set aside for the general, and this piece was a personal gift. Iizuka made his way to the general's *basha*, to thank him, delicately stepping aside to avoid the carcass of a dead horse, already stripped to skin and bone. As he gingerly edged past the foul smell, clouds of flies which had clustered round the eyes, nostrils and rump rose into the air with an angry whirr.

Yamauchi greeted him with a smile at the entrance to his tiny hut. 'I've come to thank you, general, for your kind thought.' Yamauchi pushed forward a seat, an empty ammunition box. 'I've something I'd like to show you.' The general took a notebook from his breast pocket. 'One of my father's great gifts was to compose *haiku*.[1] I dabble in it myself. Perhaps it's "the shop-boy in front of the temple gate reciting sutras"[2] and something has rubbed off on me. I'd like to read you one or two I've written lately.' He began flipping through the notebook. 'How about this one?'

Arakan wo[3]	The hills of Arakan
shide no tabiji to	I have crossed.
koe-nikeri	My journey to the next world.

Iizuka couldn't help showing his astonishment. A front-line commander shouldn't be writing pessimistic *haiku* like this. It was a swansong. He knew he was going to die in these mountains where so many of his men had been killed already. Iizuka gazed at the general's face, thin, weak and old, ravaged by malaria. Yamauchi put the notebook away, and began to speak. 'I've spent many years in America, and have some notion of their strengths and weaknesses. Isoda, the head of the Hikari Kikan, knows America as I do, and Tojo seems to have taken a dislike to officers like us who've had that experience. Mutaguchi's much the same. The whole thing's so silly . . .'[4]

Mutaguchi kept urging Yamauchi on to take Imphal, in a flurry of contradictory orders in the first three weeks of June, and on one occasion when one of Yamauchi's units had withdrawn under a fierce British

---

[1] A seventeen-syllable poem.

[2] A proverbial phrase: *monzen no kozō narawanu kyō wo yomu*, (i.e. even a shop-boy who doesn't know what the sutras mean can recite them by listening as he lingers by the temple gate.)

[3] Sticklers for prosody will notice that the first line apparently contains four syllables instead of five; but the final *n* counts as a syllable in itself, as if the name were read Arakan*u*.

[4] Iizuka Masaji, in *Hiroku Dai Tōa Senshi*, p. 238

artillery barrage he was told his men should not retreat unless 15 Army authorized it. But even in his weak state, Yamauchi would not be browbeaten. He pointed out that by the time information was sent back from sections and platoons, a unit might very well be annihilated before 15 Army gave the order to withdraw. 'There should be less pressure on 15 Division's front now', Mutaguchi signalled, 'because British pressure, including tanks, has increased against 33 Division.' 'It's a waste of time to reply', Yamauchi noted in his diary, and said nothing. On 15 June another signal came: 'The enemy is beginning to retreat on the front of Yamamoto Force. Use this opportunity to take Imphal. Crush the enemy on your front, then seize both airfields and the hills north and east of Imphal.'

This was in the realms of fantasy. But the following day came yet another: 'Secure your present positions with all strength. Occupy "Mission" and secure it during the Imphal operation.' Later the same day: 'Put your right assault column under command of Miyazaki Force.' This left Yamauchi with the equivalent of three-and-a-half battalions. He was commanding a division in name only. To complete the denudation, on 22 June, he was told to send 300 transport units to hold the British coming from the north towards Ukhrul. This was a strength equivalent to two of his present battalions: troops under his direct divisional command now numbered a battalion and a half.

The following day, Major Usui arrived from 15 Army Headquarters bearing a letter from Kunomura. Yamauchi was dismissed. With effect from 10 June, he was to be attached to Army General Staff headquarters in Tokyo, and would be replaced by Lieutenant-General Shibata Ryūichi. With a fever of 38°C, Yamauchi was running operations from his bed, and lacked the energy to dispute his transfer.

> 23 June... I can't help but be sorry to be transferred in the very midst of operations. In particular, for not being able to build up the division again after it's taken such a beating. But the order's from Imperial GHQ so there's nothing I can do about it. I suppose it is because I didn't do things as 15 Army wanted.[1]

Uehara's poison gas

When Yamauchi's 15 Division was driven off the heights of Nungshigum, his forces both west and east of the Imphal-Kohima road were left open to IV Corps' probing attacks by three divisions, trying to prise away the Japanese grip. 5 Division's 9 Brigade (Salomons) established itself at Sengmai, two miles south of Kanglatongbi, a village which was the site of a

---

[1] Takagi, *Funshi*, p. 304

reinforcement camp and ordnance depot, but less well endowed for defence than Sengmai, though a defensive perimeter had been hastily flung round it. As soon as they reached the road and cut it – 10 April – Yamauchi's infantry began to raid the perimeter, so the depot's largely non-combatant garrison was evacuated south. They were attacked in error by British planes as they came out, and in the chaos much of the stores material was abandoned. The Japanese spread west of the road – Yamauchi had the cutting of the Silchar track in mind – instead of plunging straight down for Imphal. They also occupied the height called Mapao in the hills east of the road from which they could threaten the Kangla airstrip, itself only a couple of miles from Imphal.

But Yamauchi's depleted numbers were not equal to all the tasks they had been set, and it was evident to Scoones that they constituted Mutaguchi's weakest point. He therefore decided to destroy 15 Division, and sent 23 Indian Division (Roberts) against Ukhrul which the Japanese had begun to use as a supply depot. 5 Indian Division was to advance beyond Kanglatongbi towards Kohima and also, once Salomons's 9 Brigade was relieved by 63 Brigade of 17 Division after the withdrawal from the Tiddim road, to cut up the Iril Valley alongside Nungshigum and force the Japanese off the hills between the River Iril and the main road – the hills of Mapao, the 'Hump' and Molvum, some of them 5000 feet high.

Roberts was tempted by the thought that if he could move up through Yaingangpokpi and break through Litan fast enough, he might well not simply reach Ukhrul but capture 15 Division Headquarters, Yamauchi and all, which was then (correctly) supposed to be at Kasom. The Seaforths of I Brigade (King) worked their way through the hills and came down into Kasom on 15 April, just too late. Yamauchi had taken himself – or rather been taken – off to the north to the village of Shongpel. Joined by 37 Brigade (Collingridge), King made for Shongpel but once again Yamauchi eluded him.

At the same time, 123 Brigade (Evans) of 5 Indian Division was laying siege to a stronghold the Japanese had built along the ridge between Mapao and Molvum, just east of Kanglatongbi. No advance northwards was possible while they were there, and Evans could not dislodge them. Briggs, commanding 5 Division, realized it was futile to batter away at the positions – the 'Hump' alone was attacked seven times during the month of May by 3/ 14 Punjab – and decided to bring Evans's brigade round on the main road through Sengmai and send it into the hills from Kanglatongbi, a turning move which might outflank the Japanese by breaking into the ridge from the north.

While 89 Brigade (Crowther) from 7 Division (given to Briggs to compensate for the loss of 161 Brigade operating round Kohima) tried to move up the road and against Hill 3813 just east of Kanglatongbi, Evans's three battalions,[1] supported by 28 Field Regiment, Royal Artillery and air-

---

[1] 2 Suffolk, 3/2 Punjab, 1/17 Dogra.

strikes, tried to no avail to make an impression on the Japanese. Briggs, urged on by Scoones, knew it was increasingly important to break through towards Kohima, and was forced to leave the Japanese entrenched on their heights and concentrate on the road. He brought 9 Brigade round into Kanglatongbi again to back up Evans and kept Evans's 123 Brigade edging its way forward through the foothills alongside the road to the east, just below Molvum.

The British themselves, though in much greater strength than Yamauchi's depleted division, were feeling the effects not only of casualties but of rain and stringency. The full force of the monsoon hit their positions round Kanglatongbi and in the hills nearby from 27 May onwards; and their artillery ammunition was rationed. 5 Division's artillery was restricted to six rounds per day per gun, at the very time that 2 Divisional artillery was pouring thousands of rounds a day into Satō's positions round Kohima.[1]

2 Suffolk (Menneer), supported by tanks, put in assaults on smaller hills, nicknamed Isaac and James, close to Modbung during the first week in June. As happened at Kohima, the tanks had to be winched up the slopes by Engineers, but it was difficult to keep them in position. The rains had turned the slopes into a grease-pan and one tank slid over the hillside. The Suffolks sustained nearly forty casualties on 7 July, but came back to the attack the next day, backed by a Hurricane strike and tanks, one of which was hit. The setback was temporary. Soon 5 Division's prongs between the Iril Valley and the Kohima Road winkled out the Japanese hill positions one by one, or forced the defenders to flee. First 23 Division, then 20 Division, after its transfer to the Litan area, began to destroy 51 and 67 Infantry Regiments. IV Corps successfully drove a wedge between the two halves of 15 Division and started to annihilate it piecemeal.[2]

On the heights of Modbung, the Japanese infantry battalion (II/60 – Matsumura) had no anti-tank guns, nor did it have any defence against a strange-looking gun positioned on the slopes of Ekban, two miles south of Modbung. The nature of this was revealed when two sections of 6 Company/II Battalion/60 Infantry Regiment were hammered by a barrage which sent a pillar of flame rising from trenches close by and ten seconds later the Japanese heard shells coming over. Lance-Corporal Muragishi listened to the shells' flight and the echoing which followed, and judged the gun to be an anti-aircraft gun brought up from Imphal, where it would be of no further use, since there were no Japanese planes in the skies to be

---

[1] Brett-James, *Ball of Fire*, p. 346

[2] But not cheaply. In an attack on a roadblock near MS 113, in mid-June, D Company of 2 West Yorks lost all its officers and twenty seven men. And of the forty-seven survivors who returned, under their CSM, twenty had been wounded. The following week the 3/9 Jats lost thirty-three officers and men killed and 111 wounded. (Brett-James, *Ball of Fire*, pp. 351, 353.)

shot down. The bunkers on the hill were blown up, and fragments of shattered flesh fell all round Muragishi, who scrabbled away furiously at the hillside to dig himself in. To put one's head out of the trench was almost suicidal, but Muragishi peeped out during a brief pause in the shelling and saw what looked like a great mass of black iron coming along the ridge fifty yards away. It spat red and white flame, and he screamed 'Tanks!', despite his sheer disbelief that a tank could climb the 45° slope of their hill. The tank halted by a trench it had already shelled, and turned its gun on the Japanese corpses lying there, pumped a few more rounds in them to make sure, and slowly began to move towards Muragishi. He counted four tanks in all, on the hillside, and knew he could do nothing about it. There were no anti-tank guns in the entire battalion. Ten seconds, and one of the tanks was almost on the edge of the trench.

To Muragishi's amazement, Lance-Corporal Uehara, beside him, suddenly heaved his body up out of the trench and dashed at the tank, hissing to his companion, 'I'll get that tank! Leave it to me!' Muragishi saw his right fist clutching what looked like a big, round, glass ball. The tank was a few yards away, and Uehara hurled the ball at it. At once, the ball shattered against the front of the tank, which was enveloped in a white vapour, like steam, which was sucked inside.

In seconds, the lid of the gun-turret was pushed up and the tank crew hurled themselves out of the tank and down the slope, rolling over and over to escape the smoke. Uehara scrambled on to the turret and threw a grenade. A fiery red pillar rose up from the interior and suddenly the great iron lump was booming and flaming. The grenade had ignited the ammunition.

What Muragishi had witnessed was a rare instance of the use of poison gas in the Second World War. The gas bomb flung by Uehara was relatively new to the Burma battlefield and there were not many available. It was, in fact, a German invention, one of the few examples of useful military collaboration between Germany and Japan. A Japanese submarine had brought samples and drawings to Japan. The Japanese called it '*chibi-dan*', the 'tich-bomb', and it consisted of a thick glass ball the size of a baseball containing at its core prussic acid gas in liquid form. When a tank's armour plating shattered the glass on impact, the liquid gasified at once in the atmosphere, producing a stream of white smoke which was drawn into the crew space and asphyxiated the occupants. The gas had enormous killing power; 0.4 mgs in the blood was lethal.

The Japanese also used a TA-DAN against tanks. This is so called as a kind of acronym formed by taking the sounds of the first and last characters of the phrase *TA*i-sensha-senkō-*DAN*, 'anti-tank perforating shell', which worked by emitting a gas at ultra-high temperature. When

301

the shell made a slight penetration of the armour on impact, the gas was released and burned its way into the tank.[1]

The adventures of Lieutenant Shima

The *chibi-dan* in much greater numbers might indeed have proved a formidable anti-tank weapon in the hands of Japanese infantry. But in the event it was nothing more than a last desperate throw, characteristic of the mood and situation of 15 Division in June 1944. The fate of its Independent Mountain Artillery Unit is another example. During the phase of the battle when Mutaguchi planned a drive towards Imphal from Ukhrul, using 15 and 31 Divisions, men of that unit were sent along in support of an infantry attack, under the command of Shima Tatsuo, a cadet officer (*minarai shikan*) who was acting company commander because every officer senior to him had been killed. When he received orders to move, he had been living on bamboo shoots, parsley and lizards for a month and had almost no strength left.

His battery commander, Captain Imaizumi, told him to take the forty-five men who remained, and three guns. The report was that the infantry had only two mines, and were faced by ten British tanks moving south. As Imaizumi's flaccid hand sought a farewell grasp, Shima felt repelled by him and by the tired clichés with which he coaxed consent. Imaizumi was disliked, gave orders like a mad dog and was known to monopolize the dry biscuit ration. . .[2]

Shima found the infantry, a hundred men under a Captain Mori, holding a 4000-foot high hill covered in dense jungle, called Height 105A, halfway between Ukhrul and Imphal. Mori couldn't help opening his eyes wide when he saw that his support was commanded by a cadet. But he was glad to see him and they decided on trenches and gun-emplacements, and set the observer detachment measuring distances.

The ten tanks soon came into sight, and Shima could see the leading tank commander standing up in his turret, surveying the terrain in a deliberate, leisurely fashion. Shima's No. 2 gun kept the caterpillar tracks in its panoramic sights and the section leaders watched for his signal. 'Fire!' His right hand fell, and Sergeant Nishiura's No. 1 Squad scored a bullseye on the leading tank. The column slowed, and No. 2 and No. 3 Squads hit the

[1] When I was first told about the use of the *chibi-dan* I was sceptical, believing that if the British had known poison gas was being used against them, they would have turned it into a first-rate anti-Japanese propaganda weapon, naturally enough. But my informant, Mr Kuzuma of the Kyōtō Shimbun, insisted that he had interviewed Muragishi, whose account appears in his *Sakimori no shi, Inpāru-hen* (Poems of the Guards – Imphal section), Kyoto, 1979, pp. 280–6

[2] This account is based on Shima Tatsuo, '*Jigoku kaidō no tatakai*' (The battle in Hell Road), in *Jitsuroku Taiheiyō Sensō*, III, pp. 178–88

second and third tanks. But the other seven did not turn tail; instead their guns swivelled on to the Japanese mountain guns and in an instant Shima and his men felt as if heaven and earth had exploded simultaneously.

Then, through the fire and smoke they heard aircraft, saw bombs drop, and heard machine guns open up until the earth shook. Rain, however, saved Shima. The planes made off, and the British withdrew in the downpour, leaving four of their tank-skeletons behind. Shima had lost a gun, and half his men. The rest, covered with mud from head to foot, shifted the gun emplacement in a sullen rage. Shima was amazed to hear the company's old sweat, Warrant Officer Takeda, a Singapore veteran, mutter audibly, 'We should withdraw, too!' He and Shima, an ex-student, had never got on. Shima felt a reprimand was in order, but contented himself with saying awkwardly, 'Don't be daft! Deserters get shot!' Takeda was not impressed. 'What are we supposed to do with a couple of guns and 23 men? If we don't scarper now, we'll all be Buddhas tomorrow (*Dabutsu da ze!*)'

Shima was no natural warrior. To himself he admitted that at heart he was a coward. He had been in battle for just three months, and at the beginning, whenever he heard a shell, 'I'd have hidden in the belly of a horse'. But he was in command now, and it made a difference. 'We'll be told to withdraw tomorrow, I imagine. In the meanwhile, we have three boxes of ammo for the guns. Don't upset the men.' But Shima was putting a brave face on it. As he told himself, the tragedy of the battlefield was not what you felt in the roar and blaze of the guns – that was a moment's shudder of horror – but the grief of deepest night when you could be tempted to an abyss of despair which knew no limits.

Dawn stabbed through gaps in the clouds like white swords, and with it came the planes, puttering overhead like a car engine about to break down. Soon the shelling began, but when that stopped a twin-engine bomber flew over the infantry, profusely scattering petrol. Then it turned, came back over, and deliberately fired incendiary bullets. Dispersed in their foxholes, enveloped in black smoke, the infantry screamed and writhed in agony, but Shima had no time to linger on the horror as a cry went up from his own men – 'Tanks!' – eleven all told, including six small tanks. One of Mori's infantry dashed forward carrying an armour-piercing mine, another clambered on the leading tank, opened the lid and was shot by British infantry as he tried to drop a grenade inside. Two tanks were stopped, then the rest found Shima's position and began to pound it, but in the whirlwind of metal fragments and clods of earth the mountain guns replied, and two more tanks burst into flames. The other seven came on, spitting out red tongues like wounded animals, spattering the Japanese now with machine-gun fire.

'Sir, five shots left!' shouted Sergeant Nishiura. Shima realized he was at the end of this battle over open sights and gave the order to destroy the aiming device and leave one shot in the barrel. Each man was to keep one grenade. Then a stick of bombs straddled the guns as Captain Mori came up.

Shima's body flew up into the air, then the back of his head struck something hard. When he came to, everything was over. The company had been decimated; only five were left. Shima had survived because his head had hit an ammunition box and he was otherwise unhurt. He knew he had to report to battery headquarters, but now lines of British tanks, trucks and jeeps were moving south and he and his men started off through a trackless jungle.

Then Nishiura pointed out something odd. Neither Warrant Officer Takeda nor Corporal Iwasaki had been seen during the tank battle. Nishiura spat out a spiteful accusation – 'They beat it!' It was true, though, and Shima was wild with rage. He'd bring them in. And he'd see off Imaizumi! How could their own captain have pulled back without warning them? Shima remembered how Takeda had always groused about his inefficiency, and always in his hearing. But now things were different. He had fought his best for two days, and was like a sword frozen hard. He had survived without deserting. He had finally got used to war and the kind of death it brings. He had learned that you exist in the paper-thin space between one piece of flying metal and another, and his self-respect and pride increased when he realized he'd made a stand.

One of his men, Lance-Corporal Hanada, was seriously wounded in the abdomen, and by dawn of the next day, after they'd spent the night getting past a line of British sentries, he was dead. Pfc Doi, with a wound in the back, walked along supported by Nishiura and Kobayashi, but he knew he was keeping them back, and whispered pitifully, 'That's long enough, put me down. Go on, get walking.' Shima replaced Kobayashi and they went on walking, but Doi, who seemed to be moving mechanically, slipped noiselessly down from their shoulders and fell on his face. He had died as he walked along. Shima joined hands, said a prayer, and the three walked on, passing burned-out Japanese trucks, big 8-wheelers, lying by the roadside, open ammunition boxes, corpses lying athwart the tracks, all the paraphernalia of retreat. And the living: little groups of two or three, emaciated, riddled with disease, skin taut on the bone, and long filthy hair, clutched at their legs as they passed, sobbing and moaning, 'Give us water!' 'Take me with you!'

Shima and his two men knew they were done for if they let themselves be trapped by the coiling limbs, and they forged on, on the dim edge of consciousness. Shima's long sword tangled in his legs, but he did not throw it away. The mess-tin and helmet went first. 'Stay awake! Keep walking!' he croaked hoarsely at Nishiura and Kobayashi, until his voice went. Then he beat feebly at them with a bamboo stick. Hatred moved him. He would not collapse until he had hold of Imaizumi and Takeda. If they could reach Sibong, he was sure there was a Japanese position there. So on they went, up and down, along winding paths, branches flicking leaves into their mouths as they stumbled past, all sensation in their legs dulled. But there were now other dangers beside the British. Where corpses lay with bellies blown open by near-misses, packs were scattered, their contents emptied by thief-soldiers hidden in the trees. And it was not just the dead they preyed on. 'That's what we've come to,' Shima thought, 'just to stay alive, we even kill those on our own side.' Soon he and the other two were rifling the packs of the corpses as well, without any feeling of shame. But to no purpose, there wasn't a scrap of food in any of them.

By this time, the British had driven Yamamoto Force back from the Shenam Saddle and the Japanese were making for Tamu. But Shima had no means of knowing this and climbed up a steep slope hoping to see Sibong below him. He could see the river winding in and out and was certain it passed through Sibong. He decided on one last effort, when he heard the sound of tanks behind him, and pitched headlong into a stream.

When he stood up, he realized there were two other Japanese there beside his men. They were Warrant Officer Takeda and Iwasaki, who had fled from the battle. Iwasaki was already dead. Takeda had been wounded in the back. He told Shima that Captain Imaizumi had been killed by Japanese soldiers scrounging for food, and warned him it was dangerous to linger.

Shima found his hatred had gone. Revenge on Takeda had been the foundation of his long march. He had lived for his anger and now knew that it no longer mattered. The three of them left the dying Takeda behind and trudged on. The corpses began to multiply again: the moist air of Assam and the monsoon rains were picking them clean, and many were already skeletons. He saw men lying in pools of rain identifiable only by their uniforms, bones glistening white, with only the hair on their heads moving like grass in the water, faces gazing up at the sky through voided black sockets. He remembered the foolish dreams he had had when he first came to Burma, of a triumphant return to Japan and his chest covered with medals. That was a fever, a madness which had gone. There were no more *banzais*, only farewells and separation.

His consciousness slipped from him. He was lying down, now. He stretched out his hand for the pistol at his side. He couldn't find it anywhere. Had Nishiura and Kobayashi taken it away, fearing he would kill himself? There was a rumble of tanks in the distance. This time, he did not stand up to fight, or to run. He fell into a deep sleep. When he woke, he was in a British prisoner-of-war camp.

Shenam — Palel (iii)
(see map facing p. 314)

Yamamoto decided to have one last go at Palel when the commander of 213 Infantry Regiment, Colonel Nukui Chikamitsu, returned from hospital on 12 June. With survivors from I/60 Regiment and II/51 Regiment – about 160 men in all – a company of his own regiment, eighty engineers and a hundred men from No. 1 Anti-tank Battalion and two mountain guns, he was told to cut through the hills north of the road, through Khudei Khunou, and attack the main base and airfield at Palel. His reconnaissance found the British installed on the ridge between Langgol and the hills north of Palel, but north-east of Palel there were no positions, and plenty of cover. His attempt shows the impossibility of preventing small groups of dedicated Japanese from infiltrating the hills east of Palel, though 48 Brigade of 17 Division had swept those hills early in May and the process had been repeated by 1 Brigade of 23 Division at the end of the month.

Nukui was in Langgol on 16 June and left for Palel five days later but was caught in the open by British bombers and took heavy losses, particularly among his engineers. He was bombed, too, when he withdrew to Khudei Khunou, and the British guns found him there on 26 June and plastered his force regularly at ten-minute intervals during the night. And although Japanese shelling at maximum range hit the airfield at Palel, aircraft kept taking off and landing and Nukui could not stop them. He decided to scrap the idea of hitting the airfield with his force as a whole and to send in instead a *kirikomitai* (commando raid) in lightening attacks. Captain Inoue Sukezō was to take thirteen men and break into the airfield on 2 July, while WO Yamada, a week later, was to take nine men and wreck the depots in the town.

These attacks paid off. Inoue set fire to thirteen fighters and reconnaissance aircraft, and returned safely on 4 July; Nukui observed with grim satisfaction that fighter activity in the days following was greatly reduced. On the night of 9 July, Yamada got among the weapons stores and fuel depots at Palel, bombed them, set them ablaze, and returned with all his men on 10 July. It was, as the British Army commander recalls, 'a very fine effort' (though he thought there were seven Japanese involved, and puts the figure of aircraft destroyed at eight).[1]

But it was Yamamoto's last throw. When he heard Nukui had used *kirikomo* tactics, not his whole force, he ordered a unit temporarily attached to him from 31 Division to move up to the front line. The unit did not budge. His supplies were running out, the villagers bitterly resented his foraging, and his men had to make do with half a pint of gruel a day from what rice they had left, mixed with grasses and powdered *miso* (bean paste). The seventy-two head of buffalo which had been used to carry supplies were slaughtered for food.

On 13 July, he was ordered by 15 Army to withdraw from the Shenam-Tengnoupal area into the Kabaw Valley, towards Mawlaik and Yazagyo. He set up HQ at Chamol, and ordered Nukui to cover his withdrawal. On the evening of 23 July, Nukui's engineers blew the last bridge at Sibong. One mountain gun held off the advancing British who

[1] Slim, *Defeat into Victory*, p. 334

were puzzled that the gun could never be spotted, and which they never captured. The reason was simple: the disappearing gun was under the command of Lt Tonda Hiroshi, who gave the Japanese infantry time to withdraw, staying well to the front himself. When he had fired his last round, he dismantled the gun, and vanished down the trail, his men bringing along only the barrel and the firing pin.

As Yamamoto's HQ pulled out of Chamol on 24 July, the British broke into the village but they did not press him hard, and he was able to collect stragglers from 15 and 31 Divisions and the battered remnants of the INA. By this time, rations were down to 48 grams a day, and Moreh proved useless for foraging. Not even unhulled rice, not even vegetables, were to be found.

Like the other generals, Yamamoto was fed up with Mutaguchi. When Fujiwara came up with him again from 15 Army HQ to advise on withdrawal, Yamamoto was explicit: 'So far I have obeyed Army orders,' he told him, 'but from today I move according to my own judgment.'[1] Fujiwara brought orders for him to hold Moreh until 31 July, but after seeing the area was clear of stragglers, Yamamoto moved out a day early and went the whole way back to Sittaung on the Chindwin, reaching it on 2 August. He was ordered to halt the British advance and cover the retreat of the main body of 33 Division, placing his HQ at Yazagyo. He ignored the order, but sent an infantry company from Nukui Force to Yazagyo as a token resistance to the oncoming British. His earlier behaviour with Itō and Ueda showed how fierce he could be with subordinates when they objected to his own unreasonable demands in the fighting on the Shenam Saddle. Now he had had enough himself.

Kohima Phase Four:
Satō dismissed

Satō was right in suspecting that Mutaguchi wanted to use his starving and tattered forces for a fresh offensive. An order arrived on 25 June telling him to assemble his troops at Mintha and attack Palel. He would have Yamamoto Force attached to him. Satō was still looking for food. Humine Field Hospital, where he had been told to leave his casualties, had no food. In Mintha and the hills to the west there was almost none. He decided to send the main body of the division to gather unhulled rice; the remainder were to make for the Chindwin.

On 7 July, Mutaguchi cancelled his previous order, and told Satō to send three battalions of infantry and one artillery battalion to Myochit, where they would come under Yamamoto's command. Satō sent two battalions of 138 Regiment, II/124 Regiment and mountain artillery to Myochit. How-

---

[1] Recollections of Fujiwara, in OCH, *Inpāru Sakusen*, II, p. 175

ever, when the force got there, they refused to budge, in spite of Yamamoto's insistence.

Two days after the new order, Satō received an Army order dated 7 July, dismissing him from the command of the division. His successor was to be Lieutenant-General Kawada Tsuchitarō, and Satō was to be attached to Burma Area Army in Rangoon. 'Proceed to new appointment without awaiting arrival of successor' he was told on 10 July.

Satō was overjoyed at the prospect. As he saw it, he was being moved to a general headquarters higher up the scale than 15 Army, where he could express his views to Kawabe. He sent him a signal in advance – 'The entire army is on the banks of the Chindwin, in an impossible situation' – said farewell to the division and set out for 15 Army headquarters at Kuntaung.

He asked to see Kunomura. It was Kunomura's turn to be coy. Giving out that he was sick, he refused to see Satō, who promptly called on Colonel Kinoshita, the GSO I, rehearsed again for his ears the irresponsibility of 15 Army, and told him to get supplies up the Chindwin at once. Without calling on Mutaguchi, he left Kuntaung on 13 July, and sailed down the Chindwin to Kalewa. He went on the rampage here, too, and told the L of C unit to expedite supplies to 31 Division.

Satō reached Rangoon on 22 July. He had already resolved to ask for a court-martial, in the course of which he intended to show up 15 Army and its peccant staff in public and, within the bounds of legality, justify the rightness of his own actions. Indeed, a court-martial seemed likely, as Mutaguchi had, weeks before, already told Kawabe that he thought Satō had over-reached himself. The occasion was Mutaguchi's fury when he learned the real strength of Miyazaki Force, which came under direct 15 Army command on 4 June. '31 Division Commander is contravening Army intentions on strength and duties of Miyazaki Force... This time I fear we have a case that must be dealt with by military law.'[1] Mutaguchi signalled Satō to revise the strength of Miyazaki Force in accordance with Army orders. Satō merely threw the signal into the waste-paper basket, with the phrase, 'It's far too late for that', and finally broke off wireless contact with Mutaguchi. On the other hand, by his order of 2 June, telling Satō to move to Ukhrul, Mutaguchi had earlier covered Satō's withdrawal, because he did not want a scandal: it was unheard of, in the history of the Japanese Army, for a divisional commander to retreat from the battle line under his own authority, in direct contravention of an Army order.

Satō began to collect the documentation for his trial. 'I had listened to all the signal traffic which passed between Army and its divisions', he recalled later,

and was able to form an opinion on the likely upshot of the

[1] Kawabe's diary, OCH, *Inpāru Sakusen*, II, p. 114

Imphal campaign. Given the situation at the start, Army's inability to command, and the true condition of the troops in the front line, I realized that there could be no hope of success after the middle of May, and Army was only carrying on for reasons of face. The strength of every division was drained, and all we could do was wait to be massacred. I thought I had to make them bring that insane Imphal operation to a halt.

The Army commander was not a man who listened to reports on the reality of the situation, or expressions of opinion. I signalled Burma Area Army to cancel the operation, but that was fruitless. So I was forced to bring about that cancellation by starting my own division moving to the rear, causing the front to collapse, however much Lieutenant General Mutaguchi might want to soldier on.

By so doing, I saved my division from futile annihilation, and the rest of 15 Army from destruction.[1]

He was to be denied his platform. Kawabe had already decided, on 3 July, to end the Imphal operation. His headquarters was preoccupied with the crisis on its northernmost front, facing China, Stilwell, and Wingate's hard-pressed (and misused) columns. And it would have to plan 15 Army's retreat. The last thing Kawabe wanted was the court-martial of one of his own generals on his hands. There would be no profit in it, and it would expose to all the world the shame of his Army command. It was decided to treat the affair medically. Satō was judged to be 'mentally disturbed under the stress of the acute war situation' (*karetsu na senkyoku-ka ni okeru seishin sakuran*). The heads of the Adjutant-General's departments at Southern Army and Burma Area Army conferred with an emissary from the War Ministry, and it was decided not to proceed with a prosecution. On 23 November 1944, Satō was placed on the waiting list, and the next day transferred to the reserve.

U-GO comes to an end

When Kunomura ordered 31 Division on 26 June to join in the offensive against Palel, it was not merely because Satō's weary men happened to be conveniently in the area. Satō's refusal to co-operate with the joint attack by 15 and 31 Divisions against Imphal from the north and east, and his insistence on moving south for rations, meant that one of Mutaguchi's last plans to take Imphal had foundered. In fact, when he returned to GHQ in Kuntaung on 7 June after talking to Kawabe, Mutaguchi knew that his

[1] ibid., p. 101

gamble had failed. But there were ways of recouping his losses. If 31 Division could be brought to battle in the Shenam-Palel area, and 33 Division under its new commander put in another attack on Imphal from the south, it should be possible to stabilize the front. Tanaka had succeeded in imparting a sense of urgency to Yanagida's battered regiments, and Mutaguchi hoped that even if Imphal were not taken, he could achieve the capture of Bishenpur. Tanaka had already shown his mettle by ordering Major Saitō, commanding I/214 Regiment, into a night attack on 18 May, during which Saitō himself and 360 (out of 380) men of his battalion were killed. Ten days later, the twenty survivors made another attack, to avenge their battalion commander, and were wiped out themselves. He was luckier than Yamauchi's successor at the head of 15 Division, Shibata. Shibata realized that he too would have to be a fire- eater, and spiritedly ordered his men to advance. But to dejected soldiers, near to starvation and stuck in waterlogged trenches, the summons fell on deaf ears. Their morale was rock-bottom, and the most they would do was return the enemy's fire when attacked, and even then, only under the fierce tongue-lashings of the new divisional commander. If Kawabe then ordered the campaign to be stopped, Mutaguchi would at least be able to say he had almost achieved the defensive position that the various higher commands had hoped for, though it was far less than he had desired himself. It should be possible to withdraw to a line passing from the Tiddim area through the hills north-west of Mawlaik to the heights on the west bank of the Chindwin.[1]

Kinoshita drafted the plan. Mutaguchi considered it for a while in silence, then abruptly told Kunomura to signal it to Rangoon. It should have met with a sympathetic reception, because Kawabe's impressions of the front had shown him how remote success was. 'When I returned to Rangoon [he later wrote], I kept seeing groups of soldiers leaving for the front line in the pouring rain, and the faces of the Indians of the Indian National Army I had committed to the battle for Palel. If I could have viewed the battle situation calmly and coldly, I would have cancelled the operation there and then.'[2] But Kawabe also wrote that there was a larger personality than his own dominating his judgment; and, oddly enough, he did not mean the Emperor or Tojo. 'As long as one man's hand could be raised to hold a weapon, I knew the fight must go on. The destiny of both India and Japan depended on this battle. Subhas Chandra Bose is the key.'[3] He therefore replied at once to Mutaguchi's signal:

---

[1] Kojima Noboru, *Taiheiyō Sensō*, II, p. 163

[2] ibid., p. 166

[3] Kawabe had visited Bose on his return from 15 Army, and was impressed by the fiery passion with which Bose proclaimed he intended to fight on and free India, whatever the temporary setbacks. And when Naka visited him on 12 July, to report the cancellation of the Imphal operation, Bose declared he wanted his men to stay on the Indian frontier, not to be withdrawn south of Mandalay. (OCH, *Inpāru Sakusen*, II, p. 156)

I am surprised to receive these pessimistic representations from
15 Army. As Area Army Commander, I must repeat that our
duty only permits us to take the offensive. You are requested
to struggle on and put heart and soul into fulfilling your duty.
As for 31 Division, you are to take it in hand with the utmost
severity.[1]

This signal removed all reticence from Mutaguchi's mind. Far from
struggling on to fulfil his duty, he was now more in a state of mind for
one last throw, and did not care whether it succeeded or not. It was
characteristic of the way the Japanese conducted this campaign that
while Kawabe was urging Mutaguchi on to yet greater efforts, he was
sending signals to Southern Area Army and Tokyo, looking for authority to cancel everything. And while Mutaguchi, in the depths of his
own heart, already knew the bitterness of final defeat, he was whipping
his sodden, hungry remnants into battle once more.[2]

He gave his last order for an attack. 15 Division was to move on Palel
from Thoubal, what was left of 31 Division from Myochit, while 214
Regiment of 33 Division would attack Imphal from the south.
Mutaguchi had reshuffled his pack several times, but this time it was
barely a forlorn hope. 15 Division's staff had already been locked in
debate whether they should fight on or do what Satō had done. In the
upshot, their men simply drifted away from the battlefield. 33 Division
was surrounded by Cowan's 17 Indian Division and was quite incapable
of detaching 214 Regiment for Palel. And 31 Division had already
thrown away its weapons. There was no reaction to his order, and
Mutaguchi resigned himself to the inevitable. He gave the order to
retreat on 9 July.

Kawabe was giving orders, too, from his bed. Prostrate from amoebic
dysentery, he heard on 25 June that the British had broken through the
Japanese hold on the Kohima-Imphal road. This meant the operation
was over. The next day he was told Satō had passed through Humine on
his retreat from Ukhrul, and the signal came from Mutaguchi with the
ominous phrase: 'if by a thousand and one chance we have to move
over to the defensive . . .'

---

[1] Mutaguchi's post-war recollections, OCH, *Inpāru Sakusen*, II, p. 149

[2] There seems little doubt that Mutaguchi was quite unhinged by this time (whatever the
doubts on his sanity before). 'He had a little clearing made near his tactical headquarters'
recalls Takagi Toshirō, 'and stood bamboo in it pointing in the four directions of the compass,
which he then decorated. Early in the morning, he would approach the bamboo and call on
the eight hundred myriad gods of Japan. His batman said that he would get up in the middle
of the night and shout out "There's some strange thing under the floor of my hut, get troops
here at once and chase it away!" The batman promptly had the place scoured by troops, who
of course found nothing untoward.' (Takagi Toshirō, '*Mubō!* Inpāru Sakusen' – ('The insane
operation at Imphal') – in *Shōwa-shi tanbō* (Enquiries into the history of the Shōwa period)
Vol. 4, ed. Mikuni Ichirō, 1974, p. 105

He told Colonel Aoki to go at once to GHQ Southern Army to report that a crisis had been reached. Armed with a personal letter to Lieutenant-General Kimura, Terauchi's Chief of Staff, Aoki left Rangoon for Manila by plane on 29 June.[1] Southern Army was as Janus-faced as Kawabe. Viewing the seizure of Imphal as the highest priority in Burma, it even suggested the withdrawal of troops covering the Arakan coast to reinforce Mutaguchi, on 20 June. By an ironic coincidence, it was the day selected by the Royal Navy to mount a large-scale attack on the Andaman Islands, a hint that the British might be contemplating a seaborne landing against Burma across the Bay of Bengal. Southern Army followed Kawabe's example: it referred back. Colonel Miyama Yōzō was sent off to Tokyo to enquire about Imperial GHQ's views on the future course of operations in Burma. Tokyo looked at the collapse of the Imphal front, the menace from the Hukawng Valley and Yunnan to the far north, and the capture of Myitkyina and conveyed its views through Miyama on 29 June.

Colonel Aoki arrived in Manila on 1 July 1944. He added his own verbal report to Kawabe's letter, and a signal went off at once from Manila to Tokyo, making clear Kawabe's views that the Imphal operation should be cancelled. Tokyo agreed. The order went out from Manila on 2 July:

> GOC Burma Area Army will henceforth crush the enemy's plans for a road-link between India and China, in the area west of the Salween River and North Burma, and will plan a battle of resistance in the area west of the Chindwin against the enemy in the Manipur area.

Kawabe received the signal at 2.30 am on 3 July, on his sick-bed. He could hardly speak, his eyes were sunken, his cheeks emaciated, his body drained of energy by dysentery. So Mutaguchi's dream, which had been Kawabe's main preoccupation for a year, and had brought about the deaths of tens of thousands of his men, had been pricked like a bubble. Kawabe writhed in anguish on his bed, unable to sleep, waiting for dawn.[2]

Even now, he lacked the ability to order a full-scale withdrawal. Signalling to Mutaguchi an expectation of a change in duty, he asked whether he expected to take Palel. The reason behind this was that if 15 Army were to pull back to the Chindwin, he feared that a follow-up through Palel by the British forces would destroy it completely. He

---

[1] According to Kojima Noboru, *Taiheiyō Sensō*, II, p. 168, bad weather held him up and he did not leave until 3 July.

[2] Ushiro, *Hiroku Taiheiyō Sensō*, III, p. 207

wanted to be sure the British could be halted along that axis. A signal was sent cancelling the Imphal operation on 5 July. But that, too, contained a pious hope that Mutaguchi would secure a defensive position along the Chindwin by holding the road from Palel.[1]

Incredibly, as we have seen, Mutaguchi had decided on one last assault on Palel with what remained of his Army, putting three infantry battalions and an artillery battalion from 31 Division, then at Myochit, under the command of Yamamoto Force. When he received Kawabe's signal on 5 July, he judged that his attack on Palel was in conformity with it, in spite of the cancellation of the Imphal operation, and on 7 July ordered 33 Division to supply a force of three infantry battalions to join in. He told 15 Division to take the offensive towards Imphal in order to put pressure on the British elsewhere.

Kawabe received Mutaguchi's report on his plans of attack and was nonplussed. It did not seem to accord with the cancellation, nor with taking up a defensive position on the Chindwin. And it seemed to ignore the true condition of the Japanese divisions. In particular, as 33 Division was under hard pressure from 17 Indian Division, to take a strong force from it now was to put the withdrawal of the entire division at risk.

Kawabe signalled Mutaguchi on 11 July to stop his prospective attack on Palel. Burma Area Army was beginning to replan the future course of events in Burma, though it had already lost the strength to decide them.

The tatterdemalion divisions staggered back along the mountain roads. Weapons gone, clutching a stick in one hand and a rice tin in the other, the Japanese stumbled painfully through the torrential rain. The lucky casualties were taken to the Chindwin on horse-drawn sledges, others bounced to and fro on sodden stretchers. The more seriously wounded lay by the side of the tracks. The pain from untended wounds, the frantic hunger, and the inward racking of malaria and dysentery pushed them inexorably to the moment when they would beg passers-by for a hand-grenade with which to finish themselves off.

Some were too weak even to ask for that and lay with the maggots of putrefaction squirming and wriggling in eyes, noses, mouths. Even the walking wounded were too exhausted to brush off the white worms that gathered in their long matted hair, so that they gave the odd appearance of hoary sages tottering down the jungle tracks, pursued by agonized cries of 'Soldiers... give me a grenade... A grenade, soldier!'

They were soldiers no longer. As the historian Kojima Noboru writes, '15 Army, once released from battle, was no longer a body of soldiers, but a herd of exhausted men.'[2] As they pressed on down the Kabaw Valley, a

---

[1] Recollections of Lt-Col. Fuwa, Staff Officer of Burma Area Army, in OCH, *Inpāru Sakusen*, II, p. 153

[2] Kojima Noboru, *Taiheiyō Sensō*, II, p. 169

trap for every bacillus of dysentery, typhus and malaria, their generals tried to keep a semblance of organized movement. Kawada, Satō's newly-appointed successor at 31 Division, wielded a six-foot long stick and padded along in socks, scolding and encouraging officers and men alike.

At Sittaung, they waited to be taken across the Chindwin, and British planes swooped down on them. The river banks were heaped with corpses, and it was impossible to tell whether the piles of mud and blood, eaten up by maggots, were the corpses of human beings, or heaps of earth. Some were already picked clean, and as the British planes flew off, their place was taken in the sky by hovering flocks of vultures.

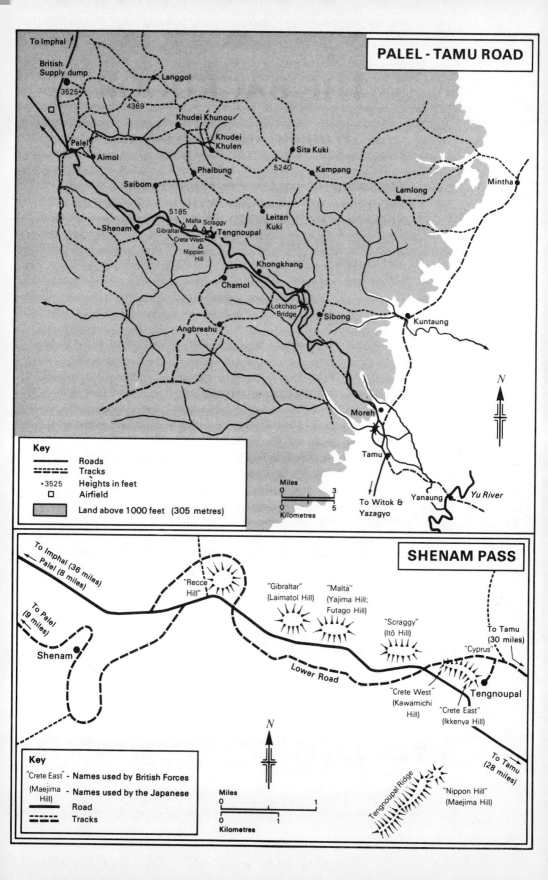

PALEL - TAMU ROAD

To Imphal

British
Supply dump
•3525
□
Palel
Aimol
Langgol
4369
Khudei Khunou
Khudei
Khulen
Sita Kuki
Phalbung
Saibom
5240
Kampang
Mintha
Lamlong
5185
Shenam
Malta Scraggy
Gibraltar △△△
Crete West △
Tengnoupal
Nippon
Hill
Leitan
Kuki
Khongkhang
Chamol
Lokchao
Bridge
Sibong
Kuntaung
Angbreshu
Moreh
N
Tamu

Key

——	Roads	
-----	Tracks	
•3525	Heights in feet	
□	Airfield	
▒	Land above 1000 feet (305 metres)	

Miles
0   3
Kilometres
0   5

To Witok &
Yazagyo
Yanaung
Yu River

SHENAM PASS

To Imphal (36 miles)
Palel (8 miles)

To Palel
(9 miles)

Shenam

"Recce
Hill"

"Gibraltar"
(Laimatol Hill)

"Malta"
(Yajima Hill;
Futago Hill)

"Scraggy"
(Itō Hill)

To Tamu
(30 miles)

"Cyprus"

Lower Road

"Crete West"
(Kawamichi
Hill)

"Crete East"
(Ikkenya Hill)

Tengnoupal

To Tamu
(28 miles)

N

Key

"Crete East"	- Names used by British Forces
(Maejima Hill)	- Names used by the Japanese
——	Road
-----	Tracks

Miles
0   1
Kilometres
0   1

Tengnoupal Ridge

"Nippon Hill"
(Maejima Hill)

5. THE BACKDOOR

Wingate and Stilwell

Operation THURSDAY — Stilwell and Tanaka's
'Chrysanthemums' — the Chindits fly in — Takemura.
meets the Chindits — Fergusson at Indaw — the death
of Wingate — 'White City' and 'Blackpool' — Stilwell
burns up the Limeys and crucifies GALAHAD —
Mogaung: Calvert takes umbrage — Myitkyina:
Mizukami's suicide

Operation THURSDAY

On the evening of 5 March, 1944, Colonel Sakuma Takanobu[1], commander
of 214 Infantry Regiment of 33 Division, was leading his regiment to
Yazagyo in the Kabaw Valley. He had passed through the village of Kantha
when he heard the sounds of engines shaking the night air. Sakuma was on
horseback and glanced up. Huge transport aircraft, red and green
navigation lights clearly visible, were passing overhead in what seemed an
endless procession. 'Must be going to bomb Rangoon', he supposed and
then, not giving them another thought, spurred his horse on.[2]

A few nights later, another regimental commander, Colonel Matsumura
Hiroshi of 60 Infantry Regiment, 15 Division, found his sleep shattered by
the throb of aircraft, a big formation not far off. He and his men came out
from the jungle and looked up at the bright moonlit sky. Four or five
transport planes, at a height of about 2500 feet, were flying north-east, each
one towing two or three gliders. The implications were serious, Matsumura
felt at once, but he could not help but be impressed by the spectacle. In that
clear sky, the formations looked magnificent. 'But what are they making for
behind our lines?'

---

[1] Kojima (*Eirei no tani*, p. 157) reads his personal name as Takanobu, but another reading
is Takayoshi, as in Takagi, *Inpāru*, p. 18

[2] Hamachi Toshio, *Inpāru sai-zensen*, p. 25

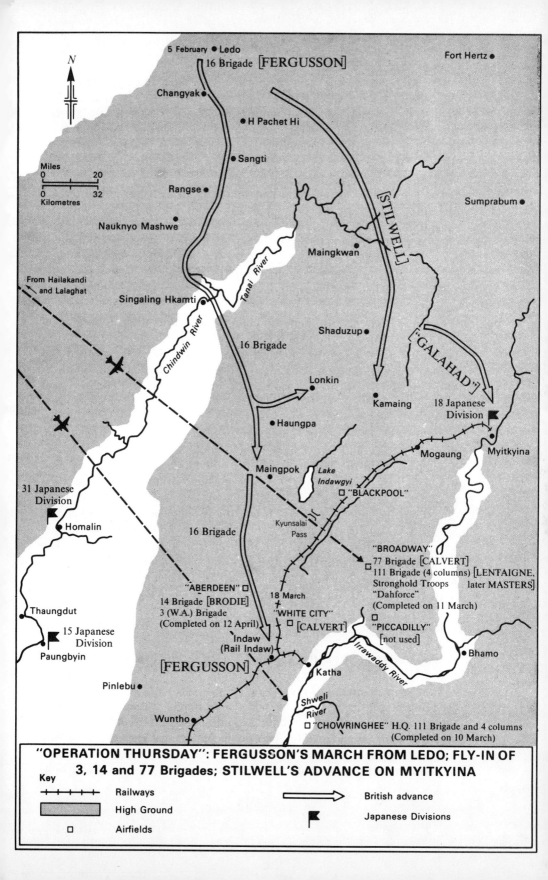

Miles
0 — 20
0 — 32
Kilometres

5 February ● Ledo
16 Brigade [FERGUSSON]

Fort Hertz ●

Changyak ●

● H Pachet Hi

● Sangti

[STILWELL]

Sumprabum ●

Rangse ●

Nauknyo Mashwe ●

Tanai River

Maingkwan ●

Chindwin River

From Hailakandi and Lalaghat

Singaling Hkamti ●

16 Brigade

Shaduzup ●

"GALAHAD"

Lonkin ●

Kamaing ●

18 Japanese Division ◣

Myitkyina ●

● Haungpa

Mogaung ●

31 Japanese Division ◣

Homalin ●

Maingpok ●

Lake Indawgyi

□ "BLACKPOOL"

16 Brigade

Kyunsalai Pass

"BROADWAY" □
77 Brigade [CALVERT]
111 Brigade (4 columns) [LENTAIGNE,
Stronghold Troops   later MASTERS]
"Dahforce"
(Completed on 11 March)

Thaungdut ●

15 Japanese
Division ⚑

Paungbyin ●

"ABERDEEN" □
14 Brigade [BRODIE]
3 (W.A.) Brigade
(Completed on 12 April)

18 March

"WHITE CITY" □
[CALVERT]

"PICCADILLY"
[not used]

● Bhamo

Irrawaddy River

Indaw
(Rail Indaw)

[FERGUSSON]

Katha ●

Pinlebu ●

Shweli River

Wuntho ●

□ "CHOWRINGHEE" H.Q. 111 Brigade and 4 columns
(Completed on 10 March)

**"OPERATION THURSDAY": FERGUSSON'S MARCH FROM LEDO; FLY-IN OF
3, 14 and 77 BRIGADES; STILWELL'S ADVANCE ON MYITKYINA**

Key

+‑+‑+‑+‑+‑+   Railways

░░░░░░   High Ground

□   Airfields

⟹   British advance

◣   Japanese Divisions

Had he but known it, Matsumura had been fairly close to the man in whose head lay the answer to that question. Just before he had reached Tonhe, his crossing-point on the Chindwin, on 3 March 1944, Orde Wingate, now a major-general, stood on the opposite bank, upstream from Singkaling Hkamti, watching the crossing of Brigadier Fergusson's 16 Brigade. It was the start of Operation THURSDAY, the code name for Wingate's Second Expedition into Burma.

The LONGCLOTH penetration had subsisted on air supply. His second operation was to do the same, but was taken a step further: with the exception of one Brigade (16, Fergusson) which would march in, his columns would be flown in by glider to their destination, establish strongholds far in the Japanese rear, and build airstrips into which transport planes would then fly in vehicles and artillery. The purpose was not to bring the Japanese to a head-on confrontation in battle: it was to sever their supply routes.

Nor was it intended to help the main British effort to push back again into Central Burma. The idea was to cut off those divisions – 18 in North Burma, 56 in Yunnan, which faced General Stilwell's US-equipped and trained Chinese divisions and make North Burma safe, as far south as Mogaung and Myitkyina, for the building of the road from Ledo in Assam to Kunming in China. Stilwell held that his Ledo road would be a substitute for the road north from Rangoon, which had been in Japanese hands for nearly two years. It would enable him to send supplies from Calcutta up through Assam and into China, which would help form sixty Chinese divisions to fight the Japanese; and the pipe-line accompanying the road would fuel the long-range B29 bombers which would strike at Formosa (Taiwan), Korea, and later still the Japanese mainland and so contribute directly to the defeat of Japan. It was the promise of aircraft to support Stilwell's venture that made the use of air supply and transport feasible on a large scale in Burma. US aircraft diverted from their main use had been instrumental in rescuing the British divisions in Arakan in February 1944, and were used again when Imphal was isolated. Their C47 Douglas transports (Colonels Alison and Cochran) would draw Wingate's gliders over the frontier hills, over the Chindwin, and deposit them round the upper reaches of the railway leading from Mandalay to Myitkyina. Their small L5s would carry commanders to confer with each other and with headquarters and fly out the wounded (one of the greatest griefs of the first expedition had been the need to abandon the wounded).

That Wingate managed even to get his new force accepted, let alone off the ground, is little short of a miracle. To his immediate superiors – at one time or another they included Slim, Mountbatten, Giffard and Auchinleck – he was arrogant and insufferable. To his juniors – at least those who did not find risible the Biblical rhetoric of his orders of the day – he was an inspired military genius, and the boldest among them (Calvert, Fergusson) knew he was a winner. What hit hardest in India was his successful appropriation of forces. Ready access to Mountbatten, and even to Churchill himself, in a crisis, meant that Wingate would ruthlessly ask for – and get – most of what he wanted. The new force for Operation THURSDAY would consist of six brigades, not one as in 1943, each brigade consisting of four battalions. To get this number, Wingate was given – after much fierce debate and heart-burning – 70 British Division, trained for the Middle East under Major-General Symes, who, with outward good grace and a very natural inner resentment, made way for Wingate and was named Deputy Commander, Special Force. Wingate naturally used many of those who had proved their worth in LONGCLOTH, and this too caused offence (but was undoubtedly sensible). He also split his brigades into columns. The basis of the column was an infantry company – Gurkhas or British county regiments – provided with an RAF officer to signal for supplies and air-strikes, and Burma Rifles units who interpreted for them, negotiated with village headmen, and generally acted as an intelligence spearhead. The racial spectrum of Wingate's second expedition was much wider. Although, unlike every other formation in Burma apart from 2 Division, he had no Indian contingents,[1] Special Force of 1944 was given the title 3 Indian Division, for security reasons. It contained a West African brigade and an American unit – 2832 strong – with the uninspiring nomenclature 5307 Composite Unit (Provisional). This unit trained with Wingate in the jungles of Central India, and was the only American infantry force on the mainland of Asia.

But it was the air component which made the most striking difference from LONGCLOTH. The American Air Commando in support of Special Force had at its disposal thirteen Dakotas (C47s), twelve Commando transports (C46), twelve Mitchell medium bombers (B25), thirty Mustang fighter-bombers (P51), a hundred light planes (L5)[2] and six helicopters. The men would be carried in 225 gliders. Movement through the jungle would be, as before, on foot, with pack-mules carrying supplies, ammunition and wireless sets.[3]

These allocations were not accepted with universal acclaim. As Commander-in-Chief, India, General Auchinleck considered the breaking-up of 70 British Division highly undesirable, to put it mildly. It was battle-seasoned (it had been in the siege of Tobruk) and would, if left intact, alter the balance of forces in Arakan heavily in favour of the British.[4] Why

---

[1] 'Second-rate troops' in Wingate's view (R. Callahan, *Burma 1942–1945*, p. 101)

[2] 'These planes were to become the lynchpin of the whole operation and were a bigger factor in sustaining morale than anything else' (Richard Rhodes-James, *Chindit*, p. 81)

[3] Kirby, *War Against Japan*, III, p. 38, n.3

[4] Wingate approved of its artillery and RAC components, but thought its infantry needed bringing up to scratch.

destroy a perfectly good division, which could play a part in a major offensive, and dissipate its strength in guerrilla activities? Why not wait until 82 West African Division arrived? It was based on porter-transport and was jungle-trained. And how could the Indian L of C provide the extra fuel for Wingate's air force, when it was already strained to the limit by the commitment to 11th Army Group in Assam and to Stilwell at Ledo? Auchinleck despatched a telegram, in three parts, to Quebec, where Churchill was conferring with Roosevelt and the Chiefs of Staff. Churchill had long since mistrusted Auchinleck as too deliberate and cautious, and dismissed the telegram with some acerbity; and on 25 August 1943 South-East Asia Command was set up which meant that Mountbatten became responsible for Wingate – though India Command was still the source of supply and the ground for training.

There were objections from other quarters to the allocation of the Americans. General Stilwell had long desired to see American infantry operate in his command, and when they were placed under Wingate he exploded. 'After a long struggle, we get a handful of US troops and by God they tell us they are going to operate under *Wingate*! We don't know how to handle them but that exhibitionist does! He has done nothing but make an abortive jaunt to Katha, cutting some railroad that our people had already cut, got caught east of the Irrawaddy and come out with a loss of 40 per cent. Now he's the expert. That is enough to *discourage Christ*.'[1] In the end, Stilwell prised the Americans, codenamed a little more picturesquely as GALAHAD, from Wingate and used them in his offensive against Myitkyina. In his crucifixion of them and the exhausted Chindit columns at the end of the campaign, he was to earn *their* undying hatred too.[2]

Stilwell and Tanaka's Chrysanthemums

THURSDAY's mission was, from the first, to help Stilwell. With three, later five, Chinese divisions, trained at Ramgarh in India where India Command

[1] Tuchman, *Sand Against the Wind*, p. 385

[2] Stilwell's pathological anglophobia is well known. It was partly because he took too seriously what he took to be the affected vowels of British officers, partly the result of wanting to fight the American War of Independence all over again. But it would be wrong to assume he was unique in this respect. When Masters went to see Lentaigne at Shaduzup, 'Stilwell's staff!' Lentaigne burst out to him, 'He's difficult enough, but they're impossible. There's one chap who keeps whispering in Stilwell's ear that the Chindits do nothing but march away from the enemy and drink tea, by Jove, eh what?' And even the incredibly brave and hard-working 'Burma surgeon', Dr Gordon Seagrave, constantly betrays a loathing of the British colonial presence in Burma, which even extended to their use of sweeper-served commodes, the ubiquitous 'thunderboxes', which he obviously regarded as yet one more weapon, fully satisfying 'the inner desires of the colonial English', to humiliate and abuse Indians by forcing them to carry out the most servile and demeaning of tasks. (Seagrave, *Burma Surgeon Returns*, p. 132)

paid and fed them, and US officers trained them and supplied them with US equipment, Stilwell's aim was to march into North Burma from Ledo in Assam, drawing his engineers and the Ledo road behind him as he went, and driving back the Japanese 18 Division down the Hukawng Valley. The Kachin Levies, operating from Fort Hertz, were to act as scouts and guerrillas operating south towards Myitkyina. And it was fondly hoped that the Chinese would co-operate by advancing into Burma from Yunnan where the Japanese 56 Division, as tough and experienced as the 18th, blocked their path. It is easy to criticize the Chinese unwillingness to budge. But they had been fighting the Japanese four years longer than their new allies, much of the most valuable part of their country was under occupation by twenty-five Japanese divisions and they little relished the prospect of re-establishing the British in Burma from which, as the Chinese had witnessed, they had been so rudely and summarily ejected in 1942.

After numerous plans for 1944 had been examined and discarded, Mountbatten finally decided on 14 January that Stilwell should advance from Ledo to Shaduzup and then into the area Mogaung-Myitkyina from where his road would branch into China. IV Corps would patrol actively west of the Chindwin – and east of it where feasible – one advance would be made in Arakan and Akyab taken; and Wingate's Long Range Penetration forces would cut the L of C of the Japanese opposing Stilwell.

Patrols of 38 Chinese Division (Sun Li-jen) clashed with a reconnaissance company of 18 Division (Tanaka Shinichi) in the Hukawng Valley on 30 October 1943. 18 Division's codename was Kiku (Chrysanthemum – the Imperial flower) and it considered itself among the best – if not the best – in the Japanese Army. After Mutaguchi declared for Operation U-GO in September, Tanaka knew that he need expect no reinforcements from that quarter. His 114 Regiment was transferred to Yunnan, also, to stiffen 56 Division's resistance to the Chinese armies. Nonetheless, he would hold the Hukawng Valley. It was an awful place. Like the Kabaw Valley, its name meant 'Valley of Death'.[1] From fifteen to fifty miles across, east to west, it extended north to south for 130 miles, a kind of basin criss-crossed by many rivers, easily turned into a marshy quagmire by the monsoon, a nest for cholera and malaria. Tanaka had no wish to commit all his force to this hellhole, so he sent up Colonel Nagahisa's 56 Regiment to face Sun Li-jen. It would be enough.

Tanaka soon found his confidence misplaced. At Yubang Ga, a crossing-point on the Tanai River, Nagahisa surrounded 38 Chinese Division, which promptly formed itself into a box with heavy weapons and tanks and supplied from the air. Nagahisa put in attack after attack, but failed to make an impact, and finally withdrew to lick his wounds. Sun was cockahoop. For years the Chinese had been defeated in their own country,

---

[1] Though the reference is to a massacre, not the climate.

and fought on desperately, feeling they were no match for the Japanese. Now they had stood and fought, and licked one of the finest Japanese regiments. Stilwell came to Sun's rescue with an artillery barrage on 24 December, and under his direct supervision – he spent the whole day in the command post – the Chinese finally drove the Japanese from the river crossing and out of their jungle positions covering it. It cost nearly 800 casualties, and the Chinese celebrated not only by firing rifles in the air, but by parading the heads of Japanese on bamboo poles.[1]

Tanaka was enraged. He decided to make an advance right up the Hukawng to Shingbwiyang, Stilwell's advanced headquarters, but Mutaguchi would not permit an offensive that might divert supplies from Imphal, and told him to hold Maingkwan, further south in the centre of the valley. This meant that Stilwell could move south with little resistance, and he expected 38 Division, after its victory, and 22 Division to follow up the Japanese fast. But Sun had already complained that Stilwell's deputy, General Boatner, had put him at risk by seriously underestimating Japanese strength in the Hukawng, and he wanted Boatner removed. In theory, the Chinese should have obeyed Stilwell's orders, but this was yet another instance where his fantastically absurd triple command simply failed to pay off. He had been named Chief of Staff to Chiang Kai-shek in March 1942. He was also commanding officer of the US forces in the China-Burma-India theatre, and Deputy Supreme Commander, South-East Asia. They were roles demanding diplomacy, a gift for high command, and *entregent*. Stilwell had none of these things. He was happiest as a field commander, and he loved the ordinary Chinese soldier, the *ping*, every bit as much as he detested the Chinese Government and its President, whom he derisively nicknamed 'Peanut'. 'Peanut' knew quite well what Stilwell's opinion of him was. He also had no intention of allowing Stilwell to fritter away these wonderful new Chinese divisions with their fresh uniforms and equipment in Burma, when they might be needed later on for his own internal purposes in China (he had been fighting the Chinese Communists as well as the Japanese). So the two Chinese divisions moved slowly down the Hukawng, and came to a halt on 29 January 1944.

Stilwell got hold of Sun and castigated him, threatening to resign his command and tell Washington why, with all that that implied: the stopping of supplies to China. The ironic thing about Stilwell's anger at Sun's decision is that, at that very moment, Stilwell was in the midst of planning a mission of members of his staff to Washington to subvert Mountbatten. The ambitious young American general, Albert Wedemeyer, had gone to the Chiefs of Staff with Mountbatten's AXIOM Mission, to change SEAC's policy to a maritime one, aiming at diverting resources from Burma into a seaborne invasion of Sumatra and Malaya as the quickest

---

[1] Tuchman, op.cit., p. 420

way of recapturing Singapore and opening a way into the South China Sea. Stilwell wanted none of this, and he felt Mountbatten was using Chiang Kai-shek's reluctance to push hard into North Burma as a lever for going slow on Burma altogether. Stilwell, although he was Mountbatten's deputy, sent his deputy, Boatner, to Roosevelt who promptly devised a telegram, with Boatner dictating the terms, inviting Churchill to pressurize Mountbatten to carry out immediately a vigorous campaign in Upper Burma. Himself a protagonist of a seaborne invasion, Churchill would not be drawn; but the Joint Chiefs of Staff, tit for tat, rejected AXIOM when Wedemeyer put the case to them.

In the meanwhile, GALAHAD was about to play its part. Colonel Rothwell Brown's sixty light tanks had chased the Japanese from Taro, about twenty-five miles down the Tanai River from Shingbwiyang, and so covered the flank of the Hukawng operation. Brigadier Frank Merrill arrived in command of GALAHAD on 19 February 1944. The presence of this Japanese-speaking officer, a protégé of Stilwell's, at the head of the force, prompted a journalist to dub the men 'Merrill's Marauders'. However melodramatic, it was an improvement on 5307 Composite Unit (Provisional) and the noun was not inappropriate for the tough, battle-scarred hooligans whom Merrill commanded. In India they had behaved like delinquents. Alongside the Chinese, in the Hukawng, they showed they could fight.

Stilwell was delighted to have them and ordered an attack on Maingkwan. GALAHAD was divided into two combat teams armed with light weapons, mortars and bazookas. An air strike on 3 March acted as their artillery, and they were lucky enough to have a very courageous Nisei[1] with them, Sergeant Roy Matsumoto, who crawled up to the Japanese positions and listened to conversations; and also clipped himself onto their telephone wires. That was how he heard 18 Division ordering its units at Maingkwan to withdraw on 5 March.

GALAHAD was bedevilled by its ignorance of racial types. In Guadalcanal or New Guinea, everything was relatively simple. There were white men, natives and Japanese. Here in Burma it was not easy to tell Burmese from Chinese from Japanese, and once the Chinese took off their US helmets they looked startlingly like Japanese in their gaiters and scruffy uniforms. A company of Lieutenant-Colonel McGee's II Battalion was on patrol one day and met what it took to be a group of friendly Chinese, who suddenly opened up on them with machine guns. But this uneasy suspicion did not slow up GALAHAD's advance: four days after leaving Maingkwan, they were in Warazup. The whole of the Hukawng Valley was in Stilwell's hands.

---

[1] American of Japanese descent.

The Chindits fly in

It was at this juncture that Special Force flew in. There had been a last-minute panic on the airfield at Lalaghat. Disobeying orders not to overfly the three landing-grounds – 'Piccadilly', 'Broadway', 'Chowringhee' – in case the Japanese were alerted to their whereabouts, an American pilot thought he should give one last secret check. The photographs he returned with showed that one of them, 'Piccadilly', had been blocked by tree trunks. Had Special Force been more alive to the varieties of photographic intelligence, its headquarters would have put in a request for regular overflights at 20,000 or 30,000 feet, which were regularly carried out by Spitfires and Mosquitos of the Army Photographic Intelligence Unit. That unit was never asked to keep an eye on the landing zones, but 'Piccadilly' was known as the site, photographed for *Life* magazine, June 1943, from which wounded men had been flown out in Dakotas from Wingate's first expedition, and the APIU glanced at it occasionally when on the lookout for Force 136 and other forces operating behind the Japanese lines. But no regular inspection was asked for, or maintained.[1]

At any rate, there it was. 'Piccadilly' was out. Slim was present to see the expedition off and a hurried last-minute conference took place. Calvert, whose 77 Brigade was to fly into both 'Piccadilly' and 'Broadway', accepted the hazards involved in taking his entire Brigade into one strip. Wingate reported to Slim, who gave his verdict: 'The operation will go on.'[2]

Wingate opted to use 'Broadway' alone that night, and to send in Lentaigne's 111 Brigade to 'Chowringhee' later. Loads were switched, pilots rebriefed and a code word arranged with Calvert to alert Headquarters to his failure ('Soya Link') or success ('Pork Sausage'). The entire debate, decision and change of plan took no more than seventy minutes. The first Dakota moved off at 6.12 pm.[3] Calvert thought the risk had to be taken: there were only a few nights of full moon available, and the Japanese were massing for the offensive against Imphal. A delay might involve the Chindits being turned back into IV Corps' battle, and the

---

[1] Private information from David Wilson, formerly G2, Army Photographic Intelligence Section, covering Bengal and Burma. 3 Tactical Air Force reported extensions to Japanese airfields round Indaw on 8 March; and cf. Bidwell, *The Chindit War*, p. 104, and Slim, *Defeat into Victory*, pp. 261–2

[2] There has been debate over this. In some photographs of the conference Slim does not appear, and it has been assumed that Wingate took the responsibility alone. Slim's verdict is made quite clear in the Indian Official History (*Reconquest of Burma*, I, p. 337) and is cogently argued by Ronald Lewin (*Slim*, p. 163). Wingate was naturally anxious lest the Japanese, having blocked one airfield, and thereby induced a descent on the other two, might have prepared an ambush at 'Broadway', or 'Chowringhee'. He was convinced the Chinese had betrayed his secret: their security was notoriously lax (Tulloch, *Wingate in Peace and War*, p. 148).

[3] Tulloch, op.cit., pp. 200–01

opportunity to carry out Long Range Penetration on this massive scale might be gone forever.[1]

The first gliders to land emptied out Alison and a team of controllers who placed landing lights – petroleum flares – to define the strip, but the follow-up was too fast. Some of the first gliders had crashed (there were two trees on the main runway, and ditches, which the photographs had not shown) and were still blocking the runaway, and the successive waves came in and hit them. Calvert looked at the jammed glider path, realized that many of the gliders had failed to arrive, and that he had casualties: thirty killed, twenty-one wounded. He sent the signal: 'Soya Link'.[2]

Wingate received the signal at 2.30 am and told Tulloch gloomily that it looked as if the operation had failed. Tulloch disagreed, told Wingate to get some sleep, and woke him four hours later with the news that 'Pork Sausage' had been sent. Calvert had cleared his strip, and realized his casualties were not as bad as he had feared, though of the 61 gliders which took off that night, only 35 reached 'Broadway'. Seventeen landed in various parts of Assam and six had the bad luck to come down into Japanese-held areas. One even landed close to 15 Division Headquarters, then at Pinlebu. But Lieutenant Brockett, of the US Engineers, had his two bulldozers intact, and began at once to clear the strip for planes. It worked. After dusk, USAAF Brigadier-General Old landed with the first Dakotas. Sixty-three more flew in, then a hundred each for the next few nights, bringing field and anti-aircraft guns. On the second night, Wingate himself came in. Lentaigne's 111 Brigade started its fly-in at 'Chowringhee' on the night of the 6th.

The flights went on. Nearly 600 sorties were made, and at the end of it over 9000 men and nearly 1400 mules, as well as two troops of artillery, had been landed, in the very heart of Japanese-held Burma. 'Our first task is fulfilled', went Wingate's Order of the Day on 11 March. 'We have inflicted a complete surprise on the enemy. All our columns are inserted in the enemy's guts... The enemy will react with violence. We will oppose him with the resolve to reconquer our territory of Northern Burma... This is not the moment, when such an advantage has been gained, to count the cost. This is a moment to live in history. It is an enterprise in which every man who takes part may feel proud one day to say I WAS THERE.'[3]

[1] Calvert, *The Chindits*, p. 27

[2] ibid., p. 28

[3] Sykes, *Orde Wingate*, pp. 522–3. Not everyone was at home with Wingate's Scriptural rhetoric. 'The officers, with the contempt of sentimentality that they always affected, were apt to laugh at these stirring little pieces, and they were apt to convey some of this cynicism to the men. This was dangerous as the men for the most part worshipped Wingate and it was a direct blow at their idol. I think that secretly we were rather ashamed of our scorn.' (Rhodes-James, *Chindit*, p. 79.)

Surprise was achieved. And that in itself is quite extraordinary. Mutaguchi's own plans against India derived from Wingate's penetration of 1943, yet it never seems to have occurred to him that the threat might be renewed – as a reconnaissance in force, perhaps, but not on a larger scale. There seems to have been no contingency planning. When the reports of the landings came to him, he was contemptuous, and not to be diverted from his own great project. The gliders which had dropped into Japanese territory gave the first indication of the scope of THURSDAY, although it cannot have been easy to extract the information. Iizuka Masaji, of the Yomiuri Shimbun, was told of the interrogation of a glider pilot, a second-lieutenant, whose machine had hit an air pocket.[1] The tow-rope had parted and he made a forced landing in the mountains, near Paungbyin, where the locals took him prisoner and handed him over to the Japanese 15 Division Headquarters. The glider had hit a teak tree coming down, on impact a branch had struck him in both eyes, and he was blind, otherwise he would never have let himself be taken. The other seventeen in the glider had escaped into the jungle. The pilot gave only his name and the address of his family, and when pressed to reveal both the airfield he had left and his destination, replied simply, 'There is something called Bushidō in the Japanese Army, or so I've heard. The English too have the soldier's spirit. I would rather die than betray my country.' But of course the glider's measurements were taken, and from other interrogations it became clear that each transport plane towed two of them, around eighty [sic] had left from a base west of Imphal, and their objective was a sandy area in the jungle, which they were to find by flying east, passing over Paungbyin, and turning north at right angles after twice crossing the Irrawaddy. Sixty machines were supposed to have reached this objective, and the Divisional Commander, Yamauchi, estimated each to hold nine men and thought the force might be between 700 and 800 strong. Mutaguchi received his signal to this effect on 9 March.[2]

It is perhaps fair to point out that not every Japanese commander was taken aback by THURSDAY. When the formation flew over the airfield at Indaw, where there was not a single fighter or anti-aircraft gun to oppose them, Lieutenant Narabayashi woke the sleeping Chief of Staff of 5 Air Division, Suzuki, who merely said, 'So they've come at last'. The Japanese Air Force, and its commander in Burma, Major-General Tazoe, were pretty sure that Wingate would put in another appearance, and would be airborne. Otherwise, why had they left air-strips behind in the jungle in 1943, and agents in the villages? To find the answer, the Japanese had infiltrated agents into India, who reported back that aircraft made from wood were being produced at airfields near Calcutta. These were gliders,

---

[1] *Hiroku Dai Tōa Senshi*, p. 24

[2] OCH *Inpāru Sakusen*, II, p. 152

without a doubt, and, linking them with the jungle air-strips, Tazoe drew the obvious conclusion.

On the morning of 6 March, Tazoe flew to Maymyo from Shwebo. He wanted a word with Mutaguchi before returning to his headquarters at Kalaw in the Shan States. He was worried about sightings of red and black smoke in the sky the previous day. There was a flap on at Maymyo, bustle everywhere, and an aircraft burning in a corner of the field. There had been an air-raid thirty minutes before, and soldiers were still trying to beat out the flames. The airfield battalion commander brought him the latest news from 5 Air Division. Enemy airborne units had landed in several spots near Katha (north of Mandalay). The railway at Mawlu had been destroyed, and heavy fighting was in progress.

Tazoe took his adjutant, Lieutenant Iizuka, with him and went to see Mutaguchi. If he didn't strike at once, Tazoe said, the Allied airborne landings could soon blossom into a tremendously strong unit in the very heart of the Japanese rear communications. They would cut off Myitkyina, and once that was taken, nothing would prevent Stilwell's road going through to China, which meant enormous pressure on the Japanese armies in China and quite possibly direct raids by US China-based planes on Japan herself. Given these implications, Mutaguchi should hurl against them every unit he could, even if this meant postponing the Imphal operation.

'You worry too much,' the unmoved Mutaguchi replied. Tazoe had become flushed with the force of his own arguments. 'You're an airman, so naturally you think it's important. What kind of strength can they muster? Your 5 Air Division would know if they had a hundred or two hundred gliders, so we know what the limits are. And how are they going to supply the men they've dropped? While they're scuttling around Katha, I'll be into Imphal and cut the line to Ledo. They'll simply wither on the vine.'

Tazoe realized that Mutaguchi simply did not consider airborne operations as crucial, in spite of the German success in Crete in 1941. 'There are a couple of paratroop or glider divisions in India,' Mutaguchi went on. 'Let them use them. That's still not very important, if they drop them in the middle of Burma when the battle's happening elsewhere.'

'You don't realize the transport capacity of these planes,' Tazoe countered. 'With 300 aircraft they can shift 1800 tons a day. If they only manage 20% of that, that means 30,000 tons a month, the equivalent of using 100 trucks a day. Look what's happened in Arakan. They were landing steel planking to make runways, and receiving and despatching planes in twenty-four hours.'

Mutaguchi let Tazoe go on, until his patience gave out. 'Let them do what they like with their airborne units. I'll cut at their very roots in Ledo. I've never lost a battle yet. The gods are with me, Tazoe. Leave it to me. How is your air umbrella for my river crossings? Just get me safely across the Chindwin, that's all I ask.' There was no arguing with Mutaguchi's divine inspiration, so Tazoe flew to Rangoon to reason with Kawabe. Kawabe took the landings more seriously, but, he told Tazoe, it was unthinkable to cancel Imphal now. Perhaps he would do better to leave it to Mutaguchi.

Tazoe's airfields had been liberally plastered by Cochran's air commando before the landings began, but in spite of the planes destroyed on the ground, he could muster enough for a riposte and on 10 March, he attacked 'Chowringhee' with twenty fighters and two light bombers, and 'Broadway' on 13 March with fifty-five fighters and three light bombers. But by the 13th, 'Broadway' could answer back, and Tazoe's planes were met by anti-aircraft guns and Spitfires.

Neither Kawabe nor Mutaguchi had any contingency plans for an airborne invasion, and their reaction to the Chindits was, first, to use whatever units happened to be in the area of the landings, and, second, to bring up the Tenasserim garrison, 24 Independent Mixed Brigade. If the reaction was rapid enough to hit the Chindits before they consolidated their strongholds, they could be eliminated. *Fukuro no nezumi*, Mutaguchi called them – a mouse in a bag.

The landings had established a kind of arc at distances of between thirty and forty miles round Indaw from where the railway went north to Myitkyina, and roads led west to 15 Army's crossing-points. In addition, another brigade – 16 (Fergusson) – had left Ledo on 5 February to march to its destination – also Indaw, though the Japanese were not aware of this until he was almost on it. Clearly, Indaw was the focus of the airborne invasion, and Mutaguchi on 10 March despatched to Indaw two infantry companies formed from units of 18 Division stationed in the area Mandalay-Maymyo, under one of his Headquarters staff, Lieutenant-Colonel Nagahashi. Their orders were simply to attack the enemy where they found him. They found Calvert, and put in a night attack on him at Henu ('White City') on 17 March. Calvert lit up the night sky with star shells and poured mortars and machine-gun fire into the hapless Japanese, most of whom were killed in the first few minutes. Nagahashi himself died from his wounds.

Calvert was told that Nagahashi's men had nothing more lethal than mortars, when Brigade Headquarters arrived at the railway block. The South Staffords, under Major Ron Degg – a former coal miner who had risen from the ranks – were already astride the railway. Degg had asked for a supply drop of picks and shovels to dig positions, barbed wire to enclose them, and food and ammunition. A drop was arranged but fell on the hillside nearer to Brigade Headquarters. It took a week to bring it in – Calvert used elephants – and in the meanwhile, Degg and his men had to improvise. Calvert got in touch with him by walkie-talkie and directed him

Colonel Omoto, CO 51 Infantry Regiment, Japanese 15 Division, with his
ADC, watches the progress of the battle for Nungshigum.
(Richard Storry Estate)

Link up of advance guards of XXXIII Corps and IV Corps on the Imphal-
Kohima Road, June 1944. *(Imperial War Museum)*

Major-General (later Sir) Douglas Gracey, GOC 20 Indian Division.
Photograph taken in Saigon, 1945, during command of British forces in French
Indo-China. *(Imperial War Museum)*

The investiture at Imphal. The XIV Army commander and his three corps
commanders were knighted by the Viceroy, Lord Wavell, on the Imphal Plain
after the Japanese defeat. Front row, left to right: Lieutenant-General Sir
William (later Field-Marshal Viscount) Slim, Lieutenant-General Sir Philip
Christison (XV Corps), Lieutenant-General Sir Geoffrey Scoones (IV Corps),
and Lieutenant-General Sir Montagu Stopford (XXXIII Corps).
(Imperial War Museum)

The Burmese temple guardian or Chinthe. This was the mythical beast chosen by Wingate as the symbol of his expeditions. *(P. Woodward)*

Orde Wingate sitting in a Dakota. The interior has been adapted to carry mules. *(Imperial War Museum)*

Major (later Brigadier) Bernard Fergusson (Lord Ballantrae), column commander in first Wingate expedition and commander 16 Brigade in Operation THURSDAY. *(Imperial War Museum)*

British troops marching through Monywa, 16 March 1945.
(Imperial War Museum)

Dead Japanese lying in the Shweli River, February 1945.
(Imperial War Museum)

Three battalion commanders of 5 Brigade, 2 Division. Left to right:
Lieutenant-Colonel Somerville Macalester (Camerons), Lieutenant-Colonel
O. G. W. White (Dorsets), Lieutenant-Colonel T. A. Irvine (Worcesters).
(Imperial War Museum)

Stuart tanks move up to cross the Irrawaddy, at the XXXIII Corps bridgehead
at Myinmu. *(Imperial War Museum)*

During the Irrawaddy crossings the 4/15 Punjab land at Nyaungu.
(Imperial War Museum)

'Tit Pagoda', a celebrated landmark during the Irrawaddy crossings.
(P. Woodward)

Major-General T. W. ('Pete') Rees, GOC 19 Indian Division, directing the battle for Mandalay, 9 March 1945. *(Imperial War Museum)*

along a ridge until he saw the battle: the Japanese were concentrated round a small pagoda atop a hillock close to the railway. They had penetrated Degg's positions and as Calvert and some of Brigade Headquarters ran across the valley they noticed a number of dead and wounded. Calvert realized that fast action was needed to restore the situation and gave the order to charge. Major Freddie Shaw, whose 3/6 Gurkha Rifles were Calvert's reserve, was to give covering fire:

> So, standing up, I shouted out 'Charge!' in the approved Victorian manner, and ran down the hill with Bobbie (Squadron Leader Robert Thompson) and the two orderlies. Half of the South Staffords joined in. Then, looking back, I found a lot had not. So I told them to bloody well 'Charge, what the hell do you think you're doing.' So they charged. Machine-gunners, mortar teams, all officers – everybody who was on that hill.[1]

Not to be outdone, the Japanese charged too. The result was a vicious free-for-all round the pagoda, 'everyone shooting, bayoneting, kicking at everyone else, rather like an officers' guest night.'[2] A young South Staffords officer, Lieutenant Cairns, had his arm hacked off by a Japanese officer. Cairns shot the officer, picked up his sword with his remaining arm and laid about him with it until he collapsed. Calvert knelt down beside him. 'Have we won, sir? Was it all right? Did we do our stuff? Don't worry about me.' Then he died.[3] Only one Japanese officer was involved in this ferocious fight – Second Lieutenant Kiyomizu, leading three sections of his platoon to Mawlu under the orders of Major Takemura, II/51 Regiment of 15 Division. Takemura had told him he estimated the airborne strength at Mawlu to be around 1000 men, but Kiyomizu had not anticipated how strong their positions were as he made for Pagoda Hill, nor the immense fire-power from mortars and Spitfire machine guns which would decimate his men. Pointing out that this would be the regiment's first contact with the enemy, Takemura told him that he expected his section to fight well, because this battle would have an effect on the morale of the rest of the regiment. Kiyomizu accepted this. His men dropped their packs for the attack and came in lightly armed through the morning mist. He attacked Pagoda Hill as soon as the mist lifted and he saw half-a-dozen airborne troops moving about. He was flailing around with his sword when bullets struck him in the right arm and genitals.[4] He screamed with pain and fell.

[1] Calvert, *Prisoners of Hope*, new edn., 1971, p. 52

[2] ibid., p. 52

[3] 'Just as the Japanese were being driven behind the pagoda', according to Calvert (*The Chindits*, p. 49); 'the following morning' according to Lieutenant Durant (Bidwell, *The Chindit War*, p. 122). Cairns was awarded the VC.

[4] Hamachi, op.cit., p. 46

Calvert's men killed forty-two Japanese, including – Calvert claims – four officers, in this first fierce encounter, but at the price of twenty-three dead and sixty-four wounded. It was characteristic of much of the Chindit fighting. The philosophy of the columns was to avoid frontal encounters, and the men might march for days without seeing or hearing a Japanese. Then, when the battle broke, it was a question of bloody hand-to-hand combat of the most ferocious kind.

It was renewed by the probing of Japanese patrols from Mawlu against the block on three successive nights, 18, 19 and 20 March. But by this time, Calvert had had a good supply drop, was digging and wiring, and sending out Gurkha commando platoons to lay mines round the Japanese positions south of Mawlu. Meanwhile, Lentaigne's 111 Brigade was assembling from its two dropping zones, two battalions at 'Chowringhee', two at 'Broadway'. Those dropped at 'Chowringhee' had to cross the Irrawaddy before reaching their zone of operations, but alterations to the flight plan resulting from the non-use of 'Piccadilly' meant changes in departure times, and put Lentaigne behind schedule. He put his Headquarters Column and 30 Column together and worked west, while No. 40 Column and the mules and heavy weapons of 30 Column were still on the left bank of the Irrawaddy. So he sent them to join Morris Force which was to strike east until it hit the Chinese border and work up to Myitkyina from the south. It was 26 March before Lentaigne crossed the railway at Wuntho and made for Pinlebu, which was the depot area for Yamauchi's 15 Division. The march west and the exhausting twelve hours trying (unsuccessfully) to get the mules to swim had told on Lentaigne, who was older than most of the men in the operation; and his exhaustion in turn began to tell on his powers of command.[1]

Takemura meets the Chindits

Further to the north-west, another column was exhausted before it reached its battleground. This was Fergusson's 16 Brigade, the only brigade to march in the whole way. Fergusson had left Ledo on 5 February, seeking a path somewhere between the forces massing on the Chindwin and 18 Division resisting Stilwell in the Hukawng Valley. So he made across the Patkai Hills down to the upper reaches of the Chindwin (Tanai) near Singkaling Hkamti, at a widening distance of thirty to sixty miles west of Stilwell, in the direction of Indaw. His orders were to capture Indaw and its two airfields – not, as he had previously been told, by bypassing it and coming round upon it from the south-east, but directly. He was to set up a stronghold at 'Aberdeen' on the way.

[1] Rhodes-James, *Chindit*, p. 77

The Backdoor

The idea of the stronghold was central to Wingate's conception of the Second Chindit Expedition. Its basic purpose was to draw Japanese forces upon itself, act as a centre for Brigade columns and a shelter for their wounded, and a strip for planes. But perhaps Wingate can phrase his idea best himself:

OBJECT OF THE STRONGHOLD

The Stronghold is a *machan*[1] overlooking a kid tied up to entice the Japanese tiger.
The Stronghold is an asylum for Long Range Penetration Group wounded.
The Stronghold is a magazine of stores.
The Stronghold is a defended air-strip.
The Stronghold is an administrative centre for loyal inhabitants.
The Stronghold is an orbit round which columns of the Brigade circulate. It is suitably placed with reference to the main objective of the Brigade.
The Stronghold is a base for light planes operating with columns on the main objective.[2]

To assault well dug-in and well-defended Japanese positions required a massive concentration of guns; much better tempt the enemy out into the open by sticking a thorn in his flesh, miles away from where he could bring munitions and men by wheeled transport:

The ideal situation for a Stronghold is the centre of a circle of thirty miles radius consisting of closely wooded and very broken country, only passable to pack transport owing to great natural obstacles... this centre should ideally consist of a level upland with a cleared strip for Dakotas, a separate supply dropping area, taxi-ways to the Stronghold, a neighbouring friendly village or two, and an inexhaustible and uncontaminatable supply of water within the Stronghold.
...The motto of the Stronghold is NO SURRENDER.[3]

A brave vision, accurately envisaged. Fergusson's 'Aberdeen' was to be such a site, and he was told to set it up on 12 March, after a gruelling slog. He had already fulfilled his promise to Stilwell to eliminate Japanese units at Lonkin on his flank: two columns, 900 men, were already assigned to that job. With 3000 others, and 400 mules, Fergusson's men drew close to

[1] Hindustani: 'dais', 'platform'.
[2] Calvert, *Prisoners of Hope*, p. 282
[3] ibid., p. 283

Indaw in single file, as they had moved since they set out. 'Aberdeen' was set up in two strongholds either side of the River Meza, a mile north of the village of Manhton, whence ran a road which ended up at Indaw and Calvert's stronghold at Henu, 'White City'.

12 Battalion, Nigeria Regiment, was to act as garrison for 'Aberdeen' when Fergusson left it. He expected to have another one soon, and to have 14 Brigade (Brodie) as immediate back-up as soon as the Nigerians were in position. Originally 14 Brigade was intended to relieve another Chindit brigade after two months, the period Wingate anticipated they might be used in the field. Now, as Fergusson understood it, Brodie was to help him take Indaw. Wingate had confided to him, on a visit on 23 March, that he feared he might lose 14 and 23 Brigade to the battle in the Imphal Plain, and he intended to use them in his own way first. As we have seen, 23 Brigade (Perowne) was withdrawn from the main Chindit operation and acted in collaboration with 2 and 7 Divisions in defeating the Japanese at Kohima. 14 Brigade was still available. On 24 March, Fergusson left 'Aberdeen'.

His columns at Lonkin had not caught up with him, and he therefore had three battalions with which to take Indaw. They were exhausted after their incredible march from India, and he should have rested them first.[1] 17 and 71 Columns (II Battalion/Leicester Regiment) were already in the hills south-east of Indaw, the proud recipients of Wingate's congratulatory signal to them when they reached the Chindwin: 'Well done, Leicesters. Hannibal eclipsed.'[2]

But once they became aware they were not dealing with a few airborne companies but a massive force which could not be suppressed by the local garrisons, the Japanese began to react. First of all, on 11 March, III Battalion (Yamashita)/114 Infantry Regiment of 18 Division, which had been in the Sagaing area near Mandalay, was told to restore the situation at Henu and in the hills north-east of Mawlu. Yamashita came up south of Henu on 17 March, took over what was left of Nagahashi's companies, attacked Calvert on the 21st, and was repulsed with heavy casualties.

Takemura Battalion (II/51 Infantry Regiment) left Hsipaw at 9.20 pm on 7 March, and moved in trucks by night to Mandalay, reaching it three days later. The delay was imposed by the need to avoid Allied aircraft.[3] The battalion stocked up with ammunition and left Mandalay on the 10th for Sagaing, reaching Indaw on 15 March. His men were delighted to find

---

[1] As he admits, in *The Wild Green Earth*, p. 99

[2] ibid., p. 57

[3] I have preferred this timetable for Takemura – relevant to Fergusson's plans for Indaw – because it is derived from the recollections of one of the section commanders involved (Hamachi Toshio, *Inpāru sai-zensen*, p. 26) and the details are more circumstantial than those given in OCH *Inpāru Sakusen*, II, p. 153, where Takemura's date of departure is given as 12 March, and his arrival in the Indaw area as 27 March.

groves of trees, with papayas and mangoes in abundance. Takemura gave 7 Company (Ite) the role of reserve, told 5 Company (Matsumura) and 8 Company (Iwasaki) to start reconnoitring the enemy's positions round Mawlu, and sent 6 Company (Sakazawa) to Katha. Sunset was at 9 pm when Sakazawa left for Katha on 15 March, and the moon came up at 1.35 am. His men clambered onto trucks in Indaw station in the darkness and made for Katha. An interesting place for them, not merely as an old royal capital but also as a town with many Buddhist associations: they heard temple bells sounding along the river bank as they approached it, and they thought how good it would be to die in a place consecrated to Buddha, where they could see the orange-robed monks coming and going at the temple gates and watch their silhouettes at prayer, where the pagoda stood on a hillock against the sky and the Irrawaddy snaked slowly along amid the dense luxuriant jungle. Perhaps the British airborne troops could hear the temple bells too?

Although they did not know it, Takemura's men were about to encounter Fergusson's 16 Brigade, and they were every bit as exhausted as his men of the Leicesters and Queens. They had marched from Thailand after what seemed like endless months of back-breaking road works, and each man had on his back between 65 and 70lbs of kit which tugged at his shoulders and spinal column: twenty days' rations, four hand-grenades, 240 rounds of rifle ammunition, sixty rounds in reserve, great-coat, tent, blanket, water-bottle, mess-tin, gas-mask, pick and shovel.[1] Whenever they got up after resting, their legs buckled under them, they became dizzy and lost their balance. Staggering under this burden, Sakazawa's men were brought to a petrified halt as they made their way through the hills alongside the Irrawaddy, by a sound which seemed to them like the waves of the sea breaking over the forest. It was a host of wild monkeys chattering away in the distance as they swarmed up from the valley floor to the tops of the hills. Sakazawa reached Katha on 16 March, the same day Southern Area Army, alerted by Kawabe in Rangoon, notified Imperial General Headquarters in Tokyo of Stilwell's advance down the Hukawng and Wingate's airborne landings. The signal estimated the number of men dropped in the Katha area as around 1000, and reported that they were making airstrips at Inywa and Mohnyin.[2]

As Sakazawa came out of the forest, Mustangs broke through a gap in the clouds, swooped low, and raked the area with machine-gun fire. 'We've been spotted!' yelled one of his men, 'Let's get back!' There was no going

---

[1] 'The total weight on the man when we first set out was about 72lb', writes Fergusson of the first Chindit operation, 'half the weight of the average man, and more in proportion to a man's weight than the load carried by a mule. The Everest pack fitting alone weighed 6lb; seven days' rations 14lb... The man also carried rifle and bayonet, *dah* or *kukri*, three grenades, ground-sheet, spare shirt and trousers, four spare pairs of socks, balaclava, jack-knife, rubber shoes, housewife, toggle-rope, canvas life-jacket, mess-tin, ration bags, water bottle, *chagal* (canvas water-bottle) and many statutory odds and ends.' (*Beyond the Chindwin*, p. 249.)

[2] Hamachi, op.cit., p. 26

back: at that moment Lance Corporal Hakabe ran up and reported enemy troops from a nearby group of huts, moving in their direction. The platoon vanished into the forest and watched. About 800 yards away, a group of men with packs on their backs and rifles appeared. Hamachi, the Japanese section commander, told his men to hold their fire, then, when the enemy group had come to within 5–600 yards, he gave the order to get ready to fire. At 300 yards he rapped out 'Fire!' realizing this gave a good opportunity to Hakabe, the section's LMG expert, who reckoned a hundred bulls for a hundred shots. Rifles and LMGs spat fire together. The eight men were taken by surprise, but recovered at once, and four of them dashed forward, careless of Japanese bullets. 'They may be the enemy, but they've got guts,' Hamachi thought; then one of them, hit by LMG fire, gave a scream of pain and fell, blood pouring from him. 'Got him!' one of Hamachi's men called, 'Got him!', and went on firing. 'Hakabe, we're firing high – 250 yards, shoot lower!' Hakabe was standing upright, swinging his LMG from left to right as he sprayed the oncoming British. Two or three fell, the rest dropped to the ground, began to crawl forward, then panicked and ran off. 'Cease fire! Take the rest alive!' Hamachi yelled, and took his section in pursuit. To the fury of the pursuers, the survivors managed to escape. They searched the pockets and packs of the dead, shared out the cigarettes, chewing gum and tinned rations, and started off again. The going was hard, and they had to hack their way through thorns and creepers. Finally, after making less than two miles through the jungle, they returned to the Company where Hamachi was told the enemy airborne force was now estimated at around 10,000 men. 'Ignorance is bliss', he thought. If he'd really gone after those men, his section might have got more than it bargained for . . . Sakazawa told him that two days before they got to Katha, Japanese troops concealed in a dyke by the bank of a river eighty yards wide had kept under observation a group of British airborne troops crossing the river by raft. The raft carried guns, ammunition and mules, and the Japanese waited till it was in midstream before firing. The quiet of the river was turned into an inferno with the sound of rifles, the screams of wounded men, and the braying of the pack-animals. 'We've got you, you hairy foreign bastards!'[1] the Japanese shouted as they poured bullets into the raft. The river ran red with blood, and the British soldiers who survived the first burst hurled themselves into the river and dived under, disappearing in the weeds on the river-bed. It was a matter of a few seconds; then, some minutes later, British gun fire began to probe the river bank and fighter planes strafed it. The Japanese returned to their Company. It was learned the following day that they had bumped into part of a unit, 5–600 strong, which was on its way, split into several columns, from Katha to the area west of Indaw.[2]

[1] '*Kutabare, ketome ga!*' (Hamachi, op.cit., p. 32)

[2] i.e. part of Lentaigne's 111 Brigade.

At 2.10 pm on 17 March, Sakazawa was ordered to return to Takemura Battalion's position at Indaw. Matsumura and Iwasaki Companies were locked in combat with airborne troops at Mawlu, and Ite and Takemura Battalion Headquarters troops had discovered British troops in the jungle close to the railway garrison unit's position at Indaw. This put Takemura in a quandary. He had intended to move to Mawlu to join the battle there, but his forces were split north and south by this incursion into his rear. He decided to put in a night commando raid on the British near Indaw. His men's spirits had been at a low ebb, looking for the enemy and not finding him; now, suddenly, their morale shot up, they were spoiling for a fight.

Eight lorry-loads of Japanese infantry drove west through the darkness, headlights weaving through the forest. The intense heat of the day had given way to a thick mist, the rapid change of temperature seemed to induce fatigue, and the men shivered with cold. A crescent moon cast a pale light, and the only sounds were the vibrations of the engines and the clatter of the bodywork. Soon they were in the enemy area, and the noises disappeared, as the Japanese kept their ears open for the sound of the hunter's whistle which, they were told, was used by the British to signal to their men. And, too, for the sound of mules. When they heard whinnying, they knew the enemy was near. Hamachi waited with the other section commanders for dawn, and as the sky lightened, he saw in the morning mist nine pack animals in the thick grass in front of him, and an armoured car. Nearby were scattered mortars, machine-guns, boxes of ammunition, packs, carbines, W/T sets, compasses and watches. When the sky was clear, Sakazawa's company dived into this treasure-trove and made off with their booty, captured without a shot being fired.

Then Battalion Headquarters came through: 'British troops discovered.' At once, through the morning mist, Takemura's men put in an attack. The enemy was thrown off balance by the two assault sections, but soon reacted with grenades. Then Battalion Headquarters came into the battle, and the British were driven back, leaving prisoners in Takemura's hands: two glider pilots, British soldiers, and Kachins. To the surprise of the Japanese, they appeared unaffected by being taken prisoner, an unthinkable condition for a Japanese soldier. The Japanese were intrigued by the racial differences of their prisoners, particularly the gleaming white teeth and high noses of the Englishmen, who seemed aristocratic; but their hair was longer than usual, as they had been wandering in the jungle for some time, and they were in a state close to exhaustion. The Kachins seemed to have had the warlike spirit knocked out of them: their faces twitched, as if their nerves were on edge. A bad smell rose from their bodies which were covered in mud and sweat. The entire body of one of the prisoners was covered with some kind of skin disease, and his sores were suppurating – Burma north of Wuntho had a reputation for epidemic diseases. The Japanese were still at the height of their battle anger, and threatened the

prisoners, jabbing at them with their bayonets. Then the battalion interpreter came up and began to question them, only to find that the glider
pilots, who told him the British always won in the end, steadfastly refused
information. The interpreter tried cajoling, moderating his tone, but he got
no further. Then, as everyone, both friend and foe, was watching him, he
lost patience and began to beat them angrily with a stick. 'Go on, bash
them good and hard!' the Japanese shouted, standing around in a ring. The
pilot who was being beaten stumbled forward a pace or two. At that
instant, the skin on his face burst open like a pomegranate and blood
poured from the wound, dripping on to his chest and down to his feet. His
lips were twisted with pain as he looked up at the sky. The interpreter's
rage increased, and without a second's pause he struck down with the stick
from brow to chin and shattered the pilot's jaw. Hamachi watched this
piece of cruelty, and then averted his gaze.[1]

As they picked through the captured weapons, Hamachi was fascinated
by a light automatic which seemed to be made with great precision – he
thought what an inferior weapon the old Japanese 38 infantry rifle was,
both from the point of view of weight and action. The scale of the airborne
rations amazed him, too: corned beef, bread, jam, sugar, coffee, tea,
cigarettes, tinned fruit, butter, cheese. It was an apt reflection of the
material might of the British Empire. He contrasted it mentally with the
Japanese rations, foraged locally, made bearable with pickled plums and
salt, with a piece of dried cod thrown in as makeweight. Then there were
the watches, compasses and specially printed maps of central and northern
Burma in coloured silk which the prisoners carried.

On the afternoon of 19 March, Takemura's men came back to their base
at Indaw. Reports came through from Colonel Sasaki, in command of 5
Railway Regiment and the Mawlu garrison, that he had been attacked by
strong enemy airborne forces, and that the iron bridge north of Indaw at
Nanhsiaing had been blown up. Indaw had been a peaceful place until
Mutaguchi had dreamed up his Imphal operation. Now it had become a
military depot, where 33 Division's rations were stored – twenty days'
rations for men, ten days' supply of ammunition, 4000–6000 regimental
gun shells, 4500 mortar bombs for 15 and 31 Divisions, twelve mortar
bombs for 18 Division in the far north, rifle ammunition, river crossing
materials, boats, and so on, all camouflaged under trees or hidden in the
forest. Between forest and railway lay the crude houses of the locals, many
of them friendly to the Japanese. Some of the Railway Regiment was
quartered in these huts; and 118 Field Hospital was set up nearby.

---

[1] Hamachi, p. 36. But the 'Aberdeen' garrison apparently could also be rough with prisoners.
Fergusson's anti-aircraft guns shot down seven planes in two days and took a pilot prisoner.
'He was a chatty creature, this pilot', writes Fergusson, 'and once he had recovered from a
misunderstanding with the butt of a Nigerian rifle, which made contact with his mouth, he
produced a lot of useful information.' (*Wild Green Earth*, pp. 90–1)

The arrival of the Chindits put an end to the Japanese feeling of security in Indaw. The locals soon became aware that the railway was cut, the constant presence of Allied aircraft in the skies and the burning of Japanese depots indicated on which side military strength now lay, and they began to greet the Japanese with coolness instead of smiles.[1]

The discrepancy in air strengths was patently obvious. In June 1943, British aircraft in eastern India numbered 503, US aircraft 337; by the end of the year the joint total was up to 1000 and by summer 1944 to 1500. The Japanese air force in Burma, No.4, No. 5 and No. 12 air groups,[2] had 69 fighters, 92 light and heavy bombers, a total of 161. No wonder that Tazoe could do nothing about Satō's despairing call for air supply. No wonder either, that Mutaguchi felt one feature of the Chindit operation would actually tell to his advantage: the Allied air command would be so involved flying in men, guns and rations across the Irrawaddy that they would not be present in force at his crossing-points on the Chindwin.

Fergusson at Indaw

Takemura Battalion's first clash with the Chindits in the Indaw area on 17 March was not necessarily an indication to the Japanese that it was going to be the objective of an Allied assault. As far as they could gather from their prisoners, they were a group detached from the main body; and the build-up near Mawlu suggested that that was where the strength lay. Nonetheless, Indaw's stocks were vital to the progress of hostilities in North Burma, and it was there that reinforcements were sent after that first holding action. As the scale of Operation THURSDAY became clearer to the Japanese, particularly to Burma Area Army in Rangoon, the reinforcements began to arrive.

II Battalion of 21 Field Artillery Regiment which, like Takemura Battalion, belonged to 15 Division, was ordered to make speed to Indaw. It had just arrived in Maymyo on its way to the Chindwin crossings. A staff officer, Lieutenant-Colonel Hashimoto Hiroshi, was despatched to Indaw to take command of the units likely to arrive there; more were soon on the way, and the command became too extensive for a mere colonel. The Tenasserim garrison, 24 Independent Mixed Brigade, Kawabe's defence against a possible British seaborne landing across the Gulf of Martaban against Moulmein, was ordered north to Mandalay on 14 March and placed under Mutaguchi's command. On 19 March, II Battalion/146 Infantry Regiment (Wakiyama) of 56 Division, then in Wanting forming a front against the Chinese in Yunnan, was told to move south down the railway

---

[1] Hamachi, op.cit., p. 39

[2] *Hikōdan*, or air brigade, of nine or more squadrons.

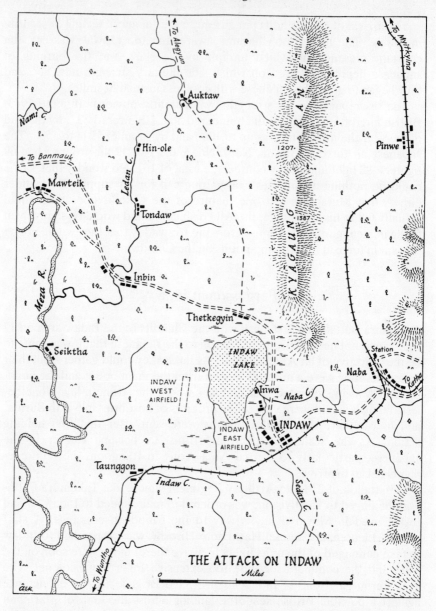

THE ATTACK ON INDAW

through Myitkyina and attack the Chindits in Mawlu from the north. II Battalion/29 Infantry Regiment (Harada) of 2 Division, which was coming up from Java and Sumatra to garrison the coast of the Bay of Bengal, was despatched by rail and air to Pegu as a contingency reinforcement. It was then sent forward to Mandalay.

The commander of 24 Independent Mixed Brigade, Major-General Hayashi Yoshihide, with 139 Independent Infantry Battalion, 141 Independent Infantry Battalion, and his brigade artillery, engineers and signals, left Moulmein on 18 March by rail for Mandalay. The main body of his brigade reached Indaw between 26 and 31 March. Colonel Ichikari brought II Infantry Regiment of 2 Division there on the 22nd, and Harada's battalion arrived on the 26th. Hayashi acted promptly, even though his disparate units had hardly time to receive orders. Harada was sent at once to the hills east of Indaw, and on the night of the 26th he occupied Thetkyegin on the north side of Lake Indaw. Three other battalions were thrown into the battle at Indaw in rapid succession. The speed of advance was creditable, given the vulnerability of Burma Area Army's communications, but it also had the result that there was a lack of a strong command structure even when General Hayashi arrived: infantry and artillery were not properly co-ordinated, and reconnaissance was poor. And the technique of the Stronghold ensured that whenever Hayashi's forces were drawn on to one of them, the concentration of artillery and dive bombing led to heavy Japanese casualties. On the other hand, their mere presence in Indaw frustrated Fergusson's plans to take it.

He had put his men through an agony of a march, merely to cover the first seventy miles to the Chindwin. Over the inadequately mapped terrain, where slopes could have gradients of one in two, which the tropical storms converted into landslides of mud, and where the climate of the valleys was torrid and the fly-plagued heights at night could chill to the bone, it would have been hazardous to take even a patrol.[1] Fergusson brought 4000 men and 500 laden mules over it. From their roadhead just before Tagap Ga on the Ledo Road to Hkalah Ga was a distance of thirty-five miles. It took them nine whole days. Wingate flew in to his Chindwin crossing-point on 2 March and watched two columns of the Queen's Regiment, creased with fatigue, get smartly across the river in a couple of hours. Indaw then lay 150 miles ahead as the crow flies, but crows were of little help in such country – it might mean another 300 miles up and down the razorback ridges, and it soon became evident that Fergusson was not going to be there on the date Wingate had fixed: 15 March. His two-column detour to Lonkin on behalf of Stilwell left him with six columns with which to take Indaw. He set up his stronghold at a village twenty miles west of Calvert at 'White City', and twenty-five miles northwest of his objective.[2]

---

[1] The extremes of fatigue had their toll later. Two men were found asleep when they should have been on sentry-go, and were subjected to the special punishment which Wingate, without any legal sanction whatever, had authorized for the Chindit columns. The men were flogged, and the column commander was tried by court-martial after the war as a result. He was exonerated: no glasshouse sentence could have rivalled the conditions under which the men were already living. (Bidwell, *The Chindit War*, pp. 136–7)

[2] ibid., pp. 134–6

It was christened 'Aberdeen', excellent from the point of view of water and friendly villagers, poor as an airfield. Wingate visited him there on 20 March, told him that he was bringing his reserve brigades into Burma as soon as he could, and that Fergusson was to scrap his original order of sporadically attacking the Japanese in the area of Indaw and Banmauk, and should instead leave at once for Indaw, take Indaw East airfield and hold it. According to Shelford Bidwell this was because Wingate's mind, not fixed on one particular plan, had veered back to TARZAN, a plan by which 26 Indian Division would be flown into an airfield in Northern Burma, thereby transforming the elaborate raids of the Chindits into something more ambitious and permanent.[1] That meant seizing Indaw with all speed, and, as we have seen, he had hoped Fergusson would be there on 15 March, instead of which the ferocious march across the Patkais and onwards to 'Aberdeen' had delayed Fergusson by five days. But 16 Brigade moved out of 'Aberdeen' to take Indaw, its commander assuming that 14 Brigade (Brodie) would collaborate in his attack; whereas Wingate had already ordered Brodie to march south-west, not south-east, from Indaw, establish his own stronghold and airstrip and harass the Japanese line of communications which led from Indaw to Homalin on the Chindwin, thereby contributing not to Stilwell's campaign, but to Slim's in Imphal.[2]

Fergusson's second-in-command at Rear Brigade Headquarters, Colonel F. O. ('Katie') Cave, certainly had the impression that, after 16 Brigade captured Indaw, its airfield was to be used to fly in more troops. In fact, on Wingate's own instructions, he went to Force Headquarters and read the entire Operation Order to see how 16 Brigade's role fitted in with the rest. 'Roughly speaking, we were going to move down to Indaw and capture the airfield which could then be used for flying in more troops.' But, he added, 'how long it remained the latest thing I don't know; as far as I can make out, Wingate was always changing the plan, and I often wondered who was in the know, and who really knew which the latest plan was.'[3]

This business of the role of Indaw, its effect on Fergusson's campaigns, and the implications for its assessment of Wingate as a commander, have been the object of much study, but surely Shelford Bidwell is right when he calls it a misunderstanding 'which did not, in fact, affect the course of events'.[4] The crucial thing for Fergusson was that the Japanese had reinforced Indaw when he arrived, and that would have been the case whether he had Brodie's help or not. He himself was always absolutely convinced that Indaw was to be held for a fly-in by at least one fresh

[1] ibid., p. 138

[2] ibid., p. 139

[3] Diaries of Colonel F. O. Cave, OBE, MC, p. 48, Imperial War Museum

[4] Bidwell, op.cit., p. 142

division. Nearly twenty years after the event, he wrote to Derek Tulloch, who had been Wingate's Brigadier, General Staff, at Headquarters in 1944:

> Although details are hazy in my mind after all these years, two points are crystal clear in my recollections...
>
> A. Throughout the campaign up to my failure at Indaw, I was in no doubt that Wingate intended me to think that the capture of the airfield would result in the introduction of either one or two non-Chindit divisions there.
>
> B. Equally, I was in no doubt that after I had brought the Indaw Japs to battle, the arrival on the field from the West of 14 Brigade (though not yet at full strength) was to be counted on.[1]

In this connection, there is a curious remark in Cave's diaries. Cave flew down to watch 16 Brigade cross the Chindwin near Singkaling Hkamti:

> I enjoyed the trip in the air flying over the most amazing tangled country and over high hills skirting the west bank of the Chindwin, until at last we dropped down and came to a river that flowed into the Chindwin close to Singkaling Hkamti. Here we were right down to ground level, banking round the corner and thoroughly enjoying ourselves. There was nothing; just river and jungle; each corner that we rounded revealed the same familiar scene, until suddenly after turning one corner we found a scene of great activity, many people about on the sandbank, and a continuous flow of small craft across the river. We did one quick look round and then planted ourselves down on a suitable-looking bit of sand... What fun it was, and how one felt one was taking part in something almost historical. Rather a long trudge over soft sand to Brigade Headquarters where I found Wingate about to leave, so nothing much happened until after he had gone. He appeared to be in one of his better moods, but stressed the need for getting the aircraft away from the sandbank to avoid giving things away. I asked him if he would tell Bernard [Fergusson] his plans for pinching our reinforcements for the use of other brigades. His only reply was, 'I don't think you need worry your brigadier with that.' Needless to say, I promptly did so. However there is nothing more to be said about the matter, although it was one which occupied me for many a week or more to come.[2]

[1] Imperial War Museum Archives

[2] Cave Diaries, loc.cit.

It was not clear what 'reinforcements' are referred to, and of course on this same occasion Wingate swam in the Chindwin with Fergusson and brought him up to date. So either in his talk with Wingate on 2 March 1944 – in which he warned Wingate he could not reach the Banmauk-Indaw area before 20 March – or with Cave the day after, Fergusson should have been *au fait* with the most recent planning. Wingate was more concerned that Fergusson was going to be late on target, and an exasperated comment at a supply drop conference at Imphal on 16 March seems to indicate that his conception of the role of 16 Brigade was not clear. 'I remember,' writes Cave, 'the problem of Strongholds cropped up, and I knew that no one really knew what he wanted to do with 16 Brigade, nor with 111 Brigade, and so I asked him "Is it your intention that 16 Brigade and 111 Brigade should have their Strongholds more or less at the same place and use the same airstrip?" He said, "My dear Cave, how the hell can I tell until I have seen the place?"'[1] After Cave visited Fergusson at Manhton on the march to 'Aberdeen' – flown in by C64 – he returned to Rear Headquarters at Lalaghat and told Tulloch that 16 Brigade's Stronghold would be empty as Fergusson was being bustled on to Indaw, and that 12 Battalion Nigerian Regiment (Hughes) should be got there to garrison it as fast as possible. Tulloch told him that the whole plan of campaign had been changed, that Wingate had decided to move in 14 Brigade at once to 'Aberdeen', whence they could move out to their appointed place. When Cave protested that the Japanese might move on 'Aberdeen' first, Tulloch got on the phone to Wingate who remained adamant: 14 Brigade should go in before the Nigerians.

Fergusson, fully convinced that Brodie's men would join in the Indaw battle, 'hoping hourly to get news of them', pressed on to Indaw.[2] Wingate's insistence on timing prevented him waiting for his two columns sent against Lonkin, 51 and 69, now ten days behind the main body: the Chinese had been dilatory in replacing them. Fergusson compounded this numerical weakness by mistakes of his own. He had failed to see that his troops were rested before the assault; and he had not sent reconnaissance ahead to check the lie of the land between 'Aberdeen' and Indaw, so that he was horrified when he learnt it was waterless. Mid-March in North Burma is torrid and dry and Fergusson had four columns of men, plus his own Headquarters column, and several hundred mules to water. After a brisk encounter with a unit of the Burma National Army together with some Japanese at the village of Auktaw about six miles north of Indaw, 45 Column (Cumberlege) and the Leicesters (17 Column, Wilkinson) realized that the men and mules would have to reach the lake at Indaw before they found water. Cumberlege was told to take his men into Thetkegyin, a

[1] ibid., p. 59

[2] Fergusson, *The Wild Green Earth*, p. 114

village on the north side of the lake, while Fergusson moved on Indaw directly with the Leicesters. 45 Column found Thetkegyin occupied by the Japanese who made Cumberlege's men pay heavily for their attempts to get through to the precious water. Wingate and Fergusson had agreed on a plan by which the Kyagaung Ridge overlooking the town of Indaw and its lake would provide the approach march. The road to Banmauk would be cut by another column, to stop the Japanese reinforcing from the west; and a further column would loop round and come up at Indaw from the south. This task devolved on the Queen's, who were attacked by lorried infantry, lost their mules in the mêlée, and so could not carry their heavy weapons. Their colonel was wounded into the bargain. Fergusson realized they had ceased to be a major factor in his attack, and told them to harass the Japanese as best they could. The 45 Recce Regiment which made up 45 and 54 Columns had an appalling accident when an explosive bullet ignited a mule carrying flame-throwing fuel.[1] Crazed by the pain and flames, the mule hurled itself against a dump of mortar bombs and ammunition and exploded the lot.

---

[1] Flame-throwers were a conspicuous feature of Special Force equipment. They are an ugly weapon, and present dreadful hazards to the user as well as the victims. 'I saw one of the flame-thrower men hit and be set on fire. "Oh God, I can't...", came a cry from the flames.' (Calvert, *Prisoners of Hope*, p. 234). One use of them, almost in revenge, is referred to by James Baggaley, a subaltern in Fergusson's 16 Brigade. Another subaltern from a sister column had been caught by the Japanese and shot with three of his men. His arms were crossed as if to protect his face, and were badly slashed, as if a Japanese had tried to cut him across the head with a sword. Baggaley was disgusted at the brutality of this attack, and said so to a fellow-officer who was a regular soldier and reacted differently. 'He calmly condoned an incident that filled me with horror. He seemed to bear neither malice nor hatred towards our opponents for this crime...' But Baggaley was appalled by it, and his appetite for revenge was satiated on a party of five Japanese ambushed later by two flame-thrower operators. The weapon was nicknamed 'lifebuoy' from its shape and carried on the back like a rucksack, from which came a pipe and nozzle. Baggaley gave the signal to fire:

> The flames leapt up from the fuel as it pitched on the undergrowth and foliage, and within seconds the trees were ablaze. One Jap took a burst of flame full in his back and, with a piercing scream, disintegrated. The others ran about in circles trying to find a way through the inferno, but there was only one exit and we were waiting for them. They found it and came rushing towards us. One man half raised his arms in surrender, but I'm afraid he was just too late, and received a jet of fire full in the face; he went down writhing. The others were very soon human fire-balls. They dashed madly backwards and forwards in all directions, and the flame-throwers went after them. As the flames clung to them, and consumed their bodies, their screaming and shrieking ceased and they fell to the ground, charred heaps of flesh and bones. Except one. Only the bottom half of his body was burning, and he was rolling over and over on the ground trying to beat out the flames, screaming horribly all the time. I raised my rifle. Then I heard one of the men say quietly: "Let the --er die slowly. He's one of the --ers who killed my wounded mate ..." Suddenly I thought of that subaltern a few hours back. I lowered my rifle.'

Walking back from the scene, Baggaley could not understand what sadistic instinct had made him lower his rifle, when a squeeze on the trigger would have put an end to abominable suffering. And the man with the flame-thrower had gloated; yet Baggaley knew him for a kind and sensitive man. (*A Chindit Story*, pp. 96–97)

The death of Wingate

Fergusson was unable to get any sense from his rear W/T link at 'Aberdeen', and Rear Brigade Headquarters, with Cave, had been packed off from their location near Imphal just before the Japanese closed the road out of the Plain. They were moved right back to Sylhet in Assam, and meanwhile Fergusson was left without wireless contact for twenty-four hours. There was even a rumour that 'Aberdeen' had been suddenly overwhelmed by the Japanese, and the US light plane force decamped to Taro, on the strength of the rumour (Paul Rebori, its commander, was later sacked by Cochran for not verifying the rumour). Fergusson knew that Indaw was held by a couple of thousand Japanese, perhaps more; and he had 1800 men. And the Japanese in Indaw would be expecting him. He attributed this later to 111 Brigade moving from 'Broadway' on its way to Pinlebu, and asking villagers en route about Indaw as if that were their objective instead. But, as we have already seen, Takemura had already been alerted to the presence of Chindits in the Indaw area before this, by pure chance. So Indaw would probably have been strengthened anyway.

Even so, even with only three columns available to him, Fergusson might still have taken Indaw. The Second Leicesters, led by Colonel Wilkinson with his wounded arm in a sling, reached the edge of the airfield before they bumped into the Japanese. They dug in on the banks of a stream, the Inwa Chaung, which saved them from 45 Recce Regiment's pathetic fight at Thetkegyin to fill its water-bottles; and held out for three days against Japanese frontal attack. First Air Commando gave them razor-close bombing support and if the rest of 16 Brigade had had equal luck – and better mapping and intelligence – they might have gone into Indaw and taken the airstrip. As it was, Fergusson felt compelled to withdraw his scattered forces and turn back to 'Aberdeen', to recoup strength and try again. 'They had attacked as clutching fingers from all sides, and not as a fist', is Calvert's accurate summary.[1] It became clear that 'Aberdeen' was not under threat, and the Nigerians were arriving to garrison it. But to Fergusson's great anger, the much-awaited 14 Brigade was moving south down the Taung and Meza valleys and not towards him at Indaw at all. It later occurred to him that the plan he and Wingate had agreed upon had never reached Force Headquarters, and so the staff there would be merely puzzled by his insistent signals about Brodie's columns.[2] The man in whose head the plan lay, according to Fergusson, was now a corpse on a hillside in Assam. For, on 24 March, Orde Wingate's plane flew into the reverse slope of a hillside on leaving Imphal, and all its occupants were killed. Fergusson knew that not only his own plans were

---

[1] Calvert, *Prisoners of Hope*, p. 97

[2] Bidwell, op.cit., pp. 147–8; Fergusson, *The Wild Green Earth*, pp. 116–17

not heard of. The entire operation was now at risk: 'Wingate was dead, and his Plan with him.'[1]

The Official History suggests that Wingate's orders (23 March) for 14 Brigade to move south to Alezu, twenty-one miles south-west of Pinlebu, to interrupt Japanese communications between Wuntho and the Chindwin, were either a misinterpretation of, or disregard for, Slim's wishes.[2] Other writers have echoed this. 'The 14th Brigade began to fly in on the night of the 23rd/24th,' wrote the late Arthur Swinson, 'but Wingate went against Slim's orders instructing its commander, Ian Brodie, to cut enemy communications between Wuntho and the Chindwin. Unhappily, he forgot to tell Fergusson of this plan, and the latter therefore expected the Brigade to help him at Indaw, as promised.'[3]

The authors of the pro-Wingate *requisitoire* against the Official History point out that Slim agreed to release 14 Brigade to Wingate on 21 March but that his reservations about using it against the communications to Imphal as opposed to those against Stilwell referred to Slim's view of the long-term objective of Special Force: 'For 14 Brigade to operate against the Japanese Fifteenth Army communications would hardly be to change Wingate's main object, on which the three original Chindit brigades were still operating and were about to be joined by 3 West African Brigade.'[4]

In the fluid state of operations round Imphal in April, Slim was perfectly prepared, *himself*, to contemplate the use of Special Force astride Mutaguchi's lines to the Chindwin. And Wingate, naturally, had contingency plans for changes in circumstance. Plan A devoted his energies to Stilwell, the role laid down for him by XIV Army orders of 4 February 1944; he also had his Plan B, which included fulfilling his commitment to Stilwell, but also the use of 14 and 23 Brigades against the Japanese lines to the Chindwin.[5] He would have been a fool not to envisage the latter possibility; and if Fergusson got into difficulties at Indaw, it was perfectly within Wingate's power to direct Brodie's 14 Brigade on to him *then*. Fergusson's later grievance against Wingate, Mead and Thompson suppose, arose because he was shown Wingate's operation order to Brodie, of which, until then, he had been unaware. It hurt all right. 'At times the truth was simply not in him',[6] was a bitter phrase from his final verdict in print, and 'I stand by every word of that carefully considered

[1] ibid., p. 117

[2] Kirby, *War Against Japan*, III, pp. 212, 218

[3] 'Wingate's Last Campaign', *History of the Second World War*, Purnell, vol.V, No.10, p. 2053

[4] Sir Robert Thompson and Brigadier P. W. Mead, 'Memorandum on *The War Against Japan*, Vol. III, in its judgment on Wingate', lodged in the Imperial War Museum, 78/12/L, 1978.

[5] Tulloch, *Wingate in Peace and War*, pp. 193–4

[6] Fergusson, *Trumpet in the Hall*, p. 177

judgement', he wrote ten years later.[1] His exasperation is understandable, since the defeat at Indaw rankled. But it is clear from 'Katie' Cave's diaries that he did not meet Wingate on 23 March, the day the operation order was issued, though he says he did.[2] Wingate was prevented from passing on the new dispositions for the best of reasons: the following day he was dead.

It should be noted that there were positive results from Fergusson's incursion into the Indaw area, though he did not seize it. He discovered the massive dumps which the Japanese built up in the area from which to supply their forward divisions. He told Cave about them, and Cave on his return called on Cochran at Hailakandi and asked him to lay on a bombing raid, which he did, 'but reported that there had not been any visible result from it'.[3] There seems no doubt, though, that the strike *was* effective, though upon supplies to 18 Division and not to Mutaguchi at Imphal: 'All Japanese troops were disposed for the Imphal operation, all arrangements made, all supplies, etc. dumped. The Chindits affected none of this, and none of those troops were diverted.'[4] Major Usui, 15 Army's Staff Officer (Supply), Major-General Okada, 15 Division's Chief of Staff, and Major Ushiro, Burma Area Army's Staff Officer (Supply) were interrogated about the effects of the Chindit operations on Japanese supply and declared that 2 Transport Headquarters' plans were completely frustrated by them, and that as a result neither 15 nor 31 Division received additional supplies for emergencies once their 25-day allocation ran out.[5] It is interesting, incidentally, that parties to the debate on Indaw do not appear to have noticed that Slim clearly believed Brodie *had* helped Fergusson in his attack: 'Fergusson's 16 Brigade', he writes, '*supported by part of Brodie's 14 Brigade*, moved out of 'Aberdeen' and attempted to seize Indaw by surprise.'[6]

Wingate's death at such a moment, with Stilwell moving down on Myitkyina, IV Corps locked in a battle with three Japanese divisions at Imphal, and Wingate's own operation already well under way, was one of those tragic events that create their own myth, so that the very basic facts seem hard to ascertain. The weather, for instance. 'Curiously, the night Wingate was killed,' wrote Cave, 'I was up at the same time and in much the same area, and I am not conscious of any bad weather. There was a thunderstorm about, but my recollection is that it was very local and there was no difficulty in getting round it. I was surprised to hear that he had

---

[1] Private communication to the author, 16 October, 1980

[2] Fergusson, *Wild Green Earth*, p. 98

[3] Cave, *Diaries*, p. 65

[4] Interrogation of General Kimura, Lieutenant-General Naka, and Major Kaetsu, *Burma Command Intelligence Summary*, No. 13, 28 March 1946.

[5] *Reply to Questionnaire on Operation of 3 Indian Division*, p. 26

[6] Slim, *Defeat into Victory*, p. 270; my italics.

crashed. A long time later, we learned that his plane had been found in the hills west of Imphal, some miles off its proper route, and that although it was heading for Sylhet the plane was found pointing eastwards as though it had been making for Imphal again.'[1]

'The wreckage was eventually found on the reverse side of a ridge,' writes Slim, 'so it was unlikely that the aircraft had flown into the hill. The most probable explanation is that it had suddenly entered one of those local storms of extreme turbulence so frequent in the area. These were difficult to avoid at night, and once in them an aeroplane might be flung out of control, or even have its wings torn off.'[2]

Flying Officer Joe Simpson, of 194 Squadron, RAF, based on Agartala, was at Imphal at the same time as Wingate's plane took off. 'On March 23rd,' he writes, 'I was at Imphal after two trips between Dohazari and Imphal and was waiting to go back to Agartala. I was told to hang on because I might have to go via Comilla, as Wingate was waiting to go. As it turned out, he decided not to go by RAF and so I was despatched. The weather was particularly bad – I made a note that we came back via Silchar. We found a hole and circled down through it until we were below the cloud and thence home.

As we came out of the bottom I clearly recall seeing a Mitchell coming down through the cloud and said: "Look at that silly so-and-so, he's too near the hills!" I have never really known where or when Wingate crashed, but I think it was about this day and place.'[3]

Wilfred Russell, who quotes Simpson's account in his history of 194 Squadron RAF, points out that this disposes of the tale, current at the time, that the RAF would not fly Wingate out of Imphal because the weather was too bad, so he turned to the Americans who were ready to take him in any weather. Wingate's biographer, Christopher Sykes, says, 'Stories were told afterwards that Wingate was advised against flying because of storms, and that with characteristic impetuosity, he overruled his American pilot, Lieutenant Hodges. All this is imagined. There was no reason to fear a difficult journey either to Lalaghat or Comilla. There were isolated storms, but in the main the weather was fine.' He adds a footnote from Air Marshal Sir John Baldwin, commander of Third Tactical Air Force: 'It was quite a good flying day and the isolated storms could be avoided.'[4] (It was to see Baldwin that Wingate flew to Imphal in the first place.)[5]

---

[1] Cave, *Diaries*, p. 22

[2] Slim, op.cit., pp. 268–9

[3] Wilfred Russell, *The Friendly Firm, A History of 194 Squadron, Royal Air Force*, 1972, p. 40

[4] Sykes, *Orde Wingate*, p. 534

[5] 'Baldwin flew off in his own aircraft for Comilla immediately after the B25. He remembers that the weather that evening was good apart from a few thunderclouds, and his log book confirms this fact. Baldwin says that he saw the B25 in the evening light flying on a level course up to within six minutes of the crash.' (Calvert, *Chindits*, pp. 85–9)

As far as the conditions on the airfield were concerned, a brisk note from one of the last men to see Wingate alive, Frank Thomas, reads: 'March 24th, '44. Wingate took off in Mitchell bomber (B25) in pissing rain.'[1] Thomas was on duty at the all-weather airstrip at Imphal, and remembers that the American pilot of the B25 was told by the senior airfield controller (Squadron-Leader John B. Hewitson) that weather conditions were 10/10ths all over. Hodges replied, 'The old man [Wingate] wants to go, so I guess I'd better take him.' Wingate was pacing up and down the area round the control tower in the torrential rain, in complete disregard of the soaking he was receiving, obviously itching to be off. It does not seem that he overruled Hodges, but his impetuosity and urge to be off are totally in character, and his death, in this way, seems in complete conformity with his life.

Slim's problem was how to replace Wingate. He was ten days into the Imphal battle by this time, and it was IV Corps that was in the forefront of his mind. But if Wingate's Operation THURSDAY were to succeed as its author had planned, it was vital that his leadership should fall on someone in sympathy with his ideas and difficult personality, dedicated to the success of the enterprise, and able to defend Special Force against hostility in the higher echelons of command. Slim chose Brigadier W. D. Lentaigne, the commander of 111 Brigade, who regarded Wingate as an upstart, held his theories in contempt, and thought them unsound and unproven.[2] Lentaigne had already shown himself to be physically inadequate for the severe trials of the campaign.[3] Under his command, the momentum slowed, and the great concept dimmed. In the end, the Chindits were villainously misused, and he was powerless to prevent it.

The natural question is, how on earth could this happen? There were a number of possible successors to Wingate. The second-in-command was Major-General W. G. Symes, an able officer, who had had to step down for Wingate in the first place when his 70 Division was split up to make the columns of Special Force. There was Derek Tulloch, Brigadier General Staff at Rear Headquarters, who had known Wingate since their days as cadets together at Woolwich. There was Calvert, perhaps the most dedicated to Wingate's theories of all the brigade commanders, who had run the Bush Warfare School in Burma in 1942 and had led a column into Burma in 1943. And there was Lentaigne, a gallant Gurkha officer who had fought the whole way up through Burma in the defeat of 1942, an able regimental officer and a brave man, who had raised his own 111 Brigade on

---

[1] Private communication.

[2] Bidwell, *The Chindit War*, p. 161

[3] Rhodes-James, *Chindit*, p. 87

Chindit principles in 1943 as part of the expansion of Wingate's Long Range Penetration Groups.

Slim did not act without advice. Tulloch's steady, unflappable behaviour at Lalaghat when the news arrived that 'Piccadilly' was blocked minutes before take-off, had impressed him, so he phoned Tulloch on the 26th to discuss who should take over. Tulloch had been promised command by Wingate in the event of anything happening to him.[1] Wingate had, of course, no right to do this, and in any case Tulloch ruled himself out because he had never commanded a Chindit column in the field. The same thing applied to Symes, and Calvert was no doubt considered a man of flair and dash on the battlefield, but perhaps not apt for higher command – a mistake, since Calvert was not only fanatically brave, and full of invention, but a trained Royal Engineer capable of detailed planning. Tulloch went over the possibilities with Slim, then told him that of all the candidates for command, Lentaigne was 'the one most in tune with Wingate'.[2]

Tulloch, in his own account of the phone call ('the most difficult telephone conversation I have ever had in my life')[3] does not give his reasons for this extraordinary statement, which could not be more at variance with the facts. Lentaigne had been imposed on Wingate, to whom he was anathema, Fergusson wrote later.[4] But Tulloch is probably right in thinking that Slim had come to the same conclusion: Lentaigne, like Slim, was a Gurkha officer, and Slim wanted someone with the same regimental background as himself, who would not be so painfully difficult and unorthodox as Wingate, and would not threaten him with telegrams direct to Churchill whenever his desires were thwarted. The next day Tulloch flew to Comilla to discuss the future of Wingate's plans with Slim and Irwin, Slim's Brigadier General Staff. Slim badly wanted Special Force to move back from its Strongholds to help his battle against Mutaguchi at Imphal and proposed that all the Chindits should be concentrated in the Kalewa area to hit 15 Army's communications close to the battle. Tulloch demurred, pointing out that both Calvert and Fergusson were engaged in battle and could not break contact, and that the configuration of the Zibyu Hills near the Chindwin would make it far too easy to attack the Chindits on their approach march. So the plan was scrapped, rightly so, because it would have meant Calvert leaving 'White City', his stranglehold on Japanese supplies to North Burma, which was preventing Kawabe reinforcing his 18 Division against Stilwell. A compromise was reached – already envisaged by Wingate's contingency planning – by which 14 and 111 Brigade would move west and block the roads supposed to be used by

[1] So had two others of Wingate's subordinates (Slim, *Defeat into Victory*, p. 269)

[2] Bidwell, op.cit., p. 160

[3] Tulloch, *Wingate in Peace and War*, p. 236

[4] Fergusson, *Trumpet in the Hall*, p. 179

15 and 31 Divisions; but Tulloch later blamed himself for not backing Slim's plan to the hilt, as it would have saved Special Force from later being taken over by Stilwell and so misused by him that 90% of its casualties were incurred under his command.[1]

At any rate, Lentaigne was flown out of Burma on 30 March to take command of the Chindits. He was, as one of the commanders who saw him at the time obsērved, a very worried man, who expected both 'Broadway' and 'White City' to fall to the Japanese in a couple of days – events that never occurred – and utterly failing to inspire confidence. Symes was understandably furious at being passed over and it is clear from his diary that he apportions the blame for this equally between Tulloch and Slim. He was at Force HQ when Tulloch phoned Slim to announce a burnt-out plane had been spotted and that Wingate must be presumed to have crashed:

25th March (Saturday)
Tulloch then rang up Army HQ to tell Slim and returned to me saying that (1) as he was completely in the picture Gen. Slim had said that he was to take command (2) that it meant no reflection on me (3) that he (Tulloch) had suggested that as Lentaigne was more in Gen. Wingate's mind than anyone else, he should be withdrawn from the field at the earliest possible time and take command of the operations (4) that Gen. Slim had agreed.

An astonishing message and an astonishing way of conveying it. I have known and sensed that Tulloch has been in opposition to me all the time and has made no effort to keep me in the picture. Reason I don't know other than that he knows I disagree with some – or most – of the administrative methods. Anyhow there was no object, profit or decorum in arguing so I summoned the Anson and flew to Comilla after lunch to see Slim. I saw him at 4 and asked him where I stood. He professed that he didn't know I was in these parts before. He then told me that until he had told Tulloch to take command he didn't know I was there. *Then* Tulloch told him and he didn't alter it because he didn't know what my status was. He then told me that the suggestion re Lentaigne came from Tulloch (but hedged afterwards) and he had agreed because he hadn't thought about me at all. I pointed out that by his action he had superseded me and had created a difficult situation. He said that he hadn't meant that at all and had made the decision hurriedly and had not had time to think it out...

Symes then went on to see Giffard, who told him Slim wanted to put in Lentaigne. 'I didn't like the way it was done, there was a lot of evasive action

---

[1] Tulloch, op.cit., p. 239

and I told Giffard so', he noted the next day.[1] Symes next made a formal protest to the Chief of Imperial General Staff in London, and asked to be relieved as deputy commander. Tulloch, who had not worked for that particular result, found himself appointed to Symes's job; ironically enough, as Symes did not value Tulloch much.[2] Nor, in the upshot, did Lentaigne, who bypassed him and relied more on Brigadier Neville Marks, a brilliant administrator who ran the Chindit supply organization. Morris, commanding officer of the 4/9 Gurkhas, then leading his own mini-column called Morris Force on the other side of the Irrawaddy, was promoted to lead 111 Brigade. But Morris was involved in pushing his 1300 men up fast to Myitkyina via Bhamo, so a compromise was reached, whereby Morris was left *in situ* but promoted to Brigadier,[3] and the actual command of 111 Brigade devolved on its brigade major, John Masters – a Gurkha officer like Lentaigne – who henceforth had the uncomfortable task of ordering into battle as column commanders men senior in rank to himself.

Lentaigne was present at a meeting at Jorhat on 3 April attended by Mountbatten, Slim and Stilwell, Baldwin, Boatner and Stopford. The situation on IV Corps front was gloomy, and Stilwell, perturbed lest his railhead at Ledo be taken by Japanese advancing from Kohima, offered Slim a Chinese division to reinforce the Imphal front, an offer which was politely refused. Slim did, however, permanently remove one of Special Force brigades, 23, to operate with Stopford on the flanks of Kohima, but he assured Stilwell that Lentaigne's other brigades would remain on the lines of communication of the Japanese forces facing him, and he should go all out for Myitkyina.[4] If Stilwell's own line of communication were cut, it would not be for more than ten days. It was also agreed, with Mountbatten's consent, that two Chindit Brigades (14 and 111) would operate towards the Chindwin, to relieve the pressure on IV Corps.[5] Lentaigne flew to 'Aberdeen' to meet his brigade commanders and told them there would be pressure to divert them to the Imphal front, which Calvert and Fergusson both opposed.[6] Fergusson wanted another crack at Indaw, and Calvert naturally thought 'White City' and 'Broadway' should continue to function. There was discontent even in Lentaigne's own Brigade, where it was felt they were 'at the beck and call of anyone who felt in need of help and our strategic plan would be discarded'.[7]

[1] Symes Diaries, Imperial War Museum.

[2] Bidwell, op.cit., p. 160

[3] He was, says Bidwell (op.cit., p. 187) 'overbearing, tactless and authoritarian, the last man to be entrusted with the political and military subtleties of clandestine warfare.' Morris was later to command 62 Brigade of 19 Indian Division.

[4] Slim, *Defeat into Victory*, pp. 272–3

[5] Kirby, *War Against Japan*, III, p. 247

[6] He only paid one further visit to the forces in the field (Bidwell, op.cit., p. 169)

[7] Rhodes-James, op.cit., p. 92

Six days later, Slim's orders to Lentaigne about the two brigades operating on the road west from Indaw were cancelled. He would let Stopford keep Perowne's 23 Brigade, but Special Force as a whole would otherwise maintain its original role of helping Stilwell. More than that, they would come directly under Stilwell's command. Lentaigne was to set up an advanced Headquarters at Shaduzup, next to Northern Combat Area Command's Headquarters. Perhaps he had already decided that 'Broadway' and 'White City' were no longer tenable, perhaps his own move north naturally made him feel the Chindit operation should be closer to Stilwell. At any rate, the order was given to abandon 'White City' and establish another block on the railway near Hopin, closer to Mogaung. This was not a wise move. Long Range Penetration succeeds only if it is remote from the front, where its aid consists of cutting supplies and communications, and that can be done far to the rear. In addition, Calvert had not only established a solid position on the block at Henu: the Japanese had thrown everything at him they could to dislodge him, and had failed. 'Broadway' was attacked on 27 March: it had already been strafed and bombed by twenty Oscar fighters on 13 March, when the radar was wrecked and four light aircraft were damaged. Five Spitfires took off against the Japanese, and downed four of them with the help of anti-aircraft guns, for the loss of one of their own number. They returned for another dog-fight on the 18 March, when three Spitfires were destroyed on the ground, and two Oscars were shot down.[1] A few days later, twelve Japanese medium bombers came over and dropped anti-personnel and 500lb bombs with great accuracy. Then, on the 27th, the infantry moved in. Colonel Claud Rome, who was in charge at 'Broadway', had artillery under his command, was surrounded by a belt of barbed wire, and had developed a system of bunkers for defence. As for amenities, he had a hospital, shops for the local Burmese, and even a chicken farm. He decided to let in the Dakotas to fly away the wounded who were collected at 'Broadway' from the battles at 'White City', and the last one took off at 10.30 pm. Fifteen minutes later, the Japanese attacked his perimeter; a Japanese section got inside but was eliminated at dawn on the 28th. The next day Rome mortared the Japanese who were digging in on the north side of his position, against which the Japanese retaliated with two battalion guns to shell the garrison. In their turn, they were put out of action by the Chindits' troop of 25-pounders, which killed all the Japanese gun crews. The battle continued until the end of the month with infantry charges, sniping, and finally an air strike by Cochran's Mustangs guided by an RAF pilot who had checked the Japanese positions on the ground, been flown out to India, gave his information to Cochran and then led the Mustangs in. By 1 April, the Japanese had accepted defeat at 'Broadway', which was left in peace until Calvert was told to withdraw on 13 May.[2]

---

[1] See Calvert, *Chindits*, p. 82; Bidwell dates it as 16 March (op.cit., p. 128)

[2] Calvert, op.cit., pp. 82–3

'White City' and 'Blackpool'

The block at 'White City' was attacked on 6 April. Major-General Hayashi, the commander of 24 Independent Mixed Brigade, had moved to Sepein near Mawlu on 1 April with the intention of clearing the block. He shelled it for three hours from 10 pm on the 6th and then sent his men against the south-east corner, defended by the Lancashire Fusiliers, Gurkhas, and the newly arrived 6 Nigerian Regiment. Calvert's machine guns were sited to fire along the perimeter wire and with the barrage from his sixteen 3-inch mortars, the Japanese were repulsed. They brought up bangalore torpedoes, up to fifteen feet long, to explode his wire, but none went off. Mustangs flew in after dawn and strafed the Japanese forming-up areas. Then, surprisingly, Japanese aircraft intervened: twenty-seven medium bombers hit the garrison, and the perimeter wire was broken in several places. The shelling was more to be feared than the bombing, and was a constant factor in the lives of the garrison. Calvert himself recalls lying in his dug-out and shivering, partly through fear and partly through the frustration of not being able to hit back on the move.

His tension was relieved by a visit to the Nigerians, one of whom had decided that a box-full of grenades was preferable to his rifle, as he had successfully flattened the head of a marauding Japanese with it. When his fellow-Nigerians put in a bayonet-charge, he wielded his box. Calvert noticed that the Nigerians tended to decorate their dugouts with Japanese heads.[1] The Nigerians kept on coming in by plane in the intervals of the shelling, and soon Calvert had roughly seven battalions in and around 'White City' against Hayashi's eight. He found the Japanese artillery not very effective against the dugouts he had instructed his men to build, but their 6-inch mortar, with its four-a-half feet high bomb, which took over half a minute to complete its trajectory, was devastating.[2]

Two small tanks were also employed against the garrison, but a 2-pounder anti-tank gun put one out of action immediately and the second promptly withdrew. Calvert was more insistent on ammunition being dropped than food, as it was consumed at a great rate: of Vickers MG ammunition alone, 700,000 rounds were dropped into 'White City'. The machine-gunners were ordered never to fire less than a whole belt at a time.[3]

Hayashi's attacks went on until 11 April, but on the 10th Lentaigne flew in and told Calvert that Gillmore and his Nigerians would take over the garrison of the block while Calvert with 3/9 Gurkhas, 7 Nigerian Battalion (Vaughan), 450 bearded troopers of 45 Recce Regiment from 16 Brigade[4]

[1] Calvert, *Fighting Mad*, p. 21

[2] Calvert, *Chindits*, p. 99

[3] ibid., p. 101

[4] As an interesting example of how vague memory can be, Calvert calls them 'Devonshires' in *Fighting Mad* (1964) and 'bearded Cornishmen' in *Chindits* (1973).

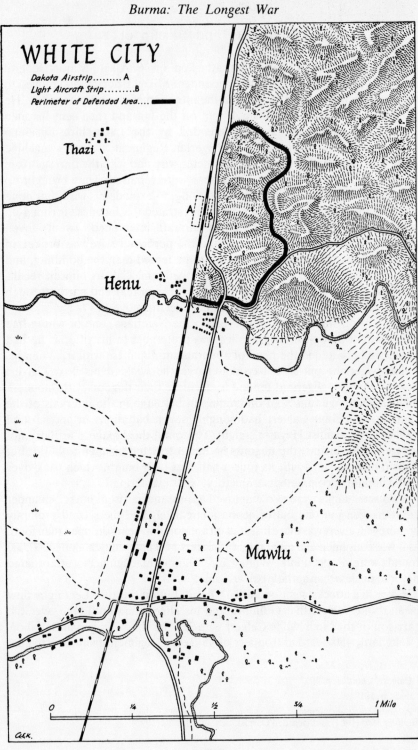

WHITE CITY

Dakota Airstrip..........A
Light Aircraft Strip..........B
Perimeter of Defended Area....

Thazi

Henu

Mawlu

0   ¼   ½   ¾   1 Mile

and the Lancashire Fusiliers – about 2400 men – was to leave 'White City' and act as a striking force round it – the principle of the 'floater column' much enlarged. Calvert was glad to be up and doing instead of acting as a sitting target, and he decided to attack the village of Sepein just south of Mawlu, which he was sure was the Japanese headquarters. He set up his own headquarters at the nearby village of Thayaung, cleared an airstrip to take out his wounded and put in his infantry at dawn on the 13th. A company of Vaughan's Nigerians were to neutralize the Japanese in Mawlu while 3/6 Gurkhas took on Sepein. For four hours the Nigerians were hit by small-arms, mortars and even dive-bombers but they held on to the corner of Mawlu they had seized until Vaughan pulled them back at dusk, sending in a final cascade of 3-inch mortar bombs as a farewell gesture. But the Japanese at Sepein – or rather just on the outskirts (Calvert had got their location wrong) – were too well dug-in and surrounded by lantana scrub: neither a 25-pounder barrage nor a Mustang strike could budge them.

Calvert had, in fact, attacked too soon, and had done exactly what Fergusson did at Indaw – gone in without adequate reconnaissance. Lentaigne had told him to act fast, and he did so; and his attack certainly relieved pressure on 'White City'. Gillmore told him, from inside the block, that he could not guarantee to hold unless the enemy were shifted from his perimeter, so Calvert decided to bring his forces up and squeeze the Japanese between himself and 'White City'. The distance between his men and the block was half-a-mile, and it contained 2000 Japanese who had not realized Calvert's force had moved so close to them during the night: Calvert had forbidden his men to light fires. Realizing they were now threatened from front and rear, the Japanese turned on Calvert, and in their turn they were attacked by the Nigerians streaming out of 'White City'.

Calvert's headquarters were caught in a Japanese counter-attack, and it was his mules which suffered. The Japanese machine guns scythed through the grass about two feet above the ground, and Calvert watched in helpless fascination as rows of bullet holes were stitched across the mules' bodies, bringing them and the W/T sets they carried crashing to the ground. Calvert was so close to the Japanese that they could hear his voice as he called in Cochran's Mustangs for the strike timed at 1.00 pm – the Japanese machine guns began to fire in the direction of his voice. Then the planes came in, bombed and machine-gunned with precise accuracy, and silenced them.[1]

Utterly exhausted, Calvert decided not to go into the block but to return to his headquarters at Thayaung. He then found out that his great friend, Ian MacPherson, commander of the Gurkhas who acted as defence for Brigade headquarters, had been killed; and he would have gone back into

[1] Calvert, *Fighting Mad*, p. 186

the battle to look for him had not his brigade-major, Francis Stuart, thrust a revolver into his stomach and threatened to shoot him if he didn't return to headquarters.[1] He had lost nearly seventy dead and 150 wounded.[2] But he had inflicted far greater losses on Hayashi, and the block was not attacked again. Calvert estimated that 24 Independent Mixed Brigade sustained 3000 casualties in this second battle for 'White City', whereas losses to the garrison were small. He could, therefore, have held it indefinitely, whatever field artillery the Japanese used against it for, as he points out, 3000 Japanese dug in at Myitkyina, without the Chindits' air supply, resisted a force of 30,000 Allied troops for seventy days.

But Lentaigne was alert to the difficulties posed by the monsoon, when air supply would be hazardous; and the dirt airstrips could not be converted into all-weather airfields. Lentaigne's more orthodox military training also told him that if he were to hold the Railway Corridor while Stilwell came down on Myitkyina from the north, he would have to concentrate his men, not disperse them in columns. So the order went out to abandon 'White City' and 'Broadway', and to build a new stronghold – codenamed 'Blackpool' – about sixty miles further north, near Hopin, and thirty miles south of Mogaung itself. This would be 111 Brigade's job, and 77 Brigade would act as a mobile force in conjunction with it as Calvert led it towards Mogaung. 14 Brigade was to play a similar role. When the Chinese reached Mogaung, by benefit of Special Force, the campaign in North Burma would be over. Not before time, because Wingate had said that the maximum effective operating period for his force was ninety days. The men of GALAHAD had been told the same thing.

To Calvert and his Brigade, the idea of abandoning the two positions they had fortified so strongly and defended with such élan and tenacity was unbearable, and Calvert's signals to Lentaigne began to acquire an air of insubordination. Lentaigne flew into 'Broadway' on 8 May to explain why it was necessary to go north. There were only four Chindit brigades in the area now, as 23 had never joined them and Fergusson's exhausted 16 had been flown out. 111 Brigade, under John Masters, was already in position at 'Blackpool'; 14 Brigade would operate to his west, together with the Nigerians in 'White City', who would be out in a few days, when Rome also would evacuate 'Broadway'. Calvert knew his men should be relieved, after the last ferocious two months. So did Lentaigne. But the commitment to Stilwell was primary, so Special Force made for Hopin. It would not be easy, because the Japanese had now sent a new division to the Chindit area. And to free Mutaguchi's energies for Imphal and Kohima alone, a new Army formation had been set up on 9 April, with headquarters in

---

[1] ibid., p. 187, *Chindits*, p. 105

[2] The figures are those given in *Fighting Mad*, p. 187. *Chindits* gives them as 100 killed and over 200 wounded.

Maymyo, under Lieutenant-General Honda Masaki. This 33 Army, codenamed KON, was to take control of the battle against Stilwell and the Chinese, keep the supply road to China cut, and deal once and for all with the now nearly 6000 men of Operation THURSDAY. There was an adjustment to the British command too: Special Force would now come directly under Stilwell.

Stilwell, to give him credit, wanted none of it. He did not want Wingate's men, because he was not at all sure they would accept his orders; and he did not want them to give up 'White City'. He also feared that if they moved north, they would draw in their wake Japanese forces, and he already had enough on his hands with Tanaka's 18 Division dodging his Chinese and disputing every inch of the way to Myitkyina.[1] He had not been able to persuade Chiang Kai-shek to intervene from Yunnan with what was codenamed 'Yoke Force', the Chinese divisions which Chiang was supposed to contribute to the war in Burma, but which he refrained from committing to battle on the grounds that a Japanese offensive north of the Yangtze was in the offing and that he was also threatened by the Communists in North China. Chiang was faced by precisely one Japanese division – 56 (Matsuyama) – and in his perspective, whatever the Western Allies may have thought about his dilatoriness, Burma cannot have loomed very large.

So Stilwell really was relying on his US-trained Chinese divisions from India, and on GALAHAD. On 27 March he flew to Chungking to put pressure on Chiang to release Yoke Force, and came back with the promise of two divisions to strengthen his drive on Myitkyina – Slim had signalled him on 23 March to 'get Yoke in' to relieve pressure on the Imphal front where, as Stilwell inevitably phrased it, 'Limeys have wind up'.[2]

His own advance had been going well. The Chinese 66 Regiment took the Jambu Bum, the ridge separating the Hukawng Valley from the Mogaung Valley on 19 March, which was Stilwell's sixty-first birthday. Both events were celebrated by the presentation to the General of a large chocolate cake – in itself a tribute to American supply – in the middle of the jungle: Stilwell cut the cake and passed out pieces to officers and men as they filed past. GALAHAD's curve through the hills to outflank the Japanese 18 Division (Tanaka) had almost succeeded, and Stilwell needed to keep the war of movement going, to press Tanaka down towards Kamaing, and so to the Irrawaddy and the railway to Myitkyina. By the middle of April 1944, Stilwell had managed to deploy five Chinese di-

---

[1] Bidwell, *The Chindit War*, p. 208
[2] *The Stilwell Papers*, p. 265

visions in North Burma. With GALAHAD, they faced the wily and battle-hardened veterans of 18 Division, consisting now of three under-strength regiments.

Sun Li-jen felt free to move south again on 19 May, saying to his US liaison officer 'We go on to take Kamaing now'.[1] His 112 Regiment worked through the jungle round the town, came out behind Tanaka, and occupied a major supply centre, with eight warehouses crammed with food and ammunition. One of Tanaka's subordinate commanders, Aida, abandoned his position in the village of Lavon seven miles east of Kamaing, and left Tanaka's flank wide open. If Sun's 112 could hold this block of the road leading south to Mogaung then Tanaka's whole division would be in the net. Chinese 22 and 38 Divisions came in on Tanaka from all sides, in spite of monsoon rains and heavy flooding.

In command of that part of 111 Brigade which was west of the Irrawaddy, John Masters received the order to establish a block of the railway in the Hopin area with misgivings. Neither he nor Lentaigne had much faith in Wingate's person or doctrines, as we have seen, but Masters did accept that the characteristic Chindit operation demanded jungle mobility, and a permanent block destroyed that. And what Calvert had done in 'White City' with great success, because it was so far in the rear of the Japanese front line, would be much harder close to where they were fighting for their lives. Masters's men had been in the field for forty-five days – half Wingate's postulated time-span for a Chindit operation – and although he made a speech to them to make them think they would be drawing on their reserves of strength, both officers and men had in mind the end of a kind of contract period, beyond which their exertions and discomforts would cease.[2] It was going to be increasingly difficult to spur them into holding on after the time when they had been told their fight would be over. 'Whether this is a gallant frame of mind is rather doubtful', writes one of 111 Brigade's officers, 'but the British soldier has long since ceased to be consciously gallant and his sacrifice consists of involuntary acts in battle, not a state of mind.'[3]

Command nourished Masters. Ruthless, competent, flamboyant, he disguised himself in Burmese clothing when 111 Brigade had almost reached the site that was to be 'Blackpool' near the village of Namkwin, and looked around. He would not be actually straddling the line, as 'White City' was, but near enough to intercept traffic. There was water, a suitable gun emplacement for 25-pounders and space for an airstrip. Unfortunately, 111

---

[1] Romanus and Sunderland, *Stilwell's Command Problems*, pp. 215, 216

[2] Masters, *The Road past Mandalay*, p. 219

[3] Rhodes-James, op.cit., p. 109

Brigade had no time in which to settle in at its leisure. As soon as the King's Own and the Cameronians, now down to twenty-five men per platoon instead of forty, arrived on 8 May, the Japanese attacked them. There was a Japanese railway detachment at Pinbaw, five miles up the line, and they came in at them five nights in a row. Outclassed and outnumbered, the Japanese were repulsed with machine guns and mortars, as they had been at 'White City', one machine gun firing at a Japanese platoon enough rounds to kill a battalion. But the Chindits who fought were also the labourers who dug trenches and levelled the strip, which the Japanese belaboured with a single 75-mm gun from Pinbaw. Gliders and C-47s crashed and were set on fire, until by 13 May Masters had his own anti-aircraft guns and three 25-pounders with which to retaliate; as well as the 'long-range artillery' provided by Cochran's Mustangs.[1]

111 Brigade were not isolated in 'Blackpool', but it is clear that they felt they were. 77 Brigade was in the hills to the east – 111 Brigade assumed they were resting – and 14 Brigade arrived, slowly, to take up positions west of 'Blackpool'. Masters flew out by light plane to see Stilwell and Lentaigne and ask him to urge Brodie to move his 14 Brigade faster into position. 'The "White City" had been evacuated thirteen days earlier, and 14 Brigade was supposed to come straight up. My brigade had marched 140 route miles in 14 days to establish this block. Surely those bloody nitwits could cover 120 miles in thirteen days? Where the *hell* were they? Where were the West Africans?' Lentaigne assured him Brodie was doing what he could, and told Masters he could abandon 'Blackpool' if he found 111 Brigade was on the verge of destruction. Not the most heartening of orders.[2]

The monsoon added to Masters's worries. It turned the foxholes into the trenches of Passchendaele, with trees blown to pieces and human fragments sticking up out of the damp earth, from which rose the smell of putrefaction from the Brigade's dead, or from the spilled entrails of the Japanese corpses hanging on the wire. The proximity of the Japanese artillery, more severe than Calvert had found at Mawlu, was beginning to make 'Blackpool' untenable. It was not the sort of battle for which the Long Range Penetration Groups had been trained. On 17 May, the positions of the King's Own in 'the Deep' (Masters had named his posts after positions in the cricket-field) were systematically probed by at least twelve pieces of Japanese heavy artillery; the second-in-command stumbled into Masters's command post and reported direct hits on machine guns and their crews; he doubted if they could hold when the Japanese infantry came in. Masters put a call through to the Cameronians and told them to take over 'the Deep' at once. The men of the King's Own passed him, as they

---

[1] ibid., p. 125

[2] Masters, *The Road past Mandalay*, p. 243

were relieved, their eyes wandering, jaws sagging wide. He was sure the attack would come at once, but the Japanese waited for an hour until the night was black and thick with dense rain. These were men of the 53 Division under Major-General Takeda – not by any means the tough young warriors from the hills of Kyūshū, but older men, late conscripts, and townsmen nearly all, from Kyoto. Nonetheless, they fought hard, and it was four in the morning before the Cameronians knew they had driven back the last mad assault.

A week later, Takeda put in a mass assault with his 128 Regiment. Neither Brodie's 14 Brigade nor the Nigerians, who had successfully ambushed a Japanese company probing the Kyunsalai Pass and decimated it, could get down to the railway valley in time to help Masters. The difficulty of the jungle and the monsoon's full force made their advance pitifully slow, and no one seems to have told them of the track that Masters himself had used down the ridge to Namkwin.[1]

Nor could Calvert help. He formed his men into three battalions, and then found the Namyin Chaung impossible to cross. It was in spate, had flooded the surrounding paddy fields, and the Japanese had prudently removed all the country boats. The only reinforcements to come from that quarter were 900 men of the 4/9 Gurkhas under the command of a cavalryman, Major Harper of the Deccan Horse, who got his men across the Namyin just before it flooded. After that, there was nothing. On the night of 24 May, after intense fighting, a Cameronian subaltern spoke over the phone to Brigade Headquarters: 'Most of my men are wounded, I am wounded. And if I don't get help I've had it!'[2] The story was the same round the whole of 'Blackpool's' perimeter; and Japanese artillery was now so close to the strip that dropping supplies meant that even those planes which succeeded in coming close often dropped their rations and ammunition to the Japanese. On one occasion, Masters watched Japanese anti-aircraft fire tear an engine from a C47 which crashed in flames. On another occasion, the block itself was raided by Zero fighters. 'Further retention of this block entails loss of brigade. Commander asks permission to withdraw,' was the signal drafted by Masters that night. In the early hours of the next dawn, his signals officer enciphered it, and was about to send it when the order was shouted to stand to. The Japanese had penetrated the perimeter and taken a small hill feature inside the block from which they poured machine-gun fire. Even the defiant gallantry of the Cameronians could not eject them, and Masters realized that he would have to pull out with the Japanese actually in his positions. He was short of food, but worse, his ammunition was desperately low. He decided to bring the Brigade out to the west and make for the Bumrawng Bum, the hills

---

[1] Bidwell, *The Chindit War*, p. 233

[2] Rhodes-James op.cit., p. 141

over which they had first moved from 'Aberdeen'. As they moved out, shells and mortar bombs burst in the middle of the retreating wounded. Richard Rhodes James, the cipher officer, found himself praying helplessly, as a stretcher was hit and the casualty and stretcher-bearers were blown into the air. A severed head gazed up at him from the track. Some of the stretcher-bearers, vulnerable beyond endurance, threw down their charges and fled. Some of the wounded, who knew they would not survive the march out, or who were too terribly mauled by shell fragments, were shot by their friends. Masters himself described their grisly condition:

> The first man was quite naked and a shell had removed the entire contents of his stomach. Between his chest and pelvis there was a bloody hollow, behind it his spine. Another had no legs and no hips, his trunk ending just below the waist. A third had no left arm, shoulder or breast, all torn away in one piece. A fourth had no face and whitish liquid was trickling out of his head into the mud...[1]

One column was then misdirected by a staff officer from Headquarters and was only just put back on the right track in time. A man in front was hit in the thigh and ran down the path shouting for help, recalls Richard Rhodes-James.

> I passed him and felt like a murderer. Why not stop and help him?... One man had been wounded in the leg and was dragging himself across the paddy towards the path along which we were moving. On looking back at this moment afterwards, I reflected how gallant it would have been to have rescued him. At the time, I was conscious only of men pressing me from behind and the need to keep going.[2]

It took three days for 111 Brigade to reach Mokso Sakan, the village in the hills from which they had set out to reconnoitre Blackpool. They were met by Nigerians who cut steps in the trail to help them on and took over the wounded. The Brigade now numbered 2000 men capable of fighting, and 130 wounded. At the top of the pass they halted, and waited for rations to be brought up from Lake Indawgyi, from where an improvised service of flying-boats was started with a base on the Brahmaputra. The men were exhausted, battle-shocked, and furious with 14 Brigade whose dilatory movement had almost let the Japanese wipe out 'Blackpool's' garrison. '14 Brigade could have saved us', wrote Richard Rhodes-James.[3] Masters was angry with Lentaigne, too. Why did he not come and visit them, and see for himself how shot they were?[4]

[1] Masters, *The Road past Mandalay*, p. 259

[2] Rhodes-James op.cit., pp. 144–5

[3] ibid

[4] Masters, *The Road past Mandalay*, p. 267

They were so spent and drained that, at any rate, no further operations could be called for. Then came the incredible order: 111 Brigade was to move out, and attack Mogaung from the west while 77 Brigade took it from the east.

Stilwell burns up the Limeys and crucifies GALAHAD

This was the end product of a tussle between Lentaigne and the vitriolic Stilwell, which ultimately involved Slim and Mountbatten. Stilwell did not like Wingate from the start, and termed the Chindit operation 'shadow-boxing'. But that did not set him apart from many British generals, who took the same view. What he was mad about was that they had failed him. Morris Force – that part of 111 Brigade east of the Irrawaddy – had failed to make an impression on Stilwell's battle for Myitkyina, though, since they were only 1300 strong and Stilwell's Chinese and GALAHAD, numbering in all 5,500 men, had also not yet succeeded in taking Myitkyina, the criticism seems harsh. 111 Brigade, without authorization, had abandoned its block at 'Blackpool', leaving Stilwell vulnerable to the reinforcement by 2–3000 Japanese who could thereby move up to Mogaung.

Boatner, on behalf of Stilwell, began to wear Morris down. He was told, on 25 May, to clear the Japanese from the village of Waingmaw on the east bank of the Irrawaddy opposite Myitkyina. The Japanese were there in company strength, the area was flooded, and Morris Force could not take Waingmaw. Increasingly impatient, Boatner invoked the Supreme Commander. Mountbatten had ordered Myitkyina to be taken at all costs, he signalled, so Morris must accept casualties. Aware that Boatner was reading from a map and unaware of the conditions on the ground, Morris described Waingmaw. The whole countryside was flooded chest-high. There were few approaches to Waingmaw, and the Japanese had these covered with machine guns. He was losing a third of a platoon daily, from sickness, and those that were left were so exhausted they fell asleep even under Japanese fire. By 14 July, Morris Force consisted of exactly three platoons. Lentaigne insisted that they be brought out. The Chinese objected, Stilwell refused. A week later, Lentaigne repeated the request, ironically suggesting that when the numbers were down to 25 officers and men, the moment for evacuation might have arrived. Stilwell finally agreed.[1]

But, of course, his Chinese had been longer in the field than either Chindits or the US troops of GALAHAD, and he did not want to evacuate the latter while the Chinese were still embattled; though, as he frequently complained himself, their advance had not been energetic, and secret

---

[1] Romanus and Sunderland, *Stilwell's Command Problems*, pp. 243–4

orders from Chiang Kai-shek were husbanding their strength. He used one against the other. How could he evacuate GALAHAD when he was at the same time insisting that the rain-sodden and battle-weary Chindits should stay operational?

Weariness was hitting even the best of the Americans by this time, including Cochran's pilots. 'We were showing signs of wear and tear', admitted Cochran. 'My fighter pilots were getting sick with extreme fatigue. Some were losing their desire to fight and fly. It was the same with the bomber pilots. The transport and light-plane flyers were losing their fire, were growing ill. They had some of the heaviest of the evacuation jobs. We had harder work than ever in winding up the job, and wore ourselves out, wore ourselves ill.'[1]

The Americans on the ground were in even worse case. GALAHAD had performed miracles of marching and endurance in support of Stilwell's Chinese. In the Kamaing valley, it had trekked sixty miles through jungle to seize the road at Walawbum and intercept Tanaka's 18 Division. Alongside a regiment of the Chinese 38 Division, it had then had a slogging match with Tanaka which resulted in 1500 Japanese dead being left on the battlefield. It was on this occasion that Mountbatten, on a visit to Stilwell, was taken round a tour of the battlefield: 'Louis has been up, but didn't like the smell of the corpses', Stilwell chortled in a letter to his wife.[2] GALAHAD then repeated its encirclement tactics at Inkangahtawng twenty miles north of Kamaing. Two battalions moved through the hills and came out on the road on 23 March. The Japanese beat them back into the hills, and they stood and fought at Nhpum Ga, a sharp ridge up the Tanai valley at the end of a group of hills, with only one water point. The Japanese of 18 Division formed a task force under Colonel Maruyama to pursue GALAHAD and began to assault the perimeter from all sides, taking the water-point from the Americans on 30 March.

GALAHAD had command problems, too. Brigadier-General Merrill, Stilwell's friend and appointee, was flown out with heart trouble on 31 March, and Colonel Frank Hunter, who had, in effect, trained the force in Central India, and was a regular infantry officer of great calibre and strength of purpose, took over and tried to break through to the be-leaguered men at Nhpum Ga from Hsamshingyang, a clearing in the jungle three miles to the north. The garrison had plenty of food and ammunition but was hard hit by the lack of water and the smell of decomposition from their dead pack animals.

Then the Japanese simply disappeared. General Tanaka was beginning to worry more and more about holding Myitkyina, and did not want to disperse his efforts in the hills above Kamaing. GALAHAD had lost 59

[1] Lowell Thomas, *Back To Mandalay*, p. 243
[2] B. Tuchman, *Sand Against the Wind*, p. 434

killed, and 379 men were evacuated with wounds or sickness. As the historian Riley Sunderland puts it, 'the fighting edge of the most mobile and most obedient force that Stilwell had was worn dull.'[1]

Tanaka's purpose was to hold the area Kamaing-Mogaung – a linear distance of around thirty miles – as long as possible. There would be no attack on Myitkyina, he reasoned, as long as 18 Division lay astride Stilwell's southward thrust in the Mogaung Valley. He determined to hold Kamaing until the monsoon came, and then withdraw gradually while Stilwell's forces were trapped in the flooded valleys. His guess was a shrewd one: though he could not shift the roadblock at Seton, a few miles south of Kamaing, which 112 Chinese Regiment held against all his counter-attacks, Tanaka knew that by mid-June the rainfall in the valley would be an inch a day, and tanks would be unable to move. On the other hand, he was in pretty dire straits himself, with his men's rations down to one-eighth of the rice they needed, his trucks immobile through lack of petrol, and his guns rationed to four rounds a day. On 16 June, the Chinese pushed him out of Kamaing, into the hills south and west. On the same day, the 114 Chinese Regiment linked up with Gurkhas at the appropriately named village of Gurkhaywa, just north of Mogaung, in a large enveloping movement that cut off elements of Tanaka's 56 and 114 Infantry Regiments in the hills west of Kamaing. The remnants of Lentaigne's Chindits now had an overland connection to Stilwell, and, through him, back to India.

Tanaka wanted to continue the fight in the Mogaung valley, and asked Honda at 33 Army to urge 53 Division to help him break the Chinese stronghold at Seton. Honda agreed, and for three days, Tanaka and the Kyoto soldiers of 53 Division tried to prise apart the fingers of 112 Chinese Regiment, now reinforced by the 113th. They failed, and Honda told Tanaka to withdraw his division to Sahmaw, on the railway below Mogaung. He did so, and with half his original strength, and that half riddled with malaria and in the grip of famine, he moved out of the Mogaung valley.

The American historians of the China-Burma-India Theatre speculate interestingly on the effect of Tanaka's long-drawn-out resistance for the future, not of the Burma campaign, but of the history of Asia. Had Stilwell taken Myitkyina in mid-1944 and opened the road to China then, Chiang Kai-shek could have had back his experienced troops from North Burma, and their artillery, in 1944, with incalculable effects on his ability to resist the Communists in 1945.

As it was, Stilwell's timetable had slowed down, and he relied on GALAHAD to speed things up. The force now had 1400 men out of its original figure of 2997, and three combat teams were made up from these

---

[1] Romanus and Sunderland, op.cit., p. 191

men, with stiffening from the Chinese. Merrill took command again, and indicated to his battalion commanders that the capture of Myitkyina was the end of the road: after that, the men would be evacuated. The plan was not to approach Myitkyina from Mogaung, but to put a force across the hills of the Kumon range, with the help of the Kachins, and strike at Myitkyina from the north. Animals and men used vestigial tracks rather than regular paths, and many of the pack animals fell down the mountain-side. Dealing with the mules, unloading them when they slipped, carrying the loads back to the track, wore out GALAHAD far more than combat. 'The mule leaders', wrote Charlton Ogburn, 'became virtually dehumanized.' GALAHAD's men had already marched 500 miles, and the route was purgatory for them. At one point they had to climb a 6000-foot pass, at the summit of which a cold bitter wind hit them. Most of them kept on because they believed in Merrill's incentive: this was to be the last battle.

On the way, K Force (3 Battalion GALAHAD plus 88 Chinese Regiment) lost its commander, Colonel Kinnison, from scrub typhus, one of 149 casualties to the lethal mite during the march, most of whom died. Small forces of Japanese holding mountain villages were destroyed, and Hunter pushed on, releasing a pre-arranged signal to Stilwell and the USAAF General Old in the Mogaung valley: 48 hours before Myitkyina on 14 May, 24 hours before on 15 May. On 16 May, Hunter was two miles from the airfield at Myitkyina. He sent Kachin scouts from Dick D'Silva's Kachin Levy company on ahead to spy out the land. They came back with the welcome news that the airfield was lightly held. So was the town. Colonel Maruyama had two weak battalions of 114 Infantry Regiment in Myitkyina, around 700 men in all, if we include the men of 15 Airfield Battalion in the north and south airstrips, about 300 men from service units and over 300 sick in the army hospital. The Japanese were still using the stretch of railway between Mogaung and Myitkyina, and as Hunter and GALAHAD's I Battalion bivouacked by the Namkwi River, they heard the sound of a steam-engine puffing through the night.

At 10.00 am on 17 May, Hunter took his battalion towards Pamati, the ferry point on the Irrawaddy just west of Myitkyina, while sending the 150 Chinese Regiment to the airfield. A Japanese sniper shot at them as they moved across the dead flat terrain. Otherwise their surprise was complete. Hunter signalled Merrill at GALAHAD Headquarters at Nanbum: IN THE RING. He was at the airfield. In a few minutes the Japanese were driven off the airfield, Hunter put up picquets, and sent his second codeword: MERCHANT OF VENICE.[1]

It was the signal to fly in supplies, and the men eagerly awaited their food and ammunition. But Stilwell's staff had decided otherwise. He saw it as vital to hold the strip, so the first plane brought in a company of 879

---

[1] Ian Fellowes Gordon, *The Battle for Naw Seng's Kingdom*, p. 120

Engineer Aviation Battalion. Then came a battery of .50 anti-aircraft artillery, then Chinese infantry.

Merrill and Hunter were itching to go on into the town and take it. These supplies were defensive in their purpose, and the fault was compounded by General Stratemeyer, in command of USAAF for India-Burma, who insisted on flying in two British troops of the 69 Light Anti-Aircraft Regiment.

The monsoon was a fortnight away, Stilwell noted in his diary for 18 May 1944. But it did not prevent him exulting over Hunter's splendid achievement: WILL THIS BURN UP THE LIMEYS! he added. It was indeed a sweet moment of victory for him. As the American historians Romanus and Sunderland point out, he had gone into Myitkyina despite all the prognostications of the pessimists, his planes were landing on its airstrip, the Chinese were flying in to lift the Japanese blockade of Yunnan, his forces had driven a hard 500 miles into Burma and defeated one of the toughest divisions in the Japanese Army, the victors of Singapore: 'The brilliant seizure of Myitkyina air strip was the height of Stilwell's career and the grand climax of the North Burma Campaign.'[1] They must have had their tongues in their cheeks: it was very soon to turn into a horrendous anti-climax. The Joint Chiefs of Staff in Washington got the message: a new directive was issued on 2 June 1944 giving priority to aircraft flying the Hump into China, while SEAC exerted ground and air pressure against the Japanese to exploit the Ledo Road when completed. The plans for a seaborne invasion of Sumatra (Operation CULVERIN) were shelved for good. The airfield proved a worthy prize for the Hump route, and between its capture and October 1944, 14,000 transport flights were made from it, bringing 40,000 tons of cargo to China.[2]

Unfortunately, Maruyama was still in Myitkyina itself. A first attempt to clear him, by two Chinese battalions, ended in disaster. They lost their way and began firing on each other, an action repeated on the 20th, with three battalions involved instead of two. Hunter realized the rest of GALAHAD must come in if he was going to take the town, and although they had not eaten for days, the other two GALAHAD combat units moved off to join him. As they came on to the airstrip, Merrill, who came in on 17 May, noticed that none of his men could walk properly. Almost every one of them had jungle sores, foot-rot and dysentery. One platoon had even cut away the trouser-seats of their uniforms so that dysentery would not delay them in battle. They were, he recorded, 'a pitiful but still a splendid sight'.[3]

[1] Romanus and Sunderland, op.cit., p. 228

[2] ibid., p. 229

[3] ibid., p. 230

It is not difficult to see why Merrill suffered another heart attack the day the Chinese began fighting each other. His deputy, Colonel John MacCammon, was promoted to Brigadier-General and put in charge of the reorganized Myitkyina Task Force, and Hunter kept the depleted GALAHAD – exactly the same decision the Japanese made for their garrison, and equally wrong. MacCammon lasted a week, then was replaced by Stilwell's deputy and Chief of Staff, Brigadier-General Hayden Boatner.

The Japanese build-up was fast. Maruyama's force was 3000 strong within a week; soon the garrison numbered 4500. These men, seriously underestimated by Stilwell's G2, his son Colonel Joseph Stilwell, were about to snatch victory from Stilwell's hands.[1] The situation was, in fact, perfectly redeemable even at this late hour. The British 36 Division (Festing) was ready to fly in – as it later did, to take the Railway Corridor – and could have been put into Myitkyina airfield at short notice. The men were fit and ready for battle and were the obvious force with which to replace Hunter's exhausted men. The US historians say that Stilwell decided against this, 'giving no reason in his diary'.[2] He hardly needed to. After 'burning up' the Limeys, and with a dozen war correspondents describing to the world his great American triumph, it was unthinkable for Stilwell to call on the British to pick his chestnuts out of the fire. He preferred to call on his Ledo Road engineers if necessary. 'I will probably have to use some of our engineer units to keep an American flavour in the fight', he signalled to General Marshall.[3] Another thing his diary omits to mention is the stinging report on his staff work that the dedicated Hunter presented to him. Hunter had been an infantry instructor at Fort Benning and was not merely a brave and humorous leader, but an officer who knew the rules. His letter stated plainly that Stilwell's staff, from Boatner down, discriminated against GALAHAD in favour of the Chinese, that GALAHAD had been over-extended and its men were dropping from sickness and disease.[4] That this was desperately true was evident in the two-and-a-half months the siege lasted, instead of the couple of days it might have taken with proper planning and accurate intelligence. During a Japanese counter-attack on 27 May, Colonel McGee's men of M Force persistently fell asleep during the battle, and McGee himself fainted three times. He asked that his unit be relieved, but he was wasting his time: Stilwell needed the presence of US troops, apparently in any condition whatsoever. When the replacements arrived from the States, things were even worse. Some

---

[1] The nepotism of NCAC extended to the liaison officers with the Chinese, two of whom were Stilwell's sons-in-law.

[2] Romanus and Sunderland, op.cit., p. 233. Kirby, *War Against Japan*, iii, p. 404, says Stilwell did ask for 36 Division, and Mountbatten agreed; but the division was timed to move in early July.

[3] ibid., p. 233

[4] ibid., p. 237

replacements were found by scouring hospitals in the rear, and men were sent back to Myitkyina who should have been in hospital beds. Of one such group of 200, ten were re-evacuated sick at once. The engineers were no better, many of them never having used a rifle since basic training. They had recognition problems. A young officer led a company towards a group of what he took to be men in Chinese uniforms. One of them beckoned him forward, then hurled himself to the ground and let a Japanese machine gun scythe the air above him. The company was destroyed.[1]

Then 2600 volunteers were shipped from America to Bombay where they arrived on 25 May, were rushed to Ramgarh for a week and formed into two battalions known as 'New Galahad'. When the officers at Myitkyina took them over, they realized this would not do, and reformed this force as three battalions, mixing old and new. 'These green soldiers were flown into Myitkyina during the monsoon rains and stepped off the transports into a nightmare', wrote John Paton Davies, the US diplomat who was Stilwell's political adviser. 'They entered a battlefield of mud from which the veterans of the airfield victory were being flown out by the scores, wounded and diseased. For an American to qualify for evacuation on account of sickness, he had to maintain a temperature of 102 degrees for three consecutive days. So desperate was the need for anyone who could pull a trigger. GALAHAD survivors were vomiting most of their K rations and some fell asleep during battle.'[2] The battle then sorted them out. Fifty of them were categorized as psychopathic cases, some officers were declared unfit, and Boatner wrote to Stilwell on 15 June of the disorganization and fear of the US units: 'They are in many cases simply terrified of the Japs.'[3] The II Battalion commander of the original GALAHAD, Lieutenant-Colonel Osborne, was sure some of the men evacuated to the rear were malingering. 'GALAHAD is just shot'[4] Stilwell was compelled to admit to himself, and later '*US troops are shaky*. Hard to believe. Either all our officers are rotten, or else Boatner is getting hysterical. I'll have to go down.'[5]

He did go down, and was lucky to return, for the hatred of his own men had reached such a pitch. Lieutenant Charlton Ogburn, an officer in GALAHAD, described him as 'bloodless and coldhearted without a drop of human kindness', and records that one of his men nearly shot him, and was sorry he didn't: 'I had him in my rifle sights. I coulda squeezed one off and no one woulda known it wasn't a Jap that got the son of a bitch.'[6]

---

[1] ibid., p. 240

[2] J.C. Davies, *Dragon by The Tail*, p. 293

[3] ibid., p. 242

[4] Diary, 30 May, 1944, *The Stilwell Papers*, p. 279

[5] ibid., 15 June, 1944, p. 287

[6] C. Ogburn, *The Marauders*, p. 279

Mogaung: Calvert takes umbrage

Apart from the sycophants on his staff, who laughed at his caustic anti-British wit, and distant admirers like General Marshall, the universal verdict on Stilwell is not kind. And it is – almost – universal: the Chinese detested him, the British – with the possible exception of Slim – loathed him, his own men hated and feared him. His orders had annihilated GALAHAD, and bade fair to do the same to the surviving Chindits. But in its last battle, Special Force carried off a great coup: down to a strength of 2000 men, Calvert's 77 Brigade took Mogaung, cutting the railway to Myitkyina for the last time. Lentaigne signalled him on 27 May that Stilwell's Chinese had put a block at Seton behind 18 Division in Kamaing, and Calvert was detailed to take Mogaung. Would he give a date? Calvert said he would take it by 5 June.

Colonel Claud Rome, who had been in command at 'Broadway', went forward with 3/6 Gurkhas and took the heights overlooking Mogaung on 31 May. This promptly changed Honda's plans for the relief of Myitkyina by 53 Division. It was possible to move in and out of Myitkyina in spite of the American and Chinese encirclement, as Major Mihashi had shown. Staff Officer (Intelligence) of 33 Army, he had penetrated the defences, talked with Mizukami and Maruyama, then returned to report. It was perfectly feasible for Takeda's 53 Division, once 111 Brigade had abandoned 'Blackpool', to move through Mogaung and reinforce Myitkyina. In fact, Honda ordered him to do just that, then cancelled the order when Takeda was within a few miles of his goal. Honda by that time judged that 18 Division's need was the greater, and since the rescue of 18 Division bulked larger in his mind than that of Myitkyina, he sent Takeda towards Kamaing; then told him to fend off the Chindit descent on Mogaung.

The Mogaung River closes Mogaung on the north, the Namyin Chaung, which flows into it, on the west; the Wettauk Chaung borders it on the south-east, where a bridge crosses the Chaung at the village of Pinhmi. The South Staffords destroyed some ammunition dumps on their way down to the Wettauk Chaung, where they halted to let the Lancashire Fusiliers pass through and take the bridge. The road from Pinhmi was several feet above the level of the watery march round it. On one side of the road ran a ditch four feet deep, with jungle on the other side. The Japanese had dug in on high ground just beyond the bridge from which they could cover the bridge itself and the approaches from Pinhmi. It was here that Calvert's first setback occurred. After a slow and fruitless attempt to approach the bridge along the ditch, Calvert arrived, and after a conference with the Fusiliers' Commanding Officer, Major David Monteith, it was decided that two platoons, under the cover of heavy mortaring (the Brigade had no artillery), would rush the Japanese positions across the bridge. W. F. Jeffrey describes what happened:

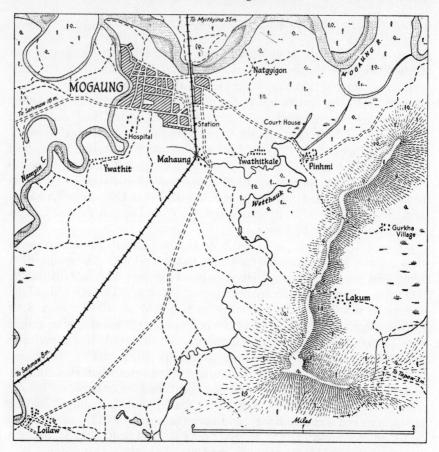

The faces of the men in the ditch were tired and grim: some of
them pressing each others' hands. My own belly was turning over
and over and tying itself into knots... the attack went in down
the road. It was suicidal. The Japanese held their fire until the
platoon reached the bridge, then the machine guns from the
hidden bunkers caught them in the open.[1]

The next day Mustangs were whistled up to bomb and machine-gun the
bridge. The third plane made for the village instead of the bridge and
bombed a fatigue party unloading mules. The carnage was horrible. Men
and mules lay kicking and screaming on the ground, the Fusiliers shook
angry fists at the plane and cursed the pilot as he came in to machine-gun –
this time, fortunately, on the bridge. The Fusiliers quivered when planes

---

[1] W. F. Jeffrey, *Sunbeams like Swords*, pp. 142–3

came over again – the bombing had shaken them, and some cracked under the strain.[1]

The following day the Gurkhas opened the road over the bridge by making a detour and coming on the bunkers from behind, not an easy thing to do since the open countryside between the ridge from where Calvert commanded the battle and Mogaung itself was criss-crossed with interlocking fire from bunkers, and snipers were everywhere. One of them hit Major Archie Wavell, the Viceroy's son, in the wrist and almost ripped his hand off. Wounded as he was, Wavell walked back holding on to his hand, hanging on by a sinew, and waited his turn to be evacuated, in spite of Lentaigne's urgent signals that he was to be flown out at once.[2]

In the fight for Pinhmi Bridge, the Brigade lost about 130 killed and wounded.

Some Japanese strongpoints were dug in beneath Burmese houses, and for these flame-throwers were used, since the loopholes were covered with metal grills against grenades. The delay at the bridge had given Takeda time to bring more men into Mogaung. Soon four battalions of 53 Division were facing Calvert who, naturally, began to wonder where the Chinese were who were supposed to collaborate in the attack.

On 13 June, Calvert's battalion commanders told him that they were down to company strength each, and the attacks through the eternal mud and rain were bringing exhaustion in their wake. Two days later, he began to pull his men back to the Pinhmi area to recuperate, then halted the withdrawal on information from his outposts that the Japanese were also pulling out from the river sector. Were they leaving Mogaung? No such luck. Takeda was merely taking up positions on the railway line to get his men above the flooded areas, and they continued to shell 77 Brigade from the village of Naungkyaiktaw, jutting out into the open paddy midway between Pinhmi and the railway station. Calvert lost up to fifteen men a day from their very accurate shelling directed from this village. From the station to the bridge over the Mogaung River the Japanese were very securely dug-in, in eight strong bunkers which Calvert tried to dominate by subjecting them to daily bombing. But the constant shelling and the appalling onset of trench foot in the flooded trenches meant that Calvert's estimate of his force at 550 'fit' men kept dwindling. Of his contingent from the South Staffords, only *one* subaltern still survived *in situ* of those who

---

[1] ibid., p. 145

[2] Bidwell, *The Chindit War*, p. 269. Lentaigne ordered him to be flown out immediately and threatened Calvert with dismissal from his command if he failed to ensure this. Calvert supposes this was for two reasons. It may not have been known to the Viceroy that Operation Thursday had a different philosophy for its wounded from that adopted in the first Wingate expedition: they were to be evacuated where possible, not abandoned. And on the map it looked as if Calvert, whose offensive had come to a standstill, might be surrounded and taken prisoner, in which case Archie Wavell might fall into the hands of the Indian National Army who might torture him to bring pressure on the Viceroy. (Calvert, *Prisoners of Hope*, p. 211)

had landed at 'Broadway' weeks before, and he had been wounded four times. The rest were dead, or had been evacuated with wounds.

Calvert decided he simply had to eliminate Naungkyaiktaw, which he guessed held about a hundred Japanese.[1] For fifteen minutes just before dawn on 18 June, after a night raid by Mustangs to soften up resistance, 400 mortar shells rained down on Naungkyaiktaw, with an *obbligato* of 2" and 4.2" bombs and machine guns. The Lancashire Fusiliers and the seventy survivors of the King's Liverpool then moved in with the flame-throwers of Major Blain's detachment (Bladet), a dozen of whom had been dropped in by parachute. The Japanese stood it for a while, then broke out of their positions and sprinted east round the paddy then towards the railway station 400 yards west, Calvert's machine guns catching forty of them as they ran across the open ground.[2] It was at the end of this day, during which a hundred Japanese were killed in Naungkyaiktaw, that a very odd episode occurred. The Lancashire Fusiliers, in occupation of positions taken from the Japanese, were cooking an evening meal when a tired seven-man patrol walked in and shed their rifles and equipment. One of the Fusiliers idly glanced up from his dinner and saw the patrol was Japanese: they had not realized their billet was in enemy hands. The Fusiliers grabbed for their weapons and shot it out, eliminating the lost patrol for ever.[3]

The same evening, the Chinese began to arrive, crossing the Mogaung River in ranger boats provided by the Chindits. They were men of I Battalion, 114 Regiment under a Major P'ang, 'a tough little Hakka from Kwangtung' whom Calvert took to at once.[4] Calvert had volunteers from Hong Kong in his brigade – he had served in China himself in the 1930s – and the Chinese were made more than welcome, though Calvert was put out to find that they were not at all keen on frontal attack. Nor, in fact, did they need to be. Acutely conscious of his diminishing numbers, Calvert wanted to finish off Mogaung in short order, and indeed some of his officers in the Lancashire Fusiliers eagerly enquired from the US liaison officer with the Chinese when they would begin to attack, only to be nonplussed by the answer that the Chinese had been fighting for years, and a week more or less did not mean much to them.[5]

Their caution made good sense, as Calvert later found out. During his final attack, he was amazed to find the Chinese had withdrawn from his left flank, which left the Lancashire Fusiliers wide-open. But there was a

---

[1] His estimate in *The Chindits* (p. 142). His earlier work, *Prisoners of Hope*, gives their figure as 'forty to fifty' (p. 218).

[2] Calvert, *Prisoners of Hope*, p. 218

[3] ibid., pp. 220–1; *Fighting Mad*, pp. 197–8

[4] Calvert, *Prisoners of Hope*, p. 223

[5] Jeffrey, op.cit., p. 160

reason. The Chinese had moved forward close to the Japanese positions during the night, not with the intention of staying there, but to leave behind, concealed in the rubble, two observers who pinpointed Japanese bunker positions when the Japanese came out to relieve themselves under cover of darkness. They rejoined their unit before dawn, and the Chinese then brought forward their 81-mm mortars and knocked out the positions from a range of 200 yards, taking them at a minimim cost in casualties to themselves. (It was, in fact, Calvert's own doctrine of compensating for weakness in numbers by weight of material, which his own impatience occasionally made him forget.[1])

This final attack of Calvert's was timed for 24 June, and aimed at the railway bridge over the Mogaung River and the area of Natyigon on its south bank. If he held this, he had the key to Mogaung. The arrival of the Chinese – Colonel Li, P'ang's commanding officer, turned up the next day with another battalion and a battery of 75s – meant that Calvert now had artillery, though his infantry strength was terribly low: Lancashire Fusiliers and King's Liverpool 110, South Staffords 180, Gurkha Rifles 230. He proposed a mortar barrage of 1000 bombs, plus the 75s, after which the infantry would move across the open space, Gurkhas on the right, South Staffords on the left, with the flame-throwers and the Lancashire Fusiliers in reserve. Seventy US planes were to attack Natyigon the previous night.

The mortar barrage began promptly, but it did not silence the Japanese. They answered with a heavy counter-barrage that hit not only the mortar positions but headquarters and infantry forming-up places, causing heavy casualties, so the troops moved up closer to their own barrage. The Gurkhas swept forward along the bank of the Mogaung River and made for the railway bridge. One of their young officers, Captain Michael Almand, an ex-cavalryman, ran ahead of his company to silence a Japanese machine-gun post at the approach to the bridge. Like almost everyone in the Brigade, Almand was plagued by trench foot and he could barely run at all, but he waded through the mud and hurled grenades at the Japanese gun until it was silenced. He paid for that silence with his life, and was awarded a posthumous VC. The other VC of the campaign went to another Gurkha, Rifleman Tulbahadur Pun, also of the 3/6 Gurkha Rifles.

'The Chinese were full of admiration', wrote Lieutenant Durant of the South Staffordshire machine-gun company, 'but thought we were quite mad, for with oriental patience they would have taken a week to do the same attack and probably suffered five per cent of our casualties.'[2] Indeed,

---

[1] Of Major P'ang, Calvert later wrote, 'After many years of campaigning [he had become] cautious and frugal in the expenditure of the lives of his men. This at times is a virtue, but at other times frugality at the wrong period causes greater loss spread over a longer period.' (*Prisoners of Hope*, p. 224). He adds later '[Colonel] Li told me that he thought our troops were bunched up too close together, and that if we spread them more we would have fewer casualties and could rest more of them at a time. There was some truth in this.' (p. 231)

[2] Quoted in Bidwell, *The Chindit War*, pp. 272–3

yes. And the casualties were heavy, on both sides. Calvert lost 47 officers killed or wounded, and 729 other ranks, i.e. around 800 battle casualties after coming under Stilwell. To think out a further advance when firing from a Japanese strongpoint in a house where the railway joined the Pinhmi road, Calvert called his infantry commanders for a quick conference in a large bomb crater close to where Japanese hit by flame-throwers were lying. Calvert could hear them screaming, and smell the odour of their cooking flesh.[1] The Chinese had not, as he had been assured by their US liaison officer, taken the railway station, and his men on the railway embankment were being picked off from behind as a result. More fire was brought to bear. The Fusiliers poured 200 mortar shells on to the Japanese strongpoint, while the South Staffords PIATS and anti-tank grenades blasted holes in the house wall. The flame-throwers had a go, and the defenders fled.

By noon Calvert's Brigade had taken every one of its objectives, and began to dig in, as Japanese shelling started up again. His men were, as he puts it, 'absolutely exhausted and finished', but they had won.[2] The Japanese shelling was, apart from some desultory sniping, the last throw. Gurkhas and Chinese moved forward with much precaution into the rest of the town on the 26th and 27th. It was empty. 'Good news from Mogaung', wrote Stilwell in his diary for 27 June 1944, *'we have it.'*[3] The BBC news announcement from Stilwell's headquarters that the Chinese had taken Mogaung naturally roused Calvert and his officers to fury. Colonel Li, who was not responsible for the bulletin, apologized to Calvert, 'If anyone has taken Mogaung,' he said, 'it is your Brigade, and we all admire the bravery of your soldiers.' Even in post-combat depression, Calvert's mischief could not forego the riposte. 'Chinese reported taking Mogaung', he signalled to Headquarters. 'My Brigade now taking umbrage.'[4]

So, too, but with less cause, was Stilwell. His publicity had jumped the gun over Myitkyina. The whole world had been told of the capture, on 17 May, of the first town in Burma to be retaken from the Japanese. It was now nearly the end of July, the Japanese were still entrenched in Myitkyina, while GALAHAD and the Chinese were still battering away at it from the western airstrip. Holding Boatner – now sick with malaria – responsible for its stalemate, he replaced him with Brigadier-General Wessels, on 26 June. Three days later – a change long overdue – Hunter was put in command of all US troops at Myitkyina. As Stilwell saw it, Lentaigne had failed to keep 111 Brigade against the Japanese; now Calvert, after taking Mogaung, was refusing to obey orders. Stilwell told

[1] Calvert, *Prisoners of Hope*, p. 235

[2] ibid., p. 236

[3] *The Stilwell Papers*, p. 283

[4] Calvert, *Fighting Mad*, p. 198

him to move down the railway towards Hopin, near the old site of 'Black-pool', to deal with remnants of 18 and 53 Divisions in retreat from Kamaing and Mogaung.[1] They had established themselves at Sahmaw and Tungni, west of the Namyin River, in an attempt to block further moves south by Stilwell's men. Two hills dominating the road between these two villages became the scene of bitter fighting. One, above Sahmaw, was nick-named 'Hill 60' after a famous battleground of the First World War. The other was Point 2171, which was assigned as the objective for 111 Brigade.

Calvert was told to move to Myitkyina with his survivors formed into one unit. His reply was to close wireless communications with Chindit Headquarters at Shaduzup and march his men to Kamaing, from where he expected them to be evacuated to India. Even this march, through waist-deep mud, was so atrocious that two of the Lancashire Fusiliers died of exhaustion.[2] Calvert's Brigade was naturally terrified of being asked to join in the siege of Myitkyina, hence Calvert's wish to avoid going there at all costs. But he later admitted it was a mistake. It would have been easier to reach Myitkyina and be evacuated from there.[3]

Calvert then went to Headquarters himself, to meet a harassed Lentaigne, who had been defending him against Stilwell's charges of dis-obedience. The threat of a court-martial hung in the air. As he drove in a jeep to Stilwell's headquarters the following day, Colonel Alexander, the Force's GSO1 (Operations) kept telling him not to hold his punches but to give Stilwell hell, while Lentaigne begged him to consider the other Brigades and to watch his tongue. Stilwell sat at a table with his son, Lieutenant-Colonel Stilwell, and General Boatner. Calvert and he shook hands.

'Well, Calvert, I have been wanting to meet you for some time.'

'I have been wanting to meet you too, sir.'

'You send some very strong signals, Calvert.'

'You should see the ones my brigade-major won't let me send.'

It was the right note. Stilwell burst out laughing. 'I have just the same trouble with my own staff officers when I draft signals to Washington.'[4] The ice was broken, and Calvert went into a long recital of the bitter battles of Mogaung. It became obvious from Stilwell's repeated, 'Why wasn't I told?', that his sycophantic staff had played down the British role, and that the true nature of the battle had been kept from him. He had not

---

[1] 53 Division had suffered 1600 casualties in its fight against Calvert. (*War Against Japan*, III, p. 410, n.4)

[2] Calvert, *Prisoners of Hope*, p. 251

[3] ibid., p. 249

[4] ibid., p. 252

even been aware that 77 Brigade was the same body of men who had been flown in four months before. Calvert returned to his men, and began moving them out to India. They had done enough.

Calvert's decision was only one episode in the long struggle between Stilwell and SEAC (of which he himself was Deputy Commander) about the fate of the Chindits. Relations between him and Lentaigne had deteriorated so much that early in June, Slim was sent up to Stilwell's headquarters by Mountbatten to sort things out. Stilwell, who had taken over Special Force on 17 May, now wanted to be rid of them. 'Stilwell complained to me', wrote Mountbatten, 'that units of the Force had disobeyed his order to carry on an advance... since he no longer felt able to command the Force, he wished it to be withdrawn.'[1] Finding 'Stilwell bitter and Lentaigne indignant', Slim heard them both out, and, perhaps, naturally, came to a Sir Roger de Coverley conclusion: 'Stilwell's orders on the face of it were sound enough and it was quite obvious that the Chindits had not carried all of them out. It was equally clear that in their present state of exhaustion, after the casualties they had suffered... they were physically incapable of doing so.'[2] Stilwell quoted the achievement of GALAHAD. Slim countered that GALAHAD had been behind Japanese lines for a shorter time, and their battle casualties were higher. When Stilwell complained that Morris Force had not contributed to the fall of Myitkyina: 'Why accuse a unit a few hundred strong', Slim replied, 'of failing to do what 30,000 men – Stilwell's Chinese divisions and GALAHAD – had not done?' Slim persuaded Stilwell to talk matters over with Lentaigne, allow his force to recuperate, and keep it under command until the fall of Myitkyina. A reasonable compromise, on the surface; but Slim anticipated Myitkyina would fall by the end of June. It did not, and the longer the siege lasted, the shorter grew Stilwell's temper, the more furious his resentment against the shortcomings of Special Force. Finally, on 30 June, Mountbatten himself flew in to Shaduzup.

The command situation itself had changed by this time. Stilwell reminded Mountbatten on 20 May that when Kamaing was reached – the Chinese 22 Division took it on 16 June – the agreement reached at the Cairo Conference came to an end. This had specified, as an attempt to sort out the jurisdictional cobwebs, that Stilwell should act operationally under Slim, Commander-in-Chief XIV Army, even though he (Stilwell) was theoretically Slim's superior officer as Deputy Supreme Commander, South-East Asia. Holding this post, he refused to come under the command of General Giffard, Commander-in-Chief 11 Army Group, under whom Slim operated. Stilwell could not stand Giffard at any price. Mountbatten accepted this, but tried to solve an insoluble situation by

[1] Mountbatten, *Report to Combined Chiefs of Staff*, para. 177, p. 63
[2] Slim, *Defeat into Victory*, p. 279

asking the Chiefs of Staff to provide him with an overall commander for the Allied Land Forces, South-East Asia. In fact Lieutenant-General Sir Henry Pownall, his Chief of Staff, was at that very moment lobbying in London for such an appointment, and was trying to get the man he thought best equipped for the job, Lieutenant-General Oliver Leese, sent out to Ceylon.[1] But Leese was in Italy, in command of Eighth Army, and fully involved in operations. So as a temporary measure Mountbatten agreed to place Stilwell's forces directly under his own command: 'I now became', his despatch comments, 'virtually Commander-in-Chief of the Allied Land Forces', a job which he was not personally supposed to undertake, and with which his staff could not cope.[2]

Mountbatten and Stilwell came to an arrangement. The men of 77 and 111 Brigades should be medically examined. Those unfit to fight should be withdrawn at once, the rest as soon as the emergency in Stilwell's command ended. Morris Force was to remain east of Myitkyina, 14 Brigade and the West Africans would come out later, depending on conditions and the availability of replacements i.e. as soon as 36 Division was in the field again. It had been withdrawn from Arakan to re-fit before being allocated to Stilwell's Northern Combat Area Command. Mountbatten also recommended GALAHAD should be withdrawn, but, he observes, 'my advice was not taken'.[3] Both Slim and Mountbatten had attempted a compromise which, as Slim recognizes, was inadequate: it would have been better to have withdrawn both Chindits and GALAHAD at once, 'they had shot their bolt... both were asked to do more than was possible.'[4] But there was a complicated balance of interests to maintain, as Pownall later noted in his diary:

> On the one hand we must convince the Americans that the British under US Command have not run out on them and not pulled their full weight – on the other hand, it is both criminal and a folly to drive men beyond breaking point at the instance of a subordinate commander, whether British or American. Whatever happens we are in danger of this affair embittering Anglo-US relations. If we pull them out, the Americans (especially Stilwell) will say we ratted on them. If we leave them in, the British commanders and troops will know why, and will say so.[5]

[1] Pownall was also trying to negotiate the removal of Admiral Sir James Somerville, Commander-in-Chief Eastern Fleet and Naval Commander-in-Chief, SEAC, who was senior to Mountbatten in the naval hierarchy and resented being subordinate to him in SEAC.

[2] Mountbatten, *Report to the Combined Chiefs of Staff*, paras 171–3, p. 62

[3] ibid., para. 179, p. 63

[4] Slim, op.cit., p. 280

[5] Pownall, *Diaries*, pp. 182–3

These wrangles did not, perhaps, provide the right atmosphere for raising the question of Noel Coward, but he was very close to Mountbatten, whose role as commander of the destroyer *Kelly* he had played in the film *In Which We Serve*. When he came out to SEAC to entertain the troops, Coward generously offered to go up to Ledo and play for the Americans. Stilwell's refusal to airlift him and his company offended Mountbatten who considered it, he told US General Wheeler, a slap in the face. The upshot of a flurry of signals between Kandy and Ledo was that Coward was admitted to Ledo where his performance apparently fell flat, to Stilwell's undisguised pleasure. 'If any more piano players start this way', he wired to General Dan Sultan, his deputy in command of the China-Burma-India Theatre, 'you know what to do with the piano.'[1]

The medicals were a slap in the face for 77 and 111 Brigades, too. The Chindits were, in effect, being treated as malingerers, though John Masters claims that, in despair at his men's condition, he insisted to Lentaigne that his men be examined and all the unfit sent out at once.[2] At various places in the jungle, the men of 111 Brigade were auscultated, probed and fingered. Its four-and-a-half battalions then numbered 2200 men, and the doctors judged 118 of them fit for action: seven British officers, twenty-one other ranks and ninety Gurkhas. Masters amended the figure to 119, to include himself, and then ordered the rest to move to Kamaing. They had fought long past the prescribed period set by Wingate, long past the limits of endurance, and even in their final hours had shown gallantry of the highest kind, as when the 3/9 Gurkhas assaulted Point 2171. Under Captain Jim Blaker, the Gurkhas took five-and-a-half hours to clamber up the hill, and when they reached the summit, they found it ringed with mortars and machine guns. Blaker ordered them to charge, but the machine-guns halted them and scattered them into the thick jungle of the slopes. Blaker then went on alone, yelling: 'Come on, C Company!', until machine-gun bullets crashed into his stomach. He sank down against a tree and turned his head towards the men who were pressing themselves into the hillside below him. 'Come on, C Company. I'm going to die. Take the position!' The Gurkhas rose, and swept the hill with bayonets. Blaker was awarded an immediate VC, but his exhausted comrades did not have the strength to bury him, and he and his dead Gurkhas were bundled over the steep slope, down into the jungle beneath, where a Graves Registration Unit discovered their bodies three months later, tall bamboos growing through them.[3]

On 8 July, the medical report justified all the brigades' complaints. All ranks were physically and mentally worn out, and all had lost an average of up to three stones. Most had had at least three bouts of malaria, and the

---

[1] Tuchman, *Sand Against the Wind*, p. 452

[2] Masters, *Road past Mandalay*, p. 278

[3] ibid., p. 776

monsoon rains and fetid ground had given them foot-rot, septic sores, and prickly heat. Deaths from cerebral malaria and typhus were on the increase. Loss of weight and post-malarial anaemia meant that any approach march would wear them out so much that they would not be fit to fight without one or two days' rest.

Incredibly, Stilwell insisted to Mountbatten that Lentaigne's orders to 111 Brigade to withdraw from action contravened the agreement. Both 77 and 111 Brigade were, he averred, to stay in the battle zone until Taungni, south of Sahmaw, was cleared of Japanese. Fortunately Mountbatten stayed firm: all the medically unfit were to leave at once, and a timetable was to be drawn up for the evacuation of the rest. No, said Stilwell, 111, 14 and 3 West African Brigades must help 72 Brigade (36 Division) to clear Taungni before he let them go. The physically unfit could go anyway, he had already released 77 Brigade and Morris Force. So Mountbatten sent up yet another circus from Kandy: Giffard's Chief of Staff, Major-General I. S. O. Playfair, and the two American generals Wedemeyer and Merrill. A face-saving arrangement – yet another! – was reached, permitting 111 Brigade to evacuate once 72 Brigade had passed through the artillery position it was guarding. 14 and 3 Brigades would help in the Taungni fighting, but Lentaigne would inform Stilwell of their fitness.

When Masters reported his evacuation of the unfit to Stilwell, in a fit of sarcasm he asked for orders for the remainder: he was reduced to a company. But Stilwell would not be bested. Whether he recognized the sarcasm or not, he promptly signalled Masters to cover a battery of Chinese medium artillery at Pahok. When they reached it, the Chinese battery commander and his US liaison officer puzzled at the new arrivals, said they did not need guarding, the Japanese were in headlong retreat and, anyway, 36 British Division had already passed through on its way south to deal with them. Not to be gainsaid, Masters reorganized the defences, much to the disgust of the Chinese who just wanted a quiet time. Ten days later, on 1 August 1944, Masters and his remnants were allowed to leave Burma.

It was a good day for Stilwell, too: he was promoted to four-star general. As if to congratulate him, the Japanese garrison commander at Myitkyina ordered Colonel Maruyama to leave the town, where the Japanese had gone on doggedly resisting even after a massive land and air blitz on 12 July. When General Wessels ordered a fresh attack on 3 August, he was met by resistance from a small rearguard and 187 sick men. By late afternoon, the town was in his hands. The oil pipelines and the road from Ledo could now be brought right through to Myitkyina. The tail-end of the Chindits did as they were bid. 36 Division drove the Japanese from Sahmaw and 3 West African Brigade relieved them there. They then marched on Taungni, and took it on 9 August. 14 Brigade re-took Point 2171, which the Japanese had re-occupied after Masters's frightful struggle for it; and both brigades were flown out to India between 17 and 27 August. Operation THURSDAY was at an end.

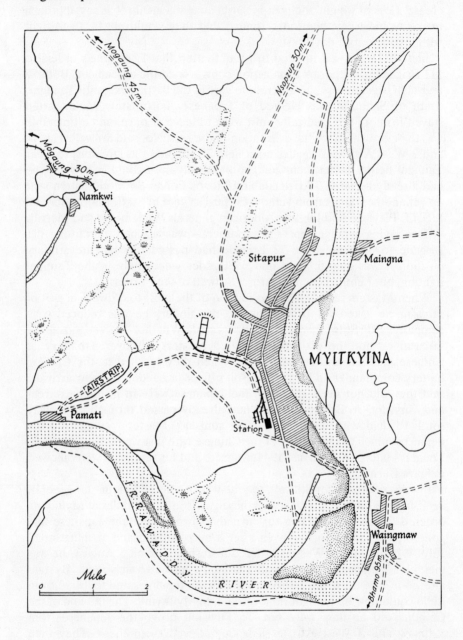

Myitkyina: Mizukami commits suicide

When Stilwell's men burst into Myitkyina, they found 187 prisoners, in the last stages of sickness and exhaustion, and learned that the commander of the garrison, Major-General Mizukami, had taken his own life. It was an unnecessary sacrifice.

The situation inside Myitkyina was a little less monolithic than the besiegers supposed. In fact, there was a basic disagreement between the two senior officers about the purpose of the siege. Colonel Maruyama, Commanding Officer of the 114 Infantry Regiment, was in charge of the defence of Myitkyina before the attack on the town began, and his orders were to facilitate the future operations of 33 Army 'by securing the vital areas in the vicinity of Myitkyina' (*Mītokīna fukin no yōchi wo kakuho seyo*).[1] He understood by this that he was not to defend Myitkyina street by street and house by house, but to go on fighting on the other side of the Irrawaddy if necessary to impede Stilwell's progress. If he continued to cut the Ledo-Kamaing route, he would have done his duty. When the commander of 56 Division Infantry Group, Major-General Mizukami, arrived to command the garrison, he explained this to him. But Mizukami apparently kept his own counsel and did not put forward a view of his own. Then, on 10 July, a signal came from 33 Army: 'Major-General Mizukami will defend Myitkyina to the death' (*Mizukami shōshō wa Mītokīna wo shishu subeshi*).[2] This was not Maruyama's wider understanding of 'the Myitkyina area' but the town of Myitkyina itself. It was odd, too, in that it referred to Mizukami personally and not to 'the Myitkyina garrison' or 'the Mizukami unit.' This was no accident. 'This order was drafted by Colonel Tsuji', recalls the Staff Officer (Intelligence) at 33 Army Headquarters, Major Noguchi. 'He wept as he did it, and then without saying a word, handed it over to us staff officers. We were struck by a feeling of intense sorrow as we read it, and then Abe, as I remember, altered the words "Major-General Mizukami" to "the Mizukami unit" (*Mizukami butai*). Tsuji took it back, and said "No, let it stand. It's all right as it is", and kept his original wording.'

When Honda's 33 Army was set up in April, the former GSOI at Rangoon, Colonel Katakura, who had already shown himself to be a thorn in Kawabe's and Mutaguchi's flesh over the Imphal planning, was conveniently shunted upstairs as Chief of Staff of the new Army. Under him came Tsuji Masanobu, one of the legendary figures in the Japanese Army since the days of the China Incident. Tsuji was involved in every major campaign, Nomonhan, Guadalcanal, Singapore and now Burma. His

---

[1] Sagara Shunsuke, *Kiku to Tatsu* (18 Division and 56 Division) Tokyo, 1972, (15th ed. 1978) p. 137

[2] ibid., p. 137

egotistic account of the Malayan campaign makes it seem as if every success was attributable to his foresight and energy, and he was thought to have the ear of the Imperial family. He was also a savage, and was (quite reliably) reputed to have eaten the liver of an American pilot and handed it round to his appalled colleagues.[1] This thrusting fire-eater, tears or no, now effectively consigned Mizukami to death.

Mizukami let no indication of his feelings escape, and we only have events, and Maruyama's account, from which to judge. Towards the end of July, seeing the destruction of the garrison to be imminent, Maruyama said to Mizukami that they ought, instead of hastening on their own annihilation to no purpose, to withdraw their men as fast as possible to the Mayan hills east of the Irrawaddy and plan further resistance there. Mizukami seemed, by his silence, not to disapprove of this, and Maruyama gave orders to the survivors – the garrison had had 1000 casualties since the end of May – to cross the Irrawaddy by night, in three nightly contingents, on 1, 2, and 3 August. It is in these terms that the official Japanese history describes the order, but the divisional historian Sagara points out that since Mizukami was still in command, it seems odd that the initiative should have come from Maruyama.[2]

Mizukami had already signalled to Honda that he expected to hold Myitkyina for two months. But Honda was puzzled when a second telegram came from Myitkyina: 'when the enemy puts in his all-out attack, anticipate difficulties in long-term resistance due to weakness of position, and shortages of food and ammunition.' 33 Army staff deduced that the second signal represented Maruyama's views. Hence the 10 July signal, the purpose of which was to indicate that 33 Army intended soon to start an offensive against the Chinese in the Lungling area, and that preparations for the defence of Bhamo and Namkham were complete.[3] The context of this offensive was, simply, that Honda had been informed by Southern Area Army that Mutaguchi's Imphal operations had been halted on 3 July, and that when the Imphal front crumbled, the Allies might then turn their attention to the Salween.

Tsuji himself attributes Maruyama's insistence on withdrawing from Myitkyina across the Irrawaddy to a respect for the regimental flag. This is by no means as odd as it seems. 'I don't want to think Maruyama was a coward', Tsuji later wrote. 'His state of mind was, rather, that he couldn't bear the thought either of having his flag (*gunki*) captured, or burning it, and that, even at the risk of being called a coward, he wanted to use the flag as a core round which his regiment could be rebuilt. The fate of his men and the regiment were linked together by

---

[1] Private information from Lieutenant-General Fujiwara.

[2] Sagara, op.cit., p. 138

[3] Tsuji's recollections, ibid.

the flag. Regimental commanders come and go, but the flag is the heart of the regiment.'[1]

Whether or not that was Maruyama's motivation is not really the point; it is a smoke screen put up by Tsuji to distract attention from the fact that a more carefully worded order from 33 Army would have prolonged the siege of Myitkyina as far as it would go, and have saved Mizukami from a futile suicide as well. When he was ready, Mizukami signalled Honda that he could no longer continue to hold Myitkyina and that the siege was entering its final phase. He had evacuated the wounded by raft down the Irrawaddy and asked for them to be looked after in Bhamo. Ordering his garrison to withdraw, and then killing himself, was, of course, Mizukami's way of flouting 33 Army's order 'defend Myitkyina to the death'.

The men themselves – well, their officers at any rate – were taken aback when the order to retreat came. So much so that Major Nakanishi Tokutarō, III Battalion commander, asked Maruyama to show him the written order. As Nakanishi saw it, his battalion's annihilation was only a question of time, in which case he preferred to be given an order for one last all-out attack. Maruyama then told him that their job was not to fight to the end in the streets of Myitkyina but to continue a delaying action in the hills across the Irrawaddy. 'That's what he said', Nakanishi recalls. 'But I think he'd simply lost the will to fight.'[2]

Matsuyama, the general commanding 56 Division, was full of anguish as he became aware of what 33 Army was asking of the men who had been under his command. One of the garrison Medical Officers, Lieutenant Maruyama, remembers his signal to the beleaguered garrison: 'My heart breaks when I see your men going to their deaths without a grain of rice or a single round of ammunition being sent to them, but I hope you will fight to the last for the glorious tradition of the Imperial Army and the honour of the sons of Kyūshū'. (56 Division was raised in Fukuoka and Nagasaki.) Lieutenant Maruyama thought that the receipt of that signal crystallized the garrison commander's intentions. Then another signal came, from Southern Area Army – or even higher up? – 'You are specially promoted two ranks to the rank of full general'. Mizukami knew what that meant – it was almost a posthumous honour. Irony or black humour, it was hard to know which. Then a second: 'You have become a "god of the army" (*gunshin*).'[3]

Lieutenant Maruyama remembers the confusion which arose in the various units about the order to withdraw. He was only 500 yards from the enemy, and Mizukami and about ten men went down to the river bank. Crossing the Irrawaddy was only going from one death to another, they

---

[1] Tsuji Masanobu, *Jūgo tai-ichi* (Fifteen to one), 1962, p. 82

[2] Sagara, op.cit., p. 140

[3] ibid., p. 141

knew, but even so, after sixty days cooped up in the garrison defences, going to the river bank was itself a kind of freedom. The country boat that was to take them rode on the waters as they made their way through the tall grass to the brink. They rested on a hillock crowned with a few trees until dawn on the 3rd. Mizukami seemed to be praying for the success of the crossing. As day broke, a fine rain began to fall. Lieutenant Maruyama left the general for a few moments and made his way through the jungle to the point of embarkation. In the direction of the river, he could hear occasional explosions – hand-grenades, the sound of his comrades hastening on the inevitable end. General Mizukami went to sit with his back against a tree.

Suddenly there was the sound of a pistol shot. It came from where Mizukami had sat down, and Lieutenant Maruyama sprinted in that direction with Captain Shūgyō. The general's orderly was nervous, in tears. The general's body was inclined forward, in a north-easterly direction, supported by the tree-trunk, looking towards Japan. This was a ceremonial suicide. The general's despatch case lay in front of him, with a piece of notepaper on top, held down by a little stone: 'The survivors of the Myitkyina garrison are ordered to proceed south.' The lieutenant felt his pulse, crying out 'General! General!', but there was no point.

Lieutenant Horie ran off to report the general's death to Colonel Maruyama who, he said on his return, did not express a single word of grief over the general. Maruyama immediately readied the 700 survivors for their escape. An officer patrol had already reconnoitred the path. On the adjutant's orders, one of the general's fingers was cut off and wrapped in a bandage. A hole was dug, grass and leaves piled over it.

There are a number of discrepancies in Japanese accounts of the evacuation of Myitkyina. The official history bases itself on Colonel Maruyama's notes, and says that he gave the order to leave on 1 August 1944, and on that night and the following two nights – the moon being nearly full – the survivors crossed the Irrawaddy. The first to cross were General Mizukami's brigade headquarters and the walking wounded. Maruyama himself crossed on the last night, with the last units. The men concealed country boats under the river banks during the day and crossed to the far bank in a sequence laid down beforehand, then assembled in the jungle on the opposite side, as star-shells and tracer continued to light up the sky over Myitkyina.[1]

Sergeant Nishiyama Hideo was one of those responsible for the embarkation, and his recollections are rather different. He believes either that Maruyama's memory is at fault, or that a certain varnishing has taken place. The first night, he says, the walking wounded did get across, but it was in the company of the regimental adjutant, Lieutenant Hirai, and

---

[1] OCH *Irawaji Kaisen*, p. 59

officers and NCOs in charge of the records of meritorious service, and about twenty comfort girls; and General Mizukami and his headquarters. On the second night Colonel Maruyama crossed with his regimental flag, and the officers of regimental headquarters. On the last night, the rest of the officers and men. It is clear that Maruyama, according to this account, was not in the rear party. If Nishiyama's memory serves him right, the sky was clouded on that night, the moon could not be seen, and there were no star-shells or tracer.

Nor was Mizukami's suicide in the thinly wooded spot on the east bank, as Maruyama claims, but on an island in midstream called Nonthalon. The ambiguities are inevitable, given the lapse of time, and apart from the official account giving a favourable gloss to Maruyama's conduct, the discrepancy in the suicide accounts can be resolved by a supposition that Mizukami crossed to the east bank with his group, re-embarked and landed on Nonthalon because that was considered as being still inside the Myitkyina perimeter, i.e. he was still obeying the order given to him personally 'to die in Myitkyina'.[1]

When Lieutenant Horie, carrying Mizukami's relics, finally reached headquarters at Bhamo, he was greeted characteristically by Colonel Tsuji. 'You were told to fight to the last man! What are you doing here? You should be ashamed to be alive!' The 18 Divisional commander, Lieutenant-General Tanaka Shinichi, a martinet and disciplinarian himself, turned to Tsuji and yelled at him: 'That's enough, Tsuji! You'd do better to have some sympathy for a change!'[2] But Tsuji's sympathy, even if he had any, would have been a little late for Mizukami, who should never have been saddled with responsibility for Myitkyina in the first place. The main body of the defence was provided by Maruyama's 114 Regiment, and he could well have been left in command of the garrison. As infantry group commander of 56 Division, Mizukami brought 1500 men with him. He also brought with him the strong feudal spirit of the samurai of North Kyūshū, which would not allow him to interpret an order. Brought in to command the garrison, told to hold it to the death, he did exactly that; but his paternalistic attitude to his men ensured that he saved as many of them as he could. He makes an interesting contrast with 'Vinegar Joe' Stilwell.

[1] Sagara, op.cit., pp. 144–5
[2] ibid, p. 146

385

6. THE BASTION

The Irrawaddy crossings;
back to Mandalay

New generals, new plans — Bridgeheads across the
Irrawaddy — Mandalay

New generals, new plans

As the armies drew apart, sparring for the next round, they began to strip
themselves for the fight. Mutaguchi had sacked his three divisional generals in the course of Operation U-GO. Now he was to go himself. On 30
August 1944, he was transferred to the General Staff in Tokyo, and
replaced by Lieutenant-General Katamura, the commander of 54 Division
in Arakan, which was in turn taken over by Miyazaki, the stubborn little
survivor of Kohima. The same day, Kawabe received his comeuppance,
too, and was moved to Tokyo. The staffs suffered a similar fate, some
being kicked upstairs, others being shunted aside. Naka was given command of 18 Division. The staff officers responsible in Rangoon for Lines of
Communication (Kurahashi) and Operations (Fuwa) were removed, as
were Mutaguchi's staff: Lieutenant-General Kunomura was put in command of 2 Guards Division, his staff officers for Operations (Hirai)
and Lines of Communication (Usui) went elsewhere. Only Fujiwara (Intelligence) survived until the end of December, when he became an instructor at the Military Academy. At the head of Burma Area Army,
Tokyo now placed an interesting combination: shrewdness, strategical skill
and flexibility in the person of Lieutenant-General Kimura Hyōtarō, head
of the Ordnance Administration Headquarters (Heiki gyōsei honbu) in
Tokyo, who had also been at one time Vice-Minister of War under Tojo;
and tenacity and toughness in the shape of Lieutenant-General Tanaka
Shinichi, from the command of 18 Division in North Burma, as his Chief of
Staff. Some of it looks like shuffling chess-pieces around, but by and large
it was a pretty thorough sweep-out, unprecedented in the Japanese Army
at such a high level.

The Allies began to moult, as well. After renewed pressure from Chiang Kai-shek, who had found him intolerable for so long – it was mutual – Roosevelt agreed to remove Stilwell. 'I liked him', wrote Slim, 'There was no one I would rather have had commanding the Chinese Army that was to advance with mine. Under Stilwell it *would* advance. We saw him go with regret...'[1] That is a personal point of view, and although Slim makes it clear he refers to Stilwell as 'a fighting soldier', his 'we' is less than broad. The British Chief of the Imperial General Staff in London, Brooke (later Lord Alanbrooke) dismissed him as having 'little military knowledge and no strategic ability of any kind... he did a vast amount of harm...'[2] Whatever Stilwell's qualities and defects, his departure meant his absurd command structure could be dismantled. His role as advisor to Chiang Kai-shek was taken over by the ambitious and conceited Lieutenant-General Albert Wedemeyer. 'Good God – to be ousted in favour of Wedemeyer – that would be a disgrace', Stilwell had prophetically anticipated in June.[3] Lieutenant-General Daniel Sultan would command the Northern Combat Area Command (NCAC) and Mountbatten's Principal Administrative Officer, Lieutenant-General Raymond Wheeler, was to become Deputy Supreme Commander, SEAC.

The land forces command was also rationalized. Since Stilwell, after the capture of Kamaing, had refused to come under any direction other than Mountbatten's, the latter had in effect been combining his own job with that of Commander-in-Chief Allied Land Forces, a role he was not equipped to handle. Lieutenant-General Sir Oliver Leese was finally winkled out of command of Eighth Army and took over control of NCAC, XV Corps, Lines of Communication troops, and XIV Army. Slim noticed that on his arrival on 12 November 1944, Leese was accompanied by his own staff from Eighth Army, with 'a good deal of desert sand in its shoes and... rather inclined to thrust Eighth Army down our throats'.[4] Eleventh Army Group ceased to exist, and Giffard went home. His congé was long overdue, Pownall had already noted months before: 'He is a tired man... has been long abroad and he dislikes Mountbatten so much that he won't "play"... And Mountbatten feels that he cannot project his own energy and drive through so passive a man as Giffard.'[5] Slim, who had understood Giffard's reticence, said he saw him go with grief, but it was a gesture of friendly politeness: Giffard's time was up.[6] So was Pownall's. He had long felt he had come to the end of his usefulness in Ceylon, and was con-

---

[1] Slim, *Defeat into Victory*, p. 384

[2] Bryant, *The Turn of the Tide*, p. 506

[3] Diary for 22 June 1944, *The Stilwell Papers*, p. 283

[4] Slim, op.cit., p. 385

[5] Bond, ed., *Chief of Staff*, pp. 166–7

[6] Slim, op.cit., p. 385

sistently pessimistic about the chances of SEAC contributing anything useful to the war against Japan, though he was, as Chief of Staff, a handy counterbalance to Mountbatten's restless and volatile enthusiasm. He was replaced by Lieutenant-General Frederick (Boy) Browning, fresh from the defeat of his parachute forces at Arnhem: 'rather nervy and highly strung', commented Pownall.[1] Leese's arrival and the new command structure meant that Slim at XIV Army did not need to be responsible for Christison and XV Corps operations in Arakan, and could occupy himself with planning for the invasion of Central Burma. What he had in mind for this explains one final change in command.[2] Of his two Corps Commanders, Scoones at IV Corps had borne the strain of action for longer than Stopford. He had taken the Corps out to rest at Ranchi after the defeat of Mutaguchi, and early in October brought his headquarters back to Imphal in readiness for the new campaign. Throughout the battle for Imphal, he had been steady, farsighted – as Slim called him – and slow off the mark; and Slim's new ideas demanded a IV Corps Commander who would have, above all, dash and spirit. Fortunately, in December, Scoones was offered the job of Commander-in-Chief, Central Command, in India, which enabled Slim to replace him by Messervy, GOC 7 Indian Division, the very man 'not too calculating of odds' for the cavalry charge that was going to cut the Japanese in two.[3]

In this way, defeat for the Japanese and victory for the Allies in 1944 led on both sides to a massive recasting. As a final flourish, Wavell came to Imphal in December and, on behalf of the King, knighted Slim and his three Corps Commanders, Christison, Scoones and Stopford. It only needed the master of the tournament to say: 'let battle commence'.

Both sides scrapped not only their hierarchies, but also their plans. SEAC considered three possibilities:

(i) XIV Army crossing the Chindwin and making a limited offensive on the other side while NCAC, absorbing British and Indian divisions, would join up with the Chinese from Yunnan and secure North Burma up to a line Katha-Mongmit-Lashio. In other words, forget everything except securing a land route to China.

(ii) NCAC and the Yunnan Chinese to strike further south, as far as Maymyo, and link up there with XIV Army which would take Mandalay.

---

[1] Bond, ed., *Chief of Staff*, p. 193

[2] Lewin, *Slim*, p. 206

[3] Slim, op.cit., p. 388

(iii) Rangoon to be captured by a joint seaborne and airborne operation.

All three were more ambitious than the directive by the Chiefs of Staff in London, drawn up in June 1944, which merely prescribed the development of the *air* link to China in support of operations in the Pacific; maximum pressure to be exerted during the monsoon with the aim of developing an *overland* link with China. As Slim viewed it, their directive enshrined the US view of the campaign, and even if aid to China were put first, it seemed to him that the capture of Rangoon by clearing the Japanese out of Burma was the best way to do that. Naturally, he preferred SEAC's second proposition, since it gave pride of place to XIV Army. He undervalued the third, because he thought the theatre would never get the equipment for an amphibious attack on Rangoon. In the end, Mountbatten opted for a combination of the second and third plans. The offensive, codenamed CAPITAL, envisaged XIV Army occupying Central Burma between Chindwin and Irrawaddy, and taking Mandalay; NCAC and the Chinese advancing to a line Thabeikkyin-Mogok-Lashio; an advance in Arakan to seize airfields from which an advance on Rangoon could be covered; and lastly Operation DRACULA, a sea and airborne capture of Rangoon by March 1945.

Slim had doubts whether SEAC had the manpower and equipment for Mandalay and Rangoon; and his own mission, of taking Central Burma up to a line Pakokku-Mandalay, could well be bedevilled by dwindling numbers in his British battalions. The shortfall was made up to some extent by releasing anti-aircraft gunners, no longer needed, into infantry units. Giffard had suggested to him a plan involving airborne advances to secure Kalewa and Kalemyo and the Shwebo area, but he argued that planes were best used to supply his troops rather than carry them, and Giffard agreed.

Messervy, at IV Corps, was to have the so far unused 19 Indian Division, under another general with North African experience, Major-General T. W. ('Pete') Rees;[1] 7 Indian Division (now under Geoffrey Evans); and 255 Tank Brigade. XXXIII Corps had 2 Division (Nicholson, since Glover's departure, 5 July 1944), 20 Indian Division, 268 Brigade and 254 Tank Brigade. XXXIII Corps' right flank would be protected down the west bank of the Chindwin by the Lushai Brigade and 28 East African Brigade. 11 East African Division, which had marched down the Kabaw Valley sweeping it of the remnants of 15 Army, would be flown out to India to rest, as soon as Stopford was across the Chindwin at Kalewa. 5, 17 and 23 Divisions were for the time being out of the battle; but not for long. The

---

[1] who had been most unfairly sacked by his Corps Commander, Gott, from command of the 10 Indian Division because he disagreed with Gott's dispositions for Tobruk. By a strange coincidence, this happened two days before the 8 Army commander, Ritchie, dismissed Messervy from the command of 7 Armoured Division in the same battle. (John Connell, *Auchinleck*, pp. 610–11)

physical condition of the troops left much to be desired. The Japanese were certainly retreating in a catastrophic state to the Chindwin; but XXXIII Corps statistics show an uneasy picture. 'Of its average weekly July-November strength of 88,500', writes Raymond Callahan, 'about half were maintained forward of Imphal in pursuit of the Japanese. Total casualties, however, came to 50,300, of whom only *forty-nine* were killed in action [my italics]. More than half the 47,000 who went sick had to be evacuated back to India. Even with mepacrine, there were over 20,000 cases of malaria.'[1]

The Japanese, too, had altered their perspective. The war was going badly for them in the Pacific. The US naval assault was already beginning to lap at the approaches to Japan itself, and had destroyed the Japanese fleet at the Battle of Leyte in the Philippines. And in South-East Asia, where minds had contemplated for a time the heady dream of the offensive into India and the launching of Subhas Chandra Bose into Bengal, the posture was now one of defence, with Thailand and the Malayan Peninsula as the outer periphery of a self-sufficient military zone which would block the progress of the Allied forces toward Singapore and the South China Sea, even though it was cut off from the Japanese islands by relentless US submarine warfare against its shipping lanes. Burma's role in this was to continue the attempt to block the reinforcement of China, though this would lie more in attempting to cut the Ledo Road than intercepting aircraft across the Hump, for which there were now not enough fighter planes. The occasional shooting down of the transport aircraft, which the Japanese termed *tsuji-giri* ('cutting down a casually-met stranger') or *akago no te wo hineru* ('twisting a baby's arm') was no longer, since the fall of Myitkyina airfield, the easy game it had been.

On 2 July 1944, Southern Area Army issued Operation Order 101 instructing Kawabe to continue to resist the British west of the Chindwin and Stilwell's forces in North Burma and west of the Salween, thus keeping the link between India and China cut. Within weeks this was out-of-date, and Terauchi had to think again. He waited until the command shake-up settled down and on 26 September gave the new GOC-in-C in Rangoon, Lieutenant-General Kimura, a very much reduced role. He was to ensure the stability and security of *southern* Burma as the northern flank of the South-East Asian defence zone. The duty of cutting the Allies' India-China link remained, *dekiru kagiri* – 'as far as possible' – and he was to plan *jikatsu jisen* for his command. This phrase was much in use at the time for Japanese forces overseas. It meant subsisting on your own and fighting on your own. No help was to be expected from Japan, the armies must learn

---

[1] Callahan, *Burma 1942–1945*, p. 141

to live off the land where they were. Seaborne supplies to Rangoon were already a trickle, and Allied bombing had reduced the effectiveness of the Burma-Siam Railway. Kimura's job as head of ordnance in Tokyo had accustomed him to organizing factories under difficulties, and he was obviously expected to make what he could of the factories around Rangoon. But Burma was not an industrial country. It was a forlorn hope.

What is interesting about these plans is the shift of *real* attention, on both sides, from the China link to a confrontation in Central or Southern Burma. Victory at Imphal had shown Slim that what he must do was not capture towns but bring the Japanese Army to battle and destroy it. Kimura knew that he had as good as lost North Burma, and he had received the last reinforcements he was going to get – 49 Division. Still, he had three Armies, 15, 28, and 33, grouping ten divisions in all (2, 15, 18, 31, 33, 49, 53, 54, 55, 56). In addition, he had a (much reduced) tank regiment, two independent mixed brigades (one badly mauled by the Chindits), lines of communication and administration troops – about 100,000 men, and Bose's INA. He also had seven battalions of the Burma National Army under Aung San, the young anti-British revolutionary turned Major-General. But Japanese intelligence was aware that the success of the British and the ineptitude of the Japanese military was putting strains on the loyalty of those Burmese who, a year ago, had been overjoyed to receive their independence at Japanese hands.

Some reinforcements had reached him. A conference of Lines of Communication staff officers in Singapore had put the number of men available for Burma as 60,000 with whom there could be sent weapons and ammunition for three divisions, 45,000 tons of supplies, 500 lorries, and 2000 pack animals. The problem was to get them there. Under constant attack by Allied aircraft, the Burma-Siam Railway, in a good month, could carry a maximum of 15,000 tons. Maritime transport was therefore used. Sixty vessels under No. 38 Harbour Unit at Rangoon ran the gauntlet of British submarines and aircraft. Between June and October 1944, around 30,000 fresh troops arrived in Burma to shore up the depleted divisions. But it was a temporary expedient, because by November the war in the Philippines and tension in French Indo-China decided Terauchi to pull out some of the troops he had sent to Burma; and the morale of those that stayed in Burma, under the impact of the climate and fearful battle conditions, began to slip. They were flung into battle without adequate preparation, stragglers dragged behind their units, deserters began to slip off into the Burmese villages. In the end, the divisions received about 2000 reinforcements each. 15 Army's divisions received ten–twelve guns each in November, and 14 Tank Regiment's new light and medium tanks brought its total up to twenty. Kimura's Chief of Staff laid down in round numbers that a division should be 10,000 men; but often they were reduced to half that number.

In October, Burma Area Army defined its aims. It was to secure a line linking Lashio, the Mandalay area, the Irrawaddy south of Mandalay, Yenangyaung, and Rangoon. It expected the front of the decisive battle to be on the banks of the Irrawaddy downstream from Mandalay, or the triangle area of the Irrawaddy delta. Its dispositions for this battle were:

(i) 33 Army (18 and 56 Divisions) to hold a line from Lashio to the Monglong mountains north-east of Mandalay and halt the enemy on it. To try and cut the India-China land link, as far as that was possible. The operation was to be called Operation DAN (which means 'to cut').

(ii) 15 Army (15, 31 and 33 Divisions) was to secure the heights north of Madaya, the Sagaing bridgehead, and the Pakokku area. Enemy attacks would be halted on the banks of the Irrawaddy. The operation to be called BAN ('plate').

(iii) 28 Army (54 and 55 Divisions, and an independent mixed brigade to be formed at Yenangyaung) was to seek out the enemy advance and hold it at a distance. If things went badly, it would hold a zone comprising Yenangyaung, the southern frontier hills, Bassein and Rangoon. The operation was to be called KAN ('completion').

28 and 33 Armies were to co-operate for the success of BAN, so that was clearly where the priority lay, though 15 Army was in a worse condition than the other two. Boundaries were fixed. The line Mogok-Sumsai-Kalaw divided 15 Army from 33 Army, and the line Pagan-Kyaukpadaung from 28 Army. The latter line was to affect the coming battle in a way that Kimura could not have foreseen.

Kimura placed 2 Division, removed from coastal duties in Arakan, and 49 Division in rear areas between Pyinmana and Pegu, along the main road and rail artery from Mandalay south to Rangoon, as strategic reserves. 53 Division was placed under command of 15 Army, with the proviso that Kimura himself might, in an emergency, place it directly under his own command.

Map manoeuvres were conducted by Kimura's staff during which the following issues arose:

(i) Could 15 Army hold its present line against a superior Allied force as it moved into a dry-season offensive?
The line was Indaw-Zibyu Range-Kalewa, and 15 Army estimated that there was a greater risk of internal collapse from a

The Intelligence Officer of 63 Brigade, 17 Indian Division, searching Japanese corpses at Meiktila, 23 February 1945. *(Imperial War Museum)*

Lieutenant-General (later Sir) Frank Messervy, GOC IV Corps.
(Imperial War Museum)

Major-General D. T. ('Punch') Cowan (left), GOC 17 Indian Division,
conferring with Brigadier R.C.O. Hedley, commanding 48 Brigade. Meiktila,
28 February 1945. *(Imperial War Museum)*

Colonel Tsuji Masanobu, staff officer in Lieutenant-General Honda's 33 Army, in post-war civilian dress. (In Tsuji's *Underground Escape*)

The Rangoon-Mandalay Road near Milestone 137 where 28 Army Headquarters broke out towards the Sittang, June 1945. *(Lieutenant-Colonel Tsuchiya Eiichi)*

Lieutenant-Commander Tsutsumi Shinzō, 13 Naval Guard Force. (Taken in 1940 at age 25, rank Sub-Lieutenant.) *(Mr Tsutsumi Shinzō)*

Kayabuki Norimasa, the Japanese Muslim agent who worked against the British in Arakan. (A recent photograph taken on a flight from Jeddah.) *(Mr Kayabuki)*

Five Chinese and Korean comfort girls captured during the Sittang breakout. In the cage at Penwegon. *(Imperial War Museum)*

Japanese soldier carrying white flag at a surrender parley near Waw.
(Imperial War Museum)

Lieutenant-General Numata Takazō, Chief of Staff to Field-Marshal Terauchi at Southern Army Headquarters, arrives in Rangoon to discuss surrender arrangements. He is accompanied by Rear-Admiral Chūdō, Imperial Japanese Navy. *(Imperial War Museum)*

British troops cheer the news of the surrender. *(Imperial War Museum)*

The Beaten. Major Wakō Hisanori, a staff officer from 28 Army, hands over his sword before negotiations with Lieutenant-Colonel O. C. Smyth, CO 1/10 Gurkha Rifles. Lieutenant Bert Corey (centre, glasses) interprets.
(Imperial War Museum)

The Beaten. Major-General W. A. Crowther, Cowan's successor as GOC
17 Indian Division, accepts the surrender of Lieutenant-General Kawada
Tsuchitarō, GOC 31 Division. *(Imperial War Museum)*

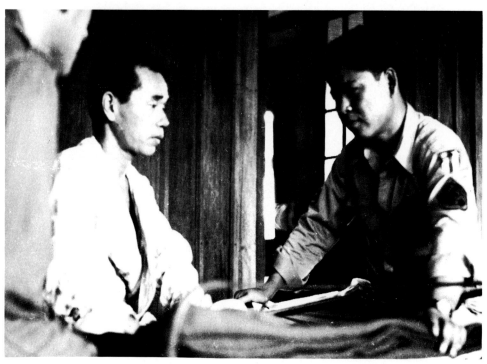

The author (left) and US Nisei Sergeant Tabata interrogate POW Lieutenant
Naito. *(Imperial War Museum)*

rapidly continuing retreat than from an attempt to hold the British offensive for two months.

(ii) 15 Army had lost most of its mobility, and with that, its fighting strength. Could it take up a counter-offensive position in the dry season on the banks of the Irrawaddy after withdrawing for more than 300 miles?

15 Army thought that if it pulled 31 Division into the Shwebo Plain ahead of the rest, it could secure the Plain, and 15 and 53 Divisions could withdraw along both banks of the Irrawaddy. 33 Division could make for Monywa after crossing the Chindwin at Kalewa. By avoiding a front in the Shwebo Plain in this way, it should be possible to bring the divisions to the east bank of the Irrawaddy.

(iii) The third problem was crucial: was the Irrawaddy to be defended on the far bank, the near bank, or behind the near bank? This caused the most prolonged debate, and they finally settled on a plan to distribute forces directly along the river bank, along its southern shore (i.e. the 'east' bank). This gave 15 Army a front of 250 miles to defend; and behind it, the rice (the Delta) and oil (Yenangyaung) that Kimura needed to keep his army going.

A thousand yards wide, the Irrawaddy had many islands in midstream, and at Sagaing, opposite Mandalay, it swung west at right-angles. The Japanese decided to hold a strong point in this curve, based on the Sagaing hills.

It was realized that, with 15 Army's vastly decreased firepower and mobility, there was no chance of it repelling the enemy during a crossing. Further north, it was considered absolutely vital to hold the point where 15 Army and 33 Army's fronts met in the Monglong hills, and reinforcements were to be rushed there if the enemy threatened to break through to the south.

I have given the Japanese thinking at some length, because it had a vital effect on the clinching battle of the campaign. It can be seen from the disposition of both sides that if the Allies were confident of being able to move and be protected from the air, the Japanese were not: they had 64 planes with which to defend Burma, compared with an RAF and USAAF strength of 1200. The Allies were obsessed by roads and supplies, as were the Japanese. Both Slim and Kimura feared there would be little more in the way of reinforcements, though Slim hoped for some once the war against Germany was over. In the meanwhile he could see his British battalions being stripped by the departure of men on long overdue leave and repatriation.

For both of them, naturally, the Irrawaddy was the central factor. Psychologically it was, as Major-General Iwakuro, 28 Army Chief of Staff pointed out, 'the line of change of the hearts of the Burmese people'. But it will be clear from the Japanese debates that Kimura never considered meeting XIV Army in a mass confrontation on the Shwebo Plain, as Slim was sure he would. It was Slim's greatest mistake, but he perceived he was wrong before the year was out, and rapidly readjusted. That readjustment produced the master-stroke of the Burma campaign: the drive on Meiktila, which scissored Kimura's army in two, and in the end lost him the whole of Burma.

Given the amount of information at the disposal of commanders in North Africa, Italy and North-West Europe from decoded signals intelligence (ULTRA), it may seem surprising that Slim could be in doubt about what Kimura was planning. In the first book which revealed the extent of ULTRA information, Group-Captain Winterbotham states categorically, 'Slim was getting all he needed to know from London, Washington and Australia.'[1] Winterbotham asserts Slim told him that intelligence from ULTRA had been invaluable throughout the campaign and was crucial in the Imphal battles, by showing first that the Japanese supply position was desperate and second that the Japanese air force had dwindled so as to be practically useless. Hence the uninterrupted airlift of supplies to Imphal, and the unharmed fly-in of 5 Division.

Now the Japanese supply position and the order of battle of its air divisions was known from captured documents and agents' reports. ULTRA was hardly crucial by itself, and the surrounding of 7 Division at Sinzweya and the narrow escape of 17 Division at Tiddim would surely have been avoided if signals intelligence had been available early enough on the same ample scale on which it was used in Normandy. In fact, Slim was less than flattering about the intelligence at his disposal. Admittedly *Defeat into Victory* was published in 1956, years before it was possible to mention ULTRA. But this does not affect the nature of his comments:

> I had throughout been conscious that... our intelligence... was far from being as complete or as accurate as in other theatres. We never made up for the lack of methodically collected intelligence or the intelligence organization which should have been available to us when the war began. We knew something of the Japanese intentions, but little of the dispositions of their reserves, and practically nothing about one of the most important factors that a general has to consider – the character of the opposing commanders.[2]

[1] *The Ultra Secret*, 1975, p. 228.

[2] Slim, op.cit., p. 221. Cf. Ronald Lewin, *Ultra Goes to War*, 1980, p. 139: 'In South-East Asia, moreover, SLUs [Special Liaison Units] now serviced Mountbatten, Slim, Stilwell and the US bomber commands in India and China, drawing on a world-wide information loop that linked Bletchley, SEAC, Washington and Brisbane.'

'I had not at my disposal,' he wrote later of the Imphal battles, 'the sources of information of the enemy's intentions that some more fortunate commanders in other theatres were able to invoke'[1] a fairly clear, if veiled, reference to ULTRA.

Nor is this hindsight. At the very time he was trying to assess the intentions of Burma Area Army in September 1944, Slim wrote to General Playfair, of Mountbatten's staff in Ceylon, that he was concerned about the lack of information coming out of Burma. He wanted twenty Z patrols sent into Burma to bring out fresh intelligence, and he had learned that only two such patrols were going in 'and although this is better than nothing it is not sufficient as I am about to start this autumn's campaign with woefully little intelligence of enemy on my front.'[2] Z patrols were small parties of Burmese or Burmese-speakers – often no more than two – equipped with radio and a simple cipher and armed with revolver and carbine, who were dropped into Japanese-held territory by parachute, or flown in by helicopter. In other words, they were not all that different from the patrols of V Force, save that the latter were led by British officers. It is characteristic of Slim that he should value direct information taken on the spot, of this kind, which might often be less useful or detailed than that provided by captured documents.

Scoones at IV Corps was equally disparaging of the information supplied to him:

> I feel sure (he wrote in June 1944) that the Jap is going to have a final smack for Imphal from both the Bishenpur and Tamu directions. Reinforcements have undoubtedly reached Ouvry's front [i.e. 23 Division, Major-General Ouvry Roberts] and there is some indication that these too may belong to 53 Division. Incidentally the arrival of this Div or elements of it unheralded on this front is a pretty poor chit for our higher intelligence organization.
>
> I sent in a long letter the other day setting out my views on the amount of money and manpower which we are wasting on these hush-hush organizations and which, so far as I am concerned, produce nothing useful.[3]

For other armies, prisoner-of-war interrogation might provide detailed tactical information before or during the battle, but the number of Japanese POWs taken in Burma was tiny, at any rate until morale began to crack in

[1] ibid., p. 289

[2] PRO, WO 203. There were of course static agents equipped with radio transmitters. One such was a doctor at Kohima who found himself in the middle of the battle and was compelled to act as MO for the Assam Regiment during the siege, which reduced his intelligence effectiveness to nil. But it was not the function of static agents to operate in battle zones; he was just unlucky.

[3] Letter dated 24 June 1944, PRO, WO 203/56.

the monsoon of 1945; and no rank higher than captain was ever captured, which limited the usefulness of the knowledge they had anyway. On the other hand, they could be excellent indicators of morale and unit identification. Documents were another matter: captured operation orders and maps provided crucial intelligence in Arakan (it will be recalled that 7 Indian Division was in possession of 'Tokuta's' plans when Tanahashi burst into its HQ at Sinzweya and found them). The same is true of Kohima and Imphal, where Major Richard Storry's mobile section of the Combined Services' Detailed Interrogation Centre (CSDIC) kept up a constant flow of intelligence to Corps HQ, and was there throughout the siege. Later still, at Meiktila and in the battle of the Breakout, the strengths and intentions of the Japanese were crystal-clear from their own documents.

The exploitation of these resources should have been more immediate and more extensive than it was. There were simply not enough linguists to go round. When Cowan went into Meiktila in what was arguably the most crucial armoured thrust of the entire campaign, he had, among his 11,000 men, precisely two who could speak and read the enemy's language. Stanley Charles and George Kay solved Cowan's constant anxiety – what forces were the Japanese putting up against him? – by tireless interrogation of prisoners and endless scouring of the battlefield for identifications from corpses – paybooks, photographs, identity discs, diaries, maps. A single document taken at Meiktila, for instance, gave a complete breakdown of the order of battle of 15 Army. But the linguists were rare birds. A few were old Japan hands who had ended up in India after Pearl Harbour. Most were classics and modern language students from the universities, trained at the School of Oriental Studies in London and then appointed to a division or corps headquarters in Burma. But their rarity meant that many documents had to be flown out to India, where a long-range picture was built up, whereas, for what Slim and Scoones were after, prompt decipherment on the spot was needed and one translator and one inter-rogator per division were far too few.[1]

Bridgeheads across the Irrawaddy

On 3 December 1944, thirty miles north of Kalewa, on the banks of the Chindwin at Mawlaik, a brigade of 20 Division started to cross the river. The East Africans of 11 Division battered a bridgehead through Kalewa and the rest of 20 Division passed through it aiming for Monywa. The Japanese offered little resistance, which was surprising, even given their battered state, because the east bank of the Chindwin at this point is

[1] Private correspondence, S. T. Charles. And cf. Evans and Brett-James, *Imphal*, pp. 76–83, p. 89

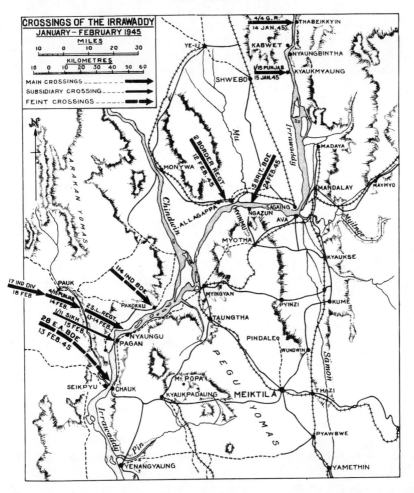

thick jungle covering steep hills and ridges, which could have put a brake on Stopford similar to the delaying action of Miyazaki earlier on the Kohima-Imphal road. 2 Division came through the bridgehead on 19 December to relieve the East Africans and push on to Shwebo, about forty miles north-west of Mandalay. As they fanned out from the east bank of the Chindwin, Slim's troops began to find that the balance, in terms of numbers and lines of communications, was tipping slightly against them. Kimura could place over five divisions in their path, not counting the odd brigade and administrative tail; and the Allies were now the ones at the end of tenuous lines of supply facing an enemy with a railway leading to railheads at Alon and Myingyan. They were also coming out of the jungle: Central Burma was made up of low hills and flat level plain, hot and dusty under the December sun. It was ideal country for tank warfare, and Slim was sure that when he concentrated his divisions in the Shwebo Plain, a triangle formed by the Irrawaddy as it flowed south then bent sharp west, to where the Chindwin flows into it north of Myingyan, he would be able to inflict a decisive defeat on Kimura.

As we have seen, Kimura had no intention of giving battle in the Shwebo Plain. He was a good strategist, but his isolation from Japan and a penurious existence at the end of the South-East Asia supply lines meant that his armies were to be fighting not for strategic advantage but for their lives. Soon they were doing just that. Five days before 20 Division began to cross the Chindwin, 19 Division, so far unblooded, came out of its Sittaung bridge-head making for Pinlebu and Pinbon. It had no artillery or motor transport because there had not been enough boats at the crossing, but Rees remembered Slim's instructions to IV Corps to take risks for the sake of speed, and in eight days he was across the Zibyu hills. Four days later, on 16 December, he had linked up with 36 Division coming down the Railway Corridor at Rail Indaw: NCAC and XIV Army fronts now ran together.[1]

Rees's rapid progress made Slim think again. Would the Japanese not have made greater efforts to block him, if they were going to hold XIV Army west of the Irrawaddy? The Burmese in the villages through which 19 Division passed told the same story: most of the Japanese had gone. If they were simply slipping away under the impact of his offensive, then there would be no battle of confrontation, which was what he sought. So Kimura would have to be trapped in another way, behind the Irrawaddy if not before it. He therefore devised a plan to send a strong force behind Kimura, at a point he least expected, and grip his communications network. There was an obvious spot: the area of Meiktila and Thazi, where there were dumps supplying 15 Army and 33 Army, airfields, hospitals and rail and road links with Rangoon. If Kimura could be persuaded that XIV Army was aiming at Mandalay, as seemed natural enough, then Slim could switch enough of his forces into Meiktila to compel Kimura to fight to get it back. When one of the official historians (Brigadier M. R. Roberts) asked him where he got the notion of going for Meiktila rather than Shwebo, Slim answered that it arose naturally out of staff discussions at XIV Army.[2] He did not know who first mentioned the name Meiktila. It is a characteristically modest disclaimer. But it hides perhaps an obvious source. To get at Meiktila you have to jump the Irrawaddy. The best place from which to do that, on the map, is Pakokku on the west bank. As early as March 1944, Wingate had proposed to Mountbatten and Slim that one possibility of using the reserve Chindit brigades would be to send them via Pakokku into Meiktila.[3] It was in

[1] Lewin, *Slim*, p. 212

[2] Evans, *Slim*, p. 187

[3] 'The most profitable sphere for this (i.e., 23) Brigade, assuming all goes well and 14 Bde is successfully introduced into PAKOKKU; will be in the MEIKTILA area to exploit the situation generally. If this is done, we may confront the Japanese at the beginning of the monsoon with a front stretching from PAKOKKU to LASHIO, with almost the entire length of the CHINDWIN in our hands.' Wingate, 'Forecast of Possible Development of THURSDAY by Commander Special Force', 13 March 1944. (PRO, WO 203/187, LRP Correspondence.)

fact the impact of this idea that inspired Mountbatten to signal to his AXIOM Mission under Wedemeyer, in Washington, that the whole of Burma *could* be taken, provided there was ample air supply and air support. Wedemeyer was naturally dumbfounded, since AXIOM's purpose was to soft-pedal the idea of a land offensive across Burma. But General Arnold, Chief of the USAAF, thought it a splendid idea and authorized the sending of 400 transport aircraft to SEAC on the strength of it. The US historians point out that it was this sudden gift of riches in the air which radically transformed the future of the war in Burma. Perhaps this is a debt from Slim to Wingate, on either score.[1]

But how to get to Pakokku? Slim knew the answer to that already. The short way into Burma across the Chindwin is from Kalewa to Yeu and Shwebo, which lands you just north-west of Mandalay. There is another way, longer, more difficult and so less obvious: down the valley of the River Myittha, past the Chin Hills, Gangaw, Tilin and Pauk, which brings you out about thirty miles west of Pakokku. 2 Burma Brigade had used this route during the retreat of 1942. Slim's capture of the Shwebo Plain could go ahead: that was Operation CAPITAL. Operation EXTENDED CAPITAL would use the main body of IV Corps, moving secretly down the Myittha Valley so that Kimura would not suspect a switch of strength, put it across at Pakokku and take Meiktila by an armoured thrust.[2] In the lead would be Cowan's 17 Indian Division, now returned from resting in India, one brigade of which could be airborne.

All that was necessary was to get the armour down the Myittha Valley. Slim's engineers had already performed miracles. Indeed miracles were almost casually quotidian. The longest Bailey Bridge in the world now spanned the Chindwin at Kalewa. A fleet of boats and rafts was ready to carry men and supplies down the Chindwin to where it joined the Irrawaddy near Myingyan, a return to the superiority of traditional river transport in Burma. Eight hundred tons a day were planned to be available by 1 May 1945, using this route.[3] Major-General 'Bill' Hasted, XIV Army's chief engineer, guessed that he could put a road down the Myittha in forty-two days, and that bithess was the way to do it. Bithess was extensively used to make runways for airstrips, and consisted of hessian in rolls fifty yards long by one yard wide, treated with bitumen so that it looks like a long carpet of oilcloth. The strips are laid to overlap by eight inches and the road, levelled and packed tight, is cambered by laying the two

[1] Tulloch, *Wingate in Peace and War*, pp. 211–13. Romanus and Sunderland, *Stilwell's Command Problems*, p. 99

[2] Lewin, *Slim*, p. 215

[3] Evans, *Slim*, p. 190

outside strips first and then building the road up from edge to centre. It is expensive. Every yard of road takes a gallon of petrol and a gallon of diesel. But it works. A hundred miles of bithess road took a thousand vehicles a day.[1]

Lieutenant-Colonel J. H. Williams ('Elephant Bill') had already helped 11 East African Division down the waterlogged Kabaw Valley by laying tree trunks. By December 1944, four roads fit for motor transport were available to the Chindwin, and Williams's elephants had built every bridge on them.[2] The elephants were now conscripted for the Myittha project, but not as bridge or road-builders. They were to be part of IV Corps' deception plan.[3] Williams was asked to go forty miles up the Yeu River, contact six elephant camps, and get their headmen to bring their elephants across the Chindwin to give the appearance of a large force crossing. Williams mentioned casually that one of his officers, Finch, knew the valley down which IV Corps was to travel. Messervy realized that someone who knew the terrain, in command of elephants, would be far more use to him than a mere ruse. So Finch and his elephants went down the Myittha, too. Deception went on in other ways. To make Kimura's intelligence organizations think that IV Corps was still making for Mandalay, signals were sent from a bogus Corps Headquarters at Tamu to 19 Division, which had by then been taken under the umbrella of XXXIII Corps.

Slim needed aircraft, too. From 16 December, his Army's needs had been worked out at 750 tons a day, rising to 1200 tons from March, when the Meiktila operation would be in full swing. He was flabbergasted one morning in his headquarters at Imphal to hear aircraft passing overhead in large numbers and to learn that they were Dakotas he had been allocated – three squadrons – which had been suddenly ordered to China. He needed 7000 sorties a day, and every plane he could lay his hands on, and to lose seventy-five without notice was a hard blow.[4] The complication was the situation in China. To forestall the use of US advanced airfields in China from which Chennault's planes were ultimately to bomb the Japanese islands, the Japanese Expeditionary Force in China mounted Operation ICHI-GO (No. 1) aimed at capturing the airfields. It was the one campaign in 1944 in which they had some success, and Wedemeyer, now adviser to Chiang, decided to airlift the Chinese divisions out of Burma to reinforce the central front in China, using the

---

[1] Lewin, *Slim*, p. 217

[2] J. H. Williams, *Elephant Bill*, p. 279

[3] Slim, op.cit., p. 398

[4] Lewin, *Slim*, p. 217

Dakotas on loan to Slim to do it. 'The noise of their engines', wrote Slim, 'was the first intimation that anyone in Fourteenth Army had of the administrative crisis now bursting upon us.'[1]

It meant working out afresh every loading calculation for Meiktila, and although reducing the air-lift to 15 Corps in Arakan helped to restore the lost tonnage, the delay left less time to complete the Army's tasks before the 1945 monsoon.

Wedemeyer's 'retrieval' happened on 10 December. Nine days later Slim was heartened to learn that his northernmost prong was going well. By that day Rees's 19 Division was at Wuntho, and by the 23rd had covered nearly 200 miles from the Chindwin, making their road as they went, winching lorries up slopes when they could not climb them unaided. To the right of Rees, 268 Brigade had marched on Oil Indaw[2] and on to the Mu River which flowed down to Shwebo. XXXIII Corps took over these two formations on 26 December, while its southernmost divisions, 2 and 20, moved on Yeu and Monywa respectively. Slim had expected some resistance to 2 Division at Pyingaing, the point at which the Zibyu Range petered out, but there was none until some miles further east. After breaking through a roadblock with the co-operation of Gurkhas from 20 Division who came round behind it, and chasing away a Japanese de-molition party about to blow the Kabo weir on which the irrigation of the plain depended, 2 Division reached Yeu on 2 January 1945. The Mu River, which lay between it and Shwebo, was crossed the following day, and a bridgehead established. Engineers then bridged the river to allow the main body of the division to cross. Within a week they were forcing their way into Shwebo from the northwest.

They were not, though, the first into the town: 19 Division had attacked from the east on the 7th. The defenders were 2 Division's old opponents from Kohima, the now reconstituted 31 Division. 58 Infantry Regiment (Inage) was at Kanbalu to the north of the town, and 124 Infantry Re-giment (Hirunuma) was in Shwebo itself, with 138 Infantry Regiment (Torikai) at Sagaing, just opposite Mandalay. As tourists, Torikai's men were undoubtedly the luckiest, though they did not have much time to appreciate it. Just before Sagaing lies a great pagoda surrounded by 120 Buddhas in alcoves round its base. Plants grow from the great dome which is shaped exactly like a breast. (The architect is said to have asked the Queen, his patron, what design she preferred, whereupon she thrust her own breast out of her dress and asked what better shape there could be.) The whole area is a complex of shrines, one of which contains a reclining Buddha like the massive couched figure at Pegu. The link between Sagaing

---

[1] Slim, op.cit., p. 396

[2] So called to differentiate it from Rail Indaw, the Chindits' former objective in the Railway Corridor.

and Mandalay was the magnificent Ava Bridge, its red girders resting on terracotta and grey-brown abutments, but this was destroyed during the 1942 retreat – the two central spans had gone – and the Japanese had not had time to rebuild it.

There was also a composite artillery unit under the command of Lieutenant-Colonel Oyabe, with 31 Division's mountain guns and a battalion from 21 Field Regiment of 15 Division. Hirunuma used mines and prepared positions to delay 19 Division's advance, but received orders to pull back south on 1 January. They managed to leave Kanbalu in good order, but in a night battle at Kinu chaos ensued and they were in a mess by the time they reached Shwebo, leaving the way open for Rees's hot pursuit.

On the morning of 7 January, a patrol of the 5 Baluch (64 Brigade) entered Shwebo. The rest of the battalion followed, the same night, beating 2 British Division by a whisker. Rees received a signal from the Corps Commander, urging him to put the Japanese 31 Division 'in the bag', and he sent a battalion to cut the Japanese retreat. The battalion was then ordered to halt, Rees acting on the orders of the Corps Commander, as the offensive into the town itself was the responsibility of 2 Division. That was in the original plan. 19 Division was to block Shwebo on the south and east. The Japanese history, describing this switch of roles when Rees was poised to take the town himself, admits that there may have been tactical reasons for Stopford's order to halt 19 Division, such as the undesirability of committing a large body of troops to street fighting, and the need to prevent Allied units firing on each other by mistake. But it suspects also that there may have been a desire on the part of the British corps commander to ensure that a totally British unit – 2 Division – entered Shwebo first. At all events, Shwebo fell to XXXIII Corps, with Japanese casualties of fifty-eight killed and ten prisoners.[1]

Lieutenant-General Katamura never had any intention of making Shwebo a last-man last-round battle. His order to 31 Division to withdraw to the Irrawaddy was issued on 10 January, and Hirunuma's regiment moved by night over forty miles south to occupy Indaw. A rear party resisted in the northern part of Shwebo until the 10th. To the soldiers of XXXIII Corps, the ability of the individual Japanese soldier to resist had been diminished by the shattering defeats at Imphal and Kohima. In command of 2 Dorset,

---

[1] The British official history refers to 64 Brigade being in Shwebo on 8 January, the Indian history puts the Baluch patrol in on the 7th, Evans refers to 2 and 19 Divisions capturing Shwebo 'by 5 January'. In fact, the minutes of Stopford's conference with his divisional commanders on 20 December 1944 give 'to capture Shwebo' as 19 Division's task, but Stopford ordered 2 Division to take it, on 5 January. Evans, *Slim*, p. 191; *Reconquest of Burma*, II, p. 490; Kirby, *War against Japan*, IV, p. 177

Lieutenant-Colonel White noticed, after a skirmish at the Irrawaddy crossing, that the Japanese he was fighting were 'obvious reinforcements, big chaps but seemingly overfed and from their showing of that morning lacking the guts of their predecessors, our old opponents of the District (sic) Commissioner's bungalow.'[1] This was not a universal reaction. During the Durham Light Infantry's securing of its bridgehead west of the village of Ngazun, the Japanese commander had ordered a unit of thirty-five men to oppose the Durhams to the last man and the last round. The British battalion duly found thirty-five bodies in their fox-holes. The morning after their attack, when the tanks of 3 Carabiniers were in support of the infantry, a Japanese officer jumped from concealment on to the top of a tank in which the tank commander was standing with his turret open. The Japanese beheaded the tank commander instantly with his sword, thrust the body aside and climbed down into the tank, where he stabbed the gunner to death. He was about to seize the gunner's pistol but the driver made a grab for it, and after a struggle shot the officer. On the flank of the Durham Light Infantry, where the Royal Berkshires were attacking, a Japanese who had lost his weapons simply made for the British company commander and sank his teeth in his throat.[2]

From Shwebo, 19 Division turned east to the Irrawaddy, and prepared to cross at two places north of Mandalay: Kyaukmyaung forty miles north of the city, and Thabeikkyin, fifteen miles further upstream, from which a road ran into the Monglong Range and the town of Mogok. Rees put across the Irrawaddy tanks of 254 Tank Brigade as well as his own three infantry brigades, 62, 64 and 98. The Japanese were sure that the division and its tanks would be the major thrust against Mandalay, and they threw 15 Division and 53 Division against the bridgeheads to pinch them out.

These divisions were, of course, seriously under strength. 15 Division had been reinforced, but even so it did not number more than 4500 men with 10–12 guns. Lieutenant-General Shibata put a battalion at Kabwet and one at Kyaukmyaung and spread the rest of his strength down the east bank of the Irrawaddy – 67, 51 and 60 Regiments, reading from north to south. Thabeikkyin was defended by III Battalion, 58 Infantry Regiment of 31 Division, which was temporarily put under his command. Further south, at Singu, was 119 Regiment of 53 Division, also attached to 15 Division for the Mandalay battle. The main body of 53 Division was deployed south of Singu. (After its battering by the Chindits, the entire 53 Division numbered only around 4000 men.)[3]

Rees's 62 Brigade (Morris) failed to get across the Irrawaddy by using country boats on 11 January, at Kyaukmyaung, but shifted their crossing-point and made it safely on the night of the 14th. 98 Brigade (Jerrard)

[1] White, *Straight on for Tokyo*, p. 201

[2] Rissik, *The D.L.I. at War*, p. 204

[3] OCH, *Irawaji Kaisen*, p. 72

established its bridgehead between 14 and 16 January against very light opposition, and 64 Brigade (Bain), the last to leave the Shwebo area, crossed over on 16 and 17 January. The Japanese, sensing the rapidity of Rees's build-up, sent against him I Battalion (Yoshioka), 60 Infantry Regiment and 67 Infantry Regiment, but in spite of repeated night attacks at the end of January, 19 Division refused to be budged. More, Rees intended to move south fast, and 1/6 Gurkha Rifles with the tanks (Stuarts) of 7 Light Cavalry took Thila and Steamer Point, though five tanks were damaged by Japanese 37 mm anti-tank guns. It was clear that 19 Division was superior in fire-power to anything the Japanese put against it, and Rees decided to change the axis of his advance. He had been moving down the main road; now he intended to use a route of cart tracks and village paths closer to the river, along which he was sure the Japanese would not expect his main thrust. His GSO(1), John Masters, who had joined Rees after recuperating from 111 Brigade's excoriating experiences under Stilwell, claims the credit for suggesting this transfer to Rees over a long night's session of whisky, tea, boiled sweets and cake (Rees's wife sent him a cake once a fortnight from England). But the heavy fire thrown at 7 Light Cavalry in a defile on the main road on 26 February from artillery, mortars and Japanese medium tanks in prepared positions was no doubt as important a factor. Until that defile were taken, or he could go round it, Rees's way to Mandalay was blocked.[1]

Not, of course, that Rees and 19 Division were meant to take Mandalay at all, or at any rate not first. Rees was to isolate Mandalay from the north and east, then draw Japanese from the city on to his guns, to facilitate its taking from the south, and south-west. When the battle for the city itself started, he was to establish his division in the northern outskirts and stop the Japanese escaping eastwards. But Rees, almost certainly, knowing how fast his division could move – they had covered 400 miles, air-supplied, from the Chindwin to Shwebo in just under five weeks – must have intended to be first into Mandalay.

There were still Japanese on the west bank, though, who might prove awkward. 15 Division held a bridgehead at Kabwet, and Rees sent 98 Brigade against it on 25 January, using tanks and a heavy air and artillery barrage on the Japanese defenders. These were Captain Kumano's I Battalion, 51 Infantry Regiment, and they numbered no more than 200 men.[2] Each of his companies was down to thirty men apiece, but they had fire support from the main body of the regiment on the opposite bank. By the time the battalion was reduced to half its strength from the constant air and land bombardment, its officers came to Kumano and begged – since they were obviously going to die anyway – to put in one last massive suicide

---

[1] Masters, *The Road past Mandalay*, pp. 297–300. Perrett, *Tank Tracks to Rangoon*, p. 182

[2] OCH, *Irawaji Kaisen*, p. 68

attack. That was not their duty, retorted Kumano. 'We are here to block the crossing, and as long as one soldier is alive to resist and delay the British even by one day, then we fight on as we are.'[1] Even when Kumano decided they would have to leave Kabwet village, they came on the river-bank about half-a-mile to the west and renewed their attacks. It was only the deterioration of 15 Division on the east bank which finally compelled Kumano to rejoin his regiment. In the bitter fighting for Kabwet, which reduced the Japanese positions to a single thick-walled pagoda by 30 January, the 2 Royal Berkshires lost a hundred officers and men.[2]

With a canny mixture of dash and caution, Rees advanced where the Japanese proved weak, and took it steady when they offered stiff re-sistance. 'If the Japanese are obviously pulling out fast', ran his Operation Instruction No 14, 'act boldly and go fast while the going is good, and take risks.' But, he added, 'I do not intend to incur unnecessary casualties in any ill-prepared rushes at organized defences.'[3] Such defences were set up by the Japanese at the feature called Kidney, a hill between Shwepyi and Pinle-In, through which the best road passed. Rees put 64 Brigade as his left flank along the main road, and took the main body of the division, tanks in front, artillery behind, through the boggy strip of land between Kidney and the river. His brigades began to leapfrog south, and a mobile column – Stiletto – was formed to exploit towards Mandalay ahead of the rest of the division. This was based on the divisional reconnaissance battalion – 1/15 Punjab – armoured with C Squadron of 7 Cavalry, and a troop of 150 RAC with Lee medium tanks. Rees had a sharp encounter with the second-in-command of 254 Tank Brigade, the parent formation of his armour. Rees was, it appeared, making incorrect use of the tanks, and putting them at unnecessary risk along the riverside tracks, where often they would be limited to a single tank front. The squadron commander was prepared to have a go, but the colonel from brigade was not. Perhaps, Rees queried smoothly, the cavalry should be excused from this war, as it was becoming dangerous? Masters, who reported the interview, discreetly left with the young squadron commander.[4] In the upshot, after the dis-astrous encounter with Japanese guns in a defile with the hills on one side and marsh on the other, when two of 7 Cavalry's Stuarts were knocked out, they were not used on that road axis again.[5]

---

[1] ibid., p. 70

[2] Kirby, *War against Japan*, IV, p. 186, no. 2. Kumano's diary gives an account of the battle for Kabwet, but his memory for dates plays him false: he is about a week out in his reckoning. (OCH *Irawaji Kaisen* p. 71)

[3] *Reconquest of Burma*, II, p. 344, n. 7

[4] Masters, *The Road past Mandalay*, pp. 299–300

[5] Perrett, op.cit., p. 182

Stiletto, under the command of Major Parker of 150 RAC, set off towards Mandalay on 6 March, and made eight miles the first day. They did not, of course, outstrip their ebullient little general, who was up front – or further – as usual, and when the tanks were halted by a *chaung* told the sappers to heave three three-ton trucks on their sides to fill the *chaung*. The tanks went across on top of them. The engineer officer on the spot, who (naturally) had not thought of this somewhat prodigal expenditure of motor transport himself, was vividly rebuked by his general. With infantry clinging to their superstructure, the tanks plunged south, until the country opened up before them so that they could now ride two abreast. The attack went in along the main road, too, and Japanese pressure slackened on the brigade on Rees's left flank as it became clear they would soon be cut off from Mandalay. The brigadier, obviously under strain after three days and nights of heavy fighting, phoned Rees to say his men were exhausted and his vehicles needed repairs: he would start again the following morning. Rees would have none of it. 'Keep up the pressure', the brigadier was told, and his protests were drowned in a crisp order not to stop anywhere but to keep advancing through the night.

So confident was Rees that his momentum would carry him right into the city that he detached 62 Brigade to take Maymyo, about thirty miles away in the hills to the east. The division's leading tanks were at Powa Taung, five miles north of the city, by late afternoon on 7 March. The thousand-foot high Mandalay Hill and its wreath of pagodas was in sight. Though it was in no way the strategic prize that the taking of Rangoon would represent, it bore a name known throughout the world. Its temple-covered summit, with the stairway roofed in corrugated iron leading to the top, lay just north of the massive bastion of Fort Dufferin. It was a religious centre, the ancient Burmese capital, and the prestige of the Victorian conquerors of nineteenth-century Burma was linked with it. Rees's tanks came to a halt, having covered twenty-six miles that day: some of them were already out of petrol. He was, of course, impatient to move the battle into the city. But it was not going to be a push-over. Both hill and fort were held by Japanese to whom GOC 15 Army, Katamura, had given the simplest order: defend Mandalay to the death.

15 Division held Mandalay and had a new commander, Major-General Yamamoto Seiei,[1] who had been Chief of Staff at 33 Army and had seen the desperate defence of Lameng and Tengyueh. As a staff officer he had felt responsible for the annihilation of units in those towns, and saw no point in it: 'Fighting to the last man is, from the point of view of command, the very worst option.'[2] He asked 15 Army what exactly the order meant,

---

[1] No connection with Major-General Yamamoto Tsunoru, commander of 33 Division Infantry Group at Palel.

[2] OCH *Irawaji Kaisen*, p. 138

and received the cold signal back: 'Literally what it says.' Raging inwardly, Yamamoto accepted the order '15 Division will defend Mandalay to the last man' and he signalled back, 'leave it to us' (*go anshin are*). He even wrote a poem and distributed it to the defenders, to stiffen their resolve:

Kimi ga tame	For their sovereign
Waga tsuwamono yo	Our warriors will fall
Tomo ni chire	Defending to the end
Tsutome hataseri	This town of Mandalay . . .
Mandarē no sato.	

He should never, of course, have been given such an order at all. A holding action was all 15 Army was capable of, and in spite of Mandalay's import-ance as a communications centre for road, rail and river, the higher command in Burma already intended to confine itself to holding southern Burma only. 'Strategically, I never considered Mandalay worth any serious defence', General Kimura admitted. 'The only reason it was held at all was for its prestige value.'[1]

Kimura's lack of motivation did not, needless to say, diminish the courage of Mandalay's defenders, nor the thickness of its superb walls. Fort Dufferin was about 2000 square yards of ground, containing the teak-built palace of King Thibaw, Government House, Jail, Club, even a polo ground. Round its square hulk ran a moat seventy-five yards wide, bridged in five places, and planted with lotus. A main gate sat firmly in the centre of each side, protected by a massive buttress. The brick walls were thirty feet thick at the bottom, narrowing to twelve at a height of twenty-three feet. In their turn, they were protected by three-foot-thick brick castella-tions, and by buttresses every hundred yards. The jungle war was about to turn into a medieval siege.

Japanese depots – food, MT spares, weapons, ammunition – were at Tonbo, about ten miles south-east, and though a desperate attempt had been made to move them south, a fair amount remained. There was simply not enough transport. 67 Infantry Regiment was on Mandalay Hill and the north side of the city, 60 Infantry Regiment to the west and south, and 15 Division headquarters in the Fort.

Rees ordered 98 Brigade to take Mandalay Hill, as the necessary preli-minary to taking the city. Jerrard at first told his Royal Berkshires to do the job, but the Commanding Officer of the 4/4 Gurkhas asked that his men should do it: he had been five years in Burma, attached to the Burma Rifles until 1942, and he had intimate knowledge of the hill and its paths. Jerrard inclined, and the Gurkhas climbed the north-eastern end of the hill in the darkness and attacked the summit the following morning. They took

---

[1] SEATIC Bulletin, No. 242

it, but there were still Japanese resisting on the hill, and eleven days of fighting, bombing and fire lay ahead.[1]

Rees's own crisp clear voice broadcast a general's eye account over the BBC:[2]

I'm now in the northern suburbs of Mandalay. The fighting is going on. Mandalay Hill is just to the south-east of me. Our troops have got on to the top. On the way up they've killed a fair number of Japanese, captured material. So far the number of corpses reported [is] twenty to thirty Japs, [?] machine guns. The Gurkhas are the people who got up there first. They, in some extraordinary way, managed to get round last night in spite of a very fatiguing day marching south through the dust. They worked their way round and got a small detachment up first, then more, and now they're busy clearing the top of the hill. We're sending up a company of the Royal Berkshire Regiment to assist. They're now on the way. Meanwhile, right at the bottom of the mountain, at the north end there's still stubborn fighting going on, Japanese in machine-gun nests and anti-tank defences there, and at the moment Gurkhas and Baluchis, supported by British tanks are dealing with that. The rest of the Royal Berkshires are just behind me, and their last company is just slogging in from the north, very dusty, in very good spirits. We had to send them back yesterday evening in the dust to clear a village near which I had my headquarters last night, when they kindly cleared it for me. They had British tanks and Bombay Grenadiers to help them, and at least fifty corpses were seen before they finished the Japanese. At first the Japanese resisted, very like hornets, but when they saw that the game was really up, then they scattered and ran like rabbits. There are similar parties in various villages that we've overrun, because we've outstripped them, and they're small disorganized parties from all sorts of units, mixed bodies. They are trying to get back, and whenever they run into our troops, they put up this sort of show. Now in Mandalay itself, the south-west, the Frontier Force Regiment are busy cleaning the place. There are Japs about there still, a certain amount of shooting, but it isn't clear yet whether they're going to offer stubborn house-to-house resistance. We've had some 105 shells at us this morning. Not many, and we haven't had any for some time now. Now here it's a very sunny, hot morning, it's very dusty, the troops are very dusty and they're pouring with sweat. For some

[1] Masters, *The Road past Mandalay*, p. 306
[2] Recorded 9 March 1945 (Imperial War Museum)

days now they've been going all out, they've been going more than all out. They've had a negligible amount of sleep, but their spirit and *élan* is tremendous. I've never, never seen such enthusiasm and it's that, undoubtedly, that is carrying them through, because they feel the prize is really worth the effort.

19 Division was not on its own: two other divisions, 2 and 20, were involved in the taking of Mandalay, 20 Division by severing the Japanese road and rail arteries leading to Rangoon, and 2 Division by looping round at the bend in the Irrawaddy and coming upon the city from the south.

Through no fault of their own, 2 Division had not been able to move as fast as they wanted. After Yeu and Shwebo were taken, Stopford had called a halt because his corps, 400 miles from its railhead, looked as if it were going to outstrip its supplies. 19 Division had been completely on air supply and this was now confined to two brigades; in the case of 2 Division, to one brigade, even though the clearing of Yeu and Shwebo had put a handy group of airfields into Stopford's hands. It was 24 February before 2 Division, which had cleared the Shwebo Plain and pushed troops forward towards Sagaing, opposite Mandalay, gathered its forces to cross the Irrawaddy. 268 Brigade took over the Sagaing sector, leaving the Division a front of fifteen miles from which to select its crossings. The river was far wider than it had been for 19 Division, as it flows, between Thabeikkyin and Kyaukmyaung, through a gorge which narrows it to 500 yards. As the country opens out, the river widens, being around 1500 to 2000 yards just below Mandalay, and where it meets the Chindwin, at Myingyan, it can extend to 4500 yards. It can rise capriciously, too. As the temperature also rises in the Central Plain in February and March, and as the river's speed can be four knots, boatmen's tempers are likely to fray. However thinly spread the Japanese were on the south, or east bank, 2 Division had to employ every device of surprise and deception to avoid being decimated by machine-gun fire while they were in the water.

One way of diverting the attention of the Japanese was, of course, to make landings simultaneously at widely separated spots. This is what happened in the case of 20 Division, which had fought its way down the east bank of the Chindwin, meeting opposition from 213 Regiment of 33 Division at Budalin and Monywa. Budalin, a beautiful town of many pagodas, surrounded by flat, open countryside, was occupied by III Battalion (Major Yazu), 213 Regiment who moved twenty miles north of Monywa on 1 January 1945. Yazu noticed how few natural tank obstacles the terrain offered, a problem worsened by the fact that he had neither anti-tank guns nor battalion guns. He did what he could to form defensive positions.

There was no local labour, as the inhabitants of the villages had all fled. Four days later, 32 Brigade (Mackenzie) began its attack on Budalin.

Yazu's battalion had only 100 men, and he stood little chance against a whole brigade in such an open position. His losses began to mount and he was soon boxed into a perimeter 100 yards square. He was ordered to move out on the night of the 9th, and slipped through Mackenzie's encirclement with forty survivors. Yazu was convinced his men were allowed to escape through the chivalrous abstention from attack of his opposite number, Captain Cherrington, of 1 Northamptons. 'The British front line units did not fire a single shot at my battalion in spite of recognizing the withdrawal', he wrote many years later to the Northamptons' Commanding Officer, Lieutenant-Colonel (later Brigadier) D. E. Taunton. (Cherrington, who was awarded a DSO for his bravery at Budalin, was killed some days later at Monywa.) 'I felt that the British commander must have intentionally overlooked our retreat. I was keenly impressed by the knightly spirit. With the aid of flare-bombs fired by the British, my battalion with many wounded men were able to withdraw safely towards the south... Now that I have learnt that you were the British commander, I would like to express again my sincere appreciation for sparing our lives.'[1] Taunton was interested by the suggestion but sceptical, and honesty compelled him to reply to Yazu that he was lucky to have picked a route which took him clear of positions held by Gurkhas also involved in Budalin. 'I feel sure that the reason you were not fired on was that by the light of flares it is not easy to distinguish clearly friend from foe and knowing there were Gurkhas behind you, our fire was withheld rather than risk casualties to our own troops... If you had not gone that night, I doubt if you would have escaped on the 10th!'

Yazu had asked for the order to evacuate, signalling to his regiment on the morning of the 8th that he was almost out of food and ammunition. The signal in reply told him to keep contact with the enemy, and wait until the night of the 9th, when he was to withdraw and protect the regiment's left flank. 'Those thirty-six hours', he remembered later, 'seemed like thirty-six years.'[2] Even so, he might not have survived that long in what Mackenzie called 'a platoon battle' if a torrential downpour had not altered Gracey's plans. 20 Division's motor transport was brought to a standstill, ration distribution stopped, and he put everyone on half-rations.[3] 'If armour were available, the place would have fallen in 24 hours', claims the official Indian Army History. Mackenzie moved off to Monywa, the last riverside port on the Chindwin, on 10 January. An earlier attempt to seize Monywa by a surprise *coup* failed when a convoy of infantry and carriers

---

[1] Letter dated 26 September, 1967, Imperial War Museum Archives.

[2] OCH *Irawaji Kaisen*, p. 56

[3] 'Summary of results of main operations since leaving Manipur', Gracey Papers, 26.

was ambushed, losing nearly all the vehicles. 32 and 80 Brigades treated its capture a little more cautiously. They cut all approaches to it by 19 January, and occupied the west bank of the Chindwin facing it. Between 18 and 20 January, massive air attacks hit the town – the first time Hurricane rocket strikes were used in Burma – and 32 Brigade moved in slowly. They were in occupation by the 22nd. Their task was rendered easier by the fact that the defenders, 213 Infantry Regiment (Kawara), though holding a good water supply and not being in the least diffident about using temple groves as defensive positions, was ordered by 33 Division commander to give up its two mountain guns, needed across the Irrawaddy at Sameikkon, and had to fight without direct artillery support. The bombing and strafing by close on 200 planes wrecked the town, but 32 Brigade found that Japanese machine-gun fire met its first probing attacks: there were craters all round the bunkers, but the bunkers themselves were intact. Kawara succeeded in retreating through 20 Division's screen on the night of the 21st.

The 33 Divisional commander, Lieutenant-General Tanaka Nobuo, twice visited the regiment during the battle for Monywa, intent on keeping up his division's morale. But it did not avail his division much. Their days of defending the Irrawaddy line were already numbered, as 20 Division had taken Myinmu on the same day that Monywa fell. The Japanese were sure the British would cross at Myinmu, and as 19 Division were already in this bridgehead, it would certainly make them think the main objective was Mandalay. To keep them guessing, Slim decided that IV Corps' crossing should be simultaneous, so 7 Division, which was to establish a bridgehead for IV Corps through which the force for Meiktila should pass, crossed within twenty-four hours of 20 Division. The area chosen for 20 Division was at a bend in the Irrawaddy west of Myinmu near the village of Allagappa, where the river was 1500 yards wide, and the opposite point was steeply banked, a drawback as far as getting vehicles off the beach was concerned, but likely to be less heavily defended. Corporal Dillon, of the 2 Border Regiment (100 Brigade) gave an account of one of the patrols which reconnoitred the crossing:

> There were three of us on this patrol. Sergeant Harewood, Private Bennion and myself. We drew four days' rations and blacked our faces with dirty grease from the cookhouses. At about seven o'clock in the evening, before the moon rose, we shoved off in a rubber boat. Halfway across, some parachute flares lit everything up but we lay flat in the boat for fifteen minutes and nobody saw us. We got to the other side and let the air out of the boat and pulled it up to the shore very cautiously, crawling on our stomachs. Then we carried it across the track into a pea field. We had just hidden it near a tree, when a party of Japs came along

and started digging bunkers only ten yards away from us. They posted one sentry on the track we'd just crossed and another on a track that joined it, a few yards in front. We were just between the two, and at the side there was a village so we went into a huddle and decided to get back to the beach and try further up. We took an hour-and-a-half crawling at twenty yards to the track and just as we got there two Japs came within an arm's length of us so we crawled back again. Then we thought the only thing was to bluff our way out so we got to the other track and stood up and sauntered across a few yards from the sentry. After that we went on to our first round and hid for the rest of the night in some elephant grass near the lake and had our first rations.

Some Japs came down at first light to water the mules five yards away from us but we didn't see anything else all day. We finished our water during the night. We couldn't risk going to the lake to get more so that night we made for some paddy fields.

It wasn't like water, more like mud, but we enjoyed it. Then we went on to a road junction to watch for Jap supplies.

After a couple of hours, a bullock cart drove past drawn by three mules with a Jap sitting astride the shafts and a lot of empty ammunition boxes banging about in a cart. We followed it nearly to a village and heard more carts coming in and out. So that meant the Japs had a supply dump there. Next morning we moved off on to some high ground overlooking the river to see if the Japs were digging in there. I'd just started climbing a tall tree to have a look around when Bennion saw some Japanese biscuits and sweets on the other side of the tree and a cigar still smoking, so we did a quick move to the left and lay up and watched. That night we moved six miles south, watching the tracks to see if the Japs were using them and early the next morning we saw footmarks of some Japs who'd marched up in threes and turned left. Suddenly, while we were following the footmarks, a Jap artillery gun opened fire over our heads from a hundred yards away, so we pinpointed the gun on our map and observed it all day. By now our lips were cracking with thirst, so that night we got right back to the paddy fields and got right down on our stomachs and drank the dirty water. Then we opened two tins of cheese, but they were both bad. That left us only sardines. The next day we drank all our water again and finished our food, and we took a bearing on the place where we'd left the boat. When we got there that night, we found a party of Japs still there with a sentry on each of the tracks. We were crazy to go in, it was a suicide job, but I think we were fuddled after five nights without sleep. Sergeant Harewood led us across the track, straight to the tree where the boat was hidden. A miracle that was. It took us an hour to get the grass off it without making a rustle. Then Bennion and the sergeant dragged it down to the other track, inch by inch, and I went forward and gave a low whistle when the sentry's head was turned. We got it down to the water's edge, and we'd just blown it up when five Japs came down to the river, about ten yards away on our left. We rolled into the water and stayed there with our stens ready for ten minutes until the Japs'd filled their water carriers and gone away. Then another lot came down five yards away on our right, and went away again. So we didn't wait to blow the boat right up. We shoved off as quick as we could. It was a terrible boat to manoeuvre. After an hour and a half, we'd only got forty yards off the shore and we were afraid the moon would come up any minute and when we did get back we found that two Vickers guns had been trained on us ever since we were halfway across because *they* thought we were Japs. Indian gunners came round and laughed and patted us on the shoulder and said '*Tikh hai, Sahib!*' *Tikh hai* is Hindustani for OK. We were *tikh hai* all right after the officer in charge had given us a cigarette and some rum, and that was the end of the patrol.

Trains of ranger-boats, powered by outboard motors, were used, not the up-to-date landing craft which would have been available in Europe. The Japanese artillery was softened up by a raid of fifty Liberators on 12 February, followed by a squadron of Lightnings which took out four guns and scattered the others. The Japanese mortared the beaches, but by 15 February 100 Brigade was over the Irrawaddy.

The Northamptons of 32 Brigade were less lucky. The outboard motors driving their chain of ranger-boats broke down and the troops drifted downstream for about half a mile past their intended beachhead, finally landing where Japanese fire opposed them. Elsewhere the Japanese burned grass concealing 9/14 Punjab near their beachhead and tried to drive them into LMG fire. But the biter was bit, the wind changed and fanned the flames towards the Japanese.

Beachheads were shelled, and on one occasion the Japanese airforce put in a rare appearance. Sixteen Oscars bombed and strafed 100 Brigade's beaches and the ferry it was running across to the other shore. Jitter parties attacked the perimeters at night. An officer of the 9/14 Punjab noticed something very curious about Japanese morale in the course of one of these attacks. Late on 17 March the battalion was attacked, and the battle went on until five the next morning, a small party of Japanese having penetrated B Company's forward trenches at 3.00 am. They were all killed, and when a body count was taken at dawn, the Punjabis found the

Japanese battalion commander, Captain Moritani, among the dead, together with five officers and 36 other ranks. Two of the dead officers had committed suicide, being badly wounded in the legs. One Japanese drowned himself to avoid being captured. The Punjabis took two prisoners, and found it significant that while the Japanese battalion commander and three old sergeants lay *inside* the Punjabi perimeter, other officers and a first-class private had died on the wire, and second-class privates had all been killed in the background.[1]

At Talingon, about a mile inland, the Japanese brought up medium tanks, and as 20 Division had no armour across, this could have been crucial. Fortunately, the Oscars' attack had caused the RAF to institute a cab-rank over the beachheads, and on 20 February, a Hurricane spotted a tank near Paunggadaw. The tank had been camouflaged, but not well enough, and the Hurricane blasted it. Then others became visible, and the RAF needled them out one by one until thirteen tanks had been destroyed. The Japanese brought no more against the beachhead.

It took 20 Division three weeks of fighting to cross the Irrawaddy and establish its beachheads, but in doing so it drew troops from Mandalay, and also prevented reinforcements being brought from the east against IV Corps' crossing. In suicide attacks by two battalions against the bridge-head, the Japanese of 33 Division lost 953 men out of 1200. Five hundred Japanese bodies were buried by bulldozer between 21 and 26 February.[2]

Further upstream, 2 Division crossed at Ngazun on 24 February. 7 Worcesters had bad luck on the first night, seventeen of their boats filling with water or being sunk by Japanese fire. Soon the Worcesters' Commanding Officer himself was in the water, and by midnight the battalion was back on the bank it started from. The Camerons came under sniper fire, got little over a company across and had a steep cliff to assault on the other side. The Royal Welch Fusiliers at first only managed to get two platoons across. Brigadier West realized his main beachhead was a flop, and told the Dorsets to move 5000 yards across country to Myittha, cross behind the Camerons, and open out their bridgehead. The Dorsets' Commanding Officer (White) found the inexperienced sapper engineer who manoeuvred his boat from one sandbank to another in ever-decreasing circles more of a trial than the Japanese, and his last view of the shore was 'the agonized look on General Nicholson's face as he saw us depart in this manner, strangely reminiscent of the "Owl and the Pussycat".'[3] His party were

---

[1] *The Crossing of Irrawaddi* (sic) 9/14 Punjab; Gracey Papers, 51, in Liddell Hart Archive.

[2] Slim, op.cit., p. 421

[3] White, *Straight on for Tokyo*, p. 236. The Dorsets' CO describes the speed of the Irrawaddy at this point as 4 knots. The Indian Official History (*Reconquest of Burma*, II, p. 278) says it

lucky though: they had no casualties at all, whereas some of the men crossing in DUKWS (amphibious trucks) drifted close to a Japanese medium machine gun which opened up on them in the water. The machine-gun nest proved almost impossible to winkle out. 2 Division artillery shelled them, a troop of Grant tanks tried to blow them out of the ground, then a strike of Hurricanes had a go, all to no effect. In the end, 4 Brigade's Lancashire Fusiliers, supported by a troop of Carabiniers, silenced them, but the troop leader died in the attempt. 2 Division's perilous crossing, which at one moment looked like ending in failure, finally succeeded. 5 and 6 Brigade were on the east bank, with tanks, by 26 February, and began to march east towards Ava and Mandalay.

So much for the crossing of XXXIII Corps. IV Corps' crossing, with 7 Division in the van, was timed, as we have seen, to go ahead at roughly the same time as 20 Division's near Myinmu, to distract and puzzle the Japanese command. It was much further down the Irrawaddy, and there had been an elaborate system of deception before Evans's brigades hit the beaches. The deception scheme, given the operational name CLOAK, was to conceal the composition of IV Corps, to prevent the Japanese knowing there was a Corps coming down the Gangaw (Myittha) Valley, to make them assume Pakokku would be a crossing-point and then cross elsewhere, and to make them think that the Corps, when finally across the river, was aimed at the oil-fields of Yenangyaung and not at Meiktila.[1] The crossing was to be made by 7 Division, and 17 Indian Light Division and 255 Tank Brigade would pass through its bridgeheads and make a dash across the hot, dusty, desert area between the east bank and Meiktila before the Japanese assessed what was happening. 17 Division and the tank brigade were to observe wireless silence until they were deployed across the river, and 28 East African Brigade – whose presence was meant to make the Japanese think that 11 East African Division was involved – was to make a feint crossing at Seikpyu, south of the main crossing area, to deceive the Japanese into thinking the attempt was directed against Chauk.

Along a thin thread of road down the Gangaw Valley, 28 East African Brigade pressed on ahead of the main body, while behind it 7 Division was stretched out in a long file that led over 350 miles as far back as Kohima. The advance began on 19 February. Tanaka (33 Division) intended to block the track, and in one three-mile stretch, his men felled hundreds of trees. This was a formidable obstacle, but artillery vehicles and ten elephants towed them away, and the division only lost a day's

was 2½ knots. Either way it could carry off badly handled boats, and shifting shoals were a further complication.

[1] IV Corps Operation Instruction No. 124, 25 January 1945, *Reconquest of Burma*, II, p. 499

march. By 10 February, after a hot march through swirling, red laterite dust, the division was on the Irrawaddy.[1]

Facing them, along fifty miles of the river bank, the Japanese had spread out four battalions of 72 Independent Mixed Brigade, 2 INA Division reported vaguely as being between 5000 and 10,000 strong, between Chauk and Nyaungu, with 214 Regiment around Pakokku on the west bank. 72 IMB was under the command of 28 Army (Sakurai) whose zone of operations had hitherto been in Arakan. Now it was responsible for an area of the lower Irrawaddy, and its Army boundary with 15 Army ran close to the village of Nyaungu, a fact which turned out to be of some importance for the crossing. Nyaungu was the narrowest point of the Irrawaddy in the area and Evans and his staff had made a particularly thorough study of aerial photographs to choose the best crossing point. Maps were not too reliable, since the position of sandbanks changed from year to year, and the presence of fresh sandbanks across the direct route meant that oblique instead of direct courses would have to be taken, thus producing what Slim called 'the longest opposed river crossing in any theatre of the Second World War'.[2] Two or three miles downstream lay the old capital of Burma, Pagan, a dramatic sight with its 1200 red and white pagodas and temples silhouetted against the sky. Neither Pagan nor Nyaungu offered the shortest route to Meiktila from the Irrawaddy. That was undoubtedly at Pakokku, which had the extra advantage of a metalled road leading directly to it from Pauk where the Gangaw Valley debouched on to the plain. But this made it, precisely, too obvious a choice, though 7 Division intended to put pressure on it, to keep the Japanese guessing. In addition, the narrowest crossing, at Nyaungu – three-quarters of a mile – meant that there would be a more rapid turn-round of boats and rafts, and Evans's men could be across sooner.[3] The crossing could be easily observed. Along the east bank of the Irrawaddy ran 100-foot high cliffs, and if anyone wanted a higher observation point, it was easy enough to climb one of the many pagodas. The Japanese also carried out one of their rare aerial reconnaissances over the Gangaw Valley at the end of January, and reported a long line of vehicles between Tilin and Pauk. Tanaka saw the report, but, since it was not repeated, decided that the sighting was not of much importance.

Evans intended to use 33 Brigade for the crossing, and as a result it had been kept in the rear and not involved in the fighting on the flanks of the divisional advance like 89 or 114 Brigades; and from the latter brigade he took the newly arrived 2 Battalion, South Lancashire Regiment which had experience in seaborne landings and had taken part in the seizure of

---

[1] Slim, op.cit., p. 422

[2] ibid., p. 425

[3] Evans, *The Desert and the Jungle*, p. 141

Madagascar from the Vichy French. The South Lancashires would provide his assault battalion. The dates he had thought of were 12 or 13 February, but he was dismayed to find the assault craft in such bad shape when they reached Pauk that he was forced to postpone until the 14th.[1]

To find out about the opposite bank, Evans used a Sea Reconnaissance Unit to test the river conditions, and a Special Boat Section, with frogmen, to cross over in the darkness and reconnoitre. One officer was killed in Nyaungu village on such a patrol, but the event did not seem to arouse Japanese suspicions. Nor did the clearing of the village of Myitche by 1/11 Sikhs or the battle for the crossroads at Kanhla which cleared the ground between Pakokku and Myitche. The Sikhs also put a small patrol across the river at Pagan, and reported that the southern edge of the village was empty of Japanese.

On the morning of 14 February, not all the knowledge acquired and past experience could avert accidents in such a massive operation. The very battalion selected for its experience of such actions, the South Lancashires, went hideously amiss. They were to be the dawn embarkation, and in the half-light there was chaos. The first flight was to be silent, so the men were not to start their outboard motors until well out into the river. When they got there, some failed to start, and some of the boats sprang leaks. Desperate to get at least part of his force across, the commanding officer ordered the boats to move, whether they were in sequence or not. As a result the reserve company found itself in the lead, but the current bore it downstream, and the rest, thinking this was the right course, tried to follow. As they came level with the enemy positions, machine guns opened up on them and in a matter of minutes two company commanders had been killed and several boats sunk. The defenders on the far bank were not Japanese, but INA troops under Captain Chander Bhan of Major Dhillon's 4 Guerrilla Regiment (Nehru Brigade), made up largely of Tamils who had been recruited in Malaya. At this time, the INA Commander-in-Chief, Subhas Chandra Bose, was at Meiktila.[2] Only the arrival of cab-rank aircraft, keeping the machine-gunners' heads down, enabled the survivors to be brought back. But that landing – C Beach – was a fiasco.[3]

The Corps Commander spotted the mêlée of sinking boats and struggling men. He went over the crossing-point in a light plane and took it into Division Headquarters at 6.30 am, two-and-a-half hours after the crossings began. 'What's happening?', he asked Evans. 'All our boats are going the wrong way – they're coming back, and there's a good deal of firing going on.' This was the first intimation Evans had that things were not going according to plan – odd enough in itself. He took off to have a

[1] ibid., p. 146

[2] Shah Nawaz Khan, *INA and its Netaji*, p. 154

[3] Slim, op.cit., pp. 427–8

look. His plane was walloped in the air by the explosions of tank guns firing just 200 feet below him, but it stayed up.[1] Light planes did, in fact, save many of the wounded from the catastrophe into which the boats had led them. Americans piloting L5s picked them up off the sandbanks and brought them to safety, while USAAF Mustangs, Mitchells and Thunderbolts pasted the Japanese guns and machine-gun nests, the RAF providing cover for the bombers and reconnaissance.

At 9.45 am, 4/15 Punjab (Conroy) were sent across, took command of the isolated South Lancashire company which had crossed successfully in the small hours before the main body, and stayed to guard the beaches. The next day the South Lancashires made a successful crossing into the beachhead. 89 Brigade crossed over and began to deploy south towards Pagan, and Indian Engineers were ferrying mules across the river on rafts powered by outboard motors. The fiasco of the previous day was forgotten. 1 Burma Regiment attacked a system of tunnels and catacombs which the Japanese were using on the river bank covering Nyaungu. An air-strike was summoned, the guns and tanks opened up, and even napalm bombs were used, which set the town ablaze but left the Japanese as they were. In the end, the decision was taken simply to seal up the entrances to the tunnels, burying the Japanese alive. The town was reported clear on 16 February.[2]

Six miles south of the main crossing, another disaster was narrowly averted. Here 1/11 Sikhs were to make a feint to draw Japanese away from Nyaungu. Their orders were changed to make it a real crossing when the news came that the far bank was not occupied. The Sikhs ferried stores and equipment to an island in midstream in the pitch-dark on 12 February. At eleven the next morning, a report came in which contradicted the previous one and said the position – Pagan – was now occupied. At 4 am on 14 February, the Sikhs decided to risk their crossing of the next stage from the island and came under machine-gun fire from the far bank. The Burmese boatmen immediately panicked, the Sikh official account scornfully reports, 'and cowered in the bottom of the boats'.[3] It is difficult to feel anything other than sympathy for them, brought under the fire of one side while being more or less press-ganged by the other. At any rate, after the boats had got out of hand and were being swept away by the current, the Burmese were 'persuaded' to row the Sikhs back to the island.

The Sikhs' problem, what to do next, was solved for them. A small boat was observed leaving the Pagan side of the river. The men in it raised a white flag, and when they landed on the island said they belonged to the Indian

---

[1] Evans, *The Desert and the Jungle*, p. 151

[2] *Reconquest of Burma*, II, p. 286

[3] ibid., II, p. 287

National Army and their unit wanted to surrender. The INA, under the overall command of the 28 Army, was positioned precisely at the boundary between 28 and 15 Armies, and a very ineffective seal it proved to be. A party of Sikhs crossed over to Pagan, took the surrender of the INA unit, and the rest of the Sikhs crossed without interference. 'This incident was, I think,' writes Slim dismissively, 'the chief contribution the Indian National Army made to either side in the Burma War.'[1]

114 Brigade took Pakokku on the west bank, as another deception measure, and 28 East African Brigade's feint at Chauk was so successful that the Japanese reacted violently to it and drove the East Africans back several miles on the west bank. Fearing this could develop into a threat on his route down the Gangaw Valley through Pauk to Nyaungu, the Corps Commander sent reinforcements to halt the Japanese. This was a minor set-back, and in spite of all the various *contretemps* which, at any one moment, must have seemed as if they were going to ruin the vast enterprise, 7 Division was across the Irrawaddy in the third week of February. On 17 February, Slim's strategic plan began to take shape. The bridgehead, 6000 yards wide and 4000 yards deep, received 17 Indian Division. Sensing what was happening, the Japanese tried desperately to pinch them out. A flight of Oscars raided the bridgehead, to no effect, units of 33 Division which had crossed from Pakokku moved against Nyaungu to be bloodily thrown back by 33 Brigade, and units of 72 Independent Mixed Brigade coming up from Yenangyaung tried in vain to batter a way through 89 Brigade (Crowther) advancing south from Pagan. It was too late. On 21 February, the tanks of 255 Tank Brigade, and Cowan's motorized infantry, were poised for the assault.

These crossings of the Irrawaddy, with their multiplicity of engineering triumphs and disasters, their combination of improvisations and meticulous planning, constitute almost a campaign in themselves. In five weeks, Slim had put two Army Corps across one of the widest rivers in the world. As his biographer points out, 'it serves to emphasize his achievement if one draws a contrast with Montgomery's advantage at the Rhine Crossing. Behind his 21 Army Group lay the vast and efficient road and rail network of North-West Europe. He had airborne divisions on his immediate front. His technical equipment – the continuous smoke-screen, amphibious vehicles, etc. – was lavish and up-to-date. An enormous artillery pool, rich in ammunition, gave him unlimited support. Compared with the Irrawaddy, the Rhine is narrow and its behaviour readily calculable.'[2]

---

[1] Slim, op.cit., p. 429. This incident is *not* mentioned in the Indian Army Official History, which merely states Pagan was evacuated (*Reconquest of Burma*, II, p. 288.)

[2] Lewin, *Slim*, p. 221

Mandalay

Rees's 19 Division, the first to cross, was also the first to achieve its object: the recapture of Mandalay.

The 4/4 Gurkhas had taken the summit of Mandalay Hill, but in the subterranean chambers bored in the hillside the Japanese defenders survived and came out to snipe at the attackers who were waiting for them to emerge, thumbs ready to press the buttons of vigilant machine guns. It was the engineers who solved the problem, and in a particularly gruesome way. Under the surface of this hill, with its temples dedicated to an ideal of tranquillity and non-violence, they burst open the concrete casings with explosive, poured petrol through the gaps and then fired Very lights into them. Anti-tank projectiles were used to blow down steel doors, through which petrol drums were rolled and exploded with grenades. This ghastly inferno was the key to victory. By 12 March, Mandalay Hill was clear.[1] It would have been cleared earlier, the Indian Army Official History states, but 'Major-General Rees had decided not to bomb the sacred places, the pagodas, though [a] lot of machine-gun fire was poured on the garrison from the air.'[2] Rees had served in Mandalay as a young officer, and no doubt knew its importance as a religious centre. But the casuistical distinction between aerial bombardment and explosives igniting petrol drums is not easy to follow. Or perhaps the purpose was aesthetic rather than moral: when Compton Mackenzie toured Mandalay in 1947 in preparation for his Indian Army History, a Gurkha battalion commander explained to him the difficulties of removing the Japanese without destroying the hill, and, he commented, he could wish that 'the Americans had always been as scrupulous in Italy... I could not help contrasting the lot of Mandalay Hill with that of Cassino.'[3]

Fort Dufferin was next. 5·5 inch howitzers breached the walls, Thunderbolts bombed the bridge on the south side of the moat, 8/12 Frontier Force Regiment and 1/6 Gurkhas probed the approaches. But the Japanese reacted strongly. Their guns stopped the tanks accompanying the Gurkhas and the attack came to a halt. For several days the British guns continued to pound the walls, but the 50-foot earth ramparts behind them simply absorbed the shells.

Rees then decided to use a tactic remarkably similar to those of the Japanese *ninja*, the silent, invisible killers of *samurai* fiction. 'Exercise Duffy', as it was called, was meant to achieve a secret entry into the fort, to establish a foothold which could then be exploited. Rees was insistent that it was to be inexpensive in terms of casualties:

---

[1] Masters, *The Road past Mandalay*, p. 307

[2] *Reconquest of Burma*, II, p. 354

[3] Mackenzie, *All Over the Place*, p. 110

The operation I intend is one of surprise; a silent start and rapid seizing of the bridgehead, NOT the forcing of an entry at all costs by bludgeon methods. If the surprise operation at reasonably light cost is not possible owing to enemy vigilance and preparations, then it will not be pressed home at all costs.[1]

The operation was entrusted to 1/15 Punjab and 8/12 Frontier Force of 64 Brigade (Flewett). They were to leave behind their steel helmets and change their boots for rubber-soled shoes. They would be brought to the walls in the darkness by engineers manning assault boats, with scaling ladders at the ready, and six manpack flame-throwers and a machine-gun company would augment their firepower when the attack went in, which was at 10 pm on 17 March. They reached the north-east and north-west corners of the Fort in the darkness, but as they made for the breaches the guns had opened, the Japanese opened fire, sinking one of the boats. In the early hours of the 18th, a platoon which had a foothold on the railway bridge in the north-west corner (the railway ran right through the west side of the Fort) was met by automatic fire and driven back. The flame-throwers never got near enough to be of use. Realizing that any of his men caught on the walls by the morning light would be mercilessly shot down, Rees called off the attack at 3.30 am.[2]

After the failure of 'Exercise Duffy', the battering began again. The RAF bombed the north wall, to little purpose, and 6-inch howitzers made seventeen more breaches in the north and east walls, on the theory that the Japanese could only man a small number of breaches and in the end would not be able to defend them all. B25s used skip-bombing with 2000lb bombs, the kind of thing that had been used against the Mohne Dam. The result was a 15-foot hole in the wall, and nothing more.[3] Rees described for the BBC, again, a typical day's assault on the Fort in the earlier phase – 10 March – :

Let's get under cover. The Frontier Force are attacking Mandalay Fort now. You can probably hear the noise of the shelling, mortaring, shooting. I'm fairly close to the walls myself, standing, looking half round a concrete wall. Our chaps are advancing steadily, bunching a little more than I'd like to see them. They're going very well. The tanks are advancing, firing very hard at the walls. You can see where our medium guns, firing direct, have

[1] *Reconquest of Burma*, II, p. 359

[2] Kirby, *War against Japan*, IV, p. 299

[3] *Reconquest of Burma*, II, p. 361

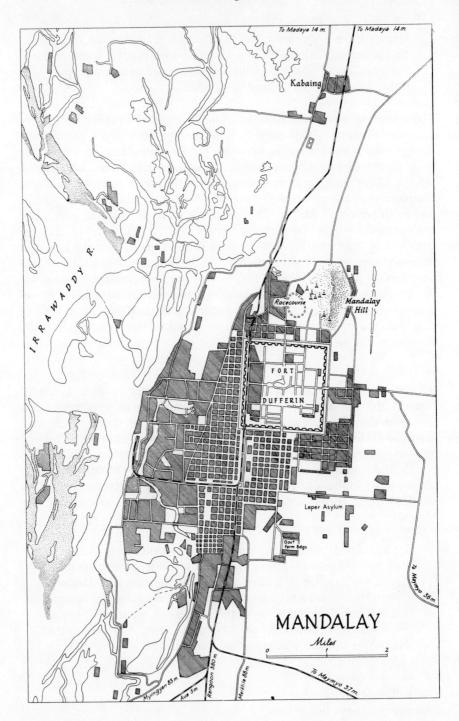

made breaches in the walls of the fort. You can see the bullets flicking the ground just ahead of me. I think actually they're our own tank bullets. The tank Besa's co-axial firing just ahead of the infantry, smothering the operation. I can see one of our infantry running across now, just near the fort wall.

I'll get my glasses on.

I can see the breach, but there's a big moat, this side. I can now see some of our leading infantry. They've just doubled to behind a concrete shelter which the sappers have built before the war, because we're standing now in the sapper lines just north of Mandalay Fort, actually called Fort Dufferin, with a palace in- side.

Tremendous lot of noise going on. A whole lot of smoke now, near the wall itself, which is a very good thing for our infantry. I'm not quite sure which of the firing is the enemy firing. I can see some of our infantry running round the tanks. Not always a wise thing to stand near a tank. Now I can see more of our infantry going across now, they're running across near the tanks, they're in slouch hats, Australian hats, Gurkha hats, very clear to see.

Rees's instructions from the Corps Commander to avoid unnecessary damage to Mandalay were proving increasingly difficult to observe. Slim was confident the Fort could be bypassed, and considered its capture to be a matter of news value rather than military advantage.[1] Rees did not want a repetition of the stalemate at Myitkyina, and sought desperately for ways of substituting cunning for the bludgeon of artillery and air strikes. 'Duffy' had failed, but he remembered that, as the Governor of Burma's Military Secretary in pre-war days, he had explored the Fort and discovered a culvert which went beneath the moat. He decided to find it again, and an assault unit was got ready to follow a Burmese who knew the plan of the Mandalay sewers. Sappers found that it *was* possible to approach the Fort from underneath, as they waded through the sewers, up to their thighs in mud.[2]

It would have been a nauseatingly filthy attack. Happily, it was not necessary. In the early afternoon of 20 March, after yet another air-strike had taken place, four Anglo-Burmans[3] – civilian prisoners held by the Japanese – carrying a white flag and a Union Jack came out of the north gate. Already harassed by the incursion of 17 Division into Central Burma, and not wishing to see the morale of his troops deteriorate, the GOC 15

[1] Slim, op.cit., p. 469

[2] Frank Owen, *The Campaign in Burma*, HMSO, 1946, p. 124

[3] 'Six Burmans' '. . . from the east gate' (*War Against Japan*, IV, p. 300)

Army, Katamura, relaxed his order to the defenders. 51 and 60 Infantry Regiments were ordered to put in a final attack on 19 Indian Division and then withdraw. The order was given on 18 March. 60 Regiment occupied the Government Farms Buildings area (called in the Japanese texts 'the Agricultural College') on the south edge of the city. During the night of 19 March, the main body of 15 Division withdrew from Mandalay. They were as well informed as Rees: they came out through a drain under the moat.[1]

Slim was at Monywa when the news came through. Air Vice-Marshal Vincent at once detailed a Sentinel light plane from the L5 detachment of 194 Squadron, RAF, to fly him into Mandalay to take the salute at the victory parade, escorted by two Spitfires.[2]

2 British Division got in on the act; but only just. Brigadier Michael West, of 5 Brigade, had been told to link up with his opposite number from 19 Division in Mandalay, and he drove up on 21 March, taking Colonel White, the Commanding Officer of the Dorsets, with him, a troop of Grant tanks, and some armoured carriers. There was no one at the crossroads rendezvous, except a puzzled military policeman, who sent them on to the Fort. They drove through the shambles of the city – White was oppressed by its air of desolation – past the ruins of King Thibaw's Palace, and on to the parade ground where they found 19 Division drawn up on the site of Government House, in the presence of Slim, Messervy, and three divisional commanders. 'It was perhaps most fitting', White wrote later, 'that the Dorsets gate-crashed this party to represent the 2nd Division, as we and the troop of the 3rd Dragoon Guards with us were the only troops of the Division to fight in Mandalay itself.' All the more appropriate since the Dorsets wore the battle honour 'Ava' for the Burma War of 1824–6, during which they had not entered Mandalay. By another odd coincidence, the fourth Marquis of Dufferin and Ava, who was with a Field Broadcasting Unit, was killed in an ambush between Ava and Fort Dufferin on 23 March.[3] The flag was hoisted over Fort Dufferin, as soon as 72 Brigade went in, by Rees himself – according to Slim – or by a gunner of 134 Medium Regiment, Royal Artillery – according to the Official History. The ceremony was repeated by Slim at the formal parade to make sure everyone realized that more than one division had collaborated in the capture: 'The capture of Mandalay had been as much the result of operations at Meiktila and elsewhere as of those around the city itself. Every one of my divisions had played its part; it was an Army victory. I thought it would be good for everyone to have that fact demonstrated.'[4]

[1] OCH, *Irawaji Kaisen*, p. 142

[2] Wilfrid Russell, *The Friendly Firm. A History of 194 Squadron, Royal Air Force*, 1972, p. 65

[3] White, *Straight on for Tokyo*, p. 262, 266–7. The first marquis gave his name to the Fort in Mandalay. He was Viceroy of India when upper Burma was annexed in 1886. (Kirby, *War Against Japan*, IV, p. 290, n.3)

[4] Slim, op.cit., p. 470; *Reconquest of Burma*, II, p. 363

7. THE BATTERING-RAM

The capture and siege of Meiktila

Tanks to Meiktila — the Capture — the Siege —
Setting up the board again

Tanks to Meiktila

Slim's dismissal of the strategic value of Mandalay does not do justice to the situation in which the Japanese found themselves when it fell. The higher command were uncomfortably aware of the saying 'who rules Mandalay rules Burma' and that it would have an impact on their already shaky relationship with the Burma National Army. On the purely military level, it represented the disruption of the Lines of Communication to 15 and 33 Armies; and the taking of Maymyo isolated 56 Division in the Northern Shan States. But it was the seizure of Meiktila which finally destroyed any chance Kimura had of rectifying the situation in Central Burma.

The Indian Army Official History places the capture of Mandalay *after* the battle for Meiktila in its narrative; the Japanese does the very opposite and that instinct is surely right. For Slim it was 'the vital thrust',[1] for Evans 'the decisive battle'.[2] Evans, of course, had prepared the platform for the assault. East of the bridgehead, at Pakokku, and west of it at Seikpyu, he kept the Japanese from pinching it out, and captured Myingyan on the Irrawaddy near the confluence with the Chindwin, so that Slim's forces could be supplied down-river from Kalewa. Myingyan later became a main supply base for XIV Army. It was not easy to take. The Japanese withdrew on it from Pakokku, and some indication of the hard fighting needed to wrest it from them is shown by the fact that two VCs were won by Evans's men – both Sikhs of 4/15 Punjab – in taking it.[3]

Cowan's 17 Division crossed the Irrawaddy on 17 February 1945, and broke out of the bridgehead four days later. As 255 Armoured Brigade spearheaded the assault there was, inevitably, a cavalry flavour to the

---

[1] Slim, *Defeat into Victory*, p. 235

[2] Evans, *Slim,* p. 196

[3] Evans, *The Desert and the Jungle*, p. 156

occasion. The Brigade consisted of 116 Regiment Royal Armoured Corps – a Gordon Highlanders territorial unit converted originally from infantry to an anti-tank role, then turned into an armoured regiment – Indian Cavalry, 9 Cavalry (Royal Deccan Horse) and 5 Lancers (Probyn's Horse) which liked to think of itself as an Indian Army version of the Blues. They were commanded by an adventurous colonel from Hodson's Horse, Miles Smeeton, tall and skinny, with a conspicuous Roman nose, who has left a vivid account of the Meiktila battle in his book *A Change of Jungles.*[1] Their motorized infantry was the 4/4 Bombay Grenadiers. The Brigade was commanded by Claud Pert, a cavalry commander of rare distinction, and an international polo player, who had been second-in-command of 254 Independent Indian Tank Brigade during the siege of Imphal.

Long before the full plans for Meiktila matured in his mind, Slim came to see the Brigade at Imphal in September 1944. Once XIV Army was in the open country of Central Burma, there would be full scope for armour, and as he was shown round the Brigade, he turned to the Brigade Major, Alasdair Tuck, and asked him what was the most important thing about the use of armour. Tuck gave him the usual training pamphlet reply – mobile striking power, saving of infantry lives – when Slim stopped him and said, 'Those are expected of it, but the *most* important thing is *reliability.*' Mechanical failure could make them a burden. 'How reliable are those Shermans?' he went on. 'Very, sir,' Tuck replied. 'Given sufficient fuel, some essential spares and some time at night to do maintenance on them.' 'You had better be right,' Slim growled and stumped off to his jeep.[2]

The tanks moved on their own tracks longer than they should have done to get to the starting-point. The tank transporters which brought them down the valleys from Imphal were well past their best and often broke down. (Oddly enough, the Tank Transporter Squadron were nearly all members of the same theatrical touring company in England, who had joined up en masse, actors, electricians, and stage-hands, and they would often run two trailers together and put on a show.) But these worn vehicles rumbling over tracks consisting at times of sawn-off tree-stumps and holes in the ground occasionally had to be towed in by the Shermans, so that the tanks ended up doing a third of the journey on their own tracks. After doing 210 miles, the transporters finally gave up the ghost at Mawle. The drawback of the tanks moving on their own – though it was faster – was that they tore up the one-way track into deep dust, and this caused a particularly unpleasant accident when Smeeton's jeep-driver came alongside to give him a message, skidded in the dust toward the Command

[1] Miles Smeeton, *A Change of Jungles*, 1962. Also under command was B Squadron, 11 Light Cavalry.

[2] Colonel Alasdair Tuck, 'Notes on 255 Independent Tank Brigade's part in the Capture and Holding of Meiktila in 1944', 18 pp with maps; privately communicated to the author, 1979. (Tuck was Brigade-Major during the battle.)

Sherman, put his hand out to fend the vehicle off, and was pulled into the tank suspension.

Leaving the Gordons behind as armour for 7 Division, 255 Brigade began to cross the Irrawaddy on 18 February. As one of the Deccan Horse tanks was in the water, a Japanese fighter zoomed in on it and machine-gunned its raft. The sappers manning the raft jumped overboard and clung to the sides as the raft circled slowly in the river. The tank crew blazed away on their anti-aircraft Browning on the turret at two planes which followed. These turned out to be Hurricanes pursuing the Oscar, and the Brigade second-in-command, Colonel Ralph Younger, who was having his morning shave at the time, was jumping up and down on the bank with fury (neither side sustained any damage). . .

It was eighty miles from the beachhead at Nyaungu to Meiktila, and the going was tough, the tanks sliding into dry ravine beds and clambering up the other side, then forging through deep dust. They had passed through jungle: this was war in the desert. The first day they made only fifteen miles.

The first resistance came the next day when the village of Oyin had to be taken. Astride one of the two roads passing through Taungtha that led to Meiktila, Oyin offered the classic shelter to the Japanese snipers of 16 Infantry Regiment (2 Division), a mud bank and a cactus hedge, tall trees and houses with spaces dug out beneath them. The 5/6 Rajputs were the tanks' infantry screen and were soon held up by enemy fire. The infantry, as Smeeton knew, wanted the tanks to clean up the village to make their advance simpler, but the tanks themselves, separated from infantry, felt ungainly and vulnerable; and although they carried a telephone on the outside, the theory of tank/infantry communication was not so simple. As the leading tank went ahead through Oyin, a Japanese suddenly rushed out from hiding, hurled himself under the squadron commander's tank and detonated a box of explosive that killed himself and the Sikh driver, and brought the tank to a halt.[1]

That was the usual pattern of suicide attacks against tanks. The box was wood, and filled with picric acid. It had a pull igniter, and a single Japanese, with this strapped to his chest, would fling himself on the engine louvres or between the tracks, then pull the string. The tanks' safety depended on alert crews and watchful infantry.[2] Smeeton watched the faces of the Japanese as they ran, and was taken aback at 'their anguished look of determination and despair, pitting their puny strength against such tremendous force. This desperate form of courage was something that we knew little of and saw with amazement, admiration and pity. . .'[3]

[1] Smeeton, op.cit., p. 89

[2] *Tuck, MS*, p. 12

[3] Smeeton, op.cit., p. 90

Smeeton grew more and more curious about the nature of the Japanese. When the fight for Oyin was over, with some 200 Japanese dead, for seventy Rajput casualties, the Rajput company commander killed and a tank commander shot through the head,[1] he walked back into the village and past the foxholes where the Japanese corpses now sat, some broken with bullets, others with uniforms smouldering and – he noticed – 'surprisingly good-looking, sturdy and young'. It was a corrective to the propaganda cartoons he had been used to, and he recognized their bravery without difficulty: 'If a British regiment had fought against such odds as they had fought, the story would live forever in their history, but it was not unusual for the Japanese to fight like this. . .'[2] Tuck thought this tenacity indicated the number of Japanese they would have to kill: the lot.[3]

The Oyin action took place on 22 February, the day on which Allied aircraft flew over Meiktila and dropped leaflets. Yoshiichi Shigemitsu, a *gunzoku*[4] attached to Burma Area Army Headquarters who was in Meiktila at the time, picked one up and read it. It was a warning notice. 'When we say we'll bomb Mandalay, we'll bomb it. When we say we'll bomb Amanapura,[5] we'll bomb it. The Allied air forces have decided to bomb Lines of Communication installations at Meiktila on 23 February. Non-combatants and those who value their lives are urged to be three miles away when we come.'[6]

Yoshiichi did not know about Mandalay or Amarapura, but he took the threat seriously. Documents were evacuated, and men told to stick to their posts. At 2 pm on the 23rd, enemy aircraft showed up, but there were only three of them, and their 100lb bombs dropped on the officers' quarters either did not go off or missed. Then, for some reason Yoshiichi could not fathom, they strafed villagers' huts about a mile east of the Japanese lines.

That night, cars began to arrive in Meiktila from all directions for an important staff meeting. Lieutenant-General Numata Takazō, the Chief of Staff of Southern Army, had come to Meiktila from Saigon to discuss future plans with the Chiefs of Staff of the armies in Burma, presided over by Lieutenant-General Tanaka Shinichi, now Kimura's Chief of Staff, who ran an advanced tactical headquarters at Kalaw in the Shan States.

[1] Smeeton held the view that tank manoeuvring was often hampered by excess of caution, and refused to let his tank commanders close their turrets. As a result, five of them were shot through the head, but he thought the advantage of manoeuvre worth the risk.

[2] ibid., p. 91

[3] *Tuck MS*, p. 12

[4] Civilian attached to the Army.

[5] (sic) for Amarapura.

[6] Yoshiichi Shigemitsu, *Gunzoku Biruma monogatari*, pp. 212–13

Yoshiichi was given the duty of looking after the conference members, and realized how tight the security was when he was told that, even to bring them tea, he was the only one allowed inside, and would have to indicate when they were ready for tea to another man waiting fifty yards away. Sentries marched up and down in front of the conference centre, a big building 200 yards from the officers' quarters by the lake, and also stood at the front and rear entrances. Yoshiichi told his unit commander he thought the news of the conference had leaked out, and that was why the bombing raid was so derisory. Perhaps the British intended a real raid on the day of the conference. He was told not to concern himself.[1]

Mandalay was invested, Allied bridgeheads were across the Irrawaddy knocking in 31 Division's defence lines, the link-up between 28 Army and 15 Army was delayed, the Japanese in Central Burma were *happō fusagari* – 'blocked in on all sides' – and the conference tackled all these problems. The main issue was, could 15 Army mount an offensive on the west bank of the Irrawaddy (a little late to discuss by now)? Burma Area Army had privately indicated it hoped this was possible. Not a mass battle in the Shwebo Plain – Kimura had already decided against that – but an offensive forward from the strong point at Sagaing, since 15 Army had been reinforced by 18 Division and 72 Independent Mixed Brigade. The gain would be great if such an offensive could be sustained for two weeks from about 10 March.

15 Army indicated its willingness to act along these lines, and proposed an attack across the Irrawaddy from north of Myingyan by 33 Division, with 72 Independent Mixed Brigade, and from north of Mandalay by 18 and 53 Divisions, hoping to surround the British forces in a pocket in the lower reaches of the Mu River. 53 Division would hold the south (i.e. east) bank of the Irrawaddy in strength between Myingyan and Mandalay.[2]

These were pipe-dreams, as were Tanaka's hope that 15 Army would retain sufficient elasticity to operate on both banks of the Irrawaddy, and his request to Numata for extra air support, to which Numata said nothing. The situation was changing far more rapidly than they envisaged. As they were spinning these futile plans in Meiktila, the advance guard of 17 Division and 255 Tank Brigade were smashing into Taungtha from the south-west against light opposition. That brought them within forty-three miles of where the conference was taking place. Probyn's Horse arrived in the afternoon, with 63 Brigade, and said they had contested every village between Welaung and Taungtha, in one of them killing sixty-five Japanese.

---

[1] Yoshiichi, *Gunzoku Biruma Monogatari*, pp. 213–14. 'The Japanese records are uncertain about the exact date of this conference but suggest that it took place on 23 February', says the British Official History (*War Against Japan*, IV, p. 272, n.3). It seems clear enough from Yoshiichi's book and *Irawaji Kaisen* that the staff officers assembled on the evening of 23 February, and the conference took place the following day.

[2] OCH, *Irawaji Kaisen*, p. 152

Nonetheless, the Brigade Major of 255 Tank Brigade was uneasy: he felt that the Brigade should not be stopping for these engagements but should cut a swathe through this Japanese screen and push on to Meiktila regardless of opposition. There was no doubt the tanks could do it. But it would leave the road uncleared, and the Japanese in the roadside villages would simply close in when they had passed and ambush the soft-skinned transport bringing up the infantry behind them. This became clear to Tuck as he found the triangle between the roads leading to Taungtha from Welaung to the west and Mahlaing to the east 'crawling with Jap snipers in rough scrubby country'.[1] The 7 Baluch cleared it, and killed over 100.

Of all this, Tanaka's conference remained blissfully unaware, though Cowan's force was now three days out from its bridgehead, and the engagement at Oyin had been fought on the 22nd. It so happens that the Sakyō Battalion which fought that battle against Probyn's Horse carried no wireless sets, and not only was the conference not informed of it, it knew nothing of Taungtha either. Had intelligence come through from 53 Division, it would have put a stop at once to speculations about attacks on XIV Army on the west bank of the Irrawaddy.

As it was, three hours after the staff officers had dispersed to their respective formations, an urgent signal came in to Meiktila from a small unit stationed south of Myingyan: 'The enemy at Pakokku has crossed the river and entered Taungtha. The force at Taungtha is estimated at 80 in 8 vehicles led by 2 tanks.' Early the following day (25 February), a second report arrived: 'Enemy at Taungtha appears to be moving to Mahlaing. 4 tanks in front, 20 trucks, about 300 men.' If they hurried, they could be in Meiktila three hours from now, Yoshiichi thought, as he noticed the estimates had increased.[2] He was, naturally enough, somewhat perturbed. Meiktila had no defences, there were few weapons, the Lines of Communication men were unarmed; but the garrison did contain two airfield battalions (52 and 84) and 36 Field Anti-Aircraft Battalion for the defence of its airfields, the most valuable in Central Burma. It was largely a hospital area, for casualties or Lines of Communication troops, the site of 107 Lines of Communication Hospital. An emergency meeting was called of the Lines of Communication officers, and reports sent at once to the nearest combatant units, and those troops in Meiktila who belonged to other units were told to remain in the town, and a *tōbatsu* (punitive force) company was formed from them. There were about 4000 troops in Meiktila, but their combat strength was low.[3] Yoshiichi, who was told to

---

[1] *Tuck MS*, p. 14

[2] Yoshiichi, *Gunzoku Biruma Monogatari*, p. 212–13

[3] 'These totalled some twelve thousand men', writes Slim *(Defeat into Victory*, p. 442) but this figure is quite unreal for the town itself, and is an approximation for the forces later assembled to extrude 17 Division.

transmit these orders, called on the four officers who were still billetted in quarters, and found that large numbers of men had left early that morning. He told the officers as politely as he could that they could not rejoin their units, and that if they left Meiktila without permission they would be guilty of desertion.

'Isn't there some mistake?' queried one of the officers. 'How can the enemy be so close in these back areas?' Yoshiichi told them of the two reports that had come in. They would have been less sceptical had 53 Division's report been sent on, which mentioned the figure of 2000 vehicles and tanks being observed en route for Meiktila. That emergency signal had been sent from 53 Division north of Taungtha in the afternoon of 24 February.[1] An officer on duty from 53 Division in the Mount Popa area reported seeing an armoured column moving east, and gave the figures as 'tanks and lorries, at least 2000 vehicles', but the date and time of the report are not known.[2] 53 Division transmitted the report, and other formations received the signal on 24 February, as Lieutenant-General Tanaka, GOC 33 Division, noted in his diary that day. But he, too, was sceptical: 'The figure is far too high', he noted, because he had received another report from Colonel Sakuma, in command of 214 Regiment near the bridgehead area, which spoke of thirty tanks and 300 lorries.[3] That same day, Major Miura Sukezō, a staff officer of 33 Division, had also been on Mount Popa and reported similar numbers at once by telephone to 15 Army Headquarters. A staff officer – whom he does not name – came to the phone and when he heard Miura's figures simply said 'don't be such a fool!' and rang off.[4] So the scepticism was considerable at *both* headquarters in the first instance.

The Japanese were caught short here, just as Slim had been over Kohima, and similar action was taken. There were no combatant units, so Major-General Kasuya, GOC No. 2 Field Transport, took command. So this vital Lines of Communication centre, the site of four airfields at all four points of the compass, fell to be defended by those troops regarded by the rest of the Japanese Army as most distant from the idea of battle: transport troops. Since the Allies had used airborne troops, and proved themselves capable of long-range penetration, it is astonishing that Kimura's headquarters had no provisional plan for the defence of this place, only eighty miles from the banks of the Irrawaddy.

15 Army Headquarters received 53 Division's message on the 25th. That it should take a day for a signal of such importance to filter through to higher command says little for the sense of urgency of 15 Army's new staff. Colonel

[1] OCH *Irawaji Kaisen*, p. 162
[2] ibid., p. 564
[3] ibid., p. 564
[4] OCH, *Irawaji Kaisen*, pp. 564–5

Tsuji Masanobu, then on secondment to 15 Army Headquarters, took the signal to be an indication of a new phase in the battle for Burma. He had been put into a small tent on his arrival at Katamura's headquarters, and was feeling with pleasure the cold sand between his toes in the early morning as he stood before his camp table and basin to wash in cold water, when Wakizaka, a staff officer, came up with the sheet of signal paper. It referred to 'at least 100 tanks' and 'about 1000 trucks' being observed, and was from 53 Division's Chief of Staff.[1] Tsuji urged Katamura to throw everything into the defence of Meiktila. Katamura agreed. This was on the 27th. In reply to a signal from 15 Army in this sense, Kimura's GHQ in Rangoon replied: 'Enemy in Meiktila area not to be over-estimated... keep to your objective of the battle for the Irrawaddy shore.' Katamura was not to be outfaced, and wired back: 'Meiktila situation transformed. Whether this is merely local disturbance of battlefield will in the end be known by facts. Army cannot treat present situation as local disturbance.'[2] The terms of the signals showed the mutual lack of confidence and respect between the two Army commanders. The Japanese histories say this was supposedly due to a faulty transmission of signals, or at any rate to a suspicion on the part of Burma Area Army that somewhere between itself and its subordinate formations a 'natural' figure of 200 (natural because the Japanese in Burma had got used to local battles in mountain areas) had had an extra 0 added to it by mistake. Kimura's Chief of Staff, Tanaka Shinichi, who had been in Meiktila a couple of days before, recalled that there had been a similar flap over the Wingate expedition in 1943, and the Imphal operation had gone ahead in spite of it. If Burma Area Army sent up 49 Division from reserve (it was two regiments short), it should be enough to deal with a similar incursion to Meiktila without distorting arrangements for dealing with the threat to the Irrawaddy shore.

The Japanese signals people themselves reject the theory of the mistaken 0. Major Koga Shunji, a staff officer of 49 Division who once commanded the Signals detachment at Burma Area Army GHQ, regards it as impossible: 'Especial care is demanded in the treatment of numbers in signals, and codes for numbers and numerical abbreviations are duplicated. So it's absolutely impossible to put 200 instead of 2000 or vice-versa. And the head of the signals operating team at the time was Lieutenant Suzuki, who committed suicide at the end of the war. He was recognized as devoted to his duty and for him to drop a zero, arbitrarily, is quite unthinkable.'[3]

It has also been suggested by Major Kōno Kōichi, chief staff officer (Intelligence) at Burma Area Army in Rangoon, that the signals detachment there might simply, on its own initiative, have cancelled the last

---

[1] Tsuji Masanobu, *Jugō tai-ichi* p. 225

[2] OCH, *Irawaji Kaisen*, p. 163

[3] ibid., p. 164

zero from the message before it was handed in to the staff. Either way, signals or staff, the responsibility for misreading the intelligence seems to lie with the receiver, Burma Area Army, and not the sender, 15 Army.

Katamura decided to go ahead with his 'Plan for the Battle of Meiktila'. The main body of 15 Army artillery, and an infantry force consisting of 18 Division and a regiment from each of 15 and 33 Divisions would take the offensive at Meiktila, timed to begin on 10 March, while all divisions on the Irrawaddy front would go on the defensive. Kasuya would take command of the units now in Meiktila and secure the Station area. There was strong disagreement at Burma Area Army over this. Tanaka passionately advocated keeping to the already determined plan, but Kimura swept his opposition aside, and accepted Katamura's proposals. Katamura hustled 18 Division down from the Shan States, and transferred to the Meiktila area most of 31 Division's heavy guns, 14 Tank Regiment, 119 Infantry Regiment, and 214 Regiment from 33 Division. Clearly this was going to weaken – and very rapidly – these divisions' ability to hold their front, but he was convinced the crisis at Meiktila was crucial.

Meiktila: the capture

By 2 pm on 26 February, the Deccan Horse were on the airstrip at Thabutkon, fifteen miles from Meiktila, to the north. They had made it across open country intersected by sandy *chaung* beds across which the tanks had to tow the lorries. The air-strip was vital to Cowan's plan. 99 Brigade (Torver) which he had left behind at Palel was now flown in, after the divisional sappers had readied the strip. The brigade was complete by 2 March without casualties, and petrol was air-dropped for the tanks, though Thabutkon came under sporadic rifle and machine-gun fire for a day or two.[1]

A slight hitch occurred on the 27th. The armoured cars of 16 Cavalry were patrolling forward to Meiktila when they hit strong opposition eight miles from the town. The Japanese had blown a *chaung* bridge and laid mines, and had dug and wired positions for 150 yards on either side of the road. They had plenty of machine guns, and were backed by 75s and 105s. 63 Brigade, with Probyn's Horse and 129 Field Regiment, moved forward to tackle the position, and a classic textbook engagement took place. Men of the 9 Border Regiment and A Squadron of Probyn's Horse hooked round north of the Japanese, overran their guns, and set up a block behind them. The armoured cars of 16 Cavalry attempted a frontal attack on the bridge, withdrew when fired on at point-blank range, and called on the USAAF Thunderbolts for an airstrike. The armoured cars then left the

---

[1] Perrett, *Tank Tracks to Rangoon*, p. 165

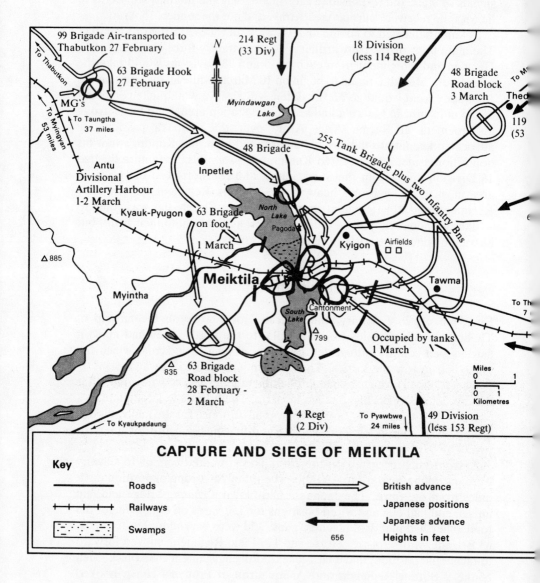

CAPTURE AND SIEGE OF MEIKTILA

Key

————	Roads
+++++	Railways
Swamps	Swamps

British advance
Japanese positions
Japanese advance
656 Heights in feet

way open for C Squadron of Probyn's Horse to attack the bridgehead on
with a battalion of infantry, the Shermans came across the gap in the road
through the mines and snipers and the Japanese broke. As they fled back
towards Meiktila, A Squadron opened up on them from their roadblock.

434

The action accounted for eighty Japanese and a number of guns, though Alasdair Tuck recalls one gruesome casualty in the USAAF.

255 Brigade had a very pleasant American liaison officer with whom Tuck was friendly, and he could not forbear asking him some time later why his jeep stank so much. The American told him he had watched a Thunderbolt pilot pull out too late after dive-bombing the Japanese, and his tail had hit the ground. The liaison officer had collected the pilot's remains in a sandbag and put them in his jeep tool bin as he knew the boy's parents in America would want them. Tuck begged him to bury them and send back the dog tags with a map reference so the bones could be collected later. At first the American demurred, but after another twenty-four hours of Central Burma heat he did it.

That day, 28 February, Cowan was poised to attack Meiktila. He *had* to take it, since its airfields were essential to keep him supplied. The road link with the bridgehead was severed after the Japanese retook Taungtha where they had fought with 48 Brigade until it joined Cowan for the attack on Meiktila. The geometry of the lakes decided the pattern of the assault. On a map, the north and south lakes of Meiktila, linked by a narrow strip of water, look like a balloon with a hand clutching it in the middle. The north lake bends to the west, and the 'bag' of the south lake covers the southern approaches to the town. The road and railway from Thazi, twelve miles away, come in from the east. It is a branch line which continues to Myingyan since the Mandalay-Rangoon main line does not run directly through Meiktila. The road from Mandalay, about eighty miles to the north, passes out north-east of the town between the north and east airstrips. Roads run south-west to Kyaukpadaung and the oil-fields, and north-west to Mahlaing and Taungtha. The town itself straddles the neck of water between the lakes, but the Japanese Lines of Communication area was between two and three miles north of this, beside the North Lake. In peacetime, Meiktila is a beautiful spot. From its elegant red-brick buildings, and pleasant villas set among shady trees, you can see the cone of Mount Popa in the distance to the south-west, the trees are full of birds and butterflies, and the dawn skies a blaze of orange and gold, making the tall golden pagoda on high ground overlooking the town glow in the sun. In March and April it is torrid, and the lakes are shallow, but the presence of water adds a little coolness. There are hillocks of 6–900 feet around it, but the river flowing along the edge of the town produces cliffs to the east. The river is almost dry in February and March, but there are occasional wells in the villages. What forest there is is not luxuriant, as elsewhere in Burma, and the shrub thorns can make walking painful and hazardous. The cactus, unlike the cactus at home, was so tough and spindly that it reminded the Japanese of barbed wire. The red soil was hard, and digging in it arduous. East of the town the land has been developed, to the west it is sparsely cultivated. The ferocious heat of March, April and May and scarcity of water mean that little grows apart from cotton, peanuts, and beans, as opposed to the flat land round Mandalay, Shwebo or Kyaukse, where rice is grown, and tobacco, onions and other vegetables. On the other hand, Japan itself in midsummer can be stifling and worse than Meiktila at 40°C. To the Japanese convalescing there, Meiktila, even in February, was an oasis.

It is an appropriate term. Just as Mandalay turned the jungle war into a medieval castle siege, Meiktila turned it into a desert battle – very aptly for the British, since its Corps Commander, Frank Messervy, had commanded 7 Armoured Division in the Western Desert in North Africa.

Cowan was not to be allowed to fight his way into Meiktila unobserved. Too much depended on it, both for Messervy and Slim, for them to resist the itch to be on the spot, so Cowan planned and fought, with his Corps Commander and Army Commander breathing down his neck. Slim saw Meiktila's formidable defences rather than its beauty.[1] The houses and ammunition dumps offered strong positions, the lakes which covered the approaches from the west and south turned the roads into narrow causeways which hostile guns could close and which gave tanks no room for manoeuvre; and they would be slowed up by the irrigation ditches in the countryside around. The main built-up area in the town was some 1200 yards across, including the railway station. An 800-foot hill rose south-east of the town, about 1000 yards long by 500 yards deep, where the road and rail bridge ran, and some brick bungalows lay to the south of this. Over 3000 yards further west, the railway bridged the Mordaing Chaung, the main lake feeder.[2]

Slim came up to watch the assault with a grave burden on his mind. On 23 February, Chiang Kai-shek had asked for all US[3] and Chinese forces to leave Burma for China, where he planned an offensive. Pending their return, they were not to advance beyond the line Lashio-Hsipaw-Kyaukme, which lay eighty miles north-east of Mandalay where – he advised Mountbatten, who protested – XIV Army should halt. 36 Division would still be marching down to relieve 19 Division in the old capital once it was taken, but with most of NCAC vacated of enemy, Kimura could transfer his troops from there and send them south. The aircraft Slim needed for Meiktila and elsewhere would have to supply 36 Division and ferry the Chinese out. He did not learn this until the tanks were well on their way to Meiktila.

Mountbatten argued that he could not afford to release transport aircraft from North Burma, and that the aircraft were allotted to Burma as a whole, not merely to NCAC. It was unthinkable that 36 Division should undertake all NCAC's commitments once the Chinese withdrew, and at the same time

[1] Slim, op.cit., pp. 442–3

[2] *Tuck MS*, p. 17

[3] In infantry terms, 5332 Brigade known as MARS Brigade, the successor to GALAHAD.

lose transport aircraft.[1] The British Chiefs of Staff endorsed this view to the US Joint Chiefs of Staff, and Churchill sent a personal message to General Marshall on 30 March, emphasizing the need for Slim to keep his aircraft until Rangoon had fallen. Marshall, to SEAC's great relief, replied that there was no intention of removing air resources from South-East Asia before 1 June, or the capture of Rangoon, whichever came first. This was, of course, an extra spur for Slim. He *had* to be in Rangoon not later than May, because he could not afford to be stranded between Meiktila and Rangoon, as the monsoon broke, without a port to bring him supplies, and with his aircraft vanishing into the blue.[2]

All these things were on his mind as he flew in with Messervy in a USAAF B25 – the RAF had refused to take him as Thabutkon airfield was still said to be unsafe: 'I was told that the RAF would be delighted to fly any of my staff anywhere at any time, but not me, not to Meiktila, not now.'[3] Slim found Thabutkon peaceful, though there was firing some distance away, and the occasional Japanese corpse on the edge of the strip. Cowan's jeeps then brought him and Messervy into 'the bitterest fighting of the battle'.[4]

Cowan planned a wide loop north of the town by 255 Tank Brigade, while 48 Brigade hit the strong position at the side of the north lake where the Japanese installations were. 63 Brigade put a road block on the road to Chauk south-west of the town to prevent reinforcements coming up from Yenangyaung, and then went in from the west. The tanks would come in from their semi-circular loop, take the eastern airfields and reach the town through the cantonment area. A couple of miles behind 63 Brigade, the massed divisional artillery, screened by an infantry battalion, covered the entire operation.

The main thrust came from the east, where Cowan put the artillery and air-strikes at the disposal of the tank brigade, which had a battery of self-propelled 25-pounders under command. They took the height overlooking the east of Meiktila, Point 859, and the infantry followed them up as they assaulted the town after a very heavy and accurate air bombardment. But Kasuya's resistance, though a last-minute improvisation, was ferocious. Artillery fire met the tanks, and a bunker system and scores of snipers poured fire into the advancing infantry. The attack went in as far as the railway station, but Cowan did not want his tanks to harbour among the ruins, as night approached, and therefore ordered them to pull back two miles on the outskirts of Meiktila. Patrols were left behind to hold the positions won, but inevitably, in the hours of darkness, the Japanese infiltrated back again into some of the areas they had lost.

---

[1] Mountbatten, *Report*, pp. 134–5

[2] Lewin, *Slim*, p. 224

[3] Slim, op.cit., p. 446

[4] ibid., p. 447

As the battle developed, Alasdair Tuck noticed that although Kasuya did not seem to be short of infantry weapons, including 75s and 105s, there was little heavy anti-aircraft which could have been used in an anti-tank role, nor were there anti-tank mines. But the Japanese used anti-aircraft machine guns and 250 kg aerial bombs in a special way, as Tuck heard later. The guns did have armour-piercing shot, which could be disquieting at fifty yards range, but the anti-aircraft machine gun shells stuck in the armour without penetrating, so that by the end of the day the tanks began to look like pin-cushions. At one point of the assault, when Probyn's Horse tried to move through the wooded area between the railway line and an irrigation canal, on the banks of which the Japanese had dug themselves in, they were even threatened by a vast fire. The wooded area was used by the Japanese as a petrol dump, and as the tanks approached it, the defenders fired into the petrol barrels which exploded and turned the woods into a sheet of flames.[1]

Slim left Cowan, and went to the north side of the town, where two platoons of 1/7 Gurkhas of 48 Brigade were edging forward against what looked like innocent grassy hummocks but from which, as Slim could see through his binoculars 500 yards away, the characteristic smoke of hot machine guns rose in wisps. He could make out loopholes in the hummocks, and hear the firing of the automatics as the Gurkhas moved in, dash by dash, covered by occasional shelling from a single Sherman tank concealed in a hollow, and then by mortars. The tank would edge forward, fire a couple of rounds, then withdraw into its hollow out of sight of the bunkers. Slim and his party moved away from the pagoda terrace and concealed themselves behind a clump of cactus to get a better view, as the tank began to fire, first with grenades, then with solid shot, at the loopholes in the bunkers. Then the tank worked round a spinney behind the bunkers, and began firing again. The 'overs' came straight towards Slim, Messervy and the visiting American general whose bomber had flown them in. Flinging themselves flat on the ground they survived without a scratch, luckier than one of the US aircrew who hurled himself straight into a cactus hedge and emerged, in Slim's description, like 'a blood-stained pin-cushion'.

The Gurkhas closed in, thrust tommy-guns through the loopholes and sprayed the interior of the bunkers. Half-a-dozen Japanese sprinted from this shelter and were brought down by the automatics. Slim noticed that one of them was much taller than the rest, and the tank gun, with unnecessary emphasis, Slim thought, finished him off. It was not the place for an Army Commander-in-Chief and one of his Corps commanders, and was the nearest to close fighting Slim had been since he took over XIV Army. He relished particularly the fact that this piece of classic tank-cum-infantry

[1] *Tuck MS*, pp. 19–20

collaboration was done by a Gurkha regiment of which he was honorary Colonel.[1]

The next day, 2 March, 48 Brigade knocked the Japanese from house to house until they were pinned with their backs to the South Lake, while 63 Brigade cleared them from the west of the town. On 255 Tank Brigade's front, the Japanese had come back into the railway station in Meiktila East during the night 1/2 March, and had devised a way they hoped would destroy the tanks. In the open ground across the tanks' approach routes, they dug a series of holes and installed a man in each of them. Between his knees he held a fused 250 kg aerial bomb, nose uppermost, and clutched a brick in his hand, the idea being to wait until a tank was on top of him, then smack the brick down on the bomb cap and blow himself and the tank to kingdom come. The area had become a human anti-tank minefield.

Then, in one of the coolest actions of the battle, Alan Wakefield, a colonel of the Deccan Horse, took a hand. He was not commanding a tank formation but was on intelligence duties with the brigade and had attached himself to his old regiment. They had been over this ground the day before, and he now noticed that it was covered in pock marks in regular lines. He told the tanks to stop and cover him with their guns, then went forward and began to shoot each human mine in the head. Every now and then he would pause to reload, then move on to the next series of pock marks. None of the Japanese detonated their bombs – Wakefield was not a tank, and they had been told to do it only for tanks – and he remained miraculously unscathed by fire from the Japanese in the railway station. It was bravery worthy of a VC, Tuck thought as he watched, but Wakefield was a Lieutenant-Colonel on his own and so nobody put him in for it. The ground was clear, and the tanks rolled on.[2]

By 3 March, organized resistance from Kasuya's scratch garrison had come to an end, and 17 Division began winkling out the last snipers, grenading bunkers, and wiping out small parties attempting to escape. A group of escapers, east of Point 859, were caught by 255 Tank Brigade which killed sixty-five of them, and twelve guns were destroyed or captured, in addition to those taken in the early phase of the battle.[3] Two wide sweeps by mobile columns – tanks, armoured cars and light infantry – were made, destroying guns and mortars, and these continued on the 4th and 5th. Over 2000 Japanese bodies were counted in the town area when the battle was over, forty-seven prisoners were taken, quite a high figure, and forty-eight guns were captured.[4] Tuck thought the number of dead was

[1] Slim, op.cit., pp. 449–50

[2] *Tuck MS*, p. 21

[3] *Tuck MS*, p. 22

[4] Mountbatten, *Report*, p. 131

higher than the body-count, partly because the Japanese were not in a running mood, and often infiltrated their old positions. Even the sick in hospital, he wrote,

> unable to get arms, sharpened bamboo poles and hardened the points in a fire to use as improvised bayonets. None surrendered. All fought to the end, except a very very few who were picked up unconscious or otherwise incapacitated and made prisoner and some of these managed to commit suicide. Bodies were popping up in the lake for weeks afterwards. A great many Japs were buried in underground bunkers and tunnels, the entrances and exits of which had been stove in. The few still alive committed suicide or dug themselves out some ten days later too weak from thirst or starvation to do much damage, but prepared to 'have a go' before being shot or overpowered.[1]

The strengthening of the transport personnel and the convalescent casualties was undoubtedly due to the arrival of 49 Division's first contingent, 168 Infantry Regiment. Code-named OKAMI ('Wolf'), 49 Division was never employed as a fighting unit after its arrival in Burma in August 1944, but was placed under direct command of Burma Area Army and used as a stock for reserves. Its 153 Regiment had already been in action against the East Africans at Seikpyu on 14 February, and later at Letse. 168 Regiment fought alongside 56 Division against four Chinese armies in Yunnan and North Burma in August 1944, incurring losses of over 600 from the 3521 men with which it had left Japan. Orders to withdraw south to Meiktila were received on 4 February 1945. The regiment concentrated in Kyaukse and advance elements arrived in Meiktila on 27 February: regimental headquarters, parts of I and II battalions and two companies of mountain artillery, totalling 300 men.[2]

'We'll be all right now', Yoshiichi and his friends said to themselves as Yoshida Regiment (168) marched into Meiktila behind their regimental flag, 'OKAMI Division's a tough unit, isn't it?' 'Yes, they've made it just in time!' The men showed no signs of fatigue as they made for the Mahlaing road.[3] At the end of 28 February, Yoshida Regiment were fighting hard against 48 Brigade at the road fork east of the North Lake, but by nightfall were withdrawn west of the Lake. They watched as Cowan's artillery and air strikes reduced Meiktila to rubble, and saw the fish rise, white bellies upwards on the reddened surface of the South Lake. When 17 Division's

---

[1] *Tuck MS*, p. 23

[2] SEATIC Bulletin No. 244, 1946, p. 46

[3] Yoshiichi, *Gunzoku Biruma Monogatari*, p. 237

attacks were renewed, Yoshida Regiment fought alongside a single field gun placed west of the lake. They received the full impact of 63 Brigade's onslaught on the morning of 2 March with 20 tanks. The field piece halted the tanks but it was not long before the British found its range and destroyed it. By 2 pm what was left of I Battalion and Regimental Headquarters was overrun and Colonel Yoshida, the regimental commander, was killed. The rest of the regiment fought on, with Andō Composite Battalion (the hospital casualties)[1] but systematic resistance was gradually battered to pieces, and the survivors left the town for the south and east.

The bright clear sunlight of 3 March brought no relief. The Kikuchi Mountain Artillery Battalion destroyed two tanks at a distance of 250 yards, using *Ta-Dan*,[2] but the other tanks kept coming and from behind the blazing wrecks poured fire on the two mountain guns, shattering the gun apron, then destroying the guns and their crews with direct hits. The Mountain Artillery Battalion had one gun left by this time, and Second Lieutenant Suganami got three tanks with it in the afternoon, then rushed to his death with the rest of his men, screaming '*Banzai!*' as he fell, followed later by the battalion commander, Captain Kikuchi, who died of his wounds. Grenades burst at the entrance of Major-General Kasuya's trench, and Captain Iwamura, in command of the Mixed Transport Company, found his trench straddled by a tank. The tanks withdrew at nightfall, but the infantry stayed, and the garrison exchanged shots with them among the blazing buildings. Kasuya had earlier given the expected order: '*Mēkutēra heitan wo shishu seyo*' – 'defend Meiktila to the death' – but by this time without any contact with higher formations, he felt his men had done enough.[3] 'Go out east and make for Thazi', he ordered the few survivors, thirty or forty of them, whom he could contact. They split into small groups and made their way through gaps in Cowan's defences. Kasuya got away to Thazi, then moved to Kemapyu, where he was put in command of Shan States Lines of Communication.[4]

'The capture of Meiktila in four days and the annihilation of the garrison... was a magnificent feat of arms', comments Slim.[5] And he showed his appreciation: Messervy flew into Meiktila and decorated

---

[1] Of the 700 sick in Meiktila in February, 200 severe cases had been evacuated to the rear and Andō Composite Battalion was formed from the remaining 500 who could walk.

[2] Armour-piercing shells which released an intense heat on impact and burnt their way through tank armour.

[3] OCH, *Irawaji Kaisen*, p. 174–5

[4] Information from Major Kaetsu, staff officer at Burma Area Army GHQ, but at the time on the strength of Headquarters 49 Division. Kaetsu saw Kasuya at Chiengmai, in Thailand, in June 1945. The general was still Officer Commanding No. 2 Transport Command, and Kaetsu thought the survivors of the Meiktila garrison were with him, engaged on Lines of Communication duties. (Burma Command Intelligence Summary No. 1, (1) 'The fate of the Meiktila Garrison', Rangoon, 1946.)

[5] Slim, op.cit., p. 452

Brigadier Claud Pert, commanding 255 Tank Brigade, with an immediate DSO for an outstanding feat of cavalry leadership. The Japanese had done well, too, as is evident from Slim's pages, which are quoted in the official Japanese history. But that not everyone on their side thought so is evident from the bitter comment made by Second Lieutenant Iwahara Kanichi, of No 2 Field Transport GHQ. 'They say we were routed, all the units who were in Meiktila, and that we did nothing. That's very hard to take. 168 Regiment to start with, the rear echelon units, even the sick, fought to the death, and the survivors should see to it that that goes down in history.'[1] The reason for this feeling is possibly that the Japanese were now arriving from all directions, and finding that all was to do again. The capture was over. The siege was about to begin.

The siege

When they learned that a force was breaking out from the Nyaungu bridgehead, the Japanese believed that it was a raiding force like one of the Wingate columns or that it might be making for the bridgeheads higher up the Irrawaddy. Cowan's rapid seizure of Meiktila caught them unawares. Their reaction was fast, but unco-ordinated. There seems to have been a difference of attitude towards Meiktila in Kimura's headquarters at Rangoon between the rear areas staff and the operations staff. The former were concerned that a vital supply base for 15 and 33 Armies was lost, as well as a transport route for petrol supplies to Central Burma from the oil-fields at Yenangyaung. The latter pooh-poohed their anxieties: 'Don't worry about Meiktila. We'll destroy the enemy within a week, by using 49 Division.' Their unconcern, one of the rear staff officers thought, was because none of Kimura's operational staff officers had any infantry training. If they only assumed, he wondered, that the British had 100 tanks there, and each tank one gun, weren't those 100 guns superior to the entire divisional artillery of 49 Division?[2] (A good question, because 49 Division in fact lost forty-six guns at Meiktila.)[3]

Kimura had, as we have seen, already despatched 49 Division to Meiktila, and 168 Regiment was almost destroyed there. Advance Divisional Headquarters left Pegu on 27 February and reached Pyawbwe on the 29th. By 6 March, 106 Regiment was north of Pyawbwe and ready to take part in the battle. So, too, were the survivors of the capture of Meiktila. When Lieutenant-General Takehara Saburō, GOC 49 Division, arrived at Mindan, about four miles south of Pyawbwe, on the morning of

---

[1] OCH, *Irawaji Kaisen*, p. 176

[2] Ushiro Masaru, *Biruma senki*, *(The War in Burma)*, p. 114

[3] SEATIC Bulletin, No. 244, p. 48

4 March, he realized that Meiktila was already occupied, most of the Japanese garrison killed or wounded, and one of his regimental commanders (Yoshida) already dead. The British seemed to be staying in Meiktila, not advancing beyond it. There was no news of the survivors of Yoshida (168) Regiment.

Then, the next day, a report came in from Major Kanda of 168: 'Approx. 400 men now concentrated in Thazi Station, Yoshida Regiment follow-up units plus survivors escaped from Meiktila. Now defending area Thazi.' Takehara had been too late to frustrate the British assault on Meiktila, and now had to plan its recapture, from the south and south-west.[1]

Other divisions were laid under contribution: elements of 33 Division were to attack from the north (Colonel Sakuma's 214 Regiment, whose acquaintance with Cowan was long and painful), 18 Division from the north-east, and a regiment of 2 Division from the east. It was like an octopus, stabbed in the eye, drawing in its tentacles frantically to pull off the weapon.

The battle can now be taken in two segments: from 6 March to the attacks on the airfields and the change of higher command from 15 Army to 33 Army; and from 10/12 March to the order to pull back from Meiktila issued by Lieutenant-General Honda on 28 March.

Kimura had already planned to bring 18 Division down from North Burma, where it was to leave a regiment at Mongmit to delay the advance of 36 British Division, and move to Mandalay. The 18 Division Commander, Naka, was then told to make for Kume, roughly halfway between Mandalay and Thazi. He was at Kume on 4 March, and was then ordered to recapture Meiktila, using not only his own division but the nine tanks of 14 Tank Regiment, the Naganuma Artillery Group – forty-nine guns – and two battalions of 214 Regiment (Sakuma), 33 Division. North of Meiktila, at Pindale, 119 Regiment, 53 Division, would cover him as he assembled his forces and likewise come under his command. Sakuma had left Taungtha on 3 March. Naka told him to move south-west of Meiktila and attack the town in conjunction with 49 Division. On the 7th, he was in the area of the west airfield. Naka himself, whose 55 Regiment was already at Wundwin, north-east of Meiktila, would attack from the north and east. 18 Mountain Artillery Regiment and 56 Regiment would cover the road from Mahlaing.[2]

At the time he got his orders, Naka had no idea what British formations were facing him. Neither did 15 Army. They told him it was either 5 or 7 Indian Division, and his function was to block its exit westward and, with 49 Division, destroy it.

[1] OCH, *Irawaji Kaisen*, p. 641

[2] Kirby, *War Against Japan*, IV, p. 295

Cowan did not simply sit in Meiktila and wait for all this to happen. The policy was aggressive defence. He secured the town, then formed forces with which he mounted a series of attacks on the roads leading out. 99 Brigade (Torver) was to defend Meiktila, its airfield and supply dumps. At each of six points round the South Lake, a single infantry company with mortars and machine guns would act as static defence, three provided by 99 Brigade, one each by 48 and 63 Brigades, and one by 17 Division's Headquarters Battalion. Two battalions defended the airfield and the dump.

Five columns swept out from Meiktila on 6 March along the roads radiating out from the town, to Mahlaing, Zayetkon, Pyawbwe, Thazi and Wundwin, only the latter column being heavily resisted by Japanese on the move west of Wundwin. A second series of sweeps between 8 and 12 March met strong opposition at Yindaw, ten miles south of Meiktila, and ten miles north-west where roadblocks halted 48 Brigade which came under heavy fire from the guns of Naganuma Force installed near Myindawgyan Lake. On 13 and 14 March, a third sweep encountered resistance on the road to Pyawbwe, seven miles out, where after a day's long battle eighty-four Japanese dead were counted. Four days later, C Squadron of the Deccan Horse ran into trouble at Shawbyugan to the north-east where the Japanese had softened the hard, dry ground by opening irrigation sluices round the village. The tanks tried to avoid being bogged down, and were thereby drawn into an area covered by anti-tank guns which knocked out five tanks, putting C Squadron completely out of action.

One of the toughest engagements occurred as the result of a signal from Colonel Sakuma. He signalled Naka about noon on 9 March that his Force had occupied the west airfield and secured the Mahlaing road at MS 8 with one battalion. Naka hustled 56 Regiment and 18 Divisional engineers to MS 6 and ordered it to be secured, with artillery support. The order came down to Colonel Fujimura of 56 Regiment, who detailed his I Battalion (Captain Ikejima) to go ahead with a regimental gun and occupy MS 6. Ikejima gaily marched out, without maps (the Japanese were woefully undermapped for much of the Meiktila operation), making for the south-west from Myindawgan Lake, and reached MS 6 on the morning of 10 March.

He set his men to digging in at once, but a strong force moved out of Meiktila towards him. Ikejima counted seventeen tanks. They were on their way to extricate a 400-vehicle soft-skinned convoy which had been cut off by Sakuma's advance at Mahlaing. The ground was hard, there had been no time to erect defences, the gunners were not prepared, and Ikejima had to slug it out in the open with the British tanks. To cap it all, reinforcements arrived from 255 Tank Brigade in Meiktila and Ikejima was forced off the road. Naganuma's artillery intervened in the course of the afternoon and rescued him.

Unaware of Ikejima's plight, Naka was busy planning a further development. 55 Regiment (Yamazaki) was to occupy the south side of the lake at Myindawgan and attack southward, while 56 Regiment (Fujimura) would seize the area round MS 4 on the Mahlaing Road, with co-operation from the heavy artillery and mountain guns. Sakuma was to attack south-west Meiktila, while 119 Regiment (53 Division) remained in reserve. The notion was obviously to envelop Meiktila from the north and west, and the Japanese began to move on the night of the 10th. The order was quashed when Naka heard what had happened to Ikejima's battalion. He drafted an order to Fujimura to occupy the high ground north of the Mahlaing road during the night. Staff officers were despatched with the revised orders but, in the Japanese phrase, *ya wa sude ni tsuru wo hanarete ita* – the arrow had already left the bow.[1] The staff did not know the terrain, and it was hard to find the units in the darkness.

Fujimura had his engineers preparing roadblocks in the area of MS 5 and 6, and infantry anti-tank teams were readied. The battle began on the morning of the 11th. Covered by 47 mm anti-tank guns, Fujimura tried to block the advance of the column coming out from Meiktila. It was no use. Overpowered, his battalion and company commanders casualties, he lifted the roadblocks. The engineers planned to destroy the tanks with suicide squads, but they were attacked by the infantry marching alongside the tanks and sustained over 200 casualties. Only two platoon commanders survived the battle. The Japanese anti-tank battalion exacted its price, though. Half-a-dozen tanks were knocked out and set ablaze. The battle ended towards evening when the British column withdrew into Meiktila, leaving Fujimura and the engineers with a third of the strength with which they had begun the day.

Sakuma bumped into British tanks on the morning of the 11th, about four miles west of Meiktila, and was subjected to a heavy barrage, but the British did not pursue their advantage, and withdrew. This engagement of 10/11 March was later described by 18 Division officers as 'the bloodiest of the whole battle': they lost regimental guns and anti-tank guns and over 400 men.[2]

As a result of the failure of his plan, Naka turned his attention to the other side of Meiktila and the east airfields. Cowan's land link with the Nyaungu bridgehead had been broken at Taungtha, and he was completely dependent on air supply; if he lost control of the airfields, everything would have to be dropped to him, at a time when he was using up petrol and ammunition in enormous quantities. Naka, too, was perturbed. 31 Di-

---

[1] OCH, *Irawaji Kaisen*, p. 182

[2] SEATIC Bulletin, No. 244, p. 28

vision's front on the Irrawaddy had broken, he was told, and the British were moving on Myotha and thereby threatening him from the north.

Patrols had already probed the airfield on the night of 9/10 March, and had been taken aback. They had been able to move around freely on the parts of the airfield where planes landed during the day. There were no strong British positions on the Wundwin road side of the airfield, and they deduced that the presence of trucks in the daytime meant this was the dump area, the 'soft core' of the defence. Naka planned an action against the airfield on 16 March. However, characteristic of the Japanese lack of co-ordination in their arrangements, Mori Special Force had a go first.

This unit, officially termed 5 Guerrilla Unit, had been formed to act behind the Allied lines if the Ledo Road were completed, to sabotage oil pipe installations, and was in training near Toungoo when the British attacked Meiktila. Commanded by Colonel Komatsubara Yukio, a Japanese intelligence expert who had run secret operatives into Siberia from Manchuria, and later worked for the Hikari Kikan[1], Mori Special Force was under the command of 49 Division, which had its own plans for the eastern airfield.

Now 18 Division, though it knew 49 Division's wireless frequency, had not established contact with it. Overland contact was slow and laborious. An 18 Division officer and a warrant officer were sent to 49 Division Headquarters at Yindaw on 16 March and did not return until the 19th. No liaison officer ever came from 49 Division. The boundary between the two divisions who were, of course, under different Army Commands, 18 under 15 Army, 49 under 33 Army, ran through the village of Tawma south-east of the airfield. Some attacks were known beforehand, when messages were passed via the Army Headquarters. Some were not, and Komatsubara's attack on the airfield was one of these.

With Force Headquarters and 17 Guerrilla Company, Komatsubara installed himself at the north-east end of the airfield, and attacked the field itself at 3 am on 15 March, destroying one aircraft on the ground and blowing up several fuel tanks. He repeated the attack three times on succeeding nights, using different points of penetration, but on the 18th the force was heavily counter-attacked and he himself badly wounded. His other company, 16 Guerrilla, made for the south-west corner of Meiktila and sent raiding parties into the tank harbour areas, finally withdrawing to Pyawbwe on the 27th.[2]

This was the first series of attacks on the airfield, involving around 500 men, and, damage apart, it was a tricky time for the defenders, as 15

---

[1] The Japanese liaison unit with the Indian National Army.

[2] SEATIC Bulletin, No. 244, p. 32

March was the day selected for the fly-in of 9 Brigade (5 Division). 5 Division had been brought out of reserve, and Slim committed 161 Brigade to help Evans at the bridgehead and 9 Brigade, which had trained as airborne troops, was the easiest to ferry in to help Cowan, 5 Division still being at Jorhat, 700 miles away. Brigadier Salomons brought his men into Meiktila from the airfield at Palel, the American pilots flying fifty-four sorties on the first day. Brigade Tactical Headquarters and 3/2 Punjab were the first to arrive and were somewhat taken aback, not by the Japanese anti-aircraft fire, but by the sounds of battle and puffs of smoke on the airfield below. 'Get out quick, for God's sake', the pilots yelled to them as they came in to land; then paused to photograph the Japanese corpses lying near the aircraft before taking off again. Only one Dakota was hit.[1]

The rest of 9 Brigade arrived over the next three days, under a curtain of Japanese shelling and sniping from Komatsubara's men. In the circumstances, the brigade survived miraculously. Another Dakota was destroyed on 16 March and six men wounded while escaping from it. In all, the Brigade had twenty-two casualties over 142 aircraft sorties.

Then 18 Division took a hand. At 4 am on 16 March, two battalions of 55 Infantry Regiment (Yamazaki) dug themselves in a hundred yards from the perimeter wire. The Japanese histories speak of them 'occupying the airfield', but they had no time to dig themselves in properly and were forced to use irrigation ditches as trenches where a squadron of Probyn's Horse encircled them and gunned them out. Yamazaki expected field and mountain artillery support, but it was not laid on in time, and as the wires to the heavy artillery were cut, no message got through to them. Kimura, one of the battalion commanders, became a casualty, and the Japanese were gradually driven off north of the main road.

On the evening of 17 March, 9 Brigade took over the static defence of Meiktila and released 99 Brigade for a mobile role. But even with 9 Brigade guarding the airfield, Cowan judged that the constant raids and shelling were making it unusable for supply aircraft, and asked for supplies to be dropped to him from the 18th onwards. The Japanese were, in fact, using their artillery like virtuosos. When a column from 48 Brigade attacked Kinde on 22 March, they lost three tanks and the Japanese followed them as they withdrew, right to the Brigade's harbour area, where a 75 mm gun was manhandled to within fifteen yards of a forward Gurkha post. This was 49 Artillery Regiment, commanded by Colonel Uga, who brought 49 Division's guns right into the front line. That day, Uga's mountain artillery destroyed three trucks and halted several others. Wearing a white headband like the samurai, Uga fought his eight guns at a hundred yards from the approaching tanks, then hit them with *Ta-Dan*. But Naganuma Force, too, made life uncomfortable for the defenders. Jack Scollen, an artillery

---

[1] Brett-James, *Ball of Fire*, p. 402

observer with B Flight, 656 Squadron RAF, who spent the siege spotting Japanese gun positions for 311 Battery of 129 Field Regiment, Royal Artillery, and was a veteran of the North African and Sicily campaigns, was caught in Kyigon by sustained artillery fire:

The Japs shelled us steadily for two and a half hours, keeping us in our slit trenches all the time, apart from a short break of about ten minutes. I had just landed after an early morning sortie when they began to fire shell after shell into our box – slowly at first, presumably while they were ranging, and then in bursts of very rapid fire. Usually you can hear the swish of a shell for a second or two before it arrives – in time to dive for cover – but these shells seemed to be fired at very short range and we found later that the Japs had brought up two guns into a valley little more than half a mile from our perimeter and during darkness they had made an observation post in a tree overlooking our box, which explained the uncomfortable accuracy of their fire. We all had slit trenches – and pretty deep ones, too (I slept in mine) – and although several rounds landed within twenty or thirty yards of my trench and much nearer some of the others, none of us was injured. One shell missed a trench in which one of our men was sheltering by no more than a yard. His kit was riddled with splinters and he had a lot of earth thrown over him but he was quite unhurt. After crouching, bent up, in my trench for what seemed hours, I grew stiff and sore, very bad-tempered and madly hungry, too (I had had no breakfast before my sortie) and when the shelling stopped I was very glad to stretch my legs again. I had a quick breakfast and we were all congratulating ourselves on our lucky escapes when it all began again. We did not know until later about the tree O.P. and we assumed then that one of the Japs must have had us under observation all the time. We dived back into our holes and soon I was as stiff and sore and bad-tempered – and scared – as before.

The new arrivals of 9 Brigade were soon introduced to Uga's skills. On 23 March, Lieutenant-Colonel K. Bayley of the 2 West Yorks, who had succeeded Salomons in command of 9 Brigade, was standing in the approach trench to the Brigade command post, on the very edge of the box, talking to his Brigade Major, W. S. Armour, and Captain Leslie-Smith, the intelligence officer. A shell hit just outside the command post, killing Bayley's batman. Bayley himself was wounded in the back and knocked down the steps into the post; Armour was hit in the arm and back; Leslie-Smith was unhurt.

Armour's odyssey to hospital was hair-raising. The dressing station to which he was taken was shelled, and he was wounded again. He was taken to a Dakota to be evacuated, and a Japanese anti-tank gun fired at it straight down the runway and set it ablaze. Armour was wounded again, in the head, and unable to speak. He heard the RAMC orderlies discussing whether they should take his body out of the burning Dakota: they assumed he was dead. 'Anyhow, you can't let the so-and-so burn. Let's take the body out', he heard, to his relief.[1]

Bayley took over from Salomons on 23 March. Salomons, who had commanded 9 Brigade for more than a year through hard fighting around Imphal, had led his Brigade in the Meiktila box for a week and had grown increasingly resentful about the way Cowan was handling it. But Cowan was in no mood to be crossed, and relieved Salomons of his command, to the great distress of his men. Cowan had disagreements with his tank commanders, too. 'Punch Cowan was a splendid Infantry General but he did not really understand the tank problems and he or his staff kept on asking for *one* tank to accompany an infantry patrol. It took some time for it to sink in that a troop of three was the minimum tank team, if we were not to get too many knocked out. A single tank cannot cover itself while it manoeuvres, nor tow itself out of action. We on the other hand fully realized that if we could save infantry lives by sacrificing machines and crews, it was our job to do so. All we asked was that it was on a really worthwhile task.'[2] Tuck thought too much was asked of the RAF Regiment Commando, too. The Japanese sent endless patrols in on it at night, the Squadron-Leader and all his officers were killed in night skirmishes and morale was at rock bottom.

Cowan was, though few knew it, under very great personal strain at the height of the battle. He and Slim had been young Gurkha officers together after the First World War, and his son joined their old battalion, the 1/6 Gurkhas. Slim had spoken to the son when he visited Mandalay, but a few days later young Cowan died of wounds in the assault on the city. It was in the throes of this great grief that Cowan conducted his hardest-fought and most crucial battle.[3]

The Japanese High Command was in a crisis of another sort. At 15 Army's strong urging, Kimura had altered its role from a defensive position in the

---

[1] Brett-James, op.cit., p. 404

[2] *Tuck MS*, p. 25

[3] It was not the only tragic loss of a son by a father in a commanding position on the British side. Sir George Sansom, the world-famous Japanese historian, who had been in Singapore during the invasion of Malaya and later became commercial counsellor at the British Embassy in Washington, lost his son in the battle for Imphal. The extra twist of tragedy in his case was that the son was the child of a first marriage to a Japanese woman, and died fighting in the Japanese Army. (Private information from Professor Hosoya Chihiro)

battle for the Irrawaddy into an offensive directed at the retaking of Meiktila.[1] When the collapse of the Irrawaddy front threw 15 Army into disarray, Kimura decided to remove the Meiktila operation from its command, and put Lieutenant-General Honda Masaki of 33 Army in control. 18 Division having been despatched to Meiktila, Honda's army now consisted only of 56 Division, and his headquarters was in Hsipaw, controlling operations against 36 British Division and the southward NCAC offensive. On 12 March, Kimura signalled to Honda that he was to hand over the 33 Army command to the 56 Divisional GOC, Matsuyama, and take his headquarters staff only with all speed to 'Yamato Village' – the codename used for a location ten miles east of Thazi on the road to Kalaw. No explanation was given for the order, and Honda and his staff were naturally puzzled, but on the principle of 'theirs not to reason why', they left Hsipaw that day. 'We thought it a pretty appalling example of high command', Lieutenant-Colonel Tanaka Hiroatsu recalled later, 'sending an Army Headquarters buzzing here and there without giving them the slightest notion of what the purpose was, or what their duty was.'[2] To avoid Allied aircraft they moved by night and rested by day, but the planes found them nonetheless and they were bombed daily. They reached 'Yamato Village', a villa in the middle of a teak forest, on 16 March. That night, the Chief of Staff of Burma Area Army, Lieutenant-General Tanaka Shinichi, arrived with two of his staff, Yamaguchi and Kōno, and explained to Honda the state of the emergency.

He was to take command of 18 and 49 Divisions from 18 March, and destroy the British armoured forces in Meiktila. Honda was perplexed. Even if he recaptured Meiktila, had not the Irrawaddy battle already gone so badly that there was not much point in doing so? Burma Area Army would have been better occupied, he thought, in strengthening the position at Toungoo and drawing everyone to the south. And here he was, with only a headquarters staff, no preliminary information on the area, no signals unit, no infantry, not even operational maps. On 18 March, with great misgivings, he started planning, under his army's new title of *Kesshō-gun* –'the army of the decisive battle'.[3] Honda moved his headquarters a little closer to the battle, to Hlaingdet, east of Thazi, at the exit from the Shan Plateau, then to Thazi itself. Colonel Tsuji now returned to 33 Army from 15 Army and gave the staff an idea of what was happening in Meiktila. Advised by Tsuji, Honda planned to use 18 Division to attack Meiktila from the north-east and 49 Division from the south-east on 22

---

[1] 15 Army Tactical Headquarters was at this time at Nankan, in the foothills south-east of Kyaukse, and had been bombed on 9 March, when its chief staff officer, Colonel Tanaka Tetsujirō, had been killed.

[2] OCH, *Irawaji Kaisen*, p. 606

[3] *Sittan; Mei-go Sakusen*, p. 52

March, the boundary between the two being a line east-west along the Thazi-Myingyan railway. Major Abe Mitsuo, Honda's staff officer (Operations) was sent off to contact 49 Division and convey the plan to them. Naka – 18 Division GOC – later complained that Honda was almost as bad as Kimura in terms of directions to his divisions. Kimura pushed them around piecemeal at Meiktila, without a prearranged plan, and once Tsuji left Meiktila to rejoin 33 Army on 16 March, there was no higher staff direction. Honda simply said, 'You're back under my command, get on with what you were doing', and gave no further instructions. As the Japanese Official History points out, Naka seems to have forgotten the directive about the operation of 22 March.[1] It was assumed that the east airfield was in 18 Division's hands since the morning of 16 March. 33 Army had not yet learned that the British had retaken it later in the day. The news came just before the attack went in, but by then it was too late. 18 Division made for the airfield and 49 Division attacked the town. A determined effort to penetrate 48 Brigade's perimeter was made on the night of 22 March, on the south-east corner of the defence system, held by 1/7 Gurkhas and 4 Frontier Force Regiment. The Japanese used two 75 mm guns, but the wired-in positions held, and by dawn the attackers moved back, leaving 195 dead behind them.[2]

The irrepressible Colonel Uga had a trick up his sleeve for this attack. During an action near Tawma on the 22nd, the British had attacked with a force of ten tanks and been repulsed. 'We had been trying to keep them out of artillery range of the airfield', Alasdair Tuck recalls, 'and they captured one of our Shermans that had been put out of action and was unable to be recovered. They got this tank going again and, although it had a jammed turret and could only fire forward, very gallantly attacked positions covering 17 Division Headquarters on the east side of the lake two nights running.'[3]

It was in fact Uga who had got hold of the Sherman, had it repaired, and realized that it could be used for the next night attack. 106 Regiment (Totoki) of 49 Division was to lead the division's assault on the night of 22 March, and the captured Sherman was driven from Kandan in pride of place, with Uga's mountain guns in support, and a company of engineers. 48 Brigade's box was stormed by 500 Japanese under an umbrella of fire from Uga's guns and the captured tank, with Uga doing his usual stunt of bringing the guns right up to the perimeter. The attackers took a corner of the box, but 48 Brigade's fire was so intense under the light of flares, and

---

[1] ibid., pp. 63–4

[2] *Reconquest of Burma, II*, p. 329

[3] *Tuck MS*, pp. 26–7

the defence system of barbed wire and trenches so effective, that the Japanese were held there. Totoki lost 200 men, before he was finally forced back to Kangyi. The Japanese account says the Sherman blew itself up[1] and was abandoned, but Tuck's version is rather different. 'The first night', he says, 'it got stuck and was withdrawn by dawn. On the second, after plunging around firing in the dark, it overturned and was destroyed.'[2]

Jack Scollen heard this happen. The tank men were worried about how it might be used against them, and they asked him to go up in his light plane and locate it, but Uga had hidden it with great care. 'A few nights later', Scollen remembers,

> a very determined attack began on the south side of our perimeter. It developed into the noisiest bit of fighting of the kind that I had heard for a long while – mortar bombs and grenades, machine guns and rifles and every now and then sharp bursts of fire from the field guns they had brought up to support their attack made an absolute pandemonium in the midst of which we could hear the yells and shouts of the Japs as they charged again and again.
>
> Presently we heard the unmistakeable sound of a tank approaching. I was lying watching and listening with a tank officer and I asked him if he thought it was their lost tank or a Jap. He couldn't tell at first (in the dark we could only go by the noise). Verey lights rose and fell all the time but we could not catch sight of the tank. It came nearer and nearer along the road and then it sounded as though the driver were trying to turn it round.
>
> Its engine was roaring and the tank officer beside me said 'It's ours all right. The bugger can't get it out of second gear.' Then there was a tremendous noise and the grinding and rattling sounds stopped suddenly.
>
> Next morning we found the tank lying upside down in a deep ditch beside the road.[3]

Uga's incredible bravery in handling his mountain guns forward led to the inevitable end. 'He had fought like a god', says the Japanese Official History, 'was severely wounded by a shell fragment, and died as he was being carried to the rear.'[4] But Uga's was not the only type of artillery

---

[1] OCH, *Irawaji Kaisen*, p. 197. They use the term *jibaku* which means both 'to scuttle' and 'to carry out a suicide attack'.

[2] *Tuck MS*, p. 27

[3] John Scollen, MS account of the battle of Meiktila, privately communicated to the author, 1979.

[4] OCH, *Irawaji Kaisen*, p. 198. Another commander who took risks, Miles Smeeton, was also wounded but less lethally. While out on one of Cowan's armoured sweeps, he was hit in the nose by a bullet or shell splinter that pierced it through. He gingerly felt the place, convinced 'the whole apparatus had gone', only to be reassured by another tank man that most of it was still *in situ*. Smeeton, op.cit., p. 89

tactic used by the Japanese at Meiktila. They were expert at camouflaging their guns, and firing from considerable distances. The art of spotting them became a highly prized talent, and Jack Scollen's light plane was much in demand. All the more so because he was not dependent on the main airfield but flew from a strip of land beside the lake. It was not the best of strips, as it had a sideways slope, but Austers and L5s used it without difficulty, and severe wound cases were evacuated from it.

To locate the Jap guns that were firing into Meiktila was not easy [Scollen remembers].[1] It required a vast amount of patience and not a little luck because their guns were almost always dug deep down under cover where they could not be seen from the air and even their flashes were difficult to spot. One day (25 March) I was cruising about North of Meiktila, looking for a single Jap gun that had been giving us a great deal of trouble by firing odd rounds into the town at irregular intervals. We had all tried to spot him but without success and he was such a nuisance that we were pressed to keep on trying so that he could be put out of action. I searched for well over an hour in all the suspected areas but could not find a trace of him though I kept getting reports over the radio that he had fired again. He always seemed to fire just when for some reason or other I could not observe him but more than once I felt a 'thump' in my seat from his blast as he fired. And then, just as I was about to give it up and go back and land, I spotted him.

I had been airborne for nearly two hours and therefore had little petrol left; the light was beginning to fail; and I had already told the guns that I was going back. As I turned south to leave the area where I had been searching I turned round in my seat to keep an eye on the area through the back of the perspex roof of the cockpit as I flew away. And then I saw him. There was the unmistakeable red muzzle flash of a field gun – a sight that was familiar from flash-spotting days – and I shouted over the radio that I had got him and gave orders for the guns to get into action again. I kept my eye on the spot where I had seen the flash and the gunsmoke as I swung the plane round to fly back to give fire orders and observe the fall of shot. The gun was deep in some bushes and even when I was right overhead I could see neither the gun nor its crew.

I had very little time left and had to engage the target with all speed. I was firing medium guns and put down about twenty 100 lb shells all round the target. I saw two of them fall into the actual

---

[1] Scollen MS, p. 156

clump of bushes in which the gun was hidden. I could not see
what effect they had but their explosions covered the target area
and the gun did not fire into Meiktila again. This was the first
time that anyone of the flight had spotted and engaged a gun in
this way and as an ex-Flash Spotter I felt rather good that I had
got him.

Setting up the board again

By the time Scollen found that gun, the Japanese in Meiktila had only
three more days to go. In the week since 33 Army had taken over responsibility for the battle, the casualties on either side had been such that,
Colonel Tsuji worked out, the Japanese could not possibly prevail.

Enemy losses, he reckoned, were 50 tanks destroyed, and about 300
casualties. Japanese losses were 50 guns destroyed, and 2500 casualties.
That meant that, in order to destroy an enemy tank, the Japanese needed
to sacrifice one gun and fifty men. Enemy tanks must be at least 100, so to
destroy them all the Japanese required 100 guns and 5000 men. Putting the
Army's entire strength together, there were no more than twenty guns.

All this figuring was for the benefit of Lieutenant-General Tanaka
Shinichi, Kimura's Chief of Staff, on a visit to 33 Army Headquarters.
Several minutes of silence followed, as the burly general turned over the
alternatives in his mind. 'On my own responsibility', he finally said, 'I'll
revise Burma Area Army's operations orders. 33 Army will now cover 15
Army's retreat.' 'I'd like that in writing – or by signal – from Burma Area
Army', replied Honda, but he accepted the change of role: he no longer
commanded 'the army of the decisive battle' but an army of resistance.[1] 15
Army, in total disarray, was streaming south from Mandalay and the
Irrawaddy bend, fleeing towards the safety of the Shan Hills and Toungoo.

To intercept this southward exodus – chiefly of 31 and 33 Divisions –
Gracey's 20 Division moved from their bridgehead area towards Kyaukse,
and southwards in the general direction of Meiktila, killing lavishly as they
went. In the six weeks between mid-February and the end of March,
Gracey's division killed more than 3000 Japanese, and captured 50 guns.[2]
A column of tanks and infantry was to cover the seventy miles through
Pyinzi and Pindale to Wundwin, about seventeen miles north-east of
Meiktila. The column, under Lieutenant-Colonel Barlow and therefore
called Barcol, destroyed the Japanese forces garrisoning these towns and
villages, and exploited down the road to Meiktila to make contact with 17
Division. Gracey then directed him north to Kume, where he drove 300

[1] Tsuji, *Jūgo tai-ichi,* p. 255

[2] Mountbatten, *Report,* p. 140

Japanese into the hills, killing over 100 of them. To all intents and purposes, by the end of March, the area south from Mandalay to Wundwin was in XXXIII Corps' hands, and the two Corps were ready to switch.

On the northern front, against the Chinese and 36 Division, the Japanese positions were crumbling. With the transfer of 33 Army Headquarters to the Meiktila battle, and the use of 18 Division there, 56 Division could attempt little more than delaying actions. After a fierce battle on 19 February for Myitson where the engineers built a timber bridge across the fast-flowing Shweli River, 500 yards across, 36 Division (Festing) took Mongmit and set up an airfield there, and on 19 March was in Mogok, the source of Burma's rubies. Festing pushed on fast across the Monglong Hills and the advance guard of his 26 Brigade (Jennings) was in Namsaw on 29 March. East of his advance, 50 Division of General Liao's New Chinese Sixth Army sauntered into Hsipaw, where Honda had once had his headquarters. Chiang Kai-shek had told his generals they were not to advance beyond the area Lashio-Hsipaw, but he agreed, under pressure from Mountbatten, to let them go as far as Kyaukme, where they would contact 36 Division. This was a *quid pro quo* for Mountbatten's release of the US infantry and cavalry regiments of Mars Force (Brigadier-General Willey) – against the objections of Leese, who said it would have a bad effect on Slim's battle – and the withdrawal of the Chinese in June-July. On 30 March, Festing's 26 Brigade was in contact with the Chinese regiment of Mars Brigade. Lashio had fallen on 7 March, and the line Lashio-Hsipaw was now secure. Festing's men then left the command of NCAC and came under XIV Army which promptly sent them off to Mandalay to relieve 19 Division, wanted for further operations down the Irrawaddy. The last link with China was open, and a convoy arrived in Kunming on 4 February 1945, carrying 75 mm and 105 mm guns and supplies for the Chinese. The city greeted them with fireworks, and the Governor of Yunnan, the old warlord General Lung Yun, gave a banquet in their honour graced by the presence of the opera star Lily Pons and her husband, the musician André Kostelanetz. (Neither of them knew that Lung Yun was in regular correspondence with the Japanese Commander-in-Chief in China, General Okamura.) The Chinese began to fly home in May. Five or six thousand Japanese troops still remained in the hills of the Shan States, able, should need arise, to cover the retreat towards Siam of the forces fighting round Mandalay and Meiktila. A body of US-officered guerrillas, about 2500 strong, named Detachment 101, was given the job of neutralizing these Japanese forces to prevent them interfering with Slim's southward advances.[1]

---

[1] Romanus and Sunderland, *Time Runs Out in CBI*, p. 141; Allen, *End of the War in Asia*, p. 220; Kirby, *War Against Japan*, IV, p. 194; Mountbatten, *Report*, p. 134

Only one resource now remained to Kimura, once the Irrawaddy bridgeheads between Allagappa and Sagaing were secured by Stopford's XXXIII Corps, and once it became clear that Cowan was not going to release his grip on Meiktila: to strike at IV Corps' bridgehead at Nyaungu, from where reinforcements for 17 Division were due to break out. This was to be the role of Lieutenant-General Sakurai's 28 Army. In their Arakan fastnesses, even after the failure of Operation HA-GO, Sakurai and his staff had little regard for Kimura and his GHQ in Rangoon, the city which Sakurai had taken three years before. But for Kimura Arakan had become a backwater, and he needed 28 Army to act as a stop-gap in the oil-field area of Yenangyaung and along the Irrawaddy. So the pieces began to be pushed around the board, renamed and renumbered.

28 Army had lost 2 Division to Burma Area Army in May 1944. 55 Division replaced it in the Delta, a move screened by the activity of Sakura Force (Major-General Sakurai Tokutarō) in the Mayu and Kaladan Valleys between July and September 1944. Sakura Force rejoined the division in the Prome area at the end of December, the same month in which 72 Independent Mixed Brigade (Kantetsu Force) was organized at Yenangyaung under Major-General Yamamoto Tsunoru, who had commanded 33 Division Infantry Group at Shenam-Palel.

The 28 Army commander, Lieutenant-General Sakurai Shōzō, had long expected to pull Burma Area Army's chestnuts out of the fire in the Irrawaddy area and he had begun to build defence positions round Mount Popa between October and December 1944. Mount Popa, 500 feet above sea-level, dominated the flat plain for miles around, and its slopes offered excellent defence positions, as well as concealing the infamous hamadryad, the only snake which will pursue and attack a human being. Sakurai put Colonel Furuya, CO 112 Infantry Regiment, in command of Kanjō Force to defend Popa, using two of his own infantry battalions and a battalion of 5 Heavy Field Artillery brought up from Tenasserim. Three infantry battalions of 55 Division, with artillery and engineers, were constituted as Shinbu Force under Major-General Nagazawa Kanichi to hold the south-west area of the Delta, while 54 Division (Miyazaki) held Arakan between the Irrawaddy and the coast, just north of Shinbu.

In this way, 28 Army attempted to co-ordinate a defence line from the Bay of Bengal, through the Arakan Hills, across the Irrawaddy, and across to the Rangoon road.[1] Its headquarters was at Taikkyi, on the road leading north from Rangoon along the east bank of the Irrawaddy. As it happened, Sakurai was denuding his Arakan forces just as they came under renewed

---

[1] *Burma Command Intelligence Summary*, No. 1, 'The History of Japanese 28 Army'; *Dai nijūhachi-gunsenshi* (Campaign history of 28 Army), ed. Tsuchiya Eiichi, privately printed, Tokyo, 1977.

pressure from Christison's 15 Corps. Two African divisions, 81 West African, 82 West African, were pushing through the *chaung*-and-jungle territory parallel with the coast while 25 Indian Division with 3 Commando Brigade, a squadron of medium tanks, a medium artillery regiment, a naval bombardment force of three cruisers, and 200 planes of 224 Group RAF, at long last took Akyab. This massive sledgehammer was poised to fall on 3 January 1945, but an artillery observation officer, seeing no sign of activity on the island as he flew over, landed to verify, and was told by the inhabitants that the Japanese had gone. Christison went to have a look himself, taking with him Air Vice-Marshal the Earl of Bandon, command-ing 224 Group. It was true, the Japanese had decamped, leaving the vital airfields, which had been the aim of so many strategic plans and desperate battles since December 1942, there for the taking. Christison called off the bombardment, but had the landings carried out, presumably to give the men a little work-out. Mountbatten and Slim had urgently requested Akyab to be taken at all costs, to bring air-strikes and supply close to the Rangoon advance when it came. Toungoo was now within reach, and when Ramree and Cheduba were taken by 26 Indian Division (Chambers) on 21 and 26 January respectively, Rangoon itself came within range. Mountbatten had the part of Arakan he wanted, and the rest would fall soon, as the pressure increased from the Irrawaddy bridgeheads.[1]

Attempts to cut IV Corps' supply line to Meiktila by retaking the bridgehead at Nyaungu failed and 7 Division's capture of Myingyan en-sured that river-borne supplies could reach the bridgeheads down the Chindwin and, with Taungtha taken, that the road to Meiktila was open again. Messervy set up IV Corps' headquarters there, ready for the next stage of his advance on Rangoon.

The threat to Messervy's lifeline at Mt Popa from the Japanese and the Indian National Army was blunted by 2 Division whose advance converged with that of 268 Brigade and 7 Division at Kyaukpadaung, the last major point on the east bank before the oilfields at Yenangyaung. Desperate attacks by Furuya's Kanjō Force at Pyinbin, halfway between Nyaungu and Welaung, failed to sever IV Corps' L of C. The Indian National Army's Division covered the right flank of the Mt Popa defences but despite support from Koba's 154 Regiment the INA men lost heart and began to surrender to the British in large numbers. The Dorset battalion commander noticed they were different from the fanatics who had fought against him in the Tamu area a year before, and he assumed they were made up of sepoys who had enlisted largely in order to reach the front and surrender at the first opportunity. But they did not find it easy to escape:

The Japanese had an unpleasant habit of slashing with their

---

[1] Kirby, *War Against Japan*, IV, pp. 141–2

swords the arms of those caught deserting. When we captured the 2nd Indian National Army Division headquarters and read some of their Part II orders (in English), the number of admissions to hospital with sword slashes showed clearly those who had been unfortunate enough to be discovered in the act of returning to their own side.[1]

Further east, Gracey's 20 Division was again on the move. A battalion of 32 Brigade was in Zayatkon on 10 April and turned south without a pause to Natmauk. Two of his brigades were still at Wundwin and Meiktila, but 32 Brigade was already far advanced on the road to Magwe, on the east bank *south* of Yenangyaung, which it reached on 19 April; and 1 Northampton, under direct divisional command, was sent to link up with 268 Brigade west of Mount Popa to cut off the Japanese remaining there. So, far from threatening IV Corps' communications to Meiktila, Sakurai's 28 Army was now finding its own defence positions round the oil-fields threatened from all sides. The multiple probes down the Irrawaddy were now the responsibility of Stopford's XXXIII Corps, which returned 19 Division to Messervy and took over Evans's 7 Division to act with Gracey in a push down to Rangoon through Prome. The supply situation then became acute, and it was decided to fly out the two British divisions: 2 and 36. Nicholson's men were all out of Burma by 26 April, 5 Brigade being last to leave; and the Indian battalions of 36 Division were exchanged for Gracey's British battalions. This left only Indian Army formations in the dash for Rangoon. Messervy, with 5, 17 and 19 Divisions, now began his southward advance from Meiktila.

[1] White, *Straight on for Tokyo*, pp. 275–6

8. THE BATTUE

The pursuit : Pyawbwe to Rangoon

The battle for Pyawbwe — DRACULA in the wings —
DRACULA descends on Rangoon — the birds have
flown

The battle for Pyawbwe

You can reach Rangoon from Meiktila in a day, with a decent car and pretty hard driving all the way. The distance is 338 miles, and it's sensible to take two days over it, stopping overnight at Pyinmana. In 1945 XIV Army took thirty-six days over the trip, from the end of March when Meiktila was cleared and Messervy had set up his Corps headquarters there, to 6 April, when Cowan's 17 Division vanguard – 1/7 Gurkhas with tanks – came to a halt at Hlegu, twenty-seven miles from Rangoon.

There is another way to Rangoon, taking the road which leads for a while along the east bank of the Irrawaddy, through Taungtha, Yenangyaung and Prome, a distance of 441 miles. Slim intended to use both routes. XXXIII Corps – 7 and 20 Divisions, with 268 Brigade – was to take this route, while IV Corps – 5 and 17 Divisions leapfrogging over each other, with 255 Brigade – was to take the shorter route. 19 Division was to secure the Mandalay-Meiktila area, then protect the left flank of IV Corps' thrust south. The Japanese, Slim was sure, did not have enough forces to stop him on *both* routes. One Corps was bound to get through.

It was essential to capture Rangoon before the monsoon set in. That was the prime factor. While IV Corps was still engaged in bitter fighting at Meiktila, a meeting was held at Monywa on 22 March to discuss the delay in Slim's advance that resulted from the withdrawal of transport aircraft to China. For Mountbatten was already looking beyond Rangoon in his forward planning, indeed beyond Burma, which was, in his mind, merely a staging-post in the retaking of Malaya and Singapore. The Chiefs of Staff worked on the assumption that Rangoon would be in British hands before 1 June. On that basis, they had authorized an operation to seize an island off the Kra Isthmus as a stepping stone to Malaya. The island was called Phuket, and some wag on Mountbatten's planning staff, with a rudimentary sense of humour and an inadequate knowledge of the romanization of Siamese, christened it Operation ROGER. After ROGER was to come ZIPPER, a landing of four or five divisions in the area Port-Swettenham – Port Dickson on the west coast of Malaya, in October 1945. The next stage, MAILFIST, was the capture of Singapore, as soon as possible after the success of ZIPPER.

So Mountbatten's timetable was very tight, and he could take no risk whatever as far as Rangoon was concerned. It *must* be in his hands some time in May.[1] He had never been fully confident that it would be taken in time by Slim's overland advance, and an amphibious and airborne assault had been planned to take it from the sea, with paratroop landings at Elephant Point, to silence the Japanese guns at the entrance to the Rangoon River. The top Army commanders – Giffard, Leese and Slim – had opposed this, assuming it meant the withdrawal of strength from XIV Army at a time when every man and every ton of supplies was vital for its own advance.

Churchill had told Mountbatten in Cairo, whither he had summoned him in October 1944, that the Germans were putting up a stiffer resistance than had been anticipated, which meant that the resources for a seaborne and airborne seizure of Rangoon – DRACULA – would not be available for some time. That fact, and Army opposition on the spot, put DRACULA in jeopardy. At a meeting with his Commanders-in-Chief on 14 February 1945, Mountbatten was told that the overland columns might be in Rangoon by mid-April, rendering DRACULA unnecessary.[2] Nine days later, in Calcutta, Leese reported his great confidence in XIV Army's progress, and said he thought DRACULA was not necessary, and that there was no need to divert forces from ROGER to carry it out. Such a diversion was the only way of mounting DRACULA, if nothing was forthcoming from Europe. The decision was therefore taken not to mount the 'modified' DRACULA. 'The only factor that was not taken into account in arriving at this decision,' the Indian Official History drily remarks, 'was the possibility of the stubbornness of Japanese resistance to the advance of the Fourteenth Army.'[3]

At the meeting in Monywa, Leese expressed doubts that XIV Army would reach Rangoon before the rains made movement difficult. Four days later he signalled Mountbatten that he thought part of the forces for ROGER should be diverted to a 'modified' DRACULA, given that the Chiefs of Staff had said ROGER could not be launched until the fall of Rangoon was imminent.[4] Slim, too, was now not so sure XIV Army would make it.

---

[1] Mountbatten, *Report*, p. 145, para 500

[2] *Reconquest of Burma*, II, p. 417

[3] ibid., p. 419

[4] Mountbatten, *Report*, p. 145, para. 499

He had been impressed by the fierce Japanese resistance in Meiktila, and 'I could not contemplate with anything but dismay', he later wrote, 'a repetition of the Meiktila battle, around Rangoon at the end of a most precarious supply line, in the midst of the rains.'[1] So he, too, urged that an amphibious-cum-airborne assault should be put into Rangoon as XIV Army neared its prize, 'a hammering at the back door while I burst in at the front', as he put it.[2] On 2 April, the Calcutta decision was reversed, and orders went out to mount an operation against Rangoon using one division, while a parachute battalion dropped at Elephant Point. This was to be done by 5 May at the latest.

On 30 March, Cowan started to move south out of Meiktila.

The Japanese 33 Army, under Lieutenant-General Honda Masaki, planned to intercept IV Corps' advance twenty-six miles south of Meiktila, at Pyawbwe. 18 Division was to be the mainstay of the defence, with 49 Division holding the road between Pyawbwe and Meiktila. In fact, no one else was available. 31 and 33 Divisions of 15 Army, or rather their ragged remnants, were making for the shelter of the Shan hills, east of the main road. 53 Division was retreating across country from Taungtha and reached Yanaung, just west of Pyawbwe, ten days after leaving Taungtha, on 6 April. It could hardly have chosen a worse moment. 17 Division's mechanized metal fist was about to hit it hard.

Cowan put 99 Brigade into Thazi, east of Meiktila, and told it to move south on Pyawbwe from there. 48 Brigade was to go straight down the main road from Meiktila, and 63 Brigade was to bypass Pyawbwe on the west and come in at it from the south-west. It was a classic pincer movement of the type beloved of the Japanese themselves in their more mobile past, but Cowan added an extra flavour. Under Brigadier Claud Pert, he sent 'Claudcol' to move across country south-west of Meiktila, cutting through the villages west of Pyawbwe – Yindaw, Ywadin, Yanaung, Ywadan – and then curve in eastwards towards the main road, cutting it between Pyawbwe and Yamethin. In this way, Pyawbwe would be almost completely surrounded.

'Claudcol' consisted of two squadrons, A and C, of Probyn's Horse, two armoured car squadrons of 16 Light Cavalry, a self-propelled gun battery, engineers, and supporting infantry: 4/4 Bombay Grenadiers and 6/7 Rajputs. It was a formidable little force. Pert took it out of Meiktila on 4 April and struck at Yindaw.

Round the village of Yindaw ran a high *bund* and a ditch, both effective anti-tank obstacles. On one side of the village was a lake, which meant that for an armoured column the main road was the only choice. The place was strongly held by around 1000 men from 49 Division, with anti-tank guns,

---

[1] Slim, *Defeat into Victory*, p. 481
[2] ibid., p. 481

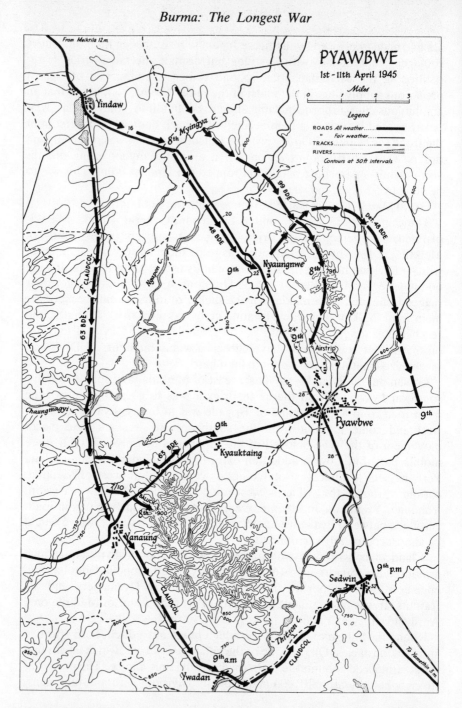

who fought for three days against bombardment from the air and shelling
from the ground. The Rajputs attacked the northern part of the *bund* and

were driven back by withering fire, with many casualties. The tanks could not get into the village to help them, and had to content themselves by giving support with air-burst HE fired into the trees. The attack was called off when the Rajputs lost two of their company commanders, and Pert, mindful of the need not to be bogged down, decided to bypass Yindaw. The mopping-up could be left to 5 Division who were coming up behind.[1]

'Claudcol' took Yanaung on 8 April, and fell upon the unhappy remnants of Takeda's 53 Division. They were in a pathetic state. All the firepower they had left was two anti-tank guns, two battalion guns, thirty-eight grenade-throwers, eleven heavy and twenty-seven light machine guns – no field or heavy artillery at all. They were exhausted by the long march from Taungtha and had had no time to construct defences. As the Japanese put it, it was like a praying mantis defending itself with its pincers (*tōrō no ono no mukau ni mo nita*)[2] and 'Claudcol' made mincemeat of them, killing 230 men and destroying their anti-tank guns. As they began to gather themselves together, Honda ordered them to move south and start defence works on the Sinthe Chaung where he expected them to make a stand with 49 Division at Thatkon.

Meanwhile 'Claudcol' moved on to Ywadan, surprising the Japanese holding it, killing over 200 and capturing four guns. Pert sent a detachment south to Yamethin and began to move up the main road to Pyawbwe from the south.

What Pert did not know was that the GOC 33 Army, Honda himself, had set up his headquarters near Pyawbwe. He had called on Takehara, commanding 49 Division, at Yindaw, and heard from him that a strong armoured column was moving south, bypassing Yindaw. Honda, whose army was now about the strength of a division, desperately tried to secure Pyawbwe by ordering 119 Infantry Regiment (53 Division) to move on it and by sending Inudō Guerrilla Force to cut the main road. But 119 Regiment did not arrive in time and Inudō was rudely thrust aside by Cowan's armour.

Pert's column had already destroyed or scattered a reinforcement convoy of eleven lorries moving up from Yamethin, and it put paid to Honda's few remaining tanks as they withdrew for the night from Pyawbwe. The leading Japanese tank spotted the line of burning lorries, hesitated, then came on, having no reason to suspect British armour south of Pyawbwe. Miles Smeeton describes what happened:

> As it came opposite us I leaned forward and touched Bahadur Singh's shoulder. A dagger of flames shot from the barrel of his

---

[1] Perrett, *Tank Tracks to Rangoon*, p. 219

[2] *Sittan; Mei-go Sakusen*, p. 197

gun, the enemy tank glowed redly, and immediately with a great belch of flame blew up.

At the sight of the explosion ahead of it the second tank turned right-handed and came bucketing up towards us, then seeing for the first time a great wall of Shermans in front of it, the driver pulled it sharply to the right and drove down the line of tanks and only a few yards from them, while the gunners struggled to depress their guns, for it had a low silhouette, in order to destroy it. As it ran the gauntlet of the line of guns, the lowering muzzles, lit by the blaze on the road, looked as if they were saluting its last moments, and the long flashes reached out over it as it passed, as if they were firing a *feu de joie*. If it had stayed so close to the tanks it might have escaped by its nearness, but it cut back to the road, was hit, caught fire, and upset.

A third tank on the road withdrew at such a pace that it overshot the bend at a high bridge and crashed into a dry stream bed, where it landed upside down.[1]

'Claudcol' moved up to Pyawbwe, destroying *en route* a column of thirty-nine trucks and staff cars. As they closed up, they could hear the tank guns of the Royal Deccan Horse in support of 48 and 99 Brigades on the north side of the town. The infantry were losing heavily to Japanese automatic fire, which the Deccan Horse could not silence, the Japanese trenches being on the reverse slope. At last, impatient at not being able to intervene effectively, Captain Sheodan Singh decided to risk taking his tanks over the crest, not knowing what guns, if any, the defenders had on the other side. The risk was worth it, the infantry rallied and the Japanese were pushed back to a defence point at the waterworks, which was taken the next day. The whole of the western area of Pyawbwe was in 63 Brigade's hands on 10 April, and on the 11th the Japanese withdrew.

Pert missed his chance of putting Honda and his staff into the bag. 33 Army headquarters had sited itself in an unnamed village a thousand yards south of Pyawbwe. One side was covered by vineyards, and the terrain was one of sunken roads and terraces, and so poor ground for tank manoeuvres. Katamura, who was shepherding his battered divisions through the hills east of the road, called on Honda and thanked him for returning Sakuma Force (214 Infantry Regiment) to its original formation, 33 Division, even though he was in the midst of a difficult battle. Then he made off for Toungoo, where Kimura had told him to prepare a second line of defence if Pyawbwe should fall.[2]

---

[1] Smeeton, *A Change of Jungles*, pp. 108–9

[2] Tsuji, *Jūgo tai-ichi* (Fifteen to One) p. 258

As Honda and his staff, Colonel Tsuji among them, were taking a meal, they heard heavy gunfire to the south-west. They looked round in the direction of the firing and were appalled to see ten tanks approaching, raising clouds of dust. Tsuji could hardly credit that they might be Japanese tanks; they would not be moving in daylight like this. He grabbed his binoculars and, sure enough, they were British M4 medium tanks. They had obviously sliced right through 53 Division and were storming up the road to complete the encirclement of Pyawbwe. Then they swung off the road and began to cut across the vineyard, aiming straight for 33 Army headquarters. Shells and machine-gun bullets began to fall around Honda and his men, and flames started to shoot up from the transport park. It was not the first time Honda had been within range of small arms fire, but he had never before been the target of direct attack by enemy armour.[1]

The officers and men were thrown into a panic by the 'unexpected guests', as Tsuji called 'Claudcol's' tanks. They were Intendance Branch officers, medical officers and some medical staff, about 300 men in all, and they scattered in all directions. Tsuji cast about for some way of restoring their morale. There were few places of concealment, other than the natural folds of the terrain. But his eye fell on the well in the middle of the encampment. This was headquarters' water-point and washing-point. He had not been able to free himself from sweat and grime for days, and an idea suddenly struck him. He stripped off his uniform, and began to sluice his naked body with water, raising the well-bucket high and pouring the cold water on his head, forgetting both the dusty heat and the battle.

The Intendance chief ran up, panting, pale-faced, helmet thrust firmly on his head, armed to the teeth. 'What's happening?' Tsuji asked. 'I'm having a cold shower. Won't you join me?' And he began to rub himself down with a towel. He saw men gather round him, flabbergasted, smiling in spite of themselves. They might be being fired at, but their panic had gone. Honda, on the other hand, had been more concerned with the future. Crouched in a foxhole, he was writing his will.[2]

The gunfire poured into the vineyards and headquarters area until night fall, then suddenly the enemy seemed to break off. Honda and Tsuji were lucky. In spite of the fact that a wireless intercept service at Monywa was regularly breaking the Japanese signals and passing on to Slim – among other things – the locations of the various Japanese headquarters, 17 Division had not been alerted to Honda's presence in the front line at Pyawbwe. Quite simply, 33 Army's wireless communications had ceased to function, there were no signals to intercept, and

[1] ibid., p. 259
[2] ibid., p. 260–1

Pert had no idea his tanks had Honda in their sights. As at Yindaw, not wanting to be diverted from the main battle, Pert broke off what seemed to be a minor action and made for Pyawbwe.

Honda's lack of wireless meant that he had to use liaison officers to take his orders to the divisions under his command, such as they were. To get in touch with the defenders of Pyawbwe, 18 Division, Tsuji selected 2/Lieutenant Fujimoto, a young officer graduate from the Nakano School. Fujimoto, aged 23, had been working with the Intelligence staff of 33 Army, and Tsuji had noticed how calm he was under fire. 'Fujimoto!' he called, 'you're to take this written order to the commander of 18 Division. And try and find out where 49 Division is, and make contact with them.'

Fujimoto's face was expressionless. He put aside his uniform and dressed in a *longyi*, the sarong-like garment worn by all Burmese. He tucked the Army order into the knotted waist, put a hand grenade inside his shirt, and made his way slowly out of the village with Tsuji's former batman Pfc. Miyaji, who was similarly disguised. In the blaze of noon, they passed through the British tanks, and walked north until their shapes vanished in the gunsmoke. Tsuji watched them go, and thought they looked just like a couple of Burmese escaping from the noise of battle.

As they came into Pyawbwe itself, Indian troops surrounded them. Fujimoto could not risk being searched, so he let them come closer, then pulled out his grenade and threw it. As the grenade exploded and tore apart the group of Indians, Fujimoto and Miyaji hared off. Within a few minutes they had reached 18 Division headquarters. Fujimoto handed over the Army order to Lieutenant-General Naka, listened to what Naka had to say about the division's circumstances and future plans, and went straight back across the battlefield. On the way, he came upon 49 Division, and before nightfall ambled into 33 Army headquarters, nonchalantly munching a banana.

Thanks to Fujimoto, Honda managed to convey to 18 and 49 Divisions the change of plan he had in mind. They were, as Tsuji puts it, to exchange space for time. There would be no nonsense about holding territory for the sake of holding it. They were to play for time, delaying Messervy if possible until the monsoon arrived, bogged down his tanks, and put a stop to his air supplies. By 14 April, Honda reported that 18 Division now numbered 3100 men with four mountain guns; 49 Division had 1600 men with one mountain gun; 53 Division had 1600 men; Ichikari Unit (4 Infantry Regiment of 2 Division, down from the Mandalay area) had 800 men with one regimental gun. Army Heavy Artillery could muster precisely three 15 cm howitzers. 119 Regiment, which strictly belonged to 53 Division, was taken under direct Army command. This gave Honda another 500 men, with one more mountain gun. His whole Army strength was therefore less than 8000 men, half the size of a division. With it he was, if he obeyed Kimura's wild, ignorant orders emanating from Rangoon, to stop the mechanized armoured might of XIV Army.

Slim now had 312 miles to go and three weeks to do it in. And Pyawbwe was Kimura's last real throw. There would be other fights, some of them bitter, before IV Corps broke through to Rangoon. But Pyawbwe, as Slim says, was one of the most decisive battles of the Burma war. 'It shattered Honda's army, but it did more – it settled the fate of Rangoon.'[1] It was the last heavily defended position between Meiktila and the sea.

DRACULA in the wings

The Royal Navy decided the timetable for DRACULA. For an amphibious force to be safely landed at the mouth of the Rangoon River, it was thought essential to keep at a distance any possible incursions by elements of the Japanese Fleet (highly unlikely, in fact) and, to ensure this, a carrier force of two cruisers, four destroyers and four escort carriers (21 Aircraft Carrier Squadron, Commodore G. N. Oliver) provided fighter cover for the convoys. Close tactical air support was the RAF's province, and 224 Group had a wing in Kyaukpyu and one in Akyab from which long-range fighters could operate. Eight Liberator squadrons and four Mitchell squadrons, all from the USAAF, were to provide heavy bombing support.

Further out to sea, Vice-Admiral Walker's 3 Battle Squadron from Trincomalee would cover the whole operation by striking at airfields on the Andaman Islands. The very presence of this force should have been enough to frighten off any Japanese naval opposition. Walker had two battleships, the *Queen Elizabeth* and the Free French *Richelieu*, two escort carriers, four cruisers and six destroyers. This massive naval screen bombed Car Nicobar and Port Blair on 30 April, on the same day that Commodore Poland's destroyers sank a convoy of eleven craft with one escort vessel carrying a thousand Japanese troops across the Gulf of Martaban to Moulmein. This was D minus 2.[2]

Admiral Power's real scruples about DRACULA were derived from the likely difficulties to be encountered, not by his battleships or cruisers, but by the landing craft from the Akyab and Kyaukpyu convoys. Once the monsoon set in, the sea approaches to Rangoon could be tricky, and he would only agree to DRACULA if it were carried out by the first week in May, at the latest. 26 Indian Division (Major-General H. M. Chambers), which was to provide the assault troops, was part of XV Corps, which had experience of co-operation with the Navy in the war of *chaungs* and little

---

[1] Slim, op.cit., p. 496

[2] Mountbatten, *Report*, p. 156, n.1 and charts pp. 148–9

ports which was characteristic of operations in the Arakan. All kinds of vessels had been involved, destroyers, minesweepers, motor-launches, and they were taken often into uncharted waters, backed up by bombardment support from cruisers out at sea. It was estimated that 23,000 rounds of naval gunfire had been fired between 4 January and 13 March 1945 in support of Christison's clearing of the Arakan coastline, the recapture of Akyab, and the taking of the islands of Ramree and Cheduba. The navy had been carriers, too, and had lifted 54,000 men, 1000 vehicles, 14,000 tons of stores, and 800 animals in the same period.[1] So DRACULA was an exercise for forces which knew and trusted each other after long experience, and Chambers knew his men would be put down where he wanted them. But he could not have naval bombardment from the cruisers. The seas round the mouth of the Rangoon River were so shallow that the nearest they could come was twenty-five miles off shore. This re-emphasized the need for airfields inland from which the squadrons of 221 Group would co-operate with the landings. Mountbatten had told Leese that XIV Army would have to capture suitable airfields in Southern Burma to guarantee an air umbrella from the landward side. He wanted Pyinmana and Toungoo, and they would have to be in Messervy's hands by 25 April, even at the risk – he stressed this – of very heavy casualties, because DRACULA risked incurring even heavier casualties if the air support were not forthcoming.[2]

In the event, 5 Division, which had taken over the pursuit of Honda's 33 Army from 17 Division after the capture of Pyawbwe, was well on time, though it was held up by serious opposition at Yamethin thirteen miles further south. An advance guard had already passed through Yamethin and reported little opposition: there were only about a hundred Japanese in the town. But a group of 4–500 closed in on the town from the hills to the east after the vanguard had passed through, and blocked the road to such effect that 123 Brigade (Denholm-Young) did not free the town until 14 April.

Honda had sent 18 and 49 Divisions[3] to make defensive positions at the Sinthe Chaung, south of Yamethin, but 5 Division's advance guard was already probing at the defences while the mopping-up continued at Yamethin, and Honda's troops had no time to install themselves properly. About thirty miles south of Yamethin, a hilly feature about 700 feet high called the Shwemyo Bluff runs alongside the main road, offering a perfect vantage-point over it for many miles, and it was assumed the Japanese

[1] ibid., p. 147

[2] ibid., p. 146, para. 506

[3] The British Official History (Kirby, *War Against Japan*, IV, 384, n.2) says that Honda had lost touch with 49 Division when its remnants withdrew from Yindaw, but, as we have seen, his liaison officer had in fact made contact with it and conveyed his intentions, during the battle for Pyawbwe.

would hold it and the Sinthe Chaung in force. In the event, Denholm-Young's brigade hooked on to the Bluff after a wide flanking movement to the east, and his Punjabis and Dogras drove the defenders off. The Sinthe Chaung proved less of an obstacle than Honda had hoped – it was almost dry – but Japanese mines and snipers made the progress of 161 Brigade and its accompanying tanks slow. To keep the momentum of his advance going, Mansergh sent 9 Brigade forward along the railway instead of the road, using bullock carts, as it was an airborne brigade and not equipped with motor transport. On 20 April, 161 Brigade was in Pyinmana, Pert's tanks well in front, with a troop of engineers equipped with Valentine bridge-layers to deal with *chaungs* and demolished bridges. They might have had a considerable problem at Pyinmana, where the Sinthe Chaung bridge four miles north, at MS 248, had been heavily mined and was ready to blow up. As it turned out, the Japanese sapper charged with the job fell asleep, and was still asleep when Colonel Blackater's 116 Regiment's tanks (Gordon Highlanders) rumbled into Pyinmana. He woke up and wandered round in a daze, not having anticipated such a rapid change in his situation, then took to his heels.[1]

His Army commander was little better off. A Squadron of 116 Regiment RAC, with the 3/9 Jats and Bombay Grenadiers, attacked a village just south of Pyinmana. It was supposed to be a headquarters, and they thought a big prize was in their grasp. Honda had distributed his headquarters group of around 300 men on either side of the road, a group west of it with the medicals, intendance and ordnance staff, and east of it his staff, including Tsuji, and Major-General Sawamoto, his Chief of Staff. He himself was in a small wood in the centre of this group. He had been reinforced at Pyinmana by the advance guard of Chū Force, elements of 55 Division under the command of the old bully Lieutenant-General Hanaya, whom Tsuji had known from Manchuria days. The vanguard was Colonel Yoshida's 144 Regiment – around battalion strength, thought Tsuji, with two mountain guns. 53 Division, without a single gun, was placed next to them, east of the road, and Naka's 18 Division further east, across the Sittang. 49 Division's whereabouts were unknown, so of the four divisions nominally under Honda's command at this stage, Tsuji reckoned he had a strength of an artillery battalion and four infantry battalions. They were in position by 18 April.

Tsuji placed two of his staff officers on either side of the town, north and south, to guide in any units retreating from Yamethin and any reinforcements coming up from Toungoo. The previous day, Hanaya had come along and presented Honda with a bottle of beer he had brought with him from Arakan. Honda did not drink it. Instead, the next day, he

---

[1] His subsequent fate is diversely reported: 'He managed to escape' reported Blackater (Perrett, *Tank Tracks to Rangoon*, p. 226); 'he was killed before he was aware of our sudden arrival' (Brett-James, *Ball of Fire*, p. 416).

summoned the officers and men of his headquarters, told them to put out their mess-tin lids, and went gravely round them all, putting a tiny drop of the liquid into each lid. Tsuji had not tasted or smelt Japanese beer for a long time, and a smell was about all there was. But he knew it was a kind of libation to death. Honda was indicating that perhaps their last moment had come. There could be worse places to die, thought Tsuji, with the little temples close by, and their thatched roofs. The village had only about twenty huts, and little groves of conifers, which made good camouflage from marauding fighters.

On 19 April Tsuji was just sitting down, getting ready to write out the next Army order, when he heard sounds of small arms fire and shelling from Pyinmana, a mile or so to the north. About ten aircraft flew over, tank guns joined in, and Pyinmana was soon engulfed in black smoke. The sun was blood-red in the east, and he could not remember when the enemy had attacked with such ferocity so early in the morning. Then four or five trucks came tearing out of Pyinmana like stampeding horses, and as they did so the medicals' area began to be plastered with shellfire from tank guns. The tanks were coming up just behind the trucks, about twenty of them. Headquarters was up a side road, and Tsuji could not understand why the tanks were making for it. Then he spotted Hanaya's empty car. It had been left on the south side of Pyinmana, the tanks had seen it, and come on from there.

Soon the temples were ablaze. Tsuji and Tanaka, one of his staff officers, jumped into a foxhole big enough for one of them. A shell just missed them, but set a temple close by on fire. Tsuji could feel the heat burn into his back. A tank halted. It was in the middle of dried paddy, about ten yards from the edge of the wood. Its gun was turned in their direction, the turret opened, and one of the tank crew raised himself up, and looked around, smiling.

They had no idea of 33 Army's condition, obviously, but by the light of the burning temples, Tsuji began to draft Army orders. He got Honda and Sawamoto to sign them. The next problem was how to get them to the 'divisions'. Fujimoto and two other subalterns at once volunteered to go through the British encirclement. They had not had a drop of water since morning, nor a grain of rice. There was a rotten melon lying close by, Tsuji picked it up, hacked it with his knife, and distributed it among them. After the day's sweat, it tasted delicious.

Each of the three picked an orderly, and the three groups made off for the north side of the wood, sliding over the ground between the British tanks. Tsuji waited for a burst of rifle-fire, but nothing came. Next, how to get headquarters out of its predicament? Tsuji was resigned to the fact that by now the British would know, from wounded prisoners, that 33 Army headquarters was in their grasp. When dawn came, they would be annihilated.

There seemed to be about fifty tanks spread round, and sentries were posted in between them. But wasn't it common sense to suppose the British would put their strong point to the south, to cut off the Japanese line of retreat? Tsuji counted the enemy tanks, from the edge of the wood, and decided on a plan. Headquarters would break through the encirclement to the north, then make a right angle turn when they were clear and march east to the railway line. Then they would move south along the railway. The seriously wounded would be carried on stretchers, the rest would walk, Honda would be in the middle, each man carrying nothing but a grenade. Everything else would be burnt or thrown away. They would move off at ten.

If they once reached the railway, Tsuji felt they had a chance. Tanks could not move along the line, and there was no fear of losing their way. About forty men had been killed during the day's fighting, and about sixty wounded, ten of them badly. Hair and fingers were cut from the dead, to be taken home to Japan. The weakest point of vigilance at the perimeter was sniffed out, and 33 Army headquarters began to inch its way forward on its collective belly. Sounds from the British positions made Tsuji think they were already anticipating in whisky their triumph to come. Voices were raised in laughter. He slid by. Finally they were all through, not a man had been left behind. When they got to the paddy-fields, they formed up into units, and, moving by compass, turned east, changing over the stretcher-bearers to give them a rest.

Suddenly shapes loomed up ahead of them in the darkness. Tsuji grasped his sword and moved closer, assuming they would be British and he would have to cut his way through them. But it was an officer patrol from 18 Division. Tsuji told them to wait while he wrote out a signal for them, concealing the light from his torch as he scribbled. Whether his three teams had got through or not, an extra precaution was always useful.

Nobody felt safe until they sensed the railway beneath their feet. It was exactly midnight. They drank their fill from the *chaung* under the railway bridge, and replenished their water-bottles. And the wounded allowed themselves, for the first time, to groan aloud in their pain. Tsuji was elated. He decided to leave a farewell present to the enemy. He took his signal-pad and writing case, and wrote:

> *Go kurō sama*: sorry to cause you so much trouble.
> This spot is where Lt-General Honda was. Try harder next time.

Sayōnara.[1]

---

[1] Slim never realized Honda had simply walked out. 'His staff car was faster than our tanks', he wrote (*Defeat into Victory*, p. 498).

They were in luck. By next morning they had found a Burmese village with pigs and chickens. They could judge where the spot they had left was and, sure enough, with the dawn, it was battered by shellfire. Fire away to your heart's content, thought Tsuji. Around noon his three liaison teams returned, also along the line of the railway.[1]

If Honda had had any doubts that the British were after him personally, they were set to rest at the conference between British and Japanese generals held in Rangoon in February 1946. When the proceedings were over, a British colonel took him on one side, and said, 'You know, in the Pyinmana battle, the British went into the attack with the conviction that you, the commander of 33 Army, were there. We wondered how you gave us the slip. I'd like you to explain to me, in detail, just how you did it. You see, we knew from agents' reports that you were at the Manwet pagoda.'[2]

DRACULA descends on Rangoon

'I considered it vital that the Toungoo airfields should be in our possession by 25 April if efficient close air support was to be given to DRACULA', wrote Mountbatten.[3] Toungoo was sixty-nine miles south of Pyinmana, 187 north of Rangoon. The plan for it was that 63 Brigade of 17 Division should concentrate on seizing the airfields, while 255 Tank Brigade and 123 Brigade of 5 Division should take the town, followed by 161 Brigade.[4] In the upshot, the tanks were on Toungoo airfield just after ten in the morning on 22 April. Coming up behind them, 7 Yorks and Lancs which had rejoined 123 Brigade found the town almost deserted. Allied aircraft had bombed the town the day before, but Honda had placed his headquarters there, and Slim had not expected it to fall so easily into his hands.[5]

Kimura's idea had been that 15 Army, after a helter-skelter along mountain tracks east of the Mandalay–Rangoon road, would come out at Toungoo and take over from 33 Army the second line of defence. But Katamura's men never got there. It was at this point that Force 136 and the armed Karens played a crucial role. Moving into the hills east of Kyaukse, 15 Army had come down west of Kalaw and Loikaw and then turned west along the road leading from Kemapyu on the Salween, through Mawchi, to Toungoo, the so-called Mawchi Road. Slim's orders to the Karens, awaiting the signal to rise, indicated that 13 April was the moment they were

---

[1] Tsuji, *Jūgo tai-ichi*, pp. 264–75

[2] *Sittan; Mei-go Sakusen*, p. 216

[3] Mountbatten, *Report*, p. 153, para. 531

[4] *Reconquest of Burma* II, p. 400

[5] Slim, op.cit., p. 500

waiting for: Operation CHARACTER. Some Force 136 groups dropped ahead of XIV Army's advance had either been ambushed and killed or had failed to rouse the local inhabitants; and when officers were dropped into the Karenni between 21 and 25 February their reception was lukewarm, since the Karens feared Japanese reprisals.[1] But when the British showed they meant business, and sent in more officers and weapons, the number of Levies soon rose to several hundreds. As the Japanese came down the hill tracks and roads, they were ambushed by the Karen Levies, 'bridges were blown ahead of them, their foraging parties were massacred, their sentries stalked, their staff cars shot up.'[2] By the time they reached Mawchi, the Levies were prepared almost to stage a pitched battle with them. In the event, 15 Army failed to reach Toungoo on time, its forward elements, 15 Division (Lieutenant-General Yamamoto Seiei) arriving east of the town on 19 April, the same day Honda's 33 Army was swept aside at Pyinmana. Kimura's Chief of Staff, Lieutenant-General Tanaka Shinichi, went up to Toungoo to put some life into the defence of the place, with little success. A 15 Division staff officer, Major Yamanaka, got through to Toungoo to confer with him, and Tanaka told him his division was to collect every unit under its command and get them into Toungoo to hold it against the British forces coming south. Easier said than done, thought Yamanaka. 15 Army and 15 Division had sited their tactical headquarters at MS 14 east of Toungoo on the Mawchi road. But that was all there was of them. Their units simply hadn't turned up yet. Tanaka was in a fury and upbraided Yamanaka, then left Toungoo to go north and get in touch with Honda. He returned to Rangoon on 21 April, the day before 5 Division crashed into Toungoo. Honda's remnants were making the same speed as Katamura's: it was 27 April before they reached the Toungoo area, down the east bank of the Sittang, by which time the British thrust was miles to the south, on the edge of Pegu. All that Katamura could do was harry the Rangoon road L of C, if he could get near it, while Honda ploughed his weary way south along the Sittang.[3]

The Japanese Air Force decided, a little late in the day, to take a hand. 161 Brigade harboured north of Toungoo on the night of 23 April, ready to resume the advance the next day. Eight Japanese fighters swooped down on it, strafing and bombing. The Brigade suffered over thirty casualties, but its move was not halted. With armour in front, and the 4 Royal West Kents, the Brigade crossed the Pyu Chaung, where a concealed Japanese 75-mm gun destroyed A Squadron commander's tanks. The Japanese had blown the road and rail bridges across it, but the sappers put two scissors bridges over the 120-foot gap, under constant sniper fire, about a mile

---

[1] Kirby, *War Against Japan*, IV, p. 249–250

[2] Slim, op.cit., p. 499

[3] *Sittan; Mei-go Sakusen*, p. 245

upstream. This served to put the advance guard across while the sappers set up a Bailey bridge for the main road.[1]

Eager to be in the lead, 17 Division was naturally perturbed that 5 Division seemed to be disobeying orders. Not content with charging through Pyu and taking the surrender of the 1st INA Division – 150 officers and 3000 men who were promptly put to work restoring the Toungoo airfields – 5 Division's advance guard bowled merrily down the road another twenty miles into the village of Penwegon. They repeated an earlier experience with Japanese demolitions. The demolition party at Penwegon was as fast asleep as the solitary sapper at the Sinthe Chaung. 'They never woke', Slim drily comments.[2]

17 Division passed through 5 Division at Penwegon on 25 April.[3] The next day it was just north of Nyaunglebin, with a hundred miles still to go. Here the armoured advance guard hit a curious mixture of retreating Japanese, including, of all things, horsed cavalry. As one of the Indian Army's leading cavalry officers, this must have given Claud Pert considerable satisfaction. By dusk they had killed a hundred Japanese, captured a hundred horses, and taken in charge two trains and three engines.[4]

At Pyinbongyi, on the edge of the Moyingyi Reservoir, the Japanese intended to block the road. The Reservoir itself was six miles across, and the land west of the road was marshy, so the armour was confined to the road itself. As the Stuart tanks of 7 Light Cavalry approached Pyinbongyi, their commander, Lt Harpartap Singh, sensed something suspicious about the village. It stretched for half a mile on both sides of the road, and there was no villager in sight. A bridge had been blown, and on the other side of it an overturned vehicle blocked the road.

Lt Singh did not know it, but this was IV Corps' first contact with Kimura's odds-and-sods. In a last-minute desperate attempt to improvise the defence of Rangoon, the Japanese civilians in the city, clerks, administrators and businessmen had been formed into 105 Independent Mixed Brigade (Kani Group) under Major-General Matsui, incorporating elements of naval guard units and anchorage units, 82 Airfield Battalion, Anti-Aircraft units, and all the administrative tail that gathers round a large headquarters. The civilians were hurriedly militarized and put into uniforms. On 27 April, Kimura ordered Matsui to send a force to defend Payagyi and Pegu, the town at the vital crossroads between the Sittang and the main road to Rangoon. If Pegu were lost, then Rangoon was completely cut off from the Japanese defending Tenasserim, whither all the

---

[1] Perrett, op.cit., p. 228

[2] Slim, op.cit., p. 501

[3] Slim, op.cit., p. 501; *Reconquest of Burma*, II. p. 402; '28th April', according to Kirby, *War Against Japan*, IV p. 389

[4] Kirby, op.cit., p. 389

remaining forces in the Shan and Karen Hills were now making. Matsui was also to hold the road to Waw and prevent XIV Army moving on to Moulmein. He created a forward unit, the Payagyi Defence Force, to garrison the village of Payagyi a few miles north of Pegu. Like the rest of Kani Group it was a mixed bag, L of C staff, a marine transport battalion, an NCOs training school, railway staff, two field A/A companies and a battalion (138) of 24 Independent Mixed Brigade, all under the command of Colonel Nemoto, who, until a few weeks before, had been in charge of 38 Anchorage Unit, down in the Rangoon docks.

The defence force contained enough engineering expertise to make life difficult for an armoured column. Lt Singh decided not to risk his tanks dashing through the deceptively quiet village of Pyinbongyi, just north of Payagyi, and called for artillery. 18 Field Regiment obliged, then the Shermans of the Royal Deccan Horse moved in, B Squadron on the left and C on the right, with two infantry companies of 6/7 Rajput. Although C Squadron was held up in swampy terrain, the tanks had no losses but the infantry were badly hit. 1/3 Gurkhas were brought up as reinforcements. The overturned vehicle itself turned out to be not merely a block but a huge booby-trap. 255 Brigade had just acquired a Sherman tank-bulldozer, which moved forward to shove the obstacle out of the way, when explosives detonated under it, blowing the Sherman and accompanying engineers into the air.[1]

The Japanese repeated the performance at the next village, Payagale, where tanks and infantry had to go up and down through the village twice before it was cleared. A tank of B Squadron, Royal Deccan Horse, was hit by an aerial bomb which blew the engine clean out of it. The infantry came to the crew's rescue as the Japanese were closing in on them. On the other flank, A Squadron lost two tanks, one to another buried bomb, another to a 75-mm gun. The defenders also used pole charges, and the suicide attacks continued until late afternoon.

Payagyi was the next stop, and it was rumoured to be heavily defended, so an air-strike and artillery barrage was poured into it on 29 April, followed by 63 Brigade. They found the village empty, and pushed on towards Pegu. The tanks were now in country heavy with memories. This was where 7 Armoured Brigade had fired its first shots against the Japanese in the 1942 campaign. The only survivor of those battles was the Stuart tank nicknamed 'The Curse of Scotland' which was still in use as the command vehicle of 7 Light Cavalry.[2] Along the road from Payagyi to Waw, where 17 Division had retreated from the Sittang Bridge, Cowan sent tanks and a company of 1/3 Gurkhas to set up a road-block. This cut the only escape route by road available to whatever Japanese were left between Pegu

[1] Perrett, op.cit., pp. 229–30

[2] ibid., p. 232

and Rangoon. It was the road which led from Rangoon, via Pegu, through Waw and across the Sittang at Mokpalin to Moulmein.

The Japanese thought the road was still open. At 8.30 pm on 28 April a Japanese convoy closed up on the block, where the Gurkhas had dug themselves in round the vehicles, a troop of armoured cars and a troop of Stuart tanks. Three tanks and three armoured cars opened fire at point-blank range on the convoy, a staff car followed by three trucks of infantry. It was a massacre, marred only by the death of the Gurkha company commander who was hit by return fire from the staff car before the occupants – two Japanese colonels and a high-ranking INA officer – were wiped out.[1]

Cowan was racing against time. Not against the Japanese, but against the rains and DRACULA. There had already been several 'mango showers', light rain which was the usual precursor of the monsoon which should in theory still be a couple of weeks away. And Slim had already told his Corps commanders, Messervy and Stopford, on 20 April, that DRACULA was going in on 2 May. They were to regard the information as secret, divulging it to no one except the chief staff officers at Corps and divisional headquarters. It had a particular significance for Cowan. In a sense, he was playing a return match with an almost too accurate pattern. He had been Smyth's Chief of Staff when 17 Division was broken at the Sittang Bridge in 1942. He had had a recent sharp reminder of those days when a British officer had walked into 48 Brigade headquarters at Kadok, just north of Pyinbongyi, and announced that he had been captured at Singapore, had been a POW ever since, and had just been released by the Japanese because the road to Waw was blocked and the Japanese could not therefore remove their prisoners along it to the Sittang. They were sheltering in a village north-east of Pegu, over 400 of them. It was the worst of bad luck that some of these men were killed by Allied aircraft on the very threshold of liberation. Planes swooping low had seen merely the colour of their uniforms which – given the date of their capture – was khaki, not the by-now-universal jungle green. So the aircraft took them for a Japanese column and strafed them, killing and wounding several.[2] Some of the prisoners were men from the 17 Division who had been held in Rangoon Gaol, including its chief medical officer, Colonel Mackenzie. Cowan had taken over command after Smyth left, and fought back the whole way through Burma to the borders of India. Five of the battalions in his division had been with him then and had stayed with him the entire time 17 Division had fought its way back from Imphal, down the Tiddim Road and

---

[1] ibid., p. 232; *Reconquest of Burma*, II, p. 403

[2] Slim, op.cit., p. 502. The Official History denies this. 'They had scattered to avoid RAF attacks', it says (Kirby, *War Against Japan*, IV, 390. n.5), 'but were all found during the next two days.'

across the Irrawaddy to Meiktila. What could be more dramatically appropriate than that his division should be the spearhead of XIV Army as it triumphantly re-entered the capital city of Burma?

Messervy had already planned the capture of Rangoon, and issued his operation instructions on 28 April. He intended 17 Division to approach from the north, and 5 Division to come in from the north and north-east, taking the southward turn at Zayatkwin. But first Pegu had to be taken.

Cowan's armour was on the edge of the town, on the night of 29 April, just over fifty miles from his goal. Pegu is a big place, one of the most important towns in the whole of Burma, and contains an enormous reclining statue of the Buddha, about 200 feet long, and a large number of pagodas. It straddles the Pegu River, which is bridged by two railway bridges and a road bridge at MS 49. The railway bridges are to the north of the town, but the road is in the centre, surrounded by a heavily built-up area. Cowan told 255 Brigade to capture the village of Kamanat, south-east of the town, and then turn north-east to meet 63 Brigade which would come down the main road and meet them at the road bridge in the centre of the town. Meanwhile 48 Brigade was to cross the river to the west bank at the little hamlet of Okpo and seize the railway station. In this way both sides of the town would fall, while 99 Brigade acted as long-stop at Payagyi.

The defenders were commanded by Major-General Matsui himself, who had arrived in Pegu on 28 April. He had received an order from Kimura, the day before, to defend both Payagyi and Pegu and also – which gave him pause – to destroy or burn all immovable installations in Rangoon, electricity generators, wharf installations, heavy A/A guns and so on. It was on his orders that the POWs fit to walk had been sent out of Rangoon on 25 April. He had left instructions with the last Japanese units remaining in the city to let the other 1100 go when they left. Matsui found Colonel Kawano's marines in Pegu when he arrived, and Lieutenant-Colonel Kaneko's A/A men. The others had not yet arrived. He was not surprised. Most of the transport had been commandeered by units leaving Rangoon for Moulmein, and he had had to call into use every kind of beat-up vehicle being repaired in the city. Even so, many of the men would have to make it on foot.

At 10.30 am on 30 April, 4 Frontier Force Regiment was told to set up a bridgehead on the Pegu River, to allow 48 Brigade to cross to the west bank and reach the station. The battalion left at one o'clock and A Company made for the railway bridge nearest the town, while D Company cleared the villages on the east bank as far as Okpo. As A Company approached the bridge, the Japanese blew it. The company commander ordered a platoon to give him covering fire, and went forward to look at the damage. There were two girders still intact. He told his platoon to keep firing, and ordered an artillery concentration on the bridgehead area.

Another platoon was then ordered to cross by the remaining girders in single file. Under fire from dug-outs on the far bank, the platoon made it in twos and threes, with some casualties. The platoon commander told them to fix bayonets and they charged the Japanese positions. The counter-attack was fierce, and a second platoon was unable to join the first until nightfall. D Company tried its luck at the other bridge and found it was blown. There were two Japanese tanks installed on the railway line, too. D Company decided to wait until the following morning on the east bank. A Company was counter-attacked during the night but beat off all attacks, and to their surprise the Japanese had vanished by the morning of 1 May. A Company then moved south along the railway to help D Company's crossing.

The station area was then shelled. The Japanese troops holding it fled westwards and B and C Companies moved in. 1/10 Gurkhas and 7/10 Baluch met stiff opposition in the area of the main road bridge, 1/3 Gurkhas and 4/4 Bombay Grenadiers attacking from the east made little progress, and the tanks of Royal Deccan Horse were held up by a *nullah* (a deep, dried-up ditch). During the night of 30 April, patrols were sent into the town and they reported that numbers of vehicles were moving to and from the main road bridge area, and guns were being towed away westward. The Japanese had, in fact, withdrawn completely from east Pegu. The next day, 17 Division cleared the west of the town, and regrouped for the advance on Rangoon.

The tenacious Japanese defence of the early hours of the battle for Pegu, and the blowing of the bridges, meant that Matsui was capable of a much longer resistance to Cowan's brigades, even if he could not hold him indefinitely. And Cowan was now bedevilled by another enemy. The monsoon arrived, a fortnight before it was expected. On 29 April,[1] Pegu was deluged in torrential rain, like the rest of Lower Burma. At once, the airfields so recently captured began to be affected. 221 Group was forced to withdraw every close-support squadron but one from Toungoo.[2] The heavy rains kept the tanks and trucks confined to the main road. And any possibility of fording the Pegu River and so ignoring the bridge demolitions disappeared as the waters rose in flood.

Slim, whose plane had flown over the battle and been shot at by Japanese anti-aircraft fire[3], promptly put the whole of IV Corps on half-rations. He was right to conserve supplies. But Cowan had lost the race for

---

[1] So Mountbatten. The afternoon of 1 May, according to Slim (*Defeat into Victory* p. 505)

[2] Mountbatten, *Report*, p. 155, para. 539

[3] And hit. One of his US staff officers, Major Fullerton, lost a leg as a result. 'I often wonder,' wrote Messervy, who was also in the plane, 'what we would have done had we got to Rangoon. I feel that if we had found the airfield clear and possible for landing we would probably have done so and Bill Slim could have personally re-occupied Rangoon. What fun that would have been!' (*War Against Japan*, IV, p. 399)

Rangoon anyway. DRACULA had been put in on 2 May, the same day he resumed his advance through the deluge. Those two days in Pegu made all the difference. Had Matsui's men not resisted with such fanatical zeal, 17 Division might well have beaten DRACULA to it. Why, then, did Matsui suddenly withdraw and leave the road open?

He had received an order from Kimura on 30 April: 'Your brigade will return with all speed to Rangoon and defend it to the death.'[1] Matsui was no fool. He knew what the implications of the last part of his 27 April order were. Nonetheless, it was not up to him to question an order from Burma Area Army, and he ordered his men to withdraw from Pegu. Colonel Kawano had been killed in the fighting, and as Matsui withdrew his men began to be harried by 17 Division down the road towards Hlegu. At this rate, thought Matsui, he was going to be annihilated. Far better to move off the road, leave it to the crushing weight of the British armour, and move into the hills of the Pegu Yomas, where he could concentrate his men round Paunggyi and ready them for this impossible task of 'defending Rangoon to the death'.[2]

Of course it was already too late. The six assault convoys of DRACULA had set off from Akyab and Kyaukpyu on Ramree Island between 5 pm on 27 April and 5 am on the 30th, to cover the 480-odd miles to Rangoon. Early in the morning of 1 May, a Force 136 detachment and a Visual Control Post were dropped five miles west of Elephant Point. Half an hour later the parachute battalion (a composite battalion of 50 Indian Parachute Brigade, the re-formed survivors of Sangshak) was dropped from thirty-eight Dakotas. The drop went well, but the parachuted Gurkhas were unlucky later. They marched to within two-and-a-half miles of their objective, the guns at Elephant Point, which was being bombed by Liberators. Some of the bombs fell short and caused over thirty casualties among the paratroops, at which the Visual Control Post cancelled the bombing. Late afternoon saw the Gurkhas, after a trudge through the same torrential rain which had bogged down 17 Division, on top of the Japanese gunners. There were thirty-seven of them, and only one survived. The landing craft could now come in, once a channel had been swept through the mines.[3]

Aircraft flying over the city the previous day sent back reports that they had seen English words painted on the roof of Rangoon Gaol. Two phrases, in fact. One was JAPS GONE. The other, in unmistakable RAF slang,

---

[1] *Sittan; Mei-go Sakusen*, p. 343

[2] Komiya Tokuji, a young officer in a Rangoon A/A Unit, believes Matsui had no intention of returning to fight for Rangoon. If he did, why did he free the POWs? More likely, he intended to defend Pegu, then withdraw towards the Sittang. Komiya also believes it was not by accident or forgetfulness that Kimura failed to inform 28 Army he was going to leave Rangoon. To do so was deliberately to disregard Terauchi's orders to hold it, and he knew 28 Army knew this. (*Sensō to ningen no kiroku. Biruma-sen. Zenpen.* Records of man and war. The war in Burma, I, p. 110, 112)

[3] Kirby, *War Against Japan*, IV, p. 394

EXTRACT DIGIT.[1] The first phrase might be a trick. The second, hardly. Nonetheless, it was decided to go through with DRACULA as planned. Minesweepers swept the approaches and laid marker buoys, and at 2.15 am on 2 May the convoys were ready to lower their landing craft. The Navy had been right about the risk of worsening conditions. The landing craft had thirty miles to go in sheeting rain and with a heavy swell. The bombers came over and saturated the beachheads, but the landings were unopposed. Chambers's 26 Division was soon in force on both east and west banks.

One man took the gaol rooftop message seriously. This was Wing-Commander Saunders, commanding 110 Squadron, who made a reconnaissance flight over Rangoon on the afternoon of 2 May. From the air, the city seemed empty of Japanese, and he decided to have a look. He took his Mosquito over Mingaladon airfield and tried to put it down, but found to his dismay that Allied bombing had been so effective that the runway was full of craters. Nonetheless, he landed, damaging the Mosquito enough to prevent him taking off again. He and his navigator made their way to the gaol. The POWs remaining, over 1000 of them, told him the Japanese guards had left on the night of 29 April.[2] With superb panache, Saunders walked out of the gaol, made his way to the docks, and commandeered a sampan, in which he blithely sailed down the Rangoon River to meet the incoming launches of 26 Division, which picked him up on the morning of 3 May. 'We were rather pleased about this in Fourteenth Army', Slim remembers. 'If we could not get to Rangoon first ourselves, the next best thing was for someone from 221 Group, which we regarded in all comradeship as part of the Fourteenth Army, to do it.'[3]

At 4.30 pm on 6 May, 1/7 Gurkhas of 48 Brigade linked up with a column of Lincolns from 26 Division at Hlegu. They were just twenty-seven miles north of Rangoon.

The birds have flown

So the birds had flown the coop. Even as late as the end of the battle for Meiktila, Slim was sure Rangoon would be hotly defended. 'It was difficult

[1] 'Japs gone. Exdigitate.' Slim, op.cit., p. 506

[2] Kirby, op.cit., IV, p. 396

[3] Slim, op.cit., p. 507. The historian of 26th Division is, of course, aware of the feelings roused by the contemplation of the laurels snatched at the last minute from Fourteenth Army's brow, but is unrepentant. The capture of Rangoon, he writes, was a proper reward 'for the two gruelling years of obscurity in the Arakan where, though well out of the play of the limelight, the Division had been doing an indispensable job in disrupting the Japanese supply lines and building up the air and sea communications necessary to nourish the main body of South-East Asia forces fighting their way down the interior of Burma.' (*Tiger Head*, p. 36, in *Reconquest of Burma*, II, p. 427, n.52)

to get information of Japanese intentions,' he wrote, 'but there was certainly at this time no evidence that they would on our approach evacuate the city.'[1] He learnt on 24 April that Kimura was moving his headquarters to Moulmein, but this did not tell him all he wanted to know. Was Rangoon to be totally abandoned, or would Kimura leave a suicide garrison there? Intelligence reported that Kimura would fight hard to hold the communications centre of Pegu, but not that by 22 April he had decided to evacuate Rangoon in spite of orders from Field-Marshal Terauchi in Saigon to hold the city.[2]

There was every good reason why Slim should not know this; most of the Japanese higher command in Rangoon did not know it either. By 25 April, Brigadier Gwyn at HQ Allied Land Forces South-East Asia reported a drop of 3000 men in an area within twenty-five miles' radius of Rangoon, reducing the known totals to 11,300. The next day he signalled a further possible drop to 9450. Three days later he was able to use ULTRA information to report that HQ Burma Area Army had left, and that destruction of installations showed that the Japanese had accepted the loss of the city. He ventured the possibility that the Japanese might attempt total withdrawal from Rangoon towards Pegu if transportation facilities permitted, and that the numbers of troops of all kinds in the area might, by the time DRACULA was launched, be reduced to 8000.[3]

Even Kimura's fellow-officers, who lacked Mountbatten's and Slim's privilege of reading his coded signals, did not know that Burma Area Army headquarters was going to abandon Rangoon. Kimura was not, though, a 'last-ditcher' by temperament, and he intended to hold south-east Burma as a block to any Allied advance into Siam as long as he could. The way to do this, he reasoned, was to concentrate what forces he had left in Tenasserim, the borders of which ran with those of Siam and, in the south, Malaya. If he could shepherd the divisions coming from the north – the battered 15, 31 and 33, and the still tough and triumphant 56 – and Sakurai's 28 Army from Arakan and the Irrawaddy Valley, then he could still create an effective barrier. But he did not see the point of trying to control a force in Tenasserim from Rangoon. Traffic from Rangoon to Tenasserim either had a perilous passage by sea across the Gulf of Martaban, or had to make its way overland via Pegu and the Sittang River. Either way, if XIV Army was on his approaches in Lower Burma, it meant running the gauntlet. Far better to cut his losses and put his headquarters in Moulmein.

---

[1] Slim, op.cit., p. 487

[2] Mountbatten, *Report,* p. 154, para. 535

[3] Signal 25 April 1945: 'Changes in Japanese Order of Battle since 3 April 1945'; signal 26 April 1945 54015/1; ULTRA-based signal 29 April 1945: 'Japanese Order of Battle April 1943 to August 1945' (PRO, WO 208/1057)

Terauchi had wired him from Saigon on 20 April to hold the capital. It was easy to give last-man last-round orders if you were reclining in that French-provincial-city-lost-in-the-tropics which was Saigon. It rather paralleled the kind of orders Kimura had given Honda from the comparative ease of Rangoon. Now the boot was firmly transferred. 'I admired the sentiment expressed in the message', Kimura later recalled with smooth irony, 'but I was at the same time astounded by the complete ignorance of the actual situation shown by the staff of Southern Army. It should have been clear to them that Burma Area Army could not allow itself to be cut off in Rangoon. But headquarters both in Rangoon and Singapore were so afraid of the prospect of Rangoon becoming the base of an all-out attack on Malaya that they were capable of issuing such fantastic orders as the one which instructed me to make Rangoon the graveyard of the Burma Area Army. My decision to abandon Rangoon was and is eminently justifiable.'[1]

Terauchi was not the only one who disagreed. There was hostility to the move on Kimura's own doorstep. His Chief of Staff, Lieutenant-General Tanaka Shinichi, had just returned from his tour of the Toungoo front during the morning of 23 April. He was appalled when he realized the mood of the entire headquarters staff was for getting out at once. When Kimura told him that it was obvious the Allied armoured thrusts from Prome and Toungoo would probably be in the city by 27 April and headquarters should not be caught up in the maelstrom which would result, Tanaka said he could see that there might be a time when Burma Area Army might have to conduct operations from Moulmein, but that time was not yet. The only way to restore its bankrupt authority over all the armies under command was to stay in Rangoon and fight. A withdrawal of Burma Area Army headquarters would be taken everywhere as an indication that Rangoon was to be abandoned. Kimura flatly rejected his arguments. Then the air-raid warning sounded, they both went off to their shelter and continued the dispute there.[2]

Tanaka had long made it clear that he thought Rangoon should be fought for street by street, house by house, even temple by temple if that became necessary. He had said as much to the Burmese Premier, Ba Maw. 'We have over a million troops in South-East Asia,' Tanaka had told him, 'and we will throw every soldier into the battle.'[3] Tanaka's resolution was brought home to Ba Maw as he saw the hill on which the Shwe Dagon Pagoda was built being fortified and mined, and explosives being buried under the big business blocks in the city. Ba Maw went to see Kimura and told him that if a shrine so sacred in Burmese and Buddhist history as the Shwe Dagon should be used for gun emplacements, the consequences for

---

[1] Allen, *Sittang: The Last Battle*, p. 31

[2] *Sittan; Mei-go Sakusen*, p. 233

[3] Allen, op.cit., p. 29

Japan's relations with the rest of South-East Asia would be catastrophic. Kimura was noncommittal, but Ba Maw at least gleaned the impression that he was not convinced a scorched-earth policy was appropriate for Burma. Ba Maw decided to bring the matter up at the highest level when he was invited to speak on the Japanese radio in Tokyo late in 1944. He impressed on Koiso, the new Japanese Prime Minister, and on Field-Marshal Sugiyama, the Chief of the Imperial General Staff, that Rangoon should not become a battlefield. Sugiyama said he understood how he felt about the city, particularly about the Shwe Dagon Pagoda. 'We will do our utmost to spare your cities,' he agreed, 'but I warn you that if, no matter how or through whom, the enemy should come to suspect that we will not defend Rangoon or any other big town, we will fight anywhere regardless of the consequences.'

It may seem an odd warning. It was both a promise and a hint to Ba Maw to keep his mouth shut about it. Sugiyama had a shrewd idea that members of Ba Maw's government were already in secret contact with the British and were only waiting for a chance to change sides.[1]

True to his determination to fight on, Tanaka refused to sign the draft order for the move to Moulmein when the senior staff officer, Colonel Aoki Takeki, brought it to him. Aoki explained that Burma Area Army's W/T sets had already been moved the day before, and the GOC's flight to Moulmein had already been decided. Everything was ready to go. Tanaka stormed off again to Kimura, and angrily asked him to reconsider. Kimura steadily refused. The Burmese Government and the Japanese Embassy had already been notified and were preparing to leave. Tanaka still refused to sign the draft order, which had been drawn up at top speed while he was away in Toungoo. Since Kimura himself had already sanctioned it, Tanaka's refusal was no more than a formality anyway.[2]

Almost to the last, Ba Maw was unsure if Tanaka would fight for the city. The Japanese Ambassador, Ishii Itarō, told him Tanaka intended to fight to the bitter end. It was on 21 April that he was told that all the Burmese ministers and their families who wanted to join the Japanese in their retreat would have to leave on the night of 23 April. Ba Maw called his last cabinet meeting and broke the news. Five of his ministers agreed to accompany him. He asked those remaining to carry on the administration and then said goodbye.

Tanaka's absence in Toungoo was providential. Three of the staff had gone with him, Yamaguchi (Operations), Takagi (Intelligence), and Ushiro (Rear L of C). The day before they were due to return, Aoki called the rest of the staff together and discussed the situation with them. The general consensus was that evacuation was unavoidable. No one advocated

---

[1] ibid., p. 30

[2] *Sittan; Mei-go Sakusen*, p. 233

holding Rangoon to the last, and Aoki drafted the evacuation order and took it to Kimura. Kimura's mind was made up anyway, and he signed the order without more ado. It might have been awkward for Aoki that he did not wait for Tanaka's return, but 22 April was the day that Messervy's armour burst through Toungoo, and the fall of Pegu was clearly imminent. If it fell, the land route to Moulmein would be cut, so a day's grace, even half a day's, could be vital.

The notification was not as systematic as it should have been. Major-General Matsui, Commander-in-Chief of the hastily assembled Rangoon Defence Force, was still conscripting Japanese residents in Rangoon on 26 April, the same day most of the headquarters staff left by car, and three days after Kimura had gone by plane. In theory, Matsui should even have incorporated the sick, and he did go through the motions of making a battalion out of the 500 casualties lying in the L of C Hospital, but they were so obviously useless as a fighting force that he put them into a boat and packed them off to Moulmein. He did not know, at the time, that Kimura had gone. When he heard that headquarters staff had left their buildings (they used the Rangoon University campus), Matsui at once sent round a squad from his defence force. They found a chaos of scattered documents, including nominal rolls of awards for merit, which were lying about on office floors. Boxes of cigarettes intended for the troops had been broken into by local Burmese who had rifled the buildings.

When the squad returned with its report, Matsui was speechless. 'I'm the Rangoon garrison commander', he raged inwardly, 'and they've skipped out without saying a word!'[1] It was then he decided to deal with the prisoners of war. The fit he sent off with Captain Sumida, the gaol commandant, towards the Sittang, giving him secret instructions to let them go if circumstances demanded it. A message was left for the unfit. 'From tomorrow, 30th April,' Matsui told them, 'you are free to move as you wish. Enough food and medical supplies have been left behind for you. The British-Indian forces will soon be in Rangoon and you can wait for them or not as you choose.' A message to this effect was pinned to the main gate of Rangoon Gaol. After that Matsui went off with his men to fight for Pegu. There had been an order to destroy all port installations but there were not enough explosives and all he could arrange was to blow up part of a bridge.

Women and children had mostly already gone, but there were about a hundred left at the very end. Colonel Aoki said they should go out with the last troops, but it was obvious they would not be able to keep pace with marching soldiers, so Captain Shirasawa, adjutant of 73 L of C Area, went down to the docks to find a boat for them. All that was left was a wooden boat, which he took over and put the women in, together with the boxes of

---

[1] Allen, op.cit., p. 35

ashes of the men who had been killed in the recent campaigns. They had been stored in Rangoon awaiting shipment back to Tokyo and the Yasukuni Shrine. There were 40,000 of these boxes, in thirty-seven large chests. Unlike the convoy of eleven boats which had been decimated in the preparations for DRACULA, this one reached Moulmein without a hitch.

In the period of about ten days between the departure of Burma Area Army and the arrival of the British, looting broke out in the city. The Japanese stockpiles of stores, weapons and ammunition had not all been transferred to Moulmein in time, and they were picked clean. Bands of dacoits descended on the wealthier houses by the lakes and wrenched apart fittings. Taps, valves, switches, lamps, everything was ripped away. Manhole covers were stolen from the roads, parts taken from stationary cars and lorries, the streets became clogged with rubbish, the alleys with excrement. Here and there the streets were carpeted with millions of Japanese occupation rupee notes, pleasingly designed in green and red, and now worth no more than their value as paper.

Oddly enough, the leader of the Provisional Government of Free India and the Indian National Army seemed to have more conscience about the state of Rangoon than did either the Japanese commander or the Burmese premier. Bose anticipated the city would be vulnerable to pillage on a grand scale once the Japanese left, and as there was still a sizeable Indian population there, he instructed Major-General Loganathan ('Uncle') to stay behind in command of 5000 men to maintain order until the British turned up to start a new administration.

One thing Bose did not lack, and that was courage. He would have fought on, but his ministers persuaded him he could do more if he continued the struggle from Bangkok. In May 1945 it still looked as if the war in Asia might go on for years, so Bose sent off his women's unit, the Rani of Jhansi Regiment, in a convoy of lorries on 24 April. On the way to the Sittang, Bose's convoy was strafed by British planes, and his car skidded into an eight-foot ditch on the road to Waw. There was no bridge at Waw and the Japanese were ferrying men across. General Isoda, the head of the Hikari Kikan, the body responsible for liaison between the Japanese and the INA, politely indicated to Bose that he should cross first. Bose rounded on him. 'Go to hell, Isoda!' he shouted. 'I will not cross until the girls have gone over first.' The commander of the women's unit, Janaki Thevers, was appalled two days later when she asked Bose to remove his heavy boots so that she could wash his socks. He had, by this time, been marching instead of riding. His feet were a mass of blisters, but he refused a car, and that same night covered fifteen miles at the head of his column.[1]

[1] Shah Nawaz Khan, *INA and its Netaji*, p. 205

He let his temper slip when he thought of Ba Maw, the same man for whom he had expressed great admiration in Tokyo in November 1943, when they were the leading personalities of the Greater East Asia Conference. Isoda managed to get some lorries up from Moulmein and came to meet Bose. There was space for his staff and the Rani of Jhansi women. The men would have to follow on foot. In a rage Bose turned on Isoda: 'Do you think I am Ba Maw of Burma that I will leave my men and run for safety? I have told you time and time again that I will not go unless my men have gone on ahead.' He reached Moulmein on 1 May, as the Gurkha paratroops were dropping on Elephant Point.

It is not, then, true that Kimura left Ba Maw and Bose in the lurch, as Tsuji declares.[1] But Kimura's flight left a bad taste in the mouth of his officers and men. Aida Yūji recalled being in hospital and seeing a man with his right hand missing marked as 'fit for service'. The MO heard him whisper how monstrous it was to send a cripple to the front, and shouted at him, 'He may not be able to fire a rifle, but he can still pull a horse's reins! Everyone is needed at the front, even those who are as little use as he is. Those are the General's orders.' The same General had, Aida knew, met a contingent of new officer reinforcements and told them the front line was no pushover. 'You've led a pretty sheltered life so far,' he said. 'If you're going to be of any use, you must be ready and resolute. Off you go. And see you die like men.' 'Die like men!' Aida repeated to himself. 'Because I intend to escape to a safe spot by aeroplane!'

'It was a great disgrace in the history of the Burma campaign', a 28 Army staff officer said, 'that the Commander-in-Chief ran away with his staff officers, ignoring the fact that two or three weeks before he had boasted that, as far as Burma was concerned, Southern Army need have no fears, he would hold it.' Two days before his retreat, Kimura had apparently said to Sakurai, C-in-C 28 Army, when the plan for its guerrilla warfare in the Pegu Yomas was being discussed, 'Don't worry, we'll keep the line north of Toungoo till the end of the monsoon.'[2]

Ba Maw's departure did not go smoothly. For one thing, his daughter was about to give birth; and secondly the Japanese arrangements broke down. Colonel Hiraoka, his liaison officer with Kimura, was in charge of these, and arranged for him to have a platoon of soldiers as escort. With the ministers and their families travelling with him, this meant that thirty lorries would be needed for the group, and Lieutenant-Colonel Okamoto, who was to accompany them, put in a requisition for these to one of the Rear L of C staff officers, Major Uemura. When the time came, Uemura had done absolutely nothing.

---

[1] Tsuji, *Jūgo tai-ichi*, p. 291

[2] Allen, op.cit., pp. 32–3

Inevitably I had to hunt around for local vehicles (says Okamoto) and just as inevitably there were delays. I left Rangoon two days after the group, and when I reached the Sittang crossing I met our Ambassador Mr Ishii and the Consul-General Mr Shimazu. They were held up there and had not been able to get across.

I went along to talk to the river crossing unit and got them priority to go over.

Among the ministers, other than Ba Maw, there were some who were absolutely worn out because they had no cars. Some were walking along the road from Pegu. Cars kept going past them, but they were all overloaded and wouldn't stop to pick them up. They really were a pathetic sight.

Once he was across the Sittang and had gone on a bit, Ba Maw stopped and said he would go no further. He intended to stay put. If he went to Moulmein, he said, he'd be assassinated. I went on ahead to Moulmein, to Burma Area Army headquarters, and explained what had happened. I asked for instructions. There was no need to worry, they said, if Ba Maw could be settled in Mudon. I was to stay with him. I went straight back and told Ba Maw what headquarters had said, and went with him to Mudon.[1]

Ba Maw was now distraught. His car was driving through the night towards Kyaikto, sixteen miles beyond the Sittang crossing, when his daughter Tinsa felt her first labour pains, and they reached a house just in time for her delivery.[2]

The Burmese government had escaped the British; so had Bose's government; so had Kimura's headquarters. But there was an entire Japanese army – Sakurai's 28 – marooned in the hills north of Pegu. They would have to be got out.

---

[1] *Sittan; Mei-go Sakusen*, p. 240

[2] Ba Maw, *Breakthrough in Burma*, pp. 397–8. There remains an interesting footnote to Britain's recapture of her great imperial city and an illustration of how easily society forgets its debts. The Union Jack was raised over Rangoon by an Indian soldier, Mohammed Munsif Khan. After Partition, Khan worked for the Pakistan embassy in Peking, and later joined his son in England. As the result of an administrative error, he was stopped by an immigration officer at Heathrow airport and the Home Office refused his application to stay. In protest against the Home Office order to deport him, he returned his decorations. They included, of course, the Burma Star. (*Sunday Times*, 27 June 1982.)

9. THE BREAKOUT

The Japanese breakout from the Pegu Yomas; across the Sittang

Life in the Yomas — Honda goes round the bend —
Sussing it out — Lieutenant Levy produces an ace from
his sleeve — Saito and Shinbu Force — Sakurai makes
for home — The odyssey of Tsutsumi Shinzō

Life in the Yomas

The first thing 28 Army had to do in the Pegu Yomas was to survive. This should not have been such a problem. The Yomas were not like the massive ranges of North Burma, thousands of feet high. Seen from the Mandalay-Rangoon road they are a line of low-lying hills which seem to offer little difficulty in crossing. But the appearance is deceptive. They rise to around 1800 feet and run for about eighty miles north to south and are over thirty miles across, between the level of Toungoo and Prome, and the southern edge which points down at Rangoon from the level of Pegu. They are thickly forested, mainly with bamboo, there are few tracks – including elephant tracks – and these are precipitous. Likewise there are few villages. Here and there are large stretches of swamp, which turn into lakes of mud during the monsoon, which was precisely the period 28 Army spent in them. The plan had originally envisaged a two-month period, from the beginning of May to the end of June, by which time the Army would break out from the hills across the Sittang Valley, into Tenasserim. But not all its units assembled fast enough, and it was nearly the end of July before the Army was ready to move out. This meant an extra month in the Yomas, which knocked their commissariat arrangements askew.

Major Yamaguchi, of 28 Army staff, had been in charge of these. A resourceful, brisk and energetic man, he had conveyed into the hills not only ammunition but enough food supplies to give the men two months' rations. When food started to run short, it was necessary to restrict these to 250 grammes a day, and to send out foraging parties. This was a hazardous business now. On the western side of the foothills, where the parties made their way down towards the villages between the Yomas and the Prome-Rangoon road, the Burma National Army was now collaborating with the British. They harried the Japanese foragers, and if the parties were small enough, the villagers killed them. The foraging was often undisciplined. The troops were desperate and took what they wanted by force, a sure sign of an army that does not think it is coming back. Gradually Japanese resourcefulness had to take the place of Burmese resources.

One thing the Yomas offered in abundance was bamboo. Now bamboo was something the Japanese had dealt with for millennia. They could house themselves with it, they could write with it, they could even eat it. Bamboo tubes of all sizes make Japanese writing brushes, *fude*, and also the pots in which the brushes stand. Japanese architecture employs wood more successfully than any other national architecture – the oldest and most beautiful wooden buildings in the world are the Hōryūji temple buildings in Nara – and bamboo is a distinctive component. Bamboo is a perennial symbol in Japanese painting, along with the cherry and the plum. And you can eat *takenoko*, bamboo shoots. It was the best time of the year for picking bamboo shoots, and 28 Army's standard diet was a gruel of rice and bamboo shoots, with the latter increasing in proportion as the ration of rice grew smaller and smaller. This un-Lucullan diet was supplemented by what wild life the hills provided: snakes, snails and lizards, and grasses. Colonel Saitō, senior staff officer of Shinbu Force, had already, in anticipation of the conditions he expected to find in the Yomas, begun to experiment with grasses while the Force was still in Arakan. He had logged more than ten varieties of *nogusa*, edible grasses. When Shinbu Force first went into the Yomas they were reasonably well supplied. Unhulled rice (*momi*) was taken with them, vegetables for vitamins and poultry for fats. It was only when these were exhausted that the grasses had to be used, and necessity expanded the varieties of edible grasses to thirty-eight.

28 Army also found that the fish in the Mezali *chaung* were excellent. Sakurai himself fished for these during the lulls in the monsoon rain, and particularly aimed for a fish he could not name, rather like a carp, which was a foot long and quite delicious. There was game, too. Sakurai's adjutant, Ozaki, had the foresight to bring a shotgun with him, and discovered flocks of pheasants to add to the pot. There were hens, too. The men trailed these to small woods, and moved in to catch them after sundown.

The bamboo shoots in the diet kept down beri-beri, but it meant eating a great deal more bamboo than they would normally have eaten in Japan, perhaps ten times the yearly average. And there was the question of taste, which meant salt. More than taste, in fact: life itself. Men who work hard under tropical heat conditions lose salt from their bodies in large amounts. If this is not replaced, heat exhaustion follows, then heat cramps and dehydration. The Indian Army had faced this problem and had worked out that the average man who had unlimited water (water was not one of 28 Army's problems – not as far as drinking was concerned, at any rate) would sweat a litre an hour. To replace the salt lost in that sweat, 2 grammes of salt per working hour were needed to maintain what was called 'sodium chloride balance', and half a gramme for every hour of rest. A man doing an eight-hour day would, therefore, need 24 grammes of salt a day. Ample supplies could have been stored in the Yomas from Rangoon, if only stocks had been properly distributed before Kimura fled the city. But that had not been done, so Sakurai's men had to find substitutes. One ingenious method consisted of making a sour sauce from mangoes and eating it with rice. Grass, lizards and sour mango sauce – it may have kept body and soul together, but that was about all. And the diet was common to everyone. When a final staff meeting of formations under 28 Army command was held on 25 June, the colonels and generals dined together after it, and their meal was field rations and bamboo shoots.

They lived in bamboo as well as on it. The Yomas began to sprout whole villages of bamboo huts, the pillars and walls of bamboo, the roofs of leaves and grasses. The rain came through, of course, but it was better than nothing. The 28 Army staff quartet, who had been students at the Military Academy together – Tsuchiya, Yamaguchi, Fukutomi, Okudaira – shared a hut. It was quite a complex little affair: a staff room, an office with a fireplace scooped out of the earth floor in true Japanese fashion, and a bedroom. This was after 28 Army had moved further into the hills from Tanbingon, where they had settled on 28 April after moving headquarters from Taikkyi on the main Rangoon-Prome road. But Tanbingon was just in the western foothills near the end of a motorable track and therefore not out of reach of British armour should the tanks decide to explore the edges of the Yomas. At the beginning of June it was thought prudent to move further into the interior, and 28 Army HQ shifted its ground to Mezali (Pinmezali on British maps). Unfortunately for them, they were still on mapped tracks, and the maps showed a bungalow at Pinmezali, which the British deduced might be used for Army headquarters. So they began to shell it.

'The first shells came over at Mezali', Okudaira noted in his diary for 11 June.[1] 'It was 7.30 in the evening, and nine rounds were fired. At 1 am on the 10th, nine more rounds. At 7.30 am, nine more rounds. At 3 pm and 7 pm, four rounds each. At 10 pm, three rounds. On the 13th, they came smack into headquarters. The staff *basha* had foxholes dug in it for just such an occasion, and Yamaguchi and Fukutomi dived straight for the floor. No one was harmed.' The staff judged it was random firing, but they also deduced that it showed that the British, after their wild dash down to Rangoon down the Prome and Toungoo roads, were now beginning

[1] *Nanso*, '30th anniversary of the Breakout' edition, Tokyo, July, 1975, p. 6

seriously to turn their attention to the Japanese in the Pegu Yomas. In fact, long-distance guns had begun to find them from 21 May, as Sakurai recalls it. The shelling occurred regularly every day at the same time, and Sakurai supposed they were the objects of an artillery exercise. They got used to it, and began to time it, looking at their watches and saying 'five minutes now to the shelling', then counting the shells and finally saying 'shelling over' once the standard number of rounds had been fired. Then they would come out of their foxholes.[1]

So bamboo fed and sheltered them. It was also to save their lives more directly. 28 Army headquarters listened in to British wireless signals. They did this sparingly, because dry batteries were scarce, but it was clear from the traffic that boats were being destroyed on the banks of the Sittang every day to prevent a future Japanese crossing. If no country boats were available when they reached the river, then 28 Army would have to find other ways of crossing. This meant bamboo again. Sakurai was lucky in his choice of Senior Staff Officer. Okamura had been an Engineer, and Sakurai said to him, 'You can stop being a staff officer for the time being and get back to being an engineer. How do we cross the Sittang?' Rafts were the answer, and Okamura began testing lengths of bamboo in the streams of the Yomas. He found that twenty-four bamboo poles, each sixteen feet long, were buoyant enough to support ten men. A sixteen-foot pole was an awful hindrance on the march so it was agreed that every other man should carry an eight-foot pole. They could be put together later, once the river bank was reached.

How? Yamaguchi heard that Okamura was perplexed by the lack of rope in the Yomas. Without it, the bamboo was useless. 'Some of our men have watched the Burmese', he told Okamura. 'They make rope by stripping the bark off certain trees which have a broad leaf and look rather like mountain maples.' Okamura got his river-crossing unit to work on this bark-rope. It was surprisingly effective: not so strong as manila, but tougher than hemp palm rope, and the trees it grew on were everywhere.[2] Okamura's unit was at Thabyu, deeper into the Yomas than headquarters at Mezali and on the edge of the North Zamayi Reserved Forest, which became the source of what Okamura, with some justification, called 'the rope of life'. He went to see the Army commander and asked him to issue an order that every man was to make his own rope from the bark, at least two yards long, which was to be wound round the waist. If larger rafts were not used, then Okamura calculated that three lengths of bamboo about four inches thick, bound with this rope, would be an adequate individual raft which could support one man and his rifle and pack. Models of these rafts were built and tried out by the staff officers themselves in the streams

---

[1] Sakurai, 'Biruma sensen: teki-chū toppa', *Bungei Shunjū*, Nov. 1955, pp. 62–7
[2] Allen, *Sittang*, p. 154

of the Yomas. Tests were also carried out with single lengths of bamboo to find out how long they had to be to carry a man across 110 yards of river. Other rafts were contrived for those who would not risk the single bamboo. There were some car inner-tubes which, combined with bamboo in a basket-type container, made buoyancy rafts for individuals and groups. They could be carried on the back, and a piece of bamboo twenty inches long would give all the extra buoyancy needed.

More complex were the catamaran-style rafts. Bamboo poles were wrapped round with tents, making a primitive canoe. Secured together, two of these provided a small vessel which would take four men across a river. There would be *chaungs* in the Yomas to cross as well as the Sittang, and it was vital to find out their depth and strength of current, even their location: a map in Burma did not have to be very old before *chaungs* found new channels, and villages which had appeared on the edges of streams had been moved elsewhere. In Shinbu Force, Saitō had the perfect answer to this problem. He had Kitamura.

Nine years before, Kitamura had won the 1500 metres at the Los Angeles Olympics. He was one of the finest long-distance swimmers in the world, and now, a lieutenant in 55 Division, 'the champ' (*ōja*) was about to find a use for his skills that would not attract admiring applause from the stands but might save thousands of his comrades' lives. In the utmost secrecy, and with reserves of what seemed inexhaustible energy, Kitamura went back and forth from the headquarters of Shinbu Force, slipping through Burmese guerrilla camps and British positions, sliding into the water under the reeds to note the strength of the current and remembering the spots where the *chaungs* were fordable, and how far unfit men could cope with them at the height of the monsoon. He also trained the men, who hero-worshipped him.

Honda goes round the bend

The two Armies east of the Sittang were to protect Sakurai's breakout by holding or diverting British attention at the crucial moment. Matsuyama's 56 Division, under the grandiose name of Phoenix Group (*Ōtori Shūdan*) had come down into the Southern Shan States from the Chinese border and was, single-handed, replacing 15 Army. Matsuyama was to send commando units from 113 Infantry Regiment's positions on the Mawchi Road (between Toungoo and Kemapyu on the Salween) east of the Palaw Bridge, to harass British communications north of Toungoo and south of it at Lamebya. Its boundary lay along an east-west line through Pyu.

South of that, to Nyaunglebin, was the breakout area. From Nyaunglebin south again, to Pegu, 33 Army was to harass lines of communication by commando raids. 9 Brigade of 5 Indian Division had already advanced to

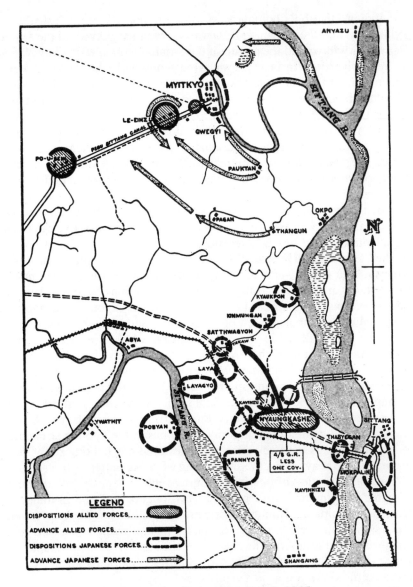

Battle of the Sittang Bend, July 1945

the Sittang, and its patrols intercepted parties of Japanese moving south into Tenasserim – broken fragments of 31 and 33 Divisions of 15 Army, and 18, 49 and 53 Divisions of 33 Army. Its duties were taken over by 7 Division on 22 June leaving 20 Division with 268 Brigade and 22 (East African) Brigade on the banks of the Irrawaddy to clear up the resistance to XXXIII Corps by 28 Army, from Prome southwards.

7 Indian Division's boundary with 17 Division ran from just north of Pyinbongyi and the Moyingyi Reservoir across to Myitkyo and the Sittang. Between Myitkyo and the mouth of the Sittang, Honda's 33 Army planned a strong diversion. In fact, Burma Area Army had asked it to do a great deal more, and offence was taken when the chore was refused. Or rather Tanaka Shinichi took offence. At the end of May, Honda's Chief of Staff, Major-General Sawamoto Rikichirō, went to Moulmein to report to Burma Area Army headquarters. 'In spite of the brave fight put up by all ranks,' he told Kimura, 'we were unable to destroy the enemy's armoured forces, and unavoidably compelled Burma Area Army to abandon Rangoon. For this disgrace I would like to apologize from the bottom of my heart.'

'No, that was my fault,' replied Kimura, 'because my direction of the battle was poor (*watakushi no tōsui ga mazukatta kara da*). I've caused you a great deal of hardship. But you did well.'

Then Lieutenant-General Tanaka, Kimura's Chief of Staff, chipped in. 'Burma Area Army wants 33 Army to attack at once on the west bank of the Sittang and retake Rangoon. What condition is your Army in?' Sawamoto was taken aback. He knew from recent experience how remote from reality was Tanaka's view of 33 Army strength, and the casualties that had been the result for 33 Army's men. If the whole strength of 33 Army units were put together, there would be three infantry battalions and one company of artillery; and they had spent the last forty days in an exhausting retreat. There was no question of such a force retaking Rangoon from a triumphantly victorious army like Slim's. 'If you order us to attack, we will do our best,' he answered, 'even though it destroys us in the process. But frankly, at the moment, I regret my Army hasn't the fighting strength for it. If you order us to attack after we've restored our fighting strength and given us some heavy guns, there's nothing we'd like better.'

'It's not a question of fighting strength,' replied Tanaka, 'but of the will to fight.' Sawamoto kept a guard on his tongue, and said nothing. The tension was palpable. Kimura quietly drew him aside into the next room. 'I understand you perfectly well,' he said. 'What Tanaka's just said represents what Southern Army has been demanding. We think it's stupid, too, and I've sent Ichida (Vice-Chief of Staff) to Southern Army to voice precisely the views you've just expressed.'

Then they talked about a number of things. The order '33 Army will carry out delaying tactics between Pyinmana and Toungoo' had enabled 33 Army to leave Toungoo, and saved it from being massacred. Sawamoto was deeply impressed when he learnt Kimura had sent that order personally.[1]

---

[1] *Sittan; Mei-go Sakusen*, p. 323; 33 Army strengths at the time: 18 Division 2000; 55 Division group 1000; 53 Division 600; 49 Division 300; total 3900 (*Sittan; Mei-go Sakusen*, p. 312)

Needless to say, Tanaka's recollections of this exchange are somewhat different. He says Sawamoto told him that 33 Army no longer had the will to fight.

> 'Don't you mean – has no fighting strength?' I asked him, offering him the chance of correcting it. Sawamoto replied, 'No will to fight, that's the fact.'
>
> 'Does GOC 33 Army accept that? Isn't it the principle of army and divisional command that you see your men have the will to fight to the last man?'
>
> Finally Kimura looked unhappy at my strong expressions, hummed and ha-ad a bit, until finally everything ended in a non-committal fashion.
>
> I could not help showing my anger, because I took it that what Sawamoto said was an indirect means of conveying that 33 Army was refusing to carry out a difficult task.[1]

At any rate, Sawamoto returned from Moulmein with twenty truckloads of weapons and clothing, and the news that Tsuji was soon to be transferred.

Lower down the scale in 33 Army, Honda's men were occupied in dumping supplies in readiness for 28 Army if and when it succeeded in breaking across the Sittang. At Salugyaung, just below Shwegyin on the east bank, 60 tons of food were stored, together with spare clothing, enough medical supplies for 3000 men for a month, and a month's supply of batteries and wireless valves. East of the ferry at Okpo, sixty tons of food were left at Zibyaung; ninety tons at Kyaikto, south-east of Mokpalin; sixty tons at Paan, south-east of Bilin; and 120 tons at Thaton, south-east of Paan. To convey these stores by 20 July was no less difficult than military operations. The heavy monsoon rains radically alter the landscape of the lower Sittang, which is a fairly prosperous area, with a number of villages and small towns. The land between the main road running from Pegu north to Daiku, and the line of the Sittang, is intersected by canals, by a railway line (Pegu-Waw-Abya-Nyaungkashe-Mokpalin) and a number of roads, and contains the large Moyingyi Reservoir. The railway crossed the Sittang River at the village called Sittang, where the bridge had been blown in 1942. All this terrain is very low-lying, and the maps mark many parts of it with the warning 'Usually flooded from June to October'. The warning was particularly apt in the summer of 1945. The monsoon rain acting directly on the paddy fields and the overflowing of rivers and *chaungs* turned the land east of Waw into a large shallow lake, right up to the Sittang itself. The only way to move about was to use country boats, or to walk along the railway embankment, which was built up higher than the

---

[1] ibid., p. 323

surrounding countryside. Infantry patrols found their work difficult and uncomfortable. The British were also more vulnerable than the Japanese, because they moved on the flooded west bank, while the Japanese could observe them from the heights on the east bank.

Along this bank, besides food dumps, 53 Division collected river-crossing materials. Ten outboard motors were assembled, eight collapsible dinghies, and other boats of all shapes and sizes. And attempts were made to bridge the *chaungs*.

Not without risk, as Aida Yūji found. He had already run the gauntlet of horrors while escaping through the foothills of the Shan States. With a lieutenant who had befriended him – they were both university graduates and glad to be away from the old sweats of the regiment – he found himself four days' march behind the main body of the regiment. They stopped at one spot where other units had passed through on their way to a rendezvous, so on the assumption they were on the right track they decided to bed down for the night. The place was cheerful and pleasant with swarms of fireflies glinting in the dusk and tiny rivulets gurgling in the hollows (this was before the monsoon had set in). The quiet was an uneasy quiet, though. There were many corpses lying around, burned by the torrid heat and picked at by vultures.

Not only the dead, but the dying. A couple of men from 56 Division lay under an awning near them. Aida gave them water, but it was a waste of time, they could not swallow, and it trickled down their chins. Aida and the lieutenant were dozing off when they heard a weird choked scream. The light was fading, and they crawled carefully forward in the direction of the sound, clutching their carbines. Some yards away was a group of about fifty Burmese, men, women and children. Aida could see they were raiding the corpses, but was surprised that there should be anything to make it worthwhile. Most of the dead were nearly naked and had nothing save an occasional wrist-watch, wrapped in a condom for protection against the rain.

Ah, perhaps there was something else. Aida started back in fear and disgust. The Burmese were knocking the teeth out of the dead mouths. He watched as they placed a head on a rock, dropped a large stone on it, and broke open the face. They had a claw hammer. Once the face was broken open they began to pull out the gold teeth. Aida then understood the screams he had heard. The two dying men from 56 Division had been killed by having their heads smashed open in this way. The screams were the last expulsion of breath from their throats. He and the lieutenant could do nothing against so many, and had to wait until the night came down and darkness absorbed the horror.

Other deaths were on their way. Aida's company, once 300-strong, was now reduced to ten men, and the duty it was given by 128 Regiment was to guard several thousand yards of front line with a light machine gun and a few rifles. The machine gun kept jamming, and they had to use pig's fat to lubricate it. Most of their ammunition was used up anyway, and it did not look as if any more were coming through.

One day Aida went off to collect stores for their position, which was in a Burmese *kyaung* or temple. On the way back he found the crossing had altered, the bridge across to the temple had been swept away and engineers were trying to rig up a substitute. In the meanwhile they were ferrying men across by a steel wire slung to the opposite bank. The water was chest-high, and the theory was that if you clung to the wire hard enough you could pull yourself to the other side, though the current was strong and fast.

They were about to have a go when a Burmese country boat sped past, with helpless occupants screaming as the river bore them relentlessly seawards. In a few seconds, the boat disappeared into the muddy waters. Still, Aida and his friends were carrying supplies and they could not wait until the engineers completed their bridge. The main weight lay in a new stock of boots, and it was the younger and raw recruits who were told to get on with transporting these. The old hands had simply crossed carrying their own packs and little else. Aida and his friend Yoshimura, also a student, from Wakayama, volunteered to get the boots across. They made containers out of the tents they were carrying and put sixty pairs in each. Yoshimura went first, with the tent and boots strapped to his back. He made about ten paces into the water, with great confidence, then came to a stop:

> It looked as if the river had suddenly gone deeper near where he was and the brown torrent was swirling up to his chest. The water began to seep into the tent on his back, and made it swell up like a balloon. He couldn't budge an inch. For what seemed a very long time Yoshimura gripped the steel wire in desperation and withstood the pressure of the water. Then in a second he was on his back, his feet floating. I shall never forget how he looked as he stared at us straight in the eyes. He made no sound, but his eyes held ours, in a look of despair, pleading for help.

The engineers began to string themselves out along the wire to him, but it was too late. It was impossible to undo in time the knots that bound the tent:

> The next instant, Yoshimura's hand let go, and he was in the maelstrom of waters. He seemed to somersault a dozen yards downstream, and his feet whirled in the air. That was the last we saw of him.[1]

No one used the wire after that. Aida and the rest waited until the engineers rigged up a raft.

[1] Aida Yūji, *Prisoner of the British*, p. 12

The area in which Aida and his friends brought up supplies is on the opposite bank from what is called 'The Sittang Bend'. In this curl of the river on 3 July Honda attempted to draw the fire of IV Corps. The 2000 men of 53 Division, and another 1000 from 18 Division, attacked the villages of Nyaungkashe and Abya. The British positions were defended by 4/8 Gurkhas of 89 Brigade,[1] and they found the flood waters a problem, so much so that some areas were described as 'too deep for Gurkhas to operate'. But the Japanese are no taller, and the flood waters incommoded them, too. They managed to cut the Gurkhas' communications at Nyaungkashe, which meant 7 Division had to lay on air supply to a dropping zone constantly under fire. The Japanese cut the railway line and the canal and tightened their grip on the village until they were three-quarters of the way round it. The Japanese artillery observers overlooked every move and the Gurkha casualties soon became very heavy.

IV Corps' original plan had been that the Japanese artillery positions would by now be in British hands. Mansergh's 5 Indian Division had been ordered to capture Kyaikto, seventeen miles south of Mokpalin on the east bank of the Sittang, before the monsoon began. It was a tall order, with tidal *chaungs* and flooded paddy to cross, and strong natural defensive positions to face. Patrols found Mokpalin very strongly held. The sappers could not build a reliable line of communication from Waw to the Sittang – a distance of seventeen miles – through the waterlogged country, though they managed to make a jeep track along the railway. There were no armoured landing craft to attempt a crossing, and artillery could only be deployed in inadequate amounts. Aircraft operating from airfields in Central Burma were often prevented from flying because heavy rain put the strips out of action. Nor could a water line of communication be extended to Kyaikto, where there were no beach exits. So the idea of assaulting the east bank was given up. The Japanese must have known what was intended, because, as an extra precaution, they blew up another span of the Sittang Bridge.[2]

Further north, in the Myitkyo area, the Japanese attempted to reach the line of the Pegu-Sittang canal between Abya and Myitkyo and were only cleared from their positions by desperate attacks from 3/6 Gurkhas and a massive series of air strikes. Every plane that IV Corps had at its disposal was sent in support of 89 Brigade, and the Japanese made no further move in this area. But in Nyaungkashe they were more successful. 4/8 Gurkhas had suffered eighty-five casualties (twenty-five killed) by 6 July. While the Japanese remained astride the railway between Abya and Nyaungkashe, it was impossible either adequately to supply the Gurkhas or to evacuate

---

[1] 89 Brigade of 7 Indian Division began to relieve 9 Brigade of 5 Division on 21 June, two days after the Japanese started shelling Nyaungkashe and sending strong patrols into the area.

[2] *IV Corps Narrative of Operations May – August, 1945*, p. 6

their casualties, and the number of casualties from shelling and sniping made the retention of Nyaungkashe a dubious proposition. On the night of 7/8 July the Gurkhas were withdrawn. It was long overdue. The previous night they had been shelled for half-an-hour by 150 shells from Japanese 105 mm artillery, two shells hitting the regimental aid post and killing several of the wounded.

Lt Arthur Adamson, who flew as 7 Division's Air observer for the artillery from June until August over the whole Sittang Bend area, says that the positioning of 4/8 Gurkhas at Nyaungkashe was over-optimistic. 'The village was isolated except for a very long rail link, which was easily cut by small parties of Japanese. Worst of all it was overlooked from high ground rising from the east bank of the Sittang, only about 4000 yards away. The Gurkhas successfully held off the Japanese infantry attacks but the Japanese had concentrated a lot of artillery in the dense jungle on these slopes. They were always exceedingly good at concealing their artillery: these positions made them impossible to spot. While I was flying over the area they kept silent. As soon as I turned away they fired on Nyaungkashe, to my intense frustration, and that of the E Troop officers of 500 Bty on the ground, anxious to return the fire. When aircraft were not about and at night they poured shells into the 4/8 Gurkha positions.'[1]

These assaults were not mounted by the division to which Aida belonged, but by the tougher and more experienced 18 Division who were also mounting what they called 'tactical guerrilla warfare' against the British L of C near Pegu. These consisted of four groups of fifteen men each who had no luck in trying to penetrate the cordon of Burmese round the British positions. The division also put in a battalion-strength attack on British positions at Satthwagyon and the railway bridge east of Abya on the night of 26 July, and had a spectacular success four nights later, on the 30th, when observers watched an enormous conflagration reach into the sky at the southern end of Abya, as fire begin to lick round the station area, and spread to the whole village. The Japanese battalion commander signalled at dawn, 'Attack successful. More than half village in flames. Main body concentrated in area SE of railway bridge east of Abya by dawn. No casualties. About one company left east of Abya.' That battalion was lucky in its Abya raid. The Sittang Bend operations caused casualties, but not heavy ones in comparison with what was happening elsewhere. The Japanese official history puts them at 320.

The figure is low because, I think, the Japanese had the sense to realize they would not gain from endless struggle in the flooded terrain round Nyaungkashe. When the Gurkhas came out they moved in a hollow square, with their wounded, their mortars and their wireless in the middle, through a corridor set up by 4/15 Punjab and another Gurkha company in

[1] Private correspondence.

the village of Satthwagyon. They could not bring out the guns, three 25-pounders which had been heavily and accurately shelled by the Japanese, more accurately than usual, the gunners noticed. The troop disabled the 25-pounders and marched out with the Gurkhas. These three were the only guns ever lost by 7 Division artillery 'and even the extreme circumstances did not do much to sugar the pill'.[1]

The withdrawal was difficult because the wounded had to be carried out on stretchers, but the Gurkhas were surprised they got away without interference. The reason was quite simple. The Japanese were doing the same thing. The Japanese had achieved their objective, but they too – no taller than the Gurkhas – were finding it impossible terrain to fight over. When RAF planes came over Nyaungkashe and then over Laya to the north-west along the railway they came as low as 100 feet and saw no sign of Japanese. 89 Brigade also thought Myitkyo was too expensive to hold on to, and the Japanese moved into it on 9 July but they did not develop any thrust to Pegu from it. They, too, were beginning to find it inconvenient to move through flooded paddy with reeds growing to chest height and occasionally submerging the entire body. They could not use bullock carts, and were having to patrol by boat. They came back into Nyaungkashe on 10 July, the day they moved into Myitkyo, as 89 Brigade handed over to 33 Brigade, but there was little activity. Sporadically, patrol clashes kept occurring for the next few weeks, the final attack coming on 2 August when the Japanese occupied Satthwagyon for a day and then evacuated it.[2]

It still seems odd that Honda should have begun his offensive in the Sittang Bend so early. Perhaps he thought an early attack might draw IV Corps forces down into the area long enough for Sakurai to profit from the switch. But the crucial fighting in the Bend lasted only a week, though there was sporadic fighting into August. Even if IV Corps had switched considerable strength into Honda's area, there still remained ten days in which to bring it back before 28 Army left the Yomas. Only 7 Indian Division was involved, and Honda failed to divert forces from the breakout area. Perhaps his judgment was not what it was. He was a pretty sick man by this time, and his unhappy experiences with the location of his headquarters were being repeated. At first he used a temple in a street on the north side of Bilin which had remained free from air attack. But when the Japanese took it over, they noticed that the local Burmese started to avoid the area, and one day about twenty bombers came over and plastered it, the temple went up in smoke, the staff operations room was destroyed, and some of his staff were killed or wounded. There were other dangers, too. Tsuji was ambushed when driving to an airfield on his way to Southern Army in Saigon, severely wounded, and brought back to

---

[1] *IV Corps Narrative of Operations, May – August 1945*, p. 2

[2] Kirby, *War Against Japan*, V, p. 45

headquarters covered in blood. The road between 33 Army and Burma Area Army in Moulmein ceased to be safe for single vehicles.

Honda knew the date on which Sakurai intended to break out, which makes his own 'X-Day' date of 3 July even more incomprehensible. The poor condition of the wireless sets and batteries in the Yomas meant that the staffs relied more and more on officer patrols. Honda needed to know what Sakurai intended, and sent an officer patrol into the Yomas to locate him. The patrol consisted of Captain Mikuriya and WO Fujimoto, with a few men, who reached 28 Army headquarters after weeks of hard going. Sakurai told him to tell Honda he could use whatever diversion Honda could provide, and intended to break out across the Mandalay Road on 20 July. Honda's orders to start guerrilla forays towards the Pegu road were issued on 25 June after the return of this information, but it is clear that he spent his efforts too early.

Sussing it out

Kitamura was not the only one to risk his way past British and Burmese vigilance during those sodden weeks. 28 Army had a very efficient espionage system and it was put to full use in reconnoitring the paths out of the Yomas, the British Army strengths near proposed crossing-points, and the conditions likely to be encountered either side of the Sittang. Major-General Iwakuro, Sakurai's Chief of Staff, was an old hand at secret warfare. He had once been a party to the Japanese Army's negotiations with Frank Walker, Roosevelt's postmaster-general, in an endeavour to reach the President's ear without the interference either of Japanese diplomats or the State Department. He was also a founder of the Nakano School, the Tokyo institution for training spies and saboteurs, and had for a time headed the Iwakuro Kikan, the successor to the F Kikan (Fujiwara) which liaised with the INA. Both Lieutenant-General Hanaya and his infantry group commander in Arakan, Major-General Sakurai Tokutarō, had experience of intelligence work in China and Manchuria and believed in the use of secret agents.

On their doorstep, in Akyab, they had a very efficient set-up for penetrating into India. The successor to the Iwakuro Kikan was called the Hikari Kikan ('Lightning Organization') and it had a branch in Akyab under Captain Hattori. Hattori was a graduate in political science from Waseda University and a product of the Nakano School as well, and he had a regular service of agents who slipped across the Indian frontier into Chittagong and also into the hill-tracts around Mowdok, where the primitive tribesmen, Mru and Kamui, sent him news of the movements of 82 West African Division down the Kaladan Valley.

501

Hattori also had on his books Japanese civilians (*shokutaku*) with religious connections in the area. One of these was a Buddhist priest of the ultra-nationalist Nichiren sect, Maruyama Gyōryō, who spoke Urdu and recruited agents from the Kaladan Valley to work in Bengal. Maruyama had worked in India before the war and set up a network of Arakanese who went in and out of the war zones with considerable freedom, tipping him off whenever there was a risk of his being taken by the British. They respected his cool courage during air-raids and artillery barrages, when it was his habit to beat his priest's drum and intone aloud the invocation *Namu myōhō renge kyō* ('We pray the Lotus Sutra of the Wonderful Law') which has a mesmeric effect like a rosary when constantly repeated.

Kayabuki was an even odder bird. A Muslim, he was one of the very few Japanese to have performed the *hajj*, the pilgrimage to Mecca, and had been a student at the Al Azhar University in Cairo until the outbreak of war in Europe in 1939. As a *hajji*, Kayabuki enjoyed the same reverence among Arakanese Muslims as Maruyama did among the non-Muslims, and between them they were able to use religious enthusiasm in the service of the Japanese Empire. Kayabuki's agents walked freely from Japanese-held areas into British, and one of them even strolled into a British Army headquarters, looked around, noticed what might be useful to Kayabuki, and strolled out again unhindered.[1]

Another civilian agent, Mizushima, married a Karen wife, who pleaded with him to take her when she realized he was going to leave the Delta with Shinbu Force and not return for a long time – perhaps for ever. It was obvious that even if he disguised himself and continued living with her in Bassein, where life had been very pleasant, sooner or later the British would catch up with him when they returned. The couple were useful to Colonel Saitō in the foothills of the Yomas, watching the assembly areas of the Burma National Army and reporting them. But it was not long before the villagers began to gossip about them, the Burma National Army decided to pull them in for questioning, and one day surrounded a village where they were known to be. Mizushima sensed there were other people there besides the villagers, and when three or four strangers made a move to take him, he pulled out a pistol. He intended to ensure that neither he nor his wife fell into Burmese (and therefore British) hands, pointed the gun at her and fired. As her body slid to the earth he put the next bullet in his own brain.[2]

Besides these, 28 Army had its own organizations specifically trained with the Pegu Yomas in mind, at a time when Sakurai thought it might be a base for guerrilla activity against the British. *Hayate Tai* ('Rushing Wind Unit') is one of these. Set up at 28 Army HQ in Taikkyi in October 1944,

[1] Kayabuki's conversations with the author, Durham 1980.

[2] Allen, *Sittang*, pp. 14–15

its aim at first was the gathering of long-range rather than short-term tactical intelligence. Recruits were selected for their facial resemblance to Burmese, ability to mix with Burmese, and high standard of mental and physical fitness. Four Japanese characters summed up the ideal: *Kōshin menkei* ('A Japanese heart in a Burmese skin') and care was taken to imitate Burmese ways in everything. Burmese curry is usually too hot for Japanese palates accustomed to subtle flavourings of vegetables and fish, but the *Hayate Tai* recruits grew accustomed to it, and to Burmese ways of micturition and defecation. The Japanese army hair-style, head shaved almost bald like a Buddhist priest ('*maru bōzu*' – real bonze-style) was abandoned, and their hair was allowed to grow as long as they liked. Naturally they walked barefoot or wore Burmese sandals, as well as the *engyi* and *longyi* (shirt and sarong-type skirt). Below the *longyi* their legs might be hairier than Burmese legs, so they plucked them out, hair by hair, to achieve the smoothness of the Burmese skin.

Hayate Tai's commanding officer was Major Hachisuka Mitsuo, of 28 Army staff. Small and tanned enough to be taken for a Burmese, he was resilient, humorous, broad-shouldered, muscular and very tough. Over 160 trainees passed through his hands in the few months of the unit's existence. Twenty-one were kept by 28 Army, the rest were sent either to 54 Division, where they formed a unit called *Kusunoki Tai*, after the great hero of Japanese medieval war chronicles, Kusunoki Masashige; or to 55 Division's Shinbu Force where they adopted the name used by the defiant samurai of the Meiji period, *Shinpū Tai* ('The Wind from Heaven Unit').[1] Casualty rates for *Hayate* were high. By the time the unit disbanded in Moulmein when the Japanese surrendered, it was down to 34 men.

Hachisuka ranged far afield, taking some of his men right into the Karenni, close to the border with Thailand, up into the Shan Hills and down along the banks of the Salween. By the time they got back they learned that their parent formation, 28 Army, had already packed its bags and was making its way into the Pegu Yomas. Soon they were being sent into the western foothills and then into the villages along the Mandalay-Rangoon road to report weather conditions and numbers of men and guns.

The British positions were not enclosed in tight wired perimeters and you could walk in and out of the villages without much difficulty. One *Shinpū* group made its way into Penwegon, noticed how strongly held it was, and came back with a report that there were 4000 men in the village with sixty guns and ten tanks, with several hundred Burmese guerrillas in the surrounding area. There was a military police unit there, where Japanese prisoners were held. The *Shinpū* infiltrator moved round

---

[1] The name *Shinpū*, read with another possible pronunciation, is more familiar to British readers as *kamikaze*. The implication is the same.

Penwegon after nightfall and had a whispered conversation with some of the Japanese in the POW cage. He was lucky. A Burmese he spoke to penetrated his disguise and realized he was a Japanese, but did not betray him to the British.

A Kempei (military police) sergeant and private, one of six Kempei groups sent out from 28 Army by Colonel Tsuchiya with instructions to report back by 17 July, reconnoitred the Kun Chaung and the village of Kanyutkwin, just north of Penwegon. They took longer to the swollen Kun Chaung than they anticipated, through waterlogged paddy and tall elephant grass, and went across the road two miles towards the Sittang. They then turned back and as they walked through Kanyutkwin again the private was stopped and questioned by a patrol of Indian troops. He was wearing the usual agent's get-up, Burmese clothes, and a bag containing a pistol and grenades. The Indians were singularly unimpressed by his answers and took him prisoner. The sergeant made himself scarce.[1]

These reconnaissances told Tsuchiya that what he had feared was true: the rains were altering the tracks and *chaungs* almost beyond recognition. The move into the Yomas had been slow. The move out was going to be no picnic either.

Lieutenant Levy produces an ace from his sleeve

Inevitably, for the British after the fall of Rangoon, there was a sense of completion, a feeling that nothing remained but sweeping-up, the aftermath of achievement rather than achievement itself. Yet no one at the time suspected that the war against Japan might not go on for a few more years. There were still campaigns to organize: Operation ZIPPER to retake Malaya and Singapore, the invasion of Siam across the border hills of Burma, and the final defeat of the tens of thousands of Japanese who still remained in south-east Burma and were hoping to turn it into a fortress. Imphal had destroyed 15 Army. Meiktila had destroyed 33 Army. Now the last Army remaining more or less intact, 28 Army, was to be destroyed in the Battle of the Breakout.

The Allied forces which dealt with this were themselves undergoing radical changes in command. Slim left XIV Army for leave in the UK on 9 June, leaving Lieutenant-General Sir Philip Christison to take over temporary command. XIV Army HQ moved to India and a new formation, XII Army, set up its headquarters in Rangoon under Lieutenant-General Sir Montagu Stopford (24 May). Messervy, who was knighted on 5 July, then handed over command of IV Corps to Lieutenant-General F. S. ('Gertie') Tuker, former GOC of 4 Indian Division in North Africa.

[1] Allen, op.cit., pp. 163–4

Cowan, who had been longer in Burma than any other senior officer and had commanded 17 Division since March 1942, left the Division in June 1945, to be succeeded by Major-General Crowther, commanding 89 Brigade of 7 Division. In Crowther's zone of operations, facing 28 Army along the Mandalay-Rangoon road, the commander of 63 Brigade, Burton, was succeeded by Miles Smeeton, who left Probyn's Horse with great regret:

> It was a fine brigade, but I found it very difficult to leave Probyn's. They had been very good to me... it was a time that we were going to remember more than any other time in our lives... you have to accept the fact that, like the captain of a ship, you are now removed from the close fellowship of the ordinary soldier and his officers, which in war-time a colonel with a regiment could still retain. On the whole I think that, after the command of a regiment, being a brigadier is a dreary business.

He may have thought so at the start. But being the brigadier of 63 Brigade in the last days of the war turned out to be quite an exciting business. XII Army took over 7 and 20 Divisions operating in the fast-fading fighting in the Irrawaddy Valley, with 255 and 268 Brigades, and IV Corps, now responsible for the Sittang Valley – 5 and 17 Divisions – and 19 Division attempting to move its brigades out as prongs along the roads to the Salween, 64 Brigade to Kalaw and Taunggyi, and 62 Brigade to Mawchi. Had the war continued, these roads would have offered XII Army a route into Chiengmai in northern Siam. IV Corps also fought the battle of the Sittang Bend which was, like the Breakout, waged under some of the most atrocious conditions of the entire war.

> Probably the monsoon of 1945 was the worst of all. Pouring rain alternated with sweltering oppressive heat whenever a break in the clouds resulted in a few weeks of sunshine.[1]

It was, of course, infinitely worse for the Japanese, as they made their way across endless flooded paddy or up and down the mud slides which the hill tracks became, across streams which in a matter of days had turned into torrents.

> Added to these difficulties were myriads of biting insects, prickly heat and jungle sores which made life about as pleasant as the medieval concept of purgatory. Fighting, though on a small scale, was nearly always bitter since the Japanese fought desperately for

---

[1] Kirby, op.cit., V. 37

survival against opponents determined to ensure that few if any of them would live to fight another day.[1]

Not that, in its later stages, the Breakout was an infantry battle. On the British side, 'it was largely a gunners' battle'.[2] The reason for this was quite simple. As at similar crucial moments in the battles for Imphal-Kohima and Meiktila, captured Japanese documents, translated in the field one or two days after they were taken, revealed the entire movement plans of Shinbu Heidan (and by inference of the rest of 28 Army), its ammunition and health states, its numbers and so on. All that was missing was the actual date of D-Day (X Day in Japanese parlance) and this was supplied, according to the Official History, which does not refer to Signals intercept intelligence,[3] on 18 July when a Japanese officer and a Kempei Tai sergeant acting as liaison officers were captured.

On 2 July 1945, in the eastern foothills of the Pegu Yomas just north of the village of Myogyaung and a few miles south-west of 17 Indian Division headquarters at Penwegon, a patrol of 1/7 Gurkhas (48 Brigade) bumped a small Japanese force and a brisk engagement followed, leaving nineteen Japanese dead.[4] By this time Shinbu Heidan had formed up in the Yomas just west of Myogyaung, and the dead were obviously a patrol sent out to reconnoitre routes to the Mandalay road and the Sittang. The Gurkhas, upon whom had been impressed the value of captured documents, searched the bodies, and picked up the usual souvenirs – photographs, paybooks, an occasional name-seal, watches – and a despatch bag, the leather of which was soaked through from the monsoon rain. In a short time the bag was lying on a table in the village of Penwegon, the headquarters of 17 Indian Division, its contents being gingerly removed and dried.

At division headquarters was a small detachment of translators and interrogators from CSDIC,[5] consisting of Lieutenant Levy and a US Nisei sergeant, Katsu Tabata. Levy had only recently arrived from the CSDIC Mobile Section headquarters in Pegu, and had become reconciled to chatting to the occasional half-dead prisoner and deciphering the unit numbers on paybooks. It looked as if nothing was ever likely to happen on 17 Division's front, and rumour was that the Division was going to move in the direction of Siam, sooner or later. In the meantime, it rained. There had been plenty of excitement for his predecessors, Stanley Charles and

---

[1] ibid.

[2] *IV Corps Narrative of Operations May – August 1945*, 'The Artillery Aspect', p. 3

[3] It was published in 1969, five years before Group-Captain F. W. Winterbotham's *The Ultra Secret* triggered off a series of revelations about cipher intelligence.

[4] Kirby, op.cit., V, p. 44

[5] Combined Services Detailed Interrogation Centre

George Kay, who had handled the prisoners and documents at the battle of Meiktila. With the rueful assurance that no such *trouvailles* were going to come his way, Lt Levy sorted out the papers in the despatch bag. He put the maps on one side. They were very delicate things, made of fine tissue paper glued together to make up a large sheet, which had been placed over a British Army map and pencilled through. The Japanese were short of maps, and used copies of the British maps where they could.

He glanced through the inevitable diary, written in a scribble he knew he would find it hard to decipher, and looked for something more plainly written. There was an operation order among the papers, which he put beside the battered typewriter as he began to type out the translation. Charles had remained behind for a few days to show him the ropes, and looked over his shoulder as he typed. After a few lines, he hissed, 'Christ! this is red-hot!' and dashed off to notify the Divisional staff of the material coming off the machine.

The order bore the signature Nagazawa Kanichi, and was dated 14 June 1945. It had been captured just over a fortnight after being issued, and was the operation order for the entire Shinbu Force (Major-General Nagazawa had suceeded Sakurai Tokutarō as 55 Division Infantry Group commander) to move to the Mandalay Road and the Sittang River. The force was to move between a line drawn through the villages of Kintha, Penwegon and Kyaukkyi to the north and Myogyaung, Mukh Ram, and Hill 852 to the south. Divided into three columns, the Force would advance along precisely defined routes noted by contour heights, *chaung* crossing-points and capital letters of names shown on the accompanying map. The points they would need to attack and hold were described, including the bridge on the railway by the Kun Chaung and – Levy noted with heightened interest – the village of Penwegon itself. The road was to be broken by demolitions in a number of places to prevent reinforcements reaching it. No firing was to be permitted, to prevent confusion among the marching columns: 'cold steel will be the order of the day', wrote Nagazawa. They would avoid familiar routes, and all three columns would make a feint in the direction of Toungoo. No wireless would be used until the Sittang was crossed. Communication would be by visual signals and runners. Rations would include salt and dried and salted fish, which would be carried even if it meant cutting down on rice.

Soldiers of *Shinpū Tai* (Hachisuka's *Hayate Tai* attached to 55 Division) would collect country boats on the banks of the Sittang, and three-to-four-man sampans would be built from bamboo the troops carried with them, with tyres, tubes, drums and tins. They would carry twice the usual amount of ammunition, and no weapons were to be abandoned without the column commander's permission. The order went into even further detail for the veterinary units. Bullocks and horses were to be taken over the Sittang as time permitted. Priority was for casualties and stores.

Each horse had to have with it a spare set of shoes and fifty nails, and a week's fodder on the basis of one kilogram per day.

It was a peach of a document from the intelligence point of view. It opened up the conditions in the Yomas and Japanese intentions with amazing clarity. But then Levy began to build up a more detailed picture from the other documents in the bag. They were scribbled messages to reconnaissance units asking for details of the swampy terrain either side of the Sittang, the width and speed of the river at certain points, the depth of the water, the state of the river banks, whether there was jungle near the villages, the height of miscanthus, whether there were landmarks like a pagoda which could be used, whether the present names corresponded with those on the map, if demolitions were to be carried out on a bridge, whether it was made of wood, iron or concrete, how many bays it had, where the signal lines were, if the roads flooded at the height of the monsoon, whether rice and salt could be got from the villagers on the Shan Plateau, how frequent enemy air activity was in the Sittang Valley, areas where dense mist occurred. Finally, the passwords. These were, rather unoriginally, *Kami*, and its countersign, *Kaze*.

By 7 July the documents had been distributed in translation from 17 Division headquarters. A fresh and more accurate translation was made at headquarters IV Corps in Pegu on 10 July, and the operation order was finally vetted and retranslated at Mountbatten's Rear Headquarters in Delhi on 16 July. A fortnight before Sakurai's 28 Army burst out from the Yomas, its entire course of development along the Shinbu Force front was totally known to the enemy through whose thinly held line it proposed to pass.

Messervy had this mountain of information to weigh up before he left IV Corps' headquarters. Information from the 19 Division sector, where documents and prisoners had begun to reveal similar plans, told him that the main breakout sector for 28 Army Headquarters and 54 Division would be around Pyu. Little if anything was likely to happen south of Nyaunglebin, or north of Toungoo, so he focused his attention on the area between Pyu and Nyaunglebin. 17 Division held a front of seventy-four miles along this part of the main road, and Messervy decided to reinforce one stretch of this, between the Pyu Chaung and the Kun Chaung, where it was expected that Sakurai himself would try to cross. This was to be the preserve of Flewforce, under Brigadier Flewett of 64 Brigade (19 Division) whose headquarters controlled three battalions of infantry, a tank detachment, a detachment of medium guns and two artillery batteries. Neither 20 nor 7 Division were likely to be too hard pressed during the Breakout, it was believed, and three battalions were milked from them as 17 Division reserves.

It is perhaps hard to imagine the effort that was put into slaughtering Sakurai's 28 Army, since the end of the war was only a little more than three weeks away when the Breakout came. But to the officers and men of IV

Corps it was by no means clear that the end was so close, and they saw themselves as facing further formations of Japanese as they moved into Siam or Malaya. It was a matter of simple necessity to kill as many as possible before they escaped the net flung round them in the Pegu Yomas. Messervy intended to do just this. He saw two main areas as killing grounds, one between the Yomas and the Sittang, and one between the mouths of the Sittang and the Salween Rivers. The discovery of the Shinbu operation order almost guaranteed the success of the first killing ground without much infantry intervention. That document turned it into a gunners' battle. The guns could fire along fixed lines at targets set weeks before. The RAF would complete the task (no USAAF planes were involved at this stage of the campaign).

The forces assembled in the Yomas before Sakurai concentrated his men for a single all-out effort had managed to escape into the Sittang Valley in dribs and drabs. 17 Division had allowed them to get across the main road, had them followed to the Sittang, then called up artillery fire and air-strikes to destroy them on the river line. The PBF (Patriotic Burma Forces, as Aung San's Burma National Army was now called by the British) would deal with any survivors as they tried to make their way south along the Sittang east bank or the Shwegyin Chaung. But it was impossible to cover the whole area and small groups got through. Had Sakurai decided to filter his men through in the same way he might have been more successful. But he estimated that the Mandalay-Rangoon Road would not be held as strongly as it was. There would be a battalion at each important spot, he thought, and armoured units were in Pegu. 7 Division was there, 17 Division in Payagyi (he was wrong in this), 19 Division in Toungoo and, he believed, 20 Division (he was wrong in this too). He did not realize the ring of steel around him was so complete, and thought that if a mass breakout occurred, IV Corps would not be able to deal with it at every crossing-point simultaneously. He was not over-sanguine about numbers. But he believed half his force would survive the attempt, which was more than they would do if they stayed and rotted in the Yomas until the end of the monsoon.

Interestingly, Crowther, in his new seat at 17 Division, had begun to think along similar lines. The penny-packet treatment might be all right for small parties. But the captured documents showed that a massive crossing by the whole of 28 Army would take place, and Crowther thought this needed a radical change of plan. 'I consider a better plan', he wrote in his Operation Instruction No. 17 (16 July 1945) 'is to destroy the Jap as he crosses the road or comes within range of the road and then to follow the remnants up to the Sittang.' 17 Division could not be present in force at *every* crossing-point, but strong ambushes could be laid at likely places (the captured maps had shown him these). On the (correct) assumption that the Japanese would move at night, the ambushes would be laid in the hours of darkness. There would be no slow trailing: the Japanese would be fired on the instant they came within range of the guns.[1]

Saitō and Shinbu Force

Colonel Saitō Hiroo had a great contempt for the commander and staff of Burma Area Army. 'They had no battle experience. They made plans and drew up maps and operation orders without any inkling of what conditions in the front were like. Womanisers!' The last comment is rather strange. The Japanese Army was not a puritanical organization. But Saitō was born in Paris and had been brought up in a French mission school in Japan, and four years in the Military Academy in Tokyo and service in Manchuria had not blunted the sharpness of a fine sensibility. Stranger still, he warmed to the toughness of the older members of 55 Division staff. The old bully Hanaya, who used to slap his senior officers in the face in front of their men till the blood ran, greeted him with 'Another bloody greenhorn!' when he reported at Akyab in 1943 to join the 55 Division as a lieutenant-colonel. 'You think you know all the answers. Well, you don't, you have a hell of a lot to learn, and I'm going to see you learn it.' And he admired Colonel (later Major-General) Iwakuro Hideo, the Chief of Staff who was the brains behind 28 Army's intelligence organization and had commanded a Guards tank regiment in the attack on Singapore. He contrasted the atmosphere in 28 Army, where the staff knew the front-line units and worked with them, with Burma Area Army where the staff were totally unaware of the condition of front-line units, of strengths they could put in the field, and of the speed of the British advance. Those two young staff majors, Kōno and Kaetsu, full of self-confidence and professionally capable, but lacking in campaign experience, were working out paper plans without knowing what it was like to command a unit of fighting soldiers. That was why he smiled derisively when he heard that Kimura had talked of crushing the British assault on Central Burma on the banks of the Irrawaddy, that the British would be defeated at Meiktila, and later that they could be held north of Rangoon till the autumn of 1945.

His own Division, 55, had been adversely affected by the move to Pyinmana of the main body of the infantry under Hanaya, to pull Kimura's chestnuts out of the fire (too late). Even so, Saitō knew that if he acted promptly he could ensure the rest of the division was not cut off by the British advance down into the Irrawaddy Delta. He and

---

[1] *Reconquest of Burma*, II, pp. 454–55; Allen, op.cit., Appendix A, pp. 239–46

Nagazawa called at 28 Army Headquarters on 15 April and were given a rundown of the whole Burma situation by Sakurai and Iwakuro.

A few small parties were to be left behind at Gwa, Kyause and Pagoda Point. The rest of the Division, under its code name of Shinbu Force, was to concentrate at Henzada and Bassein ready to move out of the Delta. The plan at first had been to move up towards the oil-fields and join in the battle there, but when the news that Kimura had abandoned Rangoon came through, Shinbu was split into three groups under three colonels, Inoue, Kimura and Murayama, and told to make for the foothills of the Yomas in the area east of Okkan and Letpadan. Headquarters was to leave Henzada on 5 May, but two days beforehand they were notified by 28 Army that the latest defence line had been broken through, so they moved at once and were in their concentration area the next day.

The rest of the Force was to move out of Arakan, across the Irrawaddy and into the Yomas before the British caught them in a pincer movement from Rangoon in the south and Prome in the north. To shield them, Inoue was to hold the area Minhla-Letpadan until 12 May, using an infantry battalion, four 25-pounders and six mountain guns. In the event, Inoue moved into the Yomas too soon, much to General Nagazawa's fury. But the Force got across, and between 23 and 25 May was strung out across the Yomas along a line linking Letpadan and Myogyaung on the eastern slopes.

Saitō was relieved to have got rid of the women. Unlike some of the other breakout units, which had comfort girls escaping with them, Saitō had the foresight to use the boats still in the Delta to get them out by sea. Captain Asanaga, a veteran of the Bias Bay and Java battles, who had spent the summer of 1943 fighting British gunboats on the Mayu River, was put in charge of forty motor-boats run by crews taken from 4 Shipping Engineer Regiment. Saitō had casualties loaded into them, and eighty comfort girls, who then ran the gauntlet across the Gulf of Martaban to Moulmein, ten days after Rangoon had fallen into British hands. The Force wireless operators worked in shifts listening for the signal they had arrived – the boats themselves were to keep wireless silence for forty-eight hours. All the boats reached safety, though some of them ended up at Ye, about 180 miles south of Moulmein. Other comfort girls were not so lucky. Nor were the Japanese nurses, who stuck with 28 Army to the bitter end.

Saitō paid a visit to 28 Army headquarters on 3 June, and reported to Nagazawa on his return that Sakurai wanted him to carry out some minor guerrilla activity in the area Letpadan-Tharrawaddy-Hmawbi. 'Since it doesn't seem to be known yet whether the initial breakout will be in the early part of July or the middle, we will have to do something about our rations. Somehow or other we will have to lay in stocks of food for a month.'[1]

[1] Allen, op.cit., p. 151

Shinbu Force was to concentrate at Mayan, about twenty miles west of the Rangoon road and railway which ran parallel to the eastern foothills of the Yomas. If possible, they were to slip through British positions. If not, they would fight their way through, though Saitō was unsure how reliable a column commander like Inoue was without adequate field experience of battle. Saitō carried out buoyancy tests with bamboo on the Pegu River, as Okamura was doing for 28 Army in the *chaungs* of the Yomas. He used Kitamura, the Olympic champion, to reconnoitre rivers, and his own ingenuity to keep up morale. He devised Japanese names for the collections of *bashas* that passed for villages in the Yomas, so that the allusion might strike a spark of hope in the sodden soldiers who were making for them (on the same principle as Wingate's 'White City', 'Piccadilly', and 'Aberdeen'). Seventeen miles east of Letpadan was Asahi ('Rising Sun') village, a track junction five miles to its south-east was Hikari ('Light') village, and two spots in the western foothills were Akatsuki ('Dawn') and Tsukimi ('Moon-viewing'). Towns in the prefectures of Shikoku, the division's home base, gave their names to other villages – Matsuyama, Yoshino, Kōchi, Kotohira. Then there were names with deeper allusions: a village was called Misogi, the Japanese term for ritual purification, an ablution linked with the notion of praying to the gods for a state of great beauty and strength, as if the men's bodies would be washed free of all evil by plunging into a cascade in the depths of the mountains. In this village, Saitō's men wrote their wills. Then came Shinpei village. Compounded of Shin ('god') and hei ('soldier'), the name implied that after purification the soldier was nearer to God, transcending the issue of life and death. Lastly, came Point 2256 which was called Kachidoki Village. Kachidoki is a Japanese word for 'battle-cry', and the sequence was that at this point the purified soldier, all unworthy thoughts shed, was now on the brink of success. Kachidoki was where Shinbu Force finally concentrated before it broke out of the Yomas. Other names were used for simple deception purposes. The Mandalay Road became Hakone Yama, one of Japan's tourist attractions, the Sittang was called the Japan Alps, and the track east from it became Japan's fabled highway, the Tōkaidō.

On 26 June 1945, Saitō attended an Army conference at headquarters in 'Katori Village'. A mere name in the depths of the forest, Sakurai had moved here to be out of reach of British guns, but it was a devil to find, and the representatives from 105 Independent Mixed Brigade, Matsui's force of odds-and-sods in flight from Rangoon, which would break out on the southernmost fringe of 28 Army, and from 54 Division, took a week to reach it. 54 Division had broken off the fighting at Paukkaung on 17 June, and withdrawn further into the hills. Its commander, Miyazaki, told the staff officer who would represent him at the conference, Major Murata, that he thought the breakout should be at the end of July, or even later. He also did not want to break out *south* of Toungoo. He thought the Sittang would be wider, and they would have to abandon any guns larger than battalion guns, and simply get the men across. If they make us go south of Toungoo, he said, we'll lose two-thirds or more of our men.

28 Army staff listened to Murata's points, but without enthusiasm. They did not want to change either routes or timing. They did not consider that the abandonment of artillery mattered much at this stage. It was never hoped to bring guns of any size across the Mandalay Road to the Sittang, though, incredibly, some Japanese gunners had manhandled their pieces into the Yomas. 54 Division had abandoned its 75s by the time it got to the eastern side of the Yomas, and was finding communication difficult. RAF planes had strafed the divisional signals unit north of Thayetmyo on 29 April and smashed its sets to pieces. Miyazaki was not insensible of Iwakuro's main case: the point was to get the *men* across. Miyazaki had sworn to retrieve his men from Arakan across the Irrawaddy without losing a single one of them, and he had already lost heavily at Kama.

He was also haunted by what had happened earlier in 1945 to his 121 Regiment on Ramree Island. Nagazawa was then its regimental commander – he always irritated Saitō by comparing 55 Division unfavourably to 54 even after he had been appointed to command 55 Division Infantry Group – and the order to the garrison to leave Ramree had been postponed too long. It was cut to pieces by the British. 'It'll be a repeat performance of Ramree Island', Miyazaki told Murata. 'We'll lose most of our men.' He based this judgment on what he was sure the banks of the Sittang would be like when they were reached. 'How does he know this?' was the natural question put to Murata by Iwakuro, Sakurai's Chief of Staff. All Murata could lamely answer was that the judgment was based on a single officer reconnaissance report. He was a Kempei captain, and he had been over the whole area round Toungoo, and reported on his return that the Sittang was already flowing fast and was 220 yards across. 'Our information is different', answered Iwakuro, 'and anyway we need 54 Division as a shield for the left flank of the main body of 28 Army.'[1]

Murata was not the only one to raise objections. When the date scheduled as X-Day was given as 20 July, many formations thought it optimistically early, but accepted it. Saitō did not. 'If that is Army's order, we will carry it out,' he said. 'But if possible I would like the date to be 23 July.' Sakurai sympathized with this, surprisingly enough since he had already notified Honda of the date, and the information was in Honda's hands by liaison officer, as we have seen, the day the Pegu Yomas conference opened. Should we not re-study the date, he queried? Okamura chipped in, much to Saitō's annoyance. Saitō remembered he had been an instructor at the Military Academy, but doubted if he had had much front-line experience. 'Everything has been decided', said Okamura. 'Let's keep

[1] ibid., p. 76–7

it as the 20th, it's a Friday.' The weak flippancy seemed out of place to Saitō. 28 Army staff thought it over and gave their answer the following day. X-Day would be 20 July.

It was not mere stubborness which made Iwakuro want to adhere to his dates and routes in spite of Miyazaki's objections. He and Sakurai both knew that when the chance of a breakout in June had been lost (and the slow concentration of forces in the Yomas made that certain) then the crossing would have to be made in the worst of the monsoon. South of Toungoo, it was quite true that both banks would be a swamp, the river would be much wider, the current much faster. But because of this, the enemy's control would be less tight: they would think the conditions impossible and not be able to move themselves. And although movement would be difficult across swampy terrain, enemy armour would be absolutely prevented from following up their tracks.[1]

Saitō had his own view of 28 Army's desire to see the Sittang breakout operation speedily done with. He had a great respect for Sakurai, who was the general who had captured Rangoon in the first place. When the British retook it, Sakurai knew how stunned Terauchi at Southern Army must have been. He knew he could not retake it, but he wanted his Army to be active in the Tenasserim operations late in 1945, to maintain the bastion that Terauchi wanted South-East Burma to become. He was therefore, Saitō was sure, acting rather with Southern Army in Saigon in mind, not Kimura in Moulmein. He could understand this. But he could have done with those extra three days. So could Miyazaki. And he had to knuckle under to the refusal to change routes. Miyazaki listened to Murata's report on his return. 'We have no choice, then,' he said. 'We must move in accordance with the Army plan. Since they make it a matter of principle to hold on to the idea of moving south of Toungoo, we shall have to make our divisional plan on that basis.'[2] But it was with a heavy heart and a brooding conviction that he was going to lose a lot of men.

Sakurai makes for home

Communications and hunger were Sakurai's greatest anxieties in the Pegu Yomas. Disease, in two frightening forms, was added later. First, he had to get his units under command. The baby-faced staff captain Tsukamoto was sent to liaise with Miyazaki, the commander of 54 Division, who in turn had sent a liaison officer to find 28 Army HQ. Tsukamoto reported on 18 June that he had found Miyazaki, to Sakurai's great relief: 54 Division was his largest force, around 9000 men. Miyazaki, the skilful commander of

[1] Sakurai, 'Biruma sensen: teki-chū toppa', *Bungei Shunjū*, Nov. 1955, p. 64

[2] Allen, op.cit., p. 78

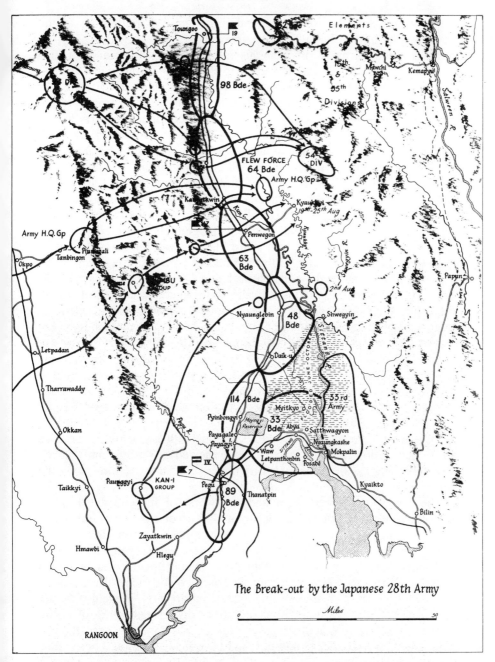

The Break-out by the Japanese 28th Army

the rearguard in 31 Division's retreat from Kohima, led his men out of Arakan in two groups, one across the An Pass, the other from Taungup, leaving the field clear for Christison's XV Corps to move in. Meanwhile his

515

infantry group, under Major-General Koba, moved south from Mount Popa to join him as he crossed the Irrawaddy.

Gracey cut Miyazaki off from his intended crossing-point by taking Allanmyo on 20 April, and moved on to Prome on 3 May, while Evans's 7 Division closed the gap east of the river. In ten days, as Miyazaki put his men across the Irrawaddy at Kama, he lost most of his transport and artillery, and 1400 men were killed. 7 Division continued to harry him as he moved into the western foothills of the Yomas at Paukkaung, by which time his men were living on unpolished rice, salt and water. Even in these conditions, Miyazaki struck back. Three guns of his Mountain Gun Battalion found a British artillery unit, five guns strong, at Yebyu, halfway between Prome·and Paukkaung, on 6 June. The Japanese guns opened fire at once over a range of more than 6000 yards and scored a bullseye with their first round. They hit the gunners' ammunition dump, there was a huge explosion, and a fire blazed away for days.

It was a short-lived triumph. In the ranks of 54 Division, cholera broke out, one of the first to show symptoms being Colonel Murayama, CO 154 Infantry Regiment. The monsoon rains fell in a continuous sheet, foraging came to an end, and the virulent cholera began to spread, claiming hundreds of victims, including Colonel Takeda, in command of 153 Infantry Regiment; by a quirk of fate Murayama survived. Cholera was bad enough. But then plague descended on the soaking, starving Japanese. Miyazaki could not have anticipated this, because although plague spreads with relatively high humidity, it does not occur in moving camps, and 54 Division had been on the move since mid-April. On 12 June Miyazaki ordered his division to plunge deeper into the hills. In theory, they were to take a month's rations with them, but in practice their rice ration had dwindled, they gnawed at yams, and picked fragments of meat from the maggotty bones of dead cattle lying along the tracks.

The few women with them had the worst of it. Sergeant Kagehi, patrolling into the Sittang Valley for suitable river crossing-points, came across a shack with the grandiose name 'Kempei Garrison Unit' – a hut used by military policemen at some time. There were seven women in it, and when Kagehi and his five-man patrol came up the women joined their hands together in supplication and begged for food. 'Rice, please, give us a little rice!' 'I suppose they were comfort girls,' Kagehi reflected later, 'but neither we nor they could strike up a single spark of desire between us. We had about twelve pints of rice, and we gave them a cupful each in both hands, and it would have made you weep to see how overjoyed they were.'[1]

---

[1] *Uzumaku Sittan* (The swirling Sittang), History of 121 Infantry Regiment, 54 Division, Nihonkai Shimbunsha, Tottori, 1969, pp. 238–40

Miyazaki reached his assembly-point for the breakout on 17 July. The outlook was grim. His main body was to cross near Pyu, where around 600 British troops were waiting for him, and every exit from the Yomas was watched by Burmese guerillas. The water was chest-high east of the Mandalay-Rangoon road, there was no food in the villages, and no boats or rafts at the Sittang. In a desperate attempt to block 19 Indian Division's probing towards them down the road from Toungoo, Koba's engineers and 154 Infantry Regiment destroyed the Kabaung Chaung bridge south of the town. To little purpose. As 54 Division crossed the flooded paddyfields, which British guns turned into an inferno of mud and shrapnel, the men broke column and began to die by the thousand. When Miyazaki came out of the Yomas, he had just over 9000 men. By the time he concentrated in Tenasserim after the breakout, in early August, he could muster less than 4000.

Shinbu Force of 55 Division was in no better condition. As they came out of the Yomas on X-Day, 20 July, the infantry and mountain artillery which made up the left column began to pile up in the darkness just behind Force HQ, and streamed on, delaying the HQ's advance by two hours. As they moved forward at last, they heard the sounds of intense heavy and light machine-gun fire from Penwegon. It was Lt Kuroda desperately hurling himself against 17 Division HQ. Soon the waterlogged ground became a sea of mud, the water came up to their thighs, and in some places they had to cross *chaungs* in spate. The Kun Chaung was ferocious, and the men were horrified to see corpses bobbing along towards them from further upstream. Saitō saw two of his men swept away by whirlpools.

From village to village they went, trying to avoid the British guns, which, of course, knew every path the Japanese were going to take and had registered on them days before. On 27 July, after marching by compass through the night, Saitō came to a point on the track where the water was knee-high. The Machine-Gun Section commander, 2/Lt. Yamaguchi, burst out, 'I recognize that tree! The track goes south about five hundred yards from here, and there's a bullock-cart trail I've been along before. Wettu (the village they were making for) is about a mile further on, and the water goes no higher than this.' They went no more than 200 yards when the water came up to their chests. It was two days since Yamaguchi had reconnoitred this stretch of track and it showed Saitō how impossible it was to rely even on so recent reconnaissance of the waterlogged terrain up to the Sittang. He didn't want to lose his men in the water and ordered them back.

The next day, he was upbraided by Nagazawa. By 28 July the Force Commander was at the end of his tether. He shouted at Saitō that he had no confidence in him, that his control of the operation was useless. He's reflecting the mood of the men, Saitō thought, with uncanny precision. They had begun to shed heavier bits of equipment, one or two men kept bursting into wild song and would break away from the column, to wander crazily back along the path.

Not that Saitō himself was any too sure of his own sanity by this time. He had the eerie sensation of watching himself going mad. Luckily for him, he was still lucid enough to realize what was happening, and relaxed his tension by resting for three hours in the branches of a tree. It was 7 August before he reached Yele, where he was to cross the Sittang. They were attacked by Burmese guerrillas the next day, and Saitō, after a brisk exchange of gunfire, waited for dusk before chancing it. About fifty men crossed on 9 August, another 300 on the 10th, to the accompaniment of British shelling – from Penwegon, Saitō judged. The river crossing itself took them half an hour.

On the opposite bank, contact was made sporadically with other units of Shinbu Force as they made their way south from Kyaukkyi to Shwegyin, where the path was strewn with the dead and dying. British planes began to drop leaflets telling them Japan had agreed to an armistice. Nagazawa did not disbelieve this. If it were true, he wanted to get his men into Tenasserim as fast as possible, out of the lower Sittang Valley. It was the last place he wanted to be forced to linger in, if a ceasefire came. Saitō thought of the men they had passed on the way, the pathos and grief of defeat mingling with the thought of their futile sacrifice, dying beside a forsaken track in the Burmese jungle in the first few days of peace.

The thought of the dead oppressed him. 55 Division had left 3000 behind in Arakan, who had fallen in the sure belief Japan would win. Over 5000 had died round him in those terrible days in the water on the approach to the Sittang, many of them retaining, incredibly, the discipline of politeness which Japanese life demands, not complaining about the dreadful march, but whispering 'Thank you for helping me' as they slid into the last darkness.

The news that Japan might surrender would, under normal circumstances, have been treated as derisory propaganda. But the Commander-in-Chief, Lieutenant-General Sakurai himself, knew that something was afoot, even when he was planning the details of the breakout in the Pegu Yomas. Wireless communication with other units had become a near-impossibility. But 28 Army headquarters still had a working short-wave set, captured from the British. An important part of the daily routine in Katori Village, on the banks of the Zamayi Chaung, was to listen to this set and glean information from it about the enemy's condition. Not only did it help in planning, it gave Sakurai a glimpse into the outside world which placed an even greater burden on his shoulders. After they had been about a month in the hills, about the beginning of June, it was mentioned that Germany had surrendered. This had happened on 8 May, so it was news three weeks old. All-India Radio, from Delhi, also broadcast that a group of Japanese industrialists had gone to the United States to sue for peace.

He didn't dismiss it, but kept it to himself.[1] But it made it no easier to plan an operation over the next month which might well result in the deaths of half his men. Deaths which some of them had begun to anticipate, he realized, as he listened with a heavy heart to the sounds of explosions in the hills: some seriously wounded man realizing he could not submit his comrades to the intolerable burden of carrying him any further, or unable to bear the anguish of jolting his sick body through the mud until the pain became more than the mind could bear. Easier to clutch a hand-grenade to the retching stomach.

Sakurai's party was not ambushed as it came out of the Yomas, bursting across the darkness of the Mandalay Road like waves breaking, though Tsuchiya was sure they had been spotted when he saw a green signal light curve up into the sky high above the road. Then Fukutomi came up to him – 'They don't seem to have spotted us!' No, they were over smoothly enough, by 3 am on 24 July. Sakurai was less pleased than Tsuchiya. He had sensed the vanguard coming to a halt before it reached the road, and start to get bogged down, and the units coming up from behind kept moving forward until there was confusion everywhere, and screams and cries of distress from the women who, unthinkably, were still struggling along with the column. 'They're more like a mob than an army', Sakurai thought, and his point was proved when the headquarters group broke its line of march in a field of sugar-cane. Once the men found out what it was, they began to break it off and chew it – not just men, officers too. Sakurai understood why. They had been living on a few handfuls of rice and a pinch of salt for days on end – here suddenly was sweetness, and they fell upon it. He let them go on for a few minutes, then told the commanders to break it up and continue the march.

Just in time. Shells suddenly began to pour in on the column from five miles away, scattering the men in all directions. The Chief of Staff, Iwakuro, who had been conducting the march, was almost frantic with despair, but order was restored, after a time, and with difficulty. It was too late for Iwakuro, though. The strain proved too much for him. He had been moving for hours up and down the broken units of the column, yelling himself hoarse to keep the men together. It was evident he was on the verge of collapse, and his officers tried to calm him down. It was left to Fukutomi, a big, burly figure, to restrain him physically before he collapsed, but Iwakuro resisted what were well-meant attempts and pushed Fukutomi aside. Fukutomi pinioned him in a wrestler's hold, but with an access of strength – he was incubating a fever, that was obvious – Iwakuro broke away and hurled Fukutomi on his back, pressing him down into the trodden mud. The other officers and men gawped at the spectacle of two senior staff officers mixing it in this way, but it threatened to go too far,

---

[1] Sakurai; 'Biruma sensen: teki-chū toppa', p. 64

and some of them pulled Iwakuro off Fukutomi. Yano, the medical officer, quickly gave him a morphine injection, and before long he nodded off into sleep. Not only the tension of responsibility, but a violent bout of malaria, put him out of action for the next twenty-four hours.

By 26 July, 28 Army headquarters group was at Kyiyo, about two-thirds of the way to the Sittang. Here Tsuchiya received the news that Sugimoto, the colonel commanding 55 Cavalry Regiment, which acted as the Army vanguard, had been killed. And Okamura, the engineer colonel, returned from a reconnaissance to say that if 28 Army crossed where they originally intended, they would be trapped by ambushes on the river bank. They made for Kyauksang, north-east of Kyiyo, as a result, but not quickly enough. British artillery had their range and expected them to be there and before they left they had lost six killed and twenty wounded.

In the small hours of 28 July, Sakurai stood with Tsuchiya on the banks of the Sittang. Tsuchiya had marched the last few days in agony. His feet had begun to swell, sand had filtered into his boots and was bringing up great red blisters on his skin. To complete the picture, leeches as big as his thumb had clamped themselves to him.

Sakurai looked down at the strong, turbulent waters rushing past in the darkness. He had feelings no one else could share at this moment. This was the same river on which he had defeated the British so signally three-and-a-half years before. He had brought his men across it in a triumphant march, which led them to the capital of Burma, then up into the central plains. Now all that achievement was in ruins. The armies he had defeated had come back, and were now hunting *him*. He remembered what a pleasant river the Sittang could be in the dry season, with the sun on it, moving idly through the green forests – but now! As the waters thundered by he saw here and there blacker spots in the dark, not logs or tree-trunks but men. Screaming men. '*Tsuwamono da! Tasukete kure!*' [54 Division here! Help!] *Tasukete kure! Oretachi wo misuteru ki ka!*' [Help, for God's sake, don't let us go!]. But Sakurai was powerless to help. In the past, the enemy had been men, guns, planes. They had been through all that. Now the place of the guns and planes had been taken by this swirling, liquid monster into whose arms his men had to risk themselves to be free.

His staff intended to see the general safe across. Tsuchiya and Yamaguchi went up and down the bank looking for suitable spots to put the rafts down, Yamaguchi sprinting on ahead, stripped down to loin-cloth and sword. Sakurai judged the river to be 300 yards across. So much for maps. Its dry season width was 80–150 yards, and there were even fordable points. The monsoon made the river unrecognizable.

The first crossing party left at 8 pm on 27 July. Officers and men flung themselves and their rafts into the stream, and tried to get themselves over against the strengths of the current. Some were brought back to the bank two or three times.

'I crossed at 2 am on 28 July', Sakurai recalls, 'in a country boat, and landed on the east bank of the Sittang. When I looked back, I could see that some of my men had made it, but others had been swallowed up by the river, and their tired bodies were whipped away downstream. I kept praying and praying for the gods and the Buddhas to protect us.'[1]

Unusually, for that period of the monsoon, the next day was bright and clear. There was no cloud, for quite some time. The headquarters group assembled on the east bank. They were a motley lot. Iwakuro had shared the General's country boat, which had then gone back and forth to pick up the others, including comfort girls and officers' mess waitresses. The poor girls' femininity was not much in evidence. They had all cut their hair short, to look like the men, and were dressed in baggy army uniforms, soaked and mudstained after the days of tramping through the ricefields and swamps.

The next day it rained, until the sky was barely visible. It did not seem to hamper the RAF. Sakurai could hear them overhead, and headquarters remained hidden in the high reeds until night came. They had thirteen miles to go before they reached the foothills of the Shan plateau, and Tsuchiya knew what the Very lights meant as they began to march off. The British obviously had a network of agents in every village along the Sittang, and the guns began to range along the line of march of headquarters column. In spite of this, the tension of the river crossing had relaxed, and those men who had been buoyed up by it began to go sick and to beg to be left behind in the villages. Tsuchiya knew that was as good as being left behind to die.

28 Army and its subordinate formations took three weeks to cover the fifty miles of its southward trek. Sakurai's horse had drowned in the Sittang, and he made the journey on the back of an ox. 53 Division, through whose territory they were passing, did its best to welcome them. They even set up a stall at Kunzeik where *shiruko*, the Japanese delicacy of red-bean soup with rice-cake, was offered to them. Village stocks of rice were exhausted, of course, or at any rate the Burmese were behaving as if they were. Unless, that is, the Japanese had one commodity the Burmese wanted perhaps more than any other: soap. The Burmese are a clean people who bathe frequently, but water alone had not prevented many of the people in the villages across the Sittang being covered in scabies from lack of soap. Those Japanese who had soap in their packs, as some did, found that a tablet could become the currency of life.

Honda had sent one of his staff, Lieutenant-Colonel Tanaka, to go forward and wait for the 28 Army headquarters group. 33 Army itself had retreated along this path beside the Sittang only a few weeks before, it seemed to Tanaka, but you would hardly think it was the same land, or the

[1] Sakurai, op.cit., p. 67

521

same river. He was waiting at the Shwegyin Chaung from 20 July, and saw that it, too, had changed from being a tranquil country stream and had become a ruthless killer like the Sittang itself. Tanaka set to and built himself a *basha* on the edge of the track from Kyaukkyi, and sat down to wait.

The dead came first. They moved faster than the living, who were on foot. The dead came down with the current, hundreds of them, a whole multitude of soldiers borne seawards. Then, in little tattered groups, Sakurai's men began to appear, from the beginning of August. Tanaka was heartened beyond belief when Yamaguchi put in an appearance. He had not bothered to find a uniform again after crossing the river, and looked exactly as he had the night he and Tsuchiya had searched for a country boat to carry their commander across. Now there he was on the opposite bank of the *chaung*, sword swinging from his naked hips, clothed in his *fundoshi* (loincloth) and nothing else. Tanaka gave a shout, Yamaguchi waved to him, plunged straight into the Shwegyin Chaung and swam across. He looked to Tanaka exactly as he had to Tsuchiya, as he rose, dripping, from the waters of the *chaung*: a medieval warrior, a real man, a soldier from the time of the civil wars. Major Yamaguchi was a staff officer of a modern army. But underneath, there was the samurai.

The men who had survived the great killing followed Yamaguchi and Tsuchiya down through the stretch of land between the Shwegyin and the Madama Chaungs, marked on British maps as 'dense mixed forests'. Tanaka thought he had already seen the extremes of suffering in what was left of 53 Division, but nothing like these tatterdemalions with rotting feet, calves swollen to elephantine size with beri-beri, eyes burning with fever, thighs dripping with the excrement of dysentery – some of them were still carrying rifles, and ammunition hung from their belts. The thought of being near the end, of course, spurred them on. The alternative was to become like those white bones by the side of the path, with flies and bluebottles by the thousand swarming over them, and the vultures hovering over the fields, waiting to complete the task. Some of them had been wrapped in Rising Sun flags, as a last tribute. But many simply lay there in putrefying uniforms, in such numbers that it was intolerable to go into the edge of the forest to rest or eat.

Further north, Koba knew how important it was to keep his men moving. He picked for himself a switch of green bamboo, and when he saw a man dropping out of the march he moved up to him and thrashed him with the switch, bellowing *Aruke! Aruke!* ['Keep moving! Keep moving!']. His switch soon resembled a Japanese tea-whisk, or shaving-brush, but there was plenty more bamboo where that came from, and he kept renewing his stock as his men blundered past.

On 15 August, the day the Emperor of Japan announced to an appalled and barely comprehending people that the war was over, and they would have to 'endure the unendurable', Sakurai came into the headquarters of 53

Division at Shanywa. Hayashi, the 53 Division commander, was there to greet him. So, too, were Major-General Ichida, Vice-Chief of Staff, Burma Area Army, and Honda's Chief of Staff, Major-General Sawamoto. The soldiers had rigged up a wooden archway painted with the characters *Saku Kangei* ('Welcome 28 Army'). Sakurai walked through the arch. He was handed telegrams from Field-Marshal Terauchi in Saigon, and from Kimura in Moulmein, speaking of the success of the breakout operation. He gave them a brief glance, noted the fulsome congratulations, and folded them away. In the afternoon came the news of the Imperial Rescript bringing the war to an end.

It did not end for Sakurai. It could not end, until he had gathered his men into one Army again, in Tenasserim. So he pressed on south, when every fibre of his being was crying out for rest. The guns no longer sounded, and the rains were slackening off. The news that the war was over filtered through to the Burmese, too, and the villagers now came out to watch the Japanese go by. Sakurai reached Martaban, and crossed over to Moulmein on 18 August. A little group awaited him on the jetty. Tsuchiya was with him. Night had already fallen, but they could make out the figures in the group. One was Ashikawa, a senior staff officer from Burma Area Army. Another was General Kimura himself – a full general, now. In the rigidly hierarchical Japanese seniority system, he had been promoted to general in due course. By a strange coincidence, his promotion had come through five days after he had abandoned Rangoon to the British. Sakurai walked straight up to him, without ceremony, and offered a firm hand-clasp. Kimura put his arm round Sakurai's shoulders. His voice was mild and quiet. '*Nagai aida, kurō wo kakete sumanakatta.*' [It's been a long time. It's been very tough. I'm sorry.'] The two generals looked at each other in the darkness. Tsuchiya saw a strange gleam in Sakurai's eyes.[1]

Lieutenant-General Francis Tuker, in command of IV Corps during Messervy's absence, could afford to be complacent over his victory. 'Admiral Mountbatten wrote to me shortly afterwards,' he noted, 'to thank me for fighting what he described as the most successful battle of the Burma campaign. I cannot say I found the battle a difficult one; far more easy than any I had had hitherto in this war.'[2] Naturally enough: his Intelligence had given him the entire picture on a plate, and his guns and the river had done the work for him. It was, perhaps, 17 Indian Division which could feel a certain sense of fitting completion at the end of the

[1] Allen, op.cit., p. 114; Tsuchiya, 'Biruma hōmengun no higeki' (The tragedy of the Japanese Army in Burma), *Nihon Shūhō*, No. 441, April, 1958, p. 41

[2] Tuker, Personal Papers, 3 pp TS on operations with IV Corps, Archives, Imperial War Museum.

battle. In 1942, they had been drummed out of Burma by 33 and 55 Divisions of the Japanese Army, and 18 Division had helped to complete the conquest of Burma as the Black Cats retreated back into India. Since then, they had met 33 Division again at Tiddim and Bishenpur, beaten them, and driven them from Imphal. They had encountered 18 Division at Meiktila and beaten them, too. Now, as the campaign drew to a close, they had slaughtered 55 Division at the very same river on whose banks they themselves had been cut in two. They had been cheated of the recapture of Rangoon. But there was a certain geometrical tidiness as they concluded, with this last throw, their hat-trick against the Japanese Army.[1]

The odyssey of Tsutsumi Shinzō

The group which should have suffered most in Operation MAI was Kan-i Group, the Rangoon Defence Force and its assorted hangers-on. It was the most recent formation, the least 'military' of all, since it included men who only a few weeks before had been civilians, shopkeepers, clerks, businessmen and teachers in Japanese concerns in Rangoon. Its name was far more imposing than its reality : the first character, *kan*, stands for 'bold', 'adventurous', the second, *i*, for 'power' and 'authority', all qualities singularly lacking in the motley ragbag of units commanded by Major-General Matsui. Admittedly there were trained troops at the core of the brigade, naval garrison units and anti-aircraft batteries. But Kan-i was hardly the kind of force Matsui had become used to commanding. He had been regimental commander of 113 Infantry Regiment of 56 Division and had seen some hard fighting in North Burma before being promoted. In the upshot, Kan-i Force performed quite creditably. Against expectation, the percentage of its losses was slightly lower than that of the major units taking part in the breakout. And though there were some spectacular massacres, over 2000 of Matsui's men (and women) survived, of an original strength of 4173.

They were not so badly off for rations, for one thing. Many of them were weak, physically in bad shape and, on average, older than the rest of 28 Army and so more vulnerable to the horrors of the monsoon and the maladies of a Burmese summer. But they had rice, salt and meat in the shape of the bullocks which drew the ration-carts and could be slaughtered when the bulk of the rice they were pulling had diminished. On the other hand, the helter-skelter way in which they left Rangoon meant that medical supplies had been neglected. And they found the new discipline harsh. Those who could not keep up with the column were beaten and made to walk on ahead to prevent them becoming stragglers. The hardships once

---

[1] Correspondence with S. T. Charles.

they were across the Mandalay Road were the worst. Circumstances were so appalling, just at the time they thought they were nearing their destination, that the shock was fatal. So many of them were above military age, unused to physical exertion, and simply succumbed.

The most interesting of the forces which made up Kan-i Force is perhaps 13 Naval Guard Force, one of the two naval units made up from the port and shore establishments of the Imperial Japanese Navy in Burma. They broke out last of all, wanting to keep their moves independent of the Army, and found their path blocked everywhere by the enemy in a flooded countryside where it was almost impossible to move.

Slim describes their predicament:

> They amounted to about twelve hundred men in all and, strangely enough, chose to make their attempt last and alone on the 31st July. As they struggled across the road, losing heavily in the process, all our forces within reach were turned upon them. Rapidly growing fewer, as our troops and artillery took toll, they approached the Sittang, only to find their way blocked by one of our battalions and to be caught between it and another pursuing one... It took nearly a week for an Indian and Gurkha battalion to close in on the sailors, but of the four hundred to which they were now reduced... only three escaped.

That is why Japanese maps of the breakout all show blue lines leading from the Yomas tracing the escape paths of 54 Division, 28 Army, 55 Division and Kan-i Force, reading from north to south, then arching down into Tenasserim. Only one line moves from the south of the Yomas, crosses the road, then comes to a full stop between the road and the Sittang, with two Japanese characters beside it, reading *Zenmetsu*: 'wiped out', 'annihilated'.

The overall commander of naval units in Burma was Rear-Admiral Tanaka Raizō, the hero of the supply-runs to Guadalcanal, who had been relegated to this backwater employment because he had talked back to the Naval High Command in Tokyo. He had been placed under Burma Area Army on 18 February 1945, and left by car for Moulmein when Rangoon was evacuated in April. Some of his sailors, and civilians, left by minesweeper and motor-boat, but the main body of 13 Naval Guard Unit was stationed in the Irrawaddy Delta, at Myaungmya, and it seemed logical to place them under the man responsible for the defence of Arakan, Sakurai and his 28 Army. So Captain Fukami and his 600 men moved into the Pegu Yomas when 28 Army did, after sending off a couple of hundred men with the torpedo-boats and landing-craft.

The rest were in the foothills of the Yomas on 17 May and plunged into the dense jungle. By 19 May they had reached a village called Sin-Te-Sakan, a tiny spot, a cluster of bamboo huts roofed with banana leaves. They were dying of thirst and made at once for the clear stream which ran through the village. They flung themselves on it and drank without a pause, then filled their water bottles. The delicious cool water refreshed them, and they marched on, feeling as if their bodies were renewed.

They moved up the track. Higher up, about 300 yards further on, they saw something which churned their innards. A dead horse lay in the stream, half of its body submerged in the water. Its belly was distended to twice its normal size, and from its broken neck and burst rump white maggots came crawling out. Filthy black flies swarmed where the flesh had burst. It lay in the clear water they had just drunk with such delight.

They came across an Army unit under Major Nishiseko, who told them Shinbu Force headquarters was at 'Otome Village' north of where they were that day, 20 May: Hill 1581, a peak called Aukchin Taung. 'Otome' was a Japanese girl's name, not a Burmese name, and was obviously a codeword. Tsutsumi had the feeling there was something strange about some of the troops with Nishiseko, who was in a hurry to be off. Their faces seemed whiter than usual, and – yes, those bird-like voices! They were women, all of them! With their shaven heads and baggy uniforms he had taken them for raw recruits. But they were women all right. Each had a long pole with a basket suspended at either end. They carried food in the baskets, all, that is, except one of them who was carrying a baby in hers. She had covered the basket in banana leaves to shield it from the rain. The women made off, following Nishiseko, up and down the slippery mountain tracks, until they were out of sight.[1]

Tsutsumi's men moved north, from Hill 1581 to Hill 1220, then to the upper reaches of the Pegu River, still only waist-high and sixty yards wide. They crossed easily, but were stymied for a while by the Dawe Chaung, its tributary, which was only half the width but deep and fast-flowing. The sailors showed their ingenuity here. They collected rattan from the jungle, and made a rope long enough to pass to the opposite bank. Then they built a raft from bamboo poles lashed together, with a small wooden wheel in front through which the rope passed. A few men at a time, they pulled themselves across the *chaung*. It was slow, though, and took two days. Their next stop was 'Akaho Village' – another Japanese codename, which was nothing more than a hollow in the ground, high up on a mountain side. But it was a good place to stop, with plenty of bamboo shoots, sweet potatoes, edible grasses and running water, so the men rested while Fukami and Tsutsumi and a few men made contact with HQ Shinbu Force further west. They were there on 4 June, greeted with delight by Nagazawa who had known Fukami well from Arakan days, when he commanded 121 Regiment. Nagazawa introduced them to his staff, and Lieutenant-Colonel Saitō offered Tsutsumi a cigarette from a packet of *Kōa*. Tsutsumi hadn't

[1] Tsutsumi, *Tenshin*, p. 17; *Kikoku shūshū*, pp. 80–1

smoked for ages, and drew on it with gratitude. Nagazawa explained that Shinbu would spend the next three weeks preparing for the breakout over the Sittang, which was timed to start on 20 July. Fukami and Tsutsumi returned to 'Akaho' on 5 June, carrying rice with them for their men.

Fukami was perturbed about their condition. About half were sick with malaria or dysentery, and somehow or other they had to accumulate a month's ration stock to carry with them on the breakout. Tsutsumi took 220 of the fittest men down to the village of Zaungtu on the Pegu River, to forage. It was a sizeable village, and should have some rice. When they got near, they saw how the rains had changed it. It was almost an island, rising slightly above the flooded paddy. It was empty. They looked in the huts, and found only unhulled rice in large amounts, with salt and preserved fish in pots. Tsutsumi lifted the lid of one and saw the top layer was fermenting, there were maggots on it. But he was hungry enough not to be daunted, scraped the maggots off, and tasted the fish underneath. Delicious. And so was the *ngapi*, that Burmese delicacy made of prawns crushed into a paste with salt and spices, and used as a condiment. It was pungent, but the sailors had had it before and acquired the taste for it. But they couldn't carry pots of it back. They solved the problem by cutting yard lengths of bamboo, hollowing them out and stuffing the space with *ngapi*. Full of virtue, they decided to make a meal there and then. There were coconuts around, and chickens, and they ate till their eyes were bursting from their sockets, finishing off with ripe mangoes.

It was a wonderful blow-out while it lasted. But the aftermath was predictable. Their stomachs were no longer used to such food, or to such amounts. Ten of Tsutsumi's party were unable to walk, from diarrhoea or related maladies. There was little he could do, so he told the men they would stay in Zaungtu for four more days, hulling the rice, then get back to 'Akaho'. On the way back, he noticed that morale was slipping. Men began to fall out, and the sound of suicide hand-grenades was heard in the nearby forest. Others just slipped away quietly. A third of his 220 men deserted by the time the relatively fit sailors began to come out of the hills on 24 July, leaving around forty men behind with Lt Kinoshita, a young graduate of Keiō Medical School. With the notion that only enough food was needed until they reached the railway line, they left rations behind for the sick. 'You'll make it, you know!' Kinoshita said cheerily to Tsutsumi when he came to say goodbye. Then the farewell phrase, '*De wa, genki de...*' ('Well, look after yourselves'), a handshake, and they were gone. Tsutsumi was haunted for ever afterwards by the fleeting smile on Kinoshita's youthful face, and the clear limpid eyes behind which lay the sure knowledge how final that farewell was. Neither Kinoshita nor the sick were ever heard of again.[1]

---

[1] Allen, op.cit., p. 212

Sixteen RAF planes strafed them as they approached the Mandalay Road, but not a single shot met them as they crossed it. It was 3 am on 1 August. They started to cross the patch of wet grassy surface between the road and railway when the night sky was torn by green and yellow signal flares. Heavy machine guns opened up on them from both sides. Then mortars joined in. The sailors fought back with what they had, grenade-launchers, rifles, machine-guns, but there was no escaping the British 'box of fire' which was saturating the entire landscape across which they crawled. A shower of earth almost buried Tsutsumi. The guns reached a crescendo and he saw the shattered bodies of his men flying into the air in fragments. The survivors struggled on, along the banks of a steam, and where it ran sluggishly, they swam the twenty yards to the opposite bank. Then they were in a small village, screened by a grove of trees. Overhead Tsutsumi, could hear an observer plane, puzzling out where they had gone. They'll shell this village next, he thought, and moved his men over a mile further east. We'll stay here till dark, Tsutsumi told them, then meet up with the CO by moving south-east. They did so. It was a depleted Fukami Unit they rejoined. In that ambush on 1 August, the sailors lost over 400 men, including fourteen officers and petty officers.

The 148-strong remnant staggered into the village of Dalazeik on 7 August, skirmishing as they went. Dalazeik was on the banks of the Sittang, and they hoped to cross there, but the village was held by the British, who opened fire on them at once. They were down to four grenade-launchers by this time, but their fire kept the British off while they circled the village and made for the river bank. It was a fatal encounter for Commander Fukami. Grenade fragments ripped his stomach open as he led his men across the sodden fields.

They put him on a stretcher and, for two days, moved on through six-foot high elephant grass until the embankments of the river came in sight. It was 8 August when they halted. The instant they stopped, gunfire started up on three sides, north, south and west. Shots and screams echoed through the elephant grass, which hid the enemy until he was almost on them, Tsutsumi remembers. They were down to pistols, swords and bayonets, when the cry came to break off and make for a nearby wood. Tsutsumi assembled them, and was shaken to the core. Ninety-eight officers and men had lived through the move to Dalazeik. After this last brush with the enemy – Gurkhas under a British officer – 13 Naval Guard Unit now numbered seventeen men. Most of the officers, including Fukami, died that day.

The Sittang at this point was several hundred yards across, and they had to find a boat. One of his men had spotted a boat being brought across the river a little way upstream, and Tsutsumi decided to seize it, when it grew dark on the 16th. It was not so simple. They found the boat drawn up under the first floor of a hut, protected by wire netting. When they approached, someone began to take pot shots at them. They withdrew.

They spent the next day hiding in tall clumps of reeds as four columns of Indian troops filed past. The columns went on and on. They must have been a battalion strong, followed by a dozen Burmese with poles over their shoulders carrying chickens and bananas, obviously hoping for custom. The Burmese sensed what the Indians had not, and began to look across at the reeds as they passed. 'Don't fire!' Tsutsumi hissed to his men, 'Don't move, they've not seen us!' But they had. Tsutsumi shifted his men, and after an hour had passed a dozen soldiers came back with the Burmese and fired into the clump of reeds where they had been hiding.

Night came. Tsutsumi wanted that boat, and if he could not extract it from the village he would take bamboo from the cow-sheds to make a raft. Which is what he did. Rifles, pistols, grenades, packs, water-bottles were loaded on the raft. It was made with interstices in which six men could fit and swim across, clothed, to protect their bodies from the chill of the water. At 11 pm on 18 August, they pushed off into the turbulent Sittang.

They reached midstream and the current struck them. Try as they would to reach the opposite bank, the river bore them resolutely downstream, on and on, hour after hour. As slivers of light in the night sky showed the coming of dawn, Tsutsumi and his men noticed there were others in the water, struggling like themselves. Or were they? No, it was an image of struggling, nothing more. They were soldiers who had drowned in the attempt to cross the Sittang higher up, their bodies had been caught in weeds, and they were turning round and round as the river swept them on.

Then Tsutsumi's foot felt, for a brief instant, the scrape of the riverbed. He prayed and begged his mother to look after him, to watch over him, to keep him safe, the prayer of soldiers from the beginning of time, and strained against the powerful thrust of the river. 'We're almost there, lads!' he yelled out, 'Put your backs into it now!' and they were clambering up the river bank. It was 6 am on 19 August 1945. He was not to learn this for some time, but the war had already been over for four days.

The armistice hardly made a difference. They came to the edge of a village, across water meadows, and shots rang out from the huts. '*Tennō Heika Banzai!*' screamed Petty Officer Konemura as a bullet tore through his right lung. Then, softly, he murmured the Buddhist invocation, '*Namu myōhō renge kyō*' ('We pray the Lotus Sutra of the wonderful Law'), and repeated it until he died.

They skirted the village, and moved south-east. Their maps were soaked and useless now, and Tsutsumi guided them with a pocket compass. Tsutsumi is not sure how many days they walked, but the hours in the Sittang had made their feet puffy and white, save between the toes where there were raw red ulcers. They stopped in a hut in the middle of a field. To their surprise, they were not alone. A middle-aged Burmese offered them food. Such food, too, they had tasted nothing like it since Zaungtu, chicken, eggs and fluffy white rice, without stint. It was, as the Japanese phrase it, '*Jigoku de hotoke ni au*', 'like finding Buddha in hell'. They took their boots off, and one of the sailors began to pound some sesame seeds in his steel helmet, to make a soothing powder for their feet. The Burmese said he had work to do, and left.

He was gone a long time. At 3 pm, the hut suddenly became the target for a hail of gunfire. They dashed outside and began to fire back. In a pause in the shooting, Tsutsumi heard something dripping beside him, slowly, insistently, on to a piece of bamboo. A thought struck him – not everyone had come out of the hut. 'Harada!' he called out, 'Are you upstairs?' A groan answered him. 'They've done for me, Commander, I'm finished.' 'Hang on, I'll come up!' Tsutsumi answered, as he kept on firing. As it grew dark, the shooting slackened and died. Tsutsumi bounded up the stairs.

A glance was enough. Harada had fallen forward. He had been hit in the back, and great globules of blood had welled out from his jacket on to the rush matting of the floor. The ants were already beginning to crawl over the jacket as Tsutsumi gently removed it. The wound was appalling. A hole a foot wide had slit Harada's back open like a pomegranate and the raw flesh looked as if it were bursting out of the skin. Ants started to swarm round the lips of the wound. Tsutsumi brushed them away, and told one of the sailors to take Harada's gaiters and wash them. They would make a rough bandage round the body.

Harada begged for water, but Tsutsumi refused, knowing it would bring on death more quickly. He fed Harada rice-gruel but it was no use. Harada vomited it straight back. 'I can't help you, Harada,' Tsutsumi thought. 'I'm sorry, but I can't help you.' Later, a bump in the night woke them all. Harada was lying on the bottom floor, his face drained of blood. He had obviously crawled down the steps to reach the water, put his lips to the bottle for one last drink, then keeled over.

After burying Harada, they set out again on 24 August. There were four of them now. They came to the shores of a vast lake, not marked on any map, but which stretched for miles. Tsutsumi looked closer and saw it was no lake, just the result of the Sittang overflowing and obliterating the banks between patches of land. It wasn't deep, therefore, and they put together banana stalks – bananas grew in abundance – for buoyancy and pushed these little 'rafts' ahead of them as they swam through the water. They had finished off the last of their food before they began. For five days they swam, resting every fifty yards, and snatching what sleep they could at night in the branches of submerged trees. They did not dare to leave their mouths open for fear of water leeches, and to save themselves falling in the water as they slept, they strapped themselves to a branch with their gaiters. Then there were the ants. They would start to move towards the sleeping sailors from their melon-sized nests at the end of branches, and crawl over them, tormenting their hands and faces. On the fifth day the sailors heaved themselves out of the water at a low cliff on the opposite shore of the lake, and came out on a mountain path. Their feet could hardly credit the sensation of hard earth again.

The sudden joy at the physical contact with the road gave them energy to go on, after what had seemed the endless purgatory of that false lake. They begged a handful of rice from a group of soldiers by the path, and went on. After ten more days, they reached the edge of a rubber plantation. This change of forest meant, Tsutsumi knew, they must be somewhere east of the town of Shwegyin, where 28 Army forces were supposed to cross the Shwegyin Chaung on the escape to the south. They came across little groups of corpses huddled together for shelter under a tree – and others picked clean as skeletons.

Enemy aircraft flew overhead. They were dropping leaflets this time, not bombs. 'Japanese soldiers!' the leaflets said, 'The war has come to an end. If you stop for a moment under the trees, you will notice the flowers in the silence of evening. It is like old times. If you stay out in the open in Burma you will catch malaria. So come in as soon as possible.' Tsutsumi was not to be fooled. He had seen propaganda leaflets before, and walked on.

On 9 September they crossed the Shwegyin Chaung with half-a-dozen soldiers making their way south through the rubber plantations. The next day, walking through the monotonous rubber, they heard a voice calling in Japanese. It was very far off. '*Butai oran ka?*' it called, '*Butai oran ka?*' [Are there any Japanese troops here?']. Tsutsumi waited until the owner of the voice showed himself. After a while, he spotted two men wearing Japanese uniform approaching through the trees. He had told his men to scatter and lie flat in the grass nearby, and kept his eye on the two strangers. The one in front carried a Japanese Rising Sun flag, the one behind a white flag.

Tsutsumi told his men to fix bayonets. He gripped his pistol as the men came to a halt ten paces away. They were both unarmed, and the one in front, who looked to be twenty-seven or twenty-eight, had a small neat moustache.

'I am Major Wakō Hisanori,' he said in a quiet voice. 'I am a peace envoy from Burma Area Army, and I have come to inform you that the war is over. Here is the Rescript of His Majesty the Emperor declaring the war is at an end.'

When he saw them coming with their flags, Tsutsumi's first reaction was that they were prisoners of war,[1] being used by the British to coax in stragglers. Now he was less sure. He told his men to surround the pair, took the document Wakō handed over and ran his eyes over it, half doubting, half believing.

---

[1] In his earlier text, *Tenshin*, p. 44. The later text, *Kikoku shūshū* p. 200, merely mentions a suspicion they were being used (*tesaki*).

It was written in formal script, on thick paper, the Imperial Rescript ending the war, and Kimura's instructions to all units in Burma to cease fire, dated 1400 hours, 18 August, at Moulmein. Tsutsumi handed them back, saying nothing.

'I understand perfectly well what you're thinking!' Wakō burst out. 'I felt just as you do. But the war is over. That is a fact. Please believe me. That is the Emperor's order. That is the Army order.'[1]

Wakō did not seem like someone being used by the enemy. Tsutsumi noticed his men had tightened the circle, and were devouring Wakō and himself with their eyes. 'I want to read the documents to everyone', Wakō said. After reflection, Tsutsumi agreed, because he needed to know what the word '*tei-sen*' ('armistice', 'cease-fire') would mean to them. Wakō read them all, following the reading by Sakurai's order to all units under 28 Army's operational command, which ended with a warning:

> This is not a hoax by the British. The army is sending out a number of envoys in an effort to reach all of you. The reason the order is coming to you in this way is that signal communications have broken down. The enemy is continuing reconnaissance flights, but there is to be no more bombing over the entire front. The fact that you can not hear it any more will seem very strange, but it is a proof that the war is at an end. It is imperative that you trust this order, dismissing all doubt from your minds. Pass the news on to units near you. It is necessary for the future of the Empire and the Imperial Army that you bear the unbearable with patience, repress rebellious feelings, and carry out orders with sincerity. All officers are to return to their original attachments as soon as possible. A report has come from higher authority to the effect that those who lay down their arms after the Imperial Rescript will not be considered prisoners-of-war.

Sakurai's order was dated from his headquarters at Paan, 7 September 1945. Wakō finished reading, in a steady, composed voice. When he stopped, nobody spoke. Wakō sensed their anguish, knew they were thinking not only of themselves in this God-forsaken place, but of their country going through something none of them had ever dreamed of as possible. 'It is true that the war is over,' he repeated. 'Believe me, please. It is true.' Tsutsumi was in a turmoil inwardly. Yet he sensed from the style of the Rescript and the orders that they were genuine. One of his men stepped forward. 'If it's true that the war's over, then I'm going to kill myself.' The rest seemed to agree with him. Wakō cut in, his voice not steady now, but sharp. 'You will do no such thing. Suicide is out. Haven't

---

[1] *Kikoku shūshū* p. 201

you understood the meaning of His Majesty's words, and the Army order? However terrible it is, we have to endure it.' The last words were a sob in his throat.[1]

Tsutsumi could see that Wakō was weeping in his heart. He no longer had any doubts. But things were still far from simple. He told the soldiers who were with him to go with Wakō to the surrender camp. 'But I am Navy,' he told Wakō, 'and I must reach Moulmein and report to my own 13 Base HQ what has happened to Fukami Unit.'

'You make it awkward for me if you do', Wakō replied. 'Understand my point of view as an envoy. I want you all to come back with me.'

'I can't do that. I understand your point of view. But if I go into that camp I lose my freedom of movement. And I need to get to Naval HQ as soon as possible to make my report. They will need to know everything about the destruction of Fukami Unit. Fortunately PO Kiyomizu and I can still make it on foot.'

Tsutsumi would not budge. Wakō finally consented, and, as he left, he said in an aside to Tsutsumi, 'You Navy chaps had a hard time, too, didn't you?' and gave him two cigarettes, lighting one and handing it over. They were Players, and he never forgot the aroma.

Two days after he left Wakō, in the afternoon of 12 September, he and Kiyomizu heard that voice again echoing in the trees, – 'Are there any Japanese troops here? *Nihonhei wa oranu ka?*' Tsutsumi looked at Kiyomizu. 'What, again?'

'Yes, we meet again', Wakō ruefully admitted, as he came up to them. But circumstances had changed. It was Wakō now who would not budge. He had brought food up, using Burmese porters. 'Even if I pretend not to have seen you, they'll talk when they get back,' he explained, 'and the British will know I've let you go. I know how you feel, and I feel the same. But it's a question of my responsibility now. I'd be guilty of disobedience to an Army order.'[2]

They agreed to spend the night in a hut, and talked till dawn. They all set out in the direction of Shwegyin, and around noon Tsutsumi climbed up a small hill and looked to where Wakō's finger pointed. In the distance, he could see what looked like a camp on the outskirts of Shwegyin. In the clearing in the middle, there were several hundred Japanese officers and men. It was at that moment that conviction finally took over in Tsutsumi's mind: the war was over. Then everything was over, wasn't it? He felt despair, yes, but relief too.

There was a small lake at the bottom of the hill. Tsutsumi was still wearing the sword 'Kenkichi', which he had inherited from his grandfather. Resolutely, he hurled it into the lake. Better throw it away

[1] ibid., p. 205

[2] ibid., p. 207

than hand it over to the British.[1]

Later in the day, a boat pushed out from Shwegyin and crossed the *chaung* to the village of Winkanein, where Wakō, Tsutsumi and their men waited. A young British army lieutenant was in it and came up at once from the river bank. At least, Wakō said he was a British lieutenant, but it was not at all obvious. He wore nothing but a Burmese *longyi*, and a pair of wooden Burmese sandals. No uniform shirt, no badges of rank. He and Wakō seemed to be on good terms, and he saluted Tsutsumi and greeted him in Japanese. It was fluent, but ungrammatical enough to make Tsutsumi wince.

The lieutenant stared curiously at him. He had never seen such a wild-looking creature in his life. By this time Tsutsumi's jet-black hair had grown long and shaggy, his beard was matted, his stinking clothes were in tatters, and the angry light of resentment at having to surrender glittered in his eyes. He looked for all the world like Robinson Crusoe.

Tsutsumi got up and went over to the boat. Did the lieutenant know what had caused the war in the first place? Did he know American economic imperialism had started it?

'Japan would never have surrendered in normal circumstances', Tsutsumi shouted as they came to the bank.

'No, I'm sure you're right,' the lieutenant answered. 'But a new kind of bomb has been used in the past few weeks, which is different from any other kind that's ever been dropped. I daresay the Japanese would never have surrendered, otherwise.'

It was not far from this part of the Shwegyin Chaung to its confluence with the Sittang. The *chaung* ran between a luxuriant forest on either hand, and the late afternoon sunlight gleamed on the water. It was extraordinarily peaceful. As they rowed out into the middle of the *chaung*, the lieutenant, enchanted by the sunlight and the green brilliance of the trees, began to whistle. Tsutsumi made out a few bars of the Pastoral Symphony. His heart was still dark with anger, but as the notes filled the avenue of trees he felt his anger diminish, and something else took its place. Not to be outdone, he too began to whistle the symphony. He had thrown his grandfather's sword away, his country was in the agonies of defeat, he had lost friends and comrades for ever. And yet... he had come through an unbelievable odyssey, and the blood was still coursing through his veins at the end of it. Life, with all its possibilities, still lay ahead.

---

[1] ibid., p. 208. This episode does not occur in the early version, *Tenshin*.

10. THE BEATEN

The Japanese surrender

The first parleys — Major Turrell chances his arm —
The last surrender: Mountbatten and Terauchi

The first parleys

The exchange between Tsutsumi and Wakō at their first encounter illustrates the problems on both sides in Burma when the war – officially – came to an end. For most Japanese, surrender was simply unthinkable. It was so on the individual level. How much more so on the national level? Long before they could begin to endure the unendurable, they had to believe it. The first parleys were a tentative reaching out into a situation that one side, at least, had always believed to be impossible. Certain measures were taken to ease the difficulty. That last phrase that Wakō had read out from Sakurai's order, that those surrendering *after* the national capitulation would not be treated as prisoners of war, was certainly a factor Tsutsumi took into account. It was very important to him not to be thought a prisoner. And to thousands like him. Those capitulating were therefore to be called, the Allies decreed, 'Japanese surrendered personnel', or JSP, a typical bureaucratic euphemism which did, though, serve a definite purpose. It was also decided that Japanese officers should remain responsible for the maintenance and discipline of their own men. Looting from the Japanese was strictly forbidden.

Stopford in Rangoon had been told on 11 August that a Japanese surrender was highly likely. He knew, though, that in the scattered condition of the Japanese in the area under XII Army command, organized surrender was going to be far more difficult than in areas of SEAC where there had been no fighting. He ordered his men on 15 August to suspend offensive operations against the Japanese, and to ensure that the Burmese guerrillas understood that, too. On the other hand, isolated Japanese parties wandering through the jungles might have no idea of the surrender, and strict vigilance was to be maintained. Japanese surrendering were to be questioned about the location of large bodies of troops, headquarters and food supplies, though Stopford must have known this was a mere gesture.

His own intelligence staff had a shrewder idea of where the units of Burma Area Army were than Kimura himself, and the location of headquarters was no secret.[1]

Very appropriately, it fell to a unit of 17 Division to make the first contact. On 22 August a patrol of 6/15 Punjab, 17 Division infantry, met a group of eight Japanese a mile south-west of Nyaungkashe. They offered to surrender, and said that the next day a Japanese officer would be at Posabe to make formal arrangements.

Captain Charles, the intelligence officer of Miles Smeeton's 63 Brigade, kept the rendezvous and made a further arrangement for representatives from IV Corps to meet representatives of the local Japanese commander at Abya on 24 August. A Japanese captain and lieutenant came along on the 24th, and negotiated at the headquarters of 1/10 Gurkhas for an hour and three-quarters.[2] They could not surrender until their own higher command had ordered them to, they said, but they had already had a ceasefire order. They were instructed to see that fighting in the Shwegyin area came to an end, that all mines and booby traps west of the Sittang must be lifted, all troops withdrawn to the east bank of the river within five days, and the Force 136 officer they had taken prisoner released. The Japanese played it close to their chests, not revealing their dispositions, but agreeing to send more senior officers to a fresh meeting at Abya on 26 August. The Official History does not mention that they also bore a letter from the commander of the local Japanese forces, Colonel Satō, addressed to the 63 Brigade intelligence officer who had made the first contact. It expresses the Japanese attitude very well:

To: The Representative of the Commander Pegu Area, Captain Charles
From: The Commander of the Japanese Forces in the Sittang area, Colonel Satō.

1. The letter you sent me yesterday I received last night at 2000 hours (Japanese time) owing to difficulty of communications. [This obviously refers to a document Charles had conveyed to the Japanese officer at Posabe on 23 August].

2. While the overall treaty is under discussion in Tokyo, I am experiencing difficulty with the problems presented by this small sector. In order to bring about the harmonious end of hostilities in accordance with our orders, it is obviously necessary to have unity of movement, and we have so far forbidden movement of individuals.

[1] Kirby, *War Against Japan*, V, p. 252
[2] ibid., p. 252

3. The Japanese Army, in accordance with the orders of His Majesty the Emperor, has forthwith ceased military operations; further, our units, in accordance with the orders of higher formations, have been withdrawn to a line Satogyaung – BM 33 – Posabe (Nyaungkashe North-South); this was in order to avoid bringing on ourselves a senseless and mistaken struggle between the front lines.

4. If it were so ordered, the Japanese Army would fight on even in the face of total annihilation, but if it were ordered differently it has the moral resolution to endure misfortune. Therefore, your recently expressed hopes on these matters and other movements can not, in the absence of a higher ranking officer, be fulfilled on my authority. But again, as long as I receive no orders from higher formations, I will undertake no offensive action. However, while the general situation remains obscure, if our troops are challenged by small parties of your troops or by local Burmese forces, they will unavoidably have to accept battle. We would ask you, for your part, to supervise all such movements, all unnecessary artillery and air activity, and the activities of local Burmese forces.

5. We have the utmost confidence in the customary gentlemanly behaviour and honour of the armed forces of the British Empire.

6. Other similar interviews will henceforth be carried out on the orders of higher formations. I hope that the problems of this area will be solved by contact between your higher formations and the Commander-in-Chief of our army, Field Marshal Terauchi.

The officers who came to Abya had already been told that more detailed information would be available after the 26th, on which day it was expected that Terauchi's Chief of Staff, Lieutenant-General Numata, would fly to Rangoon to receive instructions from Mountbatten. Without waiting for Numata's arrival, IV Corps took its own local negotiations a step further. A lieutenant-colonel from Corps headquarters accompanied Miles Smeeton to the rendezvous at Abya. The Japanese delegation consisted of Lieutenant-Colonel Shōji of Honda's 33 Army staff, along with Lt Sawayama Yūzō, an ex-journalist on Kimura's staff who had been shanghaied into the job by the Vice-Chief of Staff with the valedictory, 'It'll make a good story when you get back to Japan.' There were three other members of the party, Saitō, the former manager of the New Asia Trading Company in Rangoon, a lance-corporal to carry the flag, and a bugler. The bugler was the most concerned. 'What do I blow, Mr Sawayama?' he asked plaintively. Sawayama did not know. The action *kōfuku* (surrender) did not exist in Japanese army regulations and there could be no ceremonial bugle call for it. 'Go and ask the colonel,' he said. Shōji did not know either.[1]

Sawayama had known something was afoot for days. Late on the night of 18 August he had been told by one of the wireless room staff that the BBC and Australian radio were giving details of Japan's surrender. He went to report this to headquarters and was told to keep it under his hat. But it was all over headquarters the following day, though everyone pretended not to have heard. The party went north through Martaban and Kyaikto, and reached 18 Division headquarters ten miles from the Sittang. Everyone was agog with the news, and fired questions at them about what was to happen – would they be sent to India? to the Burma-Siam Railway? back to Japan? They shared the HQ meal – processed bean curd with grass roots and leaves floating in it. They were told they would be joined by a staff officer from 28 Army, Lt-Col. Tsuchiya, who would discuss with them what to do if the units scattered in the breakout battle refused to believe in the surrender.[2]

They went on foot after crossing the Sittang, the officers leaving behind their swords. After an hour, they passed through Waw and came out on the railway. The flagbearer and the bugler went in front, followed by Shōji and Tsuchiya, with Sawayama and Saitō bringing up the rear. The bugler was almost in tears. 'Sir, I don't know what to blow!' 'Oh, blow what you like!' said Shōji, irritably, his mind on other things. Tsuchiya seemed in a good humour, on the other hand: 'Don't blow the charge though!'

Three hundred yards away a score of figures emerged from the drizzle, two at the head, followed by a section of Gurkhas. The officer in command gestured them to come forward. 'Are you General Kimura's envoys?' Saitō hastily came forward. 'Yes.' Then, 'Yes, *sir!*'

They were taken to a jeep train and brought to a headquarters in a Burmese house. They climbed up to the first floor and waited. After two or three minutes, a tall man came in, lazily, followed by a short thickset officer and a young lieutenant who had travelled in the jeep train with them and spoke Japanese. The Japanese straightened up. The tall man examined the faces of each of them in turn. He was clean-shaven, with a long, oval face, rather sallow, Sawayama thought, and his bloodshot, forbidding, ominous eyes gleamed fiercely at them. He sat down and gestured to them to do likewise. He was not in the least overbearing in spite of the ferocity of the eyes.

---

[1] Allen, *End of the War in Asia*, p. 3; Sawayama Yūzō, 'Hakki wo kakagete' ('Hoisting the white flag'), *Hiroku Dai Tōa Senshi*, Tokyo, 1953, pp. 367–81

[2] 'A major from 18 Division' is how Sawayama recalls this sixth member. But his memory is at fault. It was Lt-Colonel Tsuchiya Eiichi from Sakurai's HQ.

The Japanese did not know it, but Smeeton, like them, had been preoccupied with making an impression. The Gurkha headquarters were not in a Burmese house, as Sawayama recalls, but in the railway station, and the first floor was reached by a vertical ladder through a trapdoor. He did not think he would look particularly dignified if he emerged like a jack-in-the-box through this hole in the floor, and doubted if he would be able to keep his face straight if he sat at the table and waited for them as they each bobbed up in turn. The young lieutenant-colonel commanding the 4/10 Gurkhas made a suggestion. There was a cupboard-sized alcove in the room. If an army blanket were hung over the entrance to it, Smeeton could conceal himself behind it – in the wings, as it were – and sweep in from what to the Japanese might appear to be an inner office. Which is exactly what he did. He waited until the Japanese puffing from the ladder had ceased, and made a suitably dramatic entry. He thought (mistakenly) that one was a general, and was interested to note that they appeared 'neither frightened, nor proud, nor taciturn'.[1] Instead, like him, they were, if anything, anxious for everything to be done according to protocol.

The conditions were straightforward enough: the British would withdraw west of Waw, the Japanese would withdraw east of the Sittang. Would 28 Army sick and wounded, Tsuchiya enquired, be able to reach Japanese rear areas? Maps were produced, unit dispositions shown, corrections made on both sides. It took an hour, by which time Sawayama, in his soaking shirt and tunic, was beginning to nod away in the heat of the room. Then he began to observe Smeeton.

The face was not sallow, as he had thought. It was simply tanned by the sun. It was very much out of the common run of faces, very masculine, soldierly. It would twitch now and then, a tic would show in the cheek, and Smeeton would twiddle a pencil round in his fingers. He became stubborn over the question of 28 Army. He wanted it to interrupt its withdrawal south and concentrate in a camp the British had ready. Kimura wanted it to come towards Moulmein, where he would provide stocks of food and medical supplies. The British trio decided to discuss this by themselves, and retreated down the stairs. The Japanese heard footsteps on the stairs almost at once, and thought Smeeton was returning, but it turned out to be a Gurkha with a steaming pot of coffee and four big enamel mugs. They finished it off, and the Gurkha promptly brought another one, whereupon Sawayama filled his water-bottle from it, much to Shōji's and Tsuchiya's disgust.

When Smeeton did come back, his suggestion startled them. Why not go to Rangoon? It was *ultra vires*, as far as he was concerned, to change dispositions laid down about 28 Army, but they might get a different decision in Rangoon, where General Numata was expected that same day.

[1] Smeeton, *A Change of Jungles*, p. 115

539

'I understand your point of view,' he told them, 'but on the other hand I cannot ignore my own orders and give in to you just as I please.'[1] Shōji and Tsuchiya knew that 28 Army's problems might not be grasped by Numata and did not see much point. With that one issue unsettled, the Japanese party left. 'Like decrepit firemen reluctant to face the chute,' Smeeton recalls, 'they disappeared one after the other down the trap-door.'[2]

On the way out, Smeeton said to them 'I was really surprised at General Sakurai! What a reckless thing to do!' – a reference to the breakout. He also mentioned the Force 136 officer still held by a Japanese unit. They should make contact with that unit as soon as possible and have him released. The Japanese delegation had heard a rumour that the former Olympic swimmer, Kitamura Kusuo, was leading a unit still holding out in the mountains.[3] Could he be held by them? They would do their best.

On the way out, they discovered the Gurkhas had given the flagbearer and the bugler coffee, too. 'They asked us for our flag,' they said. 'We couldn't give them our national flag, could we, Mr Sawayama?' Before Sawayama could answer, Shōji said, 'Yes, you could have let them have it.' Sawayama gave Saitō a look. Attitudes were changing already.

Major Turrall chances his arm

The Force 136 officer whose fate kept cropping up in all these initial negotiations was Major Turrall, whose precipitate and entirely unauthorized attempt to bring about the surrender of the Japanese single-handed caused consternation in XII Army Headquarters in Rangoon and at Mountbatten's in Ceylon.

On the evening of 16 August 1945, Turrall appeared east of the Sittang, where his guerillas had been operating, about two nights' march north of Kanjō Force (112 Infantry Regiment, 55 Division). He was carrying a bottle of whisky, some food, and a white flag. The Japanese let him cross a *chaung* to their positions, noting that he had left on the opposite bank some Burmese with a wireless set. Turrall came up to them and called out, 'The World War is over! Let us stop this useless fighting. Please take me to the senior Japanese officer in this area!' He obviously expected them to greet him with the same delight that the news of the surrender had caused among British troops. Instead of which, they seized him and treated him not as an envoy but as a prisoner-of-war, and shared out his food and whisky among themselves. They could see the Burmese on the other bank beginning to signal with their set.

---

[1] Allen, op.cit., p. 12

[2] Smeeton, op.cit., p. 116

[3] This was not the case. I met Kitamura shortly afterwards in Rangoon Gaol.

The senior officer in the area was Colonel Furuya Sakurō, in command of Kanjō Force which, for Turrall's ill luck, happened to be even more isolated from 28 Army than the rest of its units. The reason was this. Kanjō Force had been detailed to oppose the southward thrust of XXXIII Corps towards the oil-fields area of Yenangyaung and Chauk, in co-operation with the Indian National Army (it so happened that Furuya was one of the few officers in the Japanese Army to speak Urdu, having been an attaché in India in pre-war days). But Kanjō was rudely thrust aside by Stopford's advance and made for the shelter of the Pegu Yomas. Furuya had no contact with 28 Army at the time, but he knew there existed a general plan to withdraw into the Yomas if it became necessary and then make for the Sittang Valley.

Without waiting for further orders from higher formations, Furuya decided not to linger in the Yomas, and his Force broke out on its own early in June. As a result, they were some way ahead of the rest of 28 Army and when they arrived in Kyaukkyi, the agreed rendezvous, early in July, they were bewildered to learn that the rest of Sakurai's Army was still concentrating in the Yomas. Furuya decided the best thing he could do was arrange reception areas for Sakurai between Kyaukkyi and Shwegyin in readiness for Shinbu Force which would break through the British cordon in that area.

Morale was not all that good. One man escaped from his company and Furuya later learned he had been taken by the British. And although they discovered a supply of rock salt, some of his officers were careless about replenishing stocks, and his men's feet began to come up in blisters and boils, not the happiest of skin conditions in mid-monsoon.

Turrall's captors brought him to Force headquarters, and reported that they had seen his escort go into hiding. At this time (between 5 and 24 August), though his recollection of Burmese place-names is not of the most accurate, Furuya's headquarters seems to have been about half-a-mile east of Kywegan on the Kyaukkyi-Shwegyin road, in forest so thick that 'you couldn't see the next hut if it was more than ten yards away'. He knew there were British guerrilla and espionage units in his area, and he took it for granted that Turrall was an emissary from one of these. 'I don't believe the Japanese Army has surrendered,' he told him at once, but since he had come as a peace envoy he would treat him well. He ordered his bonds to be cut and a *basha* to be made for him where he could sleep.[1] Furuya's adjutant and one of his captains, Nagai, were ordered to see that he was well fed, but a guard was to be posted by his *basha* to see that he did not escape. Nagai was told to question Turrall, using Lance-Corporal Matsumura, a Hawaiian-born Nisei, to interpret for him. They thought his

[1] Furuya, 'Popa-San no bōei to sono go no tenshin (Kanjō Heidan no omoide)' (The defence of Mt. Popa and the withdrawal afterwards – Recollections of Kanjō Force), *Nanso*, July 1965, p. 19

name was Tarō, a natural assumption for a Japanese to make, since there is such a name in Japanese, and that is how Furuya refers to him, using the Japanese characters for the name when he writes about him many years later. The confusion was understandable. Since there is no Japanese 'l' sound, Turrall's name would be transliterated as 'Tararu' and Japanese who did not know English well might use 'Tarō' as a convenience.

Through Matsumura, Turrall explained to Nagai that he had been gathering intelligence in the Tenasserim area, and then of his own accord had decided to come in and tell the Japanese that the war was over. Japan had surrendered unconditionally. The shelling and bombing in the area had come to an end. He had arranged this. 'Take me to the senior Japanese officer,' he repeated. 'I was a lieutenant in the Army in the First World War (Turrall was a good deal older than most Force 136 officers) and when the Armistice was declared I went off and told the Germans. I acted as a peace envoy then, and think there would be great kudos in repeating that. I would like some food, and better bedding.'[1]

Furuya was completely taken aback by 'Tarō's' assurance and briefly told him he could expect no better treatment than he had received so far. He would have to put up with it. Furuya was perplexed, but decided to postpone sending 'Tarō' under escort to 28 Army until he had had time to think it out.

Two days later, British planes flew over the Kanjō Force area and dropped showers of leaflets. They were in Mountbatten's own name:

> The Japanese Army has taken my peace envoy prisoner. This is not only contrary to the desires of your Emperor but to the Japanese code of chivalry. Japan has surrendered unconditionally. You are ordered to return the peace envoy at once.

Furuya was in a quandary. Without orders from higher command, he could not accept that Japan had surrendered. He decided to stay put and to continue to hold Turrall under close arrest. L/Cpl Matsumura continued to interrogate Turrall and during an exchange between them he punched Turrall in the face, on the pretext that he had insulted the Japanese Army.[2] Furuya was well aware that this kind of thing was not only unpleasant but inexpedient and would give rise to trouble later. He ordered Matsumura to apologize to Turrall and obtained from Turrall a note for Mountbatten to say there was no cause for concern as the Japanese were treating him

---

[1] Furuya, op.cit., p. 20

[2] I interrogated the lance-corporal at Payagyi Camp a few months after this incident. It was the same Matsumura who had acted as interpreter between Colonel Tanahashi and Brigadier Cavendish when the latter was captured at Indin in Arakan in April 1943.

properly. Turrall was not unduly put out. 'I didn't behave very well myself,' he said, 'Forget it.' The note was Furuya's precaution for later on. He had no British or Burmese signallers to call upon, obviously, and no means of getting in touch with his own headquarters, let alone Mountbatten.

A few days later, in an attempt to contact Sakurai by liaison officer, Furuya sent Major Sugiyama to find 28 Army HQ, and told him to take Turrall with him. They encountered a Japanese staff officer en route who told Sugiyama that the news of the surrender was true, and that he should return to Kanjō Force, with Turrall. Sugiyama now had two contrary duties to perform, and solved his dilemma by obeying Furuya's prior order himself and going on to contact 28 Army and also conforming with the staff officer's request by sending Turrall back under escort.

On the way back to Kanjō Force, Turrall attempted to give his escort the slip. Why he did this is not clear, but he perhaps had a suspicion that being taken back meant he might be in risk of his life. At any rate, his escort fired after him, missed, then sprinted after him and recaptured him. When he heard what had happened, Furuya broke out in a cold sweat. Had the soldier not missed Turrall, Furuya knew that he himself would be held responsible, and he saw his military career ending in a war crimes trial for the killing of a British prisoner.

Nagazawa and Shinbu Force headquarters arrived on 19 August. Furuya asked Nagazawa's advice about Turrall, who was now his prime incubus. After some discussion, they decided the best thing to do was to send him under Kempei escort to the spot where he had first made his appearance and then send him back to the British from there. Furuya saw him go with a sigh of relief. Within a short time Turrall was back across the Sittang, a luckier man than perhaps he ever realized.

The Last Surrender: Mountbatten and Terauchi

The destiny of the Japanese armies in Burma depended not only on Mountbatten but on the way Field-Marshal Terauchi and his staff at the Southern Army headquarters in French Indo-China received the news of Japan's defeat. Like Mountbatten, Terauchi was a close relative of a reigning imperial house. There was a time, a few months before, when his name had been put forward to succeed Tojo as Prime Minister, when Tojo was compelled, by Japan's worsening strategic position, to resign both as Chief of the Army General Staff and as Prime Minister in July 1944. The military element in government supported the idea, apart from Tojo himself, who vetoed it. In the end, General Koiso Kuniaki became Prime Minister and Terauchi was left at his post at Southern Army.[1]

---

[1] F. C. Jones, Hugh Borton, B. R. Pearn, *The Far East 1942–1946*, London, 1955, p. 123; and R. J. C. Butow, *Japan's Decision to Surrender*, 1954, 1967 reprint, p. 31 n. 6

The passing-over proved fatal. Not that Terauchi was particularly ambitious for political laurels, though he had in the past been War Minister. But in effect it left him to preside over the disintegration of his command, which included not merely South-East Asia, which the British were successfully campaigning to retake, but also the South Pacific and the Philippines, where the Americans were jumping from island to island, remorselessly, to bring them ever nearer to the heart of Japan itself. The loss of the Philippines and the fall of Mandalay caused Terauchi to have a cerebral haemorrhage on 10 April 1945. He should, of course, have been replaced, but his staff kept his true condition a secret.[1]

The Emperor sent him a telegram at the beginning of August: 'Come back to Japan and report. Come to Tokyo on the understanding you will not be returning to a theatre of war.'[2] Terauchi made plans to leave on the 18th or 19th, but on 10 August his headquarters reported a broadcast from Washington to the effect that Japan had surrendered. Apoplectic or not, Terauchi was remarkably swift to react, and with a shrewd look to the future. He had had the good sense to be out of Saigon's intolerable summer heat and humidity, and Southern Army General Headquarters, exactly like the British in earlier Imperial days, had withdrawn to a hill station. This was Dalat, where Soekarno and Hatta had arrived from Java to discuss plans for Indonesia's independence.[3] When he realized what the Washington broadcast implied, Terauchi summoned Soekarno and Hatta and sanctioned the independence of Indonesia at once and a transfer to the new Indonesian government of surplus weapons from the Japanese forces in Java and Sumatra. An elaborate ceremony was held on the lawn of Dalat's largest hotel, on the edge of a lake, under the shade of the palm-trees. Wearing the insignia of the Order of the Sacred Treasure, Terauchi read out a congratulatory address in his high-pitched voice. Soekarno pledged his loyalty to Japan. He and his two Indonesian colleagues returned to Jakarta blissfully unaware that their patron was on the brink of ruin: the second atomic bomb was dropped on Nagasaki, and the Russians invaded Manchuria on the same day, the eve of Terauchi's tardy gift.

On 13 August, Terauchi called a conference of his staff. The discussion was confused. If Japan *did* surrender, what was Southern Army to do? The question may seem superfluous, but it was far from being so at the time. Southern Army had long been planning a self-defence, self-subsistence policy, by which the Southern Regions would feed themselves and the occupying Japanese armies and go on fighting, whatever happened to the

---

[1] Wada Toshiaki, *Shōgen! Taiheiyō Sensō* (The Pacific War: an Eye-Witness Account) Kōbunsha, Tokyo, 1975, pp. 162–3

[2] Numata Takazō, 'Nampō Sōgun Terauchi Gensui no Shi' ('The death of Southern Army's Field-Marshal Terauchi'), *Bungei Shunjū*, November 1955, pp. 114–19

[3] Allen, op.cit., p. 76

Japanese mainland. The China Expeditionary Force had similar ideas. Some of the staff maintained this position; others said Imperial General Headquarters intended them to cease hostilities, so they should obey. Terauchi listened, said nothing at first, then 'Study the question well, gentlemen,' and stumped off to his room.

But it was not a shirking of the issue. He summoned his Chief of Staff, Lieutenant-General Numata Takazō. 'I'm not going back to Japan', he flatly announced. 'Send a signal convoking a meeting of all Area Army commanders-in-chief.'

The next night, a copy of a telegram sent by General Okamura Yasuji, C-in-C China Expeditionary Force, was received at Southern Army. It was addressed directly to the Emperor: 'We are closely united. As Your Majesty's Army, we are ready to fight to the end. We wish to continue the war.'[1] It might have swayed Terauchi to some extent. But it had been preceded by a message telling everyone to listen to a radio broadcast the next day, 15 August. Yet the impact among the staff of the telegram from China was strong enough to make one of them, Tomura, draft a signal in the same sense, giving the Emperor the state of the forces under Southern Army command, and saying they would continue the war. Tomura took it to where Terauchi was sleeping, at 1 am on 15 August. 'Has the Chief of Staff seen this telegram?' was Terauchi's reaction. 'I drafted it on General Numata's instructions,' Tomura replied, 'he has seen it.' 'Tomura, do you really understand how the Emperor thinks at the moment?' Terauchi put it to him in a serious voice. Tomura was silent. 'If His Majesty saw this telegram before dawn, he would never be able to sleep. If we assume his determination is to surrender, he probably can't sleep anyway. But would he not be distressed, if he received this telegram in my name? Don't you people understand such things?' Abashed, Tomura thought he and his colleagues had been rash and thoughtless, which was exactly what Terauchi wanted him to think. 'I will keep this telegram,' the Field-Marshal concluded. 'Just think tonight what must be going through His Majesty's mind. Think about that.'

Later that same day Terauchi and his staff went to the radio room of the news agency Dōmei Tsūshin which had the best wireless available. He listened steadily to the Emperor's speech, and at the end closed his eyes and let the tears fall. 'There is a broadcast straight after by the Prime Minister, Admiral Suzuki,' Numata told him. 'I'm going back now,' Terauchi answered, and returned to the official residence.

Numata was worried in case Terauchi might be thinking of suicide. Nothing happened, though. He had already told Gotō, the Field-Marshal's personal aide, to remove from his reach anything that might serve as an instrument of suicide.

[1] Numata, op.cit., p. 115

Then the generals and admirals turned up, on the 16th. The news had already leaked to the people in the streets of Saigon. The French, sensing their liberation was near, could not contain their excitement. The Annamites had already determined to seize their independence, and the Emperor Bao Dai had declared at Hue that a restoration of French authority was out of the question. Cambodia had proclaimed its independence. Saigon was in a turmoil. As if to warn them that Japan was still in the saddle, the Kempei kept a close watch on Japanese who seemed to be relieved that peace was in sight: they even arrested the consul-general's wife, Mrs Kōno, and interrogated her for several hours at their headquarters until they were compelled to release her.

In this atmosphere of excitement and political disturbance, Terauchi's commanders held their debate: General Itagaki Seishirō, C-in-C 7 Area Army, in whose province lay Singapore, Lieutenant-General Kinoshita Satoshi, Vice-Admiral Fukudome Shigeru, C-in-C Southern Expeditionary Fleet, and Lieutenant-General Hanaya Tadashi, who only a few months before had been fighting for his life at Toungoo, representing Lieutenant-General Nakamura Aketo, C-in-C 18 Area Army, whose Chief of Staff he had become. Itagaki and Hanaya were both old China – or Manchuria – hands, with a heavy load of responsibility for Japan's military adventures in Asia. They might have been expected to speak with one voice. Surprisingly, the difference between them was crucial. 'We are still unaware of His Majesty's *real* intentions,' declared Itagaki. 'While this is so, should we not continue to fight with everything we have?' 'That is quite improper,' put in Hanaya. 'We have heard His Majesty's broadcast. After that, there is nothing to do but do as he says, and bring the war to an end.' The discussion was inconclusive.

As in Tokyo itself, where the indecisiveness of a vacillating Cabinet in the end forced the Emperor to make the decision for them, so, in Dalat, Terauchi made his own position clear.

> 'I received with respect the order from Imperial General Headquarters. I want the Imperial Army to end its days with honour. The forces under my command are not my forces, they belong to His Majesty. You all received the order just as I did. I am anxious that you do your utmost to send back to Japan, with honour, the officers and men of the Japanese forces.
> Does anyone have any objections?'

Everyone stood up when he had finished. 'No objections'. It was unanimous.

On the 17th, the headquarters came down into Saigon from its hill-station luxury, and greeted Prince Kanin, the Imperial envoy, the next day. After this visit, there was no room for discussion of 'the Imperial will'. Prince Kanin made it crystal clear. The war was to come to an end.

What was far from clear, in Numata's mind, was how you went about this in practice. A radio broadcast from New Delhi had already instructed Terauchi to make contact with Mountbatten by a similar radio broadcast.[1] The Japanese had stalled, saying they would reply fully when they had instructions from Tokyo. By the 23rd, it was clear that every Japanese command would comply with Imperial General Headquarters and Numata prepared to go to Rangoon to negotiate the surrender on the spot. He took with him Rear-Admiral Chūdō, the Vice-Chief of Staff, two Japanese officers including a medical lieutenant, and two civilians, Katsumori and Fujii, from the Hakuyō Trading Company, as interpreters.

Naturally enough, accounts of the negotiations differ. The British were intent on showing who was master; the Japanese, on showing they still had muscle. 'The senior representative was Lieutenant-General Numata, Chief of Staff to the Supreme Commander,' wrote Mountbatten, who was represented by Lieutenant-General F. A. M. ('Boy') Browning, his Chief of Staff. 'His attitude, and that of his officers, was entirely correct; but there can be no doubt that they had come to Rangoon feeling that they were in a position to bargain over, or at least comment on, the terms which I had laid down for the execution of the surrender.'[2]

The Japanese delegation were presented with a document which laid full responsibility on Terauchi for ordering all his forces to cease fire and ensuring the order was complied with, to remove minefields, to forbid signals between units other than in clear, and to be responsible for maintaining law and order until Allied forces arrived in the various countries of South-East Asia to take over. The Rangoon conference was merely a preliminary to the formal surrender which would take place at Singapore on 12 September. Allied POWs would be recovered, Allied aircraft would fly over Japanese-controlled territory, Allied ships would enter Japanese-controlled waters.[3]

As Mountbatten recalls it, Chūdō made difficulties by asking for separate naval arrangements, although the Tenth Area Fleet, under Vice-Admiral Fukudome, was in fact under Terauchi's direct operational control. 'But Browning was very firm: he allowed no comments on the terms laid down, and allowed only those questions that aimed at clarifying the terms as they stood.'[4]

---

[1] 'On the 20th August' says the British Official History (*War Against Japan*, V, p. 236.) 'Around the 15th', Numata, op.cit., p. 116

[2] Mountbatten, *Report*, p. 184, para. 643

[3] Kirby, *War Against Japan*, V, p. 237

[4] Mountbatten, *Report*, p. 184, para. 643

That is not how Numata remembers it. The Japanese delegation went to Rangoon with three aims in mind. They wanted to maintain their command structure; to disarm themselves and hand over surrendered weapons and armament; and to get their men back to Japan as fast as they could. When they were told that the Allies intended to disband General Headquarters at once, and that each of their Armies would be individually disarmed under Allied control, the negotiations, he says, came to a standstill. Their mood was far more desperate than they allowed it to appear. Tomura, his staff officer, turned to Numata, and said, 'General, we can only die once. If we take our lives now, even the British will take note of that. There are probably those among them who know we cannot do what is unreasonable. We have potassium cyanide with us. Should we not take our own lives now?'[1]

Numata told him their deaths might be more valuable on another occasion. There was no point in dying in haste and anger at a moment like this. As he saw it, the Allies conceded his point when they noticed the newspaper correspondents, who were there from the international press, begin to get restive and wonder when the agreement was going to be signed. The signatures were appended at 1.42 am on 28 August.

A plethora of surrenders followed Numata's visit to Rangoon. Kimura's Chief of Staff was ordered by Stopford to present himself at Rangoon to receive details for the surrender of the forces in Burma, and small British parties re-entered Mokpalin, Mergui and Tavoy, in the far south of Tenasserim. Major-General Ichida, on behalf of Kimura, signed the surrender of all forces under the command of Burma Area Army at Government House in Rangoon on 13 September, the day after General Itagaki had, with hot tears of resentment and fury in his eyes, signed for the sick Terauchi in Singapore. A ceremony was held at Judson College in Rangoon on 20 October, during which Kimura handed over his sword to Stopford, and Sakurai, Ichida, and the senior naval officer in Burma handed their swords over to senior officers of XII Army and the British Navy in Burma. Crowther had been ordered to occupy the whole of Tenasserim with his 17th Division, and Honda surrendered to him at Thaton on 25 October. The surrender of all troops in Burma was completed by 6 November – nearly 72,000 of them. The rest had moved across the hills into Siam and surrendered there. The Kempei were in gaol, Sir Reginald Dorman-Smith, the Governor, was back (for a time), and Burma was returning to a semblance of civil order.

---

[1] At Singapore, a wary American medical officer, fearful they might imitate Goering's successful suicide at Nuremberg, had the Japanese delegates' mouths probed before they entered the surrender ceremony. It was even more repellent, Numata recalls (he was part of *that* surrender, too) because the officer did not disinfect his hands, after each probe with an instrument like a shoe-horn. (Numata, op.cit., pp. 116–17)

Numata was worried about Terauchi's reaction to the evaporation of his command. Would he commit suicide? And, if he wanted to, should he be prevented anyway? To control the situation, Numata instructed Tomura to station a few Kempei in the official residence. If the Allies came to seize him, his personal aide, who slept on the floor below, was to use the Kempei to prevent them arresting the Field-Marshal. This would leave Terauchi enough time to commit suicide. Plans were made with Tomura to act as his *kaishaku*.[1] It would be unthinkable to hand the Field Marshal over to Allied hands, and Tomura decided to sleep on the floor above him.

In fact, Mountbatten did everything possible not to put pressure on Terauchi. 'I had summoned Field-Marshal Terauchi to make the formal surrender for the South-East Asia theatre, at Singapore on the 12th September,' he wrote. 'He pleaded ill-health, and asked to be excused from attending; and a member of my medical staff, who examined him, certified that it would be most unwise for the Field-Marshal to travel – and that he would not in any case be able to take part in the surrender ceremony with dignity; since he had been crippled by a stroke on the loss of Mandalay, and had never fully recovered.'[2]

It was Mountbatten's own doctor, Surgeon Captain Birt, Royal Navy, who flew to Saigon to examine Terauchi. Numata was away in Rangoon, and Terauchi was under treatment by Lieutenant-General Nagino, his physician. As Captain Birt came in, the Field-Marshal, in convalescent mood, came down the stairs and called out, 'I'm sick, you know!' (*ore wa byōki da yo!*) and blithely walked outside. There were traces of the cerebral haemorrhage, but nothing of consequence, Numata was told. Nonetheless, Captain Birt's report said that Terauchi's condition was serious, he could not walk, and could not fly in an aircraft, or ride in any vehicle. This verdict, and Mountbatten's decision not to compel Terauchi to go to Singapore for the surrender ceremony, demonstrated Mountbatten's *bushi no nasake* – 'warrior's compassion'. This was confirmed for Numata when Mountbatten accepted two swords, one gold, one silver, which Terauchi had obtained from Japan for his own personal surrender in Saigon on 30 November. Mountbatten flew there to visit the French commander, General Leclerc, and Douglas Gracey, whose 20 Division was in occupation of southern Indo-China. Terauchi came to the airport to see him off. 'You must get well again,' Mountbatten told him, 'I'd like you to be strong enough to be able to return to Japan very soon.'

But in March 1946 Mountbatten had the Field-Marshal transferred to Malaya, where he lived with a small staff in a bungalow belonging to a rubber-plantation in Rengam, near Johore Bahru. He was still sufficiently

---

[1] The 'second'. After the suicide has disembowelled himself, the *kaishaku* beheads him with a sword.

[2] Mountbatten, *Report*, p. 186

mentally aware to notice the difference since he had entered the city of Singapore as a conqueror entering a captured fortress. The gangs of Japanese soldiers labouring in the streets were painful evidence of this. A Japanese journalist describes his condition at the time in unflattering terms: 'To put it bluntly, he was already useless. Mentally and physically, he was a living corpse.'[1]

Numata accompanied him to Johore, and that was not his view. Terauchi had occasional sharp reactions. On 11 June 1946, he was having a meal with his staff when the discussion turned to the strike that Japanese soldiers were trying on in the docks in Singapore. They had been angered at seeing troops from Burma passing through Singapore on their way back to Japan, and it took the intervention of Lieutenant-General Ayabe, Chief of Staff of 7 Area Army, to pacify the cries of 'Send us home!'

And there was the case of a certain Kempei lieutenant-colonel whom the Allies had begun investigating. The colonel had come to headquarters and asked to be sent home quickly, since he was afraid he was going to be tried as a war criminal. There was no ship with a passage available, the head of Southern Army Legal Department told him, whereupon he burst out with threats: 'If they catch me, I'll blow the whole Kempei business wide open! I'll tell them everything the Kempei have done! When that happens, there'll be those among the Kempei who'll swing for it!' The Legal Department chief, Hidaka, called him a coward for trying to incriminate others in order to escape himself.

Listening to this over the meal, the Field-Marshal burst out angrily, 'Deal with that fellow at once!' He seemed excited still, after taking tea, and during the night Tomura heard a loud voice cry out from his room, 'Tomura! Tomura!' He hurried in and found the Field-Marshal's window open. The old man's eyes were open, too, but he could not speak. It was his second stroke. You'll be all right, sir!' Tomura said, and Terauchi seemed to hear him, but could only blink his eyes in reply. Tomura called the medical officer, who gave him an injection, then artificial respiration.

The sky had been cloudless until 2 am, then a massive rain storm closed the skies. During the downpour, Terauchi died.

Numata thought that Terauchi, unusually, had not been concerned about being buried in Japan. On the contrary, he had requested, 'Let me become southern earth. Bury my bones here in the south.' 'You can have any ceremony you like,' the British told Numata. 'You must take charge of it yourselves. If you need anything, money, materials, you can have whatever you want.' Numata was impressed. Terauchi was cremated in the Japanese cemetery at Singapore, and part of his ashes laid there, under a stone memorial made and raised by volunteers from his own troops; and part of them sent home to Japan.

---

[1] Wada Toshiaki, op.cit., p. 166

Why should Mountbatten have been so concerned over the fate of Field-Marshal Terauchi? Because he was a great commander, says Numata, and showed to perfection the English tradition of chivalry. There is more to it than that, in the view of Wada Toshiaki, one of the Japanese newspapermen attached to Southern Army Headquarters, who saw the war through to the capitulation in Saigon. Like Terauchi, Mountbatten was a peer of the realm, and the heir to a family with a service tradition. Terauchi's father had been Governor-General of Korea and Prime Minister of Japan. Mountbatten's father, Prince Louis of Battenberg, had served the Royal Navy faithfully until extruded from high Admiralty office by gross prejudice during the First World War, when his German origins were used against him. By a strange coincidence, he was an acquaintance of General Terauchi Seiki, the Field-Marshal's father, during the latter's tour of duty as military attaché in London.

So when news came from General Gracey that the Field-Marshal was behaving very oddly in the camp at Cap Saint-Jacques, where Japanese forces in Indo-China were concentrated before going home, Mountbatten took notice. Finally, thinking that he should extend a helping hand to the mad old Field-Marshal, as far as it lay in his power, he decided to keep a close watch on him personally, and had him brought to Rengam, in Johore. He was under restraint there. But there was no other way of helping him.[1]

Well, yes, perhaps there is something in it. Terauchi's father had been a welcome visitor at the British Legation in Tokyo in the early years of the century. The British Minister, Colonel Sir Claude MacDonald, would warn the fledgling language attachés that they should shake hands with the General's left hand, when introduced to him, as he had lost the use of his right arm from a wound in the Satsuma Rebellion of 1877. He had been military attaché in Paris, too, and would greet the guests in Japanese or French. Francis Piggott, one of the young attachés, recalled this many years later when he brought a letter from the Secretary of State for War, Duff Cooper, to the then Minister of War in Tokyo, Count Terauchi, the old General's son.[2] It was 1936, an awkward time for the Japanese Army. Young officers had rebelled in central Tokyo, and murdered a number of leading political figures. Terauchi's drastic action in suppressing the rebellion resulted in the death sentence being passed on the ringleaders. This did not prevent him showing the utmost cordiality to his English visitors. Piggott found him physically like his father, but socially far more approachable, genial and good-humoured. He produced a magnum of champagne on Piggott's first call as military attaché in 1936, and showed him the new Diet buildings, with great scorn. 'Wouldn't two divisions be better?' he laughed. Opinion on the question, replied Piggott, in whom the

[1] ibid., p. 168
[2] F. S. G. Piggott, *Broken Thread*, p. 32

551

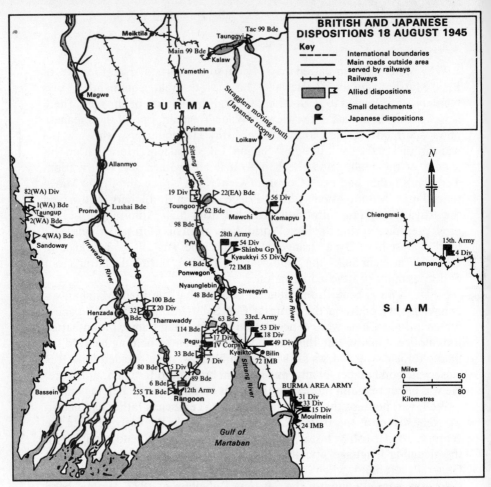

BRITISH AND JAPANESE DISPOSITIONS 18 AUGUST 1945

Key

- — — — International boundaries
- ——— Main roads outside area served by railways
- +++++ Railways
- ▨ ⚑ Allied dispositions
- ○ Small detachments
- ⚑ Japanese dispositions

soldier never took precedence of the diplomat, was probably divided.[1] Sir Robert Craigie, the British ambassador, and Piggott's chief, was not slow to see how autocratic Terauchi was. 'He treated the Diet with a fine, aristocratic contempt,' noted Craigie, 'and the Prime Minister not much better, insisting on revising all the appointments to high office in the State. Above all, he rejected the slightest taint of party politics in a prospective Cabinet minister.'[2]

Militaristic patrician though he undoubtedly was, family and personal connections with Great Britain were not lacking in Terauchi's past. And they may have helped him in those last days when the British, whose armies he had torn asunder and flung to the winds in 1942, when he conquered nearly all Europe's empires in the East, took their possessions back from him three years later and held him prisoner until he died in their captivity, a mad old man, in the rubber plantations of Malaya.

---

[1] ibid., p. 265

[2] Sir Robert Craigie, *Behind the Japanese Mask*, p. 35

11. THE BACKWASH

War and Politics in Burma

Suzuki and Aung San — Ba Maw — the conning of
Professor Asai — Force 136; Hugh Seagrim's sacrifice
— Aung San rebels

Suzuki and Aung San

Burma was incinerated by the Japanese and British armies: its whole
length and breadth twice fought over in three years, occupied by an army
more concerned with keeping its enemies on the periphery than in repair-
ing material damage to the Burmese economy, then invaded in return by
the dispossessed British, whose purpose was to destroy the Japanese and
for whom the preservation of the fabric of Burmese society could only take
second place. George Rodger describes the destruction of Mandalay in
1942, which can serve as an example of what happened to every sizeable
town in Burma:

> Mandalay, that proud city, once the capital of the Kingdom of
> Ava, steeped in tradition, now lay a heap of smouldering ruins.
> Blue-grey wisps of smoke still rose from acres of piled ashes
> where once the business and native sections stood. The entire
> district was utterly destroyed and all that remained of Mandalay
> was the stench of her dead that lay beneath the ruins. Charred
> bodies sprawled in the streets and rotting corpses floated among
> the lily-pads in the moat surrounding the rose-red walls of Fort
> Dufferin, the inner city of ancient Mandalay. Everything outside
> the walls had been demolished. A fire-blackened Pagoda still
> raised its spire as though in defiance from the smoking cinders,
> and trees, white with ash, lifted their smouldering limbs in
> supplication to the sky . . . Every temple had gone, the bazars and
> the shops had gone, and the homes of 150,000 people; Mandalay
> itself had gone.[1]

---

[1] George Rodger, *Red Moon Rising*, p. 97–8

Lt Durant's verdict on Mogaung, two years later, follows the same pattern:

> In days of peace it must have been a very pleasant place with wide tree-lined streets, some lovely pagodas and a priest's living-quarters, some large stone buildings... and very solid and well-built wooden buildings raised on props in the Burmese fashion; it was the market centre for all the natives for miles around and the centre of the north Burma sugar industry.
>
> When we went in the whole place was deserted, and the only living creatures were unkempt dogs and wildly unfriendly cats.
>
> Not one building had been left untouched by bombing, all windows were broken, roofs removed, walls cracked, and the golden pagodas were chipped or blasted to the ground. Every road was cratered and the whole town was overgrown with rank weeds and waist-high grass...[1]

The principal instrument of the recapture of Burma was the Indian Army, and the historians of that army note with some asperity that it was used for the ends of Great Britain and not for those of India, which was not consulted about its use. 'The history of the Burmese war up to June 1944 is largely a tale of the rejection of one strategic plan after another because the American and British purposes were so divergent, one seeking to utilize India for the object of keeping China in war and hitting Japan directly therefrom, the other keen to get back their old empire in South-East Asia, and thereby have a major say in the affairs of the Pacific. Indian interests were nowhere considered and Burma's aspirations were not taken account of.'[2]

Much of the air transport for the campaign was provided by the US Air Force, but for the Americans Burma was only a means to an end. US higher policy – President and State Department – favoured the folding-up of the colonial empires in the Far East, and had as little interest in maintaining a British presence in Burma as the Japanese had. Once the road back to China was established, the withdrawal of the US air arm was a matter of time; and on the level of clandestine activity, the OSS in places like Burma and Siam was instructed to keep itself at a distance from British organizations like Force 136 in case the US became accidentally compromised in British imperial policy.

At all events, when Aung San and his little Burma National Army revolted against the Japanese on 28 March 1945, there was not merely a negotiation between Burmese and British alone, but a negotiation with a

---

[1] Bidwell, *The Chindit War*, p. 273

[2] *Reconquest of Burma*, I, p. xxv

particular type of British soldier and official committed to a new view of the relationship with Burma, and not content to assume that the government-in-exile, in Simla, under the Governor Sir Reginald Dorman-Smith, would simply come back in the train of Slim's military triumph. Partly this was Mountbatten's doing, eager to ensure the smooth functioning of his military machine, and less than enthusiastic at the notion that he might have to waste men and weapons in repressing a revolt among the Burmese when it could be avoided by political means. This was the attitude he was later to demonstrate in relation to the Dutch and French when they returned to SEAC expecting their former colonies and protectorates simply to fall into their grasp, when the Indonesians and peoples of Indo-China had already evolved beyond the point when that was possible.

To a large extent, in all the countries of South-East Asia, it was the presence of the occupying Japanese armies which had wrought this difference. Japanese historians debate among themselves whether this was a genuine attempt at liberation by Japan, or whether the Japanese military simply attempted to use the resources of South-East Asia and were, in that sense, simply a substitute for the old imperialisms. A group of left-wing historians, for whom the campaigns in Asia are an expression of Japanese capital extending itself on the Asian continent and militarizing society at home in order to do so, treat the liberation of Asia as bogus. In terms of ultimate motivation, they may be right. But in the intermediate sense, a genuine liberation *did* take place and affected the post-war development of Burma. And some of the Japanese involved were not simply instruments of a military imperialist will but genuine believers in the idea of Burmese independence, just as those Japanese who founded the Indian National Army from Indian POWs in Malaya and Singapore were undoubtedly animated by the need to serve Japan's own purposes in South-East Asia and also sincerely convinced that Japan's role was to lead the rest of Asia in a movement of liberation from the European colonial powers. In the various organizations set up by the Japanese Army to carry out this task, there was a great variety of conviction and cultural depth.

The role of the Kikan in South-East Asia in the 1940s is a familiar one: it was the intermediate 'cushion' between the orders of the central authorities in Tokyo and the representatives of the various peoples who were to be used by those authorities for a particular strategic purpose. In each case, the motive of liberation was there, if remote. But for Tokyo it was not so much an ideal as a technique.

What happened in the course of events was predictable. The person who is the intermediary must, if he is to be effective, be capable not only of transmitting a strategy but also of empathy with the Asian peoples to be used. When this occurs, his own psychology is involved, his feelings may be modified after prolonged non-Japanese contacts and he will be torn between his original orders and the real nature of the relationship he has formed with other Asian peoples.

Perhaps the best idea of the polarities can be gained from a brief gaze at Colonel Suzuki Keiji, head of the Minami Kikan, which was the parent organization of the Thirty Comrades and the Burma National Army, and Major (later Lt-Colonel) Fujiwara Iwaichi, who recruited Captain Mohan Singh to the Japanese side after defeat in the jungles of northern Malaya in December 1941 and later built round him the first Indian National Army.

The independent Burma which Suzuki fought for was established, then destroyed by the returning British, then retrieved by his protégé Aung San, who took Burma out of the British Commonwealth of Nations – to the loss of both Burma and Britain – in 1948. The independence of India was conceded by the British, say some historians, because of the pressures brought by the returning INA in 1945 and 1946, and the repercussions of the British trial of its three ringleaders in 1945. I think this will not bear close scrutiny, for it ignores the powerful movement toward independence, both in India and in Britain, in the two decades leading up to 1939. And it ignores completely the mood of the British people in 1945, which returned a Labour Government to power.

But whatever the view of history upon the causality of independence, the personalities of the two Japanese officers involved are fascinating. Of the two, Suzuki was the more recalcitrant to his own higher command. Fujiwara loved his Indian colleagues with an intense passion and loyalty, and tried to intervene on their behalf with the Japanese high command when things went wrong: for instance when Mohan Singh dissolved the first INA after a squabble with the civilians of the Indian Independence League in December 1942, and was arrested by the Japanese and interned for the rest of the war. But he never encouraged them to rebel against Japanese authority, and was himself utterly devoted to the Japanese cause. When he was first given his Indian assignment in 1940, he knew next to nothing about India, as he freely admits, and found to his dismay that Army Staff GHQ only had a dozen or so books from which he could glean information.[1] His knowledge of India was therefore derived chiefly from contemporary revolutionary sources and figures like Rash Behari Bose, who had lived in Japan since 1910. Fujiwara was so distressed at the arrest of Mohan Singh and the dissolution of the first INA that he greeted the Sikh captain with tears streaming down his cheeks, and contemplated suicide for himself. 'In the depths of my heart', he later wrote, 'I realized I stood between the two armies, Japanese and Indian, and I determined I must prevent this by laying down my life.'[2] It never came to that, though he cut

[1] *F. Kikan*, Eng. trans. by Y. Akashi, *passim*; and conversations with the author.
[2] *F. Kikan*, pp. 336–7

his hair off as a relic and made his will. It is interesting that it was this traditional Japanese 'solution', rather than rebellion, which presented itself to his mind in the crisis. He had determined 'never to lie to the Indians and never to make promises that had no backing in reality'.[1]

It was on the other hand with Suzuki's urging that the young Thakins accompanying the Japanese invasion force in January 1942 proclaimed the independence of Burma at Tavoy. It was Suzuki who arranged for Aung San and Bo Yan Aung to evade the vigilance of the British police and escape to Amoy, from where they were taken to Japan. It was Suzuki who trained them and the rest of the Thirty Comrades on Hainan Island. And when war came, it was Suzuki who used them as scouts and interpreters on the flanks of Iida's 15 Army as it came into Burma from Siam.

There seems little doubt that Aung San was bound, mind and soul, to Suzuki. Shrewder in the ways of government, Ba Maw was not slow to realize that this unequivocal allegiance to Suzuki was likely to involve the nascent Burmese military forces in his downfall, which was sure to come. He knew that Suzuki aroused fear, distrust and jealousy among the other Japanese in Burma, and that sooner or later the rift would come into the open, partly because of the tensions in Suzuki's own personality. A rebel by temperament and a conformist by upbringing, an individualist who had learned with difficulty to live with others, Suzuki was also brusque, domineering, easily provoked, and could be shrill and brutal. Intensely ambitious and pragmatic, he was nevertheless ready to throw everything away for a dream. 'The dream at the moment took the conviction that he alone as the Japanese head of the Burmese forces of liberation could unite and complete the victory of the two peoples; in other words, he was the man of destiny of Burma.'[2]

One of the Thirty Comrades emphasized to Ba Maw just how close was their link with Suzuki: 'He created our little army and we were completely in his hands,' he said, 'and as we say in Burmese, we feared him from our youth, and we also loved him. So his ways with the Japanese army became ours. Moreover, we liked it so, because it made us share Bo Mo Gyo's [Suzuki's] independence and importance and feel that we were fighting for our own cause and not that of the Japanese.'[3]

Colonel Hiraoka, in charge of relations between Japanese and Burmese for 15 Army, told Ba Maw that the Japanese regarded Suzuki as their toughest problem. 'Your people are following him like children', he added, 'and that may not be good for them in the long run.' Ba Maw took the hint. He approached Aung San, and began to sow the seeds of

[1] Kojima Noboru, *Sanbō* (Staff Officers) p. 45

[2] Ba Maw, *Breakthrough in Burma*, p. 141

[3] ibid., p. 142

mistrust. How many of the Japanese higher command had he and the other Thakins got to know? None, was the answer, everything was done through Bo Mo Gyo.

When Suzuki was sent back to Tokyo, in June 1942, far from expressing condolence to Aung San, Ba Maw indicated that this was the best thing that could have happened. It meant that Aung San alone would be head of the Burma Independence Army, and could treat directly with the Japanese high command. Lack of an intermediary, however dedicated – that was real independence.

But the BIA was never to know even the limited autonomy of the INA under Bose. And it never had any crucial military operations to perform. The post-war Japanese historiography which sees the creation of this force by the Japanese as their greatest contribution to Burmese independence is really making a case for the Thirty Comrades acquiring their own instrument of power. And as Burma was occupied by strong Japanese forces, actively conducting military operations, it could hardly be effective until these forces were weakened.

Burma was declared independent in August 1943. But the Thakins were sceptical about the real content of that independence, and began to sound out the possibilities of a rapprochement with the British. There was no point, was there, in being allied to the likely losers? The likely winners, on the other hand, were far from convinced that they needed the co-operation of the Thakins. After all, there was a Burma government-in-exile, waiting its chance to return in the wake of Slim's armies. And there were those in it who regarded Aung San as a common murderer and intended to bring him to justice.

The link between Suzuki and the Thakins' Thirty Comrades had two far-reaching effects. It ensured that power of physical persuasion remained in the hands of the Thakins, and gave them a political monopoly that made life all but impossible for any opposition party. The Thakin party flag became the national flag, the Thakin party song the national anthem. It also ensured that Japanese mistrust of Suzuki was transferred to his protégés, and as a result the official proclamation of Burmese independence, with the backing of the high command and government in Tokyo, did not take place until August 1943.

Men have the defects of their qualities: Suzuki's very intensity, and his passionate commitment to the cause of independence, argue a considerable autonomy conceded to him in the first place by Imperial General Headquarters in Tokyo. They also guaranteed that the Japanese commander on the spot, and his staff, would pretty soon begin to find this private army intolerable. Which is precisely what happened.

Thakin Nu recalled that Suzuki, when they first met, began by saying, 'Don't be worried about independence. Independence is not the kind of thing you can get through begging for it from other people. You should proclaim it yourselves. The Japanese refuse to give it? Very well, then; tell them that you will... proclaim independence and set up your own government... If they start shooting, you just shoot back.'[1]

Suzuki also did not hesitate to espouse the Thakin partisanship when it came to social and communal dissension in Burma. The emphasis on blood and race – held in common with Ba Maw in his most strident pro-Japanese period – meant that when conflicts occurred between, say, Burmans and Karens or Burmans and Indians, Suzuki took the side of the Burmans. The most scandalous example of this was in Myaungmya, in the Irrawaddy Delta, where there were large Karen settlements. (The other Karen area lay between the Sittang and the Thai border, to the east.) The Burmans disliked the Karens who were in many cases Christian, had been given military training by the British,[2] and remained pro-British even after the British defeat. Aroused by increasing racial hatred and arrogance, the Suzuki-sponsored Burma Independence Army summoned the Delta Karens to surrender their firearms. Some villages complied with this order, and in their defenceless state were attacked by gangs of hooligans who followed the BIA. The Karens complained that the BIA officers not only stood and watched, but actively joined in these raids, and concluded that the purpose of the Thakins was to rob and exterminate their community.[3] Suzuki was a partisan in the massacre. One of his officers was killed in a Karen attack on a Burmese village. Suzuki promptly ordered two Karen villages, Kanazogon and Tayagon, to be razed to the ground and their inhabitants exterminated. The villages were surrounded at night and set on fire at one end. As the villagers rushed out in a panic at the other end, BIA 'troops' were waiting to cut down everyone with swords. The wounded were left to die in the flames. It was open race war after this, Ba Maw observes,[4] and the parallel is obvious with T. E. Lawrence's refusal to take prisoners and the consequent massacre of retreating Turks after the Turks had butchered the villagers of Tafas, and after the death of his companion Tallal, whose village it was.[5] These events in the Delta marred Burman-Karen relations long after the Japanese had gone.

Ba Maw

If only to secure their rear, the Japanese of 15 Army had to put a stop to

---

[1] U Nu, *Burma under the Japanese*, pp. 24–5

[2] In 1939 the Burma Defence Force contained only 472 Burmans as against 3197 Karens, Chins and Kachins. (F. Tennyson Jesse. *The Story of Burma*, p. 169)

[3] Ba Maw, op.cit., p. 188

[4] ibid., p. 189

[5] Lawrence, *Seven Pillars of Wisdom*, 1935, pp. 630–3

the depredations of the BIA. And they did so. It was purged and reconstituted as the Burma Defence Army under Aung San. Suzuki was packed
off home in the summer of 1942.[1] The Bama Baho ('Central Burmese')
Government, under Thakin Tun Oke as Chief Administrator, which came
into being on 23 March 1942, under Suzuki's patronage, was replaced by a
more extensive Civil Administration headed by Ba Maw, who had been the
first Premier of Burma under the British (1937–9) and was later imprisoned
by them for sedition. Ba Maw, the cultivated, European-educated lawyer,
was sophisticated enough to realize that, even at Area Army level, the
Japanese military structure was far from monolithic. He became very
friendly with Lieutenant-General Iida Shōjirō, the first commander-in-
chief, whom he saw as quite unlike the mentally race-bound officers who
had come to Burma from China and Korea with a pronounced master-race
complex. Of course, Ba Maw's affectation of superiority over the race-
consciousness of the Japanese military is a pose. He was as vociferously
racist as any of them at the Greater East Asia Conference in Tokyo in
November 1943 when he proclaimed, 'I seem to hear the voice of Asia
gathering her children together. It is the voice of our Asiatic blood.' And in
characteristically racist phraseology, 'This is not the time', he went on, 'to
think with our minds; this is the time to think with our blood, and it is this
thinking with the blood which has brought me all the way from Burma to
Japan.'[2] By which time, of course, he had come far along the path to
totalitarianism, with his title of Naingandaw Adipadi – 'Head of State' – of
a one-party system with a sinisterly familiar slogan: *ta-thway, ta-than, ta-
meint*, 'One Blood, One Voice, One Command'.

This was the mood in which he accepted the independence of Burma in
1943. But before he got that far he had to contend with opposition to the
very idea of independence, rooted very deeply in Terauchi's Southern
Army GHQ. The personal connection here is not hard to find. It is in
Colonel Ishii Akio, Senior Staff Officer of the General Affairs Section. In
his *Nampō Gunsei Nikki* ('Diary of Military Government in the Southern
Regions'),[3] Ishii makes it clear why he thought independence should be
refused, and military government maintained. Suzuki's hot-headed intervention came at the wrong time, when the Japanese Army was still engaged in complex operations. Any independent government would, as a
result, have to yield to over-riding military pressures, and as the Japanese
would be seen to be enforcing these, they would earn the hostility of the
population. Ishii also bore in mind – as others did – the precedent of Wang
Ching-wei in China. After he had been seduced by the Japanese from

[1] He visited Burma again in post-war days. And reunions of old members of his Minami
Kikan could still lead to hot and angry disputations thirty years later.

[2] Ba Maw, op.cit., p. 343

[3] MS in Defence Agency Archives, Tokyo.

Chiang Kai-shek's Kuomintang government in 1940 and persuaded to set up a collaborationist government in Nanking under Japanese auspices, Wang showed himself to be no less determined to preserve the prerogative of China than Chiang himself. Some Japanese thought he was simply Chiang's agent.

So Ishii took it upon himself to resist pressures towards independence. A signal from Tokyo reached Southern Army on 10 February 1942, instructing Terauchi to set up an independent Burma after the capture of Rangoon. Convinced that Burma risked becoming another Wang Ching-wei China, Ishii lobbied every visitor to Terauchi's GHQ: Lieutenant-General Iida and his staff (9 February 1942), General Sugiyama, Chief of the General Staff (23–25 March 1942), Colonel Takeda Isao (Chief of No. 8 Section, Imperial GHQ, 23–25 March 1942) and the new Chief of Staff of Southern Army GHQ, Lieutenant-General Kuroda Shigenori, who had been an advocate of early independence (30 August – 5 October 1942). Ishii's zealous and tenacious lobbying in these crucial months of 1942, no doubt helped by the aggressively vocal autonomous manoeuvres of Colonel Suzuki, and the Wild West behaviour of the infant BIA, finally convinced the advocates of early independence that they had been too hasty. It was postponed for a year. The lobbying had another effect too. It achieved the undesired object of sowing the first seeds of mistrust of Japanese motives in the minds of the younger Burmese soldiers and politicians. 'Japan did not send troops into Burma to make Burma ours,' Iida recalled. 'The Burmese were our friends, and we had to help them achieve their long-desired independence... but the very first syllable of that word was not allowed to pass our lips at the beginning.'[1] That hesitation had significant results.

Meanwhile, Ba Maw grew to know Iida:

> I had found him to be a unique type of Japanese soldier [he later wrote], human, fatherly, and very understanding, a militarist on the surface, but not altogether so deeper down; at least he always tried to see things your way too, which was what made him different from the other militarists. It gave him a good deal of inner perception, particularly of the fact that a war can be won or lost in many ways and for many reasons, one of the surest ways to lose it being to rouse the hostility and resistance of a whole people. The general was a samurai in his almost mystical devotion to his emperor, his warrior caste and code, and his country, but this very devotion which consumed him made him understand the devotion of others to their own

[1] L. Allen, 'Japanese military rule in Burma,' *Modern Asian Studies*, III 2, 1969, p. 179

gods. It was this rare, unmilitaristic quality which made him great in our eyes.[1]

Reading Iida's own account of the problems he faced, it is not difficult to see why Ba Maw found him sympathetic. What worried him most was that the people Tokyo sent out to him were men with experience of Korea and China, i.e. of a colonial state or enemy territory, and Burma should be neither of these in relation to Japan. These people were not merely the military. 'The men who came out from Japan as civilian administrators completely misunderstood the kind of military government the Army expected. They thought something in the so-called China or Manchuria style was wanted, and set to work with the intention of creating an "occupied territories administration" just as if they were in enemy country. There was ill-concealed pleasure in some quarters when they got in a mess.'[2]

Iida noticed that the Japanese companies which came to Burma in the wake of the army – concession-grabbers – were thinking of a long-term exploitation in the future, without even considering the transfer of economic power to the Burmese themselves. 'Japanese of this kind,' he wrote, 'kept pouring into Burma, and swaggered and strutted about – what kind of impression must they have made on the Burmese?'

The same was true of civilian administrators seconded from Tokyo ministries such as Commerce and Industry or Agriculture and Forestry. It was clear to Iida that they were concerned with retaining concessions, so that even when Burma achieved independence, they would inevitably remain in Japanese hands. It occurred to almost none of them to hand them over to the Burmese.

Iida argued the case with both types of civilian in terms of Japan's future relationship with an independent Burma. 'Does Japan need to take anything from Burma?' he asked them. 'The oil of Yenangyaung, the mines of Bawdwin, the Irrawaddy navigation rights – all these things which the British owned – if we give them to the Burmese, will it not be possible by doing so to ensure the Burmese have the feeling they're genuinely independent? If Japan ends up by taking these concessions, it will just mean replacing Britain by Japan – Burma will still be treated as a colony. At present the Japanese are running even small concerns, and are putting pressure on concerns run by Burmese. If we do this, we'll be even worse than the British. What Japan needs is not concessions. She needs an economically strong and independent Burma, a country which should have a feeling of trust, from her innermost heart, when she co-operates with Japan.'[3]

[1] Ba Maw, op.cit., p. 264

[2] Iida Shōjirō, quoted in *Biruma Kōryaku Sakusen*, Asagumo Shimbunsha, 1967, pp. 507–8

[3] ibid.

But the administrators and company executives kept pouring in, so that by June 1943 there were around 900 men working for the Military Government Staff and nearly 130 working officially for the Burmese administration. They were full of plans. The fast-flowing Salween should be used to generate electric power, making large-scale enterprises possible, the Shan States should be separated from Burma and turned into Japanese territory *in perpetuo*, and large-scale Japanese immigration into them encouraged; they could be linked to Japan by a railway passing through Northern French Indo-China to the China coast. Had Japan not been defeated in 1945, it is perfectly possible that some of these schemes would have been realized. The separation of the Shan States from Burma was a bitter reality Ba Maw had to accept when Burma was granted independence, as he had to accept the cession of two states, Kengtung and Mongpan, to Thailand, which had, in the nature of things, been a brisker adherent to the Japanese cause. Thailand's prompt if compulsory alliance with Japan in 1941 obtained for her the retrocession of provinces annexed by the French to Cambodia and also of those sultanates which the British had incorporated into the Federated Malay States. Ba Maw protested about the loss of Kengtung and Mongpan, but Tojo simply laughed him off.

To some extent, the concession of independence to Burma was a by-product of the first Wingate expedition, as well as of internal movements in Burma. Before Wingate, the Japanese military – or most of them – regarded the Chindwin as the outer limit of their territorial ambitions. After Wingate proved it was possible to move and support a force across the Indo-Burmese frontier, Iida's successor as C-in-C 15 Army, Mutaguchi, advocated the occupation of Imphal, the capital of Manipur State. As this idea went forward, under various forms, and with various brakes on Mutaguchi's personal ambitions, as we have seen, it became imperative to show India – i.e. Subhas Chandra Bose – that if Japan obtained a foothold there, her prime aim was to free India from the British. Burma was to be the example. Had the motive not existed of showing Bose that the intentions of liberation would be honourably fulfilled, it is doubtful whether Burma would have gained her independence in that short period of little over a year from the time of total conquest (Mandalay had been taken on 1 May 1942, Tamanthi on 30 May, Sumprabum on 17 June).

Ba Maw himself, of course, cleverly played every card in the pack. He depicts himself as the fond father of the wild, misled, but enthusiastic and patriotic Thakins, as the politician mistrusting military crudeness and racial bigotry. But he showed himself to the Japanese Government, particularly when he appeared in Tokyo in November 1943, in a military image he hoped they would recognize, 'Prussian jacket, jackboots and all', as Hugh Tinker points out.[1]

---

[1] Hugh Tinker, 'The Politics of Burma', in S. Rose, ed., *Politics in Southern Asia*, London, 1963, p. 111

Perhaps this was because the mood of the higher command in Burma had changed, the comprehensive and sympathetic Iida giving way to the narrow-minded and obsessive Kawabe, who mistrusted Ba Maw and who, like Terauchi (whose father had been Governor-General of Korea), was inclined to treat the Burmese as recalcitrant colonials. It fell to Kawabe, ironically enough, as the Japanese Commander-in-Chief in Rangoon, to convey the act of independence to Burma on 1 August 1943. On that day, one of the young Thakins, Thakin Nu, the one who made for himself (in recollection) the image of the unambitious dreamy Buddhist idealist, made a speech at the inauguration ceremony.

'History has yet to witness,' Thakin Nu proclaimed, 'a single instance in which a country, motivated by high idealism and nobility of purpose, has sacrificed its life and property solely for the liberation and welfare of oppressed peoples, and Nippon seems destined to that historic role for the first time in the chronicles of mankind.'[1]

U Nu does not quote this speech in his own book, and it was perhaps malicious and unkind for Ba Maw to recall those phrases when he came to write his own. But it is a case Ba Maw elsewhere makes himself, and which we have to consider when, campaign narratives apart, we come to make the balance-sheet for the people of Burma.

'Looking at it historically,' he wrote, 'no nation has done so much to liberate Asia from white domination, yet no nation has been so misunderstood by the very people whom it has helped either to liberate or to set an example to in many things... Japan was betrayed by her militarists and their racial fantasies. Had her Asian motives been true, had she only been faithful to the concept of Asia for the Asians that she herself had proclaimed at the beginning of the war, Japan's fate would have been very different. No military defeat could then have robbed her of the trust and gratitude of half of Asia for ever more... Even now, as things actually are, nothing can ever obliterate the role Japan has played in bringing liberation to countless peoples.'[2]

In the case of Burma, that theme has continued on into post-war Japanese historiography. Ōta Tsunezō, himself a member of the wartime military administration, has written a book from his own experience and from a collection of documents he had assembled – a hundred pages of print – to make the case for the beneficial effects of the Japanese occupation of Burma; a useful counter-balance on the Japanese side, though not official, to F.S.V. Donnison's detailed and judicious *British Military Administration in the Far East* and Hugh Tinker's *Union of Burma*. Ōta admits the physical devastation of the Burmese economy, but claims that the psychological impact of Japan on Burma outweighs this.

[1] Ba Maw, op.cit., p. 39

[2] ibid., pp. 185–6

Historically, he says, we have to look beyond the devastation of the Burmese economy, the almost total loss of the Irrawaddy Flotilla Company's vessels, of locomotives and rolling stock (he gives a Japanese figure of 85% locomotives out of commission compared with Tinker's general estimate of 48% damage to railway assets) and the laying waste or neglect of agricultural land. In spite of the economic deterioration, inevitable because Burma was a land-locked island to all intents and purposes, cut off by bombing of her sea-borne traffic, subjected to British invasion from the west and Sino-American from the north, her industrial installations damaged by air-raids, the country managed to support a Japanese force of around 200,000 men, rice production was maintained, and the people did not starve.

More than that, they acquired self-confidence, their leaders' authority was enhanced, and they learned what it was like, even on a small scale, to control the means of physical compulsion through their own armed forces. The training of the Burma National Army and the impetus given to the mature development of the Burmese independence movement are the most significant legacies of the Japanese military administration in Burma. A body of men was created, ready to assume responsibility for government and the armed forces. The original nucleus of the Burma Independence Army grew to 10,000 men under arms, and Ōta claims this was a very real factor in the background of negotiations for independence after the British returned (Ba Maw certainly makes it clear, however jejune he considers the Thakins to be, that he always had to consider the military force controlled by Aung San, though it was a negligible factor for the Japanese).

Economically, Ba Maw makes a similar case. The Burmese 'needed clothing, transport and fuels, medical supplies... machinery of all sorts, replacements, and repairs and technicians to undertake them and so on endlessly. Nearly all those supplies and services had to be brought from across the seas at a time when the American sea and air power was strangling Japanese transportation, and yet it was done.'[1]

In fact, it was not done. The evidence to the contrary is provided by Ba Maw's former Director of Press and Publicity, U Hla Pe, in his *Narrative of the Japanese Occupation of Burma*. U Hla Pe points out the ascendancy of the Japanese trading associations over the Burmese economy, the Commodity Distribution Association, the Nippon Burma Rice Union, the Nippon Burma Timber Union (the very case Iida makes). He also claims that the Japanese produced next to nothing in Burma, and imported next to nothing into Burma. The consumer goods which were distributed were those available in 1942 when the British companies left, and as these stocks dwindled they were not replaced. 'With the exception of arms and

[1] ibid., p. 273

ammunition, *sake* and comfort-women, Japanese ships could not bring anything into the country.'[1] Brigadier Smeeton vividly sums up the contrast:

> Before the war, Burma had been an advanced and prosperous country of green paddy fields and white pagodas, rich in natural resources, where the ordered rubber trees in spring burst in a convulsive effort in a few days into full leaf, and the great forests sent their teak and the earth its oil, down the rivers to the sea. A country where there was always plenty to eat and no one had to work too hard... Now it was a desolation. A desolation of the war which in three years had swept the length of the country and back again and had destroyed the oil-fields, the towns and villages and practically every bridge in the country, rail and road. A desolation of neglect, for the plantations had been untended, the paddy fields uncultivated, the oxen dispersed and killed, the elephants dead or at large in the jungle, the timber industry at a standstill and there had been no medical supplies. A desolation of the mind and of the spirit, for there had been no education, and the people were suffering from malnutrition and the Civil Service had collapsed.[2]

In the religious field, a very important one for Burma, the Japanese stressed their common religion, during the first year of occupation. But the much freer and easier structure of Japanese monasticism, in which monks take wives, was not welcomed by the Burmese *sangha*, or monastic order, which considered the Japanese as little better than sacrilegious. Admittedly many Burmese *pongyis* (monks) had played a dissident political role under British rule, but they resented the Japanese desire to use them in the control of the Burmese people, and they disliked Japanese troops billetting themselves in monasteries, and ordering *pongyis* to carry out defiling tasks such as collecting guns and disposing of bodies. They also considered Japanese emperor-worship a defilement of pure Buddhist doctrine, and public ceremonies to celebrate the spirits of the war dead as superstition: 'Burmese laymen have not yet tired of joking over sights such as a monk riding a girl's bicycle or wearing a woman's sarong round his head. It was beyond belief that a Japanese monk could be married. *Pongyis* in particular were distressed that some Japanese monks were warriors. They were deeply offended at the presumption of those warrior-monks in expecting to partake food with them.' They also disliked being asked to take part in inoculation compaigns against cholera and

[1] *U Hla Pe's Narrative of the Japanese Occupation of Burma*, recorded by U Khin, 1961, p. 55
[2] Smeeton, *A Change of Jungles*, pp. 116–7

smallpox, being appalled at the need to come in contact with a woman's body, even at the end of an inoculation syringe, as likely to harm a monk's spiritual progress. In this, as in many other ways, Japanese information on the differences between their own Buddhism and the Burmese version was grossly inadequate.[1]

Two factors produced interesting by-products. First, in Lower Burma, half the agricultural land was owned in pre-war days by Indian money-lenders (*chettyars*) who rented it out to Burmese peasant tenants. Fearing the hostility of the Burmese population when the British were no longer there to protect them, the *chettyars* and their families fled to India in the wake of the retreating Allied armies in 1942. Ba Maw's Sinyetha party (the name means 'proletariat') proclaimed itself the party of the poor man and he took the opportunity to make over the abandoned lands to the Burmese tenants. These found a ready market for the abundant rice crop in the Japanese Army, who paid in the plentiful military scrip which cost them nothing. There was no problem of exporting the rice, as it was sold on the spot, and agricultural debts came to an end.

Second is the issue of forced labour. Unspeakable suffering, disease and death, were the lot of the Burmese labourers employed on the Burma-Siam Railway; as, indeed, it was of the labour from the rest of South-East Asia, including the British, Australian and Dutch POWs. Accepting this enormous toll in life and suffering, Ba Maw makes a case for Japanese vision here:

> There was an enormous gain as well, the conquest of a vast jungle frontier which had kept two neighbouring peoples apart since time began, and this in the long reckoning of history might well be judged as outweighing everything else. If we take that histori-cal view it will be seen that few enterprises during the whole war showed more essential vision than the construction of this railroad. But with the defeat of the Japanese it vanished forever and only the most lurid wartime memories and stories remain. The region is once again a wilderness, except for a few neatly kept graveyards where many British dead now sleep in peace and dignity. As for the Asians who died there, both Burmese and Japanese, their ashes lie scattered and lost forever.[2]

In this, as in much else, whatever his criticism of the Japanese military, Ba Maw remained a fervent apologist of the Japanese intervention in the history of his country. He left Rangoon as they did in April 1945, and later

---

[1] Cf. on this, Dorothy Guyot, 'The uses of Buddhism in wartime Burma', *Asian Studies*, V11, No. 1, pp. 50–80

[2] Ba Maw, op.cit., p. 297

went to Japan where he was concealed by the Japanese Foreign Office in a Buddhist temple in the remote village of Ishiuchi in Niigata Prefecture, before he finally decided to give himself up to the British occupation authorities.

The conning of Professor Asai

It is one of the many paradoxes of the war that Ba Maw, who, as stated, made himself the dedicated apologist of the Japanese cause, and left for Japan rather than surrender to the British in 1945, should have been cordially mistrusted, even hated, by many Japanese; and that Aung San, the young student revolutionary who led their Burma National Army, turned against them in the days of their defeat and brought his army over to the side of the British. In fact the mistrust of Ba Maw went so far that Japanese high up in the Army command decided to get rid of him – permanently. General Kawabe, to start with, says he has merely 'a cold record' of the events of 1 August 1943 which aroused so many emotions among the other participants at the independence ceremony. His frigid, unfriendly glance noted that two very pro-Japanese Thakins were conspicuous by their absence, Thakin Ba Sein and Thakin Tun Oke, the men who counted for most in the first Bama Baho government of 1942. Two days after the ceremony, Ba Sein came to see him and poured out his heart for hours on the slights profferred to the Thakin party by Ba Maw's omissions. 'We have done more than anyone', he told Kawabe, 'to co-operate with the Japanese, we have exhausted our strength fighting for you, and now a bunch of know-nothings have come into the cabinet. The people are starting to call it not "Burma's independence" but "Ba Maw's independence".'[1]

Ba Sein's and Tun Oke's resentment later expressed themselves in words about Ba Maw which could have had a far more lethal effect. Colonel (later Major-General) Isomura, one of Kawabe's senior staff, had conceived a bitter dislike for Ba Maw. He was convinced, as Kawabe was, that he was far from being the wholehearted supporter of Japan which his fiery, racialist rhetoric at the Tokyo Conference proclaimed him to be. They listened sceptically to Ba Maw's celebration of Asia's awakening racial awareness and Burmese participation in this in support of Japan's sweeping away of the old colonial regimes. They were sure he was still in touch with the British.

Isomura's convictions were to have repercussions on a rather simple-minded Japanese academic who, taken in by Isomura's skill, found himself

[1] L. Allen, 'The Japanese Occupation of South East Asia (I)', *The Durham University Journal*, New Series, vol. xxxii, No. 1, Dec. 1970, p. 14

drawn into the sinister by-ways of Burmese politics, became involved in an attempt to assassinate Ba Maw, and was imprisoned for his dedication to what he conceived to be his duty to the Japanese Army.

The academic in question is Professor Asai Tokuichi,[1] author of *Biruma sensen fūdoki* (*Topography of the Burma Battle Front*), which appeared under the imprint of Tamagawa University where he was professor of geography several years ago (1980); and of a series of articles on the assassination attempt in *Seiji Keizai Shigaku* (*Political and Economic History Review*).[2]

Under the influence of the German geographer Haushofer, some Japanese geography departments had become dominated by geopolitical theories. One of these was in the Institute for Research in the Humanities *(Jinbun Kagaku Kenkyūjo)* at the University of Kyoto, where Professor Fushimi, an expert on the geography of prehistory, once made to Asai an observation which is interesting in view of later events: 'You're a *tan-saibō*, Asai.' *Saibō* is a biological term, the Japanese for 'cell' and *'tan'* means 'single' or 'simple'. It seems to have been a correct psychological observation.

Invited to South-East Asia as a geopolitical expert, Asai visited Burma, was taken on to the staff of Burma Area Army, then transferred to Southern Army in Singapore, where he met the C-in-C, Field Marshal Terauchi, an old classmate of his father at the Military Academy; a meeting which was to help him greatly when he most needed it. He was also introduced to the two Thakins, Ba Sein and Tun Oke, who had left Burma under a cloud and were living in Singapore under Southern Army's protection, as they were known to support strong rule and to look back with nostalgia on the absolutism of the old Burmese monarchy.

Ba Maw, they told him over dinner, was a British spy. The air-raids on Rangoon were guided in by him. Poor Asai never doubted them for a moment, and decided he ought to do something about it. His job in the Section for Research into Unoccupied Zones provided him with a mission to return to Burma (to investigate North Burma and Yunnan) and he and a colleague arrived in Rangoon on 20 January 1944. Everyone at GHQ was busy with the plans for the Arakan offensive and the assault on Imphal, and Asai could scarcely bear to think that while Japanese soldiers were preparing to die to defend Burma, the Burmese Premier himself was betraying them.

His suspicions were strengthened by talks with a Japanese civilian friend, from the *Shōwa Tsūsho* (Shōwa Trading Association), whom he refers to

---

[1] Misspelt and incorrectly ranked by Ba Maw as Captain Asahi. (He was in fact a *gunzoku*, a civilian attached to the Army.)

[2] Nos. 144 and 145, May and June 1978. I am indebted to Ian Gow for drawing my attention to these review articles.

as T. (Another member of the assassination group he still calls U. Both T and U are alive in Japan and he fears to open old sores. Unnecessarily: the names are known.) One night Major-General Isomura, Kawabe's deputy Chief of Staff, paid T a call. When Asai brought up the things he had heard from T, Ba Sein and Tun Oke, about Ba Maw, their supposed ally, Isomura replied simply, 'It's true'. He went on to tell Asai that the contents of a conversation between the Commander-in-Chief, Kawabe, and Ba Maw, were broadcast the next day from Calcutta. No one else had been privy to the conversation. The conclusion was obvious. Ba Maw was treating with the enemy.

Isomura had sized his man up correctly. Burning with indignation, Asai decided that Ba Maw must die.[1] Willing – of course – to fall in with Asai's project, T agreed to get some weapons, and the night of 16 February was fixed as the time to act. To ensure the assassins were not interfered with, it was thought necessary to obtain if not the collusion, at any rate the abstention, of the Burma Defence Army. At 10 pm on the night of 16th, T went to the Burmese Defence Minister and Commander-in-Chief, Major-General Aung San, for this purpose. Asai, U Kyaw Myint – a Burmese conspirator – and another Burmese, went to Ba Maw's official residence. They called at U's house on the way, and Asai said, 'We're going to kill Ba Maw now, are you coming with us?' U said, 'Yes, let's go'. They also went to the house of T's boss, the head of the Rangoon Branch of the Shōwa Trading Association. (In his text, Asai refers to him at this point simply as K, but elsewhere in the articles the name is given in full as Kishida.)[2] It seemed unwise to go to Ba Maw's residence wearing the uniform of a civilian attached to the Japanese Army, and after discussing this with Kishida they disguised themselves in Burmese clothing. But Kishida was not tempted to join them. They did not, Asai recalls, touch a drop of *sake*.

At Ba Maw's house, Asai told U Kyaw Myint to call out in Burmese to the guard: 'We know that Ba Maw is a spy for the British and we have come to kill him. Your Commander-in-Chief Aung San knows this, and is coming immediately. But first, hand over your weapons to us.' Recognizing Aung San's name, the guard handed over ten rifles, 38s supplied by the Japanese. Asai selected one. As he did so, the now nightly air-raid warning sounded.

Out of the house came Ba Maw, making for the air-raid shelter. Brandishing his rifle, Asai followed but – as Ba Maw himself relates – the Burmese Premier came out of the shelter and went back inside the house.

---

[1] His articles admit that Isomura had set him up (*Isomura shōshō wa kekka toshite wa Asai wo sosonokashita koto ni naru*). When Asai was later in a civilian internment camp in Thailand, he encountered T's boss, Mr. Kishida, who had been head of the Rangoon branch of the Shōwa Tsūshō (Shōwa Trading Association). 'They really let you in the cart, didn't they, Asai?' he said, (*Asai san ni wa kinodoku na koto wo shita*). 'He knew I'd been manipulated'.

[2] 'Ba Mō misui jiken ni tsuite no shōgen', Pt. 2, *Seiji Keizai Shigaku*, June 1978, No. 145, p.10

Asai came out, too, and dashed to the front of the house. As he did so, a first-floor window was flung open and a figure appeared in it. It was not clear whether it was Ba Maw or not, so Asai hesitated, and did not fire. He went inside, but the house was large, he did not know his way around, and he suddenly realized the plan had gone awry. He came out, and told U to go and report to Major-General Isomura.

But it was already too late for Isomura to intervene. Colonel Hiraoka, the head of the liaison organization between Ba Maw and the Japanese, who had been alerted by Ba Maw, arrived at the house, and took Asai prisoner. The military police then turned up and began to interrogate Asai. They could hardly believe it was his first attempt, since he had handled the guard so skilfully. U and T were arrested, and all three were sent to the Japanese Army gaol in Insein, north of Rangoon.

The legal upshot was interesting. Burma Area Army held a trial on 24 April 1944. It was a *gunritsu kaigi* (trial under local military law) rather than a formal *gunpō kaigi* (court martial) which it should have been. The reason was that it involved a crime committed by Japanese army-attached personnel and Burmese locals. *Gunritsu kaigi* was Southern Army law, applicable to armies of the people of occupied territories, and should not have been used to judge Japanese subjects. There was something else. Legally, Burma had been an independent country for nearly seven months when the *coup* was carried out, and it had been perpetrated against that country's first minister, the 'people's representative'. It could be held that the trial should be by Burmese law. A request was in fact sent to Kawabe, the Army Commander-in-Chief, by the Burmese Foreign Minister, Thakin Nu, to have Asai handed over, but this was refused.

U Nu, in his book, speaks of Asai being sent off to Singapore out of the way, but this is not what happened. A report on the affair was sent to the War Ministry in Tokyo by Southern Army and reached the ears of the Emperor. A friendly telegram was despatched to Ba Maw, expressing the Emperor's regrets, and Tojo, the Japanese Premier, gave vent to his anger and told Terauchi to see that Asai was severly dealt with. When Terauchi demurred, Tojo wired that he was to send Asai and his fellow assassins to Tokyo at once by plane.

'Let it lie, let it lie', Terauchi told the Staff Officer who brought him the telegram. 'It's not that important.' He crumpled the signal and threw it into the wastepaper basket. The reason was not simply that Tojo and Terauchi did not get on. Terauchi remembered the *gunzoku* Asai. Not only had his father been Terauchi's classmate. The not-so-bright Terauchi had been crammed for his mathematics examination by Asai senior, and Terauchi had not forgotten the debt. (Asai had also been a member of a military geography society in Japan called the *Kōsenkai,* with which Kawabe was connected.)

So things were fixed for him. Just as he had been manipulated into the crime, he was manipulated out of it. At the trial, a lieutenant-colonel from Kawabe's staff presided. 'A crime which causes pain to the Emperor's heart', observed this presiding judge, 'is a serious one, but I bear in mind the fact that Asai's nerves were in a damaged state as the result of malaria. I believe both T and U were merely drawn into the affair by Asai, and I find it quite remarkable that he should have the power to attract young men to himself unconditionally.' Asai was given a fifteen-year sentence, T two-and-half years, and U one year. When the three were returned to gaol, the superintendent, Uchida, told them they might only serve a third of their sentence before being paroled. In the event, the flight of Burma Area Army GHQ from Rangoon the following spring involved the transfer of the prisoners to an area of greater safety in Moulmein. Colonel Sakaguchi, the head of the legal department, with whom Asai stayed in Moulmein, told him after the surrender, 'Your name will be known to the British Army and things might go badly for you if you were taken into one of their camps. I'll set you free, and I think you should make for Thailand.' He gave Asai a few *bahts*, and Asai went down the Burma-Siam Railway into one of the camps used for Japanese civilian internees, after stopping a while in the Trocadero Hotel in Bangkok. Under the wing of the Shōwa Trading Association of which he purported to be a civilian employee, he escaped whatever vigilance of the British searchers there was, and was shipped back to Japan in June 1946. The British, he thinks, although they examined individually everyone who left the camps, were so occupied with searching for Colonel Tsuji Masanobu that they ignored the small fry. (He was right.) He returned to the study of geography, and at the time of writing his articles held a chair of geography at Tamagawa University. He has since revisited Burma with pleasure and no apparent risk.

This attempted assassination is a very curious episode indeed, and expresses fully the ambivalence of Japanese and Burmese attitudes towards each other. Ba Maw gives a brief account of it, so does U Nu, but there is an odd silence on the topic in the official Japanese war histories. The second volume of the four which deal with the land campaigns in Burma devotes a great deal of space to the negotiations leading up to Burma's independence, but neither in it, nor in the following volume, is there any reference to Professor Asai's attempt to assassinate the Prime Minister of Burma, the head of State of one of Japan's allies. Nor, even odder, is it mentioned in Ōta Tsunezō's book on the Japanese occupation, which goes into great detail. Yet Asai's attempt was known in Japanese Army and civilian circles in Rangoon, and obviously Burmese ruling circles knew of it. Surely, if any political issues at all were touched on in these military history volumes, there must be some allusion to a scandal as formidable as this? Asai's articles solve this puzzle. The president of the court who gave such a favourable judgement to Asai and his fellow-conspirators, and privately hinted to Asai that Terauchi's intervention had saved him, was Lieutenant-Colonel Fuwa Hiroshi. The historian who compiled the Burma narratives for the Defence Agency's official war histories was Lieutenant-Colonel Fuwa Hiroshi, who also told me that he did not expect to see a history of Japanese military government in South-East Asia published from the documents in the Defence Agency archives; at any rate, not for public circulation.

It seems a pity. There must be quite a lot we could still be told, whatever embarrassing revelations to Japanese and South-East Asian personalities and governments are involved. The episode itself is bound to make us sceptical of the fellow-feeling expressed by apologists for either side, Japan or Burma, depending on the dates of the expression. Ba Maw's wartime speeches are full of wild racial enthusiasm for co-operation with Japan, but his post-war autobiography lavishes scorn on the racial fantasies of the limited Japanese military mind. U Nu, likewise, in his speech on the proclamation of independence in August 1943, as we have seen, emphasizes the uniqueness of Japan's self-sacrificing role as the liberator of the Burmese people, in tones that accord ill with the naive, aloof picture of himself in *Burma under the Japanese*.

Force 136: Hugh Seagrim's sacrifice

All this is natural enough. In 1943 both Ba Maw and U Nu were acting under some constraint, and it still seemed that something was to be gained from wooing the Japanese. In the post-war period, a certain sophisticated distance from the joint past with Japan was *de rigueur*, however welcome individual Japanese returning to Burma may have been. The change was brought about by a simple military event. Once the British crossed a line running across central Burma through Mandalay, observed the Japanese general Sakurai Tokutarō, then adviser to Aung San and the Burma National Army, that line would be transformed into a psychological one: the line of rejection of the Japanese Army by the people of Burma. That is precisely what happened when Aung San, after the parade of the BNA in Rangoon on 28 March 1945, marched north as if to reinforce the Japanese fighting the Irrawaddy battle, but took his troops over to the British.

That event was no sudden volte-face. It had been prepared for several months, and the groundwork for it was laid even further back in the past by one of the bravest and best men to come out of the British forces in Burma: Major Hugh Seagrim.

When the British left Burma in the summer of 1942, they naturally left behind them agents or groups of agents to pass on information about the Japanese and Burmese who collaborated with them. Some Burmese who left with the British, or were infiltrated back into Burma after leaving on their own initiative, made contact with the Thakins as well as with pro-British elements, and a fair amount of information on the internal state of Burma was available at Simla, the headquarters of Sir Reginald Dorman-Smith, in Delhi at GHQ (India), and at Mountbatten's headquarters in Kandy.

Information came also from captured documents, some of them of long-term political interest, others of more immediate tactical value; and from the activity of V Force, a unit consisting of teams of a couple of British officers with armed Gurkhas or Karens – or other tribesmen, depending on the area in which they operated. V Force information was usually of tactical, short-term value, as its teams inserted themselves behind the Japanese lines relatively close to operational areas and observed movements of Japanese troops and transport in order to provide identifications and general 'order of battle' information. When, for instance, the operation order by the GOC Shinbu Force, Major-General Nagasawa Kanichi, was captured and translated on 17 Division's front in June 1945, revealing the plans, numbers, conditions, units, routes, ammunition and signals of 55 Division infantry group as it planned to break out of the Pegu Yomas, the information in it was confirmed by V Force units under the command of Major 'Bill' Tibbetts in Penwegon, the HQ of 17 Division. Indications from documents and prisoners made out the day of the breakout (X-Day in Japanese terminology) to be 20 July, and this was confirmed by signals intelligence. The actual movement of the Japanese formations was logged by V Force. Along one route, for instance, leading from the village of Yee in the Pegu Yomas through Penwegon itself and on to the Sittang, Captain Lindsay, one of Tibbetts's V Force officers, went into Yee and questioned the headman about the groups of Japanese moving from the Yomas through his village. This track turned out to be the main route of egress from the Yomas of Shinbu Force, along which a Japanese commando unit was to carry out an attack against Penwegon itself on the night of the 19th to secure it for the passage of the main force. Although they had agents wandering in and out of Penwegon, some of whom were caught, and some not, the Japanese did not seem to be aware that the village they were preparing to seize was in fact the heavily defended headquarters of an entire division.

At any rate, as distinct from tactical intelligence of that kind, which V Force provided in Arakan (where Lieutenant-General Irwin's son was one of its officers) and in the hills around Imphal where the Englishwoman Ursula Graham-Bower – who later married a V Force officer – had set up an extensive network of Naga informers,[1] there was long-range strategic – and therefore political – intelligence which was more strictly the province of Force 136. Force 136 was the name by which Special Operations Ex-

---

[1] Cf. Ursula Graham-Bower, *Naga Path*, passim.

ecutive was known in South-East Asia, under the command of Colin Mackenzie. It operated into Malaya, Siam, and even French Indo-China. In these countries, as in Burma – and as in Europe – its function was not primarily that of intelligence-gathering, but rather to contact nuclei of local resistance against the occupying enemy force, assess their potential, arm them if it was considered that an armed rising would assist the returning British, and lead and control the rising when it occurred. Infiltration in Malaya was chiefly by offshore submarine, and Freddie Spencer Chapman's long and lonely vigil in the jungle hills of central and northern Malaya came to an end when ex-officers of the Malayan Police contacted him in 1943. In Siam, Force 136 was instrumental in contacting the Regent, Pridi Panomyong, known for his pro-Allied sympathies, and in helping to organize a resistance movement among the Thais which would have become operative if Thailand ever became a battlefield.

The commander of Force 136 (Burma Section) from 1943 until the end of the war was John Ritchie Gardiner, a man with immense experience of pre-war Burma. Formerly of the forestry firm McGregor & Co., Gardiner had been one of two European representatives on the Municipal Council of Rangoon. In fact had the war not intervened he was due to become its Mayor in March 1942. He was, as a result, in frequent contact with Burmese politics at all levels, and knew Ba Maw and U Saw personally. U Saw appeared to him a bluff and hearty type, not over-endowed with brains, the kind of man who would have made an excellent leader of a band of dacoits. Ba Maw, on the other hand, he saw as ambitious, suave and very plausible, rather a dandy, and not particularly trustworthy. Gardiner's job was to get on with the thirty-odd members of the council, Burmese, Indians and Chinese, excellent groundwork for his later activities as head of Force 136.[1]

Partly for political, partly for racial reasons, Force 136 in Burma had two divisions (like the two sections into which SOE divided to operate in France, one for British purposes, one as liaison with de Gaulle). The 'Burmese Section' worked chiefly on the west bank of the Sittang, in liaison with guerrillas of the AFO (Anti-Fascist Organization).[2] On the east bank of the Sittang the other division was involved with the Karens, who both mistrusted the Burmese and hated the Japanese, and felt a natural affinity for the Europeans because of the long established Christian tradition in the Karenni. They suffered for this in 1942 when the Japanese Army and their Burmese auxiliaries passed northwards along the east bank of the Sittang. And they were to suffer again at the hands of the Japanese when a *tōbatsu* (punitive expedition) was organized to capture Hugh Seagrim in 1943.

[1] Correspondence with the author, 7 June 1975

[2] Later, the 'Anti-Fascist People's Freedom League' (AFPFL).

Heroic gallantry was almost a cliché in the Seagrim family. Hugh Seagrim's brother Derek – the third of five sons of the rector of the Norfolk village of Whissonsett-with-Horningtoft – was posthumously awarded the VC when commanding the 7th Battalion Green Howards in the assault on the Mareth line in March 1943. All the sons became army officers, Hugh joining the Indian Army and later the Burma' Rifles. Versatile and unconventional, an athlete and explorer of out-of-the-way places, Seagrim was a natural recruit for Noel Stevenson who was entrusted with the job of raising guerrilla levies from the hill tribes in Burma in December 1941. Assistant Superintendent in the Burma Frontier Service at Kutkai in the Northern Shan States, Stevenson had begun training Kachins for guerrilla work months before Japan came into the war. At 17 Division HQ in Moulmein, it was agreed at a conference with General Smyth that Seagrim should organize a force of Karens at Papun, based on the fifty-five military policemen of Salween District. Smyth allocated all the arms he could spare them – 200 Italian rifles and a few thousand rounds – and Seagrim started enlisting volunteers, in collaboration with George Chettle, the District Commissioner and District Superintendent of Police, to whom he confided his belief that the Japanese would go through Burma like a dose of salts. He had spent a short leave in Japan, and liked and admired the Japanese.[1]

From Papun, Seagrim moved further into the hills, to the village of Pyagawpu, where he decided that even if the Burma Army retreated, he would stay in the Karen hills and organize resistance to the Japanese. By April 1942 he was on his own, and decided to try and find Army HQ to obtain a wireless receiver and transmitter. He failed, and was ambushed by Shan bandits on the return journey. Seagrim escaped, but lost a Karen Levy officer. Communications were now his greatest problem. Whatever he did in the hills, how could he get news of it back to the Army? It was the Army's problem, too. If Seagrim still survived in those distant hills, how could they get in touch?

On February 18 1943, a Karen officer, 2/Lt Ba Gyaw, with three other Karens, was parachuted into the Karenni with instructions to contact Seagrim, the drop being 'covered' by a bombing raid on Toungoo to distract Japanese attention. But Ba Gyaw dropped without a wireless set, and attempts to drop one to him failed: at each full moon between February and October 1943, attempts were made, and all failed. In October, Major James Nimmo of Force 136, a young officer who had been employed by Gardiner's forestry firm in pre-war Burma, volunteered to be dropped in with wireless equipment, and went in on the night of October 12. Nimmo was lucky. In two days he found both

---

[1] Ian Morrison, *Grandfather Longlegs*, p. 50

Ba Gyaw and Seagrim, who was in wireless communication with India by 15 October 1943.

To make his message worthwhile, Seagrim had sent a Karen officer, Saw Po Hla, down into Rangoon in September to gather gossip and get in touch with the Karen leaders in the city. Po Hla also spoke to Karen officers of Aung San's Burma Defence Army, which contained a Karen battalion under a Sandhurst-trained officer, Hanson Kya Doe, from whom Po Hla learned that anti-Japanese feeling was strong among the Burmese of the Defence Army. He also brought back details of living conditions and whereabouts of Japanese military installations.

Seagrim lived with the Karens on terms of personal friendship, dressed as a Karen, and kept alive among them, single-handed, the flame of resistance to the Japanese and the assurance the British would return. It was obvious that the Japanese, who had conquered almost all of Burma, would not sit back and allow a British officer to maintain an autonomous area behind their lines, and, in particular, one so near to the main road and railway lines to Mandalay, which passed just west of the Karen hills. So they sent in a *tōbatsu* (or punitive expedition). The *tōbatsu* consisted of an infantry force under officers of the Kempei (Japanese military police), Captain Inoue and Lt Kurokata. The Kempei moved into the Karenni and, using their customary methods of violence, began to sow terror in the hearts of the Karens.

As he saw it, Seagrim was faced by a moral choice. The two officers sent to join him, Nimmo and McCrindle, were killed, and then his beloved Karens became the object of punitive violence because they were concealing him. He did not consider long. He voluntarily gave himself up to save his Karens from torture. His bravery impressed his captors, the men who tried him, and the Japanese doctor who saw him in prison. There was of course, no question of the sentence. Seagrim had been taken, not in British uniform, but in Karen costume, and, inevitably, was bound to be shot as a spy.

The Japanese medical officer, Kameo Susumu, who saw Seagrim when he was brought in was impressed by both his great height – he was 6 feet 4 inches tall – and by the rough and ragged Karen clothing he wore. Could this be the British major who had defied the Japanese for so long? 'I've been resolved to die for some time,' Seagrim declared. 'I'd like you to help the Karens who were taken with me. They have committed no crime.' He hated the long war between Great Britain and Japan, he told Kameo, and hoped it would soon be over. When he was interrogated, he answered briskly and in a business-like fashion, standing rigid and motionless.

His pleas for his Karens were useless. Together with twenty of them he was tried by court-martial at the gaol at Insein, north of Rangoon. 'The war between our two countries is a misfortune', he told the court-martial. 'I obey the orders of my country, as a British officer, and I have merely

577

carried out my duty. I have no complaints at being sentenced to death. But the men with me only carried out my orders, and I ask you to declare them not guilty.'[1]

He impressed his fellow-prisoners, too. 'I was strongly stirred the moment I saw him', wrote Flight-Lieutenant Arthur Sharpe, who spent March to August 1944 in the New Law Courts cells, 'his tall, proud, erect figure, his fine-cut, sun-tanned features, high forehead and deep-set kindly eyes. He had a fine beard which increased his aristocratic and unassumed appearance of superiority over ordinary men. I knew at once that I had seen an exceptional personality.'[2]

On 2 September 1944, Seagrim and seven of his Karens were sentenced to death, taken to the execution ground at Kemmendine Cemetery, blindfolded, and shot. It looked as if his efforts to create a Karen resistance had proved abortive. But Seagrim had played his part in alerting India to the importance of the nationalist movement of the young Thakins, who were growing restive under the Japanese and their puppet Ba Maw.

His Karens had established contacts in Rangoon before he died, and a channel was open for Force 136 to get in touch with those members of the Burmese government and the Burma National Army who were beginning to be resentful of Japanese rule. In December 1944, approaches were made.

At the time Slim was chiefly concerned to prevent a rising: he wanted his own forces to be much further into Burma before he could risk bringing the BNA over to the British. Too early a rising might simply allow the Japanese to deal with a rebellious Aung San at their leisure.

In the meanwhile, the organization was in place. By early 1945, teams of British officers and nearly 12,000 men under arms – Operation CHARACTER – were waiting in the hills of eastern Burma, from as far north as Maymyo down almost to the edge of Rangoon itself. All were in wireless communication with Force 136 HQ in Kandy, and up to twenty stations were operating. They were plentifully supplied with funds, as a Top-Secret operation (*Grenville* – forgery of currency) had 1,000,000 ten-rupee notes and over 1,000,000 one-rupee notes of Japanese-Burmese currency printed in England and sent out by ship.

This was part of a vast financial operation, including the printing from de la Rue's plates of nearly 10,000,000 Siamese ticals (*bahts*), 3,000,000 Nanking dollars for use in China, and sundry currencies for use in Malaya, and the Netherlands East Indies. The forgeries were treated just like real money for purposes of accountancy and loan, and Force 136 acted as banker for this purpose.

---

[1] Kameo Susumu, *Ma no Sittan-kawa* (The evil Sittang River), pp. 102–4; Author's conversation with Captain Inoue, 1946

[2] I. Morrison, op.cit., p. 151

The bulk of the forces were concentrated in the area Toungoo-Thaton where they inflicted heavy casualties on the Japanese in the aftermath of 28 Army's breakout as they hid from the RAF in villages east of the Sittang. But Force 136 guerrillas also delayed the Japanese 56 Division in the race for Toungoo with 17 and 19 Indian Divisions. 56 Division, a proud and battle-tried unit which had, almost single-handed, kept the Chinese at bay in Yunnan for over two years, had been ordered to prevent IV Corps freely using the main road south to Rangoon. Had it reached Toungoo, it might well have fortified the place sufficiently to delay IV Corps and prevent it getting into the port of Rangoon before the monsoon started. As it was, Force 136 guerrillas harried and halted Matsuyama's men and prevented them coming out of the hills.

One reason Force 136 could operate freely in this area was that many of its officers knew it intimately from pre-war days when they had been the forest lessees. New officers from Europe joined them in 1945, but the core of Force 136 was a handful of men with long experience of Burma. This ought to have made them hostile to any form of collaboration with Aung San, because they were men of the same generation and background as those in Simla with the Government-in-exile who insisted on Aung San being brought to trial for murder, in particular for the killing of a headman in Tavoy in 1942. Gardiner knew that the charges were sound and well authenticated, but if they had been proceeded with it was obvious that the BNA, after rebelling against the Japanese, would at once turn against the British, too. Gardiner had to intervene at the highest level to counter this attempt by the Burma Government-in-exile to have Aung San arraigned.[1] The dispute caused deep and bitter division in Mountbatten's headquarters and among his Civil Affairs Service Officers.

Aung San rebels

Seagrim was not, of course, the only source of information available to the British in India. Thein Pe, a Burmese communist, walked out of Burma with a friend, Tin Shwe, in 1942, saying he was disillusioned with life under the Japanese. He and his friend were naturally held at arm's length for a while, but when the British were convinced of their integrity Tin Shwe was sent back into Burma on special operations. Tin Shwe made contact with the secretary of the Communist Party of Burma, Thakin Soe, in the winter of 1943 and was picked up by submarine off the coast in February 1944. Five young Araka-nese communists came into the British lines six months later. One of them was despatched to Rangoon with a microfilm message for Thakin Soe.

---

[1] Gardiner, Correspondence with the author, 30 April 1975

In a note on the Anti-Fascist Organization and the Communist Party of Burma, probably written late in 1944, Thakin Thein Pe wrote, 'Aung San... understands his past mistakes, and means to amend them by contributing his highest share to the anti-Japanese uprising. After all he is a true patriot although he sometimes loses sight of the broader issues, blinded by one-sided nationalism. In August this year at a meeting of officers of BDA (Burma Defence Army) held in his office, Aung San said, among other things, "I learn that some of you are fixing up dates, and all to rise up against the Japanese. I congratulate you for anti-Japanese patriotism. But if you do it untimely you will be smashed up. I take the responsibility of leading this movement. When time comes, I will inform you." Yes, he is anxiously awaiting for the word from us.'[1]

Thakin Tin Shwe – referred to in Force 136 by his cover-name, Mr Lancelot – was sent into Burma late in 1943 and reached Rangoon, where he got in touch with Thakin Tan Tun, Minister for Agriculture and later of Transport in Ba Maw's government, and later general secretary of the Anti-Fascist People's Freedom League. Tin Shwe reported back in May 1944 that internally there was a struggle for power going on between Ba Maw and the Thakins, who were working with the Japanese in the hope that they would throw Ba Maw out, whereupon the Thakins would form a Government. The district officials were disillusioned with independence – 'they hate the Japanese, hate Ba Maw, hate the situation and conditions, and hate the war'.[2] The ordinary Burmese could see the Japanese were suffering from shortages, but on the other hand they also witnessed their frugality, energy and capacity for hard work, and for them independence was an important factor, which would become real once the war was over. This feeling, though, Tin Shwe added, 'is confined mostly to places where Japanese troops are not stationed. Wherever Japanese troops are stationed, they themselves are 100 per cent unpopular...'[3]

From such sources, Force 136 gradually built up a picture of conditions inside Burma, and was able to assess the extent to which Aung San was likely to move against the Japanese when the time came. Strictly speaking, that was exactly Force 136's province. Intelligence was a by-product of its activities, its real function was subversion, sabotage and the support of resistance – all of those functions which, in the end, were bound to interfere with the quiet unobtrusive gathering of information. They suffered, too, from hostility and incomprehension on their own side. XV Corps complained that Force 136 habitually used men who formerly assisted the Japanese, some of whom were wanted on criminal charges, including murder. Slim was said to be so dissatisfied with 136 that he

---

[1] H. Tinker, ed., *Burma. The Struggle for Independence*, 1983, vol. I, p. 55

[2] ibid., pp. 36–7

[3] ibid., p. 85

wanted it to cease operations in Burma and have behind-the-lines activities handed over to the American Detachment 101 of the Office of Strategic Services, confining 136 to pure intelligence work. On the other hand, Slim was not particularly well-informed about 136, nor of the extent of its networks.[1]

And, of course, although Force 136 employed officers with pre-war experience of Burma, like Gardiner, Seagrim, Nimmo and McCrindle, there were others fresh from Europe who brought to the dangers of this job loyalty and courage but also ill-informed enthusiasm. The Civil Affairs Officer at IV Corps HQ, Brigadier F.S.V. Donnison, recalls meeting one of these at Yamethin: 'He was an idealistic, cultured, sensitive person, the son of Quaker parents, and had clearly established very good relations with the Burmese members of the BNA and AFO with whom he was working. My recollection is that he found them attractive and trustworthy, and that he, very justifiably, felt it was only their loyalty and decency that had preserved his life. Having said this, it is necessary to add that he was a member of the Communist Party, which goes a long way towards explaining the rapport established with his Burmese counterparts.'[2]

Donnison also found Colin Mackenzie, the head of Force 136, secretive, and recalled that his proposals were usually met by the Chief Civil Affairs Officer, Major-General Pearce, with 'doubt, distrust or downright disapproval'. Pearce's attitude arose, says Donnison, from the conviction that the Thakins were irresponsible, disloyal and unrepresentative, and 136's support would help them to an unjustifiable share in political power once the war was over, at the same time alienating the more moderate and responsible elements in Burmese political life. Ultimately, Pearce's hostility made Mackenzie conceal his plans until they had already been approved by higher authority. On the whole, Donnison shared Pearce's views, and still thinks Force 136 ignorant of the risk it was running. 'It seemed to me that SOE were dangerously ignorant of the realities of political life in Burma, or were irresponsibly closing their eyes to them, and were playing with political fire.' He doubts, though, whether what they did appreciably altered the course of events: 'The fire had been lit by others and would have burned up the past anyway.'[3]

So a source of hostility was the Civil Affairs Service (Burma), staffed largely by men who had had responsible positions in the administration or police before the war, who were concerned to maintain the loyalties of those who sided with the British, and to exact retribution from those who had actively helped the Japanese. These CAS officers included Major-General Pearce, who had been Commissioner, Federated

---

[1] ibid., p. 136

[2] ibid., pp. 1001–02

[3] ibid., p. 1001

Shan States, and was Mountbatten's Chief Civil Affairs Officer (Burma); Brigadier Prescott, Inspector-General of Police in 1942, and later Deputy Director of Civil Affairs; and Brigadier Lindop, Deputy Civil Affairs Officer at XIV Army. The Civil Affairs organization operated under the general control of Air Chief Marshal Sir Philip Joubert, who had retired from the RAF in 1943 after being C-in-C, Coastal Command, and was re-employed as Mountbatten's Deputy Chief of Staff for Information and Civil Affairs. At these various levels of Civil Affairs policy, there was a deep-rooted opposition to Mountbatten's intentions to use the anti-Japanese feeling among the Thakins and the Burmese people in general, and this opposition focused round the treatment to be accorded to Aung San.

In the last week of March 1945, Aung San held a press conference in Rangoon. The Burmese, who were hosts at these conferences, usually offered their Japanese guests coffee with milk, but on this occasion there was nothing. Aung San usually appeared smartly dressed in his Japanese general officer's uniform. This time he wore a rather coarsely woven Burmese *longyi* and an unwashed khaki shirt. The Japanese war correspondents, who always stressed Aung San's true samurai spirit, did not criticize this apparently offhand garb. Battles were raging on the Irrawaddy shores, and they took this rough-and-ready air as token of a departure for the front.

Which, indeed is what it was supposed to be. The Burmese Army paraded under its Commander-in-Chief, then marched out of Rangoon, as if making for the battlefields in support of the hard-pressed Japanese. The British waited. They knew that this was to be the signal for Aung San and his troops to change sides. Only a few days before, on 9 March 1945, a signal was sent from Force 136 to Advanced HQ, Allied Land Forces, South-East Asia, reporting that one of their wireless stations – Station 'Terrier' – whose intelligence net stretched from Pyinmana to Toungoo, had revealed that several hundreds of Burmese, Karens and Indians of Bose's INA were awaiting orders to revolt against the Japanese, as the fighting moved closer to them. Some had already begun to desert, and the Force 136 officers in the field had transmitted their appeal: 'We can't remain passive. Either we act now or go down.'[1]

Slim, whose views on Force 136 must have undergone considerable change, welcomed the news and declared that it should encourage the rising and give it maximum support, with arms and 'Jedburgh' parties, i.e. small groups of officers with wireless sets. Unfortunately a higher command directive of 5 March 1945 forbade the issue of arms to Aung San's Anti- Fascist Organization directly, and restricted supply to 100 weapons per commissioned officer. In the field, this directive was regarded as self-

[1] ibid., p. 102

contradictory, and on 25 March 1945 Mountbatten was asked for a decision. Prescott considered that whatever military profit might be gained from arming the AFO, the long-term effects on Burmese internal security would be serious.

Two days later, on 27 March 1945, a meeting was held in Mountbatten's room in Kandy at which senior 136 officers were present. Sir Philip Joubert was not, but he had put in a memorandum to Mountbatten the day before emphasizing that whatever happened nothing should be promised or done which might hinder the trial and possible execution of members of the Burma National Army and the AFO for previous acts against the British. Mountbatten was also concerned that the rising was premature. He told the meeting it seemed likely to occur between 24 and 31 March, and wanted it delayed, because the battle was not moving south fast enough. Force 136 agreed to try and postpone the start of the rising. Mountbatten seemed to accept Joubert's misgivings – at this stage – and said those who took part in the rising should have their merits recognized but should also be told that their past actions were not forgotten, and they would have to stand trial according to the law obtaining in 1941.

After the meeting, he signalled to the Chiefs of Staff in London that although backing the rising might offend 'the more respectable elements of the population', those elements had been passive. The active elements, like Aung San, though guilty of treasonable behaviour, were likely to become national heroes and it would be to Britain's advantage if they could be seen 'to be national heroes with the British instead of against them'. And it would have serious repercussions in liberal circles in the United States if Britain were seen to be refusing help to liberation movements against the Japanese. It was vital to avoid any policy which might involve suppressing such movements by force. He intended therefore to start a propaganda campaign, once the rising began, saying the British Government's aim was to help Burma attain complete self-government.[1]

On 29 March, Slim's HQ signalled Advanced HQ, ALFSEA, that they had indications the BNA were out of Rangoon and likely to double-cross the Japanese. The army in the field had as yet received no policy directive as to how to behave towards them, and this was urgently requested.

On the same day Slim was anxiously awaiting some practical guidance, the War Cabinet's India Committee met in London, and after listening to the views of Dorman-Smith, approved a telegram to Mountbatten advising great caution. They described the possible aid from Aung San and the BNA as 'relatively unimportant' and thought it might entail 'political concessions which His Majesty's Government would not be prepared to contemplate'. If Aung San or other leaders asked about future British intentions, Force 136 was to decline to discuss political issues with them.[2]

[1] ibid., p. 200
[2] ibid., p. 203

Mountbatten held a further meeting in Kandy on 2 April, at which the acting Governor of Burma, Sir John Wise, was present, and both 136 and senior Civil Affairs officers. The rising had begun, and Mountbatten pointed out that he had initiated all necessary action himself. Major-General Pearce complained he had been kept in the dark by Force 136 about the Burmese personalities with whom they had been in touch. 136 promised to rectify this. The rest of the meeting concerned itself with the collection of arms once the rising had achieved its aim. Mountbatten refused to issue a proclamation – which had been prepared – announcing the death penalty for illicit retention of arms. He wished the problem of Burma to be treated in a sensible manner, as had been done in South Africa after the Boer War. He ordered all death sentences to be referred to himself personally. He had prepared a draft directive on a policy for the military administration of Burma, in which he insisted that it was essential to show those Burmese who had been disappointed with Japanese promises that co-operation with the British was a different matter; that the rising had taken place *before* it could have been clear to the Burmese that the British could come to their rescue; and that, therefore, they were rising for their own ends 'and not for love of us', but that if Civil Affairs were conducted so as to contrast favourably with those of the Japanese, the Burmese would agree with him that their interests and British interests were not mutually exclusive. His Civil Affairs officers must be careful to distinguish between political misdemeanours and crimes against the person – a distinction which was to be of great importance for the charge of murder against Aung San.[1]

Events in the field were overtaking all these deliberations. Aung San's closest friend among the Japanese, Captain Takahashi – known by the codename of Mr Kitajima – left Rangoon on 23 March and went after him. It was evident something was up, but there could be no question of compelling Aung San to return to Japanese allegiance by force. On the other hand, Takahashi was prepared to use powerful persuasion, because he knew how indebted Aung San felt towards the Japanese. He caught up with Aung San at Shwedaung, south of Prome, but it was too late. The Burma National Army came out in open rebellion against the Japanese on 27 March 1945.

'What do you intend to do now?' Takahashi asked Aung San. 'It would have meant the destruction of Burma', Aung San told him, 'to go on working with the Japanese.' 'What kind of deal have you made with the British?' Takahashi wanted to know. 'Our ideal is total independence for Burma', was the reply. 'No doubt that is out of the question at present, so we shall be a self-governing Dominion. We are now negotiating along those lines. If the British refuse to grant us one or the other, then we will fight

[1] ibid., p. 212

them too. We had to adopt an anti-Japanese stance to show the British we mean business. That's why we have rebelled against you.'[1]

Aung San still had to make personal contact with the British. Through agents of Force 136, he had been promised safe conduct to and from British Headquarters. Wisely enough, given the debate in the British higher commands as to whether he should be arrested or not (he must have anticipated this as a possibility), Aung San delayed taking advantage of his safe conduct until 15 May, when he crossed the Irrawaddy at Allanmyo. The next day he presented himself at XIV Army HQ in Meiktila, dressed in the full regalia of a Japanese major-general, sword and all, representing the Army of the Provisional Government of Burma.

Slim made no flowery promises. He told him he did not need his help to defeat the Japanese, and that in his view there was only one legitimate Burmese government – even though Ba Maw's independent government had been recognized by the Axis powers (naturally) and the Vatican – and that was the British Government, acting through Mountbatten. Slim recognized no provisional government, and if Aung San joined him he would have to accept Slim's orders as a subordinate commander. Aung San did not disguise his disappointment at this forthright rejection of all his claims, and demanded to be treated as an Allied Commander.

Slim admired him for refusing to be overawed, but pointed out that there was a well-substantiated charge of civil murder hanging over him, and there were those in British headquarters who would pursue this. 'I have been urged to place you on trial', he told Aung San. 'You have nothing in writing, only a verbal promise at second-hand that I would return you to your friends. Don't you think you are taking considerable risks in coming here and adopting this attitude?'

'No.' Aung San replied.

'Why not?'

'Because you are a *British* officer' came the rejoinder.[2] There could have been no reply more calculated to win over Slim, who laughed, and the two men fenced verbally for a while in high good humour about foreign rule in Burma and the dispositions of the BNA (which Aung San played close to his chest, though he agreed with Slim's claim that there were bands of men who averred they belonged to the BNA but were behaving like dacoits). Slim was even more impressed by his frankness when, to Slim's assertion, 'Go on, Aung San, you only came to us because you see we are winning!' Aung San replied, 'It wouldn't be much good coming to you if you weren't, would it?' Slim judged him to be ambitious, but a genuine patriot, and a well-balanced realist: 'The greatest impression he made on me was one of honesty... He was not free with glib assurances and he hesitated to commit himself, but I had

[1] Allen, *End of the War in Asia*, p. 18
[2] Slim, *Defeat into Victory*, p. 512

the idea that if he agreed to do something he would keep his word. I could do business with Aung San.'[1]

Slim's readiness to deal with Aung San was shared by Mountbatten, but was, to put it mildly, far from acceptable to Mountbatten's Civil Affairs Officers. Pearce expressed the view on 9 May that Aung San's record demanded he be treated as a war criminal and placed under arrest pending trial. Mountbatten replied by return signal that on no account was Aung San to be placed under arrest though he might be required to stand trial in due course.[2] To his Chief of Staff, Mountbatten sent a memorandum five days later saying that some of his Civil Affairs executive officers were not loyally carrying out his policy:

> I shall not easily forget Brigadier Prescott's astounding remarks at my meeting in Kandy, in which he implied that if certain men who happened to be members of the Thakin Party committed a murder... this should automatically outlaw the Thakin Party. The recent attempt to arrest Aung San is an indication of an attitude to the Burma National Army which runs counter to the policy laid down.[3]

To Major-General Hubert Rance, who finally succeeded Pearce as Chief Civil Affairs Officer (Burma) on 10 May 1945, Mountbatten reiterated his determination.

> I will not for one moment contemplate allowing so gross a piece of disloyalty to my expressed wish, nor such an arrant act of treachery to the Burma Defence Army, who rose on our behalf long before the Fourteenth Army or 15 Corps could give their rebellion army support, as to arrest Aung San and throw him into jail while we decide whether to try him or not![4]

At the same time, at a private meeting in Rangoon, on 16 May 1945, with Aung San, Than Tun and Ne Win, Mountbatten did not hesitate to affirm that anyone against whom charges lay might have to be arrested and stand trial.

On the very same day that Rance received that forthright signal from Kandy, another one arrived from Brigadier Lindop at XIV Army which amply underlines Mountbatten's justifiable suspicions that his policy was being sabotaged. The BNA were in many areas engaged in dacoity, Lindop

[1] Slim, *Defeat into Victory*, p. 58

[2] Tinker, ed., op.cit., p. 238

[3] ibid., p. 247

[4] ibid., p. 244

told Rance, they were a serious menace to law and order, and the ordinary villagers found them worse than the Japanese and could not understand why the British accepted them. They should be disbanded and membership of their Army made illegal. The Anti-Fascist Organization showed no desire to be loyal to the British and should be dissolved.

Similarly, to Mountbatten's suggestion that Dorman-Smith should include members of what Aung San described as the 'Provisional Government' in his Advisory Council when civil government was restored, the Governor replied that it would be a disaster to give even a semblance of recognition to Aung San and that he could not for a moment contemplate giving such an undertaking about his Advisory Council.[1] To which Mountbatten acidly rejoined that he was merely suggesting the Governor allowed Slim to tell Aung San what he would (it was presumed) eventually do in any case, 'unless indeed you propose not to invite representatives of the only elements that have risen on our side to fight the Japanese'.[2] Unless some solution were found which Aung San and his colleagues would accept, Mountbatten foresaw having to fight a civil war against 10,000 Burmese troops, when his own soldiers had better things to do. Mountbatten was, of course, looking ahead to the time when Rangoon would be the base for Operation ZIPPER, the campaign to retake Malaya and Singapore. In comparison with this object, the preoccupation of the Civil Affairs officers with crimes committed years before must have seemed trivial nit-picking. But in fairness to them, perhaps we should examine what Aung San was said to be guilty of.

According to a petition laid by Ma Ahma, on 8 April 1946, Aung San and others killed her husband, who was headman of the village of Thebyuchaung near Thaton in 1942. When Thaton was evacuated, Aung San and some of his Thakin colleagues apprehended this headman, Abdul Raschid, who was known for his loyalty to the British, tied him with ropes, and brought him to Thaton in a cart in which they had also placed a pig with the intention of humiliating him as a Muslim. They kept him without food for eight days, then took him to the football ground in Thaton. Here, according to the petition, Aung San 'speared him to death with his bayonet after crucifying him to the goal post'.[3]

The presentation of such a formal petition meant that the Governor was bound to proceed against Aung San, but it is interesting that the war was over by this time and only political issues were involved. Apart that is, from the British Government's unwillingness to allow Indian troops to be used to suppress disturbances which might arise if Aung San were to be arrested. The British Prime Minister, Clement Attlee, agreed that

[1] ibid., p. 152

[2] ibid., pp. 264–5

[3] ibid., p. 728

Dorman-Smith seemed to have no choice, and that Aung San should be arrested. On the other hand, he counselled delay, until the prosecution should have acquired clinching evidence. The problem was complicated by the fact that Tun Oke, one of the Thakins who was present when Aung San killed Abdul Raschid, was himself a member of the Governor's executive council and had referred to the incident in a public speech. It was possible that he might be, not merely a witness, but charged with being accessory to the crime. Attlee instructed he be dropped from the Executive Council, in any case, and a telegram cancelling the original instruction to arrest Aung San was sent from London, and received just in time to recall the warrant.

In the upshot, the need to incorporate the AFPFL – and therefore, necessarily, Aung San – into any future government structure, and to avoid political violence, made the British Government exercise pressure on Burma to drop the charge against Aung San, particularly once it was learnt that Abdul Raschid's widow's petition had not formally been submitted to any court. This course of action was made easier by Sir Henry Knight's taking over the governorship from Dorman-Smith who had, Attlee was convinced, 'lost his grip'.[1] Aung San at no time denied the facts of the case. Both in a public speech and in a long private conversation with Dorman-Smith on 23 May 1946, he said he had heard lurid stories about how the headman was oppressing his villagers. The country was in an absolutely lawless condition, without courts or magistrates, and he considered the case himself. Bearing in mind the need to act immediately in order to restore a semblance of authority, he decided Abdul Raschid must die. It was his own decision, and he felt he had to carry out the execution personally.[2]

Although Dorman-Smith continued to think Aung San should stand trial, his successor decided to pass a Bill under his own powers ensuring that crimes said to be committed during the war period should only be proceeded against with the Governor's express sanction. This did not eliminate the charges against Aung San, but it guaranteed they could not be raised privately or by political opponents. Knight was only a temporary stand-in. On Mountbatten's recommendation, General Rance was appointed to the Governorship of Burma in August 1946. That month, Ba Maw was back in Rangoon, having surrendered to the British occupation forces in Japan. U Saw, who had also been Premier, and was arrested by the British for sedition in 1941, was back in Burma, trying to recruit the diminished strength of his Myochit Party. He dickered with the notion of joining forces with the AFPFL, which was obviously the principal factor in

---

[1] Tinker, op. cit., p. 773

[2] The atmosphere of the times can be gauged by a more recent admission by a former subaltern in the King's Own Yorkshire Light Infantry, Gerald Fitzpatrick, that he and the officers of his battalion summarily executed 27 Burmese civilians, on suspicion of collaboration with the Japanese, during the 1942 retreat (*The Observer*, 3 June 1984, p. 5).

Burmese politics; then rejected it. In January 1947, Aung San visited London and signed an agreement with Attlee that Burma would achieve full independence within a year. Under Sir Hubert Rance, six of the nine members of the Executive Council belonged to the AFPFL, but this power was far from secure. By 1947, the Communists in Central Burma were in open rebellion. The Karens felt the British had betrayed them, because they had not obtained an autonomous Karen State. And U Saw was on the brink of taking a short cut to power.

On the morning of 19 July 1947, four young toughs in U Saw's pay burst into a Cabinet meeting, armed with tommy-guns, and slaughtered all save three of the ministers present. Aung San was among those killed. His place was taken by the speaker of the Constituent Assembly, Thakin Nu (U Nu) and a federal union constitution was approved in September. The Independent Union of Burma came into being on 4 January 1948, elected to stay outside the British Commonwealth, and was plunged almost at once into the horrors of civil war.

12. THE BACKLOG

How the armies see each other

Sex on the battlefield — Race — the aesthetic response
— 'Little Peterkin'

Sex on the battlefield

Sex on the battlefield may seem an improbable or meretricious topic, but if we are to extend the experience of war beyond the mere facts of the campaign, we need to consider it, just as we need to extend our knowledge of the individual soldier's ideas of race and class. Until most recent times, sex concerned the impact upon an army of one of the most debilitating military maladies: venereal disease. Recent research has shown what a constant problem this was for the British in India in the nineteenth century. Army and Government of India officials saw the answer in the provision of government-inspected brothels, which would channel the soldier's sexual energies into areas known to be free of infection. Religious opinion at home, and the vociferous complaints of missionaries in India, made this a difficult official posture to maintain, and certainly by the time the vast conscript armies of the Second World War arrived on the shores of India, no official brothel system existed. This does not mean the troops indulged in unsupervised licence on an unprecedented scale. Both chaplains and medical officers were encouraged to use a moral approach, to suggest that promiscuous intercourse endangered the men's future wives and children. Some of this moralizing was ineffectually hearty, but the theme in itself made sense. And the use of anti-biotics decreased the hazards for those who risked the casual encounters of Indian brothels. The lessons of other theatres were instructive. The Australians in the Syrian campaign in 1941 had 18,000 cases passing through their treatment centre, largely, it is supposed, because the army organized brothels for them, but only 65 contracted VD. In 1944, the admission rate of British troops in India was 60 per 1000. The figure may seem high, but *Field Service Hygiene Notes for India* (1945) points out that half a century earlier, in 1890, the corresponding figure had been 500, i.e. a third of the hospital admissions for that year were due to that one cause alone. At the end of the Victorian era, VD incapacitated half the troops in India.

The policy of GHQ (India) was to oppose the setting up of brothels. Interestingly enough, but perhaps not surprising, the rate of sickness among British troops was always much higher than that of Indian troops, in peace as in war. Yet the Indian troops were subject to the same temptations and pressures. The following figures show the pattern of VD cases per thousand men.

	British	*Indian*
1934	34.2	9.6
1941	64.5	27.9
1942	69.6	42.5
1943	63.9	49.4

These figures are for the Army in India, so the 1934 figures show an unfair disproportion between British and Indian, as Indian troops were then 'at home'. Nearly one in six of British other ranks was incapacitated by VD in 1943 (158 per 1000); the official history gives no figures for officers. This was reduced to 72 per 1000 in 1945, a figure higher than for West African troops in the same theatre (Indo-Burma front) which stood at 69 per 1000 and much higher than that for Indian troops (46 per 1000); though the palm – if that is the word I want – for VD statistics must go to the East Africans, who produced a figure of 83 per 1000. (In every year, interestingly, the rates for *all* diseases are higher for British than for Indians.)[1]

There was, inevitably, a fair amount of private amorous initiative, much of it of an innocuous kind. Characteristic of this is the account of 194 Squadron, Royal Air Force:

Where I think that ground crew were certainly not so well off as air crew was in the matter of the girls; and this was not entirely an officer/other rank business because of the proportion of aircrew who were NCOs. It does seem to me that aircrew did have opportunities, which were not open to ground crew, of at least seeing the popsies in the flesh on their occasional visits to that terrible and tropic city, Calcutta. And having a sight, however distant and respectful, of those many splendid women who worked so hard for the troops in canteens, on railway stations and in hospitals, amusing them as the WASBES (sic) [Women's Auxiliary Service (Burma)] did, nursing them and working for them as the QA's [Queen Alexandra's Imperial Military Nursing Service] and WACI's [Women's Auxiliary Corps (India)] did, many of them

[1] W. Franklin Mellor, *History of the Second World War: Casualties and Medical Statistics*, HMSO 1972, pp. 352–4

British wives of British businessmen, some of them Indian ladies who believed in our cause and understood the loneliness and the longings of foreign soldiers, all this did at least keep alive in those who met them the feminine presence and the ideas for which it stood.

The ground crews sweltering at Agartala or Imphal had the celluloid 'ersatz' of Joan Crawford, Bette Davis and, once in a blue moon, the actuality of the 14th Army heroine, Vera Lynn . . .

It's hard to solve this particular equation. Probably, as with the accommodation, there was really very little in it . . . And to judge by the memories of one airman from 194 who confided an exciting piece of his past to me . . . the timeless Shakespearian (sic) expertise of the British warrior abroad, be he soldier, sailor or Leading Aircraftsman, usually resulted in his getting a far better share of anything that was going than the nearest Admiral or Air Vice Marshal.[1]

A glance at SEAC's magazine might suggest that Wilfrid Russell's assurance was not universally shared; and that sexual envy could be complicated by class envy. 'A Lieutenant's Lament' evoked in cabaret style the amorous adventures of a young officer, who styled himself 'Buttercup':

I've petted with Pam way back in Poona,
I've messed around with Margie in Madras,
And on furlough in Mussoorie
Was a burning, yearning houri
Over whom I made myself an awful ass.

I've kissed Kate in a kishtie up in Kashmir,
Made lurid love to Lucy in Lahore,
While in dear old Rawalpindi
There was pretty, witty Lindy
Who took all that I could give – then asked for more . . .

This rather harmless Noel Coward-style wish-fulfilment summoned up a cry from the ranks, from 'Thwarted':

Although so far I've never been to Poona,
I've yearned for female company in Madras,
Whilst I found that all Mussoorie's
Pick of burning, yearning houris

---

[1] Wilfrid Russell, *The Friendly Firm. A history of 194 Squadron, Royal Air Force* p. 88

Were labelled: "BORs, keep off the grass."

. . . And I'm sure that on the winding road to Burma,
Whether Prome, Rangoon, or fabled Mandalay,
I shall find that a commission
Gives priority admission
To the hearts of all the charmers on the way.

So now I've reached this cynical conclusion,
(Which does little to console me, I may say);
Without pips you're not so hot,
And the ladies on the spot
Might as well be twice eight thousand miles away.[1]

An incident related by Winifred Beaumont, a nurse, emphasized the rarity of the presence of white women and (by implication) the enforced chastity of most of the troops in Burma. She was taken to a camp film show, where the projectionist suddenly turned the film (it was *Jane Eyre*) upside down. 'I laughed. Immediately every man there sprang to his feet and stared up at the balcony and me. My escort put a proprietary arm round my shoulders, and a whisper hissed round the hall: "A woman!" I experienced a wild exhilarating thrill of power. I knew every man in that great crowd saw me as a desirable woman.' In fairness to Ms Beaumont, I should add that she concludes, 'Of course, they didn't have a clear view of me!'[2]

As we have seen, British methods of dealing with sexual problems were, besides prophylaxis, propaganda: the soldier had a duty to be continent, illicit intercourse was morally wrong, venereal disease was almost certain to follow because 95% of Indian prostitutes were infected. In practice, condoms and preventive outfits were issued free to anyone who wanted them, so caution went hand-in-hand with objurgation. The soldier was instructed not merely to use a condom, but to wash his genitals after intercourse with a special solution, to insert a preventive ointment in the urethra by means of a tube, then to tie a bag round his penis for a short time to keep the ointment effective. After the Japanese surrender, when troops from SEAC reoccupied vast areas of South-East Asia the same system was more widely spread. Troops going to French Indo-China were issued with a little pamphlet of local usages and French phrases awkwardly phoneticized. They were warned to be careful about market-buying and the pamphlet added drily, 'The local woman, the *congai*, is not a good buy either.' Since the army in Burma was rarely, for any long period, an army of occupation but a battle force on the move, it does not seem to have been oppressive as far as local women were concerned. John Masters says his

---

[1] *Laugh with SEAC*, 1945, p. 62
[2] Winifred Beaumont, *A Detail on the Burma Front*, 1977 p. 110

division (19 Indian Division) recorded only one case of rape during the time it was in Burma to the end of the campaign (about nine months). Three Madrassis were given fifteen years each when found guilty. Setting aside the repellent *macho* heartiness with which he describes this, the figure itself is significant.

To some extent, of course, soldiers in rear echelons were subject to greater temptations, compounded by idleness and an easy mode of existence which contrasted greatly with the deprivations from which they had come in the United Kingdom. And at the very highest levels of command, where occasionally wives accompanied husbands, a Maughamesque attitude seems to have been, in some cases at any rate, not unknown. Mountbatten was scandalized to find that his own Air Force chief, Air Chief-Marshal Sir Richard Peirse, had seduced the wife of the Commander-in-Chief (India), Lieutenant-General Sir Claude Auchinleck. She had obviously been unprepared for Auchinleck's tireless devotion to his job and to the Indian Army, grew bored, and succumbed to Peirse's charms. She does not appear to be the only woman to have done so.

The Japanese attitude was different. There was no question of wives accompanying general officers – who would have been dumbfounded at the suggestion – even though much of the Japanese Army in Burma was, for long periods in certain areas, an army of occupation. The Siberian expedition (1918–20) taught the Japanese Army what the risk of venereal disease was. They lost 1387 men killed in that period and had 2066 wounded, but the VD casualties reached 2012. When the Japanese Army moved into China in the 1930s, a system of brothels was inaugurated, known as *ianjo* or 'comfort houses', staffed by *ianfu*, 'comfort girls', prostitutes from Korea, China and Japan. The Japanese prostitute, usually from the southernmost islands of Amakusa, off Kyushu, and known by the generic name of 'Karayuki San' had long been a feature of life in South-East Asia. But the majority of the girls in the army comfort houses were Korean. The system began in January 1938. The first house established was the Yang Chia Chia (Willow House) in Shanghai, where the L of C GHQ controlled brothels. The set-up was under the supervision of a Japanese Army medical officer, Asō Tetsuo, later head of a hospital in Fukuoka. The reason was not simply the one put forward by Army authorities in nineteenth-century India, namely that only in this way could rampant venereal disease be controlled. That was a factor, but it was also important to control the excesses of the soldiers in Shanghai and Hangchow in case they repeated their performance at Nanking where they raped at will after taking it by storm. 10 Army covered 200 miles in a month, with repeated daily battles, before it reached Nanking, and that may explain what happened there. 'No virgins after the Japanese Army passed by', was what was said, and in the Tokyo trial there were witnesses who claimed to have seen gang-rapes of one woman by thirty Japanese soldiers.

This violence was reported by foreign missionaries on the spot to diplomats in Shanghai and Nanking, and repeated by journalists for overseas consumption. The Army's prestige was at stake, and so, too, was the future of the occupation, for which it was necessary to 'win the people's hearts'. Hence the higher command's decision to institute 'comfort houses', to calm the lust of their troops and ensure that, with the control and inspection of prostitutes, venereal diseases were kept in check.

The collection of the girls was carried out in Japan by officially authorized traders who used Army funds. The price paid for a girl was 1000 yen, so after she had earned this sum she was theoretically free to return. At 2 yen per soldier, this meant freedom after 500 men. An early contingent travelled by train to Hang-Chow, which was over a two-day journey. When the curious garrisons of the wayside stations learned who they were, they asked them to pause for a while en route. Railway wagons were turned into temporary comfort houses, and at a rate of three minutes per soldier – the usual period for two yen was thirty minutes – the girls had more or less earned their liberty money by the time they reached their destination. There was no time for them to sleep, and they simply napped as best they could with a soldier riding on top of them.[1]

From the point of view of prestige again, it was felt to be undesirable to have the houses under direct Army control, so they were run by civilian traders, the Army retaining the responsibility for medical inspection. The need was calculated on the basis of one girl to forty men, so 80,000 girls were drawn into the system before the war was over.

In Japan itself, the system was treated as secret, and newspaper articles or photographs which touched upon it were stopped by the censor. There are some photographs surviving, though: a group of girls in kimono bashfully or calculatingly eyeing the camera, a pretty girl smiling happily as she wears a naval cap and reads a book, a row of wooden huts with a soldier waiting outside, and the notices displayed: 'We welcome with our hearts and bodies the brave soldiers of Japan.'

Strict rules were laid down for the use of the *ianjo*:

Army regulations for places of entertainment

1. Entry to this comfort house is authorized only for personnel attached to the Army (Army coolies excepted). Personnel entering the house must be in possession of a comfort house pass.
2. Personnel must pay the required fee in cash and obtain a receipt, in exchange for which they will be given an entrance ticket and one condom.
3. The cost of entrance tickets is as follows:

[1] Senda Natsumitsu, *Jūgun Ianfu*, (Army Comfort Girls), p. 62

N.C.Os, other ranks, attached civilians: 2 yen.[1]

4. The validity of the ticket is for the day of purchase only and if the comfort house is not entered the amount will be refunded. No refund is payable once the ticket has been handed to the attendant (*shakufu*).
5. Ticket purchasers must enter the room indicated by the number shown thereon.
6. The ticket must be handed over to the attendant upon entering the room.
7. The consumption of alcohol inside the room is strictly forbidden.
8. After use of the prophylactic solution, the user must leave the room forthwith.
9. Those who fail to observe the regulations or infringe military discipline must leave the room forthwith.
10. It is forbidden to have intercourse without the use of a condom.[2]

Some more fatherly Japanese medical officers preferred to advise young soldiers to indulge in masturbation or homosexuality, a state of affairs not alien to the samurai tradition. Nakamura Isamu, a medical lieutenant from Kokura in Northern Kyushu, is shown (on p. 168 of *Heitai Gashū – Illustration of the Soldier's Life*) instructing a class of recruits in sexual hygiene: 'No going out to comfort stations for you lot. Just show some love for your comrades in arms, and masturbate each other. You're better off doing that than going with clandestine prostitutes who're sure to be riddled with VD.'[3] The author comments on a Taiwan tour of duty that, although everyone was aware of the risks from dysentery, malaria and skin diseases, VD was not a problem because there was no opportunity to go to comfort houses.

The indication is that the system, though theoretically well supervised, was by no means always effective in preventing disease. The bureaucratic detail of the regulations Senda quotes may be the result of the efficiency of medical personnel. They could also be a joke on the part of the comfort house staff, says Itō Keiichi, who also claims that the system was not so brutalizing as we might suppose. Where love begins normally from first impressions, he says, and develops step-by-step, the relation in the battlefield is the very opposite. It starts suddenly as a purely physical

---

[1] A sergeant earned 30 yen a month in 1945, a private first class 10.50 yen, but the pay was higher overseas. Pay was every ten days, and a PFC overseas would receive 7.80 for that period.

[2] Itō Keiichi, *Heitai-tachi no rikugunshi* (The soldiers' army history), Tokyo, 1969, pp. 92–3

[3] Toda Akira, *Heitai Gashū* (Illustrations of the Soldier's life), Tokyo, 1972, p. 168

relationship, but feelings can become involved afterwards, even though speed is of the essence for the soldier, who does not know whether he will return from the next battle or not.[1]

There was also a difference in attitude between regulars and conscripts. Not, as we might expect, between tough, experienced old sweats and timid young men fresh from the household; rather the opposite. The old regular was often occupied with military chores, had an eye on promotion, and his army life had not left him much leisure for chasing women. The young conscripts fresh from civilian life might in fact have more extensive sexual experience, and therefore stronger needs. In China it sometimes happened that they would go off on their own, looking for a woman, and end up as the victim of some plain-clothes guerrilla.

In Burma, there was something else. When the tide of battle turned against the Japanese, the comfort girls were often trapped in beleaguered garrisons, and although they were told they were not under military command and could leave, they preferred to stick it out, with the soldiers. In the fighting in Yunnan in September 1944, where the garrison at Lameng was finally reduced to eighty men, who decided to commit suicide, the Japanese comfort girls said to their Korean counterparts: 'You should escape from here. You owe no duty to Japan, so save your own lives and return to your own country. You are orientals as they are, so the Chinese soldiers won't harm you. We are going to stay behind with our soldiers.' The Korean girls waved white cloths and went out to surrender. The Japanese girls swallowed the potassium cyanide with which the troops killed themselves, and the Chinese found seven Japanese female corpses among the dead when they took the town.

The girls in Myitkyina were luckier. Just before it fell, the garrison commander had rafts built and sent the wounded and the comfort girls to safety down the Irrawaddy.

Elsewhere in Burma, life was not always so hazardous. In Moulmein, engineers of a naval unit shared their bungalows with comfort girls, but they seem to have been greedy as well. Not content with what they had, they set out for the hills, where native labourers had told them there were women. They found the women, in thatched nippa huts, and paid them two or three rupees each. One of them had the sense to get a supply of disinfectant from a nurse before he left, a purple tablet which he dissolved in water. He washed himself with the solution and was safe. His friend was not so lucky, and soon swellings began to appear on his thighs. He was 'crimed' for this, being guilty of the offence of using other than Army comfort girls, and was reduced to private first class.[2]

---

[1] Itō Keiichi, op.cit., p. 208

[2] Senda, op.cit., p. 170

Since Burma was in theory a friendly country, whose people were to be won over, it was naturally desirable to avoid rape incidents. Itō Keiichi gives an account of one division in Burma in whose area the incidence of rape was high. Its men had seen long years of hard service, and although often, after six or seven years, they would be demobilised, in practice they were put on the reserve the same day they were released, so their service seemed never-ending and they never once returned home. It was not easy to enforce sexual discipline among such men, and the division decided on the extraordinary device of letting it be known that if troops raped a woman, they should kill her, so that the crime should not be discovered.

On one occasion, when three men confessed to rape, after the woman had brought a complaint, their warrant officer asked them, 'Why didn't you kill her?' to which the reply was, 'We felt sorry for her, and couldn't do it' (*Nasake ni oite dōshite mo korosenakatta*). The WO perjured himself on their behalf, but the men were sentenced, returned to Japan, and jailed. In the light of the surrender, this may not seem such a harsh outcome, but as Itō points out, it was a deep disgrace at the time and the men would never dare to return to their homes later. As it was, this sentence almost certainly saved them from death by disease or starvation along with the rest of the division.[1]

The characteristic Japanese regulations do not imply that everything was carried out with mechanical seriousness. When a soldier entered the comfort girl's room, those waiting outside would shout out, 'What's happening? What are you doing? Get a move on!', even if the man had only been there five minutes. If the girl was Burmese she would usually say, 'Master, *gowngdè-là?*' 'Was it all right, Master?'[2] These girls, and the Indian girls, stayed behind when the Japanese surrendered, and simply plied their trade for the Allied troops when they moved into Tenasserim, according to Senda Natsumitsu. Besides Moulmein, there were comfort houses in Meiktila, Mandalay, Rangoon, Toungoo, and Pyinmana. In most of them the proportion of girls was ten Koreans, four Burmese, two Indians and Chinese, and Japanese 0.8. How Senda arrives at this fraction for the Japanese is not clear, but Japanese girls were for the use of officers only. The girls were usually around twenty years old, though in the early days one medical officer complained to headquarters that prostitutes who had reached the limits of their usefulness in Japan were being sent abroad as *ianfu* and he insisted that troops of the Imperial Army were entitled to the very best.[3]

There were also in Burma geisha houses, where the girls carried out their more refined entertainment of music and classical dancing for an audience of officers, among whom each girl would have a special client. These establishments were so popular that on at least one occasion Major Ushiro, who

---

[1] Itō Keiichi, op.cit., pp. 215–16

[2] The Burmese addressed the Japanese by the English word 'Master'.

[3] Senda, op.cit., pp, 121, 171, 169

was a staff officer concerned with supply, expostulated that the queues of cars outside indicated that hard-won petrol was being used for purposes which had little to do with winning the war.

Opposition to *ianjo* and geisha establishments sometimes found a sympathetic echo in the more cultivated Japanese officer. The western-educated Colonel Saitō, of 55 Division, disparagingly referred to 'men satisfying their beastly desires' at comfort houses. And Aida Yūji, when a private in 53 Division, punctiliously saluting the Commander-in-Chief's car as it passed through the streets of Rangoon, was taken aback when he saw the car was crammed with drunken, giggling geisha.

Mutaguchi's headquarters in Maymyo had its own geisha establishment, called the Seimeisō, or 'Inn of Brightness'. It was a *ryōtei*, or restaurant, but run by the management of a brothel in the Osaka red-light district, and its mats, screens, and cooking utensils had all been transported from Japan under the guise of 'essential military equipment'. From Mutaguchi down, every officer in 15 Army HQ had his own special geisha in the Seimeisō. Although Maymyo was in the mountains of Burma, the Seimeisō was open every night serving pure Japanese *sake* and Japanese delicacies like raw tuna fish, at a time when pure *sake* was almost unobtainable in Japan. Banquets would be laid on for officers visiting HQ for conferences or reports.

Nostalgic and beautiful though the atmosphere of the Seimeisō might be, it was not always conducive to harmony. An angry rift between Mutaguchi's Chief of Staff, Major-General Kunomura, and his senior staff officer, Colonel Kinoshita, was directly attributable to the charms of the geisha. Kunomura was a more than regular visitor, and the soldiers devised any number of obscene nicknames to describe his prowess. He was fond of one particular geisha, and usually went straight to her room. On one occasion, he found Colonel Kinoshita making a pass at her. In a raging fury, he seized Kinoshita – Kunomura was a burly man, and later commanded a Guards division – and heaved him out of the room. He dragged him right outside, to where the sentry stood on guard, and slapped him across the face hard, twice, from left to right. Even in the Japanese Army, where face-slapping was part of the daily disciplining routine, it was hardly an everyday occurrence to see a Major-General slapping a Colonel across the face. But it reflects the curious mixture of spartan ideals and sybaritic behaviour that seems to have characterized the higher command of 15 Army.

Class

The effect of class differences is much harder to descry. One of Major (later Lieutenant-General) Fujiwara's observations of the different way he handled Indian soldiers from the way their British officers did is that they were surprised when he ate with them. He organized a lunch party on 17 December 1941 for the members of his 'Fujiwara Organization', civilians of the Indian Independence League, and Indian officers and NCOs. At the end, his first officer recruit, Captain Mohan Singh, stood up and thanked him for it: 'I cannot think of an occasion', he said, 'when Indian soldiers have ever had dinner together with British officers with whom we have fought side by side.'[1] There are, of course, racial as well as class overtones here, and Mohan Singh is hardly a neutral witness.

In fact, the command system of both British and Japanese armies depended on a hierarchy of distance between ranks, though this was far looser in the field than in barracks at home. In peacetime, writes Itō Keiichi, there is not much contact between the company commander and his men; nor between the men and the subalterns who in wartime are the platoon commanders.[2] The system was maintained by the British in Burma after the Japanese surrendered, because that was the easiest way to organize an efficient labour force. But the Japanese other ranks gradually began to erode the system themselves. One of these, Aida Yūji, who later became a Professor of Renaissance history in the University of Kyoto, points out that the Japanese Army had two sets of values, one dependent on rank and hierarchy, the other on the prestige of special skills, such as marksmanship.

Life in surrender camps minimized the former, and transformed the latter. The skills needed there were a talent for stealing or scrounging, being able to speak English to the guards, or to barter for cigarettes with the local Burmese. In this way, a parallel society grew up in the camps, dominated by those fittest for survival and uninhibited by memories of the old order. The officer/other rank system persisted alongside it, but it was a skeleton, manipulated by the British for their own concerns.[3]

On the other hand, it should be pointed out that the hierarchical structure of the Japanese Army was not – or so Japanese writers claim – a replica of the hierarchy of society itself. Rather it 'alleviated the dissatisfaction caused by hierarchical differences in society', says a Tokyo University Professor, Maruyama Masao; 'however exalted a status a man might have in the region of Japan he comes from', he continues, 'he must conform to the hierarchical order of the Army once he's in – that's a characteristic feature of the Japanese Army. In other countries, the officer is from the upper classes (*kizoku*), but that's not the case in Japan and that's said to be a great strength. That's interesting, but I think here, too, there is a pseudo-democratic factor in the Japanese Army. There are

---

[1] *F. Kikan*, trans. Y. Akashi, p. 86

[2] Itō Keiichi, op.cit., pp. 59–60

[3] Y. Aida, *Prisoner of the British*, pp. 148–69

differences of rank inside the structure of the Army, there's a moment of contradiction in the military hierarchy, on the theory that all men are alike under the Emperor, that a soldier's the Emperor's man, according to the *Ikkun Man-min* (one lord, and a myriad subjects) ideology... whatever his lineage or social position in his own region of Japan the son of a nobleman might be slapped across the face by the son of a peasant. This kind of pseudo-democratic system can become a solvent of the discontent which arises from difference in social status.'[1]

Major Fujiwara could congratulate himself on eating curry with his hands – however clumsily – and transcending the barriers that existed between Indians and their British officers. It is not unlike the way in which modern Japanese management techniques in British factories profit, by contrast, from the classless canteen and the classless lavatory. Did class play a role in the reactions of the British soldier to the war in the East? In terms of resentment against his officers, probably a considerable one, but that is a partly impressionistic reaction it would be difficult to quantify and substantiate. But when we read Japanese accounts of the prisoners taken after the first Wingate expedition and find the Japanese reporting that many of the men thought Wingate 'mad', does anything lie behind the observation other than the existence of an eccentric personality?[2] The Communist tank sergeant, Clive Branson, quotes a barrack-room conversation:

> Some great mental analyst should make a study of the regular soldiers in India. I took my book on Human Origins to the gunnery wing today to read during the break. A young regular, aged 23, with seven years' service, looked at the photos for a bit, read some sentences, and closed it, saying, 'those bastards write books like that to make millions out of poor soldiers'. And no explanation on my part could convince him otherwise. It all emphasizes how deeply has the sense of oppression, humiliation, and lack of human friendliness or suspicion, been driven upon their minds by the imperial army machine. I am not in the least surprised nowadays, after getting to know these fellows, why they're not interested in fighting in this war. *They don't believe in it.*[3]

It was true of the non-regular as well, according to the poet Alun Lewis's account of a visit paid to him by his brother, referred to as 'G' in his letters.

---

[1] Iizuka Kōji, *Nihon no guntai* (Japan's armed forces), 1968, p. 99

[2] 'Yūshō to jakusotai' (Brave generals and weak soldiers) in *Hiroku Dai Tōa Senshi, Biruma -hen* (Secret history of the war in East Asia: Burma), Tokyo, 1953, p. 141

[3] Clive Branson, *British Soldier in India; the letters of Clive Branson*, 1944, p. 33

Lewis was an officer in the South Wales Borderers, and was gratified that he had been able to ensure that his brother had, for a change, been able to sleep between sheets. He himself had been kept awake by the revellings in a nearby room of drunken fellow-officers. Finally he went into them and 'told them to pack it in'. Amazingly, they did so. 'Fancy people being like caricatures', he reflected, 'hundreds of them – our middle-class leaders! Still, they're not as dumb as they sound, and I don't hold it against them.'

But his brother clearly did: 'He told me how he sees things – the authentic and bitter view of the ranker who has no mercy for his superiors and revels cruelly in criticizing them – which is all he has power to do. And it is an unbalanced framework, too. G. with ten rupees a week compared with my 70 to 100 a week. I find it particularly unbearable in troopships and troop trains, where the difference in comfort is glaring and appalling...'[1]

Although the venue is Malaya not Burma, is it being over-scrupulous to suspect a class-based comment in Spencer Chapman's disparaging verdict on the inability of the British private soldier to survive in the jungle? He met two gunners and two young Argylls, the latter suffering from VD as well as beri-beri, and he gave them Vitamin B in the hope he could at least cure their deficiency disease: 'though it needed more than Vitamin B to cure their mental attitude, which was slowly but surely killing them. My experience is that the length of life of the British private soldier accidentally left behind in the Malayan jungle was only a few months, while the average NCO, being more intelligent, might last a year or even longer... They were unable to adapt themselves to a new way of life and a diet of rice and vegetables. In this green hell they expected to be dead within a few weeks – and as a rule they were...'[2]

Spencer Chapman would have been taken aback to read the story of Corporal Ras Pagani of the East Surreys who was the only man known to have escaped from the Burma-Siam Railway and to have survived. Son of an English father and a French mother, Pagani walked from the railway camp at Thanbyuzayat up into the Karen Hills where he joined Seagrim. Intending later to cross Burma to the British lines in Arakan, he was wounded by Burmese and taken to the Japanese Army. He pretended to be an American pilot who had been shot down, being sure that if they knew he had escaped from the Railway they would kill him. He was taken to Rangoon, where he spent two years, some of the time in solitary confinement, and was regularly beaten. He was finally released when the Japanese freed their prisoners after the fall of Rangoon.[3]

[1] Alun Lewis, *In the Green Tree*, 1948, p. 52

[2] F. Spencer Chapman, *The Jungle is Neutral*, p. 18

[3] Morrison, *Grandfather Longlegs*, pp. 202–10

There is a curious afterthought in Bernard Fergusson's account of the first Wingate expedition which seems to be related to the social differences between officers and men. He had to cross the Shweli River, which was breast high on himself (he was six foot one) and with a strong current running at four to five knots. His party got across to a sand bank in the middle of the river, where they were stranded. Some got across on country boats, then halfway through the night these went missing. The officers tried to persuade the men who were left to chance the current, but the hunger, the cold, the hours of waiting, and the cries of those swept downstream had unnerved them, and many refused to budge. They were taken prisoner the next day.

'It is a matter of fact', Fergusson continues, 'that those who had crossed and were with the column included all the best men, and the men whose behaviour throughout the expedition had been the most praiseworthy. It does not absolve me from my responsibility for the others to say so, but it was and is a comfort to me that among those whom I thus abandoned were few to whom our debt, and the debt of this nation, was outstanding. There were two or three whom I particularly regretted, and of these one was almost certainly drowned, and two were especially small in stature. There were two more who, had they got out, would have had to face charges at a court-martial.'[1]

It is interesting to note in this connection that one Japanese observer used height as a means of distinguishing officers and men in the British Army. Officers might read the same popular magazines as the men, but there seemed to be a total difference in the way they pronounced their words, and a glance would distinguish one from the other: 'It was their physique – particularly their stature', writes Aida Yūji. 'Among the NCOs and men, few were taller than I was – about 5 feet 6 inches. Not a few were around 5 feet 6 inches. But the officers were big men, for the most part over six feet... [They were] magnificently well-built... And there was more to it than physique. Their general attitude showed a superb self-confidence.' The reason was, in Aida's view, that British Army ranks reflected the general structure of British society. Between officers and men, in his observation, 'there was a distinction that made you wonder whether the men were considered to be fellow-Englishmen at all. The officers were "white-collar", the NCOs and men were "labourers".' There was a similar difference in their skill with weapons, too, he thought. 'The kind of people who become officers received an energetic training in sport at school. Fencing, boxing, wrestling, rugby, rowing, riding – the officer who did not play at any rate one of these sports with some skill was rather an exception.' They gave the impression of being 'tremendously lively, brisk and energetic.'

[1] Fergusson, *Beyond the Chindwin*, pp. 174–5

Aida is an historian and has an explanation for this: 'These officers are the descendants of the same bourgeoisie which carried through the bourgeois revolution. That bourgeoisie took up arms, fought against the feudal aristocracy, and ousted them from their positions of power. The working class which had fought alongside them was numerically overwhelming but afterwards, under the rule of the bourgeoisie, if the workers showed signs of getting out of hand, the bourgeoisie repressed them by force and held them in check. We had always thought of the rule of the bourgeoisie as being imposed through social structures and clever educational policies, and had not realized the part played by sheer physical strength.'[1]

Pace Aida, it is easy to over-interpret social differentiation, but Fergusson's narrative does seem to show a case when the gap between officers and men was also the gap between survival and capture. But the evidence for the impact of class is fragmentary and impressionistic and it would be foolhardy to over-deduce.

Race

The evidence for the impact of racial difference, on the other hand, is quite strong, and it stretches beyond the Burma battlefield itself to the whole of the war in the Far East. 'The issue of race', writes an American historian, 'rested at the heart of power politics in the Far East.'[2] In spite of this, and the openly racial basis of much Japanese propaganda, nothing in the war in Asia resembled the cold-blooded, rationalized and industrialized genocide of Hitler's war against the Jews. Certainly, millions of people died, through brutality, greed, ruthlessness, ineptitude, and the hazards of operations, but not as the result of a plan coldly calculated in advance and based on the prejudices of centuries.

But there were racial conflicts, and racial resentments survive between Japanese and Korean, Japanese and Chinese, British and Japanese, British and Indian. On the other hand they were never industrialized. That is why it is important to recall that among the dead of the Burma-Siam Railway there are far more thousands of helpless Asian labourers than of Allied prisoners-of-war.

The Japanese and their puppet governments made great play with racial hostility to the colonial powers. Ba Maw in particular makes embarrassing use of racial 'blood kinship' rhetoric in his address to the Great East Asia Conference in Tokyo in November 1943: 'I seem to hear the voice of Asia gathering her children together,' he proclaimed. 'It is the voice of our

---

[1] Y. Aida, op.cit., pp. 81–2

[2] W. R. Louis, *British Strategy in the Far East*, 1971

Asiatic blood. This is not the time to think with our minds; this is the time to think with our blood, and it is this thinking with the blood which has brought me all the way from Burma to Japan.'[1] This was the ideal which also inspired Major Fujiwara when he addressed the Indian POWs at Farrer Park in Singapore, in February 1942: 'Japan is fighting for the liberation of the Asiatic nations which have been so long trodden under the cruel heels of British imperialism. Japan is the liberator and friend of Asiatics.'[2]

Even the Chinese community in Singapore, which had more reason to fear and hate the Japanese than anyone on the island, felt some of the pull of this rhetoric. The brutality of the Japanese soon destroyed it: 'We were not unmindful of your claims of cousinhood, of community of blood and culture. You shamed us, your fellow-Mongols and fellow-Asiatics, by your failure to display generosity and magnanimity, and chivalry in your day of triumph.'[3] And a book published in London in 1943, written by the Eurasian Cedric Dover, warned the British public that Japan's voice was listened to in the most unlikely places, that American blacks 'saw in the then (1938) prospective clash between America and Japan their opportunity to strike for freedom'.[4] At a time when Mutaguchi was planning his invasion of India, Dover could warn his British readership that 'if the Japanese attack India seriously the confusion and anger which has already gripped millions in the country might grow into concrete and widespread support for the invaders. The Japanese army would appear as liberators.'[5]

Japan had long before claimed for herself the role of defender of the coloured peoples of the world. 'When the present conflict in Europe is over', wrote Yamagata Aritomo, the old field marshal who had been the creator of Japan's modern army, to the Prime Minister, Okuma, in August 1914, 'and when the political and economic orders are restored, various countries will again focus their attention on the Far East and the benefits and rights they might derive from this region. When that day comes, the rivalry between the white and non-white races will become violent, and who can say that the white races will not unite with one another to oppose the coloured peoples?... if the coloured races of the Orient hope to compete with the so-called culturally advanced white races and maintain friendly relations with them while retaining their own cultural identity and independence, China and Japan, which are culturally and racially alike, must become friendly and promote each other's interests.'[6]

[1] Ba Maw, *Breakthrough in Burma*, p. 343

[2] Shah Nawaz Khan, *INA and its Netaji*, p. 19

[3] H. I. Low, H. M. Cheng, *This Singapore (Our City of Dreadful Nights)*, Singapore, n.d. p. 14

[4] Cedric Dover, *Hell in the Sunshine*, London, 1943, p. 166

[5] ibid., p. 120

[6] Tsunoda et al., *Sources of Japanese Tradition*, II, 1958, p. 207

That idea lies behind Japan's insistence that her invasion of China was to shore up the central power of the Far East against western intrusion. If China could not play her part, she must be made to. In the meanwhile, Japan would take up the shield alone. The argument did not fall on deaf ears, as the recruitment of Indian prisoners-of-war by the Japanese in Singapore was to show in 1942. That resentment against racial discrimination, felt most painfully by Indian officers, played a part in this is adequately shown by evidence from both anti-British and pro-British officers. 'Indian officers were not admitted as members of a large number of clubs in Malaya,' wrote Shah Nawaz Khan, an officer of the 14th Punjab who later led a brigade of the INA against the British in Burma. 'There was an order by the Railway Authorities of the Federated Malay States that an Asiatic could not travel in the same compartment as a European, and the fact that they both held the same rank and belonged to the same unit did not seem to matter in this respect.'[1]

Exactly the same point was made by Lieutenant-Colonel Mahmood Khan Durrani, later decorated by the Viceroy of India with the George Cross for resisting Japanese torture:

> The Indian officers were insulted at every opportunity, and often we wondered if this treatment was a natural return for all the enthusiasm with which we offered to defend the British Empire. The harsh and unjust dealings of the British officers (with one exception) awakened a sense of national pride and resentment at such injustice... The biased treatment of Indians by British officers and the general discontent of Indian troops of all ranks was universal in Malaya.[2]

It should be indicated that this view is not accepted by the official British historian, who writes, 'There was no racial discrimination in Malaya, and the relations between the various communities were generally cordial; the Asians of different races, however, mixed more freely with Europeans than with one another. It can be said that pre-war Malaya was a happy, prosperous and loyal land...'[3]

Durrani's statement will simply not bear transference to the Burma context, but the racial element is very strong when the two armies, usually from the depths of a profound mutual ignorance of each other's history, assess the enemy's psychology.

Some Japanese were quite recently being asked to believe that the British took a numerically calculated revenge for those killed on the

[1] Shah Nawaz Khan, op.cit., pp. 4–5

[2] M. K. Durrani, *The Sixth Column*, pp. 2–3

[3] Kirby, *War Against Japan*, I, p. 156

Burma-Siam Railway by killing off an equivalent number of Japanese labourers in 1946, who were supposed to be buried in the Japanese cemetery in Singapore. The charge was laid in a series of articles in a popular Japanese magazine, by a Japanese, Mr Shinozaki Mamoru, who had many connections in Singapore and was instrumental in saving many Singapore Chinese from brutal treatment during the Japanese occupation. The charge was later withdrawn, after it had been demonstrated to be false, but by then the damage had been done.[1] Aida Yūji is convinced there was a considered plan by the British authorities in Burma to vent their racial contempt on the Japanese. And he has never retreated from his verdict, which was aimed as much at his countrymen's newly rediscovered Anglophilia of the 1950s as at the British themselves: 'I was obsessed', he wrote, 'by the idea that in prison camp we had glimpsed the unknown soul of the British Army and of the British. We had seen it. To us it was a frightening monster. This monster had ruled Asians for centuries and caused untold misery. . . .'[2]

The misery, as he suffered it in his own person, did not lie in being whipped or beaten, or in undergoing any of the tortures he knew were inflicted by his own army upon British and Indian captives. It consisted of being the butt of cold racial contempt, a dehumanizing indifference that Aida felt to be worse than physical violence. They did this with the Indians, too, he felt:

> They seemed simply to disregard them. Not that they were excessively contemptuous, nor did they show the caution of people coming into contact with touchy foreigners; it was rather as if they simply ignored the Indian soldiers' very existence. They hardly ever talked with us Japanese, of course, but I never once saw a British soldier, apart from some public negotiation or discussion, strike up a conversation with an Indian. I could not help but wonder how Indian troops could tolerate such an insulting attitude.[3]

Once when Aida was scrubbing a floor, a British soldier put his cigarette out on his forehead:

> Blazing with anger, I looked up at him and saw him calmly reading the paper but the expression on his face betrayed an intense

---

[1] L. Allen, 'Not so piacular', *Proc. Brit. Assoc. for Japanese Studies*, Sheffield, 1980, p. 111; and conversations with Mr Shinozaki in Kyoto, 1981

[2] Y. Aida, op.cit., p. xii. And cf. an interesting parallel in a *Sunday Times* interview with Lt-Colonel Colin Campbell Mitchell of the Argyll and Sutherland Highlanders: 'Young people with all their CND don't understand what a very nasty lot we are, the British. The rest of the world understands, the ones who've had us.'

[3] Aida, op.cit., p. 89–91

hatred. On another occasion one soldier sat down in front of me and as if by chance kicked up my chin with his boot. On another occasion a soldier made me kneel in front of him and used my shoulders as a footstool for a whole hour.[1]

Aida's section-leader cleaned out the barrack latrines. He urinated there himself on one occasion and was found by a British soldier, who shouted at him, made him kneel down, and then urinated all over his face. Some of the women auxiliaries would undress and wash in front of Japanese prisoners in total unconcern: they simply did not exist as human beings for them. Hence Aida's conclusion:

> It is true the British did not beat prisoners up or kick them or butcher people alive. They committed almost none of what are usually termed atrocities. But this does not mean that they behaved according to humanitarian principles. On the contrary they often behaved with childish vindictiveness. And yet even the most vindictive act had a façade of reasonableness, and was carried out in such a way as to avoid any accusation being made against them. And British troops were always cool and collected and carried out these actions calmly, with great indifference. From one point of view they were certainly not cruel, but from another point of view I felt that their treatment reflected the cruellest attitude a man can have towards his fellow-man.[2]

This verdict, which is not inconsistent with Aida regarding the British as honest and endowed with a highly developed sense of responsibility, has kept him from ever visiting Britain. He has been to Europe and America, but not to England. 'They made me feel like a snake that's been skinned alive.'[3]

Comparative estimates of cruelty play a great part in Aida's assessments of national character. And, of course, it is obvious that although Japan posed as the liberator of the colonized peoples of East Asia, in practice these became the unwilling prisoners of the Japanese themselves. The recent revelations by Morimura Seiichi about the medical unit in Manchuria, Unit 731, which experimented with the effects of bacteriological weapons, on living prisoners, Chinese and Russian,[4] have been matched more recently by a Japanese medical officer's account of No.4 Field

---

[1] ibid., p. 49

[2] ibid., p. 52

[3] Conversation with the author, Kyoto, 1965

[4] Morimura Seiichi, *Akuma no hōshoku* (The devil's gluttony) Tokyo, Kobunsha, 1981; and continuation 1982

Hospital at Hsenwi in North Burma, where he watched one of his colleagues carry out vivisection, without anaesthetics, on two captured Chinese agents, one being subjected to the removal of his entire inner organs, starting with the testicles, the other being injected with air into his veins to see how much he could take before he died (120 cc was the answer).[1] And Colonel Tsuji's biographer cannot rid his subject of the accusation that he cooked and ate the liver of the pilot of a downed P40, and even persuaded the unwilling Army commander, Lieutenant-General Honda, to nibble a piece.[2]

These things will not go away and, whether revisionist historians like it or not, they are part and parcel of the view of the Japanese Army during the war in East Asia which the rest of the world is likely to retain for a long time, whatever the virtues or failings of its opponents.

Oddly enough, it was the bravery rather than the cruelty of the Japanese Army which was stressed by two British generals at a meeting held in Chatham House three years after the war (September 1948), in an attempt to define the Japanese military character. The meeting was held between British diplomats with experience of Japan and the two generals who had presided over defeat and victory against the Japanese, General Percival and General Slim. In spite of their very different experiences, the two coincided fairly closely in their observations. There was no moral flag-waving or drum-beating.

Slim said he thought Japanese courage had a decidedly theatrical component. They liked an audience, and officers gave displays of swordmanship in front of their men often at the expense of British and Indian prisoners. The purpose, he thought, was to 'blood' raw combat troops, with which Percival agreed; but he added the rider that the foundation of their courage was a very high sense of patriotism. Slim ascribed it to a spiritual basis and said it had a unique quality unparalleled in other armies. The idea of an audience would persist even if the soldier was alone.

In contradistinction to the view put forward by the chairman of the meeting, Sir Paul Butler, that Japanese society was essentially a group society, in which the individual shirked responsibility and initiative, Slim said he thought Japanese courage was an individual, not a group, characteristic. It was one of the outstanding qualities of the Japanese soldier, that, when isolated, he would fight on alone and not surrender. He added that if anyone did try to surrender he would receive short shrift from his comrades.

They feared death, he said, the least of all soldiers he had ever seen. The human anti-tank mine was an instance of this. The duty involved certain

[1] Ishida Shinsaku, *Akuma no Nihon Gun-i* (The devil's medical officer), Tokyo, Yamate Shobō, 1982, pp. 175–84

[2] Sugimori Kyūei, *Sanbō; Tsuji Masanobu* (Tsuji Masanobu, Staff Officer) Kawade Shobō Shinsha, 1982, pp. 154–60

death and the men were not volunteers. Again, when the Japanese knew they were defeated, instances occurred in which they threw away their lives. On one occasion in Burma, he recalled Japanese troops trying to escape across the Irrawaddy, where the British were waiting for them on the north bank. Fifteen Japanese in full kit came down out of the hills and walked ceremoniously into the river; a completely purposeless death.

Then Slim introduced his celebrated dehumanizing metaphor, which does him little credit. In order to understand the Japanese, one must not think of them as men or even as animals, but as 'soldier ants' like those to be found in India.[1] In almost every respect they were alike. He did not think they anticipated fear before the event, and would not admit it if they did. In this connection, Percival declared that the emotion of fear grew stronger as people grew more civilized. The Japanese accepted every order without question, unlike more civilized soldiers who often questioned the wisdom of their orders.

Slim said Japanese orders were couched in totally different language from those of the British. The Japanese 33 Division, a very tough formation, was told when about to attack Imphal that the division would be annihilated, but they would win a victory. In the Arakan, they were told they would die and their bodies would lie rotting in the sand-dunes, but they would turn to grass which would wave in the breezes blowing from Japan. Their higher command was wasteful of manpower, nor did they improve in this respect as the war went on. One cause of wastage was their habit of putting reinforcements in in driblets as they arrived instead of waiting until the complete formation was available and then attacking in strength. This was due, he thought, to the excitement which overtook the Japanese in battle. Another cause was their killing their wounded when hard-pressed. The British found many field hospitals in which Japanese had been shot in their beds. And there were authenticated instances of officers killing with their swords soldiers badly wounded in battle, at the soldiers' request.

At this point Sir Paul Butler pointed out that this went against the trend of what happened in the Russo-Japanese war, where they succeeded in reducing manpower wastage from sickness to a very low percentage. Slim recognised there was a difference between what they would accept from battle and what they would accept from sickness. They were very good at vaccination and there was little smallpox, and all Japanese soldiers carried quinine. Their surgery, though, was very crude.

Japanese discipline was rigid and first-class, and only relaxed when the officers thought it should. For this reason he did not accept the idea that atrocities occurred when they were out of hand. He believed they were

---

[1] 'The individual Japanese soldier remained, as I had always called him, the most formidable fighting insect in history.' (Slim, *Defeat into Victory*, p. 381)

allowed to commit atrocities for an officially approved purpose. He did not agree that lack of control led them into acts of indiscipline. They shouted and yelled in battle but that was not lack of discipline. A diplomat intervened here to suggest that discipline in the field was therefore different from that at home. When Percival suggested that once an order was given they would not be bribed to break it, he added that in Japan, if long and complicated regulations were issued, the Japanese would not hesitate to get round them if possible. Slim said there was something similar in Burma. High command regulations from Tokyo might be treated with disrespect, but immediate orders from a superior in battle were a different matter. The men had great faith in their officers, which was not always, in his view, justified. It was a different set-up from that obtaining in the British Army. The Japanese were not 'mothered' but the officers shared everything with them. Another diplomat pointed out that many of the regiments were recruited from men from the same districts, and in the evening officers and men could meet together to discuss news from home.

Surprisingly enough – and not easily acceptable – was Slim's verdict that he did not think the Japanese treated the Burmese with excessive ruthlessness; unless, that is, their demands had been refused or they had been provoked. He referred to the case of Seagrim, who gave himself up because of the punishment inflicted on the Karens on his account. If British officers were hidden by the Burmese, there would be no limit to the atrocities, and if supplies were refused they would burn the village and bayonet the inhabitants. Atrocities, he repeated, were generally an act of policy, rather than the outcome of indiscipline.

There were political considerations, too, added Percival: the massacre of Chinese in Singapore was almost entirely confined to members of the Kuomintang. Sir Paul Butler said this confirmed his impression that the Japanese only treated colonial peoples badly if they showed political aspirations: they treated the aborigines in Formosa (Taiwan) very kindly. Slim added that they were well-behaved when under his command in Indo-China and Java after the surrender. Percival qualified this by his experience that there was usually a certain amount of drunkenness. If they were let loose in a captured town, they would nearly always get drunk, and their officers for this reason tried to keep them out of towns.

On the very puzzling issue of the Japanese attitudes to being taken prisoner and to surrender, Slim said surrender was rarer with them than with any other army. About 150,000 were killed in Burma, and 1700 taken prisoner, of whom only 400 could be described as physically fit. The rest were taken when wounded or utterly exhausted. No regular officer was captured, and none above the rank of major. For the first week, all tried to commit suicide. After that they gave up and worked docilely for their captors. They did not reconcile this with their patriotism, they simply 'chucked in their hand.' As a result, they were the only soldiers who had no instructions what to say if taken prisoner. Even when utterly exhausted they might refuse to surrender, and would merely sit lifelessly by the roadside with folded hands waiting for the British to kill them.

As a result of all this, British and Indian troops had a very ambivalent attitude towards them. They respected them very much as fighters, but hated them because of their treatment of the wounded and prisoners. Treatment of prisoners depended purely on the whim of the junior officer in charge of the men making the capture, and the prisoner might only have his hands tied, or he might be used as a target for bayonet practice. Their methods of interrogation were always brutal.

One of the diplomats asked Slim if mutilation took place. Yes, was the answer, especially of Sikhs, but there was no returning of hands, arms, etc. The Gurkhas, too, were badly treated by the Japanese and in return they treated the Japanese equally badly. He had, on the other hand, heard no verifiable stories of cannibalism and thought that it would not have been necessary in Burma anyway.[1] They appeared to ignore all the ordinary rules of war, he added; but pointed out that they should be judged by their own standards and not by British standards.

This meeting, held in September 1948, reflects a considered and unimpassioned view of an enemy by the British high command, and it says a good deal for the common sense of both Slim and Percival. But neither of them viewed the Japanese from inside, neither spoke the language, naturally enough, and their views are therefore limited by their externality. It is this which radically distorts most attempts by the British to understand their enemy. And the Japanese are no better. For the primary gulf between the two was that of language, and the inability to communicate nearly always leads to the dehumanizing of the opponent.[2] An instance of this occurs in a fragment quoted from a Chindit diary by Shelford Bidwell, who speaks of the 'physical aversion and moral horror the British felt for the Japanese soldier.' 'Somehow one can imagine,' wrote Lt Durant of the South Staffordshire Regiment, 'that one could have a drink and a cigarette and a cup of tea with a (German) prisoner, but once having met the Japs one can only imagine kicking their heads in. They look like animals, they behave like animals, and they can be killed unemotionally as swatting flies. And they need to be killed, not wounded, for as long as they breathe they're dangerous.'[3]

---

[1] Slim must have known of the Tsuji case by this time, which makes his comment odd. And he misunderstands the motivation for cannibalism if he thinks it entirely the result of hunger.

[2] The attitude persisted, between other western peoples and another eastern enemy, as William Styron observed: 'There is a continuity of events, a linkage of atrocity from war to war, that forces the conclusion that we are capable of demonstrating toward our Asian adversaries a ruthless inhumanity we would doubtless withold from those less incomprehensibly different from us, less likened to animals, or simply less brown or yellow'. Review of P. Caputo, *A Rumor of War*, in *New York Review of Books*, 23. vi. 1977, xxiv, No. 11, p. 4

[3] Bidwell, *The Chindit War*, p. 124

This reductionist metaphor, though it does not go, zoologically speaking, as far as Slim's, is constant in British evocations of the Japanese. It is a way of keeping the enemy at a distance, and, of course, a kind of *carte blanche*. There are times when the metaphor runs side by side with a puzzled acquiescence in their undoubted courage, as in Miles Smeeton's account of the battle of the breakout in July 1945:

> Whenever we caught them they still snapped back with the same vicious courage. They were so different from us, so furtive in their ways, that we still thought of them as some savage wild animal, but whatever their beliefs, their ruthless discipline or their fears, if ever a saga of courage and endurance was written by the common soldier, that of the Japanese Twenty-Eighth Army should be included.[1]

In his second book, *The Wild Green Earth*, Bernard Fergusson devotes an entire chapter to 'The Japanese as an opponent'. He echoes Slim on the solitary courage of the Japanese, though he adds, from the infantry commander's more direct experience, that there were plenty of ways of breaking it down – heavy bombing and the use of flame being two of them. The Japanese was speedy, his camouflage was excellent, his engineering good with the barest minimum of equipment, he had an eye for ground. On the other hand, the Japanese was not a born jungle-fighter any more than the British town-born soldier. He was a slave to habit, and therefore easy to ambush. He relied on noise ('The Answer to Noise is Silence' was one of Wingate's doctrines). He was a rotten shot, but handled mortars well. The British could learn a great deal from him in terms of absolute devotion to a cause and absolute disregard for one's own life. 'Nevertheless,' Fergusson concludes, 'we must not forget that he is a barbarian.' Out of eighty of Fergusson's men who reached Rangoon Jail, fifty-two died. Sixty more fell into Japanese hands who never even reached the Jail; and the twenty-eight survivors had cruel tales to tell of the way they died.[2]

Another Chindit officer carried the alienation of hatred over from the living to the dead. Major Charles Carfrae, in command of 29 Column, 7th Nigerian Regiment, at 'White City', was painstakingly telling his Nigerians they should not kill their prisoners, when one severely wounded Japanese in a truck momentarily recovered:

> A Japanese non-commissioned officer taken for dead, summoning strength by a superhuman effort of will, had shaken off the hands which lifted him and attempted to stab the nearest African

[1] Smeeton, *A Change of Jungles*, p. 111
[2] Fergusson, *The Wild Green Earth*, p. 217

with a bayonet. For a moment I saw him stand upright in the back of the truck like one risen from the dead, shouting hysterically, his tunic stiff with caked blood; then a dozen shots riddled his body.

There was no time to bury the corpses and Carfrae decided to burn them as they were, in the trucks. Soaked with petrol, the trucks soon burned but the Japanese bodies did not turn to ashes: 'When the flames died they could be seen as lumps of roasted black flesh recognisably of human shape, grotesquely crowned with steel helmets bleached white by the heat. Not one of us was emotionally moved by this revolting sight... we felt nothing but physical disgust. Our imaginations were untouched; we felt no remorse.'

As the reason for this reaction, Carfrae did not say his men were hardened against battle horrors, because they were not: 'We did not hate them. Hate is an emotion inspired by fellow-beings; and to us the Japanese were an abstraction. They were 'the enemy', the creatures of the forest whom we must destroy; the unpredictable, the robot fanatics who, it seemed to us, lacked all warmth of human feeling, who gave us no quarter and expected none... While we admired Japanese courage and tenacity, in the way that men admire the instinctive courage of animals, we also feared them, much more than we feared their bullets. Bullets we understood; but the minds and hearts of the Japanese were beyond our understanding.[1]

Captain Malcolm Monteith, of the 1st Battalion North Rhodesia Regiment, wrote a pamphlet on the East Africans in Burma which has an appendix on the Japanese. Monteith approaches them anatomically and psychologically:

> The Japanese are usually small. In colour they are a light brown, when alive; when dead their flesh resembles putty. Generally they have muscular, rather hairless bodies, thick strong legs and short arms. Their hands are like the hands of children, pudgy, smooth and small. They have broad skulls and coarse black hair, which in the case of soldiers is generally shaven. It tends to grow with the nap, as it were, from the back of the head to the front. Few Japs could grow beards to match those of the RN. The eyes of the Japanese have a peeping look, due to the double-fold in the upper lid. Their cheekbones are wide and high and their noses unobtrusive. Their teeth, which do not usually protrude, as depicted by cartoonists, have often a number of cheap-looking gold fillings. The Japanese themselves are in no sense of the word, yellow.

[1] C. A. Carfrae, TS, *Dark Company*, p. 154, Imperial War Museum Archives.

Monteith also uses the animal parallel:

> The Japanese have a peculiar animal-like quality. Even their dead look like shot game. Though bodily clean, their living habits are filthy. All their intimate possessions, such as clothing and blankets have a most distinctive smell, a legacy, presumably, from the bodies of their owners. In attack, they scream, thereby producing such a volume and quality of sound that it is difficult to believe that it emerges from human throats. In defence, after being stunned and stupefied by bombardment, they crouch in small niches and holes like trapped beasts, often weeping hysterically but fighting desperately to the last.
>
> It is impossible to predict their behaviour or reactions. One day, if surprised in the open, they will throw away their arms and take to their heels; on another they will show a fanatical tenacity in holding their ground. They display, too, a truly impressive reluctance to being taken prisoner, going to such lengths as suicide, yet when captured they eagerly betray their comrades by imparting any secret information they may possess. When in position they are invisible, eating, sleeping and performing all the natural functions by their foxholes, and yet on the march they move carelessly and are easy to surprise. They go to considerable trouble to recover their dead, yet having done so, they are just as likely to leave them unburied. They show a callous disregard for their sick and wounded and at the beginning of the campaign, the Division (11 East African Division) took several prisoners who had been abandoned to die in the rain...

From all this, Monteith concludes, 'it might perhaps be fair to say that the Japanese are the first barbarous and primitive enemy, fighting from motives of the purest patriotism, and equipped with modern arms, that the western world has encountered.'[1]

Nearly all these commentators on the Japanese character base their views on one aspect only: the antagonism of battle. The views often did not survive when the battle was over and a more humanizing contact became possible. An interesting example of this is furnished by Miles Smeeton, who was in command of an area, after the war was over, in which were a number of Japanese camps. After dining with his wife at an infantry battalion mess on the banks of the Salween, Smeeton drove back to his own HQ with her across a ferry manned by Japanese. They were unguarded, and lived in a little grass hut by the river bank, and the Japanese ferrymen dashed out of their hut and began to pull the ferry across on its

---

[1] Malcolm Monteith, *Ceylon to the Chindwin*, 1945

chain. 'In a few minutes,' he writes, 'they were heaving us back as if they were trying to beat their own record. I never ceased to wonder at them, even now.

"You see?", I said to Beryl, "Amazing isn't it? I can't imagine that I'd try under their circumstances."

"I think that you are quite proud of them now,"[1] she said, and as a matter of fact I was.'

The aesthetic response

'War', declares a memoir on Viet Nam, 'is the ultimate adventure, the ordinary man's most convenient means of escaping from the ordinary.'[2] Because of this, many of those who experience it need to make their experience permanent in writing. This is as true of the Burma campaign as of any other, but there is a strange *décalage* between the opposing sides. The reason for this lies in the fact that the Japanese people as a whole, unlike the British, had not been forced to absorb into their national temperament events like the Somme and Passchendaele. They did not have the presuppositions about the deceptiveness of war which were commonplace to the young men who joined the British forces in 1939 – or later – and who had been brought up on the assumption that the whole thing was a vast and cruel confidence trick. 'Certain attitudes habitual to poetry were prohibited,' writes Frank Kermode of the literature of the Second World War. 'People could not go to war in the manner of Brooke – "like swimmers into cleanness leaping". They knew, from the experience of their fathers, that the leap was not into cleanness. Nor did they emerge, like the men of 1914, from a long peace, informed of war only by literature.'[3]

A typical dissentient voice is that of C. Day Lewis – later to become Poet Laureate – in a brief answer to the question, 'where are the war poets?'

> They who from panic or mere greed
> Enslaved religion, markets, laws,
> Borrow our language now and bid
> Us to speak up in freedom's cause.
>
> It is the logic of our times
> No subject for immortal verse

[1] Smeeton, *A Change of Jungles*, p. 118

[2] P. Caputo, *A Rumor of War*, quoted in *New York Review of Books*, 23. vi. 1977, xxiv, No. 11, p. 3

[3] Kermode, 'The words of two wars', *Daily Telegraph*, August 1975

> That we who lived by honest dreams
> Defend the bad against the worse.[1]

Such a view is derived from the disillusion about the aims and methods of war fed by countless poets and novelists in Europe from 1929 onwards. But we will fail to understand the Japanese literature of the Second World War if we forget that the Japanese did not have that reaction available to them. The war in China had not provided it, but by August 1945 they had been through their own Passchendaeles, by the score. But to start with, they would not have found Rupert Brooke alien to them. Day Lewis's near-contemporary, the novelist Dazai Osamu, wrote in ecstasy over Pearl Harbour:

> My nature was utterly changed. I had the feeling of being utterly transparent, as if shot through by a strong ray of light. Or receiving the breath of the Holy Spirit – as if a single cold petal had melted inside my breast. From that morning on, Japan, too, had become a different country.[2]

The socialist writer, and later translator of *Lady Chatterley's Lover*, Itō Sei, exclaimed, 'In the midst of turbulent emotions, I felt a curious inner tranquillity: this is good, it's terrific. I remember the feeling of relief bubbling up inside me. The joy of having been given a direction clearly, a lightness of the whole being. It was marvellous.'[3]

'I thought it was terrific,' remembers the novelist Agawa Hiroyuki, then a student of literature at the University of Tokyo. 'Then came the announcement of the great victories, around noon. No question of moaning that if there is war some of us must die. No lamentations, that was our mood.'[4]

One of Japan's greatest writers, Shiga Naoya, reflecting a short time later on the fall of Singapore, wrote:

> We Japanese have been astounded at the spiritual and technical achievements of our armed forces, from the very start of hostilities. When we realize how much of our victory depends upon heaven, we need humility, and every day brings fresh instances of this. The confidence that heaven is with us makes us all the more humble.

[1] In *Penguin New Writing*, 1941, p. 114

[2] Quoted in Louis Allen, 'Japanese Literature of the Second World War', *Proceedings of the British Association for Japanese Studies*, Vol. 2, Part One, Sheffield, 1977, p. 118

[3] ibid., p. 134

[4] ibid.

Without our expecting it, the unanimity of the entire nation has been achieved. Pro-British or pro-American views are no longer possible in Japan. Among ourselves, we keep a modest frame of mind, we preserve harmony in the country, and not a single blemish will stain our brilliant victories. It has been a useful lesson for the God-forsaken arrogance of Britain and America. There is cause for rejoicing that hope is born among our young people.

Our spirit bright, clear and calm, we bow with reverence before the spirits of our heroic dead.[1]

The mood of 1941 was caught in one of the most famous of Japanese marching songs, which became known throughout the entire Far East:

Miyo Tōkai no sora akete	See, the sky is opening, over the Eastern sea
Kyokujitsu takaku kagayakeba	When the rising sun lights up the heavens,
Tenchi no seiki hatsuratsu to	Our hope dances on the Eight Great Islands
Kibō wa odoru ōyashima	Filled with the life and vigour of the world
O seirō no asakumo ni	Oh, in the fine bright clouds of morning
Sobiyuru Fuji no sugata koso	The shape of Fuji towers on high
Kinō muketsu yurugi naki	Firm as a rock, perfect like a vase of gold,
Waga Nippon no hokori nare.	The pride of our Japan.

It expresses a sense of glory, of Japan's beauty and greatness, rather than hostility to anyone else. A version, in a way, of 'Thanks be to God who has matched us with this hour'?

There are no British songs for the Far East. There are poems, but their mood is reflective, not despairing but certainly sombre.

The reason for the different tone of British and Japanese writing, at any rate on the onset of war, is not far to seek. The Japanese exultation in those first weeks after Pearl Harbour is that of a nation fighting for its very being. When the verb is 'to be' then every effort is permissible, every sacrifice willingly undertaken, no room for doubt is left. When the verb is 'to have', the willingness to go to the extremes of sacrifice is harder to find.[2] This is

---

[1] ibid., p. 136

[2] 'A young Chindit, whom I had met when I first arrived in Delhi, was now about to go to hospital suffering, after four months in the jungle, from jaundice, amoebic dysentery,

the difference between Dunkirk and Singapore. Both were crushing defeats. Both knocked the British temporarily out of the ring. But Dunkirk became a watchword for the future, Singapore a reminder of shame. One was fought on behalf of being, the other on behalf of having. And the difference marked the entire war.

The Japanese mood of exultation, needless to say, did not last, and the experience of Burma, particularly of Imphal and its aftermath, was a potent factor in the change. But the impact was felt chiefly in the factual reportage which came out of Burma, rather than in its fictional transposition. In terms of art, some rather surprising things occurred. One is to be found in the writings of the poet Takami Jun. Takami was an English literature graduate of Tokyo Imperial University who was attracted by the left-wing movements of the 1930s until arrested under the Peace Preservation Law in 1933. Like a number of left-wing intellectuals, he underwent a process of conversion to nationalism, and went out to China and South-East Asia on a propaganda assignment. He published a number of essay-style writings on Burma, but more interesting is his *Biruma Nikki – Burma Diary* – in which he records *inter alia* a long and fascinating interview with Ba Maw; and the occasional piece of fiction, of which I think the most illustrative is the piece 'Nowkhana', first printed in the magazine *Nihon Hyōron* in June 1943.

The first person of the story is one of a group of Japanese officers stationed in Rangoon. He is in charge of the messing arrangements for the billets, and hires cooks and boys. The servants live in a block behind the billet, which allows Takami to indulge in a little anti-British propaganda:

> The servants' living quarters behind the mess gave the impression of a solitary confinement block in a gaol. This was how the British had planned their residences: wherever they built houses there existed also 'servants quarters' of a kind which proclaims the British did not treat their Indian servants as human beings at all. If you had human feelings, you could not bear to look at them. The practice was for the servants to live there with their families, and since to look upon that filthy inhuman way of living might be injurious to the ease of mind of the white-skinned masters in their luxurious residences, a protective wall was usually set up between them and the tenement block, rather like the walls of a gaol. It was really an awful building, naked and unashamed.

malaria, and every other sort of tropical disease. He had had a beastly time. My friend said he was saddened that his men must continue fighting under such appalling conditions, and he himself felt that they were incapable of conquering Burma in this way. Some of the men were beginning to ask, "Who wants Burma anyway?"' (Cecil Beaton, *Far East*, London, 1945, p. 39)

But Takami is not writing for propaganda purposes. The story turns against himself. He and his colleagues are fed up with endless curry and rice, and the cooks seem unable to provide what is asked for, or to keep away the swarms of flies from the filthy kitchens, or to market and shop honestly. In despair, he nominates one of them, Nowkhana, as head boy, making him responsible for the others. One of his colleagues, also a writer, accuses the boys of stealing money from him. 'This shameful for Indians. This insult,' Nowkhana protests.

> I went straightaway to the third floor. The 'Master' in the middle room of the third floor was a writer. I passed on to him what Nowkhana had told me. I trusted Nowkhana, trusted the Indians, and that fact had made me get a little hot under the collar over the haste with which suspicion had been fastened on the boys, without any warning.

Then Nowkhana is caught red-handed selling tins from the billet stores. Takami goes and looks for him to confront him with this betrayal of trust:

> Nowkhana was standing in one corner of the mess-hall, looking thoroughly downcast.
> 'Nowkhana!'
> I meant to go on, 'How could you do anything like this, this rotten thing?' but when I looked at him, all I felt was the searing pain of being betrayed. I could say nothing. I picked up one of the plates from a nearby table and hurled it suddenly at the wall beside Nowkhana. It was my first outburst of violence against him, I didn't throw it *at* him, I only wanted to throw *something*. Nowkhana's eyes were moist, and he hung his head. He did not flinch when I threw the plate. He looked just as if he realized how angry I was, how justified the anger was, and how likely to get the rough side of my tongue he was. Obviously he was cursing whatever in him had finally betrayed my trust. At least, that is how I interpreted the way he looked. His whole appearance filled me with inexpressible sorrow. I too hung my head and went out.

Takami then goes along to the third floor and apologizes to his fellow writer for the mistake he had made in trusting Nowkhana with the key to the stores:

> As I did so, the writer from the room next to mine came along, and said to me, 'You were really sold on that chap Nowkhana, weren't you? You were really taken in, you know. I spotted him from the very first – he's a bad lot. You look at him now, you'll see I was right.'

My head was spinning. Even though he'd let me down badly, I still believed in Nowkhana, I still loved him. I did not want to despair of Indians. I wanted to believe in the human race.

The war is remote from this story, apart from one or two references to officers leaving for 'the front'. But that is not its purpose. It is an excellent study of how the Japanese in the Co-prosperity Sphere had begun to assume the white man's burden. The burden, in this case, is the servant problem, and the Japanese failure to make the Indians honest and do what the Japanese want them to do. That failure, and the narrator's own moral inadequacy in face of the poverty of the Indians, make an intriguing and unexpected psychological study out of what begins like a fairly orthodox *tranche de vie*. What is involved is the clash of temperaments, the pathetic will to be understood by other peoples, the dangers of an easy-going concessiveness, and the narrator's introspection, as he has his first contact with overseas India. The contact is a fiasco, but it does not end in pessimistic resignation.

It is interesting that, in the middle of a cruel and violent war, a Japanese magazine should find space for a story of that kind, which has a great deal more in common with Somerset Maugham than with any fictive representation of suffering and death in battle.

So Takami went round Burma in his curious, intrigued, exploring way, almost as if the war did not exist at all. Another Japanese work of literary art about Burma plunges directly into the battle; yet it, too, has a certain remoteness about it. This is Takeyama Michio's novel, *Biruma no tategoto* (*Harp of Burma*). The book's narrative is straightforward enough. A Japanese company in Burma was known as 'the singing company' because their captain taught them choral music, and they sang wherever they went. One of their corporals, Mizushima, was a virtuoso on the Burmese harp and played the accompaniment. Their happy faces told them apart from all the other Japanese when they were sent back to Japan.

At the war's end, they were surrounded in a Burmese village. Mizushima played the tune *Hanyu no yado* which is also that of 'Home Sweet Home'. This so moved the British troops that they came into the village and fraternized with the Japanese, all hostility at an end. They asked Mizushima to help negotiate the surrender of another company some distance away. He agreed, and went off with them. He never returned to his own company, but while they were in their surrender camp they used occasionally to see, on the edges of the camp, a yellow-robed Buddhist monk, with a parrot on his shoulder, who looked amazingly like Mizushima.

As the time drew near for their repatriation, they felt ashamed that Mizushima had not returned to the unit. Their hero had deserted them. Then the monk, who was indeed Mizushima in Burmese disguise, came near to the camp and played the harp for them. He had a letter passed to the captain, to explain what he was doing. The captain read the letter to them on board ship going home. Mizushima wrote that he had failed to persuade that other company to surrender, and they had all been killed. He had wandered south to rejoin his own company and on the way had seen hundreds of unburied Japanese bodies. He had been taken in by Kachin tribesmen, who had looked after him. The chief offered his daughter in marriage, but withdrew the offer when Mizushima could not provide evidence that he had killed and eaten men. Finally, Mizushima became a monk, deciding to imitate the tranquil cheerfulness of the Burmese and to stay behind to bury the Japanese dead.

Thematically, the story is intriguing. Its author, Takeyama Michio, had never been to Burma and knew of the campaign only at second-hand. The factual elements of the story are easily traceable. The endless numbers of bodies along 'Skeleton Road' are taken from accounts of the Imphal battles. The references to the Sittang River are drawn from the *Hiroku Dai Tōa Senshi* (*Secret History of the War in East Asia*), a series of accounts by war correspondents, published two years before.[1] From the same source comes the account of the strange cannibalistic tribe, which offers its women to Japanese in marriage, though in the original the tribe is Arakanese, and not Kachin. And the initial fraternization episode to the strains of 'Home Sweet Home' – pure fantasy – is straight from First World War narratives about Christmas in the trenches in 1914.

What is interesting is the use Takeyama has made of these sources, or rather this source, which he picked up in a second-hand bookshop in Kamakura. They have not imprinted a naturalist bent on the novel. It is, in fact, a work of fantasy, and its original public was meant to derive a message from it. It began as a children's book, and then, after a not unfamiliar pattern, was taken up by an adult readership and made into a popular film. The keynote is its anti-war theme, characteristic of Japan in the mid-1950s, but in this case quite specifically Buddhist. In a sense it is not so much a novel, more a Buddhist tract, and it reflects the admiration felt by some Japanese in Burma for what they believed was the strong and fervent Hinayana Buddhism of the Burmese, in contrast to their own pallid and moribund faith. So the book moves quite naturally out of the sphere of narrative fiction, in which the horrors of war are at one remove, into the world of religion. This translated perfectly to the screen when Ichikawa Kon, in 1956, turned it into a film of great lyrical beauty.

Just as Takeyama uses his fiction as a tract, Richard Mason in *The Wind Cannot Read* has written what is in effect a prose *Madame Butterfly* in modern dress, the difference being that it is the Japanese heroine who

---

[1] Tamura Yoshio, ed. *Hiroku Dai Tōa Senshi*; *Biruma hen* (Secret History of the War in East Asia: Burma), Tokyo, 1953

abandons her lover, not because she ceases to love him, but because a brain tumour takes her from him. Like *Biruma no tategoto*, the novel is partly based on fact. A young officer, learning Japanese in war-time India, falls in love with his pretty young Japanese teacher. She is also a news-reader on the Japanese news service broadcast from New Delhi, and when he is taken prisoner during the Imphal battle, he persuades a Japanese wireless-operator to switch on the Delhi wavelength and hears her voice. He escapes, visits her in hospital where she is operated on, and returns one night too late to find she has died suddenly. Its sentimentality will be obvious from the outline, but Richard Storry, who was with the author in Imphal during the battle, told me that he thought it had a very interesting effect on British public opinion, given the date of its publication. It came out in December 1946, very shortly after the war was over, when no one was in a mood to be sentimental, let alone affectionate, about the Japanese. And little of the writing of the war, from either side, had been able to say or describe much about the enemy, how he reacted to battle, how he carried his ordinary sentiments into it, how they survived, if at all. Now Richard Mason had, like his hero, learned Japanese, and the book makes some attempt to treat them as human beings, with a dimension beyond their cruelty. There are, too, some superbly exciting narratives, such as the narrator's capture and escape. But what is more important is the selection of a Japanese as the central figure of the book's sympathy. According to Richard Storry, the appearance of *The Wind Cannot Read* was a turning point in the re-acceptance of the Japanese as human beings in the minds of British readers. The fact that the Japanese was a heroine rather than a hero made it easier, of course, but it was the only book of its time to show the Japanese on an equally acceptable level of humanity.

Other books which used the war in Burma as background were often, like H. E. Bates's two novels, trials of inner strength undergone by the heroes without much reference to the source of those trials, the invading Japanese. *The Jacaranda Tree* (1949) is a fictional account of one party of refugee civilians escaping from Burma, where the contest is with hardship and disease. *The Purple Plain* (1947) is situated some years later, around March 1945, when an RAF plane crashes and the survivors, who are all injured in some way, have to make their way back to base. Squadron-Leader Forrester's wife had been killed, literally in his arms, by bomb blast during the London blitz as they danced in a nightclub on their honeymoon. As a result, Forrester scorns life and tries to get himself killed, merely acquiring a reputation for bravery instead. His disgust with life is cured by the sight of a crew member in flames in a plane that crash-lands on his airfield.

Bates inserts a sentimental interest, naturally enough, to help pull Forrester back: a Burmese nurse called Anna. But the core of the book is his struggle to rescue his two fellow-officers, Blore and the newly-joined

Carrington. Blore shoots himself in despair, doubting they will ever get out of the endless jungle. Carrington is wounded and needs supporting, and in the end Forrester leaves him to look for help, and stumbles across some Nagas, who bring them in. Bates's prose manages to capture not simply the landscape of Central Burma, but the detailed effects of the intense heat and colour.

> He could see the prickles of low scrub like needles in the sun. And always, all down the river-like desert between its banks of forest, there was no sound. It had the uncanniness of a forgotten place. He remembered that he had not seen in it a single bird. And thinking of that, he recalled the great dark crows... the delicate white egrets stepping like dream-birds about the paddy-fields, giving life to the blistered plain, and the small green parrots, touched with yellow or blue, with their shy sprinkling flight in the pipul trees.[1]

This notation of landscape is not absent from the book I consider to be the greatest piece of fiction to come out of the Burma war, but that is not its chief virtue. *Look Down in Mercy* (1951) by Walter Baxter is the one work of art in English which can compare with the depiction of moral catastrophe in war in the Japanese writer Ōoka Shōhei's *Fires on the Plain*. Like Robert Merle's *Weekend à Zuydcoote*, which describes the disintegration of the French Army before and during Dunkirk, Baxter's novel depicts the moral and physical breakdown of a British officer and the entire army to which he belongs, in the ghastly retreat from Lower Burma into India of 1942. It is unremittingly harsh and brutal, but wears an air of desperate conviction, and the hero, Captain Anthony Kent, passes through cowardice, seduction – both homosexual and heterosexual – abandonment of the wounded, and murder of one of his men, himself a murderer, before he finally commits suicide in the safety of India.

The enemy, in this book, is not seen personally, as in *The Wind Cannot Read*, because that is not Baxter's concern. Where the enemy does appear, it almost like anonymous brutality. One of Kent's men is caught by the Japanese when swimming in a pool:

> Venner was sitting on the rock naked, his arms around his knees and a cigarette in his mouth. Two yards behind him stood a big man; his uniform seemed very untidy. He took a delicate step forward with his left foot and something flashed behind his head and swept down in an arc from right to left. Venner's head hit his left knee, bounced on the rock and fell into the pool. A fountain

---

[1] *The Purple Plain*, p. 205

of blood shot into the air and drenched his naked body as it toppled slowly over. The big man seemed to laugh as he picked up Venner's shirt and wiped his sword. He turned and waved, two or three men stepped from their hiding places and went quickly towards him.[1]

The Japanese set fire to petrol-soaked prisoners, urinate in the face of their captives (for which an officer rebukes them), bayonet them when Kent refuses to give information (he holds out while his men are killed, but gives in when he is threatened himself). Baxter is obsessed by the infliction of pain, and by the ego's fierce, stubborn will to live, even when it has putrefied morally. Kent has a homosexual affair with his batman, Anson, and as they escape together at a river-crossing, they leave behind a wounded man who has begged to come with them:

> 'I won't shout any more, I'm sorry I've made a noise. When you're ready, please don't forget me.' Kent paddled on, holding his chin high to avoid the tiny waves. He thought to himself how ghastly it must be to be left like that, wounded and alone, but he told himself that there was nothing he could do about it, ab- solutely nothing. He tried to make himself feel sorrow for the man, but all he could feel was the joy and relief slowly filling his whole being as each moment made it more certain that he, Anthony Kent, would continue to go on living.[2]

Kent's suicide, itself partly accidental, is a way of obliterating the moral disintegration that his life has been.

The hero of Frances Clifford's *A Battle is Fought to be Won*, Anthony Gilling, is also involved in the process of self-proof, but his ordeal is much more linear than that of Baxter's Captain Kent. Gilling is a young bank clerk who has become an officer in a Burmese regiment, and is very aware of his new rawness and the experience of the old Karen subadar who is his second-in-command. He is afraid of being afraid, in a not unconventional way, and the experience of Japanese atrocity unnerves him. One of his fellow-officers is captured when wounded, and later beheaded, his head stuck on a bullock cart with a bayonet. Two of his men are castrated, their genitals lopped off and stuck in their mouths, which are then stitched up with twine.

The period is the same as *Look Down in Mercy*, and the shock of contact with a ferocious enemy is the same. But Clifford's psychology is more elementary. Gilling's inner panic is shown, time and time again, re-

---

[1] *Look Down in Mercy*, p. 48

[2] ibid., p. 185–6

lentlessly; but in counterpoint to it are the actions he performs, his objective bravery contrasting with the subjective cowardice in his mind, until at the end of the book he ensures that his men and their subadar, who, he is certain, still looks upon him with scorn, escape with their freedom while he turns to face the Japanese and hold them up, alone (the same ending as Hemingway's *For Whom the Bell Tolls*). It falls to the old subadar to praise him to the survivors.

In spite of the brutality of some of its events, *A Battle is Fought to be Won* follows an expected course to a trite conclusion, and, in fact, of all the literature in English dealing with the war in Burma, only *Look Down in Mercy* takes us to the ultimate breakdown of the very vestiges of humanity, a moral *cas-limite* which transcends the familiar narrative of adventure.

Perhaps only Laurens van der Post, in *Bar of Shadow* and *The Seed and the Sower* has made a full-scale attempt to analyze not merely his own side, but the enemy. Like nearly all the works of fiction I have mentioned, his book has been made into a film and will no doubt, like them, have a far greater resonance as a result. But there is little variety in his depiction of the Japanese, and at least one of his characters, the nightmare sergeant Hara, is described in terms of caricature which make the prose seem like nothing so much as a rendering of some propaganda cartoon:

> His arms were exceptionally long and seemed to hang to his knees but his legs by contrast were short, extremely thick and so bowed that the sailors with us called him 'Old Cutlass-legs'. His mouth was filled with big faded yellow teeth, elaborately framed in gold, while his face tended to be square and his forehead rather low and simian.

I am sure van der Post must have become aware, as he wrote this paragraph, how like a piece of propaganda it was, and so he modified it:

> Yet he possessed a pair of extraordinarily fine eyes that seemed to have nothing to do with the rest of his features and appearance. They were exceptionally wide and large for a Japanese...
> It was extraordinary how far they went to redeem this terrible little man from caricature. One looked into his eyes and all desire to mock vanished, for then one realized that this twisted being was, in some manner beyond European comprehension, a dedicated and utterly selfless person.

Van der Post has told us how Hara ruled the men of the prison camp 'with a cold, pre-determined, carefully conditioned and archaic will of steel as tough as the metal in the large two-handed sword of his ancestors dangling on his incongruous pre-historic hip.' I think the adjective 'pre-historic' sets the tone there. Is Hara anything other than van der Post's updated version of the 'inscrutable Oriental' of Mikado and Fu Manchu days ('in some manner beyond European comprehension'), whose actions are dictated not by reason but by some dim and undescribed call of the blood? Like animals and plants, his Japanese are deeply submerged in the movement of days and seasons, subject to a cosmic rhythm in a way undreamt of by European philosophy. They romanticized death and self-destruction as no other people had ever done. They rejected the claims of individuality. What inspired them was an inborn sense of the 'behaviour of the corpuscles' in their blood, 'dying every second in millions in defence of the corporate whole'.

This is all the more surprising since, of all the authors I have mentioned, van der Post is the one with most direct experience of Japanese life, in Japan itself; but his notion of them has been overtaken by his own dark gods and cosmic urges, and the idea of a blind subjection to collective ideals and natural forces.[1]

Of course van der Post's observations are only relevant to the Burma war in a general comparative sense. His book is about life as a POW in Java, and the relation of POW to gaoler is a special one from which it is risky to generalize. The same remark applies to what is perhaps the best-known of all works of fiction on the war in the Far East, *The Bridge over the River Kwai*. The fact that this novel has been prescribed for many years as a text for the A Level examination in French is a reflection of its popularity, not a cause. Pierre Boulle's original novel, *Le Pont de la Rivière Kwai*, does exactly what van der Post does – examine the mutual antagonisms of British and Japanese when the former are the prisoners-of-war of the latter, in a situation of great natural beauty and extreme human horror. But its presuppositions are quite different. Pierre Boulle is really writing a successor, in his own way, to André Maurois' highly Anglophile stories of the First World War, *Les Silences du Colonel Bramble*. A rubber planter in Malaya before the war, Boulle fought in Burma, China and French Indo-China, was taken prisoner and escaped. After the war he became a writer, and his works include the celebrated science fiction novel, *La Planète des Singes* (*Planet of the Apes*). His love of the quirkiness of the British led him to create the character of Colonel Nicholson, senior British officer in a camp on the Burma-Siam Railway. It might be thought that this, too, like *The Seed and the Sower*, is marginal to our theme, since those prisoners were taken in another war. Nonetheless, I think it is, like van der Post's stories, interesting as a confrontation between set types, Nicholson/Saitō taking the place of Lawrence/Hara and Celliers/Yonoi. Alec Guinness in David Lean's film, and that old tune 'Colonel Bogey'

---

[1] To what extent the use of two pop singers, David Bowie and Sakamoto Ryūichi, as incarnations of his national ideas, will alter or confirm the public reception of them remains to be seen.

whistled into immortality in countries which never heard it before, have imprinted on Boulle's text an almost universal myth of what the confrontation between British officer and Japanese was like in the Second World War.

That myth, attractive though it might be for British audiences, is bogus. It shows, for instance, groups of Japanese officers in a rage because they do not have the technical know-how to build a bridge. They are saved from their predicament by Nicholson's officers who design and build one for them, using it as training for their men to keep up their morale. But the real railway, which covered around 300 miles of wild, hilly jungle country, in conditions which European engineers had already examined and rejected, was designed by the Japanese, and they built it, with forced native and POW labour, in a comparatively short space of time – less than a year – and made it work. They were perfectly capable of designing and building the bridges they needed. In other words, they were not technologically inferior to their western counterparts at all.

On the other hand, Boulle saw clearly that in Nicholson's treacherous (in purely patriotic terms) dedication to the Bridge lay a need which some at any rate of the prisoners felt. The historian of the English novel, Ian Watt, who was a prisoner on the Railway himself, wrote of it:

> I had to admit that Nicholson's tranced commitment to building the bridge was a desperate response to what had been the most incessant of our frustrations as prisoners. However much we hated the Japanese and their railway, it had been difficult to go on month after month without putting something of ourselves into our work. Our lives had been one long and meaningless compromise between our notion of duty and our instinct of workmanship...[1]

The film changes the book in a number of ways. For commercial rather than aesthetic reasons, a part had to be found for an American star, hence the Americanized role of Shears, who escapes from the Railway and returns as a Force 136 commando. And the Japanese camp commandant is not merely a sadistic drunken brute, but a frustrated artist. The book itself, of course, had already changed reality. It is common knowledge that the original[2] of Colonel Nicholson was Colonel Philip Toosey, a Cheshire businessman turned soldier, who faced the Japanese with weapons totally dissimilar from those employed by Alec Guinness. 'We had already learnt,' says Ian Watt, 'that in a showdown the Japanese would always win; they had the power, and no scruples in using it.' But Toosey's behaviour

---

[1] 'Bridges over The Kwai', *The Listener*, 6. viii. 1959, p. 216 et seq.

[2] In actual fact, not in Boulle's mind.

towards them was different from Boulle's stubborn heroics. 'He was a very brave man', continues Ian Watt, 'but he never forced the issue so as to make the Japanese lose face. Instead he first awed them with an impressive display of military swagger; then proceeded to charm them with his ingratiating and apparently unshakable assumption that no serious difficulty could arise between honourable soldiers whose only thought was to do the right thing... Looked at from outside, Toosey's remarkable success obviously involved a slight increase in the degree of our collaboration with the enemy. But anybody on the spot knew that the real issue was not building the bridge, but merely how many prisoners would die, be beaten up, or break down, in the process.' Toosey's drive and panache won him the confidence of the Japanese, and at the same time his own men never accused him, as would have happened with the Colonel Nicholson of both book and film, of being 'Jap-happy'. Apparently Toosey protested when the film appeared that its distortion of what actually occurred on the Railway was insulting; but to no effect. The author himself objected to Sam Spiegel and David Lean having the bridge blown up at the end of the film. In the book, the bridge remains intact, and a train is derailed by an explosive set on the other side. The answer of the film people was natural enough: the audience would have been watching the screen for two hours in anticipation of such an event, and it would be improper, and certainly unprofitable, to thwart them of their expectations. And, in the way of these things, the myth they created has expunged, or almost, the text on which it was founded, and the horrifying reality behind that.

Nobody, on either side, has yet written a *War and Peace* of the campaigns in Burma. Is this because, as Frank Kermode claims, the First World War eroded the possibilities for literature of the Second? 'There can be few people under fifty', he wrote in 1975, 'who saw action in 1939–45 and it seems unlikely, though not of course impossible, that any of them can now provide us with a standard literary account, a myth of that war.'[1] Or is it because, as an arrogant young French historian has proclaimed, 'We historians have replaced the novelist as the witness of reality?' But Tolstoy did not take part in the battles of 1812. Sixty-three years separated Austerlitz from his masterpiece. A similar gap would produce a book written in 2005 by an author who would now be in his early twenties. Perhaps the manipulation of *Bridge over the River Kwai* was inevitable. The participants, Japanese and British, have had their say. The time has come for those who only see that distant war through the prism of history to mould it into something they want to see themselves, which may have little or nothing to do with the real emotions, the agonies and occasional joys, of the soldier in Burma between 1941 and 1945.

---

[1] Kermode, 'The words of two wars', *DailyTelegraph*, August 1975

Little Peterkin

The final question is obviously Little Peterkin's:

> 'But what good came of it at last?'
> Quoth little Peterkin:–
> 'Why, that I cannot tell,' said he,
> 'But 'twas a famous victory.'

Burma, like Blenheim, was without doubt a famous victory. Indeed, depending on which date you choose, it was a famous victory for both sides. But if we look back at what was gained by it, forty years on, answering little Peterkin becomes more difficult. Professor Raymond Callahan has looked at the motivations and rewards of those involved, and comes up with some uncompromising and not easily acceptable answers.[1]

Slim's personal achievement is unquestioned, although a clumsy attempt was made to remove him from command after his great triumph. Oliver Leese, commander of Allied Land Forces South-East Asia, proposed that Christison be promoted from XV Corps to the command of XIV Army, which in June 1945 was preparing to invade Singapore and Malaya; while Slim was to be transferred from XIV Army to the newly formed XII Army in Rangoon, whose duties were the much less exacting ones of mopping up what was left of Kimura's forces and garrisoning Burma.[2] Leese's reasons appear to have been that Slim was tired by years of continuous action and, too, lacked experience in amphibious warfare, which the invasion of Malaya demanded.

Mountbatten disagreed with Leese, who nonetheless decided to go ahead, informed Christison privately of the change – Christison's staff gave him a farewell dinner – and signalled his plans to Alanbrooke in London. Leese flew to Meiktila on 7 May to tell Slim himself. Slim was, to put it mildly, completely flabbergasted by the proposed change, but merely indicated his dissent by refusing the XII Army command, suggesting instead that he should simply resign. That Leese should, in his turn, be astonished at Slim's reaction is an indication, as Ronald Lewin points out, of his inability to grasp the realities of the situation. Slim took it he was being sacked. Leese intended, as *he* saw it, merely to make a switch in commands. The mutual misunderstanding was complete. Fortunately, Alanbrooke wired Mountbatten that no such change could take place unless Mountbatten personally recommended it to London.

---

[1] Callahan, *Burma 1942–1945*, London, 1978

[2] Cf. the excellent treatment of this episode in Lewin, *Slim*, pp. 237 et seq.

Naturally, there was no question of this, though Mountbatten also wanted Slim to cease to command XIV Army, but for another reason. He wanted him to have Leese's job at ALFSEA. In the end this was what happened. Slim took a short leave, Christison stood in for him at XIV Army – a sop to Christison's own wounded vanity – and Mountbatten, at Alanbrooke's insistence, removed Leese from the command of ALFSEA and replaced him by Slim. It was a distressing period for all concerned, and a moment of deep humiliation for Slim in the midst of his greatest triumph. But, just as he had replaced Irwin when Irwin was about to sack him, so he found he was to replace Leese, and his achievement remained untarnished. He also, when the Japanese surrender came, had sufficient awareness of his own command to ignore the arrogant directives from MacArthur and arrange matters his own way in his own time.

On a national level, the achievement was less clear. The Americans, for instance, on behalf of whose policy towards China the North Burma campaign had been fought, never succeeded in creating the Americanized Chinese Army they hoped for, and the 'great China' of American sentiment turned out to be very different from what they had envisaged. Its emergence in the post-war period, Callahan points out, convulsed American politics.

The British victory remained ambiguous. The campaign itself was, and was often seen at the time, as the wrong war, at the wrong time, in the wrong place. Once Burma had gone, the British were faced with the problem of its reconquest, an objective better achieved, as Stilwell shrewdly pointed out, at the post-war conference table than by an overland campaign, which was ruinously expensive of time, men and materials. Whether you wished to undertake it or not, depended, naturally, on what you felt it was *for*. Stilwell and the Americans were interested in keeping Nationalist China in the war to ensure that the American air forces could have continental bases from which the islands of Japan could be reached as bombing targets. Because this was America's prime aim, Churchill was forced to agree to an army campaign in North Burma to help Stilwell, because Churchill's war strategy in the Far East was dependent on American aid, as his pre-Pearl Harbour diplomatic strategy had been.

But Churchill's motivation was twofold. He intended that Britain should be seen to recover her lost territories by her own military power. The loss of Singapore, in particular, rankled. From his point of view, Burma consisted of the necessary air bases, Akyab then Rangoon, from which to mount an invasion of Malaya or, failing that, Sumatra. Afterwards it would be possible to break through the Malay barrier and sweep up the South China Sea to Borneo and Hong Kong, liberating the Netherlands East Indies en route. It was a grandiose design (of course) but perfectly feasible, given adequate air and sea forces, and enough landing craft. So Mountbatten's South-East Asia Command, formed in September 1943 to breathe new life into the dead strategies of the previous eighteen months which had, with few exceptions, produced defeat after defeat, was to plan seaborne hooks across the Bay of Bengal, move down the coast of Arakan and take Rangoon from the sea.

Here two strategies conflicted. Churchill was at the same time eager to retain as strong a British presence as possible in western Europe, and the only theatre in which the British were in overall command was in Italy. A plan to make a landing north of the point where the Allied armies were bogged down, and to take Rome, was therefore also a priority, and for this the landing craft were removed from South-East Asia and used in the Mediterranean.

In the end, it was the Japanese – specifically, Mutaguchi's dream of invading India – who compelled the British to counter-attack overland from Imphal. The Burma Road was opened by the clearing of the Japanese from North Burma in January 1945, by which time it was superfluous. In the next ten months it only carried 38,000 tons of material into Yunnan, compared with a monthly 39,000 tons carried by the airlift. But the British political goal, which Professor Callahan assumes was never a realistic one, was achieved, at any rate for the moment. For a few brief months, the military reconquest of Burma made it possible for sense to be made of that ambition of Churchill's articulated in 1937: 'My ideal is narrow and limited. I want to see the British Empire preserved for a few more generations in its strength and splendour...'

The Indian Army saw to it that the Empire in Burma was preserved, but it was to be for a matter of years, not generations. 'We will never be able to hold up our heads again in Burma', the deputy commissioner, F. H. Yarnold, had said in 1942 on leaving Mergui before the Japanese advance.[1] 'A military victory', later wrote another British civil servant in Burma, 'could not absolve the British in their civil capacity. Had there been victory in the first instance, and the Japanese been defeated on the frontiers, the Burmese and British would have been brought close together. The Empire would have been proved a working proposition. The Burmese might have been content to remain in it at least as an equal partner. But the other would not do. A ruling power through whose neglect they had been subjected to two invasions, two devastations, had not a shred of credit left.'[2] A similar impression remained with Compton Mackenzie when he toured the battlefields of Burma in 1947 to write the history of the Indian Army in the campaign: 'My immediate impression is,' he wrote, 'that we have failed completely to win the people and should get out.'[3]

---

[1] M. Collis, *Last and First in Burma*, pp. 181–2

[2] ibid., p. 182

[3] Mackenzie, *All Over the Place*, p. 84

Which is precisely what happened. Within three years of Slim's triumph, Burma was independent, and out of the Commonwealth. There is no doubt that the Japanese presence in South-East Asia had contributed to that result, even though they, too, had packed their bags and gone. They had made it impossible for the European powers to remain there on their own terms. 'Slim's great victory,' Professor Callahan concludes '– and this is the most that can be claimed for it – helped the British, unlike the French, Dutch, or, later, the Americans, to leave Asia with some dignity. That, perhaps, is no small thing.'[1]

It also enabled the Indian Army to end its long history in an apotheosis of glory. This was the military instrument which inflicted on the Japanese their greatest defeat on the continent of Asia. 'The Raj', Enoch Powell has written, '(without intending the pun) was a mirage, a dream which British and Indians dreamed together and which individuals will still dream again when they meet, long, long after other dreams and other hallucinations have succeeded it.'[2] More than a dream, it was a symbiosis, subsisting on distance, love and misunderstanding, and the Indian Army was one of the best forms of that symbiosis. The subsequent trials of the INA leaders in the Red Fort in Delhi, the derisory sentences, the political use to which the trials (inevitably) were put, then the divided Army being scissored along with the divided subcontinent, these still lay ahead as the Indian Army fought its way brilliantly and with a blitzkrieg-style panache into the capital of Burma.

Its loyalty had been sorely tried by racial discrimination in Malaya, and its raw recruits after the fall of Singapore had fallen easy prey to Japanese propaganda, by the tens of thousands. But by and large that army served its British masters splendidly in its last days before Partition put an end to it for ever. Because of Partition, there is a sad air of swansong about the valiant narratives of the last days of the united Indian Army. A passionate farewell to it exists in the pages of Anthony Brett-James's *Report My Signals* (pp. 338–43) and in John Masters's description of the movement of the Indian divisions to Rangoon down the Mandalay Road in the pre-monsoon days of 1945, slicing through Burma faster than von Rundstedt through France in 1940:

> ...past the ruins of the empire the Japanese had tried to build there, it took possession of the Empire *we* had built, in its towering rising dust clouds India traced the shape of her own future. Twenty races, a dozen religions, a score of languages passed in those trucks and tanks... The dust thickened under the trees lining the road until the column was motoring into a

[1] Callahan, op.cit., p. 164

[2] Enoch Powell, 'The imperfect dream: a return passage to India', *The Times*, 7 May 1983

thunderous yellow tunnel, first the tanks, infantry all over them, then trucks filled with men, then more tanks, going fast, nose to tail, guns, more trucks, more guns... This was the old Indian Army going down to the attack, for the last time in history, exactly two hundred and fifty years after the Honourable East India Company had enlisted its first ten sepoys on the Coromandel Coast...[1]

There *is* a magnificence in it. But it is paternal, and that was the seed of its end. Brett-James's sepoys, beloved though they are, are not his equals, or at any rate not seen to be. And for John Masters, the Army and its Empire were *his* creation, his and his forefathers'. Among its own people, the historians of that Army, in 1958, while recording its achievements with pride, nevertheless noted, as we have seen, that, although 'the fighting in these early stages [of the Burma campaign] was mainly done by Indian troops on the Assam front, and the India Command was able to mobilize the resources of the country, even to a breaking point, to bring back to life the British Empire in the East,' the Indian Army was not serving its own people, nor the interests of the people across whose territory the war was fought: 'Indian interests were nowhere considered and Burma's aspirations were not taken account of.'[2]

What was coming to an end was not just an empire or an army but one of those strange and beautiful moments in history when the geniuses of two quite dissimilar peoples lock together in hatred and love, both very deep, like that of the Jews and Austrians in the Vienna of the Habsburgs or Jews, Spaniards, and Arabs in Spain before Ferdinand and Isabella, like the flowering of the Anglo-Irish in the gifts of the Protestant Ascendancy in eighteenth-century Dublin, or the scholars of quizzical, sceptical Greece feeding the grandeur of Imperial Rome.

The end when it came had a romantic finality about it for the British, from which their national sensibility has not yet recovered. It is not hard to see why the historian John Keegan could refer to the Indian Army as 'the most durable and perhaps the most remarkable of Britain's imperial creations.'[3] Yet in its very structure we can see why Major Fujiwara had the success he did in recruiting from Indian prisoners the Azad Hind Fauj (those who did not go over to him from fear or the desire to escape, that is): it worked from top to bottom, from father to son, almost, one might say, from troop-leader to wolf-cub. The love was intense, painfully so on departure. John Osborne's depiction of that moment of bitter-sweet

---

[1] *The Road Past Mandalay*, p. 312

[2] Prasad, *Reconquest of Burma*, I, pp. xxv–xxvi

[3] In a review of P. Warner, *Auchinleck: the lonely soldier*, *The Sunday Times*, 22 xi. 1981, p. 42

nostalgia of the Indian Army officer saying farewell to his men in *Look Back in Anger* is real and sympathetic, not a blimpish caricature. But that relation lacked one fundamental of love: equality.

The Allies of the British were almost as responsible as their enemies for the impossibility of holding on to Empire. Roosevelt himself was in the lead among those Americans who had no intention of shoring up the old colonial territories with American help, military or financial, and who, in their minds and conversation, frequently gave away Indo-China, Hong Kong, and other territories. When Oliver Stanley, Colonial Secretary in the wartime British government, talked to him in January 1945, Roosevelt blithely told him, 'As to Burma... I just don't know how we will handle that situation.'[1] By military abstention and diplomatic pressure, the United States helped complete what Japan had started: the end of Europe's Empire in Asia.

Hence the sadness of the memorial to British troops at Kohima:

> When you go home
> Tell them of us, and say:
> For your tomorrow,
> We gave our today.

The men who fell in Burma did not give their today for a tomorrow that was in any sense national or imperial. And the mood of Britain herself, in 1945, would not have countenanced the use of force to suppress the new post-colonial regimes. In this sense, Professor Callahan is right when he suggests that what remains is the memory of Slim's military triumph, not any immediate political gains the government in London may have had in mind.

Nor were the Burmese people the gainers. Their country is still divided. Its hero Aung San was ruthlessly assassinated on the threshold of power, his successor U Nu excluded from it by another of the Thirty Comrades, General Ne Win. The Karens have not won their struggle to be free. The Nagas of the Assam hills are engaged in a liberation struggle against the Indian government. The Shans and Kachins are at war with the government in Rangoon,[2] the Shans struggle with the government of Thailand for the freedom to sell the opium poppy and the drugs it produces. The war has settled nothing.

And, of course, the Japanese are back. Not merely in their more acceptable role as traders, but also with a familiar piety in view. Groups of them visit Assam and Burma, picking their way, maps and cameras in hand, over the old battlefields. They consult nominal rolls, and, here and there, on

---

[1] Cf. W. R. Louis, *Imperialism at Bay*, p. 437
[2] Cf. Ian Fellowes-Gordon, *The Battle for Naw Seng's Kingdom*, London, 1971

nameless but numbered hills, in the valleys where bamboos still grow through the apertures of a shattered and rusting tank, they find heaps of bones, often dug up and reinterred by the locals. They take the bones and burn them, remove a small token amount of ash from the fire to take home to a shrine in Japan, and throw the rest into the Chindwin, the Irrawaddy, the Sittang. The Japanese soldier's intense desire that part of his body at any rate shall rest in Japanese soil is acutely felt by his wartime comrades, and this last duty is still being fulfilled. The groups are, needless to say, welcomed by the governments of India and Burma, who send escorts to guide them round the battlefields. The leader of one such group is Fujiwara Iwaichi, once a major on Mutaguchi's staff, now a Lieutenant-General (retired) in Japan's new armed forces. On a recent visit to Kohima, Fujiwara visited the graves of the British dead, and prayed over them. On his return, he wrote to the Queen to say he had done so, and that the graves were well looked after. One of his most prized possessions is the reply she sent.

Perhaps the seventeenth-century Japanese poet, Bashō, has said all that can be said about the end of wars:

Natsu-gusa ya
  tsuwamono-domo no
    yume no ato.

Summer grasses...
  all that is left of
    the dreams of soldiers...

Appendix 1

Casualty Figures

The purpose of war, writes André Malraux, is to do the utmost to ensure that fragments of metal penetrate human flesh. Using this somewhat reductionist approach, we can establish a balance sheet for the war in Burma, and set it against the cost in lives of the war in the Far East as a whole.

It was a bloody and exhausting conflict. Yet the price Japan paid for the conquest of Burma was relatively small. She took the entire country at the cost of around 2000 dead, just as the seizure of Malaya and Singapore had been achieved at a price of roughly 3500 lives. In other words, for the negligible price of 5500 lives Japan seized the greater part of Britain's empire in the Far East. On the other hand, if we forget for a moment that the British counter-offensive was largely manned by sepoys of the Indian Army, and look at the figures for losses among troops of UK origin, it becomes clear that Britain herself paid less than 5000 lives to retake Burma; and Malaya and Singapore cost her nothing, since they were reoccupied after the Japanese surrender. The balance of death between the two major powers is therefore fairly even. The greater losses are among the Indian troops, and the Chinese who were Britain's unwilling allies.

The figures are often difficult to deduce, to compare, and to square with one another. I tried to obtain figures from staff officers with recent memories and notes of the battles, in Payagyi camp in 1945, when Stanley Charles and I wrote accounts of the histories of the 15, 33 and 28 Armies and their subordinate divisions. Some of these figures were, in the nature of things, approximate; in other cases, notably that of 28 Army, they square reasonably well with those published many years after the war, or with the figures obtained by the Demobilization Bureau of Japan in the early years of the Allied occupation. But the Japanese do not necessarily divide the campaign into the same geographical areas as we do, nor do they necessarily use the same segments of time; and their categories may or may not include figures for the sick, just as our early figures for the missing include those who were taken prisoner, the notification of which may have been delayed. With these reservations in mind, the following tables and charts are an attempt to establish the relative strengths and losses of the two sides.

637

First, a comparative table divided by battles:

Operations, with dates	British and Commonwealth casualties (killed in brackets)	Japanese casualties
1st Burma 25 December 1941–12 May 1942)	13,463 (1,499)	2,431 (1,999)
1st Arakan 23 October 1942–15 May 1943)	5,057 (916)	1,100 (estimated) (400)
1st Wingate (February –June 1943)	1,138 (28)	205 (68)
II Arakan (February –July 1944)	7,951	5,335 (3,106)
II Wingate (March –August 1944)	3,786 (1,034)	5,311 (4,716)
Imphal/Kohima (March— December 1944)		
Preliminaries (Assam)	920	
Kohima	4,064	5,764
Imphal	12,603	54,879 (13,376)
Irrawaddy Crossings; *Mandalay* (January–March 1945)	10,096 (1,472)	Combined Japanese losses in these two battles for 15 Army
Meiktila (February–March 1945)	8,099 (835)	and 33 Army are 12, 912 (6,513)
Pyawbwe to Rangoon	2,166 (446)	7,015 (6,742)
Rangoon to Surrender (Breakout & Sittang Bend) May–August 1945	1,901 (435)	11,192 (9,791)
TOTALS:	71,244	106,144

Kirby gives an interesting breakdown of the British Kohima-Imphal losses as follows:

Kohima	XXXIII Corps troops	95
	2 Division	2,125
	7 Division	623
	161 Bde (5 Div)	462
	Kohima Garrison less R. W. Kent	401
	23 LRP Bde	158
	1 Assam	200 (est)
		4,064
Imphal	IV Corps troops	677
	17 Division	4,134
	20 Division	2,887
	23 Division	2,494
	5 Division (less 161 Bde)	1,603
	89 Bde	219
	50 Indian Para. Bde	589
		12,603

When the 920 casualties from the preliminary battles in Assam against 17 and 20 Divisions are included, this gives an overall total for the central front of 17,587. The Japanese figures for Sangshak roughly agree with the British: they say the British lost in killed and wounded 499 men, and 100 as POWs.

The table requires some comment. Figures for Chinese casualties are hard to deduce, since the Americans, under whose aegis they operated, do not give an overall breakdown of figures for them, and the Japanese say only vague estimates are possible. Northern Combat Area Command at the start numbered around 30,000 to 35,000 men: 22 and 28 Chinese Divisions, of roughly 12,000 men each, plus 30 Division which arrived piecemeal from China. The American infantry component, GALAHAD, was under 3000 strong, and lost heavily. Its later successor, Mars Force, was roughly the same strength. US Land Forces in SEAC by April 1945 numbered 12,097, though most of these were involved in road construction. Romanus and Sunderland give a breakdown for the battle of Myitkyina, the most important engagement of the forces under Stilwell's command, as follows:

	Killed	Wounded	Sick
Chinese	972	3184	188
US	272	955	980

In contrast, the Japanese garrison in Myitkyina, estimated at a peak figure of 3500, lost 790 killed and 1180 wounded, a total of 1970, by the end of July 1944. The Americans at the time estimated that 4075 Japanese were killed at Myitkyina. The US historians also quote a figure of 7675 Chinese being killed on the Salween front in the attempt to clear the Burma Road.

The total of Japanese casualties obtained by adding the figures in the first table is much less than the total the Japanese calculate as having died in Burma. Their overall figure is obtained by deducting the number of troops who returned to Japan after the war – 118,352 – from the total number of troops sent to Burma between 1941 and 1945 – 303,501. The resulting figure is 185,149. In other words, Japanese losses in killed are nearly thirteen times those of British and Commonwealth forces.

The British certainly underestimated the numbers of Sakurai's 28 Army in the Pegu Yomas in the summer of 1945. IV Corps (Appendix B to *Narrative of IV Corps Operations May – Aug 1945*) put Sakurai's total strength at 16,000; and XII Army estimated them, immediately after the war, as 19,000, of which the British claimed 11,000, in round figures, as killed and POWs, with 500 still remaining sick in the Yomas. Major Yamaguchi, of Sakurai's staff, gave me a detailed breakdown of the figures for that operation which put the numbers at the start at 30,872 and the numbers after the breakout at 13,953. The total lost would therefore be 16,919; with the proviso that 28 Army also listed around 4000 as still missing and 2000 as sick immediately after the surrender, which would leave the estimated figure of 11,000 killed roughly intact. The contrast with the British killed – 95 – shows the greatest discrepancy of the entire campaign. Whichever figure is taken, the proportion of losses is enormous. 'Seek life in the midst of death' was the motto Sakurai had in mind when he planned the breakout operation, and if the war had gone on there would have been some justification for rescuing even half his men to fight again, at the expense of the other half. As it is, with Japan's capitulation only a matter of days away when the operation was over, those thousands upon thousands of men died for nothing.

There are some startling contrasts in the British figures, too. The total of British and Commonwealth casualties for the war against Japan as a whole is 227,313, so the losses in Burma represent one-third of this. But the overall figure for the Far East does not mean an increase in those killed. The figure is inflated by the 127,800 described as 'missing and POW' in the final volume of the Official History. If UK figures alone are studied, it will be seen that the number of troops of UK origin who were killed in Burma is under 5000 – around a third of the total killed in Burma, and only two-thirds of the figure of Indian troops killed. Twelve times as many people (60,595) were killed in air-raids at home in the United Kingdom, and six times as many in the Merchant Navy (30,248).

The contrast is true of the Japanese as well, though not so sharply: 185,149 Japanese died in Burma, as against 241,000 who were killed by US bombing raids against the Japanese islands. They lost in Burma three-fifths of the men they sent there, which represents roughly one-twelfth of Japanese losses during the war: 2,300,000. British and Commonwealth losses (73,909, of whom 14,326 were killed) represent roughly one in thirteen of the ground troops available to SEAC, around a million men.

Sources: W. Franklin Mellor, ed., *Casualties and Medical Statistics*, HMSO, 1972. W. Kirby, *The War Against Japan*, Vols. II, III, IV and V. War History Unit, Defence Agency, *Sittan; Mei-Go Sakusen*. Ibid., *Biruma Kōryaku Sakusen*. OCH, *Arakan Sakusen*. Japanese Demobilization Bureau, Japanese Document AL 5218, Imperial War Museum Archive. 'Note on LRP casualties', WO 213/188, Public Record Office. *IV Corps Narrative of Operations May-Aug 1945*. SEATIC Bulletin No. 244 ('Short History of Japanese 49 Division'). Romanus and Sunderland, *Stilwell's Command Problems*; *Time Runs Out in CBI*. Tsuchiya Eiichi, ed. *Dai*

Appendix 1

Nijūhachi-gun Senshi (History of Japanese 28 Army) privately printed, Tokyo, 1977. *The Japanese Account of Their Operations in Burma*, published by XII Army, Rangoon, December 1945. 'Breakdown of Japanese losses in Burma'; 'Breakdown of Japanese losses in Sittang Breakout'. Tables supplied by Major (later Lt-General) Yamaguchi Tatsuru, in author's possession.

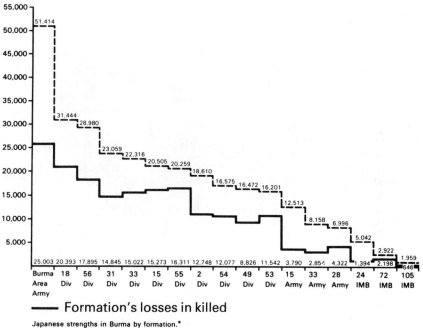

Formation's losses in killed

Japanese strengths in Burma by formation.*
*(Based on *Sittan; Mei-Go Sakusen*, pp. 501-502)

The figures include reinforcements received throughout the campaign.

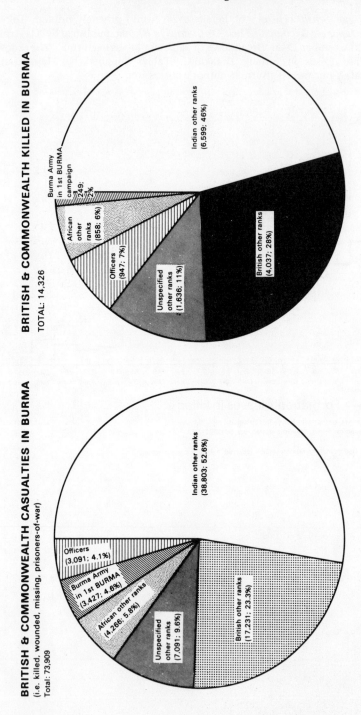

BRITISH & COMMONWEALTH KILLED IN BURMA

TOTAL: 14,326

Indian other ranks
(6,599; 46%)

British other ranks
(4,037; 28%)

Unspecified
other ranks
(1,636; 11%)

Officers
(947; 7%)

African
other ranks
(858; 6%)

Burma Army
in 1st BURMA
campaign
249;
2%

BRITISH & COMMONWEALTH CASUALTIES IN BURMA

(i.e. killed, wounded, missing, prisoners-of-war)

Total: 73,909

Indian other ranks
(38,803; 52.6%)

British other ranks
(17,231; 23.3%)

Unspecified
other ranks
(7,091; 9.6%)

African other ranks
(4,266; 5.8%)

Burma Army
in 1st BURMA
(3,427; 4.6%)

Officers
(3,091; 4.1%)

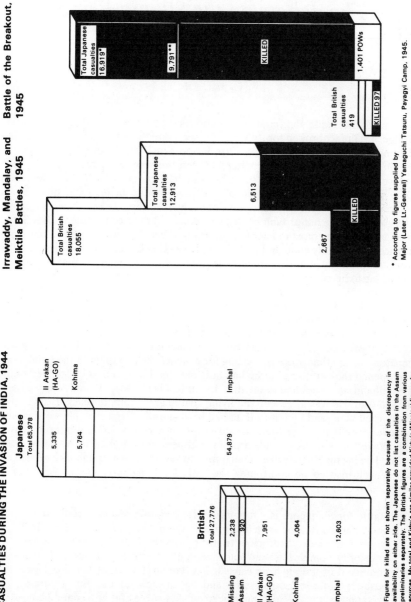

CASUALTIES DURING THE INVASION OF INDIA, 1944

Japanese
Total 65,978

II Arakan (HA-GO)   5,335
Kohima   5,764
Imphal   54,879

British
Total 27,776

Missing   2,238
Assam   920
II Arakan (HA-GO)   7,951
Kohima   4,064
Imphal   12,603

Figures for killed are not shown separately because of the discrepancy in availability on either side. The Japanese do not list casualties in the Assam preliminaries separately. The British figures are a combination from various sources. My total and Kirby's are similar provided Kirby's 'Missing' figures for the whole period are added.

Irrawaddy, Mandalay, and Meiktila Battles, 1945

Total British casualties 18,055

Total Japanese casualties 12,913

6,513

2,667

KILLED

Battle of the Breakout, 1945

Total Japanese casualties 16,919*

9,791**

KILLED

1,401 POWs

Total British casualties 419

KILLED 97

* According to figures supplied by Major (Later Lt.-General) Yamaguchi Tatsuru, Payagyi Camp. 1945.

** According to 4 Corps Narrative of Operations May-Aug 1945. Part VII

643

Appendix 2

The debate on the Sittang Bridge

The man who made the 'courageous and ghastly' decision to blow the Sittang Bridge was in fact broken for it. Major-General Smyth had one of the most gallant fighting records in the Army. A First World War VC, followed by an MC for fighting on the North-West Frontier between the wars, he had begged to go to France when war broke out in 1939, and had commanded a brigade before Dunkirk. There was no question of shattered morale in his case, none of the weakness that Wavell, the Supreme Commander in the Far East, was diagnosing everywhere as the major fault of British troops and their commanders. But Smyth was faced with the most momentous decision of his life during a period of intense physical pain. Oddly enough, his Commander-in-Chief, Hutton, was being urged to work miracles by another General in poor physical shape – Wavell himself. Returning to his command headquarters in Java after a gloomy visit to beleaguered Singapore, Wavell left Flag Staff House in Singapore around midnight on 10 February 1942 for the flying boat which would take him back to Java. His aides were loading documents into a boat at the dockside when they heard Wavell shouting. They thought he had been attacked by looters (looting had already begun in Singapore) or even by a Japanese commando. Wavell had merely grown impatient of the time spent in looking for a launch to take them to the flying boat, and opened the car door; but he had only one good eye, and as he stepped out of the lefthand side, he failed to see that the car had been stopped on the very edge of the sea-wall. He was lifted into the flying boat in great pain, his back badly torn by the barbed wire, and he felt as if he had broken a rib. Even then his worries were not over. The flying boat could not take off from the crowded harbour until dawn, and Wavell, put to sleep with aspirins and neat whisky, had to wait five hours before leaving for Batavia. The Dutch tried to keep him in hospital once he arrived, but Wavell insisted on controlling the batle for Singapore. On 11 February he signalled to Churchill:

> Battle for Singapore is not going well... Morale of some troops is not good and with none is it as high as I should like to see... The chief troubles are lack of sufficient training in some of reinforcing troops and inferiority complex which bold and skilful Japanese tactics and their command of the air have caused. Everything possible is being done to produce more offensive spirit and optimistic outlook. But I cannot pretend that these efforts have been entirely successful up to date. I have given the most categorical orders that there is to be no thought of surrender and that all troops are to continue fighting to the end.

Appendix 2

He added a word about what had happened at the dockside:

> While returning from Singapore I fell from quay in dark and have broken
> two small bones in back. Damage not serious but I shall be in hospital for
> a few days and somewhat crippled for two or three weeks probably.[1]

It was this Wavell, harassed by his injury, fearful of the collapse of British
leadership, who signalled to Hutton on 21 February, 'Why on earth should
resistance on the Sittang River collapse?. . . What is the matter that these sudden
pessimistic reports are given?'

> There seems on surface no reason whatever for decision practically to
> abandon fight for Rangoon and continue retrograde movement. You
> have checked enemy and he must be tired and have suffered heavy
> casualties. No sign that he is in superior strength. You must stop all
> further withdrawal and counter-attack whenever possible. Whole fate of
> war in Far East depends on most resolute and determined action. You
> have little air opposition at present and should attack enemy with all air
> forces available.[2]

The pressure Hutton received he passed on to Smyth. Now Smyth by this time was
a very sick man; and his sickness as well as his decision at Sittang was to haunt him.
There had been profound disagreement from the start between him and Hutton. In
the end, the concatenation of defeats and his own sickness wrecked Smyth's
chances of surviving intact the events of February 1942. Ill-luck continued to dog
him even as he left India for England: his ship was almost torpedoed in
mid-Atlantic. Back in England, he re-made his broken life. He turned author and
became an MP, and, not insignificantly, one of his most interesting works is a
defence of Percival, the general who surrendered Singapore to the Japanese in the
same month as Smyth ordered the Sittang bridge to be blown. As the years wore
on, both of them made it clear that they thought some, at any rate, of the blame for
the disasters in the Far East rested on Wavell, whose experience of Asia beyond
India was, in Percival's view, non-existent, and who crassly proclaimed to Smyth
his opinion that the Japanese were overrated as fighting men.

When Tim Carew's book, *The Longest Retreat*, was published in 1969, the
controversy over the bridge revived. 'I think too much importance has been
attached to the actual blowing of the bridge', Smyth commented, 'and not enough
to the actual situation which prevailed as a result of which the 17 Division were
caught by two Japanese divisions in the act of crossing the Sittang River.'[3] Smyth is
right about the artificiality of the importance attributed to what he terms 'this
entirely preventable disaster' since it did not prevent the Japanese reaching
Rangoon. They did what anyone who knows the geography of Lower Burma would
do, simply make north along the east bank of the Sittang until they found an easily
fordable spot. In fact they crossed at Kunzeik and reached the main road to

---

[1] Connell, *Wavell, Supreme Commander*, pp. 161–2

[2] Kirby, *War Against Japan*, II, p. 81

[3] Letter in *Times Literary Supplement*, 4.ix.1969

Rangoon from there. The blowing of the bridge, in Smyth's view, delayed the Japanese move on Rangoon by ten days. Had Smyth been able to withdraw across the Sittang at least a week before he did, and as he kept urging Hutton to allow him to do, he would have had 17 Division more or less intact on the west bank, able to act against the Japanese when they attempted their crossing.

The letter in which Smyth makes this case also scotches the old story by which a confusion of names between two brigadiers named Jones was a contributory cause to the loss of a brigade. There was no such confusion, Smyth asserts. The names certainly lead one to think such a confusion possible, until one looks into the matter closely. The brigadier commanding 48 Brigade, by then safe across on the west bank of the Sittang, was Brigadier Noel Hugh-Jones. The brigadier commanding 16 Brigade, still marooned on the east bank, was Brigadier J. K. Jones. This is how the Official History treats the episode:

> At about 4.30 am on the 23rd a staff officer of 48th Brigade spoke on the telephone over a very bad line to Brigadier Cowan (then acting as a highly unorthodox BGS to Smyth at 17 Division HQ) who was at divisional headquarters at Abya. He said that his brigadier could not guarantee to hold the bridge for more than another hour and wanted a definite order whether he should blow the bridge or not. When asked by Cowan whether 'Jonah' (the nickname for the commander of 16 Brigade) was across, the staff officer said that he was, *possibly muddling Jones with Hugh-Jones*. Cowan reported the conversation to Smyth who, *thinking that most of the division was on the western bank*, gave authority to the brigade commander to destroy the bridge, leaving it to his discretion to select the best moment. Hugh-Jones made his decision at 5.30 am.[1]

The business of the name confusion is dismissed as irrelevant by Smyth, who admits it is a generally accepted version but simply comments, 'it may have been generally accepted, but it is quite untrue.'[2]

This is how he puts it. There were only three people involved, himself, his Chief of Staff, Brigadier (later Major-General) 'Punch' Cowan, and Brigadier Noel Hugh-Jones, who advised him. The commander of 16 Brigade, Brigadier J. K. Jones, who was on the wrong side of the river, was always known as 'Jonah'. The Brigadier of 48 Brigade, Noel Hugh-Jones, was always referred to by Smyth as 'Noel'. 'I was in no doubt whatsoever when I authorized the latter, at his own request, to blow the Sittang Bridge that "Jonah" was on the wrong side of the river, and that the man I was talking to was "Noel". I knew both men well."[3] The conversation is not, therefore, between Cowan and a staff officer of brigade, as the

---

[1] Kirby, *War Against Japan*, II, pp. 71–2, (my italics). The timings are a matter of controversy. Those given in the official histories differ by at least an hour from those recorded by Lt. Bashir Ahmed Khan, who actually blew the bridge. The Japanese give two times, 0600 (*Biruma Kōryaku Sakusen*, the official history) and 0630 (the regimental history of 215 Regiment written just after the campaign). The Japanese worked on Tokyo time, which requires an adjustment of an hour and a half, giving either 0430 in the first instance or 0500 in the second, both of them tending to support Khan's version.

[2] Letter in *Times Literary Supplement*, 4.ix.1969

[3] ibid.

Official History indicates; but between Hugh-Jones and Smyth, with Smyth being aware that the other Jones – and his whole brigade – were still on the wrong side.

But this refutation of the name-confusion legend still fails to clarify Smyth's position completely. There was the further issue of time, and here the opposition between his views and those of the Army Commander, Hutton, still stands. Writing in 1957,[1] Smyth emphasized that he sent Cowan back to Rangoon to impress on Hutton the danger in which 17 Division stood of being cut off before the Sittang Bridge and to urge Hutton to give permission, first, to withdraw the division behind the line of the Bilin River immediately – the Bilin was halfway between the Salween and the Sittang – and then to allow the next stage of the withdrawal to proceed immediately, i.e. over the Sittang. 'I wanted to get across the Sittang well before the Japanese could intercept me... Even at that late stage, although I was closely engaged by two Japanese divisions, I could have made it, and would then have had the support on the other side of the Sittang of our newly arrived brigade of light tanks.'[2] In his support Smyth re-quotes the Official History on Hutton's inflexibility: 'in view of the great importance of getting 17th Division safely across the Sittang, Hutton might have been wiser, once action had been joined on the Bilin, to leave Smyth a free hand.'[3]

Smyth also emphasized that he was aware how much Hutton was under constant political pressure (as he terms it) from Wavell not to give ground. Wavell sent a signal to Hutton (17.ii.1942):

> I have every confidence in judgment and fighting spirit of you and Smyth, but bear in mind that continual withdrawal, as experience of Malaya showed, is most damaging to morale of troops, especially Indian troops. Time can be gained as effectively and less expensively, by bold counter-offensive. This especially so against Japanese.[4]

Hutton refused to accept Smyth's verdict on Wavell's pressures as political, though his own Chief of Staff, Brigadier (later Major-General) H. L. Davies,[5] backed Smyth's view in a foreword to the latter's *Before the Dawn*: 'While all his military instincts urged him to concentrate well back and fight on ground of his own choosing, the political pressure being exercised on his Army Commander (General Hutton) enforced a forward policy with which, in loyalty, General Smyth had to conform. General Smyth's clear analysis of the events leading to the disaster on the Sittang stresses once again the unwisdom of limiting the freedom of action of the executive commander.'[6]

Davies's verdict is rejected by Hutton, who was not consulted when that paragraph was written. 'It was not "political" pressure on me', Hutton affirms, 'but military necessity which enforced a forward policy'.[7] As Hutton sees it, there are seven reasons which can be put forward as contributory causes to the disaster:

[1] Smyth, *Before the Dawn*, p. 166

[2] ibid., pp. 166–7

[3] Kirby, *War Against Japan*, II, p. 76

[4] Connell, *Wavell, Supreme Commander*, p. 181

[5] Who later acted in the same capacity for Slim.

[6] Smyth, *Before the Dawn*, p. 111

[7] *Times Literary Supplement*. 2.x.1969

1) *The leakage to the Japanese on the evening of February 19 of the decision to withdraw to the Sittang.* This led the Japanese to send troops immediately to intercept Smyth's retreating column, and they accomplished the interception with speed and success.

   The 'leakage' he refers to is clarified by the Official History, which says that on the night of the 19 February 'some unit or units' sent out the withdrawal orders in clear, which gave the Japanese knowledge for which they would normally have had to fight.[1]

2) *Nearly 24 hours could have been saved by a better plan of withdrawal.* Hutton points out that both Wavell at the time and the official historian later thought the withdrawal could have been completed before the bridge was blown on the morning of the 23rd, as permission to withdraw had been given *four days earlier*, on the 19th.

3) *Lack of adequate protection for the bridgehead* . Hutton claims he sent a message to Smyth to get troops back for this purpose as soon as possible. Brigadier Ekin of 46 Brigade made the point to Smyth at the time, he affirms. This is true. When Ekin was told by Smyth that his men would be the divisional rearguard, he was sure the Japanese would not pause at the village of Kyaikto, but would bypass it and make straight for the bridge. He should therefore forestall such a move by getting straight back himself, and everything except essential fighting transport should be across the bridge on the 21st. Curiously, given his own sense of urgency, Smyth did not accept this, and would not uncover the Kyaikto area until he had more definite information about the strength and direction of the Japanese advance. There was no traffic control formation at the bridge either, so he thought it inadvisable to send so much transport back at once.[2]

4) *The bombing of British and Indian troops by their own planes.* This really grievous incident is well attested. 21 February was a hot, dry day, and as the retreating columns moved back towards the river, they stirred up clouds of thick red dust. Both on the main track – the road was nothing more than a track – and in the Boyagyi Rubber Estate east of it, the troops were bombed and machine-gunned by Japanese planes and then by Allied planes, or, as the Official History discreetly puts it, by 'aircraft carrying Allied markings'.[3] 'The one time we had the RAF in close support they were circling over the Japanese 55th Division at 100 feet and waving to them...' remembers an 8th Burma Rifles officer, 'and then roaring down over us at anything from 150 to 15 feet.'[4] The column panicked, naturally enough. Vehicles were destroyed, including ambulances loaded with wounded. Mules vanished into the jungle carrying their loads with them. There were many, many casualties. 'It is fair to add,' writes Compton Mackenzie 'that the weight of the evidence acquits the RAF and the AVG of the blame for this lamentable business.'[5] It does

---

[1] Kirby, *War Against Japan*, II, p. 77

[2] ibid., p. 66

[3] ibid., p. 67

[4] Mackenzie, *Eastern Epic*, p. 439

[5] ibid., p. 439

nothing of the kind. Air Vice-Marshal D. F. Stevenson, in command of the Allied air forces in Burma, made an exhaustive enquiry into this bombing of British troops. 'It is alleged', he writes in his despatch, 'that our troops at Mokpalin were bombed and machine-gunned by some Blenheim aircraft between 12.00 and 15.00 hours. The facts are that at the request of Army Headquarters eight Blenheims bombed Kawbein (near Bilin) in the morning and landed back at their base after mid-day... I have failed to reach a firm conclusion that our aircraft did, in fact, bomb our own troops at this time and place. The enquiry is complicated by such statements as "the attacking aircraft were identified by roundels on the underside of their wings" – our Blenheims have roundels on the upper side of the wing but certainly not on the underside, and the possibility that the Japanese used captured Blenheims during this campaign should be considered.[1] There is, moreover, a great similarity between the plan silhouette of the Japanese Army 97 medium bomber and the Blenheim, and there must have been a number of enemy bombers flying over Mokpalin about this time because the enemy effort was concentrated on the Sittang area, a few miles to the west of Mokpalin. Since, however, the country between the Rivers Sittang and Bilin is closely covered in jungle, I consider it not improbable that some crews by mistake may have bombed the wrong objective...'[2]

It is a little lame. And the point about the Blenheims simply will not wash, because the case made is about the American (AVG) Tomahawks who came in as well, together with Hurricanes. The Indian Official History takes cognizance of Stevenson's enquiry, but points out that there were British markings on the bomb fragments, as well as on the aircraft, and also that an RAF squadron leader later acknowledged to Brigadier Ekin that he had attacked his own troops because he had (wrongly) been given the Kyaikto-Mokpalin road as the western limit of the area in which he was to operate. This history emphasizes the catastrophic effect of the raid on the morale of the retreating troops, and the effect on the morrow's happenings. Nearly 200 men of the 8th Burma Rifles deserted.

The cause of the error seems, most likely, to have been the mistaken demarcation given to the RAF and AVG pilots. Reconnaissance aircraft had reported on 21 February seeing a very long column of Japanese vehicles, about 300 in all, moving through Kyaikto to Kinmun Sakan. Every plane on the Rangoon airfields was brought to bear on this column. But the Kyaikto-Kinmun Sakan road would have been the correct western limit of operations; instead, the crews were given the Kyaikto-Mokpalin road, and attacked their own men.

---

[1] The Japanese did capture a Blenheim which had been left intact on the airfield at Moulmein.

[2] Air Vice-Marshal D. F. Stevenson, 'Despatch on Air Operations in Burma and the Bay of Bengal covering the period January 1st to May 22nd, 1942', *London Gazette*, Supplement, No. 38229, 5 March 1948, p. 1723, para. 112

5) *The blocking of the bridge for two and a half hours by an overturned vehicle.* Hutton is using shorthand here: the vehicle did not overturn. It ran off the wooden planking which had been laid across the bridge, which was a railway bridge and therefore needed to be adapted for motor traffic. The Sittang bridge consisted of eleven 150-foot spans, and sappers worked throughout the night of 21 February to ready it for demolition. Then the motor transport began to cross, from about 2 am on the 22nd. It would, naturally, have been preferable to wait for dawn, particularly since the bridge was a narrow one, and only allowed for a single file of vehicles. The wooden planking had been fitted in a hurry, and planks were loose here and there, but all went well, in spite of the nervy state of half-trained drivers, for the first two hours. Then, at four in the morning, the inevitable occurred. A young Indian driver missed the gear of his three-ton lorry, and jammed his foot down, not on the brake, but on the accelerator. There was an ambulance in front of him, so he pulled the wheel over hard, the lorry swerved, and rammed the steel girders of the bridge. It took two more hours to free it. For those two hours the traffic on the bridge was at a standstill, and the Japanese used the time to catch up with the retreating columns. There was no margin of time at all, now.

6) *Upstream of the bridge a ferry service operated by three power-driven craft had been set up, Hutton says, on his instructions.* These ferry boats could have acted as a supplement to the bridge, or as a substitute if the bridge were destroyed. Japanese aircraft, unhappily, destroyed the ferry during the 22nd, which meant that once the bridge was blown, the men on the east side were condemned to swimming or rafting across.

7) *The arrangements for blowing the bridge were, in Hutton's view, inadequate, probably because of the shortage of engineers and material.* It does not, in fact, seem that Major Orgill's Malerkotla Field Company was inadequate for its task: but that task was rendered all the harder because of a shortage of fuse and electric cable, which meant that the firing point, instead of being some way on to the west bank, had to be situated on the bridge itself. Matters were complicated when a Japanese machine-gunner picked a spot for himself in the cutting through the bluff overlooking the Sittang, through which the railway line emerged on to the bridge. Any engineer checking the fuses or going to the firing point had to run the gauntlet of machine-gun fire.

These seven points made by Hutton are also, of course, to some extent, points already made by the Official Historians, and, in some cases, by Smyth himself. But the conclusion of his letter to the *Times Literary Supplement*, which lists these points, is more important.[1] The Sittang itself, on Smyth's own showing, was, Hutton affirmed, a very poor obstacle and could easily be crossed by infantry higher up. It was also so close to the only main road and rail communication with Mandalay that this could easily be interrupted once the Japanese reached it. Hutton regards this as supporting his own view that the Japanese should have been

[1] *TLS.* 2.x.1969

held, certainly east of the Sittang, and preferably east of the Salween in spite of the meagre and partially trained troops Smyth had for the purpose. But another historian of the episode, Tim Carew, points out that the Salween and the Bilin were not 'daunting obstacles', being shallow and easily fordable.[1] On the other hand, he describes the Sittang as 'one thousand yards at its widest, six hundred yards at its narrowest,... deep, fast-flowing and treacherous...' In the vicinity of the bridge, possibly. But the Sittang's worst moods are between May and October, at the height of the monsoon rains. It is tamer during the dry season – and that includes February – and a march of a few miles further up the east bank afforded easy crossing-places, as the Japanese found out.[2] I have swum in the Sittang myself, in September and October, and undoubtedly there are dangerous currents; but for desperate men?

[1] T. Carew, *The Longest Retreat*, p. 108. This is true of the Bilin River, but not of the Salween, which, as the Japanese themselves found, was a swirling maelstrom. Two Japanese war correspondents were drowned crossing it during the campaign.

[2] Against this, Roy Hudson writes, 'The Sittang is no doubt a formidable obstacle. It was 150 × 11 = 1650 feet wide, and certainly not fordable for many miles upstream. At the bridge it may even have been tidal (...Major R. W. Wood, 3 Burma Rifles, who was in Bombay Burma Trading Corporation before the war... confirms it was not only tidal but had a severe "bore" which came up the river every tide). The current in February 1942 was probably not very strong. I remember villagers trying to swim the river some 400 yards north of the bridge to escape the Japs, they were all shot dead before covering 100 yards. Also, at Shwegyin, some 30 miles north, I noted in the diary that the current was 4 knots on 7 March.' (Letter to the author, 2 Nov. 1978).

Appendix 3

Notes on the battle at Sangshak

Hope-Thomson recovered from his breakdown and later held five active commands, winning the DSO in North-West Europe. He and other officers of 50 Parachute Brigade have contested earlier narratives of the Sangshak battle on the following counts:

i. The Brigade was not told what to expect when it moved into the hills between the Kohima-Imphal road and the Chindwin. After a long training period, it had been intended to attack Akyab in January 1944, but when that operation was cancelled the Brigade was sent to the Ukhrul-Sangshak area for advanced jungle training. On 9 March, Lieut-General (later Sir) Ouvry Roberts, GOC 23 Division, addressed them, but no hint was given that a major Japanese threat was developing a few miles east of their patrolling area, as part of the assault on Kohima and Imphal. IV Corps passed on no intelligence about the massing of boats in the Homalin area, reported by RAF observers.

ii. 50 Brigade was composed of three battalions. A British battalion had been removed, after a number of scrapes with the Americans in India, and a Gurkha battalion substituted (154), which was still completing training when the order came to move to Manipur. The actual parachute strength was therefore around 2,000. The total of 3,000 was reached only at Sangshak itself, when other units came under command.

iii. Concentration was ordered, by 23 Division, at a suitable point between Sangshak and Sheldon's Corner, when it became evident that the Japanese were advancing in strength. But as the Japanese moved on the Brigade's positions at the very moment it was assembling, there was little time for reconnaissance, and the reduction of Hope-Thomson's options meant that, with all its disadvantages, Sangshak seemed the best choice. The alternative, 49 Brigade's former HQ in a river bed at MS 36, would have been, says one officer, 'suicidal'.

iv. Hope-Thomson knew that Sangshak was solid rock, but so were most of the surrounding hills so he had to accept that, as he had to accept the risk of inadequate water, though in an account of the battle Captain (later Brigadier) L. Richards, the Brigade Liaison Officer, says that the GOC 23 Division estimated the water was adequate, and as he was an RE officer they believed him. (L. Richards, *The Bloody Battle at Sangshak*, private circulation, 1984, p. 30).

v. Hope-Thomson considered occupying West Hill, but the forces he would have used – 152 Bn or 4/5 Mahrattas – were too exhausted to dig defences on

Appendix 3

their arrival from Sheldon's Corner, and in any case they would have been placed in an isolated position which the Japanese might easily have over-run. So he accepted the risk of having his Brigade HQ vulnerable to fire from that position.

vi. He also knowingly took the risk of a reduced dropping zone for air supplies, having acquired much experience of air drops.

(Correspondence with Brig. M. R. J. Hope-Thomson, DSO, OBE, MC; Brigadier P. Hopkinson; Lieut-Col. F. G. Neild, RAMC (retd), author of *With Pegasus in India: The Story of 153 Gurkha Bn*, Gurka Brigade, Singapore, 1970; Captain (later Brigadier) L. Richards, CBE; Captain Roger Sylvester).

Appendix 4

British and Japanese units in Burma, 1944

THEORETICAL STRENGTHS

British

Army:	60,000 - 100,000
Corps:	30,000 – 50,000 (an army has three corps)
Infantry Division:	13,700 (a corps has three divisions, but there were great variations)
Infantry Brigade:	2,500 (a division has three brigades, a light division might have two)
Infantry Battalion:	800 (a brigade has three battalions)
Infantry Company:	127 (a battalion has four companies)
Infantry Platoon:	32 (a company has three platoons, plus ancillary troops)
Infantry Section:	8 (a platoon has three sections)

Higher formations, divisions and upwards, contained artillery, engineers, signals and occasionally armoured components.

A British division's battalions would be entirely British troops. In an Indian division, a third would be British, the rest Indians and Gurkhas.

Japanese

The Japanese division varied greatly in strength, between 12,000 and 22,000. Its infantry, three regiments strong, was often controlled by an Infantry Brigade Group commanded by a Major-General. The strength of a Japanese infantry regiment was 2,600. Each regiment had three battalions, and three regiments made up the Infantry Brigade Group.

The Japanese in Burma did not use brigades, except in the case of independent formations like 24, 72 and 105 Independent Mixed Brigades. The Japanese regiment was the equivalent of a British brigade.

SUMMARY ORDER OF BATTLE AND CHAIN OF COMMAND*
DURING THE INVASION OF INDIA (1944)

BRITISH

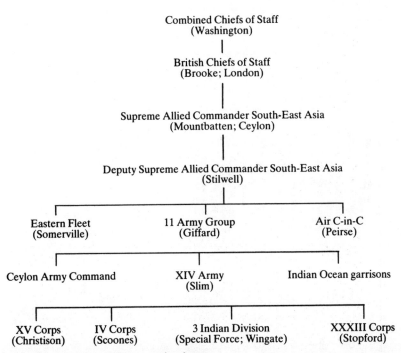

* Successors are shown after a semi-colon.

In Chinese formations, an Army was the equivalent in strength of a British division, a Chinese division of a British brigade, and a Chinese regiment of a British battalion. In the early campaigns in Burma, the Chinese had no supply or administrative system.

XV CORPS*
(Christison)

5 Indian Inf. Division
[Briggs]
(to IV Corps 19.5.44)

9 Brigade
[Evans; Salomons]
2 West Yorks
3/9 Jat
3/14 Punjab

123 Brigade
[Winterton; Evans; Denholm-Young]
2 Suffolk
2/1 Punjab
1/17 Dogra

161 Brigade
[Warren] (to XXXIII Corps)
4 Queen's Own Royal West Kent
1/1 Punjab
4/7 Rajput

7 Indian Inf. Division
[Messervy]
(to XXXIII Corps 15.5.44)

33 Brigade
[Loftus-Tottenham]
1 Queen's Royal Regt.
4/15 Punjab
4/1 Gurkha Rifles

89 Brigade
[Crowther]
2 King's Own Scot. Borderers
7/2 Punjab (later 1/11 Sikh)
4/8 Gurkha Rifles

114 Brigade
[Roberts; Dinwiddie]
1 Somerset L.I.
4/14 Punjab
4/5 Gurkha Rifles

25 Indian Inf. Division
[Davies]

51 Brigade
[Angus]
8 Yorks & Lancs
17/5 Mahratta L.I.
16/10 Baluch

53 Brigade
[Coldstream]
9 Yorks & Lancs
2/2 Punjab
4/18 Royal Gurkha R.

74 Brigade
[Hirst]
6 Ox. & Bucks. L.I.
14/10 Baluch
3/2 Gurkha Rifles

26 Indian Inf. Division
[Lomax]

4 Brigade
[Lowther]
1 Wiltshire
2/13 Frontier Force Regt.
2/17 Rajput

36 Brigade
[Thomas]
8/13 Frontier Force Regt.
5/16 Punjab
1/8 Gurkha Rifles

71 Brigade
[Bull; Cotterell-Hill]
1 Lincolnshire
5/1 Punjab
1/18 Royal Garwhali Rifles

36 Indian Inf. Division
[Festing]
(to NCAC until Dec. 44)

29 Inf. Bde. Gp.
[Stockwell]
1 Royal Scots Fus.
2 Royal Welch Fus.
2 East Lancs.
2 South Lancs.

72 Ind. Inf. Bde. Gp.
[Aslett]
6 S. Wales Borderers
10 Gloucesters
9 R. Sussex

26 Ind. Inf. Bde.
[Jennings]
2nd Buffs
1/19th Hyderabad
2/8th Punjab

81 West African Division
[Woolner]

5 West African Inf. Brigade
[Collins]
5 Gold Coast
7 Gold Coast
8 Gold Coast

6 West African Inf. Brigade
[Hayes; Cartwright]
4 Nigeria
1 Gambia
1 Sierra Leone

3 Special Service Brigade
[Nonweiler]

5 Commando

44 Royal Marine Commando

82 West African Division
(Bruce; Stockwell)

1st (W. A.) Bde.
[Swynnerton]
1st Nigeria
2nd Nigeria
3rd Nigeria

2nd (W. A.) Bde.
[Western; Wilson-Brand]
1st Gold Coast
2nd Gold Coast
3rd Gold Coast

4th (W. A.) Bde.
[Ricketts]
5th Nigeria
9th Nigeria
10th Nigeria

* Successors are shown after a semi-colon.

IV CORPS (Scoones)*

Corps Infantry	17 Indian Light Div. (Cowan)	20 Indian Inf. Div. (Gracey)	23 Indian Inf. Div. (Roberts)	50 Indian Para. Bde. (Hope-Thompson; Woods)	254 Indian Tank Bde. (R. L. Scoones)
9 Jat MG Bn.	*48 Ind. Inf. Bde.* [Cameron; Hedley]	*32 Ind. Inf. Bde.* [Mackenzie]	*1 Ind. Inf. Bde.* [McCoy; King]	152 Ind. Para. Bn.	3 Carabiniers
15/11 Sikh	9 Border	1 Northampton	1 Seaforth	153 Gurkha Para. Bn.	7 Cavalry
Chin Hills Bn.	2/5 Gurkha R.	9/14 Punjab	1/16 Punjab	50 Indian Para. MG Coy.	150 Regt. RAC (Sqn)
3 Assam Rifles	1/7 Gurkha R.	3/8 Gurkha R.	1 Patiala		3/4 Bombay Grenadiers
4 Assam Rifles					
78 Indian Inf. Coy.	*63 Ind. Inf. Bde.* [Cumming; Burton]	*80 Ind. Inf. Bde.* [Greeves]	*37 Ind. Inf. Bde.* [Collingridge; Marindin]		*19 Indian Inf. Div.* (Rees)
Kalibahadur Regt (Nepal)	1/3 Gurkha R.	1 Devon	3/3 Gurkha R.		
Gwalior Inf. (1 Coy)	1/4 Gurkha R.	9/12 Frontier Force Regt.	3/5 Gurkha R.		*62 Ind. Inf. Bde.* (Morris; Beyts)
	1/10 Gurkha R.	3/1 Gurkha R.	3/10 Gurkha R.		2nd Welch
					3/6 Rajputana
		100 Ind. Inf. Bde [James]	*49 Ind. Inf. Bde* [Esse]		4/8 Gurkha R.
		2 Border	4/5 Mahratta L.I.		
		14/13 Frontier Force Rifles	6/5 Mahratta L.I.		*64 Ind. Inf. Bde.* (Bain; Flewitt)
		4/10 Gurkha R.	5/6 Rajputana		2 Worcestershire
					5/10 Baluch
					1/6 Gurkha
					98 Ind. Inf. Bde. (Jerrard)
					2 Royal Berkshire
					8/12 Frontier Force Regt.
					4/4 Gurkha R.

(to XXXIII Corps, 26. xii. 44; to XIV Army l.iv.45)

* Successors shown after a semi-colon

657

XXXIII CORPS*
(Stopford)

Corps Infantry
- 1 Burma Regt.
- 1 Chamar Regt.
- 1 Assam Regt.
- Shere Regt. (Nepal)
- Malindra Dal Regt. (Nepal)

202 L of C Area [Ranking]

2 Division [Grover; Nicholson]

- **4 Brigade [Goschen; Theobalds; McNaught]**
  - 1 Royal Scots
  - 2 Royal Norfolk
  - 1/8 Lancs. Fus.
- **5 Brigade [Hawkins; Alston-Roberts-West]**
  - 7 Worcester
  - 2 Dorset
  - 1 Queen's Own Cameron Highlanders
- **6 Brigade [Shapland; Smith]**
  - 1 Royal Welch Fus.
  - 1 Royal Berkshire
  - 2 Durham Light Infantry

7 Division (see XV Corps)

23 Long-Range Penetration Brigade [Perowne] (see 3 Indian Division)

268 Brigade [Dyer]
- 2/4 Bombay Grenadiers
- 5/11 Bombay Grenadiers
- 17/7 Rajput

3 Special Service Brigade (see XV Corps)

Lushai Brigade [Marindin]
- 1 Bn. Royal Jat Regt.
- 8/13 Frontier Force Regt.
- 7/14 Punjab
- 1 Bihar

* Successors shown after a semi-colon

658

3 INDIAN DIVISION (SPECIAL FORCE)*

(Wingate; Lentaigne [3/9 Gurkha Rifles, attached infantry])

3 West Afr. Bde
[Gillmore; Ricketts]
6 Nigeria
7 Nigeria
12 Nigeria

14 Inf. Bde.
[Brodie]
1 Beds & Herts
7 Leicester
2 Black Watch
2 Yorks & Lancs

16 Inf. Bde.
[Fergusson]
2 Queen's Royal Regt.
2 Leicester
45 Recce Regt.

23 Inf. Bde.
[Perowne]
2 Duke of Wellington's
4 Border
1 Essex

77 Inf. Bde.
[Calvert]
1 King's Regt. (Liverpool)
1 Lancs. Fus.
1 South Staffs
3/6 Gurkha R.

111 Inf. Bde.
[Lentaigne; Morris/Masters]
2 King's Own Royal Regt.
1 Cameronians
3/4 Gurkha Rifles
4/9 Gurkha Rifles

* Successors shown after a semi-colon

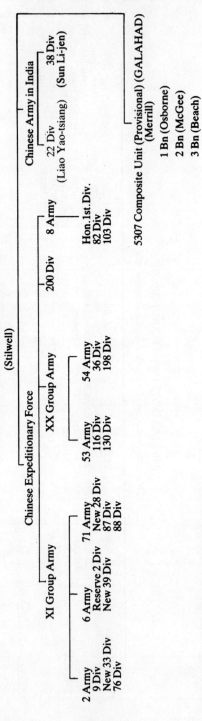

NORTHERN COMBAT AREA COMMAND
(Stilwell)

Chinese Expeditionary Force

Chinese Army in India

XI Group Army

XX Group Army

200 Div

8 Army

22 Div
(Liao Yao-tsiang)

38 Div
(Sun Li-jen)

53 Army
116 Div
130 Div

54 Army
36 Div
198 Div

Hon.1st.Div.
82 Div
103 Div

6 Army
Reserve 2 Div
New 39 Div

71 Army
New 28 Div
87 Div
88 Div

2 Army
9 Div
New 33 Div
76 Div

5307 Composite Unit (Provisional) (GALAHAD)
(Merrill)

1 Bn (Osborne)

2 Bn (McGee)

3 Bn (Beach)

(*Stilwell's Command Problems*, p. 333, adapted)

Appendix 4

SUMMARY ORDER OF BATTLE AND CHAIN OF COMMAND*
DURING THE INVASION OF INDIA (1944)

JAPANESE

IMPERIAL GENERAL HEADQUARTERS
(TOKYO; TŌJŌ)

SOUTHERN ARMY HEADQUARTERS
(SINGAPORE; TERAUCHI)

BURMA AREA ARMY
(RANGOON; KAWABE)

28 ARMY (ARAKAN; SAKURAI)	15 ARMY (MAYMYO; MUTAGUCHI)	33 ARMY (N. BURMA; HONDA)	5 AIR DIVISION [TAZOE]
55 Division [Hanaya] 55 Div. Infantry Group [Sakurai Tokutarō] 112 Infantry Regiment [Tanahashi; Furuya] 143 Infantry Regiment [Yamamoto; Yoshida]	*15 Division* [Yamauchi; Shibata] 51 Infantry Regiment [Omoto] 60 Infantry Regiment [Matsumura] 67 Infantry Regiment [Yanagizawa]	*18 Division* [Tanaka] 55 Infantry Regiment [Yamazaki] 56 Infantry Regiment [Nagahisa] 114 Infantry Regiment [Maruyama]	
54 Division [Katamura] 111 Infantry Regiment [Koba] 121 Infantry Regiment [Nagazawa] 154 Infantry Regiment [Yamamura]	*31 Division* [Sato; Kawada] 31 Div. Infantry Group [Miyazaki] 58 Infantry Regiment [Fukunaga] 124 Infantry Regiment [Miyamoto; Hirunuma] 138 Infantry Regiment [Torikai]	*53 Division* [Takeda] 119 Infantry Regiment [Asano] 128 Infantry Regiment [Okada] 151 Infantry Regiment [Hashimoto]	
2 Division [Okazaki] 4 Infantry Regiment [Ichikari] 16 Infantry Regiment [Sakai] 29 Infantry Regiment [Miyake]	*33 Division* [Yanagida; Tanaka Nobuo] 33 Div. Infantry Group [Yamamoto] 213 Infantry Regiment [Miyawaki; Nukui] 214 Infantry Regiment [Sakuma] 215 Infantry Regiment [Sasahara; Tsukada]	*56 Division* [Matsuyama] 113 Infantry Regiment [Matsui] 146 Infantry Regiment [Imaoka] 148 Infantry Regiment [Kurashige]	
(later) 72 Independent Mixed Brigade [Yamamoto]		24 Independent Mixed Brigade [Hayashi]	

* Successors are shown after a semi-colon

661

Japanese Troops in Burma, March 1944

Rangoon area under Burma Area Army	33,000
15 Army area	156,000
18, 56 Divisions' area	52,000
28 Army area	53,000
24 Independent Mixed Brigade	6,600
5 Air Division	15,500
	316,700

(Inpāru Sakusen, p. 280)

Bibliography

Primary sources

A *BRITISH MANUSCRIPT SOURCES*

I *Correspondence, reports, signals, etc. in Public Record Office*
Chiefly as follows:
DEFE 2
DEFE 3
WO 106 (C in C India)
WO 186
WO 187
WO 203 (Military HQ Far East)
WO 208 (Directorate of Military Intelligence)
WO 216 (Chief of Imperial General Staff papers)
WO 231 (Directorate of Military Training)
WO 235
WO 241 (Directorate of Army Psychiatry)
WO 345
WO 349

II *Imperial War Museum*
1 Papers collected for the official history, *The War Against Japan*.
2 Tapes of BBC Broadcasts from Burma.
3 Tapes of Thames TV interviews for 'World at War'.
4 (i) SEATIC Bulletins (interrogation reports, Japanese divisional and army histories).
   SEATIC Historical Bulletin No. 242, (Japanese generals' answers to questionnaire), Singapore, August 1946.
   SEATIC Bulletin No. 243, History of Japanese 28 Army, Singapore, October 1946.
   SEATIC Bulletin No. 244, History of Japanese 33 Army, Singapore, October 1946.
   SEATIC Bulletin No. 245, History of Japanese 15 Army, Singapore, October 1946.
   SEATIC Bulletin No. 246, *The Burma-Siam Railway*, Singapore, October 1946.
   SEATIC Interrogation Reports (Generals Kimura, Tanaka, Matsuyama, Sakurai, Shibata, Colonel Maruyama).
   (ii) *A.T.I.S. Interrogation reports*. Questions and answers on Japanese operations in South East Asia.
   (iii) Burma Command Intelligence Summary No. 13.
   Interrogation Report on Wingate I and Wingate II (Lieutenant-General Kimura, Lt-Gen. Naka, Major Kaetsu Hiroshi).

(iv) Minutes of Chatham House meeting (8 September 1948) on Japanese attitudes in wartime, with General Sir W. Slim and General Percival in attendance.

(v) Mutaguchi Renya, Lt-Gen. and Fujiwara Iwaichi, Lt-Col., Report on effect of Wingate expedition (English text, 22/ix/1951).

(vi) Taunton, Lt-Col. D. E., and Capt. Yazu, correspondence on engagement at Budalin, 1945.

(vii) Thompson, Sir Robert, and Mead, Brig. Peter, Memorandum on Wingate and the Official History.

5 Dorman-Smith papers.

6 Carfrae, Lt-Col., C. C. A., 'Dark Company', TS account of 29 Column, Second Wingate Expedition (1 Nigeria Regt) in Wingate papers (Shelford Bidwell collection).

7 Symes, Major-Gen. W. G., *Diaries*.

8 Cave, Col. F. O., OBE, MC, *Diaries*.

9 Irwin papers.

(i) Irwin, Lt-Gen., M. S., 'Notes on the Army in India and Army problems relevant to operations on the India/Burma border.'

(ii) Irwin-Wavell, Correspondence 1942–43.

(iii) Irwin, Lt-Gen. M. S., *Eastern Army Operations 1942–1943*.

(iv) Irwin, Lt-Gen. M. S., 'Note on our capacity to operate offensively against Burma.'

(v) Irwin, Lt-Gen. M. S., Notes on discussions with Mountbatten and Pownall.

(vi) Notes on morale from liaison officers.

10 Tuker, Lt-Gen. F. S., papers.

11 Minutes of a meeting held in Tokyo (25 May 1948) by Lt-Col. (later Sir) John Figgess, then British military attaché in Tokyo, and senior officers of the Japanese army and navy, on whether the Japanese planned an invasion of India.

III **Liddell-Hart Centre for Military Archives** (by kind permission of the Trustees)

1 Brooke-Popham, Air Chief Marshal Sir Robert, 'Notes on Burma by Air Chief Marshal Sir Robert Brooke-Popham.'

2 Dimoline Papers

3 Gracey Papers

(i) Report on post-war conversations with Japanese officers, Abe Kitajima and Takahashi Nagahisa.

(ii) 'Battle of Bishenpur Box'; 'Ninthoukhong', 'Potsambang'.

(iii) Correspondence with Brig. Greeves, Shenam front, 1944.

4 Hutton, Lt-Gen. Sir Thomas, 'Rangoon 1941–42. A Personal Record.' 97pp. TS.

5 Messervy Papers—Divisional Histories: 17, 19, 20, 23, 25, 26 Divisions.
XV Indian Corps, *History of Arakan Campaign 1944–45*.

IV **Individual manuscripts, narratives and notes**

1 Adamson, A. A., 'Notes on the Sittang Bend battle.'

2 Burma Command, Intelligence Summary No. 1. 'Fate of the Meiktila Garrison; History of 28 Army.' Rangoon, 1946. (Author's archives).

3 Charles, S. T., CBE, 'Notes and comments on the Meiktila battle.'

4 Escritt, C. A., Translations and notes on Burma-Siam railway.

5 Fergusson, Major (later Brigadier) Bernard (Lord Ballantrae). 'War Diary, No. 5 Column, 77 Ind. Inf. Bde. Operations February-April 1943.' (Edge papers).

6 Goodman, Cecil, TS account of 1942 exodus from Burma to India. (Private papers).

7 Hudson, Roy, 'War Diary of the Malerkotla Field Company, Sappers and Miners, Indian State Forces', 32pp. TS. Roy Hudson papers, Chiangmai, Thailand.

8 Khan, Bashir Ahmed, 'The Sittang Disaster', Draft account, B. A. Khan papers, Lahore, Pakistan.

9 Rome, Lt. (later Major) Pat, '7 Days at Kohima' (The Durham Light Infantry battle). (Private papers).

10 Scollen, J., TS account of Meiktila battle (xeroxed extract from longer account dealing with artillery observation in North Africa, Sicily and Burma).

11 Toye, Col. Hugh, 'The Indian communities of South-East Asia and the Japanese 1941–1943' (unpublished TS of paper given at St. Antony's College, Oxford, 1981).

12 Toye, Col. Hugh, 'The INA in the Japanese Disaster of 1944', (Ch. XVI of unpublished thesis, 1955–6).

13 Tuck, Col. Alasdair, 'Notes on 255 Independent Tank Brigade's part in the capture and holding of Meiktila 1944/5.'

B *JAPANESE MANUSCRIPT SOURCES*
(Where archive not stated, the documents are in the author's own archives.)

I *Defence Agency*
1 Notebook of Major Kōno Kōichi, staff officer, Burma Area Army.

2 *Kawabe Nikki* (Diary of Lt-Gen. Kawabe Masakazu).

3 Mutaguchi Renya, Lt-Gen., *Inpāru sakusen kaisōroku* (Memories of the Imphal operation), 2 vols 1947–48.

4 *Nakamura Nikki* (Diary of Lt-Gen. Nakamura Aketo, GOC Japanese forces in Thailand).

5 *Tamura Memo* (Notes of Col. Tamura, Japanese military attaché in Bangkok, 1941).

II *Private Papers*
1 Fujiwara Iwaichi, Lt-Col. (later Lt-Gen.), 'On Japanese 15 Army, 15 and 33 Divisions' (answers to British questionnaire).

2 Fujiwara Essays (xerox of Japanese text in author's possession, English translation in SEATIC Bulletin No. 242).

3 Harada, Munaji, *Nambu Biruma sakusen sentō yōkō* (Report on operations and battles in Southern Burma), 55pp. (War Diary of 215 Inf. Regt. 33 Div., 12 January–15 March 1942). Imperial War Museum.

4 Headquarters Staff, 54 Division, 'Outline of operation of the 54th Division', Phnom Penh, November 1945.

5 Headquarters Staff, 55 Division, 'Activities of Shin-i Butai' (55 Cavalry Regiment), Phnom Penh, November 1945.

6 Headquarters 55 Division Staff, 'Outline of the Quelling Operation in Burma', TS, Phnom Penh, November 1945.

Ibid., 'Outline of No. 31 Operation, 55th Division.'

Ibid., 'Outline of HA-GO Operation, 55th Division.'

Ibid., 'Activities of "Sakura" Composite Brigade.'

Ibid., 'Outline of "KOKU" Operation.'

Ibid., 'Outline of "MAI" Operation in Burma.'

 7 Hirakubo Masao, *'Indo-Biruma sakusen jūgunki'* (An account of my experiences during the operations in India and Burma). MS by a supply captain of 58 Inf. Regt., 31 Division.

 8 Katamura Shihachi, Lt-Gen. GOC-in-C 15 Army, Vice-Admiral Tanaka Raizō, 13 Naval Base, Force, Lt-Gen. Hanaya Tadashi, former commander GOC 55 Division, 'Answers to Questionnaire for S.A.C. Despatch', Nakhaun Nayok, Thailand, 1946.

 9 Interrogation of Lt.Col. Saito Hiroo, former Chief of Staff 55 Division; HQ SEATIC, Singapore, September 1946.

10 Misawa, Major, 'History of the 33 Division, Japanese Imperial Army', Japanese Burma Area Army Admin. HQ, Kokine, Rangoon, August 1946.

11 Miyazaki Shigesaburō, Lt-Gen. 'Kohima fukin no shitō keika no gaijō' (Outline of the engagements in the Kohima area), MS, Insein, December 1945.

12 *Questionnaire for Conference between the commanders of the British Forces in Burma, and the Commanders of the Japanese Forces in Burma, held at HQ Burma Command on 12 February 1946.* HQ XII Army, Rangoon, 1946.

13 SEATIC, No. 2 Mobile Section (HQ XII Army) 'Consolidated Report on Kempei taken into custody in Burma.'

14 *Sittan-kawa toppa sakusen*, pencilled MS, 30pp, by Lt-Col. Saito Hiroo, 55 Division.

15 Southern Army GHQ Staff, 'Sakusen ni kansuru kaitō (Shitsumon)' (Questions and answers on operations). Saigon, 1946.

16 Tsuchiya Eiichi, *Dai Nijūhachi-gun senshi* (War History of 28 Army), (Private circulation), Oiso, 1977.

17 Twelfth Army Intelligence Summary No. 12. 'A Short History of Japanese 54 Division.'

18 Twelfth Army Intelligence Summary No. 13. (Japanese 56 Division).

19 Yagi Tatsuo, Major, CO 55 Transport Regiment. 'Senshi shiryō' (Materials for War History), French Indo-China, 1946.

20 15 Army Staff, 'Dai Jūgo-gun kōdō ryakureki' (Movements of 15 Army). MS.

21 Yamaguchi Tatsuru, Major (later Lt-Gen.), 'Dai Nijūhachi-gun senshi no gaiyō' (Summary of the War History of 28 Army), Payagyi, 1945. (Pencil MS)

22 Yoshida Gonpachi, Major-General, 'Senshi shiryō ni kansuru kudan kaitō' (Answers relating to war history materials), Nakhaun Nayok, 1946.

23 Yoshida, Tomonaru, 'Inpāru sakusen to hōkyū' (Supply and the Imphal operation), Wakahachi-kai Bulletin, Tokyo, 1977.

Secondary Sources

(Place of publication for English-language publications is London, and for Japanese publications Tokyo, unless otherwise stated.)

A *BIBLIOGRAPHIES*
Imon, Hiroshi, *Taiheiyō Senshi Bunken Kaidai* (Bibliography of the History of the Pacific War), Shinjinbutsu Ōrai-sha, 1971.
Trager, Frank N., *Japanese and Chinese Language Sources on Burma. An Annotated Bibliogaphy*, New Haven, 1957.

B *OFFICIAL HISTORIES*

I **British**
Butler, J. R. M., and Gwyer, J. M. A., *Grand Strategy*, Vol. III, Pts. 1 & 2, HMSO, 1964.
Donnison, Brig. F. S. V., *British Military Administration in the Far East, 1943–45*, HMSO, 1956.
Ehrman, J., *Grand Strategy*, Vols. V and VI, HMSO, 1957.
Howard, Michael, *Grand Strategy*, Vol. IV, HMSO, 1972.
Kirby, Major-Gen. S. W. et al., *The War Against Japan*, Vols. II–V, HMSO, 1958, 1962, 1965, 1969.
Mackenzie, Compton, *Eastern Epic, Vol. I. Defence* (all published), Chatto & Windus, 1951.
Richards, D. and Saunders, Hilary St.G., *Royal Air Force 1939–1945*, 3 vols., new edn., HMSO, 1974–5.

II **Indian**
Prasad, B., ed., *Official History of the Indian Armed Forces in the Second World War (1939–1945)*, Orient Longmans, 1954 onwards.
> *Retreat from Burma 1941–42*
> *Arakan Operations 1942–45*
> *Reconquest of Burma 1942–45*, Vols. I and II
> *Post-war Occupation Forces: Japan and South-East Asia*

III **American**
Romanus, C. F., and Sunderland, R., *United States Army in World War II, China-Burma-India Theater,* Washington:
> *Stilwell's Mission to China*, 1953; *Stilwell's Command Problems*, 1956; *Time runs out in CBI*, 1959.

IV **Japanese**
Bōei-chō Bōei Kenshūjo Senshishitsu (War History Department, Research Center for Defence Studies, Defence Agency), *Senshi Sōsho* (War History), Asagumo Shimbunsha, 1967 onwards.
> *Biruma Kōryaku Sakusen*, (The assault on Burma), 1967
> *Inpāru Sakusen*, (The Imphal Operation), 1968.
> *Irawaji Kaisen*, (The Irrawaddy Battles), 1969.
> *Sittan Mei-go Sakusen*, (The breakout battle; French Indo-China) 1969.
> The air component has a volume to itself: *Biruma Ran-In hōmen Dai-San Kōkūgun no sakusen* (Burma and N.E.I., III Air Army Operations).
Burma is also referred to in the account of the Japanese High Command, *Dai Honei Rikugunbu* (Imperial General Headquarters, Department of the Army), Vols. 1–10.
There also exists a series of manuals derived from the above volumes, for the use of officers in training. The narrative is less complex, the mapping at times better, and there are illuminating notes which do not appear in the longer volume. Where I have preferred to rely on them they are noted in the text as Officer Cadet Histories – my own nomenclature – abbreviated to OCH before the title.
Riku-kan-pō senshi byōkan (Professors of War History, The Military Academy), *Dai Ni-ji Sekai Taisenshi* (History of the Second World War), Tokyo, 1968 onwards.

Biruma shinkō sakusen (The Invasion of Burma)
Arakan sakusen (The Arakan Operations)
Inpāru sakusen, 2 vols. (The Imphal Operation)
Irawaji kaisen (The Irrawaddy Battles)
Ichi-Oku-Nin no Showā-shi (Everyman's history of Modern Japan), *Nihon no senshi* (7), *Taiheiyo senso* (1), (Japan's war history (7), The Pacific War (1)), Mainichi Shimbunsha, Tokyo, October 1978.
XII Army, *The Japanese Account of their Operations in Burma*, December 1941 – August 1945, Rangoon, 1945.

C DESPATCHES

1 Field Marshal Sir Claude (later Viscount) Auchinleck, *Operations in the Indo-Burma Theatre based on India from 21st June 1943 to 15th November 1943*, HMSO, 1948.

2 Sir Robert Brooke-Popham, *Operations in the Far East from 12th October 1940 – 27th December 1941*, HMSO, 1948.

3 General Sir George Giffard, *Operations in Burma and North-East India from 16th November, 1943 to 22nd June, 1944*, HMSO, 1951.

4 General Sir George Giffard, *Operations in Assam and Burma, 23rd June 1944 to 12th November 1944*, HMSO, 1951.

5 Lieutenant-General Sir Oliver Leese, *Operations in Burma from 12th November 1944 to 15th August 1945*, HMSO, 1951.

6 Vice-Admiral the Earl (later Viscount) Mountbatten of Burma, *Report to the Combined Chiefs of Staff by the Supreme Allied Command South-East Asia, 1943–1945*, HMSO, 1951.

7 Air Chief Marshall Sir Keith Park, *Air Operations in South-East Asia from 1st June 1944 to the Reoccupation of Rangoon, 2nd May 1945*, HMSO, 1951.

8 Air Chief Marshal Sir Richard Peirse, *Air Operations in South-East Asia from 16th November 1943 to 31st May, 1944*, HMSO, 1951.

9 Air Chief Marshal D. F. Stevenson, *Air Operations in Burma and the Bay of Bengal, January 1st to May 22nd 1942*, HMSO, 1948.

10 General (later Field Marshal) Earl (later Viscount) Wavell, *Operations in Burma from 15th December 1941 to 20th May 1942*, HMSO, 1948. (Covers reports by Lieutenant-General (later Sir) T. J. Hutton and General the Honourable Sir Harold (later Viscount) Alexander).

11 General (later Field Marshal) Sir Archibald (later Viscount) Wavell, *Despatch by the Supreme Commander of the ABDA Area to the Combined Chiefs of Staff on the operations in the South-West Pacific 15th January 1942 to 25th February 1942*, HMSO, 1948.

12 General (later Field Marshal) Earl (later Viscount) Wavell, *Operations in Eastern Theatre, based on India, from March 1942 to December 31st, 1942*, HMSO, 1946.

13 General (later Field Marshal) Earl (later Viscount) Wavell, *Operations in India Command, 1st January 1943 to 20th June 1943*, HMSO, 1948.

14 Biennial Report of the Chief of Staff of the United States Army 1943–1945, to the Secretary of War, *General Marshall's Report. The Winning of the War in Europe and the Pacific*, Simon & Schuster, Washington, 1945.

D UNOFFICIAL HISTORIES OF THE CAMPAIGN; AND OF INDIVIDUAL BATTLES

I **American**
Callahan, Raymond, *Burma 1942–1945*, Davis-Poynter, 1978.

II **British**
Campbell, Arthur, *The Siege, A Story from Kohima*, Allen & Unwin, 1956.
Carew, Tim, *The Longest Retreat: The Burma Campaign 1942*, 1969.
Barker, A. L., *The March on Delhi*, Faber & Faber, 1963.
McKelvie, Roy, *The War in Burma*, Methuen, 1948.
Owen, Frank, *The Campaign in Burma*, HMSO.
Perrett, Bryan, *Tank Tracks to Rangoon*, Robert Hale, 1978.
Phillips, C. L. Lucas, *Springboard to Victory*.
Smith, D. E., *Battle for Burma*, Batsford, 1979.
Swinson, Arthur, *Kohima*, Cassell, 1966.
Calvert, Michael, *Prisoners of Hope*, Cape 1952; new edn, Leo Cooper 1971.
Calvert, Michael, *Fighting Mad*, Jarrolds, 1964.
Calvert, Michael, *The Chindits*, Ballantine. 1973.
Fergusson, Bernard, *Beyond the Chindwin*, Collins 1945; *The Wild Green Earth*, Collins 1946; *Return to Burma*, Collins 1962; *The Trumpet in the Hall*, Collins 1970.
Carfrae, Charles, *Chindit Column*, Kimber, 1985.

III **Japanese**
Harada Katsumasa, *Dokyumento Shōwa-shi* (A documentary history of the Shōwa period), Vol. 4, *Taiheiyō sensō* (The Pacific War); Vol. 5, *Haisen zengo* (Japan's defeat), Heibonsha, 1975.
Hattori Takushirō, *Dai Tōa Sensō Zenshi* (Complete History of the Great East Asia War), I vol. edn. Hara Shōbō, 1968.
Hayashi Saburō, *Taiheiyō sensō rikusen gaishi* (Outline history of the land campaigns of the Pacific War), Iwanami Shinsho, 25th ed. 1972 (1st ed. 1951).
Imai Seiichi et al, *Taiheiyō sensō-shi* (History of the Pacific War) Vols. 4–6. (Left-wing slant on Japanese politics at home and overseas.) Aoki Shoten, 1972.
Itō Masanori, *Teikoku Rikugun no Saigo* (The end of the Imperial Army), Vols. 1–6, Bungei Shunjū, 1st. ed. 1959, 14th ed. 1969 (unreconstructed).
Itō Masanori et al., ed., *Jitsuroku Taiheiyō Sensō*, 7 vols, Chūō Kōronsha, 1960 (Extracts and summaries of books on all aspects of the Pacific War; Vol. 3 deals with Imphal).
Kojima Noboru, *Taiheiyō Sensō* (The Pacific War), Chuhkō Shinsho, 2 vols., 1965.
Kojima Noboru, *Shiki kan* (Commanders), Bunshun Bunkō, 2 vols, 1974. (Miyazaki and Mutaguchi in Vol. 1)
Kojima Noboru, *Sanbō* (Staff Officers) Bunshun Bunkō, 2 vols, 1975. (Fujiwara and Tsuji in Vol. 1)
Takagi Toshirō, *Senshi* (Death in Battle), Bungei Shunjū, 1967. (Tanahashi and the death of Brigadier Cavendish at Indin).

E ARMY AND DIVISIONAL HISTORIES

I **British**
Brett-James, A., *Ball of Fire: The Fifth Indian Division in the Second World War*, Gale and Polden, Aldershot, 1951.

Doulton, Lt-Col. A. J. F., *The Fighting Cock, being the History of the 23rd Indian Division 1942–47*, Gale and Polden, Aldershot, 1951.

Mason, P., *A Matter of Honour: An Account of the Indian Army, its Officers and Men*, Cape, 1974.

Roberts, Brig. M. R., *Golden Arrow. The Story of the 7th Indian Division in the Second World War, 1939–45*, Gale and Polden, Aldershot, 1952.

II **Japanese**

Sagara Shunsuke, *Kiku to Ryū* (Chrysanthemum and Dragon). (Code-names for 18 and 56 Divisions respectively; the fighting in Yunnan and North Burma; Myitkyina), Kōninsha, 1972.

F   *REGIMENTAL, BATTALION AND COMPANY HISTORIES*

I **British and Indian**

Barthop, M., *The Northamptonshire Regiment*, Leo Cooper, 1974.

Birdwood, Col. F. T., *The Sikh Regiment in the Second World War*, Norwich, privately printed, 1953.

Carew, Tim, *The Royal Norfolk Regiment*, Hamish Hamilton, 1967.

Condon, Brig. W. E. H., *The Frontier Force Rifles*, Gale and Polden, Aldershot, 1953.

Holloway, R., *The Queen's Own Royal West Kent Regiment*, Leo Cooper, 1973.

Jervois, Brig. W. J., *The History of the Northamptonshire Regiment, 1934–1948* (Regimental History Committee), 1953.

Myatt, F., The Royal Berkshire Regiment, Leo Cooper, 1968.

Rissik, David, *The DLI at War*, Brancepeth, 1953.

Russell, Wilfrid, *The Friendly Firm. A History of 194 Squadron, Royal Air Force*, 194 Squadron, RAF Association, 1972.

Taylor, Jeremy, *The Devons: A History of the Devonshire Regiment, 1685–1945*, Bristol, 1951.

White, Lt-Col., O. G. W., *Straight on for Tokyo. The War History of the 2nd Battalion the Dorsetshire Regiment* (54th Foot), Gale and Polden, Aldershot, 1948.

II **Japanese**

Dai-San Chūtai Senshi Hensan Iinkai-hen, *Hohei Dai Ni-hyaku-jūgo Rentai Dai-San Chūtai Senki* (War History of No. 3 Coy. 215 Infantry Regiment), Maebashi, 1979.

Go-Hachi-Kai (58 Infantry Regimental Association), *Biruma sensen-Hohei Dai-Gojūhachi Rentai no kaisō* (Burma front – reminiscences of 58 Infantry Regiment), 1964 (private circulation).

Nanyūkai kaisōroku hensan iin (Editorial Committee, Reminiscences of Southern Friends Association), *Haruka naru pagoda* (Distant pagodas). *Yasen Kōshahō dai sanjū-roku daitai dai-îtchūtai Dai Tōa senso Kaisōroku* (Reminiscences of No 1 Coy. No. 36 Field Anti-Aircraft Artillery Battalion), 1976.

Takagi Toshirō, *Zenmetsu* (Annihilation), Bungei Shunju, 1968 (14 Tank Regiment).

Uzumaku Sittan (The swirling waters of the Sittang). *Hohei Dai-121 Rentai-shi* (History of the 121 Infantry Regiment, Tottori), Nihonkai Shimbunsha, Tottori, 1969.

G *COMMANDERS' AND SENIOR OFFICERS' ACCOUNTS; BIOGRAPHIES AND AUTOBIOGRAPHIES*

I **British and American**
Bond, Brian, ed., *Chief of Staff: The Diaries of Lt. Gen. Sir Henry Pownall*, Vol. 2, 1940–1944, Leo Cooper, 1974. (by kind permission of J.W. Pownall-Gray, Esq.).
Connell, John, *Auchinleck*, Collins, 1959.
Connell, John, *Wavell: Supreme Commander 1941–1943*, Collins, 1969.
Evans, Lt-Gen. Sir Geoffrey, *Slim as Military Commander*, Batsford, 1969.
Fergusson, Bernard, *Wavell: Portrait of a Soldier*, Collins, 1961.
Lewin, Ronald, *Slim the Standard-Bearer*, Leo Cooper, 1976.
Masters, John, *The Road Past Mandalay*, Michael Joseph, 1961.
Maule, H. R., *Spearhead General. The epic story of Sir Frank Messervy and his men at Eritrea, North Africa and Burma*, Odhams Press, 1961.
Slim, Field Marshal Viscount, *Defeat into Victory*, Cassell, 1956.
Smeeton, Brig. Miles, *A Change of Jungles*, Hart-Davis, 1962.
Smyth, Sir John, *Before the Dawn*, Cassell, 1957.
Stilwell, Lt-Gen. Joseph W., *The Stilwell Papers* (ed. T. H. White). Macdonald, 1949.
Sykes, C., *Orde Wingate*, Collins, 1959.
Terraine, J., *The Life and Times of Lord Mountbatten*, Arrow Books, 1970.
Tuchman, Barbara, *Sand Against the Wind. Stilwell and the American Experience in China 1911–1945*, New York, 1970.
Tuker, Lt-Gen. Sir Francis, *While Memory Serves*, Cassell, 1950.
Tulloch, D., *Wingate in Peace and War*, Macdonald, 1972.

II **Japanese**
Katakura Tadashi, *Inpāru sakusen hishi* (Secret history of the Imphal Operation), Keizai Ōrai-sha, 1975 (Chief Staff Officer of Burma Area Army).
Mutaguchi, Renya, Lt-Gen., *1944-nen U-Go sakusen ni kansuru Kokkai Toshokan ni okeru setsumei shiryō*, (Materials concerning Operation U-GO, 1944, in the National Library), 1964, pp. 1–32 (privately printed).
Swinson, Arthur, *Four Samurai*, Hutchinson, 1968. (Includes Honda and Mutaguchi.)
Takagi Toshirō, *Inpāru* (Imphal), Bungei Shunjū, 1968 (on Mutaguchi and Imphal).
Takagi Toshirō, *Kōmei* (Insubordination), Bungei Shunjū, 1966 (Satō and Mutaguchi).
Takagi Toshirō, *Funshi* (Death in Anger), Bungei Shunjū, 1969 (Yamauchi, 15 Division and Mutaguchi).

H *JOURNALISTS' ACCOUNTS*

I **British**
Beaton, Cecil, *Far East*, Batsford, 1945.
Burchett, W. G., *Wingate's Phantom Army*, Muller, 1946.
Curie, Eve, *Journey Among Warriors*, Doubleday, Doran, 1943.
Gallagher, O. D., *Retreat in the East*, Harrap, 1942.
Owen, Frank ed., SEAC Newspaper, *Laugh with SEAC*, Calcutta, 1945.
Rodger, George, *Red Moon Rising*, Cresset Press, 1943.

Rolo, Charles J., *Wingate's Raiders*, Harrap, 1944.
Wagg, Alfred, *A Million Died!*, Nicholson & Watson, 1943.

II **Japanese**
Mikuni Ichirō, *Shōwa-shi tanbō* (Investigations into modern Japanese history) Vols. 3–5 (interviews on the war period), Banchō Shobō, 1974.
Maruyama Shizuo, *Inpāru sakusen jūgunki* (The Imphal campaign), Iwanami Shinsho, 1984.
Tamura, Yoshio, ed. *Hiroku Dai Tōa Senshi* (Secret History of the Great East Asia War); *Biruma-hen* (Burma volume), Fuji Shobō, 1953 (25 accounts of the campaign by 15 Japanese war correspondents).

I *PARTICIPANTS' NARRATIVES*

I **Allied**
Baggaley, James, *A Chindit Story*, Souvenir Press, 1954.
Beaumont, Winifred, *A Detail on the Burma Front*, BBC, 1977.
Bower, Ursula Graham, *Naga Path*, John Murray, 1952.
Brett-James, Anthony, *Report My Signals*, Hennel Locke, 1948.
Carew, Tim, *All this and a Medal too*, Constable, 1957.
Corpe, Hilda R., *Prisoner beyond the Chindwin*, Arthur Barker, 1955.
Davis, Patrick, *A Child at Arms*, Hutchinson, 1970.
Delachet Guillon, Claude, *Daw Sein. Les dix mille vies d'une femme birmane*, Seuil, Paris, 1978.
Fellowes-Gordon, Ian, *The Battle for Naw Seng's Kingdom*, Leo Cooper, 1971 (The Kachin Levies in North Burma).
Guthrie, Duncan, *Jungle Diary*, Macmillan, 1946.
Halley, David, *With Wingate in Burma*, William Hodge, 1946.
Hanley, Gerald, *Monsoon Victory*, Collins, 1946.
Irwin, Anthony, *Burmese Outpost*, Collins, 1945.
Jeffrey, W. F., *Sunbeams like Swords*, Hodder & Stoughton, 1951.
Mains, Lt-Col. Tony, *The Retreat from Burma*, Foulsham, 1973.
Mi Mi Khaing, *Burmese Family*, Longmans, 1946.
Morrison, Ian, *Grandfather Longlegs. The life and gallant death of Major H. P. Seagrim, GC, DSO,* Faber, 1947.
Ogburn, Charlton, *The Marauders*, New York, Harper, 1959.
Rees, W. R. and Brelis, Dean, *Behind the Burma Road*, Robert Hale, 1964.
Rhodes-James, Richard, *Chindit*, John Murray, 1980.
Shaw, James, *The March Out*, Rupert Hart-Davis, 1953.
Sheil-Small, Denis, *Green shadows: a Gurkha story*, William Kimber, 1982.
Smith Dun, General, *Memoirs of the Four-Foot Colonel*, Cornell, 1980.
Williams, J. H., Lt-Col., *Elephant Bill*, Rupert Hart-Davis, 1950.

II **Japanese**
Abe Mitsuo, Lt-Col., *Sanbō* (Staff Officer), Fuji Shobō, 1953.
Aida Yūji, *Arōn Shūyōjo* (Ahlone Camp), Chūō Kōronsha, 1962, new ed. 1974. (Tr. as *Prisoner of the British*, H. Ishiguro and L. Allen, Cresset Press, 1966).
Aida Yūji, *Āron Shūyōjo Saibō* (Ahlone Camp Revisited), Bungei Shunjū, 1975.
Araki Susumu, *Biruma haisen kōki. Ippeishi no kaisō* (Wanderings after defeat in Burma. A soldier's reminiscences), Iwanami Shinsho, 1982.

Bibliography

Hamachi, Toshio, *Inpāru Saizensen* (Front-line at Imphal), Sōbunsha, 1980. (Shenam, Palel; Bishenpur.)

Kikuchi Hitoshi, *Kyōfū Inpāru saizensen* (The hurricane of battle: Imphal), Sōbunsha, 1982. (15 Division.)

Komiya Tokuji, *Sensō to ningen no kiroku. Biruma-sen zenpan*, (War and man. The War in Burma. Vol. I), Gendaishi Shuppansha, 1978. (Fall of Rangoon; Pegu Yomas.)

Kobayashi Ikusaburō, *Biruma senjo nikki* (Burma: a battlefield diary), Sōbunsha, 1981.

Kuzuma Yasuji, ed., *Sakimori no shi* (Inpāru hen) (Poems of the Guards: Imphal), Kyoto Shimbunsha, Kyoto, 1979.

Miyabe Kazumi, *Biruma saizensen* (1) (Burma front-line), Sōbunsha, 1980. (119 Inf. Regt.; 53 Division; Wingate; Meiktila; life in surrender camps).

Murata Heiji, *Inpāru sakusen. Retsu heidan Kohima no shitō* (The Imphal operation. 31 Division at Kohima), Hara Shobō, 1967.

Takami Jun, '*Biruma jūgun*' (With the Army in Burma), in *Takami Jun Nikki* (The Diary of Takami Jun) Vol. II, i, Keisō Shobō, 1966 (Poet and propagandist's account of life in occupied Burma).

Tsuji Masanobu, *Jūgo tai ichi* (Fifteen to one), Hara Shobō, 1968. (33 Army in Yunnan, North Burma, Meiktila and Pyawbwe.)

Tsuji Masanobu, *Senkō sansenri* (3000-league Odyssey), (trans. as *Underground Escape*), Robert Booth and Taro Fukuda, Tokyo, 1952.

Tsutsumi Shinzō, *Tenshin* (Retreat), privately printed, 1967.

Tsutsumi Shinzō, *Kikoku shūshū. Fukami Butai zenmetsu no ki* (Ghostly cries. The story of the annihilation of 13 Naval Guard Unit), Mainichi Shimbunsha, 1981.

Ushiro Masaru, *Biruma senki* (The War in Burma), Nippon Shuppan, Kyōtō K. K., 1953. (The author was a staff officer in Burma Area Army.)

Yoshiichi Shigemitsu, *Gunzoku Biruma Monogatari* (The story of a civilian attached to the Japanese Army), Ōshi-sha, 1973. (Hospital at Meiktila.)

J MEDICAL

I *British*

Anderson, W. M. E. & others, *Field Service Hygiene Notes*, India, 1945, Govt. of India Press, Calcutta, 1945.

Mackenzie, W., *Operation Rangoon Jail* (Account of conditions in captivity by 17 Indian Division chief medical officer, captured at Sittang Bridge, 1942).

Mellor, W. Franklin, *Casualties and Medical Statistics*, HMSO, 1970.

Short, Stanley W., *On Burma's Eastern Frontier*, Marshall, Morgan & Scott, Edinburgh, 1945.

Walker, Allan S., *Middle East and Far East*, Canberra, 1953. (Vol. 2 of Medical Series, *Australia in the War of 1939–1945*.) (Chapter 26 deals with the Burma-Siam Railway, and Chapter 27 with the prison camps in the Far East.)

II *American*

Seagrave, Gordon S., *Burma Surgeon*, Norton, New York, 1943.

Seagrave, Gordon S., *Burma Surgeon Returns*, Gollancz, 1946.

III *Japanese*

Hashimoto Takehiki, *Ruikotsu no tani* (Valley of Bones). *Biruma heitan byōin kaimetsu-ki* (The destruction of a Japanese L of C Hospital), Ōshi-sha, 1979.

Ishida Shinsaku, *Akuma no Nihon gun-i* (The Devil's M.O.), Yamamoto Shobō, 1982. (Account of vivisection of Chinese POWs in North Burma.)

Itō Keiichi, *Heitaitachi no rikugunshi* (The soldier's Army History). *Heiei to senjo seikatsu* (Life in barracks and on the battlefield), Banchō Shobō, 1969.

Kameo Susumu, *Ma no Sittan kawa* (Sittang: the devil's river), Ōshi-sha, 1980. (Pegu Yomas; INA; BNA; Breakout.)

Karube Shigenori, *Inpāru – Aru jūgun-i no shuki* (Imphal – An M.O.'s Notebook), Norima Shoten, 1979. (Gripping account of siege of Kohima and retreat of 31 Division.)

Senda Natsumitsu, *Jūgun ianfu* (Comfort girls with the Army), Futaba-sha, 1973.

K *POLITICS, RACE, MORALE*

I *Allied*

Ballhatchet, Kenneth, *Race, Sex and Class under the Raj*, Weidenfeld and Nicolson, 1980.

Bond, Brian, *British Military Policy between the two World Wars*, Clarendon Press, 1980.

Collis, Maurice, *Last and First in Burma 1941–1948*, Faber, 1956.

Dover, Cedric, *Hell in the Sunshine*, Secker & Warburg, 1943.

Keegan, John, *The Face of Battle*, Cape, 1976.

Louis, William Rogers, *British Strategy in the Far East*, Oxford U. P., 1973.

de Mendelssohn, Peter, *Japan's Political Warfare*, Allen & Unwin, 1944.

Sluimers, Laszlo, *A Method in the Madness? Aanzetten tot een vergelijkende politicologische studie van de Japonse periode in Zuidoost-Asie, 1942–1945*, Amsterdam, 1978.

Thorne, Christopher, *Allies of a Kind*, Oxford U. P., 1978.

Tinker, Hugh, ed., *Burma. The Struggle for Independence 1944–1948*, Vol. 1. *From Military Occupation to Civil Government, 1 January 1944–31 August 1946*, HMSO, 1983.

U Khin, recorded by, *U Hla Pe's Narrative of the Japanese Occupation of Burma*, Cornell, 1961.

II *Japanese*

Indo hōmen senbotsusha ikotsu shūshū seifu hakendan bunshū iinkai (Committee for documentation of the official group collecting bones of the dead in Indian areas), *Arakan no saikai* (Meeting again in Arakan); *Dai-ichi Indo hōmen ikotsu shūshū kiroku* (A record of the first bone collections in Indian areas), with envelope of maps, Tokyo, 1975.

Ichi-oku-nin no Shōwa-shi (Everyman's history of modern Japan), No. 10, Fukyoka Shashinshi (History of Photographic Censorship) Mainichi Shimbunsha, Tokyo, January, 1977.

Nihon Nyūsu Eiga-shi (History of Japanese newsreels), Ichi-oku-nin no Shōwa-shi (Everyman's history of modern Japan series), special number. Mainichi Shimbunsha, 1977.

Iizuka Kōji, *Nihon no guntai* (The Japanese Military), Hyōronsha, 1968.

Kitajima Noboru et al., *Nihon Rikungunshi* (History of the Japanese Army), Mainichi Shimbunsha, 1979. (Special issue of Ichi-oku-nin no Shōwa-shi).

Tomita Akihiro, *Heitai Gashū* (Drawings of the Soldier's Life), Banchō Shobō, Tokyo, 1972.

Tsubota Kazuo, ed., *Taiheiyō Sensō*, 2 vols, Shōwa Nihonshi (Modern Japan), Vols 4 & 5, Gyōkyōiku Tosho K. K., 1976.

L *THE ROLE OF THE INDIAN NATIONAL ARMY*

Bose, S. K., ed., *The International Netaji Seminars, Abstracts of Papers*, Netaji Bhawan, Calcutta, 1973.

Corr, Gerald H., *The War of the Springing Tigers*, Osprey, 1975.

Durrani, Mahmood Khan, *The Sixth Column*, Cassell, 1955.

Fujiwara Iwaichi, *F Kikan*, Hara Shobō, 1966. (First person account of Malaya and Burma by the Japanese major who founded the INA with Mohan Singh – (English translation by Akashi Yoji, *F. Kikan*, Japanese Army Intelligence Operations in South-East Asia during World War II), Heineman Asia, 1983.

Ghosh, Kalyan K., *The Indian National Army. Second Front of the Indian Independence Movement*, Meenakshi Prakashan, Meerut, 1969.

Hauner, Milan, *India in Axis Strategy; Germany, Japan, and Indian Nationalists in the Second World War*, German Historical Institute, 1982.

Hayashida Tatsuo, *Higeki no eiyū. Chandora Bōsu no shōgai* (Tragic Hero. The Life of S. C. Bose), Tokyo, 1968.

Imai, Takeo, *Shōwa no bōryaku*, Hara Shobō, 1967 (Japanese subversion in China and South-East Asia).

Khan, Shah Nawaz, Maj-Gen., *INA and its Netaji*, Rajkamal Publications, Delhi, 1946.

Kunizuka Kazunori, *Indoyō ni kakaru kiji* (A rainbow across the Indian Ocean), Kōbunsha, 1958.

Lebra, Joyce, *Jungle Alliance. Japan and the Indian National Army*, Asia Pacific Press, Singapore, 1971.

Singh, Mohan, *Soldier's Contribution to Indian Independence*, Army Educational Stores, New Delhi, 1974.

Sykes, Christopher, *Troubled Loyalty. A biography of Adam von Trott zu Solz*, Collins, 1968. (Chapter 14 deals with Bose.)

Toye, Hugh, *The Springing Tiger: Subhas Chandra Bose*, 1959

M *BURMA NATIONAL ARMY*

Asai Tokuichi, Prof., *Biruma sensen fūdoki (The front-line in Burma)*, Tamagawa Sensho, 1980. (Memoirs of the geography professor who tried to assassinate Ba Maw.)

Ba Maw, *Breakthrough in Burma. Memoirs of a Revolution, 1939–1946*. Yale U. P., 1968.

Collis, Maurice, *Last and First in Burma*, Faber, 1956.

Hatakeyama, Kiyoyuki, *Taisen Zenya no Chōhōsen* (Intelligence warfare on the eve of the great war), Nakano School series, Sankei shimbun shuppan-kyoku, 1967.

Nu, Thakin, *Burma under the Japanese*, tr. J. S. Furnivall, Macmillan, 1954.

Ōta Tsunezō, *Biruma in okeru Nihon gunsei-shi no kenkyū* (Studies in the History of Japanese military government in Burma), Yoshikawa Kōbunkan, 1969.

Yamamoto Masayoshi, *Biruma kōsaku to bōryaku shōkō* (A Japanese agent and saboteur in Burma), Rokko-Shuppan, 1978.

Articles

I **British, American and Indian**

Allen, L., 'Japanese Military Rule in Burma', *Modern Asian Studies*, III, 2, Cambridge, 1969, pp. 177–181.

Allen, L., 'Studies in the Japanese Occupation of South-East Asia 1942–45 (I)', *Durham University Journal*, New Series, Vol. XXXII, No. 1, Dec. 1970, pp. 1–15.

Allen, L., 'Notes on Japanese Historiography: World War II', *Military Affairs*, Kansas State University, Vol. XXXV, No. 4, Dec. 1971, pp. 173–178.

Allen, L., 'Japanese Literature of the Second World War', *Proceedings of the British Association for Japanese Studies*, Vol. 2, Sheffield, 1977, pp. 117–152.

Allen, L., 'The Historian as Little Peterkin', *Durham University Journal*, New Series, Vol. XL, Dec. 1979, pp. 89–98.

Allen, L., 'Fujiwara and Suzuki: Patterns of Asian Liberation', in W. H. Newell, ed. *Japan in Asia*, Singapore U. P., 1981, pp. 83–103.

Allen, L., 'How not to assassinate Ba Maw', *Proceedings of the British Association for Japanese Studies*, Sheffield, 1982.

Evans, Lt-Gen. Sir Geoffrey, 'Imphal: Crises in Burma', *History of the Second World War*, Purnell, No. 61, pp. 1681–1691.

Fujiwara Iwaichi, 'Burma: the Japanese Verdict', *ibid.*, pp. 1706–1707.

Ghosh, K. K., 'The Indian National Army – Motives, Problems and Significance', Paper No. 31, International Conference on Asian History, Kuala Lumpur, August 1968, pp. 1–29.

Keene, D., 'Japanese Writers and the Greater East Asia War', in *Landscapes and Portraits*, Secker & Warburg, 1972.

Lebra, Joyce C., 'Japanese Policy and the Indian National Army', Paper No. 21, International Conference on Asian History, Kuala Lumpur, August 1968, pp. 1–29.

Lebra, Joyce, 'Japanese and Western Models for the Indian National Army', *The Japan Interpreter*, V, 1972, pp. 364–375.

Lebra, Joyce C., 'The Significance of the Japanese Military Model for Southeast Asia', *Pacific Affairs*, Vol. 48, no. 2, 1975, pp. 215–229.

Mead, Brig. Peter, 'Orde Wingate and the Official Histories', *Journal of Contemporary History*, Vol. 14, January 1979, pp. 55–82.

Reid, Sir Robert, 'The Assam Rifles in Peace and War', *Blackwood's Magazine*, No. 1579, May 1947, pp. 414–412.

Sunderland, Riley, 'Burma: the Supply Solution', *History of the Second World War*, Purnell, No. 61, p. 1708.

Swinson, Arthur, 'Kohima: Turning Point in Burma', *ibid.*, pp. 1692–1704.

Thorne, Christopher, 'Racial aspects of the Far Eastern War of 1941–45', *Proceedings of the British Academy*, LXVI, 1980, pp. 329–377.

Tinker, Hugh, 'Burma: the Politics of Memory', *Pacific Affairs*, Vol. 49, No. 1, Spring 1976, pp. 108–111.

Wingate, Sybil, 'Orde Wingate and his critics', *Spectator*, 29 May 1959.

II **Japanese**

Allen, L., '*Biruma no tategoto* to *Nobi*' (*Harp of Burma* and *Fires on the Plain*), *Hikaku bungaku kenkyū*, No. 36, pp. 123–135.

Arisue Seizō, 'My Memories of Subhas Chandra Bose', (tr. Mrs. R. Sinha) *The Oracle*, I, No. 1, Calcutta, January 1979, pp. 19–24.

Asai Tokuichi, 'Bā Mo ansatsu misui jiken ni tsuite no shōgen' (Testimony on the failure of the attempt to assassinate Ba Maw), *Seiji Keizai Shigaku*, No. 144 (May 1978), pp. 1–14; No. 145 (June 1978), pp. 1–18; No. 149 (October 1978), pp. 11–22.

Gotō Shūhaku, 'Aa hikō dai-8-sentai tsubasa aru kagiri' (So long as 8 Squadron has wings) (The air war in Burma), *Maru*, No. 339, pp. 213–243, November 1974.

Ikenami Arinobu, 'Tsuji Masanobu no kōzai' (Tsuji Masanobu – for and against) *Maru*, No. 324, pp. 98–103, August 1973.

Iwahara, Kanichi, 'Sanbō to tsuwamono to shōgun to . . .' (Staff, soldiers, generals . . .), (Meiktila) *Maru*, No. 335, pp. 217–247, July 1974.

Iwakuro, Takeo, '*Indo shishi. Bōsu no saihi*' (An Indian warrior: the last days of Bose), *Bungei Shunjū*, special issue, December 1955, pp. 52–56.

Japan Times Weekly, 'Japan planned Nazi-style Rule after World War II Victory', *Japan Times Weekly*, 5 December 1981.

Kawashima Takenobu, 'Biruma dokuritsu giyūgun to Minami Kikan' (The Minami Organisation and the Burma Independence Army), *Rekishi to Jinbutsu* (Man and History), special issue on Nakano School, No. 10, October 1980, pp. 134–143.

Nagazawa, Kanichi, Major-General et al., 'Sittan toppa sakusen' (The Sittang Breakout Operation). *Nanso*, No. 31 (20th anniversary issue of the Sittang Breakout), pp. 30–48, 1965.

Nishijima Hideo, Sgt., 'Yūkon no gunzō wa naite iru' (The spirits of the dead are weeping) (114 Inf. Regt., 56 Division in North Burma), *Maru*, No. 327, pp. 229–257, November 1973.

Numata Takazō, 'Nampō Sōgun Terauchi gensui no shi' (The death of Field-Marshal Terauchi, GOC-in-C Southern Army), *Bungei Shunjū*, special issue, December 1955, pp. 114–119.

Ogawa Tadahiro, 'Inden senki' (The battle of Indin), *Nanso*, No. 34, pp. 1–28, 1972.

Sagara Shunsuke, 'Okorareru gōshō, hakkotsu kaidō ni naku' (The brave general weeps in Skeleton Road) (56 Division in North Burma, Mizukami's suicide), *Maru*, No. 336, pp. 96–101, August 1974.

Sakurai Shōzō, 'Biruma no sensen. Teki-chū toppa' (Burma front. Breaking through the enemy), *Bungei Shunjū*, special issue, December 1955, pp. 62–67.

Sakurai Shōzō, Lt-Gen. et al., 'Sittan toppa sanjūshūnen wo mukaete' (Welcoming the 30th anniversary of the Sittang Breakout), *Nanso*, No. 43, pp. 1–96, 1975.

Takasaki Tsutomu, 'Saiaku no senjo ni kiseki wa nakatta' (On the worst battlefield, no trace) (124 Inf. Regt. at Imphal), *Maru*, No. 277, pp. 245–275, November 1969.

Tsuchiya Eiichi, 'Shi no teki-chū toppa ōdan. Biruma hōmengun no higeki' (Breaking through the enemy. The tragedy of Burma Area Army), *Nihon Shūkō*, No. 441, 25 April, 1958, pp. 33–41.

Tsuchiya Eiichi, Lt-Col., 'Getsumei ni kieta nikuhaku tokkōtai' (The commandos who vanished by moonlight) (28 Army and the Irrawaddy crossings), *Maru*, No. 244, pp. 235–270, September 1962.

Yamamoto Shichihei, '*Ikkakyū shōkō no mita Teikoku rikugun*' (The Imperial Army through the eyes of a subaltern), *Shūkan Asahi*, August–September 1975 (later in book form).

Index

Note: Formations and units of the British Army and Colonial military forces are indexed under 'British Army'; those of the Indian Army and Burma military forces are indexed under 'Indian Army'. Japanese names, in text and index, are given in the Japanese sequence, i.e. surnames first.

Index

Index

Scott, Major-General J. Bruce: *59, 61, 68, 69*
Scott, Major Walter: *65, 128, 138*
Seagrave, Dr. Gordon: *66, 72*
Seagrim, Major Hugh: *573, 575–8, 579, 602, 611*
Sein, Daw: *35–6*
Shenam: *189, 193, 194, 206, 207, 210, 211, 223, 225, 245–7, 305–7, 310, 456*
Shiga, Naoya: *quoted, 617–8*
Shima, Tatsuo, Lieut.: *302–5*
Shōji, Lieut.-Colonel: *537, 538, 540*
Shwebo: *70, 74, 78, 83, 95, 127, 264, 327, 389, 393, 394, 397, 398, 399, 401–4, passim 409, 429, 436*
Shwedaung, Battle of: *63–4*
Shwegyin: *74–9 passim, 495, 509, 518, 522, 531, 533, 534, 536, 541*
Singh, Captain Mohan: *169, 556, 600*
Sittang Bridge, destruction of: *1–3, 36–44*
Slim, Lieut.-General William: commands Burcorps, *59; 61, 62, 64–9 passim, 71, 72, 73;* at Monywa, *74–6; 77, 78;* leads retreat to Imphal, *79;* takes command of XV Corps, *94; 95, 107, 109–14 passim, 119, 149, 155, 178, 187, 188, 189, 193, 196, 201, 220;* miscalculates at Kohima, *228; 229, 230, 235, 242–5 passim, 254, 318, 340;* death of Wingate, *347, 348–9; 350, 351, 352, 357, 362, 369;* in conflict with Stilwell, *376, 377;* knighted, *388; 389, 391, 393;* in renewed offensive, *397–401;* in relation to Irrawaddy crossings, *411, 416, 423, 424;* seizing of Meiktila, *425, 426, 436, 437, 438, 455, 457;* and taking of Rangoon, *459, 460, 465, 467, 476, 478, 481, 494;* hands over to Christison, *504;* and B.N.A., *555, 578, 580–3 passim, 586, 587; 609;* post-war comments on Japanese, *610–13 passim; 633, 635; quoted, 78, 93, 109, 110, 112, 113–4, 188, 201, 239, 284, 287, 347, 387, 394, 401, 437, 441, 461, 474, 525*
Smeeton, Brigadier Miles: *426, 427–8, 505, 537, 539, 540, 615–6; quoted, 463–4, 566, 613, 616*
Smith, Brigadier: *295*
Smyth, Major-General J. G.: *3, 24–34 passim, 48–50, 476, 576*
Songkram, Field-Marshal Pibun: *164, 165*
Special Force: *see* Indian Army: 3 Division
Spurlock, Lieut.: *143, 148*
Stewart, Lieut. L. A.: *254*
Stilwell, Lieut.-General J. B. (U.S.): *58, 61, 65, 66, 68, 71–2;* road from Ledo, *94, 155; 124, 156, 242, 244, 245, 264, 309, 318, 320;* in relation to Operation 'Thursday', *321–3;* in Operation 'Galahad', *323, 327, 330, 333, 339, 340, 345, 346, 349, 351, 356–9 passim, 362–8 passim, 374;* in conflict with British, *375–9, 385;* removed from command, *387; 390, 404, 631*
Stopford, Lieut.-General (*later* Sir) Montagu: *270, 275, 351, 352, 388, 397, 402, 409, 456, 458, 476, 504, 535, 541, 548*
Sueki, Hisashi, Major: *198, 199, 201–5 passim, 240*
Sugii, Mitsuru: *17, 19*
Sugita, Ichiji, Colonel: *263, 264*
Sugiyama, Gen, Field-Marshal: *175, 185, 483*

Sultan, Lieut.-General Daniel: *387*
Sun Li-jen, Lieut.-General: *65–9, 70, 71, 79, 321, 322, 358*
Suzuki, Dr: *11, 18*
Suzuki, Keiji, Colonel: *17–22 passim, 556–9 passim, 561*
Swinson, Arthur: *quoted, 245, 274–5*
Symes, Major-General G. W.: *319, 348, 349; quoted, 350–1*

Tai An-lan, General: *61*
Takagi, Toshirō: *110, 111, 260, 291*
Takahasi, Hachirō, Lieut.: *20, 22, 28, 584*
Takami, Jun: *619–21; quoted, 619, 620–1*
Takanobu, Major: *56, 57*
Takeda, Colonel: *369, 371, 516*
Takeda, Lieut.-General: *463*
Takeda no Miya Tsunenori, Prince: *153, 158, 159, 160*
Takemura, Major: *221, 222, 226, 329, 332, 333, 335, 336*
Takeuchi, Lieut.-General: *23, 24, 61, 100*
Takeyama, Michio: *621–2*
Tamu: *70, 76, 79, 82, 83, 84, 95, 188, 189, 194, 206, 207, 210, 247, 305, 395, 400, 457*
Tanahashi, Colonel: *107, 110, 111, 171, 175, 181, 182, 183, 185, 186, 396*
Tanaka, Nobuo, Major-General (*later* Lieut.-General): *275, 278–9, 280, 281, 310, 321, 322, 357, 363, 364, 411, 415, 431; quoted, 276*
Tanaka, Shinichi, Lieut.-General: *386, 428, 430, 432, 433, 450, 454, 473, 483, 484, 494; quoted, 495*
Tanaka, Tetsujirō, Col.: *201, 204, 246, 275*
Tazoe, Noboru, Major-General: *326–8, 337*
Tengnoupal: *207, 210, 211, 222, 223, 225, 306*
Terauchi, Hisaichi, General (*later* Field-Marshal): *150, 153, 165, 166, 170, 262, 312, 390, 391, 481, 482, 514, 537, 543–52 passim, 560, 561, 569, 571*
Thakin Ba Sein: *see* Ba Sein, Thakin
Thein Maung: *11, 17, 18*
Thompson, Squadron-Leader (*later* Sir) Robert: *148*
Thornton, Lieut. P.: *99, 100*
'Thursday', Operation (2nd Wingate Expedition): *specific references to, 318, 319, 320, 324, 337, 348, 357, 380; see also* 2nd Chindit Operation
Tiddim: *189, 191, 195, 196, 197, 201, 204, 206, 212, 241, 278, 299, 310, 394, 476*
Tinker, Hugh: *90, 564, 565; quoted, 84, 89, 563*
Tojo, Prime Minister: *155, 160, 163, 164, 165, 166, 168, 169, 262–4, 285, 297, 308, 310, 386, 543, 571*
Tongzang: *195, 196;* battle for, *197, 198, 201, 202; 203, 204, 212, 241*
Toungoo: *8, 25, 59, 61, 62, 64, 92, 247, 446, 450, 454, 457, 464, 468, 469, 472–4, 478, 482, 483, 484, 486, 488, 490, 492, 494, 507, 508, 509, 512, 513, 514, 517, 576, 579, 582, 598*
Trim, Lieut.-Colonel J. H.: *212, 215, 219*
Tsuchiya, Eiichi, Lieut.-Col.: *538, 539, 540*
Tsuji, Masanobu, Colonel: *381, 382, 385, 432, 450, 451, 454, 465, 466, 469, 470, 471, 472, 486, 495, 500, 572, 609*
Tsutsumi, Shinzō, Lieut.-Commander: *92, 526–34, 535*

685